THE AMERICAN PEOPLE

Creati

and a Society

THIRD EDITION

Volume Two: Since 1865

GENERAL EDITORS

Gary B. Nash
University of California, Los Angeles

Julie Roy Jeffrey
Goucher College

John R. Howe
University of Minnesota

Peter J. Frederick
Wabash College

Allen F. Davis
Temple University

Allan M. Winkler
Miami University

HarperCollins*CollegePublishers*

Executive Editor: Bruce Borland
Director of Development: Betty Slack
Developmental Editor: Elaine Silverstein
Project Editor: Susan Goldfarb
Text/Cover Design: Wendy Ann Fredericks
Photo Researcher: Leslie Coopersmith
Production Manager: Willie Lane
Compositor: Black Dot Graphics
Printer and Binder: R. R. Donnelley & Sons Company
Cover Printer: Coral Graphic Services, Inc.

Cover Illustration: Jacob Lawrence, *Parade* (1960). Hirshhorn Museum and Sculpture Garden, Smithsonian Institution, gift of Joseph H. Hirshhorn, 1966. Photo by Lee Stalsworth.

Photo credits appear on pages C-1–C-7

For permission to use copyrighted material on the following pages, grateful acknowledgment is made to the copyright holders:

939: "Little Boxes," words and music by Malvina Reynolds. © 1962 Schroder Music Co. (ASCAP). Used by permission. All rights reserved.

964–965: Quotes from Ron Kovic, *Born on the Fourth of July,* © 1976, by permission of McGraw-Hill.

1020: "I Am Woman," words by Helen Reddy, music by Ray Burton. Copyright © 1971 by Irving Music, Inc., and Buggerlugs Music Co. (BMI). All rights reserved. Reprinted by permission.

1024: Quotes from *Ms.* magazine, Tenth Anniversary Issue, August 1982.

1037: "The Times They Are A-Changin'," words and music by Bob Dylan. © 1963 Warner Bros., Inc. All rights reserved. Used by permission.

The American People: Creating a Nation and a Society,
Third Edition (Volume Two: Since 1865)

Library of Congress Cataloging-in-Publication Data

The American people : creating a nation and a society / general editors, Gary B. Nash . . . [et al.]. — 3rd ed.
p. cm.
Includes index.
Contents: v. 1. To 1877 — v. 2. Since 1865.
1. United States—History. I. Nash, Gary B.
[E178. 1. A49355 1994b]
973—dc20 93-23641
CIP

ISBN (Volume One): 0-06-501056-6
ISBN (Volume Two): 0-06-501057-4

94 95 96 9 8 7 6 5 4 3

Contents in Brief

Contents

PART VI

A Resilient People, 1945–1992 889

Recovering the Past

Maps

Charts and Tables

Preface

The Yoruba people of West Africa have an old saying: "However far the stream flows, it never forgets its source." Why, we wonder, do such ancient societies as the Yoruba find history so important, while modern American students question its relevance? This book aims to end such skepticism about the usefulness of history.

As we near the end of the twentieth century, in an ethnically and racially diverse country caught up in an interdependent global society, history is of central importance in preparing us to exercise our rights and responsibilities as free people. History cannot make good citizens, but without history we cannot understand the choices before us and think wisely about them. Lacking a collective memory of the past, we lapse into a kind of amnesia, unaware of the human condition and the long struggles of men and women everywhere to deal with the problems of their day and to create a better society. Unfurnished with historical knowledge, we deprive ourselves of knowing about the huge range of approaches people have taken to political, economic, and social life; to solving problems; and to conquering the obstacles in their way.

History has a deeper, even more fundamental importance: the cultivation of the private person, whose self-knowledge and self-respect provides the foundation for a life of dignity and fulfillment. Historical memory is the key to self-identity; to seeing one's place in the long stream of time, in the story of humankind. "It is true that history cannot satisfy our appetite when we are hungry, or keep us warm when the cold wind blows," according to the New York Chinatown History Project. "But it is also true that if younger generations do not understand the hardships and triumphs of their elders, then we will be a people without a past. As such, we will be like water without a source, a tree without roots."

When we study our own history, that of the American people, we see a rich and extraordinarily complex human story. This country, whose written history began with a convergence of Native Americans, Europeans, and Africans, has always been a nation of diverse peoples—a magnificent mosaic of cultures, religions, and skin shades. This book explores how American society assumed its present shape and developed its present forms of government; how as a nation we have conducted our foreign affairs and managed our economy; how as individuals and in groups we have lived, worked, loved, married, raised families, voted, argued, protested, and struggled to fulfill our dreams and the noble ideals of the American experiment.

Several ways of making the past understandable distinguish this book from most textbooks written in the last twenty years. The coverage of public events like presidential elections, diplomatic treaties, and economic legislation is integrated with the private human stories that underlie them. Within a chronological framework we have woven together our history as a nation, as a people, and as a society. When, for example, national political events are discussed, we analyze their impact on social and economic life at the state and local levels. Wars are described not only as they unfolded on the battlefield and in the salons of diplomats, but also on the home front, where they are history's greatest motor of social change. The interaction of ordinary Americans with extraordinary events runs as a theme throughout this book.

Above all, we have tried to show the "humanness" of our history as it is revealed in people's everyday lives. The authors have often used the words of ordinary Americans to capture the authentic human voices of those who participated in and responded to epic events such as war, slavery, industrialization, and reform movements.

Goals and Themes of the Book

Our primary goal is to provide students with a rich, balanced, and thought-provoking treatment of the American past. By this we mean a history that treats the lives and experiences of Americans of all national origins and cultural backgrounds, at all levels of society, and in all regions of the country. It also means a history that seeks connections between the many factors—political, economic, technological, social, religious, intellectual, and biological—that have molded and remolded American society over four centuries. And finally it means a history that encourages students to think about how we have all inherited a complex past filled with both notable achievements and thorny problems. The only history befitting a democratic nation is one that inspires students to initiate a frank and searching dialogue with their past.

To speak of a dialogue about the past presumes that history is interpretive. Students should understand that historians are continually reinterpreting the past. New interpretations are often based on the discovery of new evidence, but more often new interpretations emerge because historians reevaluate old evidence in the light of new ideas that spring from the times in which they write and from their personal views of the world.

Through this book, we also hope to promote class discussions, which can be organized around six questions that we see as basic to the American historical experience:

1. How have Americans developed a stable, democratic political system flexible enough to address the wholesale changes that have occurred in the last two centuries, and to what degree has this political system been consistent with the principles of our nation's founding?
2. How has this nation been peopled, from the first inhabitants to the many groups that arrived in slavery or servitude during the colonial period down to the voluntary immigrants of today? How have these waves of newcomers contributed to the American cultural mosaic, and how have they preserved elements of their ethnic, racial, and religious heritages?
3. How have economic and technological changes affected daily life, work, family organization, leisure, the division of wealth, and community relations in the United States?
4. What has been the role of our nation in the world?
5. How have the recurring reform movements in our history dealt with economic, political, and social problems in attempting to square the ideals of American life with the reality?
6. How have American beliefs and values changed over more than four hundred years of history, and how have they varied between different groups—women and men; white and black Americans; people of different regions, religions, and classes?

In writing a history that revolves around these themes, we have tried to describe two dynamics that operate in all societies. First, we observe people continuously adjusting to new developments, such as industrialization and urbanization, over which they seemingly have little control; yet we realize that people are not paralyzed by history, but rather are the fundamental creators of it. They retain the ability, individually and collectively, to shape the world in which they live and thus in considerable degree to control their own lives.

Second, we emphasize the connections that always exist between social, political, economic, and cultural events. Just as our individual lives are never neatly parceled into separate spheres of activity, the life of a society is made up of a complicated and often messy mixture of forces, events, and accidental occurrences. In this text, political and economic factors are intertwined with technological and cultural ones like strands in a rope.

Structure of the Book

Part Organization

The chapters of this book are grouped into six parts that relate to major periods in American history. Each part begins with a *comparative chronology* summarizing the political and diplomatic, social and economic, and cultural and technological events of the period.

Chapter Structure

Every chapter begins with a *personal story* recalling the experience of an ordinary or lesser-known American. Chapter 1, for example, starts with the tragic account of Opechancanough, a Powhatan tribesman whose entire life of nearly ninety years was consumed by a struggle against the land, hunger, and alien values brought by Spanish and English newcomers. This brief anecdote serves several purposes. First, it introduces the overarching themes and major concepts of the chapter, in this case the meeting in the North American wilderness of three societies—Native American, European, and African—each with different cultural values, life styles, and aspirations. Second, the personal story launches the chapter in a way that facilitates learning—by engaging the student with a human account. Last, the personal story suggests that history was shaped by ordinary as well as extraordinary people. At the end of the personal story a *brief overview* links the biographical sketch to the text by elaborating the major themes of the chapter. Students should read this crucial transition paragraph carefully to enhance their comprehension of the material to come.

We aim to facilitate the learning process for students in other ways as well. Every chapter ends with pedagogical features to reinforce and expand the presentation. A *conclusion* briefly summarizes the main concepts and developments elaborated in the chapter and serves as a bridge to the following chapter. A list of *recommended reading* provides supplementary sources for further study or research; novels contemporary to the period are often included. Finally, a *timeline* reviews the major events and developments covered in the chapter. Each graph, map, and illustration has been chosen to relate clearly to the narrative.

Special Features

A distinctive feature of this book is the two-page "Recovering the Past" section presented in each chapter. These sections introduce students to the fascinating variety of evidence—ranging from sermons, folktales, and diaries to tombstones, advertising, and popular music—that historians have learned to employ in reconstructing the past. Each "Recovering the Past" section gives basic information about the sources and their use by historians and then raises questions for students to consider as they inspect these examples.

In addition to the "Recovering the Past" sections, we have provided other elements that will facilitate learning for students. The program of *color illustrations*—paintings, cartoons, photographs, maps, and charts—reinforces important themes while presenting visual evidence for students to analyze.

The Third Edition

This third edition of *The American People* has benefited from both the helpful comments of scholars and the experience of teachers and students who used the first and second editions of the book. Some of the modifications are small, but others, like the reorganization of the chapters on the early Republic and those on the contemporary period, are substantial.

Several changes in presentation strengthen the text. For example, we have added captions to most of the maps and charts to help students understand and interpret the information presented. We have also tried to make all photo captions more informative. New tables summarize points discussed in the narrative. An example is the table in Chapter 10 titled "Significant Factors Promoting Economic Growth, 1820–1860."

Throughout the text, we have added information on the environment and environmental history. Some of this material is in Chapter 4, in the new section titled "Ecological Transformation," and in Chapter 24, in the section titled "The Dust Bowl: An Ecological Disaster." Other new sections dealing with the environment include a discussion of the problem of pollution during the industrial era of the late nineteenth century (Chapter 18); the conflict over conservation of the nation's natural resources and preservation of the wilderness during Theodore Roosevelt's administration (Chapter 21); and the impact on the environment of the economic boom of the 1950s (Chapter 27). The recommended readings at the end of each chapter are now grouped by topic in order to help students identify and categorize sources for research projects. Finally, throughout the text, we have incorporated the results of new scholarship.

Our aim has been to write a balanced and vivid history of the development of the American nation and its society. We have also tried to provide the support materials necessary to make teaching and learning enjoyable and rewarding. The reader will be the judge of our success. The authors and HarperCollins welcome your comments.

GARY B. NASH
JULIE ROY JEFFREY

Supplements

For Instructors

- ***Teaching the American People.*** Authors Julie Roy Jeffrey and Peter J. Frederick have written this guide on the basis of ideas generated in the frequent "active learning" workshops held by the authors and have tied it closely to the text. In addition to suggestions on how to generate lively class discussion and involve students in active learning, this supplement also offers a file of exam questions and lists of resources, including films, slides, photo collections, records, and audiocassettes.

- ***America Through the Eyes of Its People: A Collection of Primary Sources.*** Prepared by Carol Brown of Houston Community College, this one-volume collection of primary documents portraying the rich and varied tapestry of American life contains documents concerning women, Native Americans, African-Americans, Hispanics, and others who helped to shape the course of U.S. history. Designed to be duplicated by instructors for student use, the documents have accompanying student exercises.

- ***Discovering American History Through Maps and Views.*** Created by Gerald Danzer of the University of Illinois at Chicago—the recipient of the AHA's 1990 James Harvey Robinson Prize for his work in the development of map transparencies—this set of 140 four-color acetates is a unique instructional tool. It contains an introduction on teaching history through maps and a detailed commentary on each transparency. The collection includes cartographic and pictorial maps, views and photos, urban plans, building diagrams, and works of art.

- ***Video Lecture Launchers.*** Prepared by Mark Newman, University of Illinois at Chicago, these video lecture launchers (each 2 to 5 minutes in duration) cover key issues in American history from 1877 to the present. The launchers are accompanied by an instructor's manual.

- ***HarperCollins American History Video Laserdisc.*** This all-new HarperCollins video laserdisc features photos, film clips, and videos of major events in American history.

- ***"This Is America" Immigration Videos.*** Produced by the American Museum of Immigration, these two 20-minute videos tell the story of American immigrants, relating their personal stories and accomplishments. By showing how the richness of our culture is due to the contributions of millions of immigrant Americans, the videos make the point that America's strength lies in the ethnically and culturally diverse backgrounds of its citizens.

- ***Visual Archives of American History.*** This video laser disc provides over 500 photos and 29 minutes of film clips of major events in American history. Each photo or film clip may be instantly accessed, making this collection ideal for classroom use.

- ***Telecourse Packages.*** *The American Adventure: Beginnings to 1877* and *America in Perspective: U.S. History Since 1877*—produced and distributed by the LeCroy Center for Educational Telecommunications, Dallas County Community College District—are designed as a component of a comprehensive learning package consisting of three elements: the 26-lesson telecourse program; the text of *The American People,* Third Edition; and a telecourse study guide. *Telecourse Guide for the American Adventure: Beginnings to 1877,* Third Edition, by John A. Trickel, contains numerous studying aids and self-tests, each keyed to specific chapters and pages in *The American People,* Third Edition. *Telecourse Study Guide for America in Perspective: U.S. History Since 1877,* Second Edition, by Kenneth G. Alfers, contains essays, study guidelines, enrichment ideas, suggested reading, and practice tests, each keyed to specific pages in *The American People,* Third Edition. The study guides can be ordered through your HarperCollins representative.

- ***Transparencies.*** A set of over 40 map transparencies drawn from the text.
- ***Test Bank.*** This test bank, prepared by Charles Cook, Houston Community College, and J. B. Smallwood, North Texas State University, contains over 3500 objective, conceptual, and essay questions. All questions are keyed to specific pages in the text.
- ***TestMaster Computerized Testing System.*** This flexible, easy-to-master computer test bank includes all the test items in the printed test bank. The TestMaster software allows you to edit existing questions and add your own items. Tests can be printed in several different formats and can include figures such as graphs and tables. Available for IBM and Macintosh computers.
- ***QuizMaster.*** This new program enables you to design TestMaster generated tests that your students can take on a computer rather than in printed form. QuizMaster is available separately from TestMaster and can be obtained free through your sales representative.
- ***Grades.*** A grade-keeping and classroom management software program that maintains data for up to 200 students.

For Students

- ***Study Guide and Practice Tests.*** This two-volume study guide, created by Julie Roy Jeffrey and Peter J. Frederick, includes chapter outlines, significant themes and highlights, a glossary, learning enrichment ideas, sample test questions, exercises for identification and interpretation, and geography exercises based on maps in the text.
- ***Learning to Think Critically: Films and Myths About American History.*** Randy Roberts and Robert May of Purdue University use well-known films such as *Gone with the Wind* and *Casablanca* to explore some common myths about America and its past. Many widely held assumptions about our country's past come from or are perpetuated by popular films. Which are true? Which are patently not true? And how does a student of history approach documents, sources, and textbooks with a critical and discerning eye? This short handbook subjects some popular beliefs to historical scrutiny in order to help students develop a method of inquiry for approaching the subject of history in general.
- ***Mapping America: A Guide to Historical Geography.*** This workbook by Ken Weatherbie, Del Mar College, was revised specifically for this new edition. It contains 35 sequenced exercises corresponding to the map program in the text, each culminating in a series of interpretive questions about the role of geographical factors in American history.
- ***Mapping American History: Student Activities.*** Written by Gerald Danzer of the University of Illinois at Chicago, this free map workbook for students features exercises designed to teach students to interpret and analyze cartographic materials as historical documents. The instructor is entitled to a free copy of the workbook for each copy of the text purchased from HarperCollins.
- ***Concepts in American History.*** This slim volume, written by Robert Asher of the University of Connecticut, contains brief essays on 13 key concepts in American history, including such topics as Republicanism, nativism, feminism, and capitalism.
- ***Retracing the Past,* Third Edition.** This two-volume set of readers has been revised by Gary B. Nash and Ronald Schultz of the University of Wyoming. The readings cover economic, political, and social history, with special emphasis on the roles of women, racial and ethnic groups, and working-class people.

- ***SuperShell II Computerized Tutorial.*** Prepared by Ken L. Weatherbie, Del Mar College, this interactive program for IBM computers helps students learn major facts and concepts through drill and practice exercises and diagnostic feedback. SuperShell II provides immediate correct answers, the text page number on which the material is discussed, and a running score of the student's performance maintained on the screen throughout the session. This free supplement is available to instructors through their sales representative.
- ***TimeLink Computer Atlas of American History.*** This atlas, compiled by William Hamblin of Brigham Young University, is an introductory software tutorial and textbook companion. This Macintosh program presents the historical geography of the continental United States from colonial times to the settling of the West and the admission of the last continental state in 1912. The program covers territories in different time periods, provides quizzes, and includes a special Civil War module.

Acknowledgments

Over the years, as the first and second editions of this text were being developed, many of our colleagues read and criticized the various drafts of the manuscript. For their thoughtful evaluations and constructive suggestions, the authors wish to express their gratitude to the following reviewers:

Harry Baker, University of Arkansas at Little Rock
Michael Batinski, Southern Illinois University
Gary Bell, Sam Houston State University
Spencer Bennett, Siena Heights College
James Bradford, Texas A&M University
Jeffrey P. Brown, New Mexico State University
David Brundage, University of California, Santa Cruz
Colin Calloway, University of Wyoming
D'Ann Campbell, Indiana University
Neil Clough, North Seattle Community College
Bruce Dierenfield, Canisius College
John Dittmer, DePauw University
Gordon Dodds, Portland State University
Richard Donley, Eastern Washington University
Bernard Friedman, Indiana University–Purdue University at Indianapolis
Bruce Glasrud, California State University, Hayward
Richard Griswold del Castillo, San Diego State University
Colonel Williams L. Harris, The Citadel Military College
Robert Haws, University of Mississippi
Frederick Hoxie, D'Arcy McNickle Center for the History of the American Indian
John S. Hughes, University of Texas
Donald M. Jacobs, Northeastern University
Delores Janiewski, University of Idaho
David Johnson, Portland State University
Monte Lewis, Cisco Junior College
William Link, University of North Carolina, Greensboro
Vern Mattson, University of Nevada at Las Vegas
John McCormick, Delaware County Community College
Sylvia McGrath, Stephen F. Austin University
Norma Mitchell, Troy State University
William Morris, Midland College
Marian Morton, John Carroll University
Roger Nichols, University of Arizona
Paul Palmer, Texas A&I University
Al Parker, Riverside City College
Neva Peters, Tarrant County Junior College
James Prickett, Santa Monica College
Noel Pugash, University of New Mexico
Juan Gomez-Quiñones, University of California, Los Angeles
George Rable, Anderson College
Leonard Riforgiato, Pennsylvania State University
Randy Roberts, Purdue University
Mary Robertson, Armstrong State University
David Robson, John Carroll University
Sylvia Sebesta, San Antonio College
Herbert Shapiro, University of Cincinnati
David R. Shibley, Santa Monica College
Kathryn Kish Sklar, State University of New York at Binghamton
James Smith, Virginia State University
John Snetsinger, California Polytechnic State University, San Luis Obispo
Tom Tefft, Citrus College
John A. Trickel, Richland College
Donna Van Raaphorst, Cuyahoga Community College
Morris Vogel, Temple University
Jackie Walker, James Madison University

The authors also wish to thank the following reviewers who gave generously of their time and expertise and whose thoughtful and constructive work have contributed greatly to this edition:

Richard H. Abbott, Eastern Michigan University
Kenneth G. Alfers, Mountain View College
Gregg Andrews, Southwest Texas State University
Robert Asher, University of Connecticut, Storrs
Virginia Bellows, Tulsa Junior College
Neal A. Brooks, Essex Community College
Jeffrey P. Brown, New Mexico State University
Vincent A. Clark, Johnson County Community College
Matthew Ware Coulter, Collin County Community College
David Culbert, Louisiana State University
Robert Downtain, Tarrant County Community College
Jerrold Hirsch, Northeast Missouri State University
Richard Kern, University of Findlay
Ronald Lora, University of Toledo
George M. Lubick, Northern Arizona University
John C. Massman, St. Cloud State University
James E. McMillan, Denison University
Walter Miszczenko, Boise State University
Gerald F. Moran, University of Michigan, Dearborn
Judith Parsons, Sul Ross State University
Joseph P. Reidy, Howard University
Ellen Shockro, Pasadena City College
John A. Trickel, Richland College
Michael Wade, Appalachian State University

About the Authors

Gary B. Nash received his Ph.D. from Princeton University in 1964. He is currently Associate Director of the National Center for History in the Schools at the University of California, Los Angeles, where he teaches colonial and revolutionary American history. Among the books Nash has authored are *Quakers and Politics: Pennsylvania, 1681–1726* (1968); *Red, White, and Black: The Peoples of Early America* (1974, 1982); *The Urban Crucible: Social Change, Political Consciousness, and the Origins of the American Revolution* (1979); and *Forging Freedom: The Black Urban Experience in Philadelphia, 1720–1840* (1988). His scholarship is especially concerned with the role of common people in the making of history. He wrote Part I and served as a general editor of this book.

Julie Roy Jeffrey earned her Ph.D. in history from Rice University in 1972. Since then she has taught at Goucher College. Honored as an outstanding teacher, Jeffrey has been involved in faculty development activities and curriculum evaluation. Jeffrey's major publications include *Education for Children of the Poor* (1978); *Frontier Women: The Trans-Mississippi West, 1840–1880* (1979); and *Converting the West: A Biography of Narcissa Whitman* (1991). She is the author of many articles on the lives and perceptions of nineteenth-century women. She wrote Parts III and IV in collaboration with Peter Frederick and acted as a general editor of this book.

John R. Howe received his Ph.D. from Yale University in 1962. At the University of Minnesota his teaching interests include early American politics and relations between Native Americans and whites. His major publications include *The Changing Political Thought of John Adams* (1966) and *From the Revolution Through the Age of Jackson* (1973). His major research currently involves a manuscript entitled "The Transformation of Public Life in Revolutionary America." Howe wrote Part II of this book.

Peter J. Frederick received his Ph.D. in history from the University of California, Berkeley, in 1966. Innovative student-centered teaching of American history has been the focus of his career at California State University, Hayward, and since 1970 at Wabash College (1992–1994 at Carleton College). Recognized nationally as a distinguished teacher and for his many articles and workshops for faculty on teaching and learning, Frederick has also written several articles on life-writing and a book, *Knights of the Golden Rule: The Intellectual as Christian Social Reformer in the 1890s.* He coordinated and edited all the "Recovering the Past" sections and coauthored Parts III and IV of this book.

Allen F. Davis earned his Ph.D. from the University of Wisconsin in 1959. A former president of the American Studies Association, he is a professor of history at Temple University and Director of the Center for Public History. He is the author of *Spearheads for Reform: The Social Settlements and the Progressive Movement* (1967) and *American Heroine: The Life and Legend of Jane Addams* (1973). He is coauthor of *Still Philadelphia* (1983), *Philadelphia Stories* (1987), and *One Hundred Years at Hull-House* (1990). He is currently working on a book on masculine culture in America. Davis wrote Part V of this book.

Allan M. Winkler received his Ph.D. from Yale in 1974. He is presently teaching at Miami University, where he chairs the History Department. His books include *The Politics of Propaganda: The Office of War Information, 1942–1945* (1978); *Modern America: The United States from the Second World War to the Present* (1985); *Home Front U.S.A.: America During World War II* (1986); and *Life Under a Cloud: American Anxiety About the Atom* (1993). His research centers on the connections between public policy and popular mood in modern American history. Winkler wrote Part VI of this book.

A Visual Guide To

THE AMERICAN PEOPLE

Creating a Nation and a Society

THIRD EDITION

Gary B. Nash *University of California, Los Angeles*
Julie Roy Jeffrey *Goucher College*
John R. Howe *University of Minnesota*
Peter J. Frederick *Wabash College*
Allen F. Davis *Temple University*
Allan M. Winkler *Miami University of Ohio*

One of the most successful American history survey texts in print, *The American People* considers the rich, varied fabric of social history within a larger analytical context. Drawing on the expertise of a renowned team of authors, the text highlights the interaction of social, political, economic, cultural, religious, and technological forces in a clear, cohesive organizational framework. The text examines recurring themes in American history, including the adaptability of our political system to a changing society; liberty and authority; the reform impulse in American society; and the struggle for national unity and cultural diversity. The third edition features a stronger focus on environmental history, including a new section on The Dust Bowl of the 1930s, as well as new environmental coverage in chapters on industrialization and sections on farming. Chapter 9, "Society and Politics in the Early Republic," has been revised and reorganized to include an examination of the society and economy of pre-industrial America. Also included are new discussions and analyses of economic and demographic changes during the last decades of the 20th century. All maps and graphs in the text are now captioned for added clarity and visual appeal, allowing students to better read and comprehend them. An unparalleled pedagogical program and supplements package top off this outstanding text.

Increased Coverage of Environmental History

A stronger emphasis on **environmental history** enhances student interest and maintains currency by making connections between the progress of American society and its effect on the environment.

A farmer and his son race to find shelter from a dust storm in Cimarron County, Oklahoma, in 1936. A combination of factors, including overplanting which destroyed the natural sod of the Great Plains, resulted in the devastating dust storms of the 1930s. Without sod to protect the soil from the wind, thousands of acres of the Great Plains just blew away.

The Dust Bowl: An Ecological Disaster

The ultimate goal of the New Deal was to alter and stabilize agriculture through planning and by promoting efficiency. Some farmers profited from the agricultural legislation of the 1930s, but those who tried to farm on the Great Plains fell victim to years of drought and dust storms. Record heat waves and below-average rainfall in the 1930s turned an area from the Oklahoma panhandle to western Kansas into a giant dust bowl. A single storm on May 11, 1934, removed 300 million tons of top soil and turned day into night. Between 1932 and 1939 there was an average of fifty storms a year. Cities kept their street lights on for twenty-four hours a day. Dust covered everything from food to bedspreads and piled up in dunes in city streets and barnyards. Thousands died of "dust pneumonia." One woman remembered what it was like at night: "A trip for water to rinse the grit from our lips, and then back to bed with washcloths over our noses, we try to lie still, because every turn stirs the dust on the blankets."

A 1936 survey of twenty counties in the heart of the dust bowl concluded that 97.6 percent of the land suffered from erosion and more than 50 percent was seriously damaged. By the end of the decade 10,000 farm homes were abandoned to the elements, and 9 million acres of farmland was reduced to a wasteland. By the end of the decade three and a half million people had abandoned their farms and joined a massive migration to find a better life. Not all were forced out by the dust storms; some fell victim to large-scale agriculture, and many tenant farmers and hired hands were expendable during the depression. In most cases they not only lost their jobs, but they also were evicted from their houses. More than 350,000 left Oklahoma during the decade and moved to California, a place that seemed to many like the promised land. But the word *"Okie"* came to mean any farm migrant. The plight of these wayfarers was immortalized by John Steinbeck in his novel about the Joad family, *The Grapes of Wrath* (1939). The next year John Ford made a powerful movie based on the book staring Henry Fonda as Tom Joad. Many Americans sympathized with the plight of the embattled farm family trying to escape the dust bowl and find a better life in California; others interpreted their defeat as a symbol of the failure of the American dream.

The dust bowl was a natural disaster, but it was aided and exaggerated by human actions and inactions. The semiarid plains west of the 98th meridian were not suitable for intensive agriculture. Overgrazing, too much plowing, and indiscriminate planting over a period of sixty years exposed the thin soil to the elements. When the winds came in the 1930s, much of the land simply blew away. In the end it was a matter of too little government planning and regulation and too many farmers using new technology to exploit natural resources for their own gain.

The Roosevelt administration did try to deal with the problem. The Taylor Grazing Act of 1934 restricted the use of the public range in an attempt to prevent overgrazing, and it also closed 80 million acres of grassland to further settlement. The Civilian Conservation Corps and other New Deal agencies planted trees, and the Soil Conservation Service promoted drought-resistant crops and contour plowing, but it was too little and too late. Even worse, according to some authorities, government measures applied after the disaster of 1930 encouraged farmers to return to raising wheat

Recovering the Past

In each chapter, **Recovering the Past** Boxes put students in touch with a compelling variety of evidence—from tax lists and folk tales to diaries and tombstones—that historians have used in reconstructing and interpreting the past. Each Recovering the Past Box provides basic information about the source and its use by historians and then raises questions for students to consider as they study each reproduced example.

RECOVERING THE PAST

Popular Music

One way to recover the past is through music. Popular songs not only provide insight into attitudes and beliefs but also quickly convey the mood and feelings of an era. Through their lyrics, songwriters express the hopes and fears of a people and the emotional tone of an age. Consider, for example, the powerful message conveyed in the Democratic party adoption of "Happy Days Are Here Again" as a campaign theme during the Great Depression. The decline of pop music and the rise of rock and roll in the 1950s tells historians a great deal about the mood of that period. Similarly, the popularity of both folk music and rock in the 1960s provides another way of following social change in that turbulent decade.

The music of the 1960s moved beyond the syrupy ballads of the early 1950s and the rock and roll movement that Elvis Presley helped launch in the middle of the decade. As the United States confronted the challenges of the counterculture and the crosscurrents of political and social reform, new kinds of music began to be played.

Folk music took off at the start of the period. Building on a tradition launched by Woody Guthrie, Pete Seeger, and the Weavers, Joan Baez was one of the first to become popular. Accompanying herself on a guitar as she performed at coffee shops in Harvard Square and at the Newport Folk Festival, she soon overwhelmed audiences with her crystal-clear voice. She sang ballads, laments, and spirituals like "We Shall Overcome" and became caught up in the protest activities of the period.

Equally active was Bob Dylan, who grew up playing rock and roll in high school, then

folk music in college at the University of Minnesota. Disheveled and gravelly-voiced, he wrote remarkable songs like "Blowin' in the Wind" that were soon sung by other artists like Peter, Paul and Mary as well. His song "The Times They Are A-Changin'" (excerpted here) captured the inexorable force of the student protest movement best of all.

But the 1960s were marked by far more than folk music alone. In the early 1960s, an English group from Liverpool began to build a following in Great Britain. In early 1964, the Beatles released "I Want to Hold Your Hand" in the United States and appeared on the pop-

ular Ed Sullivan television show. Within weeks, Beatles' songs held the first, second, third, fourth, and fifth positions on the *Billboard* singles chart, and *Meet the Beatles* became the best-selling LP record to date. With *Sergeant Pepper's Lonely Hearts Club Band* a few years later, the Beatles branched out in new musical directions and reflected the influence of the counterculture with songs like "Lucy in the Sky with Diamonds" (which some people said referred to the hallucinogenic drug, LSD).

Mick Jagger and the Rolling Stones followed at the end of the decade. Another English group that changed the nature of American music, the Stones played blues-based rock music that proclaimed a commitment to drugs, sex, and a decadent life of social upheaval. Jagger was an aggressive, sometimes violent showman on stage, whose androgynous style showed his contempt for conventional sexual norms. Other artists, like Jim Morrison of the Doors and Janis Joplin, reflected the same intensity of the new rock world, and both died from drug overdoses.

Meanwhile, other groups were setting off in different directions. On the pop scene, Motown Records in Detroit popularized a new kind of black rhythm and blues. By 1960, the gospel-pop-soul fusion was gaining followers. By the late 1960s, Motown Records was one of the largest black-owned companies in America and one of the most successful independent recording ventures in
Wonder, the Temptatio
were among the group
mously popular. The Su
Ross, epitomized the
such hits as "Where Did

What songs come t
think of the 1960s? How
from that of the 1950s?
you about the period?

From "The Times They Are A-Changin'"

Come mothers and fathers
Throughout the land
And don't criticize
What you can't understand
Your sons and daughters
Are beyond your command
There's a battle
Outside and it's ragin'
It'll soon shake your windows
And rattle your walls...
For the times they are a-changin'.

Look at the lyrics for "The Times They Are A-Changin'" reprinted here. What do they tell you about the social upheaval of the 1960s? What, if anything, does the song imply can be done about the changes in the air? What other songs can you think of that give you a similar handle on the decade?

Significant Factors Promoting Economic Growth, 1820–1860

Factor	*Important Features*	*Contribution to Growth*
Abundant natural resources	Acquisition of new territories (Louisiana Purchase, Florida, trans-Mississippi West); exploitation and discovery of eastern resources	Provided raw materials and energy vital to economic transformation
Substantial population growth	Increase from 9 million in 1820 to over 30 million in 1860; due to natural increase of population and, especially after 1840, to rising immigration; importance of immigration from Ireland, Germany	Provided workers and consumers necessary for economic growth.; immigration increased diversity of work force with complex results, among them supply of capital and technological know-how
Transportation revolution	Improvement of roads; extensive canal building, 1817–1837; increasing importance of railroad construction thereafter; by 1860, 30,000 miles of tracks; steamboats facilitate travel on water	Facilitated movement of peoples, goods, and information; drew people into national economy market; stimulated agricultural expansion, regional crop specialization; decreased costs of shipping goods; strengthened ties between Northeast, Midwest
Capital investment	Investments by European investors and American interests; importance of mercantile capital and banks, insurance companies in funneling capital to economic enterprises	Provided capital to support variety of new economic enterprises, improvements in transportation
Government support	Local, state, national legislation; loans favoring enterprise; judicial decisions	Provided capital, privileges, supportive climate for economic enterprises
Industrialization	New methods of producing goods, with and without involvement of machinery	Produced more numerous, cheaper goods for mass market; transformed classes, nature of work; affected distribution of wealth, individual opportunity

working-class Americans, a third of whom lost their jobs during years of depression. Moreover, because regional economies were increasingly linked, problems in one area tended to affect conditions in others.

Factors Fueling Economic Development

What accounted for this new phase of growth and economic development? As the box suggests, the abundance of natural resources and an expanding population provided the raw materials and the human brawn and brains that supported growth and transformation. Because the size of American families gradually shrank—in 1800, the average white woman bore seven children; by 1860, the number had declined to five—immi
(discussed in detail l
played an important par
workers, new household
so essential to economi
as the capital and tech
helped to shape America

Talking Boxes

Talking Boxes bring the saga of American history into sharper focus through charts, graphs, and tables that visually summarize significant discussions and draw meaningful comparisons between trends.

Timelines

Timelines in every chapter highlight a chronological progression of important events in the American past, giving additional emphasis to text material.

TIMELINE

1789	Treaty of Fort Harmar Knox's reports on Indian affairs
1790s	Second Great Awakening begins
1794	Battle of Fallen Timbers
1795	Treaty of Greenville
1796	Congress establishes Indian Factory System
1800	Capital moves to Washington
1801	Thomas Jefferson elected president Judiciary Act New Land Act
1802	Judiciary Act repealed
1803	Marbury v. Madison Louisiana Purchase
1803-1806	Lewis and Clark expedition
1803-1812	Napoleonic Wars resume British impress American sailors
1804	Jefferson reelected
1805-1807	Pike explores the West
1806	Non-Importation Act
1807	Embargo Act Chesapeake-Leopard affair Congress prohibits slave trade James Madison elected
1808	Cherokee legal code established
1809	Tecumseh's confederacy formed Non-Intercourse Act
1810	Macon's Bill No. 2
1811	Battle of Kithtippecanoe
1812	Madison reelected West Florida annexed War declared against Great Britain
1813	Battle of the Thames
1813-1814	Creek War
1814	Treaty of Ghent Battle of Horseshoe Bend
1814-1815	Hartford Convention
1815	Battle of New Orleans U.S. establishes military posts in trans-Mississippi West
1816	James Monroe elected Second United States Bank chartered
1819	Adams-Onis Treaty with Spain Spain cedes East Florida to United States McCulloch v. Maryland
1820	Land Act Missouri Compromise
1822	Diplomatic recognition of Latin American republics
1823	Monroe Doctrine proclaimed
1824	John Quincy Adams elected
1827	Cherokee adopt written constitution

Anecdotes, Chapter Overviews, Conclusions

Chapter-opening **Anecdotes** call attention to the experiences of ordinary or lesser-known Americans, showing how their lives shaped and were shaped by events in American history.

CHAPTER 10

Currents of Change in the Northeast and the Old Northwest

For her first eighteen years, Susan Warner was little touched by the far-reaching economic and social changes that were transforming the character of the country and her own city of New York. While some New Yorkers toiled to make a living by taking in piecework, and others responded to unsettling new means of producing goods by joining trade unions to agitate for wages that would enable them to "live as comfortable as others," Susan was surrounded by luxuries and privilege. Much of the year was spent in the family's townhouse in St. Mark's Place, not far from the home of the enormously rich real estate investor and fur trader, John Jacob Astor. There Susan acquired the social graces and skills appropriate for a girl of her position and

background. She had dancing and singing lessons, studied Italian and French, and learned the etiquette involved in receiving visitors and making calls. When the hot weather made life in New York unpleasant, the Warners escaped to the cooler airs of Canaan, where they had a summer house. Like any girl of her social class, Susan realized that her carefree existence could not last forever. With her marriage, which she confidently expected some time in the future, would come significant new responsibilities as a wife and mother, but not the end of the comfortable life to which she was accustomed.

But it was not marriage and motherhood that disrupted the pattern of Susan's life but financial disaster. Sheltered as she had been from the far-reaching and unsettling economic and social changes of the early nineteenth century, Susan discovered that she, too, was at the mercy of forces beyond her control. Her father, heretofore so successful a provider and parent, lost most of his fortune during the financial panic of 1837. Like others experiencing a sharp economic reversal, the Warners had to make radical adjustments. The fashionable home in St. Mark's Place and the pleasures of New York were left behind, exchanged for a more modest existence on an island in the Hudson River. Susan turned "housekeeper" and learned how to do tasks once relegated to others: sewing and making butter, pudding sauces, and johnny cake.

The change of residence and Susan's attempt to master domestic skills did not halt the family's financial decline. Prized possessions, including the piano and engravings, all symbols of the life the Warners had once taken for granted, eventually went up for auction. "When at last the men and the confusion were gone," Susan's younger sister, Anna, recalled, "then we woke up to life."

Waking up to life meant facing the necessity of making money. But what could Susan do to reverse sliding family fortunes? True, some women labored as factory operatives, domestics, seamstresses, or schoolteachers, but it was doubtful Susan could even imagine herself in any of these occupations. Her Aunt Fanny, however, had a suggestion that was more congenial to the genteel young woman. Knowing that the steam-powered printing press had revolutionized the publishing world and created a mass readership, much of it female, Aunt Fanny told her niece, "Sue, I believe if you would try, you could write a story." "Whether she added 'that, would sell,' I am not sure," recalled Anna later, "but of course that was what she meant."

Taking Aunt Fanny's advice to heart, Susan started to write a novel that would sell. She constructed her story around the trials of a young orphan girl, Ellen Montgomery. As Ellen suffered one reverse after another, she learned the lessons that allowed her to survive and eventually triumph over adversity: piety, self-denial, discipline, and the power of a mother's love. Entitled *The Wide, Wide World,* the novel was accepted for publication only after the mother of the publisher, George Putnam, read it and told her son, "If you never publish another book, you must make *The Wide, Wide World* available for your fellow men." A modest 750 copies were printed. Much to the surprise of the cautious Putnam, if not to his mother, 13 editions were published within two years. *The Wide, Wide World* became the first American novel to sell more than a million copies. It was one of the best sellers of the century.

Long before she realized the book's success, Susan, always aware of the need to make money, was working on a new story. Drawing on her own experience of economic and social reversal, Susan described the spiritual and intellectual life of a young girl thrust into poverty after an early life of luxury in New York. Entitled *Queechy,* this novel was also a great success.

Though her fame as a writer made Susan Warner unusual, her books' popularity suggested how well they spoke to the concerns and interests of a broad readership. The background of social and financial uncertainty, with its sudden changes of fortune, so prominent in several of the novels, captured the reality and fears of a fluid society in the process of transformation. While one French writer was amazed that "in America a three-volume novel is devoted to the history of the moral progress of a girl of thirteen," pious heroines like Ellen Montgomery, who struggled to master their passions and urges toward independence, were shining exemplars of the new norms for middle-class women. Their successful efforts to

Susan Warner's life and her novels serve as an introduction to the far-reaching changes that this chapter explores. Between 1820 and 1860, as Susan Warner discovered, economic transformations in the Northeast and the Old Northwest reshaped economic, social, cultural, and political life. Though most Americans still lived in rural settings rather than in factory towns or cities, economic growth and the new industrial mode of production affected them through the creation of new goods, opportunities, and markets. In urban communities and factory towns, the new economic order ushered in new forms of work, new class arrangements, and new forms of social strife.

After discussing the factors that fueled antebellum growth, the chapter turns to the industrial world, where so many of the new patterns of work and life appeared. An investigation of urbanization reveals shifting class arrangements and values as well as rising social and racial tensions. Finally, an examination of rural communities in the East and on the frontier in the Old Northwest highlights the transformation of these two sections of the country. Between 1840 and 1860, industrialization and economic growth increasingly knit them together.

Chapter Overviews link the anecdotes to themes and topics of each chapter.

Economic Growth

Between 1820 and 1860, the American economy entered a new and more complex stage of development as it moved away from its reliance on agriculture as the major source of growth, toward an industrial and technological future. In this period of general national expansion, real per capita output grew an average of 2 percent annually between 1820 and 1840 and slightly less between 1840 and 1860. This doubling of per capita income over a 40-year period suggests that many Americans were enjoying a rising standard of living.

Though expanding, the economy was also unstable, as the Warners discovered so dramatically. Periods of boom (1822–1834, mid-1840s–1850s) alternated with periods of bust (1816–1821, 1837–1843). As never before, Americans faced dramatic and recurrent shifts in the availability of jobs and goods and in prices and wages. Particularly at risk were working-class Americans, a third of whom lost their jobs during years of depression. Moreover, because regional economies were increasingly linked, problems in one area tended to affect conditions in others.

Factors Fueling Economic Development

What accounted for this new phase of growth and economic development? As the box suggests, the abundance of natural resources and an expanding population provided the raw materials and the human brawn and brains that supported growth and transformation. Because the size of American families gradually shrank—in 1800, the average white woman bore seven children; by 1860, the number had declined to five—immigration from Europe (discussed in detail later in the chapter) played an important part in providing the new workers, new households, and new consumers so essential to economic development as well as the capital and technological ideas that helped to shape American growth.

Improved transportation played a key role in bringing about economic and geographic expansion. Early in the century, high freight rates discouraged producti
kets and the exploitation
primitive transportation hi
tlement. As one disgruntled
pointed out, "a coal min
United States not more th

valuable ores of iron and other materials, and both of them be useless...as the price of land carriage is too great to be borne by either." During the 1820s and 1830s, however, canal-building projects dramatically transformed this situation. The 363-mile-long Erie Canal, the last link in a chain of waterways binding New York City to the Great Lakes and the Northwest, was the most impressive of these new canals. The volume of goods and people it carried at low cost, the economic advantages it conferred on those within its reach (suggested by both the chart on inland freight rates and the talking box) prompted the construction of over 3,000 miles of canals by 1840, primarily in eastern and midwestern states.

Even at the height of the canal boom, politicians, promoters, and others, impressed with Britain's success with railways, also supported the construction of railroads. Railroads, unlike canals that might freeze during the winter, were capable of operating all year-round. Nor did they need large amounts of water to operate, as canals did. They could be built almost anywhere, an advantage that encouraged Baltimore merchants, envious of New York's water link to the Northwest, to begin the Baltimore & Ohio Railroad in 1828.

Despite the interest in and advantages of railroads, there were technical problems to resolve; for example, the first trains jumped their tracks and spewed sparks, setting nearby fields ablaze. But such difficulties were quickly overcome. By 1840, there were 3,000 miles of track, most in the Northeast. Another 5,000 miles were laid during the 1840s, and by the end of the 1850s, total mileage soared to 30,000.

Conclusions briefly sum up the premise behind the chapter and serve as bridges to the ensuing chapter.

CONCLUSION

The Character of Progress

Between 1820 and 1860, the United States experienced tremendous growth and economic development. Transportation improvements facilitated the movement of people, goods, and ideas. Larger markets stimulated both agricultural and industrial production. There were more goods and ample food for the American people. Cities and towns were established and thrived. Visitors constantly remarked on the amazing bustle and rapid pace of American life. The United States was, in the words of one Frenchman, "one gigantic workshop, over the entrance of which there is the blazing inscription 'NO ADMISSION HERE, EXCEPT ON BUSINESS.'"

Although the wonders of American development dazzled foreigners and Americans alike, economic growth had its costs. Expansion was cyclic, and financial panics and depression punctuated the era. Industrial profits were based partly on low wages to workers. Time-honored routes to economic independence disappeared, and a large class of unskilled, impoverished workers appeared in American cities. Growing inequality characterized urban and rural life, prompting some labor activists to criticize new economic and social arrangements. But workers, still largely unorganized, did not speak with one voice. Ethnic, racial, and religious diversity divided Americans in new and troubling ways.

Yet a basic optimism and sense of pride also characterized the age. To observers, however, it frequently seemed as if the East and the Old Northwest were responsible for the country's achievements. During these decades, many noted that the paths between the East, Northwest, and South seemed to diverge. The rise of King Cotton in the South, where slave rather than free labor formed the foundation of the economy, created a new kind of tension in American life, as the next chapter will show.

Comparative Chronologies

Comparative Chronologies, which open each part, compare the great milestones of each era in American history under the following categories: political and diplomatic; social and economic; and cultural and technological. These chronologies chart history's course and leave readers with a coherent, organized impression of events that will guide their study.

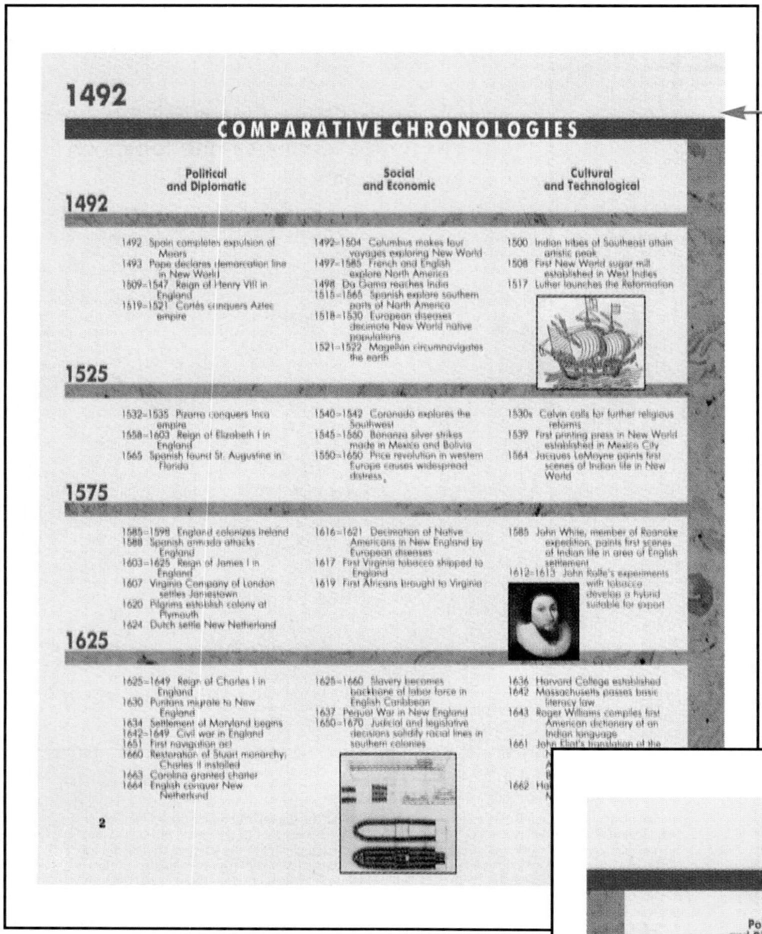

1492

COMPARATIVE CHRONOLOGIES

	Political and Diplomatic	Social and Economic	Cultural and Technological
1492	1492 Spain completes expulsion of Moors 1493 Pope declares demarcation line in New World 1509–1547 Reign of Henry VIII in England 1519–1521 Cortés conquers Aztec empire	1492–1504 Columbus makes four voyages exploring New World 1497–1585 French and English explore North America 1498 Da Gama reaches India 1515–1565 Spanish explore southern parts of North America 1518–1530 European diseases decimate New World native populations 1521–1522 Magellan circumnavigates the earth	1500 Indian tribes of Southeast attain artistic peak 1508 First New World sugar mill established in West Indies 1517 Luther launches the Reformation
1525	1532–1535 Pizarro conquers Inca empire 1558–1603 Reign of Elizabeth I in England 1565 Spanish found St. Augustine in Florida	1540–1542 Coronado explores the Southwest 1545–1560 Bonanza silver strikes made in Mexico and Bolivia 1550–1650 Price revolution in western Europe causes widespread distress	1530s Calvin calls for further religious reforms 1539 First printing press in New World established in Mexico City 1564 Jacques LeMoyne paints first scenes of Indian life in New World
1575	1585–1598 England colonizes Ireland 1588 Spanish armada attacks England 1603–1625 Reign of James I in England 1607 Virginia Company of London settles Jamestown 1620 Pilgrims establish colony at Plymouth 1624 Dutch settle New Netherland	1616–1621 Decimation of Native Americans in New England by European diseases 1617 First Virginia tobacco shipped to England 1619 First Africans brought to Virginia	1585 John White, member of Roanoke expedition, paints first scenes of Indian life in area of English settlement 1612–1613 John Rolfe's experiments with tobacco develop a hybrid suitable for export
1625	1625–1649 Reign of Charles I in England 1630 Puritans migrate to New England 1634 Settlement of Maryland begins 1642–1649 Civil war in England 1651 First navigation act 1660 Restoration of Stuart monarchy; Charles II installed 1663 Carolina granted charter 1664 English conquer New Netherland	1625–1660 Slavery becomes backbone of labor force in English Caribbean 1637 Pequot War in New England 1650–1670 Judicial and legislative decisions solidify racial lines in southern colonies	1636 Harvard College established 1642 Massachusetts passes basic literacy law 1643 Roger Williams compiles first American dictionary of an Indian language 1661 John Eliot's translation of the 1662 Ha

2

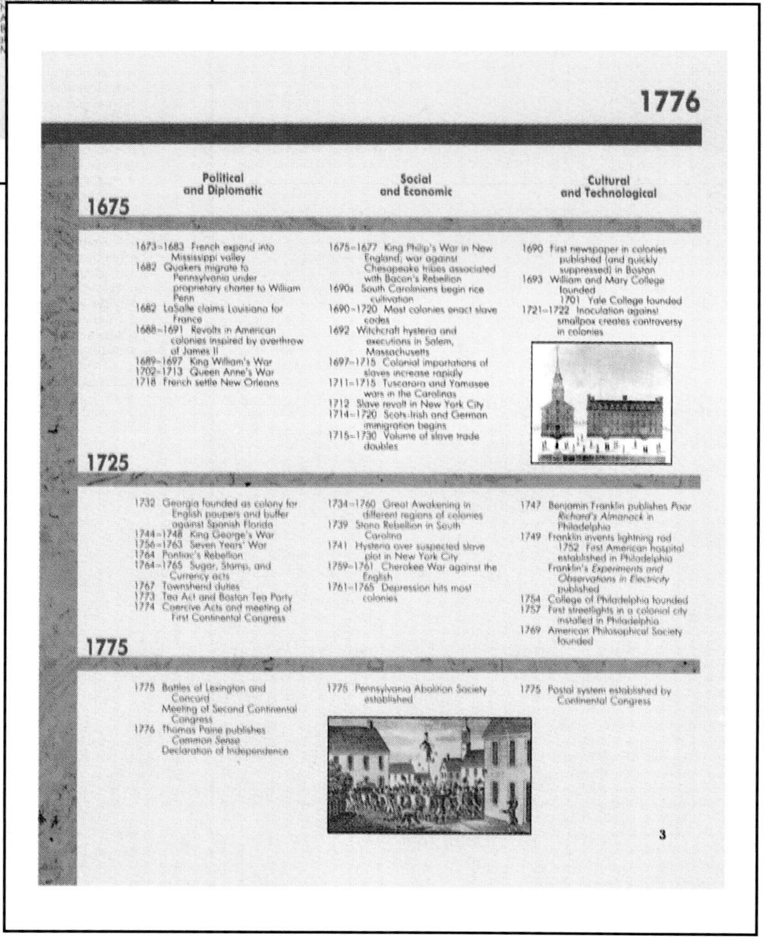

1776

	Political and Diplomatic	Social and Economic	Cultural and Technological
1675	1673–1683 French expand into Mississippi valley 1682 Quakers migrate to Pennsylvania under proprietary charter to William Penn 1682 LaSalle claims Louisiana for France 1688–1691 Revolts in American colonies inspired by overthrow of James II 1689–1697 King William's War 1702–1713 Queen Anne's War 1718 French settle New Orleans	1675–1677 King Philip's War in New England; war against Chesapeake tribes associated with Bacon's Rebellion 1690s South Carolinians begin rice cultivation 1690–1720 Most colonies enact slave codes 1692 Witchcraft hysteria and executions in Salem, Massachusetts 1697–1715 Colonial importations of slaves increase rapidly 1711–1715 Tuscarora and Yamasee wars in the Carolinas 1712 Slave revolt in New York City 1714–1720 Scots-Irish and German immigration begins 1715–1730 Volume of slave trade doubles	1690 First newspaper in colonies published (and quickly suppressed) in Boston 1693 William and Mary College founded 1701 Yale College founded 1721–1722 Inoculation against smallpox creates controversy in colonies
1725	1732 Georgia founded as colony for English paupers and buffer against Spanish Florida 1744–1748 King George's War 1756–1763 Seven Years' War 1764 Pontiac's Rebellion 1764–1765 Sugar, Stamp, and Currency acts 1767 Townshend duties 1773 Tea Act and Boston Tea Party 1774 Coercive Acts and meeting of First Continental Congress	1734–1760 Great Awakening in different regions of colonies 1739 Stono Rebellion in South Carolina 1741 Hysteria over suspected slave plot in New York City 1759–1761 Cherokee War against the English 1761–1765 Depression hits most colonies	1747 Benjamin Franklin publishes *Poor Richard's Almanack* in Philadelphia 1749 Franklin invents lightning rod 1752 First American hospital established in Philadelphia Franklin's *Experiments and Observations in Electricity* published 1754 College of Philadelphia founded 1757 First streetlights in a colonial city installed in Philadelphia 1769 American Philosophical Society founded
1775	1775 Battles of Lexington and Concord Meeting of Second Continental Congress 1776 Thomas Paine publishes *Common Sense* Declaration of Independence	1775 Pennsylvania Abolition Society established	1775 Postal system established by Continental Congress

3

Map Captions

Map Captions, added to every map in the text, help students understand and interpret the information presented graphically in the text.

City Plan of Boston, 1772
Boston's many churches became important political meeting places in the tumultuous decade leading toward the outbreak of war in 1775.

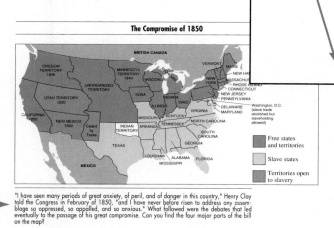

The Compromise of 1850

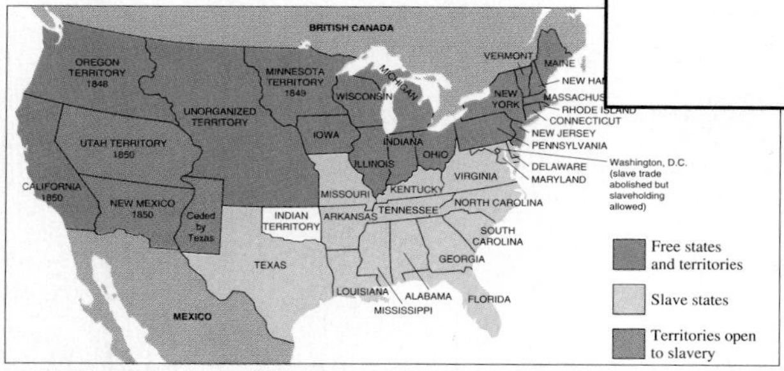

"I have seen many periods of great anxiety, of peril, and of danger in this country," Henry Clay told the Congress in February of 1850, "and I have never before risen to address any assemblage so oppressed, so appalled, and so anxious." What followed were the debates that led eventually to the passage of his great compromise. Can you find the four major parts of the bill on the map?

The Compromise of 1850

Taylor won the election by avoiding slavery issues, but as president he could no longer do so. As he was inaugurated in 1849, four compelling issues faced the nation. The rush of some 80,000 unruly gold miners to California qualified that territory for admission to the Union. But California's entry as a free state would upset the balance between slave and free states in the Senate that had prevailed since 1820.

The unresolved status of the Mexican cession in the Southwest posed a second problem. The longer the area was left unorganized, the louder local inhabitants called for an application of either the Wilmot Proviso or the Calhoun doctrine of protecting the extension of slavery. The boundary between Texas and the New Mexico Territory was also in dispute, with Texas claiming lands all the way to Santa Fe. This increased northern fears that Texas might be divided into five or six slave states.

The existence of slavery and one of the largest slave markets in North America in the nation's capital was a third problem, especially to abolitionists. Fourth, Southerners resented the lax federal enforcement of the Fugitive Slave Act of 1793. They called for a stronger act that would end the protection northerners gave runaway slaves as they fled along the underground railroad to Canada.

Although Taylor was a newcomer to politics (he had never even voted in a presidential election before 1848), he tried to tackle these problems in a statesmanlike, if evasive, manner. He thought he could sidestep the conflict over slavery in the territories by inviting California and New Mexico to apply immediately for statehood, presumably as free states. But it was not long before his efforts had alienated both southern supporters like Calhoun and mainstream Whig leaders like Clay and Webster.

Early in 1850, therefore, the old compromiser, Henry Clay, sought to regain control of

The Union Reconstructed

In April 1864, one year before Lincoln's assassination, Robert Allston died of pneumonia. His daughter, Elizabeth, was left with a "sense of terrible desolation and sorrow" as the Civil War raged around her, and she and her mother took over the affairs of their many rice plantations. With Yankee troops moving through coastal South Carolina in the late winter of 1864–1865, Elizabeth's sorrow turned to "terror" as Union soldiers arrived seeking liquor, firearms, and hidden valuables. The Allston women endured an insulting search and then fled. In a later raid, Yankee troops encouraged the Allston slaves to take furniture and other household goods from the Big Houses, some of which the blacks returned when the Yankees were gone. But before they left, the Union soldiers, in their role as liberators, gave the keys to the crop barns to the semifree slaves.

When the war was over, Adele Allston took an oath of allegiance to the United States and secured a written order commanding the blacks to relinquish these keys. She and Elizabeth made plans to return in the early summer of 1865 to resume control of the family plantations, thereby reestablishing white authority. She was assured that although the blacks had guns and were determined to have the means to a livelihood, "no outrage has been committed against the whites except in the matter of property." But property was the key issue. Possession of the keys to the barns, Elizabeth wrote, would be the "test case" of whether former masters or their former slaves would control land, labor and its fruits, and even subtle aspects of interpersonal relations.

Not without some fear, Adele and Elizabeth Allston rode up in a carriage to their former home, Nightingale Hall, to confront their ex-slaves. To their surprise, a pleasant reunion took place. The Allston women greeted the blacks by name, inquired after their children, and caught up on the affairs of those with whom they had lived closely for many years. A trusted black foreman handed over the keys to the barns. This harmonious scene was repeated elsewhere.

But at Guendalos, a plantation owned by a son absent during most of the war fighting with the Confederate army, the Allston women met a very different situation. As their carriage arrived and moved slowly toward the crop barns, a defiant group of armed ex-slaves lined both sides of the road, following the carriage as it passed by. Tension grew when the carriage stopped. A former black driver, Uncle Jacob, was unsure whether to yield the keys to the barns full of rice and corn, put there by black labor. Mrs. Allston insisted. As Uncle Jacob hesitantly began to hand the keys to her, an angry young man shouted out: "Ef yu gie up de key, blood'll flow." Uncle Jacob slowly slipped the keys back into his pocket.

The tension increased as the blacks sang freedom songs and brandished hoes, pitchforks, and guns in an effort to discourage anyone from going to town for help. Two blacks, however, left the plantation to find some Union military officers to come settle the issue of the keys, most likely on the side of the Allstons. As Adele and Elizabeth waited, word finally arrived that the Union officers, who were difficult to locate, would no doubt be found the next day and would come to Guendalos. The Allstons spent the night safely, if restlessly, in their house. Early the next morning, they were awakened by a knock at the unlocked front door. Adele slowly opened the door, and there stood Uncle Jacob. Without a word, he gave her the keys.

The story of the keys reveals most of the essential human ingredients of the Reconstruction era. Despite defeat and surrender, southern whites were determined to resume control of both land and labor. Rebellion aside, the law, property titles, and federal enforcement were generally on the side of the original owners of the land. The Allston women were friendly to the blacks in a genuine but maternal way and insisted on the restoration of the deferential relationships that existed before the war. Adele and Elizabeth, in short, both feared and cared about their former slaves.

The black freedmen likewise revealed mixed feelings toward their former owners. At different plantations, they demonstrated a variety of emotions: anger, loyalty, love, resentment, and pride. Respect was paid to the person of the Allstons but not to their property and crops. The action of the blacks indicated that what they wanted was not revenge but economic independence and freedom.

In this encounter between former slaves and their mistresses, the role of the northern federal officials is most revealing. The Union soldiers, literally and symbolically, gave the keys of freedom to the blacks but did not stay around long enough to guarantee that freedom. Although encouraging the freedmen to plunder the master's house and take possession of the crops, in the crucial encounter northern officials had disappeared. Understanding the limits of northern help, Uncle Jacob handed the keys to land and liberty back to his former owner. The blacks at Guendalos knew that if they wanted to ensure their freedom, they had to do it themselves.

The goals of the groups at the Allston plantations were in conflict. The theme of this chapter is the story of what happened to people's various dreams as they sought to form new social, economic, and political relationships during Reconstruction.

For much of the twentieth century, under the influence of prosouthern historians and Hollywood filmmakers, Reconstruction was seen as a disgraceful period in which vindictive northern Radical Republicans imposed a harsh rule of evil carpetbaggers, scalawags, and illiterate blacks on the helpless, defeated South. *Gone with the Wind* reflects this view. In 1935, the brilliant black scholar W. E. B. Du Bois challenged this interpretation, suggesting instead that an economic struggle over land and the exploitation of black workers was the crucial focus of Reconstruction. Other historians have shown the beginnings of biracial cooperation and political participation in some southern states and the eventual violent repression of the freedmen's dreams of land, schooling, and votes.

This chapter reflects this later interpretation, enriched by an awareness of the ambiguity of human motives and behavior. Amid devastation and divisions of class and race, Civil War survivors sought to put their lives back together again. Victorious but variously motivated northern officials, defeated but defiant southern planters, and impoverished but hopeful black freedmen—all had strong needs and dreams. In no way could all fulfill their conflicting goals, yet each had to try. This situation guaranteed that the Reconstruction era would be divisive, leaving a mixed legacy of human gains and losses.

The Bittersweet Aftermath of War

"There are sad changes in store for both races," the daughter of a Georgia planter wrote in her diary early in the summer of 1865, adding, "I wonder the Yankees do not shudder to behold their work." In order to understand the bittersweet nature of Reconstruction, we must look at the state of the nation in the spring of 1865, shortly after the assassination of President Lincoln.

The United States in 1865

The "Union" was in a state of constitutional crisis in April 1865. The status of the 11 states of the for-

Conflicting Goals During Reconstruction

Victorious Northern ("Radical") Republicans

- Justify the war by remaking southern society in the image of the North
- Inflict political but not physical or economic punishment on Confederate leaders
- Continue programs of economic progress begun during the war: high tariffs, railroad subsidies, national banking
- Maintain the Republican party in power
- Help the freedmen make the transition to full freedom by providing them with the tools of citizenship (suffrage) and equal economic opportunity

Northern Moderates (Republicans and Democrats)

- Quickly establish peace and order, reconciliation between North and South
- Bestow upon the southern states leniency, amnesty, and merciful readmission to the Union
- Perpetuate land ownership, free labor, market competition, and other capitalist values
- Promote local self-determination of economic and social issues, limit interference by the national government
- Provide limited support for black suffrage

Old Southern Planter Aristocracy (Ex-Confederates)

- Ensure protection from black uprising and prevent excessive freedom for former slaves
- Secure amnesty, pardon, and restoration of confiscated lands
- Restore traditional plantation-based market-crop economy with blacks as cheap labor force
- Restore traditional political leaders in the states
- Restore traditional paternalistic race relations as basis of social order

New "Other South": Yeoman Farmers and Ex-Whigs (Unionists)

- Quickly establish peace and order, reconciliation between North and South
- Achieve recognition of loyalty and economic value of yeoman farmers
- Create greater diversity in southern economy: capital investments in railroads, factories, and the diversification of agriculture
- Displace the planter aristocracy with new leaders drawn from new economic interests
- Limit the rights and powers of freedmen; extend suffrage to only the educated few

Black Freedmen

- Secure physical protection from abuse and terror by local whites
- Achieve economic independence through land ownership (40 acres and a mule) and equal access to trades
- Receive educational opportunity and foster the development of family and cultural bonds
- Obtain equal civil rights and protection under the law
- Commence political participation through the right to vote

mer Confederate States of America was unclear. They had claimed the right to secede, were successful for a time, but finally had failed. The North had denied the South's constitutional right to secede but needed four years of civil war and over 600,000 deaths to win the point. Were the 11 states part of the Union or not? Lincoln's official position had been that the southern states had never left the Union, which was "constitutionally indestructible." As a result of their rebellion, they were only "out of their proper relation" with the United States. The president, therefore, as commander in chief, had the authority to decide on the basis for setting relations right and proper again.

Lincoln's congressional opponents argued that by declaring war on the Union, the Confederate states had broken their constitutional ties and reverted to a kind of prestatehood status like territories or "conquered provinces." Congress, therefore, which decided on the admission of new states, should resolve the constitutional issues and assert its authority over the reconstruction process. In this conflict between Congress and the president was a powerful struggle between two branches of the national government. As has happened during nearly every war, the executive branch took on broad powers necessary for rapid mobilization of resources and domestic security. Many people believed, however, that Lincoln went far beyond his constitutional authority. As soon as the war was over, Congress sought to reassert its authority, as it would do after every subsequent war.

The United States in 1865: Crisis at the End of the Civil War

- *Military casualties:*

360,000	Union soldiers dead
260,000	Confederate soldiers dead
620,000	Total dead
375,000	Seriously wounded and maimed
995,000	Casualties nationwide in a total male population of 15 million (nearly 1 in 15)

- *Physical and economic crisis:* The South devastated, its railroads, industry, and some major cities in ruins, its fields and livestock wasted
- *Constitutional crisis:* Eleven ex-Confederate states not a part of the Union, their status unclear and future status uncertain
- *Political crisis:* Republican party (entirely of the North) dominant in Congress; a former Democratic slaveholder from Tennessee, Andrew Johnson, in the presidency
- *Social crisis:* Nearly 4 million black freedmen throughout the South facing challenges of survival and freedom, along with thousands of hungry demobilized white southern soldiers and displaced white families
- *Psychological crisis:* Incalculable stores of resentment, bitterness, anger, and despair throughout North and South

In April 1865, the Republican party ruled victorious and virtually alone. Although less than a dozen years old, the Republicans had made immense achievements in the eyes of the northern public. They had won the war, preserved the Union, and freed the slaves. Moreover, they had enacted most of the old Federalist-Whig economic programs on behalf of free labor and free enterprise: a high protective tariff, a national banking system, broad use of the power to tax and to borrow and print money, generous federal appropriations for internal improvements, the Homestead Act for western farmers, and an act to establish land-grant colleges to teach agricultural and mechanical skills. Alexander Hamilton, John Quincy Adams, and Henry Clay might all have applauded. Despite these achievements, the Republican party was still an uneasy grouping of former Whigs, Know-Nothings, Unionist Democrats, and antislavery idealists.

The Democratic party, by contrast, was in shambles. Republicans depicted southern Democrats as rebels, murderers, and traitors; northern Democrats as weak-willed, disloyal, and opposed to economic growth and progress. Nevertheless, it had been politically important in 1864 for the Republicans to show that the war was a bipartisan effort. A Jacksonian Democrat and Unionist from Tennessee, the tactless Andrew Johnson, had therefore been nominated as Lincoln's vice-president. In April 1865, he headed the government.

The United States in the spring of 1865 was a picture of stark economic contrasts. Northern cities hummed with productive activity, while southern cities lay in ruins. Northern factories pounded out railroad tracks and engines, steel, textiles, farm implements, and building materials. Southern factory chimneys stood silent above the rubble. Roadways and railroad tracks laced the North, while in the South railroads and roads lay in ruins. Southern financial institutions were bankrupt, while northern banks flourished. Northern farms, under increasing mechanization, were more productive than ever before, and free farmers took pride that they had amply fed the Union army and urban workers throughout the war. They saw the Union victory as evidence of the superiority of free over slave labor. By contrast, southern farms and plantations, especially those that had lain in the path of Sherman's march, were like a "howling waste." Said one resident, "The Yankees came through . . . and just tore up everything."

Despite pockets of relative wealth, the South was largely devastated as soldiers demobilized and returned home in April 1865. Rare was the family, North or South, that had not suffered a serious casualty in the war. Missing limbs and suffering from hunger (a half million southern whites faced starvation), the ragtag remains of the Confederate army experienced widespread sickness and social disorder as they traveled home. Yet, as a later southern writer, Wilbur Cash, explained, "If this war had smashed the Southern world, it had left the essential Southern mind and will . . . entirely unshaken." Many southerners wanted nothing less than to resist Reconstruction and re-

Both white southerners and their former slaves suffered in the immediate aftermath of the Civil War, as illustrated by this engraving from *Frank Leslie's Illustrated Newspaper.*

store their old world. Others, the minority who had remained quietly loyal to the Union, dreamed of a postwar period not of defiance and old values but of reconciliation and new ones.

Whatever the extremes of southern white attitudes, the dominant social reality in the spring of 1865 was that nearly 4 million former slaves were on their own, facing the challenges of freedom. After an initial reaction of joy and celebration, expressed in jubilee songs, the freedmen quickly became aware of their continuing dependence on former owners. A Mississippi woman stated the uncertainty of her new status this way:

> I used to think if I could be free I should be the happiest of anybody in the world. But when my master come to me, and says—Lizzie, you is free! it seems like I was in a kind of daze. And when I would wake up in the morning I would think to myself, Is I free? Hasn't I got to get up before day light and go into the field of work?

For Lizzie and 4 million other blacks, everything—and nothing—had changed.

Hopes Among Freedmen

Throughout the South in the summer of 1865, there were optimistic expectations in the old slave quarters. As Union soldiers marched through Richmond, prisoners in slave-trade jails chanted: "Slavery chain done broke at last! Gonna praise God till I die!" The slavery chain, however, was not broken all at once but link by link. After Union soldiers swept through an area, Confederate troops would follow, or master and overseer would return, and the slaves learned not to rejoice too quickly or openly. "Every time a bunch of No'thern sojers would come through," recalled one slave, "they would tell us we was free and we'd begin celebratin'. Before we would get through somebody else would tell us to go back to work, and we would go." Another slave recalled celebrating emancipation "about twelve times" in one North Carolina county. So former slaves became cautious about what freedom meant.

Gradually, the freedmen began to express a vision of what life beyond bondage and the plantation might be like. The first thing they did to test the reality of freedom was to leave the plantation, if only for a few hours or days. "If I stay here I'll never know I am free," a South Carolina woman said, and off she went to work as a cook in a nearby town. Some former slaves cut their ties entirely, leaving cruel and kindly masters alike. Some returned to an earlier master, but others went to towns and cities to work and to find schools, churches, and association with other

Many freed blacks, such as these young people photographed in Richmond, Virginia, gravitated to urban centers either to find work or to find family members.

blacks, where they would be safe from whippings and retaliation.

Many freedmen left the plantation in search of members of their families. The quest for a missing spouse, parent, or child, sold away years before, was a powerful force in the first few months of emancipation. Advertisements detailing these sorrowful searches filled black newspapers. For those who found a spouse or who had been living together in slave marriages, freedom meant getting married legally. Wedding ceremonies involving many couples were common in the first months of emancipation. Legal marriage was important morally, but it also served such practical purposes as establishing the legitimacy of children and gaining access to land titles and other economic opportunities. Marriage also meant special burdens for black women who took on the now familiar double role as housekeeper and breadwinner. For many newly married blacks, however, the initial goal was to create a traditional family life, resulting in the widespread withdrawal of women from plantation field labor.

Another way in which freedmen demonstrated their new status was by choosing surnames; names associated with the concept of independence, such as Washington, were common. As an indication of the mixed feelings the freedmen had toward their former masters, some would adopt their master's name, while others would pick "any big name 'ceptin' their master's." Emancipation changed black manners around whites as well. Masks were dropped, and old expressions of humility—tipping a hat, stepping aside, feigning happiness, addressing whites with titles of deference—were discarded. For the blacks, these were necessary symbolic expressions of selfhood; they proved that things were now different. To whites, these behaviors were seen as acts of "insolence," "insubordination," and "puttin' on airs."

However important were choosing names, dropping masks, moving around, getting married, and testing new rights, the primary goal for most freedmen was the acquisition of their own land. "All I want is to git to own fo' or five acres ob land, dat I can build me a little house on and call my home," a Mississippi black said. Only through economic independence, the traditional American goal of controlling one's own labor and land, could former slaves prove to themselves that emancipation was real.

During the war, some Union generals had placed liberated slaves in charge of confiscated and abandoned lands. In the Sea Islands off the coast of South Carolina and Georgia, blacks had been working 40-acre plots of land and harvesting their own crops for several years. Farther inland, most freedmen who received land were the former slaves of Cherokees and Creeks. Some blacks held title to these lands. Northern philanthropists had organized others to grow cotton for the Treasury Department to prove the superiority of free labor over slavery. In the Davis Bend section of Mississippi, thousands of ex-slaves worked 40-acre tracts on leased lands formerly owned by Jefferson Davis. In this highly successful experiment, they made profits sufficient to repay the government for initial costs, then lost the land to Davis's brother.

Many freedmen expected a new economic order as fair payment for their years of involun-

The Promise of Land: 40 Acres

Note the progression in the various documents in this chapter—from promised lands, to lands restored to whites (page 535), to work contracts (page 541), to semiautonomous tenant farms; freedom came by degrees to the freedmen.

To All Whom It May Concern

Edisto Island, August 15th, 1865

George Owens, having selected for settlement forty acres of Land, on Theodore Belab's Place, pursuant to Special Field Orders, No. 15, Headquarters Military Division of the Mississippi, Savannah, Ga., Jan. 16, 1865; he has permission to hold and occupy the said Tract, subject to such regulations as may be established by proper authority; and all persons are prohibited from interfering with him in his possession of the same.

By command of
R. SAXTON
Brev't Maj. Gen.,
Ass't. Comm.
S.C., Ga., and Fla.

tary work on the land. "It's de white man's turn ter labor now," a black preacher in Florida told a group of fieldhands. Whites would no longer own all the land, he went on, "fur de Guverment is gwine ter gie ter ev'ry Nigger forty acres of lan' an' a mule." Other freedmen were willing to settle for less: One in Virginia offered to take only one acre of land—"Ef you make it de acre dat Marsa's house sets on." Another was more guarded, aware of how easy the power could shift back to white planters: "Gib us our own land and we take care ourselves; but widout land, de ole massas can hire us or starve us, as dey please." However cautiously expressed, the freedmen had every expectation, fed by the intensity of their dreams, that the promised "forty acres and a mule" was forthcoming. Once they obtained land, family unity, and education, they looked forward to civil rights and the vote.

The White South's Fearful Response

White southerners had equally mixed goals and expectations at the war's end. Yeoman farmers and poor whites stood side by side with rich planters in bread lines, as together they looked forward to the restoration of their land and livelihood. Suffering from "extreme want and destitution," as a Cherokee County, Georgia, resident put it, white southerners responded to the immediate postwar crises with feelings of outrage, loss, and injustice. "I tell you it is mighty hard," said one man, "for my pa paid his own money for our niggers; and that's not all they've robbed us of. They have taken our horses and cattle and sheep and everything." Others felt the loss more personally, as former slaves they thought were faithful or for whom they felt great affection suddenly left. "Something dreadful has happened dear Diary," a Florida woman wrote in May 1865. "My dear black mammy has left us. . . . I feel lost, I feel as if someone is dead in the house. Whatever will I do without my Mammy?"

A more dominant emotion than sorrow, however, was fear. The entire structure of southern society was shaken, and the semblance of racial peace and order that slavery had provided was shattered. Many white southerners could hardly imagine a society without blacks in bondage. It was the basis not only of social order but of a life style the larger slaveholders, at least, had long regarded as the perfect model of gentility and civilization. Having lost control of all that was familiar and revered, whites feared everything from losing their cheap labor supply to having to sit next to blacks on trains.

The mildest of their fears was the inconvenience of doing various jobs and chores they had rarely done before, like housework. A Georgia woman, Eliza Andrews, complained that it seemed to her a "waste of time for people who are capable of doing something better to spend their time sweeping and dusting while scores of lazy negroes that are fit for nothing else are lying around idle." Worse yet was the "impudent and presumin'" new manners of former slaves, as a North Carolinian put it. Many worried that the rude behavior meant that blacks wanted social equality.

The worst fears of southern whites were rape and revenge. Impudence and pretensions of social equality, some thought, would lead to intermarriage, which in turn would produce mulattoes, "Africanization," and the destruction of the purity of the white race. The presence of black soldiers touched off fears of violence and revenge. Although demobilization occurred rapidly after Appomattox, a few black militia units remained in uniform, parading with guns in southern cities. Acts of violence by black soldiers against whites, however, were rare.

Believing that their world was turned upside down, the former planter aristocracy tried to set it right again. Their goal was to restore the old plantation order and appropriate racial relationships. The key to reestablishing white dominance were the "black codes" that state legislatures passed in the first year after the end of the war. Many of the codes granted freedmen the right to marry, sue and be sued, testify in court, and hold property. But these rights were qualified. Complicated passages in the codes explained under exactly what circumstances blacks could testify against whites or own property (mostly they could not) or exercise other rights of free people. Some rights were denied, including racial intermarriage and the right to bear arms, possess alcoholic beverages, sit on trains except in baggage compartments, be on city streets at night, or congregate in large groups.

Many of the alleged rights guaranteed by the black codes— testimony in court, for example—

The black codes, widespread violence against freedmen, and President Johnson's veto of the Civil Rights Bill gave rise to the sardonic question "Slavery Is Dead?"

were passed to induce the federal government to withdraw its remaining troops from the South. This was a crucial issue, for in many places marauding groups of whites were assaulting and terrorizing virtually defenseless freedmen. In one small district in Kentucky, for example, a government agent reported in 1865:

> Twenty-three cases of severe and inhuman beating and whipping of men; four of beating and shooting; two of robbing and shooting; three of robbing; five men shot and killed; two shot and wounded; four beaten to death; one beaten and roasted; three women assaulted and ravished; four women beaten; two women tied up and whipped until insensible; two men and their families beaten and driven from their homes, and their property destroyed; two instances of burning of dwellings, and one of the inmates shot.

Freedmen clearly needed protection and the right to testify in court against whites.

For white planters, the violence was another sign of social disorder that could be eased only by restoring a plantation-based society. More significantly, they needed the freedmen's labor. The crucial provisions of the black codes were thus intended to regulate the freedmen's economic status. "Vagrancy" laws provided that any blacks not "lawfully employed," which usually meant by a white employer, could be arrested, jailed, fined, or hired out to a man who would assume responsibility for their debts and future behavior. The codes regulated the work contracts by which black laborers worked in the fields for white landowners, including severe penalties for leaving before the yearly contract was fulfilled and rules for proper behavior, attitude, and manners. Thus southern leaders sought to reestablish their dominance. Although thwarted in perpetuating slavery or even in a program for gradual emancipation, many southerners believed, like this Texan, that "we will be enabled to adopt a coercive system of labor." A Kentucky newspaper was more direct: "The tune . . . will not be 'forty acres and a mule,' but . . . 'work nigger or starve.'"

National Reconstruction

The black codes passed by southern legislatures supported these intentions. The question facing the national government in 1865 was whether it would use its power to support the black codes and the reimposition of racial intimidation in the South or to uphold the newly sought rights of the freedmen. Would the federal government side with the democratic reform impulse in American history, which stressed human rights and liberty, or with the forces emphasizing property, order, and self-interest? Although the primary drama of Reconstruction took place in the conflict between white landowners and black freedmen over land and labor in the South, the struggle over Reconstruction policy among politicians in Washington played a significant role in the local drama, as well as the next century of American history.

The Presidential Plan

After an initially tough stand calling for punishment of the defeated Confederates for "treason," President Johnson soon adopted a more lenient policy. On May 29, 1865, he issued two proclamations setting forth his reconstruction program. Like Lincoln, he maintained that the southern states had never left the Union. His first proclamation continued Lincoln's policies by offering "amnesty and pardon, with restoration of all rights of property" to all former Confederates who would take an oath of allegiance to the Constitution and the Union of the United States. There were exceptions: ex-Confederate government leaders and rich rebels whose taxable property was valued at over $20,000. In this latter exception Johnson revealed his old Jacksonian hostility to wealthy aristocratic planters and his preference for leadership by self-made yeoman farmers like himself. Any southerners not covered by the amnesty proclamation could, however, apply for special individual pardons, which Johnson granted to nearly all applicants. By the fall of 1865, only a handful remained unpardoned.

Johnson's second proclamation accepted the reconstructed government of North Carolina and laid out the steps by which other southern states could reestablish state governments. First, the president would appoint a provisional governor, who would call a state convention representing "that portion of the people of said State who are loyal to the United States." This included those who took the oath of allegiance or were otherwise pardoned. The convention should ratify the Thirteenth Amendment, which abolished slavery, void secession, repudiate all Confederate debts, and then elect new state officials and members of Congress.

Under this lenient plan, each of the southern states successfully completed reconstruction and sent newly elected members to the Congress that convened in December 1865. Southern voters defiantly elected dozens of former officers and legislators of the Confederacy, including a few not yet pardoned. Some state conventions hedged on ratifying the Thirteenth Amendment, and some asserted their right to compensation for the loss of slave property. No state convention provided for black suffrage, and most did nothing to guarantee civil rights, schooling, or economic protection for the freedmen.

Less than eight months after Appomattox, the southern states were back in the Union, the

Promised Land Restored to Whites

Richard H. Jenkins, an applicant for the restoration of his plantation on Wadmalaw Island, S. C., called "Rackett Hall," the same having been unoccupied during the past year and up to the 1st of Jan. 1866, except by one freedman who planted no crop, and being held by the Bureau of Refugees, Freedmen and Abandoned Lands, having conformed to the requirements of Circular No. 15 of said Bureau, dated Washington, D. C., Sept. 12, 1865, the aforesaid property is hereby restored to his possession.

. . . The Undersigned, Richard H. Jenkins, does hereby solemnly promise and engage, that he will secure to the Refugees and Freedmen now resident on his Wadmalaw Island Estate, the crops of the past year, harvested or unharvested; also, that the said Refugees and Freedmen shall be allowed to remain at their present houses or other homes on the island, so long as the responsible Refugees and Freedmen (embracing parents, guardians, and other natural protectors) shall enter into contracts, by leases or for wages, in terms satisfactory to the Supervising Board.

Also, that the undersigned will take the proper steps to enter into contracts with the above described responsible Refugees and Freedmen, the latter being required on their part to enter into said contracts on or before the 15th day of February, 1866, or surrender their right to remain on the said estate, it being understood that if they are unwilling to contract after the expiration of said period, the Supervising Board is to aid in getting them homes and employment elsewhere.

freedmen were returning to work for their former masters under annual contracts, and the new president seemed firmly in charge. Reconstruction of the southern states seemed to be over. But northern Republicans were far from satisfied with President Johnson's efforts. Georges Clemenceau, a young French newspaper reporter covering the war, wondered if the North, having made so many "painful sacrifices," would "let itself be tricked out of what it had spent so much trouble and perseverance to win."

Congressional Reconstruction

As they looked at the situation late in 1865, northern leaders painfully saw that almost none of their postwar goals—moral, political, or psychological—were being fulfilled. The South seemed far from reconstructed and was taking advantage of the president's program to restore the power of the prewar planter aristocracy. The freedmen were receiving neither equal citizenship nor economic independence. And the Republicans were not likely to maintain their political power and stay in office. Would the Democratic party and the South gain by postwar elections what they had been unable to achieve by civil war?

A song popular in the North in 1866 posed the question: "Who shall rule this American Nation?"—those who would betray their country and "murder the innocent freedmen" or those "loyal millions" who had shed their "blood in battle"? The answer was obvious. Congressional Republicans, led by Congressman Thaddeus Stevens of Pennsylvania and Senator Charles Sumner of Massachusetts, thus asserted their own policies for reconstructing the nation. Many southerners believed that the Republican Congress wanted to transform the South in the North's image and to punish it by providing numerous political and economic rights for the freedmen. Although some congressional leaders did indeed have strong punitive and political motivations, as well as a strong sense of responsibility to set the freedmen on their feet, the vast majority of Republicans were moderates. Although they were branded as "radicals," only for a brief period in 1866 and 1867 did "radical" rule prevail.

Rejecting Johnson's notion that the South had already been reconstructed, Congress asserted its constitutional authority to decide on its own membership and refused seats to the newly elected senators and representatives from the old Confederate states. Congress then established the Joint Committee on Reconstruction to investigate conditions in the South. Its report documented disorder and resistance and the appalling treatment and conditions of the freedmen. Even before the report was made final in 1866, Congress passed a civil rights bill to protect the fragile rights of the blacks and extended for two more years the Freedmen's Bureau, an agency providing emergency assistance at the end of the war. President Johnson vetoed both bills, arguing that they were unconstitutional and calling his congressional opponents "traitors."

Johnson's growing anger forced moderates into the radical camp, and Congress passed both bills over his veto. Both, however, were watered down by weakening the power of enforcement. Southern civil courts, therefore, regularly disallowed black testimony against whites, acquitted whites charged with violence against blacks, sentenced blacks to compulsory labor, and generally made discriminatory sentences for the same crimes. In this judicial climate, racial violence erupted with discouraging frequency.

In Memphis, for example, a race riot occurred in May 1866 that typified race relations during the Reconstruction period. In the months before the riot, local Irish policemen frequently unleashed unprovoked brutality on black Union soldiers stationed at nearby Fort Pickering. A Memphis newspaper suggested that "the negro can do the country more good in the cotton field than in the camp" and criticized what it called the "dirty, fanatical, nigger-loving Radicals of this city" who thought otherwise.

In this inflamed atmosphere, a street brawl erupted between the police and some recently discharged but armed black soldiers. After some fighting and an exchange of gunfire, the soldiers went back to their fort. That night, white mobs, led by prominent local officials (one of whom urged the mob to "go ahead and kill the last damned one of the nigger race"), invaded the black section of the city. With the encouragement of the Memphis police, the mobs engaged in over 40 hours of terror, killing, beating, robbing, and raping virtually helpless residents and burning houses, schools, and churches. When it was over, 48 people, all but two of them black, had died in the riot. The local Union army commander took his time intervening to restore order, arguing that his troops had a "large amount of public property to guard [and] hated Negroes too." A congressional inquiry found that in Memphis, blacks had "no protection from the law whatever."

A month later, Congress proposed to the states the ratification of the Fourteenth Amendment, the single most significant act of the Reconstruction era. The first section of the amendment sought to provide permanent constitutional protection of the civil rights of freedmen by defining them as citizens. States were prohibited from depriving "any person of life, liberty, or property, without due process of law," and all people were guaranteed the "equal protection of the laws." In section 2, Congress granted black male suffrage in the South by making blacks whole people eligible to vote (thus canceling the Constitution's "three-fifths" clause). States that denied this right would have their "basis of representation reduced" proportionally. Other sections of the amendment denied leaders of the Confederacy the right to hold national or state political office (except by act of Congress), repudiated the Confederate debt, and denied claims of compensation by former slave owners for their lost property.

President Johnson urged the southern states not to ratify the Fourteenth Amendment, and ten states immediately rejected it. Johnson then went on the campaign trail in the midterm election of 1866 to ask voters to throw out the radical Republicans. Vicious name calling and other low forms of electioneering marked this first political campaign since the war's end. The president exchanged insults with hecklers and lashed out against his opponents. Democrats in both the South and the North appealed openly to racial prejudice in calling for the defeat of those who had passed the Fourteenth Amendment. The nation would be "Africanized," they charged, with black equality threatening both the marketplace and the bedroom.

Republican campaigners, in turn, called Johnson a drunkard and a traitor. Bitter Civil War memories were revived as Republicans "waved the bloody shirt" in telling voters that Democrats were traitorous rebels or draft dodgers, while Republicans were patriotic saviors of the Union and courageous soldiers. Governor Oliver P. Morton of Indiana described the Democratic party as a

A white mob burned this freedmen's school during the Memphis riot of May 1866.

"common sewer and loathsome receptacle, into which is emptied every element of treason . . . inhumanity and barbarism which has dishonored the age." Although the electorate was moved more by self-interest on other issues than by the persuasive power of these speeches, the result of the election was an overwhelming victory for the Republicans. The mandate was clear. The presidential plan of reconstruction in the seceded states had not worked, and Congress must suggest another.

Therefore, early in 1867, three Reconstruction Acts were passed. The first divided the southern states into five military districts in which military commanders had broad powers to maintain order and protect the rights of property and individuals. Congress also defined a new process for readmitting a state. Qualified voters, which included blacks and excluded unreconstructed rebels, would elect delegates to state constitutional conventions, which then would write new constitutions guaranteeing black suffrage. After the new voters of the states had ratified the constitutions, elections would be held to choose governors and state legislatures. When a state ratified the Fourteenth Amendment, its representatives to Congress would be accepted, thus completing readmission to the Union.

The President Impeached

At the same time as it passed the Reconstruction Acts, Congress also approved bills to restrict the powers of the president and to establish the dominance of the legislative branch over the executive. The Tenure of Office Act, designed to protect the outspoken secretary of war Edwin Stanton from removal by Johnson, limited the president's appointment powers. Other measures restricted his power as commander in chief. Johnson behaved exactly as congressional Republicans had anticipated, vetoing the Reconstruction Acts, issuing orders to limit military commanders in the South, and removing cabinet and other government officials sympathetic to Congress's program. The House Judiciary Committee investigated, charging the president with "usurpations of power" and of acting in the "interests of the great criminals" who had led the southern rebellion. It was evident, however, that Johnson was guilty only of holding principles, policies, and prejudices different from those of congressional leaders, and moderate House Republicans defeated the impeachment resolutions.

In August 1867, Johnson finally dismissed Stanton and asked for Senate consent. When the Senate refused, the president ordered Stanton to surrender his office, which he refused, barricading himself inside. This time the House rushed impeachment resolutions to a vote, charging the president with "high crimes and misdemeanors" as detailed in 11 offenses while in office, mostly focusing on alleged violations of the Tenure of Office Act. The three-month trial in the Senate early in 1868 featured impassioned oratory. Radical Republicans declared the president "guilty of all, and infinitely more." Evidence was skimpy, however, that Johnson had committed any crime that justified his removal. With seven moderate Republicans joining Democrats against conviction, the effort to find the president guilty as charged fell short of the two-thirds majority required by a single vote.

The moderate Republicans, satisfied with the changes wrought by the Civil War, may have feared the consequences of removing Johnson, for the next man in line for the presidency, Senator Benjamin Wade of Ohio, was a leading radical Republican. Wade had endorsed women's suffrage, rights for labor unions, and civil rights for blacks in both southern and northern states. As the moderate or regular Republicans gained strength in 1868 through their support of the presidential election winner, Ulysses S. Grant, radicalism lost much of its power within Republican ranks. Not for another 100 years would a president again face removal from office through impeachment.

Congressional Moderation

The impeachment crisis revealed that most Republicans were more interested in protecting themselves than the freedmen and in punishing Johnson rather than the South. Congress's political battle against the president was not matched by an idealistic resolve on behalf of the rights and welfare of the freedmen. As early as the state and local elections of 1867, it was clear that voters preferred moderate reconstruction policies. It is important to look not only at what Congress did during Reconstruction but also at what it did not do.

With the exception of Jefferson Davis, Congress did not imprison Confederate leaders, and only one person, the commander of the infamous Andersonville prison camp, was put to death. Congress did not insist on a long-term probationary period before southern states could be readmitted to the Union. It did not reorganize southern local governments. It did not mandate a national program of education for the 4 million ex-slaves. It did not confiscate and redistribute land to the freedmen, nor did it prevent President Johnson from taking land away from freedmen who had gained possessory titles during the war. It did not, except indirectly, provide economic help to black citizens.

What Congress did do, and that only reluctantly, was grant citizenship and suffrage to the freedmen. At the end of the Civil War, northerners were no more prepared than southerners to make blacks equal citizens. Between 1865 and 1869, several states held referendums proposing black suffrage. Voters in Kansas, Ohio, Michigan, Missouri, Wisconsin, Connecticut, New York, and the District of Columbia (by a vote of 6,521 to 35!) all turned the proposals down. Only in Iowa and Minnesota (on the third try, and then only by devious wording) did northern whites grant the vote to blacks.

Black suffrage gained support, however, after the election of 1868, when General Grant, a military hero regarded as invincible, barely won the popular vote in several states. Congressional Republicans, who had twice rejected a suffrage amendment, took another look at the idea as a way of adding grateful black votes to party rolls. After a bitterly contested fight, repeated in several state ratification contests, the Fifteenth Amendment, forbidding all states to deny the vote to anyone "on account of race, color, or previous condition of servitude," became part of the Constitution in 1870. A black preacher from Pittsburgh observed that "the Republican party had done the Negro good, but they were doing themselves good at the same time."

For political reasons, therefore, Congress gave blacks the vote but not the land, the opposite priority of what the freedmen wanted. Almost alone, Thaddeus Stevens argued that "forty acres . . . and a hut would be more valuable . . . than the . . . right to vote." But Congress never seriously considered his plan to confiscate the land of the "chief rebels" and to give a small portion of it, divided into 40-acre plots, to the freedmen, for it went against deeply held beliefs of the Republican party and the American people in the sacredness of private property. Moreover, the idea of a large propertyless class of cheap black laborers attracted northern business interests concerned with the development of southern industry and with investing in southern land.

Although most Americans, in the North as well as the South, opposed confiscation and did not want blacks to become independent landowners, Congress passed an alternative measure. Proposed by George Julian of Indiana, the Southern Homestead Act of 1866 made public lands available to blacks and loyal whites in five southern states. But the land was of poor quality and inaccessible. No transportation, tools, or seed were provided, and most blacks who might have wanted to take advantage of the offer had only until January 1, 1867, to claim their land. But that was nearly impossible for most because they were under contract to white employers until that date. Only about 4,000 black families even applied for the Homestead Act lands, and fewer than 20 percent of them saw their claims completed. The record of white claimants was not much better. Congressional moderation, therefore, left the

Reconstruction Amendments
Constitutional Seeds of Dreams Deferred for 100 Years (or More)

Substance	Outcome of Ratification Process	Final Implementation and Enforcement
	Thirteenth Amendment—Passed by Congress January 1865	
Prohibited slavery in the United States.	Ratified by 27 states, including 8 southern states, by December 1865.	Immediate, although economic freedom came by degrees.
	Fourteenth Amendment—Passed by Congress June 1866	
(1) Defined equal national citizenship; (2) reduced state representation in Congress proportional to number of disenfranchised voters; (3) denied former Confederates the right to hold office.	Rejected by 12 southern and border states by February 1867; radicals made readmission depend on ratification; ratified in July 1868.	Civil Rights Act of 1964.
	Fifteenth Amendment—Passed by Congress February 1869	
Prohibited denial of vote because of race, color, or previous servitude	Ratification by Virginia, Texas, Mississippi, and Georgia required for readmission; ratified in March 1870	Voting Rights Act of 1965.

freedmen economically weak as they faced the challenges of freedom.

Women and the Reconstruction Amendments

One casualty of the Fourteenth and Fifteenth amendments was the goodwill of the women who had been petitioning and campaigning for suffrage for two decades. They had hoped that grateful male legislators would recognize their support for the Union effort during the war and the suspension of their own demands in the interests of the more immediate concerns of preserving the Union, nursing the wounded, and emancipating the slaves. During the war, for example, the Woman's Loyal League, headed by Elizabeth Cady Stanton and Susan B. Anthony, gathered nearly 400,000 signatures on petitions asking Congress to pass the Thirteenth Amendment. They were therefore shocked to see the wording of the Fourteenth Amendment, which for the first time inserted the word *male* in the Constitution in referring to a citizen's right to vote.

Stanton and Anthony campaigned actively against the Fourteenth Amendment, despite the pleas of those who, like Frederick Douglass, had long supported woman suffrage and who also declared that this was "the Negro's hour." When the Fifteenth Amendment was proposed, they wondered why the word *sex* could not have been added to the "conditions" no longer a basis for denial of the vote. Largely abandoned by radical reconstructionists and abolitionist activists, they had few champions in Congress, however, and lost that battle too.

Disappointment over the suffrage issue was one of several reasons that led to a split in the women's movement in 1869. Anthony and Stanton continued their fight for a national amendment for woman suffrage and a long list of other rights, while other women concentrated their hopes on securing the vote on a state-by-state basis.

Life After Slavery

Union army major George Reynolds boasted to a friend late in 1865 that in the area of Mississippi under his command, he had "kept the negroes at work, and in a good state of discipline." Clinton Fisk, a well-meaning white who helped to found a black college in Tennessee, told freedmen in 1866 that they could be "as free and as happy" working again for their "old master . . . as any where else in the world." For many blacks such pronouncements sounded familiar, reminding them of white preachers' exhortations during slavery to work hard and obey their masters. Ironically, though, both Fisk and Reynolds were agents of the Freedmen's Bureau, the crucial agency intended to ease the transition from slavery to freedom for the 4 million ex-slaves.

The Freedmen's Bureau

Never in American history has one small agency—underfinanced, understaffed, and undersupported—been given a harder task than was the Bureau of Freedmen, Refugees and Abandoned Lands. Its purposes and mixed successes symbolize, as well as those of any other institution, the tortuous course of Reconstruction.

The activities of the Freedmen's Bureau included issuing emergency rations of food and providing clothing and shelter to the homeless, hungry victims of the war; establishing medical care and hospital facilities; providing funds for transportation for the thousands of freedmen and white refugees dislocated by the war; helping blacks search for and put their families back together; and arranging for legal marriage ceremonies. The bureau also served as a friend in local civil courts to ensure that the freedmen got

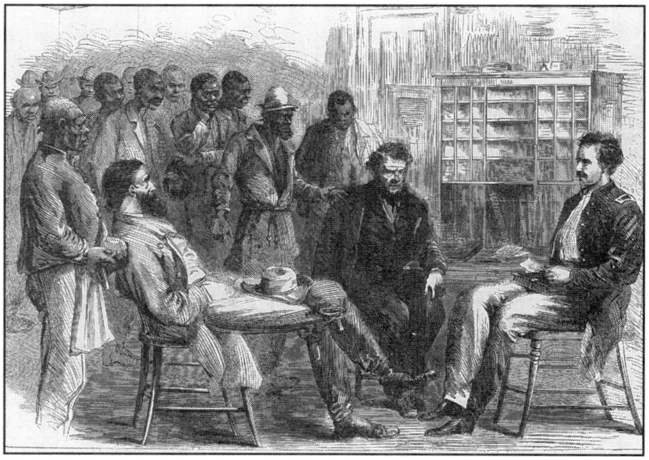

The Freedmen's Bureau had fewer resources in relation to its purpose than any agency in the nation's history. *Harper's Weekly* published this engraving of freedmen lining up for aid in Memphis in 1866.

A Freedmen's Work Contract

As you read this rather typical work contract defining the first economic relationship between whites and blacks in the early months of the postwar period, note the regulation of social behavior and deportment as well as work and "pay" arrangements. How different is this from slavery? As a freedman or woman, would you have signed such an agreement? Why or why not? What options did you have?

State of South Carolina
Darlington District
Articles of Agreement

This Agreement entered into between Mrs. Adele Allston Exect of the one part, and the Freedmen and Women of The Upper Quarters plantation of the other part *Witnesseth:*

That the latter agree, for the remainder of the present year, to reside upon and devote their labor to the cultivation of the Plantation of the former. And they further agree, that they will in all respects, conform to such reasonable and necessary plantation rules and regulations as Mrs. Allston's Agent may prescribe; that they will not keep any gun, pistol, or other offensive weapon, or leave the plantation without permission from their employer; that in all things connected with their duties as laborers on said plantation, they will yield prompt obedience to all orders from Mrs. Allston or his [sic] agent; that they will be orderly and quiet in their conduct, avoiding drunkenness and other gross vices; that they will not misuse any of the Plantation Tools, or Agricultural Implements, or any Animals entrusted to their care, or any Boats, Flats, Carts or Wagons; that they will give up at the expiration of this Contract, all Tools & c., belonging to the Plantation, and in case any property, of any description belonging to the Plantation shall be willfully or through negligence destroyed or injured, the value of the Articles so destroyed, shall be deducted from the portion of the Crops which the person or persons, so offending, shall be entitled to receive under this Contract.

Any deviations from the condition of the foregoing Contract may, upon sufficient proof, be punished with dismissal from the Plantation, or in such other manner as may be determined by the Provost Court; and the person or persons so dismissed, shall forfeit the whole, or a part of his, her or their portion of the crop, as the Court may decide.

In consideration of the foregoing Services duly performed, Mrs. Allston agrees, after deducting Seventy five bushels of Corn for each work Animal, exclusively used in cultivating the Crops for the present year; to turn over to the said Freedmen and Women, one half of the remaining Corn, Peas, Potatoes, made this season. He [sic] further agrees to furnish the usual rations until the Contract is performed.

All Cotton Seed Produced on the Plantation is to be reserved for the use of the Plantation. The Freedmen, Women and Children are to be treated in a manner consistent with their freedom. Necessary medical attention will be furnished as heretofore.

Any deviation from the conditions of this Contract upon the part of the said Mrs. Allston or her Agent or Agents shall be punished in such manner as may be determined by a Provost Court, or a Military Commission. This agreement to continue till the first day of January 1866.

Witness our hand at The Upper Quarters this 28th day of July 1865.

fair trials. Although not initially empowered to do so, the agency was responsible for the education of the ex-slaves. To bureau schools came many idealistic teachers from various northern Freedmen's Aid societies.

In addition to these many activities, the largest task of the Freedmen's Bureau was to serve as an employment agency, tending to the economic well-being of the blacks. This included settling them on abandoned lands and getting them started with tools, seed, and draft animals, as well as arranging work contracts with white landowners. As we shall see, in the area of work contracts, the Freedmen's Bureau served more to "reenslave" the freedmen as impoverished fieldworkers than to set them on their way as independent farmers.

Although some agents were idealistic young New Englanders eager to help slaves adjust to freedom, others were Union army officers more concerned with social order than social transformation. Working in a postwar climate of resentment and violence, Freedmen's Bureau agents were constantly accused of partisan Republican politics, corruption, and partiality to blacks by local white residents. But even the best-intentioned agents would have agreed with General O. O. Howard, commissioner of the bureau, in a belief in the traditional nineteenth-century American values of self-help, minimal government interference in the marketplace, the sanctity of private property, contractual obligations, and white superiority. The bureau's work served to uphold these values.

On a typical day, these overworked and underpaid agents would visit courts and schools in their district, supervise the signing of work contracts, and handle numerous complaints, most involving contract violations between whites and blacks or property and domestic disputes among blacks. One agent sent a man who had complained of a severe beating back to work with the advice, "Don't be sassy [and] don't be lazy when you've got work to do." Another, reflecting his growing frustrations, complained that the freedmen were "disrespectful and greatly in need of instruction." Although helpful in finding work for the freedmen, more often than not the agents found themselves defending white landowners by telling the blacks to obey orders, to trust their employers, and to sign and live by disadvantageous contracts.

Despite mounting pressures to support white landowners, personal frustrations, and even threats on their lives, the agents accomplished a great deal. In little more than two years, the Freedmen's Bureau issued 20 million rations (nearly one-third to poor whites), reunited families and resettled some 30,000 displaced war refugees, treated some 450,000 cases of illness and injury, built 40 hospitals and hundreds of schools, provided books, tools, and furnishings—and even some land—to the freedmen, and occasionally protected their economic and civil rights. Black historian W. E. B. Du Bois wrote an epitaph for the bureau that might stand for the whole of Reconstruction: "In a time of perfect calm, amid willing neighbors and streaming wealth," he wrote, it "would have been a herculean task" for the bureau to fulfill its many purposes. But in the midst of hunger, sorrow, spite, suspicion, hate, and cruelty, "the work of any instrument of social regeneration was . . . foredoomed to failure."

Economic Freedom by Degrees

The economic failures of the Freedmen's Bureau, symbolic of the entire congressional program, forced the freedmen into a new economic dependency on their former masters. Although the planter class did not lose its economic and social power in the postwar years, the character of southern agriculture went through some major changes. First, a land-intensive system replaced the labor intensity of slavery. Land ownership was concentrated into fewer and even larger holdings than before the Civil War. From South Carolina to Louisiana, the wealthiest tenth of the population owned about 60 percent of the real estate in the 1870s. Second, these large planters increasingly concentrated on one crop, usually cotton, and were tied into the international market. This resulted in a steady drop in food production (both grains and livestock) in the postwar period. Third, reliance on one-crop farming meant that a new credit system emerged whereby most farmers, black and white, depended on local merchants (often in competition with large landowners) for renting seed, farm implements and animals, provisions, housing, and land. These changes affected race relations and class tensions among whites.

This new system, however, took a few years to develop after emancipation. At first, most freedmen signed contracts with white landowners and worked in gangs in the fields as farm laborers very much as during slavery. Watched over by superintendents, who still used the lash, they toiled from sunrise to sunset for a meager wage and a monthly allotment of bacon and meal. All members of the family had to work to receive their rations. The freedmen resented this new form of semiservitude, preferring small plots of land of their own to grow vegetables and grains. Moreover, they wanted to be able to send their children to school and insisted on "no more outdoor work" for women. What the freedmen wanted, a Georgia planter correctly observed, was "to get away from all overseers, to hire or purchase land, and work for themselves."

Many blacks therefore broke contracts, ran away, engaged in work slowdowns or strikes, burned barns, and otherwise expressed their displeasure with the contract labor system. One white landowner expressed his frustration over having "to bargain and haggle with our servants about wages." In the Sea Islands and rice-growing regions of coastal South Carolina and Georgia, where slaves had long held a degree of autonomy, resistance was especially strong. On the Heyward plantations, near those of the Allstons, the freedmen "refuse work at any price," a Freedman's Bu-

Sharecroppers and tenant farmers, though more autonomous than contract laborers, remained dependent on the landlord for their survival.

reau agent reported, and the women "wish to stay in the house or the garden all the time." The former Allston slaves also refused to sign their contracts, even when offered livestock and other favors, and in 1869, Adele Allston was forced to sell much of her vast landholdings.

Blacks' insistence on autonomy and land of their own was the major impetus for the change from the contract system to tenancy and sharecropping. As a South Carolina freedman put it, "If a man got to go crost de riber, and he can't git a boat, he take a log. If I can't own de land, I'll hire or lease land, but I won't contract." Families would hitch a team of mules to their old slave cabin to drag it to their assigned plot of land as far away from the Big House as possible. The sharecroppers were given seed, fertilizer, farm implements, and all necessary food and clothing to take care of their families. In return, the landlord (or a local merchant) told them what to grow and how much and took a share—usually half—of the harvest. The half retained by the cropper, however, was usually needed to pay for goods bought on credit (at huge interest rates) at the landlord's store. Thus the sharecroppers were semiautonomous but remained tied to the landlord's will for economic survival.

Under the tenant system, farmers had only slightly more independence. In advance of the harvest, a tenant farmer promised to sell his crop to a local merchant in return for renting land, tools, and other necessities. He was also obligated to purchase goods on credit (at higher prices than whites paid) against the harvest from the merchant's store. At "settling up" time, the income from the sale of the crop was matched with debts accumulated at the store. It was possible, especially after an unusually bountiful season, to come out ahead and eventually to own one's own land. But tenants seemed rarely to do so; they remained in debt at the end of each year and were then compelled to pledge the next year's crop. World cotton prices remained low, and while large landowners still enjoyed profits through their large scale of operation, sharecroppers rarely received much money. When they were able to pay off their debts, landowners frequently altered the loan agreements. Thus a system of debt peonage replaced slavery, ensuring a continuing cheap labor supply to grow cotton and other staples in the South. Only a very few blacks became independent landowners—about 2 to 5 percent by 1880, but closer to 20 percent in some states by 1900.

Changes on the Barrow Plantation, 1860–1881

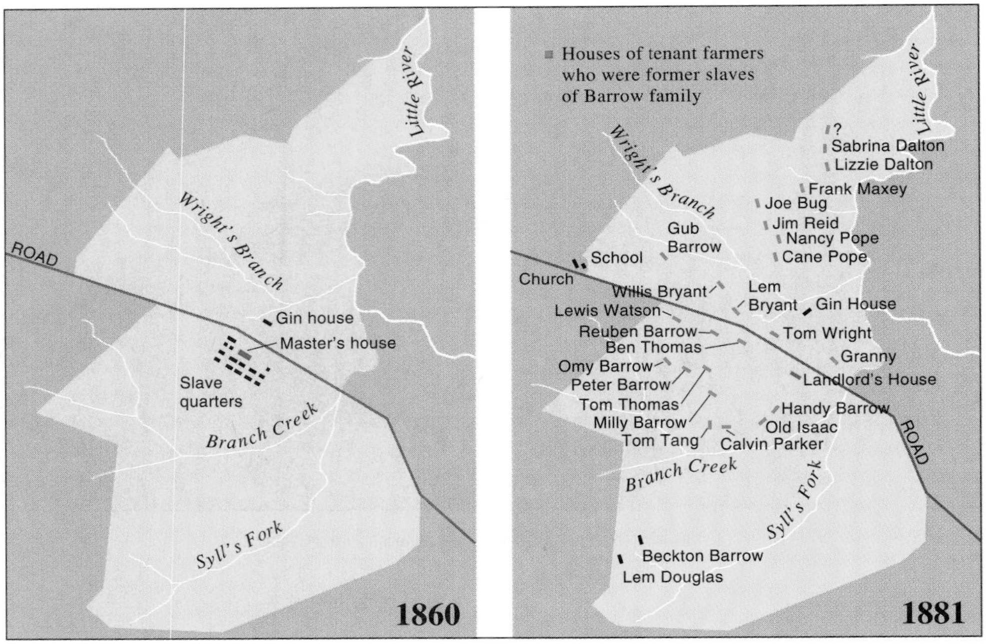

After refusing to accept labor contracts and a competitive gang system, the former slaves of David C. Barrow moved their households to 25–30-acre tenant farms, which they rented from the Barrow family in annual contracts requiring payment in cotton and other crops.

These changes in southern agriculture affected yeoman and poor white farmers as well as the freedmen. This raised the threat, always troubling to the planter class, of a coalition between poor black and pro-Unionist white farmers. As a yeoman farmer in Georgia said in 1865, "We should tuk the land, as we did the niggers, and split it, and giv part to the niggers and part to me and t'other Union fellers." But confiscation and redistribution of land was no more likely for white farmers than for the freedmen. Whites, too, were forced to concentrate on growing staples, to pledge their crops against high-interest credit from local merchants, and to face the inevitability of perpetual indebtedness. In the upcountry piedmont area of Georgia, for example, the number of whites who worked their own land dropped from nine in ten before the Civil War to seven in ten by 1880. During the same period, the production of cotton doubled.

Larger planters' reliance on cotton meant fewer food crops, which necessitated greater dependence on local merchants for provisions. In 1884, Jephta Dickson of Jackson County, Georgia, purchased over $50 worth of flour, meal, meat, syrup, and peas and corn from a local store, an almost unthinkable situation 25 years earlier, when he would have needed to buy almost no food to supplement his homegrown fare. Fencing laws seriously curtailed the livelihood of poor whites raising pigs and hogs, and restrictions on hunting and fishing reduced the ability of poor whites and blacks alike to supplement their income and diet.

In the worn-out flatlands and barren mountainous regions of the South, poor whites thus faced diminishing fortunes in the era of Reconstruction. Their antebellum heritage of poverty, ill health, and isolation worsened in the years after the war. A Freedmen's Bureau agent in South Carolina described the poor whites in his area as "gaunt and ragged, ungainly, stooping and clumsy in build." They lived a marginal existence, hunting, fishing, and growing corn and potato crops that, as a North Carolinian put it, "come up *puny,* grow *puny,* and mature *puny.*" Many poor white farmers, in fact, were even less productive than black sharecroppers. Some became farmhands, earning $6 a month (with board) from other farmers. Others fled to low-paying jobs in urban cotton mills, where they would not have to compete against blacks.

The cultural life of poor southern whites reflected both their lowly position and their pride. Their religion was emotional and revivalistic, centering on the camp meeting. Music and folklore often focused on debt and chain gangs, as well as on deeds of drinking prowess. In backwoods clearings and bleak pine barrens, men and women told tall tales of superhuman feats and exchanged folk remedies for bad health. In Alabama, there were over 90 superstitious sayings for calling rain. Aesthetic expression, in quilt making and house construction, for example, reflected a marginal culture in which everything was saved and put to use.

In part because their lives were so hard, poor whites persisted in their belief in white superiority. As a federal officer reported in 1866, "The poorer classes of white people . . . have a most intense hatred of the Negro, and swear he shall never be reckoned as part of the population." Many poor whites, therefore, joined the Ku Klux Klan and other southern white terror groups that emerged between 1866 and 1868. But however hard life was for poor whites, blacks were far more often sentenced to chain gangs for the slightest crimes and were bound to a life of debt, degradation, and dependency. The high hopes with which the freedmen had greeted emancipation turned slowly to resignation and disillusionment. Felix Haywood, a former Texas slave, recalled:

> We thought we was goin' to be richer than white folks, 'cause we was stronger and knowed how to work, and the whites . . . didn't have us to work for them anymore. But it didn't turn out that way. We soon found out that freedom could make folks proud but it didn't make 'em rich.

Black Self-Help Institutions

Felix Haywood understood the limitations of government programs and efforts on behalf of the

Sharecropping in the South, 1880

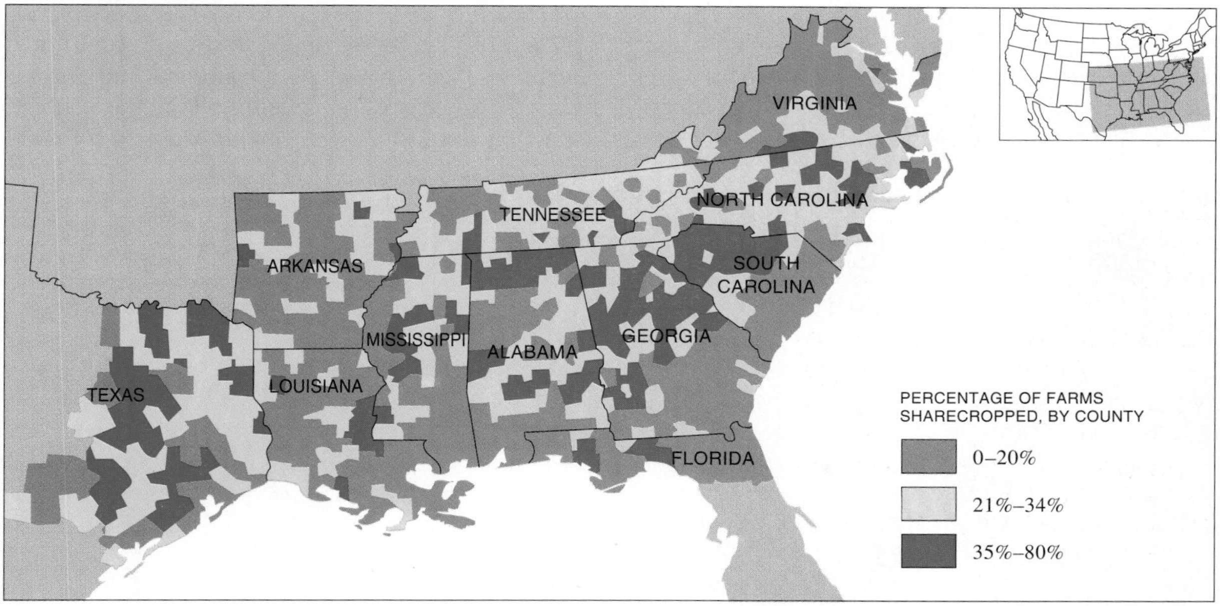

White tenant farmers as well as blacks (such as those on the Barrow plantation) were increasingly burdened with poverty and debt in a sharecropping system that had its highest concentrations in the cotton belt from South Carolina and Georgia to East Texas.

freedmen. It was clear to many black leaders, therefore, that since white institutions could not fulfill the promises of emancipation, black freedmen would have to do it themselves. Fortunately, the tradition of black community self-help survived in the organized churches and schools of the antebellum free Negro communities and in the "invisible" cultural institutions of the slave quarters. Religion, as usual, was vital. Emancipation brought an explosion in the growth of membership in black churches. The Negro Baptist church grew from 150,000 members in 1850 to 500,000 in 1870. The various branches of the African Methodist Episcopal church increased fourfold in the decade after the Civil War, from 100,000 to over 400,000 members.

Black ministers continued their tradition of community leadership. Many led efforts to oppose discrimination, some by entering politics. Over one-fifth of the black officeholders in South Carolina were ministers. Most preachers, however, focused on traditional religious themes of sin, conversion, and salvation. An English visitor to the South in 1867 and 1868, after observing a revivalist preacher in Savannah arouse nearly 1,000 people to "sway, and cry, and groan," noted the intensity of black "devoutness." Despite some efforts by urban elite blacks to restrain the emotionalism characteristic of black worship, most congregations preferred their traditional forms of religious expression. One black woman, when urged to pray more quietly, complained: "We make noise 'bout ebery ting else . . . I want ter go ter Heaben in de good ole way."

The freedmen's desire for education was as strong as for religion. A school official in Virginia echoed the observation of many when he said that the freedmen were "down right crazy to learn." A Mississippi farmer vowed, "If I nebber does do nothing more, I shall give my children a chance to go to school, for I consider education next best ting to liberty." The first teachers of these black children were unmarried northern women, the legendary "Yankee schoolmarms." Sent by groups such as the American Missionary Association, these idealistic young women sought to convert blacks to Congregationalism and to white moral values of cleanliness, discipline, and dutiful work. In October 1865, Esther Douglass found "120 dirty, half naked, perfectly wild black children" in her schoolroom near Savannah, Georgia. Eight months later, she reported that "their progress was wonderful." They could read, sing hymns, and repeat Bible verses and had learned "about right conduct which they tried to practice."

Glowing reports like this one changed as white teachers grew frustrated with crowded facilities, limited resources, local opposition, and the absenteeism that resulted from the demands of fieldwork. In Georgia, for example, only 5 percent of black children went to school for part of any one year between 1865 and 1870; this contrasted with 20 percent of white children. Furthermore, blacks increasingly preferred their own teachers, who could better understand former slaves. To ensure the training of black preachers and teachers, northern philanthropists founded

Along with equal civil rights and land of their own, what the freedmen most wanted was education. Despite white opposition and limited facilities for black schools, one of the most positive outcomes of the Reconstruction era was education in freedmen's schools.

Howard, Atlanta, Fisk, Morehouse, and other black universities in the South between 1865 and 1867.

Black schools, like churches, became community centers. They published newspapers, provided training in trades and farming, and promoted political participation and land ownership. A black farmer in Mississippi founded both a school and a society to facilitate land acquisition and better agricultural methods. These efforts made black schools objects of local white hostility. A Virginia freedman told a congressional committee that in his county, anyone starting a school would be killed and that blacks were "afraid to be caught with a book." In 1869, in Tennessee alone, 37 black schools were burned to the ground.

White opposition to black education and land ownership stimulated the rise of black nationalism and separatism. In the late 1860s, Benjamin "Pap" Singleton, a former Tennessee slave who had escaped to Canada, observed that "whites had the lands and . . . blacks had nothing but their freedom." Singleton urged them to abandon politics and migrate westward. He organized a land company in 1869, purchased public property in Kansas, and in the early 1870s took several groups from Tennessee and Kentucky to that prairie state to establish separate black towns. In following years, thousands of "exodusters" from the Lower South bought some 10,000 acres of infertile land in Kansas. There they faced both natural and human obstacles to their efforts to develop self-sufficient communities. Most were forced eventually to disband and seek relief.

By the 1880s, despairing of ever finding economic independence in the United States, Singleton and other nationalists urged emigration to Canada and Liberia. Other black leaders, notably Frederick Douglass, continued to assert that suffrage would eventually lead to full citizenship rights within the United States.

Reconstruction in the States

Douglass's confidence in the power of the ballot seemed warranted in the enthusiastic early months under the Reconstruction Acts of 1867. With President Johnson neutralized, national Republican leaders were finally in a position to accomplish their political goals. Local Republicans, taking advantage of the inability or refusal of many southern whites to vote, overwhelmingly elected their delegates to state constitutional conventions in the fall of 1867. With guarded optimism and a sense of the "sacred importance" of their work, black and white Republicans turned to the task of creating new state governments.

Republican Rule

Despite popular belief, the southern state governments under Republican rule were not dominated by illiterate black majorities intent on "Africanizing" the South by passing compulsory racial intermarriage laws, as many whites feared. Nor were these governments unusually corrupt or financially extravagant. Nor did they use massive numbers of federal troops to enforce their will. By 1869, only 1,100 federal soldiers remained in Virginia, and most federal troops in Texas guarded the frontier against Mexico and hostile Indians. Without the support of a strong military presence, then, these new state governments tried to do their work in a climate of economic distress and increasingly violent harassment.

A diverse combination of political groups made up the new governments elected under congressional Reconstruction. Labeled the "black and tan" governments by their opponents to suggest domination by former slaves and mulattoes, they were actually predominantly white, with the one exception of the lower house of the South Carolina legislature. One part of the new leadership consisted of an old Whiggish elite class of bankers, industrialists, and others interested far more in economic growth and sectional reconciliation than in radical social reforms. A second group consisted of northern Republicans who headed south out of motives similar to those prompting migration southward in our own time. These included capitalists seeking economic investment in land, railroads, and new industries; retired Union veterans seeking a warmer climate for health purposes; and missionaries and teachers pursuing an outlet for their idealism in the Freedmen's Bureau schools. Such people were unfairly labeled "carpetbaggers."

Moderate blacks made up a third group participating in the Republican state governments. A large percentage of black officeholders were mulattoes, many of them well-educated preachers, teachers, and soldiers from the North. Others, such as John Lynch of Mississippi, were self-educated tradesmen or representatives of the small landed class of southern blacks. In South Carolina, for example, of some 255 black state and federal officials elected between 1868 and 1876, two-thirds were literate and one-third owned real estate. Only 15 percent owned no property at all. This class composition meant that black leaders often supported land policies that largely ignored the economic needs of the black masses.

These black politicians were more interested in pursuing a political agenda of gaining access to government influence and education than an economic agenda of land redistribution or state aid to black peasants. They fashioned their political goals squarely in the American republican tradition. Black leaders reminded whites that they, too, were southerners and Americans, attached both to the land of the South and to the white families they had lived with for generations: "The dust of our fathers mingles with yours in the same grave yards. . . . This is your country, but it is ours too." Because of this intermingled past, blacks sought no revenge or reversal of power, only, as an 1865 petition said, "that the same laws which govern white men shall govern black men [and that] we be dealt with as others are—in equity and justice."

The primary accomplishment of Republican rule in the South was in eliminating the undemocratic features of earlier state constitutions. All states provided universal men's suffrage and loosened requirements for holding office. The basis of state representation was made fairer by apportioning more legislative seats to the interior regions of southern states. Social legislation included the abolition of automatic imprisonment for debt and laws for the relief of poverty and for the care of the handicapped. The first divorce laws in many southern states were passed, as were laws granting property rights to married women. Penal laws were modernized by reducing the list of crimes punishable by death, in one state from 26 to 5.

Republican governments undertook the task of financially and physically reconstructing the South, overhauling tax systems, and approving generous railroad and other capital investment bonds. Harbors, roads, and bridges were rebuilt. Hospitals, asylums, and other state institutions

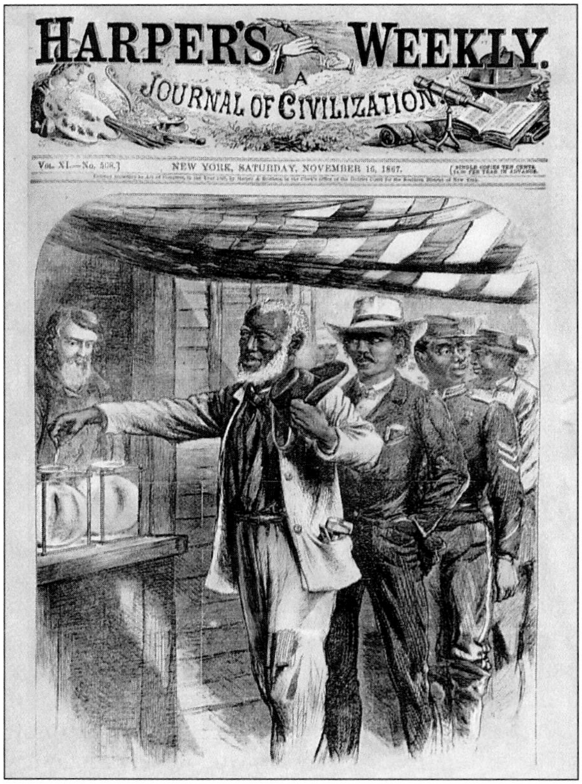

An illustration from *Harper's Weekly* from 1867 celebrates "The First Vote," as newly freed African-American males, including one still in his Union army uniform, express their political rights in the transition from slavery to freedom. Unfortunately, these rights would be short-lived in the difficult era known as "Reconstruction."

were established. Most important, the Republican governments provided for a state-supported system of public schools, absent before in most of the South. As in the North, these schools were largely segregated, but for the first time, rich and poor, black and white alike had access to education. As a result, black school attendance increased from 5 to over 40 percent, and white from 20 to over 60 percent by the 1880s. All this cost money, and the Republicans did indeed greatly increase tax rates and state debts. All in all, the Republican governments "dragged the South, screaming and crying, into the modern world."

These considerable accomplishments were achieved in the midst of opposition like that expressed at a convention of Louisiana planters, which labeled the Republican leaders the "lowest and most corrupt body of men ever assembled in the South." There was some corruption, to be sure, but mostly in land sales, fraudulent railway bonds, and construction contracts, the kind of graft that had become a way of life in American politics, South and North, in the aftermath of the Civil War. Given their lack of experience with politics, the black role was remarkable. As Du Bois put it, "There was one thing that the White South feared more than negro dishonesty, ignorance, and incompetence, and that was negro honesty, knowledge, and efficiency."

Despite its effectiveness in modernizing southern state governments, the Republican coalition did not last very long. In fact, as the accompanying map indicates, Republican rule lasted for different periods of time in different states. In some states, Virginia, for example, the Republicans ruled hardly at all. Situated in the shadow of Washington, conservatives in Virginia professed their agreement with Congress's Reconstruction guidelines while doing as they pleased. As one of the states most devastated by the war, Virginia looked almost immediately to northern investors to rebuild its cities and to develop industry. Blacks and whites alike flocked to the cities for work. In South Carolina, the unwillingness of black leaders to use their power to help black laborers contributed to their loss of political control to the Democrats. Class tensions and divisions among blacks in Louisiana helped to weaken that Republican regime as well.

Republican rule lasted the longest in the black belt states of the Deep South, where the black population was equal to or greater than the white. In Louisiana, Reconstruction began with General Ben Butler's occupation of New Orleans in 1862. Although he insisted on granting civil rights to blacks, he was quickly replaced by a succession of Republican governors in the late 1860s more interested in graft, election laws, and staying in office than in the rights and welfare of poor black Louisianans. Alabama received a flood of northern capital to develop the rich coal, iron ore, and timber resources of the northern third of the state. Republican rule in Alabama, as in other states, involved a greater role for towns and merchants, the endorsement of generous railroad bonds, and an emergent class structure that replaced the old planter aristocracy with a new industrial one.

The Return of Conservative Democratic Control in Southern States During Reconstruction

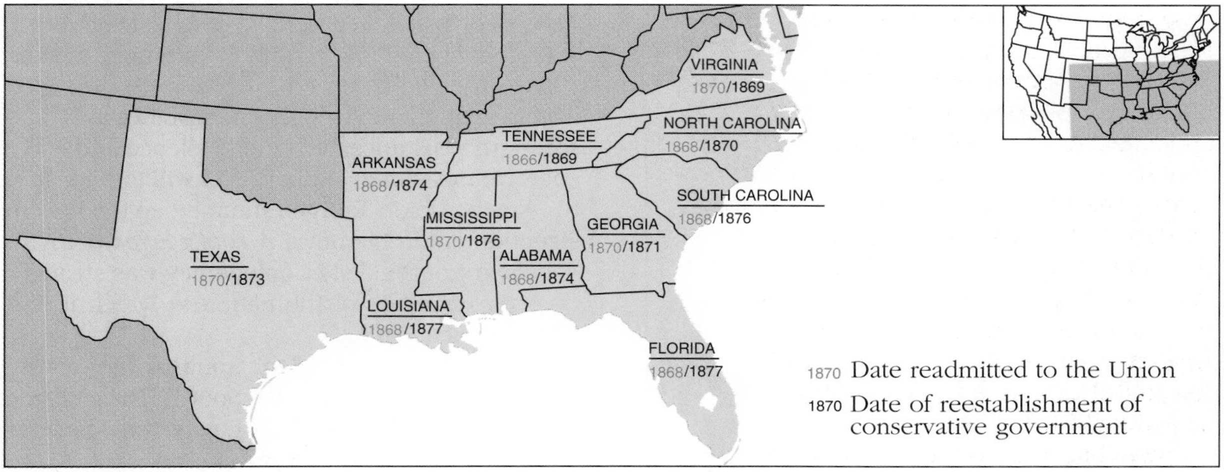

Note that the length of time Republican governments were in power to implement even moderate reconstruction programs varied from state to state. In North Carolina and Georgia, for example, Republican rule was very brief while in Virginia it never took place at all. "Redemption," the return of conservative control, took longest in the three deep South states where electoral votes were hotly contested in the election of 1876.

Violence and "Redemption"

A Georgia newspaper in 1868 charged that Republican rulers would "see this fair land drenched in blood from the Potomac to the Rio Grande rather than lose their power." In fact, it was the Democrats who used racial violence, intimidation, and coercion to restore their power. As one southern editor put it, "We must render this either a white man's government, or convert the land into a Negro man's cemetery." The Ku Klux Klan was only one of several secret organizations that used force and violence against black and white Republicans to drive them from power. The cases of North Carolina and Mississippi are representative in showing how conservative Democrats were able to regain control.

After losing a close election in North Carolina in 1868, conservatives waged a concentrated campaign of terror in several counties in the piedmont area. If the Democrats could win these counties in 1870, they would most likely win statewide. In the year before the election, several prominent Republicans were killed, including a white state senator, whose throat was cut, and a leading black Union League organizer, who was hanged in the courthouse square with a sign pinned to his breast: "Bewar, ye guilty, both white and black." Scores of citizens were flogged, tortured, fired from their jobs, or forced to flee in the middle of the night from burning homes and barns. The courts consistently refused to prosecute anyone for these crimes. Local papers, in fact, charged that "disgusting negroes and white Radicals" had committed the crimes. The conservative campaign worked. In the election of 1870, some 12,000 fewer Republicans voted in the two crucial counties than had voted two years earlier, and the Democrats swept back into power.

As shown in this Thomas Nast cartoon, "Worse than Slavery," to restore a "white man's government" and redeem the noble "lost cause," white groups such as the Ku Klux Klan and the White Leagues used every form of terror, violence, and intimidation.

In the state election in Mississippi in 1875, Democrats used similar tactics, openly announcing that "the thieves. . . , robbers, and scoundrels, white and black," in power "deserve death and ought to be killed." In what was called the Mississippi Plan, local Democratic clubs organized themselves into armed militias, marching defiantly through black areas, breaking up Republican meetings, and provoking riots to justify the killing of hundreds of blacks. Armed men were posted during voter registration to intimidate Republicans. At the election itself, anyone still bold enough to attempt to vote was either helped by gun-toting whites to cast a Democratic ballot or driven away from the polls with cannon and clubs. Counties that had earlier given Republican candidates majorities in the thousands in 1875 managed a total of less than a dozen votes!

Democrats called their victory "redemption." As conservative Democratic administrations resumed control of each state government, Reconstruction came to an end. Redemption resulted from a combination of the persistence of white southern resistance, including violence and other coercive measures, and a loss of will to persist in the North. Albion Tourgée summed up the Reconstruction era in his novel *A Fool's Errand* (1879): "The spirit of the dead Confederacy was stronger than the mandate of the nation to which it had succumbed in battle."

Congress and President Grant did not totally ignore the violence in the South. Three Force Acts, passed in 1870 and 1871, gave the president strong powers to use federal supervisors to make sure that citizens were not prevented from voting by force or fraud. The third act, known as the Ku Klux Klan Act, declared illegal secret organizations that used disguise and coercion to deprive others of equal protection of the laws. Congress created a joint committee to investigate Klan violence, which reported in 1872 in 13 huge volumes of horrifying testimony. Grant, who had supported these measures, delivered special messages to Congress proclaiming the importance of the right to vote, issued proclamations condemning lawlessness, and sent some additional troops to South Carolina. However, as reform Republicans realized that black voters supported Grant, they lost interest in defending those voters. Regular Republicans were also not very supportive, since many felt that they could do without black voters. Both groups were much more concerned with northern issues. In 1875, Grant's advisers told him that Republicans might lose important Ohio elections if he continued to protect blacks. Thus he decided that year to reject appeals by Mississippi blacks that troops be stationed in their state to guarantee free elections. Grant declared instead that he and the nation "had tired of these annual autumnal outbreaks."

The success of the Mississippi Plan in 1875, imitated a year later in South Carolina and Louisiana, indicated that congressional reports and presidential proclamations did little to stop the reign of terror against black and white Republicans throughout the South. The Force Acts were wholly inadequate and were themselves weakly enforced. Although there were hundreds of arrests, all-white juries were reluctant to find their fellow citizens guilty of crimes against blacks. The U.S. Supreme Court backed them. In two decisions in 1874, the Court threw out cases against whites found guilty of preventing blacks from voting and declared key parts of the Force Acts unconstitutional. In Hamburg, South Carolina, in 1876, several blacks were killed in a riot that started in a courtroom when a white mob came to provide its own form of "justice" to some black militiamen who had been arrested for parading on Independence Day. Although the Ku Klux Klan's power was officially ended, the attitudes (and tactics) of Klansmen would continue long into the next century.

Reconstruction, Northern Style

The American people, like their leaders, were tired of battles over the freedmen and were shifting their attention to other matters than fulfilling idealistic principles. Frustrated with the difficulties of trying to transform an unwilling South and seemingly ungrateful blacks, the easiest course was to give blacks their citizenship and the vote and move on to something else. After the interruptions of civil war and its aftermath, most Americans were primarily interested in starting families, finding work, and making money. This meant firing furnaces in the new steel plant in Wheeling, West Virginia, pounding in railroad ties for the Central Pacific in the Nevada desert, struggling to teach in a one-room schoolhouse in Vermont for $23 a month, or battling heat, locusts, and railroad rates on a family homestead in Kansas.

At both the individual and national levels, Reconstruction, northern style, meant the continuation of the enormous economic revolution of the nineteenth century. Although failing to effect a smooth transition from slavery to freedom for ex-slaves, Republican northerners were able to accelerate and solidify their program of economic growth and industrial and territorial expansion.

As Klansmen met in dark forests to plan their next raid in North Carolina in 1869, the Central Pacific and Union Pacific railroads met at Promontory Point, Utah, linking the Atlantic and the Pacific by rail. As cotton production increased again in the postbellum South, so did the making of iron and steel in the North and the settlement of the mining, cattle, and agricultural frontiers in the West. But also, as black farmers were "haggling" over work contracts with white landowners in Georgia, white workers were organizing and joining the National Labor Union in Baltimore. As Elizabeth and Adele Allston demanded the keys to their crop barns in the summer of 1865, the Boston Labor Reform Association was demanding that "our . . . education, morals, dwellings, and the whole Social System" needed to be "reconstructed." If the South would not be reconstructed, labor relations might be.

The years between 1865 and 1875 featured not only the rise (and fall) of Republican governments in the South but also the spectacular rise of working-class activity and organization. Stimulated by the Civil War to improve working conditions in northern factories, such groups as trade unions, labor reform associations, and labor parties flourished, culminating in the founding of the National Labor Union in 1866. Before the depression of 1873, an estimated 300,000 to 500,000 American workers had enrolled in some 1,500 trade unions, the largest such increase in the nineteenth century. This growth would inevitably

These two scenes vividly contrast family life during Reconstruction in the North and South. For most white northerners, as shown in this 1868 Currier & Ives print, the end of the Civil War meant renewing the good life of genteel middle-class values. For many black freedmen, however, family life was constantly threatened by the intrusion of Klan violence.

affect class tensions. In 1876, hundreds of freedmen in the rice region along the Combahee River in South Carolina went on strike to protest a 40-cent-per-day wage cut, clashing with local sheriffs and white Democratic rifle clubs. A year later, also over wage cuts, thousands of railroad workers in Pittsburgh, St. Louis, Omaha, and other northern cities went out in a nationwide wave of strikes, clashing with local police and the National Guard.

As economic relations changed, so did the Republican party. Heralded by the moderate tone of the state elections of 1867 and the national election of Grant in 1868, the Republican change was from a party of moral reform to one of material interest. In the continuing struggle in American politics between "virtue and commerce," self-interest was again winning. No longer willing to support an agency like the Freedmen's Bureau, Republican politicians had no difficulty backing huge grants of money and land to the railroads. As blacks were told to go to work and help themselves, the Union Pacific was being given subsidies of between $16,000 and $48,000 for each mile of track laid across western plains and mountains. As Susan B. Anthony and others were tramping through the snows of Upstate New York with petitions for rights of suffrage and citizenship, Boss Tweed and others were defrauding the citizen-taxpayers of New York of millions of dollars in boondoggles. As Native Americans in the Great Plains struggled to preserve their sacred Black Hills from greedy gold prospectors and U.S. soldiers, urban, state, and federal officials in the East were "mining" public treasuries by means of various forms of graft.

By 1869, the year financier Jay Gould almost succeeded in cornering the gold market, the nation was increasingly defined by materialistic "go-getters" and by sordid grasping for wealth and power. Henry Adams, descendant of two presidents, was living in Washington, D.C., during this era. As he wrote later in his autobiography, *The Education of Henry Adams* (1907), he had high expectations in 1869 that Grant, like another "great soldier" and president, George Washington, would restore moral order and peace. But when Grant announced the members of his cabinet, a group of Army cronies and rich friends to whom he owed favors, Adams felt betrayed, complaining that "a great soldier might be a baby politician."

Ulysses Grant himself was an honest man, but his judgment of others was flawed. His administration featured a series of scandals that touched several cabinet officers and relatives and even two vice-presidents. Under Grant's appointments, outright graft, as well as loose prosecution and generally negligent administration, flourished in a half dozen departments. Most scandals involved large sums of public money. The Whiskey Ring affair, for example, cost the public millions of dollars in lost tax revenues siphoned off to government officials. Gould's gold scam received the unwitting aid of Grant's Treasury Department and the knowing help of his brother-in-law.

Nor was Congress pure in these various schemes. Crédit Mobilier figured in the largest of several scandals in which construction companies for transcontinental railroads (in this case a dummy company) received generous bonds and work contracts in exchange for giving congressmen gifts of money, stocks, and railroad lands. An Ohio congressmen described the House of Representatives in 1873 as an "auction room where more valuable considerations were disposed of under the speaker's hammer than any place on earth." Henry Adams spoke for many Americans when he said that Grant's administration "outraged every rule of decency."

In *Democracy* (1880), a novel written about Washington life during this period, Adams's main character, Mrs. Madeleine Lee, sought to uncover "the heart of the great American mystery of democracy and government." What she found were corrupt legislators and lobbyists in an unprincipled pursuit of power and wealth. "Surely something can be done to check corruption?" Mrs. Lee asked her friend one evening. "Are we forever to be at the mercy of thieves and ruffians? Is a respectable government impossible in a democracy?" The answer she heard was hardly reassuring: "No responsible government can long be much better or much worse than the society it represents."

The election of 1872 marked the decline of public interest in moral issues. A "liberal" faction of the Republican party, unable to dislodge Grant and disgusted with his administration, formed a third party with a reform platform and nominated Horace Greeley, editor of the New York *Tribune*, for president. The liberal Republicans advocated free trade, which meant lower tariffs and fewer grants to railroads; honest government, which meant civil service reform; and noninterference in southern race relations, which meant the removal of federal troops from the South. Democrats, lacking notable presidential candidates, also nominated Greeley, even though he had spent much of his earlier career assailing Democrats as "rascals." Despite his wretched record, Grant easily won a second term. Greeley was beaten so badly, he said, that "I hardly knew whether I was running for the Presidency or the Penitentiary."

The End of Reconstruction

Soon after Grant's second inauguration, a financial panic, caused by overconstruction of railroads and the collapse of some crucial eastern banks, created a terrible depression that lasted throughout the mid-1870s. In these times of hardship, economic issues dominated politics, further pulling attention away from the plight of the freedmen. As Democrats took control of the House of Representatives in 1874 and looked toward winning the White House in 1876, politicians talked about such issues as new scandals in the Grant administration, unemployment and various proposals for public works expenditures for relief,

As early as 1868, three white groups—here stereotyped as apelike northern Irish workers, unrepentant ex-Confederates, and rich northern capitalists—joined hands to bring Republican Reconstruction to an end almost before it began. The immigrant's vote, the Kluxer's knife, and the capitalist's dollars would restore a "white man's government" on the back of the freedman, still clutching the Union flag and reaching in vain for the ballot box. No single image better captures the story of the end of Reconstruction than this Thomas Nast cartoon.

Novels

We usually read novels, short stories, and other forms of fiction for pleasure, for the enjoyment of plot, style, symbolism, and character development. "Classic" novels such as *Moby Dick, Huckleberry Finn, The Great Gatsby,* and *The Invisible Man,* to name a few American examples, are not only written well but also explore timeless questions of good and evil, of innocence and knowledge, or of noble dreams fulfilled and shattered. Often we enjoy novels because we find ourselves identifying with one of the major characters. Through that person's problems, joys, relationships, and search for identity we gain insights about our own.

We can also read novels as historical sources, for they reveal much about the attitudes, dreams, fears, life styles, and ordinary everyday experiences of human beings in a particular historical period. They also show how people reacted to and felt about the major events of that era. The novelist, like the historian, is a product of time and place and has an interpretive point of view.

Consider the two novels about Reconstruction quoted here. Neither is reputed for great literary merit, yet both reveal much about the various interpretations and impassioned attitudes of the post-Civil War era. *A Fool's Errand* was written by Albion Tourgée, a northerner; *The Clansman,* by Thomas Dixon, Jr., a southerner.

Tourgée was a young northern teacher and lawyer who fought with the Union army at several major battles during the Civil War. After the war, he moved to North Carolina, partly for health reasons and partly to begin a legal career. He became a judge and was an active Republican, supporting black suffrage and helping to shape the new state constitution and the codification of North Carolina laws in 1868. With jurisdiction over eight counties, Tourgée earned a reputation as one of the fairest judges in the state. Because he boldly criticized the Ku Klux Klan for its campaign of terror against blacks, his life was threatened many times. When the fearless judge finally left North Carolina in 1879, he published an autobiographical novel about his experiences.

The "fool's errand" in the novel is that of the northern veteran, Comfort Servosse, who like Tourgée seeks to fulfill humane goals on behalf of both blacks and whites in post-Civil War North Carolina. His efforts are thwarted, however, by threats, intimidation, a campaign of violent "outrages" against Republican leaders in the county, and a lack of support from the so-called wise men in Congress. Historians have verified the accuracy, down to the smallest details, of the events in Tourgée's novel. While exposing the brutality of the Klan, Tourgée features loyal southern Unionists, respectable planters ashamed of Klan violence, and even guilt-ridden poor white Klansmen who try to protect or warn intended victims.

In the year of Tourgée's death, 1905, another North Carolinian published a novel with a very different analysis of Reconstruction and its fate. Thomas Dixon was born during the Civil War. He was a lawyer, North Carolina state legislator, Baptist minister, lecturer, and novelist. *The Clansman,* subtitled *A Historical Romance of the Ku Klux Klan,* reflects turn-of-the-century attitudes most white southerners still had about Republican rule during Reconstruction. According to Dixon, once the "Great Heart" Lincoln was gone, a power-crazed, vindictive radical Congress, led by scheming Austin Stoneman (Thaddeus Stevens), sought to impose corrupt carpetbagger and brutal black rule by bayonet on a helpless South. Only through the inspired leadership and redemptive role of the Ku Klux Klan was the South saved from the horrors of rape and revenge.

Dixon dedicated *The Clansman* to his uncle, a Grand Titan of the Klan in North Carolina during the time when two crucial counties were being transformed from Republican to Democratic through intimidation and terror. No such violence shows up in Dixon's novel. When the novel was made the basis of D. W. Griffith's film classic, *Birth of a Nation,* in 1915, the novel's attitudes were firmly imprinted on the twentieth-century American mind.

Both novels convey the events and attitudes of the era by creating clearly defined heroes and villains. Both include exciting chase scenes, narrow escapes, daring rescues, and tragic, heart-rending deaths. Both include romantic subplots in which a young white southern man falls in love with a young white northern woman. In each novel, however, the author's primary purpose was to convey his views of the politics of Reconstruction. Examining brief excerpts is a poor substitute for reading the novels in their entirety. Notice the obvious differences of style and attitude in the descriptions of Uncle Jerry and Old Aleck.

what else did he do?

A Fool's Errand

Albion Tourgée (1879)

When the second Christmas came, Metta wrote again to her sister:

"The feeling is terribly bitter against Comfort on account of his course towards the colored people. There is quite a village of them on the lower end of the plantation. They have a church, a sabbath school, and are to have next year a school. You can not imagine how kind they have been to us, and how much they are attached to Comfort. . . . I got Comfort to go with me to one of their prayer-meetings a few nights ago. I had heard a great deal about them, but had never attended one before. It was strangely weird. There were, perhaps, fifty present, mostly middle-aged men and women. They were singing in a soft, low monotone, interspersed with prolonged exclamatory notes, a sort of rude hymn, which I was surprised to know was one of their old songs in slave times. How the chorus came to be endured in those days I can not imagine. It was—

'Free! free! free, my Lord, free!

An' we walks de hebben-ly way!'

"A few looked around as we came in and seated ourselves; and Uncle Jerry, the saint of the settlement, came forward on his staves, and said, in his soft voice,

"'Ev'nin', Kunnel! Sarvant, Missus! Will you walk up, an' hev seats in front?'

"We told him we had just looked in, and might go in a short time; so we would stay in the back part of the audience.

"Uncle Jerry can not read nor write; but he is a man of strange intelligence and power. Unable to do work of any account, he is the faithful friend, monitor, and director of others. He has a house and piece of land, all paid for, a good horse and cow, and, with the aid of his wife and two boys, made a fine crop this season. He is one of the most promising colored men in the settlement: so Comfort says, at least. Everybody seems to have great respect for his character. I don't know how many people I have heard speak of his religion. Mr. Savage used to say he had rather hear him pray than any other man on earth. He was much prized by his master, even after he was disabled, on account of his faithfulness and character."

The Clansman

Thomas Dixon, Jr. (1905)

At noon Ben and Phil strolled to the polling-place to watch the progress of the first election under Negro rule. The Square was jammed with shouting, jostling, perspiring negroes, men, women, and children. The day was warm, and the African odour was supreme even in the open air. . . .

The negroes, under the drill of the League and the Freedman's Bureau, protected by the bayonet, were voting to enfranchise themselves, disfranchise their former masters, ratify a new constitution, and elect a legislature to do their will. Old Aleck was a candidate for the House, chief poll-holder, and seemed to be in charge of the movements of the voters outside the booth as well as inside. He appeared to be omnipresent, and his self-importance was a sight Phil had never dreamed. He could not keep his eyes off him. . . .

[Aleck] was a born African orator, undoubtedly descended from a long line of savage spell-binders, whose eloquence in the palaver houses of the jungle had made them native leaders. His thin spindle-shanks supported an oblong, protruding stomach, resembling an elderly monkey's, which seemed so heavy it swayed his back to carry it.

The animal vivacity of his small eyes and the flexibility of his eyebrows, which he worked up and down rapidly with every change of countenance, expressed his eager desires.

He had laid aside his new shoes, which hurt him, and went barefooted to facilitate his movements on the great occasion. His heels projected and his foot was so flat that what should have been the hollow of it made a hole in the dirt where he left his track.

He was already mellow with liquor, and was dressed in an old army uniform and cap, with two horse-pistols buckled around his waist. On a strap hanging from his shoulder were strung a half-dozen tin canteens filled with whiskey.

the availability of silver and greenback dollars, and high tariffs.

No one, it seemed, talked much about the rights and conditions of southern freedmen. In 1875, a guilt-ridden Congress passed Senator Charles Sumner's civil rights bill, intended to put teeth into the Fourteenth Amendment. But the act was not enforced and was declared unconstitutional by the Supreme Court eight years later. Congressional Reconstruction, long dormant, had ended. The election of 1876 sealed the conclusion.

As their nominee for president in 1876, the Republicans turned to a former governor of Ohio, Rutherford B. Hayes, partly because of his reputation for honesty, partly because he had been an officer in the Union army (a necessity for post-Civil War candidates), and partly because, as Henry Adams put it, he was "obnoxious to no one." The Democrats chose Governor Samuel J. Tilden of New York, who achieved national recognition as a civil service reformer in breaking up the corrupt Tweed ring.

Tilden won a majority of the popular vote and appeared to have enough electoral votes for victory. Twenty more electoral votes were disputed, all but one in the Deep South states of Louisiana, South Carolina, and Florida, where some federal troops still remained on duty and where Republicans still controlled the voting apparatus. Democrats, however, had applied various versions of the Mississippi Plan to intimidate voters. To resolve the disputed electoral votes, Congress created a special electoral commission consisting of five senators, five representatives, and five Supreme Court justices, eight of whom were Republicans and seven Democrats. The vote in each disputed case was 8 to 7 along party lines. Hayes was given all 20 votes, enough to win, 185 to 184.

Outraged Democrats threatened to stop the Senate from officially counting the electoral votes, thus preventing Hayes's inauguration. The country was in a state of crisis, and some Americans wondered if civil war might break out again. But unlike the 1850s, when passions over slavery erupted, compromise was possible between northerners and southerners mutually interested in modernization of the southern economy through capital investments. They focused on a Pacific railroad linking New Orleans with the West Coast. Northern investors wanted the government to help pay for the railroad, while southerners who hoped that it would revive their economy wanted northern dollars but not northern political influence. This meant no social agencies, no federal enforcement of the Fourteenth and Fifteenth amendments, and no military occupation, not even the small symbolic presence left in 1876.

As the inauguration date approached and newspapers echoed outgoing President Grant's call for "peace at any price," the forces of mutual self-interest concluded the "compromise of 1877." The Democrats agreed to suspend resistance to the counting of the electoral votes, and on March 2, Rutherford B. Hayes was declared president. In exchange for the presidency, Hayes ordered the last remaining troops out of the South, appointed a former Confederate general to his cabinet, supported federal aid to bolster economic and railroad development in the South, and announced his intentions to let southerners handle race relations themselves. He then went on a goodwill trip to the South, where he told blacks in an Atlanta speech that "your rights and interests would be safer if this great mass of intelligent white men were let alone by the general government." The message was clear: Hayes would not enforce the Fourteenth and Fifteenth amendments, thus initiating a pattern of executive inaction not broken until the middle of the twentieth century. But the immediate crisis was averted, officially ending the era of Reconstruction.

CONCLUSION

A Mixed Legacy

In the 12 years between Appomattox and Hayes's inauguration, the diverse dreams of victorious northern Republicans, defeated white southerners, and hopeful black freedmen conflicted. There was little chance that all could be realized, yet each group could point to a modest fulfillment of its goals. The compromise of 1877 cemented the reunion of South and North, thus providing new opportunities for economic development in both regions. The Republican party achieved its economic goals and preserved its political hold on the White House, though not Congress, with two exceptions, until 1932. The ex-Confederate states were brought back into the Union, and southerners retained their firm control of southern lands and black labor, though not without struggle and some changes. To the extent that the peace of 1877 was preserved "at any price," that price was paid by the freedmen.

In 1880, Frederick Douglass summarized Reconstruction for the freedmen:

Our Reconstruction measures were radically defective. . . . To the freedmen was given the machinery of liberty, but there was denied to them the steam to put it in motion. They were given the uniform of soldiers, but no arms; they were called citizens, but left subjects; they were called free, but left almost slaves. The old master class . . . retained the power to starve them to death, and wherever this power is held there is the power of slavery.

Douglass went on to say that it was a wonder to him "not that freedmen have made so little progress, but, rather, that they have made so much; not that they have been standing still, but that they have been able to stand at all." Indeed, despite their liabilities, the freedmen had made admirable gains in education and in economic and family survival. Although sharecropping and tenancy were harsh systems, black laborers organized themselves to achieve a measure of autonomy and opportunity in their lives that could never be diminished. Moreover, the three great Reconstruction amendments to the Constitution, despite flagrant violation over the next 100 years, held out the promise that the rights of equal citizenship and political participation would yet be fulfilled.

Nevertheless, given the potential for reconstructed relations in the postwar period, there was an underlying tragedy to Reconstruction, as a short story by W. E. B. Du Bois, written a few years later, makes sadly clear. Two boyhood playmates, both named John, one black and one white, are sent from the fictional town of Altamaha, Georgia, north to school to prepare for leadership of their respective communities, the black John as a teacher and the white John as a judge and possible governor of the state. While they were away, the black and white people of Altamaha, each race thinking of its own John and not of the other, except with a "vague unrest," waited for "the coming of two young men, and dreamed . . . of new things that would be done and new thoughts that all would think."

After several years, both Johns returned to Altamaha, but a series of tragic events shattered the hopes and dreams of a new era of racial justice and harmony. Neither John understood the people of the town, and each was in turn misunderstood. Black John's school was closed because he was teaching ideals of liberty. Heartbroken and discouraged as he walked through the forest near town, he surprised the white John in an attempted rape of his sister. Without a word, black John picked up a fallen limb and with "all the pent-up hatred of his great black arm" smashed his boyhood friend to death. Within hours he was lynched.

Du Bois's story capsulizes the human cost of the Reconstruction era. The black scholar's hope for reconciliation by a "union of intelligence and sympathy across the color-line" was smashed in the tragic encounter between the two Johns. Both young men, each once filled with glorious dreams, lay dead under the pines of the Georgia forest. Dying with them were hopes that interracial harmony, intersectional trust, and equal opportunities and rights for the freedmen might be the legacies of Reconstruction. Conspicuously absent in the forest scene was the influence of the victorious northerners. They had turned their attention to other, less noble causes.

Recommended Reading

Overviews of Reconstruction

W. E. B. Du Bois, *Black Reconstruction* (1935); Eric Foner, *Reconstruction: America's Unfinished Revolution, 1863–1877* (1988); John Hope Franklin, *Reconstruction After the Civil War* (1961); Kenneth Stampp, *The Era of Reconstruction, 1865–1877* (1965).

The Freedmen's Transition: Freedom by Degrees

W. E. B. Du Bois, *The Souls of Black Folk* (1903); Barbara J. Fields, *Slavery and Freedom on the Middle Ground* (1985); Eric Foner, *Nothing but Freedom: Emancipation and Its Legacy* (1983); Robert Higgs, *Competition and Coercion: Blacks in the American Economy, 1865–1914* (1977); Jacqueline Jones, *Soldiers of Light and Love: Northern Teachers and Georgia Blacks, 1865–1873* (1980); Peter Kolchin, *First Freedom* (1972); Leon Litwack, *Been in the Storm So Long: The Aftermath of Slavery* (1980); Neil R. McMillen, *Dark Journey: Black Mississippians in the Age of Jim Crow* (1989); Clarence L. Mohr, *On the Threshold of Freedom* (1986); Donald Nieman, *To Set the Law in Motion: The Freedmen's Bureau and the Legal Rights of Blacks, 1865–1868* (1979); Claude Oubré, *Forty Acres and a Mule: The Freedmen's Bureau and Black Land Ownership* (1978); Nell I. Painter, *Exodusters: Black Migration to Kansas After Reconstruction* (1977); Roger Ransom and Richard Sutch, *One Kind of Freedom: The Economic Consequences of Emancipation* (1977); Willie Lee Rose, *Rehearsal for Reconstruction* (1964).

Reconstruction Politics: South and North

Richard H. Abbott, *The Republican Party and the South, 1855–1877* (1986); Herman Belz, *Emancipation and Equal Rights: Politics and Constitutionalism in the Civil War Era* (1978); Michael Les Benedict, *A Compromise of Principle: Congressional Republicans and Reconstruction, 1863–1869* (1974); Dan T. Carter, *When the War Was Over: The Failure of Self-Reconstruction in the South* (1985); LaWanda Cox and John Cox, *Politics, Principles, and Prejudice, 1865–1866* (1963); Richard N. Current, *Those Terrible Carpetbaggers* (1988); David Donald, *The Politics of Reconstruction* (1965); William Gillette, *Retreat from Reconstruction, 1869–1879* (1979); Stephen Hahn, *The Roots of Southern Populism* (1983); Thomas Holt, *Black over White: Negro Political Leadership in South Carolina During Reconstruction* (1977); William McFeeley, *Grant: A Biography* (1981); Eric McKitrick, *Andrew Johnson and Reconstruction* (1960); David Montgomery, *Beyond Equality: Labor and the Radical Republicans, 1862–1872* (1967); Michael Perman, *Reunion Without Compromise: The South and Reconstruction, 1865–1868* (1973); *The Road to Redemption: Southern Politics, 1869–1879* (1984); George C. Rable, *But There Was No Peace: The Role of Violence in the Politics of Reconstruction* (1984); Brooks D. Simpson, *Let Us Have Peace: Ulysses S. Grant and the Politics of War and Reconstruction, 1861–1868* (1991); Allen Trelease, *Andrew Johnson: A Biography* (1989); *White Terror: The Ku Klux Klan Conspiracy and Southern Reconstruction* (1971); Ted Tunnell, *Crucible of Reconstruction: War, Radicalism, and Race in Louisiana, 1862–1877* (1984); C. Vann Woodward, *Origins of the New South, 1877–1913* (1951) and *Reunion and Reaction* (1956).

Race Relations and the Literature of Reconstruction

Thomas Dixon, *The Clansman* (1905); W. E. B. Du Bois, *The Quest of the Silver Fleece* (1911); Howard Fast, *Freedom Road* (1944); Ernest Gaines, *The Autobiography of Miss Jane Pittman* (1971); Rayford Logan, *The Betrayal of the Negro,* rev. ed. (1965); Albion Tourgée, *A Fool's Errand* (1879); Joel Williamson, *The Crucible of Race* (1984) and *A Rage for Order: Black/White Relations in the American South Since Emancipation* (1986); C. Vann Woodward, *The Strange Career of Jim Crow,* 3d rev. ed. (1974).

TIMELINE

1865 Civil War ends
Lincoln assassinated; Andrew Johnson becomes president
Johnson proposes general amnesty and reconstruction plan
Racial confusion, widespread hunger, and demobilization
Thirteenth Amendment ratified
Freedmen's Bureau established

1865–1866 Black codes
Repossession of land by whites and freedmen's contracts

1866 Freedmen's Bureau renewed and Civil Rights Act passed over Johnson's veto
Southern Homestead Act
Ku Klux Klan formed
Tennessee readmitted to Union

1867 Reconstruction Acts passed over Johnson's veto
Impeachment controversy
Freedmen's Bureau ends

1868 Fourteenth Amendment ratified
Impeachment of Johnson fails
Ulysses Grant elected president

1868–1870 Ten states readmitted under congressional plan

1869 Georgia and Virginia reestablish Democratic party control

1870 Fifteenth Amendment ratified

1870s–1880s Black "exodusters" migrate to Kansas

1870–1871 Force Acts
North Carolina and Georgia reestablish Democratic control

1872 General Amnesty Act
Grant reelected president

1873 Crédit Mobilier scandal
Panic causes depression

1874 Alabama and Arkansas reestablish Democratic control

1875 Civil Rights Act
Mississippi reestablishes Democratic control

1876 Hayes-Tilden election

1876–1877 South Carolina, Louisiana, and Florida reestablish Democratic control

1877 Compromise of 1877; Rutherford B. Hayes assumes presidency and ends Reconstruction

1880s Tenancy and sharecropping prevail in the South
Disfranchisement and segregation of southern blacks begins

PART IV

An Industrializing People, 1865–1900

COMPARATIVE CHRONOLOGIES

1865

POLITICAL AND DIPLOMATIC

1867 Alaska purchased
1869–1874 Granger laws

SOCIAL AND ECONOMIC

1866 National Labor Union founded
1867 National Grange founded
1868 Eight-hour day for federal employees
1869 Prohibition party formed
Knights of Labor formed

CULTURAL AND TECHNOLOGICAL

1860s Bessemer and open-hearth steel processes introduced
1865 Vassar College founded
1866 Atlantic Cable laid
1867 First Horatio Alger novels published
First elevated railway in New York City
1869 First transcontinental railroad link completed

1870

POLITICAL AND DIPLOMATIC

1870 Wyoming Territory grants suffrage to women
1871 Tweed ring exposed
Indian Appropriation Act
Civil Service Commission created
1872 Grant reelected
1873 "Salary Grab" Act

SOCIAL AND ECONOMIC

1870 J. D. Rockefeller forms Standard Oil of Ohio
Chicago fire
Army suppresses Apaches
1872 Yellowstone National Park established
Montgomery Ward, first mail-order house, opens
1873 Bethlehem Steel begins production
1873–1879 Depression
1874 Women's Christian Temperance Union founded
Greenback party formed

CULTURAL AND TECHNOLOGICAL

1870 Thomas Edison invents stock ticker
1872 Expansion of public schools and higher education begins
1873 Mark Twain and Charles Dudley Warner coin the expression "Gilded Age"
1874 Barbed wire patented
First electric streetcar runs in New York City

1875

POLITICAL AND DIPLOMATIC

1875 Specie Resumption Act
United States–Hawaii commercial treaty
1877 Rutherford B. Hayes becomes president
Munn v. *Illinois*
Reconstruction ends
1878 Bland-Allison Act

SOCIAL AND ECONOMIC

1875–1876 Indian Wars in Black Hills
1877 Nez Percé Indian uprisings
Black exodusters to Kansas
Railroad strikes

CULTURAL AND TECHNOLOGICAL

1875 Wellesley College founded
First running of the Kentucky Derby
1876 Centennial Exposition in Philadelphia
Alexander Graham Bell invents telephone
First major baseball league formed
Mark Twain, *Adventures of Tom Sawyer*
1877 C. E. Hires begins making root beer
1878 Timber and Stove Act
1879 Henry George, *Progress and Poverty*
Edison perfects light bulb

1900

1880

	POLITICAL AND DIPLOMATIC		SOCIAL AND ECONOMIC		CULTURAL AND TECHNOLOGICAL
1880	James A. Garfield elected	1880s	"New South"	1880	Social Darwinism and Social Gospel
1881	Garfield assassinated; Chester A. Arthur becomes president	1882	Standard Oil Trust established	1881	Tuskegee Institute founded
1882	Chinese Exclusion Act	1883–1885	Depression	1883	Brooklyn Bridge
1883	Pendleton Civil Service Act	1884	Southern Farmers' Alliance founded	1884	W. D. Howells, *The Rise of Silas Lapham*
1884	Grover Cleveland elected				

1885

	POLITICAL AND DIPLOMATIC		SOCIAL AND ECONOMIC		CULTURAL AND TECHNOLOGICAL
1886	*Wabash* v. *Illinois*	1885	"New Immigration" begins	1888	Edward Bellamy, *Looking Backward*
1887	Dawes Severalty Act	1886	American Federation of Labor founded	1889	Andrew Carnegie, "The Gospel of Wealth"
	Interstate Commerce Act		Haymarket Riot		
1888	Benjamin Harrison elected	1887	College Settlement House Association founded		
		1888	Colored Farmers' Alliance established		
		1889	Hull House founded		
		1889–1890	Ghost Dance		
			Battle of Wounded Knee		

1890

	POLITICAL AND DIPLOMATIC		SOCIAL AND ECONOMIC		CULTURAL AND TECHNOLOGICAL
1890	Sherman Anti-Trust Act	1890	General Federation of Women's Clubs founded	1890s	Electric trolleys
	Sherman Silver Purchase Act		National American Women Suffrage Association formed	1890	Alfred Thayer Mahan, *Influence of Sea Power upon History*
	McKinley Tariff	1892	Homestead strike	1891	Hamlin Garland, *Main-travelled Roads*
1890	Yosemite National Park established	1893	Anti-Saloon League founded	1893	Stephen Crane, *Maggie: A Girl of the Streets*
1890s	Jim Crow laws and disfranchisement attempts in the South	1893–1897	Depression		World's Exposition in Chicago
1892	Populist party formed	1894	Pullman strike		City Beautiful movement
	Cleveland elected to second term		Coxey's march		
	Sierra Club founded				
1893	Hawaiian coup by American sugar growers				

1895

	POLITICAL AND DIPLOMATIC		SOCIAL AND ECONOMIC		CULTURAL AND TECHNOLOGICAL
1895	Cuban Revolution	1895	Booker T. Washington's "Atlanta Compromise" speech	1895	Elizabeth Cady Stanton, *Woman's Bible*
	United States v. *E. C. Knight*			1896	Charles Sheldon, *In His Steps*
1896	William McKinley elected			1898	Charlotte Perkin Gilman, *Women and Economics*
	Plessy v. *Ferguson*			1899	John Dewey, *School and Society*
1898	Sinking of the *Maine*				
	Spanish-American War				
	Treaty of Paris				
	Annexation of Hawaii and the Philippines				
1899–1900	Open Door notes				
1899–1902	Filipino-American War				

CHAPTER 17

The Farmer's World

In 1873, Milton Leeper, his wife Hattie, and their baby Anna climbed into a wagon piled high with their possessions and set out to homestead in Boone County, Nebraska. Once on the claim, the Leepers dreamed confidently of their future. Wrote Hattie to her sister in Iowa, "I like our place the best of any around here." "When we get a fine house and 100 acres under cultivation," she added, "I wouldn't trade with any one." But Milton had broken in only 13 acres when disaster struck. Hordes of grasshoppers appeared, and the Leepers fled their claim and took refuge in the nearby town of Fremont.

There they stayed for two years. Milton worked first at a store, then hired out to other farmers. Hattie sewed, kept a boarder, and cared for chickens and a milk cow. The family lived on the brink of poverty but never gave up hope. "Times are hard and we have had bad luck," Hattie acknowledged, but "I am going to hold that claim . . . there will [be] one gal that won't be out of a home." In 1876, the Leepers triumphantly returned to their claim with the modest sum of $27 to help them start over.

The grasshoppers were gone, there was enough rain, and preaching was only half a mile away. The Leepers, like others, began to prosper. Two more daughters were born and cared for in the comfortable sod house, "homely" on the outside but plastered and cozy within. As Hattie explained, the homesteaders lived "just as civilized as they would in Chicago."

Their luck did not last. Hattie, pregnant again, fell ill and died in childbirth along with her infant son. Heartbroken, Milton buried his wife and child and left the claim. The last frontier had momentarily defeated him, although he would try farming in at least four other locations before his death in 1905.

The same year that the Leepers established their Boone County homestead, another family tried their luck in a Danish settlement about 200 miles west of Omaha. Rasmus and Ane Ebbesen and their 8-year-old son, Peter, had arrived in the United States from Denmark in 1868, lured by the promise of an "abundance" of free land "for all willing to cultivate it." By 1870, they had made it as far west as Council Bluffs, Iowa. There they stopped to earn the capital that would be necessary to begin farming. Rasmus dug ditches for the railroad, Ane worked as a cleaning woman in a local boardinghouse, and young Peter brought drinking water to thirsty laborers who were digging ditches for the town gas works.

Like the Leepers, the Ebbesens eagerly settled on their homestead and began to cultivate the soil. Peter later recalled that the problems that the family had anticipated never materialized. Even the rumors that the Sioux, "flying demons" in the eyes of settlers, were on the rampage proved false. The real problems the family faced were unexpected: rattlesnakes, prairie fires, and an invasion of grasshoppers. The grasshoppers were just as devastating to the Ebbesen farm as they had been to the Leeper homestead. But unlike the Leepers, the Ebbesens stayed on the claim. While the family "barely had enough" to eat, they survived the three years of grasshopper infestation.

In the following years, the Ebbesens thrived. Rasmus had almost all the original 80 acres under cultivation and purchased an additional 80 acres from the railroad. A succession of sod houses rose on the land and finally even a two-story frame house, paid for with money Peter earned teaching school. By 1873, Rasmus and Ane were over 50 and could look with pride at their "luxurient and promising crop." But once more natural disaster struck, a "violent hailstorm . . . which completely devastated the whole lot."

The Ebbesens were lucky, however. A banker offered to buy them out, for $1,000 under what the family calculated was the farm's "real worth." But it was enough for the purchase of a "modest" house in town. Later, there was even a "dwelling of two stories and nine rooms . . . with adjacent park."

The stories of the Leepers and the Ebbesens, though different in their details and endings, hint at some of the problems confronting rural Americans in the last quarter of the nineteenth century. As a mature industrial economy transformed agriculture and shifted the balance of economic power permanently away from America's farmlands to the country's cities and factories, many farmers found it impossible to realize the traditional dream of rural independence and prosperity. Even bountiful harvests no longer guaranteed success. "We were told two years ago to go to work and raise a big crop; that was all we needed," said one farmer. "We went to work and plowed and planted; the rains fell, the sun shone, nature smiled, and we raised the big crop they told us to; and what came of it? Eight cent corn, ten cent oats, two cent beef and no price at all for butter and eggs—that's what came of it." Native Americans also discovered that changes in rural life threatened their values and dreams. As the Sioux leader Red Cloud told railroad surveyors in Wyoming, "We do not want you here. You are scaring away the buffalo."

This chapter explores the agricultural transformation of the late nineteenth century and highlights the ways in which rural Americans—red, white, and black—joined the industrial world and responded to new conditions. The rise of large-scale agriculture in the West, the exploitation of its natural resources, and the development of the Great Plains form a backdrop for the discussion of the impact of white settlement on western tribes and their reactions to white incursions. In an analysis of the South, the efforts of whites to create a "New South" form a contrast to the underlying realities of race and cotton. While the chapter shows that discrimination and economic peonage characterized the lives of most black southerners during this period, it also describes the rise of new black protest tactics and ideologies. Finally, the chapter highlights the ways in which agricultural problems of the late nineteenth century, which would continue to characterize much of agricultural life in the twentieth century, led American farmers to protest their place in American life and to form the Populist party.

Modernizing Agriculture

Between 1865 and 1900, the nation's farms more than doubled in number as Americans eagerly took up virgin land west of the Mississippi River. In both newly settled and older areas, farmers raised specialized crops with the aid of modern machinery and relied on the expanding railroad system to send them to market. The character of agriculture became increasingly capitalistic. Farmers, as one New Englander pointed out, "must understand farming as a business; if they do not it will go hard with them."

Rural Myth and Reality

The number of Americans still farming the land suggested the vigor of a rural tradition which pictured the farmer as a central figure for the nation. In Thomas Jefferson's words, the farmer was the "deposit for substantial and genuine virtue" and therefore fundamental to the health of the republic.

The notion that the farmer and the farm life symbolized the essence of America persisted as the United States industrialized. The popularity of inexpensive Currier and Ives prints testifies to the powerful appeal of an idealized view of country life. Healthy, well-dressed, vigorous farmers are the sturdy yeomen of Jeffersonian rhetoric. Their robust, attractive wives are content with their snug houses and the rhythms of country life. Rural children amuse themselves in pleasant diversions—skating, fishing, riding on wagons, gathering fruit. All is well in the countryside.

Other Currier and Ives prints implied that there need be no conflict between the new tech-

This 1875 Currier & Ives print provides an idyllic view of rural life. Happy children greet hunters loaded down with game, while the woman of the family looks out from her cozy cabin at the cheerful sight.

nological industrial world and rural America. Trains, representing the new order, chug peacefully through farmlands, while cheering children and trusting adults look on. Railroads bring progress but not the destruction of the land or the livelihood of those on it.

The prints obscured the reality of American agriculture. However much Americans wanted to believe that no tension existed between technological progress and rural life, it did. Farmers were no longer the backbone of the work force. In 1860, they represented almost 60 percent of the labor force; by 1900, less than 37 percent of employed Americans were farmers. At the same time, farmers' contribution to the nation's wealth declined from a third to a quarter.

Nor were farmers the independent yeomen of the rural myth, for the industrial and urban world increasingly affected them. Reliable, cheap transportation allowed them to specialize. Farmers on the Great Plains now grew most of the country's wheat, while those in the Midwest replaced that crop with corn used to feed hogs and cattle. Eastern farmers turned to vegetable, fruit, and dairy farming. Some, like Milachi Dodge from New Hampshire, gave up farming altogether. As he explained, when his "boys came home" from the Civil War, "they did not want to work on a farm, and I sold my farm out." Cotton continued to dominate the economy of the South, although farmers also raised tobacco, wheat, and rice. In the Far West, grain, fruits, and vegetables predominated.

As farmers specialized in cash crops for national and international markets, their success depended increasingly on outside forces and demands. Bankers and loan companies provided capital to expand farm operations, middlemen stored and sometimes sold produce, railroads carried farm goods to market. A prosperous American economy put money into laborers' pockets for food purchases. Even international conditions affected the American farmer. After 1870, exports of wheat, flour, and animal products rose, with wheat becoming the country's chief cash crop. Thus the cultivation of wheat in Russia and Argentina meant fewer foreign buyers for American grain while the opening of the Canadian high plains in the 1890s added another competitor. When several European countries decided between 1879 and 1883 to ban American pork imports, which they feared were infected with trichinosis, American stock raisers suffered.

Farming had become a modern business which demanded particular attitudes and skills. "Watch and study the markets and the ways of marketmen [and] learn the art of 'selling well,'" one rural editor advised his readers in 1887. "The work of farming is only half done when the crop is out of the ground."

Like other businesses of the post–Civil War era, farming increasingly depended on machinery. "It is no longer necessary for the farmer to cut his wheat with sickle or cradle, nor to rake it and bind it by hand; to cut his cornstalks with a

Agriculture in the 1880s

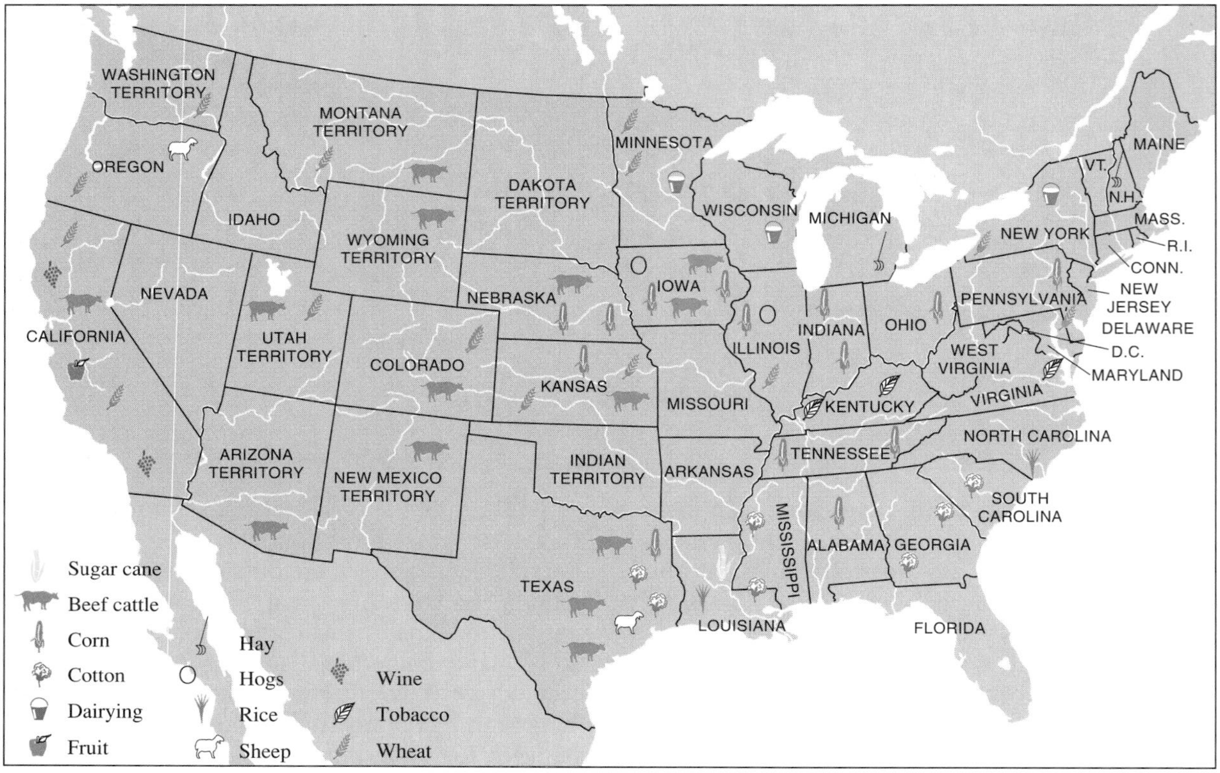

This map reveals the patterns of regional agricultural specialization in 1880.

knife and shock the stalks by hand; to thresh his grain with a flail," reported one observer. Harvesters, binders, and other new machines, pulled by work animals, performed these tasks for him.

These machines diminished much of the drudgery of farming life and made the production of crops easier, more efficient, and cheaper. Moreover, they allowed a farmer to cultivate far more land than he had been able to do with hand tools, so that by 1900 more than twice as much land was in cultivation as in 1860. But machinery was expensive, and many American farmers had to borrow to buy it. In the decade of the 1880s, mortgage indebtedness grew 2½ times faster than agricultural wealth.

New Farmers, New Farms

As farmers relied on machinery, brought new land into cultivation, raised specialized crops, and sent them to faraway markets, they operated much like other nineteenth-century businessmen. Some even became large-scale entrepreneurs. Small family farms still typified American agriculture, but vast mechanized operations devoted to the cultivation of one crop appeared, especially west of the Mississippi River. These farms with huge barns for storage of machinery and only a handful of other buildings had few gardens, trees, or outbuildings. No churches or villages interrupted the monotony of the new agricultural landscape.

The bonanza farms, established in the late 1870s on the northern plains, symbolized the trend to large-scale agriculture. Thousands of acres in size, these wheat farms required large capital investments; in fact, corporations owned many of them. Like factories, they depended on machinery, hired workers, and efficient managers. The North Dakota farm that Oliver Dalrymple operated for two Northern Pacific Railroad directors used 200 pairs of harrows and 125 seeders for planting and required 155 binders and 26 steam threshers for harvesting. At peak times, the farm's work force numbered 600 men. The results were impressive: 600,000 bushels of wheat harvested in 1882. Although bonanza farms were not typical, they dramatized the agricultural changes that were occurring everywhere on a smaller scale.

Overproduction and Falling Prices

Subscribing wholeheartedly to the rural myth Currier and Ives pictured so winningly, farmers only gradually realized that technology might backfire. As they cultivated more land with the help of machinery, they began to discover unanticipated consequences. Productivity rose 40 percent between 1869 and 1899. Almost every crop showed impressive statistical gains. But the yields for some crops like wheat were so large that the domestic market could not absorb them.

The prices farm products commanded steadily declined. In 1867, corn sold for 78 cents a bushel. By 1873, it had tumbled to 31 cents and by 1889 to 23 cents. Wheat similarly plummeted from about $2 a bushel in 1867 to only 70 cents a bushel in 1889. Cotton profits also spiraled downward, the value of a bale depreciating from $43 in 1866 to $30 in the 1890s.

Falling prices did not automatically hurt all farmers. Because the supply of money rose more slowly than productivity, all prices declined—by more than half between the end of the Civil War and 1900 (for a full discussion of the money issue, see Chapter 19). In a deflationary period, farmers were receiving less for their crops but also paying less for their purchases.

George Inness's *Lackawanna Valley*, with the reclining figure in the foreground, the train, and puffing smokestacks in the background, suggests that there need be no conflict between technology and agriculture.

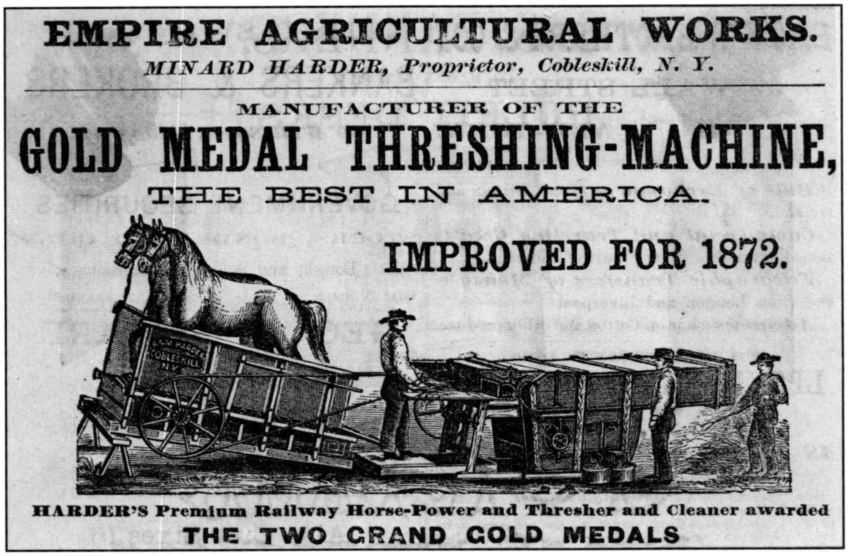

The combination of graphics and text provided a persuasive message about the excellence of the Gold Medal Threshing-Machine. The picture gave prospective purchasers an idea of the machine's appearance and size, while the text emphasized its award-winning status. Other testimonials included with the ad claimed, "It is the best machine we have ever had in the country; have threshed thirty bushels of wheat per hour, and more than double that amount of oats."

Deflation may have encouraged overproduction, however. To make the same amount of money, many farmers believed they had to raise larger and larger crops. As they did, prices fell even lower. Furthermore, deflation increased the real value of debts. In 1888, it took 174 bushels of wheat to pay the interest on a $2,000 mortgage at 8 percent. By 1895, it took 320 bushels. Falling prices thus had their greatest impact on farmers in newly settled areas who had borrowed heavily to finance their new operations.

Farming on the Western Plains: 1880s–1890s

Between 1870 and 1900, the acreage devoted to farming tripled west of the Mississippi as settlers flocked to the Great Plains (North and South Dakota, Kansas, Nebraska, Oklahoma, and Texas). In the mid–nineteenth century, emigrants had driven their wagons over the Plains believing the semiarid climate made them unsuited for cultivation. Views of the farming potential of this vast area changed after the Civil War, however.

Average Farm Acreage, 1860–1900

Region	1860	1870	1880	1890	1900
Land in Farms (1,000 acres)					
United States	407,213	407,735	536,082	623,219	841,202
North Central	107,900	139,215	206,982	256,587	317,349
South	225,514	189,556	234,920	256,606	362,036
West	12,718	16,219	26,194	47,282	96,407
Northeast	61,082	62,744	67,986	62,744	65,409
Average Acreage per Farm (acres)					
United States	199	153	134	137	147
North Central	140	124	122	133	145
South	335	214	153	140	138
West	367	336	313	324	393
Northeast	108	104	98	95	97

Source: U.S. Bureau of the Census.

This 1880 photo highlights the role of machine and animal power rather than human power during the wheat harvest. The huge wheat fields suggest the increased scale of American farming during the late nineteenth century.

Railroads, town boosters, land speculators all needed settlers to make their investments in the Great Plains profitable. To lure settlers there, they launched extravagant promotional campaigns. "This is the sole remaining section of paradise in the western world," claimed one newspaper. "All the wild romances of the gorgeous orient dwindle into nothing when compared to the everyday realities of Dakota's progress." Addressing the fear that the Plains lacked adequate rain, the article promised, "All that is needed is to plow, plant and attend to the crops properly; the rains are abundant." The rainfall, above average for the region in the 1880s, lent strength to the claim of adequate moisture.

Late-nineteenth-century industrial innovations helped settlers overcome the natural obstacles that made farming on the plains so problematic at midcentury. Because there was so little timber for fencing or housing on the plains, early emigrants had chosen to settle elsewhere. But in the 1870s, Joseph Glidden developed barbed wire as a cheap alternative to timber fencing. During a visit to a country fair, Glidden had seen a simple wooden device with protruding points that was intended to keep animals away from fences. The device suggested the possibility of making fencing wire with similar protruding barbs. Before long, he and a partner were producing hundreds of miles of barbed wire fencing that could be used to enclose fields on the Plains. Other innovations overcame some of the remaining challenges to successful agriculture. Twine binders, which speeded up grain harvesting, reduced the threat of losing crops to the unpredictable weather. And mail-order steel windmills for pumping water from deep underground wells relieved water shortages by the 1890s.

In the first boom period of settlement, lasting from 1879 to the early 1890s, tens of thousands of eager families like the Leepers and Ebbesens moved onto the Great Plains and began farming. Some made claims under the Homestead Act, which granted 160 acres to any family head or

Agricultural Productivity 1800–1900

Crop and Productivity Indicator	1800	1840	1880	1900
Wheat				
Worker-hours/acre	56	35	20	15
Yield/acre (bushels)	15	15	13	14
Worker-hours/100 bushels	373	233	152	108
Corn				
Worker-hours/acre	86	69	46	38
Yield/acre (bushels)	25	25	26	26
Worker-hours/100 bushels	344	276	180	147
Cotton				
Worker-hours/acre	185	135	119	112
Yield/acre (pounds of lint)	147	147	179	191
Worker-hours/bale	601	439	318	280

Source: U.S. Bureau of the Census.

Price of Wholesale Wheat Flour, 1865–1900

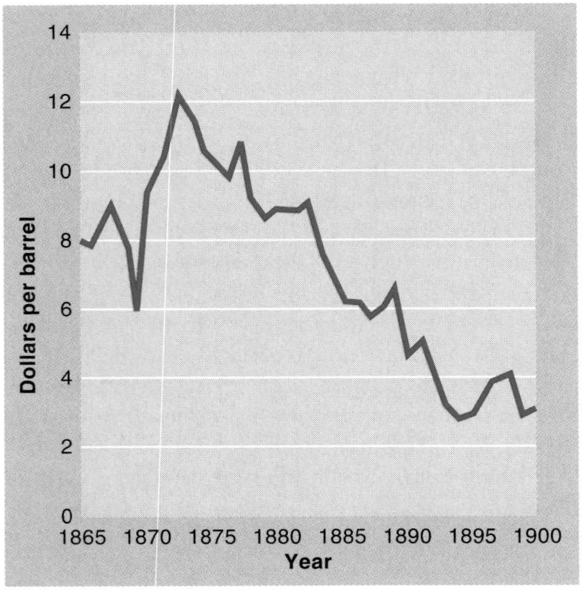

Note the plummeting price of wheat flour.

Source: U.S. Bureau of the Census.

adult who lived on the claim for five years or who paid $1.25 an acre after six months of residence. Because homestead land was frequently less desirable than land held by railroads and speculators, however, most settlers bought land outright rather than taking up claims.

The costs of getting started were thus more substantial than the Homestead Act would suggest. Western land was cheap compared with farmland in the East, but an individual farmer was fortunate if he could buy a good quarter section for under $500. The costs of machinery would often reach $700. Although some farmers thought it made better economic sense to lease rather than buy land, many rented only because they lacked the capital to purchase land and set up operations. In 1880, some 20 percent of the Plains farmers were tenants, and this percentage rose over time.

Like the Ebbesens, many of the new settlers were immigrants, making the Great Plains the second most important destination for them. The most numerous arrived from Germany, the British Isles, and Canada. Many Scandinavians, Czechs, and Poles also moved to the new frontier. Unlike the single male immigrants flocking to American cities for work, these newcomers came with their families. From the beginning, they intended to put down roots in the new country.

Life on the Plains frontier often proved difficult. Wrote Miriam Peckham, a Kansas homesteader:

> I tell you Auntie no one can depend on farming for a living in this country. Henry is very industrious and this year had in over thirty acres of small grain, 8 acres of corn and about an acre of potatoes. We have sold our small grain . . . and it come to $100; now deduct $27.00 for cutting, $16.00 for threshing, $19.00 for hired help, say nothing of boarding our help, none of the trouble of drawing

Percentage of Farms Operated by Tenants, 1880–1900

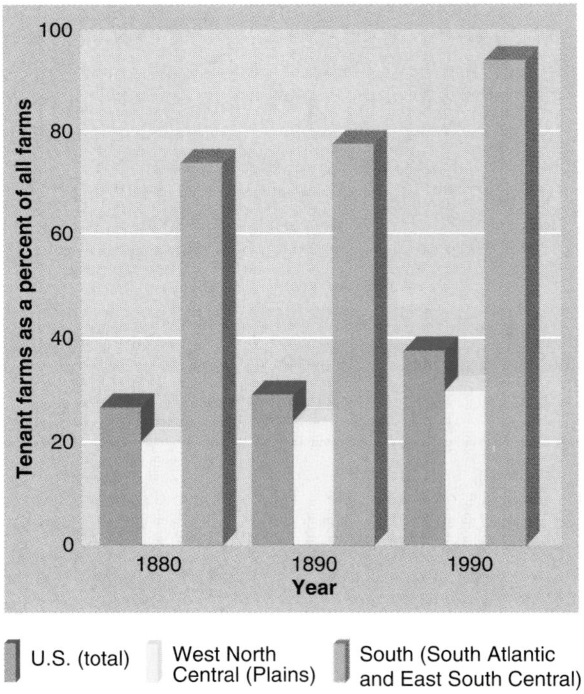

The rise in tenancy, most pronounced in the South, suggests the problems American farmers were experiencing.

Source: U.S. Bureau of the Census.

> 25 miles to market and 25 cts on each head for ferriage over the river and where is your profit. I sometimes think this a God forsaken country, the [grass]hopper hurt our corn and we have ½ a crop and utterly destroyed our garden. If one wants trials, let them come to Kansas.

Peckham's letter highlights the uncertainties of frontier life: the costs of machinery, the vagaries of crops and markets, the threat of pests and natural disasters, the shortage of cash. Unlike earlier emigrants to the Far West, who had to have the means to finance the six-month trip, many Plains pioneers took up their homesteads with only a few dollars in their pockets. Frontier diaries often revealed the marginality of early frontier operations, the loans from family in the East, the debts. Survival often depended on how well families managed to do during the crucial first years. If they succeeded in raising and selling their crops, they might accumulate the capital needed to continue. But if nature was harsh or their luck bad, or if they were unable to adjust to new conditions, the chances of failure were great.

Many settlers recoiled from a landscape without trees and the other natural markings which might make it familiar or provide a human scale. As one New England visitor observed, "It has been terrible on settlers, on the women especially, for there is no society and they get doleful and feel almost like committing suicide for want of society." This was the point many authors chose to emphasize. O. E. Rölvaag's novel *Giants in the Earth* (1927) depicts the wife of a Norwegian immigrant farmer driven to madness and death. Hamlin Garland's *Main-travelled Roads* (1891) pictures overworked, hopeless women whom the frontier defeats. His stories sprang from a "mood of resentment" after a visit to his mother "on a treeless farm."

Life on the Plains was not always so discouraging as these authors suggest. Willa Cather, who spent her childhood in Nebraska, showed both the harshness and the appeal of the prairie in her novels. Alexandra Bergson, the main character of *O Pioneers!* (1913), loves the land: "It seemed beautiful to her, rich and strong and glorious." The thousands of letters and diaries that survive from the period also provide a more positive picture of farming life. One woman reflected on the way she had softened the harsh landscape. "Our flower garden was such a vision of beauty. . . . the dreary, desolate place was blossoming in all the gorgeous beauty that God has promised to those who try." Elam Bartholomew's diary shows a life filled with human contacts and social events. In 1880, only six years after he had settled in northern Kansas, Elam's journal reveals that 1,081 people stopped at his home. His wife served 783 meals to visitors. Trips to church, parties, sings, and neighborhood get-togethers brightened family life.

The Plains frontier required many adjustments, however. Scarce water and violent changes in temperature called for resourcefulness and new modes of behavior. Without firewood, farmers learned to burn corncobs and

In 1886, Solomon Butcher took this photograph of the Rawding family in Custer County, Nebraska. The family posed with all their prized possessions in front of their sod house. While the younger Rawdings are barefoot, the women have dressed carefully for the picture. Note the glass in the windows.

twisted wheat for warmth. The log cabin, long the symbol of frontier life, disappeared as inventive settlers discovered how to build houses of sod "bricks." Although from a distance such houses often looked like mounds of earth—"homely old things," as Hattie Leeper described them—they frequently had glass windows, wooden shingles, and even plastered interiors. Dark and gloomy to our eyes, they were comfortable, cozy, and practical for the settlers. Walls, 2 to 3 feet thick, kept out the scorching summer heat and fierce cold of winter, the moaning winds, and the prairie fires. The solidity of the sod house provided a welcome contrast to the impersonal power and scale of nature.

The first boom on the Great Plains halted abruptly in the late 1880s and early 1890s. Falling agricultural prices cut profits. Then, the unusual rainfall that had lured farmers into the semiarid region near the hundredth meridian vanished. A devastating drought followed. One farmer reported in 1890 that he had earned $41.48 from his wheat crop, yet his expenses for seed and threshing amounted to $56.00. The destitute survived on boiled weeds, a few potatoes, and a little bread and butter. Although cash was scarce on the frontier, credit had not been. Many farmers had accumulated debts they now could not repay. Thousands lost their farms to creditors. Some stayed on as tenants. Homesteaders like the Leepers gave up. By 1900, two-thirds of homesteaded farms had failed. Many homesteaders fled east. In western Kansas, the population declined by half between 1888 and 1892. The wagons of those who retreated bore the epitaph of their experience: "In God We Trusted: In Kansas We Busted."

Whether individual farmers remained on the Great Plains or whether they retreated to more promising climates, collectively these new agricultural efforts had a significant long-term impact on the region's environment. When farmers removed sod to build their sod houses and broke the prairies with their ploughs in order to plant their crops, they were removing the earth's protective covering. The heavy winds so common on the prairies could lift exposed topsoil and carry it miles away. The deep plowing, which was essential for dry farming techniques introduced after the drought of the 1880s, worsened this situation. The dust bowl of the 1930s was the eventual outcome of these agricultural interventions.

Other less obvious consequences of farming and settlement on the Great Plains included a lowering of the water table level as mail-order steel windmills provided the power for pumping water from deep underground. Far from the Plains, the pine forests around the Great Lakes fell to satisfy the settlers' need for wood and the railroads voracious appetite for railroad ties.

The Early Cattle Frontier: 1860–1890

In the mid-1870s, a clash between two Plains settlers, John Duncan, a cattleman, and Peter Schmidt, a German farmer, symbolized the meeting of the farming and cattle frontiers. Duncan allowed his cattle to roam over the Plains and feed on its grasses. Some wandered onto Schmidt's property, devoured his corn, and destroyed his garden. Schmidt ran the cattle off, but he was outraged at the damage. For many years, such incidents had been rare, for few farmers were living on the Plains. As settlement increased in the 1880s and 1890s, they became more common.

Although cattle raising dated back to Spanish mission days, the commercial cattle frontier was an unexpected by-product of Union military strategy. During the war, the North had split the South and cut Texas off from Confederate cattle markets. By the war's end, herds had ballooned. Five million longhorns were roaming the Texas range. With the postwar burst of railroad construction came the means of turning these cattle into dollars. If Texas ranchers drove their steers north to towns like Abilene, Wichita, or Dodge City, they could be loaded on railroad cars for slaughtering and packinghouses in cities like Chicago and Kansas City. Thus started the first cattle drives, celebrated in stories, movies, and television. In the late 1860s and 1870s cowboys herded thousands of longhorns north with hefty profits for owners and investors.

Ranchers on the Great Plains, where grasses were ripe for grazing, bought some of the cattle and bred them with Hereford and Angus cows to create cattle able to withstand the region's severe winters. In the late 1870s and early 1880s, huge ranches appeared in eastern Colorado, Wyoming, and Montana and in western Kansas, Nebraska, and the Dakotas. These ventures, many owned by outside investors, also paid off handsomely. Be-

Frederick Remington captured the romantic aspect of the cattle frontier in this 1888 painting of a cowboy in the midst of a stampede rather than the less colorful realities of cowboy life, hard work and low pay.

cause the cattle could roam at will over the public domain, they cost owners little as they fattened up but commanded good prices at the time of sale. The cowboys (a third of them Mexican and black) who herded the steers, however, shared few of the profits. Their meager wages of $25 to $40 a month were just enough to pay for a fling in the saloons, dance halls, and gambling palaces in Dodge City or Abilene when taking the cattle to market.

By the mid-1880s, the first phase of the cattle frontier was ending as farmers moved onto the Plains, bought up public lands once used for grazing, and fenced them in. But the struggle between cattle ranchers and farmers was only one factor in the cattle frontier's collapse. Eager for fat profits, ranchers overstocked their herds in the mid-1880s. European investors added to the rush of capital into herding. Hungry cattle ate everything in sight, then grew weak as grass became scarce. As was often the case on the Plains, the weather had a part to play. A winter of memorable blizzards followed the very hot summer of 1886. Cattle, usually able to forage for themselves during the winter months, could not dig through the deep snow to the grass and died from starvation. By spring, 90 percent of the cattle were dead. As one cattleman's journal observed, "An overstocked range must bleed when the blizzards sit in judgment." Frantic owners dumped their remaining cattle on the market, getting $8 or even less per animal.

In the aftermath, the ranchers who remained stock raisers adopted new techniques. Experimenting with new breeds, they began to fence in their herds and to feed them grain during the winter months. Moreover, consumers were hungering for tender beef rather than the tough flesh of animals who roamed the land, and these new methods satisfied the market. Ranching, like farming, was becoming more a modern business and less the colorful adventure portrayed in popular culture.

Just as the ploughs and windmills of the agriculturist disrupted Plains ecology, so too did the herds of the cattle frontier. As one Texan realized, "Grass is what counts. It's what saves us all—as far as we get saved. . . . Grass is what holds the earth together." When cattlemen overstocked the range, their herds devoured the perennial grasses. In their place tough, less nutritious annual grasses sprang up, and sometimes even these grasses disappeared. Lands once able to support large herds of cattle eventually were transformed into deserts of sagebrush, weeds, and dust.

Cornucopia on the Pacific

When gold was discovered in California, Americans rushed west to find it. But as one father told his eager son, "Plant your lands; these be your best gold fields." He was right; farming eventually proved to be California's greatest asset. But farming in California neither resembled the rural life Currier and Ives depicted nor fulfilled the dreams of the framers of the Homestead Act.

Although federal and state land policies supposedly promoted "homes for the homeless," little of California's land was actually homesteaded or developed as small family farms. When California entered the Union, Mexican ranchers had vast landholdings that never became part of the public domain. Neither Mexican-Americans nor small farmers profited from the 20 years of confusion over the legitimacy of Mexican land titles. Speculators did, acquiring much of the Californios' property. Consequently, small farmers needed substantial sums to buy land. As Charles Reed observed in 1869, "Land which but two years ago could have been bought . . . for from \$1 to \$1.25 per acre cannot now be bought for less than \$10 to \$15 per acre."

By 1871, reformer Henry George described California as "not a country of farms but a country of plantations and estates." California farms were indeed substantially larger than farms in the rest of the country. In 1870, the average California farm was 482 acres, whereas the national average farm was only 153 acres. By 1900, farms of 1,000 acres or more made up two-thirds of the state's farmland.

California's landscape reflected the advent of large-scale farming. As one California visitor reported to the *New York Times* in 1887, "You go through miles and miles of wheat fields, you see the fertility of the land and the beauty of the scenery, but where are the hundreds of farm houses . . . that you would see in Ohio or Iowa?"

Small farmers and ranchers did exist, of course, but they found it difficult to compete with large, mechanized operators using cheap migrant laborers, usually Mexican or Chinese. One wheat farm in the San Joaquin Valley was so vast that workers started plowing in the morning at one end of the 17-mile field, ate lunch at its halfway point, and camped at its end that night.

The value of much of California's agricultural land, especially the southern half of the Central Valley, depended on water. Many gold rush immigrants were stunned by the brown and yellow grasses, the parched earth. By the 1870s, however, water, land, and railroad companies were taking on the huge costs of building dams, headgates, and canals and selling hitherto barren lands along with water rights, passing along the costs to settlers in the form of high prices. By 1890, over a quarter of California's farms benefited from irrigation. The irrigation ditches were a fitting symbol of the importance of technology and a managerial attitude toward the land that characterized late-nineteenth-century agriculture, particularly in California.

Although grain was initially California's most valuable crop, it faced stiff competition from farmers on the Plains and in other parts of the world. Some argued that

This New Hampshire general store, photographed at the end of the nineteenth century, contains the wide variety of nonlocal products, including bananas, that better transportation made available.

> land capable of raising Adriatic figs, Zante currants, French prunes, Malaga raisins, Batavia oranges, Sicily lemons, citrons, limes, dates and olives, and our own incomparable peaches, apricots, nectarines, pears, quinces, plums, pomegranates, apples, English and native walnuts, chestnuts, pecans and almonds, in a climate surpassing that of Italy, is too valuable for the cultivation of simple cereals.

But high railroad rates and lack of refrigeration limited the volume of fresh fruit and vegetables sent to market. As railroad managers in the 1880s realized the potential profit California's produce represented, they lowered rates and introduced refrigerated railroad cars. Fruit and vegetable production rose. In June 1888, fresh apricots and cherries successfully survived the trip from California to New York. Two years later, 9,000 carloads of navel oranges headed east. Before long California fruit was available in London. Some travelers even began to grumble that the railroads treated produce better than people. Perhaps the complaint was true. The daily eastern express contained "two sleeping cars, two or three passenger cars, and twenty cars loaded with green fruit." The comments highlighted the fact that successful agriculture in California depended on the railroad system, irrigation, and the use of machinery.

Exploiting Natural Resources

The perspective that led Americans to treat farming as a business was also evident in the ways in which they dealt with the country's abundant natural resources. Gold had been the precious metal originally drawing prospectors to California, but the discovery of other precious materials—silver, iron, copper, coal, lead, zinc, tin—lured thousands west to Colorado, Montana, Idaho, Nevada as well as to states like Minnesota. The popular conception of the miner as a hardy forty-niner searching for loose placer deposits of gold captures the early days of mining. But it does not describe the reality of late-nineteenth-century mining which relied on machinery, railroads, engineers, and a large work force for the discovery and extraction of the earth's metals and minerals. Mining was a big business with high costs and a basic dynamic that encouraged rapid and thorough exploitation of the earth's resources.

The decimation of the nation's forests went hand in hand with large-scale mining and the railroads that provided the links to markets. Both railroads and mining depended on wood—railroads for wooden ties, mines for shaft timber and ore reduction. The impact of these demands is captured by the California State Board of Agriculture's estimate in the late 1860s that one-third of the state's forests had already disappeared.

When lumber companies cut down timber, they affected the flow of streams and destroyed the habitat supporting birds and animals. Like the activities of farmers and cattle owners, the companies that stripped the earth of its forest cover were also contributing to soil erosion. The idea that the public lands belonging to the federal government ought to be rapidly developed supported such exploitation of the nation's natural resources. Often, in return for royalties, the government leased parts of the public domain to companies who hoped to extract valuable minerals, not to own the land permanently. In other cases, companies bought land, but not always legally. In 1878, Congress passed the Timber and Stone Act, which initially applied to Nevada, Oregon, Washington, and California. This legislation allowed the sale of 160-acre parcels of the public domain that were "unfit for cultivation" and "valuable chiefly for timber." Timber companies were quick to see the possibilities in the new law. They hired men willing to register for claims and then to turn them over to timber interests. By the end of the century, more than 3.5 million acres of the public domain had been acquired under the legislation, and most of it was in corporate hands.

The rapacious and rapid exploitation of resources combined with the increasing pace of industrialization to make some Americans uneasy. Many believed that forests played a part in causing rainfall and that their destruction would have an adverse impact on the climate. Others, like John Muir, lamented the destruction of the country's great natural beauty. In 1868 Muir came upon the Great Valley of California, "all one sheet of plant gold, hazy and vanishing in the distance . . . one smooth, continuous bed of honey-bloom." He soon realized, however, that a "wild, restless agriculture" and "flocks of hoofed locusts, sweeping over the ground like a fire" would destroy this vision of loveliness. Muir became a conservation champion. He played a part in the creation of Yosemite National Park in 1890 and participated in a successful effort to allow President Benjamin Harrison to classify certain parts of the public domain as forest reserves (the Forest Reserve Act of 1891). In 1892, Muir established the Sierra Club. Conservation ideas were more popular in the East, however, than in the West, where the seeming abundance of natural resources and the profit motive diminished support.

The Second Great Removal

Black Elk, an Oglala Sioux, listened to a story told by his father, who had, heard it from his father.

> A long time ago my father told me . . . that there was once a Lakota [Sioux] holy man, called Drinks Water, who dreamed what was to be; and this was long before the coming of the Wasichus [white men]. He dreamed . . . that a strange race had woven a spider's web all around the Lakotas. And he said: "When this happens, you shall live in square gray houses, in a barren land, and beside those square gray houses you shall starve."

So great was the wise man's sorrow that he died soon after his strange dream. But Black Elk lived to see it come true.

As farmers settled the western frontier and became entangled in a national economy, they clashed with the Indian tribes who lived on the land. In California, disease and violence killed 90 percent of the Native American population in the 30 years following the gold rush. Elsewhere, the struggle between Native Americans and whites was prolonged and bitter.

Black Elk, pictured here on the left, was a perceptive observer of the deleterious changes experienced by Indians during the latter part of the nineteenth century.

Background to Hostilities

As pointed out in Chapter 13, the lives of most Plains Indians revolved around the buffalo. Increased emigration to California and Oregon in the 1840s and 1850s disrupted tribal pursuits and animal migration patterns. The federal government tried, without much success, to persuade the Plains tribes to stay far away from white wagon trains and white settlers. As Lone Horn, a Miniconjou chief, explained when American commissioners at the 1851 Fort Laramie Council asked him if he would be satisfied to live on the Missouri River, "When the buffalo comes close to the river, we come close to it. When the buffaloes go off, we go off after them."

When the Civil War broke out, the tribes that President Andrew Jackson had earlier resettled in Oklahoma divided. Those who kept slaves or feared that northerners were untrustworthy sided with the Confederacy, while other tribes remained loyal to the Union. After the war, however, all were lumped together and "treated as traitors." The federal government callously nullified earlier pledges and treaties, leaving Indians defenseless against further incursions on their lands. As settlers pushed into Kansas, the tribes living in Kansas were shunted into Oklahoma.

The White Perspective

When the Civil War ended, red and white men on the Plains were at war. The shameful massacre of friendly Cheyenne at Sand Creek, Colorado, by the Colorado Volunteers in 1864 had sparked widespread hostilities. Although not all whites condoned the slaughter, the deliberations of the congressional commission authorized to make peace on the Plains revealed a constricted vision of the future of Native Americans. The commission, which included the commander of the Army in the West, Civil War hero General William T. Sherman, accepted as fact that an "industrious, thrifty, and enlightened population" of whites would occupy most of the West. All Native Americans, the commission believed, should relocate in one of two areas: the western half of present-day South Dakota, and Oklahoma. There they were to learn the ways of white society and receive instruction in agricultural and mechanical arts. The offer of annuities, food, and clothes should help placate the Indians and ease their transition from a "savage" to a "civilized" life.

At two major conferences in 1867 and 1868, Native American chiefs listened to these drastic proposals. Some agreed with the terms; others did not. As Satanta, a Kiowa chief, explained, "I don't want to settle. I love to roam over the prairies." In any case, the agreements extracted were not binding, since none of the chiefs had authority to speak for their tribes. For its part, the U.S. Senate dragged its feet in approving the treaties. Supplies promised to Indians who settled in the reserved areas failed to materialize, and wildlife proved too sparse to support them. These Indians soon drifted back to their former hunting grounds.

As General Sherman had warned, however, "All who cling to their old hunting ground are hostile and will remain so till killed off." To his brother he had written, "The more we can kill this year, the less will have to be killed the next war." Sherman entrusted General Philip Sheridan with the duty of dealing with the tribes in 1867. Sheridan introduced a new tactic of winter campaigning. The intent was to seek out the Indians who divided into small groups during the winter and to exterminate them.

The completion of the transcontinental railroad in 1869 added yet another pressure for "solving" the Indian question. Transcontinental railroads wanted rights-of-way through tribal lands and needed white settlers to make their operations profitable. They carried not only thousands of hopeful settlers to the West but miners and hunters as well.

In his 1872 annual report, the commissioner for Indian affairs, Francis Amasa Walker, addressed the two fundamental questions troubling whites: how to prevent Indians from blocking white movement and settlements throughout the Great Plains and what to do with Native Americans once they had been controlled. Walker wanted to buy the "savages" off, since they could, after all, mount 8,000 warriors in the field. With promises of food and gifts, he hoped to lure them onto reservations, where they would be subjected to a "rigid reformatory discipline."

Coercion would be necessary, since Indians, according to Walker, were "unused to manual labor, and physically unqualified for it by the habits of the chase . . . without forethought and without self control . . . with strong animal appetites and no intellectual tastes or aspirations to hold those appetites in check." The grim reservations he proposed resembled prisons more than schools. Indians could not leave the reservation without permission and could be arrested if they tried to do so. Though Walker considered himself to be a "friend of humanity" and wished to save the Indians from destruction, he also thought that their only choice was to "yield or perish."

The Tribal View

Native Americans defied such attacks on their ancient way of life and protested the violation of treaties. Black Elk remembered that in 1863, when he was only 3, his father had his leg broken in a fierce battle against the white men. "When I was older, he recalled,

> I learned what the fighting was about. . . . Up on the Madison Fork the Wasichus had found much of the yellow metal that they worship and that makes them crazy, and they wanted to have a road up through our country to the place where the yellow metal was; but my people did not want the road. It

Indian Lands and Communities in the United States

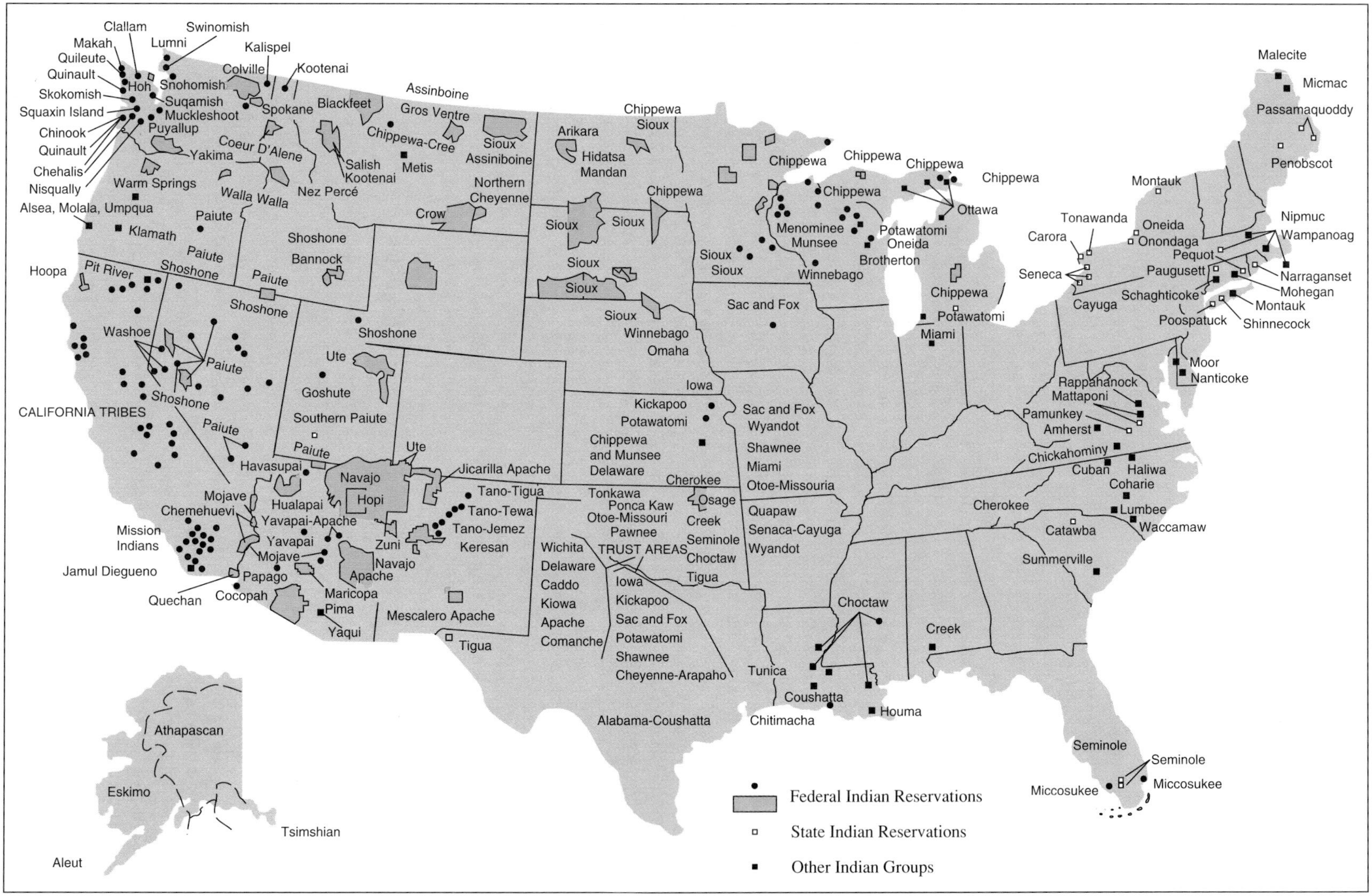

The map shows a rich variety of Indian groups, state reservations (primarily in the East), and federal reservations in the West.

> would scare the bison and make them go away, and also it would let the other Wasichus come in like a river. They told us that they wanted only to use a little land, as much as a wagon would take between the wheels; but our people knew better.

Black Elk's father and many others soon realized fighting was their only recourse. "There was no other way to keep our country." But "wherever we went, the soldiers came to kill us, and it was all our country."

Broken promises fed Indian resistance. In 1875, the federal government allowed gold prospectors into the Black Hills, part of the Sioux reservation and one of their sacred places. Chiefs Sitting Bull, Crazy Horse, and Rain-in-the-Face led the angry Sioux on the warpath. At the Battle of Little Big Horn in 1876, they vanquished General George Custer. But their bravery and skill could not permanently withstand the power of the well-supplied and well-armed U.S. Army. Elsewhere the pattern of resistance and ultimate defeat was repeated. In Texas, General Sherman vanquished Native American tribes, while in the Pacific Northwest, Nez Percé Chief Joseph surrendered in 1877.

The wholesale destruction of the buffalo was an important element in white victory. The animals were central to Indian life, culture, and religion. As one Pawnee chief explained, "Am afraid when we have no meat to offer, Great Spirit . . . will be angry & punish us." Although Plains Indians could be wasteful of buffalo in areas where the animals were abundant, white miners and hunters ultimately destroyed the herds. Sportsmen shot the beasts from train windows. Railroad crews ate the meat. Ranchers' cattle competed for grass. And demand for buffalo bones for fertilizer and hides for robes and shoes encouraged the decimation.

The slaughter, which had claimed 13 million animals by 1883, was in retrospect disgraceful. The Indians considered white men demented. "They just killed and killed because they like to do that," said one, whereas when "we hunted the bison . . . [we] killed only what we needed." But the destruction of the herds pleased whites determined to curb the movements of Native Americans. As Secretary of the Interior Columbus Delano explained in 1872, "I cannot regard the rapid disappearance of the game from its former haunts as a matter prejudicial to our management of the Indians." Rather, he said, "as they become convinced that they can no longer rely upon the supply of game for their support, they will return to the more reliable source of subsistence furnished at their agencies."

The Dawes Act: 1887

Changing federal policy also weakened Native American culture and life. In 1871, Congress ended the practice, in effect since the 1790s, of treating the tribes as sovereign nations. Other measures accompanied this attempt to undermine both tribal integrity and the prestige of tribal leaders, who would no longer be recognized as speaking for their tribes. The government urged tribes to establish court systems in place of tribal justice and extended federal jurisdiction to the reservations. Tribes were also warned not to gather for religious ceremonies.

The Dawes Severalty Act of 1887 pulled together the strands of federal Indian policy that emerged after the Civil War and set its course for the rest of the century. Believing that tribal bonds kept Indians in savagery, reformers intended to destroy them. As Theodore Roosevelt noted approvingly, the bill was a "mighty pulverizing engine to break up the tribal mass." Rather than allotting reservation lands to tribal groups, the act allowed the president to distribute these lands to individuals. By holding out the lure of private property, the framers of the bill hoped to encourage Indians to settle in one place and to farm as white men did. Those who accepted allotments would become citizens and presumably forget their tribal identity. Although Indian agents explained that Native Americans opposed the Dawes Act, Congress did not hesitate to legislate on their behalf.

Another motive was also at work. Even if each Indian family head claimed a typical share of 160 acres, millions of "surplus" acres would remain for sale to white settlers. Within 20 years of the Dawes Act, Native Americans had lost 60 percent of their lands. The federal government held the profits from land sales "in trust" and used them for the "civilizing" mission.

The Ghost Dance: An Indian Renewal Ritual

By the 1890s, the grim reality of their plight made many Native Americans responsive to the message of Paiute prophet Wovoka. Although Wovoka did not urge Native Americans to strike out against whites, his revelations predicted that natural disasters would eliminate the white race. Dancing Indians would not only avoid this destruction but also gain new strength thanks to the return to life of their ancestors. Wovoka's heartening prophecies spread from tribe to tribe. Believers expressed their faith and hope through the new rituals of ghost dancing and meditation. The more frequently they danced, the quicker whites would vanish.

Although Wovoka's prophecies discouraged hostile actions against whites, American settlers were uneasy. Indian agents tried to prevent the ghost dances and filed hysterical reports. "Indians are dancing in the snow and are wild and crazy. . . . We need protection, and we need it now." One agent determined that the Sioux medicine man Sitting Bull was a leading troublemaker and determined to arrest him. In the confusion of arrest, Indian police killed Sitting Bull.

Bands of Sioux fled the reservation with the army in swift pursuit. In late December 1890, the army caught up with the Sioux at Wounded Knee Creek. Although the Sioux had raised a flag of truce, a scuffle as they were turning over their weapons led to a bloody massacre. Using the most up-to-date machine guns, the army killed over 200 men, women, and children. An eyewitness described the desolate scene a few days later. "Among the fragments of burned tents . . . we saw the frozen bodies lying close together or piled one upon another."

Thus arose the lament of Black Elk, who saw his people diminished, starving, despairing:

> Once we were happy in our own country and we were seldom hungry, for then the two-leggeds and the four-leggeds lived together like relatives, and there was plenty for them and for us. But then the Wasichus came, and they have made little islands for us and other islands for the four-leggeds, and always these islands are becoming smaller, for around them surges the gnawing flood of the Wasichus; and it is dirty with lies and greed.

The New South

Of all the nation's agricultural regions, the South was the poorest. In 1880, southerners' yearly earnings were only half the national average. But despite poverty and backwardness, some southerners during the late nineteenth century dreamed of making the agricultural South the rival of the industrial North.

The vision of a modern, progressive, and self-sufficient South had roots in the troubled decade of the 1850s. At that time, southern intellectuals and writers had argued that the South must throw off its dependence on the North and on cotton. "The smoke of the steam engine should begin to float over the cotton fields, and the hum of spindles and the click of looms make music on all our mountain streams," insisted the editor of the New Orleans *Picayune*.

Postwar Southerners Face the Future

Too few southerners had listened. Now, after the painful war and Reconstruction, the cry for regional self-sufficiency grew sharper. Publicists of the movement for a "New South" argued that southern backwardness did not stem from the war itself, as so many southerners wished to believe, but from basic conditions in southern life, a rural economy based on cotton foremost among them. The defeat only made clearer the reality of the nineteenth century. Power and wealth came not from cotton but from factories, machines, and cities.

Henry Grady, editor of the Atlanta *Constitution* and the New South's most famous spokesman, dramatized the need for change with his story of a southerner's funeral:

> They buried him in the midst of a marble quarry; they cut through solid marble to make his grave; and yet a little tombstone they put above him was from Vermont. They buried him in the heart of a pine forest, and yet the pine coffin was imported from Cincinnati. They buried him within touch of an iron mine, and yet the nails in his coffin and the iron in the shovel that dug his grave were imported from Pittsburgh. . . . They put him away . . . in a

> New York coat and a Boston pair of shoes and a pair of breeches from Chicago and a shirt from Cincinnati, leaving him nothing to carry into the next world with him to remind him of the country in which he lived and for which he fought for four years, but the chill of blood in his veins and the marrow in his bones.

Regional pride and self-interest dictated a new course. As Grady told a Boston audience in 1886, industrial advances would allow the South to match the North in another, more peaceful contest. "We are going to take a noble revenge," he said, "by invading every inch of your territory with iron, as you invaded ours twenty-nine years ago."

In hundreds of speeches, editorials, pamphlets, articles, and books, spokesmen for the New South tried to persuade fellow southerners of the need for change. Southerners must abandon prewar ideals that glorified leisure and gentility and adopt the ethic of hard work. To lure northern bankers and capitalists, New South advocates held out attractive investment possibilities. Since the South was short of capital, northern assistance was critically important. Thus, said one beckoning New South advocate, "the profits to be reaped from investments in the South . . . appear to be fabulous." The South would be the "El Dorado of the next half century."

In a bid to attract manufacturers, several southern state governments offered tax exemptions and cheap labor based on leasing state prison convicts. Texas and Florida awarded the railroads land grants, and cities like Atlanta and Louisville mounted huge industrial exhibitions as incentives to industrial progress. Middle-class southerners increasingly accepted new entrepreneurial values. The most startling example of commitment to the vision of a New South may have come in 1886 when southern railroad companies decided to bring their tracks into line with the "standard" northern gauges. On a Sunday in May, 8,000 men equipped with sledgehammers and crowbars attacked the 2,000 miles of track belonging to the Louisville and Nashville Railroad Company and moved the western rail 3 inches to the east. On that same day, they also adjusted the iron wheels of 300 locomotives and 10,000 pieces of rolling stock to fit the new gauge.

During the late nineteenth century, northern money flowed south as dollars replaced the moral fervor and political involvement of the Civil War and Reconstruction years. In the 1880s, northerners increased their investment in the cotton industry sevenfold and financed the expansion of the southern railroad system. Northern capital helped southern cities to embark on an extended period of expansion. By 1900, some 15 percent of all southerners lived in cities, whereas only 7 percent had in 1860. (The national averages for these years were 40 percent and 20 percent, respectively.)

The city of Birmingham, Alabama, symbolized the New South. In 1870, the site of the future city was a peaceful cornfield. The next year, two northern real estate speculators arrived on the scene, attracted by the area's rich iron deposits. Despite a siege of cholera and the depression of the 1870s, Birmingham rapidly became the center of the southern iron and steel industry. By 1890, a total of 38,414 people lived in the city. Coke ovens, blast furnaces, rolling mills, iron foundries, and machine shops belched forth polluting smoke into the air where once there had been only fields. Millions of dollars of finished goods poured forth from the city's mills and factories, and eight railroad lines carried them away.

Other southern cities flourished as well. Memphis prospered from its lumber industry and the manufacturing of cottonseed products, while Richmond became the country's tobacco capital even as its flour mills and iron and steel foundries continued to produce wealth. Augusta, Georgia, was the "Lowell of the South," a leader in the emerging textile industry that blossomed in Georgia, North and South Carolina, and Alabama. Augusta's eight cotton mills employed about 2,800 workers, many of them women and children.

The Other Side of Progress

New South leaders, a small group of merchants, industrialists, and planters, bragged about the growth of the iron and textile industries and paraded statistics to prove the success of efforts to modernize. The South, one writer boasted, was "throbbing with industrial and railroad activity." But despite such optimism about matching or even surpassing the North's economic performance, the South made slow progress.

Older values persisted. Indeed, New South spokesmen paradoxically kept older chivalric values alive by romanticizing the recent past. "In the eyes of Southern people," one publication asserted, "all Confederate veterans are heroes." Loyalty to the past impeded full acceptance of a new economic order. It was significant that despite the interest in modernization, the southern school system lagged far behind that of the North.

Although new industries and signs of progress abounded, two of the new industries depended on tobacco and cotton, traditional crops long at the center of rural life. Moreover, the South did not better its position relative to the North. Whereas in 1860 the South had 17 percent of the country's manufacturing concerns, by 1904 it had only 15 percent. During the same period, the value of its manufactures grew from 10.3 percent of the total value of manufactures in the United States to only 10.5 percent. Commerce and government work still were responsible for urban growth, as they had been before the Civil War. The South's achievements were not insignificant during a period in which northern industry and cities rapidly expanded, but they could not make the South the equal of the North.

Moreover, the South failed to reap many benefits from industrialization. Southern businessmen like Richmond banker and railroad president John Skelton Williams hoped "to see in the South in the not distant future many railroads and business institutions as great as the Pennsylvania Railroad, the Mutual Life Insurance Company, the Carnegie Steel Company or the Standard Oil Company." This was not to happen. As in the antebellum period, the South remained an economic vassal of the North.

Southern businessmen grew in number, but with the exception of the American Tobacco Company, no great southern corporations arose. Instead, southerners worked for northern companies and corporations, which absorbed southern businesses or dominated them financially. By 1900, for example, five corporations directed three-quarters of the railroad mileage in the South (excluding Texas), and northern bankers controlled all five. Northerners also took over the southern steel industry.

As this happened, profits flowed north. "Our capitalists are going into your country," the Lowell *Manufacturers' Record* noted, "because they see a chance to make money there, but you must not think that they will give your people the benefit of the money they make. That will come North and enrich their heirs, or set up public libraries in our country towns." As dollars fled north, so too went the power to make critical decisions. In many cases, northern directors determined that southern mills and factories could handle only the early stages of processing, while northern factories finished the goods. Thus southern cotton mills sent yarn and coarse cloth north for completion. Southern manufacturers who did finish their products, hoping to compete in the marketplace, found that railroad rate discrimination robbed their goods of any competitive edge.

Individual workers in the new industries may have found factory life preferable to sharecropping, but their rewards were meager. The thou-

Black dockworkers load bales of cotton in this undated photograph, which is evidence not only of the kind of jobs that free blacks could secure but of the continuing dominance of cotton in southern life.

sands of women and children in factories were silent testimony to the fact their husbands and fathers could not earn sufficient wages to keep them at home. As usual, women and children earned lower wages than men. Justifying these policies, one Augusta factory president claimed that the employment of children was "a matter of charity with us; some of them would starve if they were not given employment. . . . Ours are not overworked. The work we give children is very light." Actually, many children at his factory were doing the same work as adults, for children's pay.

In general, all workers earned lower wages and worked longer hours in the South than elsewhere. Per capita income was the same in 1900 as it had been in 1860—and only half the national average. In North Carolina in the 1890s, workers were paid an average of 50 cents a day and toiled 70 hours a week. Black workers, who made up 6 percent of the southern manufacturing force in 1890 (but who were excluded from textile mills), usually had the worst jobs and the lowest wages.

Cotton Still King

Although New South advocates envisioned the South's transformation from a rural to an industrial society, they always recognized the need for agricultural change. "It's time for an agricultural revolution," Henry Grady proclaimed. "When we once decide that southern lands are fit for something else besides cotton, and then go to work in earnest to multiply and diversify our products and industries, independence and wealth will be the certain reward of our intelligent and industrious farmers."

The overdependence on "King Cotton" hobbled southern agriculture by making farmers the victims of faraway market forces and an oppressive credit system. Subdivide old cotton plantations into small diversified farms, Grady urged. Truck farming could produce "simply wonderful profits" and

> would give employment throughout the entire season, and at the end of it the fortunate farmer would have before him the assurance that diversified crops and a never-failing market alone afford, with no [fertilizer] . . . bills to settle, and no liens past or to come to disturb his mind.

A new agricultural South with new class and economic arrangements did emerge, but it was not the one Grady and others envisioned. Despite the breakup of some plantations following the Civil War, large landowners proved resourceful in holding on to their property and in dealing with postwar conditions, as Chapter 16 showed. As they adopted new agricultural arrangements, former slaves sank into debt peonage.

White farmers on small and medium-size holdings fared only slightly better than black tenants and sharecroppers. Immediately after the war, high cotton prices tempted them to raise as much cotton as they could. Then prices began a disastrous decline, from 11 cents a pound in 1875 to less than 5 cents in 1894. "At the close of the war a 500 lb. bale of cotton would bring $100," a Cherokee County, Georgia, tenant complained in 1891, "and today it will bring $32.50." Yeoman farmers became entangled in debt. Each year, farmers found themselves buying supplies on credit from merchants so that they could plant the next year's crop and support their families until harvest time. In return, merchants demanded their exclusive business and acquired a lien (or claim) on their crops. But when farmers sold their crops at declining prices, they usually discovered that they had not earned enough to settle with the merchant, who had charged dearly for store goods and whose annual interest rates might exceed 100 percent. Each year, thousands of farmers fell further behind.

The story of S. R. Simonton was typical. Between 1887 and 1895, the South Carolina farmer spent $2,681 at T. G. Patrick's furnishing house. But he could manage to pay back only $687. Like many others, Simonton lost his land and became a tenant farmer. The number of tenants inched upward, while the number of small independent farmers fell. By 1900, over half the South's white farmers and three-quarters of its black farmers were tenants. Although tenancy was increasing all over rural America, nowhere did it rise more rapidly than in the Deep South.

These patterns had baneful results for individual southerners and for the South as a whole. Caught in a cycle of debt and poverty, few farmers could think of improving agricultural techniques or diversifying crops. In their desperate attempt to pay off debts, they concentrated on cotton, despite falling prices. "Cotton brings money, and money pays debt," was the small farmer's slogan. Landowners also pressured tenants to raise a market crop. Far from diversifying, as Grady had hoped, farmers increasingly limited the number of crops they raised. By 1880, the South was not growing enough food to feed its people adequately. Poor nutrition contributed to chronic bad health and sickness.

The Nadir of Black Life

Grady and other New South advocates painted a picture of a strong, prosperous, and industrialized South, a region that could deal with the troublesome race issue without the interference of any "outside power." Grady had few regrets over the end of slavery, which he thought had contributed to southern economic backwardness. Realizing that black labor would be crucial to the transformation he sought, he advocated racial cooperation.

But racial cooperation did not mean equality. Grady assumed that blacks were racially inferior and supported an informal system of segregation. "The negro is entitled to his freedom, his franchise, to full and equal legal rights," Grady wrote in 1883. But "social equality he can never have. He does not have it in the north, or in the east, or in the west. On one pretext or another, he is kept out of hotels, theatres, schools and restaurants."

By the time of Grady's death in 1889, a much harsher perspective on southern race relations was replacing his view. In 1891, at a national assembly of women's clubs in Washington, D.C., a black woman, Frances Ellen Watkins Harper, anticipated efforts to strip the vote from blacks and appealed to the white women at the meeting not to abandon black suffrage. "I deem it a privilege to present the negro," she said, "not as a mere dependent asking for Northern sympathy or Southern compassion, but as a member of the body politic who has a claim upon the nation for justice, simple justice." This claim, she continued, was for "protection to human life," for "the rights of life and liberty," and for relief from charges of ignorance and poverty. These were "conditions which men outgrow." Women, of all people, should understand this and not seek to achieve their own right to vote at the expense of the vote for black men. "Instead of taking the ballot from his hands, teach him how to use it, and add his quota to the progress, strength, and durability of the nation."

The decision by congressional leaders in 1890 to shelve a proposed act for protecting black civil rights and the defeat of the Blair bill providing federal assistance for educational institutions left black Americans vulnerable, as Frances Harper realized. The traditional sponsor of the rights of freedmen, the Republican party, left blacks to fend for themselves as a minority in the white South. The courts also abandoned blacks. In 1878, the Supreme Court declared unconstitutional a Louisiana statute banning discrimination in transportation. In 1882, the Court voided the Ku Klux Klan Act of 1871, deciding that the civil rights protections of the Fourteenth Amendment applied to states rather than to individuals. In 1883, the provisions of the Civil Rights Act of 1875, which assured blacks of equal rights in public places, were declared unconstitutional on the grounds that the federal government did not have the right to involve itself in the racial relations between individuals.

Northern leaders did not oppose these actions. In fact, northerners increasingly promulgated negative stereotypes, picturing blacks as either ignorant, lazy, childlike fools or as lying, stealing, raping degenerates. Obviously, they could not be left to themselves or given the same rights and freedoms whites enjoyed. Instead, blacks needed the paternal protection of the superior white race. These stereotypes filled the magazines and newspapers and were perpetuated in cartoons, advertisements, "coon songs," serious art and theater, and the minstrel shows that dominated northern entertainment.

Atlanta Monthly in 1890 anticipated a strong current in magazine literature when it expressed doubts that this "lowly variety of man" could ever be brought up to the intellectual and moral standards of whites. Other magazines openly opposed suffrage as wasted on people too "ignorant, weak, lazy and incompetent" to make good use of it. *Forum* magazine suggested that "American Negroes" had "too much liberty." When this freedom was combined with natural "race traits" of stealing and hankering after white women, the *Forum* advised in 1893, black crime increased. Only lynching and burning would deter the "barbarous" rapist and other "sadly degenerated" Negroes corrupted since the Civil War by independence and too much education. The author concluded that the Negro question was "more vital" than gold, silver, or the tariff. Encouraged by northern public opinion, and with the blessing of Congress and the Supreme Court, southern citizens and legislatures sought to make blacks permanently second-class members of southern society.

In the political sphere, white southerners amended state constitutions to disenfranchise black voters. By various legal devices—the poll tax, literacy tests, "good character" and "understanding" clauses administered by white voter registrars, and all-white primary elections—blacks lost the right to vote. The most ingenious method was the "grandfather clause," which specified that only citizens whose grandfathers were registered to vote on January 1, 1867, could cast their ballots. This virtually excluded blacks. Although the Supreme Court outlawed such blatantly discriminatory laws as grandfather clauses, a series of other constitutional changes, beginning in Mississippi in 1890 and spreading to all 11 former Confederate states by 1910, effectively excluded the black vote. The results were dramatic. Louisiana, for example, contained 130,334 registered black voters in 1896. Eight years later, there were only 1,342.

In a second tactic in the 1890s, state and local laws legalized informal segregation in public facilities. Beginning with railroads and schools, "Jim Crow" laws were extended to libraries, hotels, restaurants, hospitals, asylums, prisons, theaters, parks and playgrounds, cemeteries, toilets, morgues, sidewalks, drinking fountains, and nearly every other place where blacks and whites might mingle. The Supreme Court upheld these laws in 1896 in *Plessy* v. *Ferguson* by declaring that "separate but equal" facilities did not violate the equal protection clause of the Fourteenth Amendment. The Court's decision opened the way for as many forms of legal segregation as the imaginations of southern lawmakers could devise.

Political and social discrimination made it ever more possible to keep blacks permanently confined to agricultural and unskilled labor and dependent on whites for their material welfare. In 1900, nearly 84 percent of black workers nationwide engaged in some form of agricultural labor as farmhands, overseers, sharecroppers, or tenant or independent farmers or in service jobs, primarily domestic service and laundry work. These had been the primary slave occupations. The remaining 16 percent worked in forests, sawmills, mines, and, with northward migration, in northern cities. Gone were the skilled black tradesmen of slavery days. At the end of the Civil War, at least half of all skilled craftsmen in the South had been black. But by the 1890s, the percentage had decreased to less than 10 percent, as whites systematically excluded blacks from the trades. Such factory work as blacks had been doing was also reduced, largely in order to drive a wedge between poor blacks and whites to prevent unionization. In Greensboro, North Carolina, for example, where in 1870 some 30 percent of all blacks worked in skilled trades or factory occupations, by 1910 blacks in the skilled trades had been reduced to 8 percent, and not a single black worked in a Greensboro factory. The exclusion of blacks from industry prevented them from acquiring the skills and habits that would enable them to rise into the middle class as would many European immigrants and their children by the mid–twentieth century.

Blacks did not accept their declining position passively. In the mid-1880s, they enthusiastically joined the mass worker organization the Knights of Labor (discussed in Chapter 18), first in cities such as Richmond and Atlanta, then in rural areas. As one South Carolina black explained, "We are [bound] to join something what will lead to better rights than we have." Blacks made up at least a third of the Knights' membership in the South. But southern whites feared that the Knights' policies of racial and economic cooperation might lead to social equality. "The forcing of a colored man among the white people here . . . knocked me out of the order," reported one. The Charleston *News and Courier* warned of the dangers of "miscegenation" and the possibility that the South would be left "in the possession of . . .

mongrels and hybrids." As blacks continued to join it, whites abandoned the order in growing numbers. The flight of whites weakened the organization in the South, and a backlash of white violence finally smashed it.

Against this backdrop, incidents of lynchings and other forms of violence against blacks increased. On February 21, 1891, the *New York Times* reported that in Texarkana, Arkansas, a mob apprehended a 32-year-old black man, Ed Coy, charged with the rape of a white woman, tied him to a stake, and burned him alive. As Coy proclaimed his innocence to a large crowd, his alleged victim herself somewhat hesitatingly put the torch to his oil-soaked body. The *Times* report concluded that only by the "terrible death such as fire . . . can inflict" could other blacks "be deterred from the commission of like crimes." Ed Coy was one of more than 1,400 black men lynched or burned alive during the 1890s. About a third were charged with sex crimes. The rest were accused of a variety of "crimes" related to not knowing their place: marrying or insulting a white woman, testifying in court against whites, having a "bad reputation."

IN SELF-DEFENSE

In 1876, *Harper's Weekly* published this print entitled *Self-Defense*. The white man's comment, "Ef I hadn't-er killed you, you would hev growd up to rule me," is witness to the brutal treatment meted out to blacks in the late-nineteenth-century South.

Diverging Black Responses

White discrimination and exploitation nourished new protest tactics and ideologies among blacks. For years, Frederick Douglass had been proclaiming that blacks should remain loyal Americans and count on the promises of the Republican party. But on his deathbed in 1895, his last words were allegedly, "Agitate! Agitate! Agitate!"

Among black expressions of protest, one was a woman's. In Memphis, Tennessee, Ida B. Wells, the first woman editor of an important newspaper, launched a campaign against lynching in 1892. So hostile was the response from the white community that Wells carried a gun to protect herself. When white citizens finally destroyed the press and threatened her partner, Wells left Memphis to pursue her activism elsewhere.

Other voices called for black separatism within white America. T. Thomas Fortune wrote in the black New York *Freeman* in 1887 that "there will one day be an African Empire." Three years later, he organized the Afro-American League (a precursor of the NAACP), insisting that blacks must join together to fight the rising tide of discrimination. "Let us stand up," he urged, "in our own organization where color will not be a brand of odium." The League encouraged independent voting, opposed segregation and lynching, and urged the establishment of black institutions like banks to support black businesses. As a sympathetic journalist explained, "The solution of the problem is in our own hands. . . . The Negro must preserve his identity."

While some promoted black nationalism, most blacks worked patiently but persistently within white society for equality and social justice. In 1887, J. C. Price formed the Citizens Equal Rights Association, which supported various petitions and direct-action campaigns to protest segregation. The Association also called for state laws to guarantee equal rights in the aftermath of the Supreme Court's 1883 ruling. Other blacks boycotted streetcars in southern cities, and Daniel Payne, a Methodist bishop, got off the Jim Crow car on a Florida train and, rather than riding in the segregated car, with great ceremony walked to a church conference. Other blacks petitioned Congress, demanding reparations for unpaid labor as slaves.

Efforts to escape oppression in the South, like "Pap" Singleton's movement to found black towns in Tennessee and Kansas, continued. In the 1890s, black leaders lobbied to make the Oklahoma Territory, recently opened to white settlement, an all-black state. Blacks founded 25 towns there, as well as in other states and even Mexico. But these attempts, like earlier ones, were short-lived, crippled by limited funds and the hostility of white neighbors. Singleton eventually recommended migration to Canada or Liberia as a final solution, and later black nationalist leaders also looked increasingly to Africa. Bishop Henry McNeal Turner, a former Union soldier and prominent black leader, despaired of ever securing equal rights for blacks in the United States. He described the Constitution as "a dirty rag, a cheat, a libel" and said that it ought to be "spit upon by every Negro in the land." In 1894, he organized the International Migration Society to return blacks to Africa, arguing that "this country owes us forty billions of dollars" to help. He succeeded in sending two boatloads of emigrants to Liberia, but this colonization effort worked no more successfully than those earlier in the century.

As Douglass had long argued, no matter how important African roots might be, blacks had been in the Americas for generations and would have to win justice and equal rights here. W. E. B. Du Bois, the first black to receive a Ph.D. from Harvard, agreed. Yet in 1900, he attended the first Pan-African Conference in London, where he argued that blacks must lead the struggle for liberation both in Africa and in the United States. It was at this conference that Du Bois first made his prophetic comment that "the problem of the Twentieth Century" would be "the problem of the color line."

Despite these vigorous voices of militant anger and nationalistic fervor, most black Americans continued to follow the slow, moderate self-help program of Booker T. Washington, the best-known black leader in America. Born a slave, Washington had risen through hard and faithful work to become the founder (in 1881) and principal of Tuskegee Institute in Alabama, which he personally and dramatically built into the nation's largest and best-known industrial training school. At Tuskegee, young blacks received a highly disciplined education in scientific agricultural techniques and vocational skilled trades. Washington believed that economic self-help and the familiar Puritan virtues of hard work, frugality, cleanliness, and moderation were the way to success. He spent much of his time traveling through the North to secure philanthropic gifts to support Tuskegee. In time, he became a favorite of the American entrepreneurial elite.

In 1895, Washington was asked to deliver a speech at the Cotton States and International Exposition in Atlanta, celebrating three decades of industrial and agricultural progress since the Civil War. He took advantage of that invitation, a rare honor for a former slave, to make a significant statement about the position of blacks in the South. Without a hint of protest, Washington decided "to say something that would cement the friendship of the races." He therefore proclaimed black loyalty to the economic development of the South while accepting the lowly status of southern blacks. "It is at the bottom of life we must begin, and not at the top," he declared. "In all things that are purely social we can be as separate as the fingers, yet one as the hand in all things essential to mutual progress." Although Washington worked actively behind the scenes for black civil rights, in Atlanta he publicly renounced black interest in either the vote or civil rights as well as social equality with whites. Whites throughout the country enthusiastically acclaimed Washington's address, but many blacks called his "Atlanta Compromise" a serious setback in the struggle for black rights.

Washington has often been charged with conceding too quickly that political rights should follow rather than precede economic well-being. In 1903, Du Bois confronted Washington directly in *The Souls of Black Folk,* arguing instead for the "manly assertion" of a program of equal civil rights, suffrage, and higher education in the ideals of liberal learning. A trip through the black belt of Dougherty County, Georgia, showed Du Bois the "forlorn and forsaken" condition of southern blacks. The young sociologist saw that most blacks were confined to dependent agricultural labor, "fighting a hard battle with debt" year after year. Although "here and there a man has raised his head above these murky waters . . . a pall of debt hangs over the beautiful land." Beneath all others was the cotton picker, who, with

Magazines

Weekly and monthly magazines constitute a rich primary source for the historian, offering a vivid picture of the issues of the day and useful insights into popular tastes and values. With advances in the publishing industry and an increasingly literate population, the number of these journals soared in the years following the Civil War. In 1865, only 700 periodicals were published. Twenty years later there were 3,300. As the *National Magazine* grumbled, "Magazines, magazines, magazines! The newsstands are already groaning under the heavy load, and there are still more coming."

Some of these magazines were aimed at the mass market. *Frank Leslie's Illustrated Newspaper,* established in 1855, was one of the most successful. At its height, circulation reached 100,000. Making skillful use of pictures (sometimes as large as 2 by 3 feet and folded into the magazine), the weekly covered important news of the day as well as music, drama, sports, and books. Although Leslie relied more heavily on graphics and sensationalism than modern news weeklies, his publication was a forerunner of *Newsweek* and *Time.*

Another kind of weekly magazine was aimed primarily at middle- and upper-class readers. Editors like the oft-quoted Edwin Lawrence Godkin of *The Nation,* with a circulation of about 30,000, hoped to influence those in positions of authority and power by providing a forum for the discussion of reform issues. In contrast, *Scribner's* revealed a more conservative, middle-of-the-road point of view. Both magazines, however, exuded a confident, progressive tone characteristic of middle-class Americans.

Harper's Weekly was one of the most important magazines designed primarily for middle- and upper-class readers. Established in 1857, this publication continued in print until 1916. The success of *Harper's Weekly,* which called itself a "family newspaper," rested on a combination of its moderate point of view and an exciting use of illustrations and cartoons touching on contemporary events. The popular cartoons of Thomas Nast appeared in this magazine. In large part because of the use of graphics, in 1872 the circulation of *Harper's Weekly* reached a peak of 160,000.

Illustrated here is a page from the January 16, 1869, issue of *Harper's Weekly.* The layout immediately suggests the importance of graphics. Most of the page is taken up with the three pictures. The top and bottom pictures are wood engravings based on drawings by Theodore R. Davis, one of *Harper's* best-known illustrator-reporters. The center picture was derived from a photograph.

The story featured on this page concerns a victory of General George Custer in the war against the Cheyenne tribe that the U.S. Army was waging that winter. Davis had been a correspondent in the West covering Custer's actions in 1867. But when news of Custer's victory arrived, Davis was back in New York. He thus drew on his imagination for the two scenes reproduced on this page. What kind of characterization of Native Americans does Davis give in the picture at the top of the page? What view of American soldiers does he suggest? At the bottom of the page, you can see soldiers slaughtering "worthless" horses while Cheyenne tepees burn in the background. Would the average viewer have any sympathy for the plight of the Cheyennes by looking at this picture? This "victory," in fact, involved the slaughter not only of horses but also of all males over age 8.

The editors' decision to insert a picture that had nothing to do with the incident being reported was obviously significant. As you can see, the subject is a white hunter who had been killed and scalped by Indians. What kind of special relationship were the editors suggesting by placing the picture of one dead white hunter in the center of a page that primarily covered a specific conflict between the Indians and the U.S. Army? How might the reader respond to the group of pictures as a whole? How do you? How does the text contribute to the overall view of the Indian-white relationship that the pictures suggest? By considering the choice of graphics and text, you can begin to discover how magazines provide insight, not only into the events of the day but also into the ways magazines shaped the values and perspectives of nineteenth-century men and women.

CUSTER'S INDIAN SCOUTS CELEBRATING THE VICTORY OVER BLACK KETTLE.—[SKETCHED BY THEO. R. DAVIS.]

THE INDIAN WAR.

THE Indian Peace Commission of 1867 accomplished greater harm than benefit. Treaties were entered into with the Cheyennes, Arrapahoes, Kiowas, Comanches, and at the recommendation of the Commission the Powder River country was abandoned. This latter action was construed as the result of timidity on the part of the Government, and immediately the Sioux extended their depredations to the Pacific Railroad, on the Platte, while the Indians south of the Arkansas attempted to drive the whites out of the Smoky Hill country.

Last August the Cheyennes took the war-path, and the valleys of the Saline and Solomon rivers became the theatre of a relentless savage war. It was at first supposed that the Cheyennes were about to attack a hostile tribe, but soon the mask was laid aside, and in less than a month one hundred whites fell victims to the tomahawk and scalping-knife. The chiefs of the Arrapahoes had promised to proceed to Fort Cobb and get their annuities, and thence withdraw to their reservation. Instead of fulfilling their promises, they began a series of depredations on the line between Fort Wallace and Denver, in Colorado Territory. The Kiowas and Comanches about the same time entered into an agreement at Fort Zarah to remain at peace, and left with that impression fixed on the minds of those who represented the Government. The next information was that the Kiowas and Comanches had joined the Cheyennes and Arrapahoes. General SHERIDAN, taking the practical view of the condition of affairs within the limits of his department, at once transferred his head-quarters to the field, and commenced preparations for a determined war. General SULLY'S fight near this point, FORSYTH'S gallant fight on the Arrikaree fork of the Republican, CARPENTER'S and GRAHAM'S fight on the Beaver branch of the Republican, General CARR'S decisive fight in the same vicinity, and General CUS-

THE SCALPED HUNTER.—[PHOTOGRAPHED BY WM. S. SOULE.]

CUSTER'S COMMAND SHOOTING DOWN WORTHLESS HORSES.—[SKETCHED BY THEO. R. DAVIS.]

his wife and children, would have to work from sunup to sundown to pick 100 pounds of cotton to make 50 cents. The lives of most blacks were still tied to the land of the South. If they were to improve their lives, rural blacks would have to organize.

Farm Protest

During the post–Civil War period, many farmers, both black and white, began to realize that only by organizing could they hope to ameliorate the conditions of rural life. Not all were dissatisfied with their lot, however. Farmers in the Midwest and near city markets successfully adjusted to new economic conditions and had little reason for discontent. Farmers in the South and West, by contrast, faced new problems and difficulties that led to the first mass organization of farmers in American history.

"The Purposes of the Grange: Gift for the Grangers," done in 1873, not surprisingly makes a sturdy farmer its focus. The scenes around the border picture rural life as farmers wished it to be rather than as it was.

The Grange in the 1860s and 1870s

The earliest effort to organize white farmers came in 1867 when Oliver Kelley founded the Order of the Patrons of Husbandry. At first the organization emphasized social and cultural goals. Kelley wanted to bring the country's farmers into a "cordial and social fraternity" and to encourage them "to read and think, to plant fruit and flowers, [and to] beautify their homes."

More aggressive goals soon evolved. Dudley Adams, speaking to an Iowa group in 1870, emphasized the powerlessness of the "immense helpless mob" of farmers, victims of "human vampires." Salvation, Adams maintained, lay in organization.

More and more farmers, especially those in the Midwest and the South, agreed with Adams. The depression of the 1870s (discussed in Chapter 18) sharpened discontent. By 1875, an estimated 800,000 had joined Kelley's organization, now known as the National Grange. The "Farmers' Declaration of Independence," read before local granges on July 4, 1873, captured the new activist spirit. The time had come, the declaration announced, for farmers suffering from "oppression and abuse" to rouse themselves and, by "all lawful and peaceful means," to cast off the "tyranny of monopoly." While the declaration clearly expressed rural discontent, it gave few indications that Grangers recognized the complex changes that had created their problems.

Grangers were looking for culprits close to home. Middlemen seemed obvious oppressors. They gouged farmers by raising the prices of finished goods farmers needed to buy and by lowering the prices they received for their products. Some of the Granger "reforms" attempted to bypass middlemen by establishing buying and selling cooperatives. Although many of the cooperatives failed, they indicated that farmers realized that they could not respond to new conditions on an individual basis but needed to act collectively.

Operators of grain elevators also drew fire. Midwestern farmers claimed that these merchants often misgraded their wheat and corn and paid less than its worth. But they pointed to the railroads, America's first big business, as the greatest offenders. As Chapter 18 will show, cutthroat competition among railroad companies generally brought lower rates. But even though rates dropped nationwide, the railroads often set high rates in rural areas. Moreover, railroads awarded discriminatory rebates to large shippers and put small operators at a disadvantage.

Although the Grange was originally nonpolitical, farmers recognized that confronting the mighty railroads demanded political action. Other groups also wished to see some controls imposed on the railroads. Railroad policies that favored large Chicago grain terminals and long-distance shippers over local concerns victimized many western businessmen. Between 1869 and 1874, both businessmen and farmers in Illinois, Iowa, Wisconsin, and Minnesota lobbied for state railroad laws. The resulting Granger Laws (an inaccurate name because the Grangers do not deserve complete credit for them) established the maximum rates railroads and grain elevators could charge. Other states passed legislation setting up railroad commissions with power to regulate railroad rates. In some states, legislators outlawed railroad pools, rebates, passes, and other practices that seemed to represent "unjust discrimination and distortion."

Railroad companies and grain elevators quickly challenged the new laws. In 1877, the Supreme Court upheld the legislation in *Munn* v. *Illinois* on the grounds that railroads could be regulated for the common good even though they were privately owned because their operation affected the public interest. Even so, it soon became apparent that although state commissions had authority over local rates and fares, they could not control long-haul rates. To make up for the money lost on local hauls, railroads often raised long-haul charges, thus frustrating the intent of the laws. Other complicated issues involved determining what was a fair rate, who was competent to decide that rate, and what was a justifiable return for the railroad. The tangle of questions that state regulation raised proved difficult to resolve at the local level.

Although the Granger Laws failed to solve the questions involved in attempts to control the railroads, they established an important principle. The Supreme Court decision made clear that state legislatures had the power to regulate businesses of a public nature like the railroads. But the failure of the Granger Laws and the Supreme Court's reversal of *Munn* v. *Illinois* in its 1886 decision *Wabash* v. *Illinois* led to greater pressure on Congress to continue the struggle against big business.

The Interstate Commerce Act: 1887

In 1887, Congress responded to farmers, railroad managers who wished to regulate the fierce competition that threatened to bankrupt their companies, and shippers who objected to transportation rates by passing the Interstate Commerce Act. That legislation required that railroad rates be "reasonable and just," that rate schedules be made public, and that practices such as rebates be discontinued. The act also set up the first federal regulatory agency, the Interstate Commerce Commission (ICC). The ICC had the power to investigate and prosecute lawbreakers, but the legislation limited its authority to control over commerce conducted between states.

Like state railroad commissions, the ICC found it difficult to define a reasonable rate. Moreover, thousands of cases overwhelmed the tiny staff in the early months of operation. In the long run, the lack of enforcement power was most serious. The ICC's only recourse was to bring offenders into the federal courts and engage in lengthy legal proceedings. Few railroads worried about defying ICC directions on rates. When they appeared in court four or five years later, they often won their cases from judges suspicious of new federal authority. Between 1887 and 1906, a total of 16 cases made their way to the Supreme Court, which decided 15 of them in the railroads' favor. As one railroad executive candidly admitted, "There is not a road in the country that can be accused of living up to the rules of the Interstate Commerce Law."

The Southern Farmers' Alliance in the 1880s and 1890s

The Grange declined in the late 1870s as the nation recovered from depression. But neither farm organizations nor farm protest died. Depression struck farmers once again in the late 1880s and worsened as the 1890s began. Official statistics told the familiar, dismal story of falling prices for cereal crops grown on the plains and prairies. A bushel of wheat that had sold for $1 in 1870 was worth 60 cents in the 1890s. Kansas farmers, in

1889, were selling their corn for a mere 10 cents a bushel. The national currency shortage, which usually reached critical proportions at harvest time, helped to push agricultural prices ever lower. And while prices declined, the load of debt climbed. Mortgage rates ranged between 18 and 36 percent, and shipping rates were high. It sometimes cost a farmer as much as one bushel of corn to send another one to market.

A Kansas farmer's letter reveals some of the human consequences of such trends:

> At the age of 52 years, after a long life of toil, economy and self-denial, I find myself and family virtually paupers. With hundreds of cattle, hundreds of hogs, scores of good horses, and a farm that rewarded the toil of our hands with 16,000 bushels of golden corn, we are poorer by many dollars than we were years ago. What once seemed a neat little fortune and a house of refuge for our declining years . . . has been rendered valueless.

Under these pressures, farmers turned again to organization, education, and cooperation. The Southern Farmers' Alliance became one of the most important reform organizations of the 1880s as it launched an ambitious organizational drive, sending lecturers throughout the South and onto the western plains. Eventually, Alliance lecturers reached 43 states and territories, bringing their message to 2 million farming families and organizing a far-reaching agrarian network.

An article in their newspaper, the *National Economist,* pointed out some of the Alliance's fundamental beliefs. "The agricultural population of to-day is becoming rapidly aroused to the fact that agriculture, as a class, can only be rendered prosperous by radical changes in the laws governing money, transportation, and land." The economic and social position of farmers had slipped, even though as producers the farming class was critical to national well-being. The farmer's condition was, in the words of an Alliance song, a "sin," the result of the farmer's forgetting that "he's the man that feeds them all." Alliance lecturers proposed various programs that would help realize their slogan: "Equal rights to all, special privileges to none."

On the one hand, the Alliance experimented with buying and selling cooperatives in order to free farmers from the clutches of supply merchants, banks, and other credit agencies. Although these efforts often failed in the long run, they taught the value of cooperation to achieve common goals. On the other hand, the Alliance supported legislative efforts to regulate powerful monopolies and corporations, which they believed gouged the farmer. Many Alliance members also felt that increasing the money supply was critical to improving the position of farmers and supported a national banking system empowered to issue paper money.

The Alliance also called for a variety of measures to improve the quality of rural life: better public schools for rural children, state agricultural colleges, and an improvement in the status of women. "This order has the good sense, magnanimity and moral courage," declared Hattie Huntingdon of Louisiana, "to lay aside deeply-rooted prejudices handed down from the barbaric past and admit women into its fold and proclaim to the world that it believes in equal rights to all."

By 1890, rural discontent was spreading. In the Midwest, where farmers were prospering by raising hogs and cattle on cheap grain, and in the East, where farmers were growing fruit and vegetables for urban markets, discontent was muted. But that summer in Kansas, hundreds of farmers packed their families into wagons to set off for Alliance meetings or to parade in long lines through the streets of nearby towns and villages. Floats garnished with evergreens proclaimed that the farmers' new organization focused on live issues, not the dead ones Congress debated.

Similar scenes occurred through the West and the South. A farmer's wife, Zenobia Wheeless, captured the hopeful spirit of the protest in her letter to North Carolina Alliance leader Leonidas Polk. "We rode sixteen miles . . . to hear Brother Tracy [an organizer from Texas]—started about sun-up and trotted all the way. . . . Brother Tracy's lecture was very interesting . . . it seemed that all eyes were riveted upon him." Never had there been such a wave of organizational activity in rural America. In 1890, more than a million farmers counted themselves as Alliance members.

The Alliance network also included black farmers. In 1888, black and white organizers established the Colored Farmers' Alliance, headed by a white Baptist minister, R. M. Humphrey. The Colored Farmers' Alliance recognized that black and white farmers faced common economic problems and must cooperate to ameliorate their shared plight. Few initially confronted the fact that many southern cotton farmers depended on black labor and had a different perspective from blacks. In 1891, however, cotton pickers working on plantations near Memphis, Tennessee, went on strike. White posses chased the strikers, lynched 15 of them, and demonstrated that racial tensions simmered just below the surface.

The Ocala Platform: 1890

In December 1890, the National Alliance gathered in Ocala, Florida, to develop an official platform. Most delegates felt that the federal government had failed to address the farmers' problems. "Congress must come nearer the people or the people will come nearer the Congress," warned the Alliance's president. Both parties were far too subservient to the "will of corporation and money power." Thus the platform called for the direct election of U.S. senators. Alliance members supported lowering the tariff, a much debated topic in Congress, but their justification, emphasizing the need to reduce prices for the "poor of our land," had a radical ring. Their money plank went far beyond what any national legislator was likely to consider. Rejecting the notion that only gold had value or, indeed, that precious metals had to be the basis for currency, Alliance leaders boldly envisioned a new banking system controlled by the federal government. They demanded that the government take an active economic role by increasing the amount of money in circulation in the form of treasury notes and silver. More money would lead to inflation, higher prices, and a reduction in debt, they believed.

The platform also called for the creation of subtreasuries (federal warehouses) in agricultural regions where farmers could store their produce at low interest rates until market prices favored selling. To tide farmers over until that time, the federal government would lend farmers up to 80 percent of the current local price for their products. Thus the plan would free farmers from the twin evils of the credit merchant and depressed prices at harvest time. Other demands included a graduated income tax and support for the regulation of transportation and communication networks. If regulation failed, the government was called upon to take over both networks and run them for the public benefit.

In the context of late-nineteenth-century political life, almost all these planks represented radical departures from political norms. They demanded aggressive governmental action to assist the country's farmers at a time when the government favored big business (see Chapter 19). Even though a minority of farmers belonged to the Alliance, many Americans feared that the organization was capable of upsetting political arrangements. The *New York Sun* reported that the Alliance had caused a "panic" in the two major parties. The Alliance's warning that the people would replace their representatives unless they were better represented was already coming true. Although the Alliance was not formally in politics, it had supported sympathetic candidates in the fall elections of 1890. A surprising number of these local and state candidates had won. Alliance victories in the West harmed the Republican party enough to cause President Harrison to refer to "our election disaster."

Before long, many Alliance members were pressing for an independent political party, as legislators who had courted Alliance votes conveniently forgot their pledges once elected. Alliance support did not necessarily bring action on issues of interest to farmers, or even respect. One Texas farmer reported that the chairman of the state Democratic executive committee "calls us all skunks" and observed that "anything that has the scent of the plowhandle smells like a polecat" to the Democrats. On the national level, no one had much interest in the Ocala platform. As one North Carolinian observed, "I am not able to perceive any very great difference between the two parties."

Among the first to realize the necessity of forming an independent third party was Georgia's Tom Watson. "We are in the midst of a great crisis," he argued. "We have before us three or four platforms . . . [and] the Ocala platform is the best of all three. It is the only one that breathes the breath of life." Watson also realized that electoral success in the South would depend on unity between white and black farmers.

The People's Party: 1892

In February 1892, the People's, or Populist, party was established, with almost 100 black delegates in attendance. Leonidas Polk, president of the Alliance and promoter of a political coalition between the South and the West, became the party's presidential candidate that fall. "The time has arrived," he thundered, "for the great West, the great South, and the great Northwest, to link their hands and hearts together and march to the ballot box and take possession of the government, restore it to the principles of our fathers, and run it in the interest of the people." But by the time the party met at its convention in July in Omaha, Polk had died. The party nominated James B. Weaver, Union army veteran from Iowa, as its presidential candidate, and James G. Field, a former Confederate soldier, for vice-president.

The platform preamble, written by Ignatius Donnelly, a Minnesota farmer, author, and politician, caught much of the urgent spirit of the agrarian protest movement in the 1890s:

> We meet in the midst of a nation brought to the verge of moral, political and material ruin. Corruption dominates the ballot box, the legislatures, the Congress, and touches even the ermine of the bench. The people are demoralized. . . . The fruits of the toil of millions are boldly stolen to build up colossal fortunes . . . we breed two great classes—paupers and millionaires.

The charge was clear: "The controlling influences dominating the old political parties have allowed the existing dreadful conditions to develop without serious effort to restrain or prevent them."

The Omaha platform demands, drawn from the Ocala platform of 1890, were greatly expanded. They included more means of direct democracy (direct election of senators, direct primaries, the initiative, referendum, and the secret ballot) and several planks intended to enlist the support of urban labor (eight-hour workday, immigration restriction, and condemnation of the use of Pinkerton agents as an "army of mercenaries . . . a menace to our liberties"). The People's party also endorsed a graduated income tax, the free and unlimited coinage of silver at a ratio of 16 to 1 (meaning that the U.S. Mint would have to buy silver for coinage at one-sixteenth the current official price of the equivalent amount of gold), and, rather than regulation, government ownership of railroads, telephone, and telegraph. "The time has come," the platform said, "when the railroad corporations will either own the people or the people must own the railroads."

The Populist party attempted to widen the nature of the American political debate by promoting a new vision of the government's role with respect to farmers' problems. But the tasks the party faced in attempting to win power were monumental. Success at the polls meant weaning the South away from the Democratic party, encouraging southern whites to work with blacks, and persuading voters of both parties to abandon familiar political ties. Nor were all Alliance members eager to follow their leaders into the third party. At the most basic level, the Populists had to create the political machinery necessary to function in the 1892 electoral campaign.

Despite these obstacles, the new party pressed forward. Unlike the candidates of the major parties in 1892, Benjamin Harrison and Grover Cleveland, Weaver campaigned actively. In the South, he faced rowdy audiences, rotten eggs, and rocks from hostile Democrats, who disapproved of attempts to form a biracial political coalition. The results of the campaign were mixed. Although Weaver won over a million popular votes (the first third-party candidate to do so), he carried only four states (Kansas, Colorado, Idaho, and Nevada) and parts of two others (Oregon and North Dakota), for a total of 22 electoral votes. The attempt to break the stranglehold of the Democratic party on the South had failed. Democrats raised the cry of "nigger rule" and fanned racial fears. White farmers who viewed the alliance with blacks as one of necessity voted Democratic. Intimidation tactics and violence frightened off others. Just as important, Weaver failed to appeal to city workers, who were suspicious of the party's antiurban tone and its desire for higher agricultural prices (which meant higher food prices). Nor did it appeal to people living east of the Mississippi or to farmers in the Great Lakes states. Their families enjoyed better farming weather, owed fewer debts, and were relatively prosperous. They saw little of value in the Omaha platform. Their disinterest was significant, for the growing population of the industrial northern cities, combined with the populous and prosperous Great Lake states, constituted an electoral majority by the 1890s.

Although the People's party failed to recruit a cross section of American voters in 1892, it gained substantial support. Miners and mine owners in states like Montana and Colorado and in territories like New Mexico favored the demand for coinage of silver. Most Populists, however, were rural Americans in the South and West who stood outside the mainstream of American life. Economic grievances sharpened political discontent. But Populists were often no poorer or more debt-ridden than other farmers. They did tend to lead more isolated lives, however; often their farms were far from towns, villages, and railroads. They felt powerless to affect the workings of their political, social, and economic world. Thus they responded to a party offering to act as their advocate.

Farmers who were better integrated into their world tended to believe they could work through existing political parties. In 1892, when thousands of farmers and others were politically and economically discontented, they voted for Cleveland and the Democrats, not the Populists.

Yet the Populists did not lose heart in 1892, as Chapter 19 will show. Populist governors were elected in Kansas and North Dakota, and the party swept Colorado. It was obvious that the showing of the party in the South, where even Tom Watson lost his bid for a congressional seat, stemmed from violent opposition and fraud on the part of the Democrats. For example, returns in Richmond County, Georgia, revealed a Democratic majority of 80 percent in a total vote twice the size of the actual number of legal voters.

CONCLUSION

Farming in the Industrial Age

The late nineteenth century brought turbulence to rural America. The "Indian problem," which had plagued Americans for 200 years, was tragically solved for a while, but not without resistance and bloodshed. Few whites found these events troubling. Most were caught up in the challenge of responding to a fast-changing world. Believing themselves to be the backbone of the nation, white farmers brought Indian lands into cultivation, modernized their farms, and raised bumper crops. But success and a comfortable competency eluded many of them. Some, like Milton Leeper, never gave up hope or farming. Many were caught in a cycle of poverty and debt. Others fled to the cities, where they joined the industrial work force described in the next chapter. Many turned to collective action and politics. Their actions demonstrate that they did not merely react to events but attempted to shape them.

Recommended Reading

General

Gilbert C. Fite, *The Farmer's Frontier, 1865–1900* (1966); Rodman W. Paul, with Martin Ridge, *The Far West and the Great Plains in Transition, 1859–1900* (1988); Patricia N. Limerick, *Legacy of Conquest: The Unbroken Past of the American West* (1987); Donald Worster, *Rivers of Empire: Water, Aridity, and the Growth of the American West* (1985); Henry Nash Smith, *Virgin Land: The American West as Symbol and Myth* (1950); J. B. Jackson, *The Centennial Years, 1865–1976* (1972); Annette Kolodny, *The Land Before Her: Fantasy and Experience of the American Frontiers, 1630–1860* (1984); Paul W. Gates, *History of Public Land Law Development* (1978); Alan G. Bogue, *Money at Interest: The Farm Mortgage on the Middle Border* (1955).

Regions and Groups

Fred C. Luebke, ed., *Ethnicity on the Great Plains* (1980); Howard R. Lamar, *The Far Southwest, 1846–1880* (1963); Earl Pomeroy, *The Pacific Slope: A History of California, Oregon, Washington, Idaho, Utah, and Nevada* (1965); Carlos Schwantes, *The Pacific Northwest: An Interpretive History* (1989); Richard White, *Land Use, Environment, and Social Change: The Shaping of Island County, Washington* (1980); Sue Armitage and Elizabeth Jameson, eds., *The Women's West* (1987); Sarah Deutsch, *No Separate Refuge: Culture, Class, and Gender on an Anglo-Hispanic Frontier in the American Southwest, 1880–1940* (1987); David Montejano, *Anglos and Mexicans in the Making of Texas, 1831–1986* (1987).

Mining and Cattle Frontiers

R. W. Paul, *Mining Frontiers of the Far West, 1848–1880* (1963); William S. Greever, *Bonanza West: Western Mining*

TIMELINE

1860s Cattle drives from Texas begin

1865–1867 Sioux Wars on the Great Plains

1867 National Grange founded

1869 Transcontinental railroad completed

1869–1874 Granger Laws

1873 Financial panic triggers economic depression

1874 Barbed wire patented

1875 Black Hills gold rush incites Sioux War

1876 Custer's last stand at Little Big Horn

1877 *Munn* v. *Illinois*
Bonanza farms in the Great Plains

1878 Timber and Stone Act

1880s "New South"

1881 Tuskegee Institute founded

1883–1885 Depression

1884 Southern Farmers' Alliance founded

1886 Severe winter ends cattle boom
Wabash v. *Illinois*

1887 Dawes Severalty Act
Interstate Commerce Act
Farm prices plummet

1888 Colored Farmers' Alliance founded

1890 Afro-American League founded
Sioux Ghost Dance movement
Massacre at Wounded Knee
Ocala platform
Yosemite National Park established

1890s Black disenfranchisement in the South
Jim Crow laws passed in the South
Declining farm prices

1891 Forest Reserve Act

1892 Populist party formed

1892 Sierra Club founded

1895 Booker T. Washington's "Atlanta Compromise" address

1896 *Plessy* v. *Ferguson*

Rushes (1963); Malcolm Rohrbough, *Aspen: The History of a Silver Mining Town, 1879–1893* (1986); Paula Petrik, *No Step Backward: Women and Family on the Rocky Mountain Mining Frontier, Helena, Montana* (1987); Lewis Atherton, *The Cattle Kings* (1961); Robert R. Dykstra, *The Cattle Towns: A Social History of the Kansas Cattle Trading Centers* (1970); Joseph B. Frantz and Julian E. Choate, *The American Cowboy: The Myth and the Reality* (1968).

Native Americans

William T. Hagan, *American Indians* (1979 ed.); Wilcomb E. Washburn, *The Indian in America* (1975); Ronald T. Takaki, *Iron Cages: Race and Culture in Nineteenth-Century America* (1979); Francis P. Prucha, *American Indian Policy in Crisis: Christian Reformers and the Indians* (1976); Robert M. Utley, *The Indian Frontier of the American West* (1984); Richard White, *The Roots of Dependency* (1983); Ralph K. Andrist, *The Long Death: The Last Days of the Plains Indians* (1964); John G. Neihardt, *Black Elk Speaks* (1932).

The New South

C. Vann Woodward, *The Origins of the New South, 1877–1913* (1951); Paul M. Gaston, *The New South Creed: A Study in Southern Mythmaking* (1970); Orville Vernon Burton and Robert C. McMath, Jr., eds., *Toward a New South?: Post-Civil War Southern Communities* (1982); Gavin Wright, *Old South, New South: Revolutions in the Southern Economy Since the Civil War* (1986); Robert C. McMath and Orville V. Burton, eds., *Toward a New South: Studies in Post-Civil War Southern Communities* (1982); Lawrence H. Larsen, *The Rise of the Urban South* (1985); Blaine A. Brownell and David R. Goldfield, eds., *The City in Southern History* (1977); H. N. Rabinowitz, *Race Relations in the Urban South* (1978); Morgan Kousser, *The Shaping of Southern Politics: Suffrage Restriction and the Establishment of the One-Party South* (1974); Jacqueline Jones, *Labor of Love, Labor of Sorrow: Black Women, Work, and the Family from Slavery to the Present* (1985).

Populism

Lawrence Goodwyn, *The Populist Moment: A Short History of the Agrarian Revolt in America* (1978); Sheldon Hackney, *Populism to Progressivism in Alabama* (1969); Bruce Palmer, *"Men over Money": The Southern Populist Critique of American Capitalism* (1980); Peter H. Argersinger, *Populism and Politics: William Alfred Peffer and the People's Party* (1974); Steven Hahn, *The Roots of Southern Populism: Yeoman Farmers and the Transformation of the Georgia Upcountry, 1850–1890* (1893); Robert W. Larson, *Populism in the Mountain West* (1986); Robert C. McMath, *Populist Vanguard: A History of the Southern Farmers' Alliance* (1975).

Novels

Willa Cather, *My Antonia* (1918); O. E. Rölvaag, *Giants in the Earth* (1927).

The Rise of Smokestack America

By 1883, Thomas O'Donnell, an Irish immigrant, had lived in the United States for over a decade. He was 30 years old, married, with two young children. His third child had died in 1882, and O'Donnell was still in debt for the funeral. Money was scarce, for O'Donnell was a textile worker in Fall River, Massachusetts, and not well educated. "I went to work when I was young," he explained, "and have been working ever since." However, O'Donnell worked only sporadically at the mill. New machines needed "a good deal of small help," and the mill owners preferred to hire man-and-boy teams. Since O'Donnell's children were only 1 and 3, he often saw others preferred for day work. Once, when he was passed over, he recalled, "I said to the boss . . . what am I to do; I have got two little boys at home . . . how am I to get something for them to eat; I can't get a turn when I come here. . . . I says, 'Have I got to starve; ain't I to have any work?'"

O'Donnell and his family were barely getting by even though he worked with pick and shovel when he could. He estimated that he had earned only $133 the previous year. Rent came to $72. The family spent $2 for a little coal but depended for heat on driftwood that O'Donnell picked up on the beach. Clams were a major part of the family diet, but on some days there was nothing to eat at all.

The children "got along very nicely all summer," but it was now November, and they were beginning to "feel quite sickly." It was hardly surprising. "One has one shoe on, a very poor one, and a slipper, that was picked up somewhere. The other has two odd shoes on, with the heel out." His wife was healthy but not ready for winter. She had two dresses, one saved for church, and an "undershirt that she got given to her, and . . . an old wrapper, which is about a mile too big for her; somebody gave it to her."

O'Donnell was describing his family's marginal existence to a Senate committee that was gathering testimony in Boston in 1883 on the relations between labor and capital. As the senators heard the tale, they asked him why he did not go west. "It would not cost you over $1,500," said one senator. The gap between the worlds of the senator and the worker could not have been more dramatic. O'Donnell replied, "Well, I never saw over a $20 bill . . . if some one would give me $1,500 I will go." Asked by the senator if he had friends who could provide him with the funds, O'Donnell sadly replied no.

The senators, of course, were far better acquainted with the world of comfort and leisure than with the poverty of families like the O'Donnells. From their vantage point, the fruits of industrial progress were clear. As the United States became a world industrial leader in the years after the Civil War, its factories poured forth an abundance of ever-cheaper goods ranging from steel rails and farm reapers to mass-produced parlor sets. These were years of tremendous growth and broad economic and social change. Manufacturing replaced agriculture as the leading source of economic growth between 1860 and 1900. By 1890, a majority of the American work force held nonagricultural jobs; over a third lived in cities. A rural nation of farmers was becoming a nation of industrial workers and city dwellers.

As O'Donnell's testimony illustrates, industrial growth did not benefit everyone. Although no nationwide studies of poverty existed, estimates suggest that perhaps half the American population was too poor to take advantage of the new goods of the age.

This chapter examines the new order that resulted from the maturing of the American industrial economy. Focusing on the years between 1865 and 1900, it describes the rise of heavy industry, the organization and character of the new industrial workplace, and the emergence of big business. It then examines the locus of industrial life, the fast-growing city, and its varied people, classes, and social inequities. The chapter's central theme grows out of O'Donnell's story: as the United States built up its railroads, cities, and factories, its production and profit orientation resulted in the maldistribution of wealth and power. Although many Americans were too exhausted by life's daily struggles to protest new inequalities, strikes and other forms of working-class resistance punctuated the period. The social problems that accompanied the country's industrial development would capture the attention of reformers and politicians for decades to come.

The Texture of Industrial Progress

When Americans went to war in 1861, agriculture was the country's leading source of economic growth. Forty years later, manufacturing had taken its place. During these years, the production of manufactured goods outpaced population growth. By 1900, three times as many goods per person existed as in 1860. Per capita income increased by over 2 percent a year. But these aggregate figures disguise the fact that many people did not win any gains at all.

As American manufacturing progressed, new regions grew in industrial importance. From New England to the Midwest lay the country's industrial heartland. New England was still a center of light industry, and the Midwest continued to process natural resources. Now, however, the production of iron, steel, and transportation equipment joined the older manufacturing operations there. In the Far West, manufacturers concentrated on processing the region's natural resources, but heavy industry made strides as well. In the South, the textile industry put down roots by the 1890s, although the South as a whole was far less industrialized than either the North or the Midwest.

The Rise of Heavy Industry from 1880 to 1900

Although many factors contributed to the dramatic rise in industrial productivity, the changing nature of the industrial sector itself explains many of the gains. Manufacturers before the Civil War had concentrated either on producing textiles, clothing, and leather products or on processing agricultural and natural resources like grain, hogs, or lumber. While these industries continued to be important, heavy industry, which produced goods like steel, iron, petroleum, and machinery, grew rapidly. The manufacturing of "producer's goods" (goods intended for other producers rather than consumers) provided the basis for economic growth. Farmers, who bought machinery for their farms; manufacturers, who installed new equipment in their factories; and railroads, which bought steel rails for their tracks—all contributed to rising productivity figures.

Technological innovations that revolutionized production lay behind the rise of heavy industries such as steel. Before the Civil War, the production of iron was slow and expensive. Skilled and highly paid workers turned iron ore into wrought iron, which farmers and mechanics could easily shape into tools and machines. The introduction of the Bessemer converter and the open-hearth steelmaking method in the 1870s transformed the production process. Both techniques converted iron ore into steel while reducing the need for so many skilled workers.

Dramatic changes in the steel industry resulted. Steel companies developed new forms of vertical organization that provided them with access to raw materials and markets and brought all stages of steel manufacturing, from smelting to rolling, into one mill. Production soared and prices fell. When Andrew Carnegie introduced the Bessemer process in his plant in the mid-1870s, the price of steel plummeted from $100 a ton to $50. In another two years, the price dropped to $40; by 1890, steel cost only $12 a ton.

In turn, the production of a cheaper, stronger, more durable material than iron created new goods, new demands, and new markets. Early railroads relied on iron rails that soon flattened and split. Now they consumed 1.5 million tons of hard steel rails yearly as they built new lines across the country. Steel locomotives pulled heavier and heavier loads of goods to locations far from industrial centers. Bridge builders realized the possibilities of steel-cable suspension designs, and architects such as Louis Sullivan began to use steel for the nation's first high-rise buildings. Proponents of a new foreign policy lobbied successfully for an expanded navy of steel vessels. Countless Americans bought steel in more humble forms: wire, nails, bolts, needles, and screws.

New sources of power facilitated the conversion of American industry to mass production. Because steam engines and coal were expensive, early manufacturers depended on water power. In 1869, about half the industrial power used came from water. With the opening of new anthracite coal deposits, however, the cost of coal dropped, and American industry rapidly shifted to steam. By 1900, steam engines accounted for 80 percent of the nation's industrial energy supply.

The completion of a national transportation and communications network was central to economic growth. In 1860, most railroads were located in the East and the Midwest. From 1862 on, the federal and state governments vigorously promoted railroad construction with land grants from the public domain. Eventually the railroads

This 1876 lithograph gives a good idea of the industrial character of a mining operation on the Comstock in Colorado. The Sutro Tunnel, which extended three miles into the mountain, was an example of the technological and capital requirements of the mining industry.

received over 180 million acres, an area about 1½ times the size of Texas. Similarly, counties and cities donated land for stations and terminals, bought railroad stock, made loans and grants, and gave tax breaks to railroads.

With such incentives, the first transcontinental railroad was completed in 1869. A burst of railroad construction followed. Four additional transcontinental lines and miles of feeder and branch roads were laid down in the 1870s and 1880s. By 1890, trains rumbled across 165,000 miles of tracks. As railroads crisscrossed the country, Western Union lines arose alongside them. Mass production and distribution depended on fast, efficient, and regular transportation. The completion of the national system both encouraged and supported the adoption of mass production and mass marketing.

Financing Postwar Growth

Such changes demanded huge amounts of capital and the willingness to accept financial risks. The creation of the railroad system alone cost over $1 billion by 1859 (the canal system's modest price tag was less than $2 million). The completion of the national railroad network required another $10 billion. British, French, and German investors saw American railroads as a good investment; ultimately, foreigners contributed a third of the sum needed to complete the system. Americans also eagerly supported new ventures and began to devote an increasing percentage of the national income to investment rather than consumption.

Although savings and commercial banks continued to invest their depositors' capital, investment banking houses like Morgan & Co. played a new and significant role in matching resources with economic enterprises. Investment bankers marketed investment opportunities. They bought up blocks of corporate bonds (which offered set interest rates and eventually the repayment of principal) at a discount for interested investors and also sold stocks (which paid dividends only if the company made a profit). Because stocks were riskier investments than bonds, buyers were at first cautious. But when John Pierpont Morgan, a respected investment banker, began to market stocks, they became more popular. The market for industrial securities expanded rapidly in the 1880s and 1890s. Although some Americans feared the power of investment bankers and distrusted the financial market, both were integral to the economic expansion of the late nineteenth century.

Railroads: Pioneers of Big Business

As the nature of the American economy changed, big businesses became the characteristic form of economic organization. Big businesses, with large amounts of capital, could afford to build huge factories, buy and install the latest and most efficient machinery, hire hundreds of workers, and use the most up-to-date methods. The result was more goods at lower prices. Machines costing thousands of dollars mass-produced goods costing pennies.

The railroads were the pioneers of big business and a great modernizing force in America. After the Civil War, railroad companies expanded rapidly. In 1865, the typical railroad was only 100 miles long. Twenty years later, it was 1,000. In 1888, a medium-size Boston railroad company had three times as many employees and received six times as much income as the Massachusetts state government.

The size of railroads, the huge costs of construction, maintenance, and repair, and the complexity of operations required unprecedented amounts of capital and new management techniques. No single person could finance a railroad or hope to supervise its operations involving hundreds of miles of track and hundreds of employees. Nor could any one person resolve the thorny questions such a large enterprise raised. How should the operations and employees be organized? What were the long-term and short-term needs of the railroad? What were proper rates? What share of the profits did workers deserve?

Unlike small businesses with modest overhead costs, railroads faced high constant costs of maintaining equipment and lines. In addition, railroads carried a heavy load of debt, incurred to pay for construction and expansion. The burden of regular interest payments and expenses encouraged railroads to adopt aggressive business practices and to use their equipment as intensively as possible. If 20 cars were almost as expensive to pull as 25, why not haul 25? If lower rates would lure customers, why not offer them? Railroad freight charges dropped steadily during

This depiction emphasizes the luxury, comfort, and attentive service (note the smiling black attendant who offers the diners cigars and drinks) available in a Pullman dining car. Through the window a large factory is visible. The image as a whole suggests the pride many Americans felt in industrial development.

the last quarter of the century. When two or more lines competed for the same traffic, railroads often offered lower rates than their rivals or secret rebates (cheaper fares in exchange for all of a company's business). Rate wars helped customers, but they could plunge a railroad into bankruptcy. Instability plagued the railroad industry even as it expanded.

In the 1870s, railroad leaders sought stability through eliminating ruinous competition. As George Perkins of the Chicago, Burlington, and Quincy Railroad explained, "The struggle for existence and the survival of the fittest is a pretty theory, but it is also a law of nature that even the fittest must live." Railroad leaders established "pools," informal agreements that set uniform rates or divided up the traffic. Yet pools never completely succeeded. Too often, individual companies disregarded their agreements, especially when the business cycle took a downturn.

Railroad leaders often tried to control costs and counter the late-nineteenth-century pattern of falling prices by slashing their workers' wages. Owners justified this strategy by reasoning that they had taken all the business risks. As a result, railroads faced powerful worker unrest (described later in this chapter).

The huge scale and complexity of the railroads required new management techniques. In 1854, the directors of the Erie Railroad hired engineer and inventor Daniel McCallum to devise a system to make railroad managers and their employees more accountable. In his report, McCallum highlighted the differences between large and small organizations. In a small organization, one could pay personal attention to all the details of operation. But, McCallum argued, "any system that might be applicable to the business and extent of a short road would be found entirely inadequate to the wants of a long one."

McCallum's system, emphasizing division of responsibilities and a regular flow of information, attracted widespread interest, and railroads became pioneers in rationalized administrative practices and management techniques. Their procedures became models for other businesses in decision making, scheduling, and engineering. Other large-scale businesses adopted the new procedures that effectively distributed responsibilities and separated management from operations. Because they faced similar economic conditions, big businesses also emulated the behavior of the railroads—their competitiveness, their attempts to underprice one another, their eventual interest in merger, and their tendency to cut workers' wages.

Growth in Other Industries

By the last quarter of the century, the textile, metal, and machinery industries equaled the railroads in size. In 1870, the typical iron and steel firm employed under 100 workers. Thirty years

Increase in Size of Industries, 1860–1900

Industry	Average Number of Workers per Establishment 1860	1900
Cotton goods	112	287
Glass	81	149
Iron and steel	65	333
Hosiery and knit goods	46	91
Silk and silk goods	39	135
Woolen goods	33	67
Carpets and rugs	31	214
Tobacco	30	67
Slaughtering and meatpacking	20	61
Paper and wood pulp	15	65
Shipbuilding	15	42
Agricultural implements	8	65
Leather	5	40
Malt liquors	5	26

Source: U.S. Bureau of the Census.

later, the average work force was four times as large. By 1900, more than 1,000 American factories had giant labor forces ranging between 500 and 1,000. Almost 450 others employed more than 1,000 workers. Big business had come of age.

Business expansion was accomplished in one of two ways (or a combination of both). Some owners like steel magnate Andrew Carnegie integrated their businesses vertically. Vertical integration meant adding operations either before or after the production process. Even though he had introduced the most up-to-date innovations in his steel mills, Carnegie realized he needed his own sources of pig iron, coal, and coke. This was "backward" integration, away from the consumer, in order to avoid dependence on suppliers. When Carnegie acquired steamships and railroads to transport his finished products, he was integrating "forward," toward the consumer. Companies that integrated vertically frequently achieved economies of scale through more efficient management techniques.

Other companies copied the railroads and integrated horizontally by combining similar businesses. They did not intend to control the various stages of production, as was the case with vertical integration, but rather to gain a monopoly of the market in order to eliminate competition and to stabilize prices. Horizontal integration sometimes, though not always, brought economies and thus greater profits. The control over prices that monopoly provided did boost earnings.

John D. Rockefeller used the strategy of horizontal integration to gain control of the oil market. By a combination of astute and ruthless techniques, Rockefeller bought or drove out competitors of his Standard Oil of New Jersey. Although the company never achieved a complete monopoly, by 1898 it was refining 84 percent of the nation's oil. Rockefeller reflected, "The day of individual competition [in the oil business] . . . is past and gone."

Rockefeller accurately characterized the new economic conditions. As giant businesses competed intensely, often cutting wages and prices, they absorbed or eliminated smaller and weaker producers. Business ownership became increasingly concentrated. In 1870, some 808 American iron and steel firms competed in the marketplace. By 1900, the number had dwindled to fewer than 70.

Like the railroads, many big businesses chose to incorporate. Although corporations were not new, most manufacturing firms were unincorporated in 1860. By 1900, corporations turned out two-thirds of the country's industrial goods.

Business gained many advantages by incorporating. Through the sale of stock, they could raise funds for their large-scale operations. The principle of limited liability protected investors, while the corporation's legal identity ensured its survival after the death of original and subsequent shareholders. Longevity suggested a measure of stability that heightened the attractiveness of a corporation as an investment.

The Erratic Economic Cycle

The transformation of the economy was neither smooth nor steady. Rockefeller, describing his years in the oil business as "hazardous," confessed that he did not know "how we came through them."

Two depressions, one from 1873 to 1879 and the other from 1893 to 1897, surpassed the severity of economic downturns before the Civil War. Collapsing land values, unsound banking practices, and changes in the supply of money had caused antebellum depressions. The depressions of the late nineteenth century, when the economy was larger and more interdependent, were industrial, intense, and accompanied by widespread unemployment, a phenomenon new to American life.

During expansionary years, manufacturers flooded markets with goods. The pattern of falling prices that characterized the postwar period and fierce competition between producers combined to encourage overproduction. When the market was finally saturated, sales and profits declined and the economy spiraled downward. Owners slowed production and laid off workers. Industrial workers, now an increasing percentage of the American work force, depended solely on wages for their livelihood. As they economized and bought less food, farm prices also plummeted. Farmers, like wage workers, cut back on purchases. Business and trade stagnated, and the railroads were finally affected. Eventually, the cycle bottomed out, but in the meantime, millions of workers lost employment, thousands of businesses went bankrupt, and many Americans suffered deprivation and hardship.

Pollution

Another by-product of the industrial age, widespread pollution, was less dramatic and worrisome to most Americans than the vagaries of the economic cycle. But industrial processes everywhere had an adverse impact on the environment. In the iron and steel city of Birmingham, Alabama, for example, the coke ovens poured smoke, soot, and ashes into the air. Coal tar, a by-product of the coking process, was dumped, and it made the soil so acid that nothing would grow on it.

When industrial, human, and animal wastes were disposed of in rivers, they killed off fish and other forms of marine life and the plants that were part of that ecosystem. By the late nineteenth century, major pollution of eastern and midwestern rivers as well as lakes had become pronounced.

The intellectual rationale stressed growth, development, and the rapid exploitation of the country's resources rather than conservation. As the last chapter pointed out, there were some steps taken toward protecting the environment. Presidents Grover Cleveland and Benjamin Harrison both set aside forest reserves, and there was growing interest in creating national parks. But these sorts of actions were limited in scope and impact and did not begin to touch the problems created by the rise of heavy industry and the rapid urban expansion that it stimulated.

Urban Expansion in the Industrial Age

Before the Civil War, manufacturers had relied on water power and chosen rural sites for their factories. Now as they shifted to steam power, most favored urban locations that offered them workers, specialized services, local markets, and railroad links to materials and to distant markets. Although technological innovations like electric lights (invented in 1879) and telephones (1876) were still not widespread, they further increased the desirability of urban sites. Industry, rather than commerce or finance, fueled urban expansion between 1870 and 1900.

Cities of all sizes grew. The population of New York and Philadelphia doubled and tripled.

Ten Largest Cities in the United States, 1850 and 1890

1850	1890
1. New York	1. New York
2. Philadelphia	2. Chicago
3. Baltimore	3. Philadelphia
4. Boston	4. St. Louis
5. New Orleans	5. Boston
6. Cincinnati	6. Baltimore
7. Brooklyn	7. Pittsburgh
8. St. Louis	8. San Francisco
9. Albany	9. Cincinnati
10. Pittsburgh	10. Cleveland

Source: U.S. Bureau of the Census.

Smaller cities, especially those in the industrial Midwest like Omaha, Duluth, and Minneapolis, boasted impressive growth rates. Southern cities, as we saw in Chapter 17, also shared in the dramatic growth. In the Far West during the 1880s, Spokane exploded from 350 to 20,000, and Tacoma from 1,100 to 36,000. In 1870, some 25 percent of Americans lived in cities; by 1900, fully 40 percent of them did.

A Growing Population

The American population, as a whole, was growing at a rate of about 2 percent a year, but cities were expanding far more rapidly. What accounted for the dramatic increase in urban population?

Certainly not a high birthrate. Although more people were born than died in American cities, births contributed only modestly to the urban population explosion. The general pattern of declining family size that had emerged before the Civil War continued. By 1900, the average woman bore only 3.6 children, in contrast to 5.2 in 1860. Urban families, moreover, tended to have fewer children than their rural counterparts. And urban children faced a host of health hazards like tuberculosis, diarrhea, and diphtheria. All city residents were vulnerable, but children especially so. The death rate for infants was twice as high in cities as in the countryside. In the 1880s, half the children born in Chicago did not live to celebrate their fifth birthday.

American Urban Dwellers

The swelling population of late-nineteenth-century cities came both from the nation's small towns and farms and from abroad. For foreigners and Americans alike, a combination of pressures, some encouraging them to abandon their original homes, others attracting them to the urban environment, prompted the decision to relocate.

For rural Americans, the "push" came from the modernization of agricultural life. Factories poured out farm machines that replaced human hands. By 1896, one man with machinery could harvest 18 times as much wheat as a farmer working with hand tools in 1830.

Work in the industrial city was the prime attraction. Although urban jobs were often dirty, dangerous, and exhausting, so was farmwork. Moreover, by 1890, manufacturing workers were earning hundreds of dollars more a year than farm laborers. Some industrial workers, like miners in the Far West, earned even more. Part of the difference between rural and urban wages was eaten up by the higher cost of living in the city, but not all of it.

An intangible but important lure was the glitter of city life. Rural life was often monotonous and drab. The young man who saw Kansas City as a "gilded metropolis" filled with "marvels," a veritable "round of joy," found the excitement of urban life, its culture, its amusements dazzling. Shops, theaters, restaurants, churches, department stores, newspapers, ball games, and the urban throng all amazed young men and women who had grown up on farms and in small towns.

Novelists like Theodore Dreiser and Stephen Crane captured both the fascination and the dangers of city life. Writing in a style termed literary realism, they examined social problems and cast their characters in carefully depicted local settings. Dreiser's novel *Sister Carrie* (1900) follows a typical country girl as she comes to Chicago. Carrie dreams of sharing Chicago's amusements and fantasizes a life of wealth, excitement, and ease. She finds, however, that the city's luxuries and pleasures are far beyond the reach of a mere factory employee. Only by taking lovers can she grasp the city's pleasures. Many readers were shocked that Dreiser never punished Carrie for her "sins."

The bustle and excitement of city life, suggested by this 1896 picture of Chicago, acted as a magnet for people weary of rural isolation.

In *Maggie: A Girl of the Streets* (1893), Stephen Crane's heroine did meet punishment at the story's end. As a young girl, Maggie retains her purity in the heart of New York's most appalling slums. Eventually, the city's pleasures lead to a loss of innocence. Maggie turns in despair to prostitution, and the reader is left at the novel's conclusion to guess whether Maggie has been murdered or commits suicide. Fascinating and yet repelling, the industrial city captured the imagination of American writers and American culture alike.

Southern blacks, often single and young, also fed the migratory stream into the cities. In the West and the North, blacks constituted only a tiny part of the population: 3 percent in Denver in the 1880s and 1890s, 2 percent in Boston. In southern cities, however, they were more numerous. About 44 percent of Atlanta's residents in the late nineteenth century were black, 38 percent of Nashville's. No matter where they were, however, the city offered them few rewards, little glamour, and many dangers.

The New Immigration: 1880–1900

In 1870, a "brokenhearted" Annie Sproul stole away from her parents' home in Londonderry, Ireland, to seek a new future in Philadelphia. She took all the money in the house, "leaving not the price of a loaf" behind. Probably the disgrace of a love affair prompted Annie's desperate flight, but the young woman was one of many who left their homelands in the nineteenth century in the hope of making a fortune in the New World. In the 40 years before the Civil War, 5 million immigrants poured into the United States; from 1860 to 1900, that volume almost tripled. Three-quarters of the newcomers stayed in the Northeast, and many of the rest settled in cities across the nation, where they soon outnumbered native-born whites. The American mosaic of differing cultures and races assumed new complexities.

As the flow of immigration increased, the national origin of immigrants shifted. Until 1880, three-quarters of the immigrants, often called the "old immigrants," hailed from the British Isles, Germany, and Scandinavia. Irish and Germans were the largest groups. Then the pattern slowly changed in ways that increased the ethnic and religious heterogeneity of the American people and changed the composition of the laboring class. By 1890, old immigrants composed only 60 percent of the total number of newcomers, while the "new immigrants" from southern and eastern Europe (Italy, Poland, Russia, Austria-Hungary, Greece, Turkey, and Syria) made up most of the rest. Italian Catholics and eastern European Jews were the most numerous, followed by Slavs.

Cheaper, faster, and better transportation facilitated the great tide of migration. Trains reached far into eastern and southern Europe. On transatlantic vessels, even steerage passengers could now expect a bed with blankets, cooked meals, and a communal washroom. But dissatisfaction with life at home was basic to the decision to migrate. Overpopulation, famine, and disease drove people to leave. "We could have eaten each other had we stayed," explained one Italian immigrant.

Efforts to modernize European economies also stimulated immigration. New agricultural techniques led landlords to consolidate their land, evicting longtime tenants. Younger Euro-

Immigration to the United States, 1870–1920

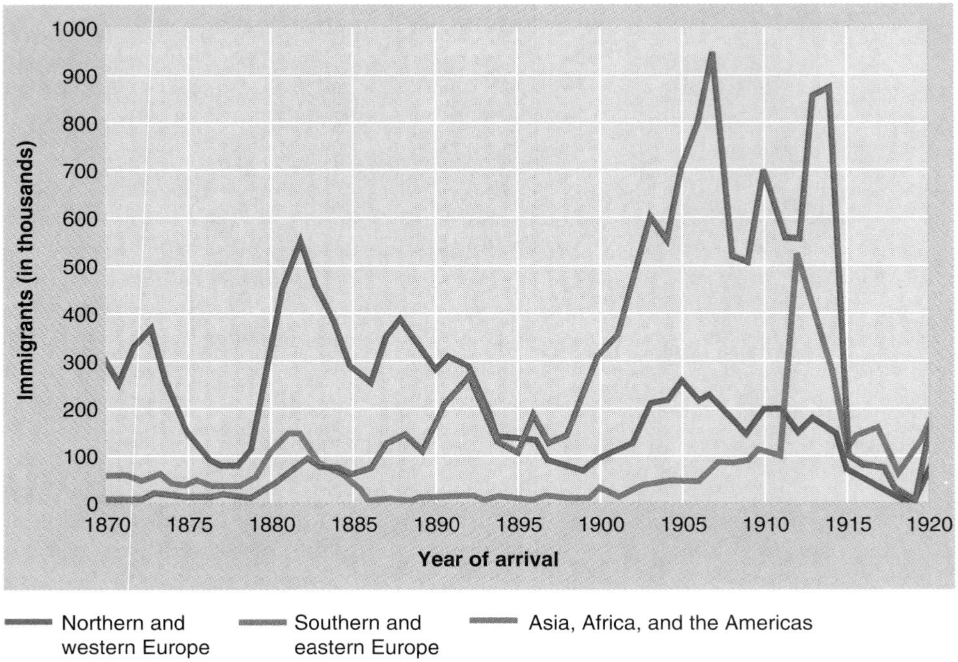

The rise of immigration from southern and eastern Europe is evident from this chart.
Source: U.S. Bureau of the Census.

pean farmers traveled in increasingly wide circles searching for work. Some emigrated to cities elsewhere in Europe. Many set out for Canada or South America. The largest share went to the United States. Similarly, artisans and craftsmen whose skills were made obsolete by the introduction of machinery pulled up stakes and headed for the United States and other destinations. Government policies pushed others to leave. In eastern Europe, especially in Russia, the official persecution of minorities and the expansion of the draft for the czar's army led millions of Jewish families and others to emigrate.

Opportunity in the "golden land" of America also lured thousands to American shores. State commissioners of immigration and American railroad and steamship companies, eager for workers and customers, wooed potential immigrants. Friends and relatives in America encouraged others to follow. Their letters described favorable living and working conditions and contained promises to help newcomers find work. One unskilled worker wrote that American cities were great places for "blast frnises and Rolen milles."

The clothes worn by these women and children, photographed as they landed at the Battery in New York City in 1907, show that they were part of the new immigration from eastern Europe and Russia.

Often passage money or pictures of friends in alluringly fashionable clothes were slipped between the pages. The phenomenon of immigrants being recruited through the reports and efforts of their predecessors has come to be known as "chain migration."

Like rural and small-town Americans, Europeans came primarily to work. Most were young, single men, who, in contrast to pre–Civil War immigrants, had few skills. Jews, however, came most often in family groups, and women predominated among the Irish. When times were good and American industry needed large numbers of unskilled laborers, migration was heavy. When times were bad and letters warned that "work is dull all over . . . no work to be got except by chance or influence," numbers fell off. Immigrants hoped to earn enough money in America to realize their ambitions at home. A surprising number, perhaps as many as a third, eventually returned to their native lands.

Adding to the stream of foreigners coming to the United States were Mexicans and Chinese laborers. Like many European countries, Mexico was in the throes of modernization. Overpopulation and new land policies uprooted many inhabitants. Gonzalo Plancarte was one. In the 1890s, Gonzalo and his father supported themselves by raising cattle in central Mexico. When the owner of the hacienda determined to turn his land over to producing goods for export, he ended the family's grazing privileges. The two men took to the road, seeking grazing lands for their herd. Their failure eventually forced them to sell their cattle. When his father died, a desperately poor Gonzalo headed for the American border. Perhaps 280,000 Mexicans crossed into the United States between 1899 and 1914, many of them finding work on the railroads and in western mines.

Overpopulation, depressed conditions, unemployment, and crop failures brought Asians, most of them from southern China, to the "Land of the Golden Mountains." "We were very much in debt because of the local warfare," explained one immigrant. "We planted each year, but we were robbed. We had to borrow. When news about the Gold Rush in California was spread by the shippers, my father decided to take the big chance."

Although only 264,000 Chinese came to the United States between 1860 and 1900, they constituted a significant minority on the West Coast.

Working-Class Immigration, 1840–1920

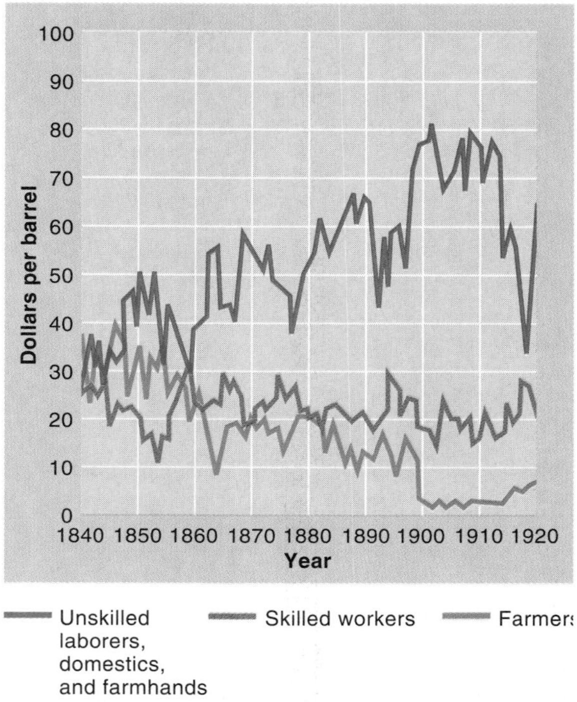

Source: U.S. Bureau of the Census.

Most were unskilled male contract laborers who promised to work for a number of years and then return to their homelands. They performed some of the hardest, dirtiest, and least desirable jobs in the West, including railroad and levee construction, mining, and factory work.

The Industrial City: 1880–1900

The late-nineteenth-century industrial city had new physical and social arrangements that attracted widespread comment. James Bryce, a Scottish visitor, noted that urban "monotony haunts one like a nightmare." Slums, which were not new, seemed disturbing because so many people lived in them. Yet these same cities also boasted of grand mansions, handsome business and industrial buildings, grandiose civic monuments, and acres of substantial middle-class homes.

By the last quarter of the nineteenth century, the jumbled arrangements of the antebellum

Downtown New York City in 1890 hosted a mixture of horse-drawn vehicles and the new "horseless carriages."

walking city, whose size and configuration had been limited by the necessity of walking to work, disappeared. Where once substantial houses, businesses, and small artisan dwellings had stood side by side, central business districts emerged. Here were banks, shops, theaters, professional firms, and businesses. Few people lived downtown, although many worked or shopped there. Surrounding the business center were areas of light manufacturing and wholesale activity with housing for workers. Beyond these working-class neighborhoods stretched middle-class residential areas. Then came the suburbs, with "pure air, peacefulness, quietude, and natural scenery." Scattered throughout the city were pockets of industrial activity surrounded by crowded working-class housing.

This new pattern, with the poorest city residents clustered near the center, is familiar today. However, it reversed the early nineteenth-century urban form, when much of the most desirable housing was in the heart of the city. New living arrangements were also more segregated by race and class than those in the preindustrial walking city. Homogeneous social and economic neighborhoods emerged, and it became more unusual than before for a poor, working-class family to live near a middle- or upper-class family.

The changing urban geography reflected the dense development of the central business district, the rise of heavy industry, and improvements in transportation. Better transportation increasingly allowed middle- and upper-class residents to live away from their work and from grimy industrial districts.

The urban transportation revolution started modestly in the 1820s and 1830s with the horse-drawn omnibus. This slow-moving vehicle accommodated only 10 to 12 passengers. Its expensive fares obliged most people to live within walking distance of their work. In the 1850s, many cities introduced horse railways. Pulling cars over rails with as many as 25 passengers, horses could cover 5 to 6 miles an hour. The horse railways, which radiated from city centers like the spokes of a wheel, allowed the city to expand outward about 4 miles. The cost of a fare limited ridership to the middle and upper classes. The introduction of cable cars, trolley cars, and subways after 1880 further extended city boundaries and broadened residential choices for the middle class.

Neighborhoods and Neighborhood Life

Working-class neighborhoods clustered near the center of most industrial cities. Here lived newcomers from the American countryside and, since

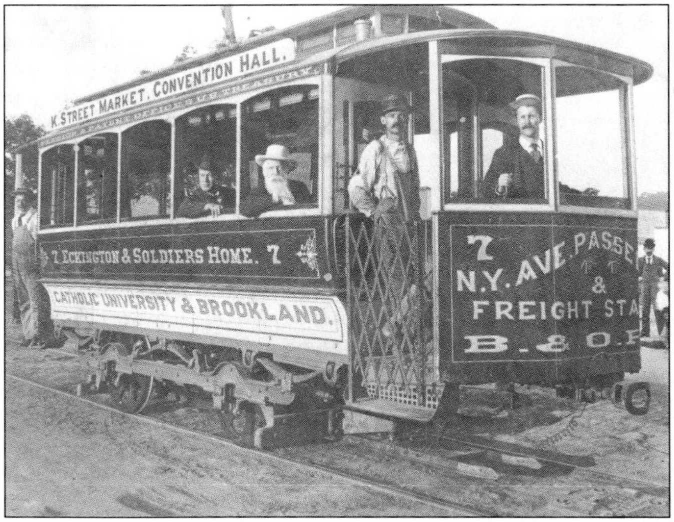

For the middle class, commuting to work from the suburbs became part of the daily routine.

most immigrants settled in cities, crowds of foreigners as well.

Ethnic groups frequently chose to gather in particular neighborhoods, often located near industries requiring their labor. In Detroit in 1880, for example, 37 percent of the city's native-born families lived in one area while 40 percent of the Irish inhabited the "Irish West Side." Over half the Germans and almost three-quarters of the Poles settled on the city's east side. Although such neighborhoods often had an ethnic flavor, with small specialty shops and foreign-language signs, they were not ethnic ghettos. Immigrants and native-born Americans often lived in the same neighborhoods, on the same streets, and even in the same houses. Toward the end of the century, when ethnic enclaves emerged, they were just that—enclaves within a neighborhood. Italians might live on one block but Jews on the next.

Working-class neighborhoods were often what would be called slums today. They were crowded and unsanitary and had inadequate public services. Many workers lived in houses once occupied by middle- and upper-class residents, now divided and subdivided to accommodate more people than the original builders had intended. Others crowded into tenements, specially constructed to house as many families as possible. Outdoor privies, often shared by several families, were the rule. Water came from outdoor hydrants, and women had to carry it inside for cooking, washing, and cleaning. When there were indoor fixtures, they frequently emptied waste directly into unpaved alleys and courts served by inadequate sewage systems or none at all. Piles of garbage and waste stank in the summer and froze in the winter. Even when people kept their own living quarters clean, their outside environment was unsanitary and unhealthy. It was no surprise that urban death rates were so high. Only at the turn of the century did the public health movement, particularly the efforts to treat water supplies with germ-killing chemicals, begin to ameliorate these living conditions.

Not every working-class family lived in abject circumstances. Skilled workers might rent comfortable quarters, and a few even owned their own homes. A study of working-class families in Massachusetts found the family of one skilled worker living "in a tenement of five rooms in a pleasant and healthy locality, with good surroundings. The apartments are well furnished and [the] parlor carpeted." The family even had a sewing machine. But the unskilled and semiskilled workers were not so fortunate. The Massachusetts survey describes the family of an unskilled ironworker crammed into a tenement of four rooms,

> in an overcrowded block, to which belong only two privies for about fifty people. When this place was visited the vault had overflowed in the yard and the sink-water was also running in the same place, and created a stench that was really frightful. . . . The house inside, was badly furnished and dirty, and a disgrace to Worcester.

Drab as their neighborhoods usually were, working families created a community life that helped to alleviate some of the dreariness of their physical surroundings. The expense of moving around the city helped encourage a neighborhood and family focus. Long hours spent at work meant that precious free time was apt to be spent close to home.

A wide range of institutions and associations came to life in urban neighborhoods. Frequently they were based on ethnic ties. They made residents feel at home in the city yet at the same time often separated them from native-born Americans and other ethnic groups. Irish associational life, for example, focused around the Roman Catholic parish church, its Irish priest, and its many clubs and group activities; Irish nationalist organizations; and ward politics. Irish saloons were convivial places for men to meet, socialize, drink, and talk politics. Jews gathered in their synagogues, Hebrew schools, and Hebrew- and Yiddish-speaking literary groups. Germans had their family saloons and educational and singing societies. While such activities may have slowed assimilation into American society and discouraged intergroup contact, they provided companionship, social life, and a bridge between life in the "old country" and life in America. Working-class men and women were far from mere victims of their environment. They found the energy, squeezed out the time, and even saved the money to support networks of social ties and associations.

Black Americans faced the most wretched living conditions of any group in the city. In the North, they often lived in segregated black neighborhoods. In southern cities, they gathered in back alleys and small streets. Many could afford only rented rooms.

However, a rich associational life tempered the suffering. Black churches enjoyed phenomenal growth. The African Methodist Episcopal Church, with a membership of 20,000 in 1856, established churches in every city and sizable town and by 1900 claimed more than 400,000 members. Often associated with churches were mutual-aid societies. By 1880, some 193 had been established in Savannah, Georgia, alone.

Some urban blacks in the late nineteenth century rose into the middle class and, in spite of the heavy odds against them, created the nucleus of professional and artistic life. Henry Ossawa Tanner gained international recognition as a painter by 1900, black educators such as George Washington Williams wrote some of the first African-American histories, and novelists such as Charles W. Chesnutt, William Wells Brown, and Paul Laurence Dunbar produced noteworthy novels and short stories.

Beyond working-class neighborhoods and pockets of black housing lay streets of middle-class houses. Here lived the urban lower middle class: clerks, shopkeepers, bookkeepers, salesmen, and small tradesmen. Their salaries allowed them to buy or rent houses with some privacy and comfort. Separate spaces for cooking and laundry work kept hot and often odorous housekeeping tasks away from other living areas. Many houses boasted up-to-date gas lighting and bathrooms. Outside, the neighborhoods were cleaner and more attractive than in the inner city. Residents could pay for garbage collection, gaslights, and other improvements.

Streetcar Suburbs

On the fringes of the city were houses for the substantial middle class and the rich, who either made their money in business, commerce, and the professions or inherited family fortunes. Public transportation sped them downtown to their offices and then back to their families. For example, Robert Work, a modestly successful cap and hat merchant, moved his family to a $5,500 house in West Philadelphia in 1865 and commuted more than 4 miles to work. The 1880 census revealed his family's comfortable life style. The household contained two servants, two boarders, his wife, and their eldest son, who was still in school. The Works' house had running hot and cold water, indoor bathrooms, central heating, and other modern conveniences of the age. Elaborately carved furniture, rugs, draperies, and lace curtains probably graced the downstairs, where the family entertained and gathered for meals. Upstairs, comfortable bedrooms provided a maximum of privacy for family members. The live-in servants, who did most of the housework, shared little of this space or privacy, however. They were restricted to the kitchen, the pantry, and bedrooms in the attic.

This photograph of a middle-class house in River Forest, Illinois, suggests the comfort available to those who could afford it and the ways in which suburban life shielded them from the squalor and ugliness of industrial life.

The Social Geography of the Cities

In industrial cities of this era, people were sorted by class, occupation, and race. The physical distances between upper- and middle-class neighborhoods and working-class neighborhoods meant that city dwellers often had little firsthand knowledge of people who were different from themselves. Ignorance led to distorted views and social disapproval. Middle-class newspapers unsympathetically described laboring men as "loafing in the sunshine" and criticized the "crowds of idlers, who, day and night, infect Main Street." Yet those "crowds of idlers" were often men who could not find work. The comments of a working-class woman to her temperance visitors in 1874 suggest the critical view from the bottom of society up: "When the rich stopped drinking, it would be time to speak to the poor about it."

The Life of the Middle Class

The sharp comments made by different classes of Americans suggest the economic polarization and social conflict that late-nineteenth-century industrialization spawned. Middle-class Americans found they had much to value in the new age: job and education opportunities, material comforts, and leisure time. Between 1865 and 1890, the average income for middle-class Americans had risen about 30 percent. Although the cost of living rose even faster than income, the difference was met by more family members' holding jobs and by taking in lodgers. By 1900, fully 36 percent of urban families owned their homes.

The expansion of American industry had raised the living standard for increasing numbers of Americans, who were better able to purchase consumer products manufactured, packaged, and promoted in an explosion of technological inventions and shrewd marketing techniques. Among the still familiar products and brands invented or mass-produced for the first time in the 1890s were Del Monte canned fruits and vegetables, National Biscuit Company (Nabisco) crackers, Van Camp's pork and beans, Wesson oil, Lipton tea, Wrigley's Juicy Fruit chewing gum, Cracker Jacks, Tootsie Rolls, the Hershey bar, shredded wheat, Aunt Jemima pancake mix, Jell-O, Campbell's soup, Fig Newtons, Canada Dry ginger ale, Coca-Cola, Pepsi-Cola, and Michelob beer. Cooked chopped meat put between two pieces of bread was first sold (for 7 cents) and called a "hamburger" in 1899.

More time for recreation like bicycling or watching professional baseball and greater access to consumer goods signaled the power of industrialism to transform the lives of middle-class Americans. Once favored with greater buying power, middle-class Americans sought to organize efficient ways of producing, purchasing, and consuming the newfound wealth. American women, agents of the rise in consumer spending, were themselves often on display as stylish objects of leisure and ostentatious wealth.

Shopping for home furnishings, clothes, and other items became an integral part of many middle-class women's lives. A plentiful supply of immigrant servant girls relieved urban middle-class wives of many housekeeping chores, and smaller families lessened the burdens of motherhood. William Dean Howells, whose literature tried to reflect life realistically, described the newly

This 1869 advertisement for a home washing machine shows an elegantly attired matron supervising her maids, who do the laundry in a well-equipped kitchen which includes a hot water heater. Few working-class Americans could afford the machine.

rich middle classes in his novel *The Rise of Silas Lapham* (1884). Howells depicted one of Lapham's two daughters, Irene, who spent her abundant leisure shopping and primping every day. Many of the goods that Irene and others bought so eagerly were to be found in the new department stores that began to appear in the central business districts in the 1870s. These stores fed women's desire for material possessions at the same time as they revolutionized retailing.

New Freedoms for Middle-Class Women

At the same time that many middle-class women enjoyed more leisure time and enhanced purchasing power, they won new freedoms. Several states granted women more property rights in marriage, adding to their growing sense of independence. Women, moreover, finally cast off confining crinolines and bustles. The new dress, a shirtwaist blouse and ankle-length skirt, was more comfortable for working, school, and sports. The *Ladies' Home Journal* recommended bicycling, tennis, golf, gymnastics—even having fewer babies—to women in the early 1890s. This "new woman" was celebrated as *Life* magazine's attractively active, slightly rebellious "Gibson girl."

Using their new freedom, women joined organizations of all kinds. Literary societies, charity groups, and reform clubs like the Women's Christian Temperance Union gave women organizational experience, awareness of their talents, and contact with people and problems away from their traditional family roles. The General Federation of Women's Clubs, founded in 1890, boasted one million members by 1920. The depression of 1893 stimulated many women to become socially active, investigating slum and factory conditions, but some began this work even earlier. Jane Addams told her graduating classmates at the Rockford, Illinois, Female Seminary in 1881 to lead lives "filled with good works and honest toil," then went off herself to found Hull House, a social settlement that did more than its share of good works.

Increased leisure time and changing styles of dress led to new freedoms and the popularity of sports for the middle class in the 1890s. These women took to the road in Crawfordsville, Indiana.

Job opportunities for these educated middle-class women were generally limited to the social services and teaching. Still regarded as a suitable female occupation, teaching was a highly demanding job as urban schools expanded under the pressure of a burgeoning population. Women teachers, frequently hired because they accepted lower pay than men, often faced classes of 40 to 50 children in poorly equipped rooms. In Poughkeepsie, New York, teachers earned the same salaries as school janitors. By the 1890s, the willingness of middle-class women to work for low pay opened up new forms of employment in office work, nursing, and clerking in department stores. In San Francisco, the number of clerical jobs doubled between 1852 and 1880. But moving up to high status jobs proved difficult, even for middle-class women.

After the Civil War, educational opportunities for women expanded. New women's colleges such as Smith, Mount Holyoke, Vassar, Bryn Mawr, and Goucher offered programs similar to those at competitive men's colleges, while state schools in the Midwest and the West dropped prohibitions against women. The number of women attending college rose. In 1890, some 13 percent of all college graduates were women; by 1900, this had increased to nearly 20 percent.

Higher education prepared middle-class women for conventional female roles as well as for work and public service. A few courageous graduates succeeded in joining the professions, but they had to overcome numerous barriers. Many medical schools refused to accept women students. As a Harvard doctor explained in 1875, a woman's monthly period "unfits her from taking

Increase in Higher Education, 1870–1900

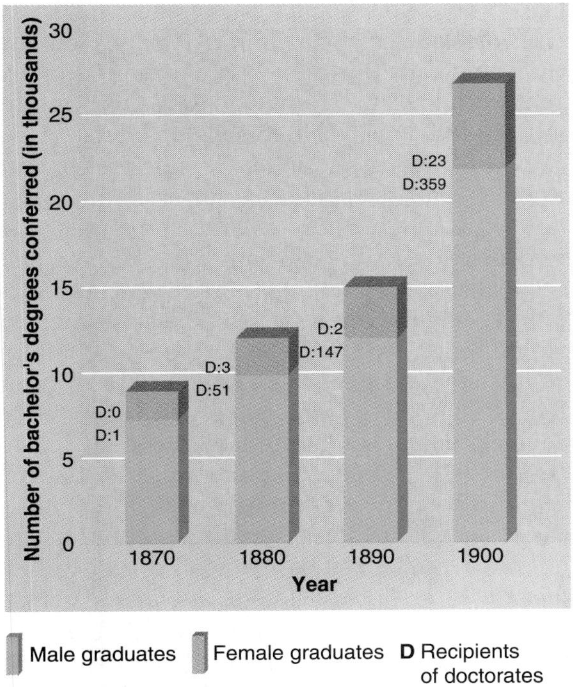

Note the rising pattern of college graduation, which suggests the professionalization of middle-class life.

Source: U.S. Department of Commerce.

those responsibilities which are to control questions often of life and death." Despite the obstacles, 2,500 women managed to become physicians and surgeons by 1880 (constituting 2.8 percent of the total). Women were less successful at breaking into the legal world. In 1880, fewer than 50 female lawyers practiced in the entire country, and as late as 1920, only 1.4 percent of the nation's lawyers and judges were women. George Washington University did not admit women to law school because mixed classes would be an "injurious diversion of attention of the students." Despite such resistance, by the early twentieth century the number of women professionals (including teachers) was increasing at three times the rate for men.

One reason for the greater independence of American women was that they were having fewer babies. This was especially true of educated women. In 1900, nearly one married woman in five was childless. Decreasing family size and an increase in the divorce rate (one out of 12 marriages in 1905) fueled men's fears that the new woman threatened the family, traditional sex roles, and social order. Theodore Roosevelt called this "race suicide" and argued that the falling white birthrate endangered national self-interest.

Arguments against the new woman intensified as many men reaffirmed Victorian stereotypes of "woman's sphere." Magazine editors and ministers borrowed from biology, sociology, and theology to support the notion that a woman's place was in the home. One male orator in 1896 attacked the new woman's public role because "a woman's brain involves emotions rather than intellect." This fact, he cautioned, "painfully disqualifies her for the sterner duties to be performed by the intellectual faculties. The best wife and mother and sister would make the worst legislator, judge and police."

Many men worried about female independence because it threatened their own masculinity. Male campaigns against prostitution and for sex hygiene, as well as efforts to reinforce traditional sex roles, reflected their deeper fears that female passions might weaken male vigor. The intensity of men's opposition to the new woman put limits on her emerging freedom.

Male Mobility and the Success Ethic

As middle-class women's lives were changing, so were men's. As the postwar economy expanded and the structure of American business changed, many new job opportunities opened up for middle-class men. The growing complexity of census classifications attests to some of them. Where once the census taker had noted only the occupation of "clerk," now were listed "accountant," "salesman," and "shipping clerk." As the lower ranks of the white-collar world became more specialized, the number of middle-class jobs increased.

To prepare for these new careers, Americans required more education. The number of public high schools in the United States increased from 160 in 1870 to 6,000 in 1900. By 1900, a majority of states and territories had compulsory school attendance laws.

Higher education also expanded in this period. The number of students in colleges and universities nearly doubled, from 53,000 in 1870 to 101,000 in 1900. Charles Eliot, president of Harvard from 1869 to 1909, led that university through a period of dynamic growth, introducing reforms such as higher faculty salaries and sabbatical leaves as well as the elective system of course selection for students. Harvard's growth reflected the rise of the university to a new stature in American life. As the land-grant state universities (made possible by the Morrill Act of 1862) continued to expand, generous gifts from wealthy businessmen helped to found leading research universities such as Stanford, Johns Hopkins, and the University of Chicago.

These developments led to greater specialization and professionalism, opening up more careers in education, medicine, law, and business. Before the Civil War, a Swedish pioneer in Wisconsin described a young man he knew, who after "working as a mason . . . laid aside the trowel, got himself some medical books, and assumed the title of doctor." But by the 1890s, with government licensing and the rise of professional schools, no longer were tradesman likely to read up on medicine and become doctors. In fact, the word *career* did not take on its modern meaning until 1893. In this period, organizations like the American Medical Association and the American Bar Association were regulating and professionalizing membership. The number of law schools doubled in the last quarter of the century, and 86 new medical schools were founded in the same period. Dental schools increased from 9 to 56 between 1875 and 1900.

The need for lawyers, bankers, architects, and insurance agents to serve business and industry expanded career opportunities. Between 1870 to 1900, the number of engineers, chemists, metallurgists, and architects grew rapidly. As large companies formed and became bureaucratized, business required many more managerial positions. As the public sector expanded, new careers in social services and government opened up as well. Young professional experts with graduate training in the social sciences filled many of them. The professional disciplines of history, economics, sociology, psychology, and political science all date from the last 20 years of the nineteenth century.

The social ethic of the age stressed that economic rewards were available to anyone who fervently sought them. Many people argued that unlike Europe, where family background and social class determined social rank, in America few barriers held back those of good character and diligent work habits. Anyone doubting this opportunity needed only to be reminded of the rise of two giants of industry. John D. Rockefeller had worked for a neighboring farmer and raised turkeys as a boy. Andrew Carnegie's mother was a washerwoman, and his father had worked himself to death in the mills within five years of reaching the United States. Both had risen spectacularly through their own efforts. Writers, lecturers, clergymen, and politicians zealously propagated the rags-to-riches tradition of upward mobility. Self-help manuals that outlined the steps to success for self-made men became widely available.

The best-known popularizer of the myth of the self-made man was Horatio Alger, Jr. Millions of boys read his 119 novels, with titles like *Luck and Pluck, Strive and Succeed,* and *Bound to Rise.* In a typical Alger novel, *Ragged Dick,* the story opens with the hero leading the low life of a shoeshine boy in the streets. Dressed in rags, he sleeps in packing crates and unwisely spends what little money he has on tobacco, liquor, gambling, and the theater. A chance opportunity to foil an attempt to cheat a gentleman results in the reward of a new suit of clothes for Dick. Before long, Dick aspires to become an office boy, "learn the business and grow up 'spectable." As he begins the process of becoming respectable, good fortune intervenes again. Dick is able to rescue a child who tumbles into the icy waters of the harbor. Her father completes the hero's transformation from Ragged Dick to Richard Hunter, Esq., by offering him a job as a clerk in his counting house. Although moralists pointed to virtuous habits as crucial in Alger's heroes, success often depended as much on luck as on pluck.

Unlimited and equal opportunity for upward advancement in America has never been as easy as the "bootstraps" ethic maintains. But the persistence of the success myth owes something to the fact that many Americans, particularly those who began well, did rise rapidly. Native-born, middle-class whites tended to have the skills, resources, and connections that opened up the most desirable jobs. Financier Jay Gould overstated the case in maintaining that "nearly every one that occupies a prominent position has come up from the ranks." In fact, the typical big businessman was a white, Anglo-Saxon Protestant from a middle- or upper-class family whose father was most likely in business, banking, or commerce.

Industrial Work and the Laboring Class

David Lawlor, an Irish immigrant who came to the United States in 1872, might have agreed with Jay Gould on the opportunities for mobility. As a child, he worked in the Fall River textile mills and read Horatio Alger in his free time. Like Alger's heroes, he went to night school and rose in the business world, eventually becoming an advertising executive.

But Lawlor's success was exceptional. Most working-class Americans labored long hours on dangerous factory floors, in cramped sweatshops, or in steamy basement kitchens for meager wages. As industrialization transformed the nature of work and the composition of the work force, traditional opportunities for mobility and even for a secure livelihood seemed to slip away from the grasp of many working-class Americans.

The Impact of Ethnic Diversity

Immigrants made up a sizable portion of the urban working class in the late nineteenth century. They formed 20 percent of the labor force and over 40 percent of laborers in the manufacturing and extractive industries. In cities, where they tended to settle, they accounted for more than half the working-class population.

The fact that more than half the urban industrial class was foreign and unskilled and often had only a limited command of English influenced industrial work, urban life, labor protest, and local politics. Eager for the unskilled positions rapidly being created as mechanization and mass production took hold, immigrants often had little in common with native-born workers or even with one another. Because of immigration, American working-class society was a mosaic of nationalities, cultures, religions, and interests, a patchwork where colors clashed as often as they complemented one another.

The ethnic diversity of the industrial work force helps explain its occupational patterns. Although every city offered somewhat different employment opportunities, generally occupation was related to ethnic background and experience.

At the top of the working-class hierarchy, native-born Protestant whites held a disproportionate share of well-paying skilled jobs. They were the aristocrats of the working class. Their jobs demanded expertise and training, as had been true of skilled industrial workers in the pre–Civil War period. But their occupations bore the mark of late-nineteenth-century industrialism. They were machinists, iron puddlers and rollers, engineers, foremen, conductors, carpenters, plumbers, mechanics, and printers.

Beneath native-born whites, skilled northern European immigrants filled most of the positions in the middle ranks of the occupational structure. The Germans, who arrived with training as tailors, bakers, brewers, and shoemakers, moved into similar jobs in this country, while Cornish and Irish miners secured skilled jobs in western mines. The Jews, who had tailoring experience in their homelands, became the backbone of the garment industry (where they faced little competition from American male workers, who considered it unmanly to work on women's clothes).

But most of the "new immigrants" from southern and central Europe had no urban industrial experience. They labored in the unskilled, dirty jobs near the bottom of the occupational ladder. They relined blast furnaces in steel mills, carried raw materials or finished products from place to place, or cleaned up after skilled workers. Often they were carmen or day laborers on the docks, ditchdiggers, or construction workers. Hiring was often on a daily basis, often arranged through middlemen like the Italian *Padrone*. Unskilled work provided little in the way of either job stability or income.

At the bottom, blacks occupied the most marginal positions as janitors, servants, porters, and laborers. Racial discrimination generally excluded them from industrial jobs, even though their occupational background differed little from that of rural white immigrants. Since there were always plenty of whites eager to work, it was not

On this Philadelphia project, blacks, like those pictured with their shovels, were hod carriers, while bricklayers were white. Black workers had few opportunities to advance up the occupational ladder.

necessary to hire blacks except occasionally as scabs during a labor strike. "It is an exceptional case where you find any colored labor in the factories, except as porters," observed one white. "Neither colored female . . . nor male laborer is engaged in the mechanical arts."

The Changing Nature of Work

The rise of big business, which relied on mechanization for the mass production of goods, changed the size and shape of the work force and the nature of work itself. More and more Americans were wage earners rather than independent artisans. The number of manufacturing workers doubled between 1880 and 1900, with the fastest expansion in the unskilled and semiskilled ranks.

But the need for skilled workers remained. New positions, as in steam fitting and structural ironwork, appeared as industries expanded and changed. Increasingly, older skills became obsolete, however. And all skilled workers faced the possibility that technical advances would eliminate their favored status or that employers would eat away at their jobs by having unskilled helpers take over parts of them. In industries as different as shoemaking, cigar making, and iron puddling, new methods of production and organization undermined the position of skilled workers.

Work Settings and Experiences

The workplace could be a dock or cluttered factory yard, a multistoried textile mill, a huge barnlike steel mill with all the latest machinery, or a mine tunnel hundreds of feet underground. A majority of American manufacturing workers now labored in factories (rather than the shops of an earlier age), and the numbers of those working in large plants dominated by the unceasing rhythms of machinery increased steadily.

Some Americans, however, still toiled in small shops and sweatshops tucked away in basements, lofts, or immigrant apartments. Even in these smaller settings, the pressure to produce was almost as relentless as in the factory, for volume, not hours, determined pay. When contractors cut wages, workers had to speed up to earn the same pay.

The organization of work divided workers from one another. Those paid by the piece competed against the speed, agility, and output of other workers. It was hard to feel any bonds with these unknown and unseen competitors. In large factories, workers separated into small work groups and mingled only rarely with the rest of the work force. The clustering of ethnic groups in certain types of work also undermined working-class solidarity.

All workers had one thing in common: a very long working day. Although the workday had fallen from the 12 hours expected in factories before the Civil War, people still spent over half their waking hours on the job—usually ten hours a day, six days a week. Different occupations had specific demands. Bakers worked 65 hours a week; canners, 77. Sweatshop workers might labor far into the night long after factory workers had gone home.

Work was usually unhealthy, dangerous, and comfortless. Although a few states passed laws to regulate work conditions, enforcement was spotty. Few owners paid attention to regulations on toilets, drinking facilities, or washing areas. Poorly ventilated mines, for example, stank of human waste and spoiled garbage. Nor did owners concern themselves with the health or safety of their employees. Women bent over sewing machines developed digestive illnesses and curved spines. In some mines, workers labored in temperatures of over 120 degrees, handled dynamite,

Factory work was usually uncomfortable and hazardous. Here workers in the Stetson hat factory, none of them with proper back support, cut fur hats to be sewn together by hand. The sexual division of labor is clear in the picture.

and died in cave-ins caused by inadequate timber supports in the mine shafts. When new drilling machinery was introduced into western mines, the shafts were filled with tiny stone particles that caused lung disease. Accident rates in the United States far exceeded those of Europe's industrial nations. Each year, 35,000 workers died from industrial mishaps. Iron and steel mills were the big killers, although the railroads alone accounted for 6,000 fatalities a year during the 1890s. Nationwide, nearly one-quarter of the men reaching the age of 20 in 1880 would not live to see 44 (compared with 7 percent today). American business owners had little legal responsibility—and some felt none—for employees' safety or health. The law placed the burden of avoiding accidents on workers, who were expected to quit if they thought conditions were unsafe.

Industrial workers labored at jobs that were also increasingly specialized and monotonous. The size of many firms allowed a kind of specialization that was impossible in a small enterprise. Even skilled workers did not produce a complete product, and the range of their skills was narrowing. "A man never learns the machinist's trade now," one New Yorker grumbled. "The different branches of the trade are divided and subdivided so that one man may make just a particular part of a machine and may not know anything whatever about another part of the same machine." Cabinetmakers found themselves not crafting cabinets but putting together and finishing pieces made by others. In such circumstances, many skilled workers complained that they were being reduced to drudges and wage slaves.

Still, industrial work provided some personal benefits. New arrangements helped humanize the workplace. Workers who obtained their jobs through family and friends found themselves in the same departments with them. In most industries, the foreman controlled day-to-day activities. He chose workers from the crowds at the gate, fired those who proved unsatisfactory, selected appropriate materials and equipment, and determined the order and pace of production. Since the foreman was himself a member of the working class who had climbed his way up, he might sympathize with subordinates. Yet the foreman could also be authoritarian and harsh, especially if the workers he supervised were unskilled or belonged to another ethnic group.

The Worker's Share in Industrial Progress

The huge fortunes accumulated by industrialists like Andrew Carnegie and John D. Rockefeller during the late nineteenth century dramatized the pattern of wealth concentration that had begun in the early period of industrialization. In 1890, the top 1 percent of American families possessed over a quarter of the wealth, while the share held by the top 10 percent was about 73 percent. Economic growth still benefited people who influenced its path, and they claimed the lion's share of the rewards.

But what of the workers who tended the machines that lay at the base of industrial wealth? Working-class Americans made up the largest segment of the labor force (more than 50 percent), so their experience reveals important facets of the American social and economic system and American values.

Statistics of increasing production, of ever more goods, tell part of the story. Figures on real wages also reveal something important. Industry still needed skilled workers and paid them well. Average real wages rose over 50 percent between 1860 and 1900. Skilled manufacturing workers, about a tenth of the nonagricultural working class

Labor Force Distribution, 1870–1900

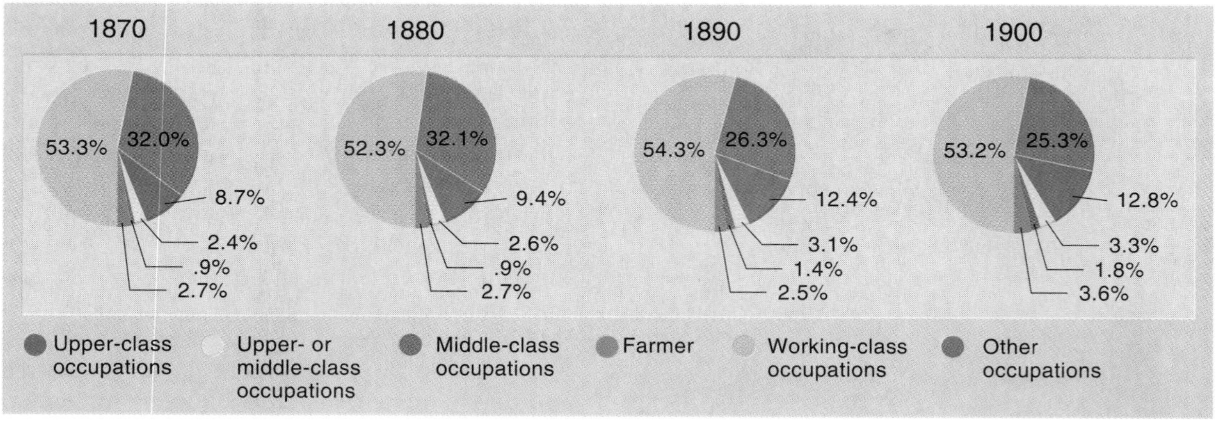

Source: U.S. Bureau of the Census.

in the late nineteenth century, saw their wages rise by about 74 percent. But wages for the unskilled increased by only 31 percent. The differential was substantial and widened as the century drew to a close.

Taken as a whole, the working class accrued substantial benefits in the late nineteenth century, even if its share of the total wealth did not increase. American workers had more material comforts than their European counterparts. But the general picture conceals the realities of working-class economic life. A U.S. Bureau of Labor study of working-class families in 1889 revealed great disparities of income: a young girl in a silk mill made $130 a year; a laborer earned $384 a year; a carpenter took home $686. The carpenter's family lived comfortably in a four-room house. Their breakfast usually included meat or eggs, hotcakes, butter, cake, and coffee. The silk worker and the laborer, by contrast, ate bread and butter as the main portion of two of their three daily meals.

For workers without steady employment, rising real wages were meaningless. Workers, especially those who were unskilled, often found work only sporadically. When times were slow or con-

Two Nineteenth-Century Budgets

Monthly budget of a laborer, his wife, and one child in 1891; his income is $23.67.

Food	$ 6.51
Rent	9.02
Furniture	3.61
Taxes and insurance	3.32
Utilities	2.94
Sundries	1.09
Tobacco	.66
Medicine	.29
Clothes	.21
Dry goods	.16
Postage	.10
Transportation	.08
	$28.01

Monthly budget of a married bank accountant with no children in 1892; his income is about $66.50.

Food	$13.22
Rent	9.88
Taxes and insurance	7.11
Utilities	4.99
Dry goods	2.45
Sundries	2.10
Transportation	1.71
Reading material	.53
Liquor and tobacco	.42
Furniture	.30
Medicine	.27
Clothes	.19
	$43.17

Source: Zunz, *The Changing Face of Inequality* (1982).

Unemployment Rates, 1870–1899

Period	Average Percent Unemployed	Peak Year	Percent Unemployed in Peak Year
1870–1879	10	1876	12–14
1880–1889	4	1885	6–8
1890–1899	10	1894	15+

ditions depressed, as they were between 1873 and 1879 and 1893 and 1897, employers, especially in small firms, laid off both skilled and unskilled workers and reduced wages. Even in a good year like 1890, one out of every five men outside of agriculture had been unemployed at least a month. One-quarter lost four months or more.

Since unemployment insurance did not exist, workers had no cushion against losing their jobs. One woman grimly recalled, "If the factory shuts down without warning, as it did last year for six weeks, we have a growing expense with nothing to counterbalance." Older workers who had no social security or those who had accidents on the job but no disability insurance had severely reduced incomes. Occasionally, kindhearted employers offered assistance in hard times, but it was rarely enough. The Lawrence Manufacturing Company compensated one of its workers $50 for the loss of a hand and awarded another $66.71 for a severed arm.

Although nineteenth-century ideology pictured men as breadwinners, many working-class married men could not earn enough to support their families alone. A working-class family's standard of living thus often depended on its number of workers. Today, two-income families are common. But in the nineteenth century, married women did not usually take outside employment, although they contributed to family income by taking in sewing, laundry, and boarders. In 1890, only 3.3 percent of married women were to be found in the paid labor force.

The Family Economy

If married women did not work for pay outside their homes, their children did. The laborer whose annual earnings amounted to only $384 depended on his 13-year-old son, not his wife, to go out and earn an extra $196, critical to the family's welfare. Sending children into the labor market was an essential survival strategy for many working-class Americans. In 1880, one-fifth of the nation's children between the ages of 10 and 14 held jobs.

Child labor was closely linked to a father's income, which in turn depended on skill, ethnic background, and occupation. Immigrant families more frequently sent their young children out to work (and also had more children) than native-born families. Middle-class reformers sentimentalized childhood and thus disapproved of parents who put their children to work. As one investigator of working-class life reported, "Father never attended school, and thinks his children will have sufficient schooling before they reach their tenth year, thinks no advantage will be gained from longer attendance at school, so children will be put to work as soon as able." Reformers believed that such fathers condemned their children to future poverty by taking them out of school. Actually, sending children to work was a means of coping with the immediate threat of poverty, of financing the education of one of the children, or even of ensuring that children stayed near their family.

Status of Young People (12–20) by Ethnicity in Detroit in 1900

Ethnic Group	In School	Working	At Home
Native white American[a]	**54.7%**	**40.4%**	**4.9%**
	56.1	16.9	27.0
Black	**50.0**	**50.0**	**0.0**
	45.5	40.9	13.6
Irish	**43.2**	**48.6**	**8.1**
	43.2	39.8	17.0
German	**30.5**	**59.5**	**10.0**
	29.2	45.1	25.8
Polish	**26.4**	**63.5**	**10.1**
	26.15	6.2	17.6
Russian	**53.3**	**30.0**	**16.7**
	17.4	60.9	21.7

[a]Born in the United States of two American-born parents.

Note: Percentage of boys is indicated in blue; percentage of girls is indicated in red.

Source: Zunz, *The Changing Face of Inequality* (1982).

Congressional Hearings

Students of history can discover fascinating materials on nineteenth-century life by exploring the published records of the American political system. The *Congressional Globe,* the proceedings of the Senate and the House, privately published from 1833 to 1873, reveals the nature of congressional deliberations in an era when debate, such as that over the Compromise of 1850 in the Senate, was the focus of the national political process. After 1873, the government published these proceedings in the *Congressional Record.* The *Record* is not a literal transcription of debate, for members can edit their remarks, insert speeches, and add supporting materials. Still, it gives a good sense of the proceedings of both the Senate and the House.

Much of the serious work of government, past and present, takes place in congressional committees. One foreign observer called Congress "not so much a legislative assembly as a huge panel from which committees are selected." The committee system is almost as old as the constitutional system itself and is rooted in the Constitution's granting of the lawmaking power to Congress. From the start, Congress divided into assorted committees to gather information, enabling members to evaluate legislative proposals intelligently.

Two kinds of committees existed in the House and Senate. Standing committees had permanent responsibility for reviewing legislative proposals on a host of financial, judicial, foreign, and other affairs. By 1892, the Senate had 44 standing committees, and the House had 50. Select committees were temporary, often charged with investigating specific problems. In the late nineteenth century, congressional committees investigated such problems as Ku Klux Klan terrorism, the sweatshop system, tenement house conditions, and relations between labor and capital. In each case, extensive hearings were held.

Congressional hearings have become increasingly important sources of historical evidence in recent years. Hearings show the Senate and the House of Representatives in action as they seek to translate popular sentiment into law. But they also reveal public attitudes themselves as they record the voices of Americans testifying in committee halls. Because one function of legislative hearings is to enable diverse groups to express their frustrations and desires, they often contain the testimony of witnesses drawn from many different social and economic backgrounds. Included here is the partial testimony of a Massachusetts laborer who appeared before the Senate Committee on Education and Labor in 1883. Because working-class witnesses like this man usually left no other record of their experiences or thoughts, committee reports and hearings provide valuable insight into the lives and attitudes of ordinary people.

Hearings also reveal the attitudes and social values of committee members. Hence, caution is needed in the use of hearings. Witnesses often have vested interests and are frequently coached and cautious in what they communicate on the stand. Committee members often speak and explore questions for other reasons, usually political, than to illuminate issues.

Despite these limitations, committee hearings are rich sources of information. In this excerpt, what can you learn about the life of the witness testifying before the committee? In what way are the values of the committee members in conflict with those of the witness? Why is the chairman so harsh toward the witness? Is he entirely unsympathetic? Why do you think the questioner overemphasizes the relationship between moral beliefs and economic realities? What kinds of social tensions does the passage reveal?

Have you observed any recent hearings of congressional investigating committees on television? Are moral behavior and hunger still topics of concern for Americans? How is the interaction between modern haves and have-nots similar to and different from those between this laborer and the committee members in 1883? Do ethical beliefs and economic realities still separate social classes?

Q. You get a dollar a day, wages?—A. That is the average pay that men receive. The rents, especially in Somerville, are so high that it is almost impossible for the working men to live in a house.

Q. What rent do you pay?—A. For the last year I have been paying $10 a month, and most of the men out there have to pay about that amount for a house—$10 a month for rooms.

Q. For a full house, or for rooms only?—A. For rooms in a house.

Q. How many rooms?—A. Four or five.

Q. How much of your time have you been out of work, or idle, for the last full year, say?—A. I have not been out of work more than three weeks altogether, because I have been making a dollar or two peddling or doing something, when I was out of work, in the currying line.

Q. Making about the same that you made at your trade?—A. Well, I have made at my trade a little more than that, but that is the average.

Q. Are you a common drunkard?—A. No, sir.

Q. Do you smoke a great deal?—A. Well, yes, sir; I smoke as much as any man.

The CHAIRMAN. I want to know how much you have got together in the course of a year, and what you have spent your money for, so that folks can see whether you have had pay enough to get rich on.

The WITNESS. A good idea.

The CHAIRMAN. That is precisely the sort of idea that people ought to know. How much money do you think you have earned during this last year; has it averaged a dollar a day for three hundred days?

The WITNESS. I have averaged more than that; I have averaged $350 or $400. I will say, for the year.

Q. You pay $10 a month rent; that makes $120 a year?—A. Yes, sir.

The CHAIRMAN. I have asked you these questions in this abrupt way because I want to find out whether you have spent much for practices that might have been dispensed with. You say you smoke?

The WITNESS. Yes, sir.

Q. How much a week do you spend for that?—A. I get 20 cents worth of tobacco a week.

Q. That is $10.40 a year?—A. Yes, sir.

Q. And you say you are not a common drunkard?—A. No, sir.

Q. Do you imagine that you have spent as much more for any form of beer, or ale, or anything of that kind, that you could have got along without?—A. No, sir.

Q. How much do you think has gone in that way?—A. About $1 or $2.

Q. During the whole year?—A. Yes, sir.

Q. That would make $11.40 or $12.40—we will call it $12—gone for wickedness. Now, what else, besides your living, besides the support of your wife and children?—A. Well, I don't know as there is anything else.

Q. Can you not think of anything else that was wrong?—A. No, sir.

Q. Twelve dollars have gone for sin and iniquity; and $120 for rent; that makes $132?—A. Yes.

Q. How many children have you?—A. Two.

Q. Your family consists of yourself, your wife, and two children?—A. Yes.

Q. One hundred and thirty-two dollars from $400 leaves you $268, does it not?—A. Yes, sir.

Q. And with that amount you have furnished your family?—A. Yes, sir.

Q. You have been as economical as you could, I suppose?—A. Yes.

Q. How much money have you left?—A. Sixty dollars in debt.

Q. How did you do that?—A. I don't know, sir.

Q. Can you not think of something more that you have wasted?—A. No, sir.

Q. Have you been as careful as you could?—A. Yes, sir.

Q. And you have come out at the end of the year $60 in debt?—A. Yes, sir.

Q. Have you been extravagant in your family expenses?—A. No, sir; a man can't be very extravagant on that much money. . . .

Q. And there are four of you in the family?—A. Yes, sir.

Q. How many pounds of beefsteak have you had in your family, that you bought for your own home consumption within this year that we have been speaking of?—A. I don't think there has been five pounds of beefsteak.

Q. You have had a little pork steak?—A. We had a half a pound of pork steak yesterday; I don't know when we had any before.

Q. What other kinds of meat have you had within a year?—A. Well, we have had corn beef twice I think that I can remember this year—on Sunday, for dinner.

Q. Twice is all that you can remember within a year?—A. Yes—and some cabbage.

Q. What have you eaten?—A. Well, bread mostly, when we could get it; we sometimes couldn't make out to get that, and have had to go without a meal.

Q. Has there been any day in the year that you have had to go without anything to eat?—A. Yes, sir, several days.

Q. More than one day at a time?—A. No.

Q. How about the children and your wife—did they go without anything to eat too?—A. My wife went out this morning and went to a neighbor's and got a loaf of bread and fetched it home, and when she got home the children were crying for something to eat.

Q. Have the children had anything to eat to-day except that, do you think?—A. They had that loaf of bread—I don't know what they have had since then, if they have had anything.

Q. Did you leave any money at home?—A. No, sir.

Q. If that loaf is gone, is there anything in the house?—A. No, sir; unless my wife goes out and gets something; and I don't know who would mind the children while she goes out.

Women in the Labor Force, 1870–1900

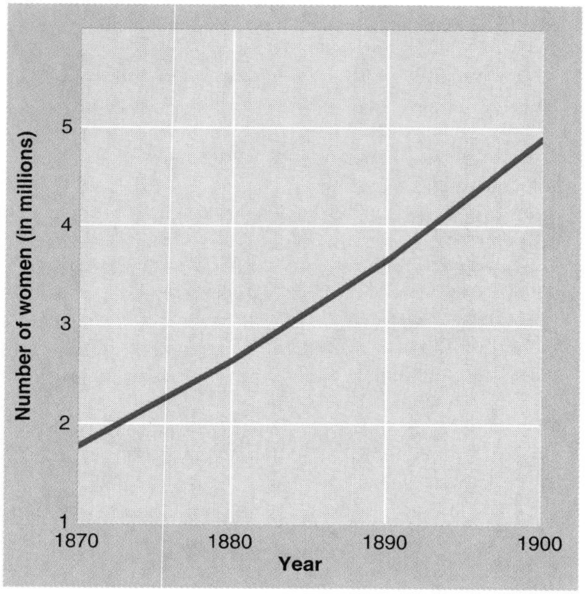

Source: U.S. Bureau of the Census.

Women at Work

Many more young people over 14 were working for wages than was the case for children. Half of all Philadelphia's students had quit school by that age. Daughters as well as sons were expected to take positions, although young women from immigrant families were more likely to work than young American women. As *Arthur's Home Magazine* for women pointed out, a girl's earnings would help "to relieve her hard-working father of the burden of her support, to supply home with comforts and refinements, to educate a younger brother." By 1900, nearly 20 percent of American women were in the labor force.

Employed women earned far less than men. An experienced female factory worker might be paid between $5 and $6 a week, while an unskilled male laborer could make about $8. Discrimination, present from women's earliest days in the work force, persisted. Still, factory jobs were desirable because they paid better than other kinds of work open to women.

Employment opportunities for women were narrow, and ethnic taboos and cultural traditions helped to shape choices. About a quarter of working women secured factory jobs. Italian and Jewish women (whose cultural backgrounds virtually forbade their going into domestic service) clustered in the garment industry, while Poles and Slavs went into textiles, food processing, and meatpacking. In some industries, like textiles, women composed an important segment of the work force. But about 40 percent of them, especially those from Irish, Scandinavian, or black families, took jobs as maids, cooks, laundresses, and nurses.

Domestic service meant low wages, unpleasant working conditions, and little free time, usually one evening a week and part of Sunday. A Minneapolis housemaid described her exhausting routine. "I used to get up at four o'clock every morning and work till ten p.m. every day of the week. Mondays and Tuesdays, when the washing and ironing was to be done, I used to get up at two o'clock and wash or iron until breakfast time." Nor could domestics count on much sympathy from their employers. "Do not think it necessary to give a hired girl as good a room as that used by members of the family," said one lady of the house. "She should sleep near the kitchen and not go up the front stairs or through the front hall to reach her room."

A servant received room and board plus $2 to $5 a week. The fact that so many women took domestic work despite the job's disadvantages speaks clearly of their limited opportunities.

The dismal situation facing working women drove some, like Rose Haggerty, into prostitution. Burdened with a widowed and sickly mother and four young brothers and sisters, Rose was only 14 when she started work at a New York paper bag factory. She earned $10 a month, but $6 went for rent. Her fortunes improved when a friend helped her buy a sewing machine. Rose then sewed shirts at home, often working as long as 14 hours a day, to support her family. Suddenly, the piecework rate for shirts was slashed in half. In desperation, Rose contemplated suicide. But when a sailor offered her money for spending the night with him, she realized she had an alternative. Prostitution meant food, rent, and heat for her family. "Let God Almighty judge who's to blame most," the 20-year-old Rose reflected, "I that was driven, or them that drove me to the pass I'm in."

Prostitution appears to have increased in the late nineteenth century, although there is no way

These domestics, in their best clothes, pose with the symbols of their work in what appears to be the parlor. The picture gives no indication that domestic work was poorly paid, exhausting, and emotionally trying.

of knowing the actual numbers of women involved. Probably most single women accepted the respectable jobs open to them. They tolerated discrimination and low wages because their families depended on their contributions. They also knew that when they married, they would probably leave the paid work force forever.

Marriage hardly ended women's work, however. Like colonial families, late-nineteenth-century working-class families operated as economic units. The unpaid domestic labor of working-class wives was critical to family survival. With husbands away for 10 to 11 hours a day, women bore the burden and loneliness of caring for children. They did all the domestic chores. Since working-class families could not afford labor-saving conveniences, housework was time-consuming and arduous. Without a refrigerator, a working-class woman spent part of each day shopping for food (more expensive in small quantities). The washing machine, advertised to do the "ordinary washing of a family in only one or two hours," was out of the question with a price tag of $15. Instead, women carried water from outside pumps, heated it on the stove, washed clothes, rinsed them with fresh water, and hung them up to dry. Ironing was a hot and unpleasant job in small and stuffy quarters. Keeping an apartment or house clean when the atmosphere was grimy and unpaved roads were littered with refuse and horse dung was a challenge.

As managers of family resources, married women had important responsibilities. What American families had once produced for themselves now had to be bought. It was up to the working-class wife to scour secondhand shops to find cheap clothes for her family. Here small domestic economies were vital to survival. "In summer and winter alike," one woman explained, "I must try to buy the food that will sustain us the greatest number of meals at the lowest price."

Women also supplemented family income by taking in work. Jewish and Italian women frequently did piecework and sewing at home. In the Northeast and the Midwest, between 10 and 40 percent of all working-class families kept boarders. Immigrant families, in particular, often made ends meet by taking single young countrymen into their homes. The cost was the added burden of work (providing meals and clean laundry), the need to juggle different work schedules, and the sacrifice of privacy. But the advantages of extra income far outweighed the disadvantages for many working-class families.

Black women's working lives reflected the obstacles blacks faced in late-nineteenth-century cities. Although few married white women worked outside the home, black women did so both before and after marriage. In southern cities in 1880, about three-quarters of single black women and one-third of married women worked outside the home. This contrasted to rates for white women of 24 and 7 percent, respectively. Since industrial employers would not hire black women, most of them had to work as domestics or laundresses. The high percentage of married black women in the labor force reflected the marginal wages their husbands earned. But it may also be explained partly by the lesson learned during slavery that children could thrive without the constant attention of their mothers.

Capital Versus Labor

Class conflict characterized late-nineteenth-century industrial life. Although workers welcomed the progress the factory made possible, many rejected their employers' values, which emphasized individual gain at the expense of collective good. While owners reaped most of the profits, bad pay, poor working conditions, and long hours were turning workers into wage slaves. Fashioning their arguments from their republican legacy, workers claimed that the degradation of the country's citizen laborers threatened to undermine the republic itself.

On-the-Job Protests

Workers and employers engaged in a struggle over who would control the workplace. Many workers staunchly resisted unsatisfactory working conditions and the tendency of bosses to treat them "like any other piece of machinery, to be made to do the maximum amount of work with the minimum expenditure of fuel." Skilled workers, like iron puddlers and glassblowers, had indispensable knowledge about the production process and practical experience and were in a key position to direct on-the-job actions. Sometimes their goal was to retain control over critical work decisions. Detroit printers, for example, struggled to hold on to the privilege of distributing headlines and white space (the "fat") rather than letting their bosses hand out the fat as a special reward and means of increasing competition among workers. Others hoped to humanize work. Cigar makers clung to their custom of having one worker read to others as they performed their tedious chores. Often workers sought to control the pace of production.

Workers also resisted owners' attempts to grasp large profits through unlimited production. Too many goods meant an inhuman pace of work and might result in overproduction, massive layoffs, and a reduction in the prices paid for piecework. Thus workers established informal production quotas. An experienced worker might whisper to a new hand, "See here, young fellow, you're working too fast. You'll spoil our job for us if you don't go slower."

A newspaper account of a glassblower's strike in 1884 illustrates the clash between capital and labor. With an eye toward bigger profits, the boss tried to increase production. "He knew if the limit was taken off, the men could work ten or twelve hours every day in the week; that in their thirst for the mighty dollar they would kill themselves with labor; they would 'black sheep' their fellows by doing the labor of two men." But his employees resisted his proposal, refusing to drive themselves to exhaustion for a few dollars more. Their goal was not riches but a decent pace of work and a respectable wage. Thus "they thundered out no. They even offered to take a reduction that would average ten percent all around, but they said, 'We will keep the forty-eight box limit.' Threats and curses would not move them."

In attempting to protect themselves and preserve the dignity of their labor, workers devised ways of combating employer attempts to speed up the production process. Denouncing fellow workers who refused to honor production codes as "hogs," "runners," "chasers," and "job wreckers," they ostracized and even injured them. As the banner of the Detroit Coopers' Union proudly proclaimed at a parade in 1880: "Each for himself is the bosses' plea / [but] Union for all will make you free."

Absenteeism, drunkenness at work, and general inefficiency were other widespread worker practices that contained elements of protest. In three industrial firms in the late nineteenth century, one-quarter of the workers stayed home at least one day a week. Some of these lost days were due to layoffs, but not all. The efforts of employers to impose stiff fines on absent workers suggested their frustration at uncooperative workers.

To a surprising extent, workers made the final protest by quitting their jobs altogether. Most employers responded by penalizing workers who left without giving sufficient notice—to little avail. A Massachusetts labor study in 1878 found that although two-thirds of them had been in the same occupation for more than ten years, only 15 percent of the workers surveyed were in the same job. A similar rate of turnover occurred in the industrial work force in the early twentieth century. Workers unmistakably and clearly voted with their feet.

Strike Activity After 1876

The most direct and strenuous attempts to change conditions in the workplace came in the form of thousands of strikes punctuating the late nineteenth century. In 1877, railroad workers staged the first and most violent nationwide industrial strike of the nineteenth century. The immediate cause of the disturbance was the railroad owners' decision to reduce wages. But the rapid spread of the strike from Baltimore to Pittsburgh and then to cities as distant as San Francisco, Chicago, and Omaha, as well as the violence of the strikers, who destroyed railroad property and kept trains idle, indicated more fundamental discontent. An erratic economy, high unemployment rates, and the lack of job security all contributed to the conflagration. Over 100 people died before federal troops ended the strike. The frenzied response of the propertied class, which saw the strike as the beginning of revolution and favored the intervention of the military, forecast the pattern of later conflicts. Time and time again, middle- and upper-class Americans would turn to the power of the state to crush labor activism.

A wave of confrontations followed the strike of 1877. Between 1881 and 1905, a total of 36,757 strikes erupted, involving over 6 million workers—three times the strike activity in France.

These numbers indicate that far more than the "poorest part" of the workers were involved. Many investigations of this era found evidence of widespread working-class discontent. When Samuel M. Hotchkiss, commissioner of the Connecticut Bureau of Labor Statistics, informally surveyed the state's workers in 1887, he was shocked by the "feeling of bitterness," the "distrust of employers," the "discontent and unrest." These sentiments exploded into strikes, sabotage, and violence, most often linked to demands for higher wages and shorter hours.

Nineteenth-century strike activity underwent important changes, however, as the consciousness of American workers expanded. In the period of early industrialization, discontented laborers rioted in their neighborhoods rather than at their workplaces. The Lowell protests of the 1830s (Chapter 10) were not typical. Between 1845 and the Civil War, however, strikes at the workplace began to replace neighborhood riots. Although workers showed their anger against their employers by turning out and often calling for higher wages, they had only a murky sense that the strike could be a weapon to force employers to improve working conditions.

As industrialization transformed work and an increasing percentage of the work force entered factories, collective actions at the workplace spread. Local and national unions played a more important role in organizing protest, conducting 60 percent of the strikes between 1881 and 1905. As working-class leaders realized more clearly the importance of collective action in dealing with their opponents and perceived that transportation had knit the nation together, they also tried to coordinate local and national efforts. By 1891, more than one-tenth of the strikes called by unionized workers were sympathy strikes. Coordination between strikers employed by different companies improved as workers tried to order capitalism by making the same wage demands. Finally, wages among the most highly unionized workers became less of an issue. Workers sought more humane conditions. Some attempted to end subcontracting and the degradation of skills. Others, like the glassblowers, struggled to enforce work rules. Indeed, by the early 1890s, over one-fifth of strikes involved the rules governing the workplace.

Labor Organizing: 1865–1900

The Civil War experience colored labor organizing in the postwar years. As one working-class song pointed out, workers had borne the brunt of that struggle. "You gave your son to the war / The rich man loaned his gold / And the rich man's son is happy to-day, / And yours is under the mold." Now workers who had fought to save the Union argued that wartime sacrifices justified efforts to gain justice and equality in the workplace.

Labor leaders quickly realized the need for national as well as local organizations to protect the laboring class against "despotic employers." In 1866, several craft unions and reform groups formed the National Labor Union (NLU). Claiming 300,000 members by the early 1870s, the organization supported a range of causes including temperance, women's rights, and the establishment of cooperatives to bring the "wealth of the land" into "the hands of those who produce it," thus ending "wage slavery."

The call for an eight-hour day reveals some of the basic assumptions of the organized labor movement. Few workers saw employers as a hostile class or felt it necessary to overturn the economic system. But they did believe bosses were often dangerous tyrants whose time demands threatened to turn citizens into slaves. The eight-hour day would curb the power of owners and allow workers the time to cultivate the qualities necessary for republican citizenship.

Many of the NLU's specific goals survived, although the organization did not. An unsuccessful attempt to create a political party and the depression of 1873 decimated the NLU and many local unions as well. Survival and the search for a job took precedence over union causes.

The Knights of Labor and the AFL

As the depression wound down, a new mass organization, the Noble Order of the Knights of Labor, rose to national importance. Founded as a secret society in 1869, the order became public and national when Terence V. Powderly, an Irish-American, was elected Grand Master Workman in 1879. The Knights of Labor sought "to secure to the workers the full enjoyment of the wealth they create." Since the industrial system denied workers their fair share as producers, the Knights of Labor proposed to mount a cooperative system of production alongside the existing system. "There is no reason," Powderly believed, "why labor cannot, through cooperation, own and operate mines, factories and railroads." Cooperative efforts would give workers the economic independence necessary for citizenship, while an eight-hour day would provide them with the leisure for moral, intellectual, and political pursuits.

The Knights of Labor opened its ranks to all American "producers," defined as all contributing members of society—skilled and unskilled, black and white, men and women. Only the idle and the corrupt (bankers, speculators, lawyers, saloonkeepers, and gamblers) were to be excluded. Membership was even open to sympathetic merchants and manufacturers. In fact, many shopkeepers joined the order and advertised their loyalty as "friend of the workingman."

This inclusive membership policy meant that the Knights potentially had the power of great numbers. The organization grew in spurts, attracting miners between 1874 and 1879 and skilled urban tradesmen between 1879 and 1885. Masses of unskilled workers joined thereafter.

Although Powderly frowned on using the strike as a labor weapon, the organization reaped the benefits of grass-roots strike activity. Local struggles proliferated after 1883. In 1884, unorganized workers of the Union Pacific Railroad walked off the job when management announced a wage cut. Within two days, the company caved in, and the men joined the Knights of Labor. The next year, a successful strike against the Missouri Pacific Railroad brought in another wave of members. Then, in 1886, the Haymarket Riot in Chicago led to such a growth in labor militancy that in that single year the membership of the Knights of Labor ballooned from 100,000 to 700,000.

The "riot" at Haymarket was, in fact, a peaceful protest meeting connected with a lockout at the McCormick Reaper Works. When the Chicago police arrived to disperse the crowd, a bomb exploded. Seven policemen were killed. Although no one knows who planted the bomb, eight anarchists were tried and convicted. Three were executed, one committed suicide, and the others served prison terms. Overheated newspaper accounts put the blame on "long-haired, wild-eyed, bad-smelling, atheistic, reckless foreign wretches, who never did an honest hour's work in their lives."

Labor agitation and turbulence spilled over into politics. In 1884 and 1885, the Knights of Labor lobbied to secure a national contract labor law that would demand work contracts and state laws outlawing the use of convict labor. The organization also pressed successfully for the creation of a federal Department of Labor. As new members poured in, however, direct political action became increasingly attractive. Between 1885 and 1888, the Knights of Labor sponsored candidates in 200 towns and cities in 34 states and 4 territories. They achieved many electoral victories. In Waterloo, Iowa, a bank janitor ousted a successful attorney to become the town's mayor. Despite local successes, no national labor party emerged. But in the 1890s, the Knights cooperated with the Populists in their attempt to reshape American politics and society.

Despite the dramatic surge in membership, the Knights of Labor could not sustain their momentum as the voice for the American laboring people. Employers, alerted by the Haymarket riot, determined to break the power of the organization. A strike against Jay Gould's southwestern railroad system in 1886 failed, tarnishing the Knights' reputation. Consumer and producer cooperatives fizzled; the policy of accepting both black and white workers led to strife and discord in the South. The two major parties proved adept at coopting labor politicians. As labor politicians became respectable, they left the rank and file to fend for themselves.

The failure of national leaders paralleled the failure of local leadership. Powderly was never able to unify or direct his diverse following. His concern with general reform issues and political action dissatisfied members pressing for better wages and work conditions. Nor could Powderly control the militant elements who opposed him. Local, unauthorized strike actions were often ill-considered and violent. Lawlessness helped neither the organization nor its members. By 1890, the membership had dropped to 100,000, although the Knights continued to play a role well into the 1890s.

In the 1890s, the American Federation of Labor (AFL), founded in 1886, replaced the Knights of Labor as the nation's dominant union. The history of the Knights pointed up the problems of a national union that admitted all who worked for wages but officially rejected strike action in favor of the ballot box and arbitration. The leader of the AFL, Samuel Gompers, had a different notion of effective worker organization. Gompers's experience as head of the Cigarmakers' Union in the 1870s and as a founder of the Federation of Organized Trades and Labor Unions in 1881 convinced him that skilled workers should put their specific occupational interests before the interests of workers as a whole. By so doing, they could control the supply of skilled labor and keep wages up.

Gompers organized the AFL as a federation of skilled trades—cigar makers, iron molders, ironworkers, carpenters, and others—each one autonomous yet linked through an executive council to work together for prolabor national legislation and mutual support during boycott and strike actions. Gompers was a practical man. He repudiated the notion of a cooperative commonwealth and dreams of ending the wage system, accepting the fact that workers "are a distinct and practically permanent class of modern society." Thus he focused on immediate, realizable "bread and butter" issues, particularly higher wages, shorter hours, industrial safety, and the right to organize.

Although Gompers rejected direct political action as a means of obtaining labor's goals, he did believe in the value of the strike. He told a congressional hearing in 1899 that unless working people had "the power to enter upon a strike, the improvements will all go to the employer and all the injuries to the employees." A shrewd organizer, he knew from bitter experience the importance of dues high enough to sustain a strike fund through a long, tough fight.

Under Gompers's leadership, the AFL grew from 140,000 in 1886 to nearly one million by 1900. Although his notion of a labor organization was elitist, he succeeded in steering his union through a series of crises, fending off challenges from socialists on his left and corporate opposition to strikes from his right. But there was no room in his organization for the unskilled or for blacks, in whom he claimed to see an "abandoned and reckless disposition."

The AFL made a brief and halfhearted attempt to unionize women in 1892. Hostile male attitudes constituted a major barrier against organizing women. Men resented women as coworkers and preferred them to stay in the home. The AFL stood firmly for the principle that "the man is the provider" and that women who work in factories "bring forth weak children." The Boston Central Labor Union declared in 1897 "the demand for female labor an insidious assault upon the home. . . . It is the knife of the assassin, aimed at the family circle." Change was slow in coming. In 1900, the International Ladies' Garment Workers Union (ILGWU) was established. Although women were the backbone of the organization, men dominated the leadership.

Working-Class Setbacks

Despite the growth of working-class organizations, workers lost many of their battles with management. Some of the more spectacular clashes reveal why working-class activism often ended in defeat and why so many workers lived precariously on the edge of poverty.

In 1892, silver miners in Coeur d'Alene, Idaho, went on strike when their employers installed machine drills in the mines, reduced skilled workers to shovelmen, and announced a wage cut of a dollar a day. The owners, supported by state militiamen and the federal government, successfully broke the strike by using scabs, but not without armed fighting. Several hundred union men were arrested, herded into huge bull pens, and eventually tried and found guilty of a wide variety of charges. Out of the defeat emerged the Western Federation of Miners (WFM), whose chief political goal was an eight-hour law for miners. The pattern of struggle in Coeur d'Alene was followed in many subsequent strikes.

Determined mine owners characteristically met strikes by shutting off credit to unionmen, hiring strikebreakers and armed guards, and paying spies to infiltrate unions. Violence was frequent, and confrontations usually ended with the arrival of state militia, the erection of bull pens, incarceration or intimidation of strikers and their local sympathizers, legal action, and elaborate blacklisting systems. In spite of this, the WFM won as many strikes as it lost.

The Homestead and Pullman Strikes of 1892 and 1894

The most serious setback to labor occurred in 1892 at the Homestead steel mills near Pittsburgh, Pennsylvania. Andrew Carnegie had recently purchased the Homestead plant and put Henry Clay Frick in charge. Together they wanted to eliminate the Amalgamated Association of Iron,

In this 1892 engraving of the Homestead strikers surrendering, done for *Harper's Weekly,* the sympathy of the artist lies with the detectives in the foreground. The strikers appear as an unruly crowd in the distance, while the detectives' kindly faces and wounds are highlighted.

Steel, and Tin Workers, which threatened to increase its organization of the steel industry. After three months of stalemated negotiations over a new wage contract, Frick issued an ultimatum. Unless the union accepted wage decreases, he would lock them out and replace them. As the deadline passed, Frick erected a formidable wood and barbed wire fence around the entire plant, with searchlight and sentry stands on it, and hired 300 armed Pinkerton agents to guard the factory. As they arrived on July 6, they engaged armed steelworkers in a daylong gun battle. Several men on both sides were killed, and the Pinkertons retreated.

Frick telegraphed Pennsylvania's governor, who sent 8,000 troops to crush both the strike and the union. Two and a half weeks later, Alexander Berkman, a New York anarchist sympathetic to the plight of the oppressed Homestead workers, attempted to assassinate Frick. The events at Homestead dramatized the lengths to which both labor and capital would go to achieve their ends.

Observing these events, Eugene Victor Debs of Terre Haute, Indiana, for many years an ardent organizer of railroad workers, wrote, "If the year 1892 taught the workingmen any lesson worthy of heed, it was that the capitalist class, like a devil-fish, had grasped them with its tentacles and was dragging them down to fathomless depths of degradation." Debs saw 1893 as the year in which organized labor would "escape the prehensile clutch of these monsters." But 1893 brought a new depression and even worse challenges and setbacks for labor. Undaunted, Debs succeeded in combining several of the separate railroad brotherhoods into a united American Railway Union (ARU). Within a year, over 150,000 railroadmen joined the ARU, and Debs won a strike against the Great Northern Railroad, which had attempted to slash workers' wages.

Debs faced his toughest crisis at the Pullman Palace Car Company in Chicago. Pullman was a model company town where management controlled all aspects of workers' lives. "We are born in a Pullman house, fed from the Pullman shop, taught in the Pullman school, catechized in the Pullman church, and when we die we shall be buried in the Pullman cemetery and go to the Pullman hell," said one worker wryly.

Late in 1893, as the depression worsened, Pullman cut wages by one-third and laid off many workers but made no reductions in rents or prices in the town stores. Forced to pay in rent what they could not recover in wages, working families struggled to survive the winter. Some parents kept their children home from school because they had no shoes or coats and could keep warm only in bed. Those still at work suffered speedups, intimidating threats, and further wage cuts. Desperate and "without hope," the Pullman workers joined the ARU in the spring of 1894 and went out on strike.

In late June, after Pullman refused to submit the dispute to arbitration, Debs led the ARU into a sympathy strike in support of the striking Pullman workers. Remembering the ill-fated railroad strike of 1877, Debs advised his lieutenants to "use no violence" and "stop no trains." Rather, he sought to boycott trains handling Pullman cars throughout the West. As the boycott spread, the General Managers Association, which ran the 24 railroads centered in Chicago, came to the Pullman's support, convinced that "we have got to wipe him [Debs] out." After hiring some 2,500 strikebreakers, the GMA appealed to the state and federal governments for military and judicial support in stopping the strike.

Governor Richard Altgeld of Illinois, sympathizing with the workers and believing that local law enforcement was sufficient, opposed the use of federal troops. But Richard Olney, a former railroad lawyer and U.S. attorney general, persuaded President Cleveland that only federal troops could restore law and order. On July 2, Olney obtained a court injunction to end the strike as a "conspiracy in restraint of trade." Two days later, Cleveland ordered federal troops in to support the injunction and crush the strikers.

Violence now escalated rapidly. Local and federal officials hired armed guards, and the railroads paid them to help the troops. Within two days, strikers and guards were fighting bitterly, freight cars were burned, and over $340,000 worth of railroad property was destroyed. The press reported "Unparalleled Scenes of Riot, Terror and Pillage" and "Frenzied Mobs Still Bent on Death and Destruction." As troops poured into Chicago, the violence worsened, leaving scores of workers dead.

Debs's resources were near an end unless he could enlist wider labor support. "Capital has combined to enslave labor," he warned other labor groups. "We must all stand together or go down in hopeless defeat." When Samuel Gompers refused his support, the strike collapsed. Debs and several other leaders were arrested for contempt of the court injunction of July 2 and found guilty. A lifelong Democrat, Debs soon became a confirmed socialist. His arrest and the defeat of the Pullman strike provided a deathblow to the American Railway Union. In 1895, the Supreme Court upheld the legality of using an injunction to stop a strike and provided management with a powerful weapon to use against unions in subsequent years. Most unions survived the difficult days of the 1890s, but the labor movement emerged with distinct disadvantages in its conflicts with organized capital.

Although in smaller communities strikes against outside owners might receive support from the local middle class, most labor conflicts ran up against the widespread middle- and upper-class conviction that unions and their demands were un-American. Many people claimed to accept the idea of worker organizations, but they would not concede that unions should participate in making economic or work decisions. Most employers violently resisted union demands as infringements of their rights to make production decisions, to hire and fire, to lock workers out, to hire scabs, or to reduce wages in times of depression. The sharp competition of the late nineteenth century, combined with a pattern of falling prices, stiffened employers' resistance to workers' demands. State and local governments and the courts frequently supported them in their battles to curb worker activism.

The severe depressions of the 1870s and 1890s also undermined working-class activism. Workers could not focus on union issues when survival itself was in question. They could not afford union dues or turn down offers of work, even at wages below union standards. Many unions collapsed during hard times. Of the 30 national unions in 1873, fewer than one-third managed to survive the depression.

A far more serious problem was the reluctance of most workers to organize even in favorable times. In 1870, less than one-tenth of the industrial work force belonged to unions, about the same as on the eve of the Civil War. Thirty years later, despite the expansion of the work force, only 8.4 percent (mostly skilled workers) were union members.

Why were workers so slow to join unions? Certainly, diverse work settings and ethnic differences made it difficult for workers to recognize common bonds. Moreover, many unskilled workers sensed that labor aristocrats did not have their interest at heart. Said one Cleveland Pole, "The [union] committee gets the money, 'Bricky' Flannigan [a prominent Irish striker] gets the whiskey, and the Polack gets nothing."

Moreover, many native-born Americans still clung to the tradition of individualism. "The sooner working-people get rid of the idea that somebody or something is going to help them," one Massachusetts shoemaker declared, "the better it will be for them." Others continued to nourish dreams of escaping from the working class and entering the ranks of the middle class. The number of workers who started their own small businesses attests to the power of that ideal, which prevented an identification with working-class causes.

The comments of an Irish woman highlight another important point. "There should be a law . . . to give a job to every decent man that's out of work," she declared, "and another law to keep all them I-talians from comin' in and takin' the bread out of the mouths of honest people." The ethnic and religious diversity of the work force made it difficult to forge a common front. No other industrial country depended so heavily on immigrants for its manufacturing labor force. The lack of common cultural traditions and goals created friction and misunderstandings. In addition, immigrants clustered in certain jobs and were insulated from other workers, both foreign-born and American. Skill differences related to ethnic group membership also clouded common class concerns.

The perspective of immigrant workers contributed to their indifference to unions and to tension with native-born Americans. Many foreigners planned to return to their homeland and had limited interest in changing conditions in the United States. Moreover, since their goal was to work, they took jobs as scabs. Much of the violence that accompanied working-class actions erupted when owners brought in strikebreakers. Some Americans blamed immigrants for both low wages and failed worker actions. Divisions among workers were often as bitter as those between strikers and employers. When workers divided, employers benefited.

The tension within laboring ranks appeared most dramatically in the anti-Chinese campaign of the 1870s and 1880s as white workers in the West began to blame the Chinese for economic hardships. A meeting of San Francisco workers in 1877 in favor of the eight-hour day exploded into a rampage against the Chinese. In the following years, angry mobs killed Chinese workers in Tacoma, Seattle, Denver, and Rock Springs, Wyoming. "The Chinese must go! They are stealing our jobs!" became a rallying cry for American workers.

Hostility was also expressed at the national level with the Chinese Exclusion Act of 1882. The law, which had the support of the Knights of Labor in the West, prohibited the immigration of both skilled and unskilled Chinese workers for a ten-year period. It was extended in 1892 and made permanent in 1902. While both middle- and working-class Americans supported sporadic efforts to cut off immigration, working-class antipathy exacerbated the deep divisions that undermined worker unity.

At the same time, many immigrants, especially those who were skilled, did support unions and cooperate with native-born Americans. Irish-Americans played important roles in the Knights of Labor and the AFL. British and Germans also helped build up the unions. Often ethnic bonds served labor causes by tying members to one another and to the community. For example, in the 1860s and 1870s, as the Molders' Union in Troy, New York, battled with manufacturers, its Irish membership won sympathy and support from the Irish-dominated police force, the Roman Catholic church, fraternal orders, and public officials.

The importance of workers' organizations lay not so much in their successful struggles and protests as in the implicit criticism they offered of American society. Using the language of republicanism, many workers lashed out at an economic order that robbed them of their dignity and humanity. As producers of wealth, they protested that so little of it was theirs. As members of the working class, they rejected the middle-class belief in individualism and social mobility.

The Balance Sheet

Except for skilled workers, most laboring people found it impossible to earn much of a share in the material bounty industrialization created. Newly arrived immigrants especially suffered from low pay and economic uncertainty. Long hours on the job and the necessity of walking to and from work left workers little free time. Family budgets could include, at best, only small amounts for recreation. Even a baseball game ticket was a luxury.

Yet this view of the harshness of working-class life partly grows out of our own standards of what is acceptable today. Since so few working-class men or women recorded their thoughts and reactions, it is hard to know just what they expected or how they viewed their experiences. But culture and background influenced their perspectives. The family tenement, one Polish immigrant remarked, "seemed quite advanced when compared with our home" in Poland. American poverty was preferable to Russian pogroms. A ten-hour job in the steel mill might be an improvement over dawn-to-dusk farmwork that brought no wages.

Studies of several cities show that nineteenth-century workers achieved some occupational mobility. One worker in five in Los Angeles and Atlanta during the 1890s, for example, managed to climb into the middle class. Most immigrant workers were stuck in ill-paid, insecure jobs, but their children ended up doing better. The son of an unskilled laborer might move on to become a semi-skilled or skilled worker as new immigrants took the jobs at the bottom. Second-generation Irish made progress, especially in the West and the Midwest. Even in Boston, 40 percent of the children of Irish immigrants obtained white-collar jobs.

Mobility, like occupation, was related to background. Native-born whites, Jews, and Germans rose more swiftly and fell less often than Irish, Italians, or Poles. Cultural attitudes, family size, education, and group leadership all contributed to different ethnic mobility patterns. Jews, for example, valued education and sacrificed to keep children in school. By 1915, Jews represented 85 percent of the free City College student body in New York City, 20 percent of New York University's student body, and one-sixth of those studying at Columbia University. With an education, they moved upward. The Slavs, however, who valued a steady income over mobility and education, took their children out of school and sent them to work at an early age. This course of action, they believed, not only helped the family but gave the child a head start in securing reliable, stable employment. The southern Italian proverb "Do not make your child better than you are" suggests the value Italians placed on family rather than individual success. Differing attitudes and values led to different aspirations and career patterns.

Two groups enjoyed little mobility. African-Americans were largely excluded from the industrial occupational structure and restricted to unskilled jobs. Unlike immigrant industrial workers, they did not have the opportunity to move to better jobs as new unskilled workers took the positions at the bottom. A study in Los Angeles suggests that Hispanic residents made minimal gains. Their experiences elsewhere may have been much the same.

Although occupational mobility was limited for immigrants, other kinds of rewards often compensated for the lack of success at the workplace.

Home ownership loomed important for groups like the Irish, for in their homeland, home ownership had been all but impossible. Ownership of a home also allowed a family to earn extra income by taking in boarders and provided some protection against the uncertainties of industrial life and the coming of old age. The Irish also proved adept politicians and came to dominate big-city government in the late nineteenth century. Their political success opened up city jobs, particularly in the police force, to the Irish. In 1886, one-third of Chicago's police force was Irish-born; many more were second-generation Irish-Americans. The Irish were also successful in the construction industry and dominated the hierarchy of the Catholic church. Irish who did not share this upward mobility could nevertheless benefit from ethnic connections and take pride in their group's achievements.

Likewise, participation in social clubs and fraternal orders compensated in part for lack of advancement at work. Ethnic associations, parades, and holidays provided a sense of identity and security that offset the limitations of the job world.

Moreover, a few rags-to-riches stories always encouraged the masses who struggled. The family of John Kearney, in Poughkeepsie, New York, for example, achieved modest success. After 20 years as a laborer, John started his own business as a junk dealer and even bought a simple house. His sons started off in better jobs than their father. One became a grocery store clerk, later a baker, a policeman, and finally, at the age of 40, an inspector at the waterworks. Another was an iron molder, while the third son was a post office worker and eventually the superintendent of city streets. If this success paled next to that of industrial giants like Andrew Carnegie and John D. Rockefeller, it was still enough to keep the American dream alive.

CONCLUSION

The Complexity of Industrial Capitalism

The rapid growth of the late nineteenth century made the United States one of the world's industrial giants. Many factors contributed to the "wonderful accomplishments" of the age. They ranged from sympathetic government policies to the rise of big business and the emergence of a cheap industrial work force. But it was also a turbulent period. Many Americans benefited only marginally from the new wealth. Some of them protested by joining unions, by walking out on strike, or by initiating on-the-job actions. Most lived their lives more quietly and never had the opportunity that Thomas O'Donnell did of telling their story to others. But middle-class Americans began to wonder about the O'Donnells of the country. It is to their concerns, worries, and aspirations that we now turn.

Recommended Reading

Industrialism and Economic Growth

Stuart Bruchey, *Growth of the Modern American Economy* (1975); Alfred W. Niemi, *U.S. Economic History: A Survey of the Major Issues* (1975); Robert L. Heilbroner, *The Economic Transformation of America* (1977); Samuel P. Hays, *The Response to Industrialism, 1885–1914* (1957); Robert Wiebe, *The Search for Order, 1877—1920* (1967); Glenn Porter, *The Rise of Big Business, 1860–1910* (1973); Olivier Zunz, *Making America Corporate, 1870–1829* (1990); Alfred D. Chandler, Jr., *The Visible Hand: The Managerial Revolution in American Business* (1977); Louis Galambos and Barbara Barron Spence, *The Public Image of Big Business in America* (1975); Edward C. Kirkland, *Dream and Thought in the Business Community, 1860–1900* (1964) and *Industry Comes of Age: Business, Labor, and Public Policy, 1860–1900* (1961); James D. Norris, *Advertising and the Transformation of American Society, 1865–1920* (1990).

Urban Growth

Zane Miller, *Urbanization of America* (1973); Sam Bass Warner, Jr., *Streetcar Suburbs: The Process of Growth in Boston,*

1870–1900 (1962); Gunther Barth, *The Rise of Modern City Culture in Nineteenth-Century America* (1980); David Goldfield, *Cotton Fields and Skyscrapers: Southern City and Region* (1989); William Cronon, *Nature's Metropolis: Chicago and the Great West* (1991); James Borchert, *Alley Life in Washington: Family, Community, Religion, and Folklife in the City, 1850–1970* (1980); Allan Spear, *Black Chicago: The Making of a Negro Ghetto, 1890–1920* (1967).

Work and Workers

Thomas J. Archdeacon, *Becoming American: An Ethnic History* (1983); Alan M. Kraut, *The Huddled Masses: The Immigrant in American Society, 1880–1921* (1982); Peter Jones and Melvin G. Holli, eds., *Ethnic Chicago* (1981); Kerby A. Miller, *Emigrants and Exiles: Ireland and the Irish Exodus to North America* (1985); Herbert G. Gutman, *Work, Culture, and Society in Industrializing America* (1976); David M. Gordon, Richard Edwards, and Michael Reich, *Segmented Work, Divided Workers: The Historical Transformation of Labor in the United States* (1982); Daniel Nelson, *Managers and Workers: Origins of the New Factory System in the United States, 1880–1920* (1975); David T. Rodgers, *The Work Ethic in Industrial America* (1978); David Montgomery, *Workers' Control in America: Studies in the History of Work, Technology, and Labor Struggles* (1970) and *The Fall of the House of Labor: The Workplace, The State, and American Labor Activism, 1865–1925* (1987); James Whiteside, *Regulating Danger: The Struggle for Mine Safety in the Rocky Mountain Coal Industry* (1990); Daniel J. Walkowitz, *Worker City, Company Town: Iron and Cotton-Worker Protest in Troy and Cohoes, New York, 1855–84* (1978); Theodore Hershberg, ed., *Philadelphia: Work, Space, Family, and Group Experience in the Nineteenth Century* (1981); Robert V. Bruce, *1877: Year of Violence* (1959); Philip S. Foner, *The Great Labor Uprising of 1877* (1977); Nell Irvin Painter, *Standing at Armageddon in the United States, 1877–1919* (1987); Leon Fink, *Workingmen's Democracy: The Knights of Labor and American Politics* (1983); Alice Kessler-Harris, *Out to Work: A History of Wage-earning Women in the United States* (1982); Julie Matthaei, *An Economic History of Women in America: Women's Work, the Sexual Division of Labor, and the Development of Capitalism* (1982); David M. Katzman, *Seven Days a Week: Women and Domestic Service in Industrializing America* (1978); Irvin G. Wyllie, *The Self-made Man in America: The Myth of Rags to Riches* (1954); Gary Scharnhorst, *Horatio Alger, Jr.* (1980); Stephan Thernstrom, *Poverty and Progress: Social Mobility in a Nineteenth Century City* (1964) and *The Other Bostonians: Poverty and Progress in the American Metropolis, 1880–1970* (1973); Clyde Griffen and Sally Griffen, *Natives and Newcomers: The Ordering of Opportunity in Mid-Nineteenth-Century Poughkeepsie* (1978); Michael P. Weber, *Social Change in an Industrial Town: Patterns of Progress in Warren, Pennsylvania, from the Civil War to World War I* (1976); Thomas Kessner, *The Golden Door: Italian and Jewish Immigrant Mobility in New York City, 1880–1915* (1977).

Novels

Theodore Dreiser, *Sister Carrie* (1900); Stephen Crane, *Maggie: A Girl of the Streets* (1893); Abraham Cahan, *The Rise of David Levinsky* (1917); Thomas Bell, *Out of This Furnace* (1976 ed.).

TIMELINE

1843–1884	"Old immigration"
1844	Telegraph invented
1850s	Steam power widely used in manufacturing
1859	Value of U.S. industrial production exceeds value of agricultural production
1866	National Labor Union founded
1869	Transcontinental railroad completed Knights of Labor organized
1870	Standard Oil of Ohio formed
1870s–1880s	Consolidation of continental railroad network
1873	Bethlehem Steel begins using Bessemer process
1873–1879	Depression
1876	Alexander G. Bell invents telephone
1877	Railroad workers hold first nationwide industrial strike
1879	Thomas Edison invents incandescent light
1882	Chinese Exclusion Act
1885–1914	"New immigration"
1886	American Federation of Labor founded Haymarket Riot in Chicago
1887	Interstate Commerce Act
1890	Sherman Anti-Trust Act
1892	Standard Oil of New Jersey formed Coeur d'Alene strike Homestead steelworkers strike
1893	Chicago World's Fair
1893–1897	Depression
1894	Pullman railroad workers strike
1900	International Ladies' Garment Workers Union founded Corporations responsible for two-thirds of U.S. manufacturing

CHAPTER 19

Politics and Reform

At the start of his best-seller *Looking Backward* (1888), Edward Bellamy likened the American society of his day to a huge stagecoach. Dragging the coach along sandy roads and over steep hills were the "masses of humanity." While they strained desperately "under the pitiless lashing of hunger" to pull the coach, at the top sat the favored few, riding well out of the dust in breezy comfort. The fortunate few, however, were constantly fearful that they might lose their seats from a sudden jolt, fall to the ground, and have to pull the coach themselves.

Bellamy's famous coach allegory introduced a utopian novel in which the class divisions and pitiless competition of the nineteenth century were replaced by a classless, caring, cooperative new world. Economic anxieties and hardships were supplanted by satisfying labor and leisure. In place of the coach, all citizens in the year 2000 walked together in equal comfort and security under a huge umbrella over the sidewalks of the city. Bellamy's outlook on American life was a middle-class reformist one. His book had enormous appeal not only because of his humane economic analysis but also because he clothed it in the form of a novel, complete with futuristic technological wonders, such as television and credit cards, a double-dream trick ending, and a love story.

The novel opens in 1887. The hero, Julian West, a wealthy Bostonian, falls asleep worrying about the effect local labor struggles might have on his upcoming wedding. When he wakes up, it is the year 2000. In the new society he discovers, through his genial guide, Dr. Leete, all citizens live in material comfort and happiness. Utopia had been achieved peacefully through the development of one gigantic trust, owned and operated by the national government. All citizens between 21 and 45 work in an industrial army with equalized pay and work difficulty. Retirement after age 45 is devoted to hobbies, reading, culture, and such minimal political and judicial leadership as is needed in a society without crime, poverty, graft, vice, lawyers, or war.

Bellamy's treatment of the role of women in the world of 2000 reflected his own era's struggle with changing gender and class relationships. On the one hand, new laborsaving gadgets relieved women of housework, and they served, like men, in the industrial army. Women married not for dependence but for love and could even initiate romantic relationships. On the other hand, the women Bellamy portrayed were still primarily responsible for shopping, supervision of domestic and aesthetic matters, and nurturing the young. In a special women's division of the industrial army, they worked shorter hours in "lighter occupations." The purpose of equality of the sexes and more leisure, the novel made clear, was to enable women to cultivate their "beauty and grace" and, by extension, to feminize culture and politics.

Bellamy's book was popular with educated middle-class Americans, who were attracted by his vision of a society in which humans were both morally good and materially well off. Readers were intrigued not only by all that was new but also by how much of the old society was preserved. The traditional male view of woman's place and purpose was one example. But Bellamy also retained such familiar values as individual taste and incentive, private property, and rags-to-riches presidents. Like most middle-class Americans of his day, he disapproved of European socialism. Although the collectivist features of Bellamy's utopia were socialistic, he and his admirers called his system "nationalism." This appealed to a new generation of Americans who had put aside Civil War antagonisms to embrace the greatness of a growing, if now economically divided, nation. In the early 1890s, with Americans buying nearly 10,000 copies of *Looking Backward* every week, over 160 Nationalist clubs were formed to crusade for the adoption of Bellamy's ideas.

The inequalities of wealth described in Bellamy's coach scene reflected a political life in which many participated but only a few benefited. The wealthiest 10 percent, who rode high on the social coach, dominated national politics, while untutored bosses held sway in governing cities. Except for token expressions of support, national political leaders ignored the cries of factory workers, immigrants, farmers, blacks, Native Americans, and other victims of the vast transformation of American industrial, urban, and agrarian life in the late nineteenth century. But as the century drew to a close, middle-class Americans like Bellamy, as well as labor and agrarian leaders, proposed various reforms. Their concern was never more appropriate than during the depression of the mid-1890s, a social upheaval in real life that mirrored the worst features and fears of Bellamy's fictional coach.

In this chapter we will examine American politics at the national and local level from the end of Reconstruction to the 1890s, a period that for the most part bolstered the rich and neglected the corrosive human problems of urban industrial life. Then we will look at the growing social and political involvement of educated middle-class reformers, who had formerly had a distaste for mass politics but now acted to effect change both locally and nationally. We will conclude with an account of the pivotal importance of the 1890s, highlighted by the Populist revolt, the depression of 1893–1897, and the election of 1896. In an age of strong national identity and pride, the events of the 1890s shook many comfortable citizens out of their apathy and began the reshaping of American politics.

Politics in the Gilded Age

In a satirical book in 1873, Mark Twain, with Charles Dudley Warner, used the expression "Gilded Age" to describe the political corruption of Grant's presidency. The phrase, with its suggestion of shallow glitter, has come to characterize social and political life in the last quarter of the nineteenth century. Ironically, although Gilded Age politics was tainted by corruption and tinted by more color than substance, the period was one of high party vitality. Politicians avoided fundamental issues in favor of the politics of mass entertainment—pomp, parades, free beer, banners, and the prattle of three-hour speeches. As a result, voter participation in national elections between 1876 and 1896 hovered at an all-time high of 73 to 82 percent of all registered voters.

Behind the glitter of Gilded Age politics, though, occurred two gradual changes that would greatly affect twentieth-century politics. The first was the development of a professional bureaucracy. In congressional committees and executive branch offices, elite specialists and experts emerged as a counterfoil to the perceived dangers of majority rule represented by high voter participation, especially by new immigrants. How else, New England poet James Russell Lowell wondered, could the culturally "better" classes temper the excesses of equality "when interpreted and applied politically by millions of newcomers alien to our traditions?" Second, after a period of close elections and party stalemate based on Civil War divisions between Democrats and Republicans, new issues and concerns fostered a party realignment in the 1890s.

Politics, Parties, Patronage, and Presidents

American government in the 1870s and 1880s clearly supported the interests of riders at the top of the coach. Although some modern observers think the national government should have tackled problems like poverty, unemployment, and trusts, few nineteenth-century Americans would have agreed. They mistrusted organized power and believed in harmony of interests and laissez-faire, a doctrine that argued that all would benefit from an economic life free of government interference. After the traumas of the Civil War era, when a strong centralized state pursued high moral causes, late-nineteenth-century political leaders favored a period of governmental passivity. This would permit the continuing pursuit of industrial expansion and wealth. As Republican leader Roscoe Conkling explained, the primary role of government was "to clear the way of impediments and dangers, and leave every class and every individual free and safe in the exertions and pursuits of life."

The Gilded Age, Henry Adams observed, was the most "thoroughly ordinary" period in American politics since Columbus. "One might search the whole list of Congress, Judiciary, and Executive during the twenty-five years 1870–95 and find little but damaged reputation." Few eras of American government were as corrupt as this one, and Adams was especially sensitive to this decline in the quality of democratic politics. His autobiography, *The Education of Henry Adams* (1907), contrasted the low political tone of his own age with the exalted political morality of the days of grandfather John Quincy Adams and great-grandfather John Adams.

As a result of the weak Johnson and Grant presidencies, Congress emerged in the 1870s as the dominant branch of government. With power in the committee system, the moral quality of congressional leadership was typified by men such as James G. Blaine and Roscoe Conkling. Despite a scandal in which he was paid for supporting favors to railroads and then lied about it afterward, Blaine was probably the most popular Republican politician of the era. A man of enormous charm, intelligence, wit, and ability, he served his country as senator from Maine and twice as secretary of state and was a serious contender for the presidency in every election from 1876 to 1892.

Blaine's intraparty foe, Roscoe Conkling, was even more typical. The *New York Times* described him as "a man by whose career and character the future will judge of the political standards of the present." A stalwart Republican who controlled the rich patronage jobs of the New York customhouse, Conkling spent most of his career in patronage conflicts with fellow party leaders. He quarreled even more with liberal Republican civil service reformers, who believed that government jobs should be dispersed for expertise and merit rather than party loyalty. Conkling could imagine no other purpose of politics and accused these genteel "mugwump" reformers of wanting the jobs for themselves. "Their real object is office and plunder." Fittingly, his career ended when he resigned from the Senate in a patronage dispute with President Garfield. Though he served in Congress for over two decades, Conkling never drafted a bill. His career was unharmed, for legislation was not Congress's primary purpose.

In 1879, a student of legislative politics, Woodrow Wilson, expressed his disgust with the degradation of Gilded Age politics in eight words: "No leaders, no principles; no principles, no parties." Little differentiated the two major parties. They diverged not over principles but patronage, not over issues but the spoils of office. At stake in elections were not laws but the thousands of government jobs at the disposal of the winning candidate and his party. In a shrewd analysis of the American political system in the late nineteenth century, an English observer, Lord James Bryce, concluded that the most cohesive force in American politics was the "desire for office and for office as a means of gain." The two parties, like two bottles of liquor, Bryce said, bore different labels, yet "each was empty."

The clear ideological party positions taken during the Civil War and Reconstruction had all but disappeared. The Republican party frequently reminded voters of its role in winning the Civil War and preserving the Union. Republican votes still came from northeastern Yankee industrial interests and from New England migrants across the Upper Midwest. The main support for Democrats still came primarily from southern whites, northern workers, and Irish Catholic and other urban immigrants. For a few years, Civil War and Reconstruction issues generated party differences. But after 1876, on national issues at least, party labels did indeed mark "empty" bottles.

One reason for avoiding issues in favor of bland platforms and careful campaigning was that the two parties were evenly matched. In three of the five presidential elections between 1876 and 1892, one percent of the vote separated the two major candidates. In 1880, for example, James Garfield defeated his Democratic opponent, General Winfield Hancock, a Reconstruction moderate and Union war hero, by only 7,018 votes. In 1884, Grover Cleveland squeaked by James G. Blaine by a popular vote margin of 48.5 to 48.2 percent. In two elections (1876 and 1888),

Although the tariff protectionist Harrison defeated Cleveland in 1888 (the results were reversed in 1892), all Gilded Age presidents were essentially "preservers" rather than innovators. None had approached the greatness of Washington, Lincoln, and the other Republican presidents hovering over Harrison and Morton in this illustration.

the electoral vote winner had fewer popular votes. Further evidence of political stalemate was that only twice, and for only two years, did one party control the White House and both houses of Congress. Although all the presidents in the era except Cleveland were Republicans, the Democrats controlled the House of Representatives in eight of the ten sessions of Congress between 1875 and 1895. As a result, political interest shifted away from Washington to states and cities.

Lord Bryce titled one of the chapters of his book on American politics "Why Great Men Are Not Chosen Presidents." Gilded Age presidents were an undistinguished group. Like Washington, D.C., itself, they played only a minor role in national life, especially when compared with industrial entrepreneurs like Carnegie and Rockefeller. None of them—Rutherford B. Hayes (1877–1881), James Garfield (1881), Chester A. Arthur (1881–1885), Grover Cleveland (1885–1889 and 1893–1897), and Benjamin Harrison (1889–1893)—served two consecutive terms. None was strongly identified with any particular issue. None has been highly regarded by historians.

Although Cleveland was the only Democrat in the group, he differed little from the Republicans. Upon his election in 1884, financier Jay Gould sent him a telegram stating his confidence that "the vast business interests of the country will be entirely safe in your hands." When Cleveland violated the expectation that presidents should not initiate ideas by devoting his entire annual message in 1887 to a call for a lower tariff, Congress listened politely and did nothing. Voters turned him out of office a year later.

Most Americans expected their presidents to take care of party business by rewarding the faithful with government positions. The scale of patronage was enormous. Garfield complained of having to dispense thousands of jobs as he took office in 1881, worrying, he said, "whether A or B should be appointed to this or that office." He is remembered primarily for being shot early in his administration by a disappointed office seeker. He achieved heroic stature only by hanging on for 2½ months before he died. Garfield's successor, Chester Arthur, was so closely identified with Conkling's patronage operation that when the shooting of the president was announced, a friend said with shocked disbelief, "My God! Chet Arthur in the White House!"

National Issues

Arthur surprised his doubters by proving himself a capable and dignified president, responsive to the growing demands for civil service reform. Four issues were important at the national level in the Gilded Age: the tariff, currency, civil service, and government regulation of railroads (see

Chapter 18). In confronting these issues, legislators tried to serve both their own self-interest and the national interest of an efficient, productive economy. Two additional issues, Indian "reform" and black rights, were submerged in these interests (see Chapter 18).

The tariff was one issue where party, as well as regional attitudes toward the use of government power, made some difference. Republicans believed in using the state to support business interests and stood for a high protective tariff. A nation demonstrated its "intelligence," one orator said, by using law to promote a "dynamic and progressive" society. The tariff would protect American businessmen, wage earners, and farmers from the competition and products of foreign labor. By contrast, Democrats stressed that a low tariff exemplified the "economic axiom . . . that the government is best which governs least." High tariffs falsely substituted the aims and actions of the state for those that should come from "individual initiative" and were a tax on consumers.

Although Democrats were identified with a low-tariff position and Republicans with a high one, in reality there was little consistency in either party's stand. In practice, politicians accommodated local interests in tariff adjustments. Democratic senator Daniel Vorhees of Indiana explained, "I am a protectionist for every interest which I am sent here by my constituents to protect."

Tariff revisions were bewilderingly complex in their acceding to these many special interests. As one senator knowingly said, "The contest over a revision of the tariff brings to light a selfish strife which is not far from disgusting." Most tariffs included a mixture of higher and lower rates that defied understanding. Since the federal government depended on tariffs and excise taxes (primarily on tobacco and liquor) for most of its revenue, there was little chance that the tariff would

A British observer of American politics, James Bryce, said in 1888 that "the American usually votes with his party, right or wrong, and the fact that there is little distinction of view between the parties makes it easier to stick to your old friends." American voters stayed with their "old friends," as this table of the evenly matched presidential elections of the Gilded Age shows. Except for 1872, the popular vote was never wider than 3 percent and in three elections was less than 1 percent.

Presidential Elections, 1872–1892

Year	Candidates	Party	Popular Vote	Electoral Vote
1872	ULYSSES S. GRANT	Republican	3,596,745 (56%)	286
	Horace Greeley	Democrat	2,843,446 (44%)	0[a]
1876	Samuel J. Tilden	Democrat	4,284,020 (51%)	184
	RUTHERFORD B. HAYES	Republican	4,036,572 (48%)	185
1880	JAMES A. GARFIELD	Republican	4,449,053 (48.5%)	214
	Winfield S. Hancock	Democrat	4,442,035 (48.1%)	155
	James B. Weaver	Greenback-Labor	308,578 (3.4%)	0
1884	GROVER CLEVELAND	Democrat	4,911,017 (48.5%)	219
	James G. Blaine	Republican	4,848,334 (48.2%)	182
		Minor parties	325,739 (3.3%)	0
1888	Grover Cleveland	Democrat	5,540,050 (48.6%)	168
	BENJAMIN HARRISON	Republican	5,444,337 (47.9%)	233
		Minor parties	396,441 (3.5%)	0
1892	GROVER CLEVELAND	Democrat	5,554,414 (46%)	277
	Benjamin Harrison	Republican	5,190,802 (43%)	145
	James B. Weaver	Populist	1,027,329 (9%)	22

[a]Greeley died before the electoral college met.

Note: Winners' names appear in capital letters.

be abolished or substantially lowered. Moreover, the surpluses produced by the tariff during the Gilded Age helped the parties finance patronage jobs as well as government programs.

The question of money was even more complicated. During the Civil War, the federal government had circulated paper money (greenbacks) that could not be exchanged for gold or silver. In the late 1860s and 1870s, politicians debated whether the United States should return to a metallic standard, which would allow paper money to be exchanged for specie. Proponents of a hard-money policy supported either withdrawing all paper money from circulation or making it convertible to specie. They opposed increasing the volume of money because they thought it would lead to higher prices. Greenbackers, who advocated soft money, argued that there was not enough currency in circulation for an expanding economy and urged increasing the supply of paper money. An inadequate money supply, they believed, led to falling prices and an increase in interest rates, which harmed farmers, industrial workers, and all people in debt.

Hard-money interests had more power and influence. In 1873, Congress demonetized silver. In 1875, it passed the Specie Resumption Act, gradually retiring greenbacks from circulation and putting the nation firmly on the gold standard. But as large supplies of silver were discovered and mined in the West, pressure was resumed for increasing the money supply by coining silver. Soft-money advocates pushed for the unlimited coinage of silver in addition to gold. A compromise of sorts was reached in 1878 with passage of the Bland-Allison Act requiring the Treasury to buy between $2 million and $4 million of silver each month and to coin it as silver dollars. Despite the increase in money supply, the period was not inflationary, but prices fell, disappointing the supporters of soft money. Their response was to push for more silver, which continued the controversy into the 1890s.

The issue of civil service reform was, Henry Adams observed, a "subject almost as dangerous in political conversation in Washington as slavery itself in the old days before the war." The worst feature of the spoils system was that parties financed themselves by assessing holders of patronage jobs, often as much as one percent of their annual salaries. Reformers, most of whom were genteel white American-born Protestants, pressed for competitive examinations, allegedly to ensure the creation of a professional, honest, nonpartisan permanent civil service. But they were motivated as well by a desire to provide "barriers against the invasion of modern barbarism and vulgarity," as Harvard culture guardian Charles Eliot Norton put it, describing the threat of dividing the spoils of office among immigrants and their urban political machine bosses.

Civil service reform had first been raised during the Grant administration, but little was accomplished. The assassination of Garfield, however, created enough public support to force Congress to take action. The Pendleton Act of 1883 established a system of merit examinations covering about one-tenth of federal offices. Gradually, more bureaucrats fell under its coverage, but parties became no more honest. As campaign contributions from government employees dried up, parties turned to other financial sources. In 1888, record corporate contributions helped to elect Benjamin Harrison.

The Lure of Local Politics

The fact that the major parties did not disagree substantially on issues like money and civil service does not mean that nineteenth-century Americans found politics dull or uninteresting. In fact, far more eligible voters turned out in the late nineteenth century than at any time since. The 78.5 percent average turnout to vote for president in the 1880s contrasts sharply with the less than 55 percent of eligible Americans who voted for president in the 1980s.

What explains the amazing nineteenth-century turnout? Americans were drawn to the polls in part by the fun and games of party parades, buttons, and banners but also by the lure of local issues. For example, Iowa corn farmers turned out to vote for state representatives who favored curbing the power of the railroads to set high grain-shipping rates. But emotional issues of race, religion, nationality, and life style often overrode economic self-interest. While Irish Catholics in New York sought political support for their parochial schools, third-generation middle-class American Protestants from Illinois or Connecticut voted for laws that would compel attendance at public schools. Nashville whites supported laws that established segregated railroad cars and other public facilities. Milwaukee German brewery workers voted against local temperance laws because they valued both their jobs and their beer. Ohio and Indiana Protestant farmers, by contrast, believing they were protecting social order and morality against hard-drinking Catholic immigrants, pushed for temperance laws.

The influx of the new immigrants, especially in the mushrooming cities, played a large role in stimulating political participation. As traditional ruling groups, usually native-born, left local government for business, where they found more money and status, urban bosses stepped in. Their power to control city government rested on an ability to deliver the votes of poor, uneducated immigrants. In return for votes, bosses like "Big Tim" Sullivan of New York and "Hinky Dink" Kenna of Chicago operated informal welfare systems. They handed out jobs and money for rent, fuel, and bail. Sullivan gave new shoes as birthday presents to all poor children in his district, as well as turkeys to poor families at Thanksgiving. Above all, party bosses provided a personal touch in a strange and forbidding environment. As one boss explained, "I think that there's got to be in every ward somebody that any bloke can come to—no matter what he's done—and get help."

New York City's Tammany Hall boss, George Washington Plunkitt, perfected the relationship of mutual self-interest with his constituents. The favors he provided in return for votes ranged from attending weddings and funerals to influencing police and the courts. His clients included not only Jewish brides, Italian mourners, and burned-out tenants but also job seekers, store owners, saloonkeepers, and madams, all of whom needed favors. State party leaders were no less effective than urban bosses in mobilizing voters. An Indiana Republican state chairman appointed 10,000 district workers in 1884 responsible for discovering the "social and political affiliation" of every single voter.

Party leaders also won votes by making political participation exciting. Nineteenth-century campaigns were punctuated by parades, rallies, and oratory. Campaign buttons, handkerchiefs, songs, and other paraphernalia generated color and excitement in political races where substantive issues were not at stake. In the election of 1884, for example, emotions ran high over the moral lapses of the opposition candidate. The Democrats made much of Blaine's record of dishonesty, chanting in election eve parades and rallies: "Blaine! Blaine! James G. Blaine! / Continental liar from the state of Maine!" Republicans, in turn, learning of an illegitimate child fathered by Grover Cleveland, answered with their own chant: "Ma! Ma! Where's my pa? / Gone to the White House, Ha! Ha! Ha!" Cleveland won, in part because a Republican clergyman unwisely called the Democrats the party of "rum, Romanism, and rebellion" on election eve in New York. The remark backfired, and the Republicans lost both New York, which should have been a safe state, and the election.

The response of voters in New York in 1884 demonstrated that local and ethnocultural issues rather than national and economic questions explained party affiliation and political behavior. New Mexico politics, for example, was marked for 20 years by the corrupt land grabs of the Santa Fe ring, a small group of Anglo-Protestant Republican bankers, lawyers, and politicians who exploited anti-Mexican and anti-Catholic sentiments. The ring controlled judges, legislators, and the business interests of the state, as well as some Spanish-speaking voters. In the late 1880s, outraged Mexican tenant farmers resorted to violence, which the ring manipulated to dispossess Mexicans, Indians, and even white squatters from enormous tracts of land. The New Mexico events showed the power of race and religion in local politics.

Voters may have been cool toward the tariff and civil service, but they expressed strong interest in temperance, anti-Catholicism, compulsory school attendance and Sunday laws, aid to parochial schools, racial issues, restriction of immigration, and "bloody shirt" reminders of the Civil War.

Party membership reflected voter interest in these important cultural, religious, and ethnic questions. Midwestern Scandinavians and Lutherans, for example, tended to be Republicans, as were northerners who belonged to Protestant denominations. These groups believed in positive government action. Since the Republican party had proved its willingness in the past to mobilize the power of the state to reshape society, people who wished to regulate moral and economic life were attracted to it. Catholics and various immigrant groups found the Democratic party more to their liking because it opposed government efforts to regulate morals. Said one Chicago Democrat, "A Republican is a man who wants you t' go t' church every Sunday. A Democrat says if a man wants t' have a glass of beer on Sunday he can have it."

These differences caused spirited local contests, particularly over prohibition. Many Americans considered drinking a serious social problem. Annual consumption of brewery beer had risen from 2.7 gallons per capita in 1850 to 17.9 in 1880. Although this increase could have been the result of changes in drinking habits, many people feared that alcoholism was on the increase. Certainly the number of saloons ballooned. In one city, saloons outnumbered churches 31 to 1. This shocked those who believed that drinking would destroy the American character, corrupt politics, and lead to poverty, crime, and unrestrained sexuality. Women especially supported temperance because they were often the targets of violent drunken men. Rather than trying to persuade individuals to give up drink, as the temperance movement had done earlier in the century, many now sought to make drinking a crime.

The battle in San Jose, California, illustrates the strong passions such efforts aroused. In the 1870s, temperance reformers put on the ballot a local option referendum to ban the sale of liquor in San Jose. Women, using their influence as guardians of morality, erected a temperance tent, where they held conspicuous daily meetings. Despite denunciations from some clergymen and heckling from some of the town's drinkers, the women refused to retreat to their homes. On election eve, a large crowd appeared at the temperance tent, but a larger one turned up at a proliquor rally. In the morning, women roamed the streets, urging men to adopt the referendum. Children were marched around to the polls and saloons, singing, "Father, dear father, come home with me now." By afternoon the mood grew ugly, and the women were harassed and threatened by drunken men. The prohibition proposal lost by a vote of 1,430 to 918.

Similarly emotional conflicts occurred in the 1880s at the state level over other issues, especially education. In Iowa, Illinois, and Wisconsin, Republicans sponsored laws mandating that children attend "some public or private day school" where instruction was in English, an early but not the last nativist movement for English-only education. The intent of these laws was to undermine parochial schools, which taught in the language of the immigrants. In Iowa, where a state prohibition law was passed as well, the Republican slogan was "A schoolhouse on every hill, and no saloon in the valley." Confident in their cause, Protestant Iowa Republicans proclaimed that

Women, often targets of drunken male violence, campaigned for temperance as well as for equal rights. Here Victoria Claflin Woodhull reads a suffrage proposal to the House Judiciary Committee in 1871. If denied the vote, she vowed that women "mean secession, and on a thousand times grander scale than was that of the South. We are plotting a revolution; we will overthrow this bogus Republic and plant a government of righteousness in its stead."

"Iowa will go Democratic when hell goes Methodist." It went Republican. But in Wisconsin, a law for compulsory school attendance was so strongly anti-Catholic that it backfired. Many voters, disillusioned with Republican moralism, shifted to the Democratic party. Campaigns like these both reflected and nourished ethnic tension and helped draw the middle class into a more active engagement with politics.

Middle-Class Reform

Generally unexcited by tariffs and the money question, middle-class Americans were moved by moral issues such as education and temperance. Moreover, many were frightened into overcoming their aversion to politics by the corruption of urban life and the violent polarizing labor upheavals of the 1880s. Although most middle-class Americans were not reformers, all worried about the social consequences of their absence from political discourse and saw the value of the sophisticated and moral thinking they could bring to national life.

Frances Willard and the Women's Christian Temperance Union (WCTU) is an example. As president of the WCTU from 1879 until her death in 1898, Willard headed the largest women's organization in the country. Although she had an academic background, most members were churchgoing white Protestant women who, like Willard, supported temperance because they believed drunkenness caused poverty and family violence. But after 1886, the WCTU reversed its position, seeing drunkenness as a result of poverty, unemployment, and bad labor conditions. Willard joined the Knights of Labor in 1887 and by the 1890s had influenced the WCTU to extend its programs in a "do-everything" policy to alleviate the problems of workers, particularly women and children.

Frances Willard typified the middle-class reformer's effort to apply both Christian principles and organizational skill to solving social problems. Her goal was nothing less than "to influence those strongholds of power, the national Congress, State Legislatures and Municipal Councils."

The Gospel of Wealth

Frances Willard called herself a Christian socialist because she believed in applying the ethical principles of Jesus to economic life. For Willard and many other educated middle-class reformers, Christianity led to a cooperative social order designed to reduce inequalities of wealth. But for most Americans in the Gilded Age, Christianity supported the competitive individualistic ethic that justified the lofty place of those who had won the race to the top.

This ethic was endorsed by prominent ministers and others, who preached sermons and wrote treatises emphasizing the moral superiority of the wealthy and justifying social class arrangements. Episcopal bishop William Lawrence wrote that it was "God's will that some men should attain great wealth." Philadelphia Baptist preacher Russell Conwell's famous sermon "Acres of Diamonds," delivered 6,000 times to an estimated audience of 13 million, praised riches as a sure sign of "godliness" and stressed the power of money to "do good."

Industrialist Andrew Carnegie expressed the ethic most clearly. In an article, "The Gospel of Wealth" (1889), Carnegie celebrated the benefits of better goods and lower prices that resulted from competition, arguing that "our wonderful material development" outweighed the harsh costs of competition. The concentration of wealth in the hands of a few leading industrialists, he concluded, was "not only beneficial but essential to the future of the race." Those most fit would bring order and efficiency out of the chaos of rapid industrialization. Carnegie's defense of the new economic order in his article and in a book, *Triumphant Democracy* (1886), found as many supporters as Bellamy's *Looking Backward.* Partly this was because Carnegie insisted that the rich were obligated to spend some of their wealth to benefit their "poorer brethren." Carnegie built hundreds of libraries, most still operating in large and small towns throughout the United States. In later years, the philanthropist turned his attentions to other projects, including world peace.

Carnegie's ideas about wealth were drawn from an ideology known as social Darwinism, based on the work of Charles Darwin, whose famous *Origin of Species* was published in 1859. Darwin had concluded that plant and animal species had evolved through a process of natural selection. In the struggle for existence, some species managed to adapt to their environment and survived. Others failed to adapt and perished. Herbert Spencer, an English social philosopher, adopted these notions of the "survival of the fittest" and applied them to human society. Progress, he said, resulted from relentless competition in which the weak failed and were eliminated while the strong climbed to the top. He believed that "the whole effort of nature is to get rid of such as are unfit, to clear the world of them, and make room for better."

When Spencer visited the United States in 1882, leading men of business, science, religion, and politics thronged to honor him with a lavish banquet at Delmonico's restaurant in New York City. Here was the man whose theories justified their amassed fortunes because they were men of "superior ability, foresight, and adaptability." Spencer warned against any interference in the economic world by tampering with the natural laws of selection. The select at the dinner heaped their praise on Spencer as founder of not only a new sociology but also a new religion.

Spencer's American followers, like Carnegie and William Graham Sumner, a professor of political economy at Yale, familiarized the American public with the basic ideas of social Darwinism. They emphasized that poverty was the inevitable consequence of the struggle for existence and that attempts to end it were pointless, if not immoral. Although Sumner's emotional hero was the middle-class "forgotten man" like his father, his writings defended the material accumulations of the wealthy. To take power or money away from millionaires, Sumner scoffed, was "like

The luxury of a fashionable home full of ornate fine art was accessible to anyone who worked hard, according to advocates of the Gospel of Wealth and social Darwinism. Successful families like the Vanderbilts, they said, represented humanity's "fittest" element. Contrast this opulent scene with those of the middle- and lower-class families pictured in Chapters 16–18.

killing off our generals in war." It was "absurd," he wrote, to pass laws permitting society's "worst members" to survive or to "sit down with a slate and pencil to plan out a new social world."

The scientific vocabulary of social Darwinism injected scientific rationality into what often seemed a baffling economic order. Underlying laws of political economy, like the laws governing the natural world, Spencer and Sumner argued, dictated all economic affairs. Social Darwinists also believed in the superiority of the Anglo-Saxon race, which they maintained had reached the highest stage of evolution. Their theories were used to justify race supremacy and imperialism as well as the monopolistic efforts of American businessmen. Railroad magnate James J. Hill said that the absorption of smaller railroads by larger ones was the industrial analogy of the victory in nature of the fit over the unfit. John D. Rockefeller, Jr., told a YMCA class in Cleveland that "the growth of a large business is merely a survival of the fittest." Like the growth of a beautiful rose, "the early buds which grow up around it" must be sacrificed. This was, he said, "merely the working out of a law of nature and a law of God."

Others questioned this rosy outlook. Brooks Adams, brother of Henry, wrote that social philosophers like Spencer and Sumner were "hired by the comfortable classes to prove that everything was all right." Fading aristocratic families like the Adamses, who were being displaced by a new industrial elite, may have felt a touch of envy and loss of status. They succeeded, however, in suggesting that social change was not as closed as the social Darwinists claimed.

Reform Darwinism and Pragmatism

A number of intellectual reformers directly challenged the gloomy social Darwinian notion that nothing could be done to alleviate poverty and injustice. With roots in antebellum abolitionism, women's rights, and other crusades for social justice, men like Wendell Phillips, Frederick Douglass, and Franklin Sanborn and women like Elizabeth Cady Stanton and Susan B. Anthony transferred their reform fervor to postbellum issues. Sanborn, for example, an Emersonian transcendentalist, founded the American Social Science Association in 1865 to "treat wisely the great social problems of the day." As the Massachusetts inspector of charities in the 1880s, he earned a reputation as the "leading social worker of his day."

A new group of reformers, however, went beyond charity work to suggest both specific social remedies and a professionalized body of social scientific research to support them. Henry George, who was not a social scientist, nevertheless observed that wherever the highest degree of "material progress" had been realized, "we find the deepest poverty." George's book, *Progress and Poverty* (1879), was an early statement of the contradictions of American life. With Bellamy's *Looking Backward,* it was the most influential book of the age, selling 2 million copies by 1905. George admitted that economic growth had produced wonders but pointed out the social costs and the loss of Christian values. His remedy was to break up landholding monopolists who profited from the increasing value of their land and rents they collected from those who actually did the work. He proposed a "single tax" on the unearned increases in land value received by landlords. In 1886, on a United Labor party ticket supported by workers, clergymen, and middle-class reformers, George ran well but unsuccessfully for mayor of New York City.

Henry George's solution may seem overly simple, but his religious tone and optimistic faith in the capacity of humans to effect change appealed to many middle-class intellectuals. Some went beyond George to develop social scientific models that justified reform energy rather than inaction. A sociologist, Lester Frank Ward, and an economist, Richard T. Ely, both found examples of cooperation in nature and demonstrated that competition and laissez-faire had proved both wasteful and inhumane. These reform Darwinists urged instead an economic order marked by caring cooperation and social regulation.

Two pragmatists, John Dewey and William James, established a philosophical foundation for reform. James, a professor at Harvard, argued that while environment was important, so was human will. People could influence the course of human events. "What is the 'cash value' of a thought, idea, or belief?" James asked. What was its result? "The ultimate test for us of what a truth means," he suggested, was in the consequences of a particular idea, in "the conduct it dictates." He made it clear that the expression of human sympathies and the aversion to both economic and international war was moral conduct with the most ethical consequences.

James and young social scientists like Ward and Ely gathered statistics documenting social wrongs and rejected the social determinism of Spencer and Sumner. They argued that the application of intelligence and human will could change the "survival of the fittest" into the "fitting of as many as possible to survive." Their position encouraged educators, economists, and reformers of every stripe, giving them an intellectual justification to struggle against the misery and inequalities of wealth found in many sectors of their society.

Settlements and Social Gospel

Jane Addams understood the gap between progress and poverty. She saw it in the misery in the streets of Chicago in the winter of 1893. For some time she had been aware that life in big cities for working-class families was bitter and hard. "The stream of laboring people goes past you," she wrote, and "your heart sinks with a sudden sense of futility." Born in a rural community in Illinois, Addams founded Hull House in Chicago in 1889 "to aid in the solution of the social and industrial problems which are engendered by the modern conditions of life in a great city."

Vida Scudder, too, "felt the agitating and painful vibrations" of the depression. This young professor of literature at Wellesley College returned from study at Oxford "kindled with the flame of social passion." Like Addams, Scudder was resolved to do something to alleviate the suffering of the poor. She and six other Smith College graduates formed an organization of college women in 1889 to work in settlement houses.

Like Addams and Scudder, other middle-class activists worried about social conditions, particularly the degradation of life and labor in America's cities, factories, and farms. They were mostly professionals—lawyers, ministers, teachers, journalists, and academic social scientists. Influenced by European social prophets like Karl Marx, Leo Tolstoy, and Victor Hugo and by Americans such as Emerson, Whitman, George, and Bellamy, most turned to the ethical teachings of Jesus for inspiration in solving social problems.

The message they began to preach in the 1890s was highly idealistic, ethical, and Christian. They preferred a society marked by cooperation rather than competition, where self-sacrifice rather than self-interest held sway and, as they liked to say, where people were guided by the "golden rule rather than the rule of gold." Like Frances Willard, they meant to apply the ethics of Jesus to industrial and urban life in order to bring about the kingdom of heaven on earth. Some preferred to put their goals in more secular terms; they spoke of radically transforming American society. Most, however, worked within existing institutions. As middle-class intellectuals, they tended to stress an educational approach to problems. But they were also practical, involving themselves in an effort to make immediate, tangible improvements by running for public office, crusading for legislation, mediating labor disputes, and living in poor neighborhoods.

The settlement house movement typified the blend of idealism and practicality characteristic of middle-class reformers in the 1890s. Addams opened Hull House, and Scudder started Denison House in Boston. A short time later, on New York's Lower East Side, Lillian Wald opened her "house on Henry Street." The primary purpose of the set-

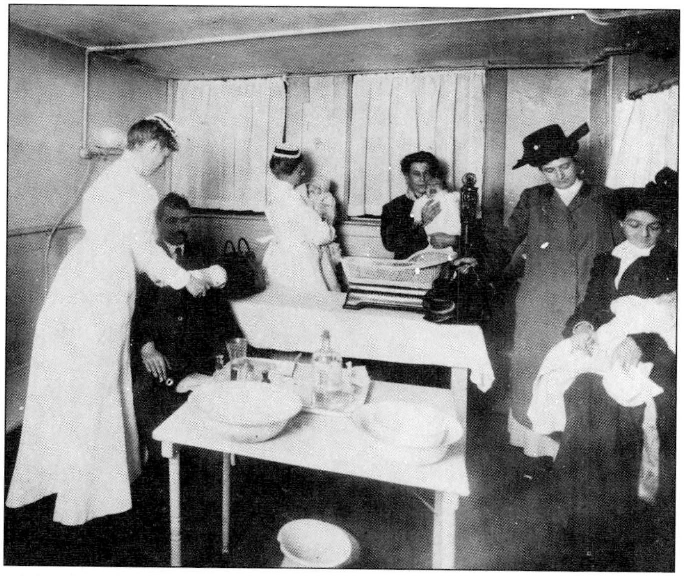

Many of the settlement houses included public health clinics, like this one at Vida Scudder's Denison House in Boston. Settlement house work, Scudder wrote, fulfilled "a biting curiosity about the way the Other Half lived, and a strange hunger for fellowship with them."

tlement houses was to help immigrant families, especially women, adapt Old World rural styles of childbearing and child care, housekeeping, and cooking to the realities of urban living in America. This meant launching day nurseries, kindergartens, boarding rooms for working women, and classes in sewing, cooking, nutrition, health care, and English. The settlements also frequently organized sports clubs and coffeehouses for young people as a way of keeping them out of the saloons.

A second purpose of the settlement house movement was to provide college-educated women with meaningful work at a time when they faced professional barriers and to allow them to preserve the strong feelings of sisterhood they had experienced in college. Settlement house workers, Scudder wrote, were like the "early Christians" in their renunciation of worldly goods and dedication to a life of service. Living in a settlement was in many ways an extension of woman's traditional role as nurturer of the weak. A third goal was to gather data exposing social misery in order to spur legislative action, such as developing city building codes for tenements, abolishing child labor, and improving safety in factories. Hull House, Addams said, was intended in part "to investigate and improve the conditions in the industrial districts of Chicago."

The settlement house movement, with its dual emphasis on the scientific gathering of facts and spiritual commitment, nourished the new academic study of sociology, first taught in divinity schools. Many organizations were founded to blend Christian belief and academic study in an attempt to change society. One was the American Institute of Christian Sociology, founded in 1893 by Josiah Strong, a Congregational minister, and economist Richard T. Ely. Similar organizations were the Christian Social Union, the Church Association for the Advancement of the Interests of Labor, and the Society of Christian Socialists.

These organizations viewed the purpose of religion as collective redemption rather than individual salvation, as exhorted by Dwight Moody in a wave of urban revivals in the 1870s. The revivals appealed to lower-class rural folk who were either drawn to the city by expectant opportunities or pushed there by economic ruin. Supported by businessmen who felt that religion would make workers and immigrants more docile, revivalists battled sin through individual conversion. The revivals helped nearly to double Protestant church membership in the last two decades of the century. Although some urban workers drifted into secular faiths like socialism, most remained conventionally religious.

In the 1890s, many Protestant ministers immersed themselves in the Social Gospel movement, which tied salvation to social betterment. Like the settlement house workers, these religious leaders sought to make Christianity relevant to industrial and urban problems. In Columbus, Ohio, Congregational minister Washington Gladden advocated collective bargaining and various forms of corporate profit sharing in books such as *Working Men and Their Employers, Social Salvation,* and *Applied Christianity.* A young Baptist minister in the notorious Hell's Kitchen area of New York City, Walter Rauschenbusch, raised an even louder voice. Often called on to conduct funeral services for children killed by the airless, diseased tenements and sweatshops, Rauschenbusch unleashed scathing attacks on the selfishness of capitalism and church ignorance of socioeconomic issues. His progressive ideas for social justice and a welfare state were later published in two landmark Social Gospel books, *Christianity and the Social Crisis* (1907) and *Christianizing the Social Order* (1912).

Perhaps the most influential book promoting social Christianity was a best-selling novel, *In His Steps,* published in 1897 by Charles Sheldon. *In His Steps* portrayed the dramatic transformations in business relations, tenement life, and urban politics made possible by the work of a few community leaders who resolved to base all their actions on a single question: "What would Jesus do?" For a minister, this meant seeking to "bridge the chasm between the church and labor." For the idle rich, it meant settlement house work and reforming prostitutes. For landlords and factory owners, it meant taking action to improve living and working conditions for tenants and laborers. Although streaked with naive sentimentality characteristic of much of the Social Gospel, Sheldon's novel prepared thousands of influential middle-class Americans for progressive civic leadership after the turn of the century.

Reforming the City

The crucial event in *In His Steps* was a city election pitting moral middle-class reformers against seedy saloon interests and corrupt urban political machines. No late-nineteenth-century institution needed reforming as much as urban government. The president of Cornell University described American city governments as "the worst in Christendom—the most expensive, the most inefficient, and the most corrupt." A Philadelphia committee found "inefficiency, waste, badly paved and filthy streets, unwholesome and offensive water, and slovenly and costly management" to have been the rule for years. New York and Chicago were even worse.

Rapid urban growth overburdened city leaders. Population increase and industrial expansion created new demands for service. Flush toilets, thirsty horses pulling street railways, and industrial users of water, for example, all exhausted the capacity of municipal waterworks built for an earlier age. As city governments struggled to respond to new needs, they raised taxes and incurred vast debts. This combination of rapid growth, indebtedness, and poor services, coupled with the influx of new immigrants, prepared fertile ground for graft and "bossism."

The rise of the boss was directly connected to the growth of the city. As immigrant voters appeared, traditional native-born ruling groups left city government for business, where more money and status beckoned. Into the resulting power vacuum stepped the boss. In an age of urban expansion, bosses dispensed patronage jobs in return for votes and contributions to the party machine. They awarded street railway, gas line, and other utility franchises and construction contracts to local businesses in return for kickbacks and other favors. They also passed on tips to friendly real estate men about the location of projected city improvements. Worse yet, the bosses received favors from the owners of saloons, brothels, and gambling clubs in return for their

New York City's William "Boss" Tweed (the heavyset man to the left) was head of the corrupt Tammany ring, which typified bossism in its cynical disregard for morality and truth. In Thomas Nast's famous cartoon "Who Stole the People's Money?" the answer is "'Twas Him."

help with police protection, bail, and influence with the courts. These institutions, however unsavory we might think them today, were vital to the urban economy and played an important role in easing the immigrants' way into American life. For many young women, the brothel was a means of economic survival. For men, the saloon was the center of social life, as well as a place for cheap meals and information about work and aid to his family.

Bossism deeply offended middle-class urban reformers, who were unkindly dubbed "goo-goos" for their insistence on purity and good government. They opposed not only graft and vice but also the perversion of democracy by the exploitation of ignorant immigrants. As one explained, the immigrants "follow blindly leaders of their own race, are not moved by discussion, and exercise no judgment of their own." Indeed, he concluded, they were "not fit for the suffrage."

The programs of urban reformers were similar in most cities. They not only worked for the "Americanization" of immigrants in public schools (and opposed parochial schooling) but also formed clubs or voters' leagues to discuss the failings of municipal government. They delighted in making spectacular exposures of electoral irregularities and large-scale graft. These discoveries led to strident calls for ousting the mayor, often an Irish Catholic, and replacing him with an Anglo-Saxon Protestant reform candidate.

Political considerations pervaded every reform issue. Many Anglo-Saxon men favored prohibition partly to remove ethnic saloon owners from politics and supported woman suffrage in part to gain a middle-class political advantage against the predominantly male immigrant community. Most urban reformers could barely hide their distaste for the "city proletariat mob," as one put it. They proposed to replace the bosses with expert city managers, who would bring honest professionalism to city government. They hoped to make government less costly and thereby lower taxes. One effect of their emphasis on cost efficiency was to cut services to the poor. Another was to disenfranchise working-class and ethnic groups, whose political participation depended on the old ward-boss system.

Not all urban reformers were elitist managerial types. Samuel Jones, for example, both opposed the boss system and had a passionate commitment to democratic political participation by the urban immigrant masses. An immigrant himself, Jones was a self-made man in the rags-to-riches mold. Beginning in poverty in the oil fields of Pennsylvania, he worked his way up to the ownership of several oil fields and a factory in Toledo, Ohio. Once successful, however, Jones espoused a different ethic from Carnegie's "Gospel of Wealth." He was, he said, a "Golden Rule man," converted by a combination of firsthand contact with the "piteous appeals" of people put out of work by the depression and by his reading of Emerson, Whitman, Tolstoy, and the New Testament.

In 1894, Jones resolved "to apply the Golden Rule as a rule of conduct" in his factory. He instituted an eight-hour day for his employees, a $2 minimum wage per day (50 to 75 cents higher than the Toledo average for ten hours), a cooperative insurance program, and an annual 5 percent Christmas dividend. He hired ex-criminals and outcasts that no one else would employ and plastered the Golden Rule all over his factory walls. Anticipating various twentieth-century industrial reforms, Jones created a company cafeteria, where he offered a hot lunch for 15 cents, a Golden Rule park for workers and their families, employee music groups, and a Golden Rule Hall, where he regularly invited both moderate and radical visionaries to speak.

In 1897, declaring that "after three years of a test I am pleased to say the Golden Rule works," Jones decided to extend his notions of cooperation and brotherhood to city government, much like Hazen Pingree had been doing in nearby Detroit. Running as a maverick Republican, Jones was elected to an unprecedented four terms as mayor of Toledo. In office, he advocated municipal ownership of natural gas, street railways, and other utilities; public works jobs and housing for the unemployed; more civic parks and playgrounds; and free municipal baths, pools, skating rinks, sleigh rides, vocational education, and kindergartens.

Few of these reforms were implemented, yet Jones's unorthodox ideas and behavior incurred the wrath of nearly every prominent citizen in Toledo. As a pacifist, he did not believe in violence or coercion of any kind. Therefore, he took away policemen's side arms and heavy clubs. When he sat as judge in police court, he regularly dismissed most cases of petty theft and drunkenness brought before him, charging that the accused were victims of an unjust social order and that only the poor went to jail for such crimes. He refused to advocate closing the saloons or brothels, and when prostitutes were brought before him, he usually dismissed them after fining every man in the room 10 cents—and himself a dollar—for permitting prostitution to exist. The crime rate in Toledo, a notoriously sinful city, decreased during his tenure, and Jones was adored by the plain people. When he died in 1904, nearly 55,000 people, "tears streaming down their faces," filed past his coffin.

The young Jane Addams was one of the college-educated women who chose to remain unmarried and pursue a career as an "urban housekeeper" and social reformer, serving immigrant families in the Chicago neighborhood near her Hull House.

The Struggle for Woman Suffrage

Women served, in Jane Addams's phrase, as "urban housekeepers" in the settlement house and good government movements, which reflected the tension many women felt between their public and private lives, between their obligations to self, family, and society. This tension was not usually expressed openly. A few women writers, however, began to vent the frustrations and restraints of middle-class domestic life. Kate Chopin's novel *The Awakening* (1899) portrayed a young woman who, in awakening to her own sexuality and life's possibilities beyond being a "mother-woman," defied conventional expectations of woman's role. Her sexual affair and eventual suicide prompted a St. Louis newspaper to say of the novel that it was "too strong drink for moral babes and should be labeled 'poison.'"

Some middle-class women, Addams and Scudder, for example, avoided marriage altogether, preferring the supportive relationships found in the female settlement house community. "Married life looks to me . . . terribly impoverished for women," a Smith College graduate observed, declaring that "most of my deeper friendships have been with women." A few women boldly advocated free love or, less openly, formed lesbian relationships. Although most preferred traditional marriages and chose not to work outside the home, the generation of women that came of age in the 1890s married less—and later—than any other in American history.

One way women reconciled the conflicting pressures between their private and public lives, as well as deflected male criticism, was to see their work as maternal. Addams called Hull House the "great mother breast of our common humanity." Frances Willard told Susan B. Anthony in 1898 that "government is only housekeeping on the broadest scale," a job men had botched, thus requiring women's saving participation. One of the leading female organizers of coal workers was "Mother" Jones, and the fiery feminist anarchist Emma Goldman titled her monthly journal *Mother Earth.* By using maternal, nurturant language to describe their work, women furthered the very arguments used against them. Many, of course, remained economically dependent on men, and all women still lacked the essential rights of citizenship. How could they be municipal housekeepers if they could not yet even vote?

In the years after the Seneca Falls Convention in 1848, women's civil and political rights advanced very slowly. Although in several western states women received the right to vote in municipal and school board elections, only the territory of Wyoming, in 1869, had granted full political equality before 1890. Colorado, Utah, and Idaho enfranchised women in the 1890s, but no other states granted suffrage until 1910. This slow pace was in part the result of an antisuffrage movement led by an odd combination of ministers, saloon interests, and men threatened in various ways by women's voting rights. "Equal suffrage," said a Texas senator, "is a repudiation of manhood."

In the 1890s, leading suffragists reappraised the situation. The two wings of the women's rights movement, split since 1869, combined in 1890 as the National American Woman Suffrage Association (NAWSA). Although Elizabeth Cady Stanton and Susan B. Anthony continued to head the association, they were both in their seventies, and effective leadership soon passed to younger, more moderate women. The new leaders concentrated on the single issue of the vote rather than dividing their energies among the many causes Stanton and Anthony had espoused. Moderate leaders were also embarrassed by Stanton's *Woman's Bible* (1895), a devastating attack on the religious argument against woman suffrage. At the NAWSA convention in 1896, despite the pleas of Anthony not to "sit in judgment" on her good friend, a resolution renouncing any connection with Stanton's book passed by a vote of 53 to 41.

Changing leadership meant a shift from principled to expedient arguments for the suffrage. Since 1848, suffragists had made their argument primarily from principle, citing, as Stanton argued at a congressional hearing in 1892, "our republican idea, individual citizenship." But Stanton's leadership was on the wane, and the younger generation shifted to three expedient arguments. The first was that women needed to vote to pass self-protection laws that would guard them against rapists, state age-of-consent laws, and unsafe industrial work. The second argument, Addams's notion of urban housekeeping, pointed out that political enfranchisement would further women's role in cleaning up morals, tenements, saloons, factories, and corrupt politics.

The third expedient argument reflected urban middle-class reformers' prejudice against non-Protestant newcomers to the city. As immigrant men arrived in America, local machine bosses saw to it that they would be able to vote. Suffragists argued that educated, native-born American women should be given the vote to counteract the undesirable influence of ignorant, illiterate, and immoral male immigrants. In a speech in Iowa in 1894, Carrie Chapman Catt, who would succeed Anthony as president of NAWSA in 1900, argued that the "Government is menaced with great danger . . . in the votes possessed by the males in the slums of the cities," a danger that could be averted only by cutting off that vote and giving it instead to women. In the new century, under the leadership of women like Catt, suffrage would finally be secured.

The Pivotal 1890s

For years, many Americans have mistakenly called the last decade of the nineteenth century the "gay nineties." This phrase suggests mustached baseball players and sporty Gibson girls, the glitter of newly lighted electric streetcars and shop windows, and the opulent dinners of rich entrepreneurs. The 1890s was, indeed, a decade of sports and leisure, the electrification of the city, and the enormous wealth of the few. But for many more Americans it was also a decade of dark tenement misery, grinding work or desperate unemployment, and poverty. As we have seen in Chapters 17 and 18, the early 1890s were marked by Populism and protesting farmers; Wounded Knee and the "second great removal" of Native Americans; lynchings, disfranchisement, and the "nadir of black life"; and the "new immigration," a changing workplace, and the devastating defeats of workers at Coeur d'Alene, Homestead, and Pullman.

The 1890s, far from gay, were years of contrasts and crises. The obvious contrast, as Bellamy had anticipated, was between the rich and the poor. As the Populist Omaha platform put it, "We breed two great classes—paupers and millionaires." Supreme Court justice John Harlan saw a "deep feeling of unrest" everywhere among people worrying that the nation was in "real danger from . . . the slavery that would result from aggregations of capital in the hands of a few." And Populist "Sockless" Jerry Simpson bluntly called the crisis a struggle between two sides: "the robbers and the robbed." On the one side, Simpson saw "the allied hosts of monopolies, the money power, great trusts, and railroad corporations, who seek the enactment of laws to benefit them and impoverish the people." On the other, he put

The contrasts between rich and poor and the threat of social upheaval are dramatically illustrated in this turn-of-the-century work, called "From the Depths."

those "who produce wealth and bear the burdens of taxation. Between these two there is no middle ground."

Simpson was wrong about the absence of a middle ground, but the gap was indeed huge between the angry Kansas orator Mary E. Lease, who in 1890 said, "What you farmers need to do is to raise less corn, and more Hell," and the wealthy Indianapolis woman who told her husband, "I'm going to Europe and spend my money before these crazy people take it." The pivotal nature of the 1890s hinged on this feeling of polarizing unrest and upheaval as the nation underwent the traumas of change. America was transforming itself from a rural to an urban society and experiencing the pressures of rapid industrialization and accompanying changes in the workplace and on farms. Moreover, the new immigration from Europe and the northward, westward, and cityward internal migrations of blacks and farmers added to the "great danger" against which Carrie Catt warned. The depression of 1893 worsened the gaps between rich and poor and accelerated the demands for reform. Government bureaucratic structures began to adapt to the needs of governing a complex specialized society, and Congress slowly shifted away from laissez-faire in order to confront national problems.

Republican Legislation in the Early 1890s

Harrison's election in 1888 was accompanied by Republican control of both houses of Congress. Though by no means reformers, the Republicans moved forward in the first six months of 1890 with legislation in five areas: pensions for Civil War veterans and their dependents, trusts, the tariff, the money question, and rights for blacks. The Dependent Pensions Act, providing generous support of $160 million a year for Union veterans and their dependents, sailed through Congress.

The Sherman Anti-Trust Act also passed easily, with only one nay vote. The bill declared illegal "every contract, combination . . . or conspiracy in restraint of trade or commerce." Although the bill was vague and not really intended to break up large corporations, the Sherman Act was an initial attempt to restrain large business combinations. But in *United States* v. *E. C. Knight* (1895) the Supreme Court ruled that the American Sugar Refining Company, which controlled more than 90 percent of the nation's sugar-refining capacity, was not in violation of the Sherman Act, which the Court said applied only to commerce, not manufacturing.

A tariff bill introduced in 1890 by Ohio Republican William McKinley generated more controversy. McKinley's bill was an attempt to make good the Republican stance on protection by raising tariff rates to higher levels than ever before. Despite heated opposition from agrarian interests, whose products were generally not protected, the bill passed the House. In the Senate, however, nearly 500 amendments extended debates until Republican leaders succeeded in modifying the bill to please some farmers, and the McKinley Tariff scraped by, 33 to 27.

Silver was even trickier. Recognizing the appeal of free silver to agrarian debtors and the new Populist party, Republican leaders feared their party might be destroyed by the issue. Senator

Major Legislative Activity of the Gilded Age

In the following table notice the kinds of issues dealt with at the different levels: mostly money, tariff, immigration, and civil service legislation at the national level and "hot button" social and value issues in the states and localities.

	National
1871	Civil Service Commission created
1873	Coinage Act demonetizes silver
	"Salary Grab" Act (increased salaries of Congress and top federal officials) partly repealed
1875	Specie Resumption Act retires greenback dollars
1878	Bland-Allison Act permits partial coining of silver
1882	Chinese Exclusion Act
	Federal Immigration Law restricts certain categories of immigrants and requires head tax of all immigrants
1883	Standard time (four time zones) established for the entire country
	Pendleton Civil Service Act
1887	Interstate Commerce Act sets up Interstate Commerce Commission
	Dawes Act divides Indian tribal lands into individual allotments
1890	Dependent Pension Act grants pensions to Union army veterans
	Sherman Anti-Trust Act
	Sherman Silver Purchase Act has government buy more silver
	McKinley Tariff sets high protective rates
	Federal Elections Bill to protect black voting rights in South fails in Senate
	Blair bill to provide support for equal education defeated
1891	Immigration law gives federal government control of overseas immigration
1893	Sherman Silver Purchase Act repealed
1894	Wilson-Gorman Tariff lowers duties slightly
1900	Currency Act puts United States on gold standard
	State and Local
1850s–1880s	State and local laws intended to restrict or prohibit consumption of alcoholic beverages
1871	Illinois Railroad Act sets up railroad commission to fix rates and prohibit discrimination
1874	Railroad regulatory laws in Wisconsin and Iowa
1881	Kansas adopts statewide prohibition
1882	Iowa passes state prohibition amendment
1880s	Massachusetts, Connecticut, Rhode Island, Montana, Michigan, Ohio, and Missouri all pass local laws prohibiting consumption of alcohol
	Santa Fe ring dominates New Mexico politics and land grabbing
1889	New Jersey repeals a county-option prohibition law of 1888
	Laws in Wisconsin and Illinois mandate compulsory attendance of children at schools in which instruction is in English
	Kansas, Maine, Michigan, and Tennessee pass antitrust laws
1889–1890	Massachusetts debates bill on compulsory schooling in English
1889–1902	Eleven ex-Confederate states amend state constitutions and pass statutes restricting the voting rights of blacks
1890–1910	Eleven ex-Confederate states pass segregation laws
1891	Nebraska passes eight-hour workday law
1893	Colorado adopts woman suffrage
1894–1896	Woman suffrage referendums defeated in Kansas and California

Sherman proposed a compromise measure that momentarily satisfied almost everyone. The Sherman Silver Purchase Act ordered the treasury to buy 4.5 million ounces of silver monthly and to issue treasury notes for it. Silverites were pleased by the proposed increase in the money supply. Opponents felt they had averted the worst, free coinage of silver. The gold standard remained secure.

Republicans were also prepared to confront violations of the voting rights of southern blacks in 1890. President Harrison told the editor of the New York *Tribune,* "I feel very strong upon the question of a free ballot." Political considerations paralleled moral ones. Since 1877, the South had become a Democratic stronghold, where party victories could be traced to fraud and intimidation of black Republican voters. "To be a Republican . . . in the South," one Georgian noted, "is to be a foolish martyr." Republican legislation, then, would honor old commitments to the freedmen and improve party fortunes in the South. An elections bill, proposed by Massachusetts senator Henry Cabot Lodge, would protect voter registration and ensure fair elections by setting up mechanisms for investigating charges of bribery and fraud. A storm of disapproval from Democrats greeted the measure, which they labeled the "Force Bill." Cleveland called it a "dark blow at the freedom of the ballot," while the Mobile *Daily Register* claimed that it "would deluge the South in blood." Senate Democrats delayed action with a filibuster.

Meanwhile, Republicans worried that they could not pass both the elections bill and the McKinley Tariff, which was languishing in the Senate. Pennsylvania senator Matt Quay, who had skillfully directed Harrison's election in 1888, proposed that if the Democrats ceased their delaying tactics so that the tariff could come to a vote, the Republicans would agree to put off consideration of the elections bill. The ploy worked, marking the end of major party efforts to protect black voting rights in the South until the 1960s. In a second setback for black southerners, the Senate defeated a bill to provide federal aid to schools in the South, mostly black, that did not receive their fair share of local and state funds. These two failed measures were the last gasp of the Republican party's commitment to the idealistic principles of Reconstruction. "The plain truth is," said the New York *Herald,* "the North has got tired of the negro."

The legislative efforts of the summer of 1890, impressive by nineteenth-century standards, fell far short of solving the nation's problems. Trusts grew more rapidly after the Sherman Act than before. Union veterans were pleased by their pensions, but southerners were incensed that Confederate veterans were not covered. Others regarded the pension measure as extravagant and labeled the 51st Congress the "billion-dollar Congress." Despite efforts to please farmers, many still viewed tariff protection as a benefit primarily for eastern manufacturers. Farm prices continued to decline, and gold and silver advocates were only momentarily silenced. Black rights were put off to another time. Polarizing inequalities of wealth remained. Nor did Republican legislative activism lead the Republicans to a "permanent tenure of power," as party leaders had hoped. Voters abandoned the GOP in droves in the 1890 congressional elections, dropping the number of Republicans in the House from 168 to 88.

Two years later, Cleveland won a presidential rematch with Harrison. His inaugural address underlined the lesson he drew from Republican legislative activism in 1890. "The lessons of paternalism ought to be unlearned," he said, "and the better lesson taught that while the people should . . . support their government, its functions do not include the support of the people."

The Depression of 1893

Cleveland's philosophy of government soon faced a difficult test. No sooner had he taken office than began one of the worst depressions ever to grip the American economy, lasting from 1893 to 1897. The severity of the depression was heightened by the growth of a national economy and economic interdependence.

The depression started in Europe and spread to the United States as overseas buyers cut back on their purchases of American products. Shrinking markets abroad soon crippled American manufacturing. Moreover, many foreign investors, worried about the stability of American currency after passage of the Sherman Silver Purchase Act, dumped some $300 million of their securities in the United States. As gold left the country to pay for these securities, the nation's supply of money declined. At the same time, falling prices hurt farmers, many of whom discovered that it cost more to raise their crops and livestock than they could recover in the market. Workers fared no better, as wages fell faster than the price of food and rent.

The collapse in 1893 was also caused by serious overextensions of the economy at home, especially in railroad construction. Farmers, troubled by falling prices, planted more and more crops, hoping somehow that the market would pick up. As the realization of overextension spread, confidence faltered, then gave way to financial panic. When the stock market crashed early in 1893, investors frantically sold their shares, companies plunged into bankruptcy, and disaster spread. People rushed to exchange paper notes for gold, reducing gold reserves and confidence in the economy even further. Banks called in their loans, which by the end of the year led to 16,000 business bankruptcies and 500 bank failures.

The decrease in available capital and diminished buying power of rural and small-town Americans (still half the population) forced massive factory closings. Within a year, an estimated 3 million Americans, 20 percent of the work force, were unemployed. Suddenly people began to look fearfully at the presence of tramps wandering from city to city looking for work. "There are thousands of homeless and starving men in the streets," one young man reported from Chicago, indicating that he had seen "more misery in this last week than I ever saw in my life before."

As in Bellamy's coach image, the misery of the many was not shared by the few, which only increased discontent. While unemployed men foraged in garbage dumps for food, the wealthy gave lavish parties sometimes costing $100,000. At one

The depression of 1893 accentuated contrasts between rich and poor. While well-to-do children enjoyed the giant Ferris wheel and other midway attractions at the Chicago World's Columbian Exposition (*left*), slum children played in filthy streets nearby (*right*).

such affair, diners ate their meal while seated on horses; at another, many guests proudly proclaimed that they had spent over $10,000 on their dresses. While poor families shivered in poorly heated tenements, the very rich built million-dollar summer resorts at Newport, Rhode Island, or grand mansions on New York's Fifth Avenue and Chicago's Gold Coast. While Lithuanian immigrants walked or rode streetcars to Buffalo steel factories to work, wealthy men skimmed across lakes and oceans in huge pleasure yachts. J. P. Morgan owned three, one with a crew of 85 sailors.

Nowhere were these inequalities more apparent than in Chicago during the World's Columbian Exposition, which opened on May 1, 1893, five days before plummeting prices on the stock market began the depression. The Chicago World's Fair was designed, as President Cleveland said in an opening-day speech, to show off the "stupendous results of American enterprise." When he pushed an ivory telegraph key, he started electric current that unfurled flags, spouted water through gigantic fountains, lit 10,000 electric lights, and powered huge steam engines, 37 in one building alone. For six months, some 27 million visitors strolled around the White City designed by Daniel H. Burnham and admired its wide lagoons, white plaster buildings modeled on classical styles, and exhibit halls filled with inventions. Built at a cost of $31 million, the fair celebrated the marvelous mechanical accomplishments of American enterprise. Its elegant design stimulated a "City Beautiful" movement that made many cities more attractive and enjoyable for their residents.

But as well-to-do fairgoers sipped pink champagne, men, women, and children in the immigrant wards of Chicago less than a mile away drank contaminated water, crowded into packed tenements, and looked in vain for jobs. The area around Jane Addams's Hull House was especially disreputable, with saloons, gambling halls, brothels, and pawnshops dotting the neighborhood. "If Christ came to Chicago," a British journalist, W. T. Stead, wrote in a book of that title in 1894, this would be "one of the last precincts into which we should care to take Him." Stead's book showed readers the "ugly sight" of corruption, poverty, and wasted lives in a city with 200 millionaires and 200,000 unemployed men.

Despite the magnitude of despair during the depression, national politicians and leaders were reluctant to respond. Only mass demonstrations forced city authorities to provide soup kitchens and places for the homeless to sleep. When an army of unemployed led by Jacob Coxey marched into Washington in the spring of 1894 to press for some form of public work relief, its leaders were arrested for stepping on the grass of the Capitol. Cleveland's reputation for callous disregard for citizens suffering from the depression worsened later that summer when he sent federal troops to Chicago to crush the Pullman strike.

The president focused his efforts on tariff reform and repeal of the Silver Purchase Act, which he blamed for the depression. Although repeal was ultimately a necessary measure to establish business confidence, in the short run all Cleveland accomplished was to worsen the financial crisis, focus attention further on silver as a panacea, and hurt his conservative wing of the Democratic party. With workers, farmers, and wealthy silver miners alienated, in the midterm elections of 1894 voters abandoned the Democrats in droves, giving both Populists and Republicans high hopes for electoral success in 1896.

The Crucial Election of 1896

The campaign of 1896, waged during the continuing depression, was one of the most critical in American history. Known as the "battle of the standards," the election was fought in part over the ratio of gold and silver as the standard national currency. Although Cleveland was in disgrace for ignoring depression woes, few leaders in either major party thought the federal government was responsible for alleviating the suffering of the people. But unskilled Slavic workers tending Pennsylvania blast furnaces, unemployed Polish meatpackers in Chicago, railway firemen in Terre Haute, Italian immigrant women in New Haven tenements, and desperate white and black tenant farmers in Georgia all wondered where relief might be found. Would either major party respond to the pressing human needs of the depression? Would the People's party succeed in setting a new national agenda for politics? Or would the established order prevail? These questions were raised and largely resolved in the election of 1896.

As the election approached, Populist leaders focused on the issues of silver and whether to fuse with one of the major parties by agreeing on a joint ticket. But fusion required abandoning much of the Populist platform, thus weakening the party's distinctive character. Under the influence of silver mine owners, many Populists became convinced that the hope of the party lay in a single-issue commitment to the free and unlimited coinage of silver at the ratio of 16 to 1. James Weaver expected both parties to nominate gold candidates, which would send disappointed silverites to the Populist standard.

In the throes of the depression in the mid-1890s, silver took on enormous importance as the symbol of the many grievances of downtrodden Americans. Popular literature captured the rural, moral dimensions of the silver movement. Although William Harvey's highly popular *Coin's Financial School* (1894) was more timely, L. Frank Baum's *Wonderful Wizard of Oz* (1900), written as a "modernized fairy tale," has had an enduring claim on the hearts of all Americans. Read carefully, one sees in Baum's classic the defense of rural values (Kansas, Auntie Em, the uneducated but wise scarecrow, and the goodhearted tin woodsman) and Populist policies (the wicked witch of the East and the magical silver shoes in harmony with the yellow brick road, in "Oz"—ounces).

The Republicans, holding their convention first, nominated William McKinley on the first ballot. A congressman from 1877 to 1891 and twice governor of Ohio, McKinley was happily identified with the high protective tariff that bore his name. Republicans were quick to cite the familiar argument that prosperity depended on the gold standard and protection and blamed the depression on Cleveland's attempt to lower the tariff. The excitement of the Democratic convention in

William Jennings Bryan, surprise nominee at the 1896 Democratic Convention, was a vigorous proponent of the "cause of humanity." His surprise nomination threw the country into a frenzy of fear and the Populist party into a fatal decision over "fusion."

July contrasted with the staid, smoothly organized Republican one, a pattern to be repeated throughout most of the twentieth century. Cleveland had already been repudiated by his party, as state after state elected convention delegates pledged to silver. Gold Democrats, however, had enough power left to wage a close battle for the platform plank on money.

The surprise nominee of the convention was an ardent young silverite, William Jennings Bryan, a 36-year-old congressman from Nebraska. Few saw him as presidential material, but as a member of the Resolutions Committee, Bryan arranged to give the closing argument for a silver plank himself. His dramatic speech swept the convention for silver and ensured his own nomination. "I come to speak to you," Bryan cried out, "in defense of a cause as holy as the cause of liberty—the cause of humanity." At the conclusion of what was to become one of the most famous political speeches in American history, Bryan attacked the "goldbugs" and promised,

> Having behind us the producing masses of this nation. . . and toilers everywhere, we will answer their demand for a gold standard by saying to them: "You shall not press down upon the brow of labor this crown of thorns, you shall not crucify mankind upon a cross of gold."

As he spoke, Bryan stretched out his arms as if on a cross, and the convention exploded with applause.

Populist strategy lay in shambles with the nomination of a Democratic silver candidate. Some party leaders favored fusion with the entire Democratic ticket. Antifusionists were outraged, in part because the Democratic vice-presidential candidate, Arthur Sewall, was an East Coast banker and a hard-money man. An unwise compromise was achieved when the Populist convention nominated Bryan but instead of Sewall chose Populist Tom Watson of Georgia as his running mate. The existence of two silverite slates damaged Bryan's electoral hopes.

During the campaign, McKinley stayed at his home in Canton, Ohio, where some 750,000 admirers came to visit him, helped by low excursion rates offered by the railroads. Republican strategy featured an unprecedented effort to reach voters through a highly sophisticated mass-media campaign, heavily financed by such major corporations as Standard Oil and the railroads. Party leaders hired thousands of speakers to support McKinley and distributed over 200 million pamphlets to a voting population of 15 million. The literature, distributed in 14 languages, was designed to appeal to particular national, ethnic, regional, and occupational groups. To all these people, McKinley was advertised as the "advance agent of prosperity."

In William McKinley's 1896 campaign, he periodically spoke to visitors gathered at his home, flailing free silver and flaunting the flag. His landslide electoral victory represented Americans' endorsement of the Republicans as the party of prosperity, tariff protection, thriving factories, and the gold standard.

From his front porch in Canton, McKinley responded to Bryan's challenge by aiming his appeal not only at the business classes but also at unemployed workers, to whom he promised a "full dinner pail." He also spoke about the money issue, declaring that "our currency today is . . . as good as gold." Free silver, he maintained, would lead to inflation and more economic disaster. Recovery depended not on money but on tariff reform, which would stimulate American industry and provide jobs—"not open mints for the unlimited coinage of the silver of the world," he said, "but open mills for the full and unrestricted labor of American workingmen."

In sharp contrast to the Republican stay-at-home policy, Bryan took his case to the people. Three million people in 27 states heard him speak as he traveled over 18,000 miles, giving as many as 30 speeches a day. Bryan's message was simple. Prosperity would return with free coinage of silver. Government policies should attend to the needs of the producing classes rather than the vested interests that believed in the gold standard. "That policy is best for this country," Bryan proclaimed, "which brings prosperity first to those who toil." But his rhetoric favored rural toilers. "The great cities rest upon our broad and fertile prairies," he had said in the "Cross of Gold" speech. "Burn down your cities and leave our farms, and your cities will spring up again as if by magic; but destroy our farms and the grass will grow in the streets of every city in the country." Urban workers were little inspired by this rhetoric, nor were immigrants impressed by Bryan's prairie moralizing.

To influential easterners, the brash young Nebraskan represented a threat to social harmony. Theodore Roosevelt wrote that "this silver craze surpasses belief. Bryan's election would be a great calamity." A Brooklyn minister declared that the Democratic platform was "made in Hell." One newspaper editor said of Bryan that he was just like Nebraska's Platte River: "six inches deep and six miles wide at the mouth." Others branded him a "madman" and an "anarchist." The New York *Mail* wrote that "no wild-eyed and rattle-brained horde of the red flag ever proclaimed a fiercer defiance of law, precedent, order, and government."

With such intense interest in the election, it was predictable that voters would turn out in record numbers. In key states like Illinois, Indiana, and Ohio, 95 percent of those eligible to vote went to the polls. When the voting was over, McKinley had won 271 electoral votes to Bryan's 176. Millionaire Mark Hanna jubilantly wired McKinley: "God's in his heaven, all's right with the world." Bryan had been defeated by the largest popular majority since Grant trounced Greeley in 1872.

Although Bryan won over 6 million votes (47 percent of the total), more than any previous Democratic winner, he failed to carry the Midwest. Nor could he make large inroads into the votes of the urban middle-classes and industrial masses, who had little confidence that the Democrats could stimulate economic growth or cope with the problems of industrialism. McKinley's promise of a "full dinner pail" was more convincing than the untested formula for free silver. Northern laborers feared that inflation would leave them even poorer than they already were, since they believed that prices and rents would rise faster than their wages, and Catholic immigrants distrusted the Protestantism of the Populists. Farmers in the established Great Lakes states enjoyed prosperous years and felt less discontented than farmers in other regions. But chance also played a part in Bryan's defeat. Bad wheat harvests in India, Australia, and Argentina drove up grain prices in the world market. Many of the complaints of American farmers evaporated amid rising farm prices.

The New Shape of American Politics

The landslide Republican victory marked the end of the political stalemate that had characterized American politics since the end of the Civil War. Republicans lost their identification with the politics of piety and strengthened their image as the party of prosperity and national greatness, which gave them a party dominance that lasted until the 1930s. The Democrats, who would remain under Bryan's leadership until 1912, took on the mantle of populist moralism but were largely reduced to a sectional party, reflecting narrow southern views on money, race, and national power. The 1896 election demonstrated that the Northeast and the Great Lakes states had acquired so many immigrants that they now controlled the entire nation's political destiny. Populists, demoralized by fusion with a losing campaign, fell apart and disappeared. A despondent Populist, Ignatius Donnelly, asked: "Will the sun of triumph never rise? I fear not." His pessimism was premature, for within the next 20 years most Populist issues were taken over and adopted by politicians of the major parties.

Another result of the election of 1896 was a change in the pattern of political participation.

Political Campaign Artifacts

Historians recover the past, as we have seen, not only through the printed words in books, diaries, magazines, tax lists, and government documents but also through such visual records as paintings, photographs, and buildings. All material objects recovered from the past, in fact, help historians understand how people lived and what they valued and thought. The products of the human experience include everything from tools to toys, farm implements to furniture, and cooking pots to clothes. Historians have learned from archaeologists and anthropologists that every object, or artifact, no matter how trivial, tells something about people's lives. We call such objects material culture.

Bryan campaign artifacts.

McKinley campaign artifacts.

Consider, for example, how material culture can provide insight into the political life of the past. Political historians tend to examine party platforms, campaign speeches, public opinion, and congressional and public voting behavior. But the study of material artifacts, such as those generated by the campaign of 1896, can also reveal much about the values and issues of American political life. The fervor of that political contest led to the production of thousands of lapel studs, pins, and other articles intended to influence American voters to cast their ballot for either Bryan or McKinley. Cloth campaign ribbons, bandannas, shirts, teacups, and even McKinley soap dolls were produced. Items such as teacups, silver spoons, and pillows were designed for the women of the family, suggesting that even though they did not vote, party leaders and manufacturers believed that women influenced men's votes.

Shown here are examples of buttons, badges, and stickpins produced during the campaign of 1896. Study the artifacts supporting Bryan's candidacy. What do they show about the ideological aspects of the Democratic campaign? What issues are voters reminded of? In what way are the artifacts supporting McKinley similar to or different from the Democratic ones? Do you see any specific attempts to refute the free silver argument? How do Republican artifacts deal with the money question? Can you find any evidence of a specific appeal to different groups of Americans? If so, which ones? Again, make a comparison between these artifacts and the ones manufactured by the Demo-crats. What general statements might you make about the campaign on the basis of these material remains? What would the buttons, bumper stickers, and other objects of the 1992 presidential election tell future historians about the parties and issues of that political campaign?

The Presidential Election of 1896

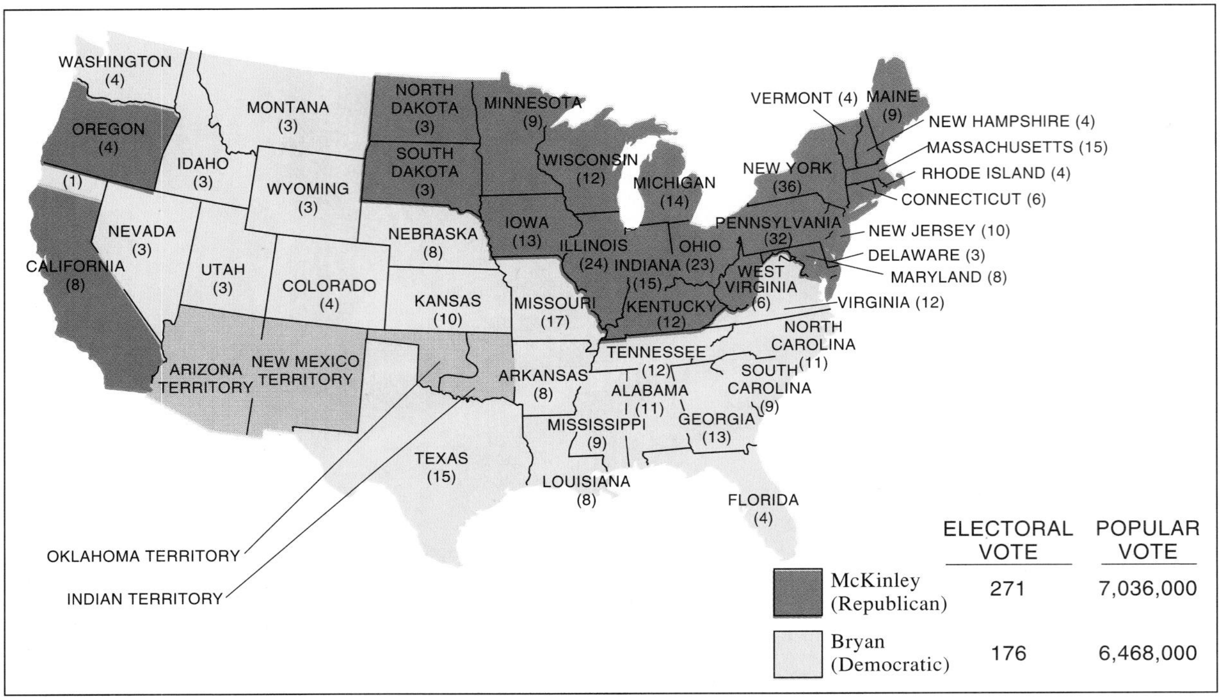

In his sweep of the densely populated urban Northeast and Midwest, McKinley beat Bryan by the largest popular vote margin since 1872. In his cabled congratulations, the first ever by a loser, Bryan, ever the "democrat," said: "We have submitted the issues to the American people and their will is law." Note that in this election California had only 8 electoral votes, fewer than the recently settled Midwestern states of Kansas or Iowa. Florida's four electoral votes were the fewest of any southern state.

Because the Republicans were so dominant, few states had vigorous two-party political battles. There seemed less and less reason to continue party activities aimed at bringing out large numbers of voters. Likewise, individual voters had less and less motivation to cast a ballot, especially since election results were so often a foregone conclusion. Many black voters in the South, moreover, were disfranchised, and middle-class good government reformers succeeded in reducing the high voter turnout achieved by urban party bosses. Thus the tremendous rate of political participation that had characterized the nineteenth century since the Jackson era gradually declined. In the twentieth century, political involvement among poorer Americans lessened considerably, a phenomenon unique among western industrial countries.

McKinley had promised that Republican rule meant prosperity, and as soon as he took office, the economy recovered. Discoveries of gold in the Yukon and the Alaskan Klondike increased the money supply, thus thwarting silver mania until the early 1930s. Industrial production returned to full capacity. In a tour of the Midwest in 1898, McKinley spoke to cheering crowds about the hopeful economic picture. "We have gone from industrial depression to industrial activity," he told citizens of Clinton, Iowa, who burst into enthusiastic applause.

McKinley's election marked not only the return of an era of economic health but also the emergence of the executive as the preeminent focus of the American political system. Just as McKinley's campaign set the pattern for the extravagant efforts to win office that have dominated modern times, his conduct as president foreshadowed the nature of the twentieth-century presidency. McKinley rejected traditional views of the president as the passive executor of laws, instead playing an active role in dealing with Congress and the press. His frequent trips away from Washington testified to his respect for public opinion. Some historians regard McKinley as the first modern president in his emphasis on the role of the chief executive in contributing to industrial growth and national power. As we shall see in Chapter 20, he began the transformation of the presidency into a potent force not only in domestic life but in world affairs as well.

CONCLUSION

Looking Forward

This chapter began with Edward Bellamy's imaginary look backward from the year 2000 at the grim economic realities and unresponsive politics of American life in the late nineteenth century. McKinley's triumph in 1896 indicated that in a decade marked by depression, Populist revolt, and cries for action to close the inequalities of wealth—represented by Bellamy's coach—the established order remained intact and politics remained as unresponsive as ever. Calls for change did not necessarily lead to change. But in the areas of personal action and the philosophical bases for social change, intellectual middle-class reformers like Edward Bellamy, Henry George, William James, Jane Addams, "Golden Rule" Jones, and many others were showing the way to progressive reforms in the new century. More Americans were able to look forward to the kind of cooperative, caring, and cleaner world envisioned in Bellamy's utopian novel.

As the year 1900 approached, people took a predictably intense interest in what the new century would be like. Henry Adams, still the pessimist, saw an ominous future, predicting the explosive and ultimately destructive energy of unrestrained industrial development, symbolized by the "dynamo" and other engines of American power. Such forces, he warned, would overwhelm the gentler, moral forces represented by art, woman, and religious symbols like the Virgin. But others were more optimistic, preferring to place their confidence in America's historic role as an exemplary nation, demonstrating to the world the moral superiority of its economic system, democratic institutions, and middle-class Protestant values. Surely the new century, most thought, would see not only the continued perfection of these values and institutions but also the spread of American influence throughout the world. Such confidence resulted in foreign expansion by the American people even before the old century had ended. We turn to that in the next chapter.

Recommended Reading

Politics in the Gilded Age

John Allswang, *Bosses, Machines, and Urban Voters* (1977); Sean Dennis Cashman, *America and the Gilded Age: From the Death of Lincoln to the Rise of Theodore Roosevelt* (1984); Harold U. Faulkner, *Politics, Reform and Expansion, 1890–1900* (1959); John A. Garraty, *The New Commonwealth, 1877–1890* (1968); Samuel P. Hays, *The Response to Industrialism, 1885–1914* (1957); Richard Jensen, *The Winning of the Midwest: Social and Political Conflict, 1888–1896* (1971); Morton Keller, *Affairs of State: Public Life in Late Nineteenth Century America* (1977); Paul Kleppner, *The Cross of*

Culture: A Social Analysis of Midwestern Politics, 1850–1900 (1970) and *The Third Electoral System, 1853–1892: Parties, Voters, and Political Cultures* (1979); H. Wayne Morgan, *From Hayes to McKinley: National Party Politics, 1877–1896* (1969); Nell I. Painter, *Standing at Armageddon in the United States, 1877–1919* (1987); William Riordon, *Plunkitt of Tammany Hall* (1963); Robert Wiebe, *The Search for Order, 1877–1920* (1967); R. Hal Williams, *Years of Decision: American Politics in the 1890s* (1978).

Middle-Class Reform and Reformers

Jane Addams, *Twenty Years at Hull House* (1910); Ruth Bordin, *Frances Willard: A Biography* (1986) and *Women and Temperance: The Quest for Power and Liberty, 1873–1900* (1981); Paul Boyer, *Urban Masses and Moral Order in America, 1820–1920* (1978); Mina Carson, *Settlement Folk: Social Thought and the American Settlement Movement, 1885–1930* (1990); Allen F. Davis, *American Heroine: The Life and Legend of Jane Addams* (1973) and *Spearheads for Reform: The Social Settlements and the Progressive Movement, 1890–1914* (1967); Robert Fogarty, *All Things New: American Communes and Utopian Movements, 1860–1914* (1990); Margaret Forster, *Significant Sisters: The Grassroots of Active Feminism* (1984); Peter J. Frederick, *Knights of the Golden Rule: The Intellectual as Christian Social Reformer in the 1890s* (1976); Richard Hofstadter, *Age of Reform: From Bryan to F.D.R.* (1955); Melvin G. Holli, *Reform in Detroit: Hazen S. Pingree and Urban Politics* (1969); Aileen Kraditor, *The Ideas of the Woman's Suffrage Movement, 1890–1920* (1965); Ralph Luker, *The Social Gospel in Black and White: American Racial Reform, 1885–1912* (1991); Arthur Mann, *Yankee Reformers in an Urban Age: Social Reform in Boston, 1880–1900* (1954); Daphne Pata, ed., *Looking Backward, 1988–1888: Essays on Edward Bellamy* (1988); John Sproat, *"The Best Men": Liberal Reformers in the Gilded Age* (1968); John L. Thomas, *Alternative America: Henry George, Edward Bellamy, Henry Demarest Lloyd and the Adversary Tradition* (1983); Ronald C. White and Charles Howard Hopkins, *The Social Gospel: Religion and Reform in Changing America* (1976).

Cultural Life, Thought, and Literature of the Late Nineteenth Century

Edward Bellamy, *Looking Backward* (1888); Burton J. Bledstein, *The Culture of Professionalism: The Middle Class and the Development of Higher Education in America* (1976); Mark C. Carnes and Clyde Griffen, eds., *Meanings for Manhood: Constructions of Masculinity in Victorian America* (1990); John Cawelti, *Apostles of the Self-made Man: Changing Concepts of Success in America* (1965); Kate Chopin, *The Awakening* (1899); Theodore Dreiser, *Sister Carrie* (1900); Peter Filene, *Him/Her/Self: Sex Roles in Modern America,* 2d ed. (1986); Richard Hofstadter, *Social Darwinism in American Thought* (1955); William Dean Howells, *A Hazard of New Fortunes* (1889) and *The Rise of Silas Lapham* (1885); Bruce Kuklick, *The Rise of American Philosophy: Cambridge, Massachusetts, 1860–1930* (1977); T. Jackson Lears, *No Place of Grace: Antimodernism and the Transformation of American Culture, 1880–1920* (1981); H. Wayne Morgan, *Unity and Culture: The United States, 1877–1890* (1971); Frank Norris, *The Octopus* (1901); Sheila Rothman, *Woman's Proper Place: A History of Changing Ideals and Practices, 1870 to the Present* (1978); Alan Trachtenberg, *The Incorporation of America: Culture and Society in the Gilded Age* (1982); Mark Twain and Charles D. Warner, *The Gilded Age* (1873); Irvin G. Wyllie, *The Self-made Man in America* (1954); Larzer Ziff, *The American 1890s: Life and Times of a Lost Generation* (1966).

Depression Politics, Populism and the Election of 1896

Gene Clanton, *Populism: The Humane Preference in America, 1890–1900* (1991); Robert F. Durden, *The Climax of Populism: The Election of 1896* (1965); Paul Glad, *McKinley, Bryan and the People (1964); Lawrence Goodwyn, Democratic Promise: The Populist Movement in America* (1976); Charles Hoffman, *The Depression of the Nineties: An Economic History* (1970); Samuel McSeveney, *The Politics of Depression: Political Behavior in the Northeast, 1893–1896* (1972); David P. Thelen, *The New Citizenship: Origins of Progressivism in Wisconsin, 1885–1900* (1972).

TIMELINE

1873 Congress demonetizes silver

1875 Specie Resumption Act

1877 Rutherford B. Hayes becomes president

1878 Bland-Allison Act

1879 Henry George, *Progress and Poverty*

1880 James A. Garfield elected president

1881 Garfield assassinated; Chester A. Arthur succeeds to presidency

1883 Pendleton Civil Service Act

1884 Grover Cleveland elected president
W. D. Howells, *The Rise of Silas Lapham*

1887 College Settlement House Association founded

1888 Edward Bellamy, *Looking Backward*
Benjamin Harrison elected president

1889 Jane Addams establishes Hull House
Andrew Carnegie promulgates "The Gospel of Wealth"

1890 General Federation of Women's Clubs founded
Sherman Anti-Trust Act
Sherman Silver Purchase Act
McKinley Tariff
Elections bill defeated

1890s Wyoming, Colorado, Utah, and Idaho grant woman suffrage

1892 Cleveland elected president for the second time; Populist party wins over a million votes
Homestead steel strike

1893 World's Columbian Exposition, Chicago

1893–1897 Financial panic and depression

1894 Pullman strike
Coxey's march on Washington

1895 *United States v. E. C. Knight*

1896 Charles Sheldon, *In His Steps*
Populist party fuses with Democrats
William McKinley elected president

1897 "Golden Rule" Jones elected mayor of Toledo, Ohio
Economic recovery begins

CHAPTER 20

Becoming a World Power

In January 1899, the United States Senate was locked in a dramatic debate over whether to ratify the Treaty of Paris concluding the recent war with Spain over Cuban independence. At the same time, American soldiers uneasily faced Filipino rebels across a neutral zone around the outskirts of Manila, capital of the Philippines. Until recent weeks, the Americans and Filipinos had been allies, together defeating the Spanish to liberate the Philippines. The American fleet under Admiral George Dewey had destroyed the Spanish naval squadron in Manila Bay on May 1, 1898. Three weeks later, an American ship brought from exile the native Filipino insurrectionary leader Emilio Aguinaldo to lead rebel forces on land while U.S. gunboats patrolled the seas.

At first, the Filipinos looked on the Americans as liberators. Although the intentions of the United States were never clear, Aguinaldo believed that, as in Cuba, the Americans had no territorial ambitions. They would simply drive the Spanish out and then leave themselves. In June, therefore, Aguinaldo declared the independence of the Philippines and began setting up a constitutional government. American officials pointedly ignored the independence ceremonies. When an armistice ended the war in August, American troops denied Filipino soldiers an opportunity to liberate their own capital city and shunted them off to the suburbs. The armistice agreement recognized American rights to the "harbor, city, and bay of Manila," while the proposed Treaty of Paris gave the United States the entire Philippine Island archipelago.

Consequently, tension mounted in the streets of Manila and along 14 miles of trenches separating American and Filipino soldiers. Taunts, obscenities, and racial epithets were shouted across the neutral zone. Barroom skirmishes and knifings pervaded the city at night; American soldiers searched houses without warrants and looted stores. Their behavior was not unlike that of the English soldiers in Boston in the 1770s.

On the night of February 4, 1899, Privates William Grayson and David Miller of Company B, 1st Nebraska Volunteers, were on patrol in Santa Mesa, a Manila suburb surrounded on three sides by insurgent trenches. The Americans had orders to shoot any Filipino soldiers found in the neutral area. As the two Americans cautiously worked their way to a bridge over the San Juan River, they heard a Filipino signal whistle, answered by another. Then a red lantern flashed from a nearby blockhouse. The two froze as four Filipinos emerged from the darkness on the road ahead. "Halt!" Grayson shouted. The native lieutenant in charge answered, "Halto!," either mockingly or because he had similar orders. Standing less than 15 feet apart, the two men repeated their commands. After a moment's hesitation, Grayson fired, killing his opponent with one bullet. As the other Filipinos jumped out at them, Grayson and Miller shot two more. Then they turned and ran back to their own lines shouting warnings of attack. A full-scale battle followed.

The next day, Commodore Dewey cabled Washington that the "insurgents have inaugurated general engagement" and promised a hasty suppression of the insurrection. The outbreak of hostilities ended the Senate debates. On February 6, the Senate ratified the Treaty of Paris, thus formally annexing the Philippines and sparking a war between the United States and Filipino nationalists.

In a guerrilla war similar to those fought later in the twentieth century in Asia and Central America, Filipino nationalists tried to undermine the American will by hit-and-run attacks. American soldiers, meanwhile, remained in heavily garrisoned cities and undertook search-and-destroy missions to root out rebels and pacify the countryside. The Filipino-American War lasted until July 1902, three years longer than the Spanish-American War that caused it and involving far more troops, casualties, and monetary and moral costs.

Bryan = not allowed to go to Cuba

How did all this happen? What brought Private Grayson to "shoot my first nigger," as he put it, halfway around the world in distant Asia? For the first time in history, regular American soldiers found themselves fighting outside North America. The "champion of oppressed nations," as Aguinaldo said, had turned into an oppressor nation itself, imposing the American way of life and American institutions on faraway peoples against their will.

The war in the Philippines marked a critical transformation of America's role in the world. Within a few years at the turn of the century, the United States acquired an empire, however small by European standards, and established itself as a world power. In this chapter we will review the historical dilemmas of America's role in the world, especially those of the expansionist nineteenth century. Then we will examine the motivations for the intensified expansionism of the 1890s and how they were manifested in Cuba, the Philippines, and elsewhere. Finally, we will look at how the fundamental patterns of modern American foreign policy were established for Latin America, Asia, and Europe in the early twentieth century. Throughout this discussion, we will see that the tension between idealism and self-interest that has permeated America's domestic history has guided its foreign policy as well.

Steps Toward Empire

The circumstances that brought Privates Grayson and Miller from Nebraska to the Philippines originated deep in American history. As early as the Puritan migration from England to Massachusetts Bay in the seventeenth century, Americans faced the dilemma of how to do good in a world that does wrong. John Winthrop sought to set up a "city on a hill" in the New World, a model community of righteous living for others in the world to behold and imitate. "Let the eyes of the world be upon us," Winthrop said, and that wish, reaffirmed during the American Revolution, became a permanent goal of American policy toward the outside world.

America as a Model Society

Nineteenth-century Americans continued to believe in the nation's special mission. The Monroe Doctrine in 1823 pointed out moral differences between the monarchical, arbitrary governments of Europe and the free republican institutions of the New World. As Spanish colonies in South and Central America followed the American Revolutionary model, Monroe warned Europe to stay out. In succeeding decades, a number of distinguished European visitors came to study "democracy in America," to see for themselves the "great social revolution" at work (see Chapter 12). They found widespread democracy, representative and responsive political and legal institutions, a religious commitment to the notion of human perfectibility, unlimited energy, and the ability to apply unregulated economic activity and inventive genius to produce more things for more people.

The model seemed irresistible. In a world that was evil, Americans believed that they stood as a transforming force for good. Many others agreed. The problem was how a nation committed to isolationism was to do the transforming. One way was to encourage other nations to observe and imitate the good example set by the United States. But often other nations preferred their own society or were attracted to competing models of modernization, as has frequently happened in the twentieth century. This implied the need for a more aggressive foreign policy.

Americans have rarely simply focused on perfecting the good example at home, waiting for others to copy it. This requires patience and passivity, two traits not prevalent in Americans. Rather, throughout history, the American people have actively and sometimes forcefully imposed their ideas and institutions on others. The international crusades of the United States, well intentioned if not always well received, have usually

Clustered in trenches against Filipino nationalists, American soldiers in the faraway Philippine Islands in 1899 were a harbinger of twentieth-century wars to come.

been motivated by a mixture of idealism and self-interest. Hence the effort to spread the exemplary American model to an imperfect world has been both a blessing and a burden, both for others and for the American people themselves.

Early Expansionism

A consistent expression of continental expansionism marked the first century of American independence. Jefferson's purchase of the Louisiana Territory in 1803 and the grasping for Florida and Canada by War Hawks in 1812 signaled an intense American interest in territorial growth. Although the United States remained "unentangled" in European affairs for most of the century, as both Washington and Jefferson had advised, the American government and people were much entangled elsewhere. To the Cherokee, Seminole, Lakota, Apache, Cheyenne, and other Native American nations, the United States was far from isolationist. Nor did the Canadians, the Spanish in Florida, or the Mexicans in Texas and California consider the Americans nonexpansionist. Until midcentury, the United States pursued its "Manifest Destiny" (see Chapter 13) by expanding across the North American continent. But in the 1850s, Americans began to look beyond their own continent. This trend was marked most significantly by Commodore Perry's visit to Japan, the expansion of the China trade, and various expeditions into the Caribbean in search of more cotton lands and a canal connecting the two oceans.

Lincoln's secretary of state, William Seward, accelerated these outward thrusts. During the Civil War, Seward was preoccupied with preventing the Confederacy from receiving foreign aid and diplomatic recognition. But once the war ended, he revived his vision of an America that would hold a "commanding sway in the world." Although restrained in his territorial ambitions, Seward believed that the United States was destined to exert commercial domination "on the Pacific ocean, and its islands and continents." His goal was that from markets, raw materials, and trade would come the "regeneration of . . . the East."

Toward this end, Seward purchased Alaska from Russia in 1867 for $7.2 million. He also acquired a coaling station in the Midway Islands near Hawaii, where missionaries and merchants were already active, and thus paved the way for American commercial expansion in Korea, Japan, and China. Moreover, he advocated the annexation of Cuba and other islands of the West Indies and tried to negotiate a treaty securing an American-built canal through the isthmus of Panama. Seward dreamed of "possession" of the entire

North and Central American continent and ultimately "control of the world." Although his larger dreams went unrealized, his interest in expansion into the Caribbean persisted among business interests and politicians after Cuba's attempted revolt against Spain in 1868.

Expansion After Seward

In 1870, foreshadowing the Philippine debates 30 years later, supporters of President Grant tried to force the Senate to annex Santo Domingo (Hispaniola), an island near Cuba. They cited the strategic importance of the Caribbean and argued forcefully for the economic value of raw materials and markets that the addition of Santo Domingo would bring. Senatorial opponents responded that expansionism violated the American principle of self-determination and government by the consent of the governed. They pointed out, moreover, that the native peoples of the Caribbean were brown-skinned, culturally inferior, non-English-speaking, and therefore unassimilable. Finally, they suggested that expansionism might involve foreign entanglements, necessitating a large and expensive navy, growth in the size of government, and higher taxes. The Senate rejected the treaty to annex Santo Domingo.

Although reluctant to add territory outright, American interests in Latin America and Asia were eager for commercial dominance. A number of statesmen asserted the United States' influence in these areas. President Hayes said in 1880 that despite a treaty with England pledging joint construction and control of a canal across either Panama or Nicaragua, he was certain that if such a canal were built, it would be "under American control" and would be considered "virtually a part of the coast line of the United States." But nothing came of diplomatic efforts with Nicaragua to smooth the way for an American-built canal except Nicaraguan suspicions of U.S. intentions.

In 1881, Secretary of State James G. Blaine sought to convene a conference of American nations to promote hemispheric peace and trade. Although motivated mostly by his presidential ambitions, his effort nevertheless led to the first Pan-American Conference eight years later. The Latin Americans may have wondered what Blaine intended, for in 1881 he intervened in three separate border disputes in Central and South America, in each case at the cost of goodwill and trust.

Ten years later, relations with Chile were harmed when several American sailors on shore leave were involved in a barroom brawl in Valparaiso. Two Americans were killed and several others injured. American pride was also injured, and President Benjamin Harrison sent an ultimatum calling for a "prompt and full reparation." After threats of war, Chile complied.

Similar incidents occurred as American expansionists pursued Seward's goals in the Pacific. In the mid-1870s, American sugar-growing interests in the Hawaiian Islands were strong enough to place whites in positions of influence over the native monarchy. In 1875, they obtained a reciprocity treaty admitting Hawaiian sugar duty-free to the United States. When the treaty was renewed and approved in 1887, the United States also gained exclusive rights to build a naval base at Pearl Harbor on the island of Oahu.

Native Hawaiians resented the growing influence of American sugar interests, especially as they contracted to bring in large numbers of Japanese sugarcane workers to replace Hawaiians killed by white diseases. In 1891, the strongly nationalist Queen Liliuokalani assumed the throne in Hawaii and promptly abolished the constitution, seeking to establish control over whites in the name of "Hawaii for the Hawaiians." In 1893, with the help of U.S. gunboats and marines, sugar planters, fearful of losing influence and of the queen's turning to Japan for political support, staged a palace coup (a revolution later called one "of sugar, by sugar, for sugar") and sought formal annexation by the friendly Harrison administration. But before final Senate ratification could be achieved, Grover Cleveland, who opposed imperial expansion, returned to the presidency for his second term and stopped the move. He was, however, unable to remove the white sugar growers from power in Hawaii. They waited patiently for a more desirable time for annexation, which came during the war in 1898.

Moving ever closer toward the fabled markets of the Far East, the United States acquired a naval station at Pago Pago in the Samoan Islands in 1878. However, it had to share the port with Great Britain and Germany. In an incident in 1889, American and German naval forces almost fought each other, but a typhoon wiped out both navies

Iolani Palace, former home of Queen Liliuokalani, was the scene of annexation ceremonies in 1898, when Hawaii became a U.S. territory. "We need Hawaii just as much and a good deal more than we did California," President McKinley said. "It is manifest destiny."

and ended the crisis. Troubles in the Pacific also occurred in the late 1880s over the American seizure of several Canadian ships in fur seal and fishing disputes in the Bering Sea. This issue was settled only by the British threat of naval action and with the ruling of an international arbitration commission, which ordered the United States to pay damages.

The United States confronted the English closer to home as it sought to replace Britain as the most influential nation in Central American affairs. In 1895, a boundary dispute between Venezuela and British Guiana threatened to bring British intervention against the Venezuelans. President Cleveland, in need of a popular political issue to deflect attention from the depression, discovered the political value of a tough foreign policy by defending a weak sister American republic against the British bully. He asked Secretary of State Richard Olney to send a message to Great Britain. Olney's note, which was stronger than Cleveland had intended, invoked the Monroe Doctrine, declared the United States as "practically sovereign on this continent," and demanded British acceptance of international arbitration to settle the dispute. The British ignored the note, and war threatened. Although England was the United States' chief rival for economic influence in the Caribbean, both sides eventually realized that war between them would be an "absurdity." The dispute was settled by agreeing to an impartial American commission to settle the boundary.

These increasing conflicts in the Caribbean and the Pacific signaled the rise of American presence beyond the borders of the United States. Yet as of 1895, the nation had neither the means nor a consistent policy for enlarging its role in the world. The diplomatic service was small, inexperienced, and unprofessional. Around the world, American emissaries kept sloppy records, issued illegal passports, involved themselves in petty local issues and frauds, and exhibited insensitive behavior toward native cultures. Not until the 1930s did a U.S. embassy official in Peking speak Chinese. The U.S. Army, numbering about 28,000 men in the mid-1890s, ranked thirteenth in the world, behind that of Bulgaria. The navy, dismantled after the Civil War and partly rebuilt under

1939 we were lower than that even Yugoslavia.

President Arthur, ranked no higher than tenth and included many ships powered by dangerously outdated boilers. These limited and backward instruments of foreign policy could not support the aspirations of an emerging world power, especially one whose rise to power had come so quickly.

Expansionism in the 1890s

In 1893, the historian Frederick Jackson Turner wrote that for three centuries, "the dominant fact in American life has been expansion." Turner observed that the "extension of American influence to outlying islands and adjoining countries" indicated that expansionism would continue. Turner's observations struck a responsive chord in a country that had always been restless, mobile, and optimistic. With the western American frontier closed, Americans would surely look for new frontiers, for mobility and markets as well as for morality and missionary activity. The motivations for the expansionist impulse of the late 1890s resembled those that had prompted people to settle the New World in the first place: greed, glory, and God. We will examine expansionism as a reflection of profits, patriotism, piety (moral mission), and politics.

Profits: Searching for Overseas Markets

Albert Beveridge of Indiana bragged in 1898 that "American factories are making more than the American people can use; American soil is producing more than they can consume. Fate has written our policy for us; the trade of the world must and shall be ours." Americans like Beveridge believed in the dream of Seward, Blaine, and others to establish a commercial empire in the islands and adjoining countries of the Caribbean Sea and the Pacific Ocean. With a strong belief in free enterprise and open markets for investing capital and selling products, American businessmen saw huge profits beckoning in the heavily populated areas of Latin America and Asia. They also believed it essential to get their share of these markets to stay competitive with European countries. The attraction was enhanced by the availability in those lands of abundant raw materials such as sugar, coffee, fruits, oil, rubber, and minerals.

Understanding that an increase in commerce required a stronger navy and coaling stations and colonies, business interests began to shape diplomatic and military strategy. As Senator Orville Platt of Connecticut said in 1893, "A policy of isolation did well enough when we were an embryo nation, but today things are different." By 1901, the economic adviser for the State Department described overseas commercial expansion as a "natural law of economic and race development."

Not all businessmen in the 1890s agreed that commercial expansion backed by a vigorous foreign policy was desirable. Some preferred traditional trade with Canada and Europe rather than risky new ventures in Asia and Latin America. Securing colonies and developing faraway markets and investment opportunities not only would require initially high expenses but also might involve the United States in wars with commercial rivals or native peoples in distant places. Some businessmen, furthermore, thought it more important in 1897 to secure recovery from the depression than little islands in Asia.

But the decrease in domestic consumption during the depression also encouraged businessmen to expand into new markets to sell surplus goods. The tremendous growth of American industrial and agricultural production in the post–Civil War years made expansionism an attractive alternative to drowning in overproduction. Many businessmen preferred new markets to cutting prices, which would redistribute wealth by allowing the lower classes to buy excess goods, or to laying off workers, which would increase social unrest. Thus, many reasons, not least the fear of overproduction and a desire to remain competitive in international markets, convinced hesitant businessmen to expand. They were led by the newly formed National Association of Manufacturers, which emphasized in 1896 "that the trade centres of Central and South America are natural markets for American products."

Despite the depression of the 1890s, products spewed from American factories at a staggering rate. The United States moved from fourth in the world in manufacturing in 1870 to first in 1900, doubling the number of factories and tripling the value of farm output, mainly cotton, corn, and wheat. The United States led the world not only in railroad construction (206,631 miles of tracks in 1900, four times more than in 1870) but also in agricultural machinery and mass-produced technological products such as sewing machines, electrical implements, telephones, cash registers, elevators, and cameras. Manufactured goods grew nearly fivefold between 1895 and 1914.

Correspondingly, the total value of American exports tripled, jumping from $434 million in 1866 to nearly $1.5 billion in 1900. By 1914, exports had risen to $2.5 billion, a 67 percent increase over 1900. The increased trade continued to go mainly to Europe rather than Asia. In 1900, for example, only 3 to 4 percent of U.S. exports went to China and Japan. Nevertheless, interest in Asian markets grew, especially as agricultural production continued to increase and prices remained low. Farmers dreamed of selling their surplus wheat to China. James J. Hill of the Great Northern Railroad promoted their hopes by printing wheat cookbooks in various Asian languages and distributing them in the Far East, hoping to fill his westward-bound boxcars and merchant ships with wheat and other grains.

Investment activity followed a similar pattern. American direct investments abroad increased from about $634 million to $2.6 billion between 1897 and 1914. Although investments were largest in Britain, Canada, and Mexico, the potential of Asia and Central America received the most attention. Central American investment increased from $21 million in 1897 to $93 million by the eve of World War I, mainly in mines, railroads, and banana and coffee plantations. At the turn of the century came the formation and growth of America's biggest multinational corporations—the United Fruit Company, Alcoa Aluminum, Amalgamated Copper, Du Pont, American Tobacco, and others. Although slow to respond to investment and market opportunities abroad, these companies soon supported an aggressive foreign policy and the expansion of America's role in the world.

American Foreign Trade, 1870–1914

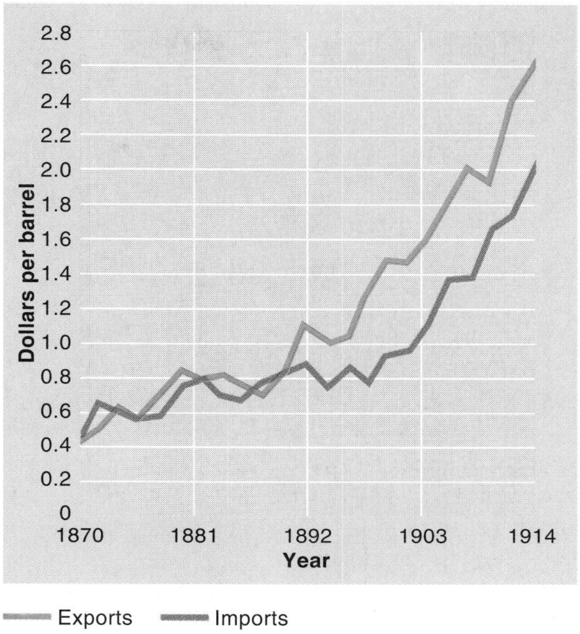

After a rather gradual increase in trade through the boom-and-bust cycles of the 1870s and 1880s, and an actual dip during the depression of 1893–1895, note the spectacular increases during the Republican era of Presidents McKinley, Roosevelt, and Taft.

Source: U.S. Bureau of the Census.

Patriotism: Asserting National Power

American interest in investments, markets, and raw materials abroad reflected a determination not to be left out of the international competition among European powers and Japan for commercial spheres of influence and colonies in Asia, Africa, and Latin America. England, France, and Germany were frequently on the verge of war as they scrambled for colonies as a measure of economic worth and national glory. In 1898, a State Department memorandum stated that the "enlargement of foreign consumption of the products of our mills and workshops has . . . become a serious problem of statesmanship as well as commerce." The memo went on to note that "we can no longer afford to disregard international rivalries now that we ourselves have become a competitor in the world-wide struggle for trade." The national state, then, had a role in supporting commercial interests.

More Americans, however, saw national glory and greatness as legitimate motivations for expansionism. In the late 1890s, a group of men cen-

Advocates of expansionism urged enlarging the U.S. Navy, part of which is pictured here in 1892. The armored warship *Maine*, soon to figure in the outbreak of the Spanish-American War, is shown in the middle foreground.

tered around Assistant Secretary of the Navy Theodore Roosevelt and Senator Henry Cabot Lodge of Massachusetts emerged as highly influential leaders of a changing American foreign policy. These vigorous and intensely nationalistic young men successfully shifted official policy from "continentalism" to what Lodge called the "large policy." By 1899, Assistant Secretary of State John Bassett Moore wrote that the United States had finally moved "into the position of what is commonly called a world power.... Where formerly we had only commercial interests, we now have territorial and political interests as well." Roosevelt agreed that economic interests should take second place to questions of what he called "national honor."

The writings of Alfred Thayer Mahan, a naval strategist and author of several books on the importance of sea power to national greatness, greatly influenced the new foreign policy elite. Mahan argued that in a world of Darwinian struggle for survival, national power depended on naval supremacy, control of sea lanes, and vigorous development of domestic resources and foreign markets. He advocated colonies in both the Caribbean and the Pacific, linked by a canal built and controlled by the United States. Strong nations, Mahan wrote, had a special responsibility to dominate weak ones. In a world of constant "strife," where "everywhere nation is arrayed against nation," it was imperative that Americans begin "to look outward." National pride and glory would surely follow.

Piety: The Missionary Impulse

As Mahan's and Roosevelt's statements suggest, a strong sense of duty and the missionary ideal of doing good for others also motivated expansionism. A statesman once boasted that "with God's help, we will lift Shanghai up and up, ever up, until it is just like Kansas City." Richard Olney agreed, saying in 1898 that "the mission of this country is . . . to forego no fitting opportunity to further the progress of civilization." Motivated by America's sense of itself as a model nation, such statements sometimes rationalized the exploitation and oppression of weaker peoples. Although the European countries had their own justifications for imperialism, Americans such as Roosevelt, Lodge, and Mahan all would have agreed with the following paraphrase of popular expansionist beliefs:

> Certain nations are more civilized than others. These nations are peopled by those who are white, Anglo-Saxon, Protestant, and English-speaking. They enjoy free enterprise and republican political institutions, meaning representative government, shared power, and the rule of law. Further evidence of the civilized nature of such nations includes their advanced technological and industrial development, large middle classes, and high de-

> gree of education and literacy. The prime examples in the world are England, Germany, and the United States.
>
> In the natural struggle for existence, the races and nations that survive and prosper, such as these, prove their fitness and superiority over others. The United States, as a matter of history, geographic location, and political genius, is so favored and fit that God has chosen it to take care of and uplift less favored peoples. This responsibility cannot be avoided. It is a national duty, or burden—the "white man's burden"—that civilized nations undertake to bring peace, progressive values, and ordered liberty to the world.

These ideas, widespread in popular thought, described America's providential sense of itself. As a missionary put it in 1885, "The Christian nations are subduing the world in order to make mankind free." Josiah Strong, a Congregational minister, was one of the most ardent advocates of American missionary expansionism. Although his book *Our Country* (1885) focused on internal threats to American social order, in a long chapter titled "The Future of the Anglo-Saxon Race," Strong made his case for an outward thrust. He argued that in the struggle for survival among nations, the United States had emerged as the center of Anglo-Saxonism and was "divinely commissioned" to spread the blessings of political liberty, Protestant Christianity, and civilized values over the earth. "This powerful race," he wrote, "will move down upon Mexico, down upon Central and South America, out upon the islands of the sea, over upon Africa and beyond." In a cruder statement of the same idea, Albert Beveridge said in 1899 that God had prepared English-speaking Anglo-Saxons to become the "master organizers of the world to establish and administer governments among savages and senile peoples."

If not so crudely, missionaries carried similar Western values to non-Christian lands around the world. China was a favorite target. The number of American Protestant missionaries in China increased from 436 in 1874 to 5,462 in 1914. The largest increase came in the 1890s. Although the missionaries were not as effective as they had hoped to be, the estimated number of Christian converts in China jumped from 5,000 in 1870 to nearly 100,000 in 1900. This tiny fraction of the Chinese population included many young reformist intellectuals who absorbed Western ideas in Christian mission colleges and went on to lead the Revolution of 1912 that ended the Manchu dynasty. Economic relations between China and the United States increased at approximately the same rate as missionary activity. The number of American firms in China grew from 50 to 550 between 1870 and 1930, while trade increased 1,500 percent.

Politics: Manipulating Public Opinion

These figures suggest how economic, religious, moral, and nationalistic motivations became interwoven in American expansionism in the late 1890s. Although less significant than the other motives, politics also played a role. For the first time in American history, public opinion over international issues loomed large in presidential politics. The psychological tensions and economic hardships of the depression of the 1890s jarred national self-confidence. Foreign adventures and the glories of expansionism provided an emotional release from domestic turmoil and promised to restore patriotic pride—and maybe even win votes.

This process was helped by the growth of a highly competitive popular press, the penny daily newspaper, which brought international issues before a mass readership. When several newspapers in New York City, notably William Randolph Hearst's *Journal* and Joseph Pulitzer's *World,* competed to see which could stir up more public support for the Cuban rebels in their struggle for independence from Spain, politicians ignored the public outcry at their peril. Daily reports of Spanish atrocities in 1896 and 1897 kept public moral outrage constantly before President McKinley as he considered his course of action. His Democratic opponent, William Jennings Bryan, entered the fray. Although in principle a pacifist, he too advocated United States intervention in Cuba on moral grounds of a holy war to help the oppressed. Bryan even raised a regiment of Nebraska volunteers to go off to the war, but the Republican administration kept him far from battle and therefore far from the headlines.

Politics, then, joined profits, patriotism, and piety in motivating the expansionism of the 1890s. These four impulses interacted to influence the Spanish-American War, the annexation of the Philippine Islands, and the foreign policy of President Theodore Roosevelt.

United States Territorial Expansion to 1900

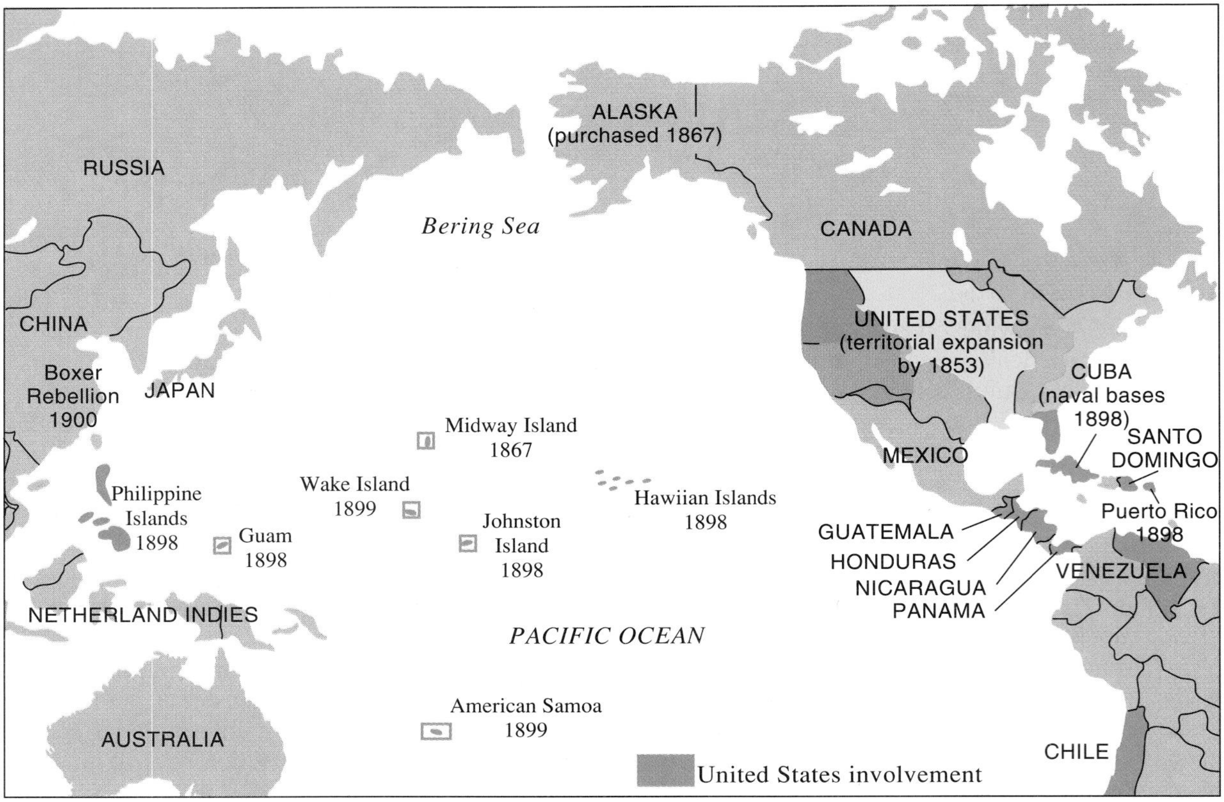

Compare this map with the one on American territorial expansionism in Chapter 13 on page 428 (represented in miniature in the United States portion of this map).

Cuba and the Philippines

Lying 90 miles off the southern tip of Florida, Cuba had been the object of intense American interest for a half century. Although successful in thwarting American adventurism in Cuba in the 1850s, Spain was unable to halt the continuing struggle of the Cuban people for relief from exploitive labor in the sugar plantations, even after slavery itself ended, and for a measure of autonomy. The most recent uprising, which lasted from 1868 to 1878, had raised tensions between Spain and the United States; it also whetted the Cuban appetite not just for reforms but for complete independence.

The Road to War

When the Cuban revolt flared up anew in 1895, the Madrid government again failed to implement reforms but instead sent General "Butcher" Weyler with 50,000 troops to quell the disturbance. When Weyler began herding rural Cuban citizens into "reconcentration" camps, Americans were outraged. An outpouring of sympathy swept the nation, especially as reports came back of the horrible suffering in the camps, with thousands dying of malnutrition, starvation, and disease. Sensationalist newspapers in the United States, competing for readers, stirred up sentiment with pages of bloody stories of atrocities. "The old, the young, the weak, the crippled—all are butchered without mercy," wrote the New York *World.*

The Cuban struggle appealed to a country convinced of its role as protector of the weak and defender of the right of self-determination. One editorial deplored Spanish "injustice, oppression, extortion, and demoralization," while describing the Cubans as heroic freedom fighters "largely inspired by our glorious example of beneficent free institutions and successful self-government." Motivated by genuine humanitarian concern and a sense of duty, many Americans held Cuba rallies to raise money and food for famine relief. They called for land reforms, and some advocated armed intervention, but neither President Cleveland nor President McKinley wanted a war over Cuba.

Self-interested motives also played a role. For many years, Americans had noted the profitable resources and strategic location of the island. American companies had invested extensively in Cuban sugar plantations. By 1897, trade with Cuba reached $27 million per year. Appeals for reform had much to do with ensuring a stable environment for further investments, as well as for the protection of sugar fields against the ravages of civil war.

The election of 1896 diverted attention from Cuba to the issues of free silver and jobs, but only temporarily. A new government in Madrid recalled Weyler and seemed ready to grant a degree of self-government to the Cubans. But these concessions were halfhearted. Conditions worsened in the reconcentration camps, and the American press kept the plight of the Cuban people before the public. McKinley, eager not to take any action that might upset business recovery from the depression, skillfully resisted the pressure for war. But his skill could not control Spanish misrule or Cuban aspirations for freedom. The fundamental causes of the war—Spanish intransigence in the face of persistent Cuban rebellion and American sugar interests and sympathies for the underdog—were seemingly unstoppable.

Events early in 1898 sparked the outbreak of hostilities. Rioting in Havana intensified both Spanish repression and American outrage. As pressures for war increased, a letter from the Spanish minister to the United States, Depuy de Lôme, calling McKinley a "weak" hypocritical politician, was intercepted by spies and made public. The American populace became enraged as Hearst's New York *Journal* called De Lôme's letter "the worst insult to the United States in its history."

Remembering the *Maine,* citizens decorated its mast in observance of the second anniversary of its sinking in Havana harbor. Secretary of the Navy John Long, upon returning to his office to discover that Assistant Secretary Roosevelt had cabled Admiral Dewey to prepare for war in the aftermath of the *Maine* explosion, wrote in his diary "I find that Roosevelt has come very near causing more of an explosion than happened to the *Maine.*"

A second event was more serious. When the rioting broke out, the U.S. battleship *Maine* was sent to Havana harbor to protect American citizens. Early in the evening on February 15, a tremendous explosion blew up the *Maine,* killing 262 men. American advocates of war, who assumed Spanish responsibility, called immediately for intervention. Newspaper publishers offered rewards for discovery of the perpetrators of the crime and broadcast slogans like "Remember the *Maine!* To hell with Spain!"

Assistant Secretary of the Navy Theodore Roosevelt, who had been preparing for war for some time, said that he believed the *Maine* had been sunk "by an act of dirty treachery on the part of the Spaniards" and that he would "give anything if President McKinley would order the fleet to Havana tomorrow." When the president did not, Roosevelt privately declared that McKinley had "no more backbone than a chocolate éclair" and continued to ready the navy for action. Although an official board of inquiry concluded that an external submarine mine caused the disaster, probably a faulty boiler or some other internal problem set off the explosion, a possibility even Roosevelt later conceded.

After the sinking of the *Maine,* Roosevelt took advantage of Secretary of the Navy John D. Long's absence from the office one day to send a cable to Commodore George Dewey, commander of the United States' Pacific fleet at Hong Kong. Roosevelt's message ordered Dewey to fill his ships with coal and, "in the event" of a declaration of war with Spain, to sail to the Philippines and make sure "the Spanish squadron does not leave the Asiatic coast." Roosevelt wrote in his diary that night that "the Secretary is away and I am having immense fun running the Navy."

Roosevelt's act was not impetuous, as Long thought, but consistent with naval policies he had been urging upon his more cautious superior for more than a year. As early as 1895, the navy had formulated plans for attacking the Philippines. Influenced by Mahan and Lodge, Roosevelt wanted to enlarge the navy, whose growth had been restricted for years. He also believed that the United States should construct an interoceanic canal, acquire the Danish West Indies (the Virgin Islands), annex Hawaii outright, and oust Spain from Cuba. As Roosevelt told McKinley late in 1897, he was putting the navy in "the best possible shape" for "when war began." His order to Dewey, then, reflected a well-thought-out strategy to implement the "large policy" necessary for the advance of civilization.

The public outcry over the *Maine* drowned out McKinley's efforts to calm the populace and avoid war. The issues had become highly political, especially with midterm elections in the fall and a presidential race only two years away. Fellow Republican Senator Lodge warned McKinley that "if war in Cuba drags on through the summer with nothing done we shall go down to the greatest defeat ever known." McKinley hoped that the Madrid government would make the necessary concessions in Cuba and sent some tough demands in March. But the Spanish response was delayed and inadequate, refusing to grant full independence to the Cubans.

On April 11, 1898, President McKinley sent an ambiguous message to Congress that seemed to call for war. Two weeks later, Congress authorized the use of troops against Spain and passed a resolution recognizing Cuban independence, actions amounting to a declaration of war. In a significant additional resolution, the Teller Amendment, Congress stated that the United States had no intentions of annexing Cuba, guaranteeing the Cubans the right to determine their own destiny. Senator George F. Hoar of Massachusetts, who later assailed the United States for its war against the Filipinos, declared that intervention in Cuba would be "the most honorable single war in all history," undertaken without "the slightest thought or desire of foreign conquest or of national gain or advantage."

"A Splendid Little War"

As soon as war was declared, Theodore Roosevelt resigned his post in the Navy Department and prepared to lead a cavalry unit in the war. Black regiments as well as white headed to Tampa, Florida, to be shipped to Cuba. One black soldier, noting the stark differences in the southern reception of the segregated regiments, commented, "I am sorry that we were not treated with much courtesy while coming through the South." Blacks were especially sympathetic to the Cuban people's struggle. As one soldier wrote in his journal, "Oh, God! at last we have taken up the sword to enforce the divine rights of a people who have been unjustly treated." Upon arriving in Puerto Rico, a white soldier wrote that it was a "wonderful sight how the natives respect us." As the four-month war neared its end in August, John Hay wrote Roosevelt that "it has been a splendid little war; begun with the highest motives, carried on with magnificent intelligence and spirit."

It was a "splendid" war also because compared with the long, bloody Civil War or even the British fight with the Boers in South Africa going on at the same time, the war with Spain was short and relatively easy. Naval battles were won almost without return fire. At both major naval engagements, Manila Bay and Santiago Bay, only two Americans died, one of them from heat prostration while stoking coal. The islands of Guam and Puerto Rico were taken virtually without a shot. Only 385 men died from Spanish bullets, but over 5,000 succumbed to tropical diseases.

The Spanish-American War was splendid in other ways, as letters from American soldiers suggest. One young man wrote that his comrades were all "in good spirits" because oranges and co-

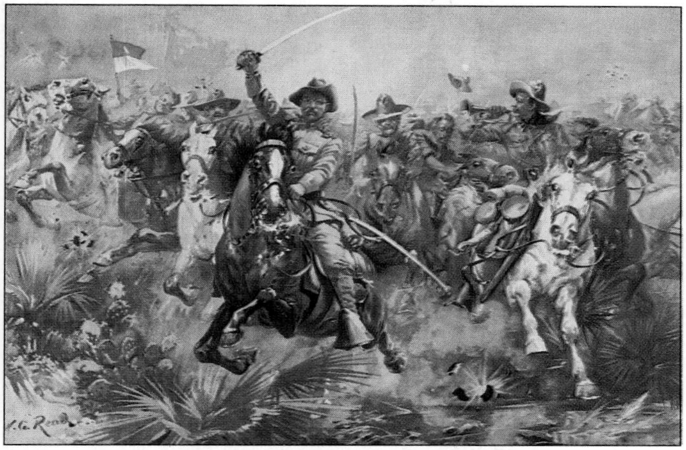

The celebrated charge of "Teddy's Rough Riders" up Kettle Hill *(left)*, which so greatly helped Roosevelt's political career, was protected by black troops like these from the 9th U.S. Cavalry *(right)*.

conuts were so plentiful and "every trooper has his canteen full of lemonade all the time." Another wrote his mother that he found Cuba not only cooler but better than Texas in many ways: "Our money is worth twice as much as Spanish money. We do not want for anything." And another wrote his brother that he was having "a lot of fun chasing Spaniards."

But for many men, the war was anything but splendid. One soldier wrote that "words are inadequate to express the feeling of pain and sickness when one has the fever. For about a week every bone in my body ached and I did not care much whether I lived or not." Another wrote:

> One of the worst things I saw was a man shot while loading his gun. The Spanish Mauser bullet struck the magazine of his carbine, and . . . the bullet was split, a part of it going through his scalp and a part through his neck. . . . He was a mass of blood.

The "power of joy in battle" that Teddy Roosevelt felt "when the wolf rises in the heart" was not a feeling all American soldiers shared. Roosevelt's brush with death at Las Guásimas and his celebrated charge up Kettle Hill near Santiago, his flank protected by black troops, made 3-inch headlines and propelled him toward the New York governor's mansion in Albany. "I would rather have led that charge," he said later, "than served three terms in the U.S. Senate." Nonetheless, no one did as much during the war as Roosevelt to advance not only his political career but also the cause of expansion and national glory.

The Philippines Debates and War

Roosevelt's ordering Dewey to Manila initiated a chain of events that led to the annexation of the Philippines. The most crucial battle of the Spanish-American War occurred on May 1, 1898, when Dewey destroyed the Spanish fleet in Manila Bay and cabled McKinley for additional troops. The president said later that when he received Dewey's cable, he was not even sure "within two thousand miles" where "those darned islands were." Actually, McKinley had approved Roosevelt's policies and knew what course of action to pursue. He sent twice as many troops as Dewey had asked for and began the process of shaping American public opinion to accept the "political, commercial [and] humanitarian" reasons for annexing all 7,000 Philippine islands. The Treaty of Paris gave the United States all of them in exchange for a $20 million payment to Spain.

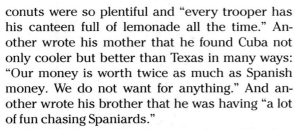

The treaty was sent to the Senate for ratification during the winter of 1898–1899. Senators for and against annexation hurled arguments at each other across the floor of the Senate as American soldiers hurled oaths and taunts across the neutral zone at Aguinaldo's insurgents near Manila. Private Grayson's encounter, as we have seen, led

The Spanish-American War

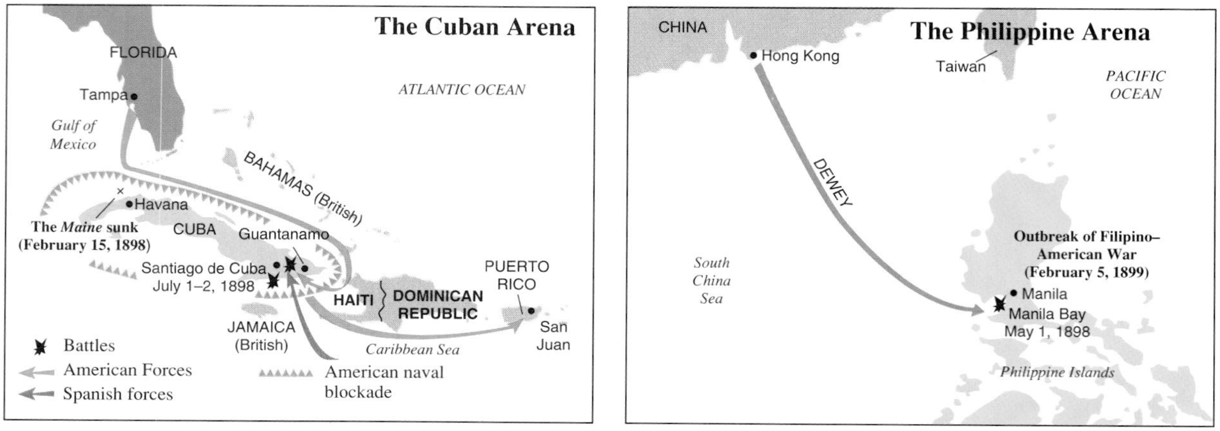

Refer to the first map in the chapter to see how far apart these two war zones were; as a result, American foreign policy was forever transformed.

to the passage of the treaty in a close Senate vote and began the Filipino-American War and the debates over what to do with the Philippines. These debates took place in a wider arena than the Senate as the entire nation joined the argument. At stake were two very different views of foreign policy and of America's vision of itself. After several months of quietly seeking advice and listening to public opinion, McKinley finally recommended annexation.

Many Democrats supported the president out of fear of being labeled disloyal. At a time when openly racist thought flourished in the United States, fellow Republicans confirmed McKinley's arguments for annexation, adding even more racist ones. Filipinos were described as childlike, savage, stunted in size, dirty, and backward. Unflattering comparisons were made to blacks and Native Americans, and policies were proposed befitting the inferior condition in which white Americans saw the Filipinos. "The country won't be pacified," a Kansas veteran of the Sioux wars told a reporter, "until the niggers are killed off like the Indians." Roosevelt called Aguinaldo a "rene-

President McKinley's Annexation Argument

In a speech to a group of expansionist Methodist ministers and missionaries in 1900, President McKinley explained his reasons for recommending annexation of the Philippines. His statement summarizes most of the reasons for expansionism. It also offers a fascinating glimpse into the inner process of presidential decision making (or at least of how a President later sought to justify a decision).

The truth is I didn't want the Philippines and when they came to us as a gift from the gods, I did not know what to do about them. . . . And one night it came to me this way—(1) that we could not give them back to Spain—that would be cowardly and dishonorable; (2) that we could not turn them over to France or Germany—our commercial rivals in the Orient—that would be bad business and discreditable; (3) that we could not leave them to themselves—they were unfit for self-government—and they would soon have anarchy and misrule over there worse than Spain's was; and (4) that there was nothing left for us to do but to take them all, and to educate the Filipinos, and uplift and civilize and Christianize them, and by God's grace do the very best we could by them, as our fellowmen for whom Christ also died. And then I went to bed, and went to sleep, and slept soundly, and the next morning I sent for the chief engineer of the War Department (our map-maker), and I told him to put the Philippines on the map of the United States, and there they are, and there they will stay while I am President!

Senator Hoar's Statement Against Imperialism

In one of the strongest anti-imperialist statements, Senator George F. Hoar of Massachusetts, who had called the war in Cuba "honorable," described the war in the Philippines in the following way.

We changed the Monroe Doctrine from a doctrine of eternal righteousness and justice, resting on the consent of the governed, to a doctrine of brutal selfishness looking only to our own advantage. We crushed the only republic in Asia. We made war on the only Christian people in the East. We converted a war of glory to a war of shame. We vulgarized the American flag. We introduced perfidy into the practice of war. We inflicted torture on unarmed men to extort confession. We put children to death. We devastated provinces. We baffled the aspirations of a people for liberty.

gade Pawnee" and said that the Filipinos had no right "to administer the country which they happen to be occupying." The attitudes favoring annexation, therefore, asserted Filipino inferiority and incapacity for self-rule while also reflecting America's proud sense of itself in 1900 as a nation of civilized order and progress.

Other Americans were not so positive about such "progress." A small but vocal group organized in the Anti-Imperialist League vigorously opposed war and annexation. Many felt displaced by the younger generation of modern expansionists. By attacking imperialism, the anti-imperialists struck out against the forces of modernism that they felt threatened their elite social position. They included a cross section of American dignitaries: ex-Presidents Harrison and Cleveland, Samuel Gompers and Andrew Carnegie, William James, Jane Addams, Mark Twain, and many others.

The major anti-imperialist arguments pointed out how imperialism in general and annexation in particular contradicted American ideals. First, the annexation of territory without immediate or planned steps toward statehood was unprecedented and unconstitutional. Second, to occupy and govern a foreign people without their consent violated the ideals of the Declaration of Independence. A third argument was that social reforms needed at home demanded American energies and money before foreign expansionism. "Before we attempt to teach house-keeping to the world," one writer put it, we needed "to set our own house in order."

Not all anti-imperialist arguments were so noble. Some were practical or downright racist. One position alleged that since the Filipinos were nonwhite, Catholic, and inferior in size and intelligence, they were unassimilable. Annexation would lead to miscegenation and contamination of Anglo-Saxon blood. Senator Ben Tillman of South Carolina argued that although whites could "walk on the necks of every colored race," he still opposed "incorporating any more colored men into the body politic." The practical argument suggested that once in possession of the Philippines, the United States would have to defend them, possibly even acquiring more territories. This would require higher taxes and bigger government in order to build and support the navy that holding such possessions demanded. Some saw the Philippines as a burden that would require American troops to fight distant Asian wars.

The last argument became fact when Private Grayson's encounter started the Filipino-American War. Before it was over in 1902, some 126,500 American troops served in the Philippines, 4,234 died there, and 2,800 more were wounded. The cost was $400 million. Filipino casualties were much worse. In addition to the 18,000 killed in combat, an estimated 200,000 Filipinos died of famine and disease as American soldiers burned villages and destroyed crops and livestock in order to disrupt the economy and deny rebel fighters their food supply. General Jacob H. Smith ordered his troops to "kill and burn and the more you kill and burn, the better you will please me." Atrocities on both sides increased with the frustrations of a lengthening war, but the American "water cure" and other tortures were especially brutal.

As U.S. treatment of the Filipinos during the war became more and more like Spanish mistreatment of the Cubans, the hypocrisy of American behavior became even more evident. This was especially true for black American soldiers

Bringing "civilization" to the Filipinos, American soldiers stand guard over captured guerrillas in 1899. Finley Peter Dunne quipped: "Twud be a disgrace f'r to lave befure we've pounded these frindless an' ongrateful people into insinsibility."

who fought in the Philippines. They identified with the dark-skinned insurgents, whom they saw as tied to the land, burdened by debt, and pressed by poverty like themselves. They were also called "nigger" from morning to night. "I feel sorry for these people," a sergeant in the 24th Infantry wrote. "You have no idea the way these people are treated by the Americans here."

The war starkly exposed the hypocrisies of shouldering the white man's burden. Upon reading a report that 8,000 Filipinos had been killed in the first year of the war, Carnegie wrote a letter, dripping with sarcasm, congratulating McKinley for "civilizing the Filipinos. . . . About 8000 of them have been completely civilized and sent to Heaven. I hope you like it." Another writer penned a devastating one-liner: "Dewey took Manila with the loss of one man—and all our institutions." One of the most active anti-imperialists, Ernest Howard Crosby, wrote a parody of Rudyard Kipling's "White Man's Burden," which he titled "The Real 'White Man's Burden'":

Take up the White Man's burden.
Send forth your sturdy kin,
And load them down with Bibles
And cannon-balls and gin.
Throw in a few diseases
To spread the tropic climes,
For there the healthy niggers
Are quite behind the times.

They need our labor question, too.
And politics and fraud—
We've made a pretty mess at home,
Let's make a mess abroad.

The anti-imperialists failed either to prevent annexation or to interfere with the war effort. However prestigious and sincere, they had little or no political power. They were seen as an older, conservative, elite group of Americans opposed to the kind of dynamic progress represented by Teddy Roosevelt and other expansionists. They were out of tune with the period of exuberant national pride, prosperity, and promise.

Expansionism Triumphant

By 1900, Americans had ample reason to be patriotic. Within a year, the United States had acquired several island territories, thereby joining the other great world powers. But several questions arose over what to do with the new territories. What was their status? Were they colonies? Would they be granted statehood or would they develop gradually from colonies to constitutional parts of the United States? Moreover, did the native peoples of Hawaii, Puerto Rico, Guam, and the Philippines have the same rights as American citizens on the mainland? Were they protected by the U.S. Constitution? The answers to these difficult questions emerged in a series of Supreme Court cases, congressional acts, and presidential decisions.

Although slightly different governing systems were worked out for each new territory, the solution in each was to define its status somewhere between subject colony and candidate for statehood. Territorial status came closest. The native people were usually allowed to elect their own legislature for internal lawmaking but had governors and other judicial and administrative officials appointed by the American president. A provincial governor, George Curry, was subsequently made governor of the New Mexico Territory, a step indicating that both the Philippines and New Mexico remained somewhere between colonies and equal states. The first full governor of the Philippines, McKinley appointee William

Howard Taft, effectively moved the Filipinos toward self-government. Final independence did not come until 1946, however, and elsewhere the process was equally slow. The question of constitutional rights was resolved by deciding that Hawaiians and Puerto Ricans, for example, would be treated differently from Texans and Oregonians. In the "insular cases" of 1901, the Supreme Court ruled that these people would achieve citizenship and constitutional rights only when Congress said they were ready. To the question "Does the Constitution follow the flag?" the answer, as Secretary of State Elihu Root put it, was, "Ye-es, as near as I can make out the Constitution follows the flag—but doesn't quite catch up with it."

McKinley's resounding defeat of Bryan in 1900 clearly revealed the optimistic, nationalistic spirit of the American people. Bryan's intentions to make imperialism the "paramount issue" of the campaign failed, in part because the country strongly favored annexation of the Philippines. A rising sense of nationhood made the Filipino-American War a popular one, and it was politically unwise to risk being branded a traitor by opposing it. In the closing weeks of the campaign, Bryan and the Democrats shied away from imperialism and the war as a "paramount issue" and focused more on economic issues—trusts, the labor question, and free silver.

But Bryan fared no better on those issues. Prosperity returned with the discovery of gold in Alaska, and cries for reform fell on deaf ears. The McKinley forces rightly claimed that under four years of Republican rule, more money, jobs, thriving factories, and manufactured goods had been created. Moreover, McKinley pointed to the

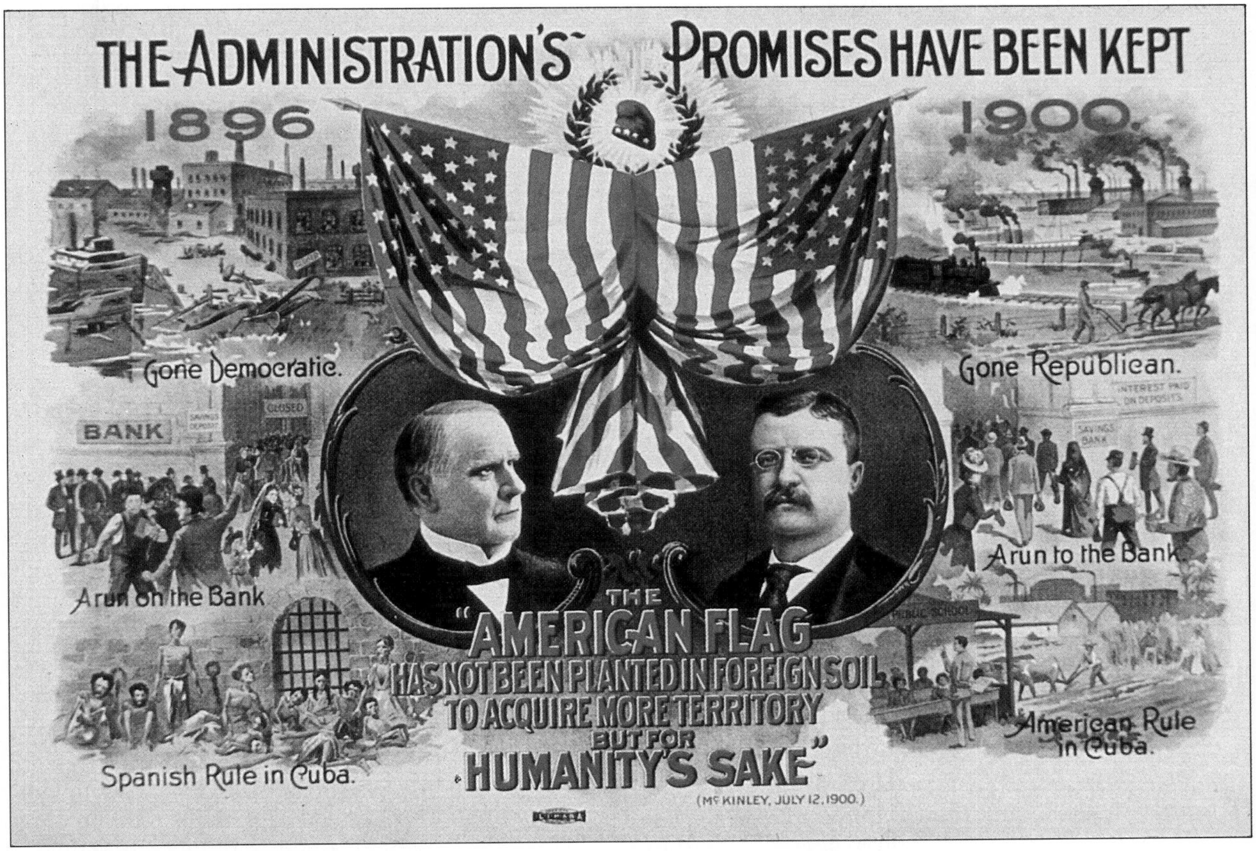

This 1900 campaign poster for McKinley makes a compelling case that four years of Republican party leadership had brought prosperity and humanity both at home and abroad. Note not only how McKinley and Roosevelt wrapped themselves in the American flag but also the dramatic contrasts the poster draws with the condition of the country and hemisphere when the Democrats left office in 1896.

Full dinner pail

tremendous growth in American prestige abroad. Spain had been kicked out of Cuba, and the American flag flew in many places around the globe. It had been a triumphant four years. As a disappointed Tom Watson put it, noting the end of the Populist revolt with the war fervor over Cuba, "The Spanish war finished us. The blare of the bugle drowned out the voice of the reformer."

He was more right than he knew. Within one year, the active expansionist Theodore Roosevelt went from assistant secretary of the navy to colonel of the Rough Riders to governor of New York. For some Republican politicos, who thought he was too vigorous, unorthodox, and independent, this quick rise to prominence as McKinley's potential rival came too fast. One way to eliminate Roosevelt politically, or at least slow him down, they thought, was to make him vice-president, which they did at the Republican convention in 1900. But six months into McKinley's second term, the president was shot and killed by an anarchist, the third presidential assassination in less than 40 years. "Now look," exclaimed party boss Mark Hanna, who had opposed putting Roosevelt on the ticket; "that damned cowboy is President of the United States!"

Roosevelt's Energetic Diplomacy

At a White House dinner party in 1905, a guest told a story about visiting the Roosevelt home when Teddy had been a baby. "You were in your bassinet, making a good deal of fuss and noise," the guest reported, "and your father lifted you out and asked me to hold you." Secretary of State Elihu Root looked up from his plate and asked, "Was he hard to hold?" Whether true or not, the story reveals much about President Roosevelt's principles and policies on foreign affairs. As president from 1901 to 1909, and as the most dominating American personality for the 15 years between 1897 and 1912, Roosevelt made much fuss and noise about the activist role he thought the United States should play in the world. As he implemented his policies, he often seemed "hard to hold." Roosevelt's energetic foreign policy in Latin America, Asia, and Europe paved the way for the vital role of the United States as a world power.

Foreign Policy as Darwinian Struggle

Roosevelt's personal principles and presidential policies went together. He was an advocate of both individual physical fitness and collective national strength. As an undersized, weak young boy who suffered humiliating drubbings by schoolmates, he undertook a rigorous program of strengthening his body through boxing and other exercise. During summers spent on his ranch in the North Dakota Badlands, Roosevelt learned to value the "strenuous life" of the cowboy. He read Darwin and understood that life among humans, as in nature, was a constant struggle for survival.

Roosevelt extended his beliefs about strenuous struggle from individuals to nations. His ideal was a "nation of men, not weaklings." To be militarily prepared and to fight well were the tests of racial superiority and national greatness. "All the great masterful races," he said, "have been fighting races." Although he believed in Anglo-Saxon superiority, he admired—and feared—Japanese military prowess. Powerful nations, like individuals, Roosevelt believed, had a duty to cultivate qualities of vigor, strength, courage, and moral commitment to civilized values. In practical terms this meant developing natural resources, building large navies, and being ever prepared to fight. "I never take a step in foreign policy," he wrote, "unless I am assured that I shall be able eventually to carry out my will by force."

Although known for his advice to "speak softly and carry a big stick," Roosevelt often not only wielded a large stick but spoke loudly as well. In a speech in 1897, he used the word war 62 times, saying that "no triumph of peace is quite so great as the supreme triumphs of war." But despite his bluster, Roosevelt was usually restrained in the exercise of force. He won the Nobel Peace Prize in 1906 for helping to end the Russo-Japanese War. The purpose of the big stick and the loud talk was to preserve order and peace in the world. "To be prepared for war," he said, "is the most effectual means to promote peace."

Roosevelt divided the world into civilized and uncivilized nations, the former usually defined as Anglo-Saxon and English-speaking. The civilized nations had a responsibility to "police" the uncivilized, not only maintaining order but also spreading superior values and institutions. This "international police power," as Roosevelt called it, was the "white man's burden." As part of this burden,

The "big stick" became a memorable image in American diplomacy as Teddy Roosevelt sought to make the United States a policeman not only of the Caribbean basin but also of the whole world. "As our modern life goes on," Roosevelt said, "and the nations are drawn closer together for good and for evil, and this nation grows in comparison with friends and rivals, it is impossible to adhere to the policy of isolation."

civilized nations sometimes had to fight wars against the uncivilized, as the British did against the Boers in South Africa and the Americans did in the Philippines. These wars were justified because the victors bestowed the blessings of culture and racial superiority on the vanquished.

A war between two civilized nations, however, as between Germany and England, would be wasteful and foolish, upsetting order in the world. Above all, Roosevelt believed in the balance of power. Strong, advanced nations like the United States had a duty to use their power to preserve order and peace. The United States had "no choice," Roosevelt said, but to "play a great part in the world." Americans could no longer "avoid responsibilities" that followed from "the fact that on the east and west we look across the waters at Europe and Asia." The 1900 census had recently shown that the United States, with 75 million people, was much more populous than Great Britain, France, or Germany. Since all these nations had many colonies in Asia and Africa, it seemed time for Americans to exercise a greater role in world affairs.

As Roosevelt looked across the oceans, he developed a highly personal style of diplomacy. Rather than relying on the Department of State, he preferred face-to-face contact and personal exchange of letters with foreign ambassadors, ministers, and heads of state. Roosevelt made foreign policy while horseback riding with the German ambassador or while discussing history with the ambassador from France. A British emissary observed that Roosevelt had a "powerful personality" and a commanding knowledge of the world. As a result, ministries from London to Tokyo respected both the president and the power of the United States.

When threat of force failed to accomplish his goals, Roosevelt used direct personal intervention as a third-party mediator. "In a crisis the duty of a leader is to lead," he said. Congress was too slow and deliberate to play a significant role in foreign affairs. When he wanted Panama, Roosevelt bragged later, "I took the Canal Zone" rather than submitting a long "dignified State Paper" for congressional debate on a suitable policy. And while Congress debated his actions, he was fond of pointing out, the building of the canal across Panama began. Roosevelt's energetic executive activism in foreign policy set a pattern followed by nearly every twentieth-century American president.

Taking the Panama Canal

In justifying the intervention of 2,600 American troops in Honduras and Nicaragua in 1906, Philander Knox, secretary of state from 1909 to 1913, said, "We are in the eyes of the world, and be-

(Above) In 1903, despite protests from the Panamanian government, the United States acquired the right to begin the enormous engineering feat of building the Panama Canal. *(Right)* A year later, a cartoonist showed the American eagle celebrating "his 128th birthday" with wings spanning the globe from Panama to the Philippines. In a prophetic anticipation of American overexpansion in the twentieth century, the eagle says, "Gee, but this is an awful stretch."

cause of the Monroe Doctrine, held responsible for the order of Central America, and its proximity to the Canal makes the preservation of peace in that neighborhood particularly necessary." The Panama Canal was not yet finished when Knox spoke, but it had already become a vital cornerstone of United States policy in the region. Three problems had to be surmounted to fulfill the long-sought goal of an interoceanic connection. First, an 1850 treaty bound the United States to build a canal jointly with Great Britain. But in 1901, John Hay, secretary of state between 1901 and 1905, convinced the British to cancel the treaty in exchange for an American guarantee that the canal, once built, would be "free and open to the vessels of commerce and of war of all nations." A second problem was where to build the canal. After considering a long but technically easy route through Nicaragua, American engineers settled on the shorter but more rugged path across the isthmus of Panama, where a French firm, the New Panama Company, had already begun work.

The third problem was that Panama was a province of Colombia and thus could not negotiate with the United States. The Colombian government was unimpressed with the share of a likely settlement the Americans would provide in buying up the New Panama Canal Company's $40 million in assets. Indeed, in 1903, the Colombian senate rejected a treaty negotiated by Hay, but mostly on nationalistic, not financial, grounds. Roosevelt, angered by this rebuff, called the Colombians "Dagoes" and "foolish and homicidal corruptionists" who tried to "hold us up" like highway robbers.

Aware of Roosevelt's fury, encouraged by hints of American support, and eager for the economic benefits the building of a canal would bring, Panamanian nationalists in 1903 staged a revolution led by several rich families and a Frenchman, Philippe Bunau-Varilla of the New Panama Canal Company. The Colombian army, dispatched to quell the revolt, was deterred by the presence of an American warship; local troops were separated from their officers, who were bought off. The bloodless revolution occurred on November 3; the next day, Panama declared its independence. On November 6, the United States officially recognized the new government in Panama. Although Roosevelt did not formally encourage the revolution, it would not have occurred without American money and support.

On November 18, Hay and Bunau-Varilla signed a treaty establishing the American right to build and operate a canal through Panama and to

Almost as fast as Truman - Israel in 1948

exercise "titular sovereignty" over the 10-mile-wide Canal Zone. The Panamanian government protested the treaty, to no avail, and a later government called it the "treaty that no Panamanian signed." Roosevelt, in his later boast that he "took the canal," claimed that his diplomatic and engineering achievement, completed in 1914, would "rank . . . with the Louisiana Purchase and the acquisition of Texas."

Policeman of the Caribbean

As late as 1901, the Monroe Doctrine was still regarded, according to Roosevelt, as the "equivalent to an open door in South America." To the United States, this meant that although no nation had a right "to get territorial possessions," all nations had equal commercial rights in the Western Hemisphere south of the Rio Grande. But as American investments poured into Central America and Caribbean islands, that policy changed to one of the primary right of the United States to dominant influence in the lands of the Caribbean basin. Order was indispensable for profitable economic activity.

This change was demonstrated in 1902, when Germany and Great Britain seized several Venezuelan gunboats and blockaded Venezuela's ports to force the government to pay defaulted debts. Roosevelt was especially worried that German influence would replace the British. He insisted that the European powers accept arbitration of the disputed financial claims and threatened to "move Dewey's ships" to the Venezuelan coast to enforce his intentions. The crisis passed, largely for other reasons, but Roosevelt's threat of force made very clear the paramount presence and self-interest of the United States in the Caribbean.

After the Spanish were expelled from Cuba, the United States supervised the island under Military Governor General Leonard Wood until 1902, when the Cubans elected their own congress and president. The United States honored Cuban independence, as it had promised to do in the Teller Amendment. But through the Platt Amendment, which Cubans reluctantly attached to their constitution in 1901, the United States obtained many economic rights in Cuba, a naval base at Guantanamo Bay, and the right of intervention if Cuban sovereignty were ever threatened. Newspapers in Havana assailed this violation of their newfound independence. One cartoon, titled "The Cuban Calvary," showed a figure representing the "Cuban people" crucified between two thieves, Wood and McKinley.

American policy intended to make Cuba a model of how a newly independent nation could achieve orderly self-government with only minimal guidance. Cuban self-government, however, was shaky. When in 1906 an internal political crisis threatened to plunge the infant nation into civil war, Roosevelt expressed his fury with "that infernal little Cuban republic." At Cuba's request, he sent warships to patrol the coastline and special commissioners and troops "to restore order and peace and public confidence." As he left office in 1909, Roosevelt proudly proclaimed that "we have done our best to put Cuba on the road to stable and orderly government." The road was paved with sugar. U.S. trade with Cuba increased from $27 million in the year before 1898 to an average of $43 million per year during the following decade. Along with economic development, American political and even military involvement in Cuban affairs continued throughout the century.

The pattern repeated itself throughout the Caribbean region. The Dominican Republic, for example, suffered from unstable governments and economic ill health. In 1904, as a revolt erupted, European creditors pressured the Dominican government for payment of $40 million in defaulted bonds. With the presence of its warships to discourage European intervention, the United States took over the collection of customs in the republic. Two years later, the United States intervened in Guatemala and Nicaragua, where American bankers controlled nearly 50 percent of all trade, the first of several interventions in those Central American countries in the twentieth century.

Roosevelt clarified his policy that civilized nations should "insist on the proper policing of the world" in his annual message in 1904. The goal of the United States, he said, was to have "stable, orderly and prosperous neighbors." A country that paid its debts and kept order "need fear no interference from the United States." A country that did not, but rather committed "chronic wrong-doing" and loosened the "ties of civilized society," would require the United States to intervene as an "international police power." This doctrine became known as the Roosevelt

Political Cartoons

One of the most enjoyable ways of recovering the values and attitudes of the past is through political cartoons. Ralph Waldo Emerson once said, "Caricatures are often the truest history of the times." A deft drawing of a popular or unpopular politician can freeze ideas and events in time, conveying more effectively than columns of type the central issues of the day and creating an immediate response in the viewer. It is this freshness that makes caricatures such a valuable source when attempting to recover the past. Cartoonists are often at their best when they are critical, exaggerating a physical feature of a political figure or capturing public sentiment against the government.

The history of political cartoons in the United States goes back to Benjamin Franklin's "Join or Die" cartoon calling for colonial cooperation against the French in 1754. But political cartoons were rare until Andrew Jackson's presidency. Even after such cartoons as "King Andrew the First" in the 1830s, they did not gain notoriety until the advent of Thomas Nast's cartoons in *Harper's Weekly* in the 1870s. Nast drew scathing cartoons exposing the corruption of William "Boss" Tweed's Tammany Hall, depicting Tweed and his men as vultures and smiling deceivers. "Stop them damn pictures," Tweed ordered. "I don't care so much what the papers write about me. My constituents can't read. But, damn it, they can see pictures." Tweed sent some of his men to Nast with an offer of $100,000 to "study art" in Europe. The $5,000-a-year artist negotiated up to a half million dollars before refusing Tweed's offer. "I made up my mind not long ago to put some of those fellows behind bars," Nast said, "and I'm going to put them there." His cartoons helped drive Tweed out of office.

The emergence of the United States as a world power and the rise of Theodore Roosevelt gave cartoonists plenty to draw about. An impetus to political cartoons was given by the rise of cheap newspapers such as William Randolph Hearst's *Journal* and Joseph Pulitzer's *World.* When the Spanish-American War broke out, newspapers whipped up public sentiment by having artists draw fake pictures of Spaniards stripping American women at sea and encouraging cartoonists to depict the "Spanish brute." Hearst used these tactics to increase his paper's daily circulation to one million copies. But by the time of the Philippines debates, many cartoonists took an anti-imperialist stance, pointing out American hypocrisy. Within a year, cartoonists shifted from depicting "The Spanish Brute Adds Mutilation to Mur-

"The Spanish Brute Adds Mutilation to Murder," by Grant Hamilton, in *Judge,* July 9, 1898.

"Liberty Halts American Butchery in the Philippines," from *Life,* 1899.

der" (1898) to "Liberty Halts American Butchery in the Philippines" (1899).The cartoons are very similar in condemning "butchery" of native populations, but the target has of course changed. Although Uncle Sam as a killer is not nearly as menacing as the figure of Spain as an ugly gorilla, both cartoons share a similarity of stance, the blood-covered swords, and a trail of bodies behind.

When Theodore Roosevelt rose to the presidency, cartoonists rejoiced. His physical appearance and personality made him instantly recognizable, a key factor in the success of a political cartoon. His broad grin, eyeglasses, and walrus mustache were the kind of features that fueled the cartoonist's imagination. A man of great energy, Roosevelt's style was as distinctive as his look. Other factors, such as the "Rough Rider" nickname, the symbol of the "big stick," and policies like "gunboat diplomacy" made Teddy the perfect target for political cartoons.

To understand and appreciate the meaning of any cartoon, certain facts must be ascertained, such as the date, artist, and source of the cartoon; the particular historical characters, events, and context depicted in it; the significance of the caption; and the master symbols employed by the cartoonist. The two remaining cartoons, "Panama or Bust" (1903) and "For President!" (1904), were both printed in American daily newspapers. Aside from the context and meaning of each cartoon, which should be obvious, note how the cartoonists use familiar symbols from Roosevelt's life and American history to underline the ironic power of their point. How many can you identify, and how are they used?

"Panama or Bust," from the *New York Times,* 1903.

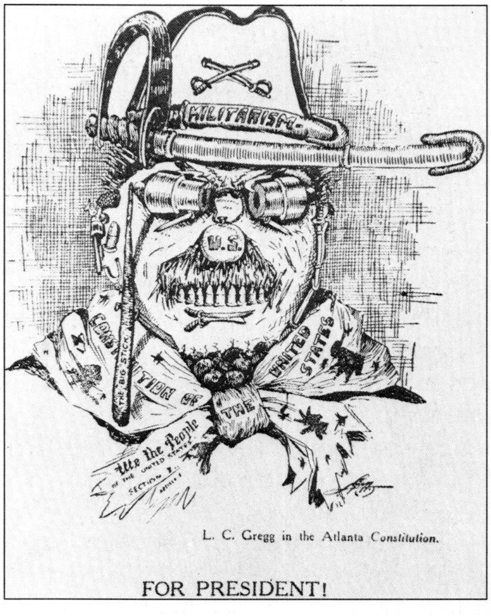

"For President!" by L. C. Gregg, in the Atlanta *Constitution,* 1904.

United States Involvement in Central America and the Caribbean, 1898–1939

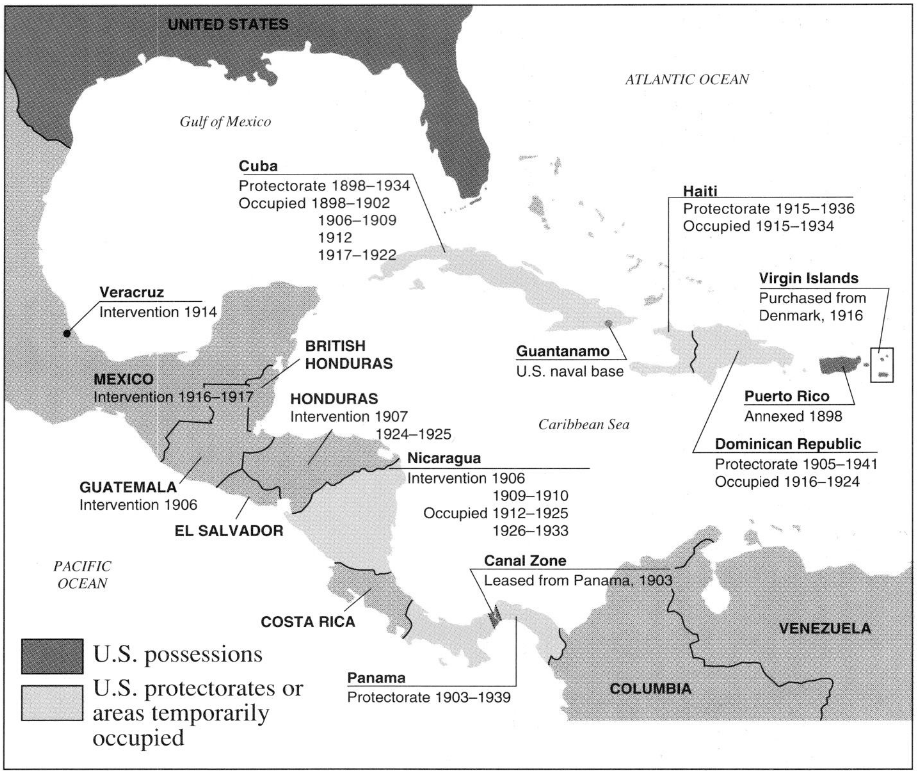

Can you update the location of further interventions in Central America and the Caribbean since the 1950s?

Corollary to the Monroe Doctrine. Whereas Monroe's doctrine had warned European nations not to intervene in the Western Hemisphere, Roosevelt's corollary justified American intervention. Starting with a desire to protect property, loans, and investments, the United States often interceded in these countries to maintain order. This meant supporting the brutal regimes of wealthy elites who owned most of the land, suppressed the poor and efforts for reform, and acted as surrogates of American policy.

After 1904, the Roosevelt Corollary was invoked in several Caribbean countries. Intervention usually required the landing of U.S. Marines to counter the threat posed by political instability and bankruptcy to American economic interests: railroads, mines, and the production of sugar, bananas, and coffee. Occupying the capital and major seaports, American marines, bankers, and customs officials usually remained for several years, until they were satisfied that stability had been reestablished. Roosevelt's successors, William Howard Taft and Woodrow Wilson, pursued the same interventionist policy. Later presidents, most recently Ronald Reagan (Nicaragua) and George Bush (Panama) would do likewise.

Opening the Door to China

Throughout the nineteenth century, American relations with China were restricted to a small but profitable trade. The British, in competition with France, Germany, and Russia, took advantage of the weak, crumbling Manchu dynasty by making trade treaties with China. These gave access to treaty ports and most-favored-nation trading privileges in various spheres of influence throughout the country. After 1898, Americans with dreams of exploiting the seemingly unlimited markets of China wanted to join the competition and enlarge their share. The United States, too, wanted favorable commercial rights and a place to sell surplus goods. Moral interests, however, including many missionaries, reminded Americans of their revolutionary tradition against European imperialism. They made clear their opposition to crass U.S. commercial exploitation of a weak nation and supported the preservation of China's political integrity against continuing interference by the European powers.

American attitudes toward the Chinese people reflected this confusion of motives. Some Americans held an idealized view of China as the center of Eastern wisdom and saw a "special relationship" between the two nations. But the dominant American attitude viewed the Chinese as heathen, exotic, backward, and immoral. The Exclusion Act of 1882 and the riots in western states against Chinese workers in the 1870s and 1880s reflected this negative stereotype. The Chinese, in turn, regarded the United States with a mixture of curiosity, resentment, suspicion, and disdain, as well as with admiration for a potential, if arrogant, guardian.

The annexation of Hawaii, Samoa, and the Philippines in 1898–1899 convinced Secretary of State Hay that the United States should announce its own policy for China. The result was the Open Door notes of 1899–1900, which became the cornerstone of U.S. policy in Asia for much of the twentieth century. The first note, focusing on customs collection issues, opened a door for American trade by declaring the principle of equal access to commercial rights in China by all nations. The second note, addressing Russian movement into Manchuria, called on all countries to respect the "territorial and administrative integrity" of China. This second principle opened the way for a larger American role in Asia, offering China protection from foreign invasions and preserving a balance of power in the Far East.

An early test of this new role came during the Boxer Rebellion in 1900. The Boxers were a society of young traditionalist Chinese in revolt against both the Manchu dynasty and the growing Western presence and influence in China. During the summer of 1900, fanatical Boxers killed some 242 missionaries and other foreigners and besieged the western quarter of Peking. Eventually, an international military force of 19,000 troops, including some 3,000 Americans sent from the Philippines, marched on Peking to end the siege.

The American relationship with China was plagued by the exclusionist immigration policy. Despite the barriers and riots, Chinese workers kept coming to the United States, entering illegally from Mexico and British Columbia. In 1905, Chinese nationalists at home boycotted American goods and called for a change in immigration policy. Roosevelt, who had a low opinion of the Chinese as a "backward" people, bristled with resentment and sent troops to the Philippines as a threat. Halfheartedly, he also asked Congress for a modified immigration bill, but nothing came of it.

Despite exclusion and insults, the idea that the United States had a unique guardian relationship with China persisted into the twentieth century. Since Japan had ambitions in China, this created a rivalry between Japan and the United States, testing the American commitment to preserve the Open Door in China and the balance of power in Asia. Economic motives in Asia, however, proved to be less significant. Investments there developed very slowly, as did the dream of the "great China market" for American grains and textiles. Although textile exports to China increased from $7 million to nearly $24 million in a decade, the China trade always remained larger in imagination than in reality.

Japan and the Balance of Power

Because of population pressures on the limited land mass of Japan, as well as war and the quest for economic opportunities, Japanese immigration to the United States dramatically increased around the turn of the century. Coming first as unmarried males working on western railroads and in Pacific Coast canneries, mines, and logging camps, immigrants from Japan increased from 25,000 in the 1890s to 125,000 between 1901 and 1908. Like the earlier Chinese immigrants, they were met with nativist hostility and discrimination. Japanese workers were barred from factory

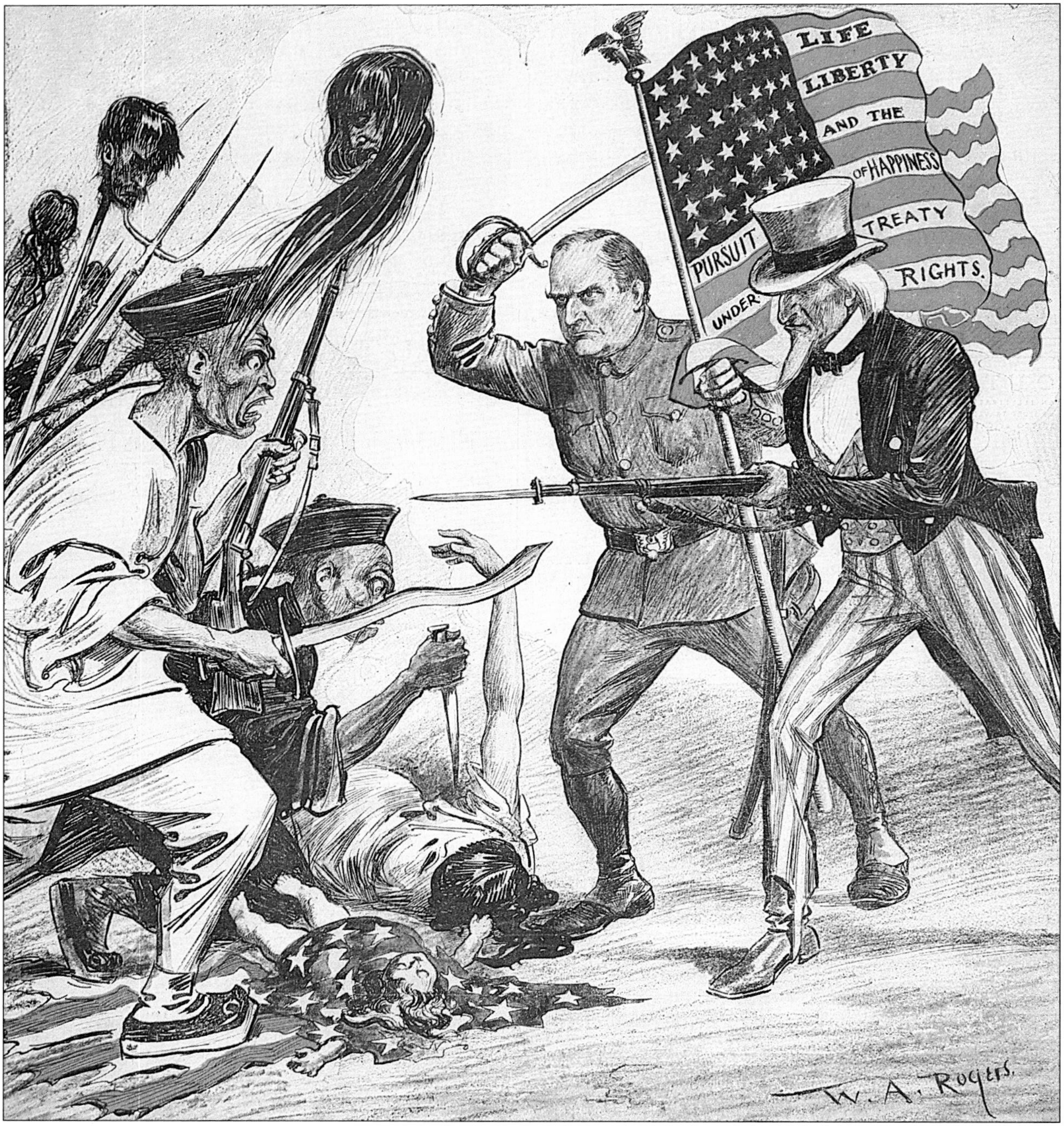

The United States' imperial role in China is supported in this cartoon showing President McKinley and Uncle Sam leading the charge against the Boxer Rebellion in 1900. What do you think is the point of view of the cartoonist?

jobs and shunted off to agricultural labor in California fields and orchards. In 1906, the San Francisco school board, claiming that Japanese children were "crowding the whites out of the schools," segregated them into separate schools and asked Roosevelt to persuade Japan to stop the emigration of its people. Though the Japanese were insulted, they agreed to limit the migration of unskilled workers to the United States in a gentleman's agreement signed in 1907. In return, the segregation law was repealed, but not without costs in relations between the two nations.

Roosevelt also relied on the use of diplomacy and negotiation in his effort to balance Asian powers against one another. The Boxer Rebellion of 1900 left Russia with 50,000 troops in Manchuria, the strongest nation in eastern Asia. Roosevelt's admiration for the Japanese as a "fighting" people and valuable factor in the "civilization of the future" contrasted with his low respect for the Russians, whom he described as "corrupt," "treacherous," and "incompetent." As Japan moved into Korea, and Russia into Manchuria, Roosevelt hoped that each would check the growing power of the other.

Because of increasing Russian strength, Roosevelt welcomed news in 1904 that Japan had launched a successful surprise attack on Port Arthur in Manchuria, beginning the Russo-Japanese War. He was "well pleased with the Japanese victory," he told his son, "for Japan is playing our game." But as Japanese victories continued, many Americans worried that Japan might play the game too well, shutting the United States out of Far Eastern markets. Roosevelt shifted his support toward Russia. When the Japanese expressed interest in an end to the war, the American president was pleased to exert his influence.

Roosevelt's goal was to achieve peace and leave a balanced situation. "It is best," he wrote, that Russia be left "face to face with Japan so that each may have a moderative action on the other."

United States Involvement in Asia, 1898–1909

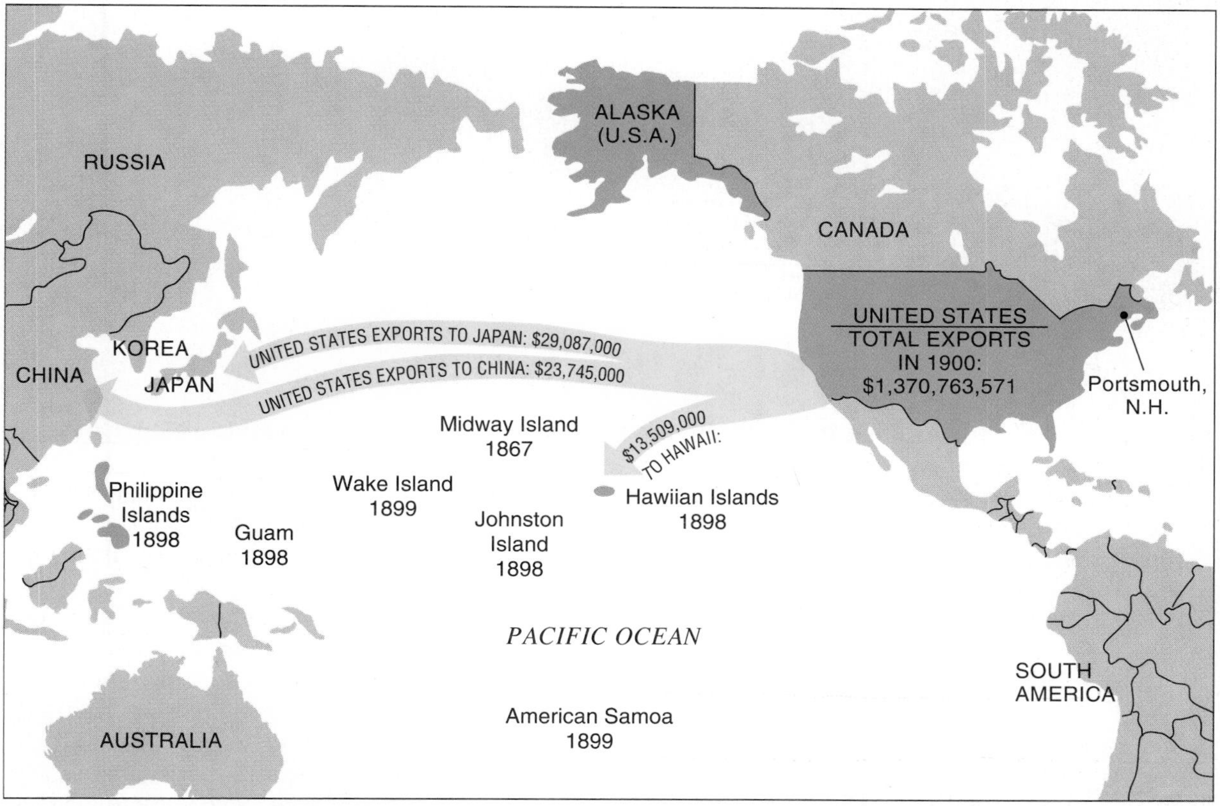

What twentieth-century events have followed the acquisition of territories in the Pacific and the development of intensified trade with East Asian countries?

President Roosevelt stands proudly at Portsmouth, New Hampshire, between Russian and Japanese representatives as they negotiated an end to the Russo-Japanese War in 1905.

The negotiations and resulting treaty were carried out in the summer of 1905 near Portsmouth, New Hampshire. No single act better symbolizes the new posture of American power and presence in the world than the signing of a peace treaty ending a war in Manchuria between Russia and Japan halfway around the globe in New Hampshire!

The Treaty of Portsmouth actually left Japan dominant in Manchuria and established the United States as the major balance to Japan's power. Almost immediately, the Japanese developed a naval base at Port Arthur, built railroads, and sought exclusive rights of investment and control in the Chinese province. In part because of his lack of respect for the Chinese, Roosevelt willingly recognized Japan's "dominance in Manchuria," as well as its control in Korea. But in return, in the Root-Takahira Agreement of 1908, he received Japan's promise to honor U.S. control in the Philippines and to make no further encroachments into China.

These agreements over territorial divisions barely covered up the tensions in Japanese-American relations. Some Japanese were angry that they had not received in the Portsmouth Treaty the indemnities they had wanted from Russia, and they blamed Roosevelt. American insensitivity to the immigration issue also left bad feelings. In Manchuria, U.S. Consul General Willard Straight aggressively pushed an anti-Japanese program of financing capital investment projects in banking and railroads. This policy, later known as "dollar diplomacy" under Roosevelt's successor, William Howard Taft, like the pursuit of markets, was larger in prospect than results. Nevertheless, the United States was in Japan's way, and rumors of war circulated in the world press.

It was clearly time for Roosevelt's version of the "big stick." In 1907, he told Secretary of State Root that he was "more concerned over the Japanese situation than almost any other. Thank Heaven we have the navy in good shape." Although the naval buildup had begun over a decade earlier, under Roosevelt the U.S. Navy had developed into a formidable force. From 1900 to 1905, outlays to the navy rose from $56 to $117 million. Such a naval spending binge was without precedent in peacetime. In 1907, to make it clear that "the Pacific was as much our home waters as the Atlantic," Roosevelt sent his new, modernized "Great White Fleet" on a goodwill tour around the World. The first stop was the Japanese port of Yokohama. Although American sailors were greeted warmly, the act may have stimulated navalism in Japan, which came back to haunt the United States in 1941. But for the time being, the balance of power in Asia was preserved.

Preventing War in Europe

The United States was willing to stretch the meaning of the Monroe Doctrine to justify sending marines and engineers to Latin America and the navy and dollars to Asia. Treaties, agreements, and the protection of territories and interests entangled the United States with foreign nations from Panama and the Dominican Republic to the Philippines and Manchuria. Toward Europe, however, the traditional policies of neutrality and nonentanglement continued. Neither the moral civilizing of unregenerate natives nor American self-interest seemed appropriate in Europe. Still, there was an American role to be played even there, and Roosevelt was eager to play it.

The most powerful nations of the world were European. Roosevelt therefore believed that the most serious threats to world peace and civilized order lay in relationships between Germany, Great Britain, and France. He established two fundamental policies toward Europe that with only minor variations would define the U.S. role throughout the century. The first was to make friendship with Great Britain the cornerstone of U.S. policy. As Roosevelt told King Edward VII in 1905, "In the long run the English people are more apt to be friendly to us than any other." Second, the crucial goal of a neutral power like the United States was to prevent the outbreak of a general war in Europe among strong nations. Toward this end, Roosevelt depended on his personal negotiating skills and began the practice of summit diplomacy.

It is difficult now to think of England as anything other than the most loyal friend of the United States outside North America. Yet throughout most of the nineteenth century, England was America's chief enemy and commercial rival. From the War of 1812 to the Venezuelan border crisis of 1895, conflict with Great Britain developed in squabbles over old debts and trade barriers, disputes over Canadian borders and fishing jurisdictions, and British interference in the American Civil War.

The Venezuelan crisis and a number of other events at the turn of the century shocked the United States and England into an awareness of their mutual interests. Both nations appreciated the neutrality of the other in their respective wars shouldering the white man's burden against the Filipinos and the Boers. Roosevelt supported British imperialism because he favored the dominance of the "English-speaking race" and believed that England was "fighting the battle of civilization." Furthermore, both nations worried about growing German power in Europe, Africa, and the Far East. As German naval power increased, England had to bring its fleet closer to home. Friendly allies were needed to police parts of the world formerly patrolled by the British navy. England therefore concluded a mutual-protection treaty with Japan in 1902 and willingly let the Americans police Central America and the Caribbean Sea.

Similarities of language and cultural traditions, as well as strategic self-interest, drew the two countries together. Roosevelt's personal style furthered the connection. He was clearly and unashamedly pro-British, and his most intimate circle of friends included many Englishmen. Although Roosevelt sometimes criticized English policies, his British bias was never in doubt. He knew, as he wrote to Lodge in 1901, that the United States had "not the least particle of danger to fear" from England and that German ambitions and militarism represented the major threat to peace in Europe. As Roosevelt left the presidency in 1909, one of his final acts was to proclaim the special American friendship with Great Britain.

German Kaiser Wilhelm II often underestimated the solidity of Anglo-American friendship and thought that Roosevelt was really pro-German, an error the American president skillfully used. He cultivated the kaiser to make him think they were friends sharing mutual interests. Wilhelm therefore sought Roosevelt's support on several diplomatic issues between 1905 and 1909. In each case Roosevelt flattered the kaiser while politely rejecting his overtures. The relationship gave Roosevelt a unique advantage in influencing affairs in Europe to prevent the outbreak of war.

The Moroccan crisis in 1905 and 1906 is illustrative. European powers competed for colonies and spheres of influence in Africa as well as in Asia. Germany in particular resented French dominance along the North African coast in Morocco and feared the recent Anglo-French entente. The kaiser precipitated a crisis in the summer of 1905 by delivering a bellicose speech in Casablanca, Morocco, intended to split the British and French and to force an opening of commercial doors in Morocco. In this endeavor he sought help from Roosevelt. The French were outraged at Wilhelm's boldness, and war threatened. Roosevelt intervened, arranging a conference in Algeciras, Spain, to avert conflict. The treaty signed in 1906 prevented war and settled the issues of commerce and police administration in Morocco favorably for the French.

Roosevelt's successful countering of meddlesome German policies continued, as did his efforts in preventing war. At the Hague conference on disarmament in 1907, the kaiser sought an agreement to reduce British naval supremacy, a superiority Roosevelt thought "quite proper." The German emperor also tried to promote German-Chinese-American entente to balance the Anglo-Japanese Treaty in Asia. Roosevelt rebuffed all these efforts. While on a European tour in 1910, the retired American president was warmly entertained and celebrated by Wilhelm, who continued to misunderstand him. Roosevelt, meanwhile, kept on urging his English friends to counter the German naval buildup in order to maintain peace in Europe.

In 1911, Roosevelt wrote that there would be nothing worse than that "Germany should ever overthrow England and establish the supremacy in Europe she aims at." German interest "to try her hand in America," he thought, would surely follow. To avert such horrors, Roosevelt's policy for Europe included cementing friendship with England and, while maintaining official neutrality, using diplomacy to prevent hostilities among European powers. The relationship between Great Britain and Germany continued to deteriorate, however, and by 1914 a new American president, Woodrow Wilson, would face the terrible reality that Roosevelt had so skillfully helped to prevent. When World War I finally broke out, no American was more eager to fight on the British side against the Germans than the leader of the Rough Riders.

CONCLUSION

The Responsibilities of Power

Since the earliest settlements at Massachusetts Bay, Americans had struggled with the dilemma of how to do good in a world that did wrong. The realities of power in the 1890s brought increasing international responsibilities. Roosevelt said in 1910 that because of "strength and geographical situation," the United States had itself become "more and more, the balance of power of the whole world." This ominous responsibility was also an opportunity to extend American economic, political, and moral influence around the globe.

As president in the first decade of the twentieth century, Roosevelt established aggressive American policies toward the rest of the world. Americans dominated and policed Central America and the Caribbean Sea to maintain order and protect its investments and other economic interests. In the Far East, Americans marched through Hay's Open Door with treaties, troops, navies, and dollars to protect the newly annexed Philippine Islands, to develop markets and investments, and to preserve the balance of power in Asia. In Europe, the United States sought to remain neutral and uninvolved in European affairs and at the same time to cement Anglo-American friendship and prevent "civilized" nations from going to war.

How well these policies worked would be seen later in the twentieth century. Whatever the particular judgment, the fundamental ambivalence of America's sense of itself as a model "city on a hill," an example to others, remained. As widening involvements around the world—the Filipino-American War, for example—painfully demonstrated, it was increasingly difficult for the United States to be both responsible and good, both powerful and loved. The American people thus learned to experience both the satisfactions and the burdens, the profits and the costs, of the missionary role.

Recommended Reading

American Expansionism: Moving Toward Empire

Robert Beisner, *From the Old Diplomacy to the New, 1865–1900* (1975); Charles Campbell, *The Transformation of American Foreign Relations, 1865–1900* (1976); John Dobson, *Reticent Expansionism: The Foreign Policy of William McKinley* (1988); Lewis Gould, *The Presidency of William McKinley* (1980); David Healy, *U.S. Expansion: Imperialist Urge in the 1890s* (1970); Walter La Feber, *The New Empire: An Interpretation of American Expansion, 1860–1898* (1963); Ernest May, *Imperial Democracy: The Emergence of America as a Great Power* (1961); H. Wayne Morgan, *America's Road to Empire: The War with Spain and Overseas Expansion* (1965); Milton Plesur, *America's Outward Thrust, 1865–1890* (1971); Emily Rosenberg, *Spreading the American Dream: American Economic and Cultural Expansion, 1890–1945* (1982); Rubin Weston, *Racism in U.S. Imperialism: The Influence of Racial Assumptions on American Foreign Policy, 1893–1946* (1972); William Widenor, *Henry Cabot Lodge and the Search for an American Foreign Policy* (1980).

The Spanish-American War and the Philippines

Robert Beisner, *Twelve Against Empire: The Anti-Imperialists, 1898–1900* (1975); Frank Freidel, *The Splendid Little War* (1958); Willard Gatewood, Jr., *Black Americans and the White Man's Burden* (1975); *"Smoked Yankees" and the Struggle for Empire: Letters from Negro Soldiers, 1898–1902* (1971); Stanley Karnow, *In Our Image: America's Empire in the Philippines* (1989); Gerald Linderman, *The Mirror of War: American Society and the Spanish-American War* (1974); Glenn A. May, *Social Engineering in the Philippines: The Aims, Execution, and Impact of American Colonial Policy, 1900–1913* (1980); Stuart Creighton Miller, *"Benevolent Assimilation": The American Conquest of the Philippines, 1899–1903* (1982); David Trask, *The War with Spain in 1898* (1981); Richard Welch, *Response to Imperialism: The United States and the Philippine-American War, 1899–1902* (1979); Leon Wolff, *Little Brown Brother: How the United States Purchased and Pacified the Philippine Islands at the Century's Turn* (1961).

Roosevelt's Energetic Foreign Policy and Relations with Asia and the Caribbean

Howard Beale, *Theodore Roosevelt and the Rise of America to World Power* (1956); Roger Daniels, *Asian Americans: Chinese and Japanese in the United States Since 1850* (1988); Raymond Esthus, *Theodore Roosevelt and the International Rivalries* (1970); Michael Hunt, *The Making of a Special Relationship: The United States and China to 1914* (1983); Walter La Feber, *Inevitable Revolutions: The United States in Central America* (1983) and *The Panama Canal* (1978); Frederick Marks II, *Velvet on Iron: The Diplomacy of Theodore Roosevelt* (1979); David McCollough, *The Path Between the Seas: The Creation of the Panama Canal, 1870–1914* (1977); Dana Munro, *Intervention and Dollar Diplomacy in the Caribbean, 1900–1920* (1964); Charles E. Neu, *An Uncertain Friendship: Theodore Roosevelt and Japan, 1906–1909* (1967); Ronald Takaki, *Strangers from a Different Shore: A History of Asian Americans* (1989); Marilyn B. Young, *The Rhetoric of Empire: American China Policy, 1895–1901* (1968).

TIMELINE

1823 Monroe Doctrine

1857 Trade opens with Japan

1867 Alaska purchased from Russia

1870 Failure to annex Santo Domingo (Hispaniola)

1875 Sugar reciprocity treaty with Hawaii

1877 United States acquires naval base at Pearl Harbor

1878 United States acquires naval station in Samoa

1882 Chinese Exclusion Act

1889 First Pan-American Conference

1890 Alfred Mahan publishes *Influence of Sea Power upon History*

1893 Hawaiian coup by American sugar growers

1895 Cuban revolt against Spanish
Venezuelan boundary dispute

1896 Weyler's reconcentration policy in Cuba
McKinley-Bryan presidential campaign

1897 Theodore Roosevelt's speech at Naval War College

1898

January	De Lôme letter
February	Sinking of the battleship *Maine*
April	Spanish-American War; Teller Amendment
May	Dewey takes Manila Bay
July	Annexation of Hawaiian Islands
August	Americans liberate Manila; war ends
December	Treaty of Paris; annexation of the Philippines

1899 Senate ratifies Treaty of Paris
Filipino-American War begins
American Samoa acquired

1899–1900 Open Door notes

1900 Boxer Rebellion in China
William McKinley reelected president

1901 Supreme Court insular cases
McKinley assassinated; Theodore Roosevelt becomes president

1902 Filipino-American War ends
U.S. military occupation of Cuba ends
Platt Amendment
Venezuela debt crisis

1903 Panamanian revolt and independence
Hay–Bunau-Varilla Treaty

1904 Roosevelt Corollary

1904–1905 Russo-Japanese War ended by treaty signed at Portsmouth, N.H.

1904–1906 United States intervenes in Nicaragua, Guatemala, Cuba

1905–1906 Moroccan crisis

1906 Roosevelt receives Nobel Peace Prize

1907 Gentleman's agreement with Japan

1908 Root-Takahira Agreement

1909 U.S. Navy ("Great White Fleet") sails around the world

1911 U.S. intervenes in Nicaragua

1914 Opening of the Panama Canal
World War I begins

1916 Partial home rule granted to the Philippines

PART V

A Modernizing People, 1900–1945

1900

COMPARATIVE CHRONOLOGIES

1900

POLITICAL AND DIPLOMATIC

1900 William McKinley reelected president
1901 McKinley assassinated; Theodore Roosevelt becomes president
1901 Socialist Party of America formed
1904 Roosevelt reelected
1906 Hepburn Act
Meat Inspection Act
Pure Food and Drug Act
1908 William Howard Taft elected president

SOCIAL AND ECONOMIC

1901 United States Steel Corporation organized
1902 Anthracite coal strike
1903–1910 Muckrakers attack social evils and corruption
1905 Industrial Workers of the World (IWW) organized
1907 Panic caused by business failures
Gentlemen's agreement stops emigration of Japanese laborers to United States
1908 *Muller* v. *Oregon*
1909 National Association for the Advancement of Colored People (NAACP) organized

CULTURAL AND TECHNOLOGICAL

1901 Frank Norris, *The Octopus*
1903 Wright brothers make first heavier-than-air flight
1904 Lincoln Steffens, *The Shame of the Cities*
1906 Upton Sinclair, *The Jungle*
1908 Frank Lloyd Wright designs Robie House in Chicago
1909 First Model T Ford produced

1910

POLITICAL AND DIPLOMATIC

1910 Mann Act
1912 Woodrow Wilson elected president
1913 Sixteenth Amendment provides for an income tax
Seventeenth Amendment provides for direct election of senators
1914 World War I begins in Europe
1915 *Lusitania* sunk
1916 Wilson reelected
1917 United States declares war on Germany and Austria-Hungary
1918 War ends in Europe
1919 Senate defeats League of Nations Treaty
Eighteenth Amendment establishes prohibition

SOCIAL AND ECONOMIC

1911 Triangle Shirtwaist Company fire
1913 Federal Reserve System established
Department of Labor separated from Department of Commerce
1914 Clayton Act
1917 Literacy test for new immigrants established
1917 Espionage Act
1918–1919 Influenza epidemic
1919 United States becomes creditor nation for first time

CULTURAL AND TECHNOLOGICAL

1910 Jane Addams, *Twenty Years at Hull House*
1911 Frederick Taylor, *The Principles of Scientific Management*
1913 First assembly line at Ford Motor Company
Armory Show, New York
1914 Panama Canal completed
1915 D. W. Griffith produces *The Birth of a Nation*
1916 Margaret Sanger organizes New York Birth Control League

1920

POLITICAL AND DIPLOMATIC

1920 Warren G. Harding elected president
Nineteenth Amendment provides for woman suffrage
1921 Washington Naval Conference
1923 Harding dies; Calvin Coolidge becomes president
Teapot Dome scandal
1924 Coolidge reelected
1928 Herbert Hoover elected president

SOCIAL AND ECONOMIC

1921 Sheppard-Towner Act
Immigration limited to 3 percent of each nationality in country in 1910
1924 Immigration limited to 2 percent of nationality in country in 1890
1925 A & W Root Beer becomes first fast-food franchise
1929 Stock market crash heralds Great Depression

CULTURAL AND TECHNOLOGICAL

1920 First commercial radio broadcast, WWJ Detroit
1922 Sinclair Lewis, *Babbitt*
1925 Scopes trial
1926 Langston Hughes, *Weary Blues*
1927 Charles Lindbergh flies alone to Paris
Sacco and Vanzetti executed
The Jazz Singer, first feature-length talking movie
1929 William Faulkner, *The Sound and the Fury*

1930

1932 Franklin Roosevelt elected president
1933 TVA and CCC created
NIRA and AAA
1935 Social security and WPA established
1936 Roosevelt reelected
1937 Wagner-Steagall Act
1939 World War II begins in Europe

1932 Bonus March
1933 Twenty-first Amendment ends prohibition
1934 Indian Reorganization Act
1935 Committee for Industrial Organization (CIO) formed
1936 United Auto Workers hold sit-down strike at General Motors plant
1938 Fair Labor Standards Act

1934–1938 Radar developed by Army Signal Corps and U.S. Navy
1935 Walt Disney releases *Flowers and Trees*, his first movie in color
1935–1943 WPA artists' and writers' projects
1936 Margaret Mitchell, *Gone with the Wind*
1938 Orson Welles's radio broadcast "The War of the Worlds"
1938 Nylon and fiberglass
1939 John Steinbeck, *The Grapes of Wrath*
New York World's Fair
First scheduled television broadcast

1940

1940 Roosevelt reelected for third term
1941 Japanese attack Pearl Harbor; Japan and Germany declare war on United States
1942 Allies invade North Africa
1943 Italy surrenders
1944 Normandy invasion
Roosevelt reelected for fourth term

1941 Roosevelt outlaws discrimination in defense industries
1942 Congress of Racial Equality (CORE) founded
1944 Bretton Woods Conference

1941 Penicillin
1942 Jet plane first tested in United States
1943 Wendell Willkie, *One World*
1944 First electronic calculator
Serviceman's Readjustment Act ("GI Bill")

CHAPTER 21

The Progressives Confront Industrial Capitalism

Frances Kellor, a young woman who grew up in Ohio and Michigan, received her law degree in 1897 from Cornell University and became one of the small but growing group of professionally trained women. Deciding that she was more interested in solving the nation's social problems than in practicing law, she moved to Chicago, studied sociology, and trained herself as a social reformer. Kellor believed passionately that poverty and inequality could be eliminated in America. She also had the progressive faith that if Americans could only hear the truth about the millions of people living in urban slums, they would rise up and make changes. She was one of the experts who provided the evidence to document what was wrong in industrial America.

Like many progressives, Kellor believed that environment was more important than heredity in determining ability, prosperity, and happiness. Better schools and better housing, she thought, would produce better citizens. Even criminals, she argued, were simply victims of environment. Kellor demonstrated that poor health and deprived childhoods explained the only differences between criminals and college students. If it were impossible to define a criminal type, then it must be possible to reduce crime by improving the environment.

Kellor was an efficient professional. Like the majority of the professional women of her generation, she never married but devoted her life to social research and social reform. She lived for a time at Hull House in Chicago and at the College Settlement in New York, centers not only of social research and reform but also of lively community. For many young people, the settlement, with its sense of commitment and its exciting conversation around the dinner table, provided an alternative to the nuclear family or the single apartment.

While staying at the College Settlement, Kellor researched and wrote a muckraking study of employment agencies, published in 1904 as *Out of Work*. She revealed how employment agencies exploited immigrants, blacks, and other recent arrivals in the city. Kellor's book, like the writing of most progressives, spilled over with moral outrage. But Kellor went beyond moralism to suggest corrective legislation at the state and national levels.

Kellor became one of the leaders of the movement to Americanize the immigrants pouring into the country in unprecedented numbers. Between 1899 and 1920, over 8 million people came to the United States, most from southern and eastern Europe. Many feared that this flood of immigrants threatened the very basis of American democracy. Kellor and her coworkers represented the side of progressivism that sought state and federal laws to protect the new arrivals from exploitation and to establish agencies and facilities to educate and Americanize them. Another group of progressives, often allied with organized labor, tried to pass laws to restrict immigration. Kellor did not entirely escape the ethnocentrism that was a part of her generation's world view, but she did maintain that all immigrants could be made into useful citizens.

Convinced of the need for a national movement to push for reform legislation, Kellor helped to found the National Committee for Immigrants in America, which tried to promote a national policy "to make all these people Americans," and a federal bureau to organize the campaign. Eventually she helped establish the Division of Immigrant Education within the Department of Education. A political movement led by Theodore Roosevelt excited her most. More than almost any other single person, Kellor had been responsible for alerting Roosevelt to the problems the immigrants faced in American cities. When Roosevelt formed the new Progressive party in 1912, she was one of the many social workers and social researchers who joined him. She campaigned for Roosevelt and directed the Progressive Service Organization, to educate voters in all areas of social justice and welfare after the election. After Roosevelt's defeat and the collapse of the Progressive party in 1914, Kellor continued to work for Americanization. She spent the rest of her life promoting justice, order, and efficiency and trying to find ways for resolving industrial and international disputes.

Frances Kellor's life illustrates two important aspects of progressivism, the first nationwide reform movement of the modern era: first, a commitment to promote social justice, to assure equal opportunity, and to preserve democracy; and second, a search for order and efficiency in a world complicated by rapid industrialization, immigration, and spectacular urban growth. But no one person can represent all facets of so complex a movement. Borrowing from populism and influenced by a number of reformers from the 1890s, progressivism reached a climax in the years from 1900 to 1914. The reform impulse seems to run in cycles in American history, and the progressive movement was one of those times in American history (others were the 1830s, the 1930s, and the 1960s) when a majority of Americans agreed that changes were needed in American society. Like most American reform movements, the progressive movement did not plot to overthrow the government; rather, it sought to reform the system in order to assure the survival of the American way of life.

This chapter traces the important aspects of progressivism, a broad and diverse movement that influenced almost all areas of American life. It examines the social justice movement, which sought to promote reform among the poor and to improve life for those who had fallen victim to an urban and industrial civilization. It surveys life among workers, a group the reformers sometimes helped but often misunderstood. Then it traces the reform movements in the cities and states, where countless officials and experts tried to reduce chaos and promote order and democracy. Finally, it examines progressivism at the national level during the administrations of Theodore Roosevelt and Woodrow Wilson, the first thoroughly modern presidents.

The Social Justice Movement

Historians write of a "progressive movement," but actually there were a number of movements, some of them contradictory but all focusing on the problems created by a rapidly expanding urban and industrial world. Some reformers, often from the middle class, sought to humanize the modern city. They hoped to improve housing and schools and to provide a better life for the poor and recent immigrants. Others were concerned with the conditions of work and the rights of labor. Still others pressed for changes in the political system to make it more responsive to their interests. Progressivism had roots in the 1890s, when many reformers were shocked by the devastation caused by the depression of 1893, and they were influenced by reading Henry George's *Progress and Poverty* (1879) and Edward Bellamy's *Looking Backward* (1888). They were also influenced by the Social Gospel movement, which sought to build the kingdom of God on earth by eliminating poverty and promoting equality (see Chapter 19).

The Progressive World View

Intellectually, the progressives were influenced by the Darwinian revolution. They believed that the world was in flux, and they rebelled against the fixed and the formal in every field. One of the philosophers of the movement, John Dewey, wrote that ideas could become instruments for change. William James, in his philosophy of pragmatism, denied that there were universal truths; ideas should be judged by their usefulness. Most of the progressives were environmentalists who were convinced that environment was much more important than heredity in forming character. Thus if one could build better schools and houses, one could make better people and a more perfect society. Yet even the more advanced reformers thought in racial and ethnic categories. They believed that some groups could be molded and changed more easily than others. Thus progressivism did not usually mean progress for blacks.

In many ways, progressivism was the first modern reform movement. It sought to bring order and efficiency to a world that had been transformed by rapid growth and new technology. Yet elements of nostalgia infected the movement as reformers tried to preserve the handicrafts of a preindustrial age and to promote small-town and farm values in the city. The progressive leaders were almost always middle-class, and they quite consciously tried to teach their middle-class values to the immigrants and the working class. Often the progressives seemed more interested in control than in reform; frequently, they betrayed a sense of paternalism toward those they tried to help.

The progressives were part of a statistics-minded, realistic generation. They conducted surveys, gathered facts, wrote reports about every conceivable problem, and usually had faith that their reports would lead to change. Their urge to document and to record came out in haunting photographs of young workers taken by Lewis Hine, in the stark and beautiful city paintings by John Sloan, and in the realist novels of Theodore Dreiser and William Dean Howells.

The progressives were optimistic about human nature, and they believed that change was possible. In retrospect, they may seem naive or bigoted, but they wrestled with many social questions, some of them old but fraught with new urgency in an industrialized society. What is the proper relation of government to society? In a world of large corporations, huge cities, and massive transportation systems, how much should the government regulate and control? How much responsibility does society have to care for the poor and needy? The progressives could not agree on the answers, but for the first time in American history, they struggled with the questions.

The Muckrakers

One group of writers who exposed corruption and other evils in American society were labeled "muckrakers" by Theodore Roosevelt. Not all muckrakers were reformers—some merely wanted to profit from the scandals—but the reformers learned from their techniques of exposé.

In part the muckrakers were a product of the journalistic revolution of the 1890s. Nineteenth-century magazines such as *Atlantic, Century,* and *Scribner's* had small, highly educated audiences.

John Sloan (1871–1951) was one of the leading members of the "ashcan" school, a group of artists that experimented with new techniques and tried to document ordinary scenes. Sloan's realistic depictions of the city, such as this 1914 painting, *Backyards, Greenwich Village,* shocked Americans just as much as the progressive era reports on child labor, prostitution, and poor housing.

The new magazines, among them *American, McClure's,* and *Cosmopolitan,* had slick formats, carried more advertising, and sold more widely. Several had circulations of more than 500,000 in 1910. Competing for readers, editors eagerly published the articles of investigative reporters who wanted to tell the public what was wrong in American society.

Lincoln Steffens, a young California journalist, wrote articles for *McClure's* exposing the connections between respectable urban businessmen and corrupt politicians. When published in 1904 as *The Shame of the Cities,* Steffens's account became a battle cry for people determined to clean up the graft in city government. Ida Tarbell, a teacher turned journalist, had grown up in western Pennsylvania, almost next door to the first oil well in the United States. She published several successful books before turning her attention to the Standard Oil Company and John D. Rockefeller. Her outraged exposé, based on years of research, revealed Rockefeller's ruthless ways and his unfair business practices.

After Steffens and Tarbell achieved popular success, many others followed. Ray Stannard Baker exposed the railroads. David Graham Phillips revealed the alliance of politics and business in *The Treason of the Senate* (1906). Robert Hunter, a young settlement worker, shocked Americans in 1904 with his book *Poverty:* setting the poverty line at $460 for a family of five, he found 10 million people living below that level. Realistic fiction also mirrored such concerns. Upton Sinclair's novel *The Jungle* (1906) described the horrors of the Chicago meatpacking industry, while Frank Norris in *The Octopus* (1901) dramatized the railroads' stranglehold on the farmers.

Working Women and Children

Nothing disturbed the social justice progressives more than the sight of children, sometimes as young as 8 or 10, working long hours in dangerous and depressing factories. Young people had worked in factories since the beginning of the industrial revolution, but that did not make the practice any less repugnant to the reformers. "Children are put into industry very much as we put in raw material," Jane Addams objected, "and the product we look for is not better men and women, but better manufactured goods."

Florence Kelley was one of the most important leaders in the crusade against child labor. Kelley had grown up in an upper-class Philadelphia family and graduated from Cornell in 1882, like Addams and Kellor a member of the first generation of college women. When the University of

Nothing tugged at the heartstrings of the reformers more than the sight of little children, sullen and stunted, working long hours in factory, farm, and mine. These children, coal miners in Pennsylvania, were carefully posed by documentary photographer Lewis Hines while he worked for the National Child Labor Committee in 1911.

Pennsylvania refused her admission as a graduate student because she was a woman, she went to the University of Zurich in Switzerland. There she married and became a socialist. The marriage failed, and some years later, Kelley moved to Chicago with her children, became a Hull House resident, and poured her considerable energies into the campaign against child labor. A friend described her as "explosive, hot-tempered, determined . . . a smoking volcano that at any moment would burst into flames." When she could find no attorney in Chicago to argue a child labor case against some of the prominent corporations, she went to law school, passed the bar exam, and argued the cases herself.

Although Kelley and the other child labor reformers won a few cases, they quickly recognized the need for state laws if they were going to have any real influence. Child labor was an emotional issue. Many businesses made large profits by employing children, and many legislators and government officials, remembering their own rural childhoods, argued that it was good for the children's character to work hard and take responsibility. Reformers, marshaling their evidence about the tragic effects on growing children of long working hours in dark and damp factories, pressured the Illinois state legislature into passing an anti–child labor law. A few years later, however, the state supreme court declared the law unconstitutional.

Judicial opposition was one factor leading reformers to the national level in the first decade of the twentieth century. Florence Kelley again led the charge. In 1899, she had become secretary of the National Consumers League, an organization that enlisted consumers in a campaign to lobby elected officials and corporations to ensure that products were produced under safe and sanitary conditions. It was not Kelley, however, but Edgar Gardner Murphy, an Alabama clergyman, who suggested the formation of the National Child Labor Committee. Like many other Social Gospel ministers, Murphy believed that the church should reform society as well as save souls. He was appalled by the number of young children working in southern textile mills, where they were exposed to great danger and condemned to "compulsory ignorance" (because they dropped out of school).

The National Child Labor Committee, headquartered in New York, drew up a model state child labor law, encouraged state and city campaigns, and coordinated the movement around the country. While two-thirds of the states passed some form of child labor law between 1905 and 1907, many had loopholes that exempted a large number of children, including newsboys and youngsters who worked in the theater. The committee also supported a national bill introduced in Congress by Indiana Senator Albert Beveridge in 1906 "to prevent the employment of children in factories and mines." The bill went down to defeat. However, the child labor reformers convinced Congress in 1912 to establish a children's bureau in the Department of Labor. Despite these efforts, compulsory school attendance laws did more to reduce the number of children who worked than federal and state laws, which proved difficult to pass and even more difficult to enforce.

The crusade against child labor was a typical social justice reform effort. Its origins lay in the moral indignation of middle-class reformers. But reform went beyond moral outrage as reformers gathered statistics, took photographs documenting the abuse of children, and used their evidence to push for legislation first on the local level, then in the states, and eventually in Washington.

Like other progressive reform efforts, the battle against child labor was only partly successful. Too many businessmen, both small and large, were profiting from employing children at low wages. Too many politicians and judges were reluctant to regulate the work of children or adults because work seemed such an individual and personal matter. And some parents, who often desperately needed the money their children earned in the factories, opposed the reformers and even broke the law to allow their children to work.

The reformers also worried over the young people who got into trouble with the law, often for pranks that in rural areas would have seemed harmless. They feared for young people tried by adult courts and thrown into jail with hardened criminals. Almost simultaneously in Denver and Chicago, reformers organized juvenile courts, where judges had the authority to put delinquent youths on probation, take them from their families and make them wards of the state, or assign them to an institution. The juvenile court often helped prevent young delinquents from adopting a life of crime. Yet the juvenile offender was frequently deprived of all rights of due process, a fact that the Supreme Court finally recognized in 1967, when it ruled that children were entitled to procedural rights when accused of a crime.

Closely connected with the anti–child labor movement was the effort to limit the hours of women's work. It seemed inconsistent to protect a girl until she was 16 and then give her the "right to work from 8 A.M. to 10 P.M., thirteen hours a day, seventy-eight hours a week for $6." Florence Kelley and the National Consumers League led the campaign. It was foolish and unpatriotic, they argued, to allow the "mothers of future generations" to work long hours in dangerous industries. "Adult females," a Pennsylvania superior court stated, "are so constituted as to be unable to endure physical exertion and exposure."

The most important court case on women's work came before the U.S. Supreme Court in 1908. Josephine Goldmark, a friend and coworker of Kelley's at the Consumers League, wrote the brief for *Muller* v. *Oregon* that her brother-in-law, Louis Brandeis, used when he argued the case. The Court upheld the Oregon ten-hour law largely because Goldmark's sociological argument detailed the danger and disease that factory women faced. Brandeis opposed laissez-faire legal concepts, arguing that the government had a special interest in protecting the health of its citizens. Most states fell into line with the Supreme Court decision and passed protective legislation for women, though many companies found ways to circumvent the laws. Even the work permitted by the law seemed too long to some women. "I think ten hours is too much for a woman," one factory worker stated. "I have four children and have to work hard at home. Make me awful tired. I would like nine hours. I get up at 5:30. When I wash, I have to stay up till one or two o'clock."

By contending that "women are fundamentally weaker than men in all that makes for endurance: in muscular strength, in nervous energy, in the powers of persistent attention and application," the reformers won some protection for women workers. But their arguments that women were weaker than men would eventually be used to reinforce gender segregation of the work force for the next half century.

In addition to working for protective legislation for working women, the social justice progressives also campaigned for woman suffrage. Unlike some supporters who argued that middle-class women would offset the ignorant and corrupt votes of immigrant men, these social reformers supported votes for all women. Addams argued that urban women not only could vote intelligently but also needed the vote to protect, clothe, and feed their families. Women in an urban age, she suggested, needed to be municipal housekeepers. Through the suffrage, they would ensure that elected officials provided adequate services—pure water, uncontaminated food, proper sanitation, and police protection. The progressive insistence that all women needed the vote helped to push woman suffrage toward the victory that would come during World War I.

Much more controversial than either votes for women or protective legislation was the movement for birth control. Even many advanced progressives could not imagine themselves teaching immigrant women how to prevent conception, especially because the Comstock Law of 1873 made it illegal to promote or even write about contraceptive devices. Margaret Sanger, a nurse who had watched poor women suffer from too many births and even die from dangerous illegal abortions, was one of the founders of the modern American birth control movement. Middle-class Americans had limited family size in the nineteenth century through abstinence, withdrawal, and abortion, as well as through the use of primitive birth control devices, but much ignorance and misinformation remained, even among middle-class women. Sanger obtained the latest medical and scientific European studies and in 1914 explained in her magazine, *The Woman Rebel,* and in a pamphlet, *Family Limitation,* that women could separate sex from procreation. She was promptly indicted for violation of the postal code and fled to Europe to avoid arrest. Birth control remained controversial, and in most states illegal, for many years. Yet Sanger helped to bring the topic of sexuality and contraception out into the open. When she returned to the United States in 1921, she founded the American Birth Control League, which became the Planned Parenthood Federation in 1942.

Home and School

The reformers believed that better housing and education could transform the lives of the poor and create a better world. Books such as Jacob

Overcrowded tenement housing depressed and angered the reformers. This carefully posed photograph, taken in New York in 1910, illustrates not only poor living conditions but also some of the immigrant habits that annoyed the reformers.

Riis's *How the Other Half Lives* (1890) horrified them. With vivid language and haunting photographs, Riis had documented the overcrowded tenements, the damp, dark alleys, and the sickness and despair that affected people who lived in New York's slums. Reformers had been trying to improve housing for the poor for years. They had constructed model tenements and housing projects and had sent "friendly visitors" to the residents to collect the rent and to teach them how to live like the middle class. Riis labored to replace New York's worst slums with parks and playgrounds. In the first decade of the twentieth century, the progressives took a new approach toward the housing problems. They collected statistics, conducted surveys, organized committees, and constructed exhibits to demonstrate the effect of urban overcrowding. Then they set out to pass tenement house laws in several cities, but the laws were often evaded or modified. In 1910, they organized the National Housing Association, and some of them looked ahead to federal laws and even to government-subsidized housing.

The housing reformers combined a moral sense of what needed to be done to create a more just society with practical ability to organize public opinion and get laws passed. They also took a paternalistic view toward the poor. Many reformers disapproved of the clutter and lack of privacy in immigrant tenements. One reformer's guide, *How to Furnish and Keep House in a Tenement Flat,* recommended "wood-stained and uncluttered furniture surfaces, iron beds with mattresses, and un-upholstered chairs. . . . Walls must be painted not papered. Screens provide privacy in the bedrooms; a few good pictures should grace the walls." But often immigrant family ideals and values differed from those of the middle-class reformers. The immigrants actually did not mind the clutter and lack of privacy. Despite the reformers' efforts to separate life's functions into separate rooms, most immigrants still crowded into the kitchen and hung religious objects rather than "good pictures" on the walls.

Ironically, many middle-class women reformers who tried to teach working-class families how to live in their tenement flats had never organized their own homes. Often they lived in settlement houses, where they ate in a dining hall and never had to worry about cleaning, cooking, or doing laundry. Some of them, however, began to realize that the domestic tasks expected of women of all classes kept many of them from taking their full place in society. Charlotte Perkins Gilman, author of *Women and Economics* (1898), dismantled the traditional view of "woman's sphere" and sketched an alternative. Suggesting that entrepreneurs ought to build apartment houses designed to allow women to combine motherhood with careers, she advocated shared kitchen facilities and a common dining room, a laundry run by efficient workers, and a roof-garden day nursery with a professional teacher.

Gilman, who criticized private homes as "bloated buildings, filled with a thousand superfluities," was joined by a few radicals in promoting new living arrangements. Most Americans, however, of all political persuasions continued to view the home as sacred space where the mother ruled supreme and created an atmosphere of domestic tranquility for the husband and children.

Next to better housing, the progressives stressed better schools as a way to produce better citizens. Public school systems were often rigid and corrupt. Far from producing citizens who would help to transform society, the schools seemed to reinforce the conservative habits that blocked change. A reporter who traveled around the country in 1892 discovered mindless teachers who drilled pupils through repetitious rote learning. A Chicago teacher advised her students, "Don't stop to think; tell me what you know." When asked why the students were not allowed to move their heads, a New York teacher replied, "Why should they look behind when the teacher is in front of them?"

Progressive education, like many other aspects of progressivism, revolted against the rigid and the formal in favor of flexibility and change. John Dewey was the key philosopher of progressive education. Having grown up in Vermont, he tried throughout his life to create a sense of the small rural community in the city. In his laboratory school at the University of Chicago, he experimented with new educational methods. He replaced the school desks, which were bolted down and always faced the front, with seats that could be moved into circles and arranged in small groups. The movable seat, in fact, became one of the symbols of the progressive education movement.

Dewey insisted that the schools be child-centered, not subject-oriented. Teachers should teach children rather than teach history or mathematics. Dewey did not mean that history and math should not be taught but that those subjects should be related to the students' experience. Students should learn by doing. They should actually build a house, not just study how others constructed houses. Students should not just learn about democracy; the school itself should operate like a democracy. Dewey also maintained, somewhat controversially, that the schools should become instruments for social reform. But like most progressives, Dewey was never quite clear whether he wanted the schools to help the students adjust to the existing world or to turn out graduates who would change the world. Although he wavered on that point, the spirit of progressive education, like the spirit of progressivism in general, was optimistic. The schools could create more flexible, better-educated, more understanding adults who would go out to improve society.

Crusades Against Saloons, Brothels, and Movie Houses

Given their faith in the reforming potential of healthy and educated citizens, it was logical that most social justice progressives opposed the sale of alcohol. Some came from Protestant homes where the consumption of liquor was considered a sin, but most favored prohibition for the same reasons they opposed child labor and favored housing reform. They saw eliminating the sale of alcohol as part of the process of reforming the city and conserving human resources.

Americans did drink great quantities of beer, wine, and hard liquor, and the amount they consumed rose rapidly after 1900, peaking between 1911 and 1915. An earlier temperance movement had achieved some success in the 1840s and 1850s (see Chapter 12), but only three states still had prohibition laws in force. The modern antiliquor movement was spearheaded in the 1880s and 1890s by the Women's Christian Temperance Union and after 1900 by the Anti-Saloon League and a coalition of religious leaders and social reformers. During the progressive era, temperance forces had considerable success in influencing legislation. Seven states passed temperance laws between 1906 and 1912.

The reformers were appalled to see young children going into saloons to bring home a pail of beer for the family and horrified by tales of alcoholic fathers beating wives and children. But most often progressives focused on the saloon and its social life. Drug traffic, prostitution, and political corruption all seemed linked to the saloon. "Why should the community have any more sympathy for the saloon . . . than . . . for a typhoid-breeding pool of filthy water, . . . a swarm of deadly mosquitoes, or . . . a nest of rats infected with bubonic plague?" an irate reformer asked.

Although they never quite understood the role alcoholic drinks played in the social life of many ethnic groups, Jane Addams and other settlement workers appreciated the saloon's importance as a neighborhood social center. Addams started a coffeehouse at Hull House in an attempt to lure the neighbors away from the evils of the saloon. In his study *Substitutes for the Saloon,* Raymond Caulkins, a young social worker, suggested parks, playgrounds, municipal theaters, and temperance bars as replacements for the saloons, where so many men gathered after work.

The progressives never found an adequate substitute for the saloon, but they set to work to pass local and state prohibition laws. As in many other progressive efforts, they joined forces with diverse groups to push for change. Their combined efforts led to victory on December 22, 1917, when Congress sent to the states for ratification, a constitutional amendment prohibiting the sale, manufacturing, or importing of intoxicating liquor within the United States. The spirit of sacrifice for the war effort facilitated its rapid ratification.

In addition to the saloon, the progressives saw the urban dance hall and the movie theater as threats to the morals and well-being of young people, especially young women. The motion picture, invented in 1889, developed as an important form of entertainment only during the first decade of the twentieth century. At first, the "nickelodeons," as the early movie theaters were called, appealed mainly to a lower-class and largely ethnic audience. In 1902, New York City had 50 theaters; by 1908, there were over 400 showing 30-minute dramas and romances.

Not until World War I, when D. W. Griffith produced long feature films, did the movies begin to attract a middle-class audience. The most popular of these early films was Griffith's *The Birth of a Nation* (1915), a blatantly racist and distorted epic of black debauchery during Reconstruction. Many early films were imported from France, Italy, and Germany; because they were silent, it was easy to use subtitles in any language. But one did not need to know the language, or even be able to read, to enjoy the action. That was part of the attraction of the early films. Many had plots that depicted premarital sex, adultery, and violence, and, unlike later films, many attacked authority and had tragic endings. *The Candidate* (1907) showed an upper-class reform candidate who gets dirt thrown at him for his efforts to clean up the town. The film *Down with Women* (1907) showed well-dressed men denouncing woman suffrage and the incompetence of the weaker sex, but throughout the film only strong women are depicted. In the end, when the hero is arrested, a woman lawyer defends him.

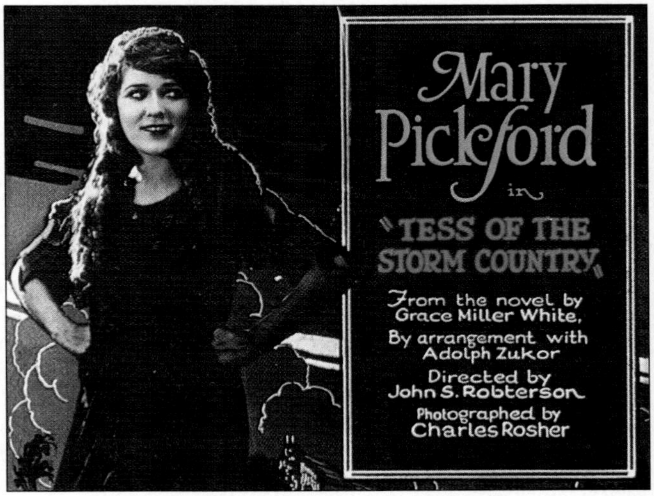

Mary Pickford, one of the superstars of the silent movies, played the heroine in a film that outraged the reformers because it dealt with the subject of unwed motherhood.

Some of the films stressed slapstick humor or romance and adventure; others bordered on pornography. The reformers objected not only to the plots and content of the films but also to the location of the theaters, near saloons and burlesque houses, and to their dark interiors. "In the dim auditorium which seems to float on the world of dreams . . . an American woman may spend her afternoon alone," one critic wrote. "She can let her fantasies slip through the darkened atmosphere to the screen where they drift in rhapsodic amours with handsome stars." It was these fantasies, in addition to the other things they imagined were going on in the dark, that disturbed the reformers. But for young immigrant women, who made up the bulk of the audience at

Documentary Photographs

As we saw in Chapter 15, photographs are a revealing way of recovering the past visually. But when looking at a photograph, especially an old one, it is easy to assume that it is an accurate representation of the past. Photographers, however, like novelists and historians, have a point of view. They take their pictures for a reason and often to prove a point. As one photographer remarked, "Photographs don't lie, but liars take photographs."

To document the need for reform in the cities, progressives collected statistics, made surveys, described settlement house life, and even wrote novels. But they discovered that the photograph was often more effective than words. Jacob Riis, the Danish-born author of *How the Other Half Lives* (1890), a devastating exposure of conditions in New York City tenement house slums, was also a pioneer in urban photography. Others had taken pictures of dank alleys and street urchins before, but Riis was the first to photograph slum conditions with the express purpose of promoting reform. At first he hired photographers, but then he bought a camera and taught himself how to use it. He even tried a new German flash powder to illuminate dark alleys and tenement rooms in order to record the horror of slum life.

Riis made many of his photographs into lantern slides and used them to illustrate his lectures on the need for housing reform. Although he was a creative and innovative photographer, his pictures were often far from objective. His equipment was awkward, his film slow. He had to set up and prepare carefully before snapping the shutter. His views of tenement

Lewis Hine, *Carolina Cotton Mill,* 1908

The reality of one-room tenement apartments (*left*) contrasted with the tidiness that reformers saw as the ideal (*right*).

ghetto streets and poor children now seem almost like clichés, but they were designed to make Americans angry, to arouse them to reform.

Another important progressive photographer was Lewis Hine. Trained as a sociologist, like Riis he taught himself photography. Hine used his camera to illustrate his lectures at the Ethical Culture School in New York. In 1908, he was hired as a full-time investigator by the National Child Labor Committee. His haunting photographs of children in factories helped to convince many Americans of the need to abolish child labor. Hine's children were appealing human beings. He showed them eating, running, working, and staring wistfully out factory windows. His photographs avoided the pathos that Riis was so fond of recording, but just as surely they documented the need for reform.

Another technique that the reform photographer used was the before-and-after shot. The two photographs shown here of a one-room apartment in Philadelphia early in the century illustrate how progressive reformers tried to teach immigrants to imitate middle-class manners. The "before" photograph shows a room cluttered with washtubs, laundry, cooking utensils, clothes, tools, even an old Christmas decoration. In the "after" picture, much of the clutter has been cleaned up. A window has been installed to let in light and fresh air. The wallpaper, presumably a haven for hidden bugs and germs, has been torn off. The cooking utensils and laundry have been put away. The woodwork has been stained, and some ceremonial objects have been gathered on a shelf.

What else can you find that has been changed? How well do you think the message of photographic combinations like this one worked? Would the immigrant family be happy with the new look and condition of their room? Could anyone live in one room and keep it so neat?

As you look at these, or any photographs, ask yourself: What is the photographer's purpose and point of view? Why was this particular angle chosen for the picture? And why center on these particular people or objects? What does the photographer reveal about his or her purpose? What does the photograph reveal unintentionally? How have fast film and new camera styles changed photography? On what subjects do reform-minded photographers train their cameras today?

most urban movie theaters, the films provided rare exciting moments in their lives. One daughter of strict Italian parents remarked, "The one place I was allowed to go by myself was the movies. I went to the movies for fun. My parents wouldn't let me go anywhere else, even when I was twenty-four."

Saloons, dance halls, and movie theaters all seemed dangerous to progressives interested in improving life in the city, because all appeared to be somehow connected with the worst evil of all, prostitution. Campaigns against prostitution had been waged since the early nineteenth century, but they were nothing compared with the progressives' crusade to wipe out what they called the "social evil." All major cities and many smaller ones appointed vice commissions and made elaborate studies of prostitution. The reports, which often ran to several thick volumes, were typical progressive documents. Compiled by experts, they were filled with elaborate statistical studies and laced with moral outrage.

The progressive antivice crusade attracted many kinds of people, for often contradictory reasons. Racists and immigration restrictionists maintained that inferior people—blacks and recent immigrants, especially those from southern and eastern Europe—became prostitutes and pimps. Social hygiene progressives published vivid accounts of prostitution as part of their campaign to fight ignorance and prudery about sex. A number of women reformers joined the campaign and argued for a single sexual standard for men and women. Others worried that prostitutes would spread venereal disease to unfaithful husbands, who would pass it on to unsuspecting wives and unborn babies, eventually wiping out humanity. Most progressives, however, stressed the environmental causes of vice. They viewed prostitution, along with child labor and poor housing, as evils that education and reform could eliminate.

Most progressive antivice reformers stressed the economic causes of prostitution. "Is it any wonder," the Chicago Vice Commission asked, "that a tempted girl who receives only six dollars per week working with her hands sells her body for twenty-five dollars per week when she learns there is a demand for it and men are willing to pay the price?" "Do you suppose I am going back to earn five or six dollars a week in a factory," one prostitute asked an investigator, "when I can earn that amount any night and often much more?"

Despite all their reports and all the publicity, the progressives failed to end prostitution and did virtually nothing to address its roots in poverty. They wiped out a few red-light districts, closed a number of brothels, and managed to push a bill through Congress (the Mann Act of 1910) that prohibited the interstate transport of women for immoral purposes. Perhaps more important, in several states they got the age of consent for women raised, and in 20 states they made the Wassermann test for syphilis mandatory for both men and women before a marriage license could be issued.

The Worker in the Progressive Era

Progressive reformers sympathized with industrial workers who struggled to earn a living for themselves and their families. The progressives sought protective legislation—particularly for women and children—unemployment insurance, and workers' compensation. But often they had little understanding of what it was really like to sell one's strength by the hour. For example, they supported labor's right to organize at a time when labor had few friends yet often opposed the strike as a weapon against management. And neither organized labor nor the reformers, individually or in shaky partnership, had power over industry. Control was in the hands of the owners and managers, and they were determined to strengthen their grip on the workplace as the nature of industrial work was being transformed.

Adjusting to Industrial Labor

John Mekras arrived in New York from Greece in 1912 and traveled immediately to Manchester, New Hampshire, where he found a job in the giant Amoskeag textile mill. He did not speak a word of English. He later remembered,

> the man who hands out the jobs sent me to the spinning room. There I don't know anything about the spinning. I'm a farmer. . . . I don't know what the boss is talking about.

Mekras didn't last long at the mill. He was one of the many industrial workers who had difficulty adjusting to factory work in the early twentieth century.

Many workers, whether they were from Greece, from eastern Europe, from rural Vermont, or from Michigan, confronted a bewildering world based on order and routine. Unlike farm or craft work, factory life was dominated by the clock, the bell tower, and the boss. The workers continued to resist the routine and pace of factory work, and they subtly sabotaged the employers' efforts to control the workplace as they had done in an earlier period (see Chapters 10 and 18). They stayed at home on holidays when they were supposed to work, took unauthorized breaks, and set their own informal productivity schedules. Often they were fired or quit. In the woolen industry, the annual turnover of workers between 1907 and 1910 was more than 100 percent. In New York needleworker shops in 1912 and 1913, the turnover rate was over 250 percent. Overall in American industry, one-third of the workers stayed at their jobs less than a year.

This industrial work force, still composed largely of immigrants, had a fluid character. Many migrants, especially those from southern and eastern Europe, expected to stay only for a short time and then return to their homeland. "Italians come to America with the sole intention of accumulating money," one Italian-American writer complained in 1905. "Their dreams, their only care is the bundle of money . . . which will give them, after 20 years of deprivation, the possibility of having a mediocre standard of living in their native country." Many men came alone—70 percent in some years. They saved money by living in a boardinghouse. In 1910, two-thirds of the workers in Pittsburgh made less than $12 a week, but by lodging in boardinghouses and paying $2.50 a month for a bed, they could save perhaps one-third of their pay. "Here in America one must work for three horses," one immigrant wrote home. "The work is very heavy, but I don't mind it," another wrote; "let it be heavy, but may it last without interruption."

About 40 percent of those who immigrated to America in the first decade of the twentieth century returned home, according to one estimate. In years of economic downturn, such as 1908, more Italians and Austro-Hungarians left the United States than entered it. For many immigrants, the American dream never materialized. But these reluctant immigrants provided the mass of unskilled labor that American industry exploited and sometimes consumed much the way other Americans exploited the land and the forests. The great pool of immigrant workers meant profits for American industry.

The nature of work continued to change in the early twentieth century as industrialists extended late-nineteenth-century efforts to make their factories and their work forces more efficient, productive, and profitable. In some industries, the introduction of new machines revolutionized work and eliminated highly paid skilled jobs. Glassblowing machines invented about 1900, for example, replaced thousands of glass-

This famous 1907 photograph, *The Steerage,* by Alfred Stieglitz, is usually used to depict the horrors of steerage and the immigrants' hope for a better life in America. It is actually a picture of a ship returning to Europe, so it is more accurately an image of the failure of the American dream.

blowers or reduced them from craftsmen to workers. Power-driven machines, better-organized operations, and, finally, the moving assembly line, perfected by Henry Ford, transformed the nature of work and turned many laborers into unskilled tenders of machines.

Coal miner John Brophy recalled his father's pride in his work as a miner. "The skill with which you undercut the vein, the judgment in drilling the coal after it has been undercut and placing the exact amount of explosive so that it would do an effective job of breaking the coal from the solid . . . indicated the quality of his work." But by the beginning of the twentieth century, undercutting machines and the mechanization of mining operations diminished miners' pride and independence.

The influence of the machine was uneven, having a greater impact in some industries than in others. While some skilled weavers and glassblowers were transformed into unskilled operators, the introduction of the machines themselves created the need for new skilled workers. In the auto industry, for example, the new elite workers were the mechanics and tool and die men who kept the assembly line running. Although these new skilled artisans survived, the trend toward mechanization was unstoppable, and even the most skilled workers were eventually removed from making decisions about the production process.

More than machines changed the nature of industrial work. The principles of scientific management, which set out new rules for organizing work, were just as important. The key figure was Frederick Taylor, the son of a prominent Philadelphia family. Taylor had a nervous breakdown while at a private school. When his physicians prescribed manual labor as a cure, he went to work as a laborer at the Midvale Steel Company in Philadelphia. Working his way up rapidly while studying engineering at night, he became chief engineer at the factory in 1880s. Later he used this experience to rethink the organization of industry.

Taylor was obsessed with efficiency. He emphasized centralized planning, systematic analysis, and detailed instructions. Most of all, he studied all kinds of workers and timed the various components of their jobs with a stopwatch. "The work of every workman is fully planned out by the management at least one day in advance," Taylor wrote in 1898, "and each man receives in most cases complete written instructions, describing in detail the task which he is to accomplish, as well as the means to be used in doing the work."

Many owners enthusiastically adopted Taylor's concepts of scientific management, seeing an opportunity to increase their profits and to take firmer control of the workplace. As Taylor himself explained, scientific management meant the "deliberate gathering in on . . . management's side of all of the great mass of traditional knowledge, which in the past has been in the heads of the workmen, and in the physical skill and knack of the workman which he has acquired through years of experience." Not surprisingly, many workers resented the drive for efficiency and control. "We don't want to work as fast as we are able to," one machinist remarked. "We want to work as fast as we think it comfortable for us to work."

Union Organizing

The progressive reformers had little understanding of the revolution going on in the factory. Samuel Gompers, head of the American Federation of Labor, however, was quick to recognize that Taylorism would reduce workers to "mere machines." Under his guidance the AFL prospered during the progressive era. Between 1897 and 1904, union membership grew from 447,000 to over 2 million, with 3 out of every 4 union members claimed by the AFL. By 1914, the AFL alone had over 2 million members. Gompers's "pure and simple unionism" was most successful among coal miners, railroad workers, and the building trades. As we saw in Chapter 18, Gompers ignored the growing army of unskilled and immigrant workers and concentrated on raising the wages and improving the working conditions of the skilled craftsmen who were members of unions affiliated with the AFL.

For a time, Gompers's strategy seemed to work. Several industries negotiated with the AFL as a way of avoiding disruptive strikes. But cooperation was short-lived. Labor unions were defeated in a number of disastrous strikes, and the National Association of Manufacturers launched an aggressive counterattack. The NAM and other employer associations provided strikebreakers, used industrial spies, and blacklisted union members to prevent them from obtaining other jobs.

The Supreme Court came down squarely on management's side, ruling in the *Danbury Hatters* case in 1908 that trade unions were subject to the Sherman Anti-Trust Act. Thus union members themselves could be held personally liable for money lost by a business during a strike. Courts at all levels sided overwhelmingly with employers. They often declared strikes illegal and were quick to issue restraining orders, making it impossible for workers to interfere with the operation of a business.

Although many social justice progressives sympathized with the working class, they spent more time promoting protective legislation than strengthening organized labor. Often cast in the role of mediators during industrial disputes, they found it difficult to comprehend what life was really like for people who had to work six days a week.

Working women and their problems aroused more sympathy among progressive reformers than the plight of working men. The number of women working outside the home increased steadily during the progressive era, from over 5 million in 1900 to nearly 8.5 million in 1920. But few belonged to unions—only a little over 3 percent in 1900—and the percentage declined by half by 1910 before increasing a little after that date with aggressive organizing in the textile and clothing trades.

Although the AFL had hired Mary Kenney as an organizer in the 1890s and accepted a few women's unions into affiliation, the policy of Gompers and the other labor leaders was generally to oppose organizing women workers (see Chapter 18). "The demand for female labor," one leader announced, "is an insidious assault upon the home. It is the knife of the assassin, aimed at the family circle."

Yet of necessity, women continued to work to support themselves and their families. Many upper-class women reformers tried to help these working women in a variety of ways. The settlement houses organized day-care centers, clubs, and classes, and many reformers tried to pass protective legislation. Tension and misunderstanding often cropped up between the reformers and the working women, but one organization in which there was genuine cooperation was the Women's Trade Union League. Founded in 1903, the league was organized by Mary Kenney and William English Walling, a socialist and reformer, but it also drew local leaders from the working class, such as Rose Schneiderman, a Jewish immigrant cap maker, and Leonora O'Reilly, a collar maker. The league established branches in most large eastern and midwestern cities and served for more than a decade as an important force in helping to organize women into unions. The league forced the AFL to pay more attention to women, helped out in time of strikes, put up bail money for the arrested, and publicized the plight of working women.

Garment Workers and the Triangle Fire

Thousands of young women, most of them Jewish and Italian, were employed in the garment industry in New York City. Most were between 16 and 25; some lived with their families, and others lived alone or with a roommate. They worked a 56-hour, six-day week and made about $6 for their efforts. New York was the center of the garment industry, with over 600 shirtwaist (blouse) and dress factories employing more than 30,000 workers. Like other industries, garment manufacturing had changed in the first decade of the twentieth century. Once conducted in thousands of dark and dingy tenement rooms, now all the operations were centralized in large loft buildings in lower Manhattan. These buildings were an improvement over the sweating labor of the tenements, but many were overcrowded, and they had few fire escapes or safety features. In addition, the owners applied scientific management techniques in order to increase their profits, making life miserable for the workers. Most of the women had to rent their sewing machines and even had to pay for the electricity they used. They were penalized for mistakes or for talking too loudly. They were usually supervised by a male contractor who badgered and sometimes even sexually harassed them.

In 1909, some of the women went out on strike to protest the working conditions. The International Ladies' Garment Workers Union (ILGWU) and the Women's Trade Union League supported them. But strikers were beaten and sometimes arrested by unsympathetic policemen and by strikebreakers on the picket lines. At a mass meeting held at Cooper Union in New York on November 22, 1909, Clara Lemlich, a young shirtwaist worker who had been injured on the picket line and was angered by the long speeches and lack of action, rose and in an emotional speech in Yiddish demanded a general strike. The entire audience pledged its agreement. The next day, all over the city, the shirtwaist workers went out on strike. "The uprising of the twenty thousand," as the strike was called, startled the nation. One young worker wrote in her diary, "It is a good thing, that strike is. It makes you feel like a grown-up person." The Jews learned a little Italian and the Italians a little Yiddish so that they could communicate. Many social reformers, ministers, priests, and rabbis urged the strikers on. Mary Dreier, an upper-class reformer and president of the New York branch of the Women's Trade Union League, was arrested for marching with the strikers. A young state legislator, Fiorello La Guardia, later to become a congressman and mayor of New York, was one of the many public officials to aid the strikers.

The shirtwaist workers won, and in part the success of the strike made the garment union one of the most powerful in the AFL. But the victory was limited. Over 300 companies accepted the union's terms, but others refused to go along. The young women went back to work amid still oppressive and unsafe conditions. That became dramatically obvious on Saturday, March 25, 1911, when a fire broke out on the eighth floor of the ten-story loft building housing the Triangle Shirtwaist Company near Washington Square in New York. There had been several small fires in the factory in previous weeks, so no one thought much about another one. But this one was different. Within minutes, the top three floors of the factory were ablaze. Many exit doors were locked. The elevators broke down. There were no fire escapes. Forty-six women jumped to their deaths, some of them in groups of three and four holding hands. Over 100 died in the flames.

Shocked by the Triangle fire, the state legislature appointed a commission to investigate working conditions in the state. One investigator for the commission was a young social worker, Frances Perkins, who in the 1930s would become secretary of labor. She led the politicians through the dark lofts, filthy tenements, and unsafe factories around the state to show them the conditions under which young women worked. The result was state legislation limiting the work of women to 54 hours a week, prohibiting labor by children under 14, and improving safety regulations in factories. One supporter of the bills in Albany was a young state senator named Franklin Delano Roosevelt.

The investigative commission was a favorite progressive tactic. When there was a problem, reformers often got a city council, a state legislature, or the federal government to appoint a commission. If they could not find a government body to give them a mandate, they made their own

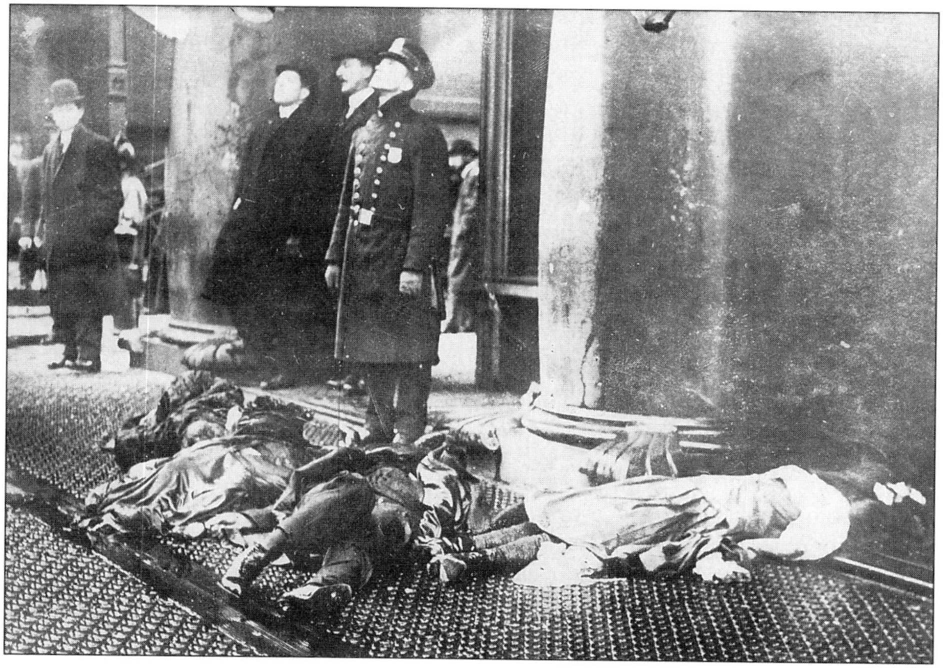

The Triangle fire shocked the nation, and dramatic photographs, such as this candid shot showing bodies and bystanders waiting for more young women to jump, helped stimulate the investigation that followed.

studies. They brought in experts, compiled statistics, and published reports.

The federal Industrial Relations Commission, created in 1912 to study the causes of industrial unrest and violence, conducted one of the most important investigations. As it turned out, the commission spent most of its time exploring a dramatic and tragic incident of labor-management conflict in Colorado, known as the Ludlow Massacre. A strike broke out in the fall of 1913 in the vast mineral-rich area of southern Colorado, much of it controlled by the Colorado Fuel and Iron Industry, a company largely owned by the Rockefeller family. It was a paternalistic empire where workers lived in company towns and sometimes in tent colonies. They were paid in company scrip and forced to shop at the company store. When the workers, supported by the United Mine Workers, went on strike demanding an eight-hour day, better safety precautions, and the removal of armed guards, the company refused to negotiate. The strike turned violent, and in the spring of 1914, strikebreakers and national guardsmen fired on the workers. Eleven children and two women were killed in an attack on a tent city near Ludlow, Colorado.

The Industrial Relations Commission called John D. Rockefeller, Jr., to testify and implied that he was personally guilty of the murders. The commission decided in its report that violent class conflict could be avoided only by limiting the use of armed guards and detectives, by restricting monopoly, by protecting the right of the workers to organize, and, most dramatically, by redistributing wealth through taxation. The commission's report, not surprisingly, fell on deaf ears. Most progressives, like most Americans, denied the commission's conclusion that class conflict was inevitable.

Radical Labor

Not everyone accepted the progressives' faith in investigations and protective labor legislation. Nor did everyone approve of Samuel Gompers's conservative tactics or his emphasis on getting better pay for skilled workers. A group of about 200 radicals met in Chicago in 1905 to form a new union as an alternative to the AFL. They called it the Industrial Workers of the World and talked of one big union. Like the Knights of Labor in the 1880s, the IWW would welcome all workers: the unskilled, and even the unemployed, women, African-Americans, Asians, and all other ethnic groups. Daniel De Leon of the Socialist Labor party attended the organizational meeting, and so did Eugene Debs. Debs, who had been converted to socialism after the Pullman strike of 1894, had already emerged by 1905 as one of the outstanding radical leaders in the country. Also attending was Mary Harris Jones, who dressed like a society matron but attacked labor leaders "who sit on velvet chairs in conferences with labor's oppressors." In her sixties at the time, everyone called her "Mother" Jones. She had been a dressmaker, a Populist, and a member of the Knights of Labor. During the 1890s, she had marched with miners' wives on the picket line in western Pennsylvania. She was imprisoned and denounced, but by 1905 she was already a legend.

Presiding at the Chicago meeting was "Big Bill" Haywood. He had been a cowboy, a miner, and a prospector. Somewhere along the way he had lost an eye and mangled a hand, but he had a booming voice and a passionate commitment to the workers. "This is the Continental Congress of the working class," he announced, adopting the rhetoric of the American Revolution. "We are here to confederate the workers of this country into a working-class movement that shall have for its purpose the emancipation of the working class from the slave bondage of capitalism." Denouncing Gompers and the AFL, he talked of class conflict. "The purpose of the IWW," he proclaimed, "is to bring the workers of this country into the possession of the full value of the product of their toil."

The IWW remained a small organization, troubled by internal squabbles and disagreements. Debs and De Leon left after a few years. Haywood dominated the movement, which played an important role in organizing the militant strike of textile workers in Lawrence, Massachusetts, in 1912 and the following year in Paterson, New Jersey, and Akron, Ohio. The IWW had its greatest success organizing itinerant lumbermen and migratory workers in the Northwest. But in other places, especially in times of high unemployment, the Wobblies, as they were called, helped the unskilled workers vent their anger against their employers.

Many American workers still did not feel, as European workers did, that they were engaged in a perpetual class struggle with their capitalist employers. Some immigrant workers, intent on earning enough money to go back home, had no time to join the conflict. Most of those who stayed in the United States were consoled by the promises of the American dream. Thinking they might secure a better job or move up into the middle class, they avoided organized labor militancy. They knew that even if they failed, their sons and daughters would profit from the American way. The AFL, not the IWW, became the dominant American labor movement. But for a few, the IWW represented a dream of what might have been. For others, its presence, though small and largely ineffective, meant that perhaps someday a European-style working-class movement might develop in America.

Reform in the Cities and States

The reform movements of the progressive era usually started at the local level, then moved to the state and finally to the nation's capital. Progressivism in the cities and states had roots in the depression and discontent of the 1890s. The reform banners called for more democracy, more power for the people, and legislation regulating railroads and other businesses. Yet often the professional and business classes were the movement's leaders. They intended to bring order out of chaos and to modernize the city and the state during a time of rapid growth.

Municipal Reformers

American cities grew rapidly in the last part of the nineteenth and the first part of the twentieth centuries. New York, which had a population of 1.2 million in 1880, grew to 3.4 million by 1900 and 5.6 million in 1920. Chicago expanded even more dramatically, from 500,000 in 1880 to 1.7 million in 1900 and 2.7 million in 1920. Los Angeles was a town of 11,000 in 1880 but multiplied ten times by 1900, and then increased another five times, to more than a half million, by 1920.

The spectacular and continuing growth of the cities caused problems and created a need for housing, transportation, and municipal services. But it was the kind of people who were moving into the cities that worried many observers. Americans from the small towns and farms continued to throng to the urban centers, as they had throughout the nineteenth century, but immigration produced the greatest surge in population. Fully 40 percent of New York's population and 36 percent of Chicago's was foreign-born in 1910; if one included the children of the immigrants, the percentage approached 80 percent in some cities. The new immigrants from eastern and western Europe, according to Francis Walker, the president of MIT, were "beaten men from beaten races, representing the worst failures in the struggle for existence." They seemed to threaten the American way of life and the very tenets of democracy.

Fear of the city and its new inhabitants motivated progressive municipal reform efforts. Urban problems seemed to have reached a crisis stage.

The twentieth-century reformers, mostly middle-class citizens like those in the nineteenth, wanted to regulate and control the sprawling metropolis, restore democracy, reduce corruption, and limit the power of the political bosses and

Immigration to the United States, 1900–1920

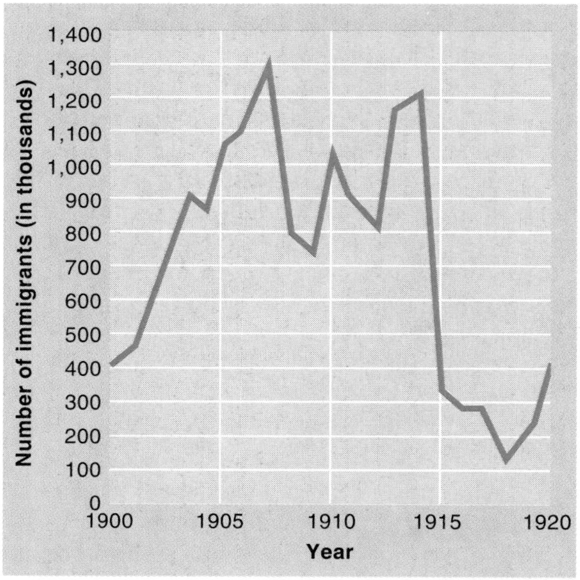

Reaching a peak in the years before World War I, immigration dropped dramatically because of the war and did not rise much during the 1920s.

Source: U.S. Bureau of the Census.

Immigrants accustomed to rural life often found American cities bewildering. These Russian Jews, immigrants to Texas from St. Petersburg, also had a difficult time adjusting to rural life in America.

their immigrant allies. When these reformers talked of restoring power to the people, they usually meant ensuring control for people like themselves. The chief aim of municipal reform was to make the city more organized and efficient for the business and professional classes who were to control its workings.

Municipal reform movements varied from city to city. In Boston, the reformers tried to strengthen the power of the mayor, break the hold of the city council, and eliminate council corruption. They succeeded in removing all party designations from city election ballots, and they extended the term of the mayor from two to four years. But to their chagrin, in the election of 1910, John Fitzgerald, grandfather of John F. Kennedy and foe of reform, defeated their candidate. In other cities, the reformers used different tactics, but they almost always conducted elaborate studies and campaigned to reduce corruption.

The most dramatic innovation was the replacement of both mayor and council with a nonpartisan commission of administrators. This innovation began quite accidentally when a hurricane devastated Galveston, Texas, in September 1900. In one of the worst natural disasters in the nation's history, over 6,000 people died. The existing government was helpless to deal with the crisis, so the state legislature appointed five commissioners to run the city during the emergency. The idea spread to Houston, Dallas, and Austin and to cities in other states. It proved most popular in small to medium-size cities in the Midwest and the Pacific Northwest. By World War I, more than 400 cities had adopted the commission form. Dayton, Ohio, went one step further: after a disastrous flood in 1913, the city hired a city manager to run the city and to report to the elected council. Government by experts was the perfect symbol of what most municipal reformers had in mind.

The commission and the expert manager did not replace the mayor in most large cities. One of the most flamboyant and successful of the progressive mayors was Tom Johnson of Cleveland. Johnson had made a fortune by investing in utility and railroad franchises before he was 40. But Henry George's *Progress and Poverty* so influenced him that he began a second career as a reformer. After serving in Congress, he was elected mayor of Cleveland in 1901. During his two terms in city hall, he managed to reduce transit fares and to build parks and municipal bath houses throughout the city. Johnson also broke the connection between the police and prostitution in the city by promising the madams and the brothel owners that he would not bother them if they would be orderly and not steal from their customers or pay off the police. His most controversial move, however, was to advocate city ownership of the street railroads and utilities (sometimes called municipal socialism). "Only through municipal ownership," he argued, "can the gulf which divides the community into a small dominant class on one side and the unorganized people on the other be bridged." Johnson was defeated in 1909 in part because he alienated many powerful business interests, but one of his lieutenants, Newton D. Baker, was elected mayor in 1911 and carried on many of his programs. Cleveland was one of many cities that began to regulate municipal utilities or to take them over from the private owners.

Cities grew so rapidly that they often ceased to work. This 1909 photograph shows Dearborn Street looking south from Randolph in Chicago. Horse-drawn vehicles, streetcars, pedestrians, and even a few early autos clogged the intersection and created the urban inefficiency that angered municipal reformers.

The City Beautiful

In Cleveland, both Tom Johnson and Newton Baker promoted the arts, music, and adult education. They also supervised the construction of a civic center, a library, and a museum. Most other American cities during the progressive era set out to bring culture and beauty to their centers. They were influenced at least in part by the great, classical White City constructed for the Chicago World's Fair of 1893 and by the grand European boulevards such as the Champs-Élysées in Paris. The architects of the "city beautiful movement" preferred the impressive and ceremonial architecture of Rome or the Renaissance for libraries, museums, railroad stations, and other public buildings. The huge Pennsylvania Station in New York was modeled after the imperial Roman baths of Caracalla, while the Free Library in Philadelphia was an almost exact copy of a building in Paris. The city beautiful leaders tried to make the city more attractive and meaningful for the middle and upper classes. The museums and the libraries were closed on Sundays, the only day the working class could possibly visit them.

The social justice progressives, especially those connected with the social settlements, were more concerned with neighborhood parks and playgrounds than with the ceremonial boulevards and grand buildings. Hull House established the first public playground in Chicago. Jacob Riis, the housing reformer, and Lillian Wald of the Henry Street Settlement campaigned in New York for small parks and for the opening of schoolyards on weekends. Some progressives looked back nostalgically to their rural childhoods and desperately tried to get urban children out of the city in the summertime to rural camps. But they also tried to make the city more livable as well as more beautiful.

Most progressives had an ambivalent attitude toward the city. They feared it, and they loved it. Some saw the great urban areas filled with immigrants as a threat to American democracy, but one of Tom Johnson's young assistants, Frederic C. Howe, wrote a book called *The City: The Hope of Democracy* (1905). Hope or threat, the progressives realized that the United States had become an urban nation and that the problems of the city had to be faced.

Reform in the States

The progressive movements in the states had many roots and took many forms. In some states, especially in the West, progressive attempts to regulate railroads and utilities were simply an extension of populism. In other states, the reform drive bubbled up from reform efforts in the cities. Most states passed laws during the progressive era designed to extend democracy and give more authority to the people. Initiative and referendum laws allowed citizens to originate legislation and to overturn laws passed by the legislature, while recall laws gave the people a way to remove elected officials. Most of these "democratic" laws worked better in theory than in practice, but their passage in many states did represent a genuine effort to remove special privilege from government.

Much progressive state legislation concerned order and efficiency, but many states passed social justice measures as well. Maryland enacted the first workers' compensation law in 1902, paying employees for days missed because of job-related injuries. Illinois approved a law aiding mothers with dependent children. Several states passed anti–child labor bills, and Oregon's ten-hour law restricting women's labor became a model for other states.

The states with the most successful reform movements elected strong and aggressive governors: Charles Evans Hughes in New York, Hoke Smith in Georgia, Hiram Johnson In California, Woodrow Wilson in New Jersey, and Robert La Follette in Wisconsin. After Wilson, La Follette was the most famous and in many ways the model progressive governor. Born in a small town in Wisconsin, he graduated from the University of Wisconsin in 1879 and was admitted to the bar. Practicing law during the 1890s in Madison, the state capital, he received a large retainer from the Milwaukee Railroad and defended the railroad against both riders and laborers who sued the company.

The depression of 1893 hit Wisconsin hard. More than a third of the state's citizens were out of work; farmers lost their farms, and many small businesses went bankrupt. At the same time, the rich seemed to be getting richer. "Men are rightly feeling that a social order like the present, with its enormous wealth side by side with appalling poverty, . . . cannot be the final form of human society," a Milwaukee minister announced. As grass-roots discontent spread, a group of Milwaukee reformers attacked the giant corporations and the street railways. Several newspapers joined the battle and denounced special privilege and corruption. Everyone could agree on the need for tax reform, railroad regulation, and more participation of the people in government.

La Follette, who had had little interest in reform, took advantage of the general mood of discontent to win the governorship in 1901. It seemed ironic that La Follette, who had once taken a retainer from a railroad, owed his victory to his attack on the railroads. But La Follette was a shrewd politician. He used professors from the University of Wisconsin, in the capital, to prepare reports and do statistical studies. Then he worked with the legislature to pass a state primary law and an act regulating the railroads. "Go back to the first principles of democracy; go back to the people" was his battle cry. The "Wisconsin idea" attracted the attention of journalists like Lincoln Steffens and Ray Stannard Baker, and they helped to popularize the "laboratory of democracy" around the country. La Follette became a national figure and was elected to the Senate in 1906.

The progressive movement did improve government and make it more responsible to the people in states like Wisconsin. For example, the railroads were brought under the control of a railroad commission. But by 1910, the railroads no longer complained about the new taxes and restrictions. They had discovered that it was to their advantage to make their operations more efficient, and often they were able to convince the commission that they should raise rates or abandon the operation of unprofitable lines. Progressivism in the states, like progressivism everywhere, had mixed results. But the spirit of reform that swept the country was real, and progressive movements on the local level did eventually have an impact on Washington, especially during the administrations of Theodore Roosevelt and Woodrow Wilson.

Theodore Roosevelt and the Square Deal

President William McKinley was shot in Buffalo, New York, on September 6, 1901, by Leon Czolgosz, an anarchist. He died eight days later, making Theodore Roosevelt, at 42, the youngest man

Theodore Roosevelt was a dynamic public speaker who used his position to influence public opinion. Despite his high-pitched voice he could be heard at the back of the crowd in the days before microphones. Note the row of reporters decked out in their summer straw hats writing their stories as the president speaks.

ever to become president. The nation mourned its fallen leader, while in many cities anarchists and other radicals were rounded up for questioning.

No one knew what to expect from Roosevelt. Some politicians thought he was too radical, but a few social justice progressives remembered his suggestion that the soldiers fire on the strikers during the 1894 Pullman strike. Nonetheless, under his leadership, progressivism reshaped the national political agenda. While early progressive reformers had attacked problems that they saw in their own communities, they gradually understood that some problems could not be solved at the state or local level. The emergence of a national industrial economy had spawned conditions that demanded national solutions.

Progressives at the national level turned their attention to the workings of the economic system. They scrutinized the operation and organization of the railroads and other large corporations. They examined the threats to the natural environment. They reviewed the quality of the products of American industry. As they fashioned legislation to remedy the flaws in the economic system, they vastly expanded the power of the national government.

A Strong and Controversial President

Roosevelt came to the presidency with considerable experience. He had run unsuccessfully for mayor of New York, served a term in the New York state assembly, spent four years as a United States civil service commissioner, and served two years as the police commissioner of New York City. His exploits in the Spanish-American War brought him to the public's attention, but he had also been an effective assistant secretary of the navy and a reform governor of New York. While police commissioner and governor, he had been influenced by a number of progressives. Jacob Riis, the housing reformer, became one of his friends and led him on nighttime explorations of the slums of New York City. He had also impressed a group of New York settlement workers with his genuine concern for human misery, his ability to talk to all kinds of people, and his willingness to learn about social problems. But no one was sure how Roosevelt would act as president. He came from an upper-class family and had associated with the important and the powerful all over the world. He had written a number of books and was one of the most intellectual presidents since Thomas Jefferson. But none of these things assured that he would be a progressive in office.

Roosevelt loved being president. He called the office a "bully pulpit," and he enjoyed talking to the people and the press. His appealing personality and sense of humor made him a good subject for the new mass-market newspapers and magazines. The American people quickly adopted him as their favorite. They called him "Teddy" and named a stuffed bear after him. Sometimes his exuberance got a little out of hand. On one occasion, he took a foreign diplomat on a nude swim in the Potomac River. You have to understand, another observer remarked, that "the president is really only six years old."

Roosevelt was much more than an exuberant 6-year-old. He was the strongest president since Lincoln. By revitalizing the executive branch, reorganizing the army command structure, and modernizing the consular service, he made many aspects of the federal government more efficient. He established the Bureau of Corporations, appointed independent commissions staffed with experts, and enlisted talented and well-trained men to work for the government. "TR," as he became known, called a White House conference on the care of dependent children, and in 1905 he even summoned college presidents and football coaches to the White House to discuss ways to limit violence in football. He angered many social justice progressives by not going far enough. In fact, on one occasion, Florence Kelley was so furious with him that she walked out of the Oval Office and slammed the door. But he was the first president to listen to the pleas of the progressives and to invite them to the White House. Learning from experts like Frances Kellor, he became more concerned with social justice as time went on.

Dealing with the Trusts

One of Roosevelt's first actions as president was to attempt to control the large industrial corporations. He took office in the middle of an unprecedented wave of business consolidation. Between 1897 and 1904, some 4,227 companies combined to form 257 large corporations. U.S. Steel, the first billion-dollar corporation, was formed in 1901 by joining Carnegie Steel with its eight main competitors. In one stroke, the new company controlled two-thirds of the market, and J. P. Morgan made $7 million for supervising the operation. The Sherman Anti-Trust Act of 1890 had been virtually useless in controlling the trusts, but a new outcry from muckrakers and progressives called for regulation. Some even demanded the return to the age of small business. Roosevelt opposed neither bigness nor the right of businessmen to make money. "Our aim is not to do away with corporations," he remarked in 1902; "on the contrary, these big aggregations are the inevitable development of modern industrialism." But he thought some businessmen arrogant, greedy, and irresponsible. "We draw the line against misconduct, not against wealth," he said.

To the shock of much of the business community, he directed his attorney general to file suit to dissolve the Northern Securities Company, a giant railroad monopoly put together by James J. Hill and financier J. P. Morgan. Morgan came to the White House to tell Roosevelt, "If we have done anything wrong, send your man to my man and they can fix it up." Roosevelt was furious, and he was determined to let Morgan and other businessmen know that they could not deal with the president of the United States as just another tycoon.

The government won its case and proceeded to prosecute some of the largest corporations, including Standard Oil of New Jersey and the American Tobacco Company. However, Roosevelt's antitrust policy did not end the power of the giant corporations or even alter their methods of doing business. More disturbing to consumers, it did not force down the price of kerosene, cigars, or railroad tickets. But it did breathe some life into the Sherman Anti-Trust Act, and it increased the role of the federal government as regulator. It also caused large firms such as U.S. Steel to diversify in order to avoid antitrust suits.

Business Mergers, 1895–1905

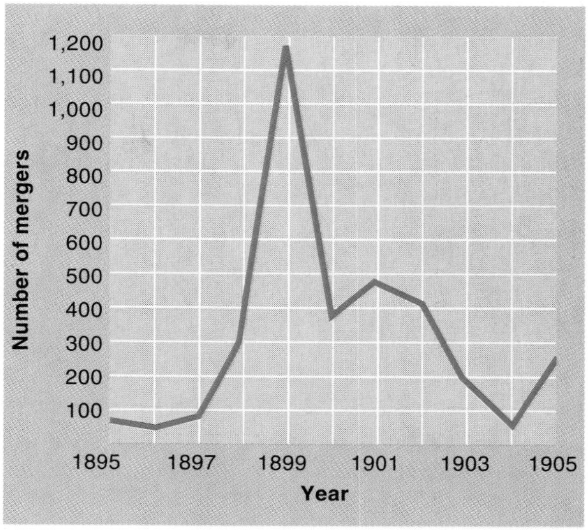

Business mergers did decline during the Roosevelt years, but they did not cease entirely and they even rose again during his second term.

Source: U.S. Bureau of the Census.

Roosevelt sought to strengthen the regulatory powers of the federal government in other ways. He steered the Elkins Act through Congress in 1903 and the Hepburn Act in 1906, which together increased the power of the Interstate Commerce Commission (ICC). The first act eliminated the use of rebates by railroads, a way that many large corporations had used to get favored treatment. The second act broadened the power of the ICC and gave it the right to investigate and enforce rates. Opponents in Congress weakened both bills, however, and the legislation neither ended abuses nor satisfied the farmers and small businessmen who had always been the railroads' chief critics.

Roosevelt firmly believed in corporate capitalism. He detested socialism and felt much more comfortable around business executives than labor leaders. Yet he saw his role as mediator and regulator. His view of the power of the presidency was illustrated in 1902 during the anthracite coal strike. Led by John Mitchell of the United Mine Workers, the coal miners went on strike to protest low wages, long hours, and unsafe working conditions. In 1901, a total of 513 coal miners had been killed. The mine owners refused to talk to the miners. They hired strikebreakers and used private security forces to threaten and intimidate the workers. George F. Baer of the Reading Railroad articulated the most extreme form of the employers' position. He argued that workingmen had no right to strike or to say anything about working conditions.

> The rights and interests of the laboring man will be protected and cared for, not by the labor agitators, but by the Christian man to whom God in His infinite wisdom has given the control of the property interests of the country, and upon the successful management of which so much depends.

Although Roosevelt had no particular sympathy for labor, he would certainly not have gone as far as Baer. In the fall of 1902, however, schools began closing for lack of coal, and it looked like many citizens would suffer through the winter. Coal, which usually sold for $5 a ton, rose to $14. Roosevelt called the owners and representatives of the union to the White House even though the businessmen protested that they would not deal with "outlaws." Finally, the president appointed a commission that included representatives of the union as well as the community. Within weeks, the miners went back to work with a 10 percent raise.

Meat Inspection and Pure Food and Drugs

Roosevelt's first major legislative reform began almost accidentally in 1904 when Upton Sinclair, a 26-year-old muckraking journalist, started research on the Chicago stockyards. Born in Baltimore, Sinclair had grown up in New York, where he wrote dime novels to pay his tuition at City College. He was converted to socialism by his reading and by his association with a group of idealistic young writers in New York. Though he knew little about Chicago, he was driven by a desire to expose the exploitation of the poor and oppressed in America. He boarded at the University of Chicago Settlement while he did research, conducted interviews, and wrote the story that would be published in 1906 as *The Jungle.*

Sinclair's novel told of the Rudkus family, who emigrated from Lithuania to Chicago filled with ambition and hope. But the American dream failed for them. Sinclair documented exploitation in his fictional account, but his description of contaminated meat drew more attention. He described spoiled hams treated with formaldehyde and sausages made from rotten meat scraps, rats, and other refuse. Hoping to convert his readers to socialism, Sinclair instead turned their stomachs and caused a public outcry for better regulation of the meatpacking industry.

Selling 25,000 copies in its first six weeks, *The Jungle* disturbed many people, including Roosevelt, who, it was reported, could no longer enjoy his breakfast sausage. Roosevelt ordered a study of the meatpacking industry and then used the report to pressure Congress and the meatpackers to accept a bill introduced by Albert Beveridge, the progressive senator from Indiana.

In the end, the Meat Inspection Act of 1906 was a compromise. It enforced some federal inspection and mandated sanitary conditions in all companies selling meat in interstate commerce. The meatpackers defeated a provision that would have required the dating of all meat. Some of the large companies supported the compromise bill because it gave them an advantage in their battle with the smaller firms. But the bill was a beginning. It illustrates how muckrakers, social justice progressives, and public outcry eventually led to reform legislation. It also shows how Roosevelt used the public mood and manipulated the political process to get a bill through Congress. Many of the progressive reformers were disappointed with the final result, but Roosevelt was always willing to settle for half a loaf rather than none at all. Ironically, the Meat Inspection Act restored the public's confidence in the meat industry and helped the industry increase its profits.

Taking advantage of the publicity that circulated around *The Jungle,* a group of reformers, writers, and government officials pushed for legislation to regulate the sale of food and drugs. Americans consumed an enormous quantity of patent medicines, which they purchased through

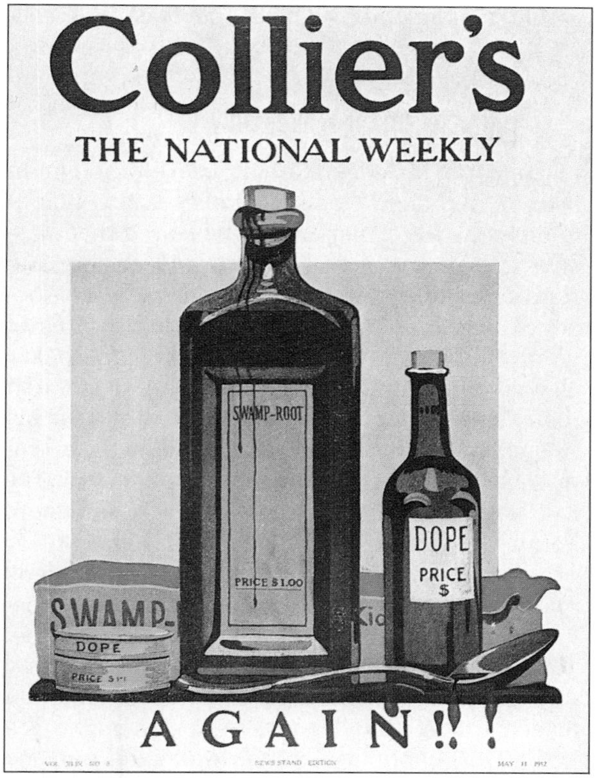

Collier's, one of the popular muckraking magazines, tried to alert the public to the dangerous drugs in patent medicines in this 1912 cover story. Magazines such as *Collier's,* with circulations approaching a million, had an immense influence during the progressive era.

the mail, from traveling salesmen, and from local stores. One article pointed out in 1905:

> Gullible Americans will spend this year some seventy-five million dollars in the purchase of patent medicines. In consideration of this sum it will swallow huge quantities of alcohol, an appealing amount of opiates and narcotics, a wide assortment of varied drugs ranging from powerful and dangerous heart depressants to insidious liver stimulants; and, far in excess of all other ingredients, undiluted fraud. For fraud exploited by the skillfulest of advertising bunco men is the basis of the trade.

Many packaged and canned foods contained dangerous chemicals and impurities. One popular remedy, Hosteter's Stomach Bitters, was revealed on analysis to contain 44 percent alcohol. Coca-Cola, a popular soft drink, contained a small amount of cocaine, and many medicines were laced with opium. Many people, including women and children, became alcoholics or drug addicts in their quest to feel better. The Pure Food and Drug Act, which passed Congress on the same day in 1906 as the Meat Inspection Act, was not a perfect bill, but it corrected some of the worst abuses, including eliminating the cocaine from Coca-Cola.

Conservation Versus Preservation

Although Roosevelt was pleased with the new legislation for regulating the food and drug industries, he always considered his conservation program his most important domestic achievement. An outdoorsman, hunter, and amateur naturalist since his youth, he announced soon after he became president that the planned protection of the nation's forests and water resources would be one of his most vital concerns. Using his executive authority he more than tripled the land set aside for national forests, bringing the total to more than 150 million acres. Because he had traveled widely in the West, Roosevelt understood, as few easterners did, the problems created by limited water in the western states. In 1902, with his enthusiastic support, Congress passed the Newlands Acts, named after Francis Newlands, its most ardent advocate from the arid state of Nevada. The National Reclamation Act (as it was officially called) set aside the proceeds from the sale of public land in sixteen western states to pay for the construction of irrigation projects in those states. Although it tended to help big farmers more than small producers, the Newlands Act federalized irrigation for the first time.

More important than conservation bills passed during Roosevelt's presidency, however, were his efforts to raise the public consciousness about the need to save the nation's natural resources. He convened a White House Conservation Conference in 1908 that included among its delegates most of the governors and representatives of seventy national organizations. A direct result of the conference was Roosevelt's appointment of a National Conservation Commission charged with making an inventory of the natural resources in the entire country. To chair the commission Roosevelt appointed Gifford Pinchot, probably the most important conservation advocate in the country. A graduate of Yale, Pinchot had studied scientific forestry management in Germany and France before becoming the forest manager of the Vanderbilt's Biltmore estate in North Carolina. In 1898 he was appointed chief of the United States Division of Forestry, and in 1900 he became the head of the Bureau of Forestry in the Department of Agriculture. An advocate of selective logging, fire control, and limited grazing on public lands, he became a friend and adviser to Roosevelt.

Pinchot's conservation policies pleased many in the timber and cattle industries at the same time they angered those who simply wanted to exploit the land. But his policies were denounced by the followers of John Muir, who believed passionately in preserving the land in a wilderness state. Muir had founded the Sierra Club in 1862 and had led a successful campaign to create Yosemite National Park in California. With his shaggy gray beard, his rough blue work clothes, and his black slouch hat, Muir seemed like an eccentric to many, but thousands agreed with him when he argued that to preserve the American wilderness was a spiritual and psychological necessity for overcivilized and overstimulated urban dwellers. Muir was one of the leaders in a "back-to-nature" movement at the turn of the century. Many middle-class Americans took up hiking, camping, and other outdoor activity, while children joined the Boy Scouts (founded 1910) and the Camp Fire Girls (1912).

The conflicting conservation philosophies of Pinchot and Muir were most dramatically demonstrated by the controversy over Hetch-Hetchy, a remote valley deep within Yosemite National Park. It was a pristine wilderness area, and Muir and his followers wanted to keep it that way. But in 1901 the mayor of San Francisco decided the valley would make a perfect place for a dam and reservoir to supply his growing city with water for decades to come. Muir argued that wilderness would soon be scarcer than water and more important for the moral strength of the nation. Pinchot, on the other hand, maintained that it was foolish to pander to the aesthetic enjoyment of a tiny group of people when the comfort and welfare of the great majority was at stake. The Hetch-Hetchy affair was fought out in the newspapers and magazines as well as in the halls of Congress, but in the end the conservationists won out over the preservationists. Roosevelt and Congress sided with Pinchot and eventually the dam was built, turning the valley into a lake. But the debate over how to use the nation's land and water would continue throughout the twentieth century.

Progressivism for Whites Only

Like most of his generation, Roosevelt thought in stereotyped racial terms. He believed that blacks and Asians were inferior, and he feared that massive migrations from southern and eastern Europe threatened the Anglo-Saxon role. But Roosevelt was a politician, so he made gestures of goodwill to most groups. He even invited Booker T. Washington to the White House in 1901, though many southerners viciously attacked him for his breach of etiquette. He also appointed several qualified blacks to minor federal posts, notably Dr. William D. Crum to head the Charleston, South Carolina, customs house in 1905. But at other times, he seemed insensitive to the needs and feelings of black Americans. This was especially true in his handling of the Brownsville, Texas, riot of 1906. Members of a black army unit stationed there, angered by discrimination against them, rioted one hot August night. Exactly what happened no one was sure, but one white man was killed and several wounded. Waiting until after the midterm elections of 1906, Roosevelt ordered all 167 members of three companies dishonorably discharged. It was an unjust punishment for an unproven crime, and 66 years later the secretary of the army granted honorable discharges to the men, most of them by that time dead.

The progressive era coincided with the years of greatest segregation in the South, but even the most advanced progressives seldom included blacks in their reform schemes. Hull House, like most social settlements, was segregated, although Jane Addams more than most progressives struggled to overcome the racist attitudes of her day. She helped found a settlement that served a black neighborhood in Chicago, and she spoke out repeatedly against lynching. Addams also supported the founding of the National Association for the Advancement of Colored People (NAACP) in 1909, the most important organization of the progressive era aimed at promoting equality and justice for blacks.

The founding of the NAACP is the story of cooperation between a group of white social justice progressives and a number of courageous black leaders. Even in the age of segregation and lynching, blacks in all parts of the country—through churches, clubs, and schools—sought to promote a better life for themselves. In Boston, William Monroe Trotter used his newspaper to oppose Washington's policy of accommodation. In Chicago, Ida Wells-Barnett, a large woman with flashing eyes, launched a one-woman crusade against lynching, organized a women's club for blacks, and founded the Negro Fellowship League to help black migrants.

The most important black leader who argued for equality and opportunity for his people was W. E. B. Du Bois. As discussed in Chapter 17, Du Bois differed dramatically with Booker T. Washington on the proper position of blacks in American life. While Washington advocated vocational education, Du Bois argued for the best education possible for the most talented tenth of the black population. While Washington preached compromise and accommodation to the dominant white society, Du Bois increasingly urged militant action to assure equality. Denouncing Washington for accepting the "alleged inferiority of the Negro," Du Bois called a meeting of young and militant blacks in 1905. They met in Canada, not far from Niagara Falls, and issued an angry statement. "We want to *pull down* nothing but we don't propose to be pulled down," the platform announced. "We believe in *taking what we can get* but we don't believe in being satisfied with it and in permitting anybody for a moment to imagine we're satisfied." The Niagara movement, as it came to be called, was small, but it was soon augmented by a group of white liberals concerned with violence against blacks and race riots in Atlanta and even in Springfield, Illinois, the home of Abraham Lincoln. Jane Addams joined the new organization, as did Oswald Garrison Villard, grandson of abolitionist William Lloyd Garrison.

In 1910 the Niagara movement combined with the NAACP, and Du Bois became editor of its journal, *The Crisis.* He toned down his rhetoric, but he

Tuskegee Institute followed Booker T. Washington's philosophy of black advancement through accommodation to the white status quo. Here students study white American history, but most of their time was spent on more practical subjects.

tried to promote equality for all blacks. The NAACP was a typical progressive organization, seeking to work within the American system to promote reform. But to Roosevelt and many others who called themselves progressives, the NAACP seemed dangerously radical.

William Howard Taft

After two terms as president, Roosevelt decided to step down. "I believe in a strong executive," he remarked in 1908. "I believe in power, but I believe that responsibility should go with power, and that it is not well that the strong executive should be a perpetual executive." But he soon regretted his decision. He was only 50 years old and at the peak of his popularity and power. Since the United States' system of government provides little creative function for former presidents, Roosevelt decided to travel and to go big-game hunting in Africa. But before he left, he handpicked his successor.

William Howard Taft, Roosevelt's personal choice for the Republican nomination in 1908, was a distinguished lawyer, federal judge, and public servant. Born in Cincinnati, he had been the first civil governor of the Philippines and Roosevelt's secretary of war. After defeating William Jennings Bryan for the presidency in 1908, he quickly ran into difficulties. In some ways, he seemed more progressive than Roosevelt. His administration instituted more suits against monopolies in one term than Roosevelt had in two. He supported the eight-hour workday and legislation to make mining safer and urged the passage of the Mann-Elkins Act in 1910, which strengthened the ICC by giving it more power to set railroad rates and extending its jurisdiction over telephone and telegraph companies. Taft and Congress also authorized the first tax on corporate profits. He also encouraged the process that eventually led to the passage of the federal income tax, which was authorized under the Sixteenth Amendment, ratified in 1913. That probably did more to transform the relationship of the government to the people than all other progressive measures combined.

Taft's biggest problem was his style. He was a huge man, weighing over 300 pounds. Rumors circulated that he had to have a special oversize bathtub installed in the White House. Easily made fun of, the president wrote ponderous prose and spoke uninspiringly. He also lacked Roosevelt's political skills and angered many of the progressives in the Republican party, especially the midwestern insurgents led by Senator Robert La Follette of Wisconsin. Many progressives were annoyed when he signed the Payne-Aldrich Tariff, which midwesterners thought left rates on cotton and wool cloth and other items too high and played into the hands of the eastern industrial interests. Even Roosevelt was infuriated when his successor reversed many of his conservation policies and fired Chief Forester Gifford Pinchot, who had attacked Secretary of the Interior Richard A. Ballinger for giving away rich coal lands in Alaska to mining interests. Roosevelt broke with Taft, letting it be known that he was willing to run again for president. This set up one of the most exciting and significant elections in American history.

The Election of 1912

Woodrow Wilson won the Democratic nomination for president in 1912. Born two years before Roosevelt, Wilson came from a very different background and would be cast in opposition to the former president during most of his political career. Wilson was the son and grandson of Presbyterian ministers. Growing up in a comfortable and intellectual southern household, he very early seemed more interested in politics than in religion. After graduating from Princeton University in 1879, he studied law at the University of Virginia and practiced law briefly before entering graduate school at the Johns Hopkins University in Baltimore. Soon after receiving his Ph.D. he published a book, *Congressional Government* (1885), that established his reputation as a shrewd analyst of American politics. He taught history briefly at Bryn Mawr College near Philadelphia and at Wesleyan in Connecticut before moving to Princeton. Less flamboyant than Roosevelt, he was an excellent public speaker with the power to convince people with his words.

In 1902, Wilson was elected president of Princeton University, and during the next few years he established a national reputation as an educational leader. Wilson had never lost interest in politics, however, so when offered a chance by the Democratic machine to run for governor of New Jersey, he took it eagerly. In his two years as governor, he showed courage as he quickly alienated some of the conservatives who had helped to elect him. Building a coalition of reformers, he worked with them to pass a direct primary law and a workers' compensation law. He also created a commission to regulate transportation and public utility companies. By 1912, Wilson not only was an expert on government and politics but had also acquired the reputation of a progressive.

Roosevelt, who had been speaking out on a variety of issues since 1910, competed with Taft for the Republican nomination, but Taft, as the incumbent president and party leader, was able to win it. Roosevelt then startled the nation by walking out of the convention and forming a new political party, the Progressive party. The new party would not have been formed without Roosevelt, but the party was always more than Roosevelt. It appealed to progressives from all over the country who had become frustrated with the conservative leadership in both major parties.

Many social workers and social justice progressives supported the Progressive party because of its platform, which contained provisions they had been advocating for years. The Progressives supported an eight-hour day, a six-day week, the abolition of child labor under age 16, and a federal system of accident, old age, and unemployment insurance. Unlike the Democrats, the Progressives also endorsed woman suffrage. "Just think of having all the world listen to our story of social and industrial injustice and have them told that it can be righted," one social worker exclaimed.

Most supporters of the Progressives in 1912 did not realistically think they could win, but they were convinced that they could organize a new political movement that would replace the Republican party, just as the Republicans had replaced the Whigs after 1856. To this end, Progressive leaders, led by Kellor, set up the Progressive Service, designed to apply the principles of social research to educating voters between elections.

The Progressive convention in Chicago seemed to many observers more like a religious revival meeting or a social work conference than a political gathering. The delegates sang "Onward Christian Soldiers," "The Battle Hymn of the Republic," and "Roosevelt, Oh Roosevelt" (to the tune of "Maryland, My Maryland"). They waved their bandannas, and when Jane Addams rose to second Roosevelt's nomination, a large group of women marched around the auditorium with a banner that read "Votes for Women." The Progressive cause "is based on the eternal principles of righteousness," Roosevelt announced. "In the end the cause itself shall triumph."

The enthusiasm for Roosevelt and the Progressive party was misleading, for behind the unified facade lurked many disagreements. Roosevelt had become more progressive on many issues since leaving the presidency. He even attacked the financiers "to whom the acquisition of untold millions is the supreme goal of life, and who are too often utterly indifferent as to how these millions are obtained." But he was not as committed to social reform as some of the delegates. Perhaps the most divisive issue was the controversy over seating black delegates from several southern states. A number of social justice progressives fought hard to include a plank in the platform supporting equality for blacks and for seating the black delegation. Roosevelt, however, thought he had a realistic chance to carry several southern states, and he was not convinced that black equality was an important progressive issue. In the end, no blacks sat with the southern delegates, and the platform made no mention of black equality.

The political campaign in 1912 became a contest primarily between Roosevelt and Wilson, with Taft, the Republican candidate and incumbent, ignored by most reporters who covered the campaign. On one level, the campaign became a debate over political philosophy, the proper relationship of government to society in a modern industrial age. Roosevelt borrowed some of his ideas from a book, *The Promise of American Life* (1909), written by Herbert Croly, a young journalist. But he had also been working out his own philosophy of government. He spoke of the "new nationalism." In a modern industrial society, he argued, large corporations were "inevitable and necessary." What was needed was not the breakup of the trusts but a strong president and increased power in the hands of the federal government to regulate business and industry and to ensure the rights of labor, women and children, and other groups. The government should be the "steward of the public welfare." He argued for using Hamiltonian means to assure Jeffersonian ends, for using strong central government to guarantee the rights of the people.

Wilson responded with a slogan and a program of his own. Using the writings of Louis Brandeis, he talked of the "new freedom." He emphasized the need for the Jeffersonian tradition of limited government with open competition. He spoke of the "curse of bigness" and argued against too much federal power. "If America is not to have free enterprise, then she can have freedom of no sort whatever." "What I fear is a government of experts," Wilson declared, implying that Roosevelt's New Nationalism would lead to regulated monopoly and even collectivism.

The level of debate during the campaign was impressive, making this one of the few elections in American history when important ideas were actually discussed. It also marked a watershed for political thought for liberals who rejected Jefferson's distrust of a strong central government. It is easy to exaggerate the differences between Roosevelt and Wilson. There was some truth in the charge of William Allen White, the editor of the Emporia *Gazette* in Kansas, when he remarked, "Between the New Nationalism and the New Freedom was that fantastic imaginary gulf that always had existed between Tweedle-dum and Tweedle-dee." Certainly in the end the things that Roosevelt and Wilson could agree on were more important than the issues that divided them. Both Roosevelt and Wilson urged reform within the American system. Both defended corporate capitalism, and both opposed socialism and radical labor organizations such as the IWW. Both wanted to promote more democracy and to strengthen conservative labor unions. Both were very different in style and substance from the fourth candidate, Eugene Debs, who ran on the Socialist party ticket in 1912.

Debs, in 1912, was the most important socialist leader in the country. Socialism has always been a minority movement in the United States; it had its greatest success in the first decade of the

Major Parties in the Presidential Election of 1912

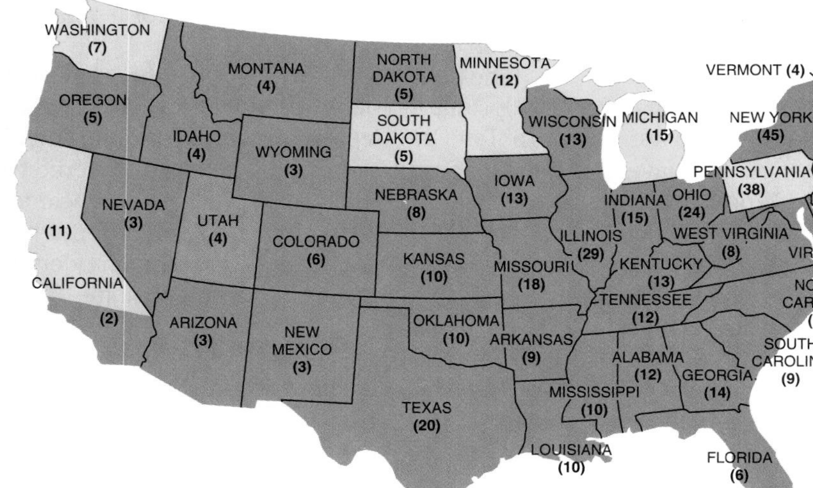

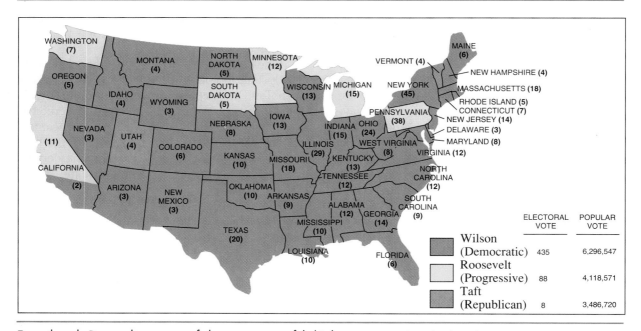

	ELECTORAL VOTE	POPULAR VOTE
Wilson (Democratic)	435	6,296,547
Roosevelt (Progressive)	88	4,118,571
Taft (Republican)	8	3,486,720

Even though Roosevelt ran one of the most successful third-party campaigns in American history, the American electoral system made it almost impossible for him to win. But Taft's overwhelming defeat was humiliating for an incumbent president. Notice how much of the electoral vote was concentrated in states east of the Mississippi.

twentieth century. Thirty-three cities including Milwaukee, Wisconsin; Reading, Pennsylvania; Butte, Montana; Jackson, Michigan; and Berkeley, California, chose socialist mayors. Socialists Victor Berger from Wisconsin and Meyer London from New York were elected to Congress. The most important socialist periodical, *Appeal to Reason,* published in Girard, Kansas, increased its circulation from about 30,000 in 1900 to nearly 300,000 in 1906. Socialism appealed to a diverse group. In the cities, some who called themselves socialists merely favored municipal ownership of street railways. Some reformers, such as Florence Kelley and William English Walling, joined the party because of their frustration with the slow progress of reform. The party also attracted many recent immigrants, who brought with them a European sense of class and loyalty to socialism.

A tremendously appealing figure and a great orator, Debs had run for president in 1900, 1904, and 1908, but in 1912 he reached much wider audiences in more parts of the country. His message differed radically from that of Wilson or Roosevelt. Unlike the progressives, socialists argued for fundamental change in the American system. The Socialist party is "organized and financed by the workers themselves," he announced, "as a means of wresting control of government and industry from the capitalists and making the working class the ruling class of the nation and the world." Debs polled almost 900,000 votes in 1912 (6 percent of the popular vote), the best showing ever for a socialist in the United States. Wilson received 6.3 million votes, Roosevelt a little more than 4 million, and Taft 3.5 million. Wilson garnered 435 electoral votes, Roosevelt 88, and Taft only 8.

Woodrow Wilson and the New Freedom

Wilson was elected largely because Roosevelt and the Progressive party split the Republican vote. But once elected, Wilson became a vigorous and aggressive chief executive who set out to translate his ideas about progressive government into legislation. Wilson was the first southerner elected president since Zachary Taylor in 1848 and only the second Democrat since the Civil War. Wilson, like Roosevelt, had to work with his party, and that restricted how progressive he could be. But he was also constrained by his own background and inclinations. Still, like Roosevelt, Wilson became more progressive during his presidency.

Tariff and Banking Reform

Wilson was not as charismatic as Roosevelt. He had a more difficult time relating to people in small groups, but he was an excellent public speaker who dominated through the force of his intellect. He probably had an exaggerated belief in his ability to persuade and a tendency to trust his own intuition too much. Ironically, his early success in getting his legislative agenda through Congress contributed to the overconfidence that would get him into difficulty later in foreign affairs. But his ability to push his legislative program through Congress during his first two years in office was matched only by Franklin Roosevelt during the first months of the New Deal and by Lyndon Johnson in 1965.

Within a month of his inauguration, Wilson went before a joint session of Congress to outline his legislative program. He recommended reducing the tariff to eliminate favoritism, freeing the banking system from Wall Street control, and restoring competition in industry. By appearing in person before Congress, he broke a precedent established by Thomas Jefferson. First on his agenda was tariff reform. The Underwood Tariff, passed in 1913, was not a free-trade bill, but it did reduce the schedule for the first time in many years.

Attached to the Underwood bill was a provision for a small and slightly graduated income tax, which had been made possible by the passage of the Sixteenth Amendment. It imposed a modest rate of 1 percent on income over $4,000 (thus exempting a large portion of the population), with a surtax rising to 6 percent on high incomes. The income tax was enacted to replace the money lost from lowering the tariff. Wilson seemed to have no interest in using it to redistribute wealth in America.

The next item on Wilson's agenda was reform of the banking system. A financial panic in 1907 had revealed the need for a central bank, but few people could agree on the exact nature of the reforms. The progressive faction of the Democratic party, armed with the findings of the Pujo Committee's investigation of the money trust, argued for a banking system and a currency controlled by the federal government. The congressional committee, led by Arsène Pujo of Louisiana, had revealed a massive consolidation of banks and trust companies and a system of interlocking directorates and informal arrangements that concentrated resources and power in the hands of a few firms such as the J. P. Morgan Company. But talk of banking reform raised the specter among conservative Democrats and the business community of socialism, populism, and the monetary ideas of William Jennings Bryan.

The bill that passed Congress was a compromise. In creating the Federal Reserve System, it was the first reorganization of the banking system since the Civil War. The bill provided for 12 Federal Reserve banks and a Federal Reserve Board appointed by the president. The bill also created a flexible currency, based on federal reserve notes, that could be expanded or contracted as the situation required. The Federal Reserve System was not without its flaws, as later developments would show, and it did not end the power of the large eastern banks; but it was an improvement, and it appealed to the part of the progressive movement that sought order and efficiency.

Despite these reform measures, Wilson was not very progressive in some of his actions during his first two years in office. In the spring of 1914, he failed to support a bill that would have provided long-term rural credit financed by the federal government. He opposed a woman suffrage amendment, arguing that the states should decide who could vote. He also failed to support an anti–child labor bill after it had passed the House. Most distressing to some progressives, he ordered the segregation of blacks in several federal departments.

Booker T. Washington had remarked on Wilson's election, "Mr. Wilson is in favor of the things which tend toward the uplift, improvement, and

Woman suffrage advocates, dressed fashionably in their long skirts and hats, gathered in Washington in 1913 to try to convince Congress and President Wilson to support a suffrage amendment.

Presidential Elections of the Progressive Era

Year	Candidates	Party	Popular Vote	Electoral Vote
1904	THEODORE ROOSEVELT	Republican	7,628,834 (56.4%)	336
	Alton B. Parker	Democratic	5,084,401 (37.6%)	140
	Eugene V. Debs	Socialist	402,460 (3.0%)	0
1908	WILLIAM H. TAFT	Republican	7,679,006 (51.6%)	321
	William J. Bryan	Democratic	6,409,106 (43.1%)	162
	Eugene V. Debs	Socialist	420,820 (2.8%)	0
1912	WOODROW WILSON	Democratic	6,296,547 (41.9%)	435
	Theodore Roosevelt	Progressive	4,118,571 (27.4%)	88
	William H. Taft	Republican	3,486,720 (23.2%)	8
	Eugene V. Debs	Socialist	897,011 (6.0%)	0
1916	WOODROW WILSON	Democratic	9,129,606 (49.4%)	277
	Charles E. Hughes	Republican	8,538,221 (46.2%)	254
	Allan L. Benson	Socialist	585,113 (3.2%)	0

Note: Winners' names appear in capital letters.

advancement of my people, and at his hands we have nothing to fear." But when southern Democrats, suddenly in control in many departments, began dismissing black federal officeholders, especially those "who boss white girls," Wilson did nothing. When the NAACP complained that the shops, offices, rest rooms, and lunchrooms of the Post Office and Treasury departments and the Bureau of Engraving were segregated, Wilson replied, "I sincerely believe it to be in their [the blacks'] best interest."

Moving Closer to a New Nationalism

How to control the great corporations in America was a question Wilson and Roosevelt debated extensively during the campaign. Wilson's solution was the Clayton Act, submitted to Congress in 1914. The bill prohibited a number of unfair trading practices, outlawed the interlocking directorate, and made it illegal for corporations to purchase stock in other corporations if this tended to reduce competition. It was not clear how the government would enforce these provisions and ensure the competition that Wilson's New Freedom doctrine called for, but the bill became controversial for another reason. Labor leaders protested that the bill had no provision exempting labor organizations from prosecution under the Sherman Anti-Trust Act. When a section was added exempting both labor and agricultural organizations, Samuel Gompers hailed it as labor's Magna Charta. It was hardly that, because the courts interpreted the provision so that labor unions remained subject to court injunctions during strikes despite the Clayton Act.

More important than the Clayton Act, which both supporters and opponents realized was too vague to be enforced, was the creation of the Federal Trade Commission (FTC), modeled after the ICC, with enough power to move directly against corporations accused of restricting competition. The FTC was the idea of Louis Brandeis, but Wilson accepted it even though it seemed to move him more toward the philosophy of New Nationalism.

The Federal Trade Commission and the Clayton Act did not end monopoly, and the courts in the next two decades did not increase the government's power to regulate business. The success of Wilson's reform agenda appeared minimal in 1914, but the outbreak of war in Europe and the need to win the election of 1916 would influence him in becoming more progressive in the next years.

Neither Wilson nor Roosevelt satisfied the demands of the advanced progressives. Most of the efforts of the two progressive presidents were spent trying to regulate economic power rather than to promote social justice. Yet the most important legacy of these two fascinating and powerful politicians was their attempts to strengthen the office of president and the executive branch of the federal government. The nineteenth-century American presidents after Lincoln had been relatively weak, and much of the federal power had resided with Congress. The progressive presidents reasserted presidential authority, modernized the executive branch, and began the creation of the federal bureaucracy, which has had a major impact on the lives of Americans in the twentieth century.

Both Wilson and Roosevelt used the presidency as a bully pulpit to make pronouncements, create news, and influence policy. For example, both presidents called White House conferences and appointed committees and commissions. Roosevelt strengthened the Interstate Commerce Commission and Wilson created the Federal Trade Commission, both of which were the forerunners of many other federal regulatory bodies. And by breaking precedent and actually delivering his annual message in person before a joint session of Congress, Wilson symbolized the new power of the presidency.

More than the increased power of the executive branch changed the nature of politics. The new bureaus, committees, and commissions brought to Washington a new kind of expert, trained in the universities, at the state and local level, and in the voluntary organizations. Julia Lathrop, a coworker of Jane Addams at Hull House, was one such expert. Appointed by President Taft in 1912 to become chief of the newly created Children's Bureau, she was the first woman ever appointed to such a position. She used her post not only to work for better child labor laws but also to train a new generation of women experts who would take their positions in state, federal, and private agencies in the 1920s and 1930s. Other experts emerged in Washington during the progressive era to influence policy in subtle and important ways. The expert, the commission, the statistical survey, and the increased power of the executive branch were all legacies of the progressive era.

CONCLUSION

The Limits of Progressivism

The progressive era was a time when many Americans set out to promote reform because they saw poverty, despair, and disorder in the country transformed by immigration, urbanism, and industrialism. The progressives, unlike the socialists, however, saw nothing fundamentally wrong with the American system. Progressivism was largely a middle-class movement that sought to help the poor, the immigrants, and the working class. Yet the poor were rarely consulted about policy, and many groups, especially blacks, were almost entirely left out of reform plans. Progressives had an optimistic view of human nature and an exaggerated faith in statistics, commissions, and committees. They talked of the need for more democracy, but they often succeeded in promoting bureaucracy and a government run by experts. They believed there was a need to regulate business, promote efficiency, and spread social justice, but these were often contradictory goals. In the end, their regulatory laws tended to aid business and to strengthen corporate capitalism, while social justice and equal opportunity remained difficult to achieve. By contrast, most of the industrialized nations of western Europe, especially Germany, Austria, France, and Great Britain, passed legislation during this period providing for old-age pensions and health and unemployment insurance.

Progressivism was a broad, diverse, and sometimes contradictory movement that had its roots in the 1890s and reached a climax in the early twentieth century. It began with many local movements and voluntary efforts to deal with the problems created by urban industrialism and moved to the state and finally the national level. Women played important roles in organizing reform, and many became experts at gathering statistics and writing reports. Eventually they began to fill positions in the new agencies in the state capitals and in Washington. Neither Theodore Roosevelt nor Woodrow Wilson was an advanced progressive, but during both their administrations, progressivism achieved some success. Both presidents strengthened the power of the presidency, and both promoted the idea that the federal government had the responsibility to regulate and control and to promote social justice. Progressivism would be altered by World War I, but it survived, with its strengths and weaknesses, to affect American society through most of the twentieth century.

Recommended Reading

General Accounts

John D. Buenker, John C. Burnham, and Robert Crunden, *Progressivism* (1977); Gabriel Kolko, *The Triumph of Conservatism* (1963); Arthur S. Link and Richard L. McCormick, *Progressivism* (1983); Robert Wiebe, *The Search for Order, 1877–1920* (1967); Richard Hofstadter, *The Age of Reform* (1955).

The Progressive Impulse

Paul Boyer, *Urban Masses and Moral Order in America, 1820–1920* (1978); Robert M. Crunden, *Ministers of Reform* (1982); Peter Conn, *The Divided Mind: Ideology and Imagination in America, 1890–1927* (1983); David Noble, *The Progressive Mind, 1890–1917* (1970); Morton White, *Social Thought in America* (1949); Robert B. Westbrook, *John Dewey and American Democracy* (1991); Susan Curtis, *Consuming Faith: The Social Gospel and Modern American Culture* (1991).

A Diversity of Progressive Movements

Allen F. Davis, *Spearheads for Reform: The Social Settlements and the Progressive Movement* (1967); Walter I. Trattner, *Crusade for Children* (1970); William L. O'Neill, *Divorce in the Progressive Era* (1963); Ruth Rosen, *The Lost Sisterhood* (1982); Mark T. Connelly, *The Response to Prostitution in the Progressive Era* (1980); Lary May, *Screening Out the Past: The Birth of Mass Culture and the Motion Picture Industry* (1980); Daniel Levine, *Poverty and Society: The Growth of the American Welfare State in International Perspective* (1988); James T. Klopenberg, *Social Democracy and Progressivism in European and American Thought* (1986); James H. Timberlake, *Prohibition and the Progressive Movement* (1963); Louis Filler, *The Muckrakers* (1976); David P. Thelen, *The New Citizenship* (1972); Bradley R. Rice, *Progressive Cities* (1977); Dewey Grantham, *Southern Progressivism* (1983); Aileen S. Kraditor, *The Ideas of the Woman Suffrage Movement, 1890–1920* (1965); August Meier, *Negro Thought in America, 1880–1915* (1963); Samuel P. Hays, *Conservation and the Gospel of Efficiency* (1959); Frederick Turner, *Rediscovering America: John Muir in His Time and Ours* (1985); David Brody, *Workers in Industrial America* (1980); Alice Kessler-Harris, *Out to Work* (1983).

National Politics

John Morton Blum, *The Progressive Presidents* (1980); John Milton Cooper, Jr., *The Warrior and the Priest* (1983); Arthur S. Lin, *Woodrow Wilson and the Progressive Era* (1954); George E. Mowry, *The Era of Theodore Roosevelt* (1958); Paolo E. Coletta, *The Presidency of William Howard Taft* (1973); Nick Salvatore, *Eugene V. Debs* (1982).

Fiction

Fiction from the period includes Theodore Dreiser, *Sister Carrie* (1900), a classic of social realism; Upton Sinclair, *The Jungle* (1906), a novel about the meatpacking industry and the failure of the American dream; David Graham Phillips, *Susan Lenox* (1917), an epic of slum life and political corruption; and Charlotte Perkins Gilman, *Herland* (1915), the story of a female utopia.

TIMELINE

1901 McKinley assassinated; Theodore Roosevelt becomes president
Robert La Follette elected governor of Wisconsin
Tom Johnson elected mayor of Cleveland
Model tenement house bill passed in New York
U.S. Steel formed

1902 Anthracite coal strike

1903 Women's Trade Union League founded
Elkins Act

1904 Roosevelt reelected
Lincoln Steffens publishes *The Shame of the Cities*

1905 Frederic C. Howe writes *The City: The Hope of Democracy*
Industrial Workers of the World formed

1906 Upton Sinclair publishes *The Jungle*
Hepburn Act
Meat Inspection Act
Pure Food and Drug Act

1907 Financial panic

1908 *Muller v. Oregon*
Danbury Hatters case
William Howard Taft elected president

1909 Herbert Croly publishes *The Promise of American Life*
NAACP founded

1910 Ballinger-Pinchot controversy
Mann Act

1911 Frederick Taylor publishes *The Principles of Scientific Management*
Triangle Shirtwaist Company fire

1912 Progressive party founded by Theodore Roosevelt
Woodrow Wilson elected president
Children's Bureau established
Industrial Relations Commission founded

1913 Sixteenth Amendment (income tax) ratified
Underwood Tariff
Federal Reserve System established
Seventeenth Amendment (direct election of senators) passed

1914 Clayton Act
Federal Trade Commission Act
AFL has over 2 million members
Ludlow Massacre in Colorado

CHAPTER 22

The Great War

On April 7, 1917, the day after the United States officially declared war on Germany, Edmund P. Arpin, Jr., a young man of 22 from Grand Rapids, Wisconsin, decided to enlist in the army. The war seemed to provide a solution for his aimless drifting. It was not patriotism that led him to join the army but his craving for adventure and excitement. A month later, he was at Fort Sheridan, Illinois, along with hundreds of other eager young men, preparing to become an army officer. He felt a certain pride and sense of purpose, and especially a feeling of comradeship with the other men, but the war was a long way off.

Arpin finally arrived with his unit in Liverpool on December 23, 1917, aboard the *Leviathan,* a German luxury liner that the United States had interned when war was declared and pressed into service as a troop transport. In England, he discovered that American troops were not greeted as saviors. Hostility against the Americans simmered partly because of the previous unit's drunken brawls. Despite the efforts of the United States government to protect its soldiers from the sins of Europe, drinking seems to have been a preoccupation of the soldiers in Arpin's outfit. Arpin also learned something about French wine and women, but he spent most of the endless waiting time learning to play contract bridge.

Arpin saw some of the horror of war when he went to the front with a French regiment as an observer, but his own unit did not engage in combat until October 1918, when the war was almost over. He took part in the bloody Meuse-Argonne offensive, which helped end the war. But he discovered that war was not the heroic struggle of carefully planned campaigns that newspapers and books described. War was filled with misfired weapons, mixups, and erroneous attacks. Wounded in the leg in an assault on an unnamed hill and awarded a Distinguished Service Cross for his bravery, Arpin later learned that the order to attack had been recalled but word had not reached him in time.

When the armistice came, Arpin was recovering in a field hospital. He was disappointed that the war had ended so soon, but he was well enough to go to Paris to take part in the victory celebration and to explore some of the famous Paris restaurants and nightclubs. In many ways, the highlight of his war experiences was not a battle or his medal but his adventure after the war was over. With a friend he went absent without leave and set out to explore Germany. They avoided the military police, traveled on a train illegally, and had many narrow escapes, but they made it back to the hospital without being arrested.

Edward Arpin was in the army for two years. He was one of 4,791,172 Americans who served in the army, navy, or marines. He was one of the 2 million who went overseas, and one of the 230,074 who were wounded. Some of his friends were among the 48,909 who were killed. When he was mustered out of the army in March 1919, he felt lost and confused. Being a civilian was not nearly as exciting as being in the army and visiting new and exotic places.

In time, Arpin settled down. He became a successful businessman, married, and reared a family. A member of the American Legion, he periodically went to conventions and reminisced with men from his division about their escapades in France. Although the war changed their lives in many ways, most would never again feel the same sense of common purpose and adventure. "I don't suppose any of us felt, before or since, so necessary to God and man," one veteran recalled.

For Edmund P. Arpin, Jr., the Great War was the most important event of a lifetime. Just as war changed his life, so too did it alter the lives of most Americans. Trends begun during the progressive era accelerated. The power and influence of the federal government increased. Not only did the war promote woman suffrage, prohibition, and public housing, but it also helped to create an administrative bureaucracy that blurred the lines between public and private, between government and business—a trend that would continue throughout the twentieth century.

Woodrow Wilson talked of a "war to end all wars" and a war "to make the world safe for democracy." His optimism, moralism, and missionary zeal helped to transform the war into a great crusade. Wilson was not alone. Many Americans, although initially reluctant, set out to defeat Germany with the same kind of commitment and enthusiasm they had once applied to promoting anti–child labor legislation and cleaning up the slums. However, not all progressives agreed that the war was the logical extension of the reform movement. Jane Addams and other pacifists saw the war as the antithesis of all they had been trying to promote. But they were a small minority; most Americans enthusiastically joined the crusade for victory. In the end, exaggerated expectations about the purposes of the war led to disappointment over the peace and fed some of the despair and intolerance that followed the armistice.

In this chapter, we travel the twisted path that led the United States into the war and share the wartime experiences of American men and women overseas and at home. We will examine not only military actions but also the impact of the war on domestic policies and on the lives of ordinary Americans. The chapter concludes with a look at the idealistic efforts to promote peace at the end of the war.

The Early War Years

Few Americans expected the Great War that erupted in Europe in the summer of 1914 to affect their lives or alter their comfortable world. When a Serbian student terrorist assassinated Archduke Franz Ferdinand of Austria-Hungary in Sarajevo, the capital of the province of Bosnia, a place most Americans had never heard of, it precipitated a series of events leading to the most destructive war the world had ever known.

The Causes of War

Despite Theodore Roosevelt's successful peacekeeping attempts in the first decade of the century (see Chapter 20), relationships between the European powers had not improved. Intense rivalries for empire turned minor incidents in Africa, Asia, or the Balkans into events that threatened world peace. A growing sense of nationalism and pride in being French or British or German was fanned by a popular press, much the way Hearst's *Journal* and Pulitzer's *World* had increased American patriotism in the years before the Spanish-American War. National rivalry, especially between Great Britain and Germany, led to military competition and a race to build bigger battleships.

As European nations armed, they drew up a complex series of treaties. Austria-Hungary and Germany (the Central Powers) became military allies, while Britain, France, and Russia (the Allied Powers) agreed to assist one another in case of attack. Despite peace conferences and international agreements, many promoted by the United States, the European balance of power rested precariously on layers of treaties that barely obscured years of jealousy and distrust.

The incident in Sarajevo destroyed that balance. The leaders of Austria-Hungary determined to punish Serbia for the assassination. Russia mobilized to aid Serbia. Germany, supporting Austria-Hungary, declared war on Russia and France. England hesitated, but when Germany invaded Belgium in order to attack France, England declared war and the slaughter began.

European Alignments, 1914

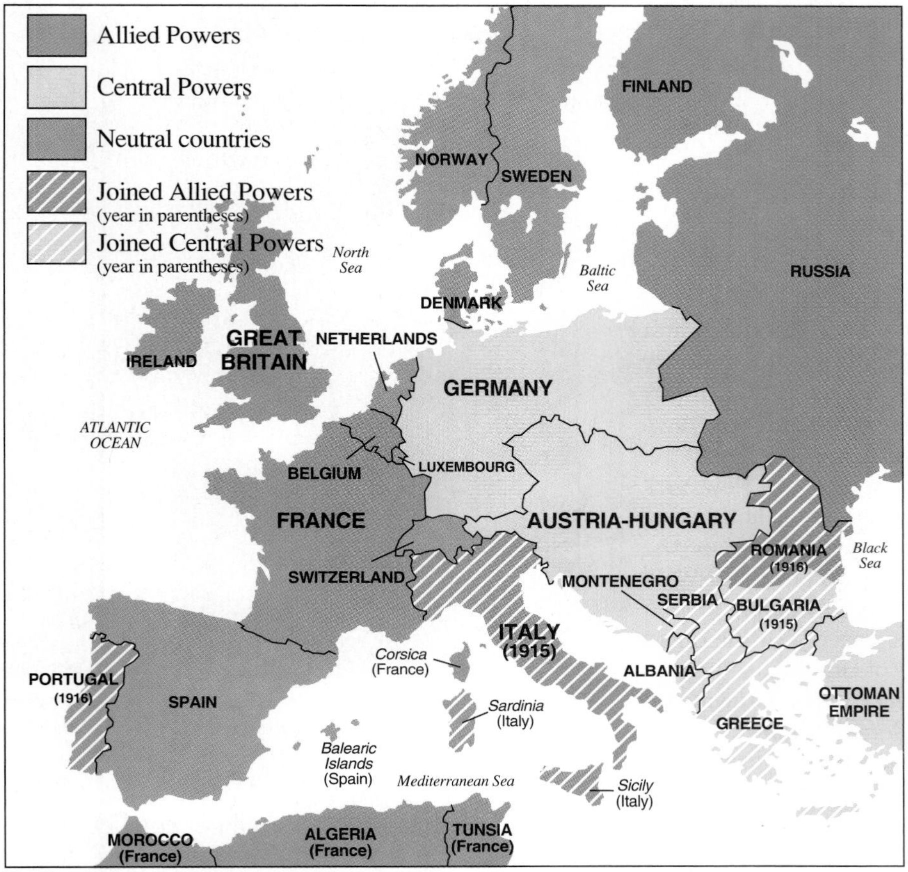

The Great War had an impact on all of Europe, even on the few countries that managed to remain neutral. Russia left the war in 1917, the same year that the United States joined the fight.

Despite much evidence to the contrary, many intelligent people on both sides of the Atlantic believed that education, science, social reform, and negotiation had replaced all-out war as a way of solving international disputes. "It looks as though we are going to be the age of treaties rather than the age of wars, the century of reason rather than the century of force," a leader of the American peace movement had declared only two years before. But as news of the German invasion of Belgium and reports of the first bloody battles began to reach the United States in late summer, it seemed to most Americans that madness had replaced reason. Europeans "have reverted to the condition of savage tribes roaming the forests and falling upon each other in a fury of blood and carnage," the *New York Times* announced.

The American sense that the nation would never succumb to the barbarism of war, combined with the knowledge that the Atlantic Ocean separated Europe from the United States, contributed to a great sense of relief after the first shock of the war began to wear off. Woodrow Wilson's official proclamation of neutrality on August 4, 1914, reinforced the belief that the United States had no major stake in the outcome of the war and would stay uninvolved. The president was preoccupied with his own personal tragedy. His wife, Ellen Axson Wilson, died of Bright's disease the day after his proclamation. Two weeks later, still engulfed by his own grief, he urged all Americans to "be neutral in fact as well as in name, . . . impartial in thought as well as in action." The United States, he argued, must preserve itself "fit and free" in order to do what "is honest and disinterested . . . for the peace of the world." But it was obvious that it was going to be difficult to stay uninvolved, at least emotionally, with the battlefields of Europe.

American Reactions

Many social reformers despaired when they heard the news from Europe. Even during its first months, the war seemed to deflect energy away from reform. "We are three thousand miles away from the smoke and flames of combat, and have not a single regiment or battleship involved," remarked John Haynes Holmes, a liberal New York minister. "Yet who in the United States is thinking of recreation centers, improved housing or the minimum wage?" Settlement worker Lillian Wald responded to the threat of war by helping to lead 1,500 women in a "woman's peace" parade down Fifth Avenue. Jane Addams of Hull House helped to organize the Woman's Peace party. Drawing on traditional conceptions of female character, she argued that women had a special responsibility to work for peace and to speak out against the blasphemy of war because women and children suffered most in any war, especially in a modern war where civilians as well as soldiers became targets.

While many people worked to promote an international plan to end the war through mediation, others could hardly wait to take part in the great adventure. Hundreds of young American men, most of them students or recent college graduates, volunteered to join ambulance units, to take part in the war effort without actually fighting. Among the most famous of them were Ernest Hemingway, John Dos Passos, and E. E. Cummings, who later turned their wartime adventures into literary masterpieces. Others volunteered for service with the French Foreign Legion or joined the Lafayette Escadrille, a unit of pilots made up of well-to-do American volunteers attached to the French army. Many of these young men were inspired by an older generation who pictured war as a romantic and manly adventure. One college president talked of the chastening and purifying effect of armed conflict, while Theodore Roosevelt projected an image of war that was something like a football game where red-blooded American men could test their idealism and manhood.

The war in Europe appealed to the sense of adventure in many young American men. However, as in all wars, the women they left behind found it hard to say good-bye.

Alan Seeger, a graduate of Harvard in 1910, was one of those who believed in the romantic and noble purpose of the war. He had been living in Paris since 1912, and when the war broke out, he quickly joined the French Foreign Legion. For the next two years, he wrote sentimental poetry, articles, and letters describing his adventures. "You have no idea how beautiful it is to see the troops undulating along the road . . . with the captains and lieutenants on horse back at the head of the companies," he wrote his mother. When Seeger was killed in 1916, he became an instant hero. Some called him "America's Rupert Brooke," after the gallant British poet who died early in the war.

Many Americans visualized war as a romantic struggle for honor and glory because the only conflict they remembered was the "splendid little war" of 1898. For them, war meant Theodore Roosevelt leading the charge in Cuba and Commodore Dewey destroying the Spanish fleet in Manila harbor without the loss of an American life. Many older Americans recalled the Civil War, but the horrors of those years had faded, leaving only the memory of heroic triumphs. As Oliver Wendell Holmes, the Supreme Court justice who had been wounded in the Civil War, remarked, "War, when you are at it, is horrible and dull. It is only when time has passed that you see that its message was divine."

The reports from the battlefields, even during the first months of the war, should have indicated that the message was anything but divine. This would be a modern war in which men died by the thousands, cut down by an improved and efficient technology of killing.

The New Military Technology

The German Schlieffen plan called for a rapid strike through Belgium to attack Paris and the French army from the rear. However, the French stopped the German advance at the Battle of the Marne in September 1914, and the fighting soon bogged down in a costly and bloody routine. Soldiers on both sides dug miles of trenches and strung out barbed wire to protect them. Thousands died in battles that gained only a few yards or nothing at all. Rapid-firing rifles, improved explosives, incendiary shells, smokeless bullets, and tracer bullets all added to the destruction. Most devastating of all, however, was the improved artillery, sometimes mounted on trucks and directed by spotters using wireless radios, that could fire over the horizon and hit targets many miles behind the lines.

The technology of defense, especially the machine gun, neutralized the frontal assault, the most popular military tactic since the American Civil War. As one writer explained: "Three men and a machine gun can stop a battalion of heroes." But the generals on both sides continued to order their men to charge to their almost certain deaths.

The war was both a traditional and a revolutionary struggle. It was the last war in which cavalry was used and the first to employ a new generation of military technologies. By 1918, airplanes, initially used only for observation, were creating terror below with their bombs. Tanks made their first tentative appearance in 1916, but it was not until the last days of the war that this new offensive weapon began to neutralize the machine gun. Poison gas, first used in 1914, added a new element of fear to a war of already unspeakable horror. But then military technicians on both sides developed the gas mask, allowing the defense to counter the new offensive weapons.

Despite the reports of carnage from the battlefields, some Americans could hardly wait to join the fighting. Theodore Roosevelt and his friend Leonard Wood, the army chief of staff, led a movement to prepare American men for war. Wood was determined that upper-class and college-educated men be ready to lead the nation into battle. In 1913, he established a camp for college men at Plattsburgh, New York, to give them some experience with military life, with order, discipline, and command. By 1915, thousands had crowded into the camp; even the mayor of New York enrolled. The young men learned to shoot rifles and to endure long marches and field exercises. But most of all, they associated with one another. Gathered around the campfire at night, they heard Wood and other veterans tell of winning glory and honor on the battlefield. In their minds at least, they were already leading a bayonet charge against the enemy, and the enemy was Germany.

Difficulties of Neutrality

Despite Wilson's efforts to promote neutrality, most Americans favored the Allied cause. About 8 million Austrian- and German-Americans lived in the United States, and some supported the cause of the Central Powers. They viewed Kaiser Wilhelm II's Germany as a progressive parliamentary democracy. The anti-British sentiment of some Irish-Americans led them to take sides not so much for Germany as against England. A few Swedish-Americans distrusted Russia so vehemently that they had difficulty supporting the Allies. A number of American scholars, physicians, and intellectuals fondly remembered studying in Germany. To them, Germany meant great universities and cathedrals, music and culture. It also represented social planning, health insurance, unemployment compensation, and many programs for which the progressives had been fighting.

For most Americans, however, the ties of language and culture tipped the balance toward the Allies. After all, did not the English-speaking people of the world have special bonds and special responsibilities to promote civilization and ensure justice in the world? American connections with the French were not so close, but they were even more sentimental. The French, everyone remembered, had supported the American Revolution, and the French people had given the Statue of Liberty, the very symbol of American opportunity and democracy, to the United States.

Other reasons made real neutrality nearly impossible. The fact that export and import trade with the Allies was much more important than with the Central Powers favored the Allies. Wilson's advisers, especially Robert Lansing and Edward House, openly supported the French and the British. Most newspaper owners and editors had close ethnic, cultural, and sometimes economic ties to the British and the French. The newspapers were quick to picture the Germans as barbaric Huns and to accept and embellish the atrocity stories that came from the front, some of them planted by British propaganda experts. Gradually for Wilson, and probably for most Americans, the perception that England and France were fighting to preserve civilization from the forces of Prussian evil replaced the idea that all Europeans were barbaric and decadent. But the American people were not yet willing to go to war to save civilization. Let France and England do that.

Woodrow Wilson also sympathized with the Allies for practical and idealistic reasons. He wanted to keep the United States out of the war, but he did not object to using force to promote diplomatic ends. "When men take up arms to set other men free, there is something sacred and holy in the warfare," he had written. Moreover, Wilson believed that by keeping the United States out of the war, he might control the peace. The war, he hoped, would show the futility of imperialism and would usher in a world of free trade in products and ideas. The United States had a special role to play in this new world and in leading toward an orderly international society. "We are the mediating nation of the world [and] we are therefore able to understand all nations."

Remaining neutral while maintaining trade with the belligerents became increasingly difficult. Remaining neutral while speaking out about the peace eventually became impossible. The need to trade and the desire to control the peace finally led the United States into the Great War.

World Trade and Neutrality Rights

The United States was part of an international economic community in 1914 in a way that it had not been a hundred years earlier during the Napoleonic Wars. The outbreak of war in the summer of 1914 caused an immediate economic panic in the United States. On July 31, 1914, the Wilson administration closed the stock exchange to prevent the unloading of European securities and panic selling. It also adopted a policy discouraging loans by American banks to belligerent nations. Most difficult was the matter of neutral trade. Wilson insisted on the rights of Americans to trade with both the Allies and the Central Powers, but Great Britain instituted an illegal naval blockade, mined the North Sea, and began seizing American ships, even those carrying food and raw materials to Italy, the Netherlands, and other neutral nations. The first crisis that Wilson faced was whether or not to accept the illicit British blockade. To do so would be to surrender one of the rights he supported most ardently, the right of free trade.

Wilson eventually backed down and accepted British control of the sea. His conviction that the destinies of the United States and Great Britain were intertwined outweighed his idealistic belief in free trade and caused him to react more harshly to German violations of international law than he did to British violators. Consequently, American trade with the Central Powers declined between 1914 and 1916 from $169 million to just over $1 million, whereas with the Allies it increased during the same period from $825 million to over $3 billion. At the same time, the United States government eased restrictions on private loans to belligerents. In March 1915, the House of Morgan loaned the French government $50 million, and in the fall of 1915, the French and British obtained an unsecured loan of $500 million from American banks. With dollars as well as sentiments, the United States gradually ceased to be neutral.

Germany retaliated against British control of the seas with submarine warfare. The new weapon, the U-boat (*Unterseeboot*), created unprecedented problems. Nineteenth-century international law obligated a belligerent warship to warn a passenger or merchant ship before attacking, but the chief advantage of the submarine was surprise. Rising to the surface to issue a warning would have meant being blown out of the water by an armed merchant ship.

On February 4, 1915, Germany announced a submarine blockade of the British Isles. Until Britain gave up its campaign to starve the German population, the Germans would sink even neutral ships. Wilson warned Germany that it would be held to "strict accountability" for illegal destruction of American ships or lives.

In March 1915, a German U-boat sank a British liner en route to Africa, killing 103 people, including one American. How should the United States respond? Wilson's advisers could not agree. Robert Lansing, a legal counsel at the State Department, urged the president to issue a strong protest, charging a breach of international law. William Jennings Bryan, the secretary of state, argued that an American traveling on a British ship was guilty of "contributory negligence" and urged Wilson to prohibit Americans from traveling on belligerent ships in the war zone. Wilson never did settle the dispute, for on May 7, 1915, a greater crisis erupted. A German U-boat torpedoed the British luxury liner *Lusitania* off the Irish coast. The liner, which was not armed but was carrying war supplies, sank in 18 minutes. Nearly 1,200 people, including many women and children, drowned. Among the dead were 128 Americans. Suddenly Americans confronted the horror of total war fought with modern weapons, a war that killed civilians, including women and children, just as easily as it killed soldiers.

The tragedy horrified most Americans. Despite earlier warnings by the Germans in American newspapers that it was dangerous to travel in war zones, the same newspapers denounced the act as "mass murder." Some called for a declaration of war. Wilson and most Americans had no idea of going to war in the spring of 1915, but the president refused to take Bryan's advice and prevent further loss of American lives by simply prohibiting all Americans from traveling on belligerent ships. Instead, he sent a series of protest

"All the News That's Fit to Print."

The New York Times.

EXTRA 5:30 A. M.

LUSITANIA SUNK BY A SUBMARINE, PROBABLY 1,260 DEAD; TWICE TORPEDOED OFF IRISH COAST; SINKS IN 15 MINUTES; CAPT. TURNER SAVED, FROHMAN AND VANDERBILT MISSING; WASHINGTON BELIEVES THAT A GRAVE CRISIS IS AT HAND

SHOCKS THE PRESIDENT

Washington Deeply Stirred by the Loss of American Lives.

BULLETINS AT WHITE HOUSE

HINTS OF CONGRESS CALL

CAPITAL FULL OF RUMORS

The Lost Cunard Steamship Lusitania

SOME DEAD TAKEN ASHORE

Several Hundred Survivors at Queenstown and Kinsale.

STEWARD TELLS OF DISASTER

One Torpedo Crashes Into the Doomed Liner's Bow, Another Into the Engine Room.

SHIP LISTS OVER TO PORT

ATTACKED IN BROAD DAY

Only 650 Were Saved, Few Cabin Passengers

Cunard Office Here Besieged for News; Fate of 1,918 on Lusitania Long in Doubt

List of Saved Includes Capt. Turner; Vanderbilt and Frohman Reported Lost

Saw the Submarine 100 Yards Off and Watched Torpedo as It Struck Ship

Loss of the Lusitania Fills London With Horror and Utter Amazement

The sinking of the *Lusitania* shocked Americans and illustrated the complexity and horror of modern warfare. In the days before radio, most Americans received their news through the newspapers. New York had fifteen daily papers in 1915, and all produced "Extra" editions to announce such dramatic events as the sinking of the *Lusitania*.

notes demanding reparation for the loss of American lives and a pledge from Germany that it would cease attacking ocean liners without warning. Bryan resigned as secretary of state over the tone of the notes and charged that the United States was not being truly neutral. Some denounced Bryan as a traitor, but others charged that if the United States really wanted to stay out of the war, Bryan's position was more logical, consistent, and humane than Wilson's. The president replaced Bryan with Robert Lansing, who was much more eager than Bryan to oppose Germany, even at the risk of war.

The tense situation eased late in 1915. After a German U-boat sank the British steamer *Arabic,* which claimed two American lives, the German ambassador promised that Germany would not attack ocean liners without warning (the *Arabic* pledge). But the *Lusitania* crisis caused an outpouring of books and articles urging the nation to prepare for war. The National Security League, the most effective of the preparedness groups, called for a bigger army and navy, a system of universal military training, and "patriotic education and national sentiment and service among the people of the United States."

Organizing on the other side were a group of progressive reformers who formed the American Union Against Militarism. They feared that those urging preparedness were deliberately setting out to destroy liberal social reform at home and to promote imperialism abroad.

Wilson sympathized with the preparedness groups to the extent of asking Congress on November 4, 1915, for an enlarged and reorganized army. The bill met great opposition, especially from southern and western congressmen, but the Army Reorganization Bill that Wilson signed in June 1916 increased the regular army to just over 200,000 and integrated the National Guard into the defense structure. Few Americans, however, expected those young men to go to war. One of the most popular songs of 1916 was "I Didn't Raise My Boy to Be a Soldier." Even before American soldiers arrived in France, however, Wilson used the army and the marines in Mexico and Central America.

Intervening in Mexico and Central America

Woodrow Wilson came to office in 1913 planning to promote liberal and humanitarian ends, not only in domestic policies but also in foreign affairs. Wilson had a vision of a world purged of imperialism, a world of free trade, but a world where American ideas and American products would find their way. Combining the zeal of a Christian missionary with the conviction of a college professor, he spoke of "releasing the intelligence of America for the service of mankind" and of enriching the world "with the products of our mines, our farms, and our factories, with the creations of our thought and the fruits of our character." With his secretary of state, William Jennings Bryan, Wilson denounced the "big stick" and "dollar diplomacy" of the Roosevelt and Taft years. Yet in the end, his administration used force more systematically than those of his predecessors. The rhetoric was different, yet just as much as Roosevelt, Wilson tried to maintain stability in the countries to the south in order to promote American economic and strategic interests.

At first, Wilson's foreign policy seemed to reverse some of the most callous aspects of dollar diplomacy in Central America. Bryan signed a treaty with Colombia in 1913 that agreed to pay $5 million for the loss of Panama and virtually apologized for the Roosevelt administration's treatment of Colombia. The Senate, not so willing to admit that the United States had been wrong, refused to ratify the treaty.

The change in spirit proved illusory. After a disastrous civil war in the Dominican Republic, the United States offered in 1915 to take over the country's finances and police force. But when the Dominican leaders rejected a treaty making their country virtually a protectorate of the United States, Wilson ordered in the marines. They took control of the government in May 1916. Although Americans built roads, schools, and hospitals, people resented their presence. In neighboring Haiti, the situation was different, but the results were similar. The marines landed at Port-au-Prince in the summer of 1915 to prop up a pro-American regime. In Nicaragua, the Wilson administration kept the marines sent by Taft in 1912 to keep the pro-American regime of Adolfo Díaz in place and acquired the right, through treaty, to intervene at any time to preserve order and protect American property. Except for a brief period in the mid-1920s, the marines remained until 1933.

Wilson's policy of intervention ran into greatest difficulty in Mexico, a country that had been ruled by dictator Porfirio Díaz, who had long welcomed American investors. By 1910, more than 40,000 American citizens lived in Mexico, and more than $1 billion of American money was invested in the country. Americans controlled 75 percent of the mines, 70 percent of the rubber, and 60 percent of the oil. In 1911, however, Francisco Madero, a reformer who wanted to destroy the privileges of the upper classes, overthrew Díaz. Two years later, he was deposed and murdered by order of Victoriano Huerta, the head of the army. This was the situation when Wilson became president.

To the shock of many diplomats and businessmen, Wilson refused to recognize the Huerta government. Everyone admitted that Huerta was a ruthless dictator, but diplomatic recognition, the exchange of ambassadors, and the regulation

A British cartoon pokes fun at the American president and his wavering policy toward Mexico.

of trade and communication had never meant approval. In the world of business and diplomacy, it merely meant that a particular government was in power. But Wilson set out to remove what he called a "government of butchers." "The United States Government intends not merely to force Huerta from power," he wrote to a British diplomat, "but also to exert every influence it can to secure Mexico a better government under which all contracts and business concessions will be safer than they have ever been."

At first, Wilson applied diplomatic pressure. Then, using a minor incident as an excuse, he asked Congress for power to involve American troops if necessary. Few Mexicans liked Huerta, but they liked even less the idea of North American interference. Hence they rallied around the dictator. As it had in 1847, the United States landed troops at Veracruz. Angry Mexican mobs destroyed American property wherever they could find it. Wilson's action outraged many Europeans and Latin Americans as well as Americans.

Wilson's military intervention succeeded in forcing Huerta out of power, but a civil war between forces led by Venustiano Carranza and those led by General Francisco "Pancho" Villa ensued. The United States sent arms to Carranza, who was considered less radical than Villa, and Carranza's soldiers defeated Villa's. When an angry Villa led what was left of his army in a raid on Columbus, New Mexico, in March 1916, Wilson sent an expedition led by Brigadier General John Pershing to track down Villa and his men. The strange and comic scene developed of an American army charging 300 miles into Mexico unable to catch the retreating villain. Not surprisingly, given the history of Mexican-American relations, the Mexicans feared that Pershing's army was planning to occupy northern Mexico. Even Carranza shot off a bitter note to Wilson accusing him of threatening war, but Wilson refused to withdraw the troops. Tensions rose. An American patrol attacked a Mexican garrison, with loss of life on both sides. Just as war seemed inevitable, Wilson agreed to recall the troops and to recognize the Carranza government. But this was in January 1917, and if it had not been for the growing crisis in Europe, it is likely that war would have resulted.

The tragedy was that Wilson, who idealistically wanted the best for the people of Mexico and Central America and who thought he knew exactly what they needed, managed to intervene too often and too blatantly to protect the strategic and economic interests of the United States. In the process, his policy alienated onetime friends of the United States. His policies would contribute to future difficulties in both Latin America and Europe.

The United States Enters the War

A significant minority of Americans opposed going to war in 1917, and that decision would remain controversial when it was reexamined in the 1930s. But once involved, the government and the American people made the war into a patriotic crusade that influenced all aspects of American life.

The Election of 1916

American political campaigns do not stop even in times of international crisis. As 1915 turned to 1916, Wilson had to think of reelection as well as of preparedness, submarine warfare, and the Mexican campaign. At first glance, the president's chances of reelection seemed poor. He had won in 1912 only because Theodore Roosevelt and the Progressive party had split the Republican vote. If supporters of the Progressives in 1912 returned to the Republican fold, Wilson's chances were slim indeed. Because the Progressive party had done very badly in the 1914 congressional elections, Roosevelt seemed ready to seek the Republican nomination.

Wilson was aware that he had to win over voters who had favored Roosevelt in 1912. In January 1916, he appointed Louis D. Brandeis to the Supreme Court. The first Jew ever to sit on the High Court, Brandeis was confirmed over the strong opposition of many legal organizations. His appointment pleased the social justice progressives because he had always championed reform causes. They made it clear to Wilson that the real test for them was whether or not he supported the anti–child labor and workers' compensation bills pending in Congress.

In August, Wilson put heavy pressure on Congress and obtained passage of the Workmen's Compensation Bill, which gave some protection to federal employees, and the Keatings-Owen Child Labor Bill, which prohibited the shipment in interstate commerce of goods produced by children under 14 and in some cases under 16. This bill, later declared unconstitutional, was a far-reaching proposal that for the first time used federal control over interstate commerce to dictate the conditions under which businesspeople could manufacture products.

To attract farm support, Wilson pushed for passage of the Federal Farm Loan Act, which created 12 Federal Farm Loan banks to extend long-term credit to farmers. Urged on by organized labor as well as by many progressives, he supported the Adamson Act, which established an eight-hour day for all interstate railway workers. Within a few months, Wilson reversed the New Freedom doctrines he had earlier supported and brought the force of the federal government into play on the side of reform. The flurry of legislation early in 1916 provided one climax to the progressive movement. The strategy seemed to work, for progressives of all kinds enthusiastically endorsed the president.

The election of 1916, however, turned as much on foreign affairs as on domestic policy. The Republicans ignored Theodore Roosevelt and nominated instead the staid and respectable Charles Evans Hughes, a former governor of New York and future Supreme Court justice. Their platform called for "straight and honest neutrality" and "adequate preparedness." In a bitter campaign, Hughes attacked Wilson for not promoting American rights in Mexico more vigorously and for giving in to the unreasonable demands of labor. Wilson, on his part, implied that electing Hughes would guarantee war with both Mexico and Germany and that his opponents were somehow not "100 percent Americans." As the campaign progressed, the peace issue became more and more important, and the cry "He kept us out of war" echoed through every Democratic rally. It was a slogan that would soon seem strangely ironic.

The election was extremely close. In fact, Wilson went to bed on election night thinking he had lost the presidency. The election was not finally decided until the Democrats carried California (by less than 4,000 votes). Wilson won by carrying the West as well as the South.

Deciding for War

Wilson's victory in 1916 seemed to be a mandate for staying out of the European war. But the campaign rhetoric made the president nervous. He had tried to emphasize Americanism, not neutrality. As he told one of his advisers, "I can't keep the country out of war. They talk of me as though I were a god. Any little German lieutenant can put us into war at any time by some calculated outrage."

People who supported Wilson as a peace candidate applauded in January 1917 when he went before the Senate to clarify the American position on a negotiated settlement of the war. The German government had earlier indicated that it might be willing to go to the conference table. Wilson outlined a plan for a negotiated settlement before either side had achieved victory. It would be a peace among equals, "a peace without victory," a peace without indemnities and annexations. The peace agreement Wilson outlined contained his idealistic vision of the postwar world as an open marketplace, and it could have worked only if Germany and the Allies were willing to settle for a draw.

The German government refused to accept a peace without victory, probably because early in 1917 the German leaders thought they could win. On January 31, 1917, the Germans announced that they would sink on sight any ship, belligerent or neutral, sailing toward England or France. A few days later, in retaliation, the United States broke diplomatic relations with Germany. But Wilson—and probably most Americans—still hoped to avert war without shutting off American trade. As goods began to pile up in warehouses and American ships stayed idly in port, however, pressure mounted to arm American merchant ships. An intercepted telegram from the German foreign secretary, Arthur Zimmermann, to the German minister in Mexico increased anti-German feeling. If war broke out, the German minister was to offer Mexico the territory it had lost in Texas, New Mexico, and Arizona in 1848. In return, Mexico would join Germany in a war against the United States. When this telegram was released to the press on March 1, 1917, many Americans demanded war against Germany. Wilson still hesitated.

As the country waited on the brink of war, news of revolution in Russia reached Washington. That event would prove as important as the war itself. The March 1917 revolution in Russia was a spontaneous uprising of the workers, housewives, and soldiers against the government of Czar Nicholas II and its inept conduct of the war. The army had suffered staggering losses at the front. The civilian population was in desperate condition. Food was scarce, and the railroads and industry had nearly collapsed. At first, Wilson and other Americans were enthusiastic about the new republic led by Alexander Kerensky. The overthrow of the feudal aristocracy seemed in the spirit of the American Revolution. Kerensky promised to continue the struggle against Germany. But within months, the revolution took a more extreme turn. Vladimir Ilyich Ulyanov, known as Lenin, returned from exile in Switzerland and led the radical Bolsheviks to victory over the Kerensky regime in November 1917.

Lenin, a brilliant lawyer and revolutionary tactician, was a follower of Karl Marx (1818–1883). Marx, a German intellectual and radical philosopher, had described the alienation of the working class under capitalism and predicted a growing split between the proletariat (the unpropertied workers) and the capitalists. Lenin extended Marx's ideas and argued that capitalist nations would eventually be forced to go to war over raw materials and markets. Believing that capitalism and imperialism went hand in hand, Lenin, unlike Wilson, argued that the only way to end imperialism was to end capitalism. The new Soviet Union, not the United States, was the model for the rest of the world to follow; communism, Lenin predicted, would eventually dominate the globe. The Russian Revolution posed a threat to Wilson's vision of the world and to his plan to bring the United States into the war "to make the world safe for democracy."

More disturbing than the first news of revolution in Russia, however, was the situation in the North Atlantic, where German U-boats sank five American ships between March 12 and March 21, 1917. Wilson no longer hesitated. On April 2, he urged Congress to declare war. His words conveyed a sense of mission about the United States' entry into the war, but Wilson's voice was low and somber. "It is a fearful thing," he concluded, "to lead this great, peaceful people into war, into the most terrible and disastrous of all wars." The war resolution swept the Senate 82 to 6 and the House of Representatives 373 to 50.

Once war was declared, most Americans forgot their doubts. Young men rushed to enlist; women volunteered to become nurses or to serve in other ways. Towns were united by patriotism.

A Patriotic Crusade

Not all Americans applauded the declaration of war. Some pacifists and socialists opposed the war, and a black newspaper, *The Messenger,* decried the conflict. "The real enemy is War rather than Imperial Germany," wrote Randolph Bourne, a young New York intellectual. "We are for peace," Morris Hillquit, a socialist leader, announced. "We are unalterably opposed to the killing of our manhood and the draining of our resources in . . . a pursuit which begins by suppressing the freedom of speech and press and public assemblage, and by stifling legitimate political criticism." "To whom does war bring prosperity?" Senator George Norris of Nebraska asked on the Senate floor.

> Not to the soldier, . . . not to the broken hearted widow, . . . not to the mother who weeps at the death of her brave boy. . . . War brings no prosperity to the great mass of common patriotic citizens. We are going into war upon the command of gold. . . . I feel that we are about to put the dollar sign on the American flag.

For most Americans in the spring of 1917, the war seemed remote. A few days after the war was declared, a Senate committee listened to a member of the War Department staff list the vast quantities of materials needed to supply an American army in France. One of the senators, jolted awake, exclaimed, "Good Lord! You're not going to send soldiers over there, are you?"

Recruiting posters helped to create a sense of purpose and patriotism, and often used pictures of attractive women to make their point. To be a soldier was to be a real man; to avoid service was to be something less than a man.

To convince senators and citizens alike that the war was real and that American participation was just, Wilson appointed a Committee on Public Information, headed by George Creel, a muckraking journalist from Denver. The Creel Committee launched a gigantic propaganda campaign to persuade the American public that the United States had gone to war to promote the cause of freedom and democracy and to prevent the barbarous hordes from overrunning Europe and eventually the Western Hemisphere.

The patriotic crusade soon became stridently anti-German and anti-immigrant. Most school districts banned the teaching of German, a "language that disseminates the ideals of autocracy, brutality and hatred." Anything German became suspect. Sauerkraut was renamed "liberty cabbage," and German measles became "liberty measles." Many families Americanized their German surnames. Several cities banned music by German composers from symphony concerts. South Dakota prohibited the use of German on the telephone, and in Iowa a state official announced, "If their language is disloyal, they should be imprisoned. If their acts are disloyal, they should be shot." Occasionally, the patriotic fever led to violence. The most notorious incident happened in East St. Louis, which had a large German population. A mob seized Robert Prager, a young German-American, in April 1918, stripped off his clothes, dressed him in an American flag, marched him through the streets, and lynched him. The eventual trial led to the acquittal of the ringleaders on the grounds that the lynching was a "patriotic murder."

The Wilson administration, of course, did not condone domestic violence and murder, but heated patriotism led to irrational hatreds and fears of subversion. Suspect were not only German-Americans but also radicals, pacifists, and anyone who raised doubts about the American war efforts or the government's policies. In New York, the black editors of *The Messenger* were given 2½-year jail sentences for the paper's article "Pro-Germanism Among Negroes." The Los Angeles police ignored complaints that Mexicans were being harassed because after learning of the Zimmermann telegram, they believed that all Mexicans were pro-German. In Wisconsin, Senator Robert La Follette, who had voted against the war resolution, was burned in effigy and censured by the faculty of the University of Wisconsin. At a number of universities, professors were dismissed, sometimes for as little as questioning the morality or the necessity of America's participation in the war.

On June 15, 1917, Congress, at Wilson's behest, passed the Espionage Act, which provided imprisonment of up to 20 years or a fine of up to $10,000, or both, for people who aided the enemy or who "willfully cause . . . insubordination, disloyalty, mutiny or refusal of duty in the military . . . forces of the United States. . . ." The act also authorized the postmaster general to prohibit from the mails any matter he thought advocated treason or forcible resistance to United States laws. The act was used to stamp out dissent, even to discipline anyone who questioned the administration's policies. Using the act, Postmaster General Albert S. Burleson banned the magazines *American Socialist* and *The Masses* from the mails.

Congress later added the Trading with the Enemy Act and a Sedition Act. The latter prohibited disloyal, profane, scurrilous, or abusive remarks about the form of government, flag, or uniform of the United States. It even prohibited citizens from opposing the purchase of war bonds. In the most famous case tried under the act, Eugene Debs was sentenced to ten years in prison for opposing the war. In 1919, the Supreme Court upheld the conviction, even though Debs had not explicitly urged the violation of the draft laws. Not all Americans agreed with the decision, for while still in prison, Debs polled close to one million votes in the presidential election of 1920. Ultimately, the government prosecuted 2,168 people under the Espionage and Sedition acts and convicted about half of them. But these figures do not include the thousands informally persecuted and deprived of their liberties and their right of free speech.

A group of amateur loyalty enforcers, called the American Protective League, cooperated with the Justice Department. League members often reported nonconformists and anyone who did not appear 100 percent loyal. People were arrested for criticizing the Red Cross or a government agency. One woman was sentenced to prison for writing, "I am for the people and the government is for the profiteers." Ricardo Flores Magon, a leading Mexican-American labor organizer and radical in the Southwest, was sentenced to 20 years in prison for criticizing Wilson's Mexican policy and violating the Neutrality Acts. In Cincinnati, a pacifist minister, Herbert S. Bigelow, was dragged from the stage where he was about to give a speech, taken to a wooded area by a mob, bound and gagged, and whipped. The attorney general of the United States, speaking of opponents of government policies, said, "May God have mercy on them for they need expect none from an outraged people and an avenging government."

The Civil Liberties Bureau, an outgrowth of the American Union Against Militarism, protested the blatant abridgment of freedom of speech during the war, but the protests fell on deaf ears at the Justice Department and in the White House. Rights and freedoms have been reduced or suspended during all wars, but the massive disregard for basic rights was greater during World War I than during the Civil War. This was ironic because Wilson had often written and spoken of the need to preserve freedom of speech and civil liberties. During the war, however, he tolerated the vigilante tactics of his own Justice Department, offering no more than feeble protest. Wilson was so convinced his cause was just that he ignored the rights of those who opposed him.

Raising an Army

How should a democracy recruit an army in time of war? The debate over a volunteer army versus the draft had been going on for several years before the United States entered the war. People who favored some form of universal military service argued that college graduates, farmers, and young men from the slums of eastern cities could learn from one another as they trained together. The opponents of a draft pointed out that people making such claims were most often the college graduates, who assumed they would command the boys from the slums. The draft was not democratic, they argued, but the tool of an imperialist power bent on ending dissent. "Back of the cry that America must have compulsory service or perish," one opponent charged, "is a clearly thought out and heavily backed project to mold the United States into an efficient, orderly nation,

Government Propaganda

All governments produce propaganda. Especially in time of war, governments try to convince their citizens that the cause is important and worthwhile even if it means sacrifice. Before the United States entered the war, both Great Britain and Germany presented their side of the conflict through stories planted in newspapers, photographs, and other devices. Some historians argue that the British propaganda depicting the Germans as barbaric Huns who killed little boys and Catholic nuns played a large role in convincing Americans of the righteousness of the Allied cause.

When the United States entered the war, a special committee under the direction of George Creel did its best to persuade Americans that the war was a crusade against evil. The committee organized a national network of "four-minute men," local citizens with the proper political views, who could be used to whip up a crowd into a patriotic frenzy. These local rallies, enlivened by bands and parades, urged people of all ages to support the war effort and buy war bonds. The Creel Committee also produced literature for the schools, much of it prepared by college professors who volunteered their services. One pamphlet, titled *Why America Fights Germany,* described in lurid detail a possible German invasion of the United States. The committee also used the new technology of motion pictures, which proved to be the most effective propaganda device of all.

There is a narrow line between education and

Liberty Bond propaganda.

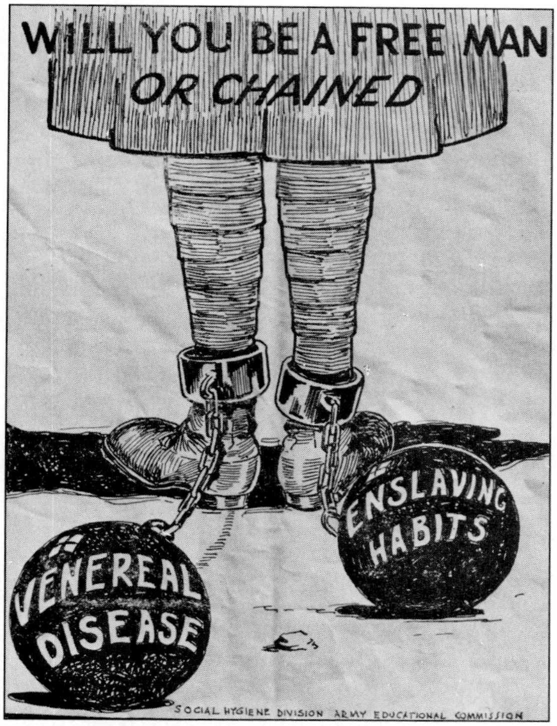

Anti-VD poster issued by the U.S. Commission on Training Camp Activities.

Scene from *Fit to Fight*.

propaganda. As early as 1910, Thomas Edison made films instructing the public about the dangers of tuberculosis, and others produced movies that demonstrated how to avoid everything from typhoid to tooth decay. However, during the war, the government quickly realized the power of the new medium and adopted it to train soldiers, instill patriotism, and help the troops avoid the temptations of alcohol and sex.

After the United States entered World War I, the Commission of Training Camp Activities made a film called *Fit to Fight* that was shown to almost all male servicemen. It was an hour-long drama following the careers of five young recruits. Four of them, by associating with the wrong people and through lack of willpower, caught venereal disease. The film interspersed a simplistic plot with grotesque shots of men with various kinds of venereal disease. The film also glorified athletics, especially football and boxing, as a substitute for sex. It emphasized the importance of patriotism and purity for America's fighting force. In one scene, Bill Hale, the only soldier in the film to remain pure, breaks up a peace rally and beats up the speaker. "It serves you right," the pacifist's sister remarks, "I'm glad Billy punched you."

Fit to Fight was so successful that the government commissioned another film, *The End of the Road,* to be shown to women who lived near military bases. The film is the story of Vera and Mary. Although still reflecting progressive attitudes, the film's message is somewhat different from *Fit to Fight.* Vera's strict mother tells her daughter that sex is dirty, leaving Vera to pick up "distorted and obscene" information about sex on the street. She falls victim to the first man who comes along and contracts a venereal disease. Mary, in contrast, has an enlightened mother who explains where babies come from. When Mary grows up, she rejects marriage and becomes a professional woman, a nurse. In the end, she falls in love with a doctor and gets married. *The End of the Road* has a number of subplots and many frightening shots of syphilitic sores. Several illustrations show the dangers of indiscriminate sex. Among other things, the film preached the importance of science, sex education, and the need for self-control.

What do the anti-VD films tell us about the attitudes, ideas, and prejudices of the World War I period? What images do they project about men, women, and sex roles? Would you find the same kind of moralism, patriotism, and fear of VD today? How have attitudes toward sex changed? Were you shown sex education films in school? Were they like these? Who sponsored them? What can historians learn from such films? Does the government produce propaganda today?

economically and politically controlled by those who know what is good for the people." Memories of massive draft riots during the Civil War also led some to fear a draft.

Wilson and his secretary of war, Newton Baker, both initially opposed the draft. In the end, both concluded that it was the most efficient way to organize military manpower. Ironically, it was Theodore Roosevelt who tipped Wilson in favor of the draft. Even though his health was failing and he was blind in one eye, the old Rough Rider was determined to recruit a volunteer division and lead it personally against the Germans. The officers would be Ivy League graduates and men trained at the Plattsburgh camp, with some places reserved for the descendants of prominent Civil War generals and a few French officers, in memory of Lafayette. There would be a German-American regiment and a black regiment (led by white officers). Roosevelt pictured himself leading this mixed but brave and virile group to France to restore the morale of the Allied troops and win the war.

The thought of his old enemy Theodore Roosevelt blustering about Europe so frightened Wilson that he supported the Selective Service Act in part, at least, to prevent such volunteer outfits as Roosevelt planned. Yet controversy filled Congress over the bill, and the House finally insisted that the minimum age for draftees should be 21, not 18. On June 5, 1917, some 9.5 million men between the ages of 21 and 31 registered, with little protest. In August 1918, Congress extended the act to men 18 to 45. In all, over 24 million men registered and over 2.8 million were inducted, making up over 75 percent of soldiers who served in the war.

The draft worked well, but it was not quite the perfect system that Wilson claimed. Most Americans took seriously their obligation of "service" during time of war. But because local draft boards had so much control, favoritism and political influence allowed some to stay at home. Draft protests erupted in a few places, the largest in Oklahoma, where a group of tenant farmers planned a march on Washington to take over the government and end the "rich man's war." The Green Corn Rebellion, as it came to be called, died before it got started. A local posse arrested about 900 rebels and took them off to jail.

Some men escaped the draft. Some were deferred because of war-related jobs, while others resisted by claiming exemption for reasons of conscience. The Selective Service Act did exempt men who belonged to religious groups that forbade members from engaging in war, but religious motivation was often difficult to define, and nonreligious conscientious objection was even more complicated. Thousands of conscientious objectors were inducted. Some served in noncombat positions; others went to prison. Roger Baldwin, a leading pacifist, was jailed for refusing military service. But Norman Thomas, a socialist, urged young men to register for the draft and to express their dissent within the democratic process.

The Military Experience

Family albums in millions of American homes contain photographs of young men in uniform, some of them stiff and formal, some of them candid shots of soldiers on leave in Paris or Washington or Chicago. These photographs testify to the importance of the war to a generation of Americans. For years afterward, the men and women who lived through the war sang "Tipperary," "There's a Long, Long Trail," and "Pack Up Your Troubles" and remembered rather sentimentally what the war had meant to them. For some, the war was a tragic event, as they saw the horrors of the battlefield firsthand. For others, it was a liberating experience and the most exciting period in their lives.

The American Doughboy

The typical soldier, according to the U.S. Medical Department, stood 5 feet 7½ inches tall, weighed 141½ pounds, and was about 22 years old. He took a physical exam, an intelligence test, and a psychological test, and he probably watched a movie called *Fit to Fight,* which warned him about the dangers of venereal disease. The majority of the American soldiers had not attended high school. The median amount of education for native whites was 6.9 years and for immigrants 4.7 years but was only 2.6 years for southern blacks. As many as 31 percent of the recruits were declared illiterate, but the tests were so primitive that they probably tested social class more than anything else. More than half the recent immigrants from eastern Europe ranked in the "inferior" category. Fully 29 percent of the recruits were rejected as physically unfit for service, which shocked the health experts.

Most World War I soldiers were ill-educated and unsophisticated young men, quite different from Ernest Hemingway's heroes or even from Edmund Arpin. They came from farms, small towns, and urban neighborhoods. They came from all social classes and ethnic groups, yet most were transformed into soldiers. In the beginning, however, they didn't look the part, because uniforms and equipment were in short supply. Many men had to wear their civilian clothes for months, and they often wore out their shoes before they were issued army boots. "It was about two months or so before I looked really like a soldier," one recruit remembered.

The military experience changed the lives and often the attitudes of many young men. Women also contributed to the war effort as telephone operators and clerk-typists in the navy and the marines. Some went overseas as army and navy nurses. Others volunteered for a tour of duty with the Red Cross, the Salvation Army, or the YMCA. Yet the military experience in World War I was predominantly male. Even going to training camp was a new and often frightening experience. A leave in Paris or London, or even in New York or New Orleans, was an adventure to remember for a lifetime. Even those who never got overseas or who never saw a battle experienced subtle changes. Many soldiers saw their first movie in the army or had their first contact with trucks and cars. Military service changed the shaving habits of a generation because the new safety razor was standard issue. The war also led to the growing popularity of the cigarette rather than the pipe or cigar because a pack of cigarettes fitted comfortably into a shirt pocket and a cigarette could be smoked during a short break. The war experience also caused many men to abandon the pocket watch for the more convenient wristwatch, which had been considered effeminate before the war.

The Black Soldier

Blacks had served in all American wars, and many fought valiantly in the Civil War and the Spanish-American War. Yet black soldiers had most often performed menial work and belonged to segregated units. Black leaders hoped it would be different this time. Shortly after the United States entered the war, W. E. B. Du Bois, the black leader and editor of *The Crisis,* urged blacks to close ranks and support the war. Although Du Bois did not speak for all blacks, he and others predicted that the war experience would cause the "walls of prejudice" to crumble gradually be-

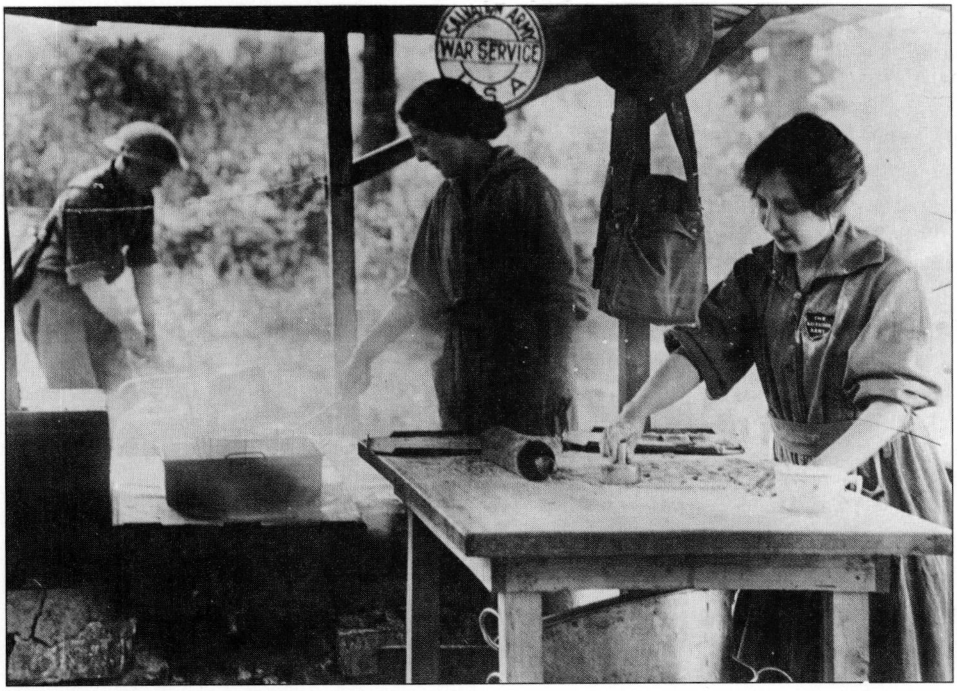

Many American women joined the great adventure by serving overseas as nurses with the Red Cross or as volunteers with the Salvation Army, but they could not join the army or navy as they did in World War II. These Salvation Army workers make doughnuts to serve with coffee to the troops.

Assigned to segregated units, black soldiers were also excluded from white recreation facilities. Here black women from Newark, New Jersey, aided by white social workers, entertain black servicemen.

fore the "onslaught of common sense." But the walls did not crumble, and the black soldier never received equal or fair treatment during the war.

The Selective Service Act made no mention of race, and African-Americans in most cases registered without protest. Many whites, especially in the South, feared having too many blacks trained in the use of arms. But this fear diminished as the war progressed. In some areas, draft boards exempted single white men but drafted black fathers. The most notorious situation existed in Atlanta, where one draft board inducted 97 percent of the African-Americans registered but exempted 85 percent of the whites. Still, most southern whites found it difficult to imagine a black man in the uniform of the U.S. Army.

White attitudes toward African-Americans sometimes led to conflict. In August 1917, violence erupted in Houston, Texas, involving soldiers from the regular army's all-black 24th Infantry Division. Harassed by the Jim Crow laws, which had been tightened for their benefit, a group of soldiers went on a rampage, killing 17 white civilians. Over 100 soldiers were court-martialed; 13 were condemned to death. Those convicted were hanged three days later before any appeals could be filed.

This violence, coming only a month after a race riot in East St. Louis, Illinois, brought on in part by the migration of southern blacks to the area, caused great concern about the handling of African-American soldiers. Secretary of War Baker made it clear that the army had no intention of upsetting the status quo. The basic government policy was of complete segregation and careful distribution of black units throughout the country.

Some African-Americans were trained as junior officers and were assigned to the all-black 92nd Division, where the high-ranking officers were white. But a staff report decided that "the mass of colored drafted men cannot be used for combatant troops." Most of the black soldiers, including about 80 percent of those sent to France, worked as stevedores and common laborers under the supervision of white noncommissioned officers. "Everyone who has handled colored labor knows that the gang bosses must be white if any work is to be done," remarked Lieutenant Colonel U. S. Grant, the grandson of the Civil War general. Other black soldiers acted as servants, drivers, and porters for the white officers. It was a demeaning and ironic policy for a government that advertised itself as standing for justice, honor, and democracy.

Over There

The conflict that Wilson called the war "to make the world safe for democracy" had become a contest of stalemate and slaughter. Hundreds of thousands had died on both sides, but victory remained elusive. To this ghastly war Americans made important contributions. In fact, without their help, the Allies might have lost. But the American contribution was most significant only in the war's final months. When the United States entered the conflict in the spring of 1917, the fighting had dragged on for nearly three years. After a few rapid advances and retreats, the war in western Europe had settled down to a tactical and bloody stalemate. The human costs of trench warfare were horrifying. In one battle in 1916, a total of 60,000 British soldiers were killed or wounded in a single day, yet the battle lines did not move an inch. By the spring of 1917, the British and French armies were down to their last reserves. Italy's army had nearly collapsed. In the east, the Russians were engaged in a bitter internal struggle, and in November, the Bolshevik Revolution would cause them to sue for a separate peace, freeing the German divisions on the eastern front to join in one final assault in the west. The Allies desperately needed fresh American troops, but those troops had to be trained, equipped, and transported to the front. That took time.

A few token American regiments arrived in France in the summer of 1917 under the command of General John J. "Black Jack" Pershing, a tall, serious Missouri-born graduate of West Point. He had fought in the Spanish-American War and led the Mexican expedition in 1916. When the first troops marched in a parade in Paris on July 4, 1917, the emotional French crowd shouted, "*Vive les Américains,*" and showered them with flowers, hugs, and kisses. But the American commanders worried about the fact that many of their soldiers were so inexperienced they did not even know how to march, let alone fight. The first

Western Front of the Great War, 1918

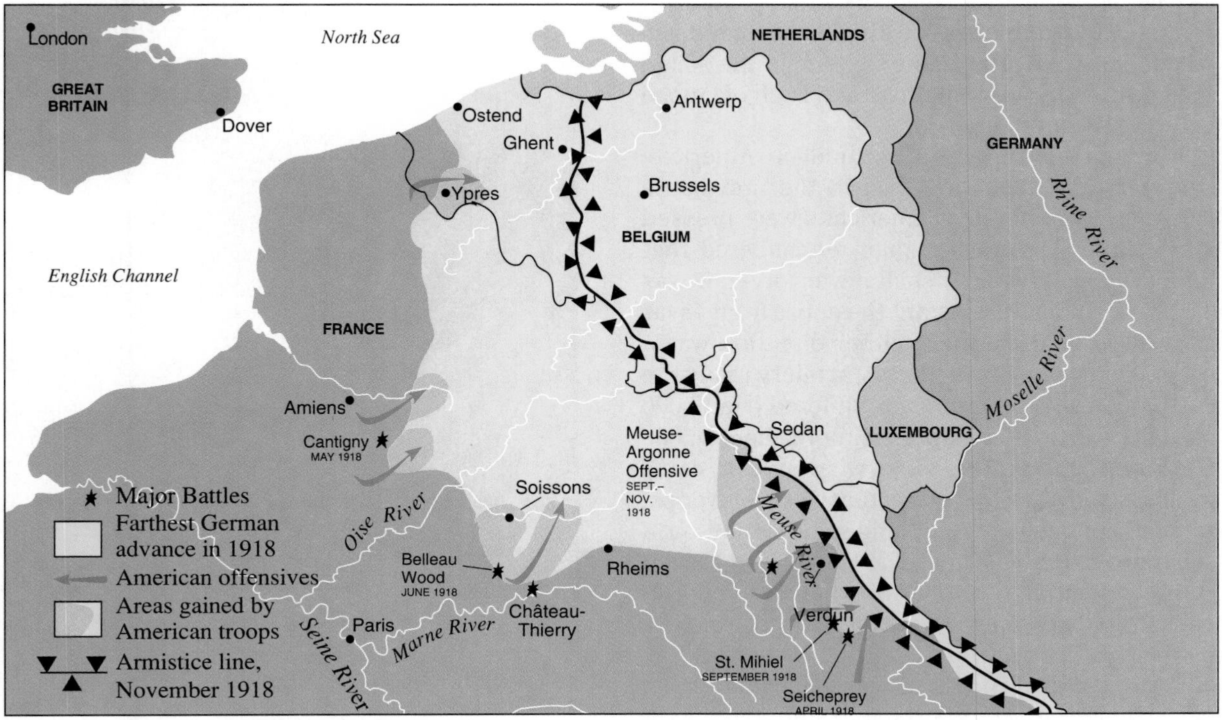

For more than three years, the war settled down to a bloody stalemate on the Western front. But in 1918 American soldiers played important roles in the Allied offensive that finally ended the war.

Americans saw action near Verdun in October 1917. By March 1918, over 300,000 American soldiers had reached France, and by November 1918, more than 2 million.

One reason that the United States forces were slow to see actual combat was Pershing's insistence that they be kept separate from the French and British divisions. An exception was made for four regiments of black soldiers who were assigned to the French army. Despite the American warning to the French not to "spoil the Negroes" by allowing them to mix with the French civilian population, these soldiers fought so well that the French later awarded three of the regiments the Croix de Guerre, their highest unit citation.

In the spring of 1918, with Russia out of the war and the British blockade becoming more and more effective, the Germans launched an all-out, desperate offensive to win the war before full American military and industrial power became a factor in the contest. By late May, the Germans had pushed to within 50 miles of Paris. American troops were thrown into the line and helped stem the German advance at Château-Thierry, Belleau Wood, and Cantigny, place names that proud survivors would later endow with almost sacred significance. Americans also took part in the Allied offensive led by General Ferdinand Foch of France in the summer of 1918.

In September, over a half million American troops fought near St. Mihiel in the first battle where large numbers of Americans were pressed into action. One enlisted man remembered that he "saw a sight which I shall never forget. It was zero hour and in one instant the entire front as far as the eye could reach in either direction was a sheet of flame, while the heavy artillery made the earth quake." The Americans suffered over 7,000 casualties, but they captured more than 16,000 German soldiers. The victory, even if it came against exhausted and retreating German troops, seemed to vindicate Pershing's insistence on a separate American army. The British and French commanders were critical of what they considered the disorganized, inexperienced, and ill-equipped American forces. They especially denounced the quality of the American high-ranking officers. One French report in the summer of 1918 suggested that it would take at least a year before the American army could become a "serious fighting force."

In the fall of 1918, the combined British, French, and American armies drove the Germans back. Faced with low morale among the German soldiers and finally the mutiny of the German fleet and the surrender of Austria, Kaiser Wilhelm II abdicated on November 8, and the Armistice was signed on November 11. More than a million American soldiers took part in the final Allied offensive near the Meuse River and the Argonne forest. It was in this battle that Edmund Arpin was wounded. Many of the men were inexperienced, and some, who had been rushed through training as "90-day wonders," had never handled a rifle before arriving in France. There were many disastrous mistakes and bungled situations. The most famous blunder was the "lost battalion." An American unit advanced beyond its support and was cut off and surrounded. The battalion suffered 70 percent casualties before being rescued.

World War I, especially on the Western front, was a war of position and defense. Troops on both sides, like these French soldiers, lived in elaborate trenches that turned into a sea of mud when it rained. The men tried to protect themselves with barbed wire and gas masks against new and terrifying technology. But there was little defense against the machine gun that mowed down the troops as they charged from their trenches.

The performance of the all-black 92nd Division was also controversial. The 92nd had been deliberately dispersed around the United States and had never trained as a unit. Its higher officers were white, and they repeatedly asked to be transferred. Many of its men were only partly trained and poorly equipped, and they were continually being called away from their military duties to work as stevedores and common laborers. At the last minute during the Meuse-Argonne offensive, the 92nd was assigned to a particularly difficult position on the line. They had no maps and no wire-cutting equipment. Battalion commanders lost contact with their men, and on several occasions the men broke and ran in the face of enemy fire. The division was withdrawn in disgrace, and for years politicians and military leaders used this incident to point out that black soldiers would never make good fighting men, ignoring the difficulties under which the 92nd fought and the valor shown by black troops assigned to the French army.

The war produced a few American heroes. Joseph Oklahombie, a Choctaw, overran several German machine gun nests and captured more than 100 German soldiers. Sergeant Alvin York, a former conscientious objector from Tennessee, single-handedly killed or captured 160 Germans using only his rifle and pistol. The press made him a celebrity, but his heroics were not typical. Artillery, machine guns, and, near the end, tanks, trucks, and airplanes won the war. "To be shelled when you are in the open is one of the most terrible of human experiences," one American soldier wrote. "You hear this rushing, tearing sound as the thing comes toward you, and then the huge explosion as it strikes, and infinitely worse, you see its hideous work as men stagger, fall, struggle, or lie quiet and unrecognizable."

With few exceptions, the Americans fought hard and well. While the French and British criticized American inexperience and disarray, they admired their exuberance, their "pep," and their ability to move large numbers of men and equipment efficiently. One British officer, surveying the abundance of American men and matériel, remarked, "For any particular work they seem to have about five times as much of both as we do." Sometimes it seemed that Americans simply overwhelmed the enemy with their numbers. They suffered over 120,000 casualties in the Meuse-Argonne campaign alone. One officer estimated that he lost ten soldiers for every German his men killed in the final offensive.

The United States entered the war late but still lost more than 48,000 service personnel and had many more wounded. Disease claimed 15 of every 1,000 soldiers each year (compared with 65 per 1,000 in the Civil War). But the British lost 900,000 men, the French 1.4 million, and the Russians 1.7 million. American units fired French artillery pieces; American soldiers were usually transported in British ships and wore helmets and other equipment modeled after the British. The United States purchased clothing and blankets, even horses, in Europe. American fliers, including heroes like Eddie Rickenbacker, flew French and British planes. The United States contributed huge amounts of men and supplies in the last months of the war, and that finally tipped the balance. But it had entered late and sacrificed little compared with France and England. That would influence the peace settlement.

Domestic Impact of the War

For at least 30 years before the United States entered the Great War, a debate raged over the proper role of the federal government in regulating industry and protecting people who could not protect themselves. Controversy also centered on the question of how much power the federal government should have to tax and control individuals and corporations and the proper relation of the federal government to state and local governments. Even within the Wilson administration, advisers disagreed on the proper role of the federal government. In fact, Wilson had only recently moved away from what he defined in 1912 as the New Freedom. But the war and the problems it raised increased the power of the federal government in a variety of ways. The wartime experience did not end the debate, but the United States emerged from the war a more modern nation, with more power residing in Washington.

Financing the War

The war, by one calculation, cost the United States over $33 billion. Interest and veterans' benefits bring the total to nearly $112 billion. Early on, when an economist suggested that the war might cost the United States $10 billion, everyone laughed. Yet many in the Wilson administration knew the war was going to be expensive, and they set out to raise the money by borrowing and by increasing taxes.

Secretary of the Treasury William McAdoo, who, like Wilson, had moved from the South to the North because of the lure of greater economic opportunities, shouldered the task of financing the war. Studying the policies that Treasury Secretary Salmon Chase had followed during the Civil War, he decided that Chase had made a mistake in not appealing to the emotions of the people. A war must be a "kind of crusade," he remarked. His campaign to sell liberty bonds to ordinary American citizens at a very low interest rate called forth patriotic sentiment. "Lick a Stamp and Lick the Kaiser," one poster urged. Celebrities such as film stars Mary Pickford and Douglas Fairbanks promoted the bonds, and McAdoo employed the Boy Scouts to sell them. "Every Scout to Save a Soldier" was the slogan. He even implied that people who did not buy bonds were traitors. "A man who can't lend his government $1.25 per week at the rate of 4% interest is not entitled to be an American citizen," he announced. A banner flew over the main street in Gary, Indiana, that made the point of the campaign clear: "ARE YOU WORTHY TO BE FOUGHT AND DIED FOR? BUY LIBERTY BONDS."

The public responded enthusiastically, but they discovered after the war that their bonds had dropped to about 80 percent of face value. Because the interest on the bonds was tax-exempt, well-to-do citizens profited more from buying the bonds than did ordinary men, women, and children. But the wealthy were not as pleased with McAdoo's other plan to finance the war by raising taxes. The War Revenue Act of 1917 boosted the tax rate sharply, levied a tax on excess profits, and increased estate taxes. Another bill the next year raised the tax on the largest incomes to 77 percent. The wealthy protested, but a number of progressives were just as unhappy with the bill, for they wanted to confiscate all income over $100,000 a year. Despite taxes and liberty bonds, however, World War I, like the Civil War, was financed in large part by inflation. Food prices, for example, nearly doubled between 1917 and 1919.

Increasing Federal Power

At first, Wilson tried to work through a variety of state agencies to mobilize the nation's resources. The need for more central control and authority soon led Wilson to create a series of federal agencies to deal with the war emergency. The first crisis was food. Poor grain crops for two years and an increasing demand for American food in Europe caused shortages. To solve the problem, Wilson appointed Herbert Hoover, a young engineer who had won great prestige as head of the Commission for Relief of Belgium, to direct the Food Administration. Hoover set out to meet the crisis not so much through government regulation as through an appeal to the patriotism of farmers and consumers alike. He instituted a series of "wheatless" and "meatless" days and urged housewives to cooperate. In Philadelphia, a large sign announced, "FOOD WILL WIN THE WAR; DON'T WASTE IT."

Women emerged during the war as the most important group of consumers. The government urged them to save, just as later it would urge them to buy. The *Ladies' Home Journal* announced, "To lose the war because we were unwilling to make the necessary efforts and the required sacrifices in regard to the food supply would be one of the most humiliating spectacles in history."

The Wilson administration used the authority of the federal government to organize resources for the war effort. The War Industries Board, led by Bernard Baruch, a shrewd Wall Street broker, used the power of the government to control scarce materials and, on occasion, to set prices and priorities. The government itself went into the shipbuilding business. The largest shipyard, at Hog Island, near Philadelphia, employed as many as 35,000 workers, but the yard did not launch its first ship until the late summer of 1918. For all the efforts of the Emergency Fleet Corporation, American ships could not be produced quickly enough to affect the outcome of the war.

The government also got into the business of running the railroads. When a severe winter and a lack of coordination brought the rail system near collapse in December 1917, Wilson put all the nation's railroads under the control of the United Railway Administration. The government spent more than $500 million to improve the rails and equipment, and in 1918 the railroads did run more efficiently than they had under private control. Some businessmen complained of "war socialism" and resented the way government agencies forced them to comply with rules and regulations. But most came to agree with Baruch that a close working relationship with government could improve the quality of their products, promote efficiency, and increase profits.

War Workers

The Wilson administration sought to protect and extend the rights of organized labor during the war, while at the same time mobilizing the workers necessary to keep the factories running. The National War Labor Board insisted on adequate wages and reduced hours, and it tried to prevent the exploitation of women and children working under government contracts. On one occasion, when a munitions plant refused to accept the War Labor Board's decision, the government simply took over the factory. When workers threatened to strike for better wages or hours or for greater control over the workplace, the board often ruled that they either work or be drafted into the army.

The Wilson administration favored the conservative labor movement of Samuel Gompers and the AFL, while the Justice Department put the radical Industrial Workers of the World "out of business." Beginning in September 1917, federal agents conducted massive raids on IWW offices and arrested most of the leaders. The government tolerated the ruthless activity of vigilante groups around the country. In Bisbee, Arizona, the local sheriff, with 2,000 deputies, rounded up 1,200 striking workers and transported them by boxcar to New Mexico. They spent two days in the desert heat without food or water before being rescued. In Butte, Montana, six masked men brutally murdered Frank Little, an IWW organizer. "Had he been arrested and put in jail for his seditious and incendiary talks," Senator H. L. Meyers of Montana suggested, "he would not have been lynched."

Samuel Gompers took advantage of the crisis to strengthen the AFL's position to speak for labor. He lent his approval to administration policies by making clear that he opposed the IWW as well as socialists and communists. Convincing Wilson that it was important to protect the rights of organized labor during wartime, he announced that "no other policy is compatible with the spirit and methods of democracy." As the AFL won a voice in homefront policy, its membership increased from 2.7 million in 1916 to over 4 million in 1917. Organized labor's wartime gains, however, would prove only temporary.

The war opened up industrial employment opportunities for black men. With 4 million men in the armed forces and the flow of immigrants interrupted by the war, American manufacturers for the first time hired African-Americans in large numbers. In Chicago before the war, only 3,000 black men held factory jobs. In 1920, more than 15,000 did.

Northern labor agents and the railroads actively recruited southern blacks, but the news of jobs in northern cities spread by word of mouth as well. By 1920, more than 300,000 blacks had joined the "great migration" north. This massive movement of people, which continued into the 1920s, had a permanent impact on the South as well as on the northern cities. As African-Americans moved north, thousands of Mexicans crossed into the United States, as immigration officials relaxed the regulations because of the need for labor in the farms and factories of the Southwest.

The war also created new employment opportunities for women. Posters and patriotic speeches urged women to do their duty for the war effort. "Not Just Hats Off to the Flag, but Sleeves Up for It," one poster announced. Another showed a woman at her typewriter, the shadow of a soldier in the background, with the message: "Stenographers, Washington Needs You."

Women responded to these appeals out of patriotism, as well as out of a need to increase their earnings and to make up for inflation, which diminished real wages. "I used to go to work when my man was sick," one woman reported, "but this is the first time I ever had to go to work to get enough money to feed the kids, when he was working regular." Women went into every kind of industry. They labored in brickyards and in

Women proved during the war that they could do "men's work." These shipyard workers even dressed like men, but the war did not change the American ideal that woman's place was in the home.

heavy industry, became conductors on the railroad, and turned out shells in munition plants. They even organized the Woman's Land Army to mobilize female labor for the farms. They demonstrated that women could do any kind of job, whatever the physical or intellectual demands. "It was not until our men were called overseas," one woman banking executive reported, "that we made any real onslaught on the realm of finance, and became tellers, managers of departments, and junior and senior officers." One black woman who gave up her position as a live-in servant to work in a paperbox factory declared:

> I'll never work in nobody's kitchen but my own any more. No indeed, that's the one thing that makes me stick to this job, but when you're working in anybody's kitchen, well you out of luck. You almost have to eat on the run; you never get any time off.

As black women moved out of domestic service, they took jobs in textile mills or even in the stockyards. Racial discrimination, however, even in the North, prevented them from moving too far up the occupational ladder.

Even though women demonstrated that they could take over jobs once thought suitable only for men, their progress during the war proved temporary. Only about 5 percent of the women employed during the war were new to the work force, and almost all of them were unmarried. For most it meant a shift of occupations or a move up to a better-paying position. Moreover, the war accelerated trends already under way. It increased the need for telephone operators, sales personnel, secretaries, and other white-collar workers, and in these occupations women soon became a majority. Telephone operator, for example, became an almost exclusively female job. There were 15,000 operators in 1900 but 80,000 in 1910, and by 1917 women represented 99 percent of all operators as the telephone network spanned the nation. In the end, the war did provide limited opportunities for some women, but it did not change the dominant perception that a woman's place was in the home. After the war was over, the men returned, and the gains made by women almost disappeared. There were 8 million women in the work force in 1910 and only 8.5 million in 1920.

The Climax of Progressivism

Many progressives, especially the social justice progressives, opposed the United States' entry into the war until a few months before the nation declared war. But after April 1917, many began to see the "social possibilities of war." They deplored the death and destruction, the abridgment of freedom of speech, and the patriotic spirit that accompanied the war. But they praised the social planning stimulated by the conflict. They approved the Wilson administration's support of collective bargaining, the eight-hour day, and protection for women and children in industry. They applauded Secretary of War Baker when he announced, "We cannot afford, when we are losing boys in France, to lose children in the United States at the same time." They welcomed the experiments with government-owned housing projects, woman suffrage, and prohibition. Many endorsed the government takeover of the railroads and control of business during the war.

For many social justice progressives who had fought hard, long, and frustrating battles trying to humanize the industrial city, the very fact that suddenly people in high places were listening and approving programs was stimulating. "Enthusiasm for social service is epidemic," one social worker wrote in the summer of 1917:

> [A] luxuriant crop of new agencies is springing up. We scurry back and forth to the national capital; we stock offices with typewriters and new letterheads; we telephone feverishly regardless of expense, and resort to all the devices of efficient "publicity work." . . . It is all very exhilarating, stimulating, intoxicating.

One of the best examples of the progressives' influence on wartime activities was the Commission on Training Camp Activities, set up early in the war to solve the problem of mobilizing, entertaining, and protecting American servicemen at home and abroad. Chairman of the commission was Raymond Fosdick, a former settlement worker. He appointed a number of experts from the Playground Association, the YMCA, and social work agencies. They set out to organize community singing and baseball, establish post exchanges and theaters, and even provide university extension lectures to educate the servicemen. The overriding assumption was that the military experience would help produce better citizens, people who would be ready to vote for social reform once they returned to civilian life.

The Commission on Training Camp Activities also incorporated the progressive crusades against alcohol and prostitution. The Military Draft Act prohibited the sale of liquor to men in uniform and gave the president power to establish zones around military bases where prostitution and alcohol would be prohibited. Some military commanders protested, and at least one city official argued that prostitutes were "God-provided means for the prevention of the violation of innocent girls, by men who are exercising their 'God-given passions.'" Yet the commission, with the full cooperation of the Wilson administration, set out to wipe out sin, or at least to put it out of the reach of servicemen. "Fit to fight" became the motto. "Men must live straight if they would shoot straight," one official announced. It was a typical progressive effort combining moral indignation with the use of the latest scientific prophylaxis. The commissioners prided themselves on having eliminated by 1918 all the red-light districts near the training camps and producing what one person called "the cleanest army since Cromwell's day." When the boys go to France, the secretary of war remarked, "I want them to have invisible armour to take with them. I want them to have armour made up of a set of social habits replacing those of their homes and communities."

France tested the "invisible armour." The government, despite hundreds of letters of protest from American mothers, decided that it could not prevent the soldiers from drinking wine in France, but it could forbid them to buy or accept as gifts anything but light wine and beer. If Arpin's outfit is typical, the soldiers often ignored the rules. Sex was even more difficult to regulate in France than liquor. Both the British and the French armies had tried to solve the problem of venereal disease by licensing and inspecting prostitutes. Clemenceau, the French premier, found the American attitude toward prostitution difficult to comprehend. On one occasion, he accused the Americans of spreading disease throughout the French civilian population and graciously offered to provide the Americans with licensed prostitutes. General Pershing considered the letter containing the offer "too hot to handle." So he gave it to Fosdick, who showed it to Baker, who remarked, "For God's sake, Raymond, don't show this to the President or he'll stop the war." The Americans never accepted Clemenceau's offer, and he continued to be baffled by the American progressive mentality.

Suffrage for Women

In the fall of 1918, while American soldiers were mobilizing for the final offensive in France and hundreds of thousands of women were working in factories and serving as Red Cross and Salvation Army volunteers near the army bases, Woodrow Wilson spoke before the Senate to ask its support of woman suffrage, which he maintained was "vital to the winning of the war." Wilson had earlier opposed the vote for women. His positive statement at this late date was not important, but his voice was a welcome addition to a rising chorus of support for an amendment to the Constitution that would permit the female half of the population to vote.

Not everyone favored woman suffrage. Many people still argued that the vote would make women less feminine, more worldly, and less able to perform their primary tasks as wives and mothers. The National Association Opposed to Woman Suffrage argued that it was only radicals who wanted the vote and declared that woman suffrage, socialism, and feminism were "three branches of the same Social Revolution."

Carrie Chapman Catt, an efficient administrator and tireless organizer, devised the strategy that finally secured the vote for women. Catt, who grew up in Iowa, joined the Iowa Woman Suffrage Association at age 28 shortly after her first husband died. Before remarrying, she insisted on a legal agreement giving her four months a year away from her husband to work for the suffrage cause. In 1915, she became president of the National American Woman Suffrage Association (NAWSA), the organization founded in 1890 and based in part on the society organized by Elizabeth Cady Stanton and Susan B. Anthony in 1869.

Catt coordinated the state campaigns with the office in Washington, directing a growing army of dedicated workers. The Washington headquarters sent precise information to the states on ways to pressure congressmen in local districts. In Washington, they maintained a file on each congressman and senator. "There were facts supplied by our members in the states about his personal, political, business and religious affiliations; there were reports of interviews;. . . there was everything that could be discovered about his stand on woman suffrage."

The careful planning began to produce results, but a group of more militant reformers, impatient with the slow progress, broke off from NAWSA to form the National Woman's Party (NWP) in 1916. This group was led by Alice Paul, a Quaker from New Jersey, who had participated in some of the suffrage battles in England. Paul and her group picketed the White House, chained themselves to the fence, and blocked the streets. They carried banners that asked, "MR. PRESIDENT, HOW LONG MUST WOMEN WAIT FOR LIBERTY?" In the summer of 1917, the government arrested more than 200 women and charged them with "obstructing the sidewalk." It was just the kind of publicity the militant group sought, and it made the most of it. Wilson, fearing even more embarrassment, began to cooperate with the more moderate reformers.

The careful organizing of the NAWSA and the more militant tactics of the NWP both contributed to the final success of the woman suffrage crusade. The war did not cause the passage of the Nineteenth Amendment, but it did accelerate the process. Fourteen state legislatures petitioned Congress in 1917 and twenty-six in 1919, urging the enactment of the amendment. Early in 1919, the House of Representatives passed the suffrage amendment 304 to 90, and the Senate approved by a vote of 56 to 25. Fourteen months later, the required 36 states had ratified the amendment, and women at last had the vote. "We are no longer petitioners," Catt announced in celebration. "We are not wards of the nation, but free and equal citizens." But the achievement of votes for women would not prove the triumph of feminism, nor the signal for the beginning of a new reform movement, that the women leaders believed at the time.

Planning for Peace

Woodrow Wilson turned U.S. participation in the war into a religious crusade to change the nature of international relations. It was a war to make the world safe for democracy—and more. On January 8, 1918, in part to counteract the Bolshevik charge that the war was merely a struggle among imperialist powers, he announced his plan to organize the peace. Called the Fourteen Points, it argued for "open covenants of peace openly arrived at," freedom of the seas, equality of trade, the self-determination of all peoples. But his most important point, the fourteenth, called for an international organization, a "league of nations," to preserve peace.

The Paris Peace Conference

Late in 1918, Wilson announced that he would head the American delegation in Paris, revealing his belief that he alone could overcome the forces of greed and imperialism in Europe and bring peace to the world. Wilson and his entourage of college professors, technical experts, and advisers set sail for Paris on the *George Washington* on December 4, 1918. Secretary of State Lansing, Edward House, and a number of other advisers were there; conspicuously missing, however, was Henry Cabot Lodge or any other Republican senator.

The Big Four in December 1919: Italy's Orlando, Britain's Lloyd George, France's Clemenceau, and the United States' Wilson.

This would prove a serious blunder, for the Republican-controlled Senate would have to approve any treaty negotiated in Paris. It is difficult to explain Wilson's lack of political insight, except that he disliked Lodge intensely and hated political bargaining and compromise. Preferring to announce great principles, he had supreme confidence in his ability to persuade and to get his way by appealing to the people.

Wilson's self-confidence grew during a triumphant tour through Europe before the conference. The ordinary people greeted him like a savior who had brought the tragic war to an end. The American president had greater difficulty convincing the political leaders at the peace conference of his genius or his special grace. In Paris, he faced the reality of European power politics and ambitions and the personalities of David Lloyd George of Great Britain, Vittorio Orlando of Italy, and Georges Clemenceau of France.

Though Wilson was more naive and more idealistic than his European counterparts, he was a clever negotiator who won many concessions at the peace table, sometimes by threatening to go home if his counterparts would not compromise. The European leaders were determined to punish Germany and enlarge their empires. Wilson, however, believed that he could create a new kind of international relations based on his Fourteen Points. He achieved limited acceptance of the idea of self-determination, his dream that each national group could have its own country and that the people should decide in what country they wanted to live.

The peacemakers carved the new countries of Austria, Hungary, and Yugoslavia out of what had been the Austro-Hungarian Empire. In addition, they created Poland, Czechoslovakia, Finland, Estonia, Latvia, and Lithuania, in part to help contain the threat of bolshevism in eastern Europe. France was to occupy the industrial Saar region of Germany for 15 years with a plebiscite at the end of that time to determine whether the people wanted to become a part of Germany or France. Italy gained the port city of Trieste but not the neighboring city of Fiume with its largely Italian-speaking population. Dividing up the map of Europe was difficult at best, but perhaps the biggest mistake that Wilson and other major leaders made was to give the small nations little power at the negotiating table and to exclude Soviet Russia entirely.

Wilson won some points at the peace negotiations, but he also had to make major concessions. He was forced to agree that Germany should pay reparations (later set at $56 billion), lose much of its oil- and coal-rich territory, and admit to its war guilt. He accepted a mandate system, to be supervised by the League of Nations, that allowed France and Britain to take over portions of the Middle East and allowed Japan to occupy Germany's colonies in the Pacific. He acquiesced when the Allies turned Germany's African colonies into "mandate possessions" because they did not want to allow the self-determination of blacks in areas they had colonized. This was not a "peace without victory," and the sense of betrayal the German people felt would later have grave repercussions. Wilson also did not win approval for freedom of the seas or the abolition of trade barriers, but he did gain endorsement for the League of Nations, the organization he hoped would prevent all future wars. The League consisted of a council of the five great powers, elected delegates from the smaller countries, and a World Court to settle disputes. But the key to collective security was contained in Article 10 of the League covenant, which pledged all members "to respect and preserve against external aggression the territorial integrity" of all other members.

Women for Peace

While the statesmen met at Versailles to sign the peace treaty hammered out in Paris and to divide up Europe, a group of prominent and successful women—lawyers, physicians, administrators, and writers from all over the world, including many from the Central Powers—met in Zurich, Switzerland. The American delegation was led by Jane Addams and included Florence Kelley of the National Consumers League; Alice Hamilton, a professor at Harvard Medical School; and Jeannette Rankin. As congresswoman from Montana (one of the few states where women could vote), Rankin had voted against the war resolution in 1917. Some of the women who gathered at Zurich had met in 1915 at The Hague, in the Netherlands, to propose an end to the war through mediation. Now they met amid the devastation of war to promote a peace that would last. At their conference they formed the Women's International League for Peace and Freedom. Electing Addams president of the new organization, they denounced the harsh peace terms, which called for disarmament of only one side and exacted great economic penalties against the Central Powers. Prophetically, they predicted that the peace treaty would result in the spread of hatred and anarchy and "create all over Europe discords and animosities which can only lead to future wars."

Hate and intolerance were legacies of the war. They were present at the Versailles peace conference, where Clemenceau especially wanted to humiliate Germany for the destruction of French lives and property. Also hanging over the conference was the Bolshevik success in Russia. Lenin's vision of a communist world order, led by workers, conflicted sharply with Wilson's dream of an anti-imperialist, free trade, capitalist world. The threat of revolution seemed so great that Wilson and the Allies sent American and Japanese troops into Russia in 1919 to attempt to defeat the Bolsheviks and create a moderate republic. But by 1920, the troops had failed in their mission. They withdrew, but Russians never forgot the event, and the threat of bolshevism remained.

Wilson's Failed Dream

Probably most Americans supported the concept of the League of Nations in the summer of 1919. A few, like former senator Albert Beveridge of Indiana, an ardent nationalist, denounced the League as the work of "amiable old male grannies who, over their afternoon tea, are planning to denationalize America and denationalize the nation's manhood." But 33 governors endorsed the plan. Yet in the end, the Senate refused to accept American membership in the League. The League of Nations treaty, one commentator has suggested, was killed by its friends and not by its enemies.

First there was Lodge, who had earlier endorsed the idea of some kind of international peacekeeping organization but who objected to Article 10, claiming that it would force Americans to fight the wars of foreigners. Chairman of the Senate Foreign Relations Committee, Lodge, like Wilson, was a lawyer and a scholar as well as a politician. But in background and personality, he was very different from Wilson. A Republican senator since 1893, he had great faith in the power and prestige of the Senate. He disliked all Democrats, especially Wilson, whose idealism and missionary zeal infuriated him.

Then there was Wilson, whose only hope of passage of the treaty in the Senate was a compromise to bring moderate senators to his side. But Wilson refused to compromise or to modify Article 10 to allow Congress the opportunity to decide whether or not the United States would support the League in time of crisis. Angry at his opponents, who were exploiting the disagreement for political advantage, he stumped the country to convince the American people of the rightness of his plan. The people did not need to be convinced. They greeted Wilson much the way the people of France had. Traveling by train, he gave 37 speeches in 29 cities in the space of three weeks. When he described the graves of American soldiers in France and announced that American boys would never again die in a foreign war, the people responded with applause.

After one dramatic speech in Pueblo, Colorado, Wilson collapsed. His health had been failing for some months, and the strain of the trip was too much. He was rushed back to Washington, where a few days later he suffered a massive stroke. For the next year and a half, the president was incapable of running the government. Protected by his second wife and his closest advisers, Wilson became irritable and depressed and unable to lead a fight for the League. For a year and a half the country limped along without a president.

After many votes and much maneuvering, the Senate finally killed the League treaty in March 1920. Had the United States joined the League of Nations, it probably would have made little difference in the international events of the 1920s and 1930s. Nor would American participation have prevented World War II. The United States did not resign from the world of diplomacy or trade, nor did the United States with that single act become isolated from the rest of the world. But the rejection of the League treaty was symbolic of the refusal of many Americans to admit that the world and America's place in it had changed dramatically since 1914.

The Divided Legacy of the Great War

For Edmund Arpin and many of his friends, who left small towns and urban neighborhoods to join the military forces, the war was a great adventure. For the next decades, at American Legion conventions and Armistice Day parades, they continued to celebrate their days of glory. For others who served, the war's results were more tragic. Many died. Some came home injured, disabled by poison gas, or unable to cope with the complex world that had opened up to them.

In a larger sense, the war was both a triumph and a tragedy for the American people. The war created opportunities for blacks who migrated to the North, for women who found more rewarding jobs, and for farmers who suddenly discovered a demand for their products. But much of the promise and the hope proved temporary.

The war provided a certain climax to the progressive movement. The passage of the woman suffrage amendment and the use of federal power in a variety of ways to promote justice and order pleased reformers, who had been working toward these ends for many decades. But the results were often disappointing. Once the war ended, much federal legislation was dismantled or reduced in effectiveness and votes for women had little initial impact on social legislation.

The Great War marked the coming of age of the United States as a world power, but the country seemed reluctant to accept the new responsibility. The war stimulated patriotism and pride in the country, but it also increased intolerance. With this mixed legacy from the war, the country entered the new era of the 1920s.

Recommended Reading

General Accounts

James Toll, *The Origins of the First World War* (1984); Frank Freidel, *Over There: The Story of America's First Great Overseas Crusade* (1964); Daniel M. Smith, *The Great Departure: The United States and World War I, 1914–1919* (1965); Ellis W. Hawley, *The Great War and the Search for Modern Order* (1979); Barbara W. Tuchman, *The Guns of August* (1962).

Diplomacy and Peace

D. F. Cline, *The United States and Mexico* (1953); P. Edward Haley, *Revolution and Intervention* (1970); C. C. Clemenden, *The United States and Pancho Villa* (1961); Robert H. Ferrell, *Woodrow Wilson and World War I* (1985); Ernest R. May, *The World War and American Isolation* (1966); N. Gordon Levin, Jr., *Woodrow Wilson and World Politics* (1968); Christopher Lasch, *The American Liberals and the Russian Revolution* (1962); C. Roland Marchand, *The American Peace Movement and Social Reform* (1973); Charles DeBenedetti, *Origins of the Modern Peace Movement* (1978).

The Battlefield Experience and Beyond

Edward M. Coffman, *The War to End All Wars: The American Military Experience in World War I* (1968); Lawrence Stallings, *The Doughboys: The Story of the AEF, 1917–1918* (1963); Arthur D. Barbeau and Florette Henri, *The Unknown Soldiers: Black American Troops in World War I* (1974); John Ellis, *The Social History of the Machine Gun* (1975); Paul Fussell, *The Great War and Modern Memory* (1975); Michael C. C. Adams, *The Great Adventure: Male Desire and the Coming of World War I* (1990).

The War at Home

David M. Kennedy, *Over Here: The First World War and American Society* (1980); Maurine W. Greenwald, *Women, War, and Work* (1980); Carol S. Gruber, *Mars and Minerva: World War I and the Uses of Higher Learning in America* (1975); Donald Johnson, *The Challenge to American Freedoms: World War I and the Rise of the American Civil Liberties Union* (1963); Frederick C. Luebke, *Bonds of Loyalty: German-Americans and World War I* (1974); Florette Henri, *Black Migration: Movement Northward, 1900–1920* (1975); Michael I. Isenberg, *War on Film* (1981); Stanley Cooperman, *World War I and the American Novel* (1970); Ronald Schaffer, *America in the Great War: The Rise of the War Welfare State* (1991).

Fiction

Erich Maria Remarque highlights the horror of the war in his classic *All Quiet on the Western Front* (1929); John Dos Passos describes the war as a bitter experience in *Three Soldiers* (1921), and Ernest Hemingway portrays its futility in *A Farewell to Arms* (1929).

TIMELINE

1914 Archduke Ferdinand assassinated; World War I begins
United States declares neutrality
American troops invade Mexico and occupy Veracruz

1915 Germany announces submarine blockade of Great Britain
Lusitania sunk
Arabic pledge
Marines land in Haiti

1916 Army Reorganization Bill
Expedition into Mexico
Wilson reelected
Workmen's Compensation Bill
Keatings-Owen Child Labor Bill
Federal Farm Loan Act
National Women's Party founded

1917 Germany resumes unrestricted submarine warfare
United States breaks relations with Germany
Zimmermann telegram
Russian Revolution
United States declares war on Germany
War Revenue Act
Espionage Act
Committee on Public Information established
Trading with the Enemy Act
Selective Service Act
War Industries Board formed

1918 Sedition Act
Flu epidemic sweeps nation
Wilson's Fourteen Points
American troops intervene in Russian Revolution

1919 Paris peace conference
Eighteenth Amendment prohibits alcoholic beverages
Senate rejects Treaty of Versailles

1920 Nineteenth Amendment grants woman suffrage

CHAPTER 23

Affluence and Anxiety

John and Lizzie Parker were black sharecroppers who lived in a "stubborn, ageless hut squatted on a little hill" in central Alabama. They had two daughters, one age 6, the other already married. The whole family worked hard in the cotton fields, but they had little to show for their labor. One day in 1917, Lizzie straightened her shoulders and declared, "I'm through. I've picked my last sack of cotton. I've cleared my last field."

Like many southern African-Americans, the Parkers sought opportunity and a better life in the North. World War I cut off the flow of immigrants from Europe, and suddenly there was a shortage of workers. Some companies sent special trains into the South to recruit African-Americans. John Parker signed up with a mining company in West Virginia. The company offered free transportation for his family. "You will be allowed to get your food at the company store and there are houses awaiting for you," the agent promised.

The sound of the train whistle seemed to promise better days ahead for her family as Lizzie gathered her possessions and headed north. But it turned out that the houses in the company town in West Virginia were little better than those they left in Alabama. After deducting for rent and for supplies from the company store, almost no money was left at the end of the week. John hated the dirty and dangerous work in the mine and realized that he would never get ahead by staying there. Instead of venting his anger on his white boss, he ran away, leaving his family in West Virginia.

John drifted to Detroit, where he got a job with the American Car and Foundry Company. It was 1918, and the pay was good, more than he had ever made before. After a few weeks, he rented an apartment and sent for his family. For the first time, Lizzie had a gas stove and an indoor toilet, and Sally, who was now 7, started school. It seemed as if their dream had come true. John had always believed that if he worked hard and treated his fellow man fairly, he would succeed.

Detroit was not quite the dream, however. It was crowded with all kinds of migrants, attracted by the wartime jobs at the Ford Motor Company and other factories. The new arrivals increased the racial tension already present in the city. Sally was beaten up by a gang of white youths at school. Even in their neighborhood, which had been solidly Jewish before their arrival, the shopkeeper and the old residents made it clear that they did not like blacks moving into their community. The Ku Klux Klan, which gained many new members in Detroit, also made life uncomfortable for the blacks who had moved north to seek jobs and opportunity. Suddenly the war ended, and almost immediately John lost his job. Then the landlord raised the rent, and the Parkers were forced to leave their apartment for housing in a section just outside the city near Eight Mile Road. While the surrounding suburbs had paved streets, wide lawns, and elegant houses, this black ghetto had dirt streets and shacks that reminded the Parkers of the company town where they had lived in West Virginia. Lizzie had to get along without her bathroom. Here there was no indoor plumbing and no electricity, only a pump in the yard and an outhouse.

The recession winter of 1921–1922 was particularly difficult. The auto industry and the other companies laid off most of their workers. John could find only part-time employment, while Lizzie worked as a domestic servant for white families. Because no bus route connected the black community to surrounding suburbs, she often had to trek miles through the snow. The shack they called home was freezing cold, and it was cramped because their married daughter and her husband had joined them in Detroit.

Lizzie did not give up her dream, however. With strength, determination, and a sense of humor, she kept the family together. In 1924, Sally entered high school. By the end of the decade, Sally had graduated from high school, and the Parkers finally had electricity and indoor plumbing in the house, though the streets were still unpaved. Those unpaved streets stood as a symbol of their unfulfilled dream. The Parkers, like most of the black Americans who moved north in the decade after World War I, had improved their lot, but they still lived outside Detroit—and, in many ways, outside America.

Like most Americans in the 1920s, the Parkers pursued the American dream of success. For them, a comfortable house and a steady job, a new bathroom, and an education for their younger daughter constituted that dream. For others during the decade, the symbol of success was a new automobile, a new suburban house, or perhaps making a killing on the stock market. The 1920s, the decade between the end of World War I and the stock market crash, has often been referred to as the "jazz age," a time when the American people had one long party complete with flappers, speakeasies, illegal bathtub gin, and young people doing the Charleston long into the night. This frivolous interpretation has some basis in fact, but most Americans did not share in the party, for they were too busy struggling to make a living.

Yet the 1920s was a time of prosperity, when many Americans sensed that a new era had dawned. Cooperation between business and government, stimulated during the war, continued, though in less dramatic fashion. The large corporation, with its sophisticated bureaucracy and new management techniques, dominated economic life. And the automobile, the radio, and the movies, as well as widespread advertising, all promoted the growth of a national mass culture and a sense of shared values. But many Americans could not afford the products advertised in the slick magazines or the expensive life styles depicted in the movies. Prohibition, immigration restriction, race relations, and the clash between old ways and new created conflict and misunderstanding.

In this chapter, we will explore some of the conflicting trends of an exciting decade. First, we will examine the currents of intolerance that influenced almost all the events and social movements of the time. We will also look at some developments in technology, especially the automobile, which changed life for almost everyone during the 1920s and created the illusion of prosperity for all. We will then focus on groups—women, blacks, industrial workers, and farmers—who had their hopes raised but not always fulfilled during the decade. We will conclude by looking at the way business, politics, and foreign policy were intertwined during the age of Harding, Coolidge, and Hoover.

Postwar Problems

The enthusiasm for social progress that marked the war years evaporated in 1919. Public housing, social insurance, government ownership of the railroads, and many other experiments quickly ended. The sense of progress and purpose that the war had fostered withered. The year following the end of the war was marked by strikes and violence and by fear that Bolsheviks, blacks, foreigners, and others were destroying the American way. Some of the fear and intolerance resulted from wartime patriotism, some from the postwar economic and political turmoil that forced Americans to deal with new and immensely troubling situations.

Red Scare

Americans have often feared radicals and other groups that seemed to be conspiring to overthrow the American way. In the 1840s, and 1890s and at other times in the past, Catholics, Mormons, Populists, immigrants, and holders of many political views have all been attacked as dangerous and "un-American." But before 1917, anarchists seemed to pose the worst threat. The Russian Revolution changed that. *Bolshevik* suddenly became the most dangerous and devious radical, while *communist* was transformed from a member of a utopian community to a dreaded, threatening subversive. For some Americans, *Bolshevik* and *German* became somehow mixed together, especially after the Treaty of Brest-Litovsk in 1918 removed the new Soviet state from the war. In the spring of 1919, with the Russian announcement of a policy of worldwide revolution and with Communist uprisings in Hungary and Bavaria, many Americans feared that the Communists planned to take over the United States. There were a few American Communists, but they never really threatened the United States or the American way of life.

However, some idealists, like John Reed, found developments in Russia inspiring. Reed, the son of a wealthy businessman, was born in Oregon and went east to private school and then to Harvard. After graduation, he drifted to New York's Greenwich Village, where he joined his classmate Walter Lippmann as well as Max Eastman, Mabel Dodge, and other intellectuals and radicals. This group converted Reed to socialism and made him understand that "my happiness is built on the misery of others." In Europe shortly after the war began, Reed was appalled by the carnage in what he considered a capitalistic war. The news of the Russian czar's abdication in 1917 brought him to Russia just in time to witness the bloody Bolshevik takeover. His eyewitness account, *Ten Days That Shook the World,* optimistically predicted a worldwide revolution. However, when he saw how little hope there was for that revolution in postwar America, he returned to the Soviet Union. By the time he died from typhus in 1920, the authoritarian nature of the new Russian regime caused him to become disillusioned.

Working-Class Protest

Reed was one of the romantic American intellectuals who saw great hope for the future in the Russian Revolution. His mentor Lincoln Steffens, the muckraking journalist, remarked after a visit to the Soviet Union a few years later, "I have been over into the future and it works." But relatively few Americans, even among those who had been socialists, and fewer still among the workers, joined the Communist party. Perhaps in all there were 25,000 to 40,000, and those were split into two groups, the American Communist party and the Communist Labor party. The threat to the American system of government was very slight. But in 1919, the Communists seemed to be a threat, particularly as a series of devastating strikes erupted across the country. Workers in the United States had suffered from wartime inflation, which had almost doubled prices between 1914 and 1919, while most wages remained the same. During 1919, more than 4 million workers took part in 4,000 strikes. Few wanted to overthrow the government; they demanded higher wages, shorter hours, and in some cases more control over the workplace.

On January 21, 1919, some 35,000 shipyard workers went on strike in Seattle, Washington. Within a few days, a general strike paralyzed the city; transportation and business stopped. The mayor of Seattle called for federal troops. Within five days, using strong-arm tactics, the mayor put down the strike and was hailed across the country as a "red-blooded patriot."

Yet the strikes continued elsewhere. In September 1919, all 343,000 employees of U.S. Steel walked out in an attempt to win an eight-hour day and an "American living wage." The average workweek in the steel industry in 1919 was 68.7 hours; the unskilled worker averaged $1,400 per year, while the minimum subsistence for a family of five that same year was estimated at $1,575. Within days, the strike spread to Bethlehem Steel. From the beginning, the owners blamed the strikes on the Bolsheviks. They put ads in the newspapers urging workers to "Stand by America, Show Up the Red Agitator." They also imported strikebreakers, provoked riots, broke up union meetings, and finally used police and soldiers to end the strike. Eighteen strikers were killed. Because most people believed the Communists had inspired the strike, the issue of long hours and poor pay got lost, and eventually the union surrendered.

While the steel strike was still in progress, the police in Boston went on strike. Like most other workers, the police were struggling to survive on prewar salaries in inflationary times. The Boston newspapers blamed the strike on Communist influence, but one writer warned that the protest could not succeed because "behind Boston in this skirmish with Bolshevism stands Massachusetts and behind Massachusetts stands America." College students and army veterans volunteered to replace the police and prevent looting in the city. The president of Harvard assured the students that their grades would not suffer. The government quickly broke the strike and fired the policemen. When Samuel Gompers urged Governor Calvin Coolidge to ask the Boston authorities to reinstate them, Coolidge responded with the laconic statement that made him famous and eventually helped him win the presidency: "There is no right to strike against the public safety by anybody, anywhere, anytime."

To many Americans, strikes were bad enough, especially strikes that dangerous radicals seemingly inspired, but bombs were even worse. The "bomb-throwing radical" was almost a cliché, probably stemming from the hysteria over the Haymarket Riot of 1886. On April 28, 1919, a bomb was discovered in a small package delivered to the home of the mayor of Seattle. The next day, the maid of a former senator from Georgia opened a package, and a bomb blew her hands off. Other bombings occurred in June, including one that shattered the front of Attorney General A. Mitchell Palmer's home in Washington. The bombings seem to have been the work of misguided radicals who thought they might spark a genuine revolution in America. But their effect was to provide substantial evidence that revolution was around the corner, even though most American workers wanted only shorter hours, better working conditions, and a chance to realize the American dream.

The strikes and bombs, combined with the general postwar mood of distrust and suspicion, persuaded many people of a real and immediate threat to the nation. No one was more convinced than A. Mitchell Palmer. From a Quaker family in a small Pennsylvania town, the attorney general had graduated from Swarthmore College and had been admitted to the Pennsylvania bar in 1893 at the age of 21. After serving three terms as a congressman, he helped swing the Pennsylvania delegation to Wilson at the 1912 convention. Wilson offered him the post of secretary of war, but Palmer's pacifism led him to refuse. He did support the United States' entry into the war, however, and served as alien property custodian, a job created by the Trading with the Enemy Act. This position apparently convinced him of the danger of radical subversive activities in America. The bombing of his home intensified his fears, and in the summer of 1919, he determined to find and destroy the Red network. He organized a special antiradical division within the Justice Department and put a young man named J. Edgar Hoover in charge of coordinating information on domestic radical activities.

As he became obsessed with the "Red Menace," Palmer instituted a series of raids, beginning in November 1919. Simultaneously, in several cities, his men rounded up 250 members of the Union of Russian Workers, many of whom were beaten and roughed up in the process. In December, 249 aliens, including the famous anarchist Emma Goldman, were deported, although very few were Communists and even fewer had any desire to overthrow the government of the United States. Palmer's men raided private homes, meeting halls, and organization offices. In Detroit, 500 people were arrested on false charges and forced to sleep or stand in a corridor of a building for 25 hours before they were released. In Boston, 800 people were rounded up, marched in chains, then held in an unheated prison on an island in the harbor.

The Palmer raids, which probably constituted the most massive violation of civil liberties in America history to this date, found few dangerous radicals but did fan the flames of fear and intolerance in the country. In Indiana, a jury quickly acquitted a man who had killed an alien for yelling, "To hell with the United States." Billy Sunday, a Christian evangelist, suggested that the best solution was to shoot aliens rather than to deport them.

Palmer became a national hero for ferreting out Communists, even though saner minds protested his tactics. Assistant Secretary of State Louis Post insisted that the arrested aliens be given legal rights, and in the end only about 600 were deported, out of the more than 5,000 arrested. The worst of the "Red Scare" was over by the end of 1920, but the fear of radicals and the emotional patriotism survived throughout the decade to color almost every aspect of politics, daily life, and social legislation.

The Red Scare promoted many patriotic organizations and societies determined to eliminate communism from American life. These organizations made little distinction between socialists, Communists, liberals, and progressives, and they found Bolsheviks everywhere. The best-known organization was the American Legion, but there were also the American Defense Society, the Sentinels of the Republic (whose motto was "Every Citizen a Sentinel, Every Home a Sentry Box"), the

United States Flag Association, and the Daughters of the American Revolution. Such groups provided a sense of purpose and a feeling of belonging in a rapidly changing America. But often what united their efforts was an obsessive fear of Communists and radicals.

Some organizations targeted women social reformers. One group attacked the "Hot-House, Hull House Variety of Parlor Bolshevists" and during the 1920s circulated a number of "spider-web charts" that purported to connect liberals and progressives, especially progressive women, to Communist organizations. In one such chart, even the Needlework Guild and the Sunshine Society were accused of being influenced by communists. The connections were made only through the use of half-truths, innuendo, and outright lies. To protest their charges did little good, for the accusers knew the truth and would not be deflected from their purpose of exterminating dangerous radicals.

The Klan, with its elaborate rituals and its white uniforms, exploited the fear of blacks, Jews, liberals, and Catholics while preaching "traditional" American values.

Ku Klux Klan

The superpatriotic societies exploited the fear that radicals and Bolsheviks were subverting the American way of life from within. The Ku Klux Klan went further. The Klan was organized in Georgia by William J. Simmons, a lay preacher, salesman, and member of many fraternal organizations. He adopted the name and white-sheet uniform of the old antiblack Reconstruction organization that was glorified in 1915 in the immensely popular but racist feature film *Birth of a Nation.* Simmons appointed himself head ("Imperial Wizard") of the new Klan.

Unlike the original organization, which took almost anyone who was white, the new Klan was thoroughly Protestant and explicitly antiforeign, anti-Semitic, and anti-Catholic. As an increasing number of second- and third-generation American Catholics began to achieve some success, even winning elections at the state and municipal level, many Protestants began to worry. The Klan declared that "America is Protestant and so it must remain." It opposed the teaching of evolution; glorified old-time religion; supported immigration restriction; denounced short skirts, petting, and "demon rum"; and upheld patriotism and the purity of women. The Klan grew slowly until after the war. In some places, returning veterans could join the Klan and the American Legion at the same table. The Klan added over 100,000 new members in 1920 alone. It grew rapidly because of aggressive recruiting but also because of the fear and confusion of the postwar period.

The Klan flourished in small towns and rural areas in the South, where it set out to keep the returning black soldiers in their "proper place," but it soon spread throughout the country, and at least half the members came from urban areas. The Klan was especially strong in the working-class neighborhoods of Detroit, Indianapolis, Atlanta, and Chicago, where the migration of African-Americans and other ethnic groups increased fear of everything "un-American." At the peak of its power, the Klan had several million members, and in some states, especially Indiana, Oregon, Oklahoma, Louisiana, and Texas, it influenced politics and determined some elections. The Klan's power declined after 1924, but widespread fear of Catholicism and everything perceived as un-American remained.

what about R.I.?

The Sacco-Vanzetti Case

One result of the Red Scare and the unreasoned fear of foreigners and radicals, which dragged on through much of the decade, was the conviction and sentencing of two Italian anarchists, Nicola Sacco and Bartolomeo Vanzetti. Arrested in 1920 for allegedly murdering a guard during a robbery of the shoe factory in South Braintree, Massachusetts, the two were convicted and sentenced to die in the summer of 1921 on what many liberals considered circumstantial and flimsy evidence. Indeed, it seemed to many that the two Italians, who spoke in broken English and were admitted anarchists, were punished because of their radicalism and their foreign appearance.

Even now, it is not clear whether Sacco and Vanzetti were guilty, but the case took on symbolic significance as many intellectuals in Europe and America rallied to their defense and to the defense of civil liberties. Appeal after appeal failed, but finally the governor of Massachusetts appointed a commission to reexamine the evidence in the case. The commission reaffirmed the verdict, and the two were executed in the electric chair on August 23, 1927. But the case and the cause would not die. On the fiftieth anniversary of their deaths in 1977, Governor Michael Dukakis of Massachusetts exonerated Sacco and Vanzetti and cleared their names.

Bartolomeo Vanzetti and Nicola Sacco, memorialized in a series of paintings by Ben Shahn, became important symbols for liberals fighting prejudice in the 1920s. (Ben Shahn. *Bartolomeo Vanzetti and Nicola Sacco,* from the Sacco-Vanzetti series of 23 paintings. 1931–1932.)

A Prospering Economy

Although the decade after World War I was a time of intolerance and anxiety, it was also a time of industrial expansion and widespread prosperity. After recovering from a postwar depression in 1921 and 1922, the economy took off. Fueled by new technology, more efficient planning and management, and innovative advertising, industrial production almost doubled during the decade, and the gross national product rose by an astonishing 40 percent. A construction boom created new suburbs around American cities, while a new generation of skyscrapers transformed the cities themselves. However, the benefits of this prosperity fell unevenly on the many social groups forming American society.

The Rising Standard of Living

Signs of the new prosperity appeared in many forms. Millions of sturdy homes and apartments were built and equipped with the latest conveniences. The number of telephones installed nearly doubled between 1915 and 1930. Plastics, rayon, and cellophane altered the habits of millions of Americans, while new products, such as cigarette lighters, reinforced concrete, dry ice, and Pyrex glass, created new demands unheard of a decade before.

Perhaps the most tangible sign of the new prosperity was the modern American bathroom. For years, the various functions we associate with the bathroom were separated. There was an outhouse or privy, a portable tin bathtub filled with water heated on the kitchen stove, and a pitcher and washbasin in the bedroom. Hotels and the urban upper class began to install cast-iron bathtubs and primitive flush toilets in the late nineteenth century, but not until the early twenties did the enameled tub, toilet, and washbasin become standard. By 1925, American factories turned out 5 million enameled bathroom fixtures annually. The bathroom, with unlimited hot water, privacy, and clean white fixtures, symbolized American affluence.

In sharp contrast to the nineteenth century, Americans had more leisure time. Persistent efforts by labor unions had gradually reduced the

Telephones in Use, 1900–1930

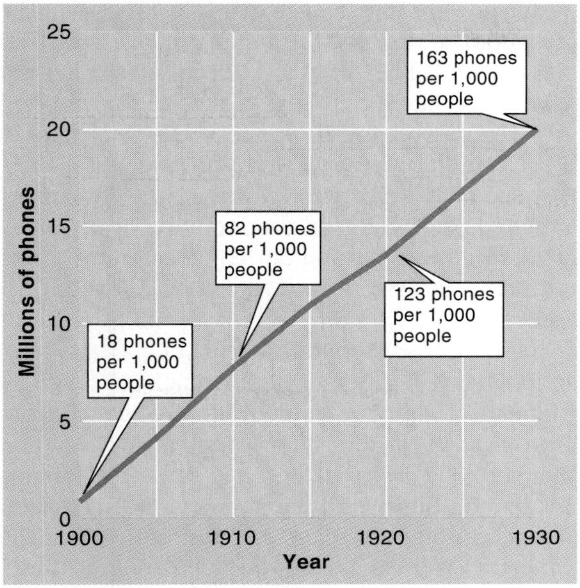

The telephone, though still a primitive instrument in the 1920s, changed business practices, social life, and even dating customs for the middle class.

Source: U.S. Bureau of the Census.

60-hour workweek of the late nineteenth century to a 45-hour week. Paid vacations, unheard of in the nineteenth century, also became prevalent. In 1916, only 16 of 389 establishments studied provided paid vacations; by 1926, some 40 percent of 250 companies gave their workers at least one week of vacation with pay.

The American diet also improved during the decade. The consumption of cornmeal and potatoes declined, while the sale of fresh vegetables increased by 45 percent. Health improved and life expectancy increased. But Americans did not share the advantages of better health and more leisure evenly. A white male born in 1900 had a life expectancy of 48 years and a white female of 51 years. By 1930, these figures had increased to 59 and 63 years, respectively. For a black male born in 1900, however, the life expectancy was only 33 years, and for the black female, 35 years. These figures increased to 48 and 47 by 1930, but the discrepancy remained.

Yet almost all Americans benefited to some extent from the new prosperity. Some took advantage of expanding educational opportunities. In 1900, only one in ten young people of high school age remained in school. By 1930, that number had increased to six in ten, and much of the improvement came in the 1920s. In 1900, only one college-age person in 33 attended an institution of higher learning; by 1930, the ratio was one in 7. Over a million people were enrolled in the nation's colleges.

The Rise of the Modern Corporation

The structure and practice of American business were transformed in the 1920s. After a crisis created by the economic downturn of 1920–1922, business boomed until the crash of 1929. Mergers increased during the decade at a rate greater than at any time since the end of the 1890s—there were more than 1,200 mergers in 1929 alone—creating such giants as General Electric, General Motors, Sears Roebuck, Du Pont, and U.S. Rubber. These were not monopolies but oligopolies (industry domination spread among a few large firms). By 1930, the 200 largest corporations controlled almost half the corporate wealth in the country. Large businesses also diversified during the decade. GE and Westinghouse began to produce household appliances and radios; Du Pont moved into plastics, paints, dyes, and film.

But perhaps the most important business trend of the decade was the emergence of a new kind of manager. No longer did family entrepreneurs make decisions relating to prices, wages, or output. Alfred P. Sloan, Jr., an engineer who reorganized General Motors, was a prototype of the new kind of manager. He divided the company into components, freeing the top managers to concentrate on planning new products, controlling inventory, and integrating the whole operation. Marketing and advertising became as important as production, and many businesses began to spend more money on research. The new manager often had a large staff but owned no part of the company. He was usually an expert at cost accounting and analyzing data. Increasingly, he was a graduate of one of the new business colleges.

Continuing and extending the trends started by Frederick Taylor before World War I, the new managers tried to keep employees working efficiently, but they used more than the stopwatch and the assembly line. They introduced pensions, recreation facilities, cafeterias, and, in some cases, paid vacations and profit-sharing plans. The managers were not being altruistic, however; "welfare capitalism" was designed to reduce worker discontent and to discourage labor unions. Planning was the key to the new corporate structure, and planning often meant a continuation of the business-government cooperation that had developed during World War I. Experts from philanthropic foundations, the National Bureau of Economic Research, and the U.S. Department of Commerce worked together hoping that they could provide a middle ground between collectivism and laissez-faire economy. All the planning and the new managerial authority failed to prevent the economic collapse of 1929, but the modern cooperation survived the Depression to exert a growing influence on American life in the 1930s and after.

Electrification

The 1920s also marked the climax of the "second industrial revolution." During the late nineteenth century, American industry had primarily manufactured goods intended for other producers. In the first quarter of the twentieth century, as industries like coal, textiles, and steel stabilized or declined, new manufacturing concerns that produced rubber, synthetic fabrics, chemicals, and petroleum arose. They focused on goods for consumers, such as silk stockings, washing machines, and cars.

Powering the second industrial revolution was electricity—a form of energy that rapidly replaced steam power after 1900. In the previous two decades, inventors such as Thomas A. Edison and George Westinghouse had developed generators for producing electric current and methods for transmitting it and using it to drive machinery. Edison's illuminating company opened the first commercial power station in New York in 1882; by the end of the century, more than 3,000 stations were supplying businesses and homes with electricity. Meanwhile, Edison's most famous invention, the electric light bulb, was rapidly replacing gas lanterns in homes and on streets.

Between 1900 and 1920, the replacement of steam power by electricity worked as profound a change as had the substitution of steam power for water power after the Civil War. In 1902, electricity supplied a mere 2 percent of all industrial power; by 1929, fully 80 percent derived from electrical generators. Less than one of every ten American homes was supplied with electricity in 1907, but more than two-thirds were by 1929. Powered by electricity, American industries reached new heights of productivity. By 1929, the work force was turning out twice as many goods as a similarly sized work force had ten years before.

Electricity brought dozens of gadgets and laborsaving devices into the home. Washing machines and electric irons gradually reduced the drudgery of washday for women, and vacuum cleaners, electric toasters, and sewing machines lightened housework. But the new machines still needed human direction and did not reduce the time the average housewife spent doing housework. For many poor urban and rural women, the traditional female tasks of carrying water, pushing, pulling, and lifting went on as they had for centuries. In many ways, the success of the electric revolution increased the contrast in American life. The "Great White Ways" of the cities symbolized progress, but they also made the darkness of slums and hamlets seem even more forbidding. The fact that many urban families could use electrical appliances whereas most rural families could not increased the tensions between rural Protestants and urban ethnic Catholics. wow!

Automobile Culture

Automobile manufacturing, like electrification, underwent spectacular growth in the 1920s. The automobile was one major factor in the postwar economic boom. It stimulated and transformed the petroleum, steel, and rubber industries. The auto forced the construction and improvement of streets and highways and caused the spending of millions of dollars on labor and concrete. In 1925, the secretary of agriculture approved the first uniform numbering system for the nation's highways, but it was still an adventure to drive from one city to another.

This promenade of pedestrians and automobiles in St. Louis, Missouri, depicts the new car culture of the 1920s. The automobile was more than a new mode of transportation; it transformed the American economy, altered the American landscape, and revolutionized life in America. Thousands of roads and highways were built during the 1920s as the growing numbers of automobile owners pressed the government for better roads.

The auto created new suburbs and allowed families to live many miles from their work. The filling station, the diner, and the tourist court became familiar and eventually standardized objects on the American scene. Traffic lights, stop signs, billboards, and parking lots appeared. Hitching posts and watering troughs became rarer, and gradually the garage replaced the livery stable. The auto changed the look of the American landscape and threatened the environment as well. Oil and gasoline contaminated streams, while piles of old tires and rusting hulks of discarded cars became a familiar sight along the highways. At the same time, the emissions from thousands and then millions of internal combustion engines polluted the air. But there was no turning back. The age of the auto had replaced the age of the horse.

The auto changed American life in other ways. It led to the decline of the small crossroads store as well as many small churches because the rural family could now drive to the larger city or town. The tractor changed methods of farming. Trucks replaced the horse and wagon and altered the marketing of farm products. Buses began to eliminate the one-room school, because it was now possible to transport students to larger schools. The automobile allowed young people for the first time to escape the chaperoning of parents. It was hardly the "house of prostitution on wheels" that one judge called it, but it did change courting habits in all parts of the country.

Gradually, as the decade progressed, the automobile became not just transportation but a sign of status. Advertising helped create the impression that it was the symbol of the good life, of sex, freedom, and speed. The auto in turn transformed advertising and design. It even altered the way products were purchased. By 1926, three-fourths of the cars sold were bought on some kind of deferred-payment plan. Installment credit, first tried by a group of businessmen in Toledo, Ohio, in 1915 to sell more autos, was soon used to promote sewing machines, refrigerators, and other consumer products. "Buy now, pay later" became the American way.

The United States had a love affair with the auto from the beginning. There were 8,000 motor vehicles registered in the country in 1900, and nearly a million in 1912. But only in the 1920s did the auto come within the reach of middle-class consumers. In 1929, Americans purchased 4.5 million cars, and by the end of that year, nearly 27 million were registered. Automobile culture was a mass movement.

The auto industry, like most American businesses, went through a period of consolidation in the 1920s. In 1908, more than 250 companies were manufacturing automobiles in the United States. By 1929, only 44 remained.

Many men contributed to the development and production of the auto—William Durant organized General Motors; Charles Kettering, an engineering genius, developed the electric self-starter; and Ransom E. Olds built the first mass-produced moderately priced light car.

Motor Vehicle Registration and Sales, 1900–1930

Year	Motor Vehicle Registration	Factory Sales
1900	8,000	4,100
1905	78,800	24,200
1910	468,500	181,000
1915	2,490,000	895,900
1920	9,239,100	1,905,500
1925	20,068,500	3,735,100
1930	26,749,800	2,787,400

Source: Historical Statistics of the United States.

Above all the others loomed a name that would become synonymous with the automobile itself—Henry Ford.

Ford had the reputation of being a progressive industrial leader and a champion of the common people. As with all men and women who take on symbolic significance, the truth is less dramatic than the stories. Ford is often credited with inventing the assembly line. In actuality it was the work of a team of engineers. But the Ford Motor Company was the first organization to perfect the moving assembly line and mass-production technology. Introduced in 1913, the new method reduced the time it took to produce a car from 14 hours to an hour and a half. It was the perfect application of Frederick Taylor's system of breaking down each operation into its components, applying careful timing, and integrating the laborer with the machine. The product of the carefully planned system was the Model T, the prototype of the inexpensive family car.

In 1914, Ford startled the country by announcing that he was increasing the minimum pay of the Ford assembly-line worker to $5 a day (almost twice the national average pay for factory workers). Ford was not a humanitarian. He wanted a dependable work force and understood that skilled workers were less likely to quit if they received good pay. Ford was one of the first to appreciate that workers were consumers as well as producers and that they might buy Model T Fords. But work in the Ford factory had its disadvantages. Work on the assembly line was repetitious and numbing. "You could drop over dead" one worker recalled, "and they wouldn't stop the line." And when the line closed down, as it did periodically, the workers were released without compensation.

Henry Ford was not easy to work for. One newspaper account in 1928 called him "an industrial fascist—the Mussolini of Detroit." He ruthlessly pressured his dealers and used them to bail him out of difficult financial situations. Instead of borrowing money from a bank, he forced dealers to buy extra cars, trucks, and tractors. He used spies on the assembly lines and fired workers and executives at the least provocation. But he did produce a car that transformed America.

The Model T, which cost $600 in 1912, was reduced gradually in price until it sold for only $290 in 1924. The "Tin Lizzie," as it was affectionately called, was light and easily repaired. Some owners claimed all one needed was a pair of pliers and some baling wire to keep it running. If it got stuck on bad roads, as it often did, it could be lifted out by a reasonably healthy man. Replacement parts were standardized and widely available. The Model T did not change from year to year, and it did not deviate from its one color, black. Except for adding a self-starter, offering a closed model, and making a few minor face-lift changes, Ford kept the Model T in 1927 much as he had introduced it in 1913. By that time, its popularity had declined as many people traded up to sleeker, more colorful, and, they thought, more prestigious autos put out by Ford's competitors, and wages at Ford dipped below the industry average. The Model A, introduced in 1927, was never as popular or as successful as the Model T, but the gigantic River Rouge factory, built especially to produce the new model, became the symbol of mass production in the new era.

The Exploding Metropolis

The automobile caused American cities to expand into the countryside. In the late nineteenth century, railroads and streetcars had created suburbs near the major cities, but the great expansion of suburban population occurred in the 1920s. Shaker Heights, a Cleveland suburb, was in some ways a typical development. Built on the site of a former Shaker community, the new suburb was planned and developed by two businessmen. They controlled the size and style of the homes and restricted buyers. No blacks were allowed. Curving roads led off the main auto boulevards, while landscaping and natural areas contributed to a parklike atmosphere. The suburb increased in population from 1,700 to 1919 to over 15,000 in 1929, and the price of lots multiplied by 10 during the decade. Other suburbs grew in an equally spectacular manner. Beverly Hills, near Los Angeles, increased in population by 2,485 percent during the decade. Grosse Point Park, near Detroit, grew by 725 percent, and Elmwood Park, near Chicago, by 716 percent. The automobile also allowed industry to move to the suburbs. Employees in manufacturing establishments in the suburbs of the 11 largest cities increased from 365,000 in 1919 to 1.2 million in 1937.

The biggest land boom of all occurred in Florida, where the city of Miami mushroomed from 30,000 in 1920 to 75,000 in 1925. One plot of

Borger, Texas, "as it was in 1926 in the middle of its rise from road crossing to an oil city," here depicted by Thomas Hart Benton, one of the best known of the regionalist painters.

land in West Palm Beach sold for $800,000 in 1923 and two years later was worth $4 million. A hurricane in 1926 ended the Florida land boom temporarily, but most cities and their suburbs continued to grow during the decade.

The census of 1920 indicated that for the first time, more than half the population of the United States lived in "urban areas" of more than 2,500. The census designation of an urban area was a little misleading because a town of 5,000 could still be more rural than urban. A more significant concept was the metropolitan area of at least 100,000 people. There were only 52 of these areas in 1900, but in 1930 there were 115.

The automobile transformed every city, but the most spectacular growth of all took place in two cities that the car virtually created. Detroit grew from 300,000 in 1900 to 1,837,000 in 1930, while Los Angeles expanded from 114,000 in 1900 to 1,778,000 in 1930. With sprawling subdivisions

Ten Largest Cities, 1900–1930[a]

1900	1930
1. New York—4,023,000	1. New York—9,423,000
2. Chicago—1,768,000	2. Chicago—3,870,000
3. Philadelphia—1,458,000	3. Philadelphia—2,399,000
4. Boston—905,000	4. Detroit—1,837,000
5. Pittsburgh—622,000	5. Los Angeles—1,778,000
6. St. Louis—612,000	6. Boston—1,545,000
7. Baltimore—543,000	7. Pittsburgh—1,312,000
8. San Francisco—444,000	8. San Francisco—1,104,000
9. Cincinnati—414,000	9. St. Louis—1,094,000
10. Cleveland—402,000	10. Cleveland—1,048,000

[a]Figures are for the entire metropolitan areas, including suburbs.

Source: U.S. Bureau of the Census.

connected by a growing network of roads, Los Angeles was the city of the future.

While cities expanded horizontally during the 1920s, sprawling into the countryside, city centers grew vertically. A building boom that peaked near the end of the decade created new skylines for most urban centers. Even cities such as Tulsa, Dallas, Kansas City, Memphis, and Syracuse built skyscrapers. By 1929, there were 377 buildings of over 20 stories in American cities. Many were started just before the stock market crash ended the building boom, and the empty offices stood as a stark reminder of the limits of expansion. The most famous skyscraper of all, the Empire State Building in New York, which towers 102 stories in the air, was finished in 1931 but not completely occupied until after World War II.

A Communications Revolution

Changing communications altered the way many Americans lived as well as the way they conducted business. The telephone was first demonstrated in 1876. By 1899, more than a million phones were in operation. During the 1920s, the number of homes with phones increased from 9 million to 13 million. Still, by the end of the decade, more than half of American homes were without phones.

The radio even more than the telephone symbolized the technological and communicational changes of the 1920s. The department stores quickly began to stock radios, or crystal sets as they were called, but many Americans in the 1920s built their own receivers. The first station to begin commercial broadcasting was WWJ in Detroit in the summer of 1920. When WWJ and KDKA in Pittsburgh broadcast the election returns in 1920, they ushered in a new era in politics. The next year WJZ of Newark, New Jersey, broadcast the World Series, beginning a process that would transform baseball and eventually football and basketball as well. Five hundred stations took to the airwaves in 1922 alone, many of them sponsored by department stores, and others by newspapers and colleges. In the same year, a radio station in New York broadcast the first commercial, an indication that the airways would be used to increase the demand for the goods the factories were producing.

Much early broadcasting consisted of classical music, but soon came news analysis and coverage of presidential inaugurals and important events. Some stations produced live dramas, but it was the serials such as "Amos 'n' Andy" that more than any other programs made radio a national medium. Millions of people scattered across the country could sit in their living rooms (and after 1927, in their cars) listening to the same program. The record industry grew just as rapidly. By the end of the decade, people in all sections of the country were humming the same popular songs. Actors and announcers became celebrities. The music, voice, and sound of the

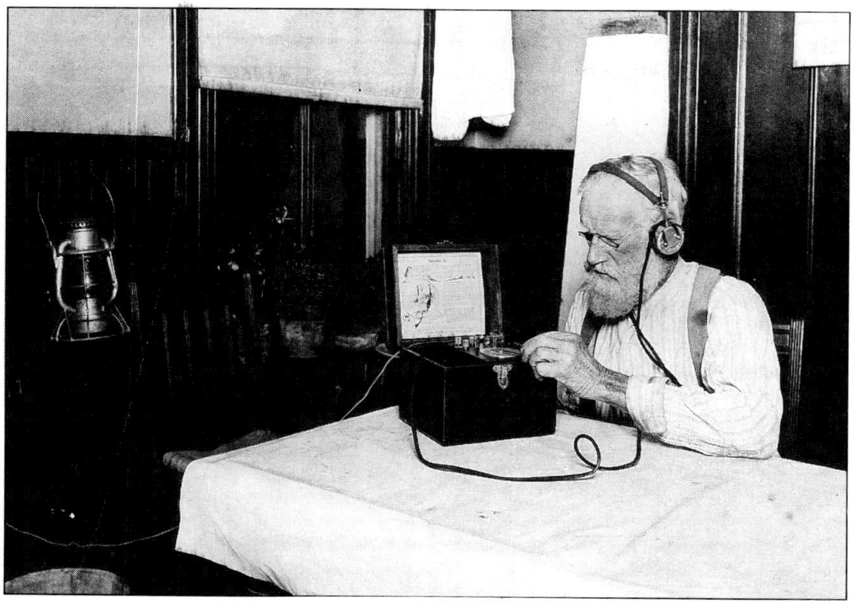

Most farmers did not own a radio until the end of the 1930s when they finally got electricity, but for those living in the cities the radio altered lives and brought a new magic of sound into 2 or 3 million households in the 1920s.

Sports figures like Jack Dempsey, depicted here by artist George Bellows, became celebrities largely because of the radio and the newspapers.

radio, even more than the sound of the automobile, marked the end of silence and, to a certain extent, the end of privacy.

Even more dramatic was the phenomenon of the movies. Forty million viewers a week went to the movies in 1922, and by 1929, that had increased to over 100 million. Men, women, and children flocked to small theaters in the towns and to movie palaces in the cities, where they could dream of romance or adventure. Charlie Chaplin, Rudolph Valentino, Lillian Gish, and Greta Garbo were more famous and more important to millions of Americans than most government officials were. The motion pictures, which before the war had attracted mostly the working class, now seemed to appeal across class, regional, and generational lines.

The movies had the power to influence attitudes and ideas. In the 1920s, many parents feared that the movies would dictate ideas about sex and life. One young college woman remembered, "One day I went to see Viola Dana in *The Five Dollar Baby.* The scenes which showed her as a baby fascinated me so that I stayed to see it over four times. I forgot home, dinner and everything. About eight o'clock mother came after me." She also admitted that the movies taught her how to smoke, and in some of the movies "there were some lovely scenes which just got me all hot 'n' bothered."

Not only movie stars became celebrities in the 1920s. Sports figures such as Babe Ruth, Bobby Jones, Jack Dempsey, and Red Grange were just as famous. The great spectator sports of the decade owed much to the increase of leisure time and to the automobile, the radio, and the mass-circulation newspaper. Thousands drove automobiles to college towns to watch football heroes perform. Millions listened for scores or read about the results the next day. One writer in 1924 called this era "the age of play." He might better have called it "the age of the spectator." The popularity of sports, like the movies and radio, was in part the product of technology.

The year 1927 seemed to mark the beginning of the new age of mechanization and progress. That was the year Henry Ford produced his fifteen millionth car and introduced the Model A. During that year, radio-telephone service was established between San Francisco and Manila. The first radio network was organized (CBS), and the first talking movie was released (*The Jazz Singer*). In 1927, the Holland Tunnel, the first underwater vehicular roadway, connected New York and New Jersey. It was also the year that Charles Lindbergh flew from New York to Paris in his single-engine plane in 33½ hours. Lindbergh was not the first to fly the Atlantic, but he was the first to fly it alone, an accomplishment that won him $25,000 in prize money and captured the world's imagina-

After his solo flight across the Atlantic, Charles Lindbergh received a hero's welcome upon his return to the United States. Here, a crowd estimated at about 4 million cheers him through the streets of New York. A couple of days earlier President Coolidge, calling Lindbergh's achievement a shining example of heroic individualism combined with American genius and industry, had presented the aviator with the Distinguished Flying Cross.

Advertising

Have you ever noticed that television commercials can often be more interesting and creative than the programs? One authority has suggested that the best way for a foreign visitor to understand the American character and popular culture is to study television commercials. Television advertising, the thesis goes, appeals to basic cultural assumptions. The nature of advertising not only reveals for historians the prejudices, fears, values, and aspirations of a people but also makes an impact on historical development itself, influencing patterns of taste and purchasing habits. One modern critic calls advertising a "peculiarly American force that now compares with such long-standing institutions as the school and church in the magnitude of its social impact."

As long as manufacturing was local and limited, there was no need to advertise. Before the Civil War, for example, the local area could usually absorb all that was produced; therefore, a simple announcement in a local paper was sufficient to let people know that a particular product was available. But when factories began producing more than the local market could ordinarily consume, advertising came into play to create a larger demand.

Although national advertising began with the emergence of "name brands" in the late nineteenth century, it did not achieve the importance it now holds until the 1920s. In 1918, the total gross advertising revenue in magazines was $58.5 million. By 1920, it had more than doubled to $129.5 million, and by 1929, it was nearly $200 million. These figures should not be surprising in a decade that often equated advertising with religion. The biblical Moses was called the "ad-writer for the Deity," and in a best-selling book, Bruce Barton, a Madison Avenue advertiser, reinterpreted Jesus, the "man nobody knows," as a master salesman. Wrote Barton: "He would be a national advertiser today."

The designers of ads began to study psychology to determine what motives, conscious or unconscious, influenced consumers. One psychologist concluded that the appeal to the human instinct for "gaining social prestige" would sell the most goods. Another way to sell products, many learned, was to create anxiety in the mind of the consumer over body odor, bad breath, oily hair, dandruff, pimples, and other embarrassing ailments. In 1921, the Lambert Company used the term *halitosis* for bad breath in an

Toothpaste advertisement.

Shaving cream advertisement.

Automobile advertisement (1929).

ad for Listerine. Within six years, sales of Listerine had increased from a little over 100,000 bottles a year to more than 4 million. The appeal to sex also sold products, advertisers soon found, as did the desire for the latest style or invention. But perhaps the most important thing advertisers marketed was youth. "We are going to sell every artificial thing there is," a cosmetic salesman wrote in 1926, "and above all it is going to be young-young-young! We make women feel young." A great portion of the ads were aimed at women. As one trade journal announced: "The proper study of mankind is man. . . , but the proper study of markets is woman."

Look at the accompanying advertisements carefully. What do they tell you about American culture in the 1920s? What do they suggest about attitudes toward women? Do they reveal any special anxieties? How are they similar to and different from advertising today?

tion. He was young and handsome, and his feat seemed to represent not only the triumph of an individual but also the triumph of the machine. Lindbergh never talked of his accomplishments in the first person; he always said "we," meaning his airplane as well. He was greeted by 4 million people when he returned to New York for a triumphant ticker-tape parade. Like many a movie star or sports hero, he had become an instant celebrity. When Americans cheered Lindbergh, they were reaffirming their belief in the American dream and their faith in individual initiative as well as in technology.

Hopes Raised, Promises Deferred

The 1920s was a time when all kinds of hopes seemed realizable. "Don't envy successful salesmen—be one!" one advertisement screamed. Buy a car. Build a house. Start a career. Invest in land. Invest in stocks. Make a fortune.

Not all Americans, of course, were intent on making a stock market killing or expected to win a huge fortune. Some merely wished to retain traditional values in a society that seemed to question them. Others wanted a steady job and a little respect. Still others hungered for the new appliances so alluringly described in ads and on the radio. Many discovered, however, that no matter how modest their hopes might be, they lay tantalizingly out of reach.

Clash of Values

During the 1920s, radio, movies, advertising, and mass-circulation magazines promoted a national, secular culture. But this new culture, which emphasized consumption, pleasure, upward mobility, even sex, clashed with traditional values of hard work, thrift, church, family, and home. Although it would be easy to see these cultural differences as a reflection of an urban-rural conflict, in fact many people clinging to the old ways had moved into the cities. Still, many Americans

John Steuart Curry was one of the 1920s regionalist painters who found inspiration in the American heartland. In *Baptism in Kansas,* he depicts a religious ritual that underscores the conflict between rural and urban values.

feared that new cultural values, scientific breakthroughs, and new ideas like bolshevism, relativism, Freudianism, and biblical criticism threatened their familiar way of life. A trial over the teaching of evolutionary ideas in high school in the little town of Dayton, Tennessee, symbolized, even as it exaggerated, the clash of the old versus the new, the traditional versus the modern, the city versus the country.

The scientific community and most educated people had long accepted the basic concepts of evolution, if not all the details of Charles Darwin's theories. But many Christians, especially those from Protestant evangelical churches, accepted the Bible as the literal truth. They believed that faith in the Gospel message was crucial to living a virtuous life on earth and, more important, going to heaven. Many of these faithful saw in the dramatic changes of the 1920s a major spiritual crisis. Resistance to the concept of evolution resulted in legislative efforts in several states to forbid its teaching. The Tennessee law enacted in 1925 became the most famous, for it made it illegal

> for any teacher in any of the universities, normal and all other public schools of the state to teach any theory that denies the story of the divine creation of man as taught in the Bible and to teach instead that man has descended from a lower order of animals.

John Scopes, a young biology teacher, broke the law by teaching evolutionary theory to his class, and the state of Tennessee brought him to trial. The American Civil Liberties Union hired Clarence Darrow, perhaps the country's most famous defense lawyer, to defend Scopes; the World Christian Fundamentalist Association engaged William Jennings Bryan, former presidential candidate and secretary of state, to assist the prosecution. Bryan was old and tired (he died only a few days after the trial), but he was still an eloquent and deeply religious man. In cross-examination, Darrow reduced Bryan's statements to intellectual rubble and revealed also that Bryan was at a loss to explain much of the Bible. He could not explain how Eve was created from Adam's rib or where Cain got his wife. Nevertheless, the jury declared Scopes guilty, for he had clearly broken the law. But the press from all over the country covered the trial and upheld science and academic freedom. Journalists like H. L. Mencken had a field day poking fun at Bryan and the fundamentalists. "Heave an egg out a Pullman window," Mencken wrote, "and you will hit a Fundamentalist almost anywhere in the United States today. . . . They are everywhere where learning is too heavy a burden for mortal minds to carry." Yet religious fundamentalism and people who held to old values and traditional beliefs continued to survive in a world fast becoming urban, modern, and sophisticated.

Immigration and Migration

Immigrants and anyone else perceived as "un-American" seemed to threaten the old ways. A movement to restrict immigration had existed for decades. An act passed in 1882 prohibited the entry of criminals, paupers, and the insane, and special agreements between 1880 and 1908 restricted both Chinese and Japanese immigration. But it was the fear and intolerance of the war years and the period right after the war that resulted in major restrictive legislation.

The first strongly restrictive immigration law passed in 1917 over President Wilson's veto. It required a literacy test for the first time (an immigrant had to read a passage in one of a number of languages). The bill also prohibited the immigration of certain political radicals. The literacy test did not stop the more than one million immigrants who poured into the country in 1920 and 1921, however.

In 1921 Congress limited European immigration in any one year to 3 percent of the number of each nationality present in the country in 1910. Congress changed the quota in 1924 to 2 percent of those in the country in 1890, in order to limit immigration from southern and eastern Europe and ban all immigration from Asia. The National Origins Act of 1927 set an overall limit of 150,000 European immigrants a year, with more than 60 percent coming from Great Britain and Germany but less than 4 percent from Italy.

Ethnicity increasingly became a factor in political alignments during the 1920s. Restrictive immigration laws, sponsored by Republicans, helped to attract American Jews, Italians, and Poles to the Democratic party. By 1924, the Democratic party was so evenly divided between northern urban Catholics and southern rural Protestants that the party voted to condemn the Ku Klux Klan, by a very small margin. How small!!

no they didn't

The immigration acts of 1921, 1924, and 1927, in sharply limiting European immigration and virtually banning Asian immigrants, cut off the streams of cheap labor that had provided muscle for an industrializing country since the early nineteenth century. At the same time, by exempting immigrants from the Western Hemisphere, the new laws opened the country to Mexican laborers who were eager to escape poverty in their own land and to work in the fields and farms of California and the Southwest.

Though they never matched the flood of eastern and southern Europeans who entered the country before World War I, Mexican immigrants soon became the country's largest first-generation immigrant group. Nearly half a million arrived in the 1920s, in contrast to only 31,000 in the first decade of the century. Mexican farm workers often lived in primitive camps, where conditions were unsanitary and health care was nonexistent. "When they have finished harvesting my crops I will kick them out on the country road," one employer announced. "My obligation is ended."

Mexicans also migrated to industrial cities such as Detroit, St. Louis, and Kansas City. Northern companies recruited them and paid their transportation. The Bethlehem Steel Corporation brought 1,000 Mexicans into its Pennsylvania plant in 1923, and U.S. Steel imported 1,500 as strikebreakers to Lorain, Ohio, about the same time. During the 1920s, El Paso, Texas, became more than half Mexican, San Antonio a little less than half. The Mexican population in California reached 368,000 in 1929, and Los Angeles was about 20 percent Mexican. Like black Americans, the Mexicans found opportunity by migrating, but they did not escape prejudice or hardship.

African-Americans migrated north in great numbers from 1915 to 1920. Reduced European immigration and industrial growth caused many northern companies to recruit southern blacks. Trains stopped at the depots in small southern towns, sometimes picking up hundreds of blacks in a single day. Lured by editorials and advertisements placed by industries in northern black newspapers such as the Chicago *Defender* and driven out of the South by an agricultural depression, many African-Americans eagerly headed north.

One young black man wrote to the Chicago *Defender* from Texas that he would prefer to go to Chicago or Philadelphia, but "I don't care where so long as I go where a man is a man." It was the young who tended to move. "Young folks just aren't satisfied to see so little and stay around on the farm all their lives like old folks did," one older man from South Carolina pointed out. Most black migrants were unskilled. They found work in the huge meatpacking plants of Chicago, East St. Louis, Omaha, and Kansas City and in the shipyards and steel mills. Only 50 African-Americans worked for the Ford Motor Company in 1916, but there were 2,500 working there in 1920 and 10,000 in 1926. The black population of Chicago increased from 44,000 in 1910 to 234,000 by 1930. Cleveland's black population grew eightfold between 1910 and 1930.

African-Americans unquestionably improved their lives by moving north. But most were like the Parkers, their dreams only partly fulfilled. Most crowded into segregated housing and faced prejudice and hate. "Black men stay South," the Chicago *Tribune* advised, and offered to pay the transportation for any who would return. In one section of Chicago, a group of white residents, fearing the encroachment of blacks, stretched across the street a banner that read: "THEY SHALL NOT PASS." Often the young black men moved first, and only later brought their wives and children, putting great pressure on many black families. Some young men, like John Parker, restrained their anger, but others, like Richard Wright's fictional Bigger Thomas, portrayed movingly in *Native Son* (1940), struck out violently against white society. The presence of more African-Americans in the industrial cities of the North led to the development of black ghettos and increased the racial tension that occasionally flared into violence.

One of the worst race riots took place in Chicago in 1919. The riot began at a beach on a hot July day. A black youth drowned in a white swimming area. Blacks claimed he had been hit by stones, but the police refused to arrest any of the white men. A group of African-Americans attacked the police, and the riot was on. It lasted four days. White youths drove through the black sections shooting blacks from car windows. Blacks returned the fire. Several dozen were killed, and hundreds were wounded. The tension between the races did not die when the riot was over.

Race riots broke out in other places as well. In the early 1920s, few cities escaped racial tension and violence. Riots exploded in Knoxville, Tennessee; Omaha, Nebraska; and Tulsa, Oklahoma. Racial conflict in Elaine, Arkansas, demonstrated that not even the rural Southwest was immune.

The wave of violence and racism angered and disillusioned W. E. B. Du Bois, who had urged African-Americans to close ranks and support the American cause during the war. In an angry editorial for *The Crisis,* he wrote:

> By God of Heaven, we are cowards and jackasses if now that the war is over, we do not marshall every ounce of brain and brawn to fight a sterner, longer, more unbending battle against the forces of hell in our own land. *We return. We return from fighting. We return fighting.* Make way for Democracy; we saved it in France, and by the Great Jehovah, we will save it in the United States of America, or know the reason why.

Marcus Garvey: Black Messiah

Du Bois was not the only militant black leader in the postwar years. A flamboyant Jamaican fed a growing sense of black pride during that time. Marcus Garvey arrived in New York at the age of 29. Largely self-taught, he was an admirer of Booker T. Washington. Although he never abandoned Washington's philosophy of self-help, he thoroughly transformed it. Washington focused on economic betterment through self-help; Garvey saw self-help as a means of political empowerment by which African peoples would reclaim their homelands from European powers.

In Jamaica, Garvey had founded the Universal Negro Improvement Association. By 1919, he had established 30 branches in the United States and the Caribbean. He also set up the newspaper *The Negro World,* the Black Cross Nurses, and a chain of grocery stores, millinery shops, and restaurants. His biggest project was the Black Star Line, a steamship company, to be owned and operated by African-Americans. Advocating the return of blacks to Africa, he declared himself the "provisional president of Africa," a title he adopted from Eamon De Valera, the first "provisional president of Ireland." He glorified the African past and preached that God and Jesus were black.

Garvey won converts, mostly among lower-middle-class blacks, through the force of his oratory and the power of his personality, but especially through his message that blacks should be proud of being black. "Up you mighty race, you can accomplish what you will," he thundered. Thousands of blacks cheered as his Universal African Legions, dressed in blue and red uniforms, marched by. They waved the red, black, and green flag and sang "Ethiopia, the Land of Our Fathers," and thousands invested their money in the Black Star Line. The line soon collapsed, however, in part because white entrepreneurs sold Garvey inferior ships and equipment. Garvey was arrested for using the mails to defraud shareholders and was sentenced to five years in prison. President Coolidge commuted the sentence. Ordered deported as an undesirable alien, Garvey left America in 1927.

Garvey's failures were as spectacular as his successes. Other black leaders, especially W. E. B. Du Bois and A. Philip Randolph, criticized and attacked him for his impractical schemes and

Marcus Garvey (*second from the right*), shown dressed in his favorite uniform, became a hero for many black Americans.

his back-to-Africa movement. But despite the exotic and romantic nature of Garvey's crusade, he convinced thousands of black Americans, especially the poor and discouraged, that they could join together and accomplish something and that they should feel pride in their heritage and their future.

The Harlem Renaissance and the Lost Generation

A group of black writers, artists, and intellectuals who settled in Harlem after the war led a movement related in some ways to Garvey's black nationalism crusade. It was less flamboyant but in the end more important. They studied anthropology, art, history, and music, and they wrote novels and poetry that explored the ambivalent role of blacks in America. Like Garvey, they expressed their pride in being black and sought their African roots and the folk tradition of blacks in America. But unlike Garvey, they had no desire to go back to Africa. They sought a way to be both black and American.

Alain Locke, the first black Rhodes scholar and a dapper professor of philosophy at Howard University, was in one sense the father of the renaissance. His collection of essays and art, *The New Negro* (1925), announced the movement to the outside world and outlined black contributions to American culture and civilization. Langston Hughes, a poet and novelist born in Missouri, went to high school in Cleveland, lived in Mexico, and traveled in Europe and Africa before settling in Harlem. He wrote bitter but laughing poems, using black vernacular to describe the pathos and the pride of black Americans. In *Weary Blues,* he adapted the rhythm and beat of black jazz and the blues to his poetry. Jazz was an important force in Harlem in the 1920s, and many prosperous whites came from downtown to listen to Louis Armstrong, Fletcher Henderson, Duke Ellington, and other black musicians. The promise of expressing primitive emotions, the erotic atmosphere, the music, and the illegal sex, drugs, and liquor made Harlem an intriguing place for many brought up in Victorian white America.

The Jamaican Claude McKay, who came to Harlem by way of Tuskegee and Kansas, wrote about the underside of life in Harlem in *Home to Harlem* (1925), one of the most popular of the "new Negro" novels. McKay portrayed two black men—one, Jake, who has deserted the white man's army and finds a life of simple and erotic pleasure in Harlem's cabarets, the other an intellectual who is unable to make such an easy choice. "My damned white education has robbed me of much of the primitive vitality, the pure stamina, the simple unwaggering strength of the Jakes of the negro race," he laments.

This was the dilemma of many of the Harlem writers: how to be both black and intellectual. They worried that they depended on white patrons, who introduced them to writers and artists in Greenwich Village and made contacts for them at New York publishing houses. Many of the white patrons pressured the black writers to conform to the white elite idea of black authenticity. The black writers resented this intrusion, but it was their only hope to be recognized. Jean Toomer, more self-consciously avant-garde than many of the other black writers, wrote haunting poems trying to explore the difficulty of black identity, and in a novel, *Cane* (1923), he sketched maladjusted, almost grotesque characters who expressed some of the alienation that many writers felt in the 1920s.

Many African-American writers felt alienated from American society. They tried living in Paris or in Greenwich Village, but most felt drawn to Harlem, which in the 1920s was rapidly becoming the center of black population in New York City. Over 117,000 white people left the neighborhood during the decade, while over 87,000 blacks moved in. Countee Cullen, the only writer in the group actually born in New York, remarked, "In spite of myself I find that I am activated by a strong sense of race consciousness." So was Zora Neale Hurston, born in Florida, who came to New York to study at Barnard College, earned an advanced degree in anthropology from Columbia University, and used her interest in folklore to write stories of robust and passionate rural blacks. Much of the work of the Harlem writers was read by very small numbers, but another generation of young black intellectuals in the 1960s still struggling with the dilemma of how to be both black and American would rediscover it.

One did not need to be black to be disillusioned with society. Many white intellectuals, writers, and artists also felt alienated from what they perceived as the materialism, conformity, and provincial prejudice that dominated American life. Many writers, including F. Scott Fitzgerald, Ernest Hemingway, E. E. Cummings, and T. S. Eliot, moved to Europe. They wanted to divorce themselves from the country they pretended to detest, but cheap rents and inexpensive food in Paris also influenced their decisions. Many of those who gathered at European cafés, drinking the wine that was illegal in the United States, wrote novels, plays, and poems about America. Like so many American intellectuals in all periods, they had a love-hate relationship with their country.

For many writers, the disillusionment began with the war itself. Hemingway eagerly volunteered to go to Europe as an ambulance driver. But when he was wounded on the Italian front, he reevaluated the purpose of the war and the meaning of all the slaughter. His novel *The Sun Also Rises* (1926) is the story of the purposeless European wanderings of a group of Americans. But it is also the story of Jake Barnes, made impotent by a war injury. His "unreasonable wound" is a symbol of the futility of life in the postwar period.

F. Scott Fitzgerald, who loved to frequent the cafés and the parties in Paris, became a celebrity during the 1920s. He was sometimes confused, even in his own mind, with the dashing heroes about whom he wrote. He epitomized some of the despair of his generation, which had "grown up to find all Gods dead, all wars fought, all faiths in man shaken." His best novel, *The Great Gatsby* (1925), was a critique of the American success myth. The book describes the elaborate parties given by a mysterious businessman, who, it turns out, has made his money illegally as a bootlegger. Gatsby hopes to win back a beautiful woman who has forsaken him for another man. But wealth won't buy happiness, and Gatsby's life ends tragically, as so many lives seemed to end in the novels written during the decade.

Paris was the place to which many American writers flocked, but it was not necessary to live in France to criticize American society. Sherwood Anderson, born in Camden, Ohio, created a fictional midwestern town in *Winesburg, Ohio* (1919) to describe the dull, narrow, warped lives that seemed to provide a metaphor for American culture. Sinclair Lewis, another midwesterner, created scathing parodies of middle-class, small-town life in *Main Street* (1920) and *Babbitt* (1922). The "hero" of the latter novel is a salesman from the town of Zenith. He is a "he-man," a "regular guy" who distrusts "red professors," foreign-born people, and anyone from New York. He lives in a world of gadgets and booster clubs and seems to be the worst product of a standardized civilization. But no one had more fun laughing at the American middle class than H. L. Mencken, who edited the *American Mercury* in Baltimore and denounced what he called the "booboisie." He labeled Woodrow Wilson a "self-bamboozled Presbyterian," and poked fun at Warren Harding's prose, which he said reminded him of "a string of wet sponges, . . . of stale bean soup, of college yells, of dogs barking idiotically through endless nights."

Ironically, while intellectuals despaired over American society and complained that art could not survive in a business-dominated civilization, literature flourished. The novels of Hemingway, Fitzgerald, Lewis, William Faulkner, and Gertrude Stein, the plays of Eugene O'Neill and Maxwell Anderson, the poetry of T. S. Eliot, Hart Crane, E. E. Cummings, and Marianne Moore, and the work of many black writers marked the 1920s as one of the most creative decades in American literature.

Women Struggle for Equality

Any mention of the role of women in the 1920s brings to mind the image of the flapper—a young woman with a short skirt, bobbed hair, and a boyish figure doing the Charleston, smoking, drinking, and being very casual about sex. F. Scott Fitzgerald's heroines in novels like *This Side of Paradise* (1920) and *The Great Gatsby* (1925) provided the role models for young people to imitate, and movie stars such as Clara Bow and Gloria Swanson, aggressively seductive on the screen, supplied even more dramatic examples of flirtatious and provocative behavior.

Without question, women acquired more sexual freedom in the 1920s. "None of the Victorian mothers had any idea how casually their daughters were accustomed to being kissed," F. Scott Fitzgerald wrote. However, it is difficult, if not impossible, to know how accustomed those daughters (and their mothers) were to kissing and enjoying other sexual activity. Contraceptives, especially the diaphragm, became more readily available during the decade, and Margaret Sanger, who had been indicted for sending birth control information through the mail in 1914, organized the first American birth control conference in 1921. Still, most states made the selling or prescribing of birth control devices illegal, and federal laws prohibited sending literature discussing birth control through the mail.

Family size declined during the decade (from 3.6 children in 1900 to 2.5 in 1930), and young people were apparently more inclined to marry for love than for security. More women expected sexual satisfaction in marriage (nearly 60 percent in one poll) and felt that divorce was the best solution for an unhappy marriage. Nearly 85 percent in another poll approved of sexual intercourse as an expression of love and affection and not simply for procreation. But the polls were hardly scientific and tended to be biased toward the attitudes of the urban middle class. Despite more freedom for women, the double standard persisted. "When lovely woman stoops to folly, she can always find someone to stoop with her," one male writer announced, "but not always someone to lift her up again to the level where she belongs."

Women's lives were shaped by other innovations of the 1920s. Electricity, running water, washing machines, vacuum cleaners, and other laborsaving devices made housework easier for the middle class. Yet these developments did not touch large numbers of rural and urban working-class women. Even middle-class women discovered that new appliances did not reduce time spent doing housework. Standards of cleanliness rose, and women were urged to make their houses more spotless than any nineteenth-century housekeeper would have felt necessary. At the same time, magazines and newspapers bombarded women with advertising urging them to buy products to make themselves better housekeepers, yet still beautiful. It must have been frustrating for those who could not afford the magic new products or whose hands and teeth and skin failed to look youthful despite all their efforts. The ads also promoted new dress styles, shorter skirts, no corsets. The young adopted them quickly, and they also learned to swim (and to display more of their bodies on the beach), to play tennis (but only if they belonged to a tennis club), and to ride a bicycle.

The revolution created by electricity remained out of reach for many rural and working-class women, who continued to use the scrub board rather than the washing machine.

More women worked outside the home. Whereas in 1890 only 17 percent of women were employed, by 1933 some 22 percent were. But their share of manufacturing jobs fell from 19 to 16 percent between 1900 and 1930. The greatest expansion of jobs was in white-collar occupations that were being feminized—secretary, bookkeeper, clerk, telephone operator. In 1930, fully 96 percent of stenographers were women. Although more married women had jobs (an increase of 25 percent during the decade), most of them held low-paying jobs, and most single women assumed that marriage would terminate their employment.

For some working women—secretaries and teachers, for example—marriage often led to dismissal. "A married woman's attitude toward men who come to the office is not the same as that of an unmarried woman," one employment agency decided. Married women are "very unstable in their work; their first claim is to home and children," concluded a businessman. Although women might not be able to work after their weddings (in one poll of college men, only one in nine said he would *allow* his wife to work after marriage), a job as a secretary could be good preparation for marriage. A business office was a good place to meet eligible men, but more than that, a secretary learned endurance, self-effacement, and obedience, traits that would make her a good wife. Considering these attitudes, it is not surprising that the disparity between male and female

Women in the Labor Force, 1900–1930

				Percent of Women in Labor Force		
Year	Women in Labor Force	Percent of Women in Total Labor Force	Women in Labor Force as Percent of Total Women of Working Age	Single	Married	Widowed or Divorced
1900	4,997,000	18.1	20.6	66.2	15.4	18.4
1910[a]	7,640,000	NA	25.4	60.2	24.7	15.0
1920	8,347,000	20.4	23.7	77.0[b]	23.0	—[b]
1930	10,632,000	21.9	24.8	53.9	28.9	17.2

[a]Data not comparable with other censuses due to a difference in the basis of enumeration.

[b]Single includes widowed and divorced.

Source: U.S. Bureau of the Census.

wages widened during the decade. By 1930, women earned only 57 percent of what men were paid.

The image of the flapper in the 1920s promised more freedom and equality for women than they actually achieved. The flapper was young, white, slender, and upper-class (Fitzgerald fixed her ideal age at 19), and most women did not fit those categories. The flapper was frivolous and daring, not professional and competent. Although the proportion of women lawyers and bankers increased slightly during the decade, the rate of growth declined, and the number of women doctors and scientists dropped. In the 1920s, women acquired some sexual freedom and a limited amount of opportunity outside the home, but the promise of the prewar feminist movement and the hopes that accompanied the suffrage amendment remained unfulfilled.

Although the flapper look of short skirts and bobbed hair appeared in the workplace in the 1920s, for most working women of the era, employed in low-paying jobs as file clerks, typists, and telephone operators, the flapper life style of freedom and equality was more illusion than reality.

Winning the vote for women did not assure equality. In most states, a woman's service belonged to her husband. Women could vote, but often they could not serve on juries. In some states, women could not hold office, own a business, or sign a contract without their husbands' permission. Women were usually held responsible for an illegitimate birth, and divorce laws almost always favored men. Many women leaders were disappointed in the small turnout of women in the presidential election of 1920. To educate women in the reality of politics, they organized the National League of Women Voters to "finish the fight." A nonpartisan organization, it became an important educational organization for middle-class women, but it did little to eliminate inequality.

Alice Paul, who had led the militant National Women's Party in 1916, chained herself to the White House fence once again to promote an equal rights amendment to the Constitution. The amendment got support in Wisconsin and several other states, but many women opposed it on the grounds that such an amendment would cancel the special legislation to protect women in industry that had taken so long to enact in the two decades before. Feminists disagreed in the 1930s on the proper way to promote equality and rights for women, but the political and social climate was not conducive to feminist causes.

Rural America in the 1920s

Most farmers did not share in the prosperity of the 1920s. Responding to worldwide demands and rising prices for wheat, cotton, and other products, many farmers invested in more land, tractors, and farm equipment during the war. Then prices tumbled. By 1921, the price of wheat had dropped 40 percent, corn 32 percent, and hogs 50 percent. Total farm income fell from $10 million to $4 million in the postwar depression. Many farmers could not make payments on their tractors. Because the value of land fell, they often lost both mortgage and land and still owed the bank money. One Iowa farmer remembered, "We gave the land back to the mortgage holder, and then we're sued for the remainder—the deficiency judgment—which we have to pay."

The changing nature of farming was part of the problem. The use of chemical fertilizers and new hybrid seeds, some developed by government experiment stations and land-grant colleges, increased the yield per acre. By 1930, some 920,000 tractors and 900,000 trucks were in use on American farms. They not only made farming more efficient, but they also released for cash crops land formerly used to raise feed for horses and mules. Production increased at the very time that worldwide demand for American farm products declined. The United States shipped abroad in 1929 only one-third the wheat it had exported in 1919, and only one-ninth the meat.

Not all farmers suffered. During the 1920s, the farming class separated into those who were getting by barely or not at all and those who earned large profits. Large commercial operations, using mechanized equipment, produced most of the cash crops. At the same time, many small farmers found themselves unable to compete with agribusiness. Some of them, along with many farm laborers, solved the problem of declining rural profitability by leaving the farms. In 1900, fully 40 percent of the labor force worked on farms; by 1930, only 21 percent earned their living from the land.

Few farmers could afford the products of the new technology. While many middle-class urban families were more prosperous than they had ever been, buying new cars, radios, and bathrooms, only one farm family in ten had electricity in the 1920s. The lot of the farm wife had not changed for centuries. She ran a domestic factory, did all the household chores, and helped on the farm as well. One farm woman on Maryland's Eastern Shore recalled that she heard a neighbor brag about making $1,000 on his cows.

> But I saw his wife pumping water for the cows to drink; she always went into the barn to help milk, washed the buckets, helped bottle the milk, and the little boy peddled it before school. The farmer made one thousand dollars, but he had not figured feed or help or interest; that was his "gross amount."

As they had done in the nineteenth century, farmers tried to act collectively. After the failure of the People's party in 1896, they gave up on direct political action but relied instead on influencing legislation in the state capital and in Washington. Most of their effort went into the McNary-Haugen Farm Relief Bill, which provided for government support for key agricultural products. The idea was for the government to buy wheat, cotton, and other crops at a "fair exchange value" and then market the excess on the world market at a lower price, thus isolating and protecting the American farmer from the worldwide swing in prices. The bill passed Congress in February 1927, only to be vetoed by President Coolidge. It passed again in revised form the next year, and again the president vetoed it. But farm organizations in all parts of the country learned how to cooperate and how to influence Congress. That would have important ramifications for the future.

The Workers' Share of Prosperity

Hundreds of thousands of workers improved their standard of living in the 1920s, yet inequality grew. Real wages increased 21 percent between 1923 and 1929, but corporate dividends went up by nearly two-thirds in the same period. The workers did not profit from the increased production they helped to create, and that boded ill for the future. The richest 5 percent of the population increased their share of the wealth from a quarter to a third, and the wealthiest one percent controlled a whopping 19 percent of all income.

Even among workers there was great disparity. Those employed on the auto assembly lines or in the new factories producing radios saw their wages go up, and many saw their hours decline. Yet the majority of American working-class families did not earn enough to move them much beyond the subsistence level. One study suggested that a family needed $2,000 to $2,400 in 1924 to maintain an "American standard of living." But in that year, 16 million families earned under $2,000. For the chambermaids in New York hotels who worked seven days a week or the itinerant Mexican migrant laborers in the Southwest, labor was so exhausting that at the end of the day, it was impossible to take advantage of new consumer products and modern life styles, even if they had the money.

While some workers prospered in the 1920s, organized labor fell on hard times. Labor union membership fell from about 5 million in 1921 to less than 3.5 million in 1929. Although a majority of American workers had never supported unions, unions now faced competition from employers' new policies. A number of large employers lured workers away from unions with promises that seemed to equal union benefits: profit-sharing plans, pensions, and their own company unions. The National Manufacturing Association and individual businesses carried on a vigorous campaign to restore the open shop. The leadership of the AFL became increasingly conservative during the decade and had little interest in launching movements to organize the large industries.

The more aggressive unions like the United Mine Workers, led by the flamboyant John L. Lewis, also encountered difficulties. The union's attempt to organize the mines in West Virginia had led to violent clashes between union members and imported guards. President Harding called out troops in 1921 to put down an "army organized by the strikers." The next year, Lewis called the greatest coal strike in history, and further violence erupted, especially in Williamson County, Illinois. Internal strife also weakened the union, and Lewis had to accept wage reductions in the negotiations of 1927.

Organized labor, like so many other groups, struggled desperately during the decade to take advantage of the prosperity. It won some victories, and it made some progress. But American affluence was beyond the reach of many groups during the decade. Eventually the inequality would lead to disaster.

The Business of Politics

"Among the nations of the earth today America stands for one idea: *Business,*" a popular writer announced in 1921. "Through business, properly conceived, managed and conducted, the human race is finally to be redeemed." Bruce Barton, the head of the largest advertising firm in the country, was the author of one of the most popular nonfiction books of the decade. In *The Man Nobody Knows* (1925), he depicted Christ as "the founder of modern business." He took 12 men from the bottom ranks of society and forged them into a successful organization. "All work is worship; all useful service prayer," Barton argued. If the businessman would just copy Christ, he could become a supersalesman.

Business, especially big business, prospered in the 1920s, and the image of businessmen, enhanced by their important role in World War I, rose further. The government reduced regulation, lowered taxes, and cooperated to aid business expansion at home and abroad. Business and politics, always intertwined, were especially allied during the decade. Wealthy financiers such as Andrew Mellon and Charles Dawes played important roles in formulating both domestic and foreign policy. Even more significant, a new kind of businessman was elected president in 1928. Herbert Hoover, international engineer and efficiency expert, was the very symbol of the modern techniques and practices that many people confidently expected to transform the United States and the world.

Harding and Coolidge

The Republicans, almost assured of victory in 1920 because of bitter reaction against Woodrow Wilson, might have preferred nominating their old standard-bearer, Theodore Roosevelt, but he had died the year before. Warren G. Harding, a former newspaper editor from Ohio, captured the nomination after meeting late at night with some of the party's most powerful men in a hotel room

Warren G. Harding (*left*) and Calvin Coolidge were immensely popular in the 1920s, but later historians have criticized them and rated them among the worst of American presidents.

in Chicago. What Harding promised no one ever discovered, but the meeting in the "smoke-filled room" became legendary. To balance the ticket, the Republicans chose as their vice-presidential candidate Calvin Coolidge of Massachusetts, who had gained attention by his firm stand during the Boston police strike. The Democrats seemed equally unimaginative. After 44 roll calls, they finally nominated Governor James Cox of Ohio and picked Franklin D. Roosevelt, a young politician from New York, as vice-president. Roosevelt had been the assistant secretary of the navy but otherwise had not distinguished himself.

Harding won in a landslide. His 60.4 percent of the vote was the widest margin yet recorded in a presidential election. More significant, less than 50 percent of the eligible voters went to the polls. The newly enfranchised women, especially in working-class neighborhoods, stayed away from the voting booths. So did large numbers of men. To many people, it did not seem to matter who was president.

In contrast to the reform-minded presidents Roosevelt and Wilson, Harding reflected the conservatism of the 1920s. He was a jovial man who brought many Ohio friends to Washington and placed them in positions of power. A visitor to the White House described Harding and his cohorts discussing the problems of the day, with "the air heavy with tobacco smoke, trays with bottles containing every imaginable brand of whiskey" near at hand. At a little house a few blocks from the White House on K Street, Harry Daugherty, Harding's attorney general and longtime associate, held forth with a group of friends. Amid bootleg liquor and the atmosphere of a brothel, they did a brisk business in selling favors, taking bribes, and organizing illegal schemes. Harding, however, was not personally corrupt, and the nation's leading businessmen approved of his policies of higher tariffs and lower taxes. Nor did he spend all his time drinking with his cronies. He called a conference on disarmament and another to deal with the problems of unemployment, and he pardoned Eugene Debs, who had been in prison since the war. Harding once remarked that he could never be considered one of the great presidents, but he thought perhaps he might be "one of the best loved." He was probably right. When he died suddenly in August 1923, the American people genuinely mourned him.

Only after Calvin Coolidge became president did the full extent of the corruption and scandals of the Harding administration come to light. A Senate committee discovered that the secretary of the interior, Albert Fall, had illegally leased government-owned oil reserves in the Teapot Dome section of Wyoming to private business interests in return for over $300,000 in bribes. Illegal activities were also discovered in the Veterans Administration and elsewhere in government. Harding's attorney general resigned in disgrace, the secretary of the navy barely avoided prison, two of Harding's advisers committed suicide, and the secretary of the interior was sentenced to jail.

Coolidge was dour and taciturn, but honest. No hint of scandal infected his administration or his personal life. Born in a little town in Vermont, he was sworn in as president by his father, a justice of the peace, in a ceremony conducted by the light of kerosene lamps at his ancestral home. To many, Coolidge represented old-fashioned rural values, simple religious faith, and personal integrity—a world fast disappearing in the 1920s. In reality, Coolidge was uncomfortable playing the rural yokel. He was ill at ease posing for photographers holding a pitchfork or sitting on a hay rig; he was much more comfortable around corporate executives.

Coolidge ran for reelection in 1924 with the financier Charles Dawes as his running mate. There was little question that he would win. The Democrats were so equally divided between northern urban Catholics and southern rural Protestants that it took 103 ballots before they nominated John Davis, an affable, corporate lawyer with little national following. A group of dissidents, mostly representing the farmers and the laborers dissatisfied with both nominees, formed a new Progressive party. They adopted the name, but little else, from Theodore Roosevelt's party of 1912. Nominating Robert La Follette of Wisconsin for president, they drafted a platform calling for government ownership of railroads and ratification of the child labor amendment. La Follette attacked the "control of government and industry by private monopoly." He received nearly 5 million votes, only 3.5 million short of Davis's total. But Coolidge and prosperity won easily.

Like Harding, Coolidge was a popular president. Symbolizing his administration was his wealthy secretary of the treasury, Andrew Mellon, who set out to lower individual and corporate taxes. In 1922, Congress, with Mellon's endorsement, repealed the wartime excess profits tax. Although it raised some taxes slightly, it exempted most families from any tax at all by giving everyone a $2,500 exemption, plus $400 for each dependent. In 1926, the rate was lowered to 5 percent and the maximum surtax to 40 percent. Only families with $3,500 income paid any taxes at all. In 1928, Congress reduced taxes further, removed most excise taxes, and lowered the corporate tax rate. The 200 largest corporations increased their assets during the decade from $43 billion to $81 billion.

"The chief business of the American people is business," Coolidge announced. "The man who builds a factory builds a temple. . . . The man who works there worships there." Coolidge's idea of the proper role of the federal government was to have as little as possible to do with the functioning of business and the lives of the people. Not everyone approved of his policies, or his personality. "No other president in my time slept so much," a White House usher remembered. But most Americans approved of his inactivity.

Herbert Hoover

One bright light in the lackluster Harding and Coolidge administrations was Herbert Hoover, who served as secretary of commerce under both presidents. Hoover had made a fortune as an international mining engineer before 1914 and then earned the reputation as a great humanitarian for his work managing the Belgian Relief Committee and directing the Food Administration. He was mentioned as a candidate for president in 1920, when he had the support of such progressives as Jane Addams, Louis Brandeis, and Walter Lippmann.

Hoover was a dynamo of energy and efficiency. He expanded his department to control and regulate the airlines, radio, and other new industries. By directing the Bureau of Standards to work with the trade associations and with individual businesses, Hoover managed to standardize the size of almost everything manufactured in the United States, from nuts and bolts and bottles to automobile tires, mattresses, and electric fixtures. He supported zoning codes, the eight-hour day in major industries, better nutrition for children, and the conservation of national resources. He pushed through the Pollution Act of 1924, the first attempt to control oil pollution along the American coastline.

While secretary of commerce, Hoover used the force of the federal government to regulate, stimulate, and promote, but he believed first of all in American free enterprise and local volunteer action to solve problems. In 1921, he convinced Harding of the need to do something about unemployment during the postwar recession. The president's conference on unemployment, convened in September 1921, marked the first time the national government had admitted any responsibility to the unemployed. The result of the conference (the first of many on a variety of topics that Hoover was to organize) was a flood of publicity, pamphlets, and advice from experts. Most of all, the conference urged state and local governments and businesses to cooperate on a volunteer basis to solve the problem. The primary responsibility of the federal government, Hoover believed, was to educate and promote. With all his activity and his organizing, Hoover got the reputation during the Harding and Coolidge years as an efficient and progressive administrator, and he became one of the most popular figures in government service.

Foreign Policy in the 1920s

The decade of the 1920s is often remembered as a time of isolation, when the United States rejected the League of Nations treaty and turned its back on the rest of the world. It is true that many Americans had little interest in what was going on in Paris, Moscow, or Rio de Janeiro, and it is also true that a bloc of congressmen was determined that the United States would never again enter another European war. But the United States remained involved—indeed, increased its involvement—in international affairs during the decade. Although the United States never joined the League of Nations, and a few dedicated isolationists, led by Senator William Borah, blocked membership in the World Court, the United States cooperated with many League agencies and conferences and took the lead in trying to reduce naval armaments and to solve the problems of international finance caused in part by the war.

Indeed, business, trade, and finance marked the decade as one of international expansion. With American corporate investments overseas growing sevenfold during the decade, the United States was transformed from a debtor to a creditor nation. The continued involvement of the United States in the affairs of South and Central American countries also indicated that the country had little interest in hiding behind its national boundaries. Yet the United States took up its role of international power reluctantly and with a number of contradictory and disastrous results.

"We seek no part in directing the destiny of the world," Harding announced in his inaugural address, but even Harding discovered that international problems would not disappear. One that required immediate attention was the naval arms race. Although moderates in Japan and Great Britain wanted to restrict the production of battleships, it was the United States, encouraged by men like William Borah, that took the lead and called the first international conference to discuss disarmament.

At the Washington Conference on Naval Disarmament, which convened in November 1921, Secretary of State Charles Evans Hughes startled the delegates by proposing a ten-year "holiday" on the construction of warships and by offering to sink or scrap 845,000 tons of American ships, including 30 battleships. He urged Britain and Japan to do the same. The delegates greeted Hughes's speech with enthusiastic cheering and applause, and they set about the task of sinking more ships than the admirals of all their countries had managed to do in a century.

The conference participants ultimately agreed to fix the tonnage of capital ships at a ratio of the United States and Great Britain, 5; Japan, 3; and France and Italy, 1.67. Japan agreed only reluctantly, but when the United States promised not to fortify its Pacific island possessions, the Japanese yielded. Retrospectively, in the light of what happened in 1941, the Washington Naval Conference has often been criticized, but in 1921 it was appropriately hailed as the first time in history that the major nations of the world had agreed to disarm. The conference did not cause World War II; neither, as it turned out, did it prevent it. But it was a creative beginning to reducing tensions and to meeting the challenges of the modern arms race. And it was the United States that took the lead by offering to be the first to scrap its battleships.

American foreign policy in the 1920s tried to reduce the risk of international conflict, resist revolution, and make the world safe for trade and investment. Nobody in the Republican administrations even suggested that the United States should remain isolated from Latin America. While American diplomats argued for an open door to trade in China, in Latin America the United States had always assumed a special and distinct role. Throughout the decade, American investment in agriculture, minerals, petroleum, and manufacturing increased in the countries to the south. The United States bought nearly 60 percent of Latin America's exports and sold the region nearly 50 percent of its imports. "We are seeking to establish a Pax Americana maintained not by arms but by mutual agreement and good will," Hughes maintained.

But the United States continued the process of intervention begun earlier. By the end of the decade, the United States controlled the financial affairs of ten Latin American nations. The marines were withdrawn from the Dominican Republic in 1924, but that country remained a virtual protectorate of the United States until 1941. The government ordered the marines from Nicaragua in 1925 but sent them back the next year when a liberal insurrection threatened the conservative government. But the American marines, and the Nicaraguan troops they had trained, had a difficult time containing a guerrilla band led by Augusto Sandino, a charismatic leader and one of Latin America's greatest heroes. The Sandinistas, supported by the great majority of peasants, came out of the hills to attack the politicians and their American supporters.

One American coffee planter decided in 1931 that the American intervention had been a disaster. "Today we are hated and despised," he announced. "This feeling has been created by employing American marines to hunt down and kill Nicaraguans in their own country." In 1934, Sandino was murdered by General Anastasio Somoza, a ruthless leader supported by the United States. For more than 40 years, Somoza and his two sons ruled Nicaragua as a private fiefdom, a legacy not yet resolved in that strife-torn country.

Mexico frightened American businessmen in the mid-1920s by beginning to nationalize foreign holdings in oil and mineral rights. Fearing that further military activity would "injure American interests," businessmen and bankers urged Coolidge not to send marines but to negotiate instead. Coolidge appointed Dwight W. Morrow of the J. P. Morgan Company as ambassador, and his conciliatory attitude led to agreements protecting American investments. Throughout the decade, the goal of U.S. policy toward Central and South America, whether in the form of negotiations or intervention, was to maintain a special sphere of influence.

The United States' policy of promoting peace, stability, and trade was not always consistent or carefully thought out, and this was especially true in its relationships with Europe. At the end of the war, European countries owed the United States over $10 billion, with Great Britain and France responsible for about three-fourths of that amount. Both countries, mired in postwar economic problems, suggested that the United States forgive the debts, arguing that they had paid for the war in lives and property destroyed. But the United States, although adjusting the interest and the payment schedule, refused to forget the debt. "They hired the money, didn't they?" Coolidge supposedly remarked.

But international debt was not the same as money borrowed at the neighborhood bank; it influenced trade and investment, which the United States wanted to promote. Practically the only way European nations could repay the United States was by exporting products, but in a series of tariff acts, especially the Fordney-McCumber Tariff of 1922, Congress erected a protective barrier to trade. This act also gave the president power to lower or raise individual rates; both Harding and Coolidge used the power, in almost every case, to raise them. Finally, in 1930, the Hawley-Smoot Tariff raised rates even further, despite the protests of many economists and 35 countries. American policy of high tariffs (a counterproductive policy for a creditor nation) caused retaliation and restrictions on American trade, which American corporations were trying to increase.

The inability of the European countries to export products to the United States and to repay their loans was intertwined with the reparation agreement made with Germany. Germany's economy was in disarray after the war, with inflation raging and its industrial plant throttled by the peace treaty. By 1921, Germany was defaulting on its payments. The United States, which believed a healthy Germany important to the stability of Europe and of world trade, instituted a plan engineered by Charles Dawes whereby the German debt would be renegotiated and spread over a longer period. In the meantime, American bankers and the American government lent Germany hundreds of millions of dollars. In the end, the United States lent money to Germany so it could make payments to Britain and France so that those countries could continue their payments to the United States.

The United States had replaced Great Britain as the dominant force in international finance, but the nation in the 1920s was a reluctant and inconsistent world leader. The United States had stayed out of the League of Nations and was hesitant to get involved in multinational agreements. However, some agreements seemed proper to sign, and the most idealistic of all was the Kellogg-Briand pact to outlaw war. The French foreign minister, Aristide Briand, suggested a treaty between the United States and France in large part to commemorate long years of friendship between the two countries, but Secretary of State Frank B. Kellogg in 1928 expanded the idea to a multinational treaty to outlaw war. Fourteen nations agreed to sign the treaty, and eventually 62 nations signed, but the only power behind the treaty was moral force rather than economic or military sanctions.

The Survival of Progressivism

The decade of the 1920s was a time of reaction against reform, but progressivism did not simply die. It survived in many forms through the period that Jane Addams called a time of "political and social sag." Progressives who sought efficiency and order were perhaps happier during the 1920s than those who tried to promote social justice, but even the fight against poverty and for better housing and the various campaigns to protect children persisted. In a sense, the reformers went underground, but they did not disappear or give up the fight. Child labor reformers worked through the Women's Trade Union League, the Consumers League, and other organizations to promote a child labor amendment to the Constitution after the 1919 law was declared unconstitutional in 1922.

The greatest success of the social justice movement was the 1921 Sheppard-Towner Maternity Act, one of the first pieces of federal social welfare legislation, the product of long progressive agitation. A study conducted by the Children's Bureau discovered that more than 3,000 mothers died in childbirth in 1918 and that more than 250,000 infants also died. The United States ranked eighteenth out of 20 countries in maternal mortality and eleventh in infant deaths. Josephine Baker, the pioneer physician and founder of the American Child Health Association, was not being ironic when she remarked, "It's six times safer to be a soldier in the trenches in France than to be born a baby in the United States."

The maternity bill called for a million dollars a year to assist the states in providing medical aid, consultation centers, and visiting nurses to teach expectant mothers how to care for themselves and their babies. The bill was controversial from the beginning. The American Medical Association, which had supported pure food and drug legislation and laws to protect against health quacks and to enforce standards for medical schools, attacked this bill as leading to socialism and interfering with the relationship between doctor and patient and with the "fee for service" system. Others, especially those who had opposed woman suffrage, argued that it was put forward by extreme feminists, that it was "inspired by foreign experiments in Communism and backed by radical forces in the country," that it "strikes at the heart of American Civilization," and that it would lead to socializing medicine and radicalizing the children.

Despite the opposition, the bill passed Congress and was signed by President Harding in 1921. The appropriation for the bill was only for six years, and the opposition, again raising the specter of a feminist-socialist-Communist plot, succeeded in repealing the law in 1929. Yet the Sheppard-Towner Act, promoted and fought for by a group of progressive women, indicated that concern for social justice was not dead in the age of Harding and Coolidge.

Temperance Triumphant

For one large group of progressives, prohibition, like child labor reform and maternity benefits, was an important effort to conserve human resources. At first, they argued for local option, whereby states, counties, or cities could decide whether or not to make the sale of alcohol illegal. Then, after 1939, they pressed for an amendment to the Constitution. The modern prohibition movement had more success than the earlier movement in translating the reformers' zeal into the passage of laws.

By 1918, over three-fourths of the people in the country lived in dry states or counties, but it was the war that allowed the antisaloon advocates to associate prohibition with patriotism. At first, the beer manufacturers supported limited prohibition, but in the end, patriotic fervor prohibited the sale of all alcoholic beverages, including beer and wine. "We have German enemies across the water," one prohibitionist announced. "We have German enemies in this country too. And the worst of all our German enemies, the most treacherous, the most menacing are Pabst, Schlitz, Blatz and Miller." In 1919, Congress passed the Volstead Act banning the brewing and selling of beverages containing more than one-half of one percent alcohol. The thirty-sixth state ratified the Eighteenth Amendment in June 1919, but the country had, for all practical purposes, been dry since 1917. One social worker confidently predicted that the Eighteenth Amendment would reduce poverty, nearly wipe out prostitution and crime, improve labor, and "substantially increase our national resources by setting free vast suppressed human potentialities."

The prohibition experiment probably did reduce the total consumption of alcohol in the country, especially in rural areas and urban working-class neighborhoods. Fewer arrests for drunkenness occurred, and deaths from alcoholism declined. But the legislation showed the difficulty of using law to promote moral reform. Most people who wanted to drink during the "noble experiment" found a way. Speakeasies replaced saloons, and people consumed bathtub gin, home brew, and many strange and dangerous concoctions. Bartenders invented the cocktail to disguise the poor quality of liquor, and women, at least middle- and upper-class women, began to drink in public for the first time. Prohibition also created great bootlegging rings, which were tied to organized crime in many cities. Al Capone of Chicago was the most famous underworld figure whose power and wealth were based on the sale of illegal alcohol. His organization alone is supposed to have grossed over $60 million in 1927; ironically, most of the profit came from distributing beer. Many supporters of prohibition slowly came to favor its repeal, some because it reduced the power of the states, others because it stimulated too much illegal activity and because it did not seem to be worth the social and political costs.

Herbert Hoover, one of the most popular politicians of the 1920s and one of the most unpopular after 1929, is seen here campaigning from the platform of his private railway car. Note the hats worn by all the men and the few women in the audience.

The Election of 1928

On August 2, 1927, President Coolidge announced simply, "I do not choose to run for President in 1928." Hoover immediately became the logical Republican candidate. Hoover and Coolidge were not especially close. Coolidge resented what he considered Hoover's spendthrift ways. "That man has offered me unsolicited advice for six years, all of it bad," Coolidge once remarked. Though lacking an enthusiastic endorsement from the president and opposed by some Republicans who thought him too progressive, Hoover easily won the nomination. In a year when the country was buoyant with optimism and when prosperity seemed as if it would go on forever, few doubted that Hoover would be elected.

The Democrats nominated Alfred Smith, a Catholic Irish-American from New York. With his New York accent, his opposition to prohibition,

Presidential Elections, 1920–1928

Year	Candidates	Party	Popular Vote	Electoral Vote
1920	WARREN G. HARDING	Republican	16,152,200 (60.4%)	404
	James M. Cox	Democratic	9,147,353 (34.2%)	127
	Eugene V. Debs	Socialist	919,799 (3.4%)	0
1924	CALVIN COOLIDGE	Republican	15,725,016 (54.0%)	382
	John W. Davis	Democratic	8,385,586 (28.8%)	136
	Robert M. La Follette	Progressive	4,822,856 (16.6%)	13
1928	HERBERT C. HOOVER	Republican	21,392,190 (58.2%)	444
	Alfred E. Smith	Democratic	15,016,443 (40.9%)	87

Note: Winners' names appear in capital letters.

and his flamboyant style, he contrasted sharply with the more sedate Hoover. On one level, it was a bitter contest between Catholic "wets" and Protestant "drys," between the urban, ethnic Tammany politician and former governor of New York against the rural-born but sophisticated secretary of commerce. Racial and religious prejudice played a role in this campaign, as it had in others. But looked at more closely, the two candidates differed little. Both were self-made men, both were "progressives." Social justice reformers campaigned for each candidate. Both candidates tried to attract women voters, both were favorable to organized labor, both defended capitalism, and both had millionaires and corporate executives among their advisers.

Hoover won in a landslide, 444 electoral votes to 76 for Smith, who carried only Massachusetts and Rhode Island outside the Deep South. But the 1928 campaign revitalized the Democratic party. Smith polled nearly twice as many votes as the Democratic candidate in 1924, and for the first time the Democrats carried the 12 largest cities.

Stock Market Crash

Hoover, as it turned out, had only six months to apply his progressive and efficient methods to running the country because in the fall of 1929, the prosperity that seemed endless suddenly came to a halt. In 1928 and 1929, rampant speculation made the stock market boom. Money could be made everywhere—in real estate and business ventures, but especially in the stock market. "Everybody ought to be Rich," Al Smith's campaign manager argued in an article in the *Ladies' Home Journal* early in 1929. Just save $15 a month and buy good common stock with it, and that money would turn into $80,000 in 20 years (a considerable fortune in 1929). Good common stock seemed to be easy to find in 1929.

John Jacob Raskob

Only a small percentage of the American people invested in the stock market, for many had no way of saving even $15 a month. But a large number got into the game in the late 1920s because it seemed a safe and sure way to make money. For many, the stock market came to represent the American economy, and the economy was booming. The New York Times index of 25 industrial stocks reached 100 in 1924, moved up to 181 in 1925, dropped a bit in 1926, and rose again to 245 by the end of 1927.

Then the orgy started. During 1928, the market rose to 331. Many investors and speculators began to buy on margin (borrowing in order to invest). Businessmen and others began to invest money in the market that would ordinarily have gone into houses, cars, and other goods. Yet even at the peak of the boom, probably only about 1.5 million Americans owned stock.

In early September 1929, the New York Times index peaked at 452 and then began to drift downward. On October 23, the market lost 31 points. The next day ("Black Thursday"), it first seemed that everyone was trying to sell, but at the end of the day the panic appeared over. It was not. By mid-November, the market had plummeted to 224, about half what it had been two months before. This represented a loss on paper of over $26 billion. Still, a month later, the chairman of the board of Bethlehem Steel could announce, "Never before has American business been as firmly entrenched for prosperity as it is today." Some businessmen even got back into the market, thinking that it had reached its low point. But it continued to go down. Tens of thousands of investors lost everything. Those who had bought on margin had to keep coming up with money to pay off their loans as the value of their holdings declined. There was panic and despair, but the legendary stories of executives jumping out of windows were grossly exaggerated.

CONCLUSION

A New Era of Prosperity and Problems

The stock market crash ended the decade of prosperity. The crash did not cause the Depression, but the stock market debacle revealed the weakness of the economy. The fruits of economic expansion had been unevenly distributed. Not enough people could afford to buy the autos, refrigerators, and other products pouring from American factories. Prosperity had been built on a shaky foundation. When that foundation crumbled in 1929, the nation slid into a major depression.

Looking back from the vantage point of the 1930s or later, the 1920s seemed a golden era—an age of flappers, bootleg gin, constant parties, literary masterpieces, sports heroes, and easy wealth. The truth is much more complicated. More than most decades, the 1920s was a time of paradox and contradictions.

The 1920s was a time of prosperity, yet a great many people, including farmers, blacks, and other ordinary Americans, did not prosper. It was a time of modernization, but only about 10 percent of rural families had electricity. It was a time when women achieved more sexual freedom, but the feminist movement declined. It was a time of prohibition, but many Americans increased their consumption of alcohol. It was a time of reaction against reform, yet progressivism survived. It was a time when intellectuals felt disillusioned with America, yet it was one of the most creative and innovative periods for American writers. It was a time of flamboyant heroes, yet the American people elected the lackluster Harding and Coolidge as their presidents. It was a time of progress, when almost every year saw a new technological breakthrough, but it was also a decade of hate and intolerance. The complex and contradictory legacy of the 1920s continues to fascinate and to influence our time.

Recommended Reading

General References

Frederick Lewis Allen, *Only Yesterday* (1931); William E. Leuchtenburg, *The Perils of Prosperity, 1914–1932* (1970); Paul Carter, *Another Part of the Twenties* (1977).

Politics and Economics

John D. Hicks, *Republican Ascendancy, 1921–1933* (1960); George Soule, *Prosperity Decade: From War to Depression* (1947); John Kenneth Galbraith, *The Great Crash, 1929* (1954); Andrew Sinclair, *The Available Man* (1965); Donald R. McCoy, *Calvin Coolidge* (1967); Oscar Handlin, *Al Smith and His America* (1958); Joan Hoff Wilson, *Herbert Hoover: The Forgotten Progressive* (1975).

Society and Culture

Robert K. Murray, *Red Scare* (1955); Frederick Hoffman, *The Twenties: American Writing in the Postwar Decade* (1955); Nathan Huggins, *Harlem Renaissance* (1971); Houston A. Baker, Jr., *Modernism and the Harlem Renaissance* (1987); George M. Marsden, *Fundamentalism and American Culture* (1980); David M. Chalmers, *Hooded Americanism: The History of the Ku Klux Klan* (1965); John Higham, *Strangers in the Land: Patterns of American Nativism, 1860–1925* (1955); Sarah Deutsch, *No Separate Refuge* (1987); Paula Fass, *The Damned and Beautiful: American Youth in the 1920s* (1977); Robert Sklar, *Movie Made America* (1975); James J. Flink, *The Car Culture* (1975); Roland Marchand, *Advertising the American Dream* (1985); William H. Chafe, *The American Woman: Her Changing Social and Economic Roles, 1920–1970* (1972); Nancy F. Cott, *The Grounding of Modern Feminism* (1987); J. Stanley Lemons, *The Woman Citizen* (1972); Ruth Schwartz, *More Work for Mother* (1983); Margaret Marsh, *Suburban Lives* (1990); Lizabeth Cohen, *Making a New Deal: Industrial Workers in Chicago, 1919–1939* (1990).

Fiction

Ernest Hemingway's novel *The Sun Also Rises* (1926) is a classic tale of disillusionment and despair in the 1920s; F. Scott Fitzgerald gives a picture of the life of the rich in *The Great Gatsby* (1925); and Claude McKay's novel *Home to Harlem* (1928) is one of the best to come out of the Harlem Renaissance.

TIMELINE

1900–1930 Electricity powers the "second industrial revolution"

1917 Race riot in East St. Louis, Illinois

1918 World War I ends

1919 Treaty of Versailles
Strikes in Seattle, Boston, and elsewhere
Red Scare and Palmer raids
Race riots in Chicago and other cities
Marcus Garvey's Universal Negro Improvement Association spreads

1920 Warren Harding elected president
Women vote in national elections
First commercial radio broadcast
Sacco and Vanzetti arrested
Sinclair Lewis, *Main Street*

1921 Immigration Quota Law
Disarmament Conference
First birth control conference
Sheppard-Towner Maternity Act

1921–1922 Postwar depression

1922 Fordney-McCumber Tariff
Sinclair Lewis, *Babbitt*

1923 Harding dies; Coolidge becomes president
Teapot Dome scandal

1924 Coolidge reelected president
Peak of Ku Klux Klan activity
Immigration Quota Law

1925 Scopes trial in Dayton, Tennessee
F. Scott Fitzgerald, *The Great Gatsby*
Bruce Barton, *The Man Nobody Knows*
Alain Locke, *The New Negro*
Claude McKay, *Home to Harlem*
5 million enameled bathroom fixtures produced

1926 Ernest Hemingway, *The Sun Also Rises*

1927 National Origins Act
McNary-Haugen Farm Relief bill
Sacco and Vanzetti executed
Lindbergh flies solo, New York to Paris
First talking movie, *The Jazz Singer*
Henry Ford produces 15 millionth car

1928 Herbert Hoover elected president
Kellogg-Briand Treaty
Stock market soars

1929 27 million registered cars in country
10 million households own radios
100 million people attend movies
Stock market crash

CHAPTER 24

The Great Depression and the New Deal

Diana Morgan grew up in a small North Carolina town, the daughter of a prosperous cotton merchant. She lived the life of a "southern belle," oblivious to the country's social and political problems, but the Depression changed that. She came home from college for Christmas vacation during her junior year to discover that the telephone had been disconnected. Her world suddenly fell apart. Her father's business had

IF·WE·WOULD·GUIDE·BY·THE
LIGHT·OF·REASON·WE·MUST

failed, her family didn't have a cook or a cleaning woman anymore, and their house was being sold for back taxes. She was confused and embarrassed. Sometimes it was the little things that were the hardest. Friends would come from out of town, and there would be no ice because her family did not own an electric refrigerator and they could not afford to buy ice. "There were those frantic arrangements of running out to the drug store to get Coca-Cola with crushed ice, and there'd be this embarrassing delay, and I can remember how hot my face was."

Like many Americans, Diana Morgan and her family blamed themselves for what happened during the Depression. Americans had been taught to believe that if they worked hard, saved their money, and lived upright and moral lives, they could succeed. Success was an individual matter for Americans. When so many failed during the Depression, they blamed themselves rather than society or larger forces for their plight. The shame and the guilt affected people at all levels of society. The businessman who lost his business, the farmer who watched his farm being sold at auction, the worker who was suddenly unemployed and felt his manhood stripped away because he could not provide for his family were all devastated by the Depression.

Diana Morgan had never intended to get a job; she expected to get married and let her husband support her. But the failure of her father's business forced her to join the growing number of women who worked outside the home in the 1930s. She finally found a position with the Civil Works Administration, a New Deal agency, where at first she had to ask humiliating questions of the people applying for assistance to make sure they were destitute. "Do you own a car?" "Does anyone in the family work?" Diana was appalled at the conditions she saw when she traveled around the county to corroborate their stories. She found dilapidated houses, a dirty, "almost paralyzed-looking mother," and a drunken father, together with malnourished children. She felt helpless that she could do nothing more than write out a food order. One day, a woman who had formerly cooked for her family came in to apply for help. Each was embarrassed to see the other in changed circumstances.

She had to defend the New Deal programs to many of her friends, who accused her of being sentimental and told her that the poor, especially poor blacks, did not know any better than to live in squalor. "If you give them coal, they'd put it in the bathtub," was a charge she often heard. But she knew "they didn't have bathtubs to put coal in. So how did anybody know that's what they'd do with coal if they had it?"

Diana Morgan's experience working for a New Deal agency influenced her life and her attitudes; it made her more of a social activist. Her Depression experience gave her a greater appreciation for the struggles of the country's poor and unlucky. Although she prospered in the years after the Depression, the sense of guilt and the fear that the telephone might again be cut off never left her.

The Great Depression changed the lives of all Americans and separated that generation from the one that followed. An exaggerated need for security, the fear of failure, a nagging sense of guilt, and a real sense that it might happen all over again divided the Depression generation from everyone born after 1940. Like Diana Morgan, most Americans never forgot those bleak years.

The Depression dominated the decade of the 1930s, and despite imaginative efforts and massive spending by Franklin Roosevelt's New Deal, not until the mobilization for World War II did the economic downturn end. Yet the legislation passed during Roosevelt's presidency had a far-reaching impact on American life. Roosevelt was an immensely popular, though controversial, president. He strengthened the role of the executive branch of the government, influenced political alignments, and defined the agenda for political debate for the next two generations.

The New Deal was not a radical movement; in fact, many have argued that it helped to preserve corporate capitalism. Yet the New Deal did establish a minimum welfare state, as the government accepted limited responsibility to manage the economy, subsidize farmers, and promote social insurance and minimum wage laws. Greater government involvement in the social welfare of the country had important consequences for the American people and nation.

This chapter explores the causes and consequences of the Great Depression. We will look at Herbert Hoover and his efforts to combat the Depression and then turn to Franklin Roosevelt, the dominant personality of the 1930s. We will examine the New Deal and Roosevelt's program to bring relief, recovery, and reform to the nation. But we will not ignore the other side of the 1930s, for the decade did not consist only of crippling unemployment and New Deal agencies. It was also a time of great strides in technology, when innovative developments in radio, movies, and the automobile affected the lives of most Americans.

The Great Depression

There had been recessions and depressions in American history, notably in the 1830s, 1870s, and 1890s, but nothing compared to the devastating economic collapse of the 1930s. The Great Depression was all the more shocking because it came after a decade of unprecedented prosperity, when most experts assumed that the United States was immune to a downturn in the business cycle. The Great Depression had an impact on all areas of American life; perhaps most important, it destroyed American confidence in the future.

The Depression Begins

Few people anticipated the stock market crash in the fall of 1929. But even after the collapse of the stock market, few expected the entire economy to go into a tailspin. General Electric stock, selling for 396 in 1929, fell to 34 in 1932; U.S. Steel declined from 261 to 21. By 1932, the median income had plunged to half what it had been in 1929. Construction spending fell to one-sixth of the 1929 level. By 1932, at least one of every four American breadwinners was out of work, and industrial production had almost ground to a halt.

Why did the nation sink deeper and deeper into depression? After all, only about 2 percent of the population owned stock of any kind. The answer is complex, but the prosperity of the 1920s, it appears in retrospect, was superficial. Farmers and coal and textile workers had suffered all through the 1920s from low prices, and the farmers were the first group in the 1930s to plunge into depression. But other aspects of the economy also lurched out of balance. Two percent of the population received about 28 percent of the national income, while the lower 60 percent got only 24 percent. Businesses increased profits while holding down wages and the prices of raw materials. This pattern depressed consumer purchasing power. American workers, like American farmers, did not have the money to buy the goods they helped to produce. There was a relative decline in purchasing power in the late 1920s, unemployment was high in some industries, and the housing and automobile industries were already beginning to slacken before the crash.

Well-to-do Americans were speculating a significant portion of their money in the stock market. Their illusion of permanent prosperity helped fire the boom of the 1920s, just as their pessimism and lack of confidence helped exaggerate the depression in 1931 and 1932.

Other factors were also involved. The stock market crash revealed serious structural weaknesses in the financial and banking systems (7,000 banks had failed during the 1920s). The Federal Reserve Board, fearing inflation, tightened credit—exactly the opposite of the action they should have taken to fight a slowdown in purchasing. Economic relations with Europe contributed to deepening depression. High American tariffs during the 1920s had reduced trade. When American investment in Europe declined in 1928 and 1929, European economies declined. As the European financial situation worsened, the American economy spiraled downward.

The federal government might have prevented the stock market crash and the Depression by more careful regulation of business and the stock market. More central planning might have assured a more equitable distribution of income. But that kind of policy would have taken more foresight than most people had in the 1920s. It certainly would have required different people in power, and it is unlikely that the Democrats, had they been in control, would have altered the government's policies in fundamental ways.

Hoover and the Depression

Initial business and government reactions to the stock market crash were optimistic. "All the evidence indicates that the worst effects of the crash upon unemployment will have been passed during the next sixty days," Herbert Hoover reported. Hoover, the great planner and progressive efficiency expert, did not sit idly by and watch the country drift toward disorder. His upbeat first statements were calculated to prevent further panic.

The Agricultural Marketing Act of 1929 set up a $500 million revolving fund to help farmers organize cooperative marketing associations and to establish minimum prices. But as agricultural prices plummeted and banks foreclosed on farm mortgages, the available funds proved inadequate. The Farm Board was helpless to aid the

To provide some relief from the deepening Depression, President Hoover urged Congress to adopt some federal public works projects, among them construction of a dam on the Colorado River in Nevada and Arizona. Hoover Dam, completed in 1936, created Lake Mead, the world's largest reservoir, with a capacity of more than 10 trillion gallons of water.

farmer who could not meet mortgage payments because the price of grain had fallen so rapidly. Nor could it help the Arkansas woman who stood weeping in the window as her possessions, including the cows, which all had names, were sold one by one.

Hoover acted aggressively to stem the economic collapse. More than any president before him, he used the power of the federal government and the office of the president to deal with an economic crisis. Nobody called it a depression for the first year at least, for the economic problems seemed very much like earlier cyclic recessions. Hoover called conferences of businessmen and labor leaders. He met with mayors and governors and encouraged them to speed up public works projects. He created agencies and boards, such as the National Credit Corporation and the Emergency Committee for Employment, to obtain voluntary action to solve the problem. Hoover even supported a tax cut, which Congress enacted in December 1929, but it did little to stimulate spending. Hoover also went on the radio in his effort to convince the American people that the fundamental structure of the economy was sound.

Unemployment Rate, 1929–1940

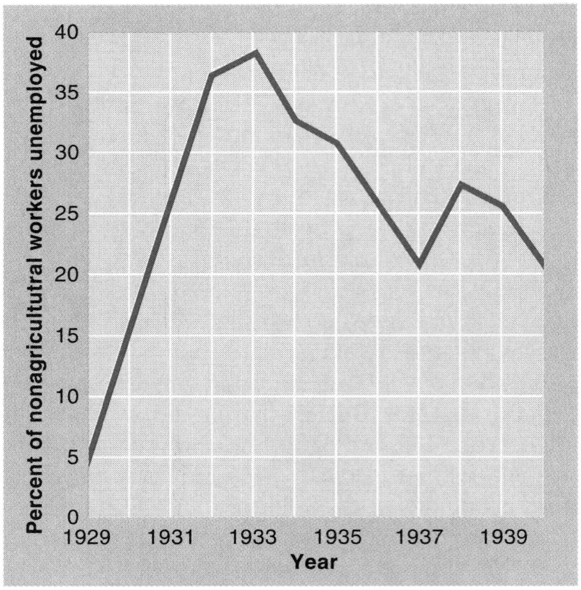

Although the unemployment rate declined during the New Deal years, the number still unemployed remained tragically high until World War II brought full employment.

Source: U.S. Bureau of the Census.

The Collapsing Economy

Voluntary action and psychological campaigns could not stop the Depression. The stock market, after appearing to bottom out in the winter of 1930–1931, continued its decline, responding in part to the European economic collapse that threatened international finance and trade. Of course, not everyone lost money in the market. William Danforth, founder of Ralston Purina, and Joseph Kennedy, film magnate, entrepreneur, and the father of a future president, were among those who made millions of dollars by selling short as the market went down.

But more than a collapsing market afflicted the economy. Over 1,300 additional banks failed in 1930. Despite Hoover's pleas, many factories cut back on production, and some simply closed. U.S. Steel announced a 10 percent wage cut in 1931. As the auto industry laid off workers, the unemployment rate rose to over 40 percent in Detroit. More than 4 million Americans were out of work in 1930, and at least 12 million by 1932. Foreclosures and evictions created thousands of personal tragedies. There were 200,000 evictions in New York City alone in 1930. While the middle class watched in horror as their life savings and their dreams disappeared, the rich were increasingly concerned as the price of government bonds (the symbol of safety and security) dropped. They began to hoard gold and to fear revolution.

There was never any real danger of revolution. Some farmers organized to dump their milk to protest low prices, and when a neighbor's farm was sold, they gathered to hold a penny auction, bidding only a few cents for equipment and returning it to their dispossessed neighbor. But everywhere people despaired as the Depression deepened in 1931 and 1932. For unemployed blacks and for many tenant farmers, the Depression had little immediate effect because their lives were already so depressed. Most Americans (the 98 percent who did not own stock) hardly noticed the stock market crash; for them, the Depression meant the loss of a job or a bank foreclosure. For Diana Morgan, it was the discovery that the telephone had been cut off; for some farmers, it was burning corn rather than coal because the price of corn had fallen so low that it was not worth marketing.

For some in the cities, the Depression meant not having enough money to feed the children. "Have you ever heard a hungry child cry?" asked Lillian Wald of the Henry Street Settlement. "Have you seen the uncontrollable trembling of parents who have gone half starved for weeks so that the children may have food?" In Chicago, children fought with men and women over the garbage dumped by the city trucks. "We have been eating wild greens," a coal miner wrote from Harlan County, Kentucky, "such as Polk salad, violet tops, wild onions . . . and such weeds as cows eat." In Toledo, when municipal and private charity funds were running low, as they did in all cities, those granted assistance were given only 2.14 cents per meal per person. In another city, a social worker noticed that the children were playing a game called "Eviction." "Sometimes they play 'Relief,' " she remarked, "but 'Eviction' has more action and all of them know how to play."

Not everyone went hungry, stood in bread lines, or lost jobs during the Depression, but almost everyone was affected, and many victims tended to blame themselves. A businessman who lost his job and had to stand in a relief line remembered years later how he would bend his head low so nobody would recognize him. A 28-year-old teacher in New Orleans was released because of a cut in funds, and in desperation she took a job as a domestic servant. "If with all the advantages I've had," she remarked, "I can't make a living, I'm just no good, I guess. I've given up ever amounting to anything. It's no use."

The Depression probably disrupted women's lives less than men's. "When hard times hit, it didn't seem to bother mother as much as it did father," one woman remembered. There were many exceptions, of course, but when men lost their jobs, their identity and sense of purpose as the family breadwinner were shattered. Some helped out with family chores, usually with bitterness and resentment. For women, however, even when money was short, there was still cooking, cleaning, and mending, and women were still in command of their households. Yet many women were forced to do extra work. They took in laundry, found room for a boarder, and made the clothes they formerly would have bought. Women also bore the psychological burden of unemployed

The worst result of the Depression was hopelessness and despair. Those emotions are captured in this painting of an unemployment office by Isaac Soyer.

husbands, hungry children, and unpaid bills. The Depression altered patterns of family life, and many families were forced to move in with relatives. The marriage rate, the divorce rate, and the birthrate all dropped during the decade. Many of these changes created tension that statistics cannot capture.

Hoover reacted to growing despair by urging more voluntary action. "We are going through a period," he announced in February 1931, "when character and courage are on trial, and where the very faith that is within us is under test." He insisted on maintaining the gold standard, believing it to be the only responsible currency, and a balanced budget, but so did almost everyone else. Congress was nearly unanimous in supporting those ideals, and Governor Franklin Roosevelt of New York accused Hoover of endangering the country by spending too much. Hoover increasingly blamed the Depression on international economic problems, and he was not entirely mistaken. The whole world was gripped by depression, but as it deepened, Americans began to blame Hoover for some of the disaster. The president became isolated and bitter. The shanties that grew near all the large cities were called "Hoovervilles," and the privies "Hoover villas." Unable to admit mistakes and to take a new tack, he could not communicate personal empathy for the poor and the unemployed.

Hoover did try innovative schemes. More public works projects were built during his administration than in the previous 30 years. In the summer of 1931, he attempted to organize a pool of private money to rescue banks and businesses that were near failure. When the private effort failed, he turned reluctantly to Congress, which passed a bill early in 1932 authorizing the Reconstruction Finance Corporation. The RFC was capitalized at $500 million, but a short time later that was increased to $3 billion. It was authorized to make loans to banks, insurance companies, farm mortgage companies, and railroads. Some critics charged that it was simply another trickle-down measure whereby businessmen and bankers would be given aid while the unemployed were ignored. Hoover, however, correctly understood the immense costs to individuals and to communities when a bank or mortgage company failed. The RFC did help shore up a number of shaky financial institutions and remained the major government finance agency until World War II. But it became much more effective under Roosevelt because it lent directly to industry.

Hoover also asked Congress for a Home Financing Corporation to make mortgages more readily available. The Federal Home Loan Bank Act of 1932 became the basis for the Federal Housing Administration of the New Deal years. He also pushed the passage of the Glass-Steagall Banking Act of 1932, which expanded credit in order to make more loans available to businesses and individuals. Hoover failed to suggest any new farm legislation, even though members of the Farm Board insisted that the only answer to the agricultural crisis was for the federal government to step in and restrict production. Hoover believed that was too much federal intervention. He maintained that the federal government should promote cooperation and even create public works. But he firmly believed in loans, not direct subsidies, and he thought it was the responsibility of state and local governments, as well as of private charity, to provide direct relief to the unemployed and the needy.

The Bonus Army

Many World War I veterans lost their jobs during the Depression, and beginning in 1930, they lobbied for the payment of their veterans' bonuses, not due until 1945. A bill passed Congress in 1931, over Hoover's veto, allowing them to borrow up to 50 percent of the bonus due them, but this concession did not satisfy the destitute veterans. In May 1932, about 17,000 veterans marched on Washington. Some took up residence in a shantytown, called Bonus City, in the Anacostia flats outside the city.

In mid-June, the Senate defeated the bonus bill, and most of the veterans, disappointed but resigned, accepted a free railroad ticket home. Several thousand remained, however, along with some wives and children, in the unsanitary shacks during the steaming summer heat. Among them were a small group of committed Communists and other radicals. Hoover, who exaggerated the subversive elements among those still camped out in Washington, refused to talk to the leaders, and finally called out the U.S. Army.

General Douglas MacArthur, the army chief of staff, ordered the army to disperse the veterans. He described the Bonus marchers as a "mob . . . animated by the essence of revolution." With tanks, guns, and tear gas, the army routed veterans who 15 years before had worn the same uniform as their attackers. Two Bonus marchers were killed, and several others were injured. "What a pitiful spectacle is that of the great American Government, mightiest in the world, chasing unarmed men, women and children with Army tanks," commented a Washington newspaper. "If the Army must be called out to make war on unarmed citizens, this is no longer America." The army was not attacking revolutionaries in the streets of Washington but was routing bewildered, confused, unemployed men who had seen their American dream collapse.

The Bonus army fiasco, bread lines, and Hoovervilles became the symbols of Hoover's presidency. He deserved better because he tried to use the power of the federal government to solve growing and increasingly complex economic problems. But in the end, his personality and background limited him. He could not understand why army veterans marched on Washington to ask for a handout when he thought they should all be back home working hard, practicing self-reliance, and cooperating "to avert the terrible situation in which we are today." He believed that the greatest problem besetting Americans was a lack of confidence. He could not communicate with these people or inspire their confidence. Willing to use the federal government to support business, he could not accept federal aid for the unemployed. He feared an unbalanced budget and a large federal bureaucracy that would interfere with the "American way." Ironically, his actions and his inactions led in the next years to a massive increase in federal power and in the federal bureaucracy.

Roosevelt and the First New Deal

The first New Deal, lasting from 1933 to early 1935, focused mainly on recovery from the Depression and relief for the poor and unemployed. Congress passed legislation to aid business, the farmers, and labor and authorized public works projects and massive spending to put Americans back to work. Some of the programs were borrowed from the Hoover administration, and some had their origin in the progressive period. Others were inspired by the nation's experiences in mobilizing for World War I. No single ideological position united all the programs, for Roosevelt was a pragmatist who was willing to try a variety of programs. More than Hoover, however, he believed in economic planning and in government spending to help the poor.

U.S. soldiers burn the Bonus army shacks within sight of the Capitol in the summer of 1932. This image of the failure of the American dream was published widely around the world.

Although confined to a wheelchair, Franklin Roosevelt gave the impression of health, vigor, and vitality. His advisors carefully arranged to have the president photographed only when he was seated or propped up behind a podium. In this 1932 photograph, taken while the president was en route to Wheeling, West Virginia, FDR shakes hands with a miner.

Roosevelt's caution and conservatism shaped the first New Deal. He did not promote socialism or suggest nationalizing the banks. He was even careful in authorizing public works projects to stimulate the economy. The New Deal was based on the assumption that it was possible to create a just society by superimposing a welfare state on the capitalistic system, leaving the profit motive undisturbed. During the first New Deal, Roosevelt believed he would achieve his goals through cooperation with the business community. Later he would move more toward reform, but at first his primary concern was simply relief and recovery.

The Republicans nominated Herbert Hoover for a second term, but in the summer of 1932, the Depression and Hoover's unpopularity opened the way for the Democrats. After a shrewd campaign, Franklin D. Roosevelt, governor of New York, emerged from the pack and won the nomination. Journalist Walter Lippmann's comment during the campaign that Roosevelt was a "pleasant man who, without any important qualifications for office, would like very much to be President" was exaggerated at the time and seemed absurd later. Roosevelt, distantly related to Theodore Roosevelt, had served as an assistant secretary of the navy during World War I and had been the Democratic vice-presidential candidate in 1920. Crippled by infantile paralysis not long after, he had recovered enough to serve as governor of New York for two terms, though he was not especially well known by the general public in 1932.

Governor Roosevelt had promoted cheaper electric power, conservation, and old-age pensions. Urged on by advisers Frances Perkins and Harry Hopkins, he became the first governor to support state aid for the unemployed, "not as a matter of charity, but as a matter of social duty." But it was difficult to tell during the presidential campaign exactly what he stood for. He did announce that the government must do something for the "forgotten man at the bottom of the economic pyramid," and he struck out at the small group of men who "make huge profits from lending money and the marketing of securities." Yet he also mentioned the need for balancing the budget and maintaining the gold standard. Ambiguity was probably the best strategy in 1932, but the truth was that Roosevelt did not have a master plan to save the country. Yet he won overwhelmingly, carrying more than 57 percent of the popular vote.

During the campaign, Roosevelt had promised a "new deal for the American people." But after his victory, the New Deal had to wait for four months because the Constitution provided that the new president be inaugurated on March 4 (this was changed to January 20 by the Twentieth Amendment, ratified in 1933). During the long interregnum, the state of the nation deteriorated badly. The banking system seemed near collapse, and the hardship increased. Despite his bitter defeat, Hoover tried to cooperate with the president-elect and with a hostile Congress. But he could accomplish little. Everyone waited for the new president to take office and to act.

In his inaugural address, Roosevelt announced confidently, "The only thing we have to fear is fear itself." This, of course, was not true, for the country faced the worst crisis since the Civil War, but Roosevelt's confidence and his ability to communicate with ordinary Americans were obvious early in his presidency. He had clever speech writers, a sense of pace and rhythm in his speeches, and an ability, when he spoke on the radio, to convince listeners that he was speaking directly to them. He instituted a series of radio "fireside chats" to explain to the American people what he was doing to solve the nation's problems. When he said "my friends," millions believed that

The Presidential Election of 1932

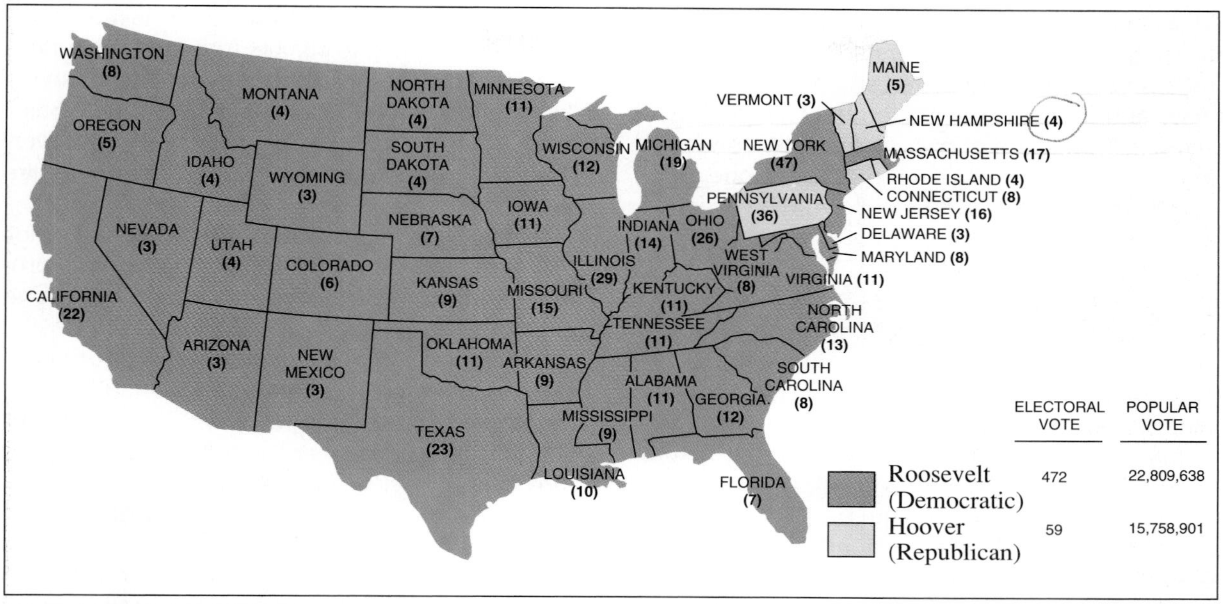

This map demonstrates the overwhelming extent of Roosevelt's landslide victory, caused largely by the economic situation.

he meant it, and they wrote letters to him in unprecedented numbers to explain their needs.

During the interregnum, Roosevelt surrounded himself with intelligent and innovative advisers. Some, like James A. Farley, a former New York State boxing commissioner with a genius for remembering names, and Louis Howe, Roosevelt's secretary and confidant since 1912, had helped plan his successful campaign. His cabinet was made up of a mixture of people from different backgrounds who often did not agree with one another. Harold Ickes, the secretary of the interior, was a Republican lawyer from Chicago and onetime supporter of Theodore Roosevelt. Another Republican, Henry Wallace of Iowa, a plant geneticist and agricultural statistician, became the secretary of agriculture. Frances Perkins, the first woman ever appointed to a cabinet post, became the secretary of labor. A disciple of Jane Addams and Florence Kelley, she had been a settlement resident, secretary of the New York Consumers League, and an adviser to Al Smith.

In addition to the formal cabinet, Roosevelt appointed an informal "Brain Trust," including Adolph Berle, Jr., a young expert on corporation law, and Rexford Tugwell, a Columbia University authority on agricultural economics and a committed national planner. Roosevelt also appointed Raymond Moley, another Columbia professor, who later became one of the president's severest critics, and Harry Hopkins, a nervous, energetic man who loved to bet on horse races and had left Iowa to be a social worker in New York. Hopkins's passionate concern for the poor and unemployed would play a large role in formulating New Deal policy.

Eleanor Roosevelt, the president's wife, was a controversial first lady. She wrote a newspaper column, made radio broadcasts, traveled widely, and was constantly giving speeches and listening to the concerns of women, minorities, and ordinary Americans. Attacked by critics who thought she had too much power and mocked for her protruding front teeth, her awkward ways, and her upper-class accent, she courageously took stands on issues of social justice and civil rights. She helped push the president toward social reform.

Roosevelt proved to be an adept politician. He was not well read, especially on economic matters, but he had the ability to learn from his advisers and yet not be dominated by them. He took ideas, plans, and suggestions from conflicting sources and combined them. He had a "flypaper mind," one of his advisers decided. There was no overall plan, no master strategy. An improviser and an opportunist who once likened himself to a football quarterback who called one play and if it did not work called a different one, Roosevelt was an optimist by nature. And he believed in action.

One Hundred Days

Because Roosevelt took office in the middle of a major crisis, a cooperative Congress was willing to pass almost any legislation that he put before it. Not since Woodrow Wilson's first term had a president orchestrated Congress so effectively. In three months, a bewildering number of bills were rushed through. Some of them were hastily drafted and not well thought out, and some contradicted other legislation. But many of the laws passed during Roosevelt's first 100 days would have far-reaching implications for the relationship of government to society. Roosevelt was an opportunist, but unlike Hoover, he was willing to use direct government action to solve the problems of depression and unemployment. As it turned out, none of the bills passed during the first 100 days cured the Depression, but taken together, the legislation constituted one of the most innovative periods in American political history.

The most immediate problem Roosevelt faced was the condition of the banks. Many had closed, and American citizens, no longer trusting the financial institutions, were hoarding money and putting their assets into gold. Using a forgotten provision of a World War I law, Roosevelt immediately declared a four-day bank holiday. Three days later, an emergency session of Congress approved his action and within hours passed the Emergency Banking Relief Act. The bill gave the president broad powers over financial transactions, prohibited the hoarding of gold, and allowed for the reopening of sound banks, sometimes with loans from the Reconstruction Finance Corporation. Within the next few years, Congress passed additional legislation that gave the federal government more regulatory power over the stock market and over the process by which corporations issued stock. It also passed the Banking Act of 1933, which strengthened the Federal Reserve System, established the Federal Deposit Insurance Corporation, and insured individual deposits up to $5,000. Although the American Bankers Association opposed the plan as "unsound, unscientific, unjust and dangerous," banks were soon attracting depositors by advertising that they were protected by government insurance.

The Democratic platform in 1932 called for reduced government spending and an end to prohibition. Roosevelt moved quickly on both. The Economy Act, which passed Congress easily, called for a 15 percent reduction in government salaries as well as a reorganization of federal agencies in order to save money. The bill also cut veterans' pensions, over their protests. However, the Economy Act's small savings were dwarfed by other bills passed the same week, which called for increased spending. The Beer-Wine Revenue Act legalized 3.2 beer and light wines and levied a tax on both. The Twenty-first Amendment, ratified on December 5, 1933, repealed the Eighteenth Amendment and ended the prohibition experiment. The veterans and the antiliquor forces, two of the strongest lobbying groups in the nation, were both overwhelmed by a Congress that seemed ready to give the president free rein.

Congress granted Roosevelt great power to devalue the dollar and to manipulate inflation. Some members argued for the old Populist solution of free and unlimited coinage of silver, while others called for issuing billions of dollars in paper currency. Bankers and businessmen feared inflation, but farmers and debtors favored an inflationary policy as a way to raise prices and put more money in their pockets. "I have always favored sound money," Roosevelt announced, "and I do now, but it is 'too darned sound' when it takes so much of farm products to buy a dollar." He rejected the more extreme inflationary plans supported by many congressmen from the agricultural states, but he did take the country off the gold standard. No longer would paper currency be redeemable in gold. The action terrified some conservative businessmen, who argued that it would lead to "uncontrolled inflation and complete chaos." Even Roosevelt's director of the budget announced solemnly that going off the gold standard "meant the end of Western Civilization."

Devaluation did not end Western civilization, but neither did it lead to instant recovery. After experimenting with pushing the price of gold up by buying it in the open market, Roosevelt and his advisers fixed the price at $35 an ounce in January 1934 (against the old price of $20.63). This inflated the dollar by about 40 percent. Roosevelt also tried briefly to induce inflation through the purchase of silver, but soon the country settled down to a slightly inflated currency and a dollar based on both gold and silver. Some experts still believed that gold represented fiscal responsibility, even morality, and others still cried for more inflation.

Relief Measures

Roosevelt believed in economy in government and in a balanced budget, but he also wanted to help the unemployed and the homeless. One survey estimated in 1933 that 1.5 million Americans were homeless. One man with a wife and six children from Latrobe, Pennsylvania, who was being evicted wrote, "I have 10 days to get another house, no job, no means of paying rent, can you advise me as to which would be the most humane way to dispose of myself and family, as this is about the only thing that I see left to do."

Roosevelt's answer was the Federal Emergency Relief Administration (FERA), which Congress authorized with an appropriation of $500 million in direct grants to cities and states. A few months later, Roosevelt created a Civil Works Administration (CWA) to put more than 4 million people to work on various state, municipal, and federal projects. Hopkins, who ran both agencies, had experimented with work relief programs in New York. Like most social workers, he believed it was much better to pay people to work than to give them charity. A woman with two daughters from Houston, Texas, wrote and asked, "Why don't they give us materials and let us make our children's clothes . . . you've no idea how children hate wearing relief clothes." An accountant working on a road project said, "I'd rather stay out here in that ditch the rest of my life than take one cent of direct relief."

The CWA was not always effective, but in just over a year, the agency built or restored a half million miles of roads and constructed 40,000

For many people, the Depression meant homeless despair. Here an Oklahoma family who have lost their farm walk with all their possessions along the highway. This compelling photograph was taken by Dorothea Lange, one of several accomplished photographers who documented the impact of the Depression for the Farm Security Administration.

schools and 1,000 airports. It hired 50,000 teachers to keep rural schools open and others to teach adult education courses in the cities. The CWA helped millions of people get through the bitterly cold winter of 1933–1934. It also put over a billion dollars of purchasing power into the economy. Roosevelt, who later would be accused of deficit spending, feared that the program was costing too much and might create a permanent class of relief recipients. In the spring of 1934, he ordered the CWA closed down.

The Public Works Administration (PWA), directed by Harold Ickes, in some respects overlapped the work of the CWA, but it lasted longer. Between 1933 and 1939, the PWA built hospitals, courthouses, and school buildings. It helped construct structures as diverse as the port of Brownsville, Texas, a bridge that linked Key West to the Florida mainland, and the library at the University of New Mexico. It built the aircraft carriers *Yorktown* and *Enterprise,* planes for the Army Air Corps, and low-cost housing for slum dwellers. One purpose of the PWA was economic pump priming—the stimulation of the economy and consumer spending through the investment of government funds. Afraid that there might be scandals in the agency, Ickes spent money slowly and carefully. Thus during the first years, PWA projects, worthwhile as most of them were, did little to stimulate the economy.

Agricultural Adjustment Act

In 1933, most farmers were desperate, as mounting surpluses and falling prices drastically cut their incomes. Some in the Midwest talked of open rebellion, even of revolution. Many observers saw only hopelessness and despair in farmers who had worked hard but were still losing their farms.

Congress passed a number of bills in 1933 and 1934 to deal with the agricultural crisis. They included the Emergency Farm Mortgage Act, designed to prevent more farm foreclosures and evictions. But the New Deal's principal solution to the farm problem was the Agricultural Adjustment Act (AAA), which sought to control the overproduction of basic commodities so that farmers might regain the purchasing power they had enjoyed before World War I. To guarantee these "parity prices" (the average prices in the years 1909–1914), the production of major agricultural staples—wheat, cotton, corn, hogs, rice, tobacco, and milk—would be controlled by paying the farmers to reduce their acreage under cultivation. The AAA levied a tax at the processing stage to pay for the program.

The act aroused great disagreement among farm leaders and economists, but the controversy was nothing compared with the outcry from the public over the initial action of the AAA in the summer of 1933. To prevent a glut on the cotton and pork markets, the agency ordered 10 million acres of cotton plowed up and 6 million little pigs slaughtered. It seemed unnatural, even immoral, to kill pigs and plow up cotton when millions of people were underfed and in need of clothes. The story circulated that in the South, mules trained for many years to walk between the rows of cotton now refused to walk on the cotton plants. Some suggested that those mules were more intelligent than the government bureaucrats who had ordered the action.

The Agricultural Adjustment Act did raise the prices of some agricultural products. But it helped the larger farmers more than the small operators, and it was often disastrous for the tenant farmers and sharecroppers, whom crop reduction made expendable. Landowners often discharged tenant families when they reduced the acres under cultivation. There were provisions in the act to help marginal farmers, but little trickled down to them. Many were simply cast out on the road with a few possessions and nowhere to go. As for large farmers, they cultivated their fewer acres more intensely, so that the total crop was little reduced. In the end, the prolonged drought that hit the Southwest in 1934 did more than the AAA to limit production and raise agricultural prices. But the long-range significance of the AAA, which was later declared unconstitutional, was the establishment of the idea that the government should subsidize farmers for limiting production.

Industrial Recovery

The flurry of legislation during the first days of the Roosevelt administration contained something for almost every group. The National Industrial Recovery Act (NIRA) was designed to help business, raise prices, control production, and put people back to work. The act established the National Recovery Administration (NRA) with the power to set fair competition codes in all industries. For a time, everyone forgot about antitrust laws and talked of cooperation and planning rather than competition. To run the NRA, Roosevelt appointed Hugh Johnson, who had helped organize the World War I draft and served on the War Industries Board. Johnson used his wartime experiences and the enthusiasm of the bond drives to rally the country around the NRA and, implicitly, around all New Deal measures. There were parades and rallies, even a postage stamp, and industries that cooperated could display a blue eagle, the symbol of the NRA. "We Do Our Part," the posters and banners proclaimed, but the results were somewhat less than the promise.

Section 7a of the NIRA, included at the insistence of organized labor, guaranteed labor's right to organize and to bargain collectively and established the National Labor Board to see that their rights were respected. But the board, usually dominated by businessmen, often interpreted the labor provisions of the contracts loosely. In addition, small businessmen complained that the NIRA was unfair to their interests. Any attempt to set prices led to controversy.

Many consumers suspected that the codes and contracts were raising prices, while others feared the return of monopoly in some industries. One woman wrote the president that she was taking down her blue eagle because she had lost her job; another wrote from Tennessee to denounce the NIRA as a joke because it helped only the chain stores. Johnson's booster campaign backfired in the end because anyone with a complaint about a New Deal agency seemed to take it out on the symbol of the blue eagle. When the Supreme Court declared the NIRA unconstitutional in 1935, few people complained. Still, the NIRA was an ambitious attempt to bring some order into a confused business situation, and the labor provisions of the act were picked up later by the National Labor Relations Act.

Civilian Conservation Corps

One of the most popular and successful of the New Deal programs, the Civilian Conservation Corps (CCC), combined work relief with the preservation of natural resources. It put young unemployed men between the ages of 18 and 25 to work on reforestation, road and park construction, flood control, and other projects. The men lived in work camps (there were over 1,500 camps in all) and earned $30 a month, $25 of which had to be sent home to their families. Some complained that the CCC camps, run by the U.S. Army, were too military, and one woman wrote from Minnesota to point out that all the best young men were at CCC camps when they ought to be home looking for real jobs and finding brides. Others complained that the CCC did nothing for unemployed young women, so a few special camps were organized for them, but only 8,000 women took part in a program that by 1941 had included 2.5 million men participants. Overall, the CCC was one of the most successful and least controversial of all the New Deal programs.

Tennessee Valley Authority

Roosevelt, like his Republican namesake, believed in conservation. He promoted flood control projects and added millions of acres to the country's national forests, wildlife refuges, and fish and game sanctuaries. But the most important New Deal conservation project, the Tennessee Valley Authority (TVA), owed more to Republican George Norris, a progressive senator from Nebraska, than to Roosevelt. During World War I, the federal government had built a hydroelectric plant and two munitions factories at Muscle Shoals, on the Tennessee River in Alabama. The government tried unsuccessfully to sell these facilities to private industry, but all through the 1920s, Norris campaigned to have the federal government operate them for the benefit of the valley's residents. Twice Republican presidents vetoed bills that would have allowed federal operation, but Roosevelt endorsed Norris's idea and expanded it into a regional development plan.

Congress authorized the TVA as an independent public corporation with the power to sell electricity and fertilizer and to promote flood control and land reclamation. The TVA built nine major dams and many minor ones between 1933 and 1944, affecting parts of Virginia, North Carolina, Georgia, Alabama, Mississippi, Tennessee, and Kentucky. Some private utility companies claimed that TVA offered unfair competition to private industry, but it was an imaginative experiment in regional planning. It promoted everything from flood control to library bookmobiles. For residents of the valley, it meant cheaper electricity and changed life styles. The TVA meant radios,

The Tennessee Valley Authority

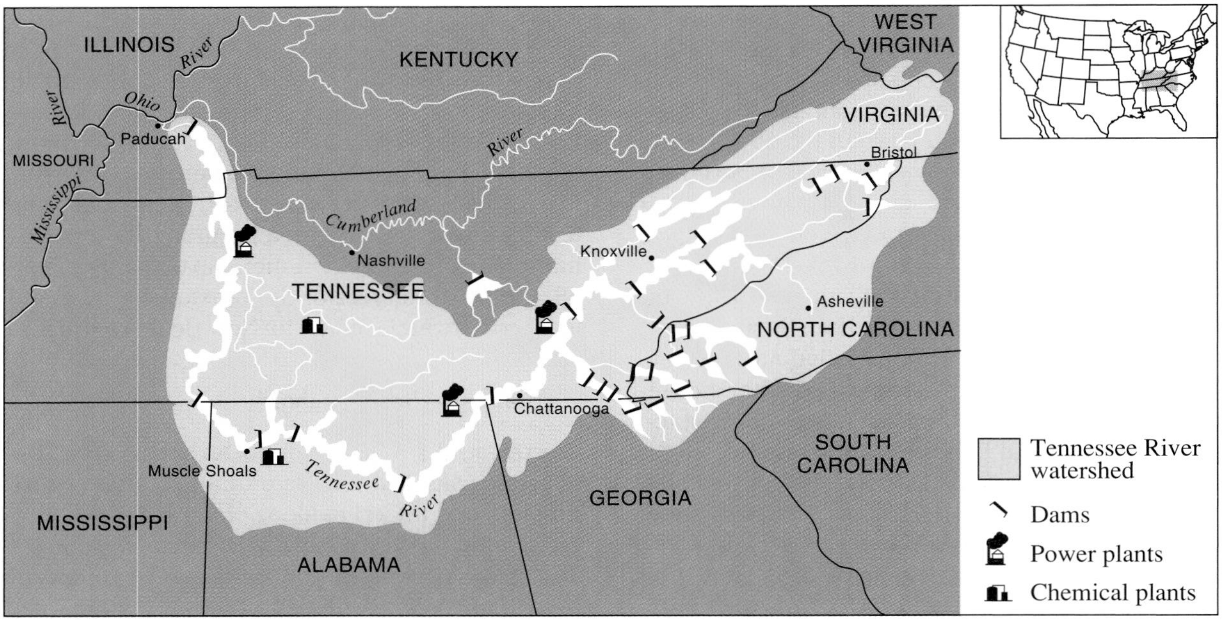

The TVA transformed the way the Tennessee valley looked; it replaced a wild river with a series of flood-control and hydroelectric dams and created a series of lakes behind the dams. It stopped short of the coordinated regional planning that some people wanted, but it was one of the most important New Deal projects.

electric irons, washing machines, and other appliances for the first time. The largest federal construction project ever launched, it also created jobs for many thousands who helped build the dams. But government officials and businessmen who feared that the experiment would lead to socialism always curbed regional planning possibilities of the TVA.

Critics of the New Deal

The furious legislative activity during the first 100 days of the New Deal helped alleviate the pessimism and despair hanging over the country. Stock market prices rose slightly, and industrial production was up 11 percent at the end of 1933. Still, the country remained locked in depression, and nearly 12 million Americans were without jobs. Yet Roosevelt captured the imagination of ordinary Americans everywhere. Hundreds of thousands of letters poured into the White House, so many that eventually 50 people had to be hired to answer them. "I've always thought of F.D.R. as my personal friend," a man wrote from Georgia. "I feel very grateful to you for all the good you have already done for all of us," another added from Missouri. "If ever there was a saint, he is one," declared a Wisconsin woman.

But conservatives were not so sure that Roosevelt was a savior; in fact, many businessmen, after being impressed with Roosevelt's early economy measures and approving programs such as the NIRA, began to fear that the president was leading the country toward socialism. Appalled by work relief programs, regional planning such as the TVA, and the abandonment of the gold standard, many businessmen were also annoyed by the style of the president, whom they called "that man in the White House."

The conservative revolt against Roosevelt surfaced in the summer of 1934 as the congressional elections approached. A group of disgruntled politicians and businessmen formed the Liberty League. Led by Alfred E. Smith and John W. Davis, two unsuccessful Democratic presidential candidates, the league stood for states' rights, free enterprise, and the "American system of the open shop." The league supported conservative or at least anti–New Deal candidates for Congress, but it had little influence. In the election of 1934, the Democrats increased their majority from 310 to 319 in the House and from 60 to 69 in the Senate (only the second time in the twentieth century that the party in power had increased its control of Congress). A few people were learning to hate Roosevelt, but it was obvious that most Americans approved of what he was doing.

Much more disturbing to Roosevelt and his advisers in 1934 and 1935 than people who thought the New Deal too radical were those on the left who maintained that the government had not done enough to help the poor. One source of criticism was the Communist party. Attracting supporters from all walks of life during a time when capitalism seemed to have failed, the Communist party increased its membership from 7,500 in 1930 to 75,000 in 1938. The Communists organized protest marches and tried to reach out to the oppressed and unemployed. While a majority who joined the party came from the working class, communism had a special appeal to writers, intellectuals, and some college students during a decade when the American dream had turned into a nightmare.

A larger number of Americans, however, were influenced by other movements promising easy solutions to poverty and unemployment. In Minnesota, Governor Floyd Olson, elected on a Farm-Labor ticket, accused capitalism of causing the Depression and startled some listeners when he thundered, "I hope the present system of government goes right to hell." In California, Upton Sinclair, the muckraking socialist and author of *The Jungle,* ran for governor on the platform "End Poverty in California." He promised to pay everyone over 60 years of age a pension of $50 a month using higher income and inheritance taxes to finance the program. He won in the primary but lost the election, and his program collapsed.

California also produced Dr. Francis E. Townsend, who claimed he had a national following of over 5 million. His supporters backed the Townsend Old Age Revolving Pension Plan, which promised $200 a month to all unemployed citizens over 60 on the condition that they spend it in the same month they received it. Economists laughed at the utopian scheme, but followers organized thousands of Townsend Pension Clubs across the country. As one Minnesota woman wrote to Eleanor Roosevelt, "The old folks who have paid taxes all their lives and built this country up will live in comfort." The plan "will banish crime, give the young a chance to work, pay off the national debt which is mounting every day."

More threatening to Roosevelt and the New Deal than Sinclair and Townsend were the protest movements led by Father Charles E. Coughlin and Senator Huey P. Long. Father Coughlin, a Roman Catholic priest from a Detroit suburb, attracted an audience of 30 to 45 million to his national radio show. At first, he supported Roosevelt's policies, but later he savagely attacked the New Deal as excessively probusiness. Mixing religious commentary with visions of a society operating without bankers and big businessmen, he roused his audience with blatantly anti-Semitic appeals. Most often the "evil" bankers he described were Jewish—the Rothschilds, Warburgs, and Kuhn-Loebs. Anti-Semitism reached a peak in the 1930s, so Jews, rather than Catholics, bore the brunt of nativist fury. Groups like the Silver Shirts and the German-American Bund lashed out against Jews. To members of these groups and others like them, Father Coughlin's attacks made sense.

Huey Long, like Coughlin, had a charisma that won support from the millions still trying to survive in a country where the continuing depression made day-to-day existence a struggle. Elected governor of Louisiana in 1928, he promoted a "Share the Wealth" program. He taxed the oil refineries and built hospitals, schools, and thousands of miles of new highways. By 1934, he was the virtual dictator of his state, personally controlling the police and the courts. Long talked about a guaranteed $2,000 to $3,000 income for all American families (18.3 million families earned less than $1,000 per year in 1936) and promised pensions for the elderly and college educations for the young. He would pay for these programs by taxing the rich and liquidating the great fortunes. Had not an assassin's bullet cut Long down in September 1935, he might have mounted a third-party challenge to Roosevelt.

The Second New Deal

Responding in part to the discontent of the lower middle class but also to the threat of various utopian schemes, Roosevelt moved his programs in 1935 toward the goals of social reform and social justice. At the same time, he departed from attempts to cooperate with the business community. "We find our population suffering from old inequalities," Roosevelt announced in his annual message to Congress in January 1935. "In spite of our efforts and in spite of our talk, we have not weeded out the overprivileged and we have not effectively lifted up the underprivileged."

Work Relief and Social Security

The Works Progress Administration (WPA), authorized by Congress in April 1935, was the first massive attempt to deal with unemployment and its demoralizing effect on millions of Americans. The WPA employed about 3 million people a year on a variety of socially useful projects. The WPA workers, who earned wages lower than private industry paid, built bridges, airports, libraries, roads, and golf courses. Nearly 85 percent of the funds went directly into salaries and wages. A minor but important part of the WPA funding supported writers, artists, actors, and musicians. Richard Wright, Jack Conroy, and Saul Bellow were among the 10,000 writers who were paid less than $100 a month. Experimental theater, innovative and well-written guides to all the states, murals painted in municipal and state buildings, and the Historical Records Survey were among the long-lasting results of these projects.

Only one member of a family could qualify for a WPA job, and first choice always went to the man. A woman could qualify only if she headed the household. But eventually more than 13 percent of the people who worked for the WPA were women, although their most common employment was in the sewing room, where old clothes were made over. "For unskilled men we have the shovel. For unskilled women we have only the needle," one official remarked.

The WPA was controversial from the beginning. Critics charged that the agency had hired Communists to paint murals or work on the state guides. For others, a lazy good-for-nothing leaning on a shovel symbolized the WPA. The initials WPA, some wags charged, stood for "We Pay for All" or "We Putter Around." Yet for all the criticism, the WPA did useful work; the program built nearly 6,000 schools, more than 2,500 hospitals, and 13,000 playgrounds. More important, it gave millions of unemployed Americans a sense that they were working and bringing in a paycheck to support their families.

The National Youth Administration (NYA) supplemented the work of the WPA and assisted

The WPA (which some wags said stood for "We Putter Around") employed many people for a great variety of jobs.

young men and women between the ages of 16 and 25, many of them students. A young law student named Richard Nixon earned 35 cents an hour working for the NYA while he was at Duke University, and Lyndon Johnson began his political career as director of the Texas NYA.

By far the most enduring reform came with the passage of the Social Security Act of 1935. Since the progressive period, social workers and reformers had argued for a national system of health insurance, old-age pensions, and unemployment insurance. By the 1930s, the United States remained the only major industrial country without such programs. Within the Roosevelt circle, Frances Perkins argued most strongly for social insurance, but the popularity of the Townsend Plan and other schemes to aid the elderly helped convince Roosevelt of the need to act. The number of people over 65 in the country increased from 5.7 million in 1925 to 7.8 million in 1935, and that group demanded action.

The Social Security Act of 1935 was a compromise. Congress quickly dropped a plan for federal health insurance because of opposition from the medical profession. The most important provision of the act was old-age and survivor insurance to be paid for by a tax of one percent on both employers and employees. The benefits initially ranged from $10 to $85 a month. The act also established a cooperative federal-state system of unemployment compensation. Other provisions authorized federal grants to the states to assist in caring for the crippled and the blind. Finally, the Social Security Act provided some aid to dependent children. This provision would eventually expand to become the largest federal welfare program.

The National Association of Manufacturers denounced social security as a program that would regiment the people and destroy individual self-reliance. In reality, it was a conservative and incomplete system. In no other country was social insurance paid for in part by a regressive tax on the workers' wages. "We put those payroll contributions there so as to give the contributors a legal, moral, and political right to collect their pensions and unemployment benefits," Roosevelt later explained. "With those taxes in there, no damn politician can ever scrap my social security program." But the law also excluded many people, including those who needed it most, such as farm laborers and domestic servants. It discriminated against married women wage earners, and it failed to protect against sickness. Yet for all its weaknesses, it was one of the most important New Deal measures. A landmark in American social legislation, it marked the beginning of the welfare state that would expand significantly after World War II.

Aiding the Farmers

The Social Security Act and the Works Progress Administration were only two signs of Roosevelt's greater concern for social reform. The flurry of legislation in 1935 and early 1936, often called the "second New Deal," also included an effort to help American farmers. Over 1.7 million farm families had incomes of under $500 annually in 1935, and 42 percent of all those who lived on farms were tenants. The Resettlement Administration (RA), motivated in part by a Jeffersonian ideal of yeoman farmers working their own land, set out to relocate tenant farmers on land purchased by the government. Lack of funds and fears that the Roosevelt administration was trying to establish Soviet-style collective farms limited the effectiveness of the RA program.

Much more important in improving the lives of farm families was the Rural Electrification Administration (REA), which was authorized in 1935 to lend money to cooperatives to generate and distribute electricity in isolated rural areas not served by private utilities. Only 10 percent of the nation's farms had electricity in 1936. When the REA's lines were finally attached, they dramatically changed the lives of millions of farm families who had been able only to dream about the radios, washing machines, and farm equipment advertised in magazines.

In the hill country west of Austin, Texas, for example, no electricity existed until the end of the 1930s. Life went on in small towns and on ranches much as it had for decades. Houses were illuminated by kerosene lamps whose wicks had to be trimmed just right or the lamp smoked or went out, but even with perfect adjustment it was difficult to read by them. There were no bathrooms, because bathrooms required running water, and running water depended on an electric pump. "Yes, we had running water," one woman remembered. "I always said we had running water because I grabbed those two buckets up and ran the two hundred yards to the house with them."

Women and children hauled water constantly—for infrequent baths, for continuous canning (because without a refrigerator, fruits and vegetables had to be put up almost immediately or they spoiled), and for washday. Washday, always Monday, meant scrubbing clothes by hand with harsh soap on a washboard; it meant boiling clothes in a large copper vat over a wood stove and stirring them with a wooden fork. It was a hot and backbreaking job, especially in summer. Then the women had to lift the hot, heavy clothes into a rinsing tub. After the clothes were thoroughly mixed with bluing (to make them white), they had to be wrung out by hand, then carried to the lines, where they were hung to dry. Tuesday was for ironing, and even in summer a wood fire was needed to heat the irons. When irons got dirty on the stove, as could easily happen, dirt got on a white shirt or blouse and it had to be washed all over again.

It was memory of life in the hill country and personal knowledge of how hard his mother and grandmother toiled that inspired a young congressman from Texas, Lyndon Johnson, to work to bring rural electrification to the area. In November 1939, the lights finally came on in the hill country, plugging the area into the twentieth century.

The Dust Bowl: An Ecological Disaster

The ultimate goal of the New Deal was to alter and stabilize agriculture through planning and by promoting efficiency. Some farmers profited from the agricultural legislation of the 1930s, but those who tried to farm on the Great Plains fell victim to years of drought and dust storms. Record heat waves and below-average rainfall in the 1930s turned an area from the Oklahoma panhandle to western Kansas into a giant dust bowl. A single storm on May 11, 1934, removed 300 million tons of topsoil and turned day into night. Between 1932 and 1939 there was an average of fifty storms a year. Cities kept their street lights on for twenty-four hours a day. Dust covered everything from food to bedspreads and piled up in dunes in city streets and barnyards. Thousands died of "dust pneumonia." One woman remembered what it was like at night: "A trip for water to rinse the grit from our lips, and then back to bed with washcloths over our noses, we try to lie still, because every turn stirs the dust on the blankets."

A farmer and his sons race to find shelter from a dust storm in Cimarron County, Oklahoma, in 1936. A combination of factors, including overplanting which destroyed the natural sod of the Great Plains, resulted in the devastating dust storms of the 1930s. Without sod to protect the soil from the wind, thousands of acres of the Great Plains just blew away.

A 1936 survey of twenty counties in the heart of the dust bowl concluded that 97.6 percent of the land suffered from erosion and more than 50 percent was seriously damaged. By the end of the decade 10,000 farm homes were abandoned to the elements, and 9 million acres of farmland was reduced to a wasteland. By the end of the decade three and a half million people had abandoned their farms and joined a massive migration to find a better life. Not all were forced out by the dust storms; some fell victim to large-scale agriculture, and many tenant farmers and hired hands were expendable during the depression. In most cases they not only lost their jobs, but they also were evicted from their houses. More than 350,000 left Oklahoma during the decade and moved to California, a place that seemed to many like the promised land. But the name Okie came to mean any farm migrant. The plight of these wayfarers was immortalized by John Steinbeck in his novel about the Joad family, *The Grapes of Wrath* (1939). The next year John Ford made a powerful movie based on the book staring Henry Fonda as

Tom Joad. Many Americans sympathized with the plight of the embattled farm family trying to escape the dust bowl and find a better life in California; others interpreted their defeat as a symbol of the failure of the American dream.

The dust bowl was a natural disaster, but it was aided and exaggerated by human actions and inactions. The semiarid plains west of the 98th meridian were not suitable for intensive agriculture. Overgrazing, too much plowing, and indiscriminate planting over a period of sixty years exposed the thin soil to the elements. When the winds came in the 1930s, much of the land simply blew away. In the end it was a matter of too little government planning and regulation and too many farmers using new technology to exploit natural resources for their own gain.

The Roosevelt administration did try to deal with the problem. The Taylor Grazing Act of 1934 restricted the use of the public range in an attempt to prevent overgrazing, and it also closed 80 million acres of grassland to further settlement. The Civilian Conservation Corps and other New Deal agencies planted trees, and the Soil Conservation Service promoted drought-resistant crops and contour plowing, but it was too little and too late. Even worse, according to some authorities, government measures applied after the disaster of 1930 encouraged farmers to return to raising wheat and other inappropriate crops, leading to more dust bowl crises in the 1950s and 1970s.

Controlling Corporate Power and Taxing the Wealthy

In the summer of 1935, Roosevelt also moved to control the large corporations, and he even toyed with radical plans to tax the well-to-do heavily and redistribute wealth in the United States. The Public Utility Holding Company Act, passed in 1935, attempted to restrict the power of the giant utility companies, the 12 largest of which controlled more than half the country's power. The act gave various government commissions the authority to regulate and control the power companies and included a "death sentence" clause that gave each company five years to demonstrate that its services were efficient. If it could not demonstrate this, the government could dissolve the company. This was one of the most radical attempts to control corporate power in American history.

In his message to Congress in 1935, Roosevelt also pointed out that the federal revenue laws had "done little to prevent an unjust concentration of wealth and economic power." He suggested steeper income taxes for wealthy groups and a much larger inheritance tax. When Congress dropped the inheritance tax provision, however, Roosevelt did not fight to have it restored. Even the weakened bill, increasing estate and gift taxes and raising the income tax rates at the top, angered many in the business community who thought that Roosevelt had sold out to Huey Long's "Share the Wealth" scheme.

The New Deal for Labor

Like many progressive reformers, Roosevelt was more interested in improving the lot of working people by passing social legislation than by strengthening the bargaining position of orga-

Distribution of Income, 1935–1936

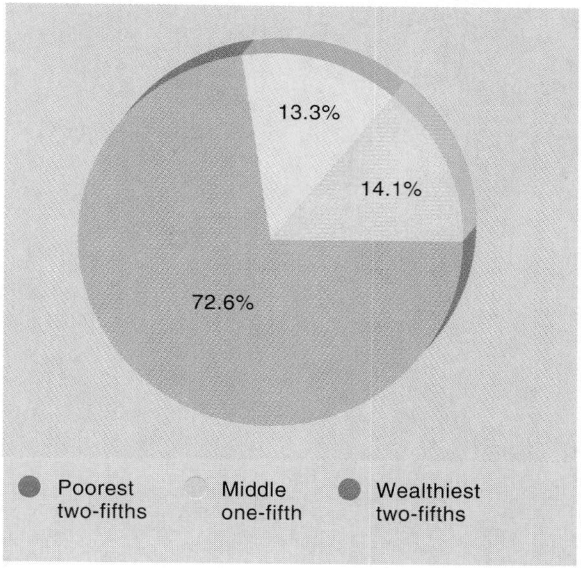

Roosevelt and the New Deal never sought consistently to redistribute wealth in America, and a great disparity in income and assets remained.

Source: U.S. Bureau of the Census.

Frances Perkins, FDR's secretary of labor, was an important defender of organized labor within the administration. As the first woman to hold a cabinet position, she was often greeted by surprised stares as she traveled around the country.

nized labor. Yet he saw labor as an important balance to the power of industry, and he listened to his advisers, especially to Frances Perkins and to Senator Robert Wagner of New York, who persistently brought up the needs of organized labor.

After strikes in San Francisco, Minneapolis, and Toledo, Roosevelt supported the Wagner Act, officially called the National Labor Relations Act, which outlawed blacklisting and a number of other practices and reasserted labor's right to organize and to bargain collectively. The act also established a Labor Relations Board with the power to certify a properly elected bargaining unit. The act did not require workers to join unions, but it made the federal government a regulator, or at least a neutral force, in management-labor relations. That alone made the national Labor Relations Act one of the most important New Deal reform measures.

The Roosevelt administration's friendly attitude toward organized labor helped to increase union membership from under 3 million in 1933 to 4.5 million by 1935. Many groups, however, were left out, including farm laborers, unskilled workers, and women. Only about 3 percent of working women belonged to unions, and women earned only about 60 percent of wages paid to men for equivalent work.

Still, many people resented the fact that women were employed at all. The Brotherhood of Railway and Steamship Clerks ruled that no married woman whose husband could support her was eligible for a job. One writer had a perfect solution for the unemployment problem: "Simply fire the women, who shouldn't be working anyway, and hire the men." The American Federation of Labor had little interest in organizing unskilled workers, but a new group of committed and militant labor leaders emerged in the 1930s to take up that task. John L. Lewis, the eloquent head of the United Mine Workers, was the most aggressive. He was joined by David Dubinsky of the International Ladies' Garment Workers and Sidney Hillman, president of the Amalgamated Clothing Workers. Both were socialists who believed in economic planning, but both had worked closely with social justice progressives. These new progressive labor leaders formed the Committee of Industrial Organization (CIO) within the AFL and set out to organize workers in the steel, auto, and rubber industries. Rather than separating workers by skill or craft as the AFL preferred, they organized everyone into an industrywide union much as the Knights of Labor had done in the 1880s. They also used new and aggressive tactics. When a foreman tried to increase production or enforce discipline, the union leaders would simply pull the switch and declare a spontaneous strike. This "brass knuckle unionism" worked especially well in the auto and rubber industries.

In 1936, the workers at three rubber plants in Akron, Ohio, went on strike without permission from the leaders. Instead of picketing outside the factory, they occupied the buildings and took them over. The "sit-down strike" became a new protest technique. After sit-down strikes against General Motors plants in Atlanta, Georgia, and Flint, Michigan, General Motors finally accepted the United Auto Workers as their employees' bargaining unit.

The General Motors strike was the most important event in a critical period of labor upheaval. A group of workers using disorderly but largely nonviolent tactics (as would the civil rights advocates in the mid-1960s) demanded their rights under the law. They helped to make labor's voice heard in the decision-making process in major industries where labor had long been denied any role. They also helped to raise the status of organized labor in the eyes of many Americans.

"Labor does not seek industrial strife," Lewis announced. "It wants peace, but a peace with justice." As the sit-down tactic spread, violence often accompanied justice. Chrysler capitulated, but the Ford Motor Company used hired gunmen to discourage the strikers. A bloody struggle ensued before Ford agreed to accept the UAW as the bargaining agent. Even U.S. Steel, which had been militantly antiunion, signed an agreement with the Steel Workers Organizing Committee calling for a 40-hour week and an eight-hour day. But other steel companies refused to go along. In Chicago on Memorial Day in 1937, a confrontation between the police and peaceful pickets at the Republic Steel plant resulted in ten deaths. In the "Memorial Day Massacre," as it came to be called, the police fired without provocation into a crowd of workers and their families, who had gathered near the plant in a holiday mood. All ten of the dead were shot in the back.

Despite the violence and management's use of undercover agents within unions, the CIO gained many members. William Green and the leadership of the AFL were horrified at the aggressive tactics of the new labor leaders. They expelled the CIO leaders from the AFL, only to see them form a separate Congress of Industrial Organization (the initials stayed the same). By the end of the decade, the CIO had infused the labor movement with a new spirit. Accepting unskilled workers, blacks, and others who had never belonged to a union before, they won increased pay, better working conditions, and the right to bargain collectively in most of the basic American industries. Jim Cole, a black butcher at one of the meatpacking plants in Chicago, tried to join the Amalgamated Butchers and Meat Cutters, an AFL union, but they turned him away because he was black. He remembered when the CIO came.

> Well, I tell you, we Negroes was glad to see it come. Sometimes the bosses or the company stooges try to keep the white boys from joining the union. They say, "You don't want to belong to a black man's organization. That's all the CIO is." Don't fool nobody, but they got to lie, spread lying words around.

America's Minorities in the 1930s

A half million African-Americans joined unions through the CIO during the 1930s, and many blacks were aided by various New Deal agencies. Yet the familiar pattern of discrimination, low-paying jobs, and intimidation through violence persisted. Lynchings in the South actually increased in the New Deal years, rising from 8 in 1932 to 28 in 1933 and 20 in 1935.

One particular case came to symbolize and dramatize discrimination against African-Americans in the 1930s. On March 25, 1931, in Scottsboro, Alabama, two young white women accused nine black men of raping them in a railroad boxcar as they all hitched a free ride. A jury of white men found all nine blacks guilty, and the court sentenced eight to die. The United States Supreme Court ordered new trials in 1933, on the grounds that the accused rapists had not received proper legal counsel. The case garnered much publicity in the United States and abroad. The youth of the defendants, their quick trial, and the harsh sentences made the "Scottsboro boys" a popular cause for many northern liberals and especially the Communist party. For many southerners, however, it was a matter of defending the honor of white women. As one observer remarked of one of the accusers, she "might be a fallen woman, but by God she is a white woman." However, evidence supporting the alleged rapes was never presented, and eventually one of the women recanted. Yet the case dragged on. In new trials, five of the young men were convicted and given long prison terms. Charges against the other four were dropped in 1937. Four of the remaining five were paroled in 1944, and the fifth escaped to Michigan.

African-Americans did not have to be accused of rape to want to flee to the North, however, and the migration of blacks to northern cities, which had accelerated during World War I, continued during the 1930s. The collapse of cotton prices forced black farmers and farm laborers to flee north for survival. But since most were poorly educated, they soon became trapped in northern ghettos, where they were eligible for only the most menial jobs. The black unemployment rate was triple that of whites, and blacks often received less per person in welfare payments.

Black leaders attacked the Roosevelt administration for supporting or allowing segregation in government-sponsored facilities. The TVA model town of Norris, Tennessee, was off limits for blacks, and AAA policies actually drove blacks off the land in the South. The CCC segregated black and white workers, and the PWA financed segregated housing projects. Some charged that NRA stood for "Negroes Rarely Allowed." Many African-Americans wrote to the president or the first lady to protest discrimination in New Deal agencies. As one woman from Georgia put it, "I can't sign my name, Mr. President, they will beat me up and run me away from here and this is my home." Blacks ought to realize, a writer in the NAACP journal *The Crisis* warned in 1935, "that the powers-that-be in the Roosevelt administration have nothing for them."

Roosevelt, dependent on the vote of the solid South and fearing that he might antagonize southern congressmen whose backing he needed, refused to support the two major civil rights bills of the era, an antilynching bill and a bill to abolish the poll tax. Yet Harold Ickes and Harry Hopkins worked to ensure that blacks were given opportunities in the CCC, the WPA, and other agencies. By 1941, black federal employees totaled 150,000, more than three times the number during the Hoover administration. Most worked in the lower ranks, but some were lawyers, architects, office managers, and engineers.

Partly responsible for the presence of more black employees was the "black cabinet," a group of more than 50 young blacks who had appointments in almost every government department and New Deal agency. The group met on Friday evenings at the home of Mary McLeod Bethune to

Eleanor Roosevelt meeting in 1937 with the National Youth Administration's executive director, Aubrey Williams, and its director of Negro activities, Mary McLeod Bethune. Eleanor Roosevelt was the most visible and the most active of all first ladies. She was both praised and attacked for her activities.

Mexican farm workers, eagerly recruited in the 1920s, often found themselves deported back to Mexico in the 1930s. That even the migrants drove cars and trucks, though old and repaired, shocked foreign observers. In much of the rest of the world autos were still owned only by the wealthy.

discuss problems and plan strategy. The daughter of a sharecropper and one of 17 children, Bethune had worked her way through the Moody Bible Institute in Chicago. She had founded a black primary school in Florida and then transformed it into Bethune-Cookman College. In the 1920s, she had organized the National Council of Negro Women. In 1934, Harry Hopkins, following the advice of Eleanor Roosevelt, appointed her to the advisory committee of the National Youth Administration. Bethune had a large impact on New Deal policy and on the black cabinet. She spoke out forcefully, she picketed and protested, and she intervened shrewdly to obtain civil rights and more jobs for black Americans.

W. E. B. Du Bois, in the meantime, had become increasingly discouraged with token appointments and the reform of race relations through integration with white society. In the 1920s, he supported a series of pan-African conferences designed to unite black people from around the world. He resigned from the NAACP and from his position as editor of *The Crisis* in 1934 and devoted his time to promoting "voluntary segregation" and a "Negro Nation within a nation." Eventually, he joined the Communist party and moved to Ghana, where he died in 1963.

Although Roosevelt appointed a number of blacks to government positions, he was never particularly committed to civil rights. That was not true of Eleanor Roosevelt, who was educated in part by Mary McLeod Bethune. In 1939, when the Daughters of the American Revolution refused to allow Marian Anderson, a black concert singer, to use their stage, Mrs. Roosevelt publicly protested and resigned her membership in the DAR. She also arranged for Anderson to sing from the steps of the Lincoln Memorial, where 75,000 people gathered to listen and to support civil rights for all black citizens.

Many Mexicans who had been actively recruited for American farms and businesses in the 1920s discovered that they were not needed in the Depression decade. Hundreds of thousands lost their jobs and drifted from the urban barrios to small towns and farms in the Southwest looking for work. By one estimate, there were 400,000 Mexican migrants in Texas alone. The competition for jobs increased ethnic prejudice. Signs inscribed "Only White Labor Employed" and "No Niggers, Mexicans, or Dogs Allowed" expressed the hate and fear that the Mexicans encountered everywhere.

Some New Deal agencies helped destitute Mexicans. A few worked for the CCC and the WPA, but to be employed, an applicant had to qualify for state relief, and that eliminated most migrants. The primary solution was not to provide aid for Mexicans but to ship them back to Mexico. Both federal and local authorities encouraged and sometimes coerced Mexican aliens into returning to Mexico. In Los Angeles and other cities, the police and immigration authorities rounded up aliens and held them illegally. A trainload of repatriates left Los Angeles every month during 1933, and officials deported thousands from other cities. One estimate placed the number sent back in 1932 at 200,000, including some American citizens.

Not all the Mexicans were repatriated, however, and some who remained adopted militant tactics to obtain fair treatment. Mexican strawberry pickers went on strike in El Monte, California, and 18,000 cotton pickers walked away from their jobs in the San Joaquin Valley in 1933. In Gallup, New Mexico, several thousand Mexican coal miners walked out on strike. They constructed a village of shacks and planned to wait out the strike. The miners, who were aided by writers and artists from Santa Fe and Taos, were evicted from their village by the city authorities. Federal agents arrested their leader, Jesus Pallares, and deported him to Mexico.

During the Depression, Native Americans also experienced hunger, disease, and despair, and their plight was compounded by years of exploitation. Since the Dawes Act of 1887 (described in Chapter 17), government policy had sought to make the Indian into a property-owning farmer and to limit tribal rights. Native Americans lost over 60 percent of the 138 million acres granted them in 1887. The government declared some of the land surplus and encouraged individuals to settle on 160 acres and adopt the "habits of civilized life." Few Native Americans profited from this system, but many whites did. Just as other progressives sought the quick assimilation of immigrants, the progressive era Indian commissioners sped up the allotment process to increase Indian detribalization. But many Native Americans who remained on the reservations were not even citizens. Finally, in 1924, Congress granted citizenship to all Indians born in the United States. The original Americans became United States citizens, but that did not end their suffering.

Franklin Roosevelt brought a new spirit to Indian policy by appointing John Collier as commissioner of Indian affairs. Collier had organized the American Indian Defense Association in 1923, but he built on the work of a group of Native American leaders, sometimes called the "Red Progressives." They included Dr. Carlos Montezuma, an Apache physician; Henry Roe Cloud, a Winnebago teacher; and Gertrude Bonnin, a Sioux writer and musician. As commissioner, Collier was primarily responsible for the passage of the Indian Reorganization Act of 1934, which sought to restore the political independence of the tribes and to end the allotment policy of the Dawes Act. "Even where a tribal group is split into factions, where leadership has broken down, where Indians clamor to distribute the tribal property, even there deep forces of cohesion persist and can be evoked," Collier wrote.

The bill also sought to promote the "study of Indian civilization" and to "preserve and develop the special cultural contributions and achievements of such civilization, including Indian arts, crafts, skills and traditions." Not all Indians agreed with the new policies. Some chose to become members of the dominant culture, and the Navajos voted to reject the Reorganization Act. Some Americans charged that the act was inspired by communism. Others argued that its principal result would be to increase government bureaucracy, while missionaries claimed that the government was promoting paganism by allowing the Indians to practice their native religions.

The paradox and contradictions of United States policy toward the Indians can be illustrated by Collier's attempt to solve the Navajo problem. Genuinely sympathetic to native Americans, he was also a modern man who believed in soil conservation, science, and progress. The Navajo lands, like most of the West, were overgrazed, and soil erosion threatened to fill the new lake behind the Hoover Dam with silt. By supporting a policy of reducing the herds of sheep and goats on Indian land and by promoting soil conservation, Collier contributed to the change in the Navajo life style and to the end of their self-sufficiency, something his other policies supported.

Women and the New Deal

Women made some gains during the 1930s, and more women occupied high government positions than in any previous administration. Besides Frances Perkins, the secretary of labor, there was Molly Dewson, a social worker with the Massachusetts Girls Parole Department and the

National Consumers League before becoming head of the Women's Division of the Democratic Committee and then an adviser to Roosevelt. Working closely with Eleanor Roosevelt to promote women's causes, she helped to achieve a number of firsts: two women appointed ambassadors, a judge on the U.S. Court of Appeals, the director of the mint, and many women in government agencies. Katharine Lenroot, director of the Children's Bureau, and Mary Anderson, head of the Women's Bureau, selected many other women to serve in their agencies. Some of these women collaborated as social workers and now joined government bureaus to continue the fight for social justice. But they were usually in offices where they did not threaten male prerogatives.

Despite the number of women working for the government, feminism declined in the 1930s. Instead of fighting for the absolute right of women to work, it became necessary to argue for married women's rights to support their families. The older feminists died or retired, and younger women did not replace them. Despite some dramatic exceptions, the image of woman's proper role in the 1930s continued to be housewife and mother.

The Last Years of the New Deal

The New Deal was not a consistent or well-organized effort to end the Depression and restructure society. Roosevelt was a politician and a pragmatist, unconcerned about ideological or programmatic consistency. The first New Deal in 1933 and 1934 concentrated on relief and recovery, while the legislation passed in 1935 and 1936 was more involved with social reform. In many ways, the election of 1936 marked the high point of Roosevelt's power and influence. After 1937, in part because of the growing threat of war but also because of increasing opposition in Congress, the pace of social legislation slowed. Yet several measures passed in 1937 and 1938 had such far-reaching significance that some historians refer to a third New Deal. Among the new measures were bills that provided for a minimum wage and for housing reform.

The Election of 1936

The Republicans in 1936 nominated a moderate, Governor Alfred Landon of Kansas. Although he attacked the New Deal, charging that new government programs were wasteful and created a dangerous federal bureaucracy, Landon only promised to do the same thing more cheaply and efficiently. Two-thirds of the newspapers in the country supported him, and the *Literary Digest* predicted his victory on the basis of a "scientific" telephone poll.

Roosevelt, helped by signs that the economy was recovering and supported by a coalition of the Democratic South, organized labor, farmers, and urban voters, won easily. A majority of black Americans for the first time deserted the party of Lincoln, not because of Roosevelt's interest in civil rights for blacks but because New Deal relief

FDR's Successful Presidential Campaigns, 1932–1944

Year	Candidates	Party	Popular Vote	Electoral Vote
1932	FRANKLIN D. ROOSEVELT	Democratic	22,809,638 (57.4%)	472
	Herbert C. Hoover	Republican	15,758,901 (39.7%)	59
	Norman Thomas	Socialist	881,951 (2.2%)	0
1936	FRANKLIN D. ROOSEVELT	Democratic	27,751,612 (60.8%)	523
	Alfred M. Landon	Republican	16,681,913 (36.5%)	8
	William Lemke	Union	891,858 (1.9%)	0
1940	FRANKLIN D. ROOSEVELT	Democratic	27,243,466 (54.8%)	449
	Wendell L. Willkie	Republican	22,304,755 (44.8%)	82
1944	FRANKLIN D. ROOSEVELT	Democratic	25,602,505 (53.5%)	432
	Thomas E. Dewey	Republican	22,006,278 (46.0%)	99

Note: Winners' names appear in capital letters.

programs assisted many poor blacks. A viable candidate to the left of the New Deal failed to materialize. In fact, the Socialist party candidate, Norman Thomas, polled less than 200,000 votes. Roosevelt won by over 10 million votes, carrying every state except Maine and Vermont. Even the traditionally Republican states of Pennsylvania, Delaware, and Connecticut, which had voted Republican in almost every election since 1856, went for Roosevelt. "To some generations much is given," Roosevelt announced in his acceptance speech; "of other generations much is expected. This generation has a rendezvous with destiny." Now he had a mandate to continue his New Deal social and economic reforms.

The Battle of the Supreme Court

"I see one-third of a nation ill-housed, ill-clad, ill-nourished," Roosevelt declared in his second inaugural address, and he vowed to alter that situation. But the president's first action in 1937 did not call for legislation to alleviate poverty. Instead he announced a plan to reform the Supreme Court and the judicial system. The Court had not only invalidated a number of New Deal measures—including the NIRA and the first version of the AAA—but other measures as well. Increasingly angry at the "nine old men" who seemed to be destroying New Deal initiatives and defying Congress's will, Roosevelt determined to create a more sympathetic Court. He hoped to gain power to appoint an extra justice for each justice over 70 years of age, of whom there were six. His plan also called for modernizing the court system at all levels, but that plan got lost in the public outcry over the Court-packing scheme.

Roosevelt's plan to nullify the influence of the older and more reactionary justices foundered. Republicans accused him of being a dictator and of subverting the Constitution. Many congressmen from his own party refused to support him. Led by Vice-President John H. Garner of Texas, a number of southern Democrats broke with the president and formed a coalition with conservative Republicans that lasted for more than 30 years. After months of controversy, Roosevelt withdrew the legislation and admitted defeat. He had perhaps misunderstood his mandate, and he certainly underestimated the respect, even the reverence, that most Americans felt for the Supreme Court. Even in times of economic catastrophe, Americans proved themselves fundamentally conservative toward their institutions, in stark contrast to Europeans, who experimented radically with their governments.

Ironically, though he lost the battle of the Supreme Court, Roosevelt won the war. By the spring of 1937, the Court began to reverse its position and in a 5-4 decision upheld the National Labor Relations Act. When Justice Willis Van Devanter retired, Roosevelt was able to make his first Supreme Court appointment, thus assuring at least a shaky liberal majority on the Court. But Roosevelt triumphed at great cost. His attempt to reorganize the Court dissipated energy and slowed the momentum of his legislative program. The most unpopular action he took as president, it made him vulnerable to criticism from opponents of the New Deal, and even some of his supporters were dismayed by what they regarded as an attack on the principle of separation of powers.

In late 1936 and early 1937, it appeared that the country was finally recovering from the long Depression; employment was up, and even the stock market had recovered some of its losses. But in August, the fragile prosperity collapsed. Unemployment shot back up nearly to the peak levels of 1934, industrial production fell, and the stock market plummeted. Roosevelt had probably helped to cause the recession by assuming that the prosperity of 1936 was permanent. He cut federal spending and reduced outlays for relief. He had always believed in balanced budgets and limited government spending, but now, facing an embarrassing economic slump that evoked charges that the New Deal had failed, he gave in to those of his advisers who were followers of John Maynard Keynes, the British economist.

Keynes argued that to get out of a depression, the government must spend massive amounts of money on goods and services. This action would increase demand and revive production. By increasing the money spent on the WPA and other agencies, Roosevelt's administration consciously practiced deficit spending for the first time in order to stimulate the economy. It was not a well-planned or well-coordinated effort, however. The economy responded slowly but never fully recovered until wartime expenditures, beginning in 1940, eliminated unemployment and ended the Depression.

The Third New Deal

Despite increasing hostility, Congress passed a number of important bills in 1937 and 1938 that completed the New Deal reform legislation. The Bankhead-Jones Farm Tenancy Act of 1937 created the Farm Security Administration (FSA) to aid tenant farmers, sharecroppers, and farm owners who had lost their farms. The FSA, which provided loans to grain collectives, also set up camps for migratory workers. Some people saw such policies as the first step toward communist collectives, but the FSA in fact never had enough money to make a real difference.

Congress passed a new Agricultural Adjustment Act in 1938 that tried to solve the problem of farm surpluses, which persisted even after hundreds of thousands of farmers had lost their farms. The new act replaced the processing tax, which the Supreme Court had declared unconstitutional, with direct payments from the federal treasury to farmers; added a soil conservation program; and provided for the marketing of surplus crops. Like its predecessor, the new act tried to stabilize farm prices by controlling production. But only the outbreak of World War II would end the problem of farm surplus, and then only temporarily.

In the cities, housing continued to be a problem. Progressive reformers had dreamed of providing better housing for the urban poor. They had campaigned for city ordinances and state laws and had built model tenements, but the first experiment with federal housing occurred during World War I. That brief experience encouraged a number of social reformers, who later became advisers to Roosevelt. They convinced him that federal low-cost housing should be part of New Deal reform.

The Reconstruction Finance Corporation made low-interest loans to housing projects, and the Public Works Administration constructed some apartments. But not until the National Housing Act of 1937 did Roosevelt and his advisers try to develop a comprehensive housing policy for the poor. The act provided federal funds for slum clearance projects and for the construction of low-cost housing. By 1939, however, only 117,000 units had been built. Most of these housing projects were bleak and boxlike, and many of them soon became problems rather than solutions. Though it made the first effort, the New Deal did not meet the challenge of providing decent housing for millions of American citizens.

In the long run, New Deal housing legislation had a greater impact on middle-class housing policies and patterns. During the first 100 days of the New Deal, at Roosevelt's urging, Congress passed a bill creating the Home Owners Loan Corporation (HOLC), which over the next two years made more than $3 billion in low-interest loans and helped over a million people save their homes from foreclosure. The HOLC also had a strong impact on housing policy by introducing the first long-term fixed-rate mortgages. Formerly, all mortgages were for periods of no more than five years and were subject to frequent renegotiation. The HOLC also introduced a uniform system of real estate appraisal that tended to undervalue urban property, especially in neighborhoods that were old, crowded, and ethnically mixed. The system gave the highest ratings to suburban developments where, according to the HOLC, there had been no "infiltration of Jews" or other undesirable groups. This was the beginning of the practice later called "redlining" that made it nearly impossible for certain prospective homeowners to obtain a mortgage in many urban areas.

The Federal Housing Administration (FHA), created in 1934 by the National Housing Act, expanded and extended many of these HOLC policies. The FHA insured mortgages, many of them for 25 or 30 years, reduced the down payment required from 30 percent to under 10 percent, and allowed over 11 million families to buy homes between 1934 and 1972. The system, however, tended to favor purchasing new suburban homes rather than repairing older urban residences. New Deal housing policies helped to make the suburban home with the long FHA mortgage part of the American way of life, but the policies also contributed to the decline of many urban neighborhoods.

Just as important as housing legislation was the Fair Labor Standards Act, which Congress passed in June 1938. Roosevelt's bill proposed for all industries engaged in interstate commerce a minimum wage of 25 cents an hour, to rise in two years to 40 cents an hour, and a maximum workweek of 44 hours, to be reduced to 40 hours. Congress amended the legislation and exempted

Key 1930s Reform Legislation

Year	Legislation	Provisions
1932	Reconstruction Finance Corporation (RFC)	Granted emergency loans to banks, life insurance companies, and railroads. (Passed during Hoover administration.)
1933	Civilian Conservation Corps (CCC)	Employed young men (and a few women) in reforestation, road construction, and flood control projects.
1933	Agricultural Adjustment Act (AAA)	Granted farmers direct payments for reducing production of certain products. Funds for payments provided by a processing tax, which was later declared unconstitutional.
1933	Tennessee Valley Authority (TVA)	Created independent public corporation to construct dams and power projects and to develop the economy of a nine-state area in the Tennessee River valley.
1933	National Industrial Recovery Act (NIRA)	Sought to revive business through a series of fair-competition codes. Section 7a guaranteed labor's right to organize. (Later declared unconstitutional.)
1933	Public Works Administration (PWA)	Sought to increase employment and business activity through construction of roads, buildings, and other projects.
1934	National Housing Act—created Federal Housing Administration (FHA)	Insured loans made by banks for construction of new homes and repair of old homes.
1935	Emergency Relief Appropriation Act—created Works Progress Administration (WPA)	Employed over 8 million people to repair roads, build bridges, and work on other projects; also hired artists and writers.
1935	Social Security Act	Established unemployment compensation and old-age and survivors' insurance paid for by a joint tax on employers and employees.
1935	National Labor Relations Act (Wagner-Connery Act)	Recognized the right of employees to join labor unions and to bargain collectively; created a new National Labor Relations Board to supervise elections and to prevent unfair labor practices.
1935	Public Utility Holding Company Act	Outlawed pyramiding of gas and electricity companies through the use of holding companies and restricted these companies to activity in one area; a "death sentence" clause gave companies five years to prove local, useful, and efficient operation or be dissolved.
1937	National Housing Act (Wagner-Steagall Act)	Authorized low-rent public housing projects.
1938	Agricultural Adjustment Act (AAA)	Continued price supports and payments to farmers to limit production, as in 1933 act, but replaced processing tax with direct federal payment.
1938	Fair Labor Standards Act	Established minimum wage of 40 cents an hour and maximum workweek of 40 hours in enterprises engaged in interstate commerce.

many groups, including farm laborers and domestic servants. Nevertheless, when it went into effect, 750,000 workers immediately received raises, and by 1940, some 12 million had had pay increases. The law also prohibited child labor in interstate commerce, making it the first permanent federal law to prohibit youngsters under 16 from working. And without emphasizing the matter, the law made no distinction between men and women, thus diminishing, if not completely ending, the need for special legislation for women.

The New Deal had many weaknesses, but it did dramatically increase government support for the needy. In 1913, local, state, and federal government spent $21 million on public assistance. By 1932, that had risen to $218 million; by 1939, it was $4.9 billion.

The Other Side of the 1930s

The Great Depression and the New Deal so dominate the history of the 1930s that it is easy to conclude that nothing else happened, that there were only bread lines and relief agencies. But there is another side of the decade. A communications revolution changed the lives of middle-class Americans. The sale of radios and attendance at movies increased during the 1930s, and literature flourished. Americans were fascinated by technology, especially automobiles. Many people traveled during the decade; they stayed in motor courts and looked ahead to a brighter future dominated by streamlined appliances and gadgets that would mean an easier life.

Taking to the Road

"People give up everything in the world but their car," a banker in Muncie, Indiana, remarked during the Depression, and that seems to have been true all over the country. Although automobile production dropped off after 1929 and did not recover until the end of the 1930s, the number of motor vehicles registered, which declined from 26.7 million in 1930 to just over 24 million in 1933, increased to over 32 million by 1940. People who could not afford new cars drove used ones. Even the "Okies" fleeing the dust bowl of the Southwest traveled in cars. They were secondhand, run-down cars to be sure, but the fact that even

The General Motors Building at the 1939 New York World's Fair. With the world hovering on the brink of war and the country still caught in the grip of depression, millions of Americans flocked to the fair to see a planned, streamlined world of the future.

many poor Americans owned cars shocked visitors from Europe, where automobiles were still only for the rich. The American middle class traveled at an increasing rate after the low point of 1932 and 1933. In 1938, the tourist industry was the third largest in the United States, behind only steel and automobile production. Over 4 million Americans traveled every year, and four out of five went by car. Many dragged a trailer to sleep in or stopped at the growing number of tourist courts and overnight cabins. In these predecessors of the motel there were no doormen, no bellhops, no register to sign. At the tourist court, all the owner wanted was the automobile license number.

The Electric Home

If the 1920s was the age of the bathroom, the 1930s was the era of the modern kitchen. The sale of electrical appliances increased throughout the decade, with refrigerators leading the way. In 1930, the number of refrigerators produced exceeded the number of iceboxes for the first time. Refrigerator production continued to rise throughout the decade, reaching a peak of 2.3 million in 1937. At first, the refrigerator was boxy and looked very much like an icebox with a motor sitting on top. In 1935, however, the refrigerator, like most other appliances, became streamlined. Sears, Roebuck advertised "The New 1935 Super Six Coldspot . . . Stunning in Its Streamlined Beauty." The Coldspot, which quickly influenced the look of all other models, was designed by Raymond Loewy, one of a group of industrial designers who emphasized sweeping horizontal lines, rounded corners, and a slick modern look. They hoped modern design would stimulate an optimistic attitude and, of course, increase sales.

Replacing an icebox with an electrical refrigerator, as many middle-class families did in the 1930s, altered more than the appearance of the kitchen. It also changed habits and life styles, especially for women. An icebox was part of a culture that included icemen, ice wagons (or ice trucks), picks, tongs, and a pan that had to be emptied continually. The refrigerator required no attention beyond occasional defrosting of the freezer compartment. Like the streamlined automobile, the sleek refrigerator became a symbol of

Household Appliance Production, 1922–1939

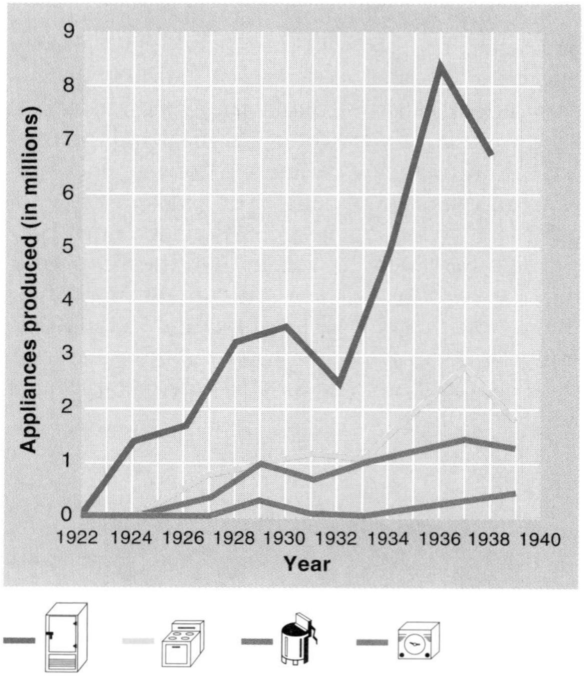

Electric appliances altered the lives of many American middle-class families during the 1930s. The replacement of the icebox with the electric refrigerator was especially dramatic.

Source: U.S. Bureau of the Census.

progress and modern civilization in the 1930s. At the end of the decade, in 1939, the World's Fair in New York glorified the theme of a streamlined future, carefully planned and based on new technology.

This reverence for technological progress contrasted with the economic despair in the 1930s, but people adapted to it selectively. For example, the electric washing machine and electric iron revolutionized washday. Yet even with labor-saving machines, most women continued to do their wash on Monday and their ironing on Tuesday. Packaged and canned goods became more widely available during the decade, and many women discovered that it was easier, and in some cases cheaper, to serve Kellogg's Corn Flakes or Nabisco Shredded Wheat than to make oatmeal, to heat Van Camp's pork and beans or Heinz spaghetti from a can than to prepare a meal, or to use commercially baked bread than to bake their own.

Ironically, despite these new conveniences, a great many middle-class families maintained their standard of living during the 1930s only because the women in the family learned to stretch and save and make do, and most wives spent as much time on housework as before. Some also took jobs outside the home to maintain their level of consumption. The number of married women who worked increased substantially during the decade. At the same time, many rural women, like those in the hill country of Texas and other remote areas, and many wives of the unemployed simply made do. They continued to cook, clean, and sew as their ancestors had for generations.

The Age of Leisure

During the Depression, many middle-class people found themselves with time on their hands and sought out ways of spending it. The 1920s was a time of spectator sports, of football and baseball heroes, of huge crowds that turned out to see boxing matches. Those sports continued during the Depression decade, although attendance suffered. Softball and miniature golf, which were cheap forms of entertainment and did not require expensive travel, also became popular. But leisure in the 1930s actually grew to be a problem, and professionals published some 450 new books on the subject. Leisure was mechanized; millions put their nickels in a slot and listened to a record played on a jukebox. Millions more played a pinball machine, a mechanized device that had no practical use other than entertainment and could end the game with one word: "Tilt."

Many popular games of the period had elaborate rules and directions. Contract bridge swept the country during the decade, and Monopoly was the most popular game of all. Produced by Parker Brothers, Monopoly was a fantasy of real estate speculation in which chance, luck, and the roll of the dice determined the winner. But one still had to obey the rules: "Go Directly to Jail. Do Not Pass Go. Do Not Collect $200." During a depression brought on in part by frenzied speculation, Americans were fascinated by a game whose purpose was to obtain real estate and utility monopolies and drive one's opponents into bankruptcy.

The 1930s was also a time of fads and instant celebrities, created by radio, newsreels, and businessmen ready to turn almost anything to commercial advantage. The leading box office attraction between 1935 and 1938 was Shirley Temple, a blond and adorable child star. She inspired dolls, dishes, books, and clothes. Even stranger was the excitement created by the birth of five identical girl babies to a couple in northern Ontario in 1934. The Dionne quintuplets appeared on dozens of magazine covers and endorsed every imaginable product. Millions of people waited eagerly for the latest news about the babies, and over 3 million traveled to see their home in Canada. The crazes over Shirley Temple and the Dionne quintuplets were products of the new technology, especially radio and the movies.

Literary Reflections of the 1930s

Though much of the literature of the 1930s reflected the decade's troubled currents, reading continued to be a popular and cheap entertainment. John Steinbeck, whose later novel *The Grapes of Wrath* (1939) followed the fortunes of the Joad family, described the plight of Mexican migrant workers in *Tortilla Flat* (1935). His novels expressed his belief that there was in American life a "crime . . . that goes beyond denunciation." "In the eyes of the hungry there is a growing wrath," he warned.

Other writers also questioned the American dream. John Dos Passos's trilogy *U.S.A.* (1930–1936) conveyed a deep pessimism about American capitalism that many other intellectuals shared. Less political were the novels of Thomas Wolfe and William Faulkner, who more sympathetically portrayed Americans caught up in the web of local life and facing the complex problems of the modern era. Faulkner's fictional Yoknapatawpha County, brought to life in *The Sound and the Fury, As I Lay Dying, Sanctuary,* and *Light in August* (1929–1932), documented the South's racial problems and its poverty as well as its stubborn pride. But the book about the South that became one of the decade's best-sellers was far more optimistic and far less complex than Faulkner's

RECOVERING THE PAST

The Movies

Just as some historians have used fiction to help define the cultural history of a decade, others in the twentieth century have turned to film to describe the "spirit of an age." On an elementary level, the movies help us appreciate changing styles in dress, furniture, and automobiles. We can even get some sense of how a particular time defined a beautiful woman or a handsome man, and we can learn about ethnic and racial stereotypes and assumptions about gender and class.

The decade of the 1930s is sometimes called the "golden age of the movies." Careful selection among the 500 or so feature films Hollywood produced each year during the decade—ranging from gangster and cowboy movies to Marx Brothers comedies, from historical romances to Busby Berkeley musical extravaganzas—could support a number of interpretations about the special myths and assumptions of the era. But one historian has argued that especially after 1934, "Not only did the movies amuse and entertain the nation through its most severe economic and social disorder, holding it together by their capacity to create unifying myths and dreams, but movie culture in the 1930s became a dominant culture for many Americans, providing new values and social ideals to replace shattered old traditions."

The year 1934 was a dividing line for two reasons. The motion picture industry, like all other industries had suffered during the Depression; 1933 marked the low point in attendance, with more than a third of the theaters in the country shut down. The next year, however, attendance picked up, heralding a revival that lasted until 1946. Also in 1934, the movie industry adopted a code for which the Catholic Legion of Decency and other religious groups had lobbied. The new code prohibited the depiction of "sex perversion, interracial sex, abortion, incest, drugs and profanity." Even married couples could not be shown together in a double bed. Although a movie could depict immoral behavior, sin always had to be punished. "Evil and good should never be confused," the code announced. Before the code, Hollywood had indeed produced graphic films, such as *The Public Enemy* (1931) and *Scarface* (1932), with a consider-

A scene from *It Happened One Night*, 1934.

A scene from *Drums Along the Mohawk*, 1939.

able amount of violence; musicals, such as *Gold Diggers* of 1933, filled with scantily clad young women; films featuring prostitutes, such as Jean Harlow in *Red Dust* (1932) and Marlene Dietrich in *Blond Venus* (1930); and other films that confronted the problems of real life. But after 1934, Hollywood concentrated on movies that created a mythical world where evil was always punished, family moral values won out in the end, and patriotism and American democracy were never questioned. Although the code was modified from time to time, it was not abandoned until 1966, when it was replaced by a rating system.

It Happened One Night (1934) and *Drums Along the Mohawk* (1939), two films out of thousands, illustrate some of the myths the movies created and sustained. Frank Capra, one of Hollywood's masters at entertaining without disturbing, directed *It Happened One Night*, a comedy-romance. A rich girl (played by Claudette Colbert) dives from her father's yacht off the coast of Florida and takes a bus for New York. She meets a newspaper reporter (Clark Gable). They have a series of madcap adventures and fall in love. But mix-ups and misunderstandings make it appear that she will marry her old boyfriend. In the end, however, they are reunited and marry in an elaborate outdoor ceremony. Afterward, they presumably live happily ever after. The movie is funny and entertaining and presents a variation on the poor-boy-marries-rich-girl theme. Like so many movies of the time, this one suggests that life is fulfilled for a woman only if she can find the right man to marry.

Claudette Colbert also stars in *Drums Along the Mohawk*, this time with Henry Fonda. Based on a 1936 novel by Walter Edmonds, *Drums* is a sentimental story about a man who builds a house in the wilderness, marries a pretty girl, fights off the Indians, and works with the simple country folk to create a satisfying life in the very year the American colonies rebel against Great Britain. *Drums* was one of a number of films based on historical themes that Hollywood released just before World War II. *The Howards of Virginia* (1940), *Northwest Passage* (1939), and most popular of all, *Gone with the Wind* (1939) were others in the same genre. Historical themes had been popular before, but with the world on the brink of war, the story of men and women in the wilderness struggling for family and country against the Indians (stereotyped as savages) proved comforting as well as entertaining.

Can a historian use movies to describe the values and myths of a particular time, or are the complexities and exaggerations too great? Are the most popular or most critically acclaimed films more useful than others in getting at the "spirit of an age"? What films popular today tell us most about our time and culture? Is there too much sex and violence in movies today? Should the government control the language, themes, and values depicted in movies? Are movies as important today as they were in the 1930s in defining and influencing the country's myths and values?

work—Margaret Mitchell's *Gone with the Wind* (1936). Its success suggested that many Americans read to escape, not to explore their problems.

Radio's Finest Hour

The number of radio sets purchased increased steadily during the decade. In 1929, slightly more than 10 million households owned radios; by 1939, fully 27.5 million households had radio sets. The radio was not just a source of music and news but a focal point of the living room. In many homes, the top of the radio became the symbolic mantel where cherished photos were displayed. Families gathered around the radio at night to listen to and laugh at Jack Benny or Edgar Bergen and Charlie McCarthy or to try to solve a murder mystery with Mr. and Mrs. North. "The Lone Ranger," another popular program, had 20 million listeners by 1939.

During the day there were soap operas. "Between thick slices of advertising," wrote James Thurber, "spread twelve minutes of dialogue, add predicament, villainy, and female suffering in equal measure, throw in a dash of nobility, sprinkle with tears, season with organ music, cover with a rich announcer sauce and serve five times a week." After school, teenagers and younger children argued over whether to listen to "Jack Armstrong, the All-American Boy" and "Captain Midnight" or "Stella Dallas" and "The Young Widder Brown."

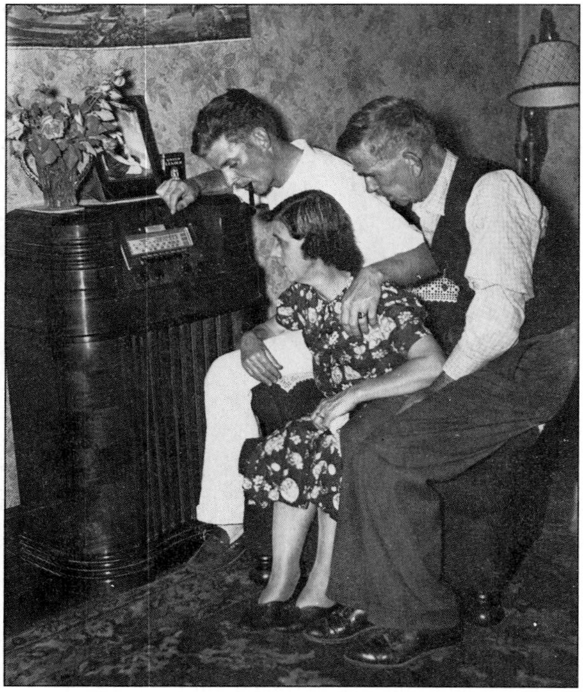

The radio played an important role in the 1930s. Here a family crowds around a typical floor model to listen to the latest news or to a favorite program.

Most families had only one radio, but everyone could join in the contests or send for magic rings or secret decoders. In Chicago's working-class neighborhoods in 1930 there was one radio for every two or three households but often families and friends gathered to listen to the radio. The reception was sometimes poor, especially in rural areas and small towns. Voices faded in and out and disappeared during storms. But the magic of radio allowed many people to feel connected to distant places and to believe they knew the radio performers personally. Radio was also responsible for one of the most widespread episodes of mass hysteria of all time. On October 31, 1938, Orson Welles broadcast "The War of the Worlds" so realistically that thousands of listeners really believed that Martians had landed in New Jersey. If anyone needed proof, that single program demonstrated the power of the radio.

The Silver Screen

The 1930s were the golden decade of the movies. Between 60 and 90 million Americans went to the movies every week. The medium was not entirely Depression-proof, but talking films had replaced the silent variety in the late 1920s, and attendance soared. Though it fell off slightly in the early 1930s, by 1934 movie viewing was climbing again. For many families, even in the depth of the Depression, movie money was as important as food money.

In the cities, one could go to an elaborate movie palace and live in a fantasy world far removed from the reality of Depression America. In small towns across the country, for 25 cents (10 cents under age 12) one could go to at least four movies during the week. There was a Sunday–Monday feature film (except in communities where the churches had prevented Sunday

Double features, newsreels, cartoons, an occasional stage show, and often a free gift of dinnerware (now called "depression glass") made the movie theater a popular place even during the Depression.

movies), a different feature of somewhat lesser prominence on Tuesday–Wednesday, and another on Thursday–Friday. On Saturday there was a cowboy or detective movie. Sometimes a double feature played, and always there were short subjects, a cartoon, and a newsreel. On Saturday there was usually a serial that left the heroine or hero in such a dire predicament that one just had to come back the next week to see how she or he survived.

The movies were a place to take a date, to go with friends, or to go as a family. Movies could be talked about for days. Young women tried to speak like Greta Garbo or to hold a cigarette like Joan Crawford. Jean Harlow and Mae West so popularized blonde hair that sales of peroxide shot up. Young men tried to emulate Clark Gable or Cary Grant, and one young man admitted that it was "directly through the movies that I learned to kiss a girl on her ears, neck, and cheeks, as well as on the mouth."

The animated cartoons of Walt Disney, one of the true geniuses of the movie industry, were so popular that Mickey Mouse was more famous and familiar than most human celebrities. In May 1933, halfway into Roosevelt's first 100 days, Disney released *The Three Little Pigs,* whose theme song "Who's Afraid of the Big Bad Wolf?" became a national hit overnight. Some people felt it boosted the nation's morale as much as New Deal legislation. One critic suggested that the moral of the story, as retold by Disney, was that the little pig survived because he was conservative, diligent, and hardworking; others felt that it was the pig who used modern tools and planned ahead who won out.

The Ambivalence of the Great Depression

The New Deal, despite its great variety of legislation, did not end the Depression, nor did it solve the problem of unemployment. For many Americans looking back on the decade of the 1930s, the most vivid memory was the shame and guilt of being unemployed, the despair and fear that came from losing a business or being evicted from a home or an apartment. Parents who lived through the decade urged their children to find a secure job, to get married, and to settle down. "Every time I've encountered the Depression it has been used as a barrier and a club," one daughter of Depression parents remembered; "older people use it to explain to me that I can't understand anything: I didn't live through the Depression."

New Deal legislation did not solve the country's problems, but it did strengthen the federal government, especially the executive branch. Federal agencies like the Federal Deposit Insurance Corporation and programs like social security influenced the daily lives of most Americans, and rural electrification, the WPA, and the CCC changed the lives of millions. The New Deal also established the principle of federal responsibility for the health of the economy, initiated the concept of the welfare state, and dramatically increased government spending to help the poor. Federally subsidized housing, minimum-wage laws, and a policy for paying farmers to limit production, all aspects of these principles, had far-reaching implications.

The New Deal was as important for what it did not do as for what it did. It did not promote socialism or redistribute income or property. It promoted social justice and social reform, but it provided little for people at the bottom of American society. The New Deal did not prevent business consolidation, and, in the end, it probably strengthened corporate capitalism.

Roosevelt, with his colorful personality and his dramatic response to the nation's crisis, dominated his times in a way few presidents have done. Yet for some people who lived through the decade, not Roosevelt or bread lines but a new streamlined refrigerator or a Walt Disney movie symbolized the Depression decade.

Recommended Reading

General Accounts

Robert S. McElvaine, *The Great Depression* (1984); Paul Conkin, *The New Deal* (1967); William E. Leuchtenburg, *Franklin D. Roosevelt and the New Deal* (1963); Anthony J. Badger, *The New Deal: The Depression Years* (1989).

The Depression

Donald Worster, *Dust Bowl* (1979); Studs Terkel, *Hard Times* (1970); Lester V. Chandler, *America's Greatest Depression* (1970); Joan Hoff Wilson, *Herbert Hoover: Forgotten Progressive* (1975); James Agee, *Let Us Now Praise Famous Men* (1941); Richard White, *The Roots of Dependency: Subsistence, Environment and Social Change Among the Choctaws, Pawnees, and Navajos* (1983).

Roosevelt and the New Deal

James MacGregor Burns, *Roosevelt: The Lion and the Fox* (1956); Frank Freidel, *Franklin Roosevelt: A Rendezvous with Destiny* (1990); Joseph Lash, *Eleanor and Franklin* (1971); Blanche Wiesen Cook, *Eleanor Roosevelt* (1992); Harvard Sitkoff, *A New Deal for Blacks* (1978); Dan T. Carter, *Scottsboro* (1969); Kenneth R. Philip, *John Collier's Crusade for Indian Reform* (1977); Abraham Hoffman, *Unwanted: Mexican Americans and the Great Depression* (1974); Roy Lubove, *The Struggle for Social Security* (1968); Richard Lowitt, *The New Deal and the West* (1984); Susan Ware, *Beyond Suffrage* (1981); Jerre Mangione, *The Dream and the Deal* (1972); Richard Pells, *Radical Visions and American Dreams* (1973); Alan Brinkley, *Voices of Protest: Huey Long, Father Coughlin and the Great Depression* (1982); Steve Fraser and Gary Gertstle, eds., *The Rise and Fall of the New Deal Order* (1989).

The Other Side of the Thirties

Siegfreid Giedion, *Mechanization Takes Command* (1948); Warren Sussman, ed., *Culture and Commitment* (1968); Andrew Bergman, *We're in the Money* (1972); William Stott, *Documentary Expression in Thirties America* (1973); Lizabeth Cohen, *Making a New Deal: Industrial Workers in Chicago, 1919–1939* (1990); Marjorie Rosen, *Popcorn Venus: Women, Movies and the American Dream* (1971).

Fiction

John Steinbeck shows Okies trying to escape the dust bowl in his novel, *The Grapes of Wrath* (1939); James Farrell describes growing up in Depression Chicago in *Studs Lonigan* (1932–1935); Richard Wright details the trials of a young black man in *Native Son* (1940).

TIMELINE

1929 Stock market crashes
Agricultural Marketing Act

1930 Depression worsens
Hawley-Smoot Tariff

1932 Reconstruction Finance Corporation established
Federal Home Loan Bank Act
Glass-Steagall Banking Act
Federal Emergency Relief Act
Bonus march on Washington
Franklin D. Roosevelt elected president

1933 Emergency Banking Relief Act
Home Owners Loan Corporation
Twenty-first Amendment repeals Eighteenth, ending prohibition
Agricultural Adjustment Act
National Industrial Recovery Act
Civilian Conservation Corps
Tennessee Valley Authority established
Public Works Administration established

1934 Unemployment peaks
Federal Housing Administration established
Indian Reorganization Act

1935 Second New Deal begins
Works Progress Administration established
Social Security Act
Rural Electrification Act
National Labor Relations Act
Public Utility Holding Company Act
Committee for Industrial Organization (CIO) formed

1936 United Auto Workers hold sit-down strikes against General Motors
Roosevelt reelected president
Economy begins rebound

1937 Attempt to expand the Supreme Court
Economic collapse
Farm Security Administration established
National Housing Act

1938 Fair Labor Standards Act
Agricultural Adjustment Act

CHAPTER 25

World War II

N. Scott Momaday, a Kiowa Indian born at Lawton, Oklahoma, in 1934, grew up on Navajo, Apache, and Pueblo reservations. He was only 11 when World War II ended, yet the war changed his life. Shortly after the United States entered the war, Momaday's parents moved to New Mexico, where his father got a job with an oil company and his mother worked in the civilian personnel office at an Army Air Force base. Like many couples, they had struggled through the hard times of the Depression. The war meant jobs.

Reading Right to Left—FIRST ROW: Britain, Canada, Australia, New Zealand, SECOND ROW: Southern Rhodesia, Newfoundland, South Africa, THIRD ROW: India, FOURTH ROW: The Colonial Empire
Reading Left to Right—FIRST ROW: U.S.A., China, U.S.S.R., Yugoslavia, SECOND ROW: Holland, France, Poland, Czechoslovakia, THIRD ROW: Greece, Norway, Belgium
FREEDOM SHALL PREVAIL!

Momaday's best friend was Billy Don Johnson, a "reddish, robust boy of great good humor and intense loyalty." Together they played war, digging trenches and dragging themselves through imaginary mine fields. They hurled grenades and fired endless rounds from their imaginary machine guns, pausing only to drink Kool-Aid from their canteens. At school, they were taught history and math and also how to hate the enemy and be proud of America. They recited the Pledge of Allegiance to the flag and sang "God Bless America," "The Star-Spangled Banner," and "Remember Pearl Harbor." Like most Americans, they believed that World War II was a good war fought against evil empires. The United States was always right, the enemy always wrong. It was an attitude that would influence Momaday and his generation for the rest of their lives.

Momaday's only difficulty was that his Native American face was often mistaken for that of an Asian. Almost every day on the playground, someone would yell, "Hi ya, Jap," and a fight was on. Billy Don always came to his friend's defense, but it was disconcerting to be taken for the enemy. His father read old Kiowa tales to Momaday, who was proud to be an Indian but prouder still to be an American. On Saturday, he and his friends would go to the local theater to cheer as they watched a Japanese Zero or a German Me-109 go down in flames. They pretended that they were P-40 pilots. "The whole field of vision shuddered with our fire: the 50-caliber tracers curved out, fixing brilliant arcs upon the span, and struck; then there was a black burst of smoke, and the target went spinning down to death."

Near the end of the war, his family moved again, as so many families did, so that his father might get a better job. This time they lived right next door to an air force base, and Scott fell in love with the B-17 "Flying Fortress," the bomber that military strategists thought would win the war in the Pacific and in Europe. He felt a real sense of resentment and loss when the B-17 was replaced by the larger but not nearly so glamorous B-29.

Looking back on his early years, Momaday reflected on the importance of the war in his growing up. "I see now that one experiences easily the ordinary things of life," he decided, "the things which cast familiar shadows upon the sheer, transparent panels of time, and he perceives his experience in the only way he can, according to his age." Though Momaday's life during the war differed from the lives of boys old enough to join the forces, the war was no less real for him. Though his youth was affected by the fact that he was male, was an Indian, and lived in the Southwest, the most important influence was that he was an American growing up during the war. Ironically, his parents, made U.S. citizens by an act of Congress in 1924, like all Native Americans living in Arizona and New Mexico were denied the right to vote by state law.

The Momadays fared better than most Native Americans, who found prejudice against them undiminished and jobs, even in wartime, hard to find. Native American servicemen returning from the war discovered that they were still treated like "Indians." They were prohibited from buying liquor in many states, and those who returned to the reservations learned that they were ineligible for veterans' benefits. Still, Momaday thought of himself not so much as an Indian as an American, and that too was a product of his generation. But as he grew to maturity, he became a successful writer and spokesman for his people. In 1969, he won the Pulitzer Prize for his novel *House Made of Dawn*. He also recorded his experiences and memories in a book called *The Names* (1976). In his writing, he stresses the Indian's close identification with the land. Writing about his grandmother, he says: "The immense landscape of the continental interior lay like memory in her blood."

Despite the fact that no American cities were bombed and the country was never invaded, World War II influenced almost every aspect of American life. The war ended the Depression. Industrial jobs were plentiful, and even though prejudice and discrimination did not disappear, blacks, Hispanics, women, and other minorities had new opportunities. Because of wartime restrictions and a shortage of consumer goods, newly affluent workers saved a substantial part of their earnings. These savings would help fuel unprecedented prosperity after the conflict's end. Like World War I, the second war expanded cooperation between government and industry and increased the influence of government in all areas of American life. The war also ended the last remnants of American isolationism. The United States emerged from the war in 1945 as the most powerful and most prosperous nation in the world. But the American people accepted the role of world leadership with ambivalence. Victory led to questioning and self-doubt, especially as Americans began to perceive the Soviet Union as a new threat to the country's security.

This chapter traces the gradual involvement of the United States in the international events during the 1930s that finally led to participation in the most devastating war the world had seen. It recounts the diplomatic and military struggles of the war and the search for a secure peace. It also seeks to explain the impact of the war on ordinary people and on American attitudes about the world, as well as its effect on patriotism and the American way of life. The war brought prosperity to some as it brought death to others. It left the American people the most affluent in the world and the United States the most powerful nation.

The Twisting Road to War

Looking back on the events between 1933 and 1941 that eventually led to American involvement in World War II, it is easy either to be critical of decisions made or actions not taken or to see everything that happened during the period as inevitable. Historical events are never inevitable, and leaders who must make decisions never have the advantage of retrospective vision; they have to deal with situations as they find them, and they never have all the facts.

Foreign Policy in the 1930s

In March 1933, Roosevelt faced not only overwhelming domestic difficulties but also international crisis. The worldwide depression had caused near financial disaster in Europe. Germany had defaulted on its reparations installments, and most European countries were unable to keep up the payments on their debts to the United States. President Hoover had agreed to a brief moratorium on war debts in 1931 and had pledged American participation in an international economic conference to be held in London in June 1933.

Roosevelt had no master plan in foreign policy, just as he had none in the domestic sphere. In the first days of his administration, he gave conflicting signals as he groped to respond to the international situation. At first, it seemed that the president would cooperate in some kind of international economic agreement on tariffs and currency. But then he undercut the American delegation in London by refusing to go along with any international agreement. Solving the American domestic economic crisis seemed more important to Roosevelt in 1933 than international economic cooperation. His actions signaled a decision to go it alone in foreign policy in the 1930s.

Roosevelt did, however, alter some of the foreign policy decisions of previous administrations. For example, he recognized the Soviet government. There were many reasons why the United States had not recognized the Soviet Union during the 1920s. The new regime had failed to accept the debts of the czar's government, but more important, Americans feared communism and believed that recognition meant approval. In reversing this nonrecognition policy, Roosevelt hoped to gain a market for surplus American grain. Although the expected trade bonanza never materialized, the Soviet Union agreed to pay the old debts and to extend rights to American citizens living in the Soviet Union. Diplomatic recognition opened communications between the two emerging world powers.

Led by Secretary of State Cordell Hull, Roosevelt's administration also reversed the earlier policy of intervention in South America. The United States continued to support dictators, especially in Central America, because they promised to promote stability and preserve American economic interests. But Roosevelt, extending the Good Neighbor policy Hoover had initiated, completed the removal of American military forces from Haiti and Nicaragua in 1934, and, in a series of pan-American conferences, he joined in pledging that no country in the hemisphere would intervene in the "internal or external affairs" of any other. The United States still had economic and trade interests in Latin America, however, and with many of the Latin American economies in disarray because of the Depression, pressures mounted to resume the policy of military intervention.

The first test case came in Cuba, where a revolution threatened American investments of more than a billion dollars. But the United States did not send troops. Instead Roosevelt dispatched special envoys to work out a conciliatory agreement with the revolutionary government. A short time later, when a coup led by Fulgencio Batista overthrew the revolutionary government, the United States not only recognized the Batista government but also offered a large loan and agreed to abrogate the Platt Amendment (which made Cuba a virtual protectorate of the United States) in return for the rights to a naval base.

The Trade Agreements Act of 1934 gave the president power to lower tariff rates by as much as 50 percent and took the tariff away from the pressure of special-interest groups in Congress. Using this act, the Roosevelt administration negotiated a series of agreements that improved trade. By 1935, half of American cotton exports and a large proportion of other products were going to Latin America. So the Good Neighbor policy was also good business for the United States. But increased trade did not solve the economic problems for either the United States or Latin America.

Another test for Latin American policy came in 1938 when Mexico nationalized the property of a number of American oil companies. Instead of intervening, as many businessmen urged, the State Department patiently worked out an agreement that included some compensation for the companies. The American government might have acted differently, however, if the threat of war in Europe in 1938 had not created a fear that all the Western Hemisphere nations would have to cooperate to resist the growing power of Germany and Italy. At a pan-American conference held that year, the United States and most Latin American countries agreed to resist all foreign intervention in the hemisphere.

Neutrality in Europe

Around the time that Roosevelt was elected president, Adolf Hitler came to power in Germany. Born in Austria in 1889, Hitler had served as a corporal in the German army during World War I. Like many other Germans, he was angered by the Treaty of Versailles. But he blamed Germany's defeat on the Communists and the Jews.

Hitler had a checkered life after the war. He became the leader of the National Socialist party of the German workers (*Nazi* is short for *National*), and in 1923, after leading an unsuccessful coup, he was sentenced to prison. While in jail he wrote *Mein Kampf* ("My Struggle"), a long, rambling book spelling out his theories of racial purity, his hopes for Germany, and his venomous hatred of the Jews. After his release from prison, Hitler's following grew. He had a charismatic style and a plan. On January 30, 1933, he became chancellor of Germany, and within months the Reichstag (parliament) suspended the constitution, making Hitler *Führer* (leader) and dictator. His Fascist regime concentrated political and economic power in a centralized state. He intended to conquer Europe and to make the German Third Reich (empire) the center of a new civilization.

In 1934, Hitler announced a program of German rearmament, violating the Versailles Treaty of 1919. Meanwhile, in Italy, a Fascist dictator, Benito Mussolini, was building a powerful military force, and in 1934, he threatened to invade the East African country of Ethiopia. These omi-

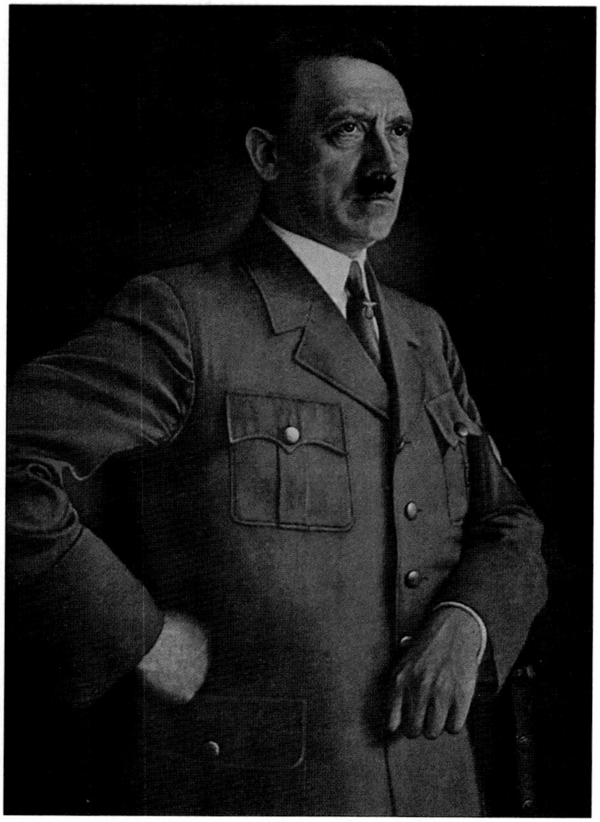

Newsreels and popular magazines such as *Life* and *Look* made Hitler's image and mannerisms familiar to all Americans.

nous rumblings in Europe frightened Americans at the very time they were reexamining American entry into the Great War and vowing that they would never again get involved in a European conflict.

Senator Gerald P. Nye of North Dakota, a conscientious and determined man who had helped expose the Teapot Dome scandal in 1924, turned to an investigation of the connection between corporate profits and American participation in World War I. His committee's public hearings revealed that many American businessmen had close relationships with the War Department. Businesses producing war materials had made huge profits. Though the committee failed to prove a conspiracy, it was easy to conclude that the United States had been tricked into going to war by the people who profited most from it.

On many college campuses, students demonstrated against war. On April 13, 1934, a day of protest around the country, students at Smith College placed white crosses on the campus as a memorial to the people killed in the Great War and those who would die in the next one. The next year, even more students went on strike for a day. Students joined organizations like Veterans of Future Wars and Future Gold Star Mothers and protested the presence of the Reserve Officer Training Corps on their campuses. One college president, who supported the peace movement, announced, "We will be called cowards . . . [but] I say that war must be banished from civilized society if democratic civilization and culture are to be perpetuated." Not all students supported the peace movement, but in the mid-1930s, many young people as well as adults joined peace societies such as the Fellowship of Reconciliation and the Women's International League for Peace and Freedom. They were determined never again to support a foreign war. But in Europe, Asia, and Africa, there were already rumblings of another great international conflict.

Ethiopia and Spain

In May 1935, Italy invaded Ethiopia after rejecting the League of Nations' offer to mediate the difficulties between the two countries. Italian dive bombers and machine guns made quick work of the small and poorly equipped Ethiopian army. The Ethiopian war, remote as it seemed, frightened Congress, which passed a Neutrality Act authorizing the president to prohibit all arms shipments to nations at war and to advise all United States citizens not to travel on belligerents' ships except at their own risk. Remembering the process that led the United States into World War I, Congress was determined that it would not happen again. Though he would have preferred a more flexible bill, Roosevelt used the authority of the Neutrality Act of 1935 to impose an arms embargo. The League of Nations condemned Italy as the aggressor in the war, and Great Britain moved its fleet to the Mediterranean. But neither Britain nor the United States wanted to stop shipments of oil to Italy or to commit its own soldiers to the fight. The embargo on arms had little impact on Italy, but it was disastrous for the poor African nation. Italy quickly defeated Ethiopia, and by 1936, Mussolini had joined forces with Germany to form the Rome-Berlin Axis.

"We shun political commitments which might entangle us in foreign war," Roosevelt announced in 1936. "We are not isolationist except in so far as we seek to isolate ourselves completely from war." But isolation became more difficult when a civil war broke out in Spain in 1936. General Francisco Franco, supported by the Catholic church and large landowners, revolted against the republican government. Germany and Italy aided Franco, sending planes and other weapons, while the Soviet Union came to the support of the Spanish republican Loyalists.

The war in Spain polarized the United States. Most Catholics and many anti-Communists sided with Franco. But many American radicals, even those opposed to all war a few months before, found the Loyalist cause worth fighting and dying for. Over 3,000 Americans joined the Abraham Lincoln Brigade, and hundreds were killed fighting fascism in Spain. "If this were a Spanish matter, I'd let it alone," Sam Levenger, a student at Ohio State, wrote. "But the rebellion would not last a week if it weren't for the Germans and the Italians. And if Hitler and Mussolini can send troops to Spain to attack the government elected by the people, why can't they do so in France? And after France?" Levenger was killed in Spain in 1937 at the age of 20.

Not everyone agreed that the moral issues in Spain were worth dying for. The U.S. government tried to stay neutral and to ship arms and equipment to neither side. The Neutrality Act, extended in 1936, technically did not apply to civil wars, but the State Department imposed a moral embargo. However, when an American businessman disregarded it and attempted to send 400 used airplane engines to the Loyalists, Roosevelt asked Congress to extend the arms embargo to Spain. While the United States, along with Britain and France, carefully protected its neutrality, Franco consolidated his dictatorship with the active aid of Germany and Italy. Meanwhile, Congress in 1937 passed another Neutrality Act, this time making it illegal for American citizens to travel on belligerents' ships. The act extended the embargo on arms and made even nonmilitary items available to belligerents only on a cash-and-carry basis.

In a variety of ways, the United States tried to avoid repeating the mistakes that had led it into World War I. Unfortunately, World War II, which moved closer each day, would be a different kind of war, and the lessons of the first war would be of little use.

War in Europe

Roosevelt had no carefully planned strategy to deal with the rising tide of war in Europe in the late 1930s. He was by no means an isolationist, but he wanted to keep the United States out of the European conflagration. When he announced, "I hate war," he was expressing a deep personal belief that wars solve few problems. Unlike his distant cousin Theodore Roosevelt, he did not view war as a test of one's manhood. In foreign policy, just as in domestic affairs, he responded to events, but he moved reluctantly (and with agonizing slowness, from the point of view of many of his critics) toward more and more American involvement in the war.

In March 1938, Hitler's Germany annexed Austria and then in September, as a result of the Munich Conference, occupied the Sudetenland, a part of Czechoslovakia. Within six months, Hitler's armies had overrun the rest of Czechoslovakia. Little protest came from the United States. Most Americans sympathized with the victims of Hitler's aggression, and eventually some were horrified at rumors of the murder of hundreds of thousands of Jews. But because newspapers avoided intensive coverage of the well-documented but unpleasant stories, many Americans did not learn of the Holocaust of the early 1940s until near the end of the war. At first, almost everyone hoped that compromises could be worked out and that Europe could settle its own problems. But that notion was destroyed on August 23, 1939, by the news of a Nazi-Soviet pact. Fascism and communism were political philosophies supposedly in deadly opposition. Many Americans had secretly hoped that Nazi Germany and Soviet Russia would fight it out, neutralizing each other. Now they had signed a nonaggression pact. A week later, Hitler's army attacked Poland, marking the official beginning of World War II. Britain and France honored their treaties and came to Poland's defense. "This nation will remain a neutral nation," Roosevelt announced, "but I cannot ask that every American remain neutral in thought as well."

Roosevelt asked for a repeal of the embargo section of the Neutrality Act and for the approval of the sale of arms on a cash-and-carry basis to France and Britain. The United States would help the countries struggling against Hitler, but not at the risk of entering the war or even at the threat

smarter than W.W. in 1914

of disrupting the civilian economy. Yet Roosevelt did take some secret risks. In August 1939, Albert Einstein, a Jewish refugee from Nazi Germany, and other distinguished scientists warned the president that German researchers were at work on an atomic bomb. Fearing the consequences of a powerful new weapon in Hitler's hands, Roosevelt authorized funds for a top-secret project to build an American bomb first. Only a few advisers and key members of Congress knew of the project, which was officially organized in 1941 and would ultimately change the course of human history.

The war in Poland ended quickly. With Germany attacking from the west and the Soviet Union from the east, the Poles were overwhelmed in a month. The fall of Poland in September 1939 brought a lull in the fighting. A number of Americans, including the American ambassador to Great Britain, Joseph Kennedy, who feared Communist Russia more than Fascist Germany, urged the United States to take the lead in negotiating a peace settlement that would recognize the German and Russian occupation of Poland. The British and French, however, were not interested in such a solution, and neither was Roosevelt.

Great Britain sent several divisions to aid the French against the expected German attack, but for months nothing happened. This interlude, sometimes called the "phony war," dramatically ended on April 9, 1940, when Germany attacked Norway and Denmark with a furious air and sea assault. A few weeks later, using armored vehicles supported by massive air strikes, the German *Blitzkrieg* swept through Belgium, Luxembourg, and the Netherlands. A week later, the Germans stormed into France. The famed Maginot line, a series of fortifications designed to repulse a German invasion, was useless, as German mechanized forces swept around the end of the line and attacked from the rear. The French guns, solidly fixed in concrete and pointing toward Germany, were never fired. The Maginot line, which would have been an effective defensive weapon in World War I, was ineffective in the new mechanized and mobile war of the 1940s. France surrendered in June as the British army fled back across the English Channel from Dunkirk.

How should the United States respond to the new and desperate situation in Europe? William Allen White, journalist and editor, and other concerned Americans organized the Committee to Defend America by Aiding the Allies, but others, including Charles Lindbergh, the hero of the 1920s, supported a group called America First. They argued that the United States should forget about England and concentrate on defending America. Roosevelt steered a cautious course. He approved the shipment to Britain of 50 overage American destroyers. In return, the United States received the right to establish naval and air bases on British territory from Newfoundland to Bermuda and British Guiana.

Winston Churchill, prime minister of Great Britain, asked for much more, but Roosevelt hesitated. In July 1940, he did sign a measure authorizing $4 billion to increase the number of American naval warships. In September, Congress passed the Selective Service Act, which provided for the first peacetime draft in the history of the United States. Over a million men were to serve in the army for one year, but only in the Western Hemisphere. As the war in Europe reached a crisis in the fall of 1940, the American people were still undecided about the proper response.

The Election of 1940

Part of Roosevelt's reluctance to aid Great Britain more energetically came from his genuine desire to keep the United States out of the war, but it was also related to the presidential campaign waged during the crisis months of the summer and fall of 1940. Roosevelt broke a long tradition by seeking a third term. He marked the increasing support he was drawing from the liberal wing of the Democratic party by selecting liberal farm economist Henry Wallace of Iowa as his running mate. The Republicans chose Wendell Willkie of Indiana. Despite his big-business ties, Willkie approved of most New Deal legislation and supported aid to Great Britain. Energetic and attractive, Willkie was the most persuasive and exciting Republican candidate since Theodore Roosevelt, and he appealed to many people who distrusted or disliked Roosevelt. Yet in an atmosphere of international crisis, most voters chose to stay with Roosevelt. He won, 27 million to 22 million, and carried 38 of 48 states.

Lend-Lease

After the election, Roosevelt invented a scheme for sending aid to Britain without demanding payment. He called it "lend-lease." He compared the situation to lending a garden hose to a neighbor whose house was on fire. Senator Robert Taft of Ohio, however, thought the idea of lending military equipment and expecting it back was absurd. He decided it was more like lending chewing gum to a friend: "Once it had been used you did not want it back." Others were even more critical. Senator Burton K. Wheeler, an extreme isolationist, branded lend-lease "Roosevelt's triple A foreign policy" (after the Agricultural Adjustment Act) because it was designed to "plow under every fourth American boy."

The Lend-Lease Act, which Congress passed in March 1941, destroyed the fiction of neutrality. By that time, German submarines were sinking a half million tons of shipping each month in the Atlantic. In June, Roosevelt proclaimed a national emergency and ordered the closing of German and Italian consulates in the United States. On June 22, Germany suddenly attacked the Soviet Union. It was one of Hitler's biggest blunders of the war, for now his armies had to fight on two fronts.

The surprise attack, however, created a dilemma for the United States. Suddenly the great Communist "enemy" had become America's friend and ally. When Roosevelt extended lend-lease aid to Russia in November 1941, many Americans were shocked. But most made a quick transition from viewing the Soviet Union as an enemy to treating it like a friend.

By the autumn of 1941, the United States was virtually at war with Germany in the Atlantic. On September 11, Roosevelt issued a "shoot on sight" order for all American ships operating in the Atlantic, and on October 30, a German submarine sank an American destroyer off the coast of Newfoundland. The war in the Atlantic, however, was undeclared, and many Americans opposed it. Eventually the sinking of enough American ships or another crisis would probably have provided the excuse for a formal declaration of war against Germany. It was not Germany, however, but Japan that catapulted the United States into World War II.

The Path to Pearl Harbor

Japan, controlled by ambitious military leaders, was the aggressor in the Far East as Hitler's Germany was in Europe. Intent on becoming a major world power yet desperately needing natural resources, especially oil, Japan was willing to risk war with China, the Soviet Union, and even the United States to get those resources. Japan invaded Manchuria in 1931 and launched an all-out assault on China in 1937. The Japanese leaders assumed that at some point the United States would go to war if Japan tried to take the Philippines, but the Japanese attempted to delay that moment as long as possible by diplomatic means. For its part, the United States feared the possibility of a two-front war and was willing to delay the confrontation with Japan until it had dealt with the German threat. Thus between 1938 and 1941, the United States and Japan engaged in a kind of diplomatic shadow boxing.

The United States did exert economic pressure on Japan. In July 1939, the United States gave the required six months' notice regarding cancellation of the 1911 commercial agreement between the two countries. In September 1940, the Roosevelt administration forbade the shipment of airplane fuel and scrap metal to Japan. Other items were added to the embargo until by the spring of 1941, the United States allowed only oil to be shipped to Japan, hoping that the threat of cutting off the important resource would lead to negotiations and avert a crisis. Japan did open negotiations with the United States, but there was little to discuss. Japan would not withdraw from China as the United States demanded. Indeed, Japan, taking advantage of the situation in Europe, occupied French Indochina in 1940 and 1941. In July 1941, Roosevelt froze all Japanese assets in the United States, effectively embargoing trade with Japan.

Roosevelt had an advantage in the negotiations with Japan, for the United States had broken the Japanese secret diplomatic code. But Japanese intentions were hard to decipher from the intercepted messages. The American leaders knew that Japan planned to attack, but they didn't know when. In September 1941, the Japanese decided to strike sometime after November unless the United States offered real concessions. The strike came not in the Philippines but at Pearl Harbor, the main American Pacific naval base, in Hawaii.

On the morning of December 7, 1941, Japanese airplanes launched from aircraft carriers attacked the United States fleet at Pearl Harbor. The surprise attack destroyed or disabled 19 ships

An exploding American battleship at Pearl Harbor, December 7, 1941. The attack on Pearl Harbor united the country and came to symbolize Japanese treachery and American lack of preparedness. Photographs such as this were published throughout the war to inspire Americans to work harder.

(including 5 battleships) and 150 planes and killed 2,335 soldiers and sailors and 68 civilians. On the same day, the Japanese launched attacks on the Philippines, Guam, and the Midway Islands, as well as on the British colonies of Hong Kong and Malaya. The next day, with only one dissenting vote, Congress declared war on Japan. Jeannette Rankin, a member of Congress from Montana who had voted against the war resolution in 1917, voted no again in 1941. She recalled that in 1917, after a week of tense debate, 50 voted against going to war. "This time I stood alone."

Corporal John J. "Ted" Kohl, a 25-year-old from Springfield, Ohio, was standing guard that Sunday morning near an ammunition warehouse at Hickam Field, near Pearl Harbor. He had joined the army two years before when his marriage failed and he could not find work. A Japanese bomb hit nearby, and Ted Kohl blew up with the warehouse. It was not until Wednesday evening, December 10, that the telegram arrived in Springfield. "The Secretary of War desires to express his deep regrets that your son Cpl. John J. Kohl was killed in action in defense of his country." Ted's younger brothers cried when they heard the news. There would be hundreds of thousands of telegrams and even more tears before the war was over.

why choose him?

December 7, 1941, was a day that "would live in infamy," in the words of Franklin Roosevelt. It was also a day that would have far-reaching implications for American foreign policy and for American attitudes toward the world. The surprise attack united the country as nothing else could have. Even isolationists and "America first" advocates quickly rallied behind the war effort.

After the shock and anger subsided, Americans searched for a villain. Someone must have blundered, someone must have betrayed the country to have allowed the "inferior" Japanese to have carried out such a successful and devastating attack. A myth persists to this day that the villain was Roosevelt, who, the story goes, knew of the Japanese attack but failed to warn the military commanders so that the American people might unite behind the war effort against Germany. But Roosevelt did not know. There was no specific warning that the attack was coming against Pearl Harbor, and the American ability to read the Japanese coded messages was no help because the fleet kept radio silence.

The irony was that the Americans, partly because of racial prejudice against the Japanese, underestimated their ability. They ignored many warning signals because they did not believe that the Japanese could launch an attack on a target as far away as Hawaii. Most of the experts, including Roosevelt, expected the Japanese to attack the Philippines or perhaps Thailand. Many people blundered, but there was no conspiracy on the part of Roosevelt and his advisers to get the United States into the war.

Even more important in the long run than the way the attack on Pearl Harbor united the American people was its effect on a generation of military and political leaders. Pearl Harbor became the symbol of unpreparedness. For a generation that experienced the anger and frustration of the attack on Pearl Harbor by an unscrupulous enemy, the lesson was to be prepared and ready to stop an aggressor before it had a chance to strike at the United States. The smoldering remains of the sinking battleships at Pearl Harbor on the morning of December 7, 1941, and the history lesson learned there would influence American policy not only during World War II but also in Korea, Vietnam, and the international confrontations of the 1980s.

The Home Front

Too often wars are described in terms of presidents and generals, emperors and kings, in terms of grand strategy and elaborate campaigns. But wars affect the lives of all people—the soldiers who fight and the women and children and men who stay home. World War II especially had an impact on all aspects of society—the economy, the movies and radio, even attitudes toward women and blacks. For many people, the war represented opportunity and the end of the Depression. For others, the excitement of faraway places meant that they could never return home again. For still others, the war left lasting scars.

Mobilizing for War

Converting American industry to war production was a complex task. Many corporate executives refused to admit that an emergency existed. Shortly after Pearl Harbor, Roosevelt created the War Production Board (WPB) and appointed Donald Nelson, executive vice-president of Sears, Roebuck, to mobilize the nation's resources for an all-out war effort. The WPB offered businesses cost-plus contracts, guaranteeing a fixed and generous profit. Often the government also financed new plants and equipment. Secretary of War Henry Stimson remarked, "If you . . . go to war . . . in a capitalist country, you have to let business make money out of the process or business won't work." Roosevelt seemed to agree.

The Roosevelt administration leaned over backward to gain the cooperation of businessmen, many of whom New Deal policies had alienated. The president appointed many business

Changing work shifts at an airplane plant in Inglewood, California, in 1942. The war suddenly meant jobs for most Americans. But it was still difficult, especially early in the war, for some groups to find employment. These workers seem to be almost entirely white and male.

executives to key positions, some of whom, like Nelson, served for a dollar a year. He also abandoned antitrust actions in all industries that were remotely war-related. The probusiness policies angered some of his supporters. "The New Dealers are a vanishing tribe," one remarked, "and the moneychangers who were driven from the temple are now quietly established in government offices."

The policy worked, however. Both industrial production and net corporate profits nearly doubled during the war. Large commercial farmers also profited. With many members of Congress supporting their demands, the farmers exacted high support prices for basic commodities. The war years accelerated the mechanization of the farm. Between 1940 and 1945, a million tractors joined those already in use. At the same time, the farm population declined by 17 percent. The consolidation of small farms into large ones and the dramatic increase in the use of fertilizer made farms more productive and farming more profitable for the large operators.

Many government agencies in addition to the War Production Board helped to run the war effort efficiently. The Office of Price Administration (OPA), eventually placed under the direction of Chester Bowles, an advertising executive, set prices on thousands of items to control inflation. The OPA also rationed scarce products. Because the OPA's decisions affected what people wore and ate and whether they had gasoline, many regarded it as oppressive. The National War Labor Board (NWLB) had the authority to set wages and hours and to monitor working conditions and could, under the president's wartime emergency powers, seize industrial plants whose owners refused to cooperate.

Membership in labor unions grew rapidly during the war, from a total of 10.5 million in 1941 to 14.7 million in 1945. This increase was aided by government policy. In return for a "no-strike pledge," the NWLB allowed agreements that required workers to retain their union membership through the life of a contract. Labor leaders, however, complained about increased government regulations and argued that wage controls coupled with wartime inflation were unfair. The NWLB finally allowed a 15 percent cost-of-living increase on some contracts, but that did not apply to overtime pay, which helped drive up wages in some industries during the war by about 70 percent. Labor leaders were often not content with the raises. In the most famous incident, John L. Lewis broke the no-strike pledge of organized labor by calling a nationwide coal strike in 1943. When Roosevelt ordered the secretary of the interior to take over the mines, Lewis called off the strike. But this bold protest did help raise miners' wages.

In addition to wage and price controls and rationing, the government tried to reduce inflation by selling war bonds and by increasing taxes. The Revenue Act of 1942 raised tax rates, broadened the tax base, increased corporate taxes to 40 percent, and raised the excess-profits tax to 90 percent. In addition, the government initiated a payroll deduction for income taxes. The war made the income tax a reality for most Americans for the first time.

Despite some unfairness and much confusion, the American economy responded to the

Military Expenditures and the National Debt, 1929–1945

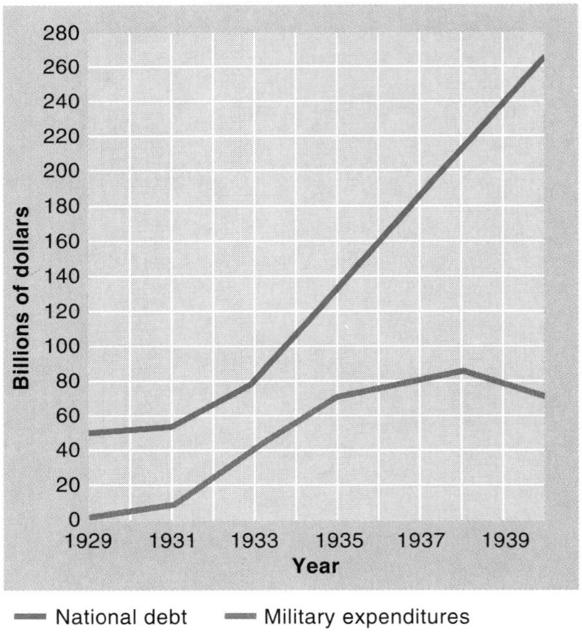

Increased taxes, the sale of war bonds, and price controls kept inflation under relative control during the war. Still, war industry not only stimulated the economy but also increased the national debt.

Source: U.S. Bureau of the Census.

Gross National Product and Unemployment, 1940–1945

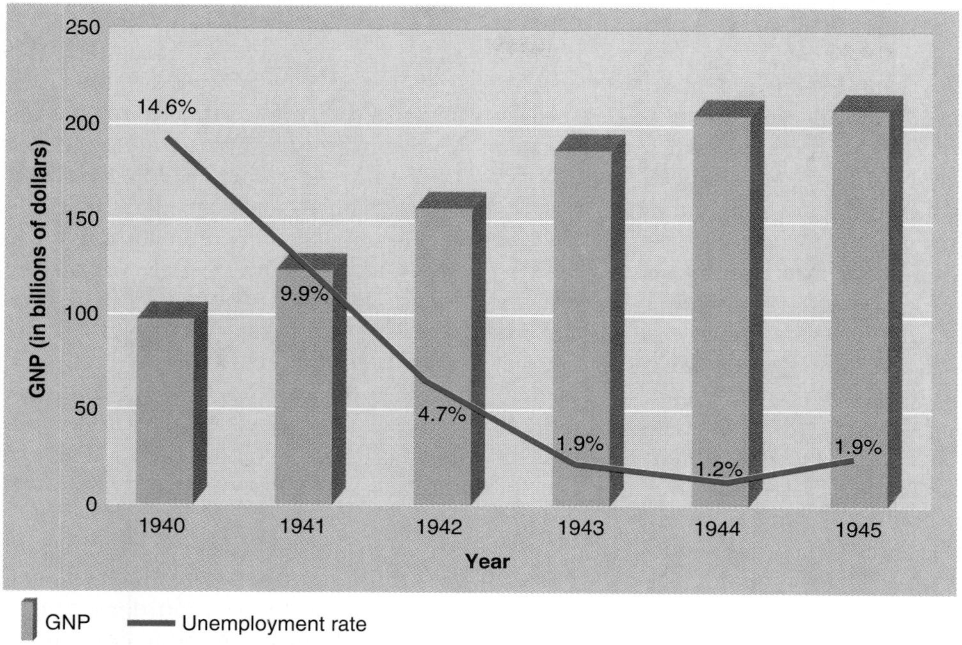

The war economy virtually wiped out unemployment and increased production to unprecedented levels.
Source: U.S. Bureau of the Census.

wartime crisis and turned out the equipment and supplies that eventually won the war. American industries built 300,000 airplanes, 88,140 tanks, and 3,000 merchant ships. In 1944 alone, American factories produced 800,000 tons of synthetic rubber to replace the supply of natural rubber captured by the Japanese. Although the national debt grew from about $143 billion in 1943 to $260 billion in 1945, the government policy of taxation paid for about 40 percent of the war's cost. At the same time, full employment and the increase in two-income families, together with forced savings, helped to provide capital for postwar expansion. In a limited way, the tax policy also tended to redistribute wealth, which the New Deal had failed to do. The top 5 percent income bracket, which controlled 23 percent of the disposable income in 1939, accounted for only 17 percent in 1945.

The war stimulated the growth of the federal bureaucracy and accelerated the trend, begun during World War I and extended in the 1920s and 1930s, toward the government's central role in the economy. The war also increased the cooperation between industry and government, creating what would later be called a military-industrial complex. But for most Americans, despite anger at the OPA and the income tax, the war meant the end of the Depression.

Patriotic Fervor

In European and Asian cities, the horror and destruction of war were everywhere. But in the United States, the war was remote. Thousands of American families felt the tragedy of war directly with the arrival of an official telegram telling of a son or husband killed in action. For most Americans, however, it was a foreign war, far removed from the reality of daily life.

The government tried to keep the conflict alive in the minds of Americans and to keep the country united behind the war effort. The Office of War Information, staffed by writers and advertising executives, controlled the news the American public received about the war. It promoted patriotism and presented the American war effort in the best possible light.

The government also sold war bonds, not only to help pay for the war and reduce inflation but also to sell the war to the American people. As had been true during World War I, movie stars and other celebrities appeared at war bond rallies. Dorothy Lamour, one of Hollywood's glamorous actresses, took credit for selling $350 million worth of bonds. Schoolchildren purchased war stamps and faithfully pasted them in an album until they had accumulated stamps worth $18.75, enough to buy a $25 bond (redeemable ten years later). Their bonds, they were told, would purchase bullets or a part for an airplane to kill "Japs" and Germans and defend the American way of life. "For Freedom's Sake, Buy War Bonds," one poster announced. Working men and women purchased bonds through payroll deduction plans and looked forward to spending the money on consumer goods after the war. In the end, the government sold over $135 billion in war bonds. While the bond drives did help control inflation, they were most important in making millions of Americans feel that they were contributing to the war effort.

Those too old or too young to join the armed forces served in other ways. Thousands became air raid wardens or civilian defense and Red Cross volunteers. They raised victory gardens and took part in scrap drives. Even small children could join the war effort by collecting old rubber, waste paper, and kitchen fats. Boys dived into lakes and rivers to recover old tires and even ripped down iron fences to aid their towns and neighborhoods in meeting their scrap quota. Some items, including gasoline, sugar, butter, and meat, were rationed, but few people complained. Even horsemeat hamburgers seemed edible if they helped win the war. Newspaper and magazine advertising characterized ordinary actions as either speeding victory or impeding the war effort. "Hoarders are the same as spies," one ad announced. "Everytime you decide *not* to buy something you help win the war."

Internment of Japanese-Americans

Cooperating with the war effort fostered a sense of pride, a feeling of community. But wartime campaigns not only stimulated patriotism but also promoted hate for the enemy. The Nazis, especially Hitler and his Gestapo, had become synonymous with evil even before 1941. But at the beginning of the war, there was little animosity toward the German people. "You and I don't hate the Nazis because they are Germans. We hate the Germans because they are Nazis," announced a character in one of Helen MacInnes's novels. But before long, most Americans ceased to make distinctions. All Germans seemed evil, although the anti-German hysteria that had swept the country during World War I never developed.

The Japanese were easier to hate than the Germans. The attack on Pearl Harbor created a special animosity toward the Japanese, but the depiction of the Japanese as warlike and subhuman owed something to a long tradition of fear of the so-called yellow peril and a distrust of all Asians.

The movies, magazine articles, cartoons, and posters added to the image of the Japanese soldier or pilot with a toothy grin murdering innocent women and children or shooting down helpless Americans. Two weeks after Pearl Harbor, *Time* magazine explained to Americans how they could distinguish our Asian friends the Chinese "from the Japs." "Virtually all Japanese are short, Japanese are seldom fat; they often dry up with age," *Time* declared. "Most Chinese avoid horn-rimmed spectacles. Japanese walk stiffly erect, hard-heeled. Chinese, more relaxed, have an easy gait. The Chinese expression is likely to be more kindly, placid, open; the Japanese more positive, dogmatic, arrogant.

The racial stereotype of the Japanese played a role in the treatment of Japanese-Americans during the war. Some prejudice was shown against German- and Italian-Americans, but Japanese-Americans were the only group confined in concentration camps, in the greatest mass abridgment of civil liberties in American history.

At the time of Pearl Harbor, about 127,000 Japanese-Americans lived in the United States, most on the West Coast. About 80,000 were nisei (Japanese born in the United States and holding American citizenship) and sansei (the sons and daughters of nisei); the rest were issei (aliens born in Japan who were ineligible for U.S. citizenship). The Japanese had long suffered from racial discrimination and prejudice in the United States.

They were barred from intermarriage with other groups and excluded from many clubs, restaurants, and recreation facilities. Many worked as tenant farmers, fishermen, or small businessmen. Others made up a small professional class of lawyers, teachers, and doctors and a large class of landowning farmers.

Although many retained cultural and linguistic ties to Japan, they posed no more threat to the country than did the much larger groups of Italian-Americans and German-Americans. But their physical characteristics made them stand out as the others did not. After Pearl Harbor, an anti-Japanese panic seized the West Coast. A Los Angeles newspaper reported that armed Japanese were in Baja, California, ready to attack. Rumors suggested that Japanese fishermen were preparing to sow mines in the harbor, blow up tunnels, and poison the water supply.

West Coast politicians and ordinary citizens urged the War Department and the president to evacuate the Japanese. The president capitulated and issued Executive Order 9066 authorizing the evacuation in February 1942. "The continued pressure of a largely unassimilated, tightly knit racial group, bound to an enemy nation by strong ties of race, culture, custom and religion, constituted a menace which had to be dealt with," General John De Witt argued, justifying the removal on military grounds. But racial fear and animosity, not military necessity, stood behind the order.

Eventually, the government built the "relocation centers" in remote, often arid, sections of the West. "The Japs live like rats, breed like rats and act like rats. We don't want them," the governor of Idaho announced. The camps were primitive and unattractive. "When I first entered our room, I became sick to my stomach," a Japanese-American woman remembered. "There were seven beds in the room and no furniture nor any partitions to separate the males and the females of the family. I just sat on the bed, staring at the bare wall."

The government evacuated about 110,000 Japanese. Those who were forced to leave their homes, farms, and businesses lost almost all their property and possessions. Farmers left their crops to be harvested by their American neighbors. Store owners sold out for a small percentage of what their goods were worth. No personal items or household goods could be transported. The Japanese-Americans lost their worldly possessions, and something more—their pride and respect. One 6-year-old kept asking his mother to "take him back to America." He thought his relocation center was in Japan.

Japanese-American children on their way to a "relocation center." For many Japanese-Americans, but especially for the children, the nightmare of the relocation camp experience would stay with them all their lives.

The evacuation of the Japanese-Americans appears in retrospect to have been unjustified. Even in Hawaii, where a much larger Japanese population existed, the government attempted no evacuation, and no sabotage and little disloyalty occurred. The government allowed Japanese-American men to volunteer for military service, and many served bravely in the European theater. The 442nd Infantry Combat Team, made up entirely of nisei, became the most decorated unit in all the military service—another indication of the loyalty and patriotism of the Japanese-Americans. In 1988, Congress belatedly voted limited compensation for the Japanese-Americans relocated during World War II.

Black and Hispanic Americans at War

The United States in 1941, even in much of the North, remained a segregated society. African-

Americans could not live, eat, travel, work, or go to school with the same freedom whites enjoyed. Black Americans profited little from the revival of prosperity and the expansion of jobs early in the war. Those who joined the military were usually assigned to menial jobs as cooks or laborers and were always assigned to segregated units with whites as the high-ranking officers. The myth that black soldiers had failed to perform well in World War I persisted. "Leadership is not embedded in the negro race yet," Secretary of War Henry Stimson wrote, "and to try to make commissioned officers . . . lead men into battle—colored men—is only to work a disaster to both."

Some black leaders found it especially ironic that as the country prepared to fight Hitler and his racist policies, the United States persisted in its own brand of racism. "A jim crow Army cannot fight for a free world," announced *The Crisis,* the journal of the NAACP. A. Philip Randolph decided to act rather than talk. The son of a Methodist minister, Randolph had worked with the first wave of African-Americans migrating from the South to the northern cities during and just after World War I. He spent years trying "to carry the gospel of unionism to the colored world." He organized and led the Brotherhood of Sleeping Car Porters, and in 1937, he finally won grudging recognition of the union from the Pullman Company.

Respected and admired by black leaders of all political persuasions, Randolph convinced many of them in 1941 to join him in a march on Washington to demand equal rights. "Dear fellow Negro Americans," Randolph wrote, "be not dismayed in these terrible times. You possess power, great power. Our problem is to harness and hitch it up for action on the broadest, daring and most gigantic scale."

The threat of as many as 100,000 black Americans marching in protest in the nation's capital alarmed Roosevelt. At first, he sent his assistants, including his wife Eleanor, who was greatly admired in the black community, to dissuade Randolph from such drastic action. Finally, he talked to Randolph in person on June 18, 1941. Randolph and Roosevelt struck a bargain. Roosevelt refused to desegregate the armed forces, but in return for Randolph's calling off the march, the president issued Executive Order 8802, which stated that it was the policy of the United States that "there shall be no discrimination in the employment of workers in defense industries or government because of race, creed, color or national origin." He also established the Fair Employment Practices Commission (FEPC) to enforce the order.

wow

By threatening militant action, the black leaders wrested a major concession from the president. But the executive order did not end prejudice, and the FEPC, which its chairman described as the "most hated agency in Washington," had limited success in erasing the color line. Many black soldiers were angered and humiliated throughout the war by being made to sit in the back of buses and being barred from hotels and restaurants. Years later, one former black soldier recalled being refused service in a restaurant in Salina, Kansas, while the same restaurant served German prisoners from a camp nearby. "We continued to stare," he recalled. "This was really happening. . . . The people of Salina would serve these enemy soldiers and turn away black American G.I.'s."

Many black Americans improved their economic conditions during the war by taking jobs in war industries. Continuing the migration that had begun during World War I, 750,000 southern blacks moved to northern and western cities in search of economic opportunity. Some became skilled workers and a few became professionals, but most did the "hard, hot, and heavy" tasks. Newcomers were often crowded into segregated housing. Racial tension and prejudice were heightened by the presence of many white southerners who had also followed the path of opportunity north and west.

Southerners were not alone in wanting to keep black Americans in their place. In Detroit, where a major race riot broke out in the summer of 1943, Polish-Americans had protested a public housing development that promised to bring blacks into their neighborhood. In one year, more than 50,000 blacks moved into that city, already overcrowded with many others seeking wartime jobs. The new arrivals increased the pressure on housing and other facilities, and the war accentuated the tension among the various groups.

The riot broke out on a hot, steamy day at a municipal park where a series of incidents led to fights between black and white young people and then to looting in the black community. Before federal and state troops restored order, 34 had been killed (25 blacks and 9 whites) and rioters had destroyed more than $2 million worth of

Even before the United States entered the war, black families like this one moved north to look for work and a better life. This massive migration would change the racial mix in northern cities.

property. Groups of whites roamed the city attacking blacks, overturning cars, setting fires, and sometimes killing wantonly. A group of young men murdered a 58-year-old black "just for the hell of it." "We didn't know him," one of the boys admitted. "He wasn't bothering us. But other people were fighting and killing and we felt like it too." Other riots broke out in Mobile, Los Angeles, New York, and Beaumont, Texas. In all these cities, and in many others where the tension did not lead to open violence, the legacy of bitterness and hate lasted long after the war.

Mexican-Americans, like most minority groups, profited during the war from the increased job opportunities provided by wartime industry. Many left their villages for the first time. Women broke away from their traditional roles and worked outside the home. Mexican-Americans labored in factories in Texas and California and replaced many of the dust bowl migrants in the fields. They joined the armed forces in unprecedented numbers and found jobs in the oil fields. On one occasion, the Fair Employment Practices Commission ordered the Shell Oil Company to promote three Mexican-Americans who had been the victims of company discrimination. Despite such attempts during the war to end unfair treatment, prejudice and discrimination were not easy to eliminate.

In California and in many parts of the Southwest, Mexicans could not use public swimming pools. Often lumped together with blacks, they were excluded from certain restaurants. Usually they were limited to menial jobs and were constantly harassed by the police, picked up for minor offenses, and jailed on the smallest excuse. In Los Angeles, the anti-Mexican prejudice flared into violence. The increased migration of Mexicans into the city and old hatreds created a volatile situation. Most of the hostility and anger focused on Mexican gang members, or *pachuchos,* especially those wearing zoot suits. The suits consisted of long, loose coats with padded shoulders, ballooned pants, pegged at the ankles, and a wide-brimmed hat. A watch chain and a ducktail haircut completed the uniform. The zoot suit had originated in the black sections of northern cities and became a national craze during the war. It was a look some teenage males adopted to call attention to themselves and shock conventional society.

The zoot-suiters especially angered soldiers and sailors who were stationed or on leave in Los Angeles. After a number of provocative incidents, violence broke out between the Mexican-American youths and the servicemen in the spring of 1943. The violence reached a peak on June 7 when gangs of servicemen, often in taxicabs, combed the city, attacking all the young zoot-suiters they could find or anyone who looked Mexican. The servicemen, joined by others, beat up the Mexicans, stripped them of their offensive clothes, and then gave them haircuts. The police, both civilian and military, looked the other way, and when they did move in, they arrested the victims rather than their attackers. The local press and the chamber of commerce hotly denied that race was a factor in the riots, but *Time* magazine was probably closer to the truth when it called the riots the "ugliest brand of mob action since the coolie race riots of the 1870s."

Social Impact of the War

Modern wars have been incredibly destructive of human lives and property, and they have social results as well. The Civil War ended slavery and ensured the triumph of the industrial North for years to come; in so doing, it left a legacy of bitterness and transformed the race question from a sectional to a national problem. World War I assured the success of woman suffrage and prohibition, caused a migration of blacks to northern cities, and ushered in a time of intolerance. World War II also had many social results. It altered patterns of work, leisure, education, and family life; caused a massive migration of people; created jobs; and changed life styles. It is difficult to overemphasize the impact of the war on the generation that lived through it.

Wartime Opportunities

More than 15 million American civilians moved during the war. Like the Momadays, many left home to find better jobs. In fact, for many Native Americans, wartime opportunities led to a migration from the rural areas and the reservations into the cities. Americans moved off the farms and away from the small towns, flocking to cities, where defense jobs were readily available. They moved west: California alone gained more than 2 million people during the war. But they also moved out of the South into the northern cities, while a smaller number moved from the North to the South. Late in the war, when a shortage of farm labor developed, some reversed the trend and moved back onto the farms. But a great many people moved somewhere. One observer, noticing the heavily packed cars heading west, decided that it was just like *The Grapes of Wrath,* without the poverty and the hopelessness.

The World War II migrants poured into industrial centers; 200,000 came to the Detroit area, nearly a half million to Los Angeles, and about 100,000 to Mobile, Alabama. They put pressure on the schools, housing, and other services. Often they had to live in new Hoovervilles, trailer parks, or temporary housing. In San Pablo, California, a family of four adults and seven children lived in an 8-by-10-foot shack. In Los Angeles, Mrs. Colin Kelley, the widow of a war hero, could find no place to live until a local newspaper publicized her plight. Bill Mauldin, the war cartoonist, showed a young couple with a child buying tickets for a movie with the caption: "Matinee, heck—we want to register for a week."

The overcrowded conditions, the uneasiness at being away from home, the volatile mixture of people from different backgrounds living close together, and the wartime situation often created tension and sometimes open conflict. Some migrants had never lived in a city and were homesick. On one occasion in a Willow Grove, Michigan, school, the children were all instructed to sing "Michigan, My Michigan"; no one knew the words because they all came from other states. One of the most popular country songs of the period, when thousands had left their rural homes to find work in the city, was "I Wanna Go Back to West Virginia."

For the first time in years, many families had money to spend, but they had nothing to spend it on. The last new car rolled off the assembly line in February 1942. There were no washing machines, refrigerators, or radios in the stores, no gasoline and no tires to permit weekend trips. Even when people had time off, they tended to stay at home or in the neighborhood. Some of the new housing developments had the atmosphere of a mining camp, complete with drinking, prostitution, and barroom brawls.

The war required major adjustments in American family life. With several million men in the service and others far away working at defense jobs, the number of households headed by a woman increased dramatically. The number of marriages also rose sharply. Early in the war, a young man could be deferred if he had a dependent, and a wife qualified as a dependent. Later, many servicemen got married, often to women they barely knew, because they wanted a little excitement and perhaps someone to come home to. The birthrate also began to rise in 1940, reversing a long decline since the colonial period as young couples started a family as fast as they could. Birthrates had been especially low during the Depression, so the shift marked a significant change. Some children were "good-bye babies," conceived just before the husband left to join the military or go overseas. The illegitimacy rate also went up, and from the outset of the war, the divorce rate began to climb sharply. Yet most of the wartime marriages survived, and many of the women left at home looked ahead to a time after the war when they could settle down to a normal life.

Women Workers for Victory

Thousands of women took jobs in heavy industry that formerly would have been considered unladylike. They built tanks, airplanes, and ships, but they still earned less than men. At first, women were rarely taken on because as the war in Europe pulled American industry out of its long slump, unemployed men snapped up the newly available positions. In the face of this male labor pool, one government official remarked that we should "give the women something to do to keep their hands busy as we did in the last war, then maybe they won't bother us."

But by 1943, with many men drafted and male unemployment virtually nonexistent, the government was quick to suggest that it was women's patriotic duty to take their place on the assembly line. A government poster showed a woman worker and her uniformed husband standing in front of an American flag with the caption: "I'm proud . . . my husband *wants* me to do my part." The government tried to convince women that if they could run a vacuum cleaner or a sewing machine or drive a car, they could operate power machinery in a factory. Advertisers in women's magazines joined the campaign by showing fashion models in work clothes. A popular song was "Rosie the Riveter," who was "making history working for victory." She also helped her marine boyfriend by "working overtime on the riveting machine."

At the end of the war, the labor force included 19.5 million women, but three-fourths of them had been working before the conflict, and some of the additional ones might have sought work in normal times. The new women war workers tended to be older, and they were more often married than single. Some worked for patriotic reasons. "Every time I test a batch of rubber, I know it's going to help bring my three sons home quicker," a woman worker in a rubber plant remarked. But others worked for the money or to have something useful to do. Yet in 1944, women's weekly wages averaged $31.21, compared with $54.65 for men, reflecting women's more menial tasks and their low seniority as well as outright discrimination. Still, many women enjoyed factory work. "Boy have the men been getting away with murder all these years," exclaimed a Pittsburgh housewife. "Why I worked twice as hard selling in a department store and got half the pay."

Black women faced the most difficult situation during the war, and often when they applied for work, they were told, "We have not yet installed separate toilet facilities" or "We can't put a

"Rosie the Riveter" became perhaps the most familiar symbol of women's contribution to the war effort during World War II. Here women rivet sections of an aircraft engine compartment. The government recruited women to work in war industries, but after the war ended it urged women to return to the traditional roles of wife and mother.

Negro in the front office." Not until 1944 did the telephone company in New York City hire a black telephone operator. Still, some black women moved during the war from domestic jobs to higher-paying factory work. Married women with young children also found it difficult to find work. They found few day-care facilities and were often informed that they should be home with their children.

Women workers often had to endure catcalls, whistles, and more overt sexual harassment on the job. Still, most persisted, and they tried to look feminine despite the heavy work clothes. In one Boston factory, a woman was hooted at for carrying a lunch box. Only men, it seemed, carried lunch boxes; women brought their lunch in a paper bag.

Many women war workers quickly left their jobs after the war ended. Some left by choice, but dismissals ran twice as high for women as for men. The war had barely shaken the notion that a woman's place was at home. Some women who learned what an extra paycheck meant for the family's standard of living would have preferred to keep working. But most women, and an even larger percentage of men, agreed at the end of the war that women did not deserve an "equal chance with men" for jobs. War work altered individual lives and attitudes, but it did not change dramatically either sex's perception of women's proper role.

Entertaining the People

According to one survey, Americans listened to the radio an average of 4½ hours a day during the war. The major networks increased their news programs from less than 4 percent to nearly 30 percent of broadcasting time. Americans heard Edward R. Murrow broadcasting from London during the German air blitz with the sound of the air raid sirens in the background. They listened to Eric Sevareid cover the battle of Burma and describe the sensation of jumping out of an airplane. Often the signal faded out and the static made listening difficult, but the live broadcasts had drama and authenticity never before possible.

Even more than the reporters, the commentators became celebrities on whom the American people depended to explain what was going on around the world. Millions listened to the clipped, authoritative voice of H. V. Kaltenborn or to Gabriel Heatter, whose trademark was "Ah, there's good news tonight." But the war also intruded on almost all other programming. Even the advertising, which took up more and more air time, reminded listeners of the war. Lucky Strike cigarettes, which changed the color of its package from green to white, presumably because there was a shortage of green pigment, made "Lucky Strike Green Has Gone to War" almost as famous as "Remember Pearl Harbor."

The serials, the standard fare of daytime radio, also adopted wartime themes. Dick Tracy tracked down spies, while Captain Midnight fought against the enemy on remote jungle islands. Superman outwitted Nazi agents, while Stella Dallas took a job in a defense plant.

Music, which took up a large proportion of radio programming, also conveyed a war theme. There were "Goodbye, Mama (I'm Off to Yokohama)" and "Praise the Lord and Pass the Ammunition," but more numerous were songs of romance and love, songs about separation and hope for a better time after the war. The danceable tunes of Glenn Miller and Tommy Dorsey became just as much a part of wartime memories as ration books and far-off battlefields.

For many Americans, the motion picture became the most important leisure activity and a part of their fantasy life during the war. Attendance at the movies averaged about 100 million viewers a week. There might not be gasoline for weekend trips or Sunday drives, but the whole family could go to the movies; and then, like Scott Momaday, they could replay them in their imaginations. Even those in the military service could watch American movies on board ship or at a remote outpost. "Pinup" photographs of Hollywood stars decorated the barracks and even tanks and planes wherever American troops were stationed.

Musical comedies, cowboy movies, and historical romances remained popular during the war, but the conflict intruded even on Hollywood. Newsreels that offered a visual synopsis of the war news, always with an upbeat message and a touch of human interest, preceded most movies. Their theme was that the Americans were winning the war, even if early in the conflict there was little evidence to that effect. Many feature films also had a wartime theme, picturing the war in the Pacific complete with grinning, vicious Japanese villains (usually played by Chinese or Korean character actors). In the beginning of these films, the Japanese were always victorious, but in the end, they always got "what they deserved."

The movies set in Europe differed somewhat from those depicting the Far Eastern war. British and Americans, sometimes spies, sometimes downed airmen, could dress up like Germans and get away with it. They outwitted the Germans at every turn, sabotaging important installations and finally escaping in a captured plane.

A number of Hollywood actors went into the service, and some even became heroes. Most, like Ronald Reagan, were employed to produce, narrate, or act in government films. The Office of War Information produced short subjects and documentaries, some of them distinguished, like John Huston's *Battle of San Pietro,* a realistic depiction of war on the Italian front. More typical were propaganda films meant to indoctrinate American soldiers into the reasons they were fighting the war. *Letter from Bataan,* a short film made in 1942, portrayed a wounded GI who wrote home asking his brother-in-law to save his razor blades because "it takes twelve thousand razor blades to make a one-thousand-pound bomb." The film ended with the announcement that the soldier had died in the hospital.

The GIs' War

GI, the abbreviation for *government issue,* became the affectionate designation for the ordinary soldier in World War II. The GIs came from every background and ethnic group. Some served reluctantly, some eagerly. A few became genuine heroes. All were turned into heroes by the press and the public, who seemed to believe that one American could easily defeat at least 20 Japanese or Germans. Ernest Pyle, one of the war correspondents who chronicled the authentic story of the ordinary GI, wrote of soldiers "just toiling from day to day in a world full of insecurity, discomfort, homesickness, and a dulled sense of danger."

Bill Mauldin, another correspondent, told the story of the ordinary soldier in a series of cartoons featuring two tired and resigned infantrymen, Willie and Joe. Joe tries to explain what the war is about, "when they run we try to ketch 'em, when we ketch 'em we try to make 'em run." In another cartoon, Willie says, "Joe, yestiddy ya saved my life an' I swore I'd pay you back. Here's my last pair of dry socks." For the soldier in the front line, the big strategies were irrelevant. The war seemed a constant mix-up; much more important were the little comforts and staying alive.

In the midst of battle, the war was no fun, but only one soldier of eight who served ever saw combat, and even for many of those the war was a great adventure (just as World War I had been). "When World War II broke out I was delighted," Mario Puzo, author of *The Godfather,* remembered. "There is no other word, terrible as it may sound. My country called. I was delivered from my mother, my family, the girl I was loving passionately but did not love. And delivered *without guilt.* Heroically my country called, ordered me to defend it." World War II catapulted young men and women out of their small towns and urban neighborhoods into exotic places where they met new people and did new things.

The war was important for Mexican-Americans, who were drafted and volunteered in great numbers. A third of a million served in all branches of the military, a larger percentage than for many other ethnic groups. Although they encountered prejudice, they probably found less in the armed forces than they had at home, and many returned to civilian life with new ambitions and a new sense of self-esteem.

Many Native Americans also served. In fact, many Indians were recruited for special service in the Marine Signal Corps. One group of Navajos completely befuddled the Japanese with a code based on their native language. "Were it not for the Navajos, the Marines would never have taken Iwo Jima," one Signal Corps officer declared. But the Navajo code talkers and all other Indians who chose to return to the reservations after the war were ineligible for veterans' loans, hospitalization, and other benefits. They lived on federal land, and that, according to the law, canceled all the advantages that other veterans enjoyed after the war.

For black Americans, who served throughout the war in segregated units and faced prejudice wherever they went, the military experience also had much to teach. Fewer blacks were sent overseas (about 79,000 of 504,000 blacks in the service in 1943), and fewer were in combat outfits, so

RECOVERING THE PAST

Oral History

World War II influenced every family in some significant way. For those who lost sons, husbands, or fathers, the war was tragic. But for others, it meant jobs, travel, adventure, and romance. The Second World War is still the subject of many movies and books, and thousands of people still collect World War II weapons, model airplanes, and other memorabilia. The generation that lived through the war is inclined to look back nostalgically and to recall the war as a wonderful period in their lives, unlike those who look back at the Vietnam War. In fact, almost as many Americans landed in France in June 1984 to celebrate the fortieth anniversary of D day as invaded Normandy on June 6, 1944. Taking former soldiers and their families back to World War battlegrounds has become a major tourist industry in Europe.

How did the war influence your family? The study of the family, "humanity's most fundamental and most durable institution," is as important for historians as the study of wars, elections, depressions, and social currents. One's own family, in fact, is a part of these events. By interviewing family members and writing about their lives, which is called oral history, the past is made both more vivid and more personal. Oral history goes beyond names and dates to the rich immediate texture of people's recollections of personal experiences and feelings. Investigating family members is an opportunity not only to "put your own family into history" but also to develop deeper relations and understanding. As such, it is an act requiring a high degree of respect and responsibility.

You can become an oral historian by asking members of your family about their World War II experience, recovering a partial history of both your family and the war. Talk to your father and mother, your grandparents, and other older relatives. Who in your family served in the armed forces? Who went overseas? Did anyone work in a war industry? Was there a "Rosie the Riveter" in your family? Did your family move during the war? For many people, the war meant jobs and the end of depression. Was that true for your family? Many young people met their future spouses during that war. Was that true in your family?

Can anyone in your family remember rationing, scrap drives, blackouts, victory gardens? Did anyone eat horsemeat or mix yellow food coloring with oleomargarine? Can anyone recall the big bands, the movie stars, the newsreels? Although there was widespread support for the war, and patriotism was popular, prejudice and hate still remained. In what ways did your family share in the patriotism or the prejudice? Whether in battles abroad or on the home front, how does the war as recalled by your family differ from the war as described in this chapter?

Look around your home. Are there any surviving memorabilia from the war—old photographs or uniforms, discharge papers, ration books, war stamps, souvenirs, magazines, or other things from the war years? Go to your library and look at a few issues of *Life* or *Look* for the 1940s. What do you notice about the advertisements and the news stories? How do they differ from magazine advertising and reporting today? What happened to the automotive industry and to professional baseball and college football during the war? What do you notice about women's dress styles? What do the two photographs shown here tell you about the American people in World War II?

Did the war mean tragedy or opportunity for your family? "World War II was a holy war and FDR a

Collecting scrap to aid the war effort.

Remembering the Good War

I was nine years old when the war started. It was a typical Chicago working-class neighborhood. It was predominantly Slavic, Polish. There were some Irish, some Germans. When you're a kid, the borders of the world are the few blocks of two-flats, bungalows, cottages, with a lot of little stores in between. My father had a tavern. In those days they put out extras. I remember the night the newsboys came through the neighborhood. Skid-row kind of guys, hawking the papers. Germany had invaded Poland: '39. It was the middle of the night, my mother and father waking. People were going out in the streets in their bathrobes to buy the papers. In our neighborhood with a lot of Poles, it was a tremendous story.

Suddenly you had a flagpole. And a marker. Names went on the marker, guys from the neighborhood who were killed. Our neighborhood was decimated. There were only kids, older guys, and women.

Suddenly I saw something I hadn't seen before. My sister became Rosie the Riveter. She put a bandanna on her head every day and went down to this organ company that had been converted to war work. There was my sister in slacks. It became more than work. There was a sense of mission about it. Her husband was Over There. . . .

There was the constant idea that you had to be doing something to help. It did filter down to the neighborhood: home-front mobilization. We had a block captain. . . .

We'd listen to the radio every night. My father would turn it on to find out what was happening. The way a kid's mind could be shaped by those dulcet voices. The world was very simple. I saw Hitler and Mussolini and Tojo: those were the villains. We were the good guys. And the Russians were the good guys too. The war was always being talked about in the bar. Everybody was a military strategist.

The big event was my brother-in-law coming home, my sister's husband. He had been a combat soldier all the way through. He had all his ribbons and medals on. He was the family hero.

Source: Mike Royko, in Studs Terkel, *"The Good War": An Oral History of World War Two*.

saint," one writer has remarked. Does your family agree? World War II may have been the last time the country was really united; those who lived through it have inevitably looked at recent events through the perspective of the war years. How did the "Good War," as Studs Terkel called it, influence the political and social views of members of your family old enough to remember it? How do their attitudes about World War II compare with their feelings about more recent American wars?

If the experience of World War II is too distant for the recollections of members of your family, ask them instead about either the Korean War or the Vietnam War. Similar questions are appropriate: ask those who went abroad to describe what the war was like and how they felt about it, and ask those who stayed at home how the war affected or changed their lives.

The accompanying brief excerpt from Studs Terkel's book *"The Good War": An Oral History of World War Two* illustrates how the world transformed the family and neighborhood of young Mike Royko, now a Chicago journalist.

Alfred Eisenstadt, *Soldier's Farewell*, Penn Station, New York, 1944.

the percentage of black soldiers killed and wounded was low. Many illiterate blacks, especially from the South, learned to read and write in the service. Blacks who went overseas began to realize that not everyone viewed them as inferior. One black army officer said, "What the hell do we want to fight the Japs for anyhow? They couldn't possibly treat us any worse than these 'crackers' right here at home." Most realized the paradox of fighting for freedom when they themselves had little freedom; they hoped things would improve after the war.

Because the war lasted longer than World War I, its impact was greater. In all, over 16 million men and women served in some branch of the military service. About 322,000 were killed in the war, and more than 800,000 were wounded. The 12,000 listed as missing just disappeared. The war claimed many more lives than World War I and was the nation's costliest after the Civil War. But because of penicillin, blood plasma, sulfa drugs, and rapid battlefield evacuation, the wounded in World War II were twice as likely to survive as in World War I. Penicillin also minimized the threat of venereal disease, but all men who served saw an anti-VD film, just as their predecessors had in World War I.

Over 300,000 American servicemen died during the war, but the government tried to protect the American people from the real cost of the battles. This photograph, published in 1943, was the first to show dead American soldiers.

Women in Uniform

Women had served in all wars as nurses and cooks and in other support capacities, and during World War II many continued in these traditional roles. A few nurses landed in France just days after the Normandy invasion. Nurses served with the army and the marines in the Pacific. They dug their own foxholes and treated men under enemy fire. Sixty-six nurses spent the entire war in the Philippines as prisoners of the Japanese. Most nurses, however, served far behind the lines tending the sick and wounded. Army nurses who were given officer rank were forbidden to date enlisted men. "Not permitting nurses and enlisted men to be seen together is certainly not American," one soldier decided.

Though nobody objected to women's serving as nurses, not until April 1943 did women physicians win the right to join the Army and Navy Medical Corps. Some people questioned whether it was right for women to serve in other capacities, but Congress authorized full military participation for women (except for combat) because of the military emergency and the argument that women could free men for combat duty. World War II thus became the first war in which women were given regular military status. About 350,000 women joined up, most in the Women's Army Corps (WACS) and the women's branch of the navy (WAVES), but others served in the coast guard and the marines. Oveta Culp Hobby, wife of a former governor of Texas and the mother of two children, directed the Women's Army Corps.

Many recruiting posters suggested that the services needed women "for the precision work at which women are so adept" or for work in hospitals to comfort and attend to the wounded "as only women can do." Most women served in traditional female roles, doing office work, cooking, and cleaning. But others were engineers and pilots. Still, men and women were not treated equally. Women were explicitly kept out of combat situations and were often underused by male officers who found it difficult to view women in nontraditional roles.

Men were informed about contraceptives and encouraged to use them, but information about birth control was explicitly prohibited for women.

Rumors charged many servicewomen with sexual promiscuity. On one occasion, the secretary of war defended the morality and the loyalty of the women in the service, but the rumors continued, spread apparently by men made uncomfortable by women's invasion of the male military domain. One cause for immediate discharge was pregnancy; yet the pregnancy rate for both married and unmarried women remained low.

Thus, despite difficulties, women played important roles during the war, and when they left the service (unlike the women who had served in other wars), they had the same rights and privileges as the male veterans. The women in the service did not permanently alter the military or the public's perception of women's proper role, but they did change a few minds, and many of the women who served had their lives changed and their horizons raised.

A War of Diplomats and Generals

Pearl Harbor catapulted the country into war with Japan, and on December 11, 1941, Hitler declared war on the United States. Why he did so has never been fully explained; he was perhaps impressed by the apparent weakness of America demonstrated at Pearl Harbor. He was not required by his treaty with Japan to go to war with the United States, and without his declaration, the United States might have concentrated on the war against Japan. But Hitler forced the United States into the war against the Axis powers in both Europe and Asia.

War Aims

Why was the United States fighting the war? What did it hope to accomplish in a peace settlement once the war was over? Roosevelt and the other American leaders never really decided. In a speech before Congress in January 1941, Roosevelt had mentioned the four freedoms: freedom of speech and expression, freedom of worship, freedom from want, and freedom from fear. For many Americans, especially after Norman Rockwell expressed those freedoms in four sentimental paintings, this was what they were fighting for. Roosevelt spoke vaguely of the need to extend democracy and to establish a peacekeeping organization, but in direct contrast to Woodrow Wilson's Fourteen Points, he never spelled out in any detail the political purposes for fighting. The only American policy was to end the war as quickly as possible and to solve the political problems it created when the time came. That policy, or lack of policy, would have important ramifications.

Roosevelt and his advisers, realizing that it would be impossible to mount an all-out war against both Japan and Germany, decided to fight a holding action in the Pacific at first while concentrating efforts against Hitler in Europe, where the immediate danger seemed greater. But the United States was not fighting alone. It joined the Soviet Union and Great Britain in what became a difficult, but ultimately effective alliance to defeat Nazi Germany. Churchill and Roosevelt got along well, although they often disagreed on strategy and tactics. Roosevelt's relationship with Stalin was much more strained, but often he agreed with the Russian leader about the way to fight the war. Stalin, a ruthless leader who had maintained his position of power only after eliminating hundreds of thousands of opponents, distrusted both the British and the Americans, but he needed them, just as they depended on him. Without the tremendous sacrifices of the Russian army and the Russian people in 1941 and 1942, Germany would have won the war before the vast American military and industrial might could be mobilized.

1942: Year of Disaster

Despite the potential of the American-British-Soviet alliance, the first half of 1942 was disastrous for the Allied cause. In the Pacific, the Japanese captured the Dutch East Indies with their vast riches in rubber, oil, and other resources. They swept into Burma, took Wake Island and Guam, and invaded the Aleutian Islands of Alaska. They pushed the American garrison on the Philippines onto the Bataan peninsula and finally onto the tiny island of Corregidor, where U.S. General Jonathan Wainwright surrendered more than 11,000 men to the Japanese. American reporters tried to play down the disasters, concentrating their stories on the few American victories and on tales of American heroism against overwhelming odds. One of the soldiers on a Pacific island picked up an American broadcast one night. "The news commentators in the States had us all win-

World War II: Pacific Theater

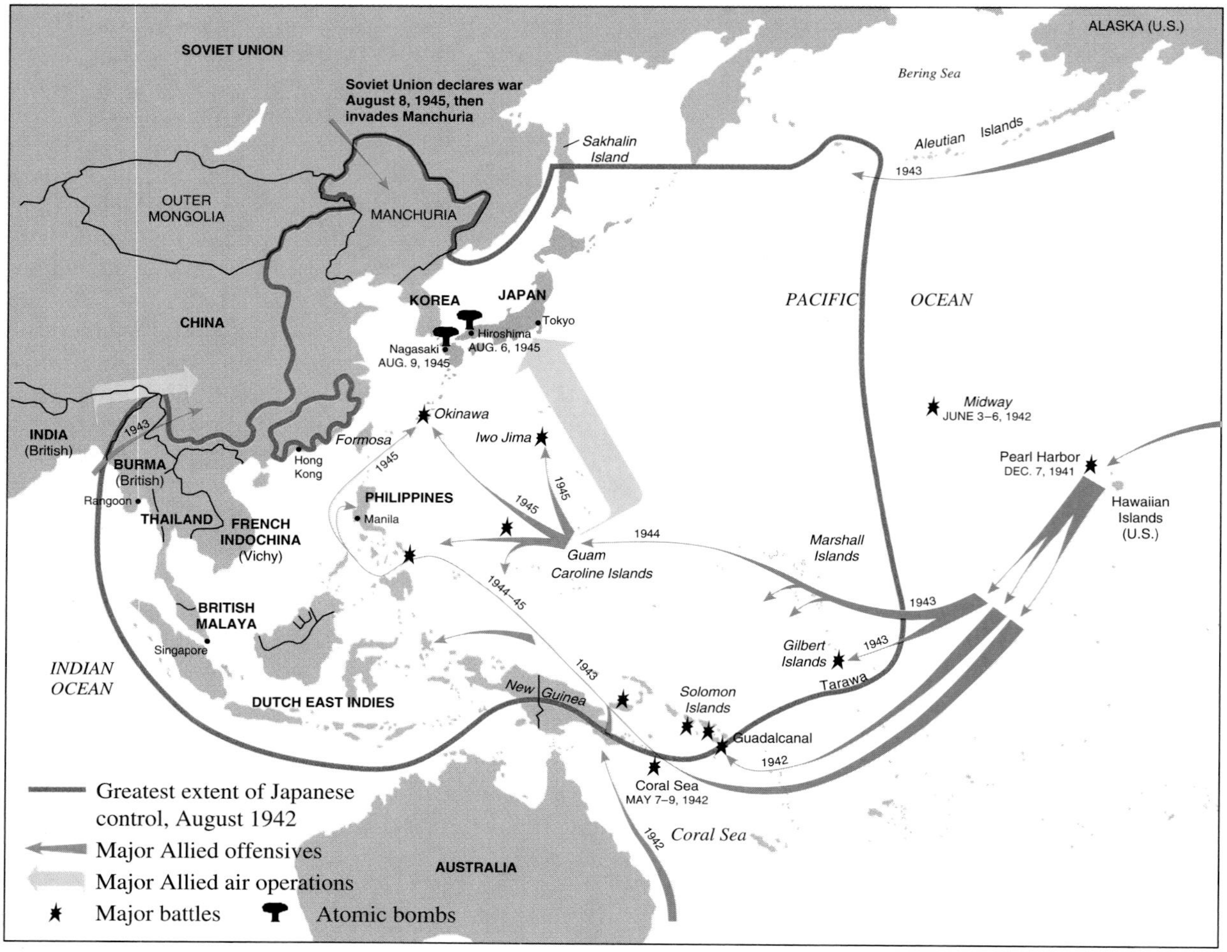

After the surprise attack on Pearl Harbor, the Japanese extended their control in the Pacific from Burma to the Aleutian Islands and almost to Australia. But after American naval and air victories at Coral Sea and Midway in 1942, the Japanese were increasingly on the defensive.

ning the war," he discovered, "their buoyant cheerful voices talking of victory. We were out here where we would see these victories. They were all Japanese."

In Europe, the Germans pushed deep into Russia, threatening to capture all the industrial centers and the valuable oil fields. For a time, it appeared that they would even take Moscow. In North Africa, General Erwin Rommel and his mechanized divisions, the Afrika Korps, drove the British forces almost to Cairo in Egypt and threatened the Suez Canal. In contrast to World War I, which had been a war of stalemate, the opening phase of World War II was marked by air strikes and troops supported by trucks and tanks covering many miles a day. In the Atlantic, German submarines sank British and American ships more rapidly than they could be replaced. For a few dark months in 1942, it seemed that the Berlin-Tokyo Axis would win the war before the United States got itself ready to fight.

The Allies could not agree on the proper military strategy in Europe. Churchill advocated tightening the ring around Germany, using bomb-

World War II: European and North African Theaters

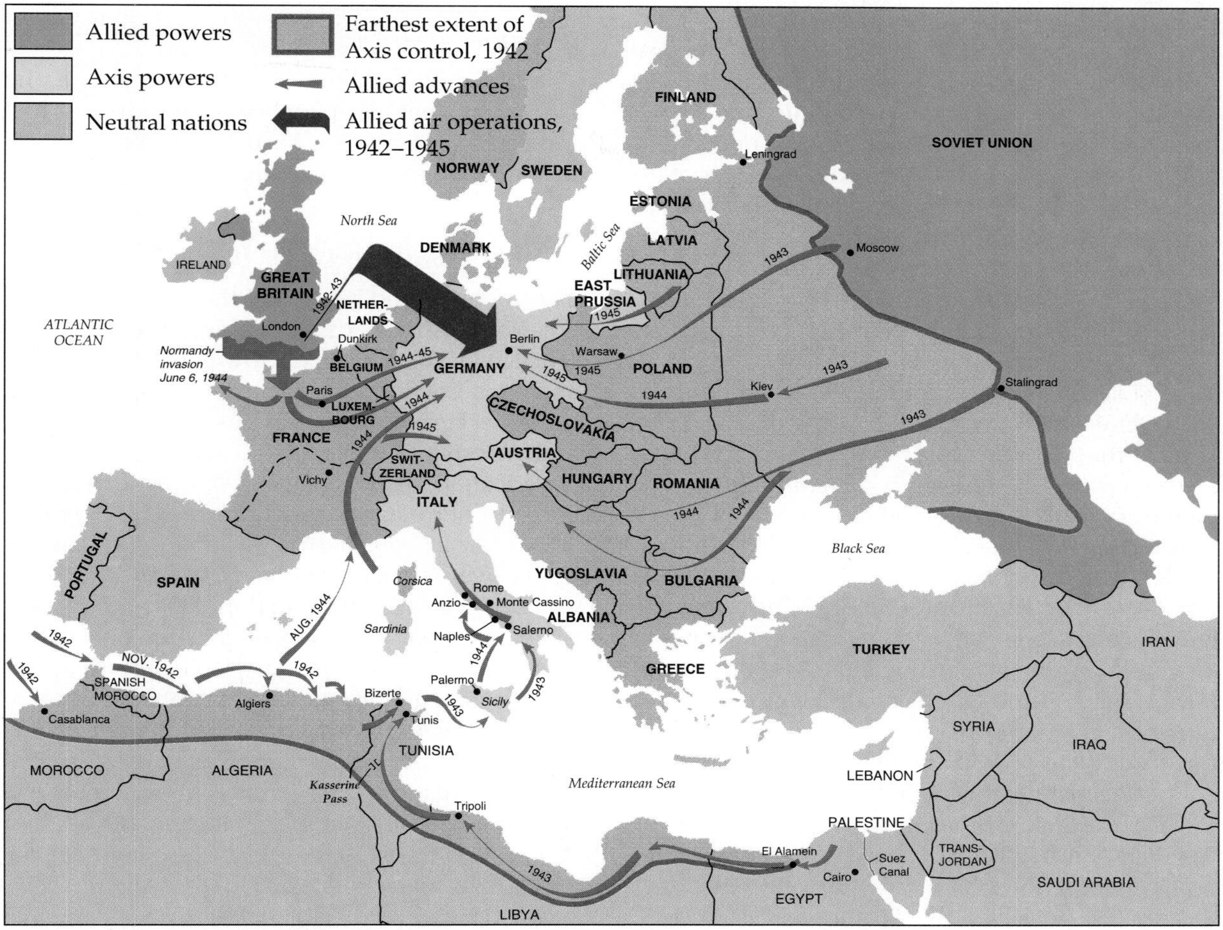

The German war machine swept across Europe and North Africa and almost captured Cairo and Moscow, but after major defeats at Stalingrad and El Alamein in 1943, the Axis powers were in retreat. Many lives were lost on both sides before the Allied victory in 1945.

ing raids to weaken the enemy and encouraging resistance among the occupied countries but avoiding any direct assault on the continent until success was assured. Remembering the vast loss of British lives during World War I, he was determined to avoid similar casualties in this conflict. Stalin demanded a second front, an invasion of Europe in 1942, to relieve the pressure on the Russian army, which faced 200 German divisions along a 2,000-mile front. Roosevelt agreed to an offensive in 1942. But in the end, the invasion in 1942 came not in France but in North Africa. The decision was probably right from a military point of view, but it taught Russia to distrust Britain and the United States. The delay in opening the second front probably contributed indirectly to the Cold War after 1945.

Attacking in North Africa in November 1942, American and British troops tried to link up with a beleaguered British army. The American army, enthusiastic but inexperienced, met little resistance in the beginning, but at Kasserine Pass in Tunisia, the Germans counterattacked and destroyed a large American force, inflicting 5,000 casualties. Roosevelt, who launched the invasion in part to give the American people a victory to relieve the dreary news from the Far East, learned that victories often came with long casualty lists.

He also learned the necessity of political compromise. To gain a cease-fire in conquered French territory in North Africa, the United States recognized Admiral Jean Darlan as head of its provisional government. Darlan persecuted the Jews, exploited the Arabs, imprisoned his opponents, and collaborated with the Nazis. He seemed diametrically opposed to the principles the Americans said they were fighting for. Did the Darlan deal mean the United States would negotiate with Mussolini? Or with Hitler? The Darlan compromise reinforced Soviet distrust of the Americans and angered many Americans as well.

Roosevelt never compromised or made a deal with Hitler, but he did aid General Francisco Franco, the Fascist dictator in Spain, in return for safe passage of American shipping into the Mediterranean. But the United States did not aid only right-wing dictators. It also supplied arms to the left-wing resistance in France, to the Communist Tito in Yugoslavia, and Ho Chi Minh, the anti-French resistance leader in Indochina. Roosevelt also authorized large-scale lend-lease aid to the Soviet Union. Although liberals criticized his support of dictators, Roosevelt was willing to do almost anything to win the war. Military expediency often dictated his political decisions.

Even on one of the most sensitive issues of the war, the plight of the Jews in occupied Europe, Roosevelt's solution was to win the war as quickly as possible. By November 1942, confirmed information had reached the United States that the Nazis were systematically exterminating Jews. Yet the Roosevelt administration did nothing for more than a year, and even then it did scandalously little to rescue European Jews from the gas chambers. Only 21,000 refugees were allowed to enter the United States over a period of 3½ years, just 10 percent of those who could have been admitted under immigration quotas. The U.S. War Department rejected suggestions that the Auschwitz gas chambers be bombed, and government officials turned down many rescue schemes. Widespread anti-Semitic feelings in the United States in the 1940s and the fear of massive Jewish immigration help to explain the failure of the Roosevelt administration to act. The fact that the mass media, Christian leaders, and even American Jews failed to mount effective pressure on the government does not excuse the president for his shameful indifference to the systematic murder of millions of people. Roosevelt could not have prevented the Holocaust, but vigorous action on his part could have saved many thousands of lives during the war.

Roosevelt was not always right, nor was he even consistent, but people who assumed he had a master strategy or a fixed ideological position misunderstood the American president.

A Strategy for Ending the War

The commanding general of the Allied armies in the North African campaign emerged as a genuine leader. Born in Texas, Dwight D. Eisenhower spent his boyhood in Abilene, Kansas. His small-town background made it easy for biographers and newspaper reporters to make him into an American hero. Eisenhower, however, had not come to hero status easily. He saw no action in World War I; he spent that war training soldiers in Texas. Even though he served as assistant to General Douglas MacArthur in the 1930s in the Philippines, he was only a lieutenant colonel when World War II erupted. General George Marshall had discovered Eisenhower's talents even before the war began. He was quickly promoted to general and achieved a reputation as an expert planner and organizer. Gregarious and outgoing, he had a broad smile that made most people like him instantly. He was not a brilliant field commander and made many mistakes in the African campaign, but he had the ability to get diverse people working together, which was crucial where British and American units had to cooperate.

The American army moved slowly across North Africa, linked up with the British, invaded Sicily in July 1943, and finally stormed ashore in Italy in September. The Italian campaign proved long and bitter. Despite the fact that the Italians overthrew Mussolini and surrendered in September 1943, the Germans occupied the peninsula and gave ground only after bloody fighting. The whole American army seemed to be bogged down for months. One soldier described the "slushy mud that reaches almost up to your knees, . . . making the roads dangerously slippery." The Allies did not reach Rome until June 1944, and they never controlled all of Italy.

Despite the decision to make the war in Europe the first priority, American ships and planes halted the Japanese advance in the spring of

Only at the end of the war did the world learn of the horrors of the Nazi concentration camps and the gas chambers.

President Roosevelt inspects General Eisenhower's troops in Sicily before returning home from the Cairo-Tehran Conference in 1943. These were two of the dominant personalities of the war years.

1942. In the Battle of Coral Sea in May 1942, American carrier-based planes inflicted heavy damage on the Japanese fleet and prevented the invasion of the southern tip of New Guinea and probably of Australia as well. It was the first naval battle in history in which no guns were fired from one surface ship against another; airplanes caused all the damage. In World War II, the aircraft carrier proved more important than the battleship. A month later, at the Battle of Midway, American planes sank four Japanese aircraft carriers and destroyed nearly 300 planes. This was the first major Japanese defeat; it restored some balance of power in the Pacific and ended the threat to Hawaii.

In 1943, the American sea and land forces leapfrogged from island to island, gradually retaking territory from the Japanese and building bases to attack the Philippines and eventually Japan itself. Progress often had terrible costs, however. In November 1943, about 5,000 marines landed on the coral beaches of the tiny island of Tarawa. Despite heavy naval bombardment and the support of hundreds of planes, the marines met heavy opposition. The four-day battle left more than 1,000 Americans dead and over 3,000 wounded. One marine general thought it was all wasted effort. He thought the island should have been bypassed. Others disagreed. No one asked the marines who stormed the beaches. Less than half of the first wave survived.

The Invasion of Europe

Operation Overlord, the code name for the largest amphibious invasion in history, the invasion Stalin had wanted in 1942, began only on June 6, 1944. It was, according to Churchill, "the most difficult and complicated operation that has ever taken place." The initial assault along a 60-mile stretch of the Normandy coast was conducted with 175,000 men supported by 600 warships and 11,000 planes. Within a month, over a million troops and more than 170,000 vehicles had landed. Such an invasion would have been impossible during World War I.

Eisenhower, now bearing the title Supreme Commander of the Allied Expeditionary Force in Western Europe, coordinated and planned the operation. British and American forces, with some units from other countries, worked together, but Overlord was made possible by American industry, which, by the war's end, was turning out an astonishing 50 percent of all the world's goods. During the first few hours of the invasion, there seemed to be too many supplies. "Everything was confusing," one soldier remembered. It cost 2,245 killed and 1,670 wounded to secure the beachhead. "It was much lighter than anybody expected," one observer remarked. "But if you saw faces instead of numbers on the casualty list, it wasn't light at all."

For months before the invasion, American and British planes had bombed German transportation lines, industrial plants, and even cities. In all, over 1.5 million tons of bombs were dropped on Europe. The massive bombing raids helped make the invasion a success, but evidence gathered after the war suggests that the bombs did not disrupt German war production as seriously as Allied strategists believed at the time. Often a factory or a rail center would be back in operation within a matter of days, sometimes within hours, after an attack. In the end, the bombing of the cities, rather than destroying morale, may have strengthened the resolve of the German people to fight to the bitter end. And the destruction of German cities did not come cheaply. German fighters and antiaircraft guns shot down 22 of 60 B-17s on June 23, 1943, and on August 17, the Americans lost 60 bombers.

The most destructive bombing raid of the war, carried out against Dresden on the night of February 13–14, 1945, had no strategic purpose. It was launched by the British and Americans to help demonstrate to Stalin that they were aiding the Russian offensive. Dresden, a city of 630,000, was a communications center. Three waves of planes dropped 650,000 incendiary bombs, causing a firestorm that swept over 8 square miles, destroyed everything in its path, and killed 135,000 civilians. One of the American pilots remarked, "For the first time I felt sorry for the population below."

With the dashing and eccentric General George Patton leading the charge and the more staid General Omar Bradley in command, the American army broke out of the Normandy beachhead in July 1944. Led by the tank battalions, it swept across France. American productive capacity and the ability to supply a mobile and motorized army eventually brought victory. But not all American equipment was superior. The American fighter plane, the P-40, could not compete early in the war with the German ME-109. The United States was also far behind Germany in the development of rockets, but that was not as important in the actual fighting as the inability of the United States, until the end of the war, to develop a tank that could compete in armament or firepower with the German tanks. The American army made up for the deficiency of its tanks in part by having superior artillery. Perhaps even more important, most of the American soldiers had grown up tinkering with cars and radios. Children of the machine age, they managed to make repairs and to keep tanks, trucks, and guns functioning under difficult circumstances. They helped give the American army the superior mobility that eventually led to the defeat of Germany.

By late 1944, the American and British armies had swept across France, while the Russians had pushed the German forces out of much of eastern Europe. The war seemed nearly over. However, just before Christmas in 1944, the Germans launched a massive counterattack along an 80-mile front, much of it held by thinly dispersed and inexperienced American troops. The Germans drove 50 miles inside the American lines before they were checked. During the Battle of the Bulge, as it was called, Eisenhower was so desperate for additional infantry that he offered to pardon any military prisoners in Europe who would take up a rifle and go into battle. Most of the prisoners, who were serving short sentences, declined the opportunity to clear their record. Eisenhower also promised any black soldiers in the service and supply outfits an opportunity to become infantrymen in the white units, though usually with a lower rank. However, Walter Bedell Smith, his chief of staff, pointed out that this was against War Department regulations and was the "most dangerous thing I have seen in regard to race relations." Eisenhower recanted, not wishing to start a social revolution. Black soldiers who did volunteer to join the battle fought in segregated platoons commanded by white officers.

The Politics of Victory

As the American and British armies raced across France into Germany in the winter and spring of 1945, the political and diplomatic aspects of the war began to overshadow military concerns. It became a matter not only of defeating Germany but also of determining who was going to control Germany and the rest of Europe once Hitler fell. The relationship between the Soviet Union and the other Allies had been badly strained during the war; with victory in sight, the tension became even greater. While the American press pictured Stalin as a wise and democratic leader and the Russian people as quaint and heroic, a number of high-level American diplomats and presidential advisers distrusted the Russians and looked ahead to a confrontation with Soviet Communism after the war. These men urged Roosevelt to make military decisions with the postwar political situation in mind.

The main issue in the spring of 1945 concerned who would capture Berlin. The British wanted to beat the Russians to the capital city. Eisenhower, however, fearing that the Germans might barricade themselves in the Austrian Alps and hold out indefinitely, ordered the armies south rather than toward Berlin. He also wanted to avoid unnecessary American casualties, and he planned to meet the Russian army at an easily marked spot to avoid any unfortunate incidents. The British and American forces could probably not have arrived in Berlin before the Russians in any case, but Eisenhower's decision generated controversy after the war. Russian and American troops met on April 25, 1945, at the Elbe River. On May 2, the Russians took Berlin. Hitler committed suicide. The long war in Europe finally came to an end on May 8, 1945, but political problems remained.

In 1944, the United States continued to tighten the noose on Japan. American long-range B-29 bombers began sustained strikes on the Japanese mainland in June 1944, and by November they were dropping firebombs on Tokyo. In a series of naval and air engagements, especially at the Battle of Leyte Gulf, American planes destroyed most of the remaining Japanese navy. By the end of 1944, an American victory in the Pacific was all but assured. American forces recaptured the Philippines early the next year, yet the American forces had barely touched Japan itself. It might take years to conquer the Japanese on their home islands.

While the military campaigns reached a critical stage in both Europe and the Pacific, Roosevelt took time off to run for an unprecedented fourth term. To appease members of his own party, he agreed to drop Vice-President Henry Wallace from the ticket because some thought him too radical and impetuous. To replace him, the Democratic convention selected a relatively unknown senator from Missouri. Harry S Truman, a World War I veteran, had been a judge in Kansas City before being elected to the Senate in 1934. His only fame came when, as chairman of the Senate Committee to Investigate the National Defense Program, he had insisted on honesty and efficiency in war contracts. He got some publicity for saving the taxpayers' dollars. The Republicans nominated Thomas Dewey, the colorless and politically moderate governor of New York, who had a difficult time criticizing Roosevelt without appearing unpatriotic. Roosevelt seemed haggard and ill during much of the campaign, but he won the election easily. He would need all his strength to deal with the difficult political problems of ending the war and constructing a peace settlement.

The Big Three at Yalta

Roosevelt, Churchill, and Stalin, together with many of their advisers, met at Yalta in the Crimea in February 1945 to discuss the problems of the peace settlements. Most of the agreements reached at Yalta were secret, and in the atmosphere of the subsequent Cold War, many would become controversial. Roosevelt wanted the help of the Soviet Union in ending the war in the Pacific so as to avoid the needless slaughter of American men in an invasion of the Japanese mainland. In return for a promise to enter the war within three months after the war in Europe was over, the Soviet Union was granted the Kurile Islands, the southern half of Sakhalin, and railroads and port facilities in North Korea, Manchuria, and Outer Mongolia. Later that seemed like a heavy price to pay for the promise, but realistically the Soviet Union controlled most of this territory and could not have been dislodged short of going to war.

When the provisions of the secret treaties were revealed much later, many people would accuse Roosevelt of trusting the Russians too much. But Roosevelt wanted to retain a working relationship with the Soviet Union. If the peace was to be preserved, the major powers of the Grand Alliance would have to work together. Moreover, Roosevelt hoped to get the Soviet Union's agreement to cooperate with a new peace-preserving United Nations organization after the war.

The European section of the Yalta agreement proved even more controversial than its Far Eastern provisions. It was decided to partition Germany and to divide the city of Berlin. The Polish agreements were even more difficult to swallow, in part because the invasion of Poland in 1939 had precipitated the war. The Polish government in exile in London was militantly anti-Communist and looked forward to returning to Poland after the war. Stalin, however, demanded that the eastern half of Poland be given to the Soviet Union to protect its western border. Churchill and Roosevelt finally agreed to the Russian demands with the proviso that Poland be compensated with German territory on its western border. Stalin also agreed to include some members of the London-based Polish group in the new Polish government. He also promised to carry out "free and unfettered elections as soon as possible." The Polish settlement would prove divisive after the war, and it quickly became clear that what the British and Americans wanted in eastern Europe contrasted with what the Soviet Union intended. Yet at the time it seemed imperative that Russia enter the war in the Pacific, and the reality was that in 1945 the Soviet army occupied most of eastern Europe.

The most potentially valuable accomplishment at Yalta was agreement on the need to construct a United Nations, an organization for preserving peace and fostering the postwar reconstruction of battered and underdeveloped countries. In 1942, a total of 26 Allied nations had subscribed to the Atlantic Charter, drafted by Churchill and Roosevelt, which laid down several principles for a lasting peace. Discussions among the Allied powers continued during the war, and Stalin agreed with Roosevelt and Churchill to call a conference in San Francisco in April 1945 to draft a United Nations charter.

Spirited debate occurred in San Francisco when the representatives of 50 nations gathered for this task. As finally accepted, amid optimism about a quick end to the war, the charter provided for a General Assembly in which every member nation had a seat. However, this General Assembly was designed mainly as a forum for discussing international problems. The responsibility for keeping global peace was lodged in the Security Council, composed of five permanent members (the United States, the Soviet Union, Great Britain, France, and China) and six other nations elected for two-year terms. The Security Council's responsibility was to suppress international violence by applying economic, diplomatic, or military sanctions against any nation that all permanent members agreed threatened the peace. In addition, the charter established an International Court of Justice and a number of agencies to promote "collaboration among the nations through education, science, and culture." Among these agencies were the International Monetary Fund, the World Health Organization, and the UN Educational, Scientific, and Cultural Organization (UNESCO).

The Atomic Age Begins

Two months after Yalta, on April 12, 1945, as the United Nations charter was being drafted, Roosevelt died suddenly of a massive cerebral hemorrhage. The nation was shocked. When an industrial worker in Springfield, Ohio, heard the news, he remarked that he was glad that "the old son of a bitch was gone"; another worker punched him in the face. Roosevelt, both hated and loved to the end, was replaced by Harry Truman, who was both more difficult to hate and harder to love. In the beginning, Truman seemed tentative and unsure of himself. Yet it fell to the new president to make some of the most difficult decisions of all time. The most momentous of all was the decision to drop the atomic bomb.

The Manhattan Project, first organized in 1941, was one of the best-kept secrets of the war. The task of the distinguished group of scientists whose work on the project was centered at Los Alamos, New Mexico, was to manufacture an atomic bomb before Germany did. But by the time the bomb was successfully tested in the New Mexico desert on July 16, 1945, the war in Europe had ended.

The scientists working on the bomb assumed that they were perfecting a military weapon. Yet when they saw the ghastly power of that first bomb, remembered J. Robert Oppenheimer, a leading scientist on the project, "some wept, a few cheered. Most stood silently." Some opposed the military use of the bomb. They realized its revolutionary power and worried about the future reputation of the United States if it unleashed this new force. But a presidential committee made up of scientists, military leaders, and politicians recommended that it be used on a military target in Japan as soon as possible.

"The final decision of where and when to use the atomic bomb was up to me," Truman later remembered. "Let there be no doubt about it. I regarded the bomb as a military weapon and never

The incredible destruction caused by the atomic bombs dropped on Japan is recalled by this 1984 Osaka department store display. The decision to drop the atomic bomb on two Japanese cities is still controversial a half century later.

had any doubt that it should be used." But the decision had both military and political ramifications. Even though Japan had lost most of its empire by the summer of 1945, it still had a military force of several million men and thousands of kamikaze planes that had already wreaked havoc on the American fleet. The kamikaze pilots gave up their own lives to make sure that their planes, heavily laden with bombs, crashed on an American ship. There was little defense against such fanaticism.

Even with the Russian promise to enter the war, it appeared that an amphibious landing on the Japanese mainland would be necessary to end the war. The monthlong battle for Iwo Jima, only 750 miles from Tokyo, had resulted in over 4,000 American dead and 15,000 wounded, and an invasion of Japan would be much more expensive. The bomb, many thought, could end the war without an invasion. But some people involved in the decision wanted to retaliate for Pearl Harbor, and still others needed to justify spending over $2 billion on the project in the first place. The timing of the first bomb, however, indicates that the decision was intended to impress the Russians and ensure that they had little to do with the peace settlement in the Far East. One British scientist later charged that the decision to drop the bomb on Hiroshima was the "first major operation of the cold diplomatic war with Russia."

On August 6, 1945, two days before the Soviet Union had promised to enter the war against Japan, a B-29 bomber dropped a single atomic bomb over Hiroshima. It killed or severely wounded 160,000 civilians and destroyed 4 square miles of the city. One of the men on the plane saw the thick cloud of smoke and thought that they had missed their target. "It looked like it had landed on a forest. I didn't see any sign of the city." The Soviet Union entered the war on August 8. When Japan refused to surrender, a second bomb was dropped on Nagasaki on August 9. The Japanese surrendered five days later. The war was finally over, but the problems of the atomic age and the postwar world were just beginning.

CONCLUSION

Peace, Prosperity, and International Responsibilities

The United States emerged from World War II with an enhanced reputation as the world's most powerful industrial and military nation. The demands of the war had finally ended the Great Depression and brought prosperity to most Americans. The war had also increased the power of the federal government. The payroll deduction of federal income taxes, begun during the war, symbolized the growth of a federal bureaucracy that affected the lives of all Americans. The war had also ended American isolationism and made the United States into the dominant international power. Of all the nations that fought in the war, the United States had suffered the least. No bombs were dropped on American factories, and no cities were destroyed. Although more than 300,000 Americans lost their lives, even this carnage seemed minimal when compared with the more than 20 million Russian soldiers and civilians who died or the 6 million Jews and millions of others systematically exterminated by Hitler.

Americans greeted the end of the war with joy and relief. They looked forward to the peace and prosperity for which they had fought. Yet within two years, the peace would be jeopardized by the Cold War, and the United States would be rearming its former enemies, Japan and Germany, to oppose its former friend, the Soviet Union. The irony of that situation reduced the joy of the hard-won peace and made the American people more suspicious of their government and its foreign policy.

Recommended Readings

General Accounts

A. Russell Buchanan, *The United States and World War II* (2 vols., 1964); Robert A. Divine, *Roosevelt and World War II* (1969); Gordon Wright, *The Ordeal of Total War* (1968).

Diplomatic and Military

Robert A. Divine, *The Reluctant Belligerent* (1979); Lloyd C. Gardner, *Economic Aspects of New Deal Diplomacy* (1964); Gaddis Smith, *Diplomacy During the Second World War* (1965); Walter LaFeber, *Inevitable Revolutions: The United States and Central America* (1983); Gordon W. Prange, *At Dawn We Slept* (1981); Waldo Heinrichs, *Threshold of War* (1988); John Dower, *War Without Mercy* (1986); Akira Iriye, *The Origins of the Second World War in Asia and the Pacific* (1988); Russell F. Weigley, *Eisenhower's Lieutenants: The Campaigns in France and Germany* (1981); Paul Fussell, *Wartime* (1989); Richard M. Dalfiume, *Desegregation of the U.S. Armed Forces* (1975); Martin J. Sherwin, *A World Destroyed* (1975); Gar Alperovitz, *Atomic Diplomacy* (1965).

The War at Home

Ross Gregory, *America 1941* (1988); John Morton Blum, *V Was for Victory* (1976); Richard Polenberg, *War and Society* (1972); Richard R. Lingeman, *Don't You Know There Is a War On?* (1970); Allan M. Winkler, *The Politics of Propaganda: The Office of War Information, 1942–1945* (1978); Gerald D. Nash, *The American West Transformed: The Impact of the Second World War* (1985); Bill Gilbert, *They Also Served: Baseball and the Homefront* (1992); Susan M. Hartman, *The Homefront and Beyond: Women in the 1940s* (1982); D'Ann Campbell, *Women at War with America* (1984); Ruth Milkman, *Gender at Work* (1987); Neil A. Wynn, *The Afro-American and the Second World War* (1976); Roger Daniels, *Concentration Camp U.S.A.* (1971); David S. Wyman, *The Abandonment of the Jews* (1984); Nicholas Lemann, *The Promised Land: The Great Black Migration and How It Changed America* (1991).

Fiction

In the *Dollmaker* (1954) Harriette Arnow tells the story of a young woman from Kentucky who finds herself in wartime Detroit; two powerful novels that tell the story of the battlefield experience are Norman Mailer, *The Naked and the Dead* (1948), and Irwin Shaw, *the Young Lions* (1948).

TIMELINE

1931–1932 Japan seizes Manchuria

1933 Hitler becomes German chancellor
United States recognizes the Soviet Union
Roosevelt extends Good Neighbor policy

1934 Germany begins rearmament

1935 Italy invades Ethiopia
First Neutrality Act

1936 Spanish civil war begins
Second Neutrality Act
Roosevelt reelected

1937 Third Neutrality Act

1938 Hitler annexes Austria, occupies Sudetenland
German persecution of Jews intensifies

1939 Nazi-Soviet Pact
German invasion of Poland; World War II begins

1940 Roosevelt elected for a third term
Selective Service Act

1941 FDR's "Four Freedoms" speech
Proposed black march on Washington
Executive order outlaws discrimination in defense industries
Lend-Lease Act
Germany attacks Russia
Japanese assets in United States frozen
Japanese attack Pearl Harbor; United States declares war on Japan
Germany declares war on the United States

1942 Internment of Japanese-Americans
Second Allied front in Africa launched

1943 Invasion of Sicily
Italian campaign; Italy surrenders
United Mine Workers strike
Race riots in Detroit and other cities

1944 Normandy invasion (Operation Overlord)
Congress passes GI Bill
Roosevelt elected for a fourth term

1945 Yalta conference
Roosevelt dies; Harry Truman becomes president
Germany surrenders
Successful test of atomic bomb
Hiroshima and Nagasaki bombed; Japan surrenders

PART VI

A Resilient People, 1945–1993

COMPARATIVE CHRONOLOGIES

1945

POLITICAL AND DIPLOMATIC

1945 Roosevelt dies; Truman becomes president
1945 First atomic bombs dropped on Japan; World War II ends
1946 Employment Act
1947 Truman Doctrine
Taft-Hartley Act
Truman establishes Federal Loyalty Program
HUAC probes movie industry
1948 Marshall Plan launched
Berlin Airlift
Truman reelected
1949 NATO established
Truman announces Fair Deal
1950 Alger Hiss convicted
Korean War begins
McCarran Internal Security Act
1951 *Dennis* v. *United States*
1952 Dwight D. Eisenhower elected president
1953 Rosenbergs executed
1953 Korean War ends
1954 Army-McCarthy hearings
1954 *Brown* v. *Board of Education*

SOCIAL AND ECONOMIC

1945–1946 Wave of strikes
1952 United States tests first hydrogen bomb
1953 Introduction of termination policy to eliminate reservations for Native Americans
1953–1954 Operation Wetback

CULTURAL AND TECHNOLOGICAL

1946 Benjamin Spock, *Baby and Child Care*
1947 Jackie Robinson becomes first African-American to play major-league baseball
1948 Kinsey publishes first report on human sexuality
1948 Bell Laboratories develops transistor
1951 J. D. Salinger, *The Catcher in the Rye*

1955

POLITICAL AND DIPLOMATIC

1956 Eisenhower reelected
Interstate Highway Act
1957 Civil Rights Act
1960 John F. Kennedy elected president
1960 Civil Rights Act
1961 Bay of Pigs invasion
1962 Cuban missile crisis
1963 JFK assassinated; Lyndon B. Johnson becomes president
1964 Civil Rights Act
War on Poverty launched
LBJ reelected

SOCIAL AND ECONOMIC

1955 AFL and CIO merge
Montgomery bus boycott
First McDonald's opens
1957 Baby boom peaks
1957 Little Rock school desegregation crisis
1960 Birth control pills made available
Sit-ins begin
SDS founded
1960s Wave of mergers in American industry
1961 Freedom rides to the South
1962 James Meredith crisis at University of Mississippi
1963 Birmingham demonstration
March on Washington
1964 Free Speech movement at Berkeley

CULTURAL AND TECHNOLOGICAL

1956 Elvis Presley hits No. 1 with "Heartbreak Hotel"
Allen Ginsberg, "Howl"
1957 First nuclear power plant opens in Shippingport, Pennsylvania
1957 Russians launch *Sputnik*
1960s Electronic calculators in office use
Jet planes used for commercial purposes
1961 Rachel Carson, *Silent Spring*
1962 Bob Dylan gains recognition with "Blowin' in the Wind"
First American orbits the earth
Michael Harrington, *The Other America*
1963 Betty Friedan, *The Feminine Mystique*

1993

1965

POLITICAL AND DIPLOMATIC

- 1965 Voting Rights Act
  Escalation in Vietnam
- 1968 Robert F. Kennedy assassinated
  Richard M. Nixon elected president
- 1969 Nixon Doctrine
- 1970 Environmental Protection Agency created
- 1971 Pentagon Papers published
- 1972 Nixon visits China
  SALT I agreement
  Watergate break-in
  Nixon reelected
- 1973 United States withdraws from Vietnam
- 1973 *Roe* v. *Wade*
- 1974 Nixon resigns; Gerald Ford becomes president
- 1974 Runaway and Homeless Youth Act

SOCIAL AND ECONOMIC

- 1965 Teach-ins begin
  Assassination of Malcolm X
- 1966 "Black Power"
- 1966 NOW founded
- 1968 Martin Luther King, Jr., assassinated
- 1968 AIM established
- 1970 Kent State and Jackson State incidents
- 1971–1975 Busing controversies
- 1973 Battle of Wounded Knee
  Arab oil embargo
- 1974 OPEC price increases

CULTURAL AND TECHNOLOGICAL

- 1965 Ralph Nader, *Unsafe at Any Speed*
- 1966 Masters and Johnson, *Human Sexual Response*
- 1969 Woodstock and Altamont rock festivals
- 1970s Electronics transform traditional industries
- 1972 *Ms.* magazine founded
  99.8 percent of American households have television sets
  Congress passes Equal Rights Amendment
- 1972–1973 Development of minicomputers
  Introduction of calculators for home use
- 1973 More than one million photocopiers in use

1975

POLITICAL AND DIPLOMATIC

- 1976 Jimmy Carter elected president
- 1977 Panama Canal treaties
- 1978 California passes Proposition 13, cutting property taxes
- 1978 *Bakke* decision
- 1979–1981 Iranian hostage crisis
- 1979 SALT II agreement
- 1980 Ronald Reagan elected president
- 1981 Sandra Day O'Connor becomes first woman Supreme Court justice
- 1981–1983 Tax cuts; deficit spending increases
- 1982 Equal Rights Amendment fails
- 1984 Geraldine Ferraro nominated for Democratic vice-president
- 1984 Reagan reelected

SOCIAL AND ECONOMIC

- 1977 Department of Energy created
  U.S. trade deficit $26.72 billion
- 1979 Three Mile Island accident
- 1980s Rise in number of deaths from AIDS

CULTURAL AND TECHNOLOGICAL

- 1976–1979 Space probes to Saturn, Pluto, Jupiter, Venus, and Mars
- 1980s Increasing sales of personal home computers
- 1982 Vietnam Veterans Memorial dedicated

1985

POLITICAL AND DIPLOMATIC

- 1986 Tax reform bill passed
- 1988 Intermediate-Range Nuclear Forces Treaty
- 1988 George Bush elected president

SOCIAL AND ECONOMIC

- 1986 Federal budget deficit hits peak of $221 billion
- 1987 Stock market crash
- 1989 Federal bailout of savings and loan industry
- 1989 One hundred thousandth case of AIDS in U.S. reported

CULTURAL AND TECHNOLOGICAL

- 1985 17 million VCRs in use; shift of film entertainment into the home
- 1986 Challenger space shuttle explodes

1990

POLITICAL AND DIPLOMATIC

- 1990 Immigration reform enacted
- 1991 Strategic Arms Reduction Treaty (START)
- 1991 Persian Gulf War
- 1992 Bill Clinton elected president

SOCIAL AND ECONOMIC

- 1990 National debt reaches $3.1 trillion

CULTURAL AND TECHNOLOGICAL

- 1990 50 million computers in use in the United States

CHAPTER 26

Chills and Fever During the Cold War

Val Lorwin was in Paris in November 1950 when word of the charges against him arrived. A State Department employee, on leave of absence after 16 years of government service, he was in France working on a book. Now he had to return to the United States to defend himself against the accusation that he was a member of the Communist party and thus a loyalty and security risk.

The accusation surprised Lorwin. It almost seemed like a tasteless joke. Yet it was no joke but a grim consequence of the Cold War. Suspicions of the Soviet Union escalated after 1945, and a wave of paranoia swept through the United States. The threat of communism was no laughing matter at home.

Lorwin was an unlikely candidate to be caught up in the fallout of the Cold War. He began to work for the government in 1935, serving in a number of New Deal agencies, then in the Labor Department and on the War Production Board before he was drafted during World War II. While in the army, he was assigned to the Office of Strategic Services, an early intelligence agency, and he was frequently granted security clearances in the United States and abroad.

Lorwin, however, did have a left-wing past as an active Socialist in the 1930s. His social life then had revolved around Socialist party causes, particularly the unionization of southern tenant farmers and the provision of aid to the unemployed. He and his wife Madge drafted statements or stuffed envelopes to support their goals. But that activity was wholly open and legal, and Lorwin had from the start been aggressively anti-Communist in political affairs.

Suddenly, Lorwin, like others in the period, faced the nightmare of secret charges against which the burden of proof was entirely on him and the chance of clearing his name slim. Despite his spotless record, Lorwin was told that an unnamed accuser had identified him as a Communist. He was entitled to a hearing if he chose, or he could resign.

Lorwin requested a hearing, held late in 1950. Still struck by the absurdity of the situation, he refuted all accusations but made little effort to cite his own positive achievements. At the conclusion, he was informed that the government no longer doubted his loyalty but considered him a security risk, grounds nonetheless for dismissal from his job.

When he appealed the judgment, Lorwin was again denied access to the identity of his accuser. This time, however, he thoroughly prepared his defense. At the hearing, a total of 97 witnesses either spoke under oath on Lorwin's behalf or left sworn written depositions testifying to his good character and meritorious service.

The issues in the hearings might have been considered comic in view of Lorwin's record, had not a man's reputation been at stake. The accuser had once lived with the Lorwins in Washington, D.C. Fifteen years later, he claimed that in 1935 Lorwin had revealed that he was holding a Communist party meeting in his home and had even shown him a party card.

Lorwin proved all the charges groundless. He also showed that in 1935 the Socialist party card was red, the color the accuser reported seeing, while the Communist party card was black. In March 1952, Lorwin was finally cleared for both loyalty and security.

Though he thought he had weathered the storm, Lorwin's troubles were not yet over. His name appeared on one of the lists produced by Senator Joseph McCarthy of Wisconsin, the most aggressive anti-Communist of the era, and Lorwin was again victimized. The next year, he was indicted for making false statements to the State Department Loyalty-Security Board. The charges this time proved as specious as before. Finally, in May 1954, admitting that its special prosecutor had deliberately lied to the grand jury and had no legitimate case, the Justice Department asked for dismissal of the indictment. Lorwin was cleared at last and went on to a distinguished career as a labor historian.

Lorwin was more fortunate than some victims of the anti-Communist crusade. People rallied around him and gave him valuable support. Despite considerable emotional cost, he survived the witch-hunt of the early 1950s, but his case still reflected vividly the ugly domestic consequences of the breakdown in relations between the Soviet Union and the United States.

The Cold War, which unfolded soon after the end of World War II and lasted for nearly fifty years, powerfully affected all aspects of American life. Rejecting for good the isolationist impulse that had governed foreign policy in the 1930s, the United States began to play a major role in the world in the postwar years. The same sense of mission that had infused America in the Spanish-American War, World War I, and World War II now impelled most Americans to see themselves struggling against communism at home and abroad. This chapter explores that continuing sense of mission and its consequences. It examines the roots of the Cold War both in the idealistic aim to keep the world safe for democracy and in the pursuit of economic self-interest that fueled American capitalism. It shows how the determination to prevent the spread of communism led American policymakers to consider vast parts of the world as pivotal to American security. And it considers the tragic consequences of the effort to promote ideological unity within the United States.

B.S.

Conflicting World Views

The Cold War was rooted in long-standing disagreements between the major powers that had been set aside during World War II. The United States and the Soviet Union had fundamentally different perceptions about the shape of the postwar world. The United States, strong and secure, was intent on spreading its vision of freedom and economic opportunity around the world. The Soviet Union, concerned about its own security after a devastating war, demanded politically sympathetic neighbors on its borders. Each nation felt threatened by the interests of the other, and actions by both sides sparked reactions that culminated in the Cold War.

The American Stance

The United States emerged from World War II more powerful than any nation ever before. No fighting had taken place on mainland American shores, and no postwar reconstruction was necessary. As the "arsenal of democracy," the United States had used its extraordinary economic might to defeat the Axis powers. Now it sought to use that might to achieve the kind of order that could sustain American aims.

American policymakers, following in Woodrow Wilson's footsteps, hoped to spread the values that provided the underpinning of the American dream. In seeking to share with other nations their conception of liberty, equality, and democracy, they did not always recognize that what they considered universal truths were rooted in specific historical circumstances in their own country and might not always flourish elsewhere. As much of the rest of the world found itself in turmoil, with empires disintegrating, civil wars unfolding, and power vacuums waiting to be filled, they assumed that they could provide the stability reconstruction required. But other nations felt threatened by that approach.

At the same time, American leaders hoped for a world where economic enterprise could thrive. With the American economy operating at full speed as a result of the war, world markets were needed once the fighting stopped. Government officials wanted to eliminate trade barriers—imposed by the Soviet Union and other nations—to provide outlets for industrial products and for surplus farm commodities like wheat, cotton, and tobacco. As the largest source of goods for world markets, with exports totaling $14 billion in 1947, the United States required open channels for growth to continue. Recollections of the Depression decade haunted leaders. "We've got to export three times as much as we exported just before the war if we want to keep our industry running at somewhere near capacity," Undersecretary of State William L. Clayton told a congressional committee in March 1945. Americans assumed that their prosperity would benefit the rest of the world. But other nations, the Soviet Union in particular, disagreed.

Soviet Aims

The Soviet Union formulated its own goals after World War II. Historically, Russia had usually had a strongly centralized, sometimes even autocratic government, and that tradition—as much as Communist ideology, with its stress on class struggle and the inevitable triumph of a proletarian state—guided Soviet policy.

During the war, the Russians had played down the notion of world revolution they knew the other allies found threatening and had mobilized support for more nationalistic goals. Still fearful of capitalist encirclement and the penetration of Western ways, as they had been since the nineteenth century, they remained confident that their Communist system would triumph, as Marxist-Leninist doctrine predicted. Yet the message was trumpeted less aggressively than before. As the struggle drew to a close, the Soviets talked little of world conquest, emphasizing socialism within the nation itself.

Rebuilding was the first priority. Devastated by the war, Soviet agriculture and industry were in shambles. But the task of reconstruction demanded internal security. At the same time, the Russians feared vulnerability along their western flank. Such anxieties had a historical basis, for in the early nineteenth century, Napoleon had reached the gates of Moscow. Twice in the twentieth century, invasions had come from the west, most recently when Hitler had attacked in 1941. The Soviets had finally repelled that offensive, but at enormous cost. Haunted by fears that the Germans would recover quickly, the Soviets demanded defensible borders and neighboring regimes sympathetic to Russian aims. Patterns for eastern European governments were not predetermined. A measure of flexibility was possible, as long as the Soviets felt they were able to maintain military and political stability in the regions closest to them.

Cold War Leadership

Both the United States and the Soviet Union had strong leadership as the Cold War unfolded. On the American side, first Harry Truman, then Dwight Eisenhower accepted the centralization of authority Franklin Roosevelt had begun, as the executive branch became increasingly powerful in guiding foreign policy. In the Soviet Union, first Joseph Stalin, then Nikita Khrushchev provided equally forceful direction.

Harry Truman served as president of the United States in the first postwar years. He was an unpretentious man who took a straightforward approach to public affairs. He was, however, ill prepared for the office he assumed in the final

Conflicting Aims During the Cold War

United States	*Soviet Union*
Spread ideological values of liberty, equality, democracy	Spread ideological values of class struggle, triumph of the proletariat
Extend the tradition of representative government	Extend the tradition of strong centralized government
Maintain stability around the world	Support revolutionary movements around the world
Fill vacuum created by the end of imperialism with regimes sympathetic to Western ideals	Support regimes sympathetic to the Soviet Union, particularly to avoid attack on its western flank
Maintain a world free for economic enterprise by eliminating trade barriers, providing markets for American exports	Rebuild the devastated Soviet economy by creating preferential trading arrangements in the region of Soviet dominance

Truman's down-to-earth directness sometimes complicated political negotiations but gained him public support. His informal appeal, reflected here, helped him win his remarkable upset victory in the presidential election of 1948.

months of World War II. His three months as vice-president had done little to school him in the complexity of postwar issues. Nor had Franklin Roosevelt confided in Truman. No wonder that the new president felt insecure. To a former colleague in the Senate, he groaned, "I'm not big enough for this job." Others agreed. Tennessee Valley Authority director David Lilienthal spoke for many who found it hard to accept the fact that Roosevelt was gone. "The country," he complained, "doesn't deserve to be left this way."

Yet Truman matured rapidly. A feisty politician, he responded ably to new challenges. Impulsive and aggressive, he made a virtue out of rapid response. At his first press conference, he answered questions so quickly that reporters could not record his responses. A sign on the president's White House desk read "The Buck Stops Here," and he was willing to make quick decisions on issues, even though associates sometimes wondered if he understood all the implications. Roosevelt had shown a masterful sense of timing during the New Deal and, on complex issues during the war, had been even more willing to delay. Truman was less inclined to wait before acting. His rapid-fire decisions had important consequences for the Cold War. Truman served virtually all of the term to which Roosevelt had been elected, then won another for himself in 1948. In 1952, war hero Dwight D. Eisenhower, who won the presidency for the Republican party for the first time in 20 years, succeeded him.

Eisenhower stood in stark contrast to his predecessor. His easy manner and warm smile made him widely popular. On occasion, in press conferences or other public gatherings, his comments came out convoluted and imprecise. Yet appearances were deceiving, for beneath his casual approach was real shrewdness. At one point, as he prepared for a session with newsmen and his aides briefed him on a delicate matter, he said, "Don't worry. . . . If that question comes up, I'll just confuse them."

Eisenhower had not taken the typical route to the presidency. After his World War II success, he served as army chief of staff, president of Columbia University, and then head of the North Atlantic Treaty Organization. Despite his lack of formal political background, he had a genuine ability to get people to compromise and to work together. Though he remained aloof from party politics, he may have entertained hopes of holding office after the war. General George Patton commented in 1943 that "Ike wants to be President so badly you can taste it," and his career choices after the war clearly kept him visible and involved in public affairs. Yet he made no move in that direction until he sought the Republican nomination in 1952.

Ike's limited experience with everyday politics conditioned his sense of the presidential role. Whereas Truman was accustomed to political infighting and wanted to take charge, Eisenhower saw things differently. The presidency for him was no "bully pulpit," as it had been for Theodore Roosevelt and even FDR. "I am not one of those desk-pounding types that likes to stick out his jaw and look like he is bossing the show," he said. "You do not lead by hitting people over the head. Any damn fool can do that, but it's usually called 'assault'—not 'leadership.'" Even so, Ike knew exactly where he wanted to go and worked behind the scenes to get there.

Though the personal styles of Truman and Eisenhower differed, as did their domestic programs (see Chapter 27), they shared a basic view that governed American foreign policy after World War II. Both subscribed to traditional American attitudes about self-determination and the superiority of American political institutions and values. Both distrusted Soviet ventures during and after the war. Truman's suspicions were obvious even before the United States entered the struggle. He commented in July 1941, "If we see that Germany is winning we ought to help Russia, and if Russia is winning we ought to help Germany." He accepted collaboration as a marriage of necessity, but he became increasingly hostile to Soviet moves as the war drew to an end. It was now time, he said, "to stand up to the Russians."

Like Truman, Eisenhower believed that communism was a monolithic force struggling for world supremacy and that the Kremlin in Moscow was orchestrating subversive activity around the globe. Like Truman, he viewed the Soviet system as a "tyranny that has brought thousands, millions of people into slave camps and is attempting to make all mankind its chattel." Both presidents perceived the issues in black and white terms. As Eisenhower declared in his 1953 inaugural address, "Forces of good and evil are massed and armed and opposed as rarely before in history. Freedom is pitted against slavery, lightness against dark." Yet Eisenhower was still a military

Eisenhower's indirect approach and low-key public image made him popular throughout the 1950s. His intent gaze and wide smile gave Americans a sense of confidence that the country was in good hands. Here "Ike" greets a delegation of Republican National Committee women during the 1952 presidential campaign.

man with a measure of caution who could practice accommodation when it served his ends.

The leader of the Soviet Union at the war's end was Joseph Stalin. Ruthless in pursuit of both national and personal ends and possessing almost absolute power, he had presided over monstrous purges against his opponents in the 1930s. Now he spoke in terms that gave the Soviets alone credit for the victory over Hitler and affirmed the superiority of Russian society. He was determined to rebuild that society, if possible with Western assistance, and to keep eastern Europe within the Russian sphere of influence.

Stalin's death in March 1953 left a vacuum in Soviet political affairs. His successor, Nikita S. Khrushchev, used his position as party secretary to consolidate his power. Purges of the party bureaucracy took place, and five years after Stalin's death, Khrushchev held the offices of both prime minister and party secretary. A peasant from a coal-mining family who had risen to the top, Khrushchev was fond of crude jokes and known for rude behavior. On one occasion, he pounded a table at the United Nations with his shoe while the British prime minister was speaking. As Khrushchev continued some of Stalin's hard-line policies, he intermittently called for "peaceful coexistence." Although the Cold War continued, there were now brief periods when relations between the two powers became less hostile.

Origins of the Cold War

The Cold War developed by degrees. Frictions that had existed since 1917, temporarily eased during World War II, began to resurface as the struggle wound down. With the Fascist threat defeated, disagreements about the shape of the postwar world brought the Soviet Union and the United States into conflict. Such conflicts caused suspicion and distrust. As confrontation followed confrontation, the two nations behaved, according to Senator J. William Fulbright, "like two big dogs chewing on a bone."

Disillusionment with the USSR

During the war, Joseph Goulden, a youngster of about 10, saw the Russians as "brave and skilled partisans." To him, "their heroic stand at Stalingrad was equal to the defense of the Alamo." Soon that comforting image began to fade. In September 1945, more than half (54 percent) of a national sample trusted the Russians to cooperate with the Americans in the postwar years. Two months later, the figure had dropped to 44 percent, and by February 1946, to 35 percent.

Americans became increasingly disillusioned with the Soviet political system. In a series of articles in *Harper's, Life,* and *The New Yorker* in 1946,

Joseph Stalin's autocratic approach to foreign and domestic affairs affronted American sensibilities. Here he stands in front of a bust of Lenin, father of the Russian Revolution.

Soviet leader Nikita Khrushchev, pictured here in a cordial meeting with Dwight Eisenhower, could turn abrasive when he chose, as when he removed his shoe and pounded it on the table during a speech at the United Nations.

author-editor John Fischer pointed to the single-minded intensity that characterized the Soviet state. In one story, he recalled a conversation with a Soviet official who argued that the United States should cease shortwave broadcasts to the Soviet Union but thought Russia should continue to transmit its messages to the American people. When the perplexed Fischer asked about the apparent contradiction, the Soviet bureaucrat responded that it was a "perfect example of reciprocity." "Your laws," he explained, "provide for free speech, and we observe them. Our laws do not, and it would be improper for you to disregard them."

As Americans soured on Russia, they began to equate the Nazi and Soviet systems and to transfer their hatred of Hitler's Germany to Communist Russia. Just as they had in the 1930s, authors, journalists, and public officials began to point to similarities between the regimes, some of them quite legitimate. Both states, they contended, maintained total control over communications and could eliminate political opposition whenever they chose. Both states used terror to silence dissidents. Russian labor camps in Siberia were now compared to German concentration camps. After the American publication in 1949 of George Orwell's frightening novel *Nineteen Eighty-four, Life* magazine noted in an editorial that the ominous figure Big Brother was but a "mating" of Hitler and Stalin. Truman spoke for many Americans when he said in 1950 that "there isn't any difference between the totalitarian Russian government and the Hitler government. . . . They are all alike. They are . . . police state governments."

The lingering sense that the nation had not been quick enough to resist totalitarian aggression in the 1930s heightened American fears. Had the United States stopped the Germans, Italians, or Japanese, it might have prevented the long, devastating war. The free world had not responded quickly enough before and was determined never to repeat the same mistake.

The Polish Question

The first clash between East and West came, even before the war ended, over Poland. Soviet demands for a government willing to accept Russian influence clashed with American hopes for a more representative structure patterned after the Western model. The Yalta Conference of February

1945 attempted to resolve the issue of a government for the postwar state (see Chapter 25), but the agreement was loosely worded and correspondingly imprecise.

When Truman assumed office, the situation was still unresolved. Averell Harriman, the American ambassador to the Soviet Union, warned that the United States faced a "barbarian invasion of Europe" unless the Soviets could be checked and American-style democracies established. Truman agreed. "We must stand up to the Russians," he said, "and not be easy with them."

Truman's unbending stance was clear in an April 1945 meeting with Soviet foreign minister Vyacheslav Molotov on the question of Poland. Concerned that the Russians were breaking the Yalta agreements, imprecise as they were, the president demanded a new democratic government there. Though Molotov appeared conciliatory, Truman insisted on Russian acquiescence. Truman later recalled that when Molotov protested, "I have never been talked to like that in my life," he himself retorted bluntly, "Carry out your agreements and you won't get talked to like that." Such bluntness sparked a hostile reaction and contributed to the deterioration of Soviet-American relations.

Truman and Stalin met face to face for the first time at the Potsdam Conference in July 1945, the last of the meetings held by the Big Three during the war. There, as they considered the Russian-Polish boundary, the fate of Germany, and the American desire to obtain an unconditional surrender from Japan, the two leaders sized each other up. It was Truman's first exposure to international diplomacy at the highest level, and it left him confident of his abilities. When he learned during the meeting of the first successful atomic bomb test in New Mexico, he became even more determined to insist on his positions, even if that angered the Soviet Union and allowed tensions to escalate.

Economic Pressure on the USSR

One major source of controversy in the last stage of the Second World War was the question of American aid to its allies. Responding to congressional pressure at home to limit foreign assistance as hostilities ended, Truman acted impulsively. Six days after V-E Day signaled the end of the European war in May 1945, he issued an executive order cutting off lend-lease supplies to the Allies. The struggle against Japan in the Pacific dragged on, and Russia had agreed to assist there, but even so, ship-loading in the United States was halted, and vessels bound for the Soviet Union and elsewhere were ordered to reverse course. Although the policy affected all nations receiving aid, it hurt the Soviet Union most of all. Secretary of State Edward Stettinius felt that the action was "particularly untimely" in view of the delicate state of the Grand Alliance. Truman had been warned of the consequences of his actions and later acknowledged that a phased end to shipments would have been preferable. By then it was too late.

The United States intended to use economic pressure in other ways as well. Russia desperately needed financial assistance to rebuild after the war and, in January 1945, had requested a $6 billion loan. Roosevelt hedged, hoping to win concessions in return. In August, the Russians renewed their application, this time for only $1 billion. Like his predecessor, the new president dragged his heels. The United States first claimed to have lost the Soviet request, then in March 1946 indicated a willingness to consider the matter—but only if Russia pledged "nondiscrimination in world commerce." In short, the United States tried to use the loan as a lever to gain access to new markets in areas traditionally dominated by the Soviet Union. Unwilling to help promote American trade in such areas, Stalin refused the offer and launched his own five-year plan instead.

Declaring the Cold War

As Soviet-American disagreements increased, both sides stepped up their rhetorical attacks. Stalin spoke out first, in 1946, asserting his confidence in the triumph of the Russian system. Capitalism and communism were on a collision course, he argued, and a series of cataclysmic disturbances would tear the capitalist world apart. The Soviet Union was prepared to strengthen its military forces, even if that meant forgoing consumer goods, to ensure its own survival in a world no longer pursuing peace. Stalin's speech was a stark and ominous statement that worried the West. Supreme Court Justice William O. Douglas called it the "declaration of World War III."

The response to Stalin's speech came not from an American but from England's former prime minister, Winston Churchill, long suspicious of the Soviet state. Speaking in Fulton, Missouri, in 1946, with Truman on the platform during the address, Churchill declared that "from Stettin in the Baltic to Trieste in the Adriatic, an iron curtain has descended across the Continent." To counter the threat, he urged that a vigilant association of English-speaking peoples work to contain Soviet designs.

Containing the Soviet Union

Containment formed the basis of postwar American policy. Troubled by the rise of a Communist superpower that threatened American interests, both political parties determined to check Soviet expansion. In an increasingly contentious world, the American government formulated rigid anti-Soviet policies. The Soviet Union responded in an equally uncompromising manner.

Containment Defined

George F. Kennan was primarily responsible for defining the new policy. Chargé d'affaires at the American embassy in the Soviet Union, he sent off an 8,000-word telegram to the State Department after Stalin's speech in February 1946. Kennan argued that Soviet-American hostility stemmed from the "Kremlin's neurotic view of world affairs," which in turn came from the "traditional and instinctive Russian sense of insecurity." The stiff Soviet stance was not so much a response to American actions as a reflection of the Russian leaders' own efforts to maintain their autocratic rule. Russian fanaticism would not soften, regardless of how accommodating American policy became. Therefore, it had to be opposed at every turn.

When it arrived in Washington, Kennan's analysis struck a resonant chord. It made his diplomatic reputation, led to his assignment to a more influential position in the State Department, and encouraged him to publish an important article, under the pseudonym "Mr. X," in *Foreign Affairs.* In that essay, he extended his former analysis and expressed his reservations about coexistence. The Russians intended to pursue their own ends for as long as they could. "The whole Soviet governmental machine, including the mechanism of diplomacy," he wrote, "moves inexorably along the prescribed path, like a persistent toy automobile wound up and headed in a given direction, stopping only when it meets with some unanswerable force." Many Americans agreed with Kennan that Soviet pressure had to "be contained by the adroit and vigilant application of counter-force at a series of constantly shifting geographical and political points."

The concept of containment provided the philosophical justification for the hard-line stance that Americans, both in and out of government, adopted. During Truman's presidency, containment was viewed as the cornerstone of all diplomatic initiatives in both Europe and Asia. All three secretaries of state—James F. Byrnes, George C. Marshall, and Dean Acheson—firmly supported the concept. Containment created the framework for military and economic assistance around the globe.

The Truman Doctrine

The Truman Doctrine represented the first major application of containment policy. The new policy was devised to respond to conditions in the eastern Mediterranean, an area that Americans had never before considered vital to their national security. The Soviet Union was pressuring Turkey for joint control of the Dardanelles, the passage between the Black Sea and the Mediterranean. Meanwhile, a civil war in Greece pitted Communist elements against the ruling English-aided right-wing monarchy. Revolutionary pressures threatened to topple the government.

In February 1947, the British ambassador to the United States informed the State Department that his exhausted country could no longer give Greece and Turkey economic and military aid. Would the United States now move into the void?

The State Department quickly developed a proposal for American assistance when Britain pulled out. But the administration needed to per-

Cold War Europe in 1950

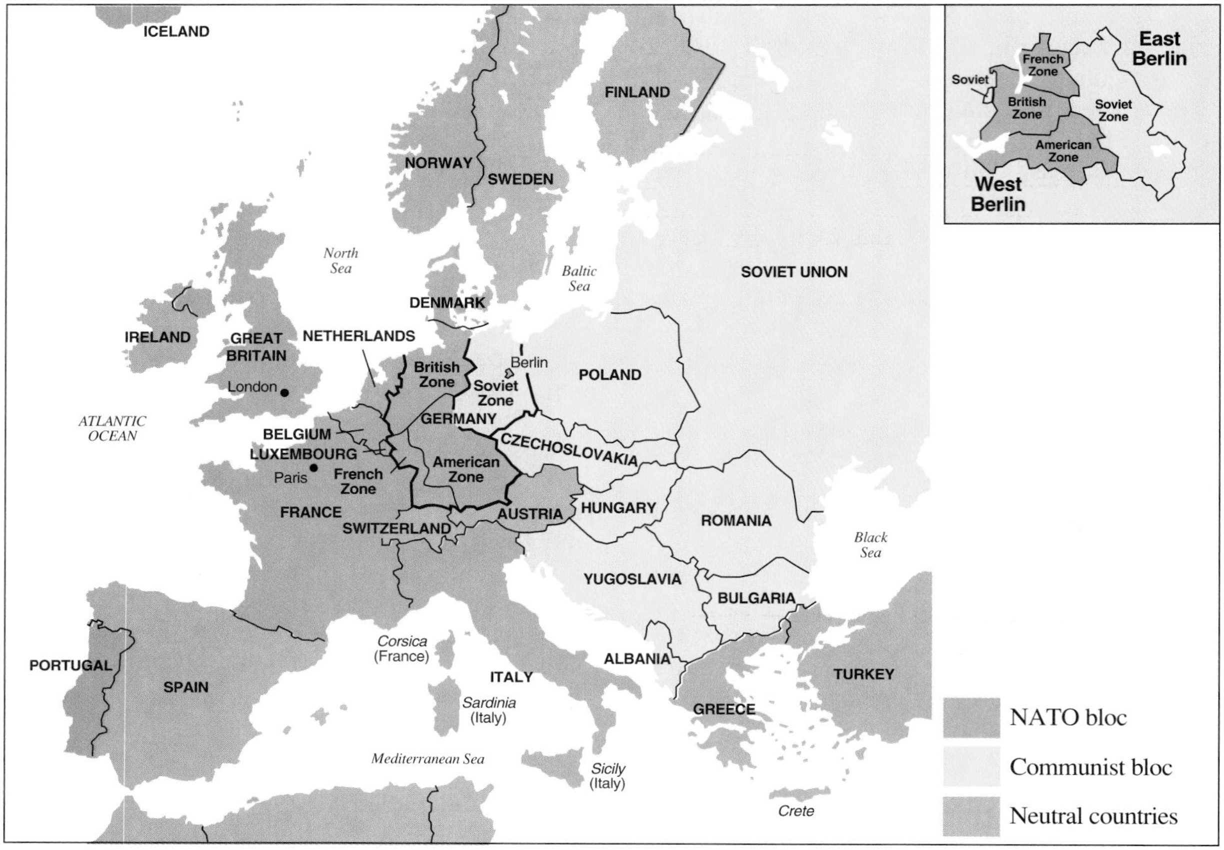

This map shows the rigid demarcation between East and West during the Cold War. Although there were a number of neutral countries in Europe, the other nations found themselves in a standoff, as each side tried to contain the possible advances of the other. The small insert map in the upper-right-hand corner shows the division of Berlin that paralleled the division of Germany itself after World War II.

suade reluctant legislators that the national interest was involved. A conservative Congress wanted smaller budgets and lower taxes rather than massive and expensive aid programs. Meeting with congressional leaders, Dean Acheson, at the time undersecretary of state, warned that "like apples in a barrel infected by one rotten one, the corruption of Greece would infect Iran and all to the east." Eager to persuade legislators of the importance of the moment, he warned in exaggerated language that a Communist victory would "open three continents to Soviet penetration." The major powers were now "met at Armageddon," as the Soviet Union pressed for whatever advantage it could get. Only the United States had the will and power to resist.

Administration leaders knew bipartisan support was necessary to accomplish such a major policy shift. Senator Arthur Vandenberg of Michigan was one of the key Republicans whose approval would help win other party members over. Sympathetic to the proposal, Vandenberg warned Democratic leaders of the need to develop public support for an interventionist policy. Quite literally, Vandenberg said, administration officials had to begin "scaring hell out of the country" if they were serious about a bold new course of containment.

Truman took Vandenberg's advice to heart and prepared to tell Americans not of the realities of the situation in Greece but of the monstrous threat to the Western vision of the world that the Soviet Union posed. On March 12, 1947, he told Congress, in a statement that came to be known as the Truman Doctrine, "I believe that it must be the policy of the United States to support free peoples who are resisting subjugation by armed minorities or by outside pressures." Unless the United States acted, the free world might not survive. "If we falter in our leadership," Truman said, "we may endanger the peace of the world—and we shall surely endanger the welfare of our own Nation." To avert that calamity, he urged Congress to appropriate $400 million for military and economic aid to Turkey and Greece.

Not everyone approved of Truman's request or of his overblown description of the situation. Autocratic regimes controlled Greece and Turkey, some observers pointed out. And where was the proof that Stalin had a hand in the Greek conflict? Others warned that the United States could not by itself stop encroachment in all parts of the world. Nonetheless, Congress passed Truman's foreign aid bill.

In its assumption that Americans could police the globe, the Truman Doctrine was a major step in the advent of the Cold War. Truman's address, observed financier Bernard Baruch, "was tantamount to a declaration of . . . an ideological or religious war." Journalist Walter Lippmann was more critical. He termed the new containment policy a "strategic monstrosity" that could embroil the United States in disputes around the world. In the two succeeding decades, Lippmann proved correct.

The Marshall Plan, NATO, and NSC-68

The next step involved extensive economic aid for postwar recovery in western Europe. At the war's end, most of Europe was economically and politically unstable, thereby offering opportunities to the Communist movement. In France and Italy, large Communist parties grew stronger and refused to cooperate with established governments. In such circumstances, administration officials believed, Russia might easily intervene. Decisive action was needed, for as the new secretary of state, George Marshall, declared, "The patient is sinking while the doctors deliberate."

Another motive was eagerness to bolster the European economy to provide markets for American goods. Western Europeans had been excellent customers earlier. In the aftermath of the war, they were able to purchase less at a time when the United States was producing much more.

Marshall revealed the administration's willingness to assist European recovery in June 1947. He asked all troubled European nations to draw up an aid program that the United States could support, a program "directed not against any country or doctrine but against hunger, poverty, desperation, and chaos." Soviet-bloc countries were welcome to participate, Marshall claimed, aware that their involvement was unlikely: since they would have to disclose economic records to join, and Communist nations maintained rigorous secrecy about their internal affairs.

The proposed program would assist the ravaged nations while providing the United States with needed markets. It would also advance the nation's ideological aims. American aid, Marshall pointed out, would permit the "emergence of political and social conditions in which free institutions can exist." The Marshall Plan and the Truman Doctrine, Truman noted, were "two halves of the same walnut."

Responding quickly to Marshall's invitation, the western European nations worked out the details of massive requests in the summer of 1947. The Soviets attended the first planning meeting but then withdrew, as American policymakers hoped and expected they would, and established their own recovery scheme for the nations in their bloc. When the multination request was finally hammered out, American officials pared it down but agreed to provide $17 billion over a period of four years to 16 cooperating nations.

Not all Americans supported the Marshall Plan. Henry A. Wallace, former vice-president and secretary of agriculture, who had broken with the administration, called the scheme the "Martial Plan" and argued that it was another step toward war. Some members of Congress feared spreading American resources too thin. But in early 1948, Congress committed the nation to funding European economic recovery, and the containment policy moved forward another step.

Closely related to the Marshall Plan was a concerted Western effort to rebuild Germany and to reintegrate it into a reviving Europe. At Yalta, as the European war drew to an end, Allied leaders had agreed on zonal occupation of Germany and on reparations Germany would pay the victors. Four zones, occupied by the Russians, Americans, British, and French, had been established for postwar administration. A year after the end of the war, however, the balance of power in Europe had shifted. With the Soviet Union threatening to dominate eastern Europe, the West moved to fill the vacuum in central Europe. In late 1946, the Americans and British merged their zones for economic purposes and began to assign administrative duties to Germans. By the middle of 1947, the process of rebuilding West German industry was under way.

Despite French fears, the United States sought to make Germany strong enough to anchor Europe. Secretary Marshall cautiously laid out the connections for Congress:

> The restoration of Europe involves the restoration of Germany. Without a revival of German production there can be no revival of Europe's economy. But we must be very careful to see that a revived Germany cannot again threaten the European community.

In mid-1948, the Soviet Union attempted to force the other nations out of Berlin, which, like Germany itself, was divided into zones after the war. Soviet refusal to allow the other Allies land access to West Berlin, located in the Russian zone of Germany, led to a U.S. and Royal Air Force airlift that flew supplies to the beleaguered Berliners. The fliers named it Operation Vittles, and it broke the Russian blockade. It delivered more than 2 million tons of supplies to the city. Operation Little Vittles, so named by Lieutenant Carl S. Halverson, provided bags of candy for the children at the same time. "The difficult we do immediately," a Seabee-Air Force boast proclaimed; "the impossible takes a little longer."

The next major link in the containment strategy was the creation of a military alliance in Europe to complement the economic program. Having justified containment in cataclysmic terms, a military presence was a logical step. In mid-1947, the Soviets had rigged elections in Hungary and

An American and British airlift in 1948 brought badly needed supplies to West Berliners isolated by a Soviet blockade of the city. By refusing to allow the Western powers to reach the city, located within the Soviet zone, the Russians hoped to drive them from Berlin, but the airlift broke the blockade.

eliminated anti-Communist opposition. The next year, Soviet troops massed on the Czechoslovakian border to keep that nation within the Russian orbit. In response, in 1949, the United States took the lead in establishing NATO, the North Atlantic Treaty Organization. Twelve nations formed the alliance, vowing that an attack against any one member would be considered an attack against all, to be met by appropriate armed force.

The Senate, formerly opposed to such military pacts, approved this time, and the United States established its first military treaty ties with Europe since the American Revolution. Congress went further than merely authorizing membership by voting military aid for its NATO allies. The Cold War had softened long-standing American reluctance to become closely involved with European affairs.

In 1949, two significant events—the success of the Communists in the Chinese civil war and the Russian detonation of an atomic device—led the United States to define its aims still more specifically. Truman asked for a full-fledged review of America's foreign and defense policy. The National Security Council, organized in 1947 to provide policy coordination, undertook the study. The important paper that resulted, NSC-68, shaped American policy for the next 20 years.

Presented to the National Security Council in 1950, NSC-68 built on the Cold War rhetoric of the Truman Doctrine, describing America's challenges in cataclysmic terms. "The issues that face us are momentous," the paper said, "involving the fulfillment or destruction not only of this Republic but of civilization itself." Conflict between East and West, the paper assumed, was unavoidable, for amoral Soviet objectives ran totally counter to American aims. Negotiation was useless, for the Soviets could never be trusted to bargain in good faith.

Having eliminated important options to resolving differences through traditional channels of diplomacy, NSC-68 now laid out the remaining alternatives. The nation could continue on its present course, with relatively limited military budgets, but would fail to achieve its objectives. If the United States hoped to meet the Russian challenge, a far more massive effort was necessary. The nation must increase defense spending from the $13 billion set for 1950 to as much as $50 billion per year and increase the percentage of its budget allotted to defense from 5 to 20 percent. The costs were huge, the document argued, but necessary if the free world was to survive.

Containment in the 1950s

Containment, the keystone of American policy throughout the Truman years, was the rationale for the Truman Doctrine, the Marshall Plan, NATO, and NSC-68. In the 1950s, however, under Eisenhower's administration, containment came under attack as too cautious to counter the threat of communism.

For most of Eisenhower's two terms, John Foster Dulles was secretary of state. A devout Presbyterian who hated atheistic communism, he sought to move beyond containment. Eager to counter the "Godless terrorism" of communism, Dulles wanted to commit the nation to a holy crusade to promote democracy and to free the countries under Soviet domination. Instead of advocating containment, the United States should make it "publicly known that it wants and expects liberation to occur."

Secretary of State John Foster Dulles viewed the Cold War as a moral struggle between good and evil. Opposed to "godless communism," he often appeared as a religious crusader for measures he believed were necessary for the survival of the free world.

The language was extreme, and the policy of liberation proved impossible to implement. Eisenhower, more conciliatory and realistic than Dulles, recognized the impossibility of changing the governments of the USSR's satellites and the need for caution. The chance to test the rhetorical liberation policy came in mid-1953, as East Germans mounted anti-Soviet demonstrations. The United States kept its distance. In 1956, when Hungarian "freedom fighters" defied Russian domination, the United States again stood back as Soviet forces smashed the rebels. Because Western action could have precipitated a more general conflict, Eisenhower refused to translate rhetoric into action. In the real world of international affairs, liberation was meaningless. Throughout the 1950s, the policy of containment, largely as it had been defined earlier, remained in effect.

American Policy in Asia, the Middle East, and Latin America

Although containment resulted from the effort to promote European stability, the United States, in a dramatic departure from its history of noninvolvement, extended the policy to meet challenges around the globe. The Communist victory in the Chinese civil war in 1949 only underscored the growing threat to the economic and social order Americans wanted in the postwar world. The Korean War, which broke out soon after, embroiled the United States in another international conflict barely five years after the end of World War II. Elsewhere in Asia, and in the Middle East and Latin America, the United States discovered the tremendous appeal of communism as a social and political system and found that ever greater efforts were required to advance American aims.

The Chinese Revolution

America's commitment to containment became stronger with the climax of the Chinese Revolution. China, an ally during World War II, had struggled against the Japanese, even as it fought a bitter civil war. The roots of the civil war lay deep in the Chinese past—in widespread poverty, disease, oppression by the landlord class, and national humiliation at the hands of foreign powers. Mao Zedong (Mao Tse-tung),* founder of a branch of the Communist party and of a Marxist study group in the early 1920s, gathered followers who wished to reshape China in a Communist mold. Opposing the Communists were the Nationalists, led by Jiang Jieshi (Chiang Kai-shek). By the early 1940s, Jiang Jieshi's regime was exhausted, hopelessly inefficient, and corrupt. Mao's movement, meanwhile, grew stronger during the Second World War as he opposed the Japanese invaders and won the loyalty of the peasant class.

After the war, the United States hoped for a coalition between Nationalists and Communists, but reconciliation proved impossible. Jiang lost city after city and finally fled in 1949 to the island of Taiwan (Formosa). There he nursed the improbable belief that his was still the rightful government of all China and that he would one day return.

The United States failed to understand the long internal conflict in China or the immense popular support Mao had generated. As the Communist army moved toward victory, the *New York Times* termed the group a "nauseous force," a "compact little oligarchy dominated by Moscow's nominees." Mao's proclamation of the People's Republic of China on October 1, 1949, fanned fears of Russian domination, for he had already announced his regime's support for the Soviet Union against the "imperialist" United States.

The Chinese question caused near hysteria in America. Staunch anti-Communists argued that the United States was to blame for Jiang's defeat by failing to provide more support. Yet Secretary of State Dean Acheson observed, "Nothing this country did or could have done within the reasonable limits of its capabilities could have changed that result."

Acheson considered granting diplomatic recognition to the new regime but backed off after the Communists seized American property, harassed American citizens, and openly allied themselves with the Russians. Like other Americans, he viewed the Chinese as Soviet puppets. The new government, Acheson remarked, was "not Chinese" and should not receive American support. At the same time, the United States de-

* Chinese names are rendered in their modern *pinyin* spelling. At first occurrence, the older but perhaps more familiar spelling (usually Wade-Giles) is given in parentheses.

Mao Zedong spearheaded the drive to reshape China according to Communist principles. Here he is shown as a heroic leader with his colleagues in arms, as their revolutionary efforts drove Jiang Jieshi from power and culminated in the creation of the People's Republic of China in 1949.

nied aid to the Nationalists on Taiwan, assuming that the Communists on the mainland would soon conquer that island as well. That position, and the entire American stance, infuriated the largely Republican lobby in the United States, which blamed Truman for having "lost" China.

Tension with China increased during the Korean War and then again in 1954 when Mao's government began shelling Nationalist positions on the offshore islands of Quemoy and Matsu. Eisenhower, now president, was by this time committed to defending the Nationalists on Taiwan from a Communist attack, but he was unwilling to respond forcefully to the shelling of Quemoy and Matsu. By resisting recommendations that the United States plunge into the conflict, he again showed an understanding that, rhetoric notwithstanding, the United States could not police the world.

The War in Korea

The Korean War marked America's growing intervention in Asian affairs. Concern about China and determination to contain communism led the United States into involvement in a long and bloody struggle in a faraway land. But American objectives were not always clear and were largely unrealized after three years of war.

The conflict in Korea stemmed from tensions lingering after World War II. Korea, long under Japanese control, hoped for independence after Japan's defeat. But the Allies temporarily divided Korea along the 38th parallel when the rapid end to the Pacific struggle allowed Soviet troops to accept Japanese surrender in the north while American forces did the same in the south. The Soviet-American line, initially intended as a matter of military convenience, rigidified after 1945, just as a similar division hardened in Germany, and in time the Soviets set up a government in the north and the Americans a government in the south. Though the major powers left Korea, they continued to support the regimes they had created. Each hoped to reunify the country on its own terms.

North Korea moved first. On June 25, 1950, North Korean forces invaded South Korea by crossing the 38th parallel. Following Soviet-built tanks, the North Korean troops steadily advanced against the South Korean soldiers. Was the invasion undertaken at Soviet command? Kim Il Sung,

The Korean War

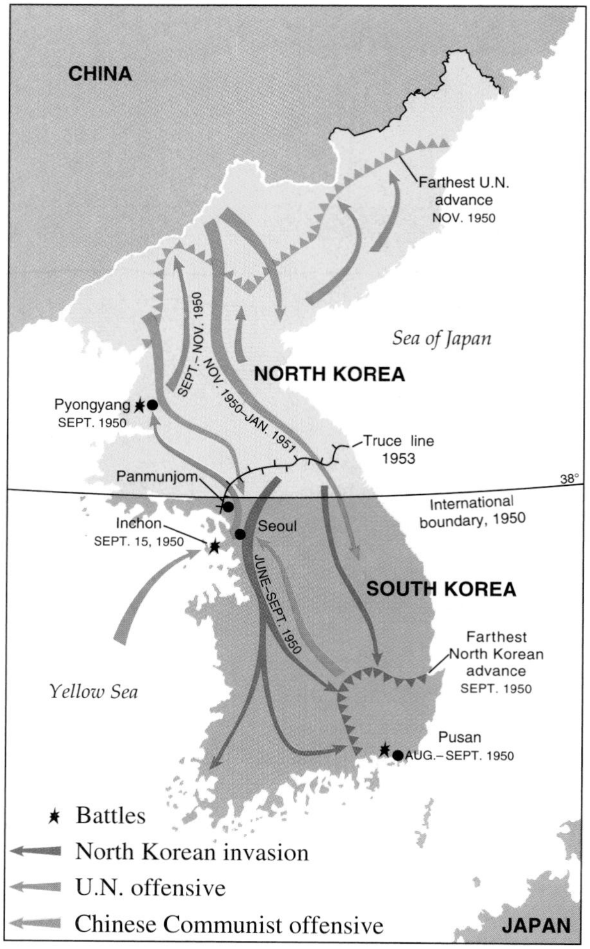

This map shows the ebb and flow of the Korean War. North Korea crossed the 38th parallel first, then the U.N. offensive drove the North Koreans close to the Chinese border, and finally the Chinese Communists entered the war and drove the U.N. forces back below the 38th parallel. The armistice signed at Panmunjom in 1953 provided a dividing line very close to the prewar line.

the North Korean leader, had visited Moscow earlier and spoken to Stalin about instability in the south. The Russians may have acquiesced in the idea of an attack, but both the planning and the timing came at the initiative of the north.

The United States was taken by surprise. Earlier, America had seemed reluctant to defend Korea, but the Communist victory in China had changed the balance of power in Asia. Certain that Russia had masterminded the North Korean offensive and was testing the American policy of containment, Truman responded vigorously. "In my generation," he announced,

> this was not the first occasion when the strong had attacked the weak. I recalled some earlier instances: Manchuria, Ethiopia, Austria. . . . Each time that the democracies failed to act it had encouraged the aggressors to keep going ahead. . . . If this was allowed to go unchallenged it would mean a third world war, just as similar incidents had brought on the second world war.

Truman readied American naval and air forces and directed General Douglas MacArthur in Japan to supply South Korea. The United States also went to the United Nations Security Council. With the Soviet Union absent in protest of the UN's refusal to admit the People's Republic of China, the United States secured a unanimous resolution branding North Korea an aggressor, then another resolution calling on members of the organization to assist the south in repelling aggression and restoring peace.

The president first ordered American air and naval forces into battle south of the 38th parallel, then American ground forces as well. Following a daring amphibious invasion that pushed the North Koreans back to the former boundary line, United Nations troops crossed the 38th parallel, hoping to reunify Korea under an American-backed government. Despite Chinese signals that this movement toward their border threatened their security, the United States pressed on. In October, Chinese troops appeared briefly in battle, then disappeared. The next month, the Chinese mounted a full-fledged counterattack, which pushed the UN forces back below the dividing line again.

The resulting stalemate provoked a bitter struggle between Douglas MacArthur and his civilian commander in chief. A brilliant but arrogant general, MacArthur called for retaliatory air strikes against China. While the administration was most concerned with the containment of communism in Europe, MacArthur argued for stronger resistance in Asia. Truman was trying to conduct a limited war; MacArthur wanted to deal the enemy a massive defeat.

MacArthur's public statements, issued from the field, finally went too far. In April 1951, he revealed his views in a letter meant to be made pub-

+ Death of Stalin

General Douglas MacArthur was a superb tactician but a supremely egotistical commander of U.N. forces in Korea. When he challenged Truman's policy, the president relieved him of his command, although, as shown in this picture, MacArthur returned home to a hero's welcome.

lic in the United States. Arguing that the American approach in Korea was wrong, he asserted that "there is no substitute for victory." When the letter appeared, Truman had no choice but to relieve MacArthur for insubordination. The decision outraged many Americans. After the stunning victories of World War II, limited war was frustrating and difficult to understand.

As the furor subsided, Truman pursued more modest goals. After another year of war, the administration was willing to settle for an armistice at the 38th parallel. Peace talks with the North Koreans began while the fighting dragged on. During the campaign of 1952, Eisenhower promised to go to Korea, and three weeks after his election, he did so. When truce talks bogged down again in May 1953, the new administration privately threatened the Chinese with the use of atomic weapons and a massive military campaign. This brought about a resumption of the peace talks.

Although the war was almost over, Anthony Ebron, a marine corporal, noted that "those last few days were pretty brutal." At the very end, he said, "we shot off so much artillery the ground shook." Finally, on July 27, 1953, an armistice was signed. The Republican administration had managed to do what the preceding Democratic administration could not. After three long years, the unpopular war had ended.

American involvement carried a heavy price: 54,000 Americans dead and many more wounded. But those figures paled beside the numbers of Korean casualties. As many as 2 mil-

The Korean War disrupted numerous families in both the north and south and led them to flee their homes. Here fleeing Korean civilians, with only the belongings they could carry with them, pass American soldiers as the bitter struggle dragged on.

lion may have died in North and South Korea, and countless others were maimed. A BBC journalist's description of napalm, a highly flammable liquid explosive first used in the war, told at least part of the story:

> In front of us a curious figure was standing, a little crouched, legs straddled, arms held out from his sides. He had no eyes, and the whole of his body, nearly all of which was visible through tatters of burnt rags, was covered with a hard black crust speckled with yellow pus. . . . He had to stand because he was no longer covered with a skin, but with a crust-like crackling which broke easily.

The war also significantly changed American attitudes and institutions. This was the first war in which United States forces fought in integrated units. President Truman, as commander in chief, had ordered the integration of the armed forces in 1948, over the opposition of many generals, and blacks became part of all military units. Their successful performance led to acceptance of military integration. The Korean War years also saw military expenditures soar from $13 billion in 1950 to about $47 billion three years later as defense spending followed the guidelines proposed in NSC-68. In the process, the United States accepted the demands of permanent mobilization. Whereas the military absorbed less than a third of the federal budget in 1950, a decade later it took half. More than a million military men were stationed around the world. At home, an increasingly powerful military establishment became closely tied to corporate and scientific communities and created a military-industrial complex that employed 3.5 million Americans by 1960.

The changes caused frustrations. With more money spent for war and defense, less was available for domestic social programs. Other frustrations resulted from the inability of many Americans to understand the constraints of limited war. Why, they asked, could they not go in with all the force necessary to the struggle? Why were American objectives not met? Why were there so few clear-cut victories?

The Korean War had important political effects as well. It led the United States to sign a peace treaty with Japan in September 1951 and to rely on that nation to maintain the balance of power in the Pacific. At the same time, the struggle poisoned relations with the People's Republic of China and ensured a diplomatic standoff that lasted more than 20 years.

Defense Expenditures, 1945–1960

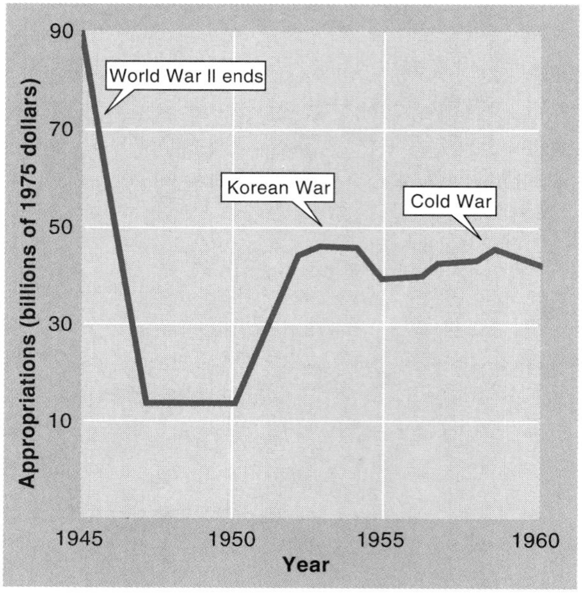

Defense spending plummeted after World War II, only to quadruple with the onset of the Korean War. After that increase, spending levels never dropped dramatically, even after the end of the war.

Source: U.S. Bureau of the Census.

Civil War in Vietnam

Indochina became another Asian battlefield in the Cold War. Since the middle of the nineteenth century, France had controlled Indochina, exploiting its supplies of rubber, tin, tungsten, and rice. During World War II, the Japanese occupied the area but allowed French collaborators to direct internal affairs. The Japanese conquest, however, shattered the image of European invincibility and encouraged an independence movement, led by the Communist organizer and revolutionary Ho Chi Minh. Using the American Revolutionary War as a model, Ho worked through his political organization, the Viet Minh, to expel the Japanese conquerors. In 1945, the Allied powers faced the decision of how to deal with Ho and his nationalist movement.

Franklin Roosevelt, like Woodrow Wilson, believed in self-determination and wanted to end colonialism. Reluctant to allow France to return, Roosevelt favored an international trusteeship scheme as a way of preparing for future Vietnamese independence. But France, believing that the nation could "only be a great power so long as our flag continues to fly in all the overseas territory," was determined to regain its colony, and by the time of his death, Roosevelt had backed down.

Ho Chi Minh and the Vietnamese, however, did not abandon national liberation. Guerrilla warfare had won them most of the countryside, and they had established the Democratic Republic of Vietnam in 1945. Although the new government enjoyed widespread support, the United States refused to recognize it. The head of the American Office of Strategic Services mission predicted that if the French returned, the Vietnamese would fight to the death.

That prediction was correct. The Vietnamese refused to capitulate as a long, bitter struggle between the French and the forces of Ho Chi Minh ensued and became entangled with the larger Cold War. President Truman was less concerned about ending colonialism than with checking growing Soviet power in Europe and around the world. He needed France to balance Russian strength in Europe, and that meant cooperating with the French in Vietnam.

While the Vietnamese battled the French, the United States watched with alarm. World War II had weakened France, and the United States doubted that it could survive a long colonial war. At the same time, the Truman administration was concerned about Vietnam itself. If France failed, the West would lose a foothold in a part of the world where a Communist revolution had already succeeded. Worse still, it would face a regime sympathetic to Moscow and the East, for Ho was a confirmed Marxist-Leninist. Though Ho did not, in fact, have close ties to the Soviet state and was committed to his independent nationalist crusade, Truman and his advisers, who saw communism as a monolithic force, assumed wrongly that Ho took orders from Moscow. Hence in 1950, the United States formally recognized a French puppet government in Vietnam. The Vietnamese viewed the Americans as France's colonialist collaborators. The United States in the Truman years did not provide direct military aid to the French, but American economic assistance freed France to use its own resources in the struggle. By 1954, the United States was paying over three-quarters of the cost of the war.

After Eisenhower took office, France's position deteriorated. Some 12,000 French troops prepared for a showdown at the fortress of Dien Bien Phu. With a French defeat looming, Eisenhower reviewed American diplomatic options. He believed in the "domino theory," which held that "you have a row of dominos set up, you knock over the first one, and what will happen to the last one is the certainty that it will go over very quickly." At a press conference in April 1954, he warned that Burma, Thailand, and Indonesia would follow if Vietnam fell, and Japan, Taiwan, the Philippines, Australia, and New Zealand might go next. "So the possible consequences of the loss," he said, "are just incalculable to the free world."

Dulles was eager to assist the French; the chairman of the Joint Chiefs of Staff even contemplated using nuclear weapons. But Eisenhower hesitated, not ready to bolt into Indochina alone. As the price for United States assistance, the French must pledge to grant Vietnamese independence at some point. England would have to cooperate in a joint assistance effort. And Congress should authorize the necessary support. Eisenhower believed that "only when there is a sudden, unforeseen emergency should the President put us into war without congressional action." Since, as he suspected, those conditions would not be met, the United States refused to intervene directly. Dien Bien Phu finally fell, and an international conference in Geneva divided Vietnam along the 17th parallel, with elections promised in 1956 to unify the country and determine its political fate.

As a result of that division, two new states emerged. Ho Chi Minh held power in the north, while in the south Premier Ngo Dinh Diem, a fierce anti-Communist, formed a separate government. Intent on taking France's place in Southeast Asia, the United States supported the Diem government and refused to sign the Geneva agreement. "We must work with these people," Eisenhower said, "and then they themselves will soon find out that we are their friends and that they cannot live without us." Shortly after this, Eisenhower dispatched a CIA unit to conduct secret missions in Vietnam. In 1956, he backed Diem's refusal to hold the national elections in Vietnam called for in the Geneva agreement. In the next few years, American aid increased and military advisers began to assist the South Vietnamese. The United States had taken its first steps toward involvement in a ruinous war halfway around the world.

The Middle East

While Cold War attitudes shaped American diplomacy in Southeast Asia, they also influenced responses to events in the Middle East. That part of the world had tremendous strategic importance as the supplier of oil for industrialized nations. During World War II, the major Allied powers occupied Iran, with the provision that they would leave within six months of the war's end. As of early 1946, both Great Britain and the United States had withdrawn, but the Soviet Union, which bordered on Iran, remained. Stalin claimed that earlier security agreements had not been honored and, further, demanded oil concessions.

Moving quickly to counter the perceived Soviet threat, the United States took the issue to the newly formed United Nations in March 1946, but still found it preferable to act independently. As Russian tanks neared the Iranian border, Secretary of State James Byrnes declared, "Now we'll give it to them with both barrels." The ultimatum threatened vigorous American action and forced the Russians to back down and withdraw.

The Eisenhower administration maintained its interest in Iran. In 1953, the CIA helped the local army overthrow the government of Mohammed Mossadegh, which had nationalized oil

The Middle East in 1949

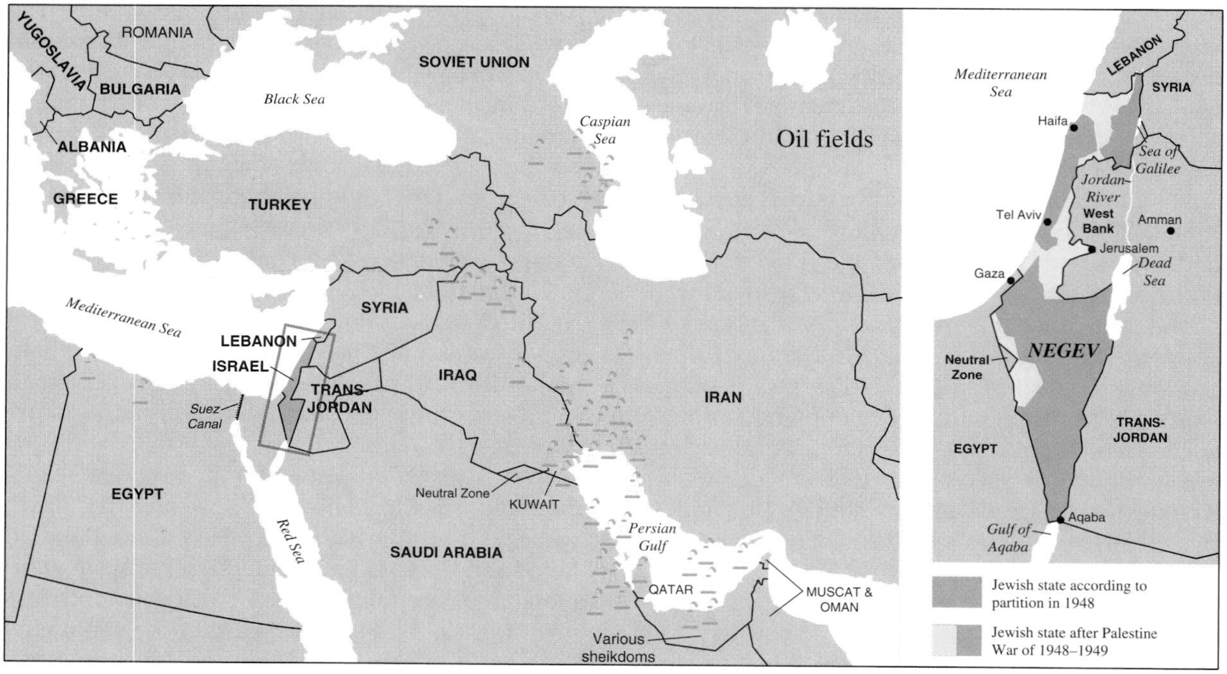

This map shows the extensive oil resources that made the Middle East such an important region, and the shifting boundaries of Israel as a result of the war following its independence in 1948. Notice how its size increased after its victory in the first of a series of Middle Eastern conflicts.

wells formerly under British control, and place the shah of Iran securely on the Peacock Throne. After the coup, British and American companies regained command of the wells, and thereafter the United States government provided military assistance to the shah.

A far more serious situation emerged west of Iran. In 1948, the United Nations attempted to partition Palestine into an Arab state and a Jewish state. Truman officially recognized the new state of Israel 15 minutes after it was proclaimed. But recognition could not end bitter animosities between Arabs, who judged they had been robbed of their territory, and Jews, who felt they had finally regained a homeland after the horrors of the Holocaust. As Americans looked on, Arab forces from Egypt, Trans-Jordan, Syria, Lebanon, and Iraq invaded Israel, but the Israelis won the war and added territory to what they had been given by the UN.

While cultivating close ties with Israel, the United States also tried to maintain the friendship of oil-rich Arab states or, at the very least, to prevent them from falling into the Soviet orbit. In Egypt, the policy ran into trouble when Arab nationalist General Gamal Abdel Nasser planned a huge dam on the Nile River to produce electricity. Nasser hoped to follow a middle course by proclaiming his country neutral in the Cold War. Although Dulles offered American financial support for the Aswan Dam project, Nasser also began discussions with the Soviet Union. Furious, the secretary of state withdrew the American offer. Left without funds for the dam, in July 1956 Nasser seized and nationalized the British-controlled Suez Canal and closed it to Israeli ships. Great Britain, whose citizens owned most of the stock in the canal company, reacted angrily. All of Europe feared that Nasser would disrupt the flow of oil from the Middle East.

Despite the American attempt to resolve the problem peacefully, Israeli, British, and French military forces invaded Egypt in October and November. Eisenhower, who had not been consulted, was irate. Realizing that the attack might push Nasser into Moscow's arms, the United States sponsored a UN resolution condemning the attacking nations and cut off oil from England and France. These actions persuaded them to withdraw.

It was not long before the United States again intervened in the Middle East. Concerned about the region's stability, Eisenhower had declared in 1957 that "the existing vacuum in the Middle East must be filled by the United States before it is filled by Russia." A year later, in line with a congressional resolution that committed the United States to stop suspected Communist aggression, he authorized the landing of 14,000 soldiers in Lebanon to prop up a right-wing government challenged from within.

Restricting Revolt in Latin America

The Cold War also affected relations in Latin America, the United States' traditional sphere of influence, and provided fresh reasons for intervention. In 1954, Dulles sniffed Communist activity in Guatemala and ordered CIA support for a coup aimed at ousting the elected government of reform-minded Colonel Jacobo Arbenz Guzmán. The right-wing takeover succeeded, restored the property of the United Fruit Company that Arbenz had seized, and demonstrated again the shortsighted American commitment to stability and private investment, whatever the internal effect or ultimate cost.

The effort in Guatemala fed anti-American feeling throughout Latin America. Many Latin Americans abhorred the interference of their northern neighbor. Dulles downplayed hostile sentiment, but when Vice-President Richard Nixon traveled to Venezuela in 1958, angry crowds stoned his car and threatened his life.

The next year, when Fidel Castro overthrew the dictatorial regime of Fulgencio Batista in Cuba, the shortsightedness of American policy became even clearer. Nationalism and the thrust for social reform were powerful forces in Latin America, as in the rest of the Third World. As Milton Eisenhower, Ike's brother and adviser, pointed out: "Revolution is inevitable in Latin America. The people are angry. They are shackled to the past with bonds of ignorance, injustice, and poverty. And they no longer accept as universal or inevitable the oppressive prevailing order." But when Castro confiscated American property in Cuba, the Eisenhower administration cut off exports and severed diplomatic ties. In response, Cuba turned to Russia for support.

Atomic Weapons and the Cold War

Throughout the Cold War period, the atomic bomb was a crucial factor in world affairs. Atomic weapons were destructive enough, but when the United States and the Soviet Union both developed hydrogen bombs, an age of overkill began. While Americans spoke casually of Dulles's policy of "massive retaliation" if the Soviet Union ever went too far, they feared a similar attack on the United States.

Sharing the Secret of the Bomb

The United States, with British aid, had built the first atomic bomb and attempted to conceal the project from its wartime ally, the Soviet Union. Soviet spies, however, discovered that the Americans were working on the bomb, and, even before the war was over, a Soviet program to create a Russian atomic bomb was under way.

The question of sharing the atomic secret was pressing in the immediate postwar years. Some people felt that Americans should guard their knowledge, arguing that the Russians would take years to duplicate their feat. But nuclear scientists knew that once others saw that the weapon could be made, it would take another nation far less time to do the same thing. Might it not be better to deal with the question of sharing before it was too late?

Secretary of War Henry L. Stimson favored cooperating with the Soviet Union. Recognizing the futility of trying to cajole the Russians while "having this weapon ostentatiously on our hip," he warned that "their suspicions and their distrust of our purposes and motives will increase." Only mutual accommodation could bring international cooperation.

But the United States never followed Stimson's advice. Truman, increasingly worried about the Soviet presence in eastern Europe, vowed to retain the technological advantage. He resisted a more flexible approach until the creation of a "foolproof method of control" over atomic weapons. Most Americans agreed.

For a time the administration contemplated a system of international arms control. Realizing by early 1946 that mere possession of the bomb by the United States did not make the Russians more malleable, Truman decided to present an atomic energy plan to the United Nations. Drafted by Dean Acheson and David Lilienthal, the plan proposed an international agency to control atomic energy. Bernard Baruch, ambassador to the UN's Atomic Energy Commission, hoping to avoid a Russian veto in the Security Council, modified the plan to establish a system of international inspection and agreement. In fact, as the Russians quickly pointed out, this plan allowed American nuclear supremacy until the international agency had gained control of the earth's fissionable material. The Russians called first for destruction of all atomic weapons, then for a discussion of controls. Negotiations collapsed.

The United States gave up on the process of sharing atomic secrets and moved toward its own internal mechanism of control. The Atomic Energy Act of 1946 established the Atomic Energy Commission to supervise all atomic energy development in the United States and, under the tightest security, to authorize all activity in the nation at large. It also opened the way to a nuclear arms race once Russia developed its own bomb.

Nuclear Proliferation

As the atomic bomb found its way into popular culture, Americans at first showed more excitement than fear. In Los Angeles, the "Atombomb Dancers" appeared at the Burbank Burlesque Theater. In 1946, the Buchanan Brothers released a record called "Atomic Power."

Anxiety lurked beneath the exuberance, though it did not surface while the United States maintained a nuclear monopoly. Then, in September 1949, reporters were called to the White House and told: "We have evidence that within recent weeks an atomic explosion occurred in the U.S.S.R." The Russians had not publicized their achievement. Rather, over the Labor Day weekend, a U.S. Air Force weather reconnaissance plane on a routine mission had picked up air samples showing higher than normal radioactivity counts. Other samples confirmed the reading, and scientists soon concluded that Russia had conducted a nuclear test.

The American public was shocked. Suddenly the security of being the world's only atomic power vanished. People wondered whether the Soviet test foreshadowed a nuclear attack. At a

The mushroom cloud resulting from an atomic blast became a familiar sight as it accompanied hundreds of nuclear tests in the postwar United States. But while the cloud was beautiful, it also filled the atmosphere with fallout that contaminated people, plants, and animals below.

meeting of the Joint Committee on Atomic Energy, legislators struggled to comprehend the implications of the news. When a thunderclap filled the air, someone in the room said, "My God, that must be Number Two!" cutting the tension for the moment. Harold C. Urey, a Nobel Prize–winning scientist, summed up the feelings of many Americans: "There is only one thing worse than one nation having the atomic bomb—that's two nations having it." The atomic genie was out of the bottle, and Americans had to accept the fact that their monopoly had disappeared.

In early 1950, Truman authorized the development of a new hydrogen superbomb, potentially far more devastating than the atomic bomb. Edward Teller, a physicist on the Manhattan Project, was intrigued with the novelty of the puzzle. During the war, as other scientists struggled with the problem of fission, he contemplated the possibility that fusion might release energy in even greater amounts. Now he had his chance to proceed.

By 1953, both the United States and the Soviet Union had unlocked the secret of the hydrogen bomb. As kilotons gave way to megatons, the stakes rose. The government remained quiet about MIKE, the first test of a hydrogen device in the Pacific Ocean in 1952, but rumors circulated that it had created a hole in the ocean floor 175 feet deep and a mile wide. A year and a half later, after the 1954 BRAVO test, Lewis Strauss, Atomic Energy Commission chairman, admitted that "an H-bomb can be made . . . large enough to take out a city," even New York. Then, in 1957, shortly after the news that the Soviets had successfully tested their first intercontinental ballistic missile (ICBM), Americans learned that the Soviets had fired the first satellite, *Sputnik*, into outer space. The apparent inferiority of American rocketry and the openness of the country to attack caused serious concern.

The discovery of radioactive fallout added another dimension to the nuclear dilemma. Fallout became publicly known after the BRAVO blast showered Japanese fishermen 85 miles away with radioactive dust. They became ill with radiation sickness, and several months later, one of them died. The Japanese, who had been the first to experience the effects of atomic weapons, were outraged and alarmed. Elsewhere people began to realize the terrible impact of the new weapons.

Authors in both the scientific and the popular press focused attention on radioactive fallout. Radiation, physicist Ralph Lapp observed, "cannot be felt and possesses all the terror of the unknown. It is something which evokes revulsion and helplessness—like a bubonic plague." Nevil Shute's best-selling 1957 novel *On the Beach,* and the film that followed, also sparked public awareness and fear. The story described a war that released so much radioactive waste that all life in the Northern Hemisphere disappeared, while the Southern Hemisphere waited for the residue to come closer and bring the same deadly end. When *Consumer Reports* warned of the contamina-

Americans sought protection from fallout in shelters that civil defense authorities told them would be just like home. Here a typical family in 1955 practices in the Kiddie Kokoon, which has beds and supplies of food and water to last for several weeks.

tion of milk with strontium-90 in 1959, the public grew even more alarmed.

One response to growing nuclear stockpiles and the threat of global destruction was the building of bomb shelters. Interest in blast shelters had arisen in the immediate postwar years, but a national program was prohibitively expensive and never got under way. The discovery of fallout, however, provoked a shelter craze. Bob Russell, a Michigan sheriff, declared that "to build a new home in this day and age without including such an obvious necessity as a fallout shelter would be like leaving out the bathroom 20 years ago." *Good Housekeeping* magazine carried a full-page editorial in November 1958 that urged the construction of family shelters. A cartoon in Pennsylvania's *Harrisburg News* showed the biblical ark, with the caption, "They Laughed at Noah!"

More and more companies advertised ready-made shelters to eager consumers. A firm in Miami reported numerous inquiries about shelters costing between $1,795 and $3,895, depending on capacity, and planned 900 franchises. *Life* magazine in 1955 featured an "H-Bomb Hideaway" for $3,000. By the end of 1960, the Office of Civil and Defense Mobilization estimated that a million family shelters had been built.

"Massive Retaliation"

As Americans grappled with the consequences of nuclear weapons, government policy came to depend increasingly on an atomic shield. The Soviet success in building its own bomb encouraged the conviction that America must beef up its atomic forces. Truman authorized the development of a nuclear arsenal but also stressed conventional forms of defense. After his election in 1952, Eisenhower found the effort fragmented and wasteful. Concerned with controlling the budget and cutting taxes, Eisenhower and the Republicans decided to rely on atomic weapons rather than combat forces as the key to American defense.

Drawing on a new breed of nuclear strategists, including Harvard's Henry Kissinger, who believed that atomic weapons might be used in military confrontations, Dulles developed the policy of "massive retaliation." The United States was willing and ready to use nuclear weapons against Communist aggression "at places of our own choosing." Eisenhower initially liked the new policy, for it left the enemy uncertain about how far the United States might go in a given situation. The policy also allowed troop cutbacks and promised to be cost-effective by giving "more bang for the buck."

Massive retaliation provided for an all-or-nothing response, leaving no middle course, no alternatives between nuclear war and retreat. Still, it was wholly consonant with the secretary of state's willingness to use extreme threats to assert the American position in the Cold War. The prospect of direct retaliation, properly used, Dulles felt, could deter Soviet challenges around the world. "The ability to get to the verge without getting into war is the necessary art," he declared. "If you cannot master it you inevitably get into war." Critics called the policy "brinkmanship" and wondered what would happen if the line were crossed in the new atomic age. Eisenhower himself was horrified when he saw reports indicating what nuclear weapons could do, and with characteristic caution he did his best to ensure that the rhetoric of massive retaliation did not lead to war.

The Cold War at Home

The Cold War also affected domestic affairs and led to the creation of an internal loyalty program that seriously violated civil liberties. Americans had feared radical subversion before and after the Russian Revolution (see Chapters 16, 21, and 22). Now the Soviet Union appeared ever more ominous in confrontations around the world. Maps showed half the world colored red to dramatize the spread of the monolithic Communist system. As Americans began to suspect Communist infiltration at home, some determined to root out all traces of communism inside the United States.

Truman's Loyalty Program

When the Truman administration mobilized support for its containment program in the immediate postwar years, its rhetoric became increasingly shrill. Picturing issues in black and white terms, spokesmen contrasted American virtues to diabolic Russian designs. For Truman, the issue confronting the world was one of "tyranny or freedom." According to Attorney General J. Howard McGrath, there were "many Communists in America," each bearing the "germ of death for society."

Such comments reflected perceptions of administration officials that a related internal threat existed. In February 1945, government agents found some classified government documents in the offices of the allegedly pro-Communist *Amerasia* magazine. A year later, a Canadian commission exposed a number of spy rings and described wartime subversion. Truman responded by appointing a Temporary Commission on Employee Loyalty. Republican gains in the midterm elections of 1946 led him to fear a congressional loyalty probe that could be used for partisan ends, especially since Republicans had accused the Democrats of being "soft on communism." Truman hoped to head off such an investigation by starting his own.

On the basis of the report from his temporary commission, Truman established a new Federal Employee Loyalty Program by executive decree in 1947. In the same week that he announced his containment policy, Truman ordered the FBI to check its files for evidence of subversive activity and then to bring suspects before a new Civil Service Commission Loyalty Review Board. Initially, the program included safeguards and assumed that a challenged employee was innocent until proved guilty. But those limits did not last long, for as the Loyalty Review Board assumed more and more power, it ignored individual rights. Employees about whom there was any doubt, regardless of proof, now found themselves under attack, with little chance to fight back.

The Truman loyalty program examined several million employees and found grounds for dismissing only several hundred. Nonetheless, it bred the unwarranted fear of subversion, led to the assumption that absolute loyalty could be achieved, and legitimated investigatory tactics that were used irresponsibly to harm innocent individuals.

The Congressional Loyalty Program

While Truman's loyalty probe investigated government employees, Congress embarked on its own program. In the early years of the Cold War, the law became increasingly explicit about what was illegal in the United States. The Smith Act of 1940 made it a crime to advocate or teach the forcible overthrow of the U.S. government. In 1949, Eugene Dennis and ten other Communist leaders were found guilty under its terms. In 1951, in *Dennis* v. *United States,* the Supreme Court upheld the Smith Act, declaring that a real danger of subversion existed in America. That action cleared the way for the prosecution of other Communist leaders. Nearly 100 were indicted in the early 1950s.

The McCarran Internal Security Act of 1950 further circumscribed Communist activity by declaring that it was illegal to conspire to act in a way that would "substantially contribute" to establishing a totalitarian dictatorship in America. Members of Communist organizations had to register with the attorney general and could not obtain passports or work in areas of national defense. Congress passed the measure over Truman's veto and provided further legal backing for the anti-Communist crusade. The American Communist party, which had never been large, even in the Depression, declined still further. Membership, numbering about 80,000 in 1947, fell to 55,000 in 1950 and 25,000 in 1954.

The investigations of the House Committee on Un-American Activities (HUAC) contributed to that decline. Intent on rooting out subversion, HUAC probed the motion picture industry in 1947 to determine the political inclinations of its members.

When hearings were scheduled, many entertainers and movie stars denounced the procedures. "Say your piece. Write your Congressman a letter! Airmail special!" Frank Sinatra warned, "Once they get the movies throttled, how long will it be before we're told what we can say and cannot say into a radio microphone?"

HUAC pressed on. Protesting its scare tactics, some people summoned by the committee refused to testify under oath. They were scapegoated for their stand. The so-called Hollywood Ten, a group of writers, were cited for contempt of court and sent to federal prison. At that, Hollywood knuckled under and blacklisted anyone with even a marginally questionable past. No one on these lists could find jobs at the studios anymore.

Congress made a greater splash with the Hiss-Chambers case. Whittaker Chambers, a former Communist who had broken with the party in 1938 and had become a successful editor of *Time,* charged that Alger Hiss had been a Communist in the 1930s. Hiss was a distinguished New Dealer who had served in the Agriculture Department before becoming assistant secretary of state. Now out of the government, he was president of the Carnegie Endowment for International Peace. He denied Chambers's charge, and the matter might have died there had not freshman congressman Richard Nixon taken up the case. Nixon finally extracted from Hiss an admission that he had once known Chambers. Outside the hearing room, Hiss sued Chambers for libel, whereupon Chambers changed his story and charged that Hiss was a Soviet spy.

Alger Hiss's conviction for perjury helped heighten American fears of communism at home. Despite damaging evidence that became public in later years, Hiss never ceased proclaiming his innocence, but he became an isolated and subdued figure, far different from the prominent government official he had once been.

With controversial evidence in hand, including several rolls of microfilmed government documents that Chambers contended Hiss had given him to pass to the Russians, HUAC sensed the possibilities of the case. In December 1948, a federal grand jury took the matter a step further. Since the statute of limitations ruled out an espionage indictment, the grand jury indicted Hiss instead for perjury, for lying under oath about his former relationship with Chambers.

The case made front-page news around the nation. Millions of Americans read about the case at about the same time they learned of Russia's first atomic explosion and the final victory of the Communist revolution in China. Chambers appeared unstable and changed his story several times. Yet Hiss, too, seemed contradictory in his testimony and never adequately explained how some copies of stolen State Department documents had been typed on a typewriter he had once owned. The first trial ended in a hung jury; the second trial, in January 1950, sent Hiss to prison for almost four years.

For many Americans, the Hiss case proved the Communist threat in the United States. It "forcibly demonstrated to the American people that domestic Communism was a real and present danger to the security of the nation," Richard Nixon declared after using the case to win a Senate seat from California and then the Republican vice-presidential nomination in 1952. The case also led people to question the Democratic approach to the problem. After Hiss's conviction but before his appeal, Dean Acheson supported his friend. Regardless of what happened, he said, "I do not intend to turn my back on Alger Hiss." Decent though his affirmation was, it caused the secretary of state political trouble. Truman too was broadly attacked for his comments about the case. Earlier he had called it a "red herring," but

Senator Joseph McCarthy's spurious charges inflamed anti-Communist sentiment in the 1950s. Here he uses a chart of Communist party organization in the United States to suggest that the nation was at risk unless subversives were rooted out.

the courts had decided otherwise. Critics questioned the strength of Truman's commitment to protect the nation from internal subversion. Ironically, his loyalty program, for all its excesses, faced charges of laxity at home. The dramatic Hiss case helped to discredit the Democrats and to justify the even worse witch-hunt that followed.

The Second Red Scare

The key anti-Communist warrior in the 1950s was Joseph R. McCarthy. Coming to the Senate from Wisconsin in 1946, McCarthy had an undistinguished career. As he began to contemplate reelection two years hence, he seized on the Communist issue. Truman had carried Wisconsin in 1948, and McCarthy saw in the Communist question a way of mobilizing Republican support. He first gained national attention with a speech before the Wheeling, West Virginia, Women's Club in February 1950, not long after the conviction of Alger Hiss. In that address, McCarthy claimed he had in his hand a list of 205 known Communists in the State Department. When pressed for details, McCarthy said first that he would release his list only to the president; then he reduced the number of names to 57.

Early reactions to McCarthy were mixed. A subcommittee of the Senate Foreign Relations Committee, after investigating, called his charge a "fraud and a hoax." Even other Republicans like Robert Taft and Richard Nixon questioned his effectiveness. Yet McCarthy persisted, for he found an anxious public primed by the Hiss case and international events. As his support grew, Republicans realized his partisan value and egged him on. Senator John Bricker of Ohio allegedly told him, "Joe, you're a dirty s.o.b., but there are times when you've got to have an s.o.b. around, and this is one of them." Taft, also from Ohio, provided similar encouragement when he advised, "If one case doesn't work, try another." McCarthy did.

McCarthy selected assorted targets. In the elections of 1950, he attacked Millard Tydings, the Democrat from Maryland who had chaired the subcommittee that dismissed McCarthy's first accusations. A doctored photograph, showing Tydings with deposed American Communist party head Earl Browder, helped bring about Tydings's defeat. McCarthy called Dean Acheson a "pompous diplomat in striped pants, with a phony British accent" and termed him the "Red Dean of the State Department." He slandered George C. Marshall, the architect of victory in World War II and a powerful figure in formulating Far Eastern policy, as a "man steeped in falsehood . . . who has recourse to the lie whenever it suits his convenience."

A demagogue throughout his career, McCarthy gained visibility through extensive press and television coverage. Playing on his tough rep-

Public Opinion Polls

In recent years, historians have used a new source of evidence, the public opinion poll. People have always been concerned with what others think, and leaders have often sought to frame their behavior according to the preferences of the populace. As techniques of assessing the mind of the public have become more sophisticated, the poll has emerged as an integral part of the analysis of social and political life. Polls now measure opinion on many questions—social, cultural, intellectual, political, and diplomatic. Because of their increasing importance, it is useful to know how to use the polls in an effort to understand and recover the past.

The principle of polling is not new. In 1824 the *Harrisburg Pennsylvanian* sought to predict the winner of that year's presidential race, and in the 1880s, the *Boston Globe* sent reporters to selected precincts on election night to forecast final returns. In 1916, *Literary Digest* began conducting postcard polls to predict political results. By the 1930s, Elmo Roper and George Gallup had developed further the field of market research and public opinion polling. Notwithstanding an embarrassing mistake by *Literary Digest* in predicting a Landon victory over FDR in 1936, polling had by World War II become a scientific enterprise.

According to Gallup, a poll is not magic but "merely an instrument for gauging public opinion," especially the views of those often unheard. As Elmo Roper said, the poll is "one of the few ways through which the so-called common man can be articulate." Polling, therefore, is a valuable way to recover the attitudes, beliefs, and voices of ordinary people.

Yet certain cautions should be observed. Like all instruments of human activity, polls are imperfect and may even be dangerous. Historians using information from polls need to be aware of how large the samples were, when the interviewing was done, and how opinions might have been molded by the form of the poll itself. Questions can be poorly phrased. Some hint at the desirable answer or plant ideas in the minds of those interviewed. Polls sometimes provide ambiguous responses that can be interpreted many ways. More seriously, some critics worry that human freedom itself is threatened by the pollsters' manipulative and increasingly accurate predictive techniques.

Despite these limitations, polls have become an ever-present part of American life. In the late 1940s and early 1950s, Americans were polled frequently about topics ranging from foreign aid, the United Nations, and the occupation of Germany and Japan to labor legislation, child punishment, and whether women should wear slacks in public (39 percent of men said no, as did 49 percent of women). Such topics as the first use of nuclear arms, presidential popularity, national defense, and U.S. troop intervention in a troubled area of the world (Indochina) remain as pertinent today as they were then.

A number of the polls included here deal with foreign policy during the Cold War in the early 1950s. How did people respond to the Russian nuclear capability? Other polls question public perceptions of Russian intentions and appropriate American responses. How do you analyze the results of these polls? What do you think is the significance of rating responses by levels of education? In what ways are the questions "loaded"? How might the results of these polls influence American foreign policy? What do you think is significant about the Indochina poll? These polls show the challenge-and-response nature of the Cold War. How do you think Americans would respond today to these questions?

Polls also shed light on domestic issues. Consider the poll on professions for young men and women taken in 1950. What does it tell us about the attitudes of the pollster on appropriate careers for men and women? Why do you think both men and women had nearly identical views on this subject? How do you think people today would answer these questions? Would they be presented in the same way? Also observe the poll on women in politics. To what extent have attitudes on this issue changed in the intervening years?

Foreign Policy Polls

December 2, 1949—Atom Bomb

Now that Russia has the atom bomb, do you think another war is more likely or less likely?

More likely	45%
Less likely	28%
Will make no difference	17%
No opinion	10%

BY EDUCATION

College

More likely	36%	Will make no difference	23%
Less likely	35%	No opinion	6%

High School

More likely	44%	Will make no difference	19%
Less likely	28%	No opinion	9%

Grade School

More likely	50%	Will make no difference	12%
Less likely	26%	No opinion	12%

May 1, 1950—National Defense

Do you think United States Government spending on national defense should be increased, decreased, or remain about the same?

Increased	63%	Same	24%
Decreased	7%	No opinion	6%

September 18, 1953—Indochina

The United States is now sending war materials to help the French fight the Communists in Indochina. Would you approve or disapprove of sending United States soldiers to take part in the fighting there?

Approve	8%	Disapprove	85%
No opinion	7%		

January 11, 1950—Russia

As you hear and read about Russia these days, do you believe Russia is trying to build herself up to be the ruling power of the world—or is Russia just building up protection against being attacked in another war?

Rule the world	70%
Protect herself	18%
No opinion	12%

BY EDUCATION

College

Rule the world	73%	Protect herself	21%
No opinion	6%		

High School

Rule the world	72%	Protect herself	18%
No opinion	10%		

Grade School

Rule the world	67%	Protect herself	17%
No opinion	16%		

February 12, 1951—Atomic Warfare

If the United States gets into an all-out war with Russia, do you think we should drop atom bombs on Russia first—or do you think we should use the atom bomb only if it is used on us?

Drop A-bomb first	66%
Only if used on us	19%
No opinion	15%

The greatest difference was between men and women—72% of the men questioned favored our dropping the bomb first, compared to 61% of the women.

Source: George H. Gallup, *The Gallup Poll: Public Opinion, 1935–1971*, vol. 2 (New York: Random House, 1972). © American Institute of Public Opinion.

Domestic Policy Polls

October 29, 1949—Women in Politics

If the party whose candidate you most often support nominated a woman for President of the United States, would you vote for her if she seemed qualified for the job?

Yes	48%	No	48%
No opinion	4%		

BY SEX

Men

Yes	45%	No	50%
No opinion	5%		

Women

Yes	51%	No	46%
No opinion	3%		

BY POLITICAL AFFILIATION

Democrats

Yes	50%	No	48%
No opinion	2%		

Republicans

Yes	46%	No	50%
No opinion	4%		

Would you vote for a woman for Vice President of the United States if she seemed qualified for the job?

Yes	53%	No	43%
No opinion	4%		

May 5, 1950—Most Important Problem

What do you think is the most important problem facing the entire country today?

War, threat of war	40%	Atomic bomb control	6%
Economic problems, living costs, inflation, taxes	15%	Strikes and labor troubles	4%
		Corruption in government	3%
Unemployment	10%	Housing	3%
Communism	8%	Others	11%

July 12, 1950—Professions

Suppose a young man came to you and asked your advice about taking up a profession. Assuming that he was qualified to enter any of these professions, which one of them would you first recommend to him?

Doctor of medicine	29%	Government worker	6%
Engineer, builder	16%	Professor, teacher	5%
Business executive	8%	Banker	4%
Clergyman	8%	Dentist	4%
Lawyer	8%	Veterinarian	3%
None, don't know	9%		

July 15, 1950—Professions

Suppose a young girl came to you and asked your advice about taking up a profession. Assuming that she was qualified to enter any of these professions, which one of them would you first recommend?

CHOICE OF WOMEN

Nurse	33%	Actress	3%
Teacher	15%	Journalist	2%
Secretary	8%	Musician	2%
Social service worker	8%	Model	2%
Dietician	7%	Librarian	2%
Dressmaker	4%	Medical, dental technician	1%
Beautician	4%	Others	2%
Airline stewardess	3%	Don't know	4%

The views of men on this subject were nearly identical with those of women.

Source: George H. Gallup, *The Gallup Poll: Public Opinion, 1935–1971*, vol. 2 (New York: Random House, 1972). © American Institute of Public Opinion.

utation, he did not mind appearing disheveled, unshaven, and half sober. He used obscenity and vulgarity freely as he lashed out against his "vile and scurrilous" enemies.

McCarthy's tactics worked because of public alarm about the Communist threat. The Korean War revealed the aggressiveness of Communists in Asia. The arrest in 1950 of Julius and Ethel Rosenberg fed fears of subversion from within. The Rosenbergs, a seemingly ordinary American couple with two small children, were charged with stealing and transmitting atomic secrets to the Russians. To many Americans, it was inconceivable that the Soviets could have developed the bomb on their own. Only treachery could explain the Soviet explosion of an atomic device.

The next year, the Rosenbergs were found guilty of espionage and sentenced to death. Judge Irving Kaufman expressed the rage of an insecure nation. "Your conduct in putting into the hands of the Russians the A-bomb," he charged, "has already caused, in my opinion, the Communist aggression in Korea, . . . and who knows but that millions more of innocent people may pay the price of your treason."

Although some argued, then and today, that hysteria had victimized the Rosenbergs, efforts to prevent their execution failed. In 1953, they were put to death, but anticommunism continued unabated.

When the Republicans won control of the Senate in 1952, McCarthy's power grew. He became chairman of the Government Operations Committee and head of its Permanent Investigations Subcommittee. He now had a stronger base and two dedicated assistants, Roy Cohn and G. David Schine. Together in early 1953, Cohn and Schine went off to Europe on a whirlwind tour of American information centers, where they briefly inspected books and articles and badgered overseas librarians to begin removing items they considered threatening from the shelves.

As McCarthy's anti-Communist witch-hunt continued, Eisenhower became uneasy. He disliked the senator but, recognizing his popularity, was reluctant to challenge him. At the height of his influence, polls showed that McCarthy had half the public behind him. With the country so inclined, Eisenhower voiced his disapproval quietly and privately.

With the help of Cohn and Schine, McCarthy pushed on, and finally he pushed too hard. In 1953, the army drafted Schine and then refused to allow the preferential treatment that Cohn insisted his colleague deserved. Angered, McCarthy began to investigate army security and even top-level army leaders themselves. When the army charged that McCarthy was going too far, the Senate investigated the complaint.

The Army-McCarthy hearings began in April 1954 and lasted 36 days. Televised to a fascinated nationwide audience, they demonstrated the power of TV to shape people's opinions. Americans saw McCarthy's savage tactics on screen. He came across to viewers as irresponsible and destructive, particularly in contrast to Boston lawyer Joseph Welch, who argued the army's case with quiet eloquence.

The hearings shattered McCarthy's mystical appeal. In broad daylight, before a national television audience, his ruthless tactics lay exposed. The Senate finally summoned the courage to condemn him for his conduct. Even conservatives turned against McCarthy because he was no longer limiting his venom to Democrats and liberals. Although McCarthy remained in office, his influence disappeared. Three years later, at the age of 48, he died a broken man.

Yet for a time he had exerted a powerful hold in the United States. "To many Americans," radio commentator Fulton Lewis, Jr., said, "McCarthyism is Americanism." Seizing upon the frustrations and anxieties of the Cold War, McCarthy struck a resonant chord. As his appeal grew, he put together a following that included both lower-class ethnic groups, who responded to the charges against established elites, and conservative midwestern Republicans. But his real power base was the Senate, where, particularly after 1952, conservative Republicans saw McCarthy as a means of reasserting their own authority. For the most part, his dominance rested on his colleagues' perception of his strength. Some members of both parties spoke out against him, but most remained silent, thus encouraging McCarthy's crusade.

The Casualties of Fear

The anti-Communist crusade promoted a pervasive sense of suspicion in American society. In the late 1940s and early 1950s, dissent no longer seemed safe. Civil servants, government workers, academics, and actors all came under attack and found that the right of due process often evaporated as the Cold War Red Scare gained ground. Old China hands lost their positions in the diplomatic service, and social justice legislation faltered.

This paranoia affected American life in countless ways. In New York, subway workers were fired when they refused to answer questions about their own political actions and beliefs. In Seattle, a fire department officer who denied current membership in the Communist party but refused to speak of his past was dismissed just 40 days before he reached the 25 years of service that would have qualified him for retirement benefits. Navajos in Arizona and New Mexico, facing starvation in the bitter winter of 1947–1948, were denied government relief because of charges that their communal way of life was communistic and therefore un-American. Black actor Paul Robeson, who along with W. E. B. Du Bois criticized American foreign policy, was accused of Communist leanings, found few opportunities to perform, and eventually, like Du Bois, lost his passport. Hispanic laborers faced deportation for membership in unions with left-wing sympathies. In 1949, the Congress of Industrial Organizations (CIO) expelled 11 unions with a total membership of more than one million for alleged domination by Communists.

Then there was Val Lorwin, introduced at the beginning of the chapter, who suffered through repeated hearings and trials on the basis of malicious and unsubstantiated accusations that threatened to destroy his career. Lorwin was named on one of McCarthy's famous lists, but like so many others, he was really a victim of the

Major Events of the Cold War

Year	*Event*	*Effect*
1946	Winston Churchill's "Iron Curtain" speech	First Western "declaration" of the Cold War
	George F. Kennan's long telegram	Spoke of Soviet insecurity and the need for containment
1947	George F. Kennan's article signed "Mr. X"	Elaborated on arguments in the telegram
	Truman Doctrine	Provided economic and military aid to Greece and Turkey
	Federal Employee Loyalty Program	Sought to root out subversion in the U.S. government
	HUAC investigation of the motion picture industry	Sought to expose Communist influences in the movies
1948	Marshall Plan	Provided massive American economic aid in rebuilding postwar Europe
	Berlin airlift	Brought in supplies when USSR closed off land access to the divided city
1949	NATO	Created a military alliance to withstand a possible Soviet attack
	First Soviet atomic bomb	Ended the American nuclear monopoly
	Communist victory in China	Made Americans fear the worldwide spread of communism
1950	Conviction of Alger Hiss	Seemed to bear out Communist danger at home
	Joseph McCarthy's first charges	Launched aggressive anti-Communist campaign in the United States
	NSC-68	Called for vigilance and increased military spending to counter the Communist threat
	Outbreak of Korean War	North Korean invasion of South Korea viewed as part of Soviet conspiracy
1953	Armistice in Korea	Brought little change after years of bitter fighting
1954	Vietnamese victory over French at Dien Bien Phu	Early triumph for nationalism in Southeast Asia
	Army-McCarthy hearings	Brought downfall of Joseph McCarthy.

larger anti-Communist crusade. He faced the same hurdles others encountered. Denials under oath made no difference. An adequate defense was almost impossible to mount. The charges themselves were often enough to smear a person, regardless of whether they were true or false. Lorwin weathered the storm and was finally vindicated, but others were less lucky. They were the unfortunate victims as the United States became consumed by the passions of the Cold War.

CONCLUSION

The Cold War in Perspective

The Cold War was the greatest single force affecting American society in the decade and a half after World War II. Tensions grew throughout the postwar years as a bitter standoff between the United States and the Soviet Union emerged. What caused the Cold War? Historians have long differed over the question of where responsibility should be placed. In the early years after the Second World War, policymakers and commentators justified the American stance as a bold and courageous effort to meet the Communist threat. Later, particularly in the 1960s, as the public started to doubt the course of American foreign policy, revisionist historians began to argue that American policy was misguided, insensitive to Soviet needs, and a contributing factor to the worsening frictions. As with most historical questions, there are no easy answers, but both sides must be weighed.

The Cold War stemmed from a competition for international influence between the two great world powers. After World War II, the American goal was to exercise economic and political leadership in the world and thus to institute capitalist economies and democratic political institutions throughout Europe and in nations emerging from colonial rule. But these goals put the nation on a collision course with nations having a different vision of what the postwar world should be like and with anticolonial movements in Third World countries around the globe. Perceiving threats from the Soviet Union, China, and other Communist powers, the United States embarked on an increasingly aggressive effort at containment, just as George Kennan had demanded, to preserve and extend its influence. The Cold War, with its profound effects at home and abroad, was the unfortunate result.

Recommended Reading

Background and Development of the Cold War

Stephen E. Ambrose, *Rise to Globalism: American Foreign Policy, 1938–1980* (3d rev. ed., 1980); Thomas H. Etzold and John Lewis Gaddis, *Containment: Documents on American Policy and Strategy, 1945–1950* (1978); John Lewis Gaddis, *The Long Peace: Inquiries into the History of the Cold War* (1987), *Strategies of Containment: A Critical Appraisal of Postwar American National Security Policy* (1982), and *The United States and the Origins of the Cold War, 1941–1947* (1972); Michael J. Hogan, *The Marshall Plan: America, Britain, and the Reconstruction of Western Europe* (1987); Walter LaFeber, *America, Russia, and the Cold War, 1945–1990* (6th ed., 1991); Thomas G. Patterson, *Meeting the Communist Threat: Truman to Reagan* (1988) and *On Every Front: The Making of the Cold War* (1979); Daniel Yergin, *Shattered Peace: The Origins of the Cold War and the National Security State* (1977).

Foreign Policy in the Eisenhower Years

H. W. Brands, Jr., *Cold Warriors: Eisenhower's Generation and American Foreign Policy* (1988); Robert A. Divine, *Eisenhower and the Cold War* (1981); Townsend Hoopes, *The Devil and John Foster Dulles* (1973).

The Korean War

Joseph C. Goulden, *Korea: The Untold Story of the War* (1982); Burton I. Kaufman, *The Korean War: Challenges in Crisis, Credibility, and Command* (1986); James A. Michener, *The Bridges at Toko-ri* (novel, 1953); David Rees, *Korea: The Limited War* (1964).

The Nuclear Threat

McGeorge Bundy, *Danger and Survival: Choices About the Bomb in the First Fifty Years* (1988); Pat Frank, *Alas, Babylon* (novel, 1959); Gregg Herken, *Counsels of War* (1985); Richard G. Hewlett and Francis Duncan, *Atomic Shield: Volume II: A History of the United States Atomic Energy Commission, 1947–1952* (1972); Richard G. Hewlett and Jack M. Holl, *Atoms for Peace and War: Eisenhower and the Atomic Energy Commission, 1953–1961* (1989); Fred Kaplan, *The Wizards of Armageddon* (1983); Walter M. Miller, Jr., *A Canticle for Leibowitz* (novel, 1959); John Newhouse, *War and Peace in the Nuclear Age* (1989); Nevil Shute, *On the Beach* (novel, 1957); Spencer R. Weart, *Nuclear Fear: A History of Images* (1988); Herbert F. York, *The Advisors: Oppenheimer, Teller, and the Superbomb* (1976).

The Anti-Communist Crusade

David Caute, *The Great Fear: The Anti-Communist Purge Under Truman and Eisenhower* (1978); Richard Freeland, *The Truman Doctrine and the Origins of McCarthyism: Foreign Policy, Domestic Politics, and Internal Security, 1946–1948* (1971); Robert Griffith, *The Politics of Fear: Joseph R. McCarthy and the Senate* (1970); David M. Oshinsky, *A Conspiracy So Immense: The World of Joe McCarthy* (1983); Ronald Radash and Joyce Milton, *The Rosenberg File: A Search for Truth* (1984); Thomas C. Reeves, *The Life and Times of Joe McCarthy: A Biography* (1982); Richard H. Rovere, *Senator Joe McCarthy* (1960); Ellen W. Schrecker, *No Ivory Tower: McCarthyism and the Universities* (1986); Allen Weinstein, *Perjury: The Hiss-Chambers Case* (1978).

TIMELINE

1945 Yalta Conference
Roosevelt dies; Harry Truman becomes president
Potsdam Conference

1946 American plan for control of atomic energy fails
Atomic Energy Act
Iran Crisis
Churchill's "Iron Curtain" speech

1947 Truman Doctrine
Federal Employee Loyalty Program
House Un-American Activities Committee (HUAC) investigates the movie industry

1948 Marshall Plan launched
Berlin Airlift
Israel created by UN
Hiss-Chambers case
Truman reelected president

1949 Soviet Union tests atomic bomb
North Atlantic Treaty Organization (NATO) established
George Orwell publishes *Nineteen Eighty-four*
Mao Zedong's forces win Chinese civil war; Jiang Jieshi flees to Taiwan

1950 Truman authorizes development of the hydrogen bomb
Alger Hiss convicted
Joseph McCarthy's Wheeling (W. Va.) speech on subversion
NSC-68
McCarran Internal Security Act

1950–1953 Korean War

1951 Japanese-American Treaty
Dennis v. *United States*

1952 Dwight D. Eisenhower elected president
McCarthy heads Senate Permanent Investigations Subcommittee

1953 Stalin dies; Khrushchev consolidates power
East Germans stage anti-Soviet demonstrations
Shah of Iran returns to power in CIA-supported coup

1954 Fall of Dien Bien Phu ends French control of Indochina
Geneva Conference
Guatemalan government overthrown with CIA help
Mao's forces shell Quemoy and Matsu
Army-McCarthy hearings

1956 Suez incident
Hungarian "freedom fighters" suppressed
Eisenhower reelected

1957 Russians launch *Sputnik* satellite

1958 U.S. troops sent to support Lebanese government

1959 Castro deposes Batista in Cuba

CHAPTER 27

Postwar Growth and Social Change

Ray Kroc, an ambitious salesman, headed toward San Bernardino, California, on a business trip in 1954. For more than a decade he had been selling "multimixers"—stainless steel machines that could make six milkshakes at once—to restaurants and soda shops around the United States. On this trip he was particularly interested in checking out a hamburger stand run by Richard and Maurice McDonald, who had bought eight of his "contraptions" and could therefore make 48 shakes at the same time.

Always eager to increase sales, Kroc wanted to see the McDonalds' operation for himself. The 52-year-old son of Slavic parents had sold everything from real estate to radio time to paper cups before peddling the multimixers, but had enjoyed no stunning success. Yet he was still on the alert for the key to the fortune that was part of the American dream. As he watched the lines of people at the San Bernardino McDonald's, the answer seemed at hand.

The McDonald brothers sold only standard hamburgers and french fries, but they had developed a system that was fast, efficient, and clean. It drew on the automobile traffic that moved along Route 66. And it was profitable indeed. Sensing the possibilities, Kroc proposed that the two owners open other establishments as well. When they balked, he negotiated a 99-year contract that allowed him to sell the fast-food idea and the name—and their golden arches design—wherever he could.

On April 15, 1955, Kroc opened his first McDonald's in Des Plaines, a suburb of Chicago. Three months later, he sold his first franchise in Fresno, California. Others soon followed. Kroc scouted out new locations, almost always on highway "strips," persuaded people to put up the capital, and provided them with specifications guaranteed to ensure future success. For his efforts, he received a percentage of the gross take.

From the start, Kroc insisted on standardization. Every McDonald's was the same—from the two functional arches supporting the glass enclosure that housed the kitchen and take-out window to the single arch near the road bearing a sign indicating how many 15-cent hamburgers had already been sold. All menus and prices were exactly the same, and Kroc demanded that everything from hamburger size to cooking time be constant. He insisted, too, that the establishments be clean. No pinball games or cigarette machines were permitted; the premium was on a good, inexpensive hamburger, quickly served, at a nice place.

McDonald's, of course, was an enormous success. In 1962, total sales exceeded $76 million. In 1964, before the company had been in operation ten years, it had sold over 400 million hamburgers and 120 million pounds of french fries. By the end of the next year, there were 710 McDonald's stands in 44 states. In 1974, only 20 years after Kroc's vision of the hamburger's future, McDonald's did $2 billion worth of business. When Kroc died in 1984, a total of 45 billion burgers had been sold at 7,500 outlets in 32 countries. Ronald McDonald, the clown who came to represent the company, became known to children around the globe after his Washington, D.C., debut in November 1963. When McDonald's began to advertise, it became the country's first restaurant to buy TV time. Musical slogans like "You deserve a break today" and "We do it all for you" became better known than some popular songs.

The success of McDonald's provides an example of the development of new trends in the 1950s in the United States. Kroc capitalized on the changes of the automobile age. He understood that a restaurant, not in the city but along the highways, where it could draw on heavier traffic, had a better chance of success. The drive-in design, catering to a new and ever-growing clientele, soon became common.

He understood, too, that the franchise notion provided the key to rapid growth. Not prepared to open up thousands of stands himself, he sold the idea to eager entrepreneurs who stood to make sizable profits as long as they remained a part of the larger whole. In numerous other product areas as well as the hamburger business the franchise method helped create a nationwide web of firms.

Finally, Kroc sensed the importance of standardization and uniformity. He understood the mood of the time, the quiet conformity of Americans searching for success. The McDonald's image may have been monotonous, but that was part of its appeal. Customers always knew what they would get wherever they found the golden arches. If the atmosphere was "bland," that too was deliberate. As Kroc said, "Our theme is kind of synonymous with Sunday school, the Girl Scouts and the YMCA. McDonald's is clean and wholesome." It was a symbol of the age.

This chapter describes the structural changes in American society in the decade and a half after World War II. We will examine how economic growth, spurred by technological advances, transformed the patterns of American life at home and at work. Self-interest triumphed over idealism as most Americans obtained material comfort previously unknown. But even as it promoted economic growth, the government was obliged to acknowledge the claims of minorities. In their protests against continuing social and economic injustice, blacks, Indians, and Hispanics highlighted the limits of the postwar American dream.

Economic Boom

In spite of anxieties about the Cold War, most Americans were optimistic after 1945. As servicemen returned home and resumed their lives, a baby boom brought unprecedented population growth. The simultaneous and unexpected economic boom had an even greater impact. Large corporations increasingly dominated the business world, but unions grew as well, and most workers improved their lives. Technology appeared triumphant, new products flooding the market and finding their way into most American homes. For the growing middle class, increased prosperity conveyed the sense that all was well in the United States.

The Peacetime Economy

The wartime return of prosperity after the Great Depression continued in the postwar years. Even though Americans feared another collapse, for the next two decades they enjoyed one of the most sustained periods of economic expansion the United States had ever known, as it solidified its position as the richest nation in the world.

The statistical evidence of economic success was impressive. The gross national product (GNP) jumped from just over $200 billion in 1945 to almost $300 billion in 1950 and by 1960 had climbed above $500 billion. Per capita income rose from $1,515 in 1945 to $2,788 in 1960. Almost 60 percent of all families in the country were now part of the middle class, a dramatic change from the class structure in the nineteenth and early twentieth century.

Personal resources fueled economic growth. During World War II, American consumers had been unable to spend all they earned because production had been concentrated in manufacturing weapons needed for war. With accumulated savings of $140 billion at war's end, consumers were ready to buy whatever they could.

McDonald's provided a model for other franchisers in the 1950s and the years that followed. The golden arches, shown here in an early version, were virtually the same wherever they appeared. Initially found along highways around the country, they were later built within cities and towns as well.

Equally important was the 22 percent rise in real purchasing power between 1946 and 1960. Families now had far more discretionary income—money to satisfy wants as well as needs—than before. At the end of the Great Depression, fewer than one-quarter of all households had any discretionary income; in 1960, three of every five did.

The United States, which produced half the world's goods, was providing new products that average Americans, unlike their parents, could afford. Higher real wages allowed people across social classes to buy consumer goods, and that consumer power, in contrast to the underconsumption of the 1920s and 1930s, spurred the economy. In the words of one government official, Adolf A. Berle, Jr., Americans were caught up in a spirit of "galloping capitalism."

The automobile industry played a key part in the economic boom. Just as cars and roads transformed America in the 1920s when mass production came of age, so they contributed to the transformation three decades later. Limited to the production of military vehicles during World War II, the auto industry expanded dramatically in the postwar period. Two million cars were made in 1946; four times as many in 1955. Customers now chose from a wide variety of engines, colors, and optional accessories. Fancy grills and tail fins distinguished each year's models.

The development of a massive interstate highway system also stimulated auto production and so contributed to prosperity. Rather than en-

Index of Weekly Wages in Manufacturing (1967 = 100)

Year	Unadjusted Wage	Adjusted for Inflation
1940	21.9	53.1
1941	25.8	59.3
1942	31.9	66.3
1943	37.6	73.5
1944	40.1	77.3
1945	38.6	72.8
1946	38.2	66.2
1947	43.5	66.0
1948	47.1	66.4
1949	47.8	68.0
1950	51.6	72.8
1951	56.3	73.5
1952	59.2	75.5
1953	62.4	79.0
1954	62.6	78.9
1955	66.4	84.3
1956	69.6	86.8
1957	71.7	86.4
1958	72.7	85.2
1959	76.8	89.3
1960	78.1	89.5

Source: U.S. Bureau of Labor Statistics.

The massive interstate highway system funded by Congress in 1956 intensified American dependence on the automobile. Despite the new network of roads, congestion continued, as increasing numbers of commuters relied on their cars.

courage the growth of a mass transit system, the Eisenhower administration underscored the American commitment to the car. Through the Interstate Highway Act of 1956 it provided $26 billion, the largest public works expenditure in American history, to build over 40,000 miles of federal highways, linking all parts of the United States.

Though highways added to the problem of pollution and triggered urban flight, the interstate complex was hailed as a key to the country's material development. Justified in part on the grounds that it would make evacuation quicker in the event of nuclear attack, the highway system made its proponents proud. President Eisenhower wrote:

> The total pavement of the system would make a parking lot big enough to hold two-thirds of all the automobiles in the United States. The amount of concrete poured to form these roadways would build . . . six sidewalks to the moon. . . . More than any single action by the government since the end of the war, this one would change the face of America.

Significantly, this massive effort helped create a nation dependent on a constant supply of cheap and plentiful oil.

House construction also contributed to economic growth. In 1940, 43 percent of all American families owned their own homes; by 1960, the figure had risen to 62 percent. Much of the stimulus came from the GI Bill of 1944. In addition to giving returning servicemen priority for many jobs and providing educational benefits, it offered low-interest home mortgages, and millions of former soldiers took advantage of the measure to buy into the American dream.

Federal policy also helped sustain the expansion, as the government played an increasingly active role in the postwar economy. It supported development by allowing businesses to buy almost 80 percent of the factories built by the government during the war for much less than they cost. Even more important was the dramatic rise in defense spending as the Cold War escalated. In 1947, when the Department of Defense was established, the defense budget stood at $13 billion. With the onset of the Korean War, it rose to $22 billion in 1951 and to about $47 billion in 1953. Between 1949 and 1960, spending for space research increased from $49 million to $401 million. As federal expenditures reached 20 percent of the GNP by the 1950s, it was clear that a major economic transformation had occurred.

Peaceful, prosperous, and productive, the country had become the "affluent society," to use economist John Kenneth Galbraith's phrase. Inflation, a problem in the immediate postwar period, slowed from an average of 7 percent per year in the 1940s to 2 to 3 percent per year in the 1950s. The concentration of income remained the same—the bottom half of the population still earned less than the top tenth—but the ranks of middle-class Americans grew. As Charles Lehman, a veteran from Missouri, later recalled:

> I was a twenty-one-year-old lieutenant with a high school education, and my only prewar experience was as a stock boy in a grocery store. But on V-J day, I *knew* it was only a matter of time before I was rich—or well-off, anyway.

The Corporate World

After 1945, the major corporations increased their hold on the American economy. Government policy in World War II had encouraged the growth of big business and produced tremendous industrial concentration. Antitrust activity was suspended in the interest of wartime production, while government contracts spurred expansion. During the war, two-thirds of all military contracts were awarded to 100 firms, and half of all contracts went to three dozen giants. In 1940, some 100 companies accounted for 30 percent of all manufacturing output in the United States. Three years later, that figure had risen to 70 percent.

Industrial concentration continued after the war. Several waves of mergers had taken place in the past, including one in the 1890s and another in the 1920s. Still another took place in the 1950s, making oligopoly—domination of a given industry by a few firms—a feature of American capitalism. At the same time, the booming economy encouraged the development of conglomerates—firms that diversified with holdings in a variety of industries. International Telephone and Telegraph, for example, purchased Avis Rent-a-Car, Continental Baking, Sheraton Hotels, Levitt and Sons Home Builders, and Hartford Fire Insurance. That pattern, widely duplicated, protected companies against instability in one particular area. It also led to the further development of finance capitalism to help put the deals together, just as the demands of consolidation in the late nineteenth century had opened the way for bankers like J. P. Morgan (see Chapter 18).

Expansion took other forms as well. Even as the major corporations expanded, so did smaller franchise operations like McDonald's, Kentucky Fried Chicken, and Burger King. Ray Kroc, introduced at the start of the chapter, provided a widely imitated pattern.

While expanding at home, large corporations also moved increasingly into foreign markets, as they had in the 1890s. But at the same time they began to build plants overseas, where labor costs were cheaper. A General Electric plant in Massachusetts might have to pay a worker $3.40 an hour, whereas a plant in Singapore paid only 30 cents an hour for the same job. In the decade after 1957, General Electric built 61 plants abroad, and numerous other firms did the same.

In the post-1945 period, the close business-government ties that had developed during the war grew stronger. Federal dollars fueled research that in turn accounted for new industrial expansion. The government underwrote 90 percent of aviation and space research, 65 percent of electricity and electronics work, and 42 percent of scientific instrument development.

Corporate planning, meanwhile, developed rapidly, as firms sought managers who could assess information, weigh marketing trends, and make rational decisions. Andrew Carnegie had pioneered such an approach in the late nineteenth century by paying meticulous attention to his costs (see Chapter 18). Now managers, trained in business schools, were even more precise in the effort to maximize profit.

The Workers' World

As corporations changed, so did the world of work. In the years after World War II, the United States reversed a 150-year trend and became less a nation of goods producers and more a country of service providers. By 1956, a majority of the American people held white-collar jobs. Between 1947 and 1957, the number of factory workers fell by 4 percent, while the number of clerical workers increased 23 percent and salaried middle-class employees rose 61 percent. Salaried rather than paid by the hour, these new white-collar workers served as corporate managers, teachers, salespeople, and office workers.

Work in the huge corporations became even more impersonal than before. In many firms, the bureaucratic style predominated, with white-collar employees seemingly dressing, thinking, and acting the same (as depicted in a popular novel and film of the 1950s, *The Man in the Gray Flannel Suit*). Money and material well-being were the prizes of corporate life. Corporations provided a secure working atmosphere and a comfortable leisure environment. The country clubs IBM built or the model homes Richfield Oil constructed were perquisites that kept employees loyal to their firms.

White-collar employees paid a price for comfort. Corporations, preaching that teamwork was far more important than individuality, indoctrinated employees and conveyed the appropriate standards of conduct. RCA issued company neckties. IBM had training programs to teach employ-

Occupational Distribution, 1940–1960

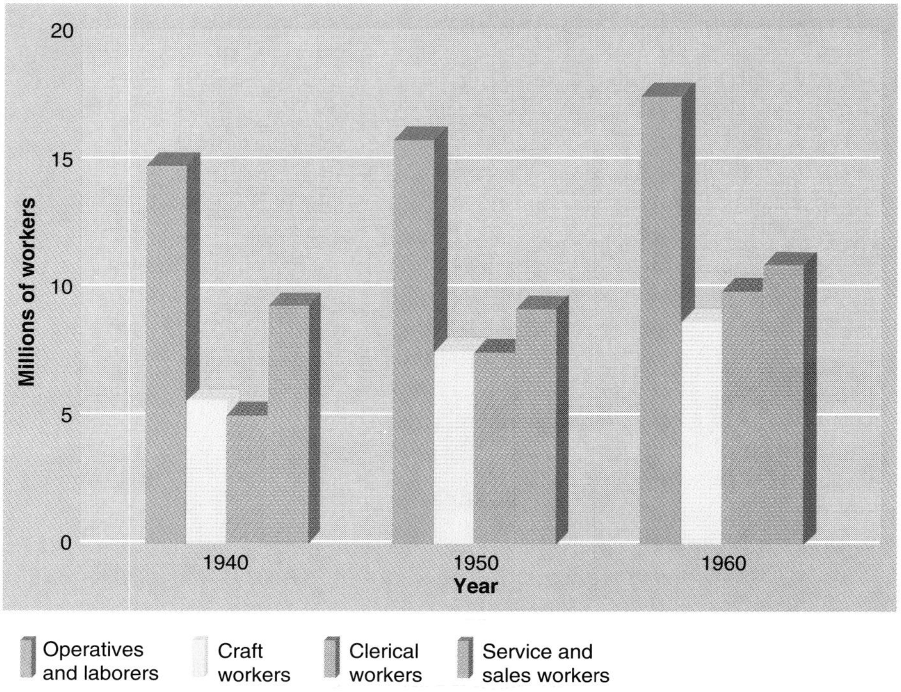

In the postwar years, the size of the work force increased considerably. In this graph, observe how all categories grew, particularly the number of clerical workers. Note, too, the increase in the number of service and sales workers between 1950 and 1960, in a trend that would continue in later years.

Source: U.S. Department of Labor.

ees the company line. Some large firms even set up training programs to show wives how their own behavior could help their husbands' careers. Just as product standardization became increasingly important, individual acceptance of company norms became necessary. "Personal views can cause a lot of trouble," an oil company recruiting pamphlet noted, suggesting that business favored moderate or conservative ideas that would not threaten the system. Author William H. Whyte described young executives whose ultimate goal was "belongingness." Social critic C. Wright Mills observed, "When white-collar people get jobs, they sell not only their time and energy but their personalities as well."

Blue-collar workers also prospered in the postwar years. Labor union strength peaked as the war ended. Rifts, present since the 1930s, healed, leading the American Federation of Labor and the Congress of Industrial Organizations to merge into the AFL-CIO in 1955. The new organization, led by building trade unionist George Meany, represented more than 90 percent of the country's 17.5 million union members.

Union activity brought real improvements in income. In 1950, General Motors and the United Automobile Workers agreed to an escalator clause to ensure that wages reflected changes in the cost of living. Five years later, autoworkers gained a guaranteed annual wage. With higher, more predictable incomes, workers were more willing to limit strike activity.

Labor peace prevailed, but at the expense of the last vestiges of autonomy in the workplace. Workers fell increasingly under the control of middle-level managers and watched anxiously as companies automated at home or expanded abroad, where labor was cheaper.

The union movement stalled in the mid-1950s. Steady wage gains were achieved with promises of labor stability and fewer strikes, and militancy, which had helped attract members, declined. The heavy industries providing workers who gravitated to the union movement were no longer growing. The unionized percentage of the nonfarm work force remained stable between 1946 and 1954 but then began to fall. Unions tried to expand their base by reaching out to new groups—less skilled minority workers and white-collar service-oriented employees—but they proved difficult to organize.

The Agricultural World

The agricultural world changed even more than the industrial world in postwar America. New technology revolutionized farming. Improved planting and harvesting machines and better fertilizers and pesticides brought massive gains in productivity.

Increasing profitability led to agricultural consolidation. In the 25 years after 1945, average farm size almost doubled. Farms specialized more in cash crops like corn or soybeans that were more profitable than hay or oats that could be used to feed animals. Demanding large-scale investment, farming became a big business. Family farms often found it difficult to compete with the technologically superior "agribusiness" and watched their share of the market fall. In response, farmers left the land in increasing numbers. At the end of World War II, farmers made up one-fourth of the nation's work force (down from one-third in 1935). Over the next 25 years, 25 million people left the rural life behind, until only 5 percent of the population remained on farms in 1970.

Population Shifts and the New Suburbs

In post–World War II America, a growing population marked prosperity's return. During the Great Depression, the birthrate had dropped to an all-time low of 19 births per 1,000 population as hard times obliged people to delay marriage and parenthood. As the Second World War boosted the economy, the birthrate began to rise again. Some

Birth and Population Rates, 1900–1960

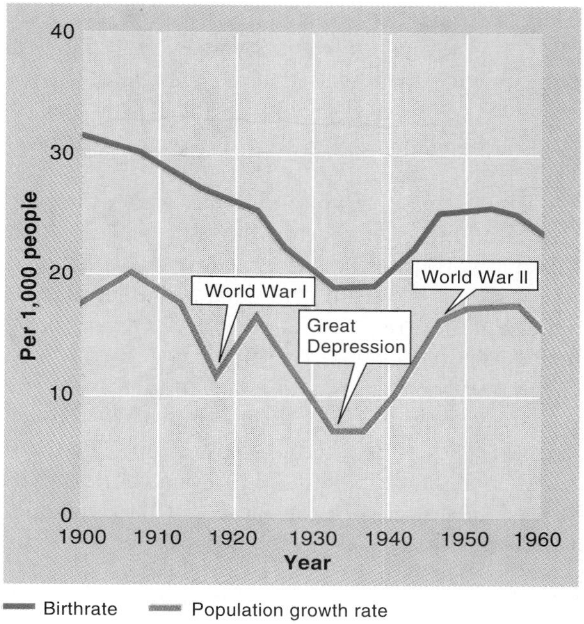

Both birth and population rates increased dramatically after the difficult years of the Great Depression. Note the baby boom that began at the end of World War II and continued for the next decade.

Source: U.S. Bureau of the Census.

experts questioned whether the trend was a long-term one. The Census Bureau cautiously claimed that it was at least partly due to "occasional furloughs," but in fact a real shift was under way.

The birthrate soared in the postwar years as millions of Americans began families. The "baby boom" peaked in 1957, with a rate of more than 25 births per 1,000. In that year, 4.3 million babies were born, one every seven seconds. While the population growth of 19 million in the 1940s was double the rise of the decade before, that increase paled against the increase in the 1950s, which totaled 29 million.

The effects of the baby boom were visible everywhere. There was Monroe Park, a community of 95 house trailers for veterans and their families at the University of Wisconsin. It was called the "state's most fertile five acres." In one week alone in 1947, five families had babies. Similar fertility was evident in communities throughout the United States.

The rising birthrate was the dominant factor affecting population growth, but the death rate was also declining. Miracle drugs, such as streptomycin and aureomycin, helped cure illnesses attacking all ages, especially the young. Life expectancy rose: midway through the 1950s, the average was 70 years for whites and 64 for blacks, compared with 55 for whites and 45 for blacks in 1920.

The baby boom shaped family and social patterns and material needs. Many women who had taken jobs during the war now left the work force to rear their children and care for their homes. The demand grew for diaper services and baby foods. When they entered school, the members of the baby boom generation strained the educational system. Between 1946 and 1956, enrollment in grades 1 through 8 soared from 20 million to 30 million. Since school construction had slowed during the Depression and had virtually halted during the Second World War, classrooms were needed. Teachers, too, were in short supply.

As Americans became more populous, they also became more mobile. For many generations, lower-class Americans had been the most likely to move; now geographic mobility spread to the middle class. Each year in the 1950s, over a million farmers left their farms in search of new employment. Other Americans picked up stakes and headed on as well. Some moved to look for better jobs. Others, like Bob Moses of Baltimore, simply wandered awhile after returning home from the war and then settled down. Moses, traveling in a 1937 Chevrolet with some high school friends, was going "nowhere in particular, just roaming. We'd see a kink in a river on the map, and head there." After regimented military life, it was good to be free.

The war had produced increasing movement, most of it westward. Although the scarcity of water in the West would require massive water projects to support population growth, war workers and their families streamed to western cities where shipyards, airplane factories, and other industrial plants were located. After the war, this migration pattern persisted, as the West and the Southwest continued to grow. Sun Belt cities like Houston, Albuquerque, Tucson, and Phoenix underwent phenomenal expansion. The population of Phoenix soared from 65,000 in 1940 to 439,000

Population Shifts, 1940–1950

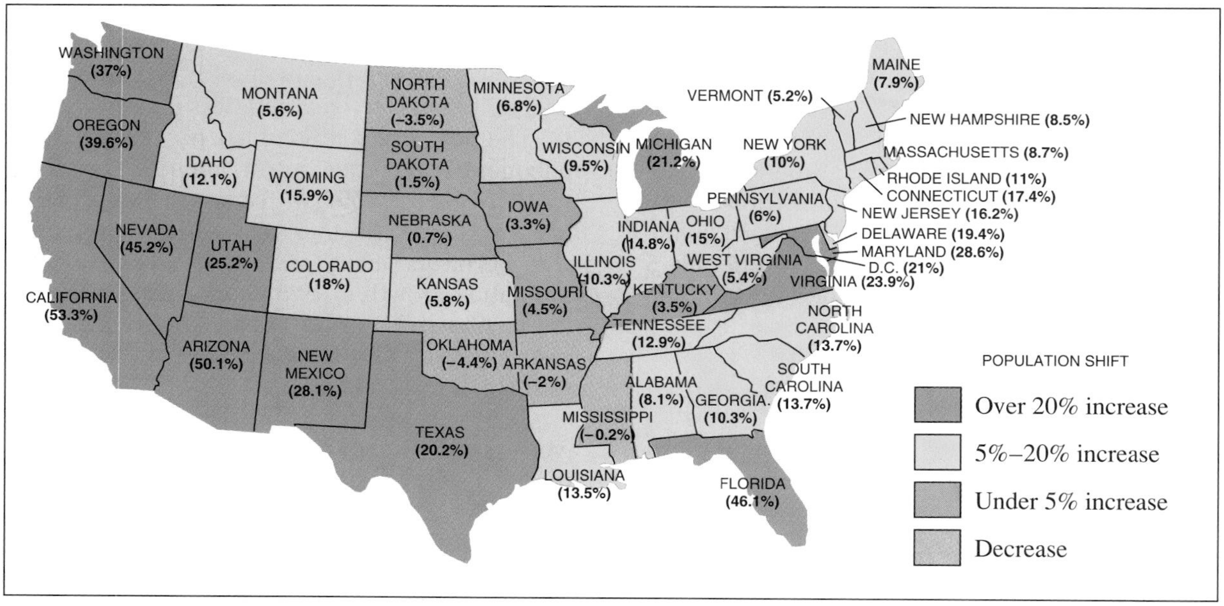

This map reveals the huge growth of population in the West and the sizable, though less extensive, increase in the Northeast and Southeast between 1940 and 1950.

Growth of Sun Belt Cities, 1920–1980
Population (in thousands)

	1920	1940	1960	1980
Los Angeles	879	2,916	6,039	7,478
Houston	168	529	1,418	2,905
Dallas	185	527	1,084	2,430
Atlanta	249	559	1,017	2,030
San Diego	74	289	1,033	1,862
Miami	30	268	935	1,626
Phoenix	29	186	664	1,509
New Orleans	398	552	907	1,256
San Antonio	191	338	716	1,072
Tucson	20	37	266	531

Source: U.S. Bureau of the Census.

in 1960. In the 1950s, Los Angeles pulled ahead of Philadelphia as the third-largest city in the United States. One-fifth of all the growth in the period took place in California's promised land; even baseball teams—the Brooklyn Dodgers and the New York Giants—left the East Coast for western shores. By 1963, in a dramatic illustration of the importance of the West, California had passed New York as the nation's most populous state.

After the war, another form of movement became even more important in the United States. Although the proportion of Americans defined as residents of metropolitan areas increased from 51 to 63 percent between 1940 and 1960, this disguised another shift. Millions of white Americans fled the inner city to suburban fringes, intensifying a movement that had begun before the war. Fourteen of the nation's largest cities, including New York, Boston, Chicago, Philadelphia, and Detroit, actually lost population in the 1950s. As central cities became places where poor nonwhites clustered, new urban and racial problems emerged.

For people of means, cities were places to work and then to leave at five o'clock. In Manhattan, south of City Hall, the noontime population of 1.5 million dropped to 2,000 during the night. The outlying regions, writer John Brooks argued, were

> draining downtown of its nighttime population, except for night watchmen and derelicts; it was becoming a part-time city, tidally swamped with bustling humanity every weekday morning when the cars and commuter trains arrived, and abandoned again at nightfall when the wave sucked back—left pretty much to thieves, policemen, and rats.

As the cities declined, the suburbs blossomed. If the decade after World War I had witnessed a rural-to-urban shift, the decades after World War II saw a reverse shift to the regions out-

Shifts in Population Distribution, 1940–1960

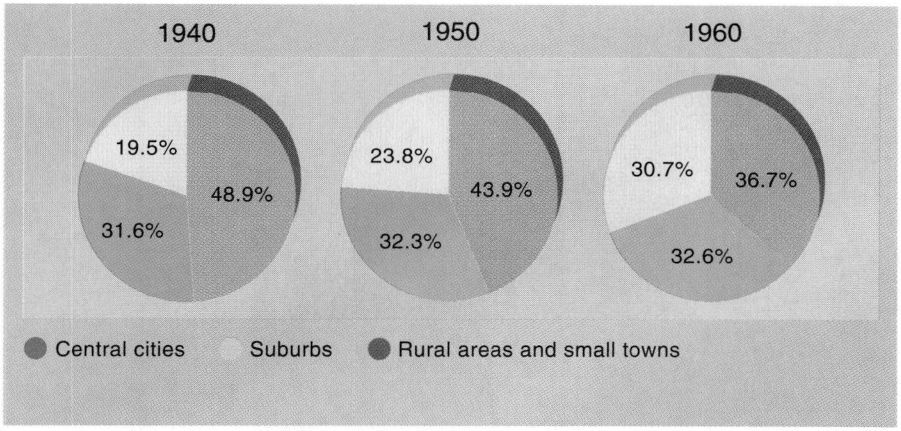

This graph shows the progressive decline in rural population, and the corresponding increase in suburban population, between 1940 and 1960.

Source: U.S. Bureau of the Census.

side the central cities, usually accessible only by car. By the end of the 1950s, a third of all Americans resided in suburbs.

Americans moved to the suburbs to buy homes that would accommodate their larger families. The number of owner-occupied houses rose from 15.2 million in 1940 to 23.5 million ten years later. Often rapidly constructed and overpriced, suburban tract houses provided the appearance of comfort and space and the chance to have at least one part of the American dream, a place of one's own. Set in developments with names like Scarborough Manor, Peppermill Village, and Woodbury Knoll, they seemed protected from the growing troubles of the cities, insulated from the difficulties of the world outside.

A key figure in the suburbanization movement was William J. Levitt, a builder eager to gamble and reap the rewards of a growing demand. Levitt recognized the advantages of mass production during World War II, when his firm constructed housing for war workers. Aware that the GI Bill made mortgage money readily available, he recognized the possibilities of suburban development. But to cash in, Levitt knew he had to use new construction methods.

Mass production was the key. Individually designed houses were a thing of the past, he believed. "The reason we have it so good in this country," he said, "is that we can produce lots of things at low prices through mass production." Houses were among them. Working on a careful schedule, Levitt's team brought precut and preassembled materials to each site, put them together, and then moved on to the next location. As on an assembly line, tasks were broken down into individual steps. Groups of workers performed but a single job, moving from one tract to another.

Levitt proved that his system worked. Construction costs at Levittown, New York, a new community of 17,000 homes built in the late 1940s, were only $10 per square foot, compared with the $12 to $15 common elsewhere. The next Levittown appeared in Bucks County, Pennsylvania, several years after the first, and another went up in Willingboro, New Jersey, at the end of the 1950s. Levitt's success provided a model for other developers.

Government-insured mortgages, especially for veterans, fueled the housing boom. So did fairly low postwar interest rates. With many American families vividly remembering the De-

Step-by-step mass production, with units completed in assembly-line fashion, was the key to William Levitt's approach to housing. But the suburban developments he and others created were marked by street after street of houses that all looked the same.

pression and saving significant parts of their paychecks, the nation had a pool of savings large enough to keep mortgage interest rates in the affordable 5 percent range.

Suburbanization transformed the American landscape. Huge tracts of former fields, pastures, and forests were now divided into standardized squares, each bearing a house with a two-car garage and a manicured lawn. Stands of trees disappeared, for it was cheaper to cut them down than to work around them. Folksinger Malvina Reynolds described the new developments she saw:

> *Little boxes on the hillside*
> *Little boxes made of ticky tacky*
> *Little boxes on the hillside*
> *Little boxes all the same.*
> *There's a green one and a pink one*
> *And a blue one and a yellow one*
> *And they're all made out of ticky tacky*
> *And they just the same.*

As suburbs flourished, businesses followed their customers out of the cities. Shopping centers led the way. At the end of World War II, there were eight, but the number multiplied rapidly in the 1950s. In a single three-month period in 1957, 17 new centers opened; by 1960, there were 3,840 in the United States. Developers like Don M. Casto, who built the Miracle Mile near Columbus, Ohio, understood the importance of location as Americans moved out of the cities. "People have path-habits," he said, "like ants."

Shopping centers catered to the suburban clientele and transformed consumer patterns. They offered easy parking and convenient late hours; if they wished, suburb dwellers could remain entirely insulated from the cities. Their new shopping patterns, however, undermined the downtown department stores and further eroded urban health.

The Environmental Impact

Fast-food restaurants, shopping centers, and suburban housing developments all had a pronounced effect on the American environment. Rapid development often took place without extensive planning, and encroached on some of the nation's most attractive rural areas. Before long, virtually every American city was ringed by an ugly highway lined with the eating places, shopping malls, and auto dealerships that catered to the suburban population. Billboard advertisements filled whatever space was not yet developed.

Responding to the increasingly cluttered terrain, architect Peter Blake ruthlessly attacked the practices of the 1950s in his muckraking book *God's Own Junkyard: The Planned Deterioration of America's Landscape,* published in 1964. The largely pictorial account indicted the careless attitudes toward the environment that led to the "uglification" of a once lovely land. After describing breathtaking natural resources, Blake declared, "The only trouble is that we are about to turn this beautiful inheritance into the biggest slum on the face of the earth." Public policy and the pursuit of private profit, coupled with general citizen indifference, he charged, led to the unconscionable desecration of the American landscape.

Despite occasional accounts like Blake's, there was little real consciousness of environmental issues in the post–World War II years. Yet the very prosperity that created the dismal highway strips in the late 1940s and 1950s was leading more and more Americans to appreciate natural environments as necessary parts of their rising standard of living. The shorter workweek provided more free time, and many Americans now had the means for longer vacations. By 1950, most wage laborers worked a 40-hour week, and 60 percent of nonagricultural workers enjoyed paid vacations, whereas few had in 1930. They began to explore mountains and rivers and ocean shores, and to ponder how they might be used for recreation. They also began to consider how to protect them. In 1958, Congress established the National Outdoor Recreation Review Commission, a first step toward consideration of environmental issues that became far more common in the next decade.

Technology Supreme

Rapid technological change occurred in the postwar years. Some developments—the use of atomic energy, for example—flowed directly from war research. Others emerged from the research and development activities sponsored by big business.

Computers led the way. Wartime advances led to large but workable calculators, followed in the postwar years by machines that contained

The ENIAC computer, first used in 1946, was a huge machine that took up an entire room. Yet it was far less powerful than the desk-top computers that became popular several decades later.

their own internal instructions and memories. In 1946, the Electronic Numerical Integrator and Calculator, called ENIAC, was built at the University of Pennsylvania. Although it contained 18,000 electronic tubes and required tremendous amounts of electricity and special cooling procedures, the machine worked. In an advertised test, it set out to multiply 97,367 by itself 5,000 times. A reporter pushed the necessary button, and the task was completed in less than half a second.

After the development of the transistor by three scientists at Bell Laboratories in 1948, the computer became faster and more reliable, and transformed American society as surely as industrialization had changed it a century before. It allowed for sophisticated forms of space exploration. Airlines, hotels, and other businesses computerized their reservation systems. Business accounting and inventory control began to depend on computers. Computer programmers and operators were in increasing demand.

Television was even more important than computers commercially. Developed in the 1930s, it became a major influence on American life after World War II. In 1946, there were fewer than 17,000 sets, but by 1960, three-quarters of all American families owned at least one set. In 1955, the average American family tuned in four to five hours each day. Some studies predicted that an American student, on graduating from high school, would have spent 11,000 hours in class and 15,000 hours before the "tube." Advertisements featuring the luxury items needed for the good life bombarded viewers, while their favorite shows often reinforced the consuming message.

Young Americans grew up to the strains of "Winky Dink and You," "The Mickey Mouse Club," and "Howdy Doody Time" in the 1950s. Older view-

Households Owning Radios and Televisions, 1940–1960

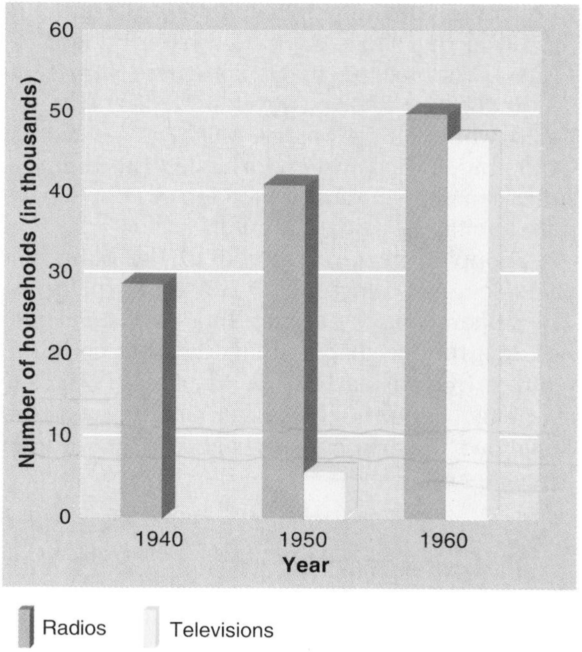

Radio became increasingly popular in the postwar years, but observe the astronomical increase in the number of households owning television sets in the decade after 1950.

Source: U.S. Bureau of the Census.

ers attended to situation comedies like "I Love Lucy" and "Father Knows Best" and live dramas such as "Playhouse 90." They watched Elvis Presley play his guitar and sing, and they danced to the rock and roll music played on "American Bandstand." Many of the programs aimed at children depicted violence and crime. Hopalong Cassidy was one of America's defenders who became a cult hero in his time. The gunslinging cowboy provided a role model that hundreds of American manufacturing firms capitalized on by making toy guns.

Americans maintained an ardent love affair with new appliances and gadgets. Tiny transistors powered not only computers and radios but also miniature hearing aids that could fit into the frame of a pair of eyeglasses. Stereophonic hi-fi sets, using new transistor components, provided better sound. By the end of the 1950s, most families had at least one automobile, as well as the staple appliances they had begun to purchase before—refrigerator, washing machine, television, and vacuum cleaner. Dozens of less essential items also became popular. There were electric can openers, electric pencil sharpeners, and electric toothbrushes. There were push-button phones and aerosol bombs, and automatic transmissions to take care of shifting car gears.

One ominous technological trend was the advent of automation. Mechanization was not new, but now it became far more widespread, threatening both skilled and unskilled workers. In 1952, the Ford Motor Company began using automatic drilling machines in an engine plant and found that 41 workers could do a job 117 had done before. The implications of falling purchasing power as machines replaced workers were serious for an economy dependent on consumer demand.

"The Mickey Mouse Club" was a popular daily feature on television in the 1950s. Millions of American children were glued to their TV sets each day after school, as they shared a common experience and absorbed the values promoted by the television networks.

The Consumer Culture

The modern American economy depended on consumption. Purchasing new goods and gadgets became easier with the expansion of consumer credit. Installment plans facilitated buying a new car, while credit cards encouraged other expenditures. The Diner's Club credit card appeared first in 1950, followed at the end of the decade by the American Express card and the BankAmericard. Consumer credit increased from \$8.4 billion in 1946 to nearly \$45 billion in 1958.

For consumers momentarily unsure about new purchases, a revitalized advertising industry was ready to convince them to go ahead. Advertising had come of age in the 1920s, as businesses persuaded customers that buying new products brought status and satisfaction. Advertising faltered when the economy collapsed in the 1930s but began to revive during the war, as firms kept the public aware of consumer goods, even those in short supply. With the postwar boom, advertisers again began to hawk their wares.

Although corporate marketing staffs maintained that customers made up their own minds, subtle manipulation was involved. Acquisitive desires were encouraged, with the means of gratification spelled out. One researcher for the J. Walter Thompson agency even quoted Benjamin Franklin, that apostle of thrift, to justify purchasing whenever possible:

> Is not the hope of being one day able to purchase and enjoy luxuries a great spur to labor and industry?

> . . . May not luxury therefore produce more than it consumes, if, without such a spur, people would be, as they are naturally enough inclined to be, lazy and indolent?

Motivational research became more sophisticated, uncovering new ways of persuading people to buy. Taking the place of radio, television played an important part in conveying the spirit of consumption to millions of Americans. Unlike radio, which could only describe new commodities, television could show them to consumers. Shows like "The Price Is Right" stressed consumption in direct ways: contestants won goods for quoting their correct retail price. Drawing on a talent honed in shopping centers and department stores, the show encouraged the acquisition of ever more material goods.

If the appeal often seemed overdone, advertisers had their defenders too. Vance Packard argued in 1957 in his best-selling book *The Hidden Persuaders* that advertisers "fill an important and constructive role in our society. Advertising, for example, not only plays a vital role in promoting our economic growth but as a colorful, diverting aspect of American life, and many of the creations of ad men are tasteful, honest works of artistry." That may have been true of some ads, but others were garish and conveyed a sense of material wealth run amok.

Americans welcomed the postwar affluence. Having weathered the poverty and unemployment of the 1930s and made sacrifices during a long war, they now intended to enjoy their newfound abundance and leisure time. Most Americans regarded all this as their due, sometimes neglecting to look beyond the immediate objects of their desire. The decade, journalist William Shannon wrote, was one of "self-satisfaction and gross materialism. . . . The loudest sound in the land has been the oink and grunt of private hoggishness. . . . It has been the age of the slob."

Consensus and Conformity

As the economy expanded, an increasing sense of sameness pervaded American society. This was the great age of conformity, when members of all social groups learned to emulate those around them rather than strike out on their own. Third- and fourth-generation ethnic Americans became much more alike. With immigration slowed to a trickle after 1924, ties to Europe weakened, and assimilation occurred. Television contributed to growing conformity by providing young and old with common, shared, visually seductive experience. Escaping the homogenizing tendencies was difficult. Sociologist David Riesman pointed out that in the classic nursery rhyme "This Little Pig Went to Market," each pig went his own way. "Today, however, all little pigs go to market; none stay home; all have roast beef, if any do; and all say 'we-we.' "

Conformity in School and Religious Life

The willingness to conform to group norms affected colleges and universities, where cautious

The supermarket, filled with convenience foods, was an important part of the consumer revolution. Suburban residents could drive to a supermarket and in aisle after aisle find all the goods that had been sold by a variety of smaller specialty stores in an earlier age.

students sought security. They joined fraternities and sororities and engaged in panty raids and other pranks but took little interest in world affairs. "I observe," Yale president A. Whitney Griswold told a graduating class in 1950, "that you share the prevailing mood of the hour, which in your case consists of bargains privately struck with fate—on fate's terms."

Americans in the postwar years discovered a shared religious sense and returned to their churches in record numbers. By the end of the 1950s, fully 95 percent of all Americans identified with some religious denomination. Church membership doubled between 1945 and 1970.

In part, church attendance reflected a desire to challenge "godless communism" at the height of the Cold War and to find some solace from the threat of annihilation in a nuclear war. Evangelist Billy Graham, often introduced as a "man with God's message for these crisis days," was in the forefront of the anti-Communist crusade. He preached to millions at his revivals, and capitalized on the media, using radio, television, and film to spread his message. "Hour of Decision" was a regular radio ministry in the 1950s, in which Graham tried to convert sinners and so save the nation. In one sermon, he declared: "Unless America at this tragic hour is willing to turn to Jesus Christ and be cleansed by the blood of Christ and know the regenerating power of the Holy Spirit, Christ will never save the nation." How could the nation be saved? "When you make your decision for Jesus Christ," Graham said, "it is America making her decision through you."

The religious resurgence had other roots as well. It resulted to some degree from the power of suggestion that led Americans to do what others did. It seemed to reinforce the importance of family life. As one slogan put it, "The family that prays together stays together." And it offered an acceptable means of escape from the anxieties of a middle-class executive's life. In the 1950s, the Full Gospel Businessmen's Fellowship not only provided religious camaraderie but also enjoyed access to the White House.

Dwight Eisenhower reflected the national mood when he observed that "our government makes no sense unless it is founded in a deeply felt religious faith—and I don't care what it is." In 1954, Congress added the words "under God" to the pledge to the flag, and the next year voted to require the phrase "In God We Trust" on all American currency. Yet religion was often devoid of piety and doctrinal understanding. In one public opinion poll, 80 percent of the respondents indicated that the Bible was God's revealed word, but only 35 percent were able to name the four Gospels and over half were unable to name even one.

Evangelist Billy Graham preached a fiery message to millions of Americans in the 1950s. On the radio, on television, and in huge revivals, he urged sinners to embrace God and so save their nation from the perils of the Communist threat.

Back to the Kitchen

World War II had interrupted traditional patterns of behavior for both men and women. As servicemen went overseas, women left their homes to work. After 1945, there was a period of adjustment as the men returned. In the 1950s, traditional gender roles were reaffirmed, even though, paradoxically, more women entered the work force than ever before.

Men, of course, expected to go to school and then find jobs to support their families. Viewing themselves as the primary breadwinners, they wanted their jobs waiting for them after the war.

For women, the situation was more difficult. Many had enjoyed working during the war and were reluctant to retreat to the home, although the government and employers persistently encouraged them to do so. In 1947, *Life* magazine ran a long photo essay called "The American Woman's Dilemma." It argued that women were caught in a conflict between the traditional expectation to stay home and the desire to have a paid job. A 1946 *Fortune* poll also captured the discontent of some women. Asked whether they would prefer to be born again as men or women, 25 percent of the women asked said they would prefer to be men. That dissatisfaction was strongest among white, well-educated, middle-class women, which was understandable, since family economic circumstances usually required black and lower-class white women to continue working outside the home.

By the 1950s, doubts and questions had been mostly suppressed. The baby boom increased average family size and made the decision to remain home easier. The flight to the suburbs gave women more to do, and they settled into the routines of redecorating their homes and gardens and transporting children to and from activities and schools.

In 1956, when *Life* produced a special issue on women, the message differed strikingly from that of nine years earlier. Profiling Marjorie Sutton, the magazine spoke of the "Busy Wife's Achievements" as "Home Manager, Mother, Hostess, and Useful Civic Worker." Married at 16, Marjorie was now busy with the PTA, Campfire Girls, and charity causes. She cooked and sewed for her family, which included four children, supported her husband by entertaining 1,500 guests a year, and worked out on the trampoline "to keep her size 12 figure."

Marjorie Sutton reflected the widespread social emphasis on marriage and home. Many women went to college to find husbands; if they succeeded, they dropped out. Almost two-thirds of the women in college stopped before completing a degree, compared with less than half the men. Women were expected to marry young, have children early, and support their husbands' careers.

Despite the reaffirmation of the old ideology that a woman's place was in the home, the 1950s were years of unnoticed but important change. Because the supply of single women workers was diminished by the low birthrate of the Depression years and by increased schooling and early marriage, older married women began entering the labor force in large numbers for the first time. In 1940, only 15 percent of American wives had jobs. By 1950, 21 percent were employed, and ten years later, the figure had risen to 30 percent. Moreover, married women now accounted for more than half of all working women, a dramatic reversal of earlier patterns.

Although many working women were poor, divorced, or widowed, many others worked to acquire the desirable new products that were badges of middle-class status. They stepped into the new jobs created by economic expansion, clustering in office, sales, and service positions, occupations already defined as female. They and their employers considered their work subordinate to their primary role as wives and mothers. Comparatively few entered professions where they would have challenged traditional notions of woman's place. As *Life* magazine pointed out in 1956, "Household skills take her into the garment trades; neat and personable, she becomes office worker and sales lady; patient and dexterous, she does well on competitive, detailed factory work; compassionate, she becomes teacher and nurse."

Black women worked as always but often lost the jobs they had won during the war. As the total percentage of women in the Detroit automobile industry dropped from 25 to 7.5, for example, jobs for black women nearly disappeared. Their median income at the end of the 1940s was less than half that of white women. Nor did they obtain white-collar work as easily as white women. But during the 1950s, they succeeded both in moving into white-collar positions and in improving their income. By 1960, more than a third of all black women had clerical, sales, service, or professional jobs, and their paychecks were 70 percent of those of white women.

Despite women's mixed experiences, society continued to view women in traditional ways. The conviction that women's main role was homemaking justified low wages and the denial of promotions. Adlai Stevenson, Democratic presidential candidate in 1952 and 1956, defined the female role in politics, telling a group of women that "the assignment for you, as wives and mothers, you can do in the living room with a baby in your lap or in the kitchen with a can opener in your hand." As in much of the nineteenth century, a woman was "to influence man and boy" in her "humble role of housewife" and mother.

Pediatrician Benjamin Spock agreed. In *Baby and Child Care* (1946), the book most responsible for the child-rearing patterns of the postwar generation, he advised mothers to stay at home if they wanted to raise stable and secure youngsters.

Movies seized on popular stereotypes and dramatized them. Doris Day, charming and wholesome, was a favorite heroine. In movie after movie, she showed how an attractive woman who played her cards right could land her man—the assumed goal of every woman.

Sexuality was a troublesome if compelling topic in the postwar years. In 1948, Alfred C. Kinsey published *Sexual Behavior in the Human Male.* Kinsey was an Indiana University zoologist who had previously studied the gall wasp. When asked to teach a course on marriage problems, he found little published material about human sexual activity and decided to collect his own. He compiled case histories of 5,300 white males, analyzed their personal backgrounds, and recorded patterns of sexual behavior.

Kinsey shocked the country with his statistics on premarital, extramarital, and otherwise illicit sexual activity. Among males who went to college, he concluded, 67 percent had engaged in sexual intercourse before marriage; 84 percent of those who went to high school but not beyond had done the same. Thirty-seven percent of the total male population had experienced some kind of overt homosexual activity. One out of every six farm boys in America had copulated with animals. Kinsey published a companion volume, *Sexual Behavior in the Human Female* (1953), that detailed many of the same sexual patterns. Although critics denounced the books, both sold widely, for they opened the door to a subject that had previously been considered taboo.

Interest in sexuality was reflected in the fascination with sex goddesses like Marilyn Monroe. With her blonde hair, breathy voice, and raw sexuality, she personified the forbidden side of the good life and became one of Hollywood's most popular stars. The images of such film goddesses corresponded to male fantasies of women, visible in *Playboy,* which first appeared in 1953. As for these men's wives, they were expected to manage their suburban homes and to be cheerful and willing objects of their husbands' desire.

Sex goddess Marilyn Monroe—shown here in *Gentlemen Prefer Blondes*—stirred the fantasies of American males in the 1950s. Despite the family orientation of suburban America, millions were captivated by her seductive appeal.

Cultural Rebels

Not all Americans fit the stereotypes of the 1950s. Some were alienated from the culture and rebelled against its values. Even as young people struggled to meet the standards and expectations of their peers, they were intrigued by Holden Caulfield, the main figure in J. D. Salinger's popular novel *The Catcher in the Rye* (1951). Holden, a sensitive student at boarding school, felt surrounded by "phonies" who threatened his individuality and independence. Holden's ill-fated effort to preserve his own integrity in the face of pressures to conform aroused readers' sympathy and struck a resonant chord in them.

Clothing

Clothing can be an important source of information about the past. The clothes people wear often announce their age, sex, and class, and frequently transmit some sense of their origin, occupation, and even their politics. The vocabulary of dress includes more than garments alone: hair styles, jewelry, and makeup all contribute to the way people choose to present themselves. Clothing can signal strong emotions; a torn, unbuttoned shirt, for example, can indicate that a person who seldom dresses that way is really upset. Bright colors can demonstrate a daring sense and a willingness to make a strong statement. By examining clothing styles in a number of different decades, we can begin to understand something of the changing patterns of people's lives.

In the 1920s, flappers and other women often dressed like children, with loose dresses usually in pastel colors ending just below the knee. Large trimmings, like huge artificial flowers, accentuated the effect. A "boyish" figure was considered most attractive. The clothes conveyed a feeling of playfulness and a willingness to embrace the freedom of the young. Men's suits in the same period were now made out of lighter materials, and looked less padded than before. As the tall, stiff collar of an earlier age disappeared and trousers became more high-waisted, men too had a more youthful look.

The Great Depression of the 1930s brought a change in style. Flappers now looked silly, especially as millions of people were starving. Advertisements and films promoted a new maturity and sophistication, more appropriate to hard times. Men's suits became heavier and darker, as if symbolically to provide protection in a bread line. Trousers were wider, and jackets were frequently double-breasted. Overcoats became longer. Women's clothes were likewise made out of heavier fabrics and used darker colors. Skirts fell, almost to the ankles on occasion, and were covered by longer coats. Clothes indicated that there was no place for the playfulness of the decade before.

As conditions improved during and after World War II, styles changed once more. In the 1940s, young teenage girls frequently wore bobby socks, rolled down to their ankles. Working women wore overalls, but with their own adornments to maintain their femininity. Rosie the Riveter, drawn by noted artist Norman Rockwell, wore her overalls proudly as she sat with a riveting gun in her lap and an attractive scarf around her hair. In the postwar years, the Man in the Gray Flannel Suit looked serious, sober, and well-tailored, ready to go work for corporate America. His female partner wanted to look equally worldly and sophisticated, and wore carefully tailored adult clothing, with the waist drawn in (often by a girdle) and heels as tall as three inches, when going out. The fashion industry helped define the decorative role women should play in supporting men as they advanced their business careers.

Then came the 1960s and an entirely new look. Casual clothing became a kind of uniform. The counterculture was a movement of the young, and clothing took on an increasingly youthful look. Skirts rose above the knee in 1963 and a few years later climbed to mid-thigh. Women began to wear pants and trouser suits. Men and women both favored jeans and informal shirts and let their hair grow longer. Men broke away from the gray suits of the preceding decade and indulged themselves in bright colors in what has been called the "peacock revolution."

Look carefully at the pictures on these pages. They show fashions from different periods and can tell

Harlem women in the 1920s.

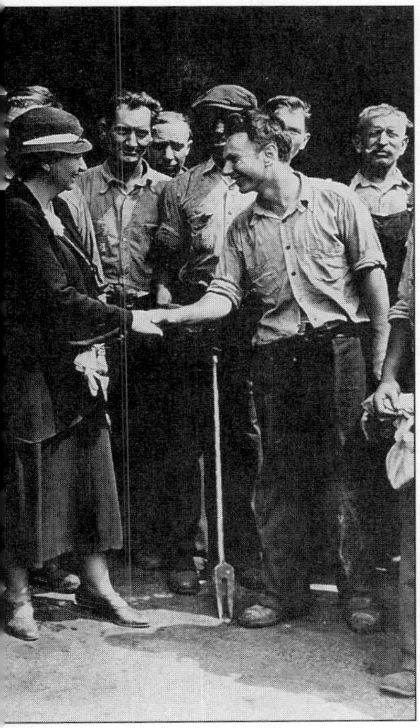

Frances Perkins with laborers in the 1930s.

World War II women at work.

A woman and child in the 1950s.

us a good deal about how these people defined themselves. Examine first the photo of the three black women from the 1920s. What kinds of adornments do you notice? What impression do these women convey?

Look at the photograph of Frances Perkins, Secretary of Labor in the 1930s. What kind of dress is she wearing? How do her clothes differ from those of the women in the 1920s? In the picture, she is talking to a number of working men. What do their clothes tell you about the kind of work they might be doing?

In the picture of two drill press operators during World War II, the women are dressed to handle the heavy machinery. Are their clothes different from those of the laborers in the preceding picture? How have the women accommodated themselves to their work, while still maintaining their individuality?

Now look at the picture of a woman in the 1950s. What kind of work might she do? What kind of flexibility do these clothes give her? What do the stylistic touches convey?

Finally, examine the photograph of the man and woman at an outdoor music festival in the 1960s. What does their clothing remind you of? Where might it come from? What impression are these people trying to create by their dress?

Countercultural dress in the 1960s.

A group of writers, often called the "beat generation," espoused unconventional values in their stories, poems, and "happenings." Confronting apathy and conformity, they insisted there were alternatives. Stressing spontaneity and spirituality, they claimed that intuition was more important than reason, Eastern mysticism more valuable than Western faith. The "beats" went out of their way to challenge the norms of respectability. They rejected materialism, engaged in overt sexual activity designed to shock, and helped popularize marijuana.

Their literary work reflected their approach to life. Finding conventional academic forms confining, they rejected them. Jack Kerouac typed his best-selling novel *On the Road* (1957), describing freewheeling trips across country, on a 250-foot roll of paper. Lacking conventional punctuation and paragraph structure, the book was a paean to the free life the beats espoused.

Poet Allen Ginsberg, like Kerouac a Columbia University dropout, became equally well known for his poem "Howl." Written during a wild weekend in 1955 while Ginsberg was under the influence of drugs, the poem was a scathing critique of the modern, mechanized culture and its effects.

Reading the poem to a group of poets in San Francisco, Ginsberg bobbed and weaved as he communicated the electric rhythm of his verse. He became a celebrity when "Howl" appeared in print in 1956. The poem developed into a cult piece, particularly after the police seized it on the grounds that it was obscene. When the work survived a court test, national acclaim followed for Ginsberg. He and the other beats would furnish a model for rebellion in the 1960s.

The popularity of Salinger, Kerouac, and Ginsberg owed much to a revolution in book publishing and to the democratization of education that accompanied the program of GI educational benefits. More Americans than ever before acquired a taste for literature, and they found huge numbers of inexpensive books available because of the "paperback revolution." The paperback, introduced in 1939, dominated the book market after World War II. By 1965, readers could choose among some 25,000 titles, available in bookstores, supermarkets, drugstores, and airplane terminals, and they purchased these cheap volumes at the rate of nearly 7 million copies per week.

The signs of cultural rebellion also appeared in popular music. Parents recoiled as their children flocked to hear a young Tennessee singer named Elvis Presley belt out rock and roll songs. Presley's sexy voice, gyrating hips, and other techniques borrowed from black singers helped make him the undisputed "king of rock and roll." A multimedia blitz of movies, television, and radio helped make songs like "Heartbreak Hotel," "Don't Be Cruel," and "Hound Dog" smash singles. Eighteen Presley hits sold more than a million copies in the last four years of the 1950s. His black leather jacket and ducktail haircut became standard dress for rebellious male teenagers.

American painters, shucking off European influences that had shaped American artists for two centuries, also became a part of the cultural rebellion. Led by Jackson Pollock and the "New York school," some artists discarded the easel, laid gigantic canvases on the floor, and then used trowels, putty knives, and sticks to apply paint, glass shards, sand, and other materials in wild explosions of color. Known as abstract expressionists, these painters regarded the unconscious as the source of their artistic creations. "I am not aware of what is taking place [as I paint]," Pollock explained; "it is only after that I see what I have done." Like much of the literature of rebellion, abstract expressionism reflected the artist's alienation from a world becoming filled with nuclear threats, computerization, and materialism.

Domestic Policy Under Truman and Eisenhower

In the prosperous postwar era, the political world reflected the structural changes taking place in the economic realm. Pressures from the expanding middle class influenced public policy. And tensions stemming from rapid growth helped shape the framework for political debate. Two dissimilar men exercised presidential leadership in the decade and a half after World War II. Democrat Harry S Truman took the same aggressive stance at home as he adopted in foreign affairs. A conservative Congress, however, blocked him at every turn. His Republican successor, Dwight D. Eisenhower, created a very different imprint. Genial and calm, even when facing an opposition

Congress himself, the war hero conveyed to Americans the feeling that everything was all right.

Reconversion

Truman's first priority when the war ended was reconversion—the transition to a peacetime economy. Servicemen wanted to come home quickly and deluged politicians with messages demanding demobilization. With such pressure, the GIs returned rapidly. The number on active duty dropped from 12 million in 1945 to 3 million in mid-1946 and to 1.6 million in mid-1947. The influx of ex-servicemen caused competition in the housing and employment markets and complicated the adjustment to civilian life.

Truman also recognized the need to keep the cap on inflation. Americans wanted to keep prices under control, but they also wished to end wartime restrictions imposed by the Office of Price Administration (OPA). In 1946, an increasingly conservative Congress extended the OPA's authority for another year but stripped it of enforcement powers. Furious, Truman vetoed the bill, even though this left the country without any control mechanism. Almost immediately, prices rose. Within a month, the cost-of-living index was up 6 points, and consumers began to demand action.

In Princeton, New Jersey, housewives calling themselves the Militant Marketers boycotted stores charging inflated prices. In Detroit, autoworkers shut down production lines for a day and congregated in Cadillac Square to protest. Eventually, Congress passed a weak bill to stem the tide, but the damage was done. A year and a half after the end of the war, the consumer price index was up almost 25 percent. One critic tartly observed that the OPA name and acronym should be changed to the Office for Cessation of Rationing and Priorities, or OCRAP.

Finally, Truman had to deal with the problem of labor unrest. Massive layoffs left 2.7 million workers without jobs by March 1946. Wage issues were also unresolved. After the wartime years of restraint, workers wanted pay increases they regarded as long overdue. Furthermore, many more of them belonged to unions. The percentage of nonagricultural workers who were union members rose from 13 percent in 1935 to 27 percent in 1940 and to 35 percent by 1945. When wage demands were refused, millions of workers walked out. In 1946, some 4.6 million workers marched on picket lines, more than had turned out ever before in the history of the United States. They struck in the automobile, steel, and electrical industries. The most serious threats came from workers on the railroads and in the soft-coal mines. When Truman argued that the national interest was compromised by strikes in those industries, he alienated many working-class Americans, a major segment of the Democratic coalition that his predecessor, Franklin Roosevelt, had put together in the 1930s.

Postwar Public Policy

Even as he grappled with the immediate problems of postwar reconversion, Truman addressed broader questions. Like Roosevelt, he believed that the federal government should move toward defined economic and social goals. To that end, less than a week after the end of World War II, Truman called on Congress to pass legislation guaranteeing all Americans jobs, decent housing, educational opportunities, and a variety of other rights. His 21-point program, he contended, would produce stability and security in the postwar era. He wanted full-employment legislation, a higher minimum wage, greater unemployment compensation, and housing assistance. During the next ten weeks, Truman sent blueprints of further proposals to Congress, including health insurance and atomic energy legislation. This liberal program soon ran into fierce political opposition.

The debate surrounding the Employment Act of 1946 hinted at the fate of Truman's proposals. The Employment Act was a deliberate effort to apply the theory of English economist John Maynard Keynes to maintain economic equilibrium and prevent depression. The initial bill committed the government to maintaining full employment by monitoring the economy and taking remedial actions in case of decline. Those actions included tax cuts and spending programs to stimulate the economy and reduce unemployment.

Liberals hailed the measure, but business groups like the National Association of Manufacturers claimed that such government intervention would undermine free enterprise and move the United States one step closer to socialism. Congress cut the proposal to bits. As finally passed, the act created a Council of Economic Advisers to make recommendations to the president, who was to report annually on the state of the economy. But it stopped short of committing the government to using fiscal tools to maintain full employment when economic indicators turned downward. The act was only a modest continuation of New Deal attempts at economic planning.

Truman Against a Conservative Congress

As the midterm elections of 1946 approached, Truman and his supporters knew they were vulnerable. Many Democrats still pined for FDR, and when they questioned what Roosevelt would have done had he been alive, the standard retort was, "I wonder what Truman would do if he were alive." Often seeming like a petty, bungling administrator, Truman became the butt of countless political jokes. Support for Truman dropped from 87 percent of those polled after he assumed the presidency to 32 percent in November 1946. Gleeful Republicans asked the voters, "Had enough?"

The voters answered that they had. Republicans won majorities in both houses of Congress for the first time since the 1928 elections, and a majority of the governorships as well. In Atlantic City, New Jersey, a Republican candidate for justice of the peace who had died a week before the election was victorious in the sweep.

After the 1946 election, Truman faced an unsympathetic 80th Congress. Republicans and conservative Democrats, dominating both houses, planned to reverse the liberal policies of the Roosevelt years. Hoping to reestablish congressional authority and cut the power of the executive branch, they insisted on less government intervention in the business world and in private life. Their goals included tax reduction and curtailment of the privileged position they felt labor had come to enjoy.

When the new Congress met, it moved to cut federal spending and reduce taxes. Robert A. Taft, Senate Republican leader, believed that cuts of $5 to $6 billion could be made to bring the budget down to $30 billion. In 1947, Congress twice passed tax-cut measures. Both times Truman vetoed them, but in 1948, another election year, Congress overrode the veto.

Congress also struck at Democratic labor policies. Republicans wanted to check labor unions, particularly their right to engage in the kind of disruptive strikes occurring immediately after the war. Early in Truman's presidency, Congress passed a bill requiring notice for strikes as well as a cooling-off period if a strike occurred. Truman had vetoed that measure. But in 1947, commanding more votes, the Republicans passed the Taft-Hartley Act, which intended to limit the power of unions by restricting the weapons they could employ. Revising the Wagner Act of 1935, the legislation spelled out unfair labor practices (such as preventing workers from working if they wished) and outlawed the closed shop whereby an employee had to join a union before getting a job. The law allowed states to prohibit the union shop, which forced workers to join the union after they had been hired. The act also gave the president the right to call for an 80-day cooling-off period in strikes affecting national security and required union officials to sign non-Communist oaths in order to use governmental machinery designed to protect their rights.

Understandably, union leaders and members were furious. As he vetoed the measure, Truman claimed that it was unworkable and unfair, then went on nationwide radio to seek public approval. He regained some of the support he had earlier lost by his aggressive antistrike position; however, Congress passed the Taft-Hartley measure over the president's veto.

The Fair Deal and Its Critics

In 1948, Truman was determined to win election in his own right. Some Democrats wanted to nominate Eisenhower or Supreme Court justice William O. Douglas, but that effort failed, leaving Truman with what most people thought was a worthless nomination. Not only was his own popularity waning, but the Democratic party itself seemed to be falling apart.

The civil rights issue—aimed at securing rights for black Americans—split the Democrats. Truman hoped to straddle the issue, at least until after the election, to avoid alienating the South. When liberals defeated a moderate platform proposal and pressed for a stronger stand on black civil rights, angry delegates from Mississippi and Alabama stormed out of the convention. They later formed the States' Rights, or Dixiecrat, party. At their own convention, delegates from 13 states nominated Governor J. Strom Thurmond of South Carolina as their presidential candidate and affirmed their support for continued racial segregation.

Meanwhile, Henry A. Wallace, for seven years secretary of agriculture, then vice-president during Roosevelt's third term and secretary of commerce after that, was mounting his own challenge. Truman had fired Wallace from his cabinet for supporting a more temperate stand on Soviet relations. Now Wallace became the presidential candidate of the Progressive party. Initially, he attracted widespread liberal interest because of his moderate position on Soviet-American affairs, his promotion of desegregation, and his promise to nationalize the railroads and major industries. But as Communists and "fellow travelers" appeared active in his organization, other support dropped off.

In that fragmented state, against the first real third-party challenges since 1912, the Democrats faced the Republicans, who coveted the White House after 16 years out of power. Once again they nominated Thomas E. Dewey, the governor of New York. Egocentric and stiff, Dewey was hardly a charismatic figure. Still, the polls uniformly picked the Republicans to win. Dewey saw little value in brawling with his opponent and campaigned, in the words of one commentator, "with the humorless calculation of a Certified Public Accountant in pursuit of the Holy Grail."

Truman, as the underdog, conducted a two-fisted campaign. He appealed to ordinary Americans as an unpretentious man engaged in an uphill fight. Believing that everyone was against him but the people, he addressed Americans in familiar language. He called the Republicans a "bunch of old mossbacks" out to destroy the New Deal. He attacked the "do nothing" 80th Congress, which he had called into special session in 1948 with instructions to live up to the Republican platform. Predictably, the legislators failed, providing Truman with handy ammunition. Speaking without a prepared text in his choppy, aggressive style, he warmed to crowds, and they warmed to him. "Give 'em hell, Harry," they yelled. "Pour it on." He did.

All the polls predicted a Republican victory. But the pollsters were wrong. On election day, despite the bold headline "Dewey Defeats Truman"

In one of the nation's most extraordinary political upsets, Harry Truman beat Thomas E. Dewey in 1948. Here an exuberant Truman holds a newspaper headline printed while he slept, before the vote turned his way.

in the *Chicago Daily Tribune,* the incumbent president scored one of the most unexpected political upsets in American history, winning 303-189 in the Electoral College. Democrats also swept both houses of Congress.

Truman won primarily because he was able to revive the major elements of the Democratic coalition that Franklin Roosevelt had constructed more than a decade before. Despite the rocky days of 1946, Truman managed to hold on to labor, farm, and black votes. The fragmentation of the Democratic party, which had threatened to hurt him severely, helped instead. The splinter parties drew off some votes but allowed Truman to make a more aggressive, direct appeal to the center, and that ultimately accounted for his success.

With the election behind him, Truman pursued his liberal program. In his 1949 State of the Union message, he declared, "Every segment of our population and every individual has a right to expect from our Government a fair deal." Fair Deal became the name for his domestic program, which included the measures he had proposed since 1945.

Some parts of Truman's Fair Deal worked; others did not. The minimum wage was raised, and social security programs were expanded. A housing program brought modest gains but did not really meet housing needs. A farm program, aimed at providing income support to farmers if prices fell, never made it through Congress. Most of his civil rights program failed to win congressional support. The American Medical Association undermined the effort to provide national health insurance, and Congress rejected a measure to provide federal aid to education.

In domestic affairs, Truman often seemed unpragmatic and too ambitious in his confrontations with a conservative and unsympathetic Congress. He frequently appeared most concerned with foreign policy as he strove to secure bipartisan support for Cold War initiatives (see Chapter 26). Committed to checking the perceived Soviet threat, he allowed his domestic program to suffer. As defense expenditures mounted, correspondingly less money was available for projects at home.

The Election of Eisenhower

In 1952, Truman had the support of only 23 percent of the American people, and all indicators pointed to a political shift. The Democrats nominated Adlai Stevenson, Illinois's able and articulate, moderately liberal governor. The Republicans turned to Dwight D. Eisenhower, the World War II hero Americans knew as Ike.

Stevenson approached political issues in intellectual terms. "Let's talk sense to the American people," he said, "Let's tell them the truth." While liberals loved his approach, Stevenson himself anticipated the probable outcome. How, he wondered, could a man named Adlai beat a soldier called Ike?

The Republicans focused on communism, corruption, and Korea as major issues and called the Democrats "soft on communism." They criticized assorted scandals surrounding Truman's cronies and friends. The president himself was

Presidential Elections, 1948–1956

Year	Candidates	Party	Popular Vote	Electoral Vote
1948	HARRY S TRUMAN	Democratic	24,105,812 (49.5%)	303
	Thomas E. Dewey	Republican	21,970,065 (45.1%)	189
	J. Strom Thurmond	States' Rights	1,169,063 (2.4%)	39
	Henry A. Wallace	Progressive	1,157,172 (2.4%)	0
1952	DWIGHT D. EISENHOWER	Republican	33,936,234 (55.1%)	442
	Adlai E. Stevenson	Democratic	27,314,992 (44.4%)	89
1956	DWIGHT D. EISENHOWER	Republican	35,590,472 (57.4%)	457
	Adlai E. Stevenson	Democratic	26,022,752 (42.0%)	73

Note: Winners' names appear in capital letters.

blameless, but some of the people near him were not. The Republicans also promised to end the unpopular Korean War.

Throughout the campaign, Eisenhower himself struck a grandfatherly pose, unified the various wings of his party, and went on to win a massive victory at the polls. He received 55 percent of the vote and carried 41 states. The new president took office with a Republican Congress as well and had little difficulty gaining a second term four years later.

"Modern Republicanism"

Eisenhower believed firmly in limiting the presidential role. Like the Republicans in Congress with whom Truman tangled, he wanted to restore balance in government and to reduce the growth of the federal government. In the process, however, he hoped to preserve gains of the preceding 20 years that even Republicans accepted. Eisenhower sometimes termed his approach "dynamic conservatism" or "modern Republicanism," which, he explained, meant "conservative when it comes to money, liberal when it comes to human beings."

Above all, economic concerns dominated the Eisenhower years. The president and his chief aides wanted desperately to preserve the value of the dollar, pare down levels of funding, cut taxes, and balance the budget after years of deficit spending.

To achieve those aims, the president appointed George Humphrey, a fiscal conservative, as secretary of the treasury. Humphrey placed a picture of Andrew Mellon, Calvin Coolidge's ultraconservative treasury head, in his office and declared, "We have to cut one-third out of the budget and you can't do that just by eliminating waste. This means, whenever necessary, using a meat axe." His words reflected the administration's approach to economic affairs. In times of economic stagnation, Republican leaders were willing to risk unemployment to keep inflation under control. The business orientation became obvious when Defense Secretary Charles E. Wilson, former president of General Motors, stated his position at confirmation hearings. "What was good for our country was good for General Motors," he declared, "and vice versa."

Eisenhower fulfilled his promise to reduce government's economic role. After support from oil interests in the campaign, the Republican Congress, with a strong endorsement from the president, passed the Submerged Lands Act in 1953. That measure transferred control of about $40 billion worth of oil lands from the federal government to the states. The *New York Times* called it "one of the greatest and surely the most unjustified give-away programs in all the history of the United States."

The administration also sought to reduce federal activity in the electric power field. Eisenhower favored private rather than public development of power. That sentiment came out clearly in a private comment about the Tennessee Valley Authority, the extensive public power and development project begun during the New Deal. "I'd like to see us sell the whole thing," he said, "but I suppose we can't go that far." Still, he opposed a TVA proposal for expansion to provide power to the Atomic Energy Commission and instead authorized a private group, the Dixon-Yates syndicate, to build a plant in Arkansas for that purpose. Later, when charges of scandal arose, the administration canceled the agreement, but the basic preference for private development remained.

Committed to supporting business interests, the administration sometimes saw its program backfire. As a result of its reluctance to stimulate the economy too much, the annual rate of economic growth declined from 4.3 percent between 1947 and 1952 to 2.5 percent between 1953 and 1960. The country suffered three recessions in Eisenhower's eight years. During the slumps, the deficits that Eisenhower so wanted to avoid increased.

Eisenhower's understated approach led to a legislative stalemate, particularly when the Democrats regained control of Congress in 1954. Opponents of the president gibed at Ike's restrained stance and laughed about limited White House leadership. One observed that Eisenhower proved that the country did not "need" a president. Another spoke of the Eisenhower doll—you wound it up, and it did nothing at all.

Yet Eisenhower understood just what he was doing and often actively pushed his favorite programs behind the scenes. By accepting the fundamental features of the welfare state the Democrats had created, he ensured its survival. For all the jokes at his expense, Eisenhower remained popular with the voters. He was one of the few presidents to leave office as highly regarded by the people as when he entered it. He was the kind of leader Americans wanted in prosperous times.

The Other America

In the years after World War II, not all Americans shared the prosperity of the growing middle class. While most Americans were unconscious of poverty, it existed in inner cities and rural areas. Nor did all Americans enjoy the same privileges, as became evident when minorities began to press for equal treatment and equal rights. Black Americans and Jews were in the forefront of the civil rights struggle. Hispanics and Native Americans, inspired by their own history of struggle as well as by the model of black protest, also became activists but moved more slowly than African-Americans.

Poverty amid Affluence

Many people in the "affluent society" lived in poverty. Economic growth favored the upper and middle classes. Although the popular "trickle-down" theory argued that economic expansion benefited all classes, little, in fact, reached the citizens at the bottom of the ladder. In 1960, according to the Federal Bureau of Labor Statistics, a yearly subsistence-level income for a family of four was $3,000 and for a family of six, $4,000. The Bureau reported that 40 million people (almost a quarter of the population) lived below those levels and nearly the same number only marginally above the line. Two million migrant workers labored long hours for a subsistence wage. Many less mobile people were hardly better off. According to the 1960 census, 27 percent of the residential units in the United States were substandard, and even acceptable dwellings were often hopelessly overcrowded in some slums.

Michael Harrington, Socialist author and critic, shocked the country with his 1962 study, *The Other America.* The poor, Harrington argued, were everywhere. He described New York City's "economic underworld," where "Puerto Ricans and Negroes, alcoholics, drifters, and disturbed people" haunted employment agencies for temporary positions as "dishwashers and day workers, the fly-by-night jobs." In the afternoon, "the jobs have all been handed out, yet the people still mill around. Some of them sit on benches in the larger offices. There is no real point to their waiting, yet they have nothing else to do."

Harrington also showed the rural poor living in what songwriter Woody Guthrie called the "pastures of plenty." The mountain folk of Appalachia, the tenant farmers of Mississippi, and the migrant farmers of Florida, Texas, and California were all caught in poverty's relentless cycle.

Black Americans and Civil Rights

Blacks became increasingly restive in the post–World War II years, particularly as economic changes affected traditional employment patterns and political shifts held out the possibility of further reform. In the South, New Deal farm legislation, the popularity of synthetic fabrics, and foreign competition robbed "King Cotton" of world markets. As cotton farmers turned to less labor-intensive crops like soybeans and peanuts, they ousted their tenants. Between 1930 and 1960, the southern agricultural population declined from 16 million to 6 million. Millions of blacks moved to southern cities, where they found better jobs, better schooling, and freedom from landlord control. Some achieved middle-class status. Still not entirely free, these southern blacks were now ready to attack Jim Crow.

Millions of African-Americans also headed for northern cities between 1940 and 1960. In the 1950s, Detroit's black population increased from 16 to 29 percent, Chicago's from 14 to 23 percent. But the experiences of African-Americans in the cities proved different from what they had expected. As author Claude Brown recalled, blacks were told that in the North, "Negroes lived in houses with bathrooms, electricity, running water, and indoor toilets. To them, this was the 'promised land' that Mammy had been singing about in the cotton fields for many years." But no one had told them "about one of the most important aspects of the promised land: it was a slum ghetto. . . . There were too many people full of hate and bitterness crowded into a dirty, stinky, uncared-for closet-size section of a great city." Since northern blacks could vote and usually voted for the Democrats, civil rights became an issue that northern Democratic leaders had to confront.

Black Americans had increased their demands for change during World War II. They had wrested some concessions (see Chapter 25) but not enough to satisfy rising black aspirations. Meanwhile, black servicemen returning from the war vowed to reject second-class citizenship and helped mobilize a grass-roots movement. At the same time, wars of national liberation inspired black American leaders. The desire for black equality appeared as part of a wider struggle. As Adam Clayton Powell, a Harlem preacher (and later congressman), warned, the black man "is ready to throw himself into the struggle to make the dream of America become flesh and blood, bread and butter, freedom and equality. He walks conscious of the fact that he is no longer alone—no longer a minority."

The racial question was dramatized in 1947 when Jackie Robinson broke the color line and began playing major-league baseball with the Brooklyn Dodgers. Sometimes teammates were hostile, sometimes opponents crashed into him with spikes flying high, but Robinson kept his frustrations to himself. A splendid first season helped ease the way, and after Robinson's trail-blazing effort, other blacks, formerly confined to the old Negro leagues, started to move into the major leagues, then into professional football and basketball.

Americans began to respond as their racial problems became entangled with Cold War politics. As leader of the "free world," America appealed for support in Africa and Asia. Discrimination in the United States was an obvious drawback in the struggle to gain new friends. Now there was another compelling reason for whites to confront racial problems at home.

A somewhat reluctant Truman supported the civil rights movement. A moderate on racial questions of race who believed in political, not social, equality, he responded to the growing strength of the black vote. He saw that black interests needed protection and realized that particularly in urban areas, black support could mean the difference between victory and defeat.

Truman first moved in 1946 when the National Emergency Committee Against Mob Violence told him of lynchings and other brutalities still taking place in the South. Disturbed by the

Jackie Robinson's electrifying play as the first black in the major leagues led to acceptance of the integration of baseball. A spectacular rookie season in 1947 opened the way for other African-Americans who had earlier been limited to the Negro leagues.

account and determined to end such terror, he appointed a Committee on Civil Rights to investigate the problem and make recommendations. The committee's report, released in October 1947, charged that black Americans remained second-class citizens in every area of American life. The first report of its type, it documented unequal treatment in education, housing, and medical care. It was time, the committee vehemently asserted, for the federal government to secure the rights of all Americans, and it set a civil rights agenda for the next two decades.

Though Truman hedged at first, the changing political situation and his own notion of justice prompted him to act. In February 1948, he sent a ten-point civil rights program to Congress—the first presidential civil rights plan since Reconstruction. When the southern wing of the Democratic party bolted later that year, he moved forward even more aggressively. First he issued an executive order barring discrimination in the federal establishment. Then he ordered equality of treatment in the military services. A committee appointed in 1948 oversaw the implementation of the policy and ended military segregation. Equal opportunities for all Americans in the navy, air force, marine corps, and, after some resistance, in the army were now promised. Manpower needs in the Korean War led to the elimination of the last restrictions, particularly when the army found that integrated units performed well.

Elsewhere the administration pushed reforms. The Justice Department, not previously supportive of NAACP litigation on behalf of equal rights for African-Americans, entered the battle against segregation and filed briefs challenging the constitutionality of restrictions in housing, education, and interstate transportation. Those helped build the pressure for change that influenced the Supreme Court. Congress, however, did little. Though Truman called for laws guaranteeing equal rights, southern Democrats like Virginia representative Howard W. Smith and Mississippi senators John Stennis and James Eastland headed committees and subcommittees responsible for considering such legislation. Liberal measures hardly had a chance.

Integrating the Schools

As the civil rights struggle gained momentum during the 1950s, the judicial system played a crucial role. The NAACP was determined to overturn the 1896 Supreme Court decision *Plessy* v. *Ferguson,* in which the Court had declared that segregation of the black and white races was constitutional if the facilities used by each were "separate but equal." The decree had been used for generations to sanction rigid segregation, primarily in the South, even though separate facilities were seldom, if ever, equal. In attempting to remove this judicial roadblock to black equality, the NAACP, working through its Legal Defense Fund, had fought and won many cases over the previous decades.

A direct challenge came in 1951 when Oliver Brown, the father of 8-year-old Linda Brown, sued the school board of Topeka, Kansas, to allow his daughter to attend a school for white children that she passed as she walked to the bus that carried her to a black school farther away. Rebuffed in the local federal court (even though the Kansas judge disagreed with segregation), the plaintiffs appealed, and the case reached the Supreme Court, whose justices were fully aware of the importance of the case. Schools in 21 states and the District of Columbia were segregated at the time, and the Court's ruling would affect them all. Adding other school segregation cases to the one before it, the Court confronted the legal questions.

On May 17, 1954, the Supreme Court released its bombshell ruling in *Brown* v. *Board of Education.* For more than a decade, Supreme Court decisions had gradually expanded black civil rights, and now the Court unanimously decreed that "separate facilities are inherently unequal" and concluded that the "separate but equal" doctrine had no place in public education. A year later, the Court turned to the question of implementation and declared that local school boards, acting with the guidance of lower courts, should move "with all deliberate speed" to desegregate their facilities.

Charged with the ultimate responsibility for executing the law was Dwight Eisenhower. Doubting that simple changes in the law could improve race relations, he once observed, "I don't believe you can change the hearts of men with laws or decisions." Privately commenting on the *Brown* ruling, he said, "I personally think the decision was wrong." Though reluctant to act aggressively, the president knew that it was his constitutional duty to see that the law was carried out.

Eisenhower moved quickly. Even while urging sympathy for the South in its period of transition, he acted immediately to desegregate the Washington, D.C., schools as a model for the rest of the country. He sought to end continuing discrimination in other areas too, mandating desegregation in navy yards and veterans' hospitals.

Even so, the South resisted. In district after district, vicious scenes occurred. White children often echoed the feelings of their parents. One Tennessee teacher heard such taunts as "If you come back to school, I'll cut your guts out." Blacks endured eggs splattered on their books, ink spread on their clothes, and worse.

The crucial confrontation erupted in Little Rock, Arkansas, in 1957. A desegregation plan, to begin with the token admission of a few black students to Central High School, was ready to go into effect. Just before the school year began, Governor Orval Faubus declared on television that it would not be possible to maintain order if integration took place. National Guardsmen, posted by the governor to keep the peace and armed with bayonets, turned away nine black students from the school. After three weeks, a federal court ordered the troops to leave. When the black children entered the school building, the white students, spurred on by their elders, belligerently opposed them, chanting such slogans as "Two, four, six, eight, we ain't gonna integrate." In the face of hostile mobs, the black children left the school.

With the lines drawn, attention focused on the moderate man in the White House. While the Guardsmen were still at the school, the president had met with the Arkansas governor and had taken a cautious stand, hoping that the crisis would dissolve of its own accord. Now, however, he faced a situation in which Little Rock whites were clearly defying the law. As a former military

National Guardsmen, under federal command, escorted black students into Central High School in Little Rock, Arkansas, in 1957. Notice the number of students and the number of soldiers as forcible integration began.

officer, Ike knew that such resistance could not be tolerated. He denounced the "disgraceful occurrence," urged those obstructing the law to "cease and desist," and finally took the one action he had earlier called unthinkable.

For the first time since the end of Reconstruction, an American president called out federal troops to protect the rights of black citizens. He ordered paratroopers to Little Rock and placed National Guardsmen under federal command. The black children entered the school and attended classes with the military protecting their rights. Thus desegregation began.

Montgomery and the Stride Toward Freedom

Meanwhile, African-Americans themselves began organizing in ways that advanced the civil rights movement. The crucial event occurred in Montgomery, Alabama, in December 1955. Rosa Parks, a 42-year-old black seamstress who was also secretary of the Alabama NAACP, sat down in the front of a bus in a section reserved by custom for whites. Tired from a hard day's work, she refused the order to move back. Told she would be arrested, she quietly remained in her seat. The bus driver called the police at the next stop, and Parks was arrested and ordered to stand trial for violating the segregation laws. Although she had not intended to challenge the law or cause a scene, her stance marked a new phase in the civil rights movement. Like Rosa Parks, ordinary black men and women would challenge the racial status quo and force both white and black leaders to respond.

In Montgomery, black civil rights officials seized the issue. E. D. Nixon, state NAACP president, told Parks, "This is the case we've been looking for. We can break this situation on the bus with your case." Though Parks knew she would lose her job, she agreed to cooperate. The next evening, resistance began. Fifty black leaders met to discuss the case and decided to organize a massive boycott of the bus system. Martin Luther King, Jr., the 27-year-old minister of the Baptist church where the meeting was held, soon emerged as the preeminent spokesman of the protest. King held a Ph.D. in philosophy in addition to religious credentials. He was an impressive figure and an inspiring speaker. In his moving speeches, he conveyed his concern at the economic and social discrimination black Americans endured. "There comes a time when people get tired . . . of being kicked about by the brutal feet of oppression," he declared. It was time to be more assertive, to cease being "patient with any-

Baptist minister Martin Luther King, Jr., emerged as the black spokesman in the Montgomery, Alabama, bus boycott and soon became the most eloquent African-American leader of the entire civil rights movement. Drawing on his religious background, he was able to mobilize blacks and whites alike in the struggle for equal rights.

thing less than freedom and justice." The black clergy was to play a vital role in mobilizing civil rights protesters in the next two decades.

Although King was arrested, as he was to be many times, grass-roots support bubbled up. In Montgomery, 50,000 African-Americans walked or formed car pools to avoid the transit system. Their actions cut gross revenue on city buses by 65 percent. Almost a year later, the Supreme Court ruled that bus segregation, like school segregation, violated the Constitution, and the boycott ended. But the mood it fostered continued, and peaceful protest became a way of life for many blacks.

Meanwhile, a concerted effort developed to guarantee black voting rights. The provisions of the Fifteenth Amendment notwithstanding, many states had circumvented the law for decades (see Chapter 16). Some required a poll tax or a literacy test or an examination of constitutional understanding. Blacks often found themselves excluded from the polls.

Eisenhower believed in the right to vote yet he harbored reservations. "I personally believe if you try to go too far too fast in this delicate field that has involved the emotions of so many millions of Americans," he declared, "you are making a mistake." As a bill worked its way through Congress, Ike helped little. He seemed unsure about specific provisions and adopted a characteristically restrained stance toward congressional actions.

Largely because of the legislative genius of Senate majority leader Lyndon B. Johnson of Texas, the civil rights bill, the first since Reconstruction, moved toward passage. With his eye on the presidency, Johnson wanted to establish his credentials as a man who could look beyond narrow southern interests. Paring the bill down to the provisions he felt would pass, Johnson pushed the measure through.

The Civil Rights Act of 1957 created a Civil Rights Commission and empowered the Justice Department to go to court in cases where blacks were denied the right to vote. The bill was a compromise measure, yet it was the first successful effort to protect civil rights in 82 years.

To plug loopholes and add enforcement mechanisms to the 1957 act, civil rights activists worked for another measure. Johnson again took the lead, and after breaking a filibuster, he helped secure the Civil Rights Act of 1960. It set stiffer punishments for people who interfered with the right to vote, but because it stopped short of authorizing federal registrars to register blacks to vote, it was generally ineffective.

The civil rights movement made important strides during the Eisenhower years, though little of the progress resulted from the president's leadership. Rather, the efforts of blacks themselves and the rulings of the Supreme Court brought significant change. The period of grass-roots civil rights activities, now launched, would continue in the 1960s.

Growing Chicano Consciousness

The effort to protest discrimination ranged beyond black protest and was, in fact, national in scope. Spanish-speaking groups coming from Cuba, Puerto Rico, Mexico, and Central America, often unskilled and illiterate, followed other less fortunate Americans to the cities. Like black Americans, they strove to improve their lives and to claim the rights enjoyed by white Americans but were less successful in their quest.

Chicanos, or Mexican-Americans, the most numerous of the newcomers, faced peculiar difficulties and widespread discrimination. During World War II, as the country faced a labor shortage at home, American farmers sought Mexican *braceros* (helping hands) to harvest their crops. A program to encourage the seasonal immigration of farm workers continued after the war when the government signed a Migratory Labor Agreement with Mexico. Between 1948 and 1964, some 4.5 million Mexicans were brought to the United States for temporary work. *Braceros* were expected to return to Mexico at the end of their labor contract, but often they stayed. Joining them were millions more who entered the country illegally.

Conditions were harsh for the *braceros* in the best of times. In periods of economic difficulty, troubles worsened. During the 1953–1954 recession, the government mounted Operation Wetback to deport illegal entrants and *braceros* who had remained in the country illegally. Deportations numbered 1.1 million. As immigration officials searched out illegal workers, all Chicanos found themselves vulnerable. They bitterly protested the violations of their rights, to little effect.

Operation Wetback did not end the reliance

Chicanos, like these in the broccoli fields of Texas, often faced grim conditions in their effort to make a living. Many were migrant workers who took temporary jobs on American farms, then moved on when their work was done, without ever enjoying the security or stability of permanent employment.

on Mexican farm laborers. A coalition of southern Democrats and conservative Republicans, mostly representing farm states, extended the Migratory Labor Agreement with Mexico. Two years after the massive deportations of 1954, a record 445,000 *braceros* crossed the border to work on American farms.

The political attacks in the heated days of the Red Scare also meant persecution for Chicano radical activists. Agapito Gómez had lived in the United States for 25 years. He had an American-born wife. Nonetheless, he found himself questioned for past union activities. In the 1930s, he had been part of a Depression relief organization and had joined the CIO. When he refused to divulge the names of people with whom he had worked, immigration officials confiscated his alien card. José Noriega found himself in the same position. He had been in the United States for more than 40 years. He too had a union past, as a member of a longshoremen's association. When questioned in 1952, like Gómez, he refused to cooperate. The government initiated deportation proceedings.

In addition to economic oppression, Chicanos in all walks of life faced discrimination in the schools, uncertain access to public facilities, and occasional exclusion from the governing process. The post–World War II years saw increasing political awareness on the part of Mexican-Americans and new aggressiveness in fighting for their rights.

Social changes lay behind many of the political developments. Jobs drew hundreds of thousands of Mexicans from rural areas into cities and trapped them in impoverished *barrios*. Mexican-Americans returning from wartime service, where they had often been racially invisible, chafed under continuing discrimination at home.

Sometimes action stemmed from a particular event. Chicanos, for example, established the American GI Forum because a Texas funeral home refused to bury a Mexican-American casualty of World War II. When the group's protest led to a burial in Arlington National Cemetery, the possibilities of concerted action became clear. The Community Service Organization was another new group that mobilized Chicanos against discrimination, as did the more radical Asociación Nacional México-Americana. And the League of United Latin American Citizens continued efforts to promote educational programs and other reforms.

Meanwhile, in the waning months of the war, a court case challenging Mexican-American segregation in the schools began. Gonzalo Méndez, an asparagus grower and a U.S. citizen who had lived in Orange County, California, for 25 years, filed suit to permit his children to attend the school reserved for Anglo-Americans, which was far more attractive than the Mexican one to which they had been assigned. A federal district court upheld his claim in the spring of 1945, and two years later, the circuit court affirmed the original ruling. With the favorable decision, other communities filed similar suits and began to press for integration of their schools.

The advance, however, came slowly. In the late 1940s, many Chicanos sought official classification as Caucasian, hoping that the change would lead to better treatment. But even when the designation changed, their status did not. They still faced discrimination and police brutality, particularly in the cities with the largest Chicano populations.

Los Angeles, with its large number of Chicanos, was the scene of numerous unsavory racial episodes. In mid-1951, on receiving a complaint about a loud record player, police officers raided a baptismal gathering at the home of Simon Fuentes. Breaking into the house without a warrant, they assaulted the members of the party. In another incident at the end of the year, in the "Bloody Christmas" case, officers removed seven Mexican-Americans from jail cells and beat them severely.

Protests continued, yet in the 1950s, Chicano activism was fragmented. Some Mexican-Americans considered their situation hopeless. While new and aggressive challenges appeared, fully effective mobilization had to wait for another day.

Native Americans and Termination

American Indians also faced great difficulties in defending their interests and securing their rights. Not only did they have to fight the forces of cultural change that were eroding tribal tradition, but they also had to resist the federal government's reversal of New Deal Indian policy.

In the postwar years, Indians faced the same technological developments affecting other Americans. As power lines reached the reservations, Indians purchased televisions, refrigerators, washing machines, and automobiles. This inevitably changed old ways of life. Indians who gravitated to the cities often had difficulty adjusting to urban life and faced discrimination much like that experienced by Mexican-Americans and blacks.

Just after the end of World War II, Native Americans achieved an important victory when Congress established the Indian Claims Commission. The commission was mandated to review tribal cases arguing that ancestral lands had been illegally taken from them through violation of federal treaties. Hundreds of tribal suits against the government in federal courts were now possible. Many of them would lead to large settlements of cash—a form of reparation for past injustices—and sometimes the return of long-lost lands.

The Eisenhower administration, determined to cut back on federal activity wherever possible, dramatically turned away from the New Deal policy of government support for tribal autonomy. In the Indian Reorganization Act of 1934, the government had stepped in to restore lands to tribal ownership and end their loss or sale to outsiders. In 1953, instead of trying to encourage Native American self-government, the administration adopted a new approach, known as the "termination" policy. The government proposed settling all outstanding claims and eliminating reservations as legitimate political entities. To encourage their assimilation into mainstream society, the government offered small subsidies to families who would leave the reservations and relocate in the cities.

The new policy victimized the Indians. With their lands no longer federally protected and their members deprived of treaty rights, many tribes became unwitting victims of people who wanted to seize their land, just as they had been throughout the nineteenth century. Though promising more freedom, the new policy caused great disruption as the government terminated tribes like the Klamaths in Oregon, the Menominees in Wisconsin, the Alabamas and Coushattas in Texas, and bands of Paiutes in Utah. At the same time, the policy spurred Indian activism and gave greater strength to the National Congress of

American Indians, their leading national organization. That group mobilized tribes as well as non-Indian organizations in opposition to the federal program. A Seminole petition to the president in 1954 summed up a general view:

> We do not say that we are superior or inferior to the White Man and we do not say that the White Man is superior or inferior to us. We do say that we are not White Men but Indians, do not wish to become White Men but wish to remain Indians, and have an outlook on all things different from the outlook of the White Man.

Not only did the termination policy foster a sense of Indian identity, but it also sparked a dawning awareness among whites of the Indians' right to maintain their heritage. In 1958, the Eisenhower administration changed the policy of termination so that it required a tribe's consent. The policy continued to have the force of law, but implementation ceased.

CONCLUSION

Qualms amid Affluence

In general, the United States during the decade and a half after World War II was stable and secure. Structural adjustments caused occasional moments of friction but were seldom visible in prosperous times. Recessions occurred periodically, but the economy righted itself after short downturns. For the most part, business boomed. Millions of middle-class Americans joined the ranks of suburban property owners, enjoying the benefits of shopping centers and fast-food establishments and other material manifestations of what they considered the good life.

Some Americans, however, did not share in the prosperity, but they were not visible in the affluent suburbs. Though black Americans and other minority groups were beginning to mobilize, their protest remained peaceful. Many still believed they could share in the American dream and remained confident that deeply rooted patterns of discrimination could be changed.

Toward the end of the 1950s, after the Soviet Union became the first nation to place a satellite in orbit, a wave of anxiety swept the nation. Some Americans began to criticize the materialism that had apparently caused the nation to fall behind. Critics began to explore questions of national purpose. Raising these questions made them more willing to criticize other shortcomings in American life. It also legitimated challenges by other groups.

Criticisms and anxieties notwithstanding, the United States—for most whites and some people of color—continued to develop according to Ray Kroc's dreams as he first envisioned McDonald's establishments across the land. The standard of living for many of the nation's citizens reached new heights, especially compared with standards in many parts of the world. Healthy and comfortable, upper- and middle-class Americans expected prosperity and growth to continue in the years ahead.

Recommended Reading

Domestic Issues

Lois W. Banner, *American Beauty* (1983); Peter Blake, *God's Own Junkyard: The Planned Deterioration of America's Landscape* (1964); David Brody, *Workers in Industrial America* (1980); James R. Green, *The World of the Worker* (1980); Samuel P. Hays, *Beauty, Health, and Permanence: Environmental Politics in the United States, 1955–1985* (1987); Kenneth T. Jackson, *Crabgrass Frontier: The Suburbanization of the United States* (1985); William E. Leuchtenburg, *A Troubled Feast* (1983); Alison Lurie, *The Language of Clothes* (1981); Zane L. Miller, *The Urbanization of Modern America* (1973); Richard

Polenberg, *One Nation Divisible: Class, Race, and Ethnicity in the United States Since 1938* (1980); David Riesman, *The Lonely Crowd: A Study of the Changing American Character* (1950); J. D Salinger, *The Catcher in the Rye* (novel, 1951); Sloan Wilson, *The Man in the Gray Flannel Suit* (novel, 1955).

Religious Developments

David Chidester, *Patterns of Power: Religion and Politics in American Culture* (1988); Peter W. Williams, *Popular Religion in America: Symbolic Change and the Modernization Process in Historical Perspective* (1980); Garry Wills, *Under God: Religion and American Politics* (1990).

Harry S Truman

Barton J. Bernstein and Allen J. Matusow, *The Truman Administration: A Documentary History* (1966); Robert J. Donovan, *Conflict and Crisis: The Presidency of Harry S Truman, 1945–1948* (1977) and *Tumultuous Years: The Presidency of Harry S Truman* (1982); Robert H. Ferrell, *Harry S. Truman and the Modern American Presidency* (1983); Alonzo L. Hamby, *Harry S. Truman and the Fair Deal* (1974); David McCullough, *Truman* (1992); Cabell Phillips, *The Truman Presidency: The History of a Triumphant Succession* (1966); Harry S Truman, *Memoirs*, 2 vols. (1955, 1956).

Dwight D. Eisenhower

Charles C. Alexander, *Holding the Line: The Eisenhower Era, 1952–1961* (1975); Stephen E. Ambrose, *Eisenhower: The President* (1984); Dwight D. Eisenhower, *Mandate for Change, 1953–1956* (1963) and *Waging Peace* (1965); Fred I. Greenstein, *The Hidden-Hand Presidency: Eisenhower as Leader* (1982); Peter Lyon, *Eisenhower: Portrait of the Hero* (1974); Herbert S. Parmet, *Eisenhower and the American Crusades* (1972); Gary W. Reichard, *The Reaffirmation of Republicanism: Eisenhower and the 83rd Congress* (1975).

Women's Role in the 1950s

Beth L. Bailey, *From Front Porch to Back Seat: Courtship in Twentieth-Century America* (1988); William H. Chafe, *The American Woman: Her Changing Social, Economic, and Political Roles, 1920–1970* (1972); John D'Emilio and Estelle B. Freedman, *Intimate Matters: A History of Sexuality in America* (1988); Sara Evans, *Born for Liberty: A History of Women in America* (1989); Betty Friedan, *The Feminine Mystique* (1963); Elaine Tyler May, *Homeward Bound: American Families in the Cold War Era* (1988).

The Civil Rights Movement

Taylor Branch, *Parting the Waters: America in the King Years, 1954–1963* (1988); David J. Garrow, *Bearing the Cross: Martin Luther King, Jr., and the Southern Christian Leadership Conference* (1986); Richard Kluger, *Simple Justice* (1975); Harvard Sitkoff, *The Struggle for Black Equality, 1954–1980* (1981).

Other Minority Struggles

Rodolfo Acuña, *Occupied America: A History of Chicanos* (3d ed., 1988); Frederick E. Hoxie, ed., *Indians in American History* (1988); Alvin M. Josephy, Jr., *Now That the Buffalo's Gone* (1982).

TIMELINE

1944 GI Bill passed

1945 World War II ends
Wave of strikes in heavy industries

1946 Truman vetoes bill extending Office of Price Administration
Prices rise by 25 percent in 18 months
Union strikes in the auto, coal, steel, and electrical industries
Employment Act
Benjamin Spock's *Baby and Child Care*

1947 Taft-Hartley Act
Jackie Robinson breaks the color line in major-league baseball

1948 Executive order bars discrimination in federal government
Armed forces begin to desegregate
"Dixiecrat" party formed
Truman defeats Dewey
Kinsey report on human sexuality
Transistor developed at Bell Laboratories

1949 Truman launches Fair Deal

1950 Asociación Nacional México-Americana formed

1951 J. D. Salinger's *Catcher in the Rye*

1952 Dwight D. Eisenhower elected president

1953 Submerged Lands Act

1954 *Brown* v. *Board of Education*

1955 Montgomery, Alabama, bus boycott begins
First McDonald's opens in Illinois
AFL and CIO merge

1956 Eisenhower reelected
Interstate Highway Act
Allen Ginsberg's "Howl"

1957 Little Rock school integration crisis
Civil Rights Act
Baby boom peaks with 4.3 million births
Soviet Union launches *Sputnik*

1959 One-third of all Americans reside in suburbs

1960 Three-fourths of all families own a TV
Civil Rights Act
GNP hits $500 billion

CHAPTER 28

The Rise and Fall of the Liberal State

Ron Kovic was an all-American boy. Born in 1946, he grew up on Long Island. Life was secure in the comfortable post–World War II years, as Kovic shared the dreams of millions of others his age. "I loved baseball more than anything else in the world," he later recalled, "playing catch-a-fly-you're-up for hours with a beat-up old baseball. We played all day long out there, running across that big open field with all our might, diving and sliding face-first into the grass, making one-handed, spectacular catches."

When baseball did not occupy him, television did. "The whole block grew up watching television," he observed. "There was Howdy Doody and Rootie Kazootie, Cisco Kid and Gabby Hayes, Roy Rogers and Dale Evans. The Lone Ranger was on Channel 7. We watched cartoons for hours on Saturdays."

Anxious moments occasionally intervened. Kovic, like others, wondered how the Russians had managed to put a satellite into space before the United States. He grew up fearing the "Communist threat" and even became persuaded that Communists "were infiltrating our schools, trying to take over our classes and control our minds." Yet that fear was but a reflection of the patriotism of his day. Like most Americans, Kovic had an unquestioning confidence in the "American way." Moreover, he had been born on the Fourth of July and could take the words of "I'm a Yankee Doodle Dandy" to heart as holiday fireworks went off.

Caught up in the spirit of the New Frontier, Kovic was stunned when President John F. Kennedy was shot. "I truly felt I had lost a dear friend," he wrote. "I was deeply hurt. . . . The pain stuck with me for a long time after he died."

Still, life went on, and Kovic remained intent on doing something for his nation. After graduating from high school, Kovic enlisted in the marines. The desire to be a hero drove him on, carried him through basic training, and stayed with him through a first tour of duty in the war in Vietnam. Proud of what he was doing, he signed up for a second tour. Only then did the conflict begin to tear him apart.

Kovic wanted to win medals, to be brave, but instead was increasingly haunted by his conduct in the war. He accidently shot and killed an American corporal and, as if to atone for his deed, plunged on even more aggressively, certain that he was "serving America in this its most critical hour, just like President Kennedy had talked about." Yet that effort, too, ended in disaster when men in his unit shot at shadowy figures moving in a village hut, only to learn that they had killed and wounded innocent children.

Later Kovic was hit in the foot and then took a 30-caliber sniper bullet in the spine. The pain in his foot vanished, but so did all sensation below his chest. Suddenly, all he could feel was "the worthlessness of dying right here in this place at this moment for nothing."

Ron Kovic returned from the war paralyzed from the chest down. As he went from hospital to hospital, seeing the muscle tone of his legs disappear, he became overwhelmed by despair, heightened by the growing opposition to the war in the United States. Kovic grew to believe that he had been trapped in a meaningless crusade and then left to dangle on his own. He became one of the many protesters who finally helped bring the war to an end.

Yet he could never forget the price he had paid. "I feel like a big clumsy puppet with all his strings cut," he wrote. Even more poignantly he observed:

I am the living death
the memorial day on wheels
I am your yankee doodle dandy
your john wayne come home
your fourth of july firecracker
exploding in the grave

Ron Kovic's passage through the 1960s and 1970s reflected that of American society as a whole. Millions of Americans shared his views as the period began. Mostly comfortable and confident, they supported the liberal agenda advanced by the Democratic party of John Kennedy and Lyndon Johnson. They endorsed the proposition that the government had responsibility for the welfare of all its citizens and accepted the need for a more active governmental role to help those who were unable to help themselves. That commitment lay behind the legislative achievements of the "Great Society," the last wave of twentieth century reform that built upon the gains of the Progressive era and the New Deal years before. Then political reaction set in, as the country, like Ron Kovic, was torn apart by the ravages of the Vietnam War. Republicans who assumed power at the end of the 1960s accepted the basic outlines of the welfare state but rejected many of the liberal initiatives of Democratic administrations as expensive failures. Under Richard Nixon and Gerald Ford, Republicans capitalized on disillusionment with federal policy and crafted a new consensus that kept them in the White House for most of the next decade and a half.

This chapter describes both the climax of twentieth-century liberalism and its subsequent decline. We will examine first the Democratic initiatives, then the Republican responses, as American politics shifted course in the 1960s and 1970s. In pondering the possibilities of reform, we will outline the various efforts to devise an effective political response to structural changes in the post–World War II economy and follow the fate of those efforts as they became intertwined with the nation's ill-conceived anti-Communist crusade in Vietnam.

The High Water Mark of Liberalism

American priorities changed as Dwight Eisenhower came to the end of his second term. The Republican administration's acceptance of New Deal and Fair Deal commitments helped to create a consensus on the major role of the federal government in American life. The Democrats who won office in the 1960s wanted to broaden that role. Dismayed at the problems of poverty, unemployment, and racism, they sought to manage the economy more effectively, eradicate poverty, and protect the civil rights of all Americans. Midway through the decade they came close to achieving their goals.

Liberal Leadership

The liberal Democratic leaders of the 1960s took an activist view of the presidency. They believed that the president should set national priorities and then work closely with Congress to ensure the passage of legislation. Whereas Eisenhower had been more comfortable working behind the scenes with legislators, first John Kennedy, then Lyndon Johnson, hoped to use the White House as a "bully pulpit" as Theodore Roosevelt had done. Kennedy encountered fierce resistance from the legislative branch; Johnson was far more successful in implementing his program.

John F. Kennedy, who won the presidency in 1960, seemed to symbolize the commitment to energetic leadership. At 43, he was the youngest man ever elected president. Son of a former ambassador to England and grandson of an Irish-American mayor of Boston, he appeared vigorous and articulate, able to make good on his campaign promise to get the country moving again.

Though Kennedy often seemed more concerned with his social life than his public responsibilities during his career in Congress, he became more focused as he aimed for the White House. Keenly aware of shifting political patterns, he recognized the need to use the techniques of advertising in his bid for the presidency. Above all he realized the power of television in taking his case to the American people.

In the 1960 campaign, Kennedy squared off against Richard Nixon, the Republican nominee,

In the election of 1960, John Kennedy, facing the camera in this picture, squared off against Richard Nixon in the first televised presidential debates. Nearly 80 million people watched Kennedy establish his credibility with a smooth performance in the four debates.

in the first televised presidential debates. Seventy million Americans turned on their sets to watch the two men in the first debate. Kennedy did what was most important on television: he projected a more dynamic image. While Nixon challenged points his opponent made, he looked worn out and ill at ease. An energetic Kennedy stared directly into the TV camera and appeared to be addressing the American people at large. Polls of radio listeners showed Nixon the winner; surveys of television viewers placed Kennedy in front. Television now would play a major role in the political process and reshape its character.

Kennedy also had the capacity to voice his aims in understandable and eloquent language. During the campaign, he pointed to "uncharted areas of science and space, unsolved problems of peace and war, unconquered pockets of ignorance and prejudice, unanswered questions of poverty and surplus" that Americans must confront, for "the New Frontier is here whether we seek it or not." He made the same point even more movingly in his inaugural address: "The torch has been passed to a new generation of Americans—born in this century, tempered by war, disciplined by a hard and bitter peace, proud of our ancient heritage." Many were inspired by his concluding call to action: "And so, my fellow Americans: Ask not what your country can do for you—ask what you can do for your country."

For Kennedy, strong leadership was all-important. The president, he believed, "must serve as a catalyst, an energizer." He must be able and willing to perform "in the very thick of the fight." Viewing himself as "tough-minded" and "hardnosed," he was determined to provide firm direction and play a leading role in creating the national agenda. Kennedy surrounded himself with talented assistants. On his staff were 15 Rhodes scholars and several famous authors. The secretary of state was Dean Rusk, a former member of the State Department who had then served as president of the Rockefeller Foundation. The secretary of defense was Robert S. McNamara, the highly successful president of the Ford Motor Company, who had proved creative in mobilizing talented assistants—"whiz kids"—and in using computer analysis to turn the company around.

Further contributing to the attractive Kennedy image were his glamorous wife Jacqueline and the glittering social occasions the Kennedys hosted. Nobel Prize winners, musicians, and artists attended White House dinners. The Kennedys and their friends played touch football on the White House lawn and charged off on 50-mile hikes. Energy, exuberance, and excitement filled the air. The administration seemed like the Camelot of King Arthur's day, popularized in a Broadway musical in 1960.

Despite his charismatic appeal, Kennedy faced real problems as president. He had won office despite seemingly insuperable odds and had become the first Catholic in the White House, but his victory over Nixon was razor-thin. The electoral margin of 303 to 219 concealed the close popular tally, in which he triumphed by less than

Glamour and grace characterized the Kennedy White House, as artists, authors, and other celebrities were invited to official functions. Here the President and First Lady greet poet Robert Frost at a party for Nobel Prize winners.

The Presidential Election of 1960

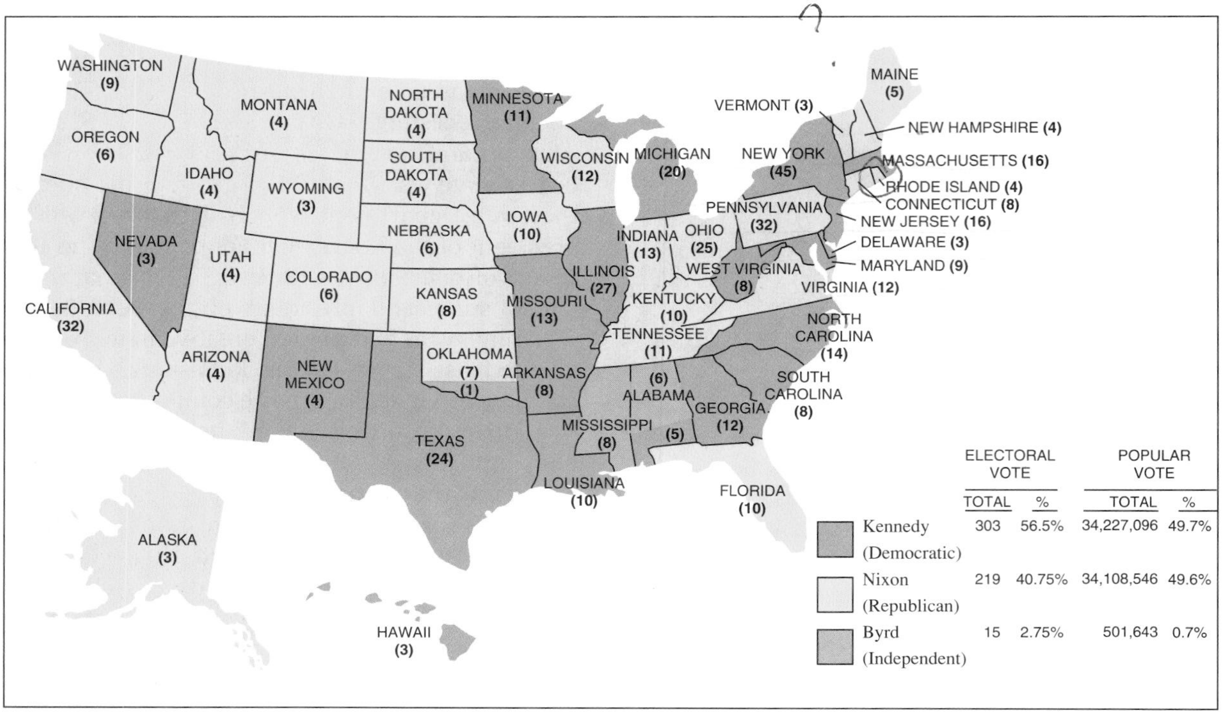

In the close election of 1960, Kennedy's strength in the industrial Northeast and the South helped him revive significant elements of the liberal Democratic coalition of the 1930s.

120,000 of 68 million votes. If but a few thousand people had voted differently in Illinois and Texas, the election would have gone to Nixon. Without an overwhelming popular mandate and without sufficient liberal support in Congress, he found it difficult to make good on his promises.

Facing reelection in 1964, Kennedy wanted not only to win the presidency for a second term but also to increase liberal Democratic strength in Congress. In November 1963, he traveled to Texas, where he hoped to unite the state's Democratic party for the upcoming election. Dallas, one of the stops on the trip, had a reputation as being less than cordial to the administration. Four weeks before, a conservative mob had abused Adlai Stevenson, ambassador to the United Nations. Now, on November 22, Kennedy had a chance to see for himself. Arriving at the airport, Henry González, a congressman accompanying the president in Texas, remarked jokingly, "Well, I'm taking my risks. I haven't got my steel vest yet." As the party entered the city in an open car, the president encountered friendly crowds. Suddenly shots rang out, and Kennedy slumped forward as bullets ripped through his head and throat. Desperately wounded, he died a short time later at a Dallas hospital. Lee Harvey Oswald, the accused assassin, was himself shot and killed a few days later by a minor underworld figure as he was being moved in the jail where he was being held.

Americans were stunned when they learned of Kennedy's death. For days people stayed at home and watched endless replays of the assassination and its aftermath on television. The images of the handsome president felled by bullets, the funeral cortege, the president's young son saluting his father's casket as it rolled by on the way to final burial at Arlington National Cemetery were all imprinted on people's minds. United

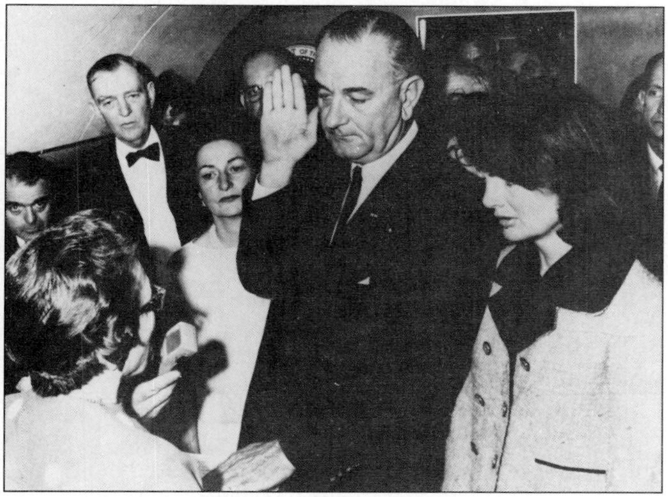

Kennedy's assassination thrust Lyndon Johnson into the presidency in an atmosphere of shocked grief and loss. Here, with Jacqueline Kennedy by his side, he takes the oath of office as he flew back to Washington on the presidential plane.

around the event, members of an entire generation remembered where they had been when Kennedy was shot, just as an earlier generation recalled Pearl Harbor.

Unexpectedly, Vice-President Lyndon B. Johnson succeeded Kennedy as president of the United States. Though less polished, Johnson was a more effective political leader than Kennedy, and brought his own special skills and vision to the presidency.

Johnson was a man of elemental force. Always manipulative, he reminded people of a riverboat gambler, according to one White House aide. Though he desperately wanted to be loved, he was, Dean Acheson once told him, "not a very likable man." There was a streak of vulgarity that contributed to his earthy appeal but offended some of his associates. Asked once why he had not responded more sympathetically to a suggestion from Richard Nixon, he said to his friends in Congress, "Boys, I may not know much, but I know the difference between chicken shit and chicken salad."

Those qualities notwithstanding, he was successful in the passion of his life—politics. Schooled in Congress and influenced by FDR, Johnson was the most able legislator of the postwar years. As Senate majority leader, he became famous for his ability to get things done. Ceaseless in his search for information, tireless in his attention to detail, he knew the strengths and weaknesses of everyone he faced. When he approached someone in the hall, one senator remarked, he was like a "great overpowering thunderstorm that consumed you as it closed in on you." He could flatter and cajole, and became famous for the "Johnson treatment." He zeroed in, according to columnists Rowland Evans, Jr., and Robert Novak, "his face a scant millimeter from his target, his eyes widening and narrowing, his eyebrows rising and falling." He grabbed people by the lapels, made them listen, and usually got his way.

Johnson ran the Senate with tight control and established a credible record for himself and his party during the Eisenhower years. He was the Democrat most responsible for keeping liberal goals alive in a conservative time, as he tried to broaden his own appeal in his quest for the presidency. Unsuccessful in 1960, he agreed to take the second spot under JFK and helped Kennedy win the election, then went into a state of eclipse as vice-president. He felt uncomfortable with the Kennedy crowd, useless and stifled in his new role. He told friends that he agreed with John Nance Garner, a former vice-president under FDR, who once observed that the vice-presidency "wasn't worth a pitcher of warm spit."

Despite his own ambivalence about Kennedy, Johnson sensed the profound shock that gripped the United States after the assassination and was determined to utilize Kennedy's memory to achieve legislative success. Even more than Kennedy, he was willing to wield presidential power aggressively, and to use the media to shape public opinion in pursuit of his vision of a society in which the comforts of life would be more widely shared and poverty eliminated.

The Changing Role of Government

The liberal agenda reflected the changing role of government. By 1960, government had become a major factor in ordinary people's lives. The New Deal and World War II had brought the unprecedented expansion of government's role. In the 1930s, the White House became an initiator of legislation and worked closely with Congress, while new agencies administered relief and recovery programs (see Chapter 24). The process continued during World War II, when the number of civilians working for the federal government more than tripled between 1940 and 1945. Though the number declined somewhat at the war's end, the government still employed close to 2.5 million people throughout the 1950s. Federal expenditures, which had stood at $3.1 billion in 1929, rose to $75 billion in 1953 and passed $150 billion in the 1960s. Defense spending rose dramatically during the Cold War years, but at the same time, the government extended old-age pensions and unemployment benefits to its citizens and took increasing responsibility for other social needs.

By 1960, most Americans accepted, even embraced, government's expanded role. The major political debate revolved around the question of how far that expansion should continue and which groups should benefit from it. Recalling the traumas of the Great Depression, Kennedy Democrats hoped to use government power to ensure stability and growth. They called for greater intervention in areas where citizens proved unable to help themselves. Demands heard in the late 1940s and the 1950s—for educational assistance, for federal health care, for more extensive welfare benefits—now became part of the political agenda in the 1960s.

The New Frontier

In office, John Kennedy sought to maintain an expanding economic system and to extend social welfare programs. As he told one of his advisers in 1962, "I want to go beyond the things that have already been accomplished. Give me facts and figures on things we still have to do." Regarding civil rights, Kennedy espoused liberal goals and social justice although his policies were limited (see Chapter 29 for a full discussion of civil rights). On the economic front, he tried to end the lingering recession by working with the business community, while controlling price inflation at the same time.

Those two goals conflicted when, in the spring of 1962, the large steel companies decided on a major price increase after steel unions had accepted a modest wage package. The angry president termed the price increases unjustifiable and on television charged that the firms pursued "private power and profit" rather than the public interest. Kennedy, determined to force the steel companies to their knees, pressed for executive and congressional action. In the end, the large companies capitulated, but they disliked Kennedy's heavy-handed approach and decided that this Democratic administration, like all the others, was hostile to business. In late May, six weeks after the steel crisis, the stock market plunged in the greatest drop since the Great Crash of 1929. Kennedy received the blame. "When Eisenhower had a heart attack," Wall Street analysts joked, "the market broke. If Kennedy would have a heart attack, the market would go up."

It now seemed doubly pressing to end the recession. Earlier a proponent of a balanced budget, Kennedy began to listen to his liberal advisers who proposed a Keynesian approach to economic growth. Budget deficits had promoted prosperity during the Second World War and might work in the same way in peacetime too. By the summer of 1962, the president had become convinced. In early 1963, he called for a $13.5 billion cut in corporate taxes over the next three years. While that cut would cause a large deficit, it would also provide capital to stimulate the economy and ultimately increase tax revenues.

Opposition mounted. Conservatives refused to accept the basic premise that deficits would stimulate economic growth and argued, as Eisenhower declared, that "no family, no business, no nation can spend itself into prosperity." Liberals, economist John Kenneth Galbraith among them, claimed that it would be better to stimulate the economy by spending for social programs rather than by cutting taxes. Why, he wondered, have "a few more dollars to spend if the air is too dirty to breathe, the water is too polluted to drink, the commuters are losing out in the struggle to get in and out of cities, the streets are filthy, and the schools are so bad that the young, perhaps wisely, stay away?" In Congress, where Democrats had thin majorities but still had to contend with conservative Southerners within the party, opponents pigeonholed the proposal in committee, and there it remained.

On other issues on the liberal agenda, Kennedy also encountered resistance. Though he proposed legislation increasing the minimum wage and providing for federal aid for education, medical care for the elderly, housing subsidies, and urban renewal, the legislative results were disappointing. His new minimum-wage measure passed Congress in pared-down form, but Kennedy did not have the votes in Congress to achieve most of his legislative program.

His inability to win necessary congressional support became even more evident in the struggle to aid public education. Soon after taking office, Kennedy proposed a $2.3 billion program of grants to the states over a three-year period to help build schools and raise teachers' salaries. Immediately, a series of prickly questions emerged. Was it appropriate to spend large sums of money for social goals? Would federal aid bring federal control of school policies and curriculum? Should assistance go to segregated schools? Should it go to parochial schools? The administration proved willing to allow assistance to segregated schools, thereby easing white southern minds. On the Catholic question, however, it stumbled to a halt. Kennedy at first insisted that he would not allow his religion to influence his actions and opposed aid for parochial schools. As Catholic pressure mounted and the administration realized that Catholic votes were necessary for passage, Kennedy began to reconsider. But in the end, the school aid measure died in the House Rules Committee.

Kennedy was more successful in securing funding for the exploration of space. As first Alan Shepard, then John Glenn, flew in space, Kennedy proposed that the United States commit itself to landing a man on the moon and returning him to earth before the end of the decade. Congress, caught up in the glamour of the proposal and worried about Soviet achievements in space, assented and increased funding of the National Aeronautics and Space Administration (NASA).

Kennedy also established the Peace Corps, which sent men and women overseas to assist developing countries. According to Kennedy aide Arthur M. Schlesinger, Jr., the Peace Corps was an effort "to replace protocol-minded, striped-pants officials by reform-minded missionaries of democracy who mixed with the people, spoke the native dialects, ate the food, and involved themselves in local struggles against ignorance and want."

If Kennedy's successes were modest, he had at least begun to set out the liberal agenda that was expanded in the following years. He had reaffirmed the importance of executive leadership in the effort to extend the boundaries of the welfare state. And he had committed himself to using modern economics to maintain fiscal stability.

The American landing on the moon in 1969 resulted from Kennedy's commitment to the space program. Here an astronaut stands next to the lunar module on the moon's surface.

The Great Society in Action

Lyndon Johnson had an expansive vision of the possibilities of reform. Using his considerable political skills, he succeeded in pushing through Congress the most extensive reform program in American history. "Is a new world coming?" the president asked. "We welcome it, and we will bend it to the hopes of man."

Johnson began to develop the support he needed the day he took office. Despite his growing ambivalence about Kennedy, he understood the profound shock gripping the nation and knew he must dispel the image of impostor. In his first public address, delivered to Congress and televised nationwide, he embraced Kennedy's liberal program. He began, in a measured tone, with the words, "All I have, I would have given gladly not to be standing here today." He asked members of Congress to work with him, and he underscored the theme "Let us continue" throughout his speech.

As a first step, Johnson determined to secure the measures Kennedy had been unable to extract from Congress. He took the bills to reduce taxes and ensure civil rights as his first and most pressing priorities, but he was interested too in aiding public education, providing medical care

Federal Aid to Education in the 1960s

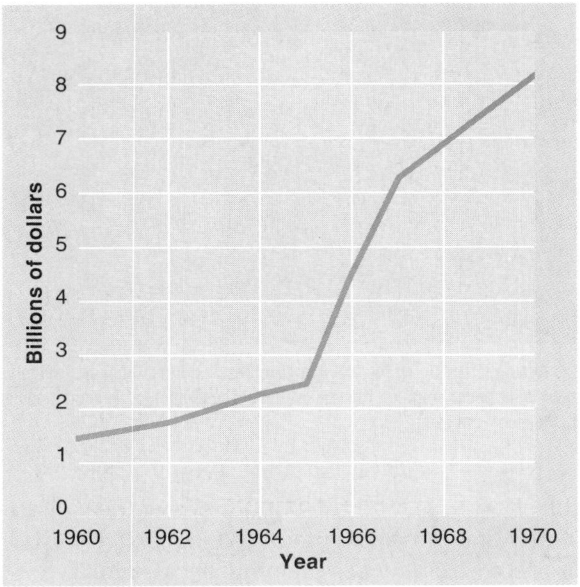

Passage of a bill to provide federal aid to education in 1965 led to rapidly increasing government support for the remainder of the decade.

Source: U.S. Bureau of the Census.

for the aged, and eliminating poverty. By the spring of 1964, the outlines of his own expansive vision were taking shape, and he had begun to use the phrase "Great Society" to describe his reform program.

Successful even before the election of 1964, his landslide victory over conservative Republican challenger Barry Goldwater of Arizona validated his approach. LBJ received 61 percent of the popular vote and an electoral tally of 486 to 52 and gained Democratic congressional majorities of 68-32 in the Senate and 295-140 in the House. Goldwater's candidacy reflected the growing power of conservatism within the Republican party and the ability of a grass-roots group to organize a successful campaign in party primaries. It also drove liberal voters into the Democratic party and gave Johnson a far more impressive mandate than Kennedy had ever enjoyed.

Johnson was an energetic leader who knew how to make things happen in the world of politics. He appointed task forces that included legislators to study problems and suggest solutions, worked with them to draft bills, and maintained close contact with congressional leaders through a sophisticated liaison staff. Not since the FDR years had there been such a coordinated effort, and it resulted in the strongest legislative program since the New Deal. It also resulted in greater gains than ever before for the liberal cause.

Civil rights reform was LBJ's first legislative priority and an integral part of the Great Society program (see Chapter 29 for a full discussion of civil rights). But other measures were equally important in extending the boundaries of government action and bolstering the foundation of the welfare state.

Following Kennedy's lead, Johnson pressed for a tax cut to stimulate the economy. He accepted the Keynesian theory that deficits, properly managed, could promote prosperity. To gain conservative support, he agreed to hold down spending; the tax bill passed.

With the tax cut in hand, the president pressed for the poverty program that Kennedy had begun to plan. Such an effort was bold and unprecedented. In the Progressive era, at the turn of the century, some legislation had attempted to alleviate conditions associated with poverty. During the New Deal, Franklin Roosevelt had proposed programs to assist the one-third of a nation that could not help itself. Now Johnson took a step that no president had taken before; in his 1964 State of the Union message, he declared an "unconditional war on poverty in America." The center of this utopian effort to eradicate poverty was the Economic Opportunity Act of 1964. It created an Office of Economic Opportunity to provide education and training for unskilled young people trapped in the poverty cycle, VISTA (Volunteers in Service to America) to assist the poor at home, and assorted community action programs to give the poor themselves a voice in improving housing, health, and education in their own neighborhoods.

Aware of the escalating costs of medical care, Johnson proposed a medical assistance plan. Both Truman and Kennedy had proposed such measures but had failed to win congressional approval. Johnson, however, succeeded. To head off conservative attacks, the administration tied the Medicare measure to the social security system and limited the program to the elderly. Medicaid met the needs of those on welfare and certain other groups who could not afford private insurance. The Medicare-Medicaid program was the most important extension of federally directed social benefits since the Social Security Act of 1935. By 1976 the two programs were paying for the medical costs of 20 percent of the American people.

Johnson was similarly successful in his effort to provide aid for elementary and secondary schools. Kennedy had met defeat when Catholics had insisted on assistance to parochial schools. Johnson, a Protestant, was able to deal with that ticklish question without charges of favoritism. His legislation allocated education money to the states based on the number of children from low-income families. Those funds would then be distributed to assist deprived children in public as well as private schools. In LBJ's expansive vision, the federal government would ensure that all shared in the promise of American life. As a result of his prodding, Congress passed a new housing act to provide rent supplements to the poor and created a Department of Housing and Urban Development. It also replaced the restrictive immigration policy, set in place in 1924 (which had limited immigration severely and favored northern Europeans), with a measure that vastly increased the ceiling on immigration and opened the door to immigrants from Asia and Latin America. The Immigration Act of 1965 also exempted from the quotas family members of United States citizens and political refugees, including at first Cuban and later Indochinese immigrants. By the late 1960s, some 350,000 immigrants were entering the United States annually; in the 1970s, the number exceeded 400,000 a year. This new stream of immigration—largely from Asia and Latin America—created a population more diverse than it had been since the early decades of the twentieth century. The consequences of this new diversity were far-ranging and affected many areas of American life, from politics, radio programming, and consumer products to street signs and public school classrooms.

Meanwhile, the federal government provided new forms of aid, such as legal assistance for the poor. It moved further in funding education, including colleges and universities in its financial grants. Congress also provided artists and scholars with assistance through the new National Endowments for the Arts and Humanities. Not since the Works Progress Administration in the New Deal had such groups been granted government aid.

At the same time, the Great Society reflected the stirring of the environmental movement. In 1962, naturalist Rachel Carson alerted the public to the dangers of pesticide poisoning and environmental pollution in her book *Silent Spring.* She took aim at chemical pesticides, particularly DDT, which had increased crop yields but had disastrous side effects. Johnson recognized the need to do something about caustic fumes in the

Immigrants, here shown being sworn in as citizens, entered the United States in vastly increased numbers after passage of the Immigration Act of 1965.

Major Great Society Programs

Date of Passage	*Program*	*Effect*
January 23, 1964 (ratified)	Twenty-fourth Amendment	Banned poll tax as prerequisite in federal elections
February 26, 1964	Tax Reduction Act	Lowered federal personal tax rates
July 2, 1964	Civil Rights Act	Banned discrimination in public accommodations; gave attorney general right to file suit to desegregate schools or other facilities; banned discrimination in employment on basis of race, color, religion, sex, or national origin
July 9, 1964	Urban Mass Transportation Act	Provided $375 million in financial aid to urban transit systems
August 30, 1964	Economic Opportunity Act	Authorized ten separate programs to be conducted by the Office of Economic Opportunity, including Job Corps and VISTA
September 3, 1964	Wilderness Preservation Act	Designated 9.1 million acres of land as national forest to be safeguarded permanently against commercial use and construction of permanent roads and buildings
April 11, 1965	Elementary and Secondary Education Act	Provided $1.3 billion in aid to elementary and secondary schools
July 30, 1965	Medicare	Provided medical care for the aged through the social security system
August 6, 1965	Voting Rights Act	Suspended literacy tests and other voter tests; authorized federal supervision of registration in states and districts where few voting-age residents had voted earlier
August 10, 1965	Omnibus Housing Act	Provided rent supplements to low-income families and federal aid to place low-income people in private housing

air, lethal sludge in rivers and streams, and the steady disappearance of wildlife. The National Wilderness Preservation System Act of 1964 set aside 9.1 million acres of wilderness, while Lady Bird Johnson, the president's wife, led a beautification campaign to eliminate unsightly billboards and junkyards along the nation's highways, and Congress passed other measures to limit air and water pollution.

A Sympathetic Supreme Court

With the addition of four new liberal justices appointed by Kennedy and Johnson, the Supreme Court supported and promoted the liberal agenda in the 1960s. Under the leadership of Chief Justice Earl Warren, the Court followed the lead it had taken in 1954 in *Brown* v. *Board of Education.* Several decisions reaffirmed the Court's support of black rights. Having disposed of the issue of school segregation, the Court moved against Jim Crow practices in other public establishments. Providing quick support for civil rights measures, the justices gave notice that the Court would no longer uphold discriminatory customs.

The Court also supported civil liberties. Where earlier judicial decisions had affirmed restrictions on members of the Communist party and radical groups, now the Court began to protect the rights of individuals with radical political views. Similarly, the Court sought to protect accused suspects from police harassment. In *Gideon* v. *Wainwright* (1963), the justices decided that poor defendants in serious cases had the

Major Great Society Programs *(continued)*

Date of Passage	*Program*	*Effect*
September 9, 1965	Department of Housing and Urban Development	Provided special programs concerned with housing needs, fair-housing opportunities, and the improvement and development of communities
September 29, 1965	National Foundation for the Arts and Humanities	Provided financial assistance for painters, actors, dancers, musicians, and others in the arts and humanities
October 2, 1965	Water Quality Act	Required states to establish and enforce water quality standards for all interstate waters within their boundaries
October 3, 1965	Immigration Act	Revision set new quotas
October 20, 1965	Air Quality Act	Amended earlier laws
October 20, 1965	Higher Education Act	Provided federal scholarships to undergraduates and others
September 9, 1966	National Traffic and Motor Vehicle Safety Act	Set federal safety standards
September 9, 1966	Highway Safety Act	Required states to set up federally approved safety programs
September 23, 1966	Minimum wage	Raised minimum wage from $1.25 to $1.40 per hour; extended coverage
October 15, 1966	Department of Transportation	Provided federal agencies to administer policies, in conjunction with state and local officials, regarding highway planning, development, and construction; urban mass transit; railroads; aviation; and safety of waterways, ports, highways; and oil and gas pipelines
November 3, 1966	Model Cities	Encouraged rehabilitation of slums

right to free legal counsel. In *Escobedo* v. *Illinois* (1964), they ruled that a suspect had to be given access to an attorney during questioning. In *Miranda* v. *Arizona* (1966), they argued that offenders had to be warned that statements extracted by the police could be used against them and that they could remain silent.

Other decisions similarly broke new ground. *Baker* v. *Carr* (1962) opened the way to reapportionment of state legislative bodies, according to the standard, defined a year later by Justice William O. Douglas's words, of "one person, one vote." This crucial ruling helped break the political control of lightly populated rural districts in many state assemblies and similarly made the United States House of Representatives much more responsive to urban and suburban issues. Meanwhile, the Court outraged conservatives by ruling that prayer could not be required in the public schools and that obscenity laws could no longer restrict allegedly pornographic material that might have some "redeeming social value.

The Great Society Under Attack

For a few years, supported by healthy economic growth, the Great Society worked as Johnson had hoped. The tax cut proved effective. After its passage, GNP rose steadily: 7.1 percent in 1964, 8.1 percent in 1965, and 9.5 percent in 1966. At the same time, the budget deficit dropped. Unemployment fell, and inflation remained under control. Medical programs provided a measure of security for the old and the poor. Education

Roots of Selected Great Society Programs

Progressive Period	*New Deal*	*Great Society*
Settlement house activity of Jane Addams and others	Relief efforts to ease unemployment (FERA, WPA)	Poverty program (OEO)
Efforts to clean up slums (tenement house laws)	Housing program	Rehabilitation of slums through Model Cities program
Progressive party platform calling for federal accident, old-age, and unemployment insurance	Social security system providing unemployment compensation and old-age pensions	Medical care for the aged through social security (Medicare)
Activity to break up monopolies and regulate business	Regulation of utility companies	Regulation of highway safety and transportation
Efforts to regulate working conditions and benefits	Establishment of standards for working conditions and minimum wage	Raising of minimum wage
Efforts to increase literacy and spread education at all levels	Efforts to keep college students in school through NYA	Assistance to elementary, secondary, and higher education
Theodore Roosevelt's efforts at wilderness preservation	Conservation efforts (CCC, TVA planning)	Safeguarding of wilderness lands
Establishment of Federal income tax	Tax reform to close loopholes and increase taxes for the wealthy	Tax cut to stimulate business activity
Theodore Roosevelt's overtures to Booker T. Washington	Discussion (but not passage) of antilynching legislation	Civil rights measures to ban discrimination in public accommodations and to guarantee right to vote

flourished as schools were built, and salaries increased in response to the influx of federal aid.

Yet Johnson's dream of the Great Society proved illusory. Some programs, like the effort to eliminate poverty, promised too much, and the administration's rhetorical oversell led to disillusionment when problems failed to disappear. Other programs, planned in haste, were simply ill-conceived and did not work. Never were the massive sums allocated to these programs that some argued were necessary to make them successful.

Factionalism also plagued the Great Society. Lyndon Johnson had reconstituted the old Democratic coalition in his triumph in 1964, with urban Catholics and southern whites joining organized labor, the black electorate, and the middle class. But diverse interests within the coalition soon clashed. Conservative white southerners and blue-collar white northerners felt threatened by the government's support of civil rights; local urban bosses, long the backbone of the Democratic party, objected to grass-roots participation of the urban poor, which threatened their own political control.

Criticisms of the Great Society and its liberal underpinnings came from across the political spectrum. There had never been widespread popular enthusiasm for much of the effort. Conservatives disliked the centralization of authority and the government's increased role in defining the national welfare. They also questioned involving the poor themselves in reform programs, arguing poor people lacked a broad vision of the nation's needs. Even middle-class Americans, generally supportive of liberal goals, sometimes grumbled that the government was paying too much attention to the underprivileged and thereby neglecting their own needs.

Radicals likewise attacked the Great Society as a warmed-over version of the New Deal. The same middle-class liberal orientation remained, they claimed, with the real intent of programs to provide the poor with middle-class values. Furthermore, because Great Society programs rested on the belief that the American system was basically sound and that economic growth would finance benefits of the American dream for all, no real effort had been made to redistribute income. Only the redistribution of wealth, in their view, could transform American life.

The Vietnam War (described in the final section of this chapter) dealt the Great Society a fatal blow. LBJ wanted to maintain both the war and his treasured domestic reform programs, but his effort to pursue these goals simultaneously produced serious inflation. The economy was already heated up as a result of the tax cut and the spending for reform. As military expenditures increased, the productive system of the country could not keep up with demand. When Johnson refused to raise taxes, in an effort to hide the costs of the war, inflation spiraled out of control. Congress finally got into the act and responded by slashing Great Society programs. As hard economic choices became increasingly necessary, many decided the country could no longer afford social reform on the scale Johnson had proposed.

The Decline of Liberalism

After eight years of Democratic rule, many Americans questioned the liberal agenda and the ability of the government to solve social problems. The war had polarized the country and the Democratic Party was under attack. Republicans, capitalizing on the alienation sparked by the Vietnam War, determined to scale down the commitment to social change. While, like Dwight Eisenhower a decade and a half before, they accepted some social programs as necessary for the well-being of modern America, they were resolved to reduce spending and cut back the federal bureaucracy. Furthermore, they were determined to pay more attention to white, middle-class Americans who disliked the social disorder they perceived as one of the consequences of rapid social change and hated the government's favoritism toward the poor and dispossessed.

Republican Leadership

Richard Nixon had long dreamed of the nation's highest office. He had failed in his first bid in 1960, and then lost in a race two years later for governor of California. His political career seemed over, as he told the press in 1962, "You won't have Nixon to kick around any more because, gentlemen, this is my last press conference." Written off for a time, he staged a comeback after the Goldwater disaster of 1964, and by 1968 seemed to have a good shot at the presidency again.

In the election, Nixon faced Vice-President Hubert H. Humphrey, who hoped to lead his seriously weakened party to victory. The turbulent Democratic convention in Chicago, where police ran amok and clubbed demonstrators, reporters, bystanders, and anyone else in the way, all on nationwide TV, made the Democrats look hopelessly disorganized and worked in Nixon's favor. But he faced a serious threat from Governor George C. Wallace of Alabama, a third-party candidate, who exploited social and racial tensions in his campaign. Appealing to northern working-class voters as well as southern whites, Wallace characterized those who had wanted to reform American life as "left-wing theoreticians, briefcase-totin' bureaucrats, ivory-tower guideline writers, bearded anarchists, smart-aleck editorial writers and pointy-headed professors." He hoped to ride into office on blue-collar resentment of social disorder and the liberal agenda.

Nixon addressed the same constituency who made up, he believed, the country's "silent majority." Capitalizing on the dismay of these Americans over campus disruptions and inner-city riots and appealing to latent racism, he promised to preserve law and order if elected. He also attacked the Great Society as a costly mistake, declaring that it was "time to quit pouring billions of dollars into programs that have failed." Intently aware of the importance of image and working closely with public-relations advisers, Nixon gave Governor Spiro Agnew of Maryland, his vice-presidential running mate, the task of leading the attack. Agnew, much like the Nixon of old, called Hubert Humphrey "squishy soft on communism" and declared that "if you've seen one city slum, you've seen them all."

When the results were in, Nixon received 43 percent of the popular vote, not quite 1 percent more than Humphrey, with Wallace capturing the rest, but enough to give the Republicans a majority in the electoral college. Sixty-two percent of all white voters had cast their votes for either Nixon or Wallace (but only 12 percent of black voters),

Policemen attacked demonstrators and bystanders alike at the turbulent Democratic convention of 1968. The senseless violence, pictured in graphic detail on national television, undermined the Democratic party and helped Nixon win the election.

suggesting the covert racial appeal had worked. Because many Americans split their tickets, the Democrats won both houses of Congress.

In and out of office, Nixon was a complex, remote man, who carefully concealed his private self. Keenly aware of the psychology of politics, he believed that "in the modern presidency, concern for image must rank with concern for substance." Thus he posed as the defender of American morality, though in private he was frequently coarse and profane. Earlier in his career he had been labeled "Tricky Dick" for his apparent willingness to do anything to advance his career. He had spent years trying to create the appearance of a "new Nixon," but to many he appeared a mechanical man, always calculating his next step.

Nixon embraced political life, but never with the exuberance of Lyndon Johnson. Physically awkward and humorless, he was most comfortable alone or with a few wealthy friends. Even at work he insulated himself, preferred written contacts to personal ones, and often retreated to a small room in the executive office building to be alone.

Philosophically, Nixon disagreed with the liberal faith in federal planning and wanted to decentralize social policy. But he agreed with his liberal predecessors that the presidency ought to be the engine of the political system. Faced with a Congress dominated by Democrats and their allocations of money for programs which he opposed, he impounded, or refused to spend, funds Congress had authorized. Later commentators would see the Nixon years as the height of the "imperial presidency."

Speaking to the "silent majority," Nixon promised to reinstitute traditional values and restore law and order. A private man, Nixon tried to insulate himself from the public and present a carefully crafted image through the national media.

Nixon's cabinet appointees, sworn in with NBC "Today" cameras relaying the ceremony directly to television viewers, were white, male Republicans. For the most part, however, he worked around his cabinet, relying on other White House staff members. In domestic affairs, Arthur Burns, a former chairman of the Council of Economic Advisers, and Daniel Patrick Moynihan, a Harvard professor of government (and a Democrat) were the most important. In foreign affairs, Henry A. Kissinger, another Harvard government professor, both talented and ambitious, directed the National Security Council staff and later became secretary of state.

Still another tier of White House officials insulated the president from the outside world and carried out his commands. None had public policy experience, but all shared an intense loyalty to their leader, a quality that Nixon prized, and a keen sense of the importance of the Nixon image. Advertising executive H. R. Haldeman, a tireless Nixon campaigner, became chief of staff. Of his relationships with the president, Haldeman remarked, "I get done what he wants done and I take the heat instead of him."

Working with Haldeman was lawyer John Ehrlichman. Starting as a legal counselor, he rose to the post of chief domestic adviser. Haldeman and Ehrlichman framed issues and narrowed options for Nixon. They came to be known as the "Berlin Wall" for the way they guarded the president's privacy. John Mitchell was known as "El Supremo" by the staff, as the "Big Enchilada" by Ehrlichman. A tough, successful bond lawyer from Nixon's New York law office, he became a fast friend and managed the 1968 campaign. In the new administration, he became attorney general and gave the president daily advice.

When Nixon resigned in disgrace midway through his second term, he was succeeded by Gerald Ford. An unpretentious middle-American Republican who believed in the traditional virtues, Ford had become vice-president in 1973 when Spiro Agnew resigned in disgrace for accepting bribes. After the appointment, Richard Rovere, a noted journalist, wrote in the *New Yorker*: "That he is thoroughly equipped to serve as Vice President seems unarguable; the office requires only a warm body and occasionally a nimble tongue. However . . . neither Richard Nixon nor anyone else has come forward to explain Gerald Ford's qualifications to serve as Chief Executive." The new president acknowledged his own limitations, declaring, "I am a Ford, not a Lincoln."

More important than his limitations were his views about public policy. Throughout his tenure in Congress, Ford had voted according to the Republican convictions he shared with his Michigan constituents. Over the years he had opposed federal aid to education, the poverty program, and mass transit. He had voted for civil rights measures only when weaker substitutes he had favored had gone down to defeat. Like his predecessor, he was determined to stop the liberal advances promoted by the Democrats in the 1960s.

The Republican Agenda

Although Nixon had come to political maturity in Republican circles, he understood that it was impossible to roll back the government's expanded role altogether. Accepting the basic contours of the welfare state, he sought to systematize and scale back its programs. Furthermore, he was determined "to reverse the flow of power and resources" away from the federal government to state and local governments, where he believed they belonged.

Despite initial reservations, Nixon was willing to use economic tools to maintain stability. The economy was faltering when he assumed office. Inflation had risen from 2.2 percent in 1965 to 4.5 percent in 1968, largely as a result of the Vietnam War. Nixon responded by reducing government spending and pressing the Federal Reserve Board to raise interest rates. Although parts of the conservative plan worked, a mild recession occurred in 1969–1970 and inflation continued. Realizing the political dangers of pursuing this policy, Nixon shifted course, imposed wage and price controls to stop inflation, and used monetary and fiscal policies to stimulate the economy. After his reelection, however, he lifted wage and price controls, and inflation began its upward course once more.

A number of factors besides the Vietnam War contributed to the troubling spiral of rising prices. Eager to court the farm vote, the administration made a large wheat sale to Russia in 1972. But government officials had miscalculated. With insufficient wheat left for the American market,

Rate of Inflation, 1947–1977

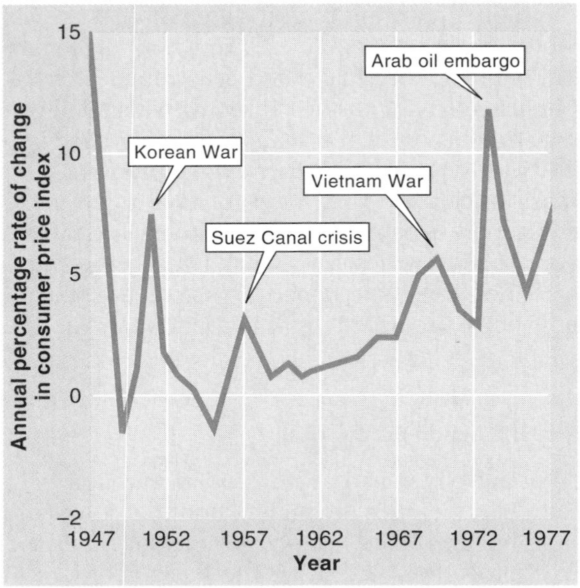

Inflation has often accompanied military spending in the postwar years. In the early 1970s, the Arab oil embargo contributed to an even higher rate.

Source: U.S. Bureau of the Census.

Oil Imports, 1973–1980

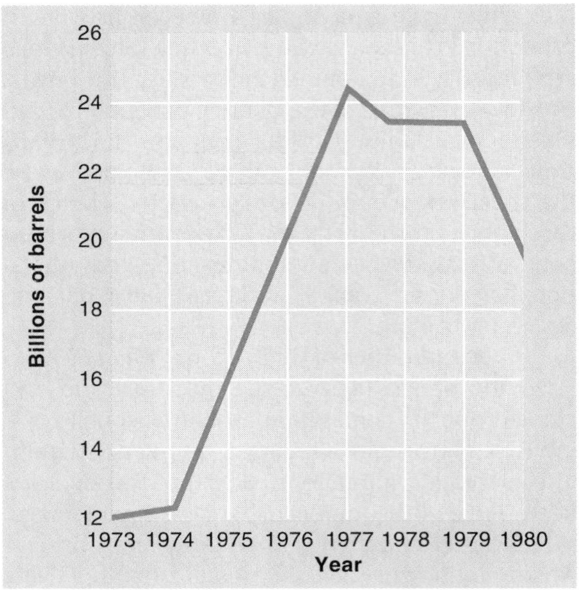

American reliance on foreign oil increased in the mid-1970s, until the United States tried to respond to price increases by reducing reliance on imports.

Source: U.S. Energy Information Administration.

grain prices shot up. Twenty-five years of grain surpluses suddenly vanished and shortages occurred. Other agricultural setbacks like corn blight compounded the problem. Between 1971 and 1974, farm prices rose 66 percent, as agricultural inflation accompanied industrial inflation.

The most critical factor in disrupting the economy, though, was the Arab oil embargo. American economic expansion had rested on cheap energy just as American patterns of life had depended on inexpensive gasoline. Although OPEC (the Organization of Petroleum Exporting Countries) had slowly raised oil prices in the early 1970s, the 1973 war between Israel, Egypt, and Syria led Saudi Arabia to impose an embargo on oil shipped to Israel's ally, the United States. Other OPEC nations quadrupled their prices. Dependent on imports for one-third of their energy needs, Americans faced shortages and skyrocketing prices. When the embargo ended in 1974, prices remained high.

The oil crisis affected all aspects of American economic life. Manufacturers, farmers, homeowners—all were touched by high energy prices. A loaf of bread that had cost 28 cents in the early 1970s jumped to 89 cents, and automobiles cost 72 percent more in 1978 than they had in 1973. Accustomed to filling up their cars' tanks for only a few dollars, Americans were shocked at paying 65 cents a gallon. In 1974, inflation reached 11 percent. But as higher energy prices encouraged consumers to cut back on their purchases, the nation also entered a recession. Unemployment climbed to 9 percent, the highest level since the 1930s. Inflation and high unemployment were worrisome bedfellows.

As economic growth and stability eluded him, Nixon also tried to reorganize rapidly expanding and expensive welfare programs. As a result of changes in welfare during the years of the Great Society, the government was spending considerably more in this area. Critics claimed that welfare was inefficient and that benefits discouraged people from seeking work. Nixon faced a dilemma. He recognized the conservative tide growing in the Sun Belt regions of the country from Florida to Texas to California, where many voters wanted cutbacks in what they viewed as excessive government programs. At the same time, he wanted to create a new Republican coalition by winning over traditionally Democratic blue-collar workers with reassurances that the Republicans would not dismantle the parts of the welfare state on which they relied.

At the urging of domestic adviser Daniel Moynihan, Nixon endorsed an expensive but feasible new program. The Family Assistance Plan would have guaranteed a minimum yearly stipend of $1,600 to a family of four, with food stamps providing about $800 more. The program, aiming to cut "welfare cheaters" who took unfair advantage of the system and to encourage recipients to work, required all participants to register for job training and to accept employment when found. Proponents, who doubtless exaggerated the number of cheaters, wanted to make it more profitable to work than to subsist on the public rolls. Though promising, the program was attacked by both liberals and conservatives and died in the Senate.

Unemployment Rate, 1940–1984

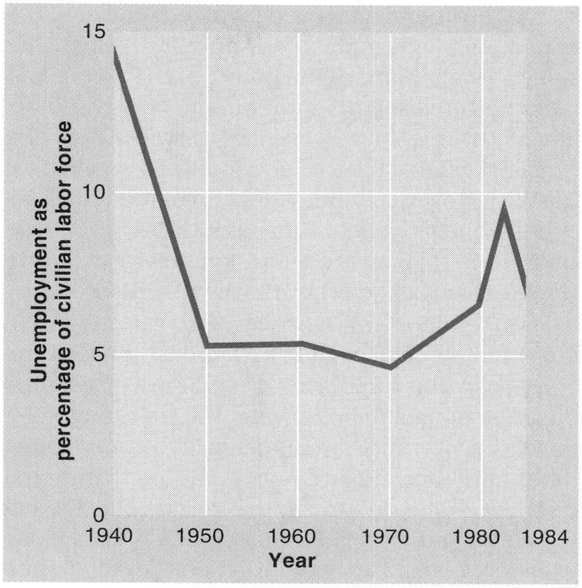

The unemployment rate, which had fallen dramatically during World War II and remained relatively constant in the 1950s and 1960s, rose at the same time inflation increased in the 1970s.

Source: U.S. Bureau of Labor Statistics.

Gasoline Prices, 1973–1980

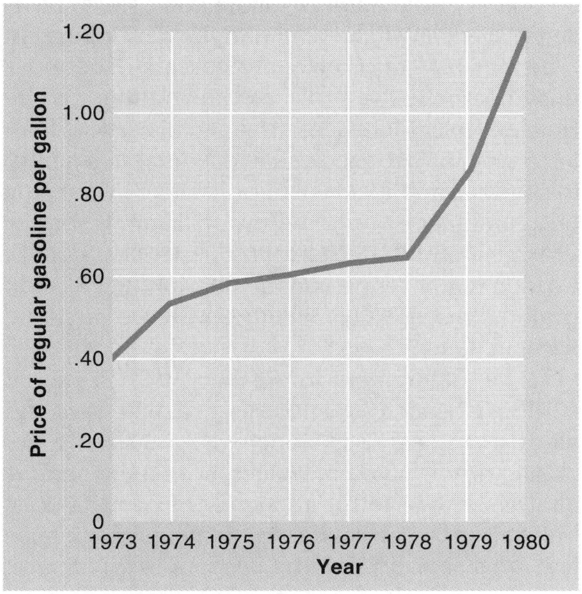

Gasoline prices rose steadily in the years following the Arab oil embargo.

Source: U.S. Energy Information Administration.

As he struggled with the economy and with what many called the "welfare mess," Nixon irritated liberals still further in his effort to restore "law and order." Political protest—and rising crime rates, increased drug use, and more permissive attitudes toward sex—created a growing backlash among working-class and many middle-class Americans (see Chapter 29 for the development of youth culture). Nixon decided to use government power to silence disruption and thereby strengthen this political constituency.

One part of the administration's campaign involved denouncing disruptive elements. Nixon lashed out at demonstrators—at one point he called the students "bums." More and more, however, he relied on his vice-president to play the part of hatchet man. As he had demonstrated during the 1968 campaign, Agnew had a gift for jugular attack. Opposition elements, students in particular, were "ideological eunuchs" who made up an "effete corps of impudent snobs." At the same time, Nixon and Agnew appealed for support to blue-collar youth, whom they described as patriotic supporters of the Vietnam War.

Another part of Nixon's effort to circumscribe the liberal approach involved attacking the communications industry. Although Nixon himself was well aware of the power of the media and used both television and radio effectively, he believed the media represented the views of the "Eastern establishment" and indulged in personal hostility toward him. After commentators responded negatively to a major address in 1969, he decided to take on the television networks. Again Agnew spearheaded the attack with relish.

Most important, however, was Attorney General John Mitchell's effort to demonstrate that the administration supported the values of citizens upset by domestic upheavals. Mitchell sought enhanced powers for a campaign on crime, sometimes at the expense of individuals' constitutional rights. He intended to send a message to the entire country that the new team in the White House would not tolerate certain actions, even if they were protected by the right to free speech.

One part of Mitchell's plan involved reshaping the Supreme Court, which had rendered increasingly liberal decisions on the rights of defendants in the past decade and a half. That shift, Republican leaders argued, had resulted in moral and ethical looseness. During his first term, Nixon had the extraordinary opportunity to name four judges to the Court, and he nominated men who shared his views. His first choice was Warren E. Burger as chief justice to replace the liberal Earl Warren, who was retiring. Burger, a moderate, was confirmed quickly. Other appointments, however, were more partisan and reflected Nixon's aggressively conservative approach. Intent on appealing to white southerners, he first selected Clement Haynesworth of South Carolina, then G. Harold Carswell of Florida. Both men on examination showed such racial biases or limitations that the Senate refused to confirm them. Nixon then appointed Harry Blackmun, Lewis F. Powell, Jr., and William Rehnquist, all able and qualified, and all inclined to tilt the Court in a more conservative direction.

Not surprisingly, the Court gradually shifted to the right. It narrowed defendants' rights in an attempt to ease the burden of the prosecution in its cases and slowed the process of liberalization by upholding pornography laws if they reflected community standards. It supported Nixon's assault on the media by ruling that journalists did not have the right to refuse to answer questions for a grand jury even if that meant revealing sources. On other questions, however, the Court did not always act as the president had hoped. In the controversial 1973 *Roe* v. *Wade* decision, the Court legalized abortion, stating that women's rights included the right to control their own bodies. This decision was one that feminists, a group hardly supported by the president, had ardently sought.

not all

Watergate and Its Aftermath

Faced with a solidly Democratic Congress, the Nixon administration found its legislative initiatives blocked. In this situation, Nixon was determined to end the stalemate by winning a second term and sweeping Republican majorities into both houses of Congress in 1972. His efforts to gain a decisive Republican victory at the polls led to excesses that brought his demise.

Nixon's reelection campaign was even better organized than the effort four years before. Sparing no expense, the president relied on aides who were fiercely loyal and prepared to do anything to win. Special counsel Charles W. Colson described himself as a "flag-waving, kick-'em-in-the-nuts, anti-press, anti-liberal Nixon fanatic." He had earlier played an important part in developing an "enemies list" of prominent figures judged to be unsympathetic to the administration. White House counsel John Dean defined his task as finding a way to "use the available federal machinery to screw our political enemies." Active in carrying out commands were E. Howard Hunt, a former CIA agent and a specialist in "dirty tricks," and G. Gordon Liddy, a onetime member of the FBI, who prided himself on his willingness to do anything without flinching.

The Committee to Re-elect the President (CREEP), headed by John Mitchell, who resigned as attorney general, launched a massive fund-raising drive, aimed at collecting as much money as it could before the reporting of contributions became necessary under a new campaign-finance law. That money could be used for any purpose, including payments for the performance of dirty tricks aimed at disrupting the opposition's campaign. Other funds financed an intelligence branch within the CREEP that had Liddy at its head and included Hunt.

Early in 1972, Liddy and his lieutenants proposed an elaborate scheme to wiretap the phones of various Democrats and to disrupt their nominating convention. Twice Mitchell refused to go along, arguing that the plan was too risky and expensive. Finally he approved a modified version of the plan to tap the phones of the Democratic National Committee at its headquarters in the Watergate apartment complex in Washington, D.C. Mitchell, formerly the top justice official in the land, had authorized breaking the law.

The wiretapping attempt took place on the evening of June 16 and ended with the arrest of those involved. They carried with them money and documents that could be traced to CREEP and incriminate the reelection campaign. Top officials of the Nixon reelection team had to decide quickly what response to make.

Reelection remained the most pressing priority, so Nixon's aides played the matter down and used federal resources to head off the investigation. When the FBI traced the money carried by the burglars to CREEP, the president authorized the CIA to call off the FBI on the grounds that national security was at stake. Though not involved in the planning of the break-in, the president was now party to the cover-up. In the succeeding months, he authorized payment of hush money to silence Hunt and others. Top members of the administration, including Mitchell, perjured themselves in court to shield the higher officials who were involved.

Nixon won the election of 1972 in a landslide, receiving 61 percent of the popular vote. In a clear indication of the collapse of the Democratic coalition, 70 percent of southern voters cast their ballots for Nixon. The president, however, failed to gain the congressional majorities necessary to support his programs.

When the Watergate burglars were brought to trial, they pleaded guilty and were sentenced to jail, but the case refused to die. Judge John Sirica was not satisfied that justice had been done, asserting that the evidence indicated that others had played a part. Meanwhile, two zealous reporters, Bob Woodward and Carl Bernstein of the *Washington Post,* were following a trail of leads on their own. Slowly they recognized who else was involved. On one occasion, when they reached Mitchell and asked him about a story tying him to Watergate, he turned on them in fury. "All that crap you're putting in the paper?" he said. "It's all been denied."

Mitchell's irritation notwithstanding, the unraveling of Watergate continued. The Senate Select Committee on Presidential Campaign Activities undertook an investigation, and one of the convicted burglars testified that the White House had been involved in the episode. Newspaper stories provided further leads, and the Senate hearings in turn provided new material for the press. Faced with rumors that the White House was actively involved, Nixon decided that he had to release Haldeman and Ehrlichman, his two closest aides, in an effort to save his own neck. On nationwide TV he declared that he would take the ultimate responsibility for the mistakes of others, for "there can be no whitewash at the White House."

In May 1973, the Senate committee began televised public hearings, reminiscent of the earlier McCarthy hearings of the 1950s. As millions of Americans watched, the drama built. John Dean, seeking to save himself, testified that Nixon knew about the cover-up, and other staffers revealed a host of illegal activities undertaken at the White House: money had been paid to the

Presidential Elections, 1968 and 1972

Year	Candidates	Party	Popular Vote	Electoral Votes
1968	RICHARD M. NIXON	Republican	31,783,783 (43.4%)	301
	Hubert H. Humphrey	Democratic	31,271,839 (42.7%)	191
	George C. Wallace	American Independent	9,899,557 (13.5%)	46
1972	RICHARD M. NIXON	Republican	45,767,218 (60.7%)	520
	George S. McGovern	Democratic	28,357,668 (37.5%)	17

Note: Winners' names appear in capital letters.

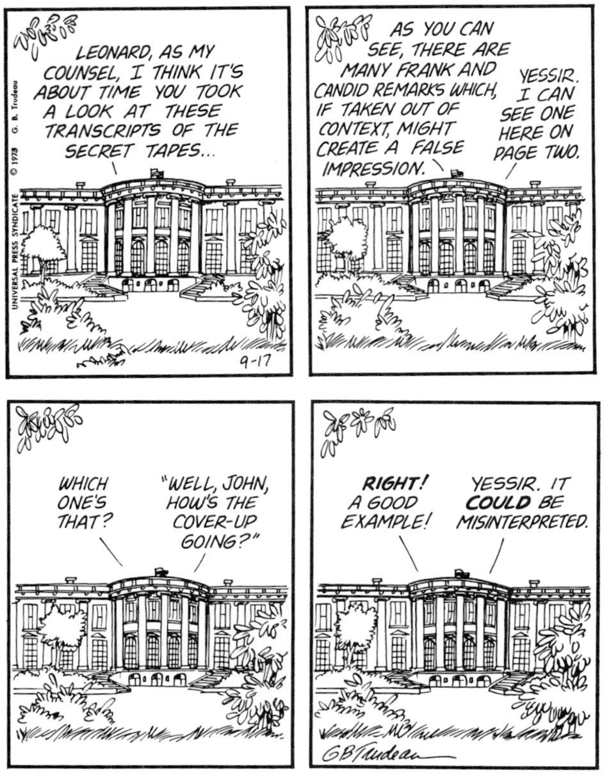

Although Nixon steadfastly denied his complicity in the Watergate affair, his tape recordings of White House conversations told a different story. In this classic "Doonesbury" cartoon from September 13, 1973, Garry Trudeau notes Nixon's efforts to head off the investigation.

burglars to silence them; State Department documents had been forged to smear a previous administration; wiretaps had been used to prevent top-level leaks. The most electrifying moment was the disclosure that the president had in his office a secret taping system that recorded all conversations. Tapes could verify or disprove the growing rumors that Nixon had in fact been party to the cover-up all along.

In an effort to demonstrate his own honesty, Nixon agreed to appoint Harvard law professor Archibald Cox as a special prosecutor in the Department of Justice. But when Cox tried to gain access to the tapes, Nixon resisted and finally fired him in what was known as the "Saturday Night Massacre." Nixon's own popularity plummeted, and even the appointment of another special prosecutor, Leon Jaworski, did not help. More and more Americans now believed that the president had played at least some part in the cover-up and should take responsibility for his acts. *Time* magazine ran an editorial headlined "The President Should Resign," and Congress considered impeachment. The first steps, in accordance with constitutional mandate, began in the House of Representatives.

In late July 1974, the House Judiciary Committee, made up of 21 Democrats and 17 Republicans, debated the impeachment case. By sizable tallies, it voted to impeach the president on the grounds of obstruction of justice, abuse of power, and refusal to obey a congressional subpoena to turn over his tapes. A full House of Representatives vote still had to occur, and the Senate would have to preside over a trial before removal could take place. But for Nixon the handwriting was on the wall.

After a brief delay, on August 5 Nixon obeyed a Supreme Court ruling and released the tapes. Despite a suspicious 18½-minute silence, they contained the "smoking gun"—clear evidence of his complicity in the cover-up. His ultimate resignation became but a matter of time. Four days later, on August 9, 1974, the extraordinary episode came to an end, as Nixon became the first American president ever to resign.

Although the power of government and of the presidency had expanded greatly in the 1960s and 1970s, the Watergate episode seemed disturbing and scandalous evidence that the appropriate balance of power had disappeared. As the scandal wound down, many began to question the centralization of power in the American political system and to cite the "imperial presidency" as the cause of recent abuses. Others simply lost faith in the presidency altogether. A 1974 survey showed that trust in the presidency had declined by 50 percent in a two-year period. Coming on the heels of Lyndon Johnson's lying to the American people about involvement in Vietnam, the Watergate affair contributed to the cumulative disillusionment with politics in Washington and to the steady decrease in political participation. Barely half of those eligible to vote bothered to go to the polls in the presidential elections 1976, 1980, and 1984. Even fewer cast votes in nonpresidential contests.

Gerald Ford: Caretaker President

In the aftermath of the Watergate affair, Washington was in turmoil. Americans wondered whether any politician could be trusted to guide public af-

Gerald Ford, a genial man, sought to reestablish confidence in the government after succeeding Nixon as president. Far different from his predecessor, he served just over two years, as his bid for reelection ended in defeat.

fairs. The new president, Gerald Ford, faced the difficult task of using his authority to restore national confidence at a time when the misuse of presidential power itself had precipitated the crisis.

Ford worked quickly to restore trust in the government. He emphasized conciliation and compromise, and he promised to cooperate both with Congress and with American citizens. The nation responded gratefully. *Time* magazine pointed to a "mood of good feeling and even exhilaration in Washington that the city had not experienced for many years."

The new feeling did not last long. The new president weakened his base of support by pardoning Richard Nixon barely a month after his resignation. Ford's decidedly conservative bent in domestic policy often threw him into confrontation with a Democratic Congress. Economic problems proved most pressing in 1974, as inflation, fueled by oil price increases, rose to 11 percent a year, unemployment stood at 5.3 percent, and gross national product declined. Home construction slackened and interest rates rose, while stock prices fell. Nixon, preoccupied with the Watergate crisis, had been unable to curb rising inflation and unemployment. Not since Franklin Roosevelt took office in the depths of the Great Depression had a new president faced economic difficulties so severe.

Like Herbert Hoover 45 years before him, the conservative Ford hoped to restore confidence and persuade the public that conditions would improve. But his campaign to cajole Americans to "Whip Inflation Now" voluntarily failed dismally. At last convinced of the need for strong governmental action, the administration introduced a tight-money policy as a means of curbing inflation. It led to the most severe recession since the Depression, with unemployment peaking at 12 percent in 1975. In response, Congress pushed for an antirecession spending program. Recognizing political reality, Ford endorsed a multibillion-dollar tax cut coupled with higher unemployment benefits. The economy made a modest recovery, although inflation and unemployment remained high, and federal budget deficits soared.

Ford's dilemma was that his belief in limited presidential involvement set him against liberals who still argued that strong executive leadership was necessary to make the welfare state work. When he failed to take the initiative, Congress intervened, and the two branches of government became embroiled in conflict. Ford vetoed numerous bills, including those creating a consumer protection agency and expanding programs in education, housing, and health. In response, Congress overrode a higher percentage of vetoes than at any time since the presidency of Franklin Pierce more than a century before.

The Carter Interlude

In the election of 1976, the nation's bicentennial year, Ford faced Jimmy Carter, former governor of Georgia. Carter, appealing to voters distrustful of political leadership, portrayed himself as an outsider. He stressed that he was not from Washington and that, unlike many of those mired in past scandals, he was not a lawyer. Carter's quest for the Democratic nomination benefited from reforms that increased the significance of primary elections in selecting a presidential candidate and decreased the influence of party professionals. Assisted by public relations experts, he effectively utilized the media, especially television, which allowed him to bypass party machiners and establish a direct electronic relationship with voters. In the election, most elements of the old Democratic coalition still held. Carter won a 50 to 48 percent majority of the popular vote and a 297 to 240 tally in the Electoral College. He did well with the working class, African-Americans, and Catholics. He won most of the South, heartening to the Democrats after Nixon's gains there. Racial voting differences, however, continued as Carter attracted less than half of all white voters but an overwhelming majority of black voters.

Carter stood in stark contrast to his recent predecessors in the White House. Rooted in the rural South, he was the first chief executive from the region in well over a hundred years. He was a graduate of the Naval Academy, trained as a manager and an engineer. A modest man by nature, he was not wholly comfortable with the pomp and incessant political activity in Washington. He hoped to take a more restrained approach to the presidency and thereby defuse its imperial stamp.

Initially, voters saw Carter as a reform Democrat committed to his party's liberal goals. When he had accepted the Democratic nomination, he had called out for an end to race and sex discrimination. He had challenged the "political and economic elite" in America and sought a new approach to providing for the poor, old, and weak.

But Carter was hardly the old-line liberal some Democrats had hoped for. Though he called himself a populist, his political philosophy and priorities were never clear. His critics charged that he had no legislative strategy at all to communicate to Congress. Rather, he responded to problems in a haphazard way and failed to provide firm direction. His status as an outsider, touted during the campaign, led him to ignore traditional political channels when he assumed power. Like Herbert Hoover, he was a technocrat in the White House at a time when liberals wanted a visionary to help them overcome hard times.

In economic affairs, Carter gave liberals some hope at first as he permitted a policy of deficit spending. When the Federal Reserve Board increased the money supply to help meet mounting deficits, which reached peacetime records in these years, inflation rose to about 10 percent a year. Seeking to reduce inflation in 1979, Carter

Jimmy Carter holds hands with his wife, Rosalyn, as they walk to his inauguration in early 1971. As much as possible, Carter tried to avoid actions that reminded people of the "imperial presidency" of the Nixon years.

slowed down the economy and cut the deficit slightly. Contraction of the money supply led to greater unemployment and many small-business failures. Budget cuts fell largely on social programs and distanced Carter from reform-minded Democrats who had supported him three years before. Yet even that effort to arrest growing deficits was not enough. When the budget released in early 1980 still showed high spending levels, the financial community reacted strongly. Bond prices fell, and interest rates rose dramatically.

Similarly, Carter disappointed liberals by his failure to construct an effective energy policy. OPEC had been increasing oil prices rapidly since 1973. Americans began to resent their dependence on foreign oil—over 40 percent was being imported by the end of the decade—and clamored for energy self-sufficiency. Carter responded in April 1977 with a comprehensive energy program, which he called the "moral equivalent of war." Critics seized on the acronym of that expression, MEOW, to describe the plan and had a field day criticizing the president. Never an effective leader in working with the legislative branch, Carter watched his proposals bog down in Congress for 26 months. Eventually, the program committed the nation to move from oil dependence to reliance on coal, possibly even on sun and wind, and established a new synthetic-fuel corporation. Nuclear power, another alternative, seemed less attractive as costs rose and accidents, like the one at Three Mile Island, occurred.

Carter further upset liberals by beginning deregulation—the removal of governmental controls in economic life. Arguing that certain restrictions established over the past century ended competition and increased consumer costs, he supported decontrol of oil and natural gas prices to spur production. He also deregulated the railroad, trucking, and airline industries.

The Continuing Cold War and Its Consequences

As executive and legislative leaders struggled to define the government's role in domestic affairs, they had to address difficult questions about America's role abroad. Politics established the shape of the welfare state; politics also affected the extent of American involvement in Cold War confrontations around the world. In the 1960s and 1970s, as the nation witnessed first the triumph, then the failure, of the liberal approach at home, it remained locked in a bitter conflict with Communist governments. In that struggle, Democrats and Republicans alike saw the world in Cold War terms and responded by increasing America's web of foreign entanglements and commitments. Involvement in the quagmire of Vietnam was the unfortunate result. Extrication from the war in the 1970s demanded the same kind of redefinition of role that was occurring on the domestic front.

Kennedy's Confrontations

John Kennedy entered office interested above all in foreign policy and determined to stand firm in the face of Russian power. Despite all the talk about a New Frontier, most of his foreign policy ideas were rooted in the past. During the campaign, Kennedy declared: "The enemy is the communist system itself—implacable, insatiable, unceasing in its drive for world domination." In his inaugural address, he eloquently described the dangers and challenges the United States faced. "In the long history of the world," he cried out, "only a few generations have been granted the role of defending freedom in its hour of maximum danger." The United States would "pay any price, bear any burden, meet any hardship, support any friend, oppose any foe, to assure the survival and success of liberty."

Kennedy's most imaginative approach to the Cold War involved the promotion of "peaceful revolution" in unaligned Third World countries. By providing nonmilitary assistance programs that increased agricultural productivity and built modern transportation and communications systems, Kennedy hoped to promote stable, pro-Western governments throughout Latin America, Africa, and Asia.

While attempts to promote social progress and pro-American governments in developing nations proceeded, Kennedy saw direct challenges from the Soviet Union almost from the beginning of his presidency. The first came at the Bay of Pigs in the spring of 1961. Cuban-American relations had been strained since Fidel Castro's revolutionary army had overthrown the dictatorial Fulgencio Batista, a longtime American ally, in

1959. As Castro expropriated private property of major American corporations, which for decades had dominated the Cuban economy, the U.S. government became increasingly concerned. More than simply economic issues were involved. American officials were convinced that a radical regime in Cuba, leaning toward the Soviet Union, provided a model for upheaval elsewhere in Latin America and threatened the venerable Monroe Doctrine.

Just before Kennedy assumed office, the United States broke diplomatic relations with Cuba. The CIA, meanwhile, was covertly training anti-Castro exiles to storm the Cuban coast at the Bay of Pigs. The American planners assumed the invasion would lead to an uprising of the Cuban people against Castro. When Kennedy learned of the plan, he approved it. The plan was bold and, Kennedy thought, would prove his toughness. He overruled the opposition of Senator J. William Fulbright, chairman of the Foreign Relations Committee, who argued that "the Castro regime is a thorn in the flesh; but it is not a dagger in the heart." Nor did he listen to the objection of marine commandant David Shoup, who claimed that Cuba could not be taken easily.

The invasion, on April 17, 1961, was an unmitigated disaster. Cuban forces kept troops from coming ashore, and there was no popular uprising to greet the invaders. The United States stood exposed to the world, attempting to overthrow a sovereign government. It had broken agreements not to interfere in the internal affairs of hemispheric neighbors and had intervened clumsily and unsuccessfully.

Although chastened by the debacle at the Bay of Pigs, Kennedy remained determined to deal sternly with the perceived Communist threat. On meeting Soviet leader Nikita Khrushchev in Vienna in June 1961, he felt cornered on the question of Berlin. The Russians were pressing for a settlement that would reflect the reality of the city's post–World War II division into eastern and western zones and prevent the flight of East Germans to the West. Fearful that the Soviet effort signaled designs on the Continent as a whole, Kennedy responded aggressively, seeking $3 billion more in defense appropriations, more men for the armed forces, and funds for a civil defense fallout shelter program, as if to warn of the possibility of nuclear war. After the Russians erected a wall in Berlin to seal off their section, the crisis eased. But Kennedy felt he had overreacted. Sensitive to his image as world leader, he believed he had come off second-best in the struggle.

The next year, Kennedy had a chance to recoup some of his lost prestige, again by running the risk of war. Fidel Castro, understandably fearful of the American threat to Cuban independence after the Bay of Pigs invasion, sought and secured Russian assistance. American aerial photographs taken in October 1962 revealed that the Soviet Union had begun to place what Kennedy saw as offensive missiles on Cuban soil. Cuba insisted that the missiles were defensive, and, in any event, they did not change the strategic balance significantly. The Soviets could still wreak untold damage on American targets from bases farther away, while American missiles stood on the borders of the Soviet Union in Turkey. But with Russian weapons installed just 90 miles from American shores, appearance was more important than reality. Kennedy was determined to confront the Russians (not the Cubans) and win.

Meeting with top staff members, the president ruled out an air strike to destroy the missile sites, but ordered a full alert. Bombers and missiles were fueled, armed with nuclear weapons, and readied to go. The fleet prepared to move, and troops stood set to invade. Kennedy himself went on nationwide TV to tell the American people about the missiles and to demand their removal. He declared that the United States would not shrink from the risk of nuclear war and announced a naval blockade around Cuba to prevent Soviet ships from bringing in additional missiles. He called the move a quarantine, for a blockade was an act of war.

As the Soviet ships steamed toward the blockade and the nations stood "eyeball to eyeball" at the brink, the American and Russian people held their breath. Americans, on the one hand, applauded the president and accepted the situation in the terms he had defined. On the other hand, they feared a cataclysmic confrontation that could bring the world to an end.

After several days, the tension broke, but only because Khrushchev called the Russian ships back and then sent a long letter to Kennedy pledging to remove the missiles if the United States ended the blockade and promised to stay out of

Cuba altogether. A second letter demanded that America remove its missiles from Turkey as well. The United States responded affirmatively to the first letter, ignored the second, and said nothing about its intention, already voiced, of removing its own missiles from Turkey. With that the crisis ended.

The Cuban missile crisis was the most terrifying confrontation of the Cold War. Soviet and Cuban forces were ready to resist invasion at all costs. Russian warheads stood ready for use. Kennedy's truculent response had led the world closer to nuclear war than it had ever been. Yet the president emerged from the crisis as a hero who had stood firm. His reputation was enhanced, as was the image of his party in the coming congressional elections. As the relief of the moment began to fade, however, critics charged that what Kennedy saw as his finest hour was in fact an unnecessary crisis. Though Kennedy had shown some restraint in not authorizing an air attack, he had neglected normal channels of diplomacy and had moved precariously close to the brink. He had avoided disaster only, as Dean Acheson observed, by "plain dumb luck," when the Russians showed restraint. One consequence of the affair was the establishment of a Soviet-American hot line to avoid similar episodes in the future. Another was Russia's determination to increase its nuclear arsenal so that it would never again be exposed as inferior to the United States.

Escalation in Vietnam

Believing that the power and prestige of the United States had been damaged by the Bay of Pigs and the confrontation over Berlin, Kennedy was determined to achieve Cold War victories in other parts of the world. Thus he willingly increased American involvement in Southeast Asia. "How do we get moving?" he queried his advisers shortly after being elected. The United States decided against entering Laos in the spring of 1961 to head off a Communist threat. In Vietnam, however, it exercised less restraint. Vietnamese leader Ho Chi Minh continued his struggle to liberate his land in what had become a bitter civil war (see Chapter 26). Unsympathetic to Ho's regime in North Vietnam, the United States steadily increased its support to South Vietnam. By the time Eisenhower left the presidency in 1961, some 675 American military advisers were assisting the South Vietnamese. After the Bay of Pigs, Kennedy decided to increase that level of assistance. By the end of 1963, the number had risen to more than 16,000.

Despite American backing, South Vietnamese leader Ngo Dinh Diem was rapidly losing support within his own country. Buddhist priests burned themselves alive in the capital of Saigon to dramatize Diem's unpopularity. American officials began to realize that Diem would never reform. After receiving assurances that the United States would not object to an internal coup, South Vietnamese military leaders assassinated Diem and seized the government.

Kennedy understood the importance of popular support for the South Vietnamese government if that country were to maintain its independence. But he was reluctant to withdraw and let the Vietnamese solve their own problems. When Kennedy met with a violent death shortly after Diem's assassination, Lyndon Johnson faced a situation in flux in Vietnam.

In 1963, Buddhist priests in Vietnam burned themselves to death in Saigon to dramatize their opposition to the Diem government. Photographs in American newspapers horrified readers and created suspicion that South Vietnam was led by a corrupt and autocratic leader.

Johnson shared many of Kennedy's assumptions about the threat of communism. His understanding of the past led him to believe that aggressors had to be stopped or their actions would lead to world war, as had been true in World War II. Like Kennedy, Johnson believed in the domino theory, which held that if one country in a region fell, others were bound to follow.

In office, Johnson was determined to oppose communism. In Latin America, this determination resulted in the support of military dictatorships and some embarrassing mistakes. In 1965, Johnson dispatched over 20,000 troops to the Dominican Republic, believing that "Castro-type elements" might win in the civil war there. In fact, the group Johnson called Communist was led by the former president, Juan Bosch, who had been overthrown by a military junta. Bosch ruefully pointed out that "this was a democratic revolution smashed by the leading democracy of the world." Johnson's claims about the threat of communism and the importance of protecting American tourists were seen as lies by some and created a wedge between his administration and liberals. That wedge would widen over the question of Vietnam. Kennedy had expanded American forces there; Johnson took the Vietnam War and made it his own. Soon after assuming office, he reached a fundamental decision that guided policy for the next four years. South Vietnam was more unstable than ever after the assassination of Diem. Guerrillas, known as Viet Cong, challenged the regime, sometimes covertly, sometimes through the National Liberation Front, their political arm. Aided by Ho Chi Minh and the North Vietnamese, the insurgent Viet Cong slowly gained ground. Henry Cabot Lodge, the American ambassador to South Vietnam, told Johnson that if he wanted to save that country, and indeed the whole region, he had to stand firm. "I am not going to lose Vietnam," Johnson replied. "I am not going to be the President who saw Southeast Asia go the way China went."

In the election campaign of 1964, Johnson posed as a man of peace. "We don't want our American boys to do the fighting for Asian boys," he declared. "We are not going to send American boys nine or ten thousand miles away from home to do what Asian boys ought to be doing for themselves." He criticized those who suggested moving in with American bombs. All the while, however, he was planning to increase American involvement in the war.

In August 1964, Johnson cleverly obtained congressional authorization for the war. North

The Vietnam War

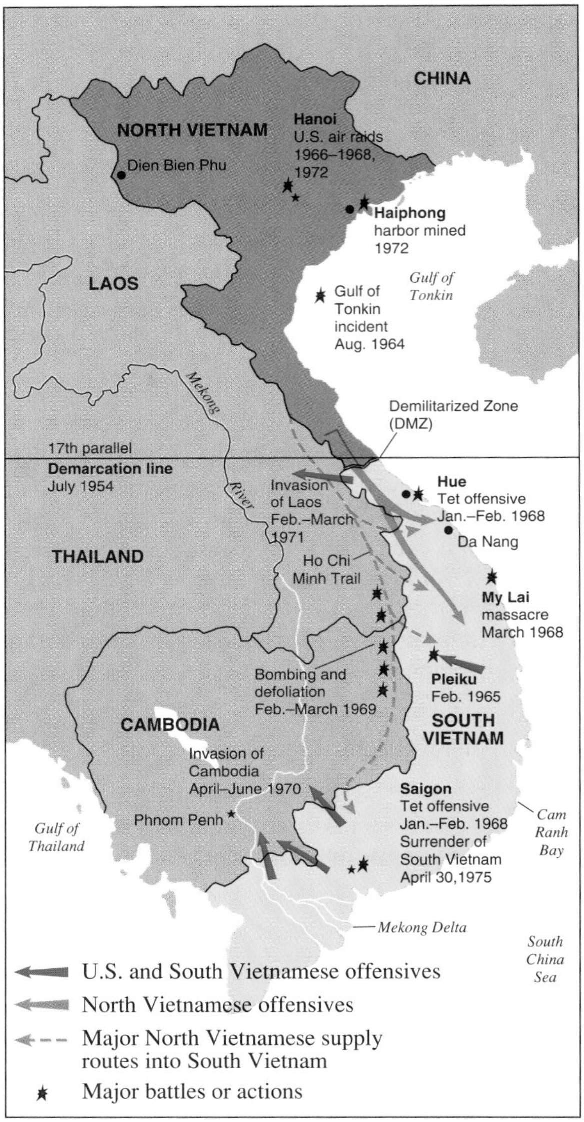

This map shows the major campaigns of the Vietnam War. The North Vietnamese Tet offensive of early 1968, pictured with red arrows, turned the tide against U.S. participation in the war and led to peace talks. The American invasion of Cambodia in 1970, pictured with blue arrows, provoked serious opposition.

Vietnamese torpedo boats, he announced, had, without provocation, attacked American destroyers in the international waters of the Gulf of Tonkin, 30 miles from North Vietnam. Only later did it become clear that the American ships had violated the territorial waters of North Vietnam by assisting South Vietnamese commando raids in offshore combat zones. With the details of the attack still unclear, Johnson used the episode to obtain from Congress a resolution giving him authority to "take all necessary measures to repel any armed attack against the forces of the United States and to prevent further aggression." Not aware that the president had been carrying the resolution around for some time, Congress passed it by a vote of 416 to 0 in the House and 88 to 2 in the Senate. It gave Johnson the leverage he sought. As he noted, it was "like grandma's nightshirt—it covered everything."

Military escalation began in earnest in February 1965, after Viet Cong forces killed 7 Americans and wounded 109 in an attack on an American base at Pleiku. Johnson responded by authorizing retaliatory bombing of North Vietnam to cut off the flow of supplies and to ease pressure on South Vietnam. A few months later, the president sent American ground troops into action, telling the American people, "We did not choose to be the guardians at the gate, but there is no one else." This marked the crucial turning point in the Americanization of the Vietnam War. Only 25,000 American soldiers were in Vietnam at the start of 1965. By the end of the year, there were 184,000, and the number swelled to 385,000 in 1966, 485,000 in 1967, 543,000 in 1968. "Remember, escalation begets escalation," Senator Mike Mansfield futilely warned the president in mid-1965.

Massive amounts of American supplies and personnel changed the character of the conflict. No longer simply military advisers in Southeast Asia, American forces became direct participants in the fight to prop up a dictatorial regime in faraway South Vietnam. Although a somewhat more effective government headed by Nguyen Van Thieu and Nguyen Cao Ky was finally established, the level of violence increased. Saturation bombing of North Vietnam continued. Fragmentation bombs, killing and maiming countless civilians, and napalm, which seared off human flesh, were used extensively. Similar destruction wracked South Vietnam. Yet the North Vietnamese and their revolutionary allies in South Vietnam pressed on. Like LBJ, they sought not compromise but victory.

U.S. Troops in Vietnam, 1965–1973

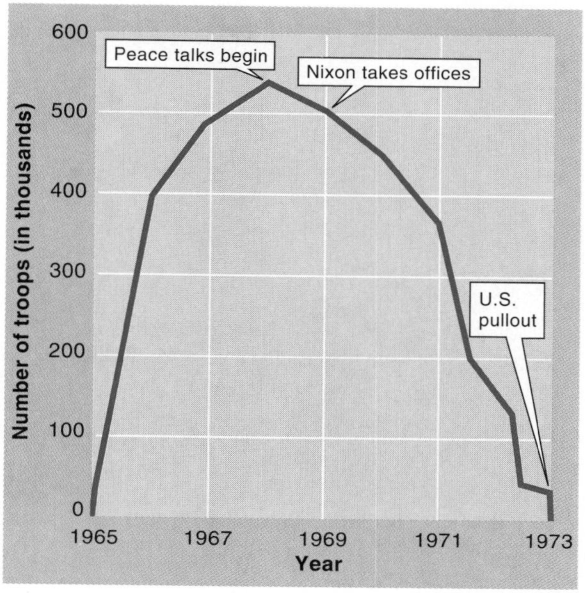

This graph shows the dramatic escalation in the number of American troops, and the corresponding decline after peace talks began and Nixon took office in 1969. The drop in the number of U.S. soldiers defused American opposition to the war.

Source: U.S. Department of Defense.

Americans began to protest their involvement in the war. As escalation began, 82 percent of the public felt that American forces should stay in Vietnam until the Communist elements withdrew. Then students began to question basic Cold War assumptions, first espoused by Truman, about the need to battle communism around the globe. The first antiwar teach-in took place in March 1965 at the University of Michigan. Others soon followed. Initially, both supporters and opponents of the war appeared at the teach-ins, but soon the sessions became more like antiwar rallies than instructional affairs. Boxer Muhammad Ali legitimated draft resistance when he declared "I ain't got no quarrel with them Viet Cong" and refused military induction. Working through Students for a Democratic Society (SDS) and other

The Vietnam War involved both ground troops and air power. Helicopters fired on enemy forces, evacuated the dead and wounded, and moved troops from one site to another.

organizations, radical activists campaigned against the draft, attacked ROTC units on campus, and sought to discredit firms that produced the destructive tools of war (see Chapter 29 for a full discussion of student activism). "Make love, not war," slogans proclaimed as more and more students became involved in political demonstrations at dozens of colleges. "Hey, hey, LBJ. How many kids did you kill today?" opponents of the war chanted. In 1967, some 300,000 people marched in New York City. In Washington, D.C., 100,000 tried to close down the Pentagon.

Working-class and middle-class Americans began to sour on the war as well. Watching nightly television reports that featured graphic representations of the death and destruction, they wondered about their nation's purposes and actions.

In early 1968, the North Vietnamese mounted the massive Tet offensive, attacking provincial capitals and district towns in South Vietnam. In Saigon, they struck the American embassy, Tan Son Nhut air base, and the presidential palace. Though beaten back, they won a psychological victory. American audiences, even more disturbed than before, came to realize that the war perhaps could not be won.

When Richard Nixon assumed office in 1969, he gave top priority to extricating the deeply divided United States from Vietnam while still finding a way to win the war. He announced the Nixon Doctrine, which asserted that the United States would aid friends and allies but would not undertake the full burden of troop defense. He thereupon embarked on the policy of Vietnamization, which entailed removing American forces and replacing them with Vietnamese ones. At the same time, Americans launched ferocious air attacks on North Vietnam. "Let's blow the hell out of them," Nixon instructed the Joint Chiefs of Staff. Between 1968 and 1972, American troop strength dropped from 543,000 to 39,000, and the reduction won political support for Nixon at home. Yet as the transition occurred, the South Vietnamese steadily lost ground to the Viet Cong.

War protests multiplied in 1969 and 1970. In November 1969, as a massive protest demonstration took place in Washington, D.C., stories surfaced about a massacre of civilians in Vietnam the year before. Journalist Seymour M. Hersh had heard rumors about an episode at My Lai and had begun to piece together an account of what had occurred. His efforts provided the American people with horrifying evidence of the war's brutality.

My Lai, a small village in South Vietnam, was allegedly harboring 250 members of the enemy Viet Cong. An American infantry company was helicoptered in to clear out the village. C Company had already had heavy combat losses, but it prepared to confront yet more enemy soldiers. Instead, it found women, children, and old men. Perhaps inured to the random destruction already wrought by the American military, perhaps concerned with the sometimes fuzzy distinction between combatants and civilians in a guerrilla war, the American forces lost control.

Lieutenant William L. Calley, Jr., a mild-mannered officer, first ordered, "Round everybody up," and then said, "Take care of 'em." When Paul Meadlo, a private from a small Indiana farm town, simply guarded the people he had collected, Calley said, "Hey, Meadlo, I said take care of 'em." At that the Americans began mowing down the civilians in cold blood. Later Meadlo recalled:

> We huddled them up. We made them squat down. . . . I poured about four clips into the group. . . . The mothers was hugging their children. . . . Well, we kept right on firing. They was waving their arms and begging. . . . I still dream about it. About the women and children in my sleep. Some days . . . some nights, I can't even sleep.

Stories of the civilian slaughter shocked Americans at home. Yet once the initial revulsion began to subside, people proved unwilling to condemn. Some sympathized with Calley, who, they argued, was simply responding to the demands of war. When Calley was court-martialed, convicted of at "least twenty-two murders," and sentenced to life imprisonment, Nixon realized that many Americans thought the sentence too harsh. He ordered Calley released from prison while the case was under appeal and announced that he would personally review it before any sentence was carried out. As the furor died down, the military reduced his sentence to ten years. Eligible for parole in six months, Calley was soon free.

While the My Lai incident led many to wonder about American conduct of the war, incidents on several college campuses made them question the use of troops at home. Nixon's policy prompted the episodes. Much as he wanted to defuse opposition to the war, he was determined not to lose the war either. As he publicized his Vietnamization initiative, he looked for other ways to achieve victory. Realizing that the Vietnamese relied on supplies funneled through Cambodia, Nixon announced that American and Vietnamese troops were invading that country to clear out the Communist enclaves there. The United States, he said, would not stand by as a "pitiful helpless giant" when there were actions it could take to stem the Communist advance.

Nixon's invasion of Cambodia brought renewed demonstrations on college campuses, some with tragic results. At Kent State, in Ohio, the response was fierce. The day after the president announced his moves, disgruntled students gathered downtown. Worried about the crowd, the local police called in sheriff's deputies to disperse the students. The next evening, groups of students collected on the college grounds. Assembling around the ROTC building, they began throwing firecrackers and rocks at the structure, which had become a hated symbol of the war. Then they set it on fire and watched it burn to the ground.

The governor of Ohio ordered the National Guard to the university. Tension grew and finally the situation exploded. Loading their guns and donning gas masks, the Guardsmen prepared to disperse the gathering mob. As the students fell back, some threw rocks or empty canisters of gas. Most, however, were so far away that they could not have reached the troops. At midday, the soldiers knelt down and aimed their rifles at the students as if to warn them to stop. Then they rose together, huddled with one another, and finally began to retreat to a different position. At the top of a hill they turned and suddenly began firing in unison at the students below.

When the firing ceased, four students lay dead, nine wounded. Two of the dead had been demonstrators, who were more than 250 feet away when shot. The other two were innocent bystanders, almost 400 feet from the troops.

Students around the country, as well as other Americans, were outraged by the attack. Many were equally disturbed about a similar attack at Jackson State University in Mississippi. Policemen and highway patrolmen poured automatic weapon fire into a women's dormitory without warning. When the shooting stopped, two people were dead, more wounded. The dead there, however, were black students at a black institution, and white America paid less attention to that attack.

In 1971, the Vietnam War made major headlines once more when the *New York Times* began

Television

In the past 40 years, television has played an increasingly important part in American life, providing historians with another source of evidence about American culture and society in the recent past.

Television's popularity by the 1950s was the result of decades of experimentation dating back to the nineteenth century. In the 1930s, NBC installed a television station in the new Empire State Building in New York. With green makeup and purple lipstick to provide better visual contrast, actors began to perform before live cameras in studios. At the end of the decade, "Amos 'n' Andy," a popular radio show, was telecast, and as the 1940s began, Franklin D. Roosevelt became the first president to appear on television. World War II interrupted the development of television, as Americans relied on radio to bring them news. After the war, however, the commercial development of television quickly resumed. Assembly lines that had made electronic implements of war were now converted to consumer production, and thousands of new sets appeared on the market. The opening of Congress could be seen live in 1947; baseball coverage improved that same year owing to the zoom lens; children's shows like "Howdy Doody" made their debut; and "Meet the Press," a radio interview program, made the transition to television.

Although sports programs, variety shows hosted by Ed Sullivan and Milton Berle, TV dramas, and episodic series ("I Love Lucy" and "Gunsmoke," for example) dominated TV broadcasting in the 1950s, television soon became entwined with politics and public affairs. Americans saw Senator Joseph McCarthy for themselves in the televised Army-McCarthy hearings in 1954; his malevolent behavior on camera contributed to his downfall. The 1948 presidential nominating conventions were the first to be televised, but the use of TV to enhance the public image of politicians was most thoroughly developed by the fatherly Dwight D. Eisenhower and the charismatic John F. Kennedy. Some argue that the TV debate in 1960 between the tanned, handsome Kennedy and a pasty-white Richard Nixon helped elect Kennedy.

In 1963, a horrified public watched as officials used vicious police dogs and thunderous fire hoses on peaceful marchers in the Birmingham civil rights demonstrations, thus arousing public opinion against southern resistance. And people throughout the United States shared the tragedy of John Kennedy's assassination in November 1963, sitting stunned before their sets trying to understand the events of his fateful Texas trip. The shock and sorrow of the American people was repeated in the spring of 1968 as they watched the funerals of Martin Luther King, Jr., and Robert Kennedy. A year later, a quarter of the world's population watched as Neil Armstrong became the first man to set foot on the moon.

This combination of visual entertainment and enlightenment made owning a television set virtually a necessity. By 1970, fully 95 percent of American households owned a TV set, a staggering increase from the 9 percent only 20 years earlier. Fewer families owned refrigerators or indoor toilets.

The implications of the impact of television on American society are of obvious interest to historians. How has television affected other communications and entertainment industries, such as radio, newspapers, and movies? What does the content of TV programming tell us about the values, interests, and tastes of the American people?

Perhaps most significant, what impact has TV had on the course of historical events like presidential campaigns, human relations, and wars? In the late 1960s, for example, television played an important part in shaping impressions of the war in Vietnam. More and more Americans began to understand the nature and impact of the war as TV newscasters brought visual images of burning huts and wounded soldiers into American living rooms every evening. As the combined Viet Cong–North Vietnamese forces attacked Saigon during the Tet offensive of 1968, American TV networks showed scenes of a kind never screened before. One such clip, on NBC News, showed the chief of the South Vietnamese National Police, General Loan, moving to the side of a Viet Cong prisoner, looking at the prisoner, lifting his gun, and calmly blowing out the captive's brains. Viewers watched the corpse drop to the ground, blood spouting from his head.

The picture you see here is a still snapshot of the execution that appeared on television and later won the Pulitzer Prize for the photographer. The picture makes a powerful impression on its own, but the impact was even stronger when the film clip on TV replayed the actual event for 20 million people.

Examine the image closely. What feelings do you see on the face of the prisoner? What is the mood of General Loan? How do you respond to such an image? Knowing that this drama involved real people, how

General Loan executing a Viet Cong suspect in Saigon.

do you think the television audience might have reacted to this segment of the evening news? How vivid does violence need to be to make a strong impression? How might such a scene have helped focus the growing frustration with the war and aid efforts to end it? Reflect on more recent incidents you have seen "live" on TV, and ponder how they have affected the history of events in your lifetime.

Television Tonight

6:30 — WTTV 4: Leave It to Beaver. Beaver tries to help a friend who has run away from home. Repeat.

6:30 — WLW-I 13: Cheyenne has a Laramie adventure in which Slim, Jess, and Jonesy work on a cattle drive. Repeat.

7:30 — WTTV 4: The Untouchables. Eliot Ness tries to deal with a late gangster's niece who has a record of the murdered hood's career. Repeat.

7:30 — WLW-I 13: Voyage to the Bottom of the Sea presents "Mutiny," in which Admiral Nelson shows signs of a mental breakdown during the search for a giant jellyfish which supposedly consumed a submarine.

7:30 — WFBM-TV 6: Members of the Indianapolis Rotary Club discuss the 1965 business outlook with former U.S. Sen. Homer Capehart.

8:00 — WFBM-TV 6: The Man from UNCLE is in at a new time and night. Thrush agents try to recapture one of their leaders before Napoleon Solo can deliver him to the Central Intelligence Agency. Ralph Taeger is guest star.

8:00 — WISH-TV 8: I've Got a Secret welcomes the panel from To Tell the Truth: Tom Poston, Peggy Cass, Kitty Carlisle, and Orson Bean.

8:30 — WLW-I 13: Basketball, I.U. vs. Iowa.

8:30 — WISH-TV 8: Andy Griffith's comedy involves Goober's attempts to fill in at the sheriff's office.

9:00 — WFBM-TV 6: Andy Williams is visited by composer Henry Mancini, Bobby Darin, and Vic Damone. Musical selections include "Charade," "Hello Dolly," and "Moon River."

9:00 — WTTV 4: Lloyd Thaxton welcomes vocal group, Herman's Hermits.

9:00 — WISH-TV 8: Lucille Ball is driven to distraction by a secret package she has been instructed not to open.

9:30 — WISH-TV 8: Many Happy Returns. Walter's plan for currying favor with the store's boss hits a snag.

10:00 — WFBM-TV 6: Alfred Hitchcock presents Margaret Leighton as a spinster who goes mad when she cannot cope with the strain of rearing an orphaned niece in "Where the Woodbine Twineth."

10:00 — WLW-I 13: Ben Casey gets help in diagnosing a boy's illness from an Australian veterinarian with terminal leukemia. The vet's knowledge of bats provides the key.

10:00 — WISH-TV 8: "Viet Nam: How We Got In—Can We Get Out?" is the topic of CBS Reports.

Source: *Indianapolis News*, January 11, 1965.

When Ohio National Guardsmen fired on a crowd of antiwar demonstrators and killed four students, even prowar Americans were shocked. This photograph shows the grief and outrage of others who survived the savage shooting of innocent bystanders.

publishing a secret Department of Defense account of American involvement in the war. The so-called Pentagon Papers, leaked by Daniel Ellsberg, a defense analyst, gave Americans a firsthand look at the fabrications and faulty assumptions that had guided the steady expansion of the struggle. Even though the study stopped with the Johnson years, the Nixon administration was furious and sought a Supreme Court injunction to halt publication of the series. By a split vote, the Court ruled against the government, and readers continued to learn more about the nightmarish war.

Vietnam remained a political football as Nixon ran for reelection in 1972. Negotiations aimed at a settlement were under way, and just days before the election, Henry Kissinger announced, "Peace is at hand." When South Vietnam seemed to balk at the proposed settlement, however, the administration responded with the most intensive bombing campaign of the war. Hanoi, the capital of North Vietnam, was hit hard; then the North Vietnamese harbors were mined. Only in the new year was a cease-fire finally signed. Kissinger shared the 1973 Nobel Peace Prize with his North Vietnamese counterpart Le Duc Tho. Tho rejected his part of the prize with the observation that the war between North and South Vietnam was not yet over, even though the American troops were finally going home. Kissinger had no such compunctions and accepted his share of the award.

After Nixon left office, the conflict in Vietnam lingered on into the spring of 1975, yet by that time, American troops had been evacuated. When at last the North Vietnamese consolidated their control over the entire country, Gerald Ford called for another $1 billion in aid, even as the South Vietnamese were abandoning arms and supplies in chaotic retreat. Congress refused, leaving the crumbling government of South Vietnam to fend for itself. Republicans hailed Kissinger for having finally freed the United States from the Southeast Asian quagmire. Antiwar critics condemned him for remaining involved for so long. The *New Republic* wryly observed that Kissinger brought peace to Vietnam in the same way Napoleon brought peace to Europe: by losing.

The long conflict had enormous consequences for American society. In foreign policy, the disillusionment with anti-Communist rhetoric undermined the entire post–World War II approach to world affairs and opened the way to a reorientation in the next two decades. In human terms, the costs were immense. In the longest war in its history, the United States lost almost 58,000 men, with far more wounded or maimed. Blacks and Chicanos suffered more than whites, since they were disproportionately represented in combat units. The nation spent over $150 billion on the unsuccessful war. Domestic reform had slowed, then stopped. Cynicism about the government had increased. American society had been deeply divided. Only time would tell whether the wounds would heal.

Détente

If the Republicans' Vietnam policy was a questionable success, accomplishments were impressive in other areas. Nixon, the Red-baiter of the past, was able to deal imaginatively and successfully with the Communist powers. In so doing, he reversed the direction of American policy since the Second World War. Bypassing Congress, often bypassing his own Department of State, the president depended most heavily on Kissinger, who grasped the complexity of the world situation, understood the tensions within the Communist realm, and exploited them to restore better American relations with both the Soviet Union and China.

Nixon's most dramatic step was opening formal relations with the People's Republic of China. In the two decades since Mao Zedong's victory on the Chinese mainland in 1949, the American position had been that Jiang Jieshi's rump government on Taiwan was the rightful government of the Chinese people; consequently, there had been no diplomatic relations with the Communist regime. In 1971, with an eye on the forthcoming political campaign, the administration began softening its rigid stand. After the Chinese invited an American table tennis team to visit the mainland, the United States eased some of the trading restrictions in force. In August 1971, Nixon announced that he intended to visit China the following year, the first American president ever to do so.

That bold step signified Nixon's understanding that the People's Republic was an established force representing the Chinese people. The president knew that the rest of the world had for years recognized the People's Republic and wanted to seat it in the United Nations. Moreover, he suspected that he could use Chinese friendship as a bargaining chip when he dealt with the Soviet Union. Finally, American leaders officially acknowledged what most nations already knew: communism was not monolithic. At home, Nixon believed that he could open a dialogue with the Chinese Communists without political harm, for he had long been a vocal critic of communism and could hardly be accused of being "soft" on it. He knew also that the press and television cover-

Nixon shifted the course of Chinese-American relations by his dramatic visit to the People's Republic. He met Chinese officials for the first time, visited the Great Wall and other sites, and then reported back enthusiastically to the American people.

age of a dramatic trip could give a boost to his image.

Nixon went to China in February 1972. He met with Chinese leaders Mao Zedong and Zou Enlai (Chou En-lai), talked about international problems, exchanged toasts, and saw some of the major sights. Wherever he went, American television cameras followed, helping to introduce the American public to a nation about which it knew little. Though formal relations were not yet restored, détente between the two countries had begun.

Nixon also used his new China policy to seek better ties with the Soviet Union. He and Kissinger hoped to be able to play one Communist state against the other, and by and large, they accomplished their aim. Several months after his trip to China, Nixon visited Russia, where he was also warmly welcomed. After several cordial meetings, the president and Soviet premier Leonid Brezhnev agreed to limit missile stockpiles, work together in space, and ease long-standing restrictions on trade. Businessmen applauded the new approach, and most Americans approved of détente.

Nixon dealt with the Communist governments with tact and skill. Using his Chinese and Russian initiatives to neutralize opposition to the phased withdrawal of troops in Vietnam, he bought time to pursue Vietnamization on his own terms.

When Gerald Ford assumed office, he followed the policies begun under Nixon. Kissinger remained secretary of state and continued to play an influential role in foreign affairs. In May 1975, an episode in another part of Southeast Asia reflected the difficulties of new policies. Cambodian forces captured the *Mayaguez,* an American merchant ship cruising inside the territorial waters of that country. When American protests went unanswered, the United States sent 350 marines to attack an island where the crew was thought to be held. The operation's cost was 41 American lives, and seemed to be a case of overkill, authorized because the United States was eager to respond vigorously after the defeat in Vietnam and to avoid the impression of weakness.

Ford continued the Strategic Arms Limitation Talks (SALT) that provided hope for eventual nuclear disarmament. He also accepted the Helsinki Accords, which defined European security arrangements and underscored basic human rights. He pursued friendly relations with China and elsewhere maintained the spirit of détente, even while rejecting the term.

Nixon's policy of détente resulted in improved relations with the Soviet Union. Here he and Soviet leader Leonid Brezhnev toast one another at the signing of the Strategic Arms Limitation Treaty.

Human Rights Diplomacy

Jimmy Carter enjoyed a number of notable successes in conducting a more modest foreign policy, though he had had little diplomatic experience when he took office. Fiercely religious, he sought to make American policy adhere to the Christian standards that were part of his personal life.

Carter's major achievement involved the Middle East, where Israel and the Arab nations had fought a series of bitter wars. When Anwar el-Sadat of Egypt and Menachem Begin of Israel began to negotiate a peace settlement in 1978, Carter invited the two adversaries to come to Camp David, in the Maryland hills. There his personal diplomacy helped bring about a peace treaty, signed in March 1979. Israel withdrew from the occupied Sinai peninsula in return for Egyptian recognition and normalized relations. After 30 years of hostilities, Israel and Egypt were at peace.

NO WAY

Jimmy Carter helped Prime Minister Menachem Begin of Israel (at the left, wearing glasses) and President Anwar el-Sadat of Egypt (in center, looking at Carter) reach agreement on a peace treaty during talks at Camp David.

At home, Carter fought for Senate acceptance of two treaties returning the Panama Canal to Panama by the year 2000. The United States had built the canal and long controlled it, but resentment had grown in Panama over the presence of a foreign power and the way in which the United States had acquired the right to build it. In the agreements, accepted by the margin of a single vote, the United States retained certain rights in the event of crisis but otherwise yielded to Panamanian demands.

In Asia, Carter successfully followed Nixon's initiatives by extending diplomatic recognition to the People's Republic of China. Attempting to modernize their economy, the Chinese sought technical assistance from the United States. American wheat farmers and businessmen eyed the Chinese market of nearly a billion people with enthusiasm, and American diplomats were eager to keep China and Russia at odds.

With the Soviet Union, Carter was less successful. Russian-American relations, the major U.S. diplomatic concern since World War II, fluctuated in the Carter years. Taking over with détente at high tide, the new president declared that the United States had finally escaped its "inordinate fear of Communism" and should forge closer ties with the Soviet state. But then his passionate belief, like Woodrow Wilson's, that morality was the "soul of . . . foreign policy" complicated his diplomatic efforts. Insistent that "our commitment to human rights must be absolute," Carter antagonized the Soviets. They charged the American president with meddling in their internal affairs when he verbally supported Russian dissidents. Consequently, Russian leaders resisted working with Carter on concrete disputes between the two superpowers.

One prickly issue was arms control. Negotiations for a more comprehensive strategic arms limitation treaty than the agreement of 1972 threatened to break down. Misjudging the Russians, the president offered new weapon reduction proposals that went further than the Soviet Union was prepared to accept. When this threw matters into confusion, Carter backed off, patient negotiation succeeded, and the SALT II strategic arms limitation agreement was reached in June 1979.

The Soviet invasion of Afghanistan in December 1979, however, complicated ratification. The Russians considered internal agitation there a threat to their security and invaded the country. After a year and a half of watching the bloody involvement, Carter responded by calling the Soviet move the most serious blow to world peace since World War II. He postponed presenting SALT II to the Senate and imposed an American boycott of the 1980 Olympic Games in Moscow. Détente was effectively dead.

Carter also stumbled in his effort to defuse a major crisis with Iran. Americans had long supported the shah of Iran. Overlooking the corruption and abuse in his regime, they viewed him as a reliable supplier of oil and defender of stability in the Persian Gulf region. In January 1979, revolutionary groups drove the shah from power. In his place sat the Ayatollah Ruholla Khomeini, an Islamic priest who returned from exile in Paris to lead a new fundamentalist Islamic regime.

When Carter admitted the shah to the United States for medical treatment in October 1979, angry Iranian students seized the American embassy in Tehran and held 53 Americans hostage. The prisoners were blindfolded, bound, and beaten. Some suffered solitary confinement and endured mock executions. In the United States, their ordeal became a national cause. Unwilling to return the shah or to apologize for past American support for his now discredited regime, Carter broke diplomatic relations and froze Iranian assets, but his actions brought no results and his popularity plummeted. The Iranians finally agreed to free the hostages in early 1981, but not until the very day Carter left office did the prisoners end their 444-day ordeal.

after Reagan election

CONCLUSION

Political Readjustment

America shifted course significantly, both at home and abroad, in the decade and a half after Dwight Eisenhower left the presidency. In the 1960s, liberal Democrats pressed for large-scale government intervention to meet the social and economic problems that accompanied the modern industrial age. Endorsing a process under way since the New Deal, they saw the triumph of their approach in Lyndon Johnson's Great Society, as the nation strengthened its commitment to a capitalist welfare state. When the Democratic party became impaled on the Vietnam War and lost the presidency, the Republicans began dismantling the Great Society programs. While accepting some provisions of the modern welfare state, they objected to the aggressive liberal effort to make the government the major player in the political game and to many of the programs aimed at the needy. On the foreign front, first the Democrats, then the Republicans, committed the nation to battling communism during the continuing Cold War, but even that cooperative approach disintegrated in the 1970s in the wake of the struggle in Vietnam.

Most Americans, like Ron Kovic, embraced the message of John Kennedy and the New Frontier in the 1960s and endorsed the Great Society programs that followed. But over time, like Kovic, they began to question the tenets of liberalism as the economy faltered, as hard economic choices had to be made, and as the country became mired in Vietnam. Slowly, as the optimism that had characterized the 1960s evaporated, a more conservative approach to both domestic and foreign problems emerged.

Recommended Reading

General Works

Peter N. Carroll, *It Seemed Like Nothing Happened: America in the 1970s* (1990); Jim F. Heath, *Decade of Disillusionment: The Kennedy-Johnson Years* (1975); Godfrey Hodgson, *America in Our Time* (1976); Allen J. Matusow, *The Unraveling of America: A History of Liberalism in the 1960s* (1984); Kurt Vonnegut, *Cat's Cradle* (novel, 1963).

John F. Kennedy and the New Frontier

Henry Fairlie, *The Kennedy Promise* (1972); James N. Giglio, *The Presidency of John F. Kennedy* (1991); Herbert S. Parmet, *Jack: The Struggles of John F. Kennedy* (1980) and *JFK: The Presidency of John F. Kennedy* (1983); Thomas C. Reeves, *A Question of Character: A Life of John F. Kennedy* (1991); Arthur M. Schlesinger, Jr., *A Thousand Days: John F. Kennedy in the White House* (1965); Theodore C. Sorensen, *Kennedy* (1965).

Lyndon B. Johnson and the Great Society

Robert A. Caro, *The Years of Lyndon Johnson: The Path to Power* (1983) and *The Years of Lyndon Johnson: Means of Ascent* (1990); Robert Dallek, *Lone Star Rising: Lyndon Johnson and His Times* (1990); Robert A. Divine, ed., *Exploring the Johnson Years* (1981) and *The Johnson Years, Volume Two: Vietnam, the Environment, and Science* (1984); Rowland Evans, Jr., and Robert Novak, *Lyndon B. Johnson: The Exercise of Power* (1966); Lyndon Johnson, *The Vantage Point: Perspectives of the Presidency* (1971); Doris Kearns, *Lyndon Johnson and the American Dream* (1976); Sar A. Levitan and Robert Taggart, *The Promise of Greatness* (1976).

Richard Nixon and Watergate

Stephen Ambrose, *Nixon: The Education of a Politician, 1913–1962* (1987); Rowland Evans, Jr., and Robert D. Novak, *Nixon in the White House* (1972); J. Anthony Lukas, *Nightmare: The Underside of the Nixon Years* (1976); Richard Nixon, *RN: The Memoirs of Richard Nixon* (1978); Jonathon Schell, *The Time of Illusion: An Historical and Reflective Account of the Nixon Era* (1975); Garry Wills, *Nixon Agonistes: The Crisis of the Self-made Man* (1969); Bob Woodward and Carl Bernstein, *All the President's Men* (1974) and *The Final Days* (1976).

Gerald Ford

John Hersey, *The President* (1975); Richard Reeves, *A Ford, Not a Lincoln* (1975).

Jimmy Carter

Jimmy Carter, *Keeping Faith: Memories of a President* (1982); Jules Witcover, *Marathon: The Pursuit of the Presidency, 1972–1976* (1977).

Vietnam

John M. Del Vecchio, *The 13th Valley* (novel, 1982); Frances FitzGerald, *Fire in the Lake* (1972); David Halberstam, *The Best and the Brightest* (1972); George C. Herring, *America's Longest War: The United States and Vietnam, 1950–1975* (1979); Stanley Karnow, *Vietnam: A History: The First Complete Account of Vietnam at War* (1983); Guenter Lewy, *America in Vietnam* (1978); Norman Mailer, *The Armies of the Night* (history as a novel, 1968); Al Santoli, *Everything We Had: An Oral History of the Vietnam War by Thirty-three American Soldiers Who Fought It* (1981); Neil Sheehan, *A Bright Shining Lie: John Paul Vann and America in Vietnam* (1988); Robert Stone, *Dog Soldiers* (novel, 1974).

TIMELINE

1960 John F. Kennedy elected president

1961 Bay of Pigs invasion fails
Khrushchev and Kennedy meet in Vienna
Berlin Wall constructed

1962 JFK confronts steel companies
Cuban missile crisis

1963 Buddhist demonstrations in Vietnam
President Diem assassinated in Vietnam
Kennedy assassinated; Lyndon B. Johnson becomes president

1964 Gulf of Tonkin Resolution
Economic Opportunity Act initiates War on Poverty
Johnson reelected

1965 Vietnam conflict escalates
Marines sent to Dominican Republic
Teach-ins begin
Department of Housing and Urban Development established
Elementary and Secondary Education Act

1966 National Traffic and Motor Vehicle Safety Act
Department of Transportation established

1967 Antiwar demonstrations

1968 Robert F. Kennedy assassinated
Antiwar demonstrations increase
Tet offensive in Vietnam
Police and protesters clash at Democratic national convention
Richard Nixon elected president
My Lai massacre

1969 Nixon Doctrine announced
Moratorium against the Vietnam War
SALT talks begin

1970 U.S. invasion of Cambodia
Kent State and Jackson State shootings

1971 *New York Times* publishes Pentagon Papers

1972 Nixon visits China and the Soviet Union
Watergate break-in
Nixon reelected
SALT I treaty on nuclear arms

1973 Vietnam cease-fire agreement
Arab oil embargo
Watergate hearings in Congress
Spiro Agnew resigns as vice-president

1974 OPEC price increases
Inflation hits 11 percent
Unemployment reaches 7.1 percent
Nixon resigns; Gerald R. Ford becomes president
Ford pardons Nixon

1975 *Mayaguez* incident
South Vietnam falls to the Communists
Unemployment reaches 12 percent

1976 Jimmy Carter elected president

1977 Carter energy program, human rights policy
Panama Canal treaties

1978 Israeli-Egyptian peace accords at Camp David

1979 Russians invade Afghanistan
Iranian revolution overthrows shah
SALT II agreement on nuclear arms

1979–1981 Iranian hostage crisis

CHAPTER 29

The Struggle for Social Reform

Ann Clarke—as she chooses to call herself now—always wanted to go to college. But girls from Italian families rarely did when she was growing up. Her mother, a Sicilian immigrant and widow, asked her brother for advice: "Should Antonina go to college?" "What's the point?" he replied. "She's just going to get married."

Life had not been easy for Antonina Rose Rumore. As a child in the 1920s, her Italian-speaking grandmother cared for her while her mother worked to support the family, first in the sweatshops, then as a seamstress. Even as she dreamed, Ann accommodated her culture's demands for dutiful daughters. Responsive to family needs, Ann fin-

ished the high school commercial course in three years. She struggled with ethnic prejudice as a legal secretary on Wall Street but still believed in the American dream and the Puritan work ethic. She was proud of her ability to bring money home to her family.

When World War II began, Ann wanted to join the WACS. "Better you should be a prostitute," her mother said. Ann went off to California instead, where she worked at resorts. When she left California, she vowed to return to that land of freedom and opportunity.

After the war, Ann married Gerard Clarke, a college man with an English background. Her children would grow up accepted with Anglo-Saxon names. Over the next 15 years, Ann devoted herself to her family. She was a mother above all, and that took all her time. But she waited for her own chance: "I had this hunger to learn, this curiosity." By the early 1960s, her three children were all in school. Promising her husband to have dinner on the table every night at six, she enrolled at Pasadena City College. It was not easy. Family still came first. A simple problem was finding time to study. When doing dishes or cleaning house, she memorized lists of dates, historical events, and other material for school. Holiday time was difficult. Ann occasionally felt compelled to give everything up "to make Christmas." Forgetting about a whole semester's work two weeks before finals, she sewed nightgowns instead of writing her art history paper.

Her conflict over her studies was intensified by her position as one of the first older women to go back to college. "Sometimes I felt like I wanted to hide in the woodwork," she admitted. Often her teachers were younger than she was. It took four years to complete the two-year program. But she was not yet done. She wanted a bachelor's degree. Back she went, this time to California State College at Los Angeles.

As the years passed and the credits piled up, Ann became an honors student. Her children, now in college themselves, were proud and supportive; dinners became arguments over Faulkner and foreign policy. Even so, Ann still felt caught between her world at home and outside. Since she was at the top of her class, graduation should have been a special occasion. But she was only embarrassed when a letter from the school invited her parents to attend the final ceremonies. Ann could not bring herself to go.

With a college degree in hand, Ann returned to school for a teaching credential. Receiving her certificate at age 50, she faced the irony of social change. Once denied opportunities, Italians had assimilated into American society. Now she was just another Anglo in Los Angeles, caught in a changing immigration wave; the city now sought Hispanics and other minorities to teach in the schools. Jobs in education were scarce, and she was close to "retirement age," so she became a substitute in Mexican-American areas for the next ten years, specializing in bilingual education.

Meanwhile, Ann was troubled by the Vietnam War. "For every boy that died, one of us should lie down," she told fellow workers. She was not an activist, rather one of the millions of quieter Americans who ultimately helped bring about change. The social adjustments caused by the war affected her. Her son grew long hair and a beard and attended protest rallies. She worried that he would antagonize the ladies in Pasadena. Her daughter came home from college in boots and a leather miniskirt designed to shock. Ann accepted her children's changes as relatively superficial, confident in their fundamental values; "they were good kids." She trusted them, even as she worried.

Ann Clarke's experience paralleled that of millions of women in the 1960s, 1970s, and 1980s. Caught up for years in traditional patterns of family life, these women began to recognize their need for something more. Like blacks, Hispanics, Native Americans, and other groups, American women struggled to transform the conditions of their lives and the rights they enjoyed within American society.

This chapter describes the reform impulse that accompanied the effort to define the government's responsibility for economic and social stability described in Chapter 28. Like earlier reform efforts, particularly those during the Progressive era and the New Deal, this modern struggle attempted to fulfill the promise of the American past and to provide liberty and equality in racial, gender, and social relations. The third reform cycle of the twentieth century, however, drew more from the militancy of those on the mudsills of society than from the pleas of middle-class activists. We will highlight the voices of the "outsiders" in the United States as we describe the still-present tension accompanying the sharp debate over power and its distribution. And we will record the continuing frustrations of integrating different groups into American society while acknowledging their integrity and identity.

The Black Struggle for Equality

The quest for equality by black Americans played a central role in the struggle for civil rights in the postwar era, although others such as Asian-Americans and Hispanic-Americans continued longstanding protest movements of their own. Stemming from an effort dating back to the Civil War and Reconstruction, the black movement had gained momentum by the mid–twentieth century. African-Americans continued to press for reform through peaceful protest and political pressure (see Chapter 27 for the gains of the 1950s). But change came slowly. Rigid segregation of public accommodations remained the rule in the South, despite victory in the Montgomery, Alabama, bus boycott of 1955. School integration occurred after the *Brown* v. *Board of Education* decision of 1954, but not without struggles like the one at Little Rock, Arkansas. In the North, urban ghettos grew, as the influx of southern blacks continued. Crowded public housing, poor schools, and limited economic opportunities fostered serious discontent.

Confrontation

A spectrum of organizations, some old, some new, spearheaded the challenge to segregation in the courts and organized nonviolent direct action that relied on grass-roots support. The National Association for the Advancement of Colored People (NAACP), founded in 1910, remained committed to overturning the legal bases for segregation. Even after the *Brown* ruling, it continued to shepherd cases through the courts. The Congress of Racial Equality (CORE), an interracial group established in 1942, promoted change through peaceful confrontation during wartime and remained active in the postwar period. In 1957, Martin Luther King, Jr., and others organized southern black clergy into the Southern Christian Leadership Conference (SCLC) after their victory in Montgomery. The Student Nonviolent Coordinating Committee (SNCC, pronounced "snick"), formed in 1960, was an offshoot of SCLC. Recruiting young Americans who had not been involved in the civil rights struggle, SNCC, far more militant than the older, gradualist organizations, provided students with a framework to participate in confrontational direct action.

The importance of grass-roots efforts for reform was evident as early as 1960 when black college students sat down at a segregated Woolworth's lunch counter and deliberately violated southern segregation laws by refusing to leave. The sit-ins captured media attention, and soon thousands of blacks were involved in the campaign. The following year, the sit-ins gave rise to freedom rides, aimed at testing southern transportation facilities, recently desegregated by a

In violation of southern law, black college students refused to leave a lunch counter, launching a new campaign in the struggle. Here the students wait patiently for service, or forcible eviction, as a way of dramatizing their determination to end segregation.

Supreme Court decision. Organized initially by CORE and aided by SNCC, the program sent groups of blacks and whites together on buses heading south and stopping at terminals along the way. The riders, peaceful themselves, anticipated confrontations that would publicize their cause and generate political support.

In North and South alike, consciousness of the need to combat racial discrimination grew. Support bubbled up from different social groups. Young people in particular, most of them students, enlisted in the effort to change restrictive patterns deeply rooted in American life. White clergy of various denominations became socially active in ways not seen since the Social Gospel movement of the late nineteenth century (when civil rights was not one of their concerns). The civil rights movement became the most powerful moral campaign since the abolitionist crusade before the Civil War. Often working together, blacks and whites vowed to eliminate racial barriers.

Participants in the movement came from every direction. Anne Moody, who grew up in a small town in Mississippi, personified the awakening of black consciousness and the new determination among ordinary black Americans to act. As a child, she had watched the passivity of blacks in the face of discrimination and struggled to understand just what the "white folks' secret" really was. She saw the murder of friends and acquaintances who had somehow transgressed the limits set for blacks. And she became frustrated at members of her own race for not doing anything about the injustices she saw. "I began to look upon Negro men as cowards," she later wrote.

> I could not respect them for smiling in a white man's face, addressing him as Mr. So-and-So, saying yessuh and nossuh when after they were home behind closed doors that same white man was a son of a bitch, a bastard, or any other name more suitable than mister.

Through her own efforts, Moody became the first of her family to go to college. Once there, she found her own place in the civil rights movement. At Tougaloo College, near Jackson, Mississippi, she joined the NAACP and also became involved in the activities of SNCC and CORE. Slowly, she noted, "I could feel myself beginning to change. For the first time I began to think something would be done about whites killing, beating, and misusing Negroes. I knew I was going to be a part of whatever happened." She participated in sit-ins where she was thrashed and jailed for her role, but she remained deeply involved. She learned how to protect herself when threatened by angry whites. Though often exhausted and discouraged, she knew that she was part of something important.

Many whites joined the struggle in the South. Mimi Feingold, a white student at Swarthmore College in Pennsylvania, had been active in northern civil rights protests and antinuclear efforts in the late 1950s, but the sit-in movement deepened her commitment. She helped picket Woolworth's in Chester, Pennsylvania, and worked to unionize Swarthmore's black dining hall workers. But these efforts were not enough. In 1961, after her sophomore year, she headed south to join the freedom rides sponsored by CORE.

Feingold's decision exposed her to frequent violence. On the freedom rides, injuries were common, as southern whites attacked civil rights workers with rocks and chains. Feingold's group had a bomb scare in Montgomery, Alabama, knowing that the last such bus to enter the state had been blown up. Like many others, Feingold went to jail as an act of conscience. In Jackson, Mississippi, where she spent a month behind bars, she heard other women screaming as local police conducted humiliating body searches.

In 1962, the civil rights movement accelerated. James Meredith, a black air force veteran and student at Jackson State College, applied to the all-white University of Mississippi and was rejected on racial grounds. Suing to gain admission, he carried his case to the Supreme Court, where Justice Hugo Black affirmed his claim. But then Governor Ross Barnett, an adamant racist, announced defiantly that Meredith would not be admitted, whatever the Court decision, and on one occasion personally blocked the way. A major riot followed; tear gas covered the university grounds; and by the riot's end, two men lay dead and hundreds hurt.

An even more violent confrontation began in April 1963, in Birmingham, Alabama, where local black leaders encouraged Martin Luther King, Jr., to launch another attack on southern segregation. Forty percent black, the city was rigidly segregated along racial and class lines. "We believed that while a campaign in Birmingham would surely be the toughest fight of our civil rights careers," King later explained, "it could, if successful, break the back of segregation all over the nation."

Though the demonstrations were nonviolent, the responses were not. City officials declared that protest marches violated city regulations against parading without a license, and, over a five-week period, they arrested 2,200 blacks, some of them schoolchildren. Police Commissioner Eugene "Bull" Connor used high-pressure fire hoses, electric cattle prods, and trained police dogs to force the protesters back. As the media recorded the events, Americans watching television and reading newspapers were horrified. The images of violence in Birmingham created mass sympathy for black Americans' civil rights struggle.

James Meredith refused to be driven from the University of Mississippi, despite the opposition of the governor and a campus riot. His perseverance paid off, as he ultimately earned his diploma.

Kennedy's Response

John Kennedy claimed to be sickened by the pictures from Birmingham but insisted that he could do nothing, even though he had courted and won black support in 1960. During the campaign, he

In Birmingham, city officials resisted peaceful demonstrators with brutal force. Here, city police use trained dogs to drive marchers back. Televised nationally, the police response appalled the American public.

announced that "if the President does not himself wage the struggle for equal rights—if he stands above the battle—then the battle will inevitably be lost." He asserted too that a "stroke of the pen" could end racial segregation in federally funded housing. That approach gained him 70 percent of the black vote, and in some states where the tally had been close, particularly Michigan and Illinois, black support made a crucial difference.

The narrowness of his victory, however, dampened his enthusiasm. Reluctant to press white southerners on civil rights when he needed their votes on other issues, Kennedy failed to propose any civil rights legislation. Nor did he fulfill his campaign promise to end housing discrimination by presidential order, despite gifts of numerous bottles of ink. Not until November 1962, after the midterm elections, did he take a modest action—an executive order ending segregation in federally financed housing. Under Robert Kennedy, the Justice Department worked to end discrimination in interstate transportation and to guarantee blacks the right to register and vote in the South. But to Martin Luther King, Jr., this was hardly enough: "If tokenism were our goal, this Administration has moved us adroitly towards its accomplishment."

Events finally forced Kennedy to take actions he had hoped to avoid. When James Meredith was refused admission to the University of Mississippi because of his color in 1962, the president, like his predecessor in the Little Rock crisis, had to send federal troops to restore control and to guarantee Meredith's right to attend. The administration also forced the desegregation of the University of Alabama and helped arrange a compromise providing for desegregation of Birmingham's municipal facilities, implementation of more equitable hiring practices, and formation of a biracial committee. And when white bombings aimed at eliminating black leaders in Birmingham caused thousands of blacks to abandon nonviolence and rampage through the streets, Kennedy readied federal troops to intervene.

The events in Birmingham raised the horrifying possibility of black revolution and helped to push Kennedy to honor the commitments he had made during the campaign. In a nationally televised address, he called the quest for equal rights a "moral issue" and asserted, "We preach freedom around the world, and we mean it. . . ; but are we to say to the world, and much more importantly, to each other that this is a land of the free except for the Negroes. . . ?" Hours after he spoke, assassins killed Medgar Evers, a black NAACP official, in his own driveway in Jackson, Mississippi.

Kennedy sent Congress a new civil rights bill, far stronger than the moderate one proposed earlier in the year. The legislation prohibited segregation in public places, banned discrimination wherever federal money was involved, and advanced the process of school integration. Polls showed that 63 percent of the nation supported his stand.

To lobby for passage of that measure, civil rights leaders, pressed from below by black activists, arranged a massive march on Washington in August 1963. Kennedy did not favor the demonstration, for he feared it would alienate Congress and provoke violence in the capital city. But his efforts to persuade the organizers to call it off failed. As Martin Luther King, Jr., pointed out, "I have never engaged in any direct action movement which did not seem ill-timed." In the end, Kennedy supported the march, which proved to be an almost festive affair. More than 200,000 people gathered from across the country and demonstrated enthusiastically. Celebrities were present: Ralph Bunche, James Baldwin, Sammy Davis, Jr., Harry Belafonte, Jackie Robinson, Lena Horne. The folk music artists of the early 1960s were there as well. Joan Baez, Bob Dylan, and Peter, Paul, and Mary sang songs associated with the movement such as "Blowin' in the Wind" and "We Shall Overcome."

The 1963 march on Washington was a high point in the civil rights movement. Several hundred thousand demonstrators lined the reflecting pool leading out from the Washington Monument and heard Martin Luther King, Jr., and other black leaders eloquently plead for racial equality.

But the high point of the day was the address by Martin Luther King, Jr., the nation's preeminent spokesman for civil rights. For many blacks and whites, he represented the struggle itself. Long interested in Gandhi's theory of nonviolent protest, he had become committed to nonviolent resistance. At the March on Washington, in a powerful speech, he proclaimed his faith in the decency of his fellow citizens and in their ability to extend the promises of the Constitution and the Declaration of Independence to every American. With all the power of a southern preacher, he implored his audience to share his faith.

"I have a dream," King declared, "that one day this nation will rise up and live out the true meaning of its creed: 'We hold these truths to be self-evident, that all men are created equal.' I have a dream that one day on the red hills of Georgia, the sons of former slaves and the sons of former slave-owners will be able to sit together at the table of brotherhood." It was a fervent appeal, and one to which the crowd responded. Each time King used the refrain "I have a dream," thousands of blacks and whites roared together. King concluded by quoting from an old hymn: "Free at last! Free at last! Thank God almighty, we are free at last!"

Despite the power of the rhetoric, not all were moved. Anne Moody, who had come up from her activist work in Mississippi to attend the event, sat on the grass by the Lincoln Memorial as the speaker's words rang out. "Martin Luther King went on and on talking about his dream," she said. "I sat there thinking that . . . we never had time to sleep, much less dream." Nor was the Congress prompted to do much. Despite large Democratic majorities, strong white southern resistance to the cause of civil rights remained, and as of November 1963, Kennedy's bill was still bottled up in committee. Not even the March on Washington had moved it along.

Civil Rights Under Johnson

Lyndon Johnson's commitment to racial justice was far stronger, although his early record on the issue was mixed. A southerner from Texas, he first voted against a series of civil rights measures in his years in the House of Representatives. But as his own career advanced, he became far more sympathetic to racial equality. By 1955, when he became Senate majority leader and eyed the White House, he was ready to play a much more active role. He made his break with the South clear when he guided the Civil Rights Act of 1957 through Congress. As president, his first legislative priority was civil rights reform. He assured black leaders that he would push for a comprehensive new law.

Reviving Kennedy's civil rights proposal, which had been sidetracked in Congress, Johnson declared in 1963, "No memorial oration or eulogy could more eloquently honor President Kennedy's memory than the earliest possible passage of the civil rights bill." After the House of Representatives passed the bill, the Senate became bogged down in a lengthy filibuster. A determined Johnson persuaded his old colleague, minority leader Everett Dirksen, to work for cloture—a two-thirds vote to cut off debate. In June 1964, the Senate for the first time imposed cloture to advance a civil rights measure, and passage soon followed. "No army can withstand the strength of an idea whose time has come," Dirksen explained.

The Civil Rights Act of 1964 outlawed racial discrimination in all public accommodations and authorized the Justice Department to act with greater authority in school and voting matters. In addition, an equal-opportunity provision prohibited discriminatory hiring on grounds of race, gender, religion, or national origin in firms with more than 25 employees. The legislation was one of the great achievements of the 1960s. The system of segregation put in place in the South in the late nineteenth century finally lost its legal sanctions. Blacks now were promised legal equality as they had been 100 years before.

Johnson realized that the Civil Rights Act of 1964 was only a starting point, since widespread discrimination still existed in American society. Despite the voting rights measures of 1957 and 1960, African-Americans still found it difficult to vote in large areas of the South. Freedom Summer, sponsored by SNCC and other civil rights groups in 1964, focused attention on the problem by sending black and white students south in a massive voter registration project in Mississippi. Early in the summer, two whites, Michael Schwerner and Andrew Goodman, and one black, James Chaney, were murdered. By the end of the summer, 80 workers had been beaten, 1,000 arrests had been made, and 37 churches had been bombed in resistance to efforts of civil rights workers to register black voters. Early in 1965, Alabama police again dramatized this classic confrontation of "soul force against physical force" as they clubbed and tear-gassed demonstrators in an aborted march from Selma to the state capital at Montgomery. Events in Selma forced President Johnson first to send the National Guard to protect another march to Montgomery, led by Martin Luther King, Jr., and second to ask Congress for a voting bill that would close the loopholes of the previous two acts. In a nationwide address, he began by saying, "I speak tonight for the dignity of man and the destiny of democracy. . . . It is wrong . . . to deny any of your fellow Americans the right to vote." Stopping at one point and raising his arms, he slowly repeated the words from the old hymn that had become the marching song of the movement: "And . . . we . . . shall . . . overcome." Once again white violence resisting peaceful, mostly black, protesters combined with the powers of the presidency to get Congress to enact long overdue constitutional rights.

The Voting Rights Act of 1965, perhaps the most important law of the decade, singled out the South for its restrictive practices and authorized the U.S. attorney general to appoint federal examiners to register voters where local officials were obstructing the registration of blacks. In the year after passage of the act, 400,000 blacks registered to vote in the Deep South; by 1968, the number reached a million.

Black Power Challenges Liberal Reform

Despite passage of the Civil Rights Act of 1964 and the Voting Rights Act of 1965, racial discrimination remained in both North and South. De facto segregated schools, wretched housing, and

The Struggle for Equal Rights

Year	Event	Effect
1947	Report of Truman's Committee on Civil Rights	Showed that blacks remained second-class citizens in America.
1948	Truman's executive order integrating the armed forces	Opened the way for equal opportunities in the armed forces.
1954	*Brown* v. *Board of Education* decision	Supreme Court ruled that "separate but equal" schools were unconstitutional; first step in ending school segregation.
1955	Montgomery bus boycott	Black solidarity tested local petty segregation laws and customs.
1957	Little Rock school integration crisis	White resistance to integration of Little Rock's Central High School resulted in Eisenhower's calling in federal troops.
	Civil Rights Act	Created Civil Rights Commission and empowered Justice Department to go to court to guarantee blacks the right to vote.
1960	Civil Rights Act	Plugged loopholes in Civil Rights Act of 1957.
	Sit-in demonstrations	Gained support for desegregation of public facilities.
1961	Freedom rides	Dramatized struggle to desegregate transportation facilities.
1962	James Meredith's attempt to attend University of Mississippi	Required federal intervention to uphold blacks' rights to attend public institutions.
1963	Effort to desegregate Birmingham, Alabama	Brutal response of police televised, sensitizing entire nation to plight of blacks.
	March on Washington	Gathered support and inspiration for the civil rights movement; scene of Martin Luther King's "I Have a Dream" speech.
1964	Civil Rights Act	Outlawed racial discrimination in public accommodations.
1965	Voting Rights Act	Allowed federal examiners to register black voters where necessary.
1971	Busing decision	Supreme Court ruled that court-ordered desegregation was constitutional, even if it employed busing.
1978	*Bakke* decision	Supreme Court declared that affirmative action was constitutional but that firm racial quotas were not.
1987	Howard Beach beatings	Racial unrest in Howard Beach, a white section of New York City, when a gang of whites beat up blacks wandering into the neighborhood, during which one was killed by a car.
1992	*Freeman* v. *Pitts* case	Supreme Court granted a suburban Atlanta school board relief from a desegregation order
	Clarence Thomas appointment	Thomas replaced Thurgood Marshall as the only African-American on the Supreme Court.

inadequate job opportunities were continuing problems. As civil rights moved north, dramatic divisions within the movement emerged.

Initially, the civil rights campaign had been integrated and nonviolent. Its acknowledged leader was Martin Luther King, Jr. But now black-white tensions flared within organizations, and King's nonviolent approach was challenged by younger black leaders tired of beatings, jailings, church bombings, and the slow pace of change when dependent on white liberal and government action. Anne Moody, the stalwart activist in Mississippi, voiced the doubts so many blacks harbored about the possibility of real change. Discouraged after months of struggle, she boarded a bus taking civil rights workers north to testify about the abuses that still remained. As she listened to the others singing the movement's songs, she was overwhelmed by the suffering she had so often seen. "We Shall Overcome" reverberated around her, but all she could think was, "I wonder. I really wonder."

One episode that contributed to many blacks' suspicion of white liberals occurred at the Democratic national convention of 1964 in Atlantic City. SNCC, active in the Freedom Summer project in Mississippi, had founded the Freedom Democratic party as an alternative to the all-white delegation that was to represent the state. Before the credentials committee, black activist Fannie Lou Hamer testified that she had been beaten, jailed, and denied the right to vote. Yet the committee's final compromise, pressed by President Johnson, who worried about losing southern support in the coming election, was that the white delegation would still be seated, with two members of the protest organization offered seats at large. That response hardly satisfied those who had risked their lives and families to try to vote in Mississippi. As civil rights leader James Forman observed, "Atlantic City was a powerful lesson, not only for the black people from Mississippi, but for all of SNCC. . . . No longer was there any hope . . . that the federal government would change the situation in the Deep South." SNCC, once a religious, integrated organization, began to change into an all-black cadre that could mobilize poor blacks for militant action. "Liberation" was replacing civil rights as a goal.

Increasingly, angry blacks argued that the nation must no longer withhold the rights pledged in its founding credo. James Baldwin, a prominent black author, wrote unless change came soon, the worst could be expected: "If we do not now dare everything, the fulfillment of that prophecy, recreated from the Bible in song by a slave, is upon us: God gave Noah the rainbow sign, No more water, the fire next time!"

Even more responsible for channeling black frustration into a new set of goals and tactics was Malcolm X, the most compelling of a number of articulate northern black leaders. Born Malcolm Little and reared in ghettos from Detroit to New York, he became intimately familiar with the sordid side of black urban life. As a young man, he wore a zoot suit, conked his hair, and hustled numbers and prostitutes in the big cities. Arrested and imprisoned, he became a convert to the Nation of Islam and a disciple of black leader Elijah Muhammad. He began to preach that the white man was responsible for the black man's condition and that blacks had to help themselves.

"The day of nonviolence is over," Malcolm X proclaimed, as many African-Americans listened enthusiastically. A compelling speaker, Malcolm made a powerful case for a more aggressive campaign for black rights.

Impatient with the moderate civil rights movement, Malcolm grew tired of hearing "all of this non-violent, begging-the-white-man kind of dying . . . all of this sitting-in, sliding-in, wading-in, eating-in, diving-in, and all the rest." The March on Washington he termed the "Farce on Washington." Espousing black separatism and black nationalism for most of his public career, he argued for black control of black communities, preached an international perspective embracing African peoples in diaspora, and appealed to blacks to fight racism "by any means necessary."

Malcolm's articulate affirmation of blackness and his justification of militant self-defense struck a resonant chord. With widespread media attention, he became the most dynamic spokesman for poor northern blacks since Marcus Garvey in the 1920s. Though he was assassinated by a black antagonist in 1965, his African-centered, uncompromising perspective helped shape the ongoing struggle against racism.

One man influenced by Malcolm's message was Stokely Carmichael. Born in Trinidad, he came to the United States at the age of 11, where he grew up with an interest in political affairs. At the Bronx High School of Science he read voraciously, attended left-wing meetings, became interested in socialism, and gravitated into black protest. Soon after arriving at Howard University, he and other students took over the Washington, D.C., chapter of SNCC. He participated in pickets and demonstrations and was beaten and jailed. Frustrated with the strategy of civil disobedience, he urged fieldworkers to carry weapons for self-defense. It was time for blacks to cease depending on whites, he argued, and to make SNCC into a black organization. His election as head of SNCC in 1966 marked a profound shift in the tactics and goals of the black struggle.

The split in the black movement was symbolized in June 1966 when Carmichael's followers challenged those of Martin Luther King, Jr., during a march in Mississippi. King still adhered to nonviolence and interracial cooperation. His movement's song, "We Shall Overcome," was drowned out by Carmichael's followers' song, "We Shall Overrun." The turning point came when Carmichael, just out of jail, jumped onto a flatbed truck to address the group. "This is the twenty-seventh time I have been arrested—and I ain't going to jail no more!" he shouted. "The only way we gonna stop them white men from whippin' us is to take over. We been saying freedom for six years and we ain't got nothing. What we gonna start saying now is Black Power!" Carmichael had the audience in his hand. As he repeated, "We . . . want . . . Black . . . Power!" the crowd roared back the same words.

Meanwhile, other blacks proposed more drastic action. The Black Panthers formed a militant organization that vowed to eradicate not only racial discrimination but capitalism as well. H. Rap Brown, who followed Carmichael as head of SNCC, became known for his statement that "violence is as American as cherry pie."

Violence accompanied the more militant calls for reform and showed that racial injustice was not a southern problem but an American one. Riots erupted in Rochester, New York City, and several New Jersey cities in 1964. In 1965, in the Watts neighborhood of Los Angeles, a massive uprising lasting five days left 34 dead, more than 1,000 injured, and hundreds of structures burned to the ground. Violence broke out again in other cities in 1966 and 1967. Now cries of "Get Whitey" and "Burn, baby, burn" replaced the peaceful slogans of the earlier civil rights movement. Martin Luther King, Jr., who had broadened his critique to include American involvement in the Vietnam War, fell before a white assassin's bullet in April 1968. Angry blacks reacted by demonstrating once more in cities around the country. As the National Advisory Commission on Civil Disobedience noted in the Kerner Report of 1968, "Our nation is moving toward two societies, one black, one white—separate and unequal."

"Southern Strategy" and Showdown on Civil Rights

Richard Nixon, elected president in 1968, was less sympathetic to the cause of civil rights than his predecessors. Eager to consolidate his political base and to underscore his allegiance to conservative groups, he felt that he had little to gain by courting black Americans. In 1968, the Republicans had won only 12 percent of the black vote, leading Nixon to conclude that any effort to woo the black electorate would endanger his attempt to obtain white southern support.

From the start, the Nixon administration sought to scale back the federal commitment to civil rights. It moved, at the start of Nixon's first term, to reduce appropriations for fair-housing enforcement. Then the Department of Justice tried to block an extension of the Voting Rights Act of 1965. Although Congress approved the extension, the administration's position on racial issues was clear. When South Carolina senator Strom Thurmond and others tried to suspend federal school desegregation guidelines, the Justice Department lent support by urging a delay in meeting desegregation deadlines in 33 of Mississippi's school districts. When a unanimous Supreme Court rebuffed the effort, Nixon disagreed publicly with the decision. His actions demonstrated his sympathy with white southern sentiment, while he avoided any blame for the integration of Mississippi's schools. Nixon also faced the growing controversy over busing as a means of desegregation, a highly charged issue in the 1970s. Transporting students from one area to another to attend school was nothing new. A century before, in 1869, Massachusetts had set aside money to send children to and from school in carriages and wagons, and over the next 50 years, public funding for student transport became lawful in all states. Parents, in fact, had usually viewed busing as an educational advantage, for their children could be moved from a one-room schoolhouse to a consolidated school. By 1970, over 18 million students, almost 40 percent of those in the United States, rode buses to school. Yet when busing became tangled with the question of integration, it inflamed passions.

The busing question first surfaced in the South. There, in the years before the Supreme Court endorsed integration, busing had long been used to maintain segregated schools. Some black students in Selma, Alabama, for example, traveled

When busing was mandated to end de facto school segregation in the North, the order frequently prompted fierce resistance. Here police provide protection for the children being bused.

50 miles by bus to an entirely black trade school in Montgomery, even though a similar school for whites stood nearby. Now, however, busing had become a means of breaking down racial barriers.

The issue came to a head in North Carolina, in the Charlotte-Mecklenburg school system. The 550-square-mile district had over 84,000 students in more than 100 schools. Twenty-nine percent of the pupils were black, and they were concentrated primarily in one section of the region. A desegregation plan involving voluntary transfer was in effect, but there, as elsewhere, many blacks still attended largely segregated schools. A federal judge ruled that the district was not in compliance with the latest Supreme Court decisions, and in 1971, the Supreme Court ruled that district courts had broad authority to order the desegregation of school systems—by busing, if necessary.

Earlier, Nixon had opposed such busing, and the Court decision did not affect his position. The fact that George Wallace had spoken out against busing and won Florida's Democratic primary in March 1972 was not lost on Nixon. The president approached Congress for a moratorium or even a restriction on busing and went on television to denounce it. Although Congress did not accede to his request, southerners knew where the president stood.

As the busing mandate spread to the North, resistance spilled out of the South. In many of the nation's largest northern cities, schools were as rigidly segregated as in the South, largely owing to residential patterns. This segregation was called *de facto* to differentiate it from the *de jure* or legal segregation that had existed in the South. Mississippi senator John C. Stennis, a bitter foe of busing, hoped to stir up the North by making it subject to the same standards as the South. "Parents," he said, "are not going to permit their children to be boxed up and crated and hauled around the city and the country like common animals." And, he informed northern colleagues, "if you have to [integrate] in your area, you will see what it means to us." Court decisions subsequently ordered many northern cities to desegregate their schools.

In Boston, the effort to integrate proved rockier than anywhere else in the North. In 1973, despite a state measure eight years earlier requiring districts to desegregate any schools more than half black, 85 percent of the blacks in Boston attended schools that had a black majority. More than half the black students were in schools that were 90 percent black. In June 1974, a federal judge ordered that busing begin. The first phase, involving 17,000 pupils, was to start in the fall of that year.

Watching the process unfold, Thomas J. Cottle, of the Children's Defense Fund of the Washington Research Project in Boston, closely followed two families, one white and one black. Though he changed their names in a report he presented in the popular press, he captured their sentiments and their words.

Clarence Charles McDonough, III, a white parent, was irate when he learned that his son Cassie was to be transferred by bus from the white school he attended to a black school farther away. "They did it to me," he screamed as Cottle visited one day.

> They went and did it to me. . . . I told you they would. I told you there'd be no running from 'em. You lead your life perfect as a pane of glass, go to church, work 40 hours a week at the same job—year in, year out—keep your complaints to yourself, and they still do it to you. They're forcing that boy to go to school miles from here in a dangerous area to a school no one knows a damn thing about, just so they can bring these other kids in, kids who don't belong here.

Black father Ronald Dearborn also had anxieties about what his son Claudell might face in a white area.

> It's a long way, even by car. Let's hope they keep those buses running fine. I'd hate to think what would happen if they broke down some night over there. If white folks don't look kindly at having black folks attending their schools, they sure won't like to see a bunch of black youngsters parked outside their home all night.

Unlike Clarence McDonough, however, he supported school desegregation. As Francine, Claudell's mother, pointed out, such steps were necessary, even if bruises were involved, for "when you're black, you know all about falling—and what you don't know this country teaches you mighty fast, even when you go to schools where everyone is black, like we did."

For both Cassie and Claudell, attendance at different elementary schools went smoothly. Reassigned high school students were less fortunate. A white boycott at South Boston High cut attendance from the anticipated 1,500 to less than 100 on the first day. Buses bringing in black students were stoned, and some children were cut. White working-class South Bostonians felt that they were being asked to carry the burden of middle-class liberals' racial views. Similar resentments and anger triggered racial episodes elsewhere. In many cases, white families either enrolled their children in private schools or fled the city altogether.

Busing became a bitter issue that reflected the volatile nature of the quest for equal rights. Given his own private views and political ends, Nixon hoped to slow down the civil rights movement, and to a degree he did. Despite that effort, he never viewed himself as a bigot but rather as a man who would do whatever was practical to assist in racial relations. "I care," he once insisted to James Farmer, a black leader appointed to the post of assistant secretary of health, education, and welfare. "I just hope people will believe that I do care." Yet actions spoke louder than words.

So it was during Gerald Ford's brief presidency. At one point, Ford asked his own attorney general, Edward H. Levi, to consider supporting antibusing advocates in a Boston court case, then accepted the advice to drop the idea. Though he never came out squarely against civil rights, Ford's lukewarm approach demonstrated a weakening of the federal commitment.

The situation was less inflamed at the college level, but the same pattern held. Blacks made significant progress until the Republican administrations in the late 1960s and 1970s slowed the movement for civil rights. Integration at the post-secondary level came easier as federal affirmative-action guidelines brought more blacks into colleges and universities. In 1950, only 83,000 black students were enrolled in institutions of higher education. A decade later, more than one million were working for college degrees. Black enrollment in colleges reached 9.3 percent of the college population in 1976, dropped back to 9.1 percent in 1980, just what it had been in 1973, then rose to 10.2 percent in 1990.

As blacks struggled on the educational and occupational fronts, some whites protested that gains came at their expense and amounted to "reverse discrimination." In 1973 and 1974, for example, Allan Bakke, a white, applied to the medical

Black Employment Shifts in the 1980s

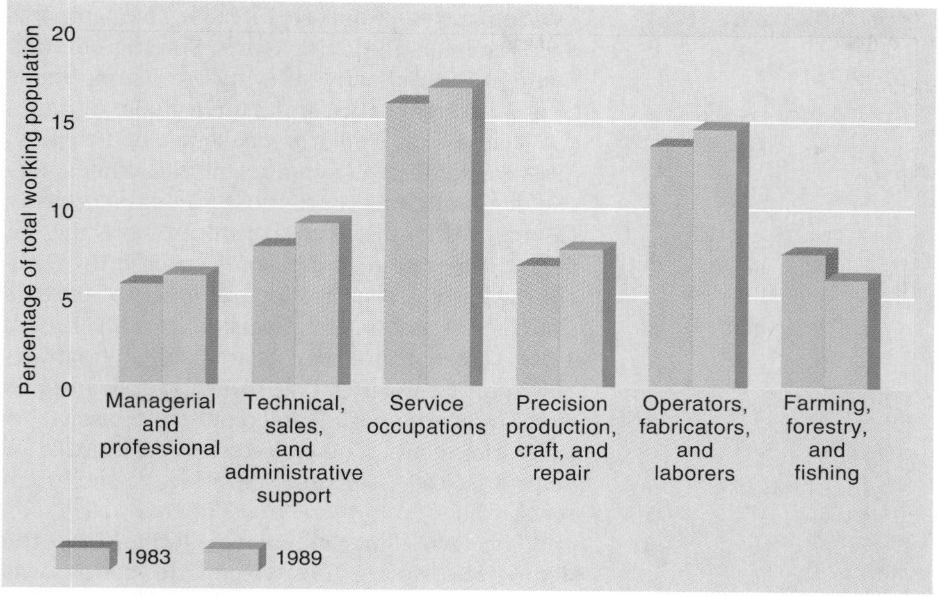

This chart shows the changes in black employment patterns in the 1980s. Note the gains in all categories except farming and related activities.

Source: Data from *Statistical Abstract of the United States,* 1991.

school at the University of California at Davis. Twice rejected, he sued on the grounds that a racial quota reserving 16 of 100 places for minority-group applicants was a form of reverse discrimination that violated the Civil Rights Act of 1964. In 1978, the Supreme Court ordered Bakke's admission to the medical school, but in a complex ruling involving six separate opinions, the Court upheld the consideration of race in admissions policies, even while arguing that quotas could no longer be imposed. The decision received widespread attention and caused many people to fear a white backlash.

Jimmy Carter, president when the *Bakke* decision was handed down, tried to adopt a more active approach than his Republican predecessors. He quickly signaled his intent to bring a large number of qualified blacks into his administration. Of 1,195 early appointees, 12 percent were black. Some, like Andrew Young, his ambassador to the United Nations, were highly visible. But his lack of support for increased social programs for the poor hurt the majority of black citizens and strained their loyalty to the Democratic party.

By the early 1980s, for the first time since Reconstruction, black voting rights had brought to political office a host of new leaders. In the election of 1982, for example, the number of black representatives in Congress increased from 18 to 21, while in state and local elective offices some 6,000 blacks served their constituents. Black political candidates won mayoral elections in the 1980s in major cities, including Detroit, Los Angeles, Cleveland, Chicago, and New York. In 1989, Douglas Wilder of Virginia became the first African-American ever to be elected governor of any state. Equally impressive were the presidential campaigns of the Reverend Jesse Jackson in 1984 and 1988. In his first effort, Jackson was a vocal, sometimes abrasive figure on the fringes of the Democratic party. But in 1988, he moved into the mainstream and dominated the primary campaign, winning 7 million votes and nearly 1,200 delegates. Though he did not win the nomination, his campaign indicated the important African-American presence in politics.

Yet cutting against the grain of those strides forward in electoral politics were backward steps in the struggle for social and economic equality.

Ratio of Median Black-to-White Family Income

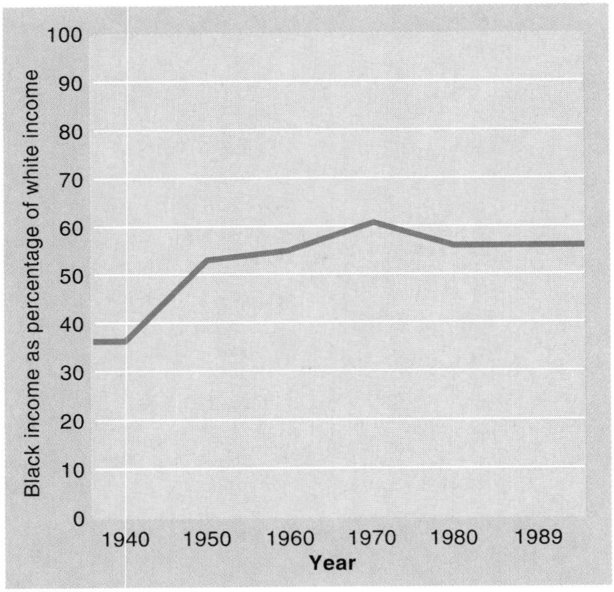

This chart shows the substantial difference between family income for blacks and whites, and reveals it has changed slowly in the past five decades.

Source: Data from U.S. Department of Labor and *Statistical Abstract of the United States,* 1991

Joseph Lattimore, a black from Chicago, observed: "As far as integrating with you—we have sang 'We Shall Overcome,' we have prayed at the courthouse steps, we have made all these gestures, and the door is not open." Sylvia Matthews, from the same city, noted, "Today it seems more acceptable to be racist. Just in the kinds of things you hear people say."

After steady progress toward integration in the 1970s and 1980s, residential and school resegregation began to occur. Racial separation in urban neighborhoods was part of the problem. More important was the erosion of the commitment to civil rights and the economic policies (discussed in Chapter 30) pursued during the Republican administrations of the 1980s and early 1990s. Ronald Reagan opposed busing to achieve racial balance, and his attorney general worked to dismantle affirmative-action programs. Initially reluctant to support extension of the enormously successful Voting Rights Act of 1965, Reagan relented only under severe criticism from Republicans as well as Democrats. He directed the Internal Revenue Service to cease banning tax exemptions for private schools that discriminated against blacks, only to see that move overturned by the Supreme Court in 1983. He also launched an assault on the Civil Rights Commission and hampered its effectiveness by appointing members who did not support its main goals.

The courts similarly weakened the commitment to equal rights. As a result of Reagan's judicial appointments, and those of his successor, George Bush, federal courts stopped pushing for school integration, and in some cases actively encouraged the pattern of separation. The Supreme Court's *Freeman* v. *Pitts* decision in the spring of 1992 granted a suburban Atlanta school board relief from a desegregation order on the grounds that it was not possible to counteract massive demographic shifts. This was the second time in two years that the Court granted a local board such relief.

The civil rights movement underscored the democratic values on which the nation was based, but the gap between rhetoric and reality remained. In an era when industrial and farming employment shrank and rents rose at a highly inflationary rate, most black families remained poor. Meanwhile, a white backlash grew. Given a wavering presidential commitment to reform in the 1970s and 1980s, only pressures from reform groups kept the faltering civil rights movement alive.

The Women's Movement

The black struggle for equality in the 1960s and 1970s was accompanied by a women's movement that grew out of the agitation for civil rights but soon developed a life of its own. That struggle, like the struggles by Hispanics and Native Americans, employed the confrontational approach and the vocabulary of the civil rights movement to create sufficient pressure for change. Using proven strategies, it sometimes proceeded even faster than the black effort.

Attacking the Feminine Mystique

Many white women joined the civil rights movement only to find that they were second-class citizens. Men, black and white, held the policy positions and relegated women to menial chores when not actually involved in demonstrations or voter drives. Many women also felt sexually exploited by male leaders. Stokely Carmichael's comment only underscored their point. "The only position for women in SNCC," he said, "is prone." In response, women learned the importance of militant, well-publicized pressure tactics in changing their own situation.

Although the civil rights movement helped spark the women's movement, broad social changes provided the preconditions. During the 1950s and 1960s, increasing numbers of married women entered the labor force, and half of all women worked. Yet, in 1963, the average working woman earned only 63 percent of what a man could expect; in 1973, only 57 percent. Just as important, many more young women were attending college. By 1970, women earned 41 percent of all B.A.'s awarded, in comparison with only 25 percent in 1950. These educated young women held high hopes for themselves. Many found that sexual liberation failed to bring equality. Feminism was compelling both in its analysis of women's problems and in the solutions it offered.

Just as in the civil rights movement, reform legislation played a part in ending sexual discrimination. Title 7 of the 1964 Civil Rights bill, as originally drafted, prohibited discrimination on the grounds of race. During legislative debate, conservatives opposed to black civil rights seized on an amendment to include discrimination on the basis of gender, in the hope of defeating the entire bill. But the amendment passed, giving women a legal tool for attacking discrimination. They discovered, however, that the Equal Employment Opportunities Commission regarded women's

Women in the Work Force, 1920–1990

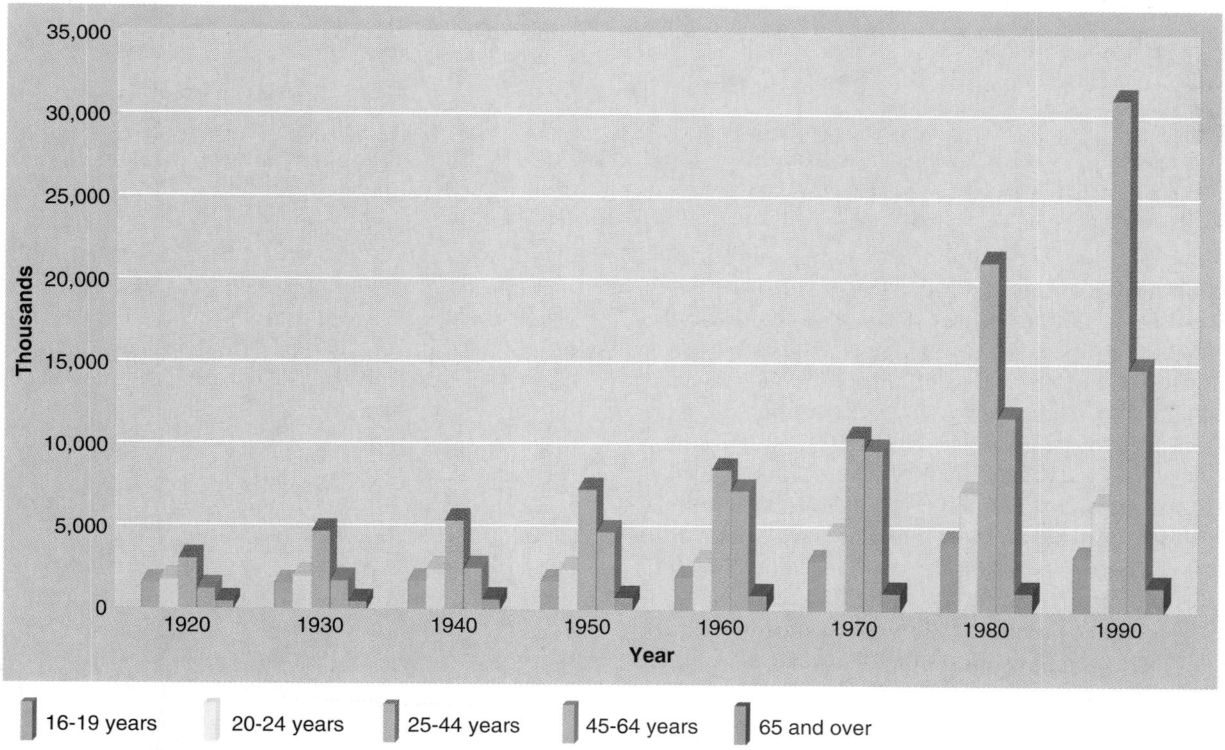

This graph shows the dramatic increase in the number of women in the work force in the 1970s, 1980s, and 1990s. Note particularly the rise in the number of working women 25–44 years old.

Source: U.S. Bureau of the Census.

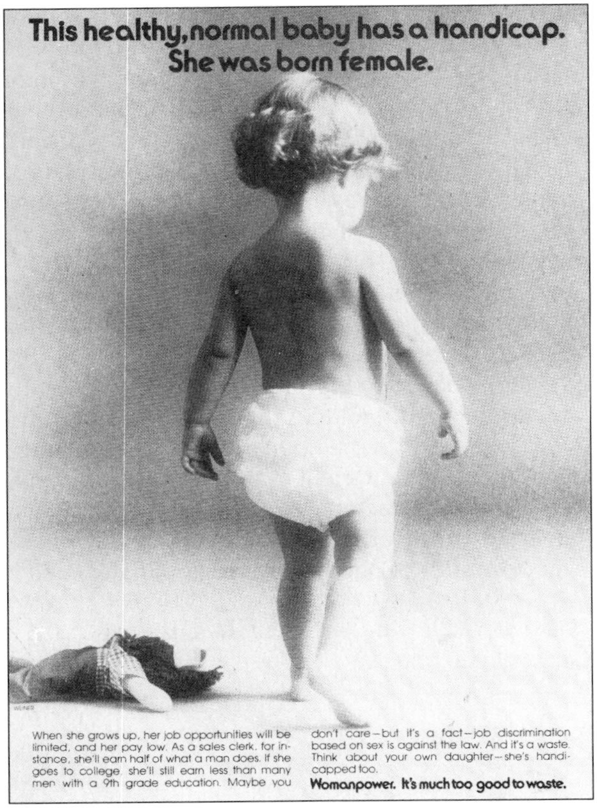
This healthy, normal baby has a handicap.
She was born female.
When she grows up, her job opportunities will be limited, and her pay low. As a sales clerk, for instance, she'll earn half of what a man does. If she goes to college, she'll still earn less than many men with a 9th grade education. Maybe you don't care—but it's a fact—job discrimination based on sex is against the law. And it's a waste. Think about your own daughter—she's handicapped too.
Womanpower. It's much too good to waste.

Awareness of racial discrimination led women to speak out against discrimination based on sex, as shown in this pointed advertisement sponsored by the National Organization for Women.

complaints of discrimination as far less important than those of blacks.

When a small group of women failed to win support from existing women's groups to pressure the commission to change its policies, they decided to form their own civil rights organization. In 1966, a group of 28 professional women, including Betty Friedan, established the National Organization for Women (NOW) "to take action to bring American women into full participation in the mainstream of American society now." By full participation the founders not only meant fair pay and equal opportunity but a new, more egalitarian form of marriage. NOW also attacked the "false image of women . . . in the media." By 1967, some 1,000 women had joined the organization, and four years later, its membership reached 15,000.

NOW was a political pressure group. To radical feminists, who had come up through the civil rights movement, NOW's agenda failed to confront adequately the problem of gender discrimination. They tried, through the technique of consciousness raising, to help women understand the extent of their oppression and to analyze their experience as a political phenomenon.

Feminism at High Tide

In 1971, Helen Reddy expressed the energy of the women's movement in a song called "I Am Woman":

I am woman, hear me roar
In numbers too big to ignore
And I know too much to go back and pretend
'Cause I've heard it all before
And I've been down there on the floor,
No one's ever gonna keep me down again.
Oh, yes, I am wise
But it's wisdom born of pain.
Yes, I've paid the price
But look how much I gained
If I have to
I can do anything.
I am strong,
I am invincible,
I am woman.

Reddy's song reflected a new militancy and sense of self-confidence among women. In the early 1970s, a survey noted that in a two-year period, the number of college students who believed women were oppressed had doubled, and the number continued to rise.

Real changes were under way in the effort to end that discrimination. A 1970 survey of first-year college students showed that men interested in such fields as business, medicine, engineering, and law outnumbered women eight to one; by 1975, the ratio had dropped to three to one. The proportion of women beginning law school quadrupled between 1969 and 1973. Women gained access to the military academies and entered senior officer ranks. In the banking industry, women's share of jobs increased from 18 to 34 percent between 1970 and 1980. According to the Census Bureau, 45 percent of mothers with preschool children held jobs away from home in 1980. That figure was four times greater than it had been 30 years before. To be sure, many employers systematically excluded women from certain positions, and women usually held "female"

Changes in Female Employment, 1940–1989
Percent of all employed women

	1940	1950	1960	1970	1980	1989
Professional and technical	13.2	10.8	12.4	15.3	16.7	14.8
Managers and administrators	3.8	5.5	5.7	3.6	6.9	11.1
Sales	7.0	8.8	7.7	7.4	6.8	13.1
Clerical	21.2	26.4	30.3	34.5	35.1	31.1
Craft workers	0.9	1.1	1.6	1.8	1.8	2.2
Operatives	18.4	18.7	15.2	15.1	10.7	7.2
Laborers	0.8	0.4	0.4	1.0	1.3	1.6
Service workers	28.9	22.9	23.7	20.5	19.5	17.7
Farmworkers	5.8	5.4	4.4	0.8	1.2	1.1

Sources: Oppenheimer, *The Female Labor Force in the United States* (1976) and *Statistical Abstract of the United States, 1991.*

jobs in the clerical, sales, and service sectors, but the progress was still unmistakable.

Legal changes brought women more benefits and opportunities. Title 9 of the Education Amendments of 1972 broadened the provisions of the Civil Rights Act of 1964. The new legislation, which barred gender bias in federally assisted education activities and programs, made the admission of women easier and changed the nature of intercollegiate athletics. By 1980, fully 30 percent of the participants in intercollegiate athletics were women, compared with 15 percent before Title 9 had become law.

A flurry of publications spread the principles of the women's movement. Gloria Steinem, author of a regular political column in *New York* magazine, first thought of herself as a professional journalist with no particular interest in women's affairs. "I certainly didn't understand that women were an 'out' group," she noted, "and I would even insist that I wasn't discriminated against as a woman." While working on a story about abortion, however, she began to see that discrimination took many forms. She realized she "had been unable to get an apartment because, the reasoning was, a single woman wasn't financially responsible—and if she was responsible, she was probably a prostitute." Steinem began writing more about women, and in 1972, she and several other women founded a new magazine. *Ms.* succeeded beyond their wildest dreams, reaching a wide audience of women who were not members of feminist organizations. In the first eight days, the 300,000 copies of the preview issue sold out. By 1973, there were almost 200,000 subscribers. Most of them were under 35, had graduated from

The women's movement spawned a number of publications that attempted to give women greater control over various aspects of their own lives. The book *Our Bodies, Ourselves* and *Ms.* magazine were two important sources in that effort.

college, and were working in professional, managerial, or technical jobs.

Among other publications that publicized the issues and concerns of the women's movement was *The New Woman's Survival Catalogue,* which provided useful advice to women readers. *Our Bodies, Ourselves,* a handbook published by a women's health collective, encouraged women to understand and control their bodies; it sold 850,000 copies between 1971 and 1976.

These new books and magazines differed radically from older women's magazines like *Good Housekeeping* and *Ladies' Home Journal.* Those publications aimed at women at home and focused on their domestic interests, needs, and sometimes fantasies. *Ms.,* in dramatic contrast, dealt with abortion, employment, and discrimination and provided a forum for the discussion of important feminist issues.

Women marched to mobilize support for ratification of the Equal Rights Amendment, but the campaign failed, as opponents aroused public fears and blocked support in a number of key states. A decade after passage, the ERA was dead.

Despite certain shared interests, women's struggle for equality was decentralized, diffuse, and often internally divided. As *Time* magazine pointed out in 1972, "The aims of the movement range from the modest, sensible amelioration of the female condition to extreme and revolutionary visions."

Groups like NOW pressed for equal employment opportunities, child care centers, and abortion reform. Women both in and out of NOW who were concerned with legal reforms worked for congressional passage, then ratification, of the Equal Rights Amendment (ERA) to the Constitution. Passed by Congress in 1972, and seemingly on the verge of ratification, it stated simply, "Equality of rights under the law shall not be denied or abridged by the United States or by any State on account of sex."

Other feminist groups adopted more radical positions. Legal changes were not enough, they argued. Fundamental changes in sexual identity were needed to end male domination and social exploitation. Shulamith Firestone, a former member of the New Left, explained in *The Dialectic of Sex* (1970) the necessity of a new society in which women were freed "from the tyranny of their reproductive biology by every means available." Moreover, traditional gender and family roles must be discarded and "the childbearing and childrearing role [diffused] to the society as a whole, men as well as women." Other socialist feminists claimed that it was not enough to strike out at male domination, for capitalist society itself was responsible for women's plight. Only through the process of revolution could women be free.

Not all women were feminists, to be sure. Many felt the women's movement was contemptuous of women who stayed at home to perform traditional tasks. Marabel Morgan was one who still insisted that the woman had a place at home by her husband's side. The wife of a Florida attorney, she argued that "it is only when a woman surrenders her life to her husband, reveres and worships him, and is willing to serve him, that she becomes really beautiful to him." In her book *The Total Woman* (1973), she counseled others to follow the 4A approach: accept, admire, adapt, appreciate. She suggested ways of meeting a husband at the door and cited approvingly the case of one woman who "welcomed her husband home

Don't amend
Just reapply usual standards

in black mesh stockings, high heels, and an apron. That's all." As of 1975, some 500,000 copies of the hardcover volume had been sold.

In politics, Phyllis Schlafly headed a nationwide campaign to block ratification of the ERA. Author of several books, she was vigorous and articulate. On the ERA she was adamant: "It won't do anything to help women, and it will take away from women the rights they already have, such as the right of a wife to be supported by her husband, the right of a woman to be exempted from military combat, and the right, if you wanted it, to go to a single-sex college." The ERA, she predicted, would lead to the establishment of coed bathrooms, the elimination of alimony, and the legalization of homosexual marriage. Women, she argued, already had legal backing enough for their rights.

Schlafly and her allies had their way. Within a few years of passage of the ERA, 35 states had agreed to the measure, but then the momentum disappeared. Even with an extension in the deadline granted in 1979, the amendment could not win support of the necessary 38 states. The opposition campaign drew on the assistance of women who felt threatened by the changes occurring and men, particularly in state legislatures, who had long been uncomfortable with the women's movement. By mid-1982, the ERA was dead.

Even so, the 1980s brought significant gains. In politics, women won mayoral races in the nation's major cities. Far more women were elected to state legislatures and to Congress. In 1981, President Ronald Reagan appointed Sandra Day O'Connor as the first woman Supreme Court justice, and in 1984, Geraldine Ferraro, a Democratic member of Congress, became the first woman vice-presidential candidate for a major party.

Despite substantial gains, women still faced serious problems. Access to new positions did not change their concentration in lower-paying jobs. In 1985, most women still served as secretaries, cashiers, bookkeepers, registered nurses, and waitresses—the same jobs most frequently held ten years before. Even when women moved into positions traditionally held by men, their progress often stopped at the lower and middle levels. Interruptions of work—to bear children or assume family responsibilities—impeded advancement. Lack of experience served as another convenient excuse for failure to promote women.

Sandra Day O'Connor became the first woman justice to sit on the United States Supreme Court. Her pre-Court career was similar to that of many other women, as she was denied numerous jobs when she emerged from law school.

Critics also became increasingly concerned about continuing wage differentials between women and men. In 1985, full-time working women still earned only 63.6 cents for every dollar earned by men. Their concentration in the so-called pink-collar positions—traditional women's jobs—made further improvement difficult. Arguments that women should receive equal pay for equal work now led to demands for equal pay for different jobs of similar value. Comparable-worth cases began to work their way through the courts.

Women were likewise worried about the erosion of their right to abortion. Despite the 1973 Supreme Court decision legalizing abortion, the issue remained very much alive. The number of abortions increased dramatically in the decade after the decision. By some estimates, 10 million lawful abortions were performed in that decade, or one for every three births. In response, "pro-life" forces mobilized. Nellie Gray organized a march on Washington every January 22 to call attention to the anniversary of the *Roe* v. *Wade* decision. "It's murder, pure and simple," she said. "Abortion means killing babies." Opponents lobbied to cut off federal funds that allowed the poor to obtain the abortions the better-off could pay for themselves; they insisted that abortions should be performed in hospitals and not in less expensive clinics; and they worked to reverse the original decision itself.

Though the Supreme Court, which included the first woman in its history, reaffirmed its judgment in 1983, the pro-life movement was not deterred. In 1989, a solidifying conservative majority on the Court ruled in *Webster* v. *Reproductive Health Services* that while women's right to abortion remained intact, state legislatures could impose limitations if they chose. With that judgment, a major legislative debate over the issue began, and numerous states began to mandate restrictions. In response, the courts heard still further cases to determine what should remain legal.

In 1992, in *Planned Parenthood* v. *Casey,* the Supreme Court reaffirmed what it termed the "essence" of the right to abortion, while permitting further state restrictions. In a narrow 5-4 decision, it upheld most provisions of a Pennsylvania law that established a 24-hour waiting period for women seeking abortions and required teenage girls to secure the permission of a parent (or a judge) before ending a pregnancy. Although the Court struck down as an undue burden a provision requiring a woman to notify her husband of her plan to have an abortion, the ruling clearly gave states greater latitude in the overall restrictive effort. It also made an abortion harder to obtain, particularly for poor women and young women. With both proponents and opponents of abortion unhappy with the decision, the issue remained very much alive.

Despite the counterattacks, the women's movement flourished in the 1970s and 1980s. In the tenth anniversary issue of *Ms.* magazine, in 1982, founding editor Gloria Steinem noted the differences a decade had made. "Now, we have words like 'sexual harassment' and 'battered women,'" she wrote. "Ten years ago, it was just called 'life.'" She also observed that "now, we are becoming the men we wanted to marry. Ten years ago, we were trained to marry a doctor, not be one." Betty Friedan, whose book *The Feminine Mystique* (1963) had helped mobilize a pervasive discontent two decades before, likewise admitted in 1983:

> I am still awed by the revolution that book helped spark. . . . I keep being surprised, as the changes the women's movement set in motion continue to play themselves out in our lives—the enormous and mundane, subtle and not so subtle, delightful, painful, immediate, far-reaching, paradoxical, inexorable and probably irreversible changes in women's lives—and in men's.

In 1991, even Blondie Bumstead, the cartoon figure who had amused readers for decades with her domestic antics, went to work. Still another mark of the success of the women's movement was the growth of a men's movement to explore questions of male identity. While women savored their gains, however, some worried that complacency was setting in. Many young women who enjoyed the fruits of the movement avoided the feminist label and shunned involvement in militant campaigns. Others remained active, convinced that only with continued pressure would women ever achieve full equality.

Hispanic Rights

Hispanics, like women, profited from the example of blacks in the struggle for equality. Long denied equal access to the American dream, they became more vocal and confrontational as their numbers increased in the postwar years. Puerto Ricans in the Northeast, Cubans in Florida, and Chicanos in California and Tejanos in Texas developed a heightened sense of solidarity and group pride as they began to assert their own rights. In 1970, some 9 million people declared they were of Spanish origin; in 1980, the figure was 14.6 million; and in 1990 it was 20.8 million, as increases far outstripped the aggregate American increase. But median household income remained less than three-fourths of that of Anglos ($31,231 compared with $22,330 in 1990), and inferior education and political weakness reinforced social and cultural separation.

César Chávez and the Politics of Confrontation

In the 1960s and 1970s, Mexican-Americans adopted confrontational tactics. They had hoped that Lyndon Johnson's poverty program would bring improved opportunities, but they soon found that most efforts were oriented toward black Americans and that bureaucrats were often less sensitive to the problems of equally exploited but less vocal groups. From this they learned the value of pressure politics in a pluralistic society. In the election of 1960, Mexican-Americans supported Kennedy, helping him win Texas. In 1961, Henry B. González was elected to Congress from San Antonio. Three years later, Elizo ("Kika") de la Garza of Texas won election to the House and Joseph Montoya of New Mexico went to the Senate. Gaining a political voice, Chicanos began to anticipate the day when it could help them improve their lives.

Direct action proved effective in winning significant changes, as César Chávez's work with migrant farmworkers of the West demonstrated. Born in Yuma, Arizona, Chávez went to California in the 1940s. There he acquired organizational skills, and two decades later, he established the United Farm Workers. Concentrating on migrant Mexican fieldhands, one of the most exploited and ignored groups of laboring people in the country, he chose a loyal cadre to conduct a door-to-door and field-to-field campaign. By 1965, his organization had recruited 1,700 members and was beginning to attract volunteer help. His intent was to present the farmworkers' struggle as part of the larger national struggle for civil rights.

Chávez first took on the grape growers of California. Calling the grape workers out on strike, the union demanded better pay and working conditions and union recognition. When the growers did not concede, Chávez launched a nationwide consumer boycott of their products. Although the Schenley Corporation and several wine companies came to terms, others held out. In 1966, the DiGiorgio Corporation agreed to permit a union election but then rigged the results. When California governor Edmund G. Brown, Sr., launched an investigation that resulted in another election, he became the first major political figure to support the long-powerless Chicano fieldhands. This time, the United Farm Workers won. Similar boycotts of lettuce and other products harvested by exploited labor also ended in success. In 1975, César Chávez's long struggle for farmworkers resulted in the successful passage in California of a measure that required growers to bargain collectively with the elected representatives of the workers. Farmworkers had never been covered by the National Labor Relations Board. Now they were guaranteed legitimate elections and representation. Farm interests continued to try to obstruct organization, but at least the workers had achieved the legal basis for representation that could help bring higher wages and improved working conditions.

César Chávez organized the United Farm Workers to give migrant Mexican workers representation in their struggle for better wages and working conditions. Here he works with laborers in his tireless campaign for their support.

Chávez himself became a national figure. The *Wall Street Journal* and *Life* and *Time* magazines ran stories about him. Before his assassination, Robert Kennedy helped rally support by visiting Chávez and his strikers in the fields. Chávez helped publicize the Chicano cause just as Martin Luther King, Jr., riveted attention on the black struggle.

Meanwhile, Mexican-Americans agitated for reform in other areas as well. In the West and Southwest, Mexican-American studies programs flourished. In 1969, at least 50 were available in California alone. They offered degrees, built library collections, and gave Chicanos access to their own past. The campuses also provided a network linking students together and mobilizing them for political action.

Beginning in 1968, Mexican-American students began to protest conditions in the secondary schools. They pointed bitterly to overcrowded and run-down institutions and to the 50 percent dropout rate that came from expulsion, transfer, or failure because students had never been taught to read. In March 1968, some 10,000 Chicano students walked out of five high schools in Los Angeles. Their actions inspired other walkouts in Colorado, Texas, and other parts of California and led to demands for Hispanic teachers, counselors, and courses and better facilities.

At the same time, new organizations emerged. A few years before, teenager David Sánchez and four Chicanos in East Los Angeles had formed a group called Young Citizens for Community Action. Gradually the organization evolved from a service club to a defensive patrol. Now known as Young Chicanos for Community Action, the group adopted a paramilitary stance. Its members became identified as the Brown Berets and formed chapters throughout the Midwest and Southwest.

Other Hispanics began to organize politically. In Texas, José Angel Gutiérrez recognized that political activism could change conditions that had existed for generations. He gained national attention at a press conference by exploding, "Kill the gringo!" Anglo-Americans feared that he meant it literally. Gutiérrez attended a rally in March 1969 at San Félipe del Río to protest the cancellation of a government-funded neighborhood project. Three months later, he and a few others went to his hometown of Crystal City, Texas, to begin organizing Hispanics at the grass-roots level. When students protested conditions at the local high school, a citizens' organization led by Gutiérrez stepped in to develop a spirit of solidarity. From that group emerged the La Raza Unida political party, which began to play a major role in the area and successfully promoted Mexican-American candidates for political offices. Throughout the 1970s, it gained strength in the West and Southwest.

Among the Chicano leaders to emerge was the charismatic Reis López Tijerina, or "El Tigre." A preacher, he became interested in land-grant issues and argued that the United States government had fraudulently deprived Chicanos of village lands. He formed an organization, La Alianza Federal de Mercedes (the Federal Alliance of Land Grants), which marched on the New Mexico state capital and occupied a number of national forests. Arrested, he stood trial and eventually served time in prison, where he became a symbol of political repression.

Rodolfo "Corky" Gonzáles was another such leader. A Golden Gloves boxing champion as a youth, he later served as a district captain for the Democratic party in Denver. He helped direct the Denver poverty programs until he was fired for being overly zealous in his support of the Chicano community. In 1966, he founded the Crusade for

Chicano leaders worked to mobilize their communities behind the campaign for equal rights. This mural in an East Los Angeles housing project helped foster a sense of Chicano pride.

Spanish-speaking students often faced serious problems in American schools. Bilingual classrooms, like the one pictured here, made learning easier for Hispanic pupils, although some critics argued that such classes slowed assimilation.

Justice to advance the Chicano cause through community organization. He too was arrested for his part in a demonstration but was subsequently acquitted.

Hispanics made a particular point of protesting against the Vietnam War. Because the draft drew most heavily from the poorer segments of society, the Hispanic casualty rate was far higher than that of the population at large. In 1969, the Brown Berets organized the National Chicano Moratorium Committee and staged antiwar demonstrations. They argued that this was a racial war, with black and brown Americans being used against their Third World compatriots. Some of the rallies ended in confrontations with the police. News reporter Rubén Salazar, active in exposing questionable police activity, was killed in one such episode in 1970, and his death brought renewed charges of police brutality.

Aware of the growing numbers and growing demands of Hispanics, the Nixon administration sought to defuse their anger and win their support. Cuban-American refugees, strongly opposed to communism, shifted toward the Republican party, which they assumed was more likely eventually to intervene against Fidel Castro. Meanwhile, Nixon courted Chicanos. Recognizing that with 5 percent more of the Mexican-American vote in Texas in 1968 he would have carried the state, political analysts advised an effort to lure Mexican-Americans into the Republican camp. By dangling political positions, government jobs, and promises of better programs for Mexican-Americans, they attempted to secure their support. The effort paid off; Nixon received 31 percent of the Hispanic vote in 1972. Rather than reward his Hispanic followers, however, the president moved to cut back the poverty program, begun under Johnson, that assisted them.

Despite occasional gains in the 1970s and 1980s, Hispanics faced continuing problems. Spanish-speaking students often found it difficult to move through the educational system. In 1987, fully 40 percent of all Hispanic high school students did not graduate. Only 31 percent of the Hispanic seniors were enrolled in college-preparatory courses. Hispanic students frequently received little help from guidance counselors. Anel Albarran, a Mexican immigrant who arrived in East Los Angeles when she was 11, applied to UCLA when a special high school teacher encouraged her and made sure that she received help in choosing the necessary courses. By contrast, her regular counselor asked her two months before graduation whether she had considered college: "All he had wanted to do during high school was give me my classes and get me out of the room." Of those Hispanics who went to college, 56 percent attended community colleges. Graduation from college was a problem as well: less than 7 percent completed a course of study. When forced to take courses that had little connection to their background and less relevance to their lives, many students became frustrated and dropped out.

A growing network of Hispanic educators and programs worked to ease the way for future students. "Ten years ago, there was no national Chicano academic community," declared Arturo Madrid, president of the National Chicano Council on Higher Education, in 1982. "Now we have a professional presence in higher education." A colleague estimated that there were 5,000 Chicano faculty members in 1980, compared with 2,000 a decade before, and the numbers continued to grow. Chicanos found themselves, like members of other minority groups, moving from the ranks of the "missing persons" to positions as "the onlys," where, Madrid noted, they served as "the only Chicano dean of this or the only Chicano professor of that." Still, those appointments, like that of Manuel T. Pacheco as president of the University of Arizona in 1991, gave them considerable visibility and influence.

Hispanics slowly extended their political gains as well. In San Antonio, Rudy Ortiz was appointed mayor pro tem in 1978, and Henry Cisneros was elected mayor in 1982. Cisneros, who held B.A., M.A., and Ph.D. degrees, was reelected the following year with 94.2 percent of the vote. At the same time, Colorado state legislator Federico Peña was elected mayor of Denver. In New Mexico, Governor Toney Anaya called himself the nation's highest elected Hispanic and worked to create a national "Hispanic force." A 1987 survey documented continued progress as Hispanics exercised their political power. The number of Hispanics holding elective offices nationwide increased 3.5 percent between 1986 and 1987. The number of Hispanic women in such offices increased 20 percent in that time. More Hispanic administrators were appointed at various levels of government. Lauro Cavazos, named U.S. secretary of education in 1988, was the most prominent.

Native American Protest

Like Hispanics, Native Americans continued to suffer second-class status as the 1960s began. But, partly inspired by the confrontational tactics of other groups, they became more aggressive in their efforts to claim their rights and to improve living and working conditions. The years not only saw a renewed aggressiveness but phenomenal population growth—from 550,000 in 1960 to 1,959,000 in 1990.

Tribal Voices

During the Eisenhower years, the federal government's policy of termination was in effect. That effort to force Indians to assimilate into mainstream American life by relocating them in cities had worked poorly. Thousands of Native Americans traded reservation poverty for urban poverty. In 1961, the United States Commission on Civil Rights observed that for Indians, "poverty and deprivation are common. Social acceptance is not the rule. In addition, Indians seem to suffer more than occasional mistreatment by the instruments of law and order on and off the reservations."

In the 1960s, Indians began to assert themselves. At a conference in Chicago in 1961, several hundred Indians asked the Kennedy administration for the right to help make decisions about programs and budgets for the tribes. A group of college-educated Indians at the conference formed a National Indian Youth Council aimed at reestablishing Indian national pride. Over the next several decades, the council helped change the attitudes of tribal leaders, who were frequently called Uncle Tomahawks and "apples" (red outside, white inside) for their willingness to sacrifice their people's needs to white demands.

Native Americans learned from the examples of protest they saw around them. Watching the development of nationalism in Third World countries and, even more important, following the progress of the civil rights revolution, they came to understand the place of interest-group politics in a pluralistic society. Finally, they were chastened by the excesses of the Vietnam War. They recognized a pattern of killing people of color that connected Indian-white relations to the excesses in the Philippines at the turn of the century and to atrocities in Korea and Vietnam.

Indians successfully promoted their own values and designs. Native American fashions became more common, museums and galleries displayed Indian art, and Indian jewelry found a new market. The larger culture came to appreciate important work by Native Americans. In 1968, N. Scott Momaday won the Pulitzer Prize for his

Poverty and discrimination marked the daily lives of most Native Americans, including the Indian children pictured here, both on reservations and in mainstream urban communities.

book *House Made of Dawn*. Vine Deloria's *Custer Died for Your Sins* (1969) had even wider readership. Meanwhile popular films like *Little Big Man* (1970) and, several decades later, the Academy Award–winning *Dances with Wolves* (1990) provided sympathetic portrayals of Indian history. Indian studies programs developed in colleges and universities. Organizations like the American Indian Historical Society in San Francisco protested traditional textbook treatment of Indians and demanded more honest portrayals.

Indian Activism

At the same time, Native Americans became more confrontational. Like other groups, they worked through the courts when they could but also challenged authority more aggressively when necessary.

Led by a new generation of leaders, Native Americans tried to protect what was left of their tribal lands. Elders reminded young people, "Once we owned all the land." For generations, federal and state governments had steadily encroached on Native American territory. "Everything is tied to our homeland," D'Arcy McNickle, a Flathead anthropologist, told other Indians in 1961.

The new activism was apparent on the Seneca Nation's Allegany reservation in New York State. Although the Seneca's right to the land was established by a treaty made in 1794, the federal government had planned since 1928 to build the Kinzua Dam there as part of a flood control project. Surveys were taken, but for years little was done. In 1956, after hearings to which the Indians were not invited and about which they were not informed, Congress appropriated funds for the project. When court appeals failed to block the scheme, the Seneca turned to President Kennedy in 1961. Kennedy, however, supported the government's right to take the land it had promised not to seize in 1794. The dam was eventually built, and although the government belatedly passed a $15 million reparations bill, money did not compensate for the loss of 10,000 acres of land that contained sacred sites, hunting and fishing grounds, and homes.

The Seneca did somewhat better in the 1970s. When New York State tried to condemn a section of Seneca land for a superhighway running through part of the Allegany reservation, the Indians again went to court. In 1981, the state finally agreed to an exchange: state land elsewhere in addition to a cash settlement in return for an easement through the reservation. That decision encouraged tribal efforts in Montana, Wyoming, Utah, New Mexico, and Arizona to resist similar incursions on reservation lands.

Native American leaders recognized that they could use the legal process in other areas as well and brought a wave of lawsuits charging violations of treaty rights. In 1967, in the first of many decisions upholding the Indian side, the U.S. Court of Claims ruled that the government had forced the Seminole in Florida to cede their land in 1823 for an unreasonably low price. The court directed the government to pay additional funds 144 years later. That decision was a source of some satisfaction to the Seminole population.

Native Americans also vigorously protested a new assault on their long-abused water rights. On the northern plains, large conglomerates, responding to the international oil shortage, vastly extended their coal strip-mining operations. Fierce legal struggles over possession of limited water resources resulted. Litigating tribes had some legal ammunition because a federal court had ruled in 1973 in a landmark case, involving the water rights of the Paiute on the Nevada-California border, that the government must carry out its obligation as trustee to protect Indian property.

Another effort involved the reassertion of fishing rights. In various parts of the nation, the Nisqually, Puyallup, Muckleshoot, Chippewa, and other Indian tribes argued that they had treaty rights to fish where they chose, without worrying about the intrusive regulatory efforts of the states. Despite pressure from other fishermen, a series of court cases provided the tribes with some of the protection they claimed by ruling that nineteenth-century treaties allowing Indians fishing rights "in common with" whites meant that Indians could take up to 50 percent of allowable limits. The cases again demonstrated the power of aggressive litigation.

The new activism took other forms as well. One important reflection of Native American militancy was the founding of the American Indian Movement (AIM) in 1968. Organized by George Mitchell and Dennis Banks, Chippewa living in Minneapolis, AIM sought to help neglected Indians in the city. It managed to get Office of Economic Opportunity funds channeled to Indian-controlled organizations. It also established patrols to protect drunken Indians from harassment by the police. As its successes became known, chapters formed in other cities.

Native American militancy was dramatized in November 1969, when a landing party of 78 Indians seized Alcatraz Island in San Francisco Bay. It was the site of a defunct federal prison, declared surplus property five years before. Pointing to the Fort Laramie Treaty of 1868, which permitted male Indians to file homestead claims on federal lands, the occupiers took over the island to protest symbolically the inability of the Bureau of Indian Affairs to "deal practically" with questions of Indian welfare. They converted the island into a cultural and educational center, but in 1971 federal officials removed them.

The American Indian Movement's armed occupation of Wounded Knee, South Dakota, site of a late-nineteenth-century massacre of the Sioux, resulted in bloodshed that dramatized unfair government treatment of Native Americans.

Other similar protests followed. In 1972, militants launched the Broken Treaties Caravan to Washington. For six days, insurgents occupied the Bureau of Indian Affairs. In 1973, AIM took over the South Dakota village of Wounded Knee, where in 1890 the U.S. 7th Calvary had massacred the Sioux. The reservation surrounding the town was mired in poverty. Half the families were on welfare, alcoholism was widespread, and 81 percent of the student population had dropped out of school. The occupation was meant to dramatize these conditions and to draw attention to the 371 treaties AIM leaders claimed the government had broken. Federal officials responded by encircling the area and, when AIM tried to bring in supplies, killed one Indian and wounded another. The confrontation ended with a government agreement to reexamine the treaty rights of the Indians, although little of substance was subsequently done.

At the same time, Native Americans devoted increasing attention to providing education and developing business and legal skills. Because roughly half of the Indian population continued to live on reservations, many tribal communities founded their own colleges. In 1971, the Oglala Sioux established Oglala Lakota College on the Pine Ridge Reservation in South Dakota. The motto "Wa Wo Ici Ya" ("We can do it ourselves") revealed the college's goal. Nearby Sinte Gleska College on the Rosebud Reservation was the first to offer accredited four-year and graduate programs. In the decade following congressional enactment of the Tribally Controlled Community College Assistance Act in 1978, 20 tribally controlled colleges from Washington to Oklahoma received regular financial support. The effort increased the number of Indians in college from a few hundred in the early 1960s to tens of thousands by 1980. Between 1980 and 1990, Native American enrollment in higher education institutions increased by over 23 percent.

Some tribal communities developed business skills, although traditional Indian attitudes hardly fostered the capitalist perspective. As Dale Old Horn, an MIT graduate and department head at Little Big Horn College in Crow Agency, Montana, explained:

> The Crow Indian child is taught that he is part of a harmonious circle of kin relations, clans and nature. The white child is taught that he is the center of the circle. The Crow believe in sharing wealth, and whites believe in accumulating wealth.

But a number of Indian groups adopted at least some of the capitalist ethos. "Now we're beginning to realize that, if we want to be self-sufficient, we're going to have to become entrepreneurs ourselves," observed Iola Hayden, the Comanche executive director of Oklahomans for Indian Opportunity. The Choctaw in Mississippi were perhaps the most successful. Before they began a drive toward self-sufficiency in 1979, their unemployment rate was 50 percent. By the middle of the 1980s, Choctaws owned all or part of three businesses on the reservation, employed 1,000 people, generated $30 million in work annually, and cut the unemployment rate in half.

Indians themselves studied law and acted as legal advocates for their own people in the court cases they were filing. In 1968, funding from the Office of Economic Opportunity helped the University of New Mexico Law School start a Native American scholarship program. Since 1971, that program has graduated 35 to 40 Indian lawyers each year. They have worked for tribes directly and have also established institutes like the Native American Rights Foundation in Boulder, Colorado. Citing precedents dating back to Chief Justice John Marshall in the 1830s and reaffirmed as recently as 1959, they have successfully argued for tribal jurisdiction in conflicts between whites and Indians on the reservations.

Government Response

Indian protest brought results. The outcry against termination in the 1960s led the Kennedy and Johnson administrations to steer a middle course, neither endorsing nor disavowing the policy. Instead they tried to bolster reservation economies and raise standards of living by persuading private industries to locate on reservations and by promoting the leasing of reservation lands to energy and development corporations. The theory was that the leases in particular might protect Indians against termination, but Indians resented relinquishing control of lands to non-Indians and feared "termination by corporation." In the 1970s, the Navajo, Northern Cheyenne, Crow, and other tribes tried to cancel or renegotiate such leases.

The Native American cry for self-determination brought Indian involvement in the poverty program of the Great Society in the mid-1960s. Two agencies, the Area Redevelopment Administration (later the Economic Development Administration) and the Office of Economic Opportunity, responded to Indian pressure by allowing Indians to devise programs and budgets and administer programs themselves. Indians were similarly involved with Great Society housing, health, and education initiatives. Even if the government guided decisions and in practice used the Indians as agents, the Indians gained more control over the administration of federal programs than they had possessed before.

Finally, in 1975, Congress passed Indian Self-determination and Education Assistance Acts. Five years earlier, Richard Nixon had declared that self-determination had replaced termination as American policy. The self-determination measure was a largely rhetorical statement of that position. The education act involved subcontracting federal services to tribal groups. Though both laws were limited, they nonetheless reflected the government's decision to respond to Indian pressure, and created a framework to guide federal policy in the decades ahead.

Social and Cultural Protest

As blacks, Hispanics, and Native Americans agitated, middle-class American society experienced an upheaval unlike any it had known before. Young people in particular rejected the stable patterns of affluent life their parents had forged in the decade before. Some embraced radical political activity; many more adopted new standards of sexual behavior, music, and dress. In time their actions spawned still other protests as Americans tried to make the political and social world more responsive than before.

The Student Movement

The demographic patterns of the post–World War II years lay behind youthful activism and helped explain the generation gap. Members of the baby boom generation came of age in the 1960s, and many of them, especially from the large middle class, moved on to some form of higher education. Between 1950 and 1964, the number of students in college more than doubled. By the end of the 1960s, college enrollment was more than four times what it had been in the 1940s. There were far more students than there were farmers, coal miners, or railroad workers. College had become a training ground for industry and corporate life; more important, it gave students time to experiment and grow before they went out into the world to make a living.

In college, some students joined the struggle for civil rights. Hopeful at first, they gradually became discouraged by the limitations of the government's commitment, despite the rhetoric of Kennedy and the New Frontier.

Out of that disillusionment arose the radical spirit of the New Left. Civil rights activists were among those who in 1960 organized Students for a Democratic Society (SDS) from the older Student League for Industrial Democracy. In 1962, SDS issued a manifesto, the Port Huron Statement, written largely by Tom Hayden of the University of Michigan. "We are people of this generation, bred in at least modest comfort, housed now in universities, looking uncomfortably at the world we inherit," it began. It went on to deplore the vast social and economic distances separating people from each other and to condemn the isolation and estrangement of modern life. The document called for a better system, a "democracy of individual participation" rooted in "self-cultivation, self-direction, self-understanding and creativity."

The first blow of the growing student rebellion came at the University of California in Berkeley. There civil rights activists became involved in a confrontation that quickly became known as the free speech movement. It began in September 1964 when the university refused to allow students to distribute protest material outside the main campus gate. The students, many of whom had worked in the movement in the South, argued that their tables were off campus and therefore not subject to university restrictions on political activity. Defiantly, they resolved to fight back. When police arrested one of the leaders, students surrounded the police car and kept it from moving all night.

Although the administration eventually sought a compromise, the university regents took disciplinary action against the student leaders. One, Mario Savio, was charged with biting a policeman on the thigh; other accusations followed. When the regents refused to drop the charges, the students occupied the administration building. Savio called the university an impersonal machine: "It becomes odious, so we must put our bodies against the gears, against the wheels . . . and make the machine stop until we're free." Folksinger Joan Baez sang "We Shall Overcome," the marching song of the civil rights movement. Then, as in the South, police stormed in and arrested the students in the building. A student strike, with faculty aid, mobilized wider support for the right to free speech.

Though the free speech movement at Berkeley was the opening blow of the student revolt, it was still basically a plea for traditional liberal reform. Students sought only the reaffirmation of a long-standing right, the right to express themselves as they chose, and they aimed their attacks at the university, not at society as a whole. Later, in other institutions, the attack broadened.

As in the civil rights movement, student protest, once launched, developed and swelled. The ferment at Berkeley spread to other campuses in the spring of 1965 as students questioned methods of college discipline, attacked conservative drinking and visitation rules, sought student involvement in university affairs, argued for curricular reform, and demanded admission of more minority students. Their success in gaining their demands changed the shape of American higher education.

The mounting protest against the escalation of the Vietnam War fueled and refocused the youth movement. Confrontation became the new tactic of radical students, and protest became a way of life. Between January 1 and June 15, 1968, hundreds of thousands of students staged 221 major demonstrations at more than 100 educational institutions.

One of the most dramatic episodes came in April 1968 at Columbia University, where the issues of civil rights and war were tightly interwoven. A strong SDS chapter urged the university to break ties with the Institute of Defense Analysis, which specialized in military research. The Students' Afro-American Society tried to stop the building of a new gymnasium, which it claimed encroached on the Harlem community and disrupted life there. Together the two groups marched on Low Memorial Library. Then the alliance split, as whites occupied one building,

In 1968, the demonstrators pictured here barricaded themselves inside Columbia University's main library to protest American involvement in the Vietnam War and the school's relations with the neighboring black community.

blacks another. Finally, the president of the university called in the police. Hundreds of students were arrested; many were hurt. A student sympathy strike followed, and Columbia closed for the summer several weeks early.

The next year, in October 1969, the Weathermen, a militant fringe group of SDS, attempted to demonstrate that the revolution had arrived with a frontal attack on Chicago, scene of the violent Democratic convention of 1968. The Weathermen, taking their name from a line in a Bob Dylan song—"You don't need a weatherman to know which way the wind blows"—came from all over the country. Dressed in hard hats, jackboots, work gloves, and other padding, they rampaged through the streets with clubs and pipes, chains and rocks. They ran into the police, as they had expected and hoped, and continued the attack. Some were arrested, others were shot, and the rest withdrew to regroup. For the next two days, they plotted strategy, engaged in minor skirmishes, and prepared for the final thrust. It came on the fourth day, once again pitting aggressive Weathermen against hostile police.

Why had the Weathermen launched their attack? "The status quo meant to us war, poverty, inequality, ignorance, famine and disease in most of the world," Bo Burlingham, a participant from Ohio, reflected. "To accept it was to condone and help perpetuate it. We felt like miners trapped in a terrible poisonous shaft with no light to guide us out. We resolved to destroy the tunnel even if we risked destroying ourselves in the process."

The rationale of the Chicago "national action" may have been clear to the participants, but it convinced few other Americans. Citizens around the country were infuriated at what they saw. In New York City, when students demonstrated in the Wall Street area in the aftermath of the Kent State affair (see Chapter 28), angry construction workers on their lunch break attacked them. Carrying signs reading "Don't worry, they don't draft faggots" and "Get the hippie! Get the traitor!" they rushed at the demonstrators with lead pipes and fists. As was so often the case, middle-class and working-class Americans found themselves on different sides.

The New Left was, briefly, a powerful force. Although activists never composed a majority, radicals attracted students and other sympathizers to their cause until the movement fragmented. But while it was healthy, the movement focused opposition to the Vietnam War and challenged inequities in American society. The impatience and frustration often evident in the student protest movement could also be seen in other areas of American life, as political upheaval was accompanied by cultural change.

The Counterculture

In the 1960s, many Americans, particularly young people, lost faith in the sanctity of the American system. "There was," observed Joseph Heller, the irreverent author of *Catch-22* (1961), "a general feeling that the platitudes of Americanism were horseshit." The protests exposed the emptiness of some of the old patterns, and many Americans, some politically active, some not, found new ways to assert their individuality and independence. As in the political sphere, the young led the way. Often drawing on the example of the beats of the 1950s, the literary figures who had rejected conventional canons of respectability, they sought new means of self-gratification and self-expression.

Surface appearances were most visible and, to older Americans, most troubling. The "hippies" of the 1960s carried themselves in different ways. Men let their hair grow and sprouted beards; men and women both donned jeans, muslin shirts, and other simple garments. Stressing spontaneity above all else, some rejected traditional marital customs and gravitated to communal living groups. Their example, shocking to some, soon found its way into the culture at large. More men grew long hair and discarded ties and jackets. Women threw off confining clothing like girdles and embraced freer fashions—miniskirts, longer dresses, slacks and jeans for casual wear.

Sexual norms underwent a revolution as more people separated sex from its traditional ties to family life. A generation of young women came of age with access to "the pill"—an oral contraceptive that was effortless to use and freed sexual experimentation from the threat of pregnancy. Americans of all social classes became more open to exploring, and enjoying, their sexuality. Scholarly findings supported natural inclinations. In 1966, William H. Masters and Virginia E. Johnson published *Human Sexual Response,* based on intensive laboratory observation of couples engaged in sexual activities. Describing the kinds of response that women, as well as men, could experience, they destroyed the myth of the sexually passive woman.

Nora Ephron, author and editor, summed up the sexual changes in the 1960s as she reflected on her own experiences. In 1962, after graduating from Wellesley College, she had moved to New York to work. Wanting a method of regular birth control, she visited the Margaret Sanger Clinic and began taking the pill. Initially she had "a hangover from the whole Fifties virgin thing," she recalled. "The first man I went to bed with, I was in love with and wanted to marry. The second one I was in love with, but I didn't have to marry him. With the third one, I thought I might fall in love." For a time she stopped taking the pill whenever she broke up with someone, but that proved inconvenient. As her doctor asked, "Who knows what's coming around the corner?" For many Americans in the 1960s, someone new was rounding the corner all the time.

The arts reflected the sexual revolution. Federal courts ruled that books like D. H. Lawrence's *Lady Chatterley's Lover,* earlier considered obscene, could not be banned. Many suppressed works, long available in Europe, now began to appear. Nudity became more common on stage and screen. In *Hair,* a rock musical, one scene featured the disrobing of performers of both sexes in the course of an erotic celebration. What had been unthinkable a decade before now became commonplace in the arts.

Paintings reflected both the mood of dissent and the urge to innovate apparent in the larger society. "Op" artists painted sharply defined geometric figures in clear, vibrant colors, starkly different from the flowing, chaotic work of the abstract expressionists. "Pop" artists like Andy Warhol, Roy Lichtenstein, and Jasper Johns made ironic comments on American materialism and taste with their representations of everyday objects like soup cans, comic strips, or pictures of Marilyn Monroe. Their paintings broke with formal artistic conventions. Some used spray guns and fluorescent paints to gain effect. Others even tried to make their pictures look like giant newspaper photographs.

Hallucinogenic drugs also became a part of the counterculture. The beats and others had experimented with drugs, but now their use spread. One prophet of the "drug scene" was Timothy Leary, who, with Richard Alpert, was doing scientific research at Harvard University on LSD. Fired from their research posts for violating a pledge to the University Health Service not to experiment with undergraduates, the two promoted the cause of LSD nationally. As Alpert drifted into a commune in New Mexico, Leary aggressively asserted that drugs were necessary to free the mind. Working through his group, the League for Spiritual Discovery, he dressed in long robes and preached his message, "Tune in, turn on, drop out."

Another apostle of life with drugs was Ken Kesey. Born and reared in Oregon, he had finished college in 1958 and entered Stanford for graduate work. There he wrote his first novel, *One Flew Over the Cuckoo's Nest,* and began participating in medical experiments at a hospital where he was introduced to LSD. With the profits from his novel, Kesey established a commune of "Merry Pranksters" near Palo Alto, California. In 1964, the group headed east in a converted school bus painted in psychedelic Day-Glo colors, wired for sound, and stocked with enough orange juice and "acid" (LSD) to sustain the Pranksters across the continent. After a series of outlandish adventures, they returned to California, where many were arrested. That only enhanced Kesey's standing in the drug culture.

Drug use was no longer confined to an urban subculture of musicians, artists, and the streetwise. Soldiers brought experience with drugs back from Vietnam. Young professionals began experimenting with cocaine as a stimulant. Taking a "tab" of LSD became part of the coming-of-age ritual for many middle-class college students. Marijuana became phenomenally popular in the 1960s. "Joints" of "grass" were passed around at high school, neighborhood, and college parties as readily as cans of beer in the previous generation.

Music became intimately connected with these cultural changes. The rock and roll of the 1950s and the gentle strains of folk music gave way to a new kind of rock that swept the country—and the world (see the Recovering the Past section of this chapter for a fuller discussion of the music of the 1960s).

The music was most important on a mid-August weekend in 1969 when some 400,000 people

Popular Music

One way to recover the past is through music. Popular songs not only provide insight into attitudes and beliefs but also quickly convey the mood and feelings of an era. Through their lyrics, songwriters express the hopes and fears of a people and the emotional tone of an age. Consider, for example, the powerful message conveyed in the Democratic party adoption of "Happy Days Are Here Again" as a campaign theme during the Great Depression. The decline of pop music and the rise of rock and roll in the 1950s tells historians a great deal about the mood of that period. Similarly, the popularity of both folk music and rock in the 1960s provides another way of following social change in that turbulent decade.

The music of the 1960s moved beyond the syrupy ballads of the early 1950s and the rock and roll movement that Elvis Presley helped launch in the middle of the decade. As the United States confronted the challenges of the counterculture and the cross-currents of political and social reform, new kinds of music began to be played.

Bob Dylan.

Joan Baez.

Folk music took off at the start of the period. Building on a tradition launched by Woody Guthrie, Pete Seeger, and the Weavers, Joan Baez was one of the first to become popular. Accompanying herself on a guitar as she performed at coffee shops in Harvard Square and at the Newport Folk Festival, she soon overwhelmed audiences with her crystal-clear voice. She sang ballads, laments, and spirituals like "We Shall Overcome" and became caught up in the protest activities of the period.

Equally active was Bob Dylan, who grew up playing rock and roll in high school, then folk music in college at the University of Minnesota. Disheveled and gravelly-voiced, he wrote remarkable songs like "Blowin' in the Wind" that were soon sung by other artists like Peter, Paul and Mary as well. His song "The Times They Are A-Changin'" (excerpted here) captured the inexorable force of the student protest movement best of all.

The Beatles.

But the 1960s were marked by far more than folk music alone. In the early 1960s, an English group from Liverpool began to build a following in Great Britain. In early 1964, the Beatles released "I Want to Hold Your Hand" in the United States and appeared on the popular Ed Sullivan television show. Within weeks, Beatles songs held the first, second, third, fourth, and fifth positions on the *Billboard* singles chart, and *Meet the Beatles* became the best-selling LP record to date. With *Sergeant Pepper's Lonely Hearts Club Band* a few years later, the Beatles branched out in new musical directions and reflected the influence of the counterculture with songs like "Lucy in the Sky with Diamonds" (which some people said referred to the hallucinogenic drug LSD).

Mick Jagger and the Rolling Stones followed at the end of the decade. Another English group that changed the nature of American music, the Stones played a blues-based rock music that proclaimed a commitment to drugs, sex, and a decadent life of social upheaval. Jagger was an aggressive, sometimes violent showman on stage, whose androgynous style showed his contempt for conventional sexual norms. Other artists, like Jim Morrison of the Doors and Janis Joplin, reflected the same intensity of the new rock world, and both died from drug overdoses.

Meanwhile, other groups were setting off in different directions. On the pop scene, Motown Records in Detroit popularized a new kind of black rhythm and blues. By 1960, the gospel-pop-soul fusion was gaining followers. By the late 1960s, Motown Records was one of the largest black-owned companies in America and one of the most successful independent recording ventures in the business. Stevie Wonder, the Temptations, and the Supremes were among the groups who became enormously popular. The Supremes, led by Diana Ross, epitomized the Motown sound with such hits as "Where Did Our Love Go."

What songs come to your mind when you think of the 1960s? How is the music different from that of the 1950s? What do the lyrics tell you about the period?

Look at the lyrics for "The Times They Are A-Changin'" reprinted here. What do they tell you about the social upheaval of the 1960s? What, if anything, does the song imply can be done about the changes in the air? What other songs can you think of that give you a similar handle on the decade?

The Supremes.

From "The Times They Are A-Changin'"

Come mothers and fathers
Throughout the land
And don't criticize
What you can't understand
Your sons and daughters
Are beyond your command
There's a battle
Outside and it's ragin'
It'll soon shake your windows
And rattle your walls . . .
For the times they are a-changin'.

While the 1969 rock festival at Woodstock represented the "dawning of the Age of Aquarius" for some Americans, for others it was an orgy of illicit and disreputable behavior, with hundreds of thousands of people smoking marijuana, removing their clothes, and reveling to the loud music.

gathered in a large pasture in upstate New York for the Woodstock rock festival. There, despite intense heat and torrential rain, despite inadequate supplies of water and food, the festival unfolded in a spirit of affection. Some people shed their clothes and paraded in the nude, some engaged in public lovemaking, and most shared whatever they had, particularly the marijuana that seemed endlessly available, while major rock groups provided ear-splitting, around-the-clock entertainment for the assembled throng.

The weekend went off without a hitch. The police chose not to enforce the drug laws and thereby avoided confrontations. The promoters had chartered helicopters to whisk away anyone suffering a drug overdose. For the most part, the gigantic crowd remained under control. Supporters hailed the festival as an example of the new and better world to come.

Other Americans, however, viewed the antics of the young with distaste. They deplored the uninhibited drug use, nudity, and sexuality, all brought into their living rooms on nightly television news shows. No matter how much the proponents hailed the "Woodstock Nation," much of America was appalled. The festival only underscored the generational polarization.

The fears of conventional Americans seemed vindicated at another festival four months later in Altamont, California. There 300,000 people gathered at a stock car raceway to attend a rock concert climaxing an American tour by the immensely popular Rolling Stones. Woodstock had been well planned; the Altamont affair was not. In the absence of adequate security, the Stones hired a band of Hell's Angels to maintain control. Those tough motorcyclists, fond of terrorizing the open road, prepared to keep order in their own way.

The spirit at Altamont was different from the start. The peace and joy of Woodstock were replaced by a lurking fear of what could go wrong. A fat man bounded onto the stage to dance naked to the music of one of the preliminary groups but clumsily trampled people around him and finally aroused the Hell's Angels, who charged him with weighted pool cues and beat him to the ground. An undercurrent of violence simmered, music critic Greil Marcus observed, as "all day long people . . . speculated on who would be killed, on when the killing would take place. There were few doubts that the Angels would do the job."

With the Stones on stage, the fears were realized. As star Mick Jagger looked on, the Hell's Angels beat a young black man to death. A musician who tried to intervene was knocked senseless. Other beatings occurred, accidents claimed several more lives, and drug-overdosed revelers found no adequate medical support. Altamont exposed the worst fears of less sympathetic Americans. *Rolling Stone,* the rock world's journal, deplored the commercial, promotional greed that had inspired the concert; other commentators feared the dark side of the counterculture, its self-indulgent, anarchic nature.

That underside could also be seen in the Haight-Ashbury section of San Francisco, where runaway "flower children" mingled with "burned-out" drug users and radical activists. Joan Didion, a perceptive essayist, wrote of American society in 1967: "Adolescents drifted from city to torn city, sloughing off both the past and the future as snakes shed their skins, children who were never taught and would never now learn the games that had held the society together." For all the spontaneity and exuberance, the counterculture's underside could not be ignored.

Gay and Lesbian Rights

Closely tied to the revolution in sexual norms that affected sexual relations, marriage, and family life was a fast-growing and increasingly militant gay liberation movement. There had always been people who accepted the "gay" life style, but American society as a whole was unsympathetic, and many homosexuals kept their preferences to themselves. The climate of the 1970s encouraged gays to "come out of the closet." A nightlong riot in 1969, in response to a police raid on the Stonewall Inn, a homosexual bar in Greenwich Village in New York, helped spark a new consciousness and a movement for gay rights. Throughout the 1970s and 1980s, homosexuals made important gains in ending the most blatant forms of discrimination against them. In 1973, the American Psychiatric Association ruled that homosexuality should no longer be classified as a mental illness, and that decision was overwhelmingly supported in a vote by the membership the next year. In 1975, the U.S. Civil Service Commission lifted its ban on employment of homosexuals.

In this new climate of acceptance, many gays who had hidden or suppressed their sexuality revealed their darkest secret. In early 1982, Dan Bradley, head of the national Legal Services Corporation, announced his own homosexuality and described the tensions of a life of concealment. "I subscribed to *Playboy* magazine—I must be the only man who subscribed to it but never read it—just to make sure that when people came to my house there was evidence of my straightness," he said. "I'd make up names of women and told people I had a lot of 'dates'—all sheer fabrication, all lies." Though he was single, he wore a wedding ring for seven years. Far more comfortable after his revelation, Bradley left his former job and worked to promote the passage of a gay civil rights bill.

Women also became more open about their sexual preferences and demanded that they not be penalized for choosing other females as partners. A lesbian movement developed, sometimes involving women active in the more radical wing of the women's movement.

Many Americans were unsympathetic to anyone who challenged traditional sexual norms. Churches and some religious groups often lashed out against gays. In 1982, James Tinney, a Pentecostal preacher who had announced his homosexuality three years before, was excommunicated from the Church of God in Christ as he prepared a revival meeting for gays in Washington. In Atlanta, the Metropolitan Community Church, part of a gay denomination, was burned after a series of attacks by vandals. Despite legislative uproar, some states refused to extend antidiscriminatory legislation to gay groups.

The discovery of AIDS (acquired immune deficiency syndrome) in 1981 changed the situation for homosexuals dramatically. The deadly new disease struck intravenous drug users and homosexuals with numerous partners more than any other groups. The growing number of deaths—

"Round up and quarantine AIDS carriers," urged the placard of one marcher in an antigay demonstration organized by the KKK in Houston in 1985. The AIDS epidemic made the gay struggle for equal rights considerably more difficult.

200,000 by 1992—suggested that the disease would reach epidemic proportions. Advertisements in the national media advised the use of condoms, and the U.S. surgeon general mailed a brochure, "Understanding AIDS," to every household in the United States. As knowledge—and misunderstanding—of the disease increased, many Americans felt that hostility toward homosexuality was justified. Still, homosexuals fought on for a greater governmental effort to find a cure for AIDS. Ironically,the disease itself began to be better understood when heterosexual sports heroes Magic Johnson and Arthur Ashe were diagnosed as having the HIV virus, and that understanding promised to help the gay cause.

The Environmental and Consumer Movements

Although many of the social movements that arose in the 1960s were defined by race, gender, and sexual preference, one further movement united many of these reformers across such boundaries. Emerging in the early 1960s, a powerful movement of Americans concerned with the environment began to revive issues raised in the Progressive era and to go far beyond them. In the mid-1960s, a Gallup poll revealed that only 17 percent of the public considered air and water pollution to be one of the three major governmental problems. By 1970, that figure had risen to 53 percent. By 1991, 78 percent of another Gallup poll considered themselves to be environmentalists.

The modern environmental movement stemmed in part from a desire in the post–World War II years for a better "quality of life." Many Americans began to appreciate that clear air, unpolluted waters, and unspoiled wilderness were indispensable to a decent existence. They worried about threats to their natural surroundings, particularly after naturalist Rachel Carson published her brilliant book *Silent Spring* in 1962. In it, she took careful aim at chemical pesticides, particularly DDT, which had increased crop yields and allowed more successful farming, yet had disastrous side effects that had been ignored. Despite opposition from the agricultural and chemical industries, her book mobilized the public. As Americans learned of the pollutants surrounding them, they became increasingly worried about pesticides, motor vehicle exhaust, and industrial wastes that filled the air, earth, and water. Earth Day in 1970 celebrated the world's natural resources and warned of continuing threats.

Public concern focused on a variety of targets. Americans were troubled in 1969 to learn how thermal pollution from nuclear power plants was killing fish in both eastern and western rivers. An article in *Sports Illustrated* aroused fishermen, sailors, and other recreational enthusiasts who had not been previously concerned. Meanwhile, DDT was threatening the very existence of the bald eagle, the nation's emblem. At the same time, a massive oil spill off the coast of southern California turned white beaches black and wiped out much of the marine life in the immediate area. An even worse oil spill occurred in Alaska in 1989 when the *Exxon Valdez* ran aground. Comedian Jay Leno joked that now fish sticks came in two styles—leaded and unleaded—but more serious observers feared that the damage was irreversible.

Concern about the deterioration of the environment increased as people learned more about substances they had once taken for granted. In 1978, the public became alarmed about the lethal effects of toxic chemicals dumped in the Love Canal neighborhood of Niagara Falls, New York. A few years later, attention focused on dioxin, one of the poisons permeating from the Love Canal, which now surfaced in other areas in more concentrated form. Dioxin, a by-product of the manufacture of herbicides, plastics, and wood preservatives, remained active after being released in the environment. Thousands of times more potent than cyanide, it was one of the most deadly substances ever made.

Equally frightening was the potential environmental damage from a nuclear accident. That possibility became more real as a result of a mishap at one of the reactors at Three Mile Island in 1979. There a faulty pressure relief valve led to a loss of coolant. Initially, plant operators refused to believe indicators showing a serious malfunction. Part of the nuclear core became uncovered, part began to disintegrate, and the surrounding steam and water became highly radioactive. An explosion releasing radioactivity into the atmosphere appeared possible, and thousands of residents of the area fled. The scenario of nuclear disaster depicted in the film *The China Syndrome* (1979) seemed frighteningly real. The worst never occurred and the danger period passed, but the

The accident at the reactor on Three Mile Island helped spark opposition to nuclear power. For people around the world, the cooling towers pictured here came to represent the horrifying possibilities of a nuclear reaction out of control.

plant remained shut down, filled with radioactive debris, a monument to a form of energy that was once hailed as the wave of the future but now appeared more destructive than any ever known.

The threat to the environment seemed even more horrifying with another nuclear accident seven years later in 1986. This time the disaster played itself out at a plant in Chernobyl in the Soviet Union. The first reports indicated as many as a thousand people had died following a huge explosion. Though the number of deaths was later scaled down, the airborne contamination affected people thousands of miles away. Europeans plowed up freshly planted crops, warned against drinking milk, and banned imports of livestock and vegetables from the east. Some scientists predicted that one million people would develop cancer, and five years after the accident, estimates of the cancer death toll ranged from 17,000 to 475,000.

Those threats underscored the arguments of grassroots environmental activists. Groups like the Clamshell Alliance in New Hampshire and the Abalone Alliance in northern California campaigned aggressively against licensing new nuclear plants at Seabrook and Diablo Canyon, respectively. While activist tactics did not always succeed in their immediate goals, they mobilized opinion sufficiently that no new plants were authorized after 1978.

Others worried about America's excessive use of water. The American West, one critic observed, had become "the greatest hydraulic society ever built in history." With massive irrigation systems, the nation's use of water rose from 40 billion gallons a day in 1900 to 393 billion gallons by 1975, though the population had only tripled. Americans used three times as much water per capita as the world's average, and far more than other industrialized societies. Pointing to the destruction of the nation's rivers and streams and the severe drawing down of the water table in many areas, environmentalists launched an angry wave of protest.

Environmental agitation produced legislative results in the 1960s and 1970s. Lyndon Johnson, whose vision of the Great Society included an "environment that is pleasing to the senses and healthy to live in," won basic legislation to halt the depletion of the country's natural resources (see Chapter 28). In the next few years, environmentalists went further, pressuring legislative and administrative bodies to regulate polluters. During Nixon's presidency, Congress passed the Clean Air Act, the Water Quality Improvement Act, and the Resource Recovery Act and mandated a new Environmental Protection Agency (EPA) to spearhead the effort to control abuses.

Despite growing national sympathy for environmental goals, the movement faced fierce political resistance in the 1980s. Ronald Reagan systematically restrained the EPA in his avowed effort to promote economic growth. James Watt, his secretary of the interior, opened forest lands, wilderness areas, and coastal waters to economic development and frankly conceded that he saw little reason to save the natural environment for future generations. George Bush initially proved more sympathetic to environmental causes, and received credit for his appointment of William K. Reilly, a crusader for stronger antipollution measures, as administrator of the Environmental Protection Agency. Ignoring the opposition of his staff to new clean air legislation, Bush delighted environmentalists by signing the measure. Later, as the economy faltered, he proved less willing to support environmental action that he claimed might slow economic growth. In 1992, he accommodated business by easing clean air restrictions. That same year, he attended a United Nations–sponsored Earth Summit at Rio de Janeiro in Brazil with 100 other heads of state. There he stood alone in his refusal to sign a biological diversity treaty framed to conserve millions of plant and animal species. Bush's opposition to any measures that might impede American growth or compromise his reelection campaign brought sharp domestic and international criticism.

Related to the environmental movement was a consumer movement. Americans throughout the twentieth century, particularly in the 1950s, their appetites whetted by advertising, had bought fashionable clothes, house furnishings, and electrical and electronic gadgets. Congress had established a variety of regulatory efforts to protect citizens from unscrupulous sellers. In the 1970s, a strong consumer movement grew, aimed at protecting the interests of the purchasing public and making business more responsible to consumers.

Leading the movement was Ralph Nader. He had become interested in the issue of automobile safety while studying law at Harvard and had pursued that interest as a consultant to the Department of Labor. His book *Unsafe at Any Speed: The Designed-in Dangers of the American Automobile* (1965) argued that many cars were coffins on wheels. Head-on collisions, even at low speeds, could easily kill, for cosmetic bumpers could not withstand modest shocks. He termed the Corvair "one of the nastiest-handling cars ever built" because of its tendency to roll over in certain situations. His efforts paved the way for the National Traffic and Motor Vehicle Safety Act of 1966.

Nader's efforts attracted scores of volunteers, called "Nader's Raiders." They turned out critiques and reports and, more important, inspired consumer activists at all levels of government—city, state, and national. Consumer protection offices began to monitor a flood of complaints as ordinary citizens became more vocal in defending their rights.

CONCLUSION

Extending the American Dream

The 1960s, 1970s, and 1980s were turbulent decades. Yet this third major reform era of the twentieth century accomplished a good deal for the groups fighting to expand the meaning of equality. Blacks now enjoyed greater access to the rights and privileges enjoyed by mainstream American society, despite the backlash the movement brought. Women like Ann Clarke, introduced at the start of the chapter, returned to school in ever-increasing numbers and found jobs and sometimes independence after years of being told that their place was at home. Native Americans and Hispanics mobilized too and could see the stirrings of change. Environmentalists created a new awareness of the global dangers the nation and the world faced.

But the course of change was ragged. The reform effort reached its high-water mark during Lyndon Johnson's Great Society and in the years immediately following, then faltered with the rise of conservatism and disillusionment with liberalism (see Chapter 28). Some movements were circumscribed by the changing political climate; others simply ran out of steam. Still, the various efforts left a legacy of ferment on which others could draw.

business that he was available and left his résumé with executive search firms that helped place people in management jobs. Nothing worked.

After nine months, the family was in serious financial trouble. Although Patterson's wife Julia had gone back to work, their combined income from her salary and his unemployment check was but a fraction of what it had been. Unable to make mortgage payments, they were forced to sell their house and move into a modest apartment in a nearby town.

The emotional costs were even greater. Embarrassed at his plight, Patterson stopped calling friends, and they ceased trying to reach him in turn. He was puzzled and hurt. Computers were hailed as the magical machines of the future, so it was hard to understand the shakedown that affected firms throughout the industry. Why was he having such trouble finding another job? Was there something wrong with him? People asked his wife, "With all the companies on Long Island, your husband can't find a job? Is he really trying? Maybe he likes not working." Despite his rational assessment of the situation, he kept coming back to the only answer that seemed to explain his failure: "It must be me."

David Patterson was not alone. Thousands of other executives faced the corporate downsizing that accompanied a continuing economic recession. Consumer confidence plummeted and pulled down countless formerly prosperous employees of firms throughout the United States. The cover of the March 2, 1987, issue of *Fortune* magazine showed the high-tech Silicon Valley's Joseph Rockom striding out a corporate door, with the caption: "Pushed Out at 45—Now What?" Although he took a sizable salary cut, Rockom landed on his feet. Others were less lucky. The cover story in the March 23, 1992, issue of *Business Week* focused on the increasingly pervasive phenomenon of "Downward Mobility," and noted in a subtitle: "Even a recovery will not bring back the thousands of jobs lost by managers and professionals." The story inside told of Allen Stenhouse, a $50,000-a-year insurance executive, who lost his job, then his house, his wife, and his place in society. It followed a number of other unfortunate executives as well, including Gerald Feldman, a $57,000 finance and administration director at an office equipment firm, who was similarly let go and had to cash in savings bonds and life insurance policies, then make plans to sell the house he and his family had lived in for 26 years.

Business Week noted the increasing difficulties these professionals, and others like them, had finding new jobs as they moved through the 1980s. At the start of the decade, 90 percent of the white-collar employees who lost their positions were quickly hired in similar jobs with the same or better pay. By the late 1980s, the figure was down to 50 percent; by 1992 it had dropped to 25 percent and was still falling. Clearly David Patterson was not alone.

Patterson and thousands of others who lost their jobs were the middle-class victims of a conservative era that was marked by greed and extravagance, especially on the part of those best off. As the nation pulled out of a recession at the start of the 1980s and the economy improved, more affluent Americans prospered most from the initiatives of the Reagan administration. The nation's economic policies widened the gaps between rich and poor, but those rifts were largely ignored by officials in power and supporters who benefited from Republican priorities. Poverty, however, became more widespread; members of minority groups encountered continued difficulty finding jobs; and finally an even worse recession in the early 1990s brought hardship to the middle and upper-middle classes as well. The national debt skyrocketed, and finally, in reaction to questions about the stability of the economy, the stock market tumbled. At the same time, cataclysmic events shook Communist governments in the USSR and eastern Europe, ending nearly a half century of Cold War.

This chapter describes the enormous changes of the 1980s and early 1990s. It covers the public policies of the new Republican majority, which promised prosperity but finally brought economic catastrophe to many of those who had formerly benefited most from the plans of Ronald Reagan and George Bush. It outlines both the economic and demographic transformations after 1980. Finally, it examines the new role of the United States in a vastly different world order.

The Conservative Transformation

In the 1980s, the Republican party established itself as the dominant force in national politics. The transformation that had begun in the Nixon era was now largely complete. The liberal agenda that had governed national affairs ever since the New Deal of Franklin Roosevelt had lost its broad appeal and gave way to a new Republican coalition determined to scale back the social welfare state and prevent what its proponents perceived as the erosion of the nation's moral values. Firmly in control of the presidency, occasionally in control of the Senate, the Republican party directed the new national agenda.

The New Politics

Conservatism became respectable in the 1980s. Two decades before, in 1964, Barry Goldwater had campaigned as the Republican candidate for president with the slogan, "In Your Heart You Know He's Right." He had been overwhelmed by the liberal landslide that gave birth to the Great Society, and political commentators had assumed that conservatism had no chance in the contemporary United States. But conservatism gained countless new adherents after the turbulence of the 1960s and the backlash of the Vietnam War. New political techniques that capitalized on national disaffection with liberal solutions to continuing social problems made the conservative movement an almost unstoppable national force.

Conservatives began with the maxim of Thomas Jefferson two centuries earlier: "That government is best which governs least." They argued that the United States in the 1980s had moved into an era of limits, as resources and economic rewards were less available than before. The dramatic economic growth of the 1960s and 1970s, they believed, left a legacy of rising inflation, falling productivity, and enormous waste and inefficiency. The liberal solution of throwing money at social problems no longer worked. They therefore sought to limit the size of government, to reduce the tax burden, and to cut back the regulations they claimed hampered business competition. In the process, they would restore the focus on individual initiative and private enterprise that many Americans felt had always been the essence of the nation's strength.

The conservative philosophy had tremendous appeal. It promised profitability to those who worked hard and showed initiative in the economic arena. It attracted middle-class Americans who were troubled that they were being forgotten in the rush to assist minorities and the poor. And it offered hope for the revival of the basic social and religious values that many citizens worried had been eaten away by rising divorce rates, legalized abortion, openly expressed homosexuality, and mass media preoccupation with sex and violence.

The new conservative coalition covered a broad spectrum. Some followers embraced the economic doctrines of the University of Chicago's Milton Friedman, who promoted the free play of market forces and an equivalent restriction of governmental activism in regulating the economy. Other supporters embraced the social and political conservatism of North Carolina Senator Jesse Helms, a tireless foe of any forms of expression—in art, dance, or literature—he deemed pornographic. Many others flocked to the Republican fold because of their conviction that civil rights activists and "bleeding heart liberals" practiced "reverse racism" with their programs of affirmative action, job quotas, and school busing to promote racially integrated schools.

The conservative coalition also drew deeply from the wells of religious fundamentalism. Millions of Americans, ranging from devout Catholics to orthodox Jews to evangelical Protestants, worried about sexual permissiveness, the ease of obtaining an abortion, the spread of gay rights, and court decisions protecting pornography as a legitimate form of free expression. They were disturbed at the increase of women working outside the home, a practice they believed eroded family life. They were particularly bothered by an increase in crime and immorality. Between 1970 and 1980, the murder rate rose 31 percent, the robbery rate 42 percent, the burglary rate 56 percent, the assault rate 79 percent, and the rape rate 99 percent. The use of drugs spread. Marijuana was not simply a fad but an institution for a broad segment of society. Cocaine use was increasingly common. In short, they objected to what they viewed as the liberalizing tendencies of American life and sought to refashion society by reaffirming traditional morality. Dedicated to the dictates of the Bible, they wanted to return religion to a central place in American life and to revive the traditional values they believed had made the country strong.

Many of these activists belonged to the so-called Moral Majority. The Reverend Jerry Falwell of Virginia and other television evangelists underscored the concerns of religious fundamentalism and developed large followings in the 1980s. Emulating Father Charles Coughlin, the radio priest of the 1930s, they appealed to audiences who knew them only on the airwaves. Listeners donated millions of dollars to support the call for the redemption from sin. Speaking electronically to enormous audiences in fiery sermons, they focused their television congregations on specific political ends. They also used their fund-raising ability to support candidates sympathetic to their cause. Moral Majority money began to fund politicians who held conservative positions on issues like school prayer, abortion, and the Equal Rights Amendment.

Conservatives also capitalized on changing political techniques more successfully than their liberal opponents. They understood the importance of television in providing instant access to the American public. John Kennedy had benefited from the first television debates, and Richard Nixon had succeeded by carefully orchestrating

The Reverend Jerry Falwell, founder of the Moral Majority, called for a crusade to revive moral values in the United States. His constituency was an important part of the new conservative movement.

apparently spontaneous interviews with ordinary citizens on the air. Now politicians became even more adept at using brief "sound bites," often no more than 15 or 30 seconds, to establish their positions.

Similarly, conservatives learned the value of negative advertising in a political campaign. Mudslinging has always been a part of the American political tradition, of course, but now carefully crafted television ads concentrated not so much on conveying a positive image of a candidate's platform but on subtly attacking an opponent's character in order to create fundamental doubt in a voter's mind.

Conservatives led the way in using public relations techniques in political campaigns. Richard Nixon had understood the value of such methods, and his 1968 campaign, described in Joe McGinniss's *The Selling of the President,* provided a model for conservative politicians in the 1980s. Polls, sometimes taken daily, mandated which part of a candidate's image needed polishing most or where one's opponent was most vulnerable. "Spin doctors" moved into action after a candidate made a public statement to put the best possible gloss on what had been said. Small wonder that Americans became increasingly cynical about politics and stayed away from the voting booth in record numbers as the twentieth century drew to a close.

Conservatives likewise led the way in raising enormous sums of money for their campaigns. Richard Viguerie was the New Right mastermind who understood how to tap the huge conservative constituency for political ends. A young Houston activist who moved east, he was determined to reorient the Republican party. "The GOP is like a stranded and disabled tank that is blocking a bridge during a battle," he said. "You've got to push it over the side so the other tanks can get through and cross over to the Promised Land." In the effort to help conservatives around the country, he organized a huge direct-mail campaign, unlike anything seen before in American politics, to raise money for right-wing causes. Viguerie's fund-raising played a major part in the rise of conservatism as a powerful political force.

But conservatives also understood the need to provide an intellectual grounding for their positions. Numerous conservative scholars worked in think tanks and other research organizations like the Hoover Institution at Stanford University or the American Enterprise Institute in Washington, D.C., that gave them a solid institutional base. Their books, articles, and reports helped elect Ronald Reagan and other politicians who shared his views, and defined the agenda for the 1980s and early 1990s.

Conservative Leadership

Ronald Reagan was more responsible than any other Republican politician for the success of the conservative cause. An actor turned politician, he had begun as radio broadcaster, then gravitated to California, where he began a movie career in Hollywood. After making a number of government films during World War II, he changed his political affiliation from Democrat to Republican and worked as a public spokesman for General Electric. His visibility and ability to articulate corporate values attracted the attention of conservatives who recognized his potential as a political candidate.

Reagan's political career began in 1966, when he was elected governor of California. He failed in his first bid for the presidency in 1976, but consolidated his strength over the next four years. By 1980, he had the firm support of the growing right, which applauded his effort to reduce the size of the federal government but bolster military might. Charging the Carter administration with a "litany of broken promises," he provided a soothing contrast to the incumbent. He showed real wit as he quibbled with Carter over economic definitions. "I'm talking in human terms and he is hiding behind a dictionary," Reagan said. "If he wants a definition, I'll give him one. A recession is when your neighbor loses his job. A depression is when you lose yours. A recovery is when Jimmy Carter loses his."

Reagan started with an enormous lead in the campaign and held it to the end. He scored a landslide victory, gaining a popular vote of 51 to 41 percent and a 489 to 49 Electoral College advantage. He also led the Republican party to control of the Senate for the first time since 1955. Reagan's strength showed in all areas of the country. He split the traditionally Democratic Jewish vote and working-class vote, though African-Americans supported Carter as before.

Ronald Reagan drew on his experience in the movies to project an appealing, if old-fashioned, image. Though he was the nation's oldest president, he gave the appearance of vitality. Here he is pictured with his wife Nancy, who was one of his most influential advisers.

In 1984, Reagan ran for reelection against Walter Mondale, Jimmy Carter's vice-president. For his running mate, Mondale selected Geraldine Ferraro, a congresswoman from New York, the first woman ever to receive a major party's nomination on the presidential ticket. Running an upbeat campaign in which he told audiences, "You ain't seen nothing yet," Reagan benefited from the economic upturn and persuaded the public that conditions were better than they had been four years before. On election day, he received 59 percent of the popular vote and swamped Mondale in the Electoral College 525 to 13, losing only Minnesota, Mondale's home state, and the District of Columbia. The Democrats, however, netted two additional seats in the Senate and managed to maintain superiority in the House of Representatives.

Reagan had a pleasing manner and a special skill as a media communicator. Relying on lessons learned in his acting days, he used television as Franklin Roosevelt had used radio in the 1930s. In prepared television speeches, or when chatting with reporters, he appeared like a trusted uncle who talked in soothing terms about concerns everyone shared. He was a gifted storyteller, who loved using anecdotes or one-liners to make his point.

For much of his presidency, Reagan enjoyed enormous popularity. People talked about a "Teflon" presidency—criticisms fell away, and disagreements over policy never diminished his personal approval ratings. As he left office, 68 percent of the American public approved of his performance over the past eight years, the highest rating for any president at the end of his term since World War II.

But Reagan had a number of liabilities that surfaced over time. He was the oldest president the nation had ever had, inaugurated two weeks before his seventieth birthday. Dwight Eisenhower, who left office at just that age, once remarked, "No one should ever sit in this office over 70 years old, and that I know." Reagan remained a full eight years beyond that. His attention often drifted, and he occasionally fell asleep during meetings. He appeared disinterested in governing. In press conferences, he was frequently unsure about what was being asked. He delegated a great deal of authority, even if that left him unclear about policy decisions. Critics often accused him of being dependent on his wife Nancy for advice, claiming that he allowed her to influence schedules and decisions, even when she relied on an astrologer to make plans (although both Reagans denied this accusation).

Worst of all, he suffered from charges of "sleaze" in his administration. In a period of several months during his last year in office, one former aide was convicted of lying under oath to

1st used in Dem. Primaries

conceal episodes of influence peddling. Another was convicted of illegally lobbying former government colleagues. Attorney General Edwin Meese escaped indictment but nonetheless came under severe criticism for improprieties that culminated in his resignation.

In 1988, Republican George Bush sought the presidency after eight years as Reagan's vice-president. A businessman who had prospered in the Texas oil industry, then served in Congress, as top envoy to China, and as head of the CIA, Bush gradually overcame his public image of a weakling who lacked the strength to govern effectively. Termed a preppy wimp by the press, Bush countered that characterization by becoming something of a pit bull and running a mudslinging campaign against his Democratic opponent, Michael Dukakis, the governor of Massachusetts, who had turned his state around after years in the economic doldrums. The son of Greek immigrants, Dukakis defeated challenges from several Democrats, including the charismatic black candidate Jesse Jackson, in the primaries, but proved unable to counter the charges of the Republican campaign.

One particularly devastating advertisement featured black convict Willie Horton, who had benefited from a Massachusetts weekend release program only to commit another brutal crime while away from prison. The advertisement, which never mentioned race directly, left viewers with the clear sense that blacks could be violent rapists, that whites needed to be cautious of blacks, and that whites would be better served by the Republican party. It was the kind of advertisement that brought political results, even as it encouraged racial polarization, and it proved a blow from which Dukakis never recovered.

On election day, many Americans, believing that neither candidate had addressed the issues, stayed home to protest the victory of style over substance. Bush claimed a 54 to 46 percent popular vote victory and carried 40 states, giving him a 426-112 electoral vote win. But he did not have

Although he trailed Democrat Michael Dukakis by 17 percentage points four months before the 1988 presidential election, George Bush rapidly overtook his opponent through effective campaigning. Bush won 85 percent of the voters who had supported Reagan in 1984.

the kind of mandate Reagan had enjoyed eight years earlier, and Democrats controlled both houses of Congress.

Bush quickly put his own imprint on the presidency. An unpretentious man, he acted like a down-to-earth resident of Main Street. "He's still plain ol' George," one Texan remarked after chatting with the chief executive at a barbecue near the end of his first year in office. Bush also made a virtue of keeping busy. "George Bush does not like to sit still," his press secretary remarked, as the president tore through golf courses and appointments from morning till night. And he maintained his own wide network of friends and political contacts through handwritten notes, telephone calls, and personal visits. More than a year and a half into his term, he was still on his political honeymoon, with a personal approval rating of 67 percent. Support grew even stronger as he presided over the Persian Gulf War in 1991. Then, as the economy faltered and the results of the war seemed suspect, approval levels began to drop.

Republican Policies at Home

Republicans in the 1980s aimed to reverse the stagnation of the Carter years and to provide new opportunities for business to prosper. To that end Reagan proposed and implemented an economic recovery program that rested on the theory of supply-side economics. This held that the reduction of taxes would encourage business expansion, which in turn would lead to a larger supply of goods to help stimulate the system as a whole. Democrats countered that a more focused effort was necessary to assist people who could not help themselves and thereby restore their purchasing power. Even George Bush was critical during his brief run for the Republican nomination in 1980, with his charge that Reagan was promoting "voodoo economics." Despite those criticisms, Republicans followed the president's lead and endorsed "Reaganomics" with its promise of a revitalized economy.

One early initiative involved pushing through regressive tax reductions. As finally passed, a 5

Federal Budget Deficits and the National Debt, 1970–1990

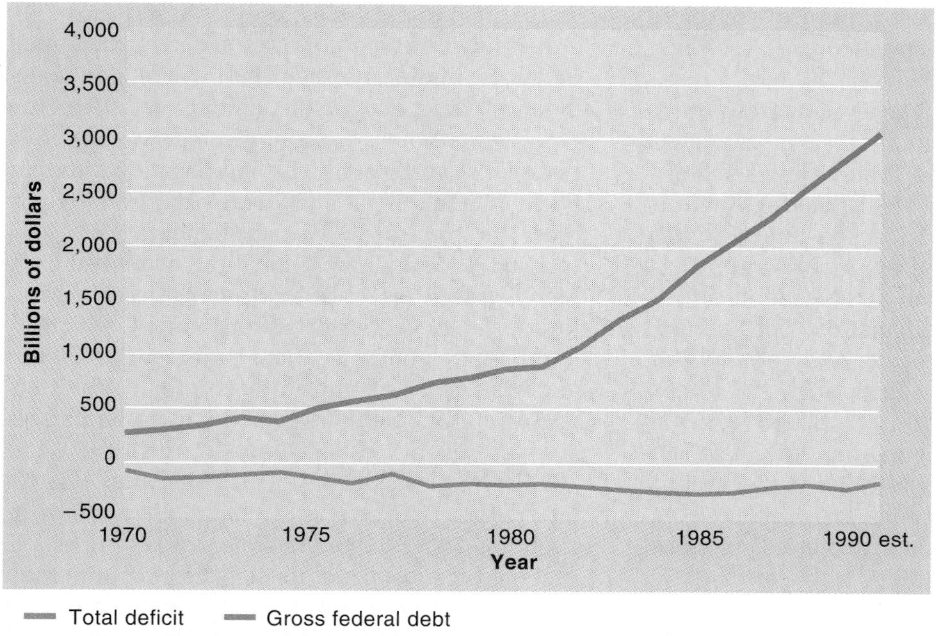

In the 1970s and 1980s, the yearly federal deficit grew steadily larger, and the gross federal debt skyrocketed, topping $3 trillion in 1990.

Source: Data from *Statistical Abstract of the United States,* 1991.

percent cut went into effect on October 1, 1981, followed by 10 percent cuts in 1982 and 1983. Although all taxpayers enjoyed some savings, the rich benefited far more than middle- and lower-income Americans. As a result of tax cuts and enormous defense expenditures, the budget deficit grew larger and ultimately ran out of control. From $74 billion in 1980 it rose to $208 billion in 1983. After a modest drop in 1984, it mounted to $221 billion in 1986. From 1987 to 1990, the budget deficit averaged $145 billion a year. Such massive deficits drove the gross federal debt—the total national indebtedness—upward from $914 billion in 1980 to $3.1 trillion in 1990. When Reagan assumed office, the per capita national debt was $4,035; ten years later, in 1990, it was about $12,400.

Faced with the need to raise more money and to rectify the increasingly skewed tax code, in 1986 Congress passed and Reagan signed the most sweeping tax reform revision since the income tax began. It lowered rates, simplified brackets, and closed loopholes to expand the tax base. Though it ended up neither increasing nor decreasing the government's tax take, the measure was an important step toward treating low-income Americans more equitably, but most of the benefits went to the richest 5 percent of Americans, whose tax rate dropped from 70 to 33 percent.

At the same time, Reagan embarked on a major program of deregulation. In a campaign more comprehensive than Jimmy Carter's, he focused on agencies of the 1970s like the Environmental Protection Agency, the Consumer Product Safety Commission, and the Occupational Safety and Health Administration. The Republican administration argued that regulations pertaining to the consumer, the workplace, and the environment were inefficient, paternalistic, and excessively expensive. Worse, they impeded business growth. Reagan cut regulations; he also appointed people like James Watt, his first secretary of the interior, who systematically relaxed enforcement of existing environmental rules in order to accommodate American business enterprise.

Meanwhile Reagan challenged the consensus fostered by the New Deal that the national government should monitor the economy and take whatever measures were necessary to assist the least fortunate citizens. He began with a fervent belief that in the United States, a person could make a mark through individual effort. He had played by the rules of the system and had won fame and fortune. Others could do the same. Underscoring his conviction, he removed Thomas Jefferson's picture from the Cabinet Room and replaced it with a portrait of Calvin Coolidge. He charged that government intruded into too many aspects of American life, and declared it was time to eliminate "waste, fraud, and abuse" by cutting programs the country did not need.

Reagan needed to make cuts in social programs, both because of the sizable tax cuts and because of the enormous military expenditures. Committed to a massive arms buildup, over a five-year period, the administration sought an unprecedented military budget of $1.5 trillion dollars. By 1985, with a budget of $300 billion, the United States was spending half a million dollars a minute on defense and four times as much as at the height of the Vietnam War. The trade-off was clear: reduced spending for social programs.

The huge cuts in social programs reversed the approach followed under Franklin Roosevelt and endorsed by liberals in the past 50 years. Republicans in the 1970s had begun to question the social policy goals of Lyndon Johnson's Great Society. Now, in the 1980s, they attacked those liberal aims head-on. Public service jobs, mandated under the Comprehensive Employment and Training Act, were eliminated, and other aid to the cities, where the poor congregated, was severely reduced. Unemployment compensation was cut back. Medicare patients were required to pay more for treatment. Welfare benefits were lowered, and food stamp allocations were reduced. Many grants for college students gave way to loans. The Legal Services Corporation, which offered legal advice to those too poor to afford lawyers' fees, was gutted. According to the Congressional Budget Office, spending on human resources fell by $101 billion between 1980 and 1982. The process continued even after Reagan left office. Between 1981 and 1992, American spending, after adjustment for inflation, fell 82 percent for subsidized housing, 63 percent for job training and employment services, and 40 percent for community services. Middle-class Americans, aided by the tax cuts, were not hurt by the slashes in social programs. But for millions of America's poorest citizens, the effect was far more harsh. Despite Republican claims of main-

Same in 1990's

taining a safety net to assist the unfortunate who would otherwise suffer serious harm, the administration's approach caused real suffering for the poor and created a growing reservoir of underclass restiveness.

As a political conservative distrustful of central government, Reagan also yearned to place more power in the hands of state and local governments and to reduce the ways in which the federal government touched people's lives. The "New Federalism" was Reagan's attempt to shift responsibilities from the federal to the state level. By eliminating federal funding and making grants to the states instead, which could spend the money as they saw fit, he hoped to restore a measure of local initiative. But the program euphemistically called "revenue sharing" never produced the desired results. As critics charged, with some justification, the proposal was merely a backhanded way of moving programs from one place to another, while eliminating federal funding. When a prolonged recession began in 1990, this policy contributed to the near-bankruptcy of a number of states and municipalities, who constitutionally could not run deficits as could the federal government but had been handed responsibility for programs formerly funded in Washington.

Meanwhile, Reagan took a decidedly conservative approach to social issues as well. He willingly accepted the support of the New Right, and strongly endorsed conservative social goals. Yet he was careful at first to provide largely symbolic support, in an effort not to compromise his economic program. He spoke out for public prayer in the schools, though he was initially unwilling to expend political capital in Congress to move the issue forward. In the same way, he showed his opposition to abortion by making sure that the first nongovernmental group to receive an audience at the White House was an antiabortion March for Life contingent.

George Bush followed directly in his predecessor's footsteps. Having forsworn his objection to "voodoo economics" as soon as he received the vice-presidential nomination, he faithfully adhered to Reagan's general economic policy while serving in that office, and continued it once he became president January 1991. In the 1988 campaign, he admonished voters to "read my lips" and promised "no new taxes." Though he backed down from that pledge in a bipartisan effort to bring the budget deficit under control, he later renounced his own agreement to modest tax increases when he went back on the campaign trail in 1992.

Like Reagan, Bush systematically prevented spending for social programs. Tireless in his criticism of the Democratic majorities in the Senate and House of Representatives, he vetoed measure after measure to assist those caught in the ravages of a troubling recession that sent unemployment rates up to 8 percent and left one of every four urban children living in poverty.

Bush was also even more outspoken in his support of conservative social goals. At the start of the 1980s, conservatives had questioned his commitment to their social agenda, and, indeed, Bush had been sympathetic to a woman's right to choice in the abortion issue. As president, however, he firmly opposed abortion, and his Supreme Court appointments, like Reagan's, guaranteed that the effort to roll back or overturn *Roe* v. *Wade* would continue (see Chapter 29).

The Republican philosophy under Reagan and Bush dramatically reversed America's domestic agenda. Liberalism in the 1960s had reached a high-water mark in a time of steady growth, when hard choices about where to spend money had been less necessary. As limits began to loom, decisions about social programs became more difficult, and millions of Americans came to believe that most of the Great Society programs had failed to conquer poverty and in fact had created lifelong welfare dependency. Conservatism offered a more attractive answer, particularly to those Americans in the middle and upper classes who were already comfortable. As Reagan left office in January 1989, *Newsweek* ran a cover story, written by sympathetic columnist George F. Will, entitled "How Reagan Changed America." Recognizing occasional limitations, Will noted Reagan's overwhelming popularity and argued that his real contribution was in setting the nation on a new course after two decades of disruptions and, allegedly, failed social programs. "Reagan, like Roosevelt," he concluded, "has been a great reassurer, a steadying captain who calmed the passengers and, to some extent, the sea."

But the transformation that Reagan effected also led to a number of serious problems that loomed in the early 1990s. As Bush assumed the presidency, his administration uncovered a scandal at the Department of Housing and Urban Development (HUD) in which highly placed Republicans received large fees from developers in return for helping wealthy clients win HUD contracts. At the same time, the new president had to deal with a crisis in the long-mismanaged savings and loan industry. The Republican deregulation policy had allowed owners of savings and loan institutions to operate without the previous restrictions, and many of them, paying themselves lavish salaries, made unwise high-risk investments that proved profitable for a while but then produced tremendous losses. To protect depositors whose assets had been lost by these questionable lending practices, Congress approved a $166 billion rescue plan (the sum soon rose above $250 billion) that committed taxpayers to bailing out the industry.

Far worse was the role Republican policy played in widening the gaps between rich and poor. Tax breaks for the wealthy, deregulation initiatives, high interest rates for investors, permissiveness toward mergers, and an enormous growth in the salaries of business executives all contributed to the shift. So did more flexible antitrust enforcement and a general sympathy for speculative finance.

The results were clear. "The 1980s," analyst Kevin Phillips observed, "were the triumph of upper America—an ostentatious celebration of wealth, the political ascendancy of the rich and a glorification of capitalism, free markets and finance." The concentration of capital increased, and the sums involved took what Phillips termed a "megaleap" forward. Now there was an extraordinary amassing of wealth at the top levels, among the dekamillionaires, centmillionaires, half-billionaires, and billionaires. "Garden-variety millionaires," Phillips noted, "had become so common that there were about 1.5 million of them by 1989." According to one study, the share of national wealth of the richest 1 percent of the nation rose from about 18 percent in 1976 to 36 percent in 1989. During the Reagan boom years, the wealthiest 1 percent of Americans expanded their

The Wealthiest Americans: Percent of National Wealth Held by the Richest 1 Percent

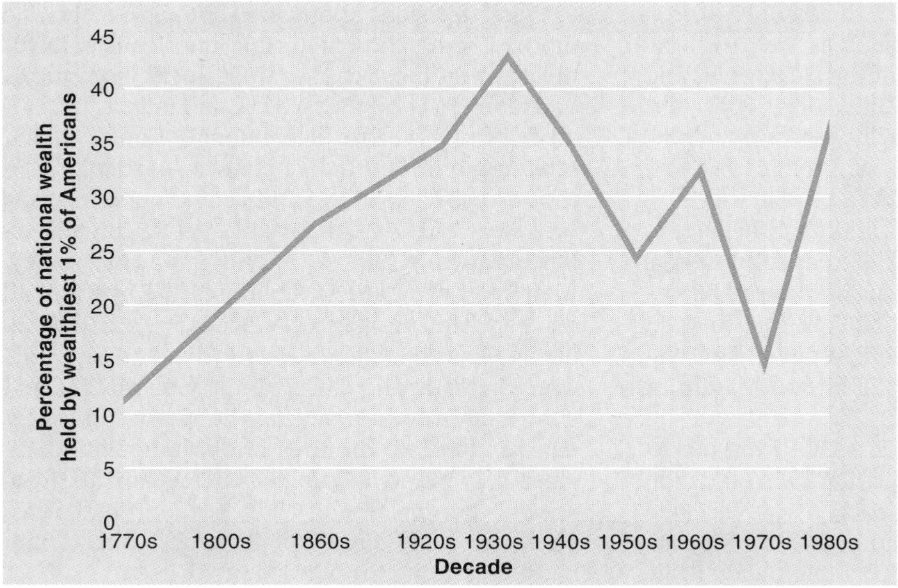

During the 1980s the percentage of national wealth held by the richest 1 percent of Americans reached the highest level since the 1930s.

Source: *New York Times*, August 16, 1992.

The Los Angeles riot of 1992 left more than 50 people dead and $1 billion in damage. Looters ransacked stores and thousands of buildings burned as poor urban dwellers protested years of neglect.

share of the nation's wealth as much as had the richest 1 percent in the entire period from 1830 to 1930 when America had changed from a nation of small farmers into an industrial giant. The net worth of the *Forbes* magazine 400 richest Americans nearly tripled between 1981 and 1989.

Meanwhile, less fortunate Americans, ranging from foreclosed farmers to laid-off industrial workers, were hurting more than they had since the Great Depression of the 1930s. A disproportionate number of women and members of minority groups lost ground in the 1980s, despite the gains of some of the luckiest in all of those groups. While white family income and net worth rose, they fell among black and Latino families. The inflation-adjusted income of families with children that were headed by adults under 30 fell by approximately 25 percent between 1973 and 1986 and even more by 1992. Middle-class Americans were smarting too. Median family and household incomes rose only slightly, after adjustment for inflation, between 1980 and 1988.

The growing disparity in wealth, resurgent racism, and the neglect of the urban poor became horrifyingly visible in the terrible rioting that swept through Los Angeles in the spring of 1992. The year before, Americans had watched a videotaped savage beating of black motorist Rodney King by white police officers, only the most dramatic of a long string of incidents involving police brutality. When a California jury, which contained no blacks, acquitted the policemen, people of all colors throughout the country were astonished and convinced that equal justice under the law had been proved unobtainable by people of color. In Los Angeles thousands reacted with uncontrolled fury. More than a decade of urban neglect lay in the background of the riot and so did tension between African-Americans and Korean shopkeepers and between black and Hispanic urban dwellers, who competed for jobs and living space in the city. As widespread arson and looting swept through many neighborhoods, the police proved unable to control the mayhem. Much of it was led by gang members but involved as well hundreds of ordinary citizens who acted irresponsibly yet with a sense that the social contract had been broken by politicians and the rich who were unresponsive to their plight. Several days later, after the riot had run its course, 51 people (most of them black and Hispanic), were dead, 2,000 injured, and $1 billion in damage done to the city. It was the worst riot in decades, more deadly even than the Watts riot 27 years before. Political candidates from both parties scurried around trying to define an urban policy, as the upheaval served notice that racial injustice and social inequality could no longer be ignored.

statistics

The Postindustrial Economy

The Los Angeles riots that shocked the country took place against the backdrop of an economy that frequently appeared more volatile than before. For decades, the Democrats had been trying to use Keynesian tools to stabilize the economy. Now, under Republican supply-side economics, the business cycle began to follow a pattern of moving from recession to boom and back to recession again. As Reagan assumed office, the economy was reeling under the impact of declining productivity, galloping inflation, oil shortages, and high unemployment. Reagan's policies brought improvement in the early 1980s, particularly for middle- and upper-income people like David Patterson, introduced at the start of the chapter. But even renewed growth and higher employment rates could not help those of lesser means, as structural changes in the national economy and the diminished role of the United States in the international economic arena led to continuing trouble in balancing budgets. The recession that gripped the country from 1990 to 1992 only underscored the need for renewed productivity, full employment, and equitable distribution of wealth.

The Shift to a Service Economy

In the 1980s, the economy underwent significant restructuring. In a trend under way for more than half a century, the United States shifted from an industrial base, where most workers actually produced things, to a service base, where most provided expertise or service to others in the work force. By the mid-1980s, three-fourths of the 113 million employees in the country worked in the service sector—as fast-food workers, clerks, computer programmers, doctors, lawyers, bankers, teachers, and public employees.

In part, that shift derived from the decline of America's industrial sector. The United States had been the world's industrial leader since the late nineteenth century. Technological and entrepreneurial ingenuity had placed the United States in a dominant economic position, one that was strengthened further by its role in the Second World War. By the 1970s, however, the United States began to lose that position. After 1973, productivity slowed in virtually all American industries; in the early 1970s, economic growth averaged 2.3 percent annually in contrast to its average of 3.2 percent in the 1950s. In the early 1980s, during the worst recession since the 1930s, economic growth virtually ceased. Real GNP fell by 0.2 percent in 1980, rose by 1.9 percent in 1981, and fell by 2.5 percent in 1982. In the midst of the Reagan boom it rose 3.0 percent in 1987 and 3.9 percent in 1988, then stagnated from 1990 to 1992 during another recession.

The causes of this decline in productivity were complex. The most important factor was a widespread and systematic failure on the part of the United States to invest sufficiently in its basic productive capacity. During the Reagan years, investment of capital in real plants and equipment within the United States gave way to speculation, mergers, and spending abroad. Gross private domestic investment in national industries rose modestly during the boom years, though most companies became caught up in an acquisition mania that consumed even more resources. At the end of the 1980s domestic investment was down—5.7 percent in 1990 and 9.5 percent in 1991. The oil crisis and rising oil prices (see Chapter 28) also contributed to the industrial decline. So too did government policies aimed at curbing inflation by keeping machines idle and environmental regulations intended to make industries change their methods of operation. Finally, the war in Vietnam diverted federal funds from support for research and development at the same time that Japan, Germany, and the Soviet Union were increasing their R & D expenditures.

While American industry became less productive, other industrial nations moved forward. German and Japanese industries, rebuilt after World War II with American aid and aggressively modernized thereafter, reached new heights of efficiency. As a result, the United States began to lose its former share of the world market for industrial goods. In 1946, the country had provided the world with 60 percent of its iron and steel. In 1978, it provided a mere 16 percent. Some of this decline was inevitable as other nations rebuilt their economies after World War II. But so efficient and cost-effective were foreign steel producers that the United States found itself importing a fifth of its iron and steel. By 1980, Japanese car manufacturers had also captured nearly a quarter of the American automobile market, and they continued to hold that substantial share in 1990. The auto industry, which had been a mainstay of economic growth for much of the twentieth century, suffered plant shutdowns and massive layoffs. In 1991, Ford lost a staggering $2.3 billion, in its worst year ever.

Workers in Transition

In the 1980s and early 1990s, American labor struggled to hold on to the gains realized by the post–World War II generation of blue-collar workers. The largest problems involved adjusting to the nation's changing economic needs. The shift to a service economy, while providing new jobs, was problematic for many American workers. Millions of men and women who had lost positions as a result of plant closings and permanent economic contractions now found themselves in low-paying jobs with few opportunities for advancement. Entry-level posts were seldom located in the central cities, where most of the poor lived. Even when new jobs were created in the cities, minority residents often lacked the skills to acquire or hold them. A basic mismatch between jobs and people in the cities became more pronounced.

Meanwhile, the trade union movement faltered as the economy moved from an industrial to a service base. Unions had been most successful in organizing the nation's industrial workers in the years since the 1930s. As the United States emerged from World War II, unions claimed 35 percent of all nonagricultural workers as members, but this percentage began to decrease steadily in the mid-1950s and continued to decline in subsequent years. Union membership rose in the public sector, but even this increase did not reverse the general decline in membership. In 1956, some 26 percent of nonagricultural workers had belonged to unions. In 1983, the figure was 20.1 percent; and by 1989, it had dropped still further to 16.4 percent. As the total number of wage and salary workers rose substantially between 1983 and 1989, the overall number of union members dropped from 17.7 to 17.0 million.

The shift from blue-collar to white-collar work contributed to the contraction. The increase in the numbers of women and young people in the work force (groups that have historically been difficult to organize) was another factor, as was the more forceful opposition to unions by managers applying the provisions of the Taft-Hartley Act of 1947, which restricted the weapons labor leaders could use.

Union Membership, 1950–1989

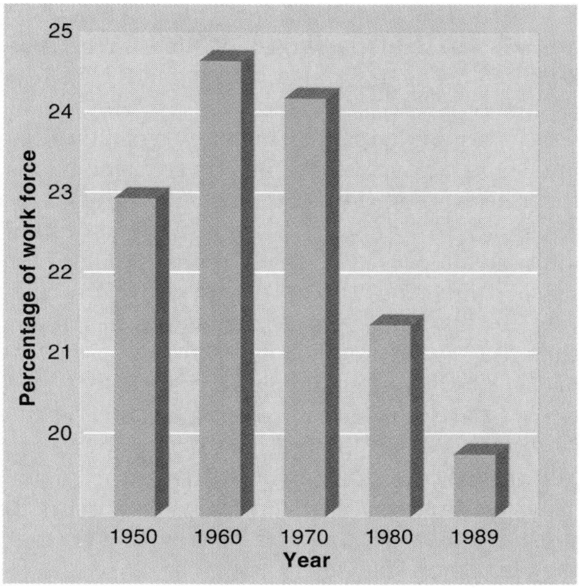

The percentage of workers belonging to unions dropped dramatically after 1960. Note the continuing decline in the 1970s and 1980s.

Source: U.S. Bureau of Labor Statistics.

Union vulnerability could be seen early in Ronald Reagan's first term, when the Professional Air Traffic Controllers Organization went out on strike. Charging that the strike violated the law and undermined the "protective services which are government's reason for being," the president fired the strikers, decertified the union, and ordered the training of new air controllers at a cost of $1.3 billion. The message was clear: government employees could not challenge the public interest. But antiunion sentiments reverberated throughout the nongovernment sector as well.

Everywhere strikers encountered hard times. In Groton, Connecticut, an affiliate of the United Auto Workers (UAW) called a strike of ship workers in 1983. After 15 months, workers accepted a "very bad" contract, leaving 43 percent of the strikers unemployed. As union leaders admitted, "No one will attempt . . . to defend the package." This pattern was repeated elsewhere. In 1992, the UAW called off a strike against Caterpillar Tractor and went back to the bargaining table after realizing that its contract demands would never be met.

To respond to increasing foreign competition and stagnant domestic productivity rates, unions found themselves forced to make concessions. In 1984, the UAW ended a strike at General Motors after winning a pledge that GM would guarantee up to 70 percent of the production workers' lifetime jobs in return for a smaller wage increase than they sought and also in return for a modification of the cost-of-living allowance that had been a part of UAW contracts since 1948. In the same way, in 1988, General Electric workers in the Midwest accepted a pay cut to save their jobs. That decision was part of a calculated effort to persuade GE to revitalize domestic plants rather than turn more actively to foreign labor.

Agricultural workers likewise had to adjust as the larger work force was reconstituted. Continuing a trend that began in the early twentieth century, the number of farmers declined steadily. When Franklin Roosevelt took office in 1933, some 6.7 million farms covered the American landscape. Fifty years later, farm families numbered only 2.4 million. In 1980, farm residents made up 2.7 percent of the total population; by 1989, that figure had fallen to 1.9 percent. Overall, the lot of American farmers improved during this half century, much of the earlier pervasive rural poverty having given way to a decent existence and sometimes considerable wealth. Part of this was attributable to the fact that as family farms disappeared, farming income became more concentrated in the hands of the largest operators. In 1983, the largest 1 percent of the nation's farmers produced 30 percent of all farm products; the top 12 percent generated 90 percent of all farm income. The top 1 percent of America's growers had average annual incomes of $572,000, although the small and medium-size farmers who were being forced off the land frequently had incomes below the official government poverty line.

The extraordinary productivity of American farmers derived in part from the use of chemical fertilizers, irrigation, pesticides, and scientific agricultural management. Equally important were the government's price support programs, initiated during the New Deal to shield struggling farmers from unstable prices and continued thereafter.

Yet that very productivity had environmental costs and led to unexpected setbacks in the 1980s. In the 1970s, as food shortages developed in many countries, the United States became the "breadbasket of the world." Farmers increased their output to meet multibillion-bushel grain orders from India, China, Russia, and other countries and profited handsomely from high grain prices caused by global shortages. Often farmers borrowed heavily to increase production, sometimes at interest rates up to 18 percent. Then, the fourfold increase in oil prices beginning in 1973 drove up the cost of running the modern mechanized farm. When a worldwide economic slump began in 1980, overseas demand for American farm products declined sharply and farm prices fell. Farmers who had borrowed money at high in-

Farm Indebtedness, 1950–1986

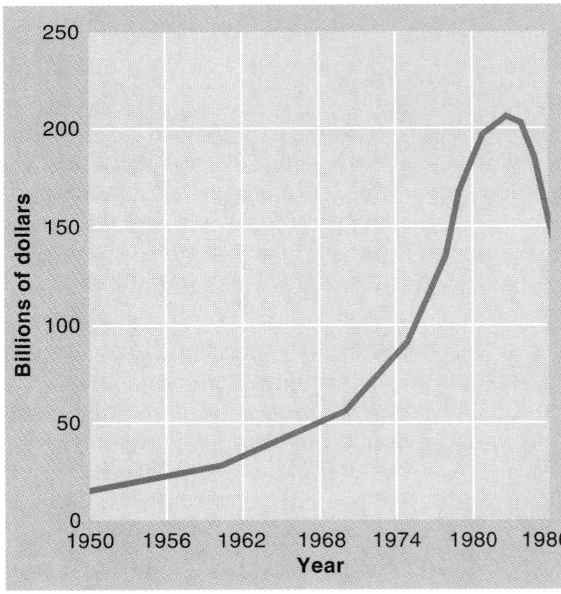

Farm indebtedness was a continuing problem in the postwar years. Even modest improvement in the early 1980s did not change the overall picture.

Source: U.S. Department of Agriculture.

terest rates, when corn sold at $3 to $4 per bushel, now found themselves trying to meet payments on these loans with corn that brought only $2 per bushel.

Thousands of farmers, caught in the cycle of overproduction, heavy indebtedness, and falling prices, watched helplessly as banks and federal agencies foreclosed on their mortgages and drove them out of business. For example, Dale Christensen, an Iowa corn grower, faced foreclosure in 1983 when the Farmers Home Administration called in his overdue payments on debts totaling $300,000. "I am 58 years old," he said. "My whole life has gone into this farm." He was one of many struggling farmers, who, in spite of government crop support programs that cost more in 1982 than all welfare programs for the poor, had to face leaving behind a livelihood that went back generations in his family.

Conditions improved little at the end of the decade. Family farms continued to disappear amid predictions that the trend would continue to the turn of the century. A drought in the Southeast in 1986 led to burned and stunted fields. An even worse drought in 1988 stretched across most of the Midwest. Devastating crops and forcing up prices, it demonstrated how vulnerable farmers remained.

The Roller Coaster Economy

During the 1980s and 1990s, the economy suffered a series of shifts. The Reagan years began with a recession that lasted for several years. The nation experienced an economic boom between 1983 and 1990 but then became mired in another equally devastating recession as the new decade began. It appeared that the United States had embarked on another cycle of boom and bust as unsettling as that which had prevailed in the early years of the twentieth century.

The recession of 1980–1982 began during Jimmy Carter's administration when the Federal Reserve Board tried to deal with mounting deficits by increasing the money supply. To counter the resulting inflation and cool down the economy, Carter cut programs but succeeded only in bringing on a recession, with substantial unemployment in the work force. Under Carter, the rate had hovered between 5.6 and 7.8 percent. During Reagan's first year, the job situation deteriorated further, and by the end of 1982, the unemployment rate had climbed to 10.8 percent, with joblessness among African-Americans over 20 percent. Nearly a third of the nation's industrial capacity lay idle, and 12 million Americans were out of work.

Inflation continued to be a problem and accompanied widespread unemployment. The rate, which reached 12.4 percent a year under Carter in 1980, fell after Reagan assumed office, to 8.9 percent in his first year and to about 5 percent during the remainder of his first term. But even the lower rate eroded the purchasing power of people already in difficulty.

The recession of 1980–1982 afflicted every region of the country. Business failures proliferated in every city and state as large and small businesses closed their doors and fired their employees. In 1982, business bankruptcies rose 50 percent from the previous year. In one week in June 1982, a total of 548 businesses failed, close to the 1932 weekly record of 612.

No area was immune from the recession. Louisville, Kentucky, had considered itself safe from the threats other areas faced but in 1982 found it was mistaken. Despite the hope that people would continue drinking and smoking in bad times as well as good, the Brown & Williamson Tobacco Corporation, manufacturer of Kool, Raleigh, and Viceroy cigarettes, closed down its Louisville branch. Then Joseph E. Seagram & Sons shut its bottling plant. General Electric released almost 10,000 of its 23,000 workers, and International Harvester closed a plant employing 6,500 people.

Detroit was one of the hardest-hit areas in the United States. An industrial city revolving around automobile manufacturing, it suffered both from Japanese competition and from the high interest rates that made car sales plummet. The Detroit unemployment rate rose to more than 19 percent. The entire city suffered from the decline. The $357 million Renaissance Center, which included a large hotel surrounded by four modern office buildings, had been expected to revitalize downtown Detroit when it opened in 1977. Instead it wallowed in red ink, and in early 1983 its owners defaulted on a huge mortgage.

Some areas initially seemed "recession-proof." The Sun Belt—the vast southern region stretching from coast to coast—prospered far more than other parts of the country. Economic growth was fostered by the availability of cheap, nonunion labor, tax advantages that state governments offered corporations willing to locate plants there, and its favorable climate. Soon, however, the Sun Belt was also suffering economic problems, and large areas began to stagnate. The unemployment rate in California in mid-1982 reached the national average of 9.5 percent, while in Texas it was 7 percent, higher than it had been for ten years. There was more joblessness in Greenlee County, Arizona, than anywhere in the country.

As the rising price of oil led to frantic drilling in many parts of the world, supplies suddenly outstripped demand. The resulting collapse in oil prices disrupted the economy in states like Texas, Oklahoma, and Louisiana. At the same time, worldwide gluts of minerals like copper added to unemployment elsewhere in the Southwest. The threat to the overextended southwestern banking system endangered the entire nation's financial structure. Since many parts of the rural South had never prospered, a gloomy economic picture spread from the Gulf states almost to California. In Jefferson County, Mississippi, 67 percent of the population lived below the poverty line.

While not all Americans suffered, virtually everyone felt the recession in some way. Everyone had a jobless friend or relative. Nobody could avoid the numerous "For Sale" signs on the lawns of houses around the country where residents, unable to meet their mortgage payments, had moved out, their faith in the American dream of home ownership badly shaken because losing a home was an attack on the status they had struggled to achieve. Everyone watched tax revenues, and then public services, decline as hard-hit Americans demanded lower taxes.

Economic conditions improved in late 1983 and early 1984, particularly for Americans in the middle and upper income ranges. The federal tax cut Reagan pushed through encouraged consumer spending, and huge defense expenditures had a stimulating effect. His effort to reduce restrictions and cut waste sparked business confidence. A voluntary Japanese quota on car exports assisted the ailing automobile industry. The stock market climbed as it reflected the optimistic buying spree. Inflation remained low, about 3 to 4 percent annually from 1982 to 1988. Interest rates likewise fell from 16.5 percent in 1982 to 10.5 percent in the same period and remained thereafter under 11 percent. Between the start of the recovery and 1988, real GNP grew at an annual rate of 4.2 percent.

But the economic upswing masked a number of problems. Poverty, in particular, remained a real concern. A 1984 survey noted a "staggering" increase in poverty in the South. The Census Bureau reported that the net worth of a typical white household was 12 times greater than the net worth of a typical black household and 8 times greater than the net worth of a typical Latino household. In 1988, the Census Bureau reported that even a 1 percent increase in the income of the typical American family in the last year had no effect on the national poverty figure, which remained virtually stationary at 13.5 percent. The figure for whites was 10.5 percent, for blacks 33.1 percent.

While many families continued to earn a middle-class income, they often did so by having two full-time income earners. They also went deeply into debt. To buy homes, young people accepted vastly higher mortgage interest rates than their parents had. Stiff credit card debts, often at 20 percent interest, were common. In the face of such circumstances, some young families barely remained in the middle class. Blue-collar workers in particular had to accept lower standards of living. Single mothers were hit hardest of all.

The huge and growing budget deficits were another reflection of fundamental economic instability. The doubts those deficits caused culminated in the stock market crash of 1987. After six weeks of falling prices, it suffered a 22.6 percent drop on Monday, October 19, almost double the 12.8 percent plunge on October 28, 1929. The deficits, negative trade balances, and exposures of Wall Street fraud all combined to puncture the bubble. The stock market revived, but the crash foreshadowed further problems.

Those problems surfaced in the early 1990s, as the country experienced another recession. The combination of extravagant military spending, the uncontrolled growth of entitlements—programs like Medicare and Medicaid which provided benefits for millions of Americans on the basis of need—and the tax cut sent budget deficits skyward. As bond traders in the 1980s speculated recklessly, bought and sold companies with an eye solely toward quick gain, and pocketed huge profits, the basic productive structure of the country continued to decline. The huge increase in the size of the national debt eroded business confidence, and this time the effects were felt not simply in the stock market but in the economy as a whole, which drifted into a downturn in 1990.

American firms suffered a serious decline. Corporate profits fell from $327 billion in 1989 to $315.5 billion in 1991. In an effort to cope with declining profits and decreased consumer demand, companies scaled back dramatically. In late 1991, General Motors announced that it would close 21 plants, lay off 9,000 white-collar employees the next year, and eliminate more than 70,000 jobs in the next several years. Hundreds of other companies did the same, trimming corporate fat but also cutting thousands of jobs. Cities where the GM plants were located wondered how they would absorb the laid-off workers. The unemployment rate rose once again. In mid-1991, it reached 7 percent, the highest level in nearly five years. About 8.7 million Americans were without jobs, up 2 million in the year since the recession began. Near the end of 1991, first-time claims for unemployment insurance increased by 79,000, more than double the number forecast. In the New York City metropolitan area, more than 400,000 jobs were lost since 1989. In Manhattan alone, job losses eliminated virtually all of the private sector growth of the 1980s. In a chilling indication of the city's economic woes, over a million New Yorkers, one out of every seven, were on the welfare rolls in July 1992. Most of the newcomers were unskilled workers who were unable to find jobs during the recession. Meanwhile, for those working, real incomes, after adjustment for inflation, began to fall. The upshot, the *New York Times* reported, was that "most Americans are entering the 1990s worse off than they were in the early 1970s." Around the nation, state governments found it impossible to balance their budgets without resorting to massive spending cuts. Reagan's efforts to move programs from the federal to the state level worked as long as funding lasted, but as national support dropped and state tax revenues declined, states found themselves in a budgetary gridlock. Most had constitutional prohibitions against running deficits, and so they had to slash spending for social services and education, even after yearly budgets had been approved.

After a number of false starts, the economy looked as though it was starting to shake off the recession in mid-1992. But deficits still haunted the nation, and grass-roots opposition to tax increases made it all the more difficult to bring the national debt under control or to balance state and local budgets. Despite some improvement, it was clear that recovery would not be dramatic and might take a long time.

The Demographic Transformation

As the American people dealt with the swings of the economy, demographic patterns changed in significant ways. The 1990 census revealed that in the previous decade the population of the United States had increased from 228 million to approximately 250 million. The rise of 9.6 percent in the 1980s, down from 11.5 percent in the 1970s, was one of the lowest rates of growth in American history. At the same time, the complexion of the country changed. As a result of increased immigration and minority birthrates significantly higher than the rate for whites, an all-time high of 25 percent of the population in 1992 was black, Hispanic, Asian, or Native American. The population shifted, as suburban growth continued, leaving ever larger minority populations in the cities. Meanwhile, the rise in the number of immigrants led to growth in states that had not been traditional magnets for newcomers from abroad.

Urban and Suburban Shifts

Urban composition changed significantly. White families continued to leave for the steadily growing suburbs, which by 1990 contained almost half the population, more than ever before. As that transformation unfolded, American cities increasingly filled with members of the nation's minorities. In 15 of the nation's 28 largest cities, minorities made up at least half the population. Between 1980 and 1990, the minority population in New York rose from 48 to 57 percent, in Chicago from 57 to 62 percent, in Houston from 48 to 59 percent, in San Diego from 31 to 41 percent. Minority representation varied by urban region. In Detroit, Washington, New Orleans, and Chicago, blacks were the largest minority, while in Phoenix, El Paso, San Antonio, and Los Angeles, Hispanics held that position, and in San Francisco, Asians outnumbered other groups.

Population Shifts, 1980–1990

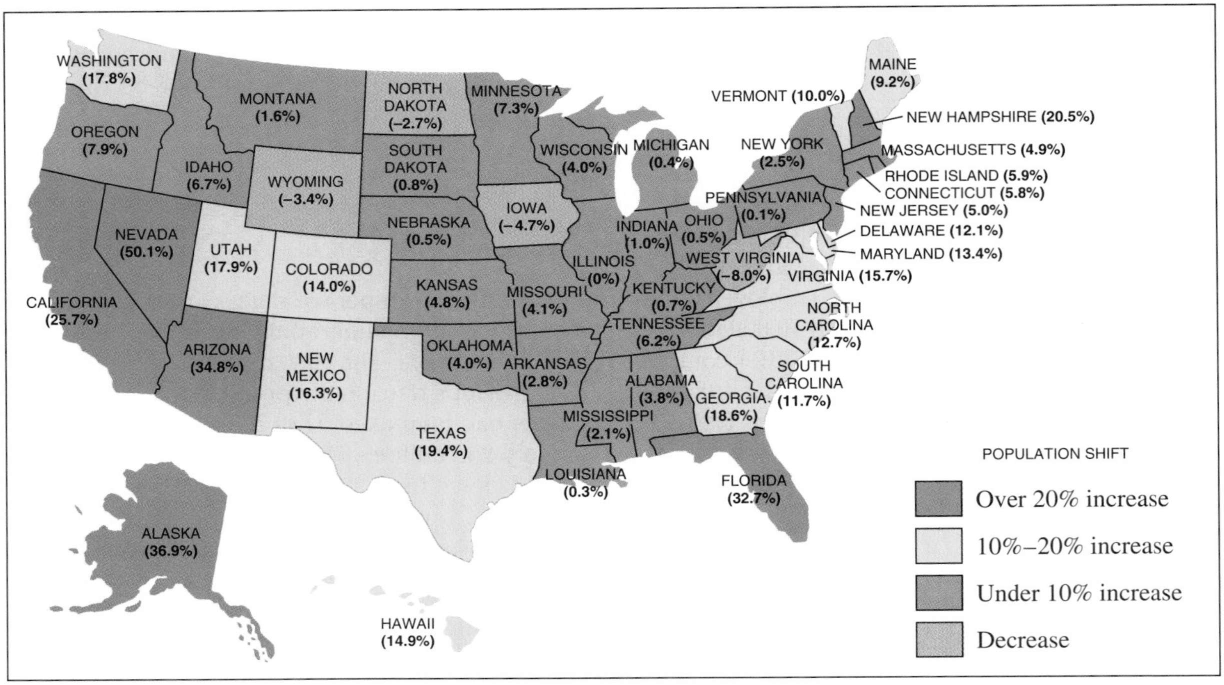

This map shows the population shifts between 1980 and 1990. Note the substantial increases in western regions of the country and the much smaller increases along the Atlantic seaboard.

In such cities, the gulf between minorities and other inhabitants widened. In Houston, for example, increasing numbers of blacks, Hispanics, and Asians lived in the suburbs, yet most less affluent minority families concentrated in the city itself. In a pattern under way since World War II, commuters from the suburbs took the better-paying jobs, while people living in the cities held lower-paying positions. A Hispanic immigrant like 27-year-old Mario Perez noted in 1991 that the increase in the number of Spanish-speaking immigrants in the nine years since he arrived made it easier to find a job, but he and others like him found it harder than in the past to secure well-paying jobs. Perez himself worked seven days a week sweeping streets downtown and tending plants for $5.50 an hour.

The New Pilgrims

Another shift occurred as the United States admitted new immigrants from a variety of foreign nations. A fifth of the decade's population growth stemmed from this immigration, which was spurred by the Immigration Act of 1965. Part of Lyndon Johnson's Great Society program, this act authorized the acceptance of immigrants impartially from all parts of the world. Because the national-origins system of the 1920s had favored western Europeans and was therefore frankly racist, most immigrants between 1930 and 1960 had come from Europe or Canada. Between 1977 and 1979, however, only 16 percent came from these areas, while 40 percent came from Asia and another 40 percent from Latin America. In the 1980s, only one of eight legal immigrants came from Europe and Canada, while 37 percent came from Asia, and 47 percent came from Mexico, the Caribbean, and Latin America. Always a nation of immigrants, the United States was once again receiving new, and very different, ethnic infusions.

As had long been true, the desire for jobs fostered immigration. But foreign crises also fueled the influx. After 1975, the United States accepted

Immigration: Volume and Sources, 1945–1989

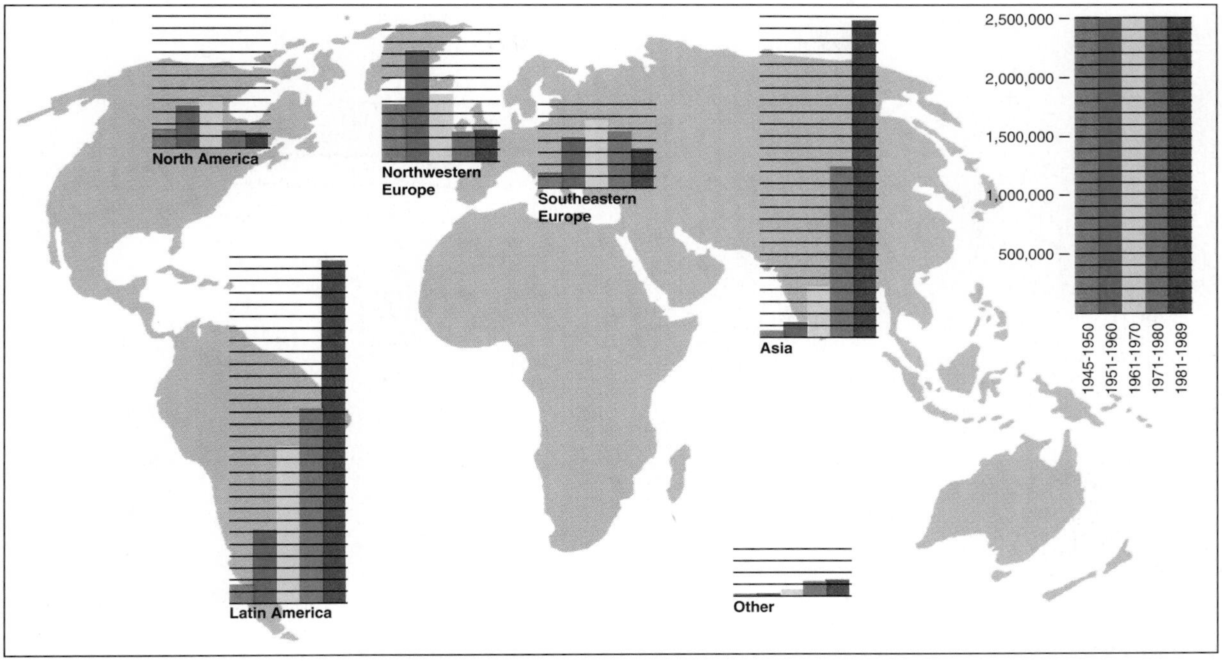

This map shows the shifting patterns of American immigration in the postwar years. In particular, note the large increase in Asian and Latin American immigration in the past several decades.

more than a half million Vietnamese refugees. In 1980, more than 160,000 arrived. That same year, the nation admitted 125,000 Cubans and Haitians to southern Florida. The official total of all immigrants in 1978 was higher than it had been in 60 years.

Millions more arrived illegally. As the populations of Latin American nations soared and as economic conditions deteriorated, more and more people looked to the United States for relief. In the mid-1970s, Leonard Chapman, commissioner of the Immigration and Naturalization Service, estimated that there might be 12 million foreigners in the nation illegally. While official estimates were lower, Attorney General William French Smith declared in 1983, "Simply put, we've lost control of our own borders."

Several legislative measures sought to rationalize the immigration process further. In 1986, Congress passed the Immigration Reform and Control Act, aimed at curbing illegal immigration while offering amnesty to aliens who had lived in the United States since 1982. Turnout for the program was less than expected until the mid-1988 deadline approached. Then 50,000 per week applied, compared with 10,000 earlier in the year, and all-night lines became common at legalization centers.

The Immigration Act of 1990 was even more important. It revised the level and preference system for admission of immigrants to the United States and refined administrative procedures for naturalization. Raising immigration quotas by 40 percent per year, the act cut back on restrictions based on ideology or sexual orientation that had been used to deny entry in the past. It also set aside a substantial number of visas for large investors, and provided for swift deportation of aliens who committed crimes. "This act recognizes the fundamental importance and historic contributions of immigrants to our country," President Bush said in signing the measure. It was

Immigration, 1970–1989

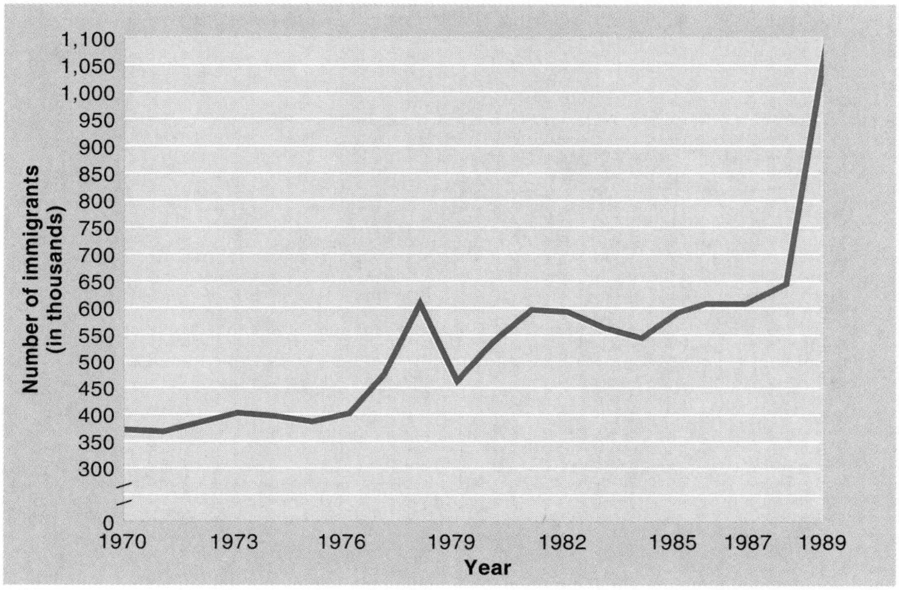

This chart shows the significant rise in immigration after 1970, as the tightly restricted quotas in force from the 1920s to 1965 were liberalized. Note the most rapid rise in the past few years, as Asians and Latin Americans have come in ever larger numbers.

Source: Data from *Statistical Abstract of the United States,* 1991.

"good for families, good for business, good for crime fighting and good for America."

The United States had once again become a refuge for people from very different parts of the world. The Sun Belt in particular, from Florida to California, felt the impact of the new Asians and Hispanics. In Los Angeles, Samoans, Taiwanese, Koreans, Vietnamese, Filipinos, and Cambodians competed for jobs and apartments with Mexicans, blacks, and Anglos, just as newcomers from different countries had contended with one another in New York City a century before. Throughout the country, in Miami, in Houston, in Brooklyn, the languages heard in the schools and on the streets changed.

These groups left a new imprint on the United States. As blacks and Hispanics became major figures in the urban equation, the number of Asians in the country doubled in the 1980s, and they exerted their own influence on the West Coast. In California, where more lived than anywhere else, they became the largest group of entering students at a number of college campuses.

Each group, each family, had its own story. Nguyen Ninh and Nguyen Viet, two brothers who remained in Vietnam after the victory of the North Vietnamese in 1975, were among the many who finally fled their war-torn country by boat. The boat sank, but they were rescued, only to be shuttled to Kuwait, then Greece, and finally to the United States, where another brother had arrived a few years before. Though they spoke no English, they immediately began to look for work. One became a carpenter's helper; the other, an attendant at a valet parking firm. With the money they earned, they helped other members of their family emigrate. Slowly they learned English, obtained better jobs, and saved enough money to purchase a home.

Professionals had an equally hard time. Frequently, training in their country of birth had little bearing in the United States. One Vietnamese

stat

Cuban "boat people, classified as refugees from Fidel Castro's Communist regime, were permitted to register for resident status.

physician who resettled in Oklahoma noted, "When I come here, I am told that I must be a beginner again and serve like an apprentice for two years. I have no choice, so I will do it, but I have been wronged to be asked to do this."

Growing Up

In the mid-1970s, the birthrate began to rise slowly after a decade and a half of decline. The baby boom, which peaked in 1960 with a rate of 24 births per 1,000 people, had created a population explosion in the years after World War II before leveling off. In 1981, the rate stood at 16, then rose to nearly 17 in 1990, as demographers viewed the new increase in births as part of a long-term trend.

But children less frequently lived in traditional homes. Despite the stereotype of the breadwinner father, the homemaker mother, and two children, the Labor Department estimated that only 7 percent of the nation's families matched that pattern in the late 1970s. Divorce shattered the mold. By 1980, the rate reached a historic peak, as the courts granted nearly 1.2 million divorces, the highest total in the nation's history. In 1990, the figure of 1.175 million was almost as high. For each 1,000 marriages there were 480 divorces, down slightly from 490 in 1980, but significantly higher than 328 per 1,000 in 1970 and 258 per 1,000 in 1960. The social stigma once attached to divorce disappeared, and the nation elected its first divorced president. "Nonfamily households" became increasingly common. Between 1980 and 1990, such households, which might be led by either a man or a woman, increased from 26 to 29 percent of the total number, while the percentage of family households declined. Single-parent families, particularly those headed by women, were now common. In 1960, 11 percent of all children lived in such homes; by 1990, the figure had reached 25 percent. For blacks, the proportion of families headed by women was three times as great as for whites. A 1986 study observed that children in such families were more likely to leave school, have children out of wedlock, and end up on welfare.

During hard times, particularly for members of the working class, new children could pose problems. An extra mouth to feed could make a difference to a family on the fringe. New children also required women of all classes to consider the relationship between family and career. Women entering the work force with long-range employment commitments had to juggle work and home schedules and find adequate child care facilities.

The rising rate of runaway children became another product of changed family life. According to some estimates, more than a million children between the ages of 10 and 17 were on the run. They left home for various reasons. Some were driven out. Others were victims of physical abuse. Still others fled violent arguments or other recession-induced strains in family life. Many returned home within a few days. Some, however, remained on city streets. In 1974, Congress passed the Runaway and Homeless Youth Act, which established telephone hot lines and temporary shelters. But the shelters served only 45,000 youths a year, leaving countless others without help.

Even more ominous was the rising death rate among the young. The Public Health Service reported in 1982 that the death rate for most Americans had dropped significantly over a 30-year period, and it continued to drop throughout the decade, but the rate for those between 15 and 24 rose steadily after 1976. Automobile accidents, murders, and suicides caused three out of four deaths for that group.

Growing Old

As concern with the problems of the young increased, awareness of the plight of the old also grew. Elderly people made up the fastest-growing age group in modern America. Between 1900 and 1980, when the population of the country tripled, the number of people over 65 rose eightfold and continued to rise in the next decade. In the 1980s, the number of Americans over 75 grew by more than 27 percent. Underlying the rapid increase was the steady advance in medical care, which in the twentieth century had increased life expectancy from 47 to 74 years. Americans watched Bob Hope celebrate his eightieth birthday, George Burns, over 90, continue to act, and Ronald Reagan, well into his 70s, govern the country. They became aware of the "aging revolution," which promised to become the most lasting of all twentieth-century social changes.

The elderly raised new issues in a nation suffering periodic recession. Many wanted to continue working and resented mandatory retirement rules that drove them from their jobs. Pleading their cause was Representative Claude Pepper of Florida, octogenarian head of the House Select Committee on Aging, who declared, "I am like an old hickory tree. The older I get, the tougher I get." Legislation in 1978 raised the mandatory retirement age from 65 to 70. That helped older workers but decreased employment opportunities for younger workers seeking jobs.

Generational resentment over jobs was compounded by the knotty problems faced by the social security system established a half century before. As more and more Americans retired, the system could not generate sufficient revenue to make the payments due without assistance from the general governmental fund. In the early 1980s, it appeared that the entire system might collapse. A government solution involving higher taxes for those still employed and a later age for qualifying for benefits rescued the fund.

At an intensely personal level, American families faced difficult decisions about how to care for older parents who could no longer care for themselves. In the past, the elderly might naturally have come into their children's homes, but attitudes and family patterns had changed. Children were fewer than in earlier generations, and as women gravitated to jobs outside, they were less able to assist in the home care of an elderly parent. Retirement villages and nursing homes provided two alternatives, but the decision to place a parent under institutional care was often excruciating.

Margaret Stump, an occupational therapist from Tenafly, New Jersey, agonized over such a decision. For six years she flew to Lima, Ohio, every three months to see her mother, who was over 90 years old. Finally, she decided to bring her to a New Jersey nursing home. "I felt that she'd be better once she got to a home," Margaret recalled. "But I knew she wanted to be in her own house. It was a very difficult decision. I had to wait until I thought she wouldn't know where she was."

The New Students

Another group of Americans faced the future more aggressively. College students were more numerous than ever before. After World War II, partly as a result of GI education benefits, higher education became broadly accessible for the first time in American history. College enrollment, which had never exceeded 1.5 million before 1945, rose to nearly 3 million in the early 1960s and reached 13.7 million in 1990. Women entered college in unprecedented numbers. Many of the students were older. A 1988 study by the College Board determined that 6 million—or 45 percent of the total undergraduate and graduate population—were at least 25 years old. The study projected that within 10 years, the older students would constitute a majority.

Students in the 1980s and 1990s were significantly more conservative. Gone was the sense of outrage and the commitment to reform that had mobilized thousands in the social struggles of the 1960s. Now students were more willing to work within the system. Howard Shapiro, a Yale senior, noted in 1983:

> If you want to change things, you have to work with those in power. I see a whole new cycle, with

> people aiming at the same good goals but in different ways. Instead of having a sit-down strike, students will meet with the administration and try to compromise.

Some students, not sure of themselves or their goals, gravitated toward various cults that recruited on campus. The Unification Church of the Reverend Sun Myung Moon grew rapidly, as did The Way International and the International Society for Krishna Consciousness. "I didn't know anything about cults when I got involved," said Heidi Feiwel, a Cornell University student who became part of The Way International. But in her freshman year, "I didn't have that many friends, and this was a source of community." By the end of her second year, her family had become concerned, and her father arranged for "deprogramming" to try to make her understand why she had become so committed to the religious group.

Most students in the 1980s coped with uncertain times by preparing for careers. Large numbers of them chose business or economics courses, while enrollment in the liberal arts dropped sharply. Conscious of the need to repay the loans that often provided their major source of support and aware of the difficulty of finding good jobs, students made choices reflecting concern for a career in a particular field rather than concern for a broad general education. Once in the working world, these young urban professionals, or "yuppies," devoted themselves to upward mobility and material gain. In the 1990s, however, many of these opportunities dried up and left students contemplating further schooling until the economy improved.

The United States in a Changed World

In the 1980s and 1990s, the United States emerged triumphant in the Cold War that had dominated world politics since the end of World War II. In the most momentous development in modern world history, communism collapsed in Eastern Europe and in the Soviet Union, and the various republics of the Soviet system embraced both capitalism and democracy. Yet the transition to a market economy was tortuous, and several of the Soviet satellite nations fragmented into separate states based on long-standing ethnic divisions. The Soviet Union itself disintegrated into its diverse republics as Marxist-Leninist doctrine and centralized authority no longer provided the cement to keep the once-unified nation together. Similar turbulence gripped the Middle East, accompanied by the rise of religious fanaticism and fundamentalism. South Africa likewise experienced breathtaking change, as black leader Nelson Mandela was freed after more than two decades of imprisonment and led the movement to end apartheid and establish a multiracial state. In the midst of this international tumult, the United States had to shift its assumptions and its traditional approach to the rest of the world and learn to operate with a new multicultural perspective.

The United States and the Cold War

The Cold War was very much alive as Reagan assumed power in 1981. In foreign affairs, the new president asserted American interests far more aggressively than Jimmy Carter. Like most of his contemporaries, Reagan believed in large defense budgets and a militant approach toward the Soviet Union. He wanted to cripple the Russians militarily and economically by forcing them to spend more than they could afford. The massive buildup in both nuclear and conventional weapons helped undermine the Communist state but ironically at the cost of tremendously destabilizing budget deficits at home.

Reagan promoted an increased atomic arsenal by arguing that a nuclear war could be fought and won. Discounting scientists' studies that showed cataclysmic destruction in the event of nuclear war, he claimed that the nation would survive. T. K. Jones, deputy undersecretary of defense for strategic and theater nuclear forces, even revived the dormant notion of nuclear civil defense. "Dig a hole, cover it with a couple of doors, and then throw three feet of dirt on top," he advised. "It's the dirt that does it. . . . If there are enough shovels to go around, everybody's going to make it." That position appeared particularly cavalier as scientists began to speculate about the "nuclear winter" that could end planetary life after a nuclear war.

While promoting defense spending and nuclear superiority during his first term, Reagan

Autobiography

As we reach our own time, the historical past most worth recovering, perhaps, is our own. Our own story is as valid a part of the story of American history as Revolutionary War soldiers, frontier women, reform politicians, and immigrant grandparents. In this increasingly computerized and depersonalized age, the person we need to recover and know is ourself, a self that has been formed, at least in part, by the entire American experience we have been studying.

Autobiography is the form of writing in which people tell their own life's history. Although written autobiographies are at least as old as the literature of the early Christians, for example, *The Confessions of St. Augustine,* the word *autobiography* dates from the late eighteenth century, around the time of the French and American revolutions. That is no accident. These momentous events represented the triumph of individual liberty and the sovereignty of the self. *The Autobiography of Benjamin Franklin,* written between 1771 and his death in 1790, and excerpted here, is a classic celebration of the American success story. Franklin's work set the standard for one autobiographical form, the memoir of one's public achievements and success. The other brief autobiographical

Autobiographical Memoirs

Benjamin Franklin

DEAR SON,

I have ever had a pleasure in obtaining any little anecdotes of my ancestors. You may remember the enquiries I made among the remains of my relations when you were with me in England and the journey I undertook for that purpose. Imagining it may be equally agreeable to you to know the circumstances of my life—many of which you are yet unacquainted with—and expecting a week's uninterrupted leisure in my present country retirement, I sit down to write them for you. Besides, there are some other inducements that excite me to this undertaking. From the poverty and obscurity in which I was born and in which I passed my earliest years, I have raised myself to a state of affluence and some degree of celebrity in the world. As constant good fortune has accompanied me even to an advanced period of life, my posterity will perhaps be desirous of learning the means, which I employed, and which, thanks to Providence, so well succeeded with me. They may also deem them fit to be imitated, should any of them find themselves in similar circumstances.

Source: *The Autobiography of Benjamin Franklin* (1771).

Elizabeth Cady Stanton

It was 'mid such exhilarating scenes that Miss Anthony and I wrote addresses for temperance, anti-slavery, educational and woman's rights conventions. Here we forged resolutions, protests, appeals, petitions, agricultural reports, and constitutional arguments; for we made it a matter of conscience to accept every invitation to speak on every question, in order to maintain woman's right to do so. To this end we took turns on the domestic watchtowers, directing amusements, settling disputes, protecting the weak against the strong, and trying to secure equal rights to all in the home as well as the nation.

It is often said, by those who know Miss Anthony best, that she has been my good angel, always pushing and goading me to work, and that but for her pertinacity I should never have accomplished the little I have. On the other hand it has been said that I forged the thunderbolts and she fired them. Perhaps all this is, in a measure, true. With the cares of a large family I might, in time, like too many women, have become wholly absorbed in a narrow family selfishness, had not my friend been continually exploring new fields for missionary labors. Her description of a body of men on any platform, complacently deciding questions in which women had an equal interest, without an equal voice, readily aroused me to a determination to throw a firebrand into the midst of their assembly.

Source: Elizabeth Cady Stanton, *Eighty Years and More: Reminiscences, 1815–1897* (1898).

memoir, from the reminiscences of Elizabeth Cady Stanton, also reflects the tone and range of this tradition.

Not all autobiographies are written late in life to celebrate one's accomplishments. The confessional autobiography, unlike most memoirs, explores the author's interior life, acknowledging flaws and failures as well as successes; it may be written at any age. The purpose of this type of autobiography is not just to reconstruct one's past to preserve it for posterity, but to find from one's past an identity in order to know better how to live one's future. The story of religious confessions and conversions is an obvious example. This form also includes secular self-examinations such as those by Maxine Hong Kingston in *The Woman Warrior* (1976), Piri Thomas in *Down These Mean Streets* (1967), or Maya Angelou in a series of five autobiographical sketches beginning with *I Know Why the Caged Bird Sings* (1969). The other two excerpts presented here are among the finest examples of confessional autobiography and suggest its variety.

These examples hardly suggest the full range of the autobiographical form or how available to all people is the opportunity to tell the story of one's life. In 1909, William Dean Howells called autobiography the "most democratic province in the republic of letters." A recent critic agrees, pointing out:

> To this genre have been drawn public and private figures: poets, philosophers, prizefighters; actresses, artists, political activists; statesmen and penitentiary prisoners; financiers and football players; Quakers and Black Muslims; immigrants and Indians. The range of personality, experience, and profession reflected in the forms of American autobiography is as varied as American life itself.

Your story, too, is a legitimate part of American history. But writing an autobiography, while open to all, is deceptively difficult. Like historians, autobiographers face problems of sources, selection, interpretation, and style. As in the writing of any history, the account of one's past must be objective, not only in the verifiable accuracy of details but also in the honest selection of representative events to be described. Moreover, as in fiction as well as history, the autobiographer must provide a structured form, an organizing principle, literary merit, and thematic coherence to the story. Many other challenges face the would-be autobiographer, such as finding a balance between one's public life and the private self and handling problems of memory, ego (should one, for example, use the first or third person?), and death.

To get an idea of the difficulties of writing an autobiography, try writing your own. Limit yourself to 1,000 words. Good luck.

Confessional Autobiographies

Black Elk

And so it was all over.

I did not know then how much was ended. When I look back now from this high hill of my old age, I can still see the butchered women and children lying heaped and scattered all along the crooked gulch as plain as when I saw them with eyes still young. And I can see that something else died there in the bloody mud, and was buried in the blizzard. A people's dream died there. It was a beautiful dream.

And I, to whom so great a vision was given in my youth,—you see me now a pitiful old man who has done nothing, for the nation's hoop is broken and scattered. There is no center any longer, and the sacred tree is dead.

Source: *Black Elk Speaks,* as told through John G. Neihardt (1932).

Malcolm X

I want to say before I go on that I have never previously told anyone my sordid past in detail. I haven't done it now to sound as though I might be proud of how bad, how evil, I was.

But people are always speculating—why am I as I am? To understand that of any person, his whole life, from birth, must be reviewed. All of our experiences fuse into our personality. Everything that ever happened to us is an ingredient.

Today, when everything that I do has an urgency, I would not spend one hour in the preparation of a book which has the ambition to perhaps titillate some readers. But I am spending many hours because the full story is the best way that I know to have it seen, and understood, that I had sunk to the very bottom of the American white man's society when—soon now, in prison—I found Allah and the religion of Islam and it completely transformed my life.

Source: *The Autobiography of Malcolm X,* with the assistance of Alex Haley (1964).

persisted in viewing the Soviet Union as an "evil empire." The administration abandoned Senate ratification of SALT II, the arms reduction plan negotiated under Carter, although it observed its restrictions. Instead the administration proposed that Russia destroy certain missiles in return for an American pledge not to deploy new weapons in Europe. The Soviet Union balked at that idea, so different from the careful negotiation accompanying previous arms talks. As the arms race escalated, new U.S. missiles were deployed in western Europe, and in both countries, military budgets soared.

Meanwhile, Reagan proposed the Strategic Defense Initiative, popularly known as "Star Wars" after a 1977 movie, to intercept Soviet missiles by means of a shield in outer space. Scientists questioned whether the proposal was technologically feasible. Economists pointed to the extraordinary sums it would cost just to find out. The public developed its own acronyms for the extravagant project: DUMB—for "Defensive Umbrella," WACKO—for "Wistful Attempts to Circumvent Killing Ourselves," and WIMP—for "Western Intercontinental Missile Protection," among others. But the administration still pressed ahead with the project, supported by a reluctant Congress.

In his second term, however, Reagan softened his rigid position toward the Soviet Union. Mikhail Gorbachev, the new Russian leader, watched his own economy collapsing under the pressure of the superheated arms race and realized the need for greater accommodation with the West. He understood that the only way the Soviet Union could survive was through arms negotiations with the United States that would help reduce his overextended budget. He therefore proposed a policy of *perestroika* (restructuring the economy) and *glasnost* (political openness to encourage personal initiative). His overtures opened the way to better relations with the United States.

Concerned with his own place in history, Reagan agreed to meet with Gorbachev, and the two heads of state developed a close working relationship. Summit meetings in Switzerland and Iceland led to an Intermediate-Range Nuclear Forces Treaty in 1987 that provided for withdrawal and destruction of 2,500 Soviet and American nuclear missiles in Europe. The two nations had not yet resumed détente, but ties were better than they had been in some time.

George Bush maintained Reagan's comfortable relationship with Mikhail Gorbachev. Initially he sought to maintain high military expenditures and proceed cautiously in what his advisers called a policy of "status-quo-plus," but he found the rapid pace of world events required a personal meeting. The two leaders met at a first summit at Malta in late 1989, then again in the United States in mid-1990. Together they signed agreements reducing the number of long-range nuclear weapons to a maximum of 1,600 rockets and 6,000 warheads, ending their manufacture of

Soviet leader Mikhail Gorbachev met with Ronald Reagan at a series of summits, including this one in Iceland, as relations between the two powers improved.

Boris Yeltsin, leader of Russia, the largest of the republics in what had been the Soviet Union, became the most influential leader after Gorbachev's fall. But Yeltsin's efforts at economic reform met with serious opposition and left him vulnerable as well.

chemical weapons, and easing trade restrictions between the two nations. The Strategic Arms Reduction Treaty (START) they signed in 1991 dramatically decreased the number of long-range weapons stockpiled during years of international hostility. "The Cold War is now behind us," Gorbachev declared at Stanford University. "Let us not wrangle over who won it." But the victor was clear, and in the final years of the twentieth century, the United States would clearly be the dominant force.

Hailed around the world for his part in ending the Cold War, Gorbachev encountered trouble from opposition groups within the Soviet Union. In mid-1991, a conservative coup, led by those who opposed *glasnost* and *perestroika* and felt Gorbachev was changing the Soviet Union too quickly, drove him from Moscow. Gorbachev survived this right-wing challenge, but he could not resist those who wanted to go even further to establish democracy and capitalism. The forces he had unleashed within the Soviet Union finally tore the USSR apart. In the turbulence that followed the coup, Boris Yeltsin, head of Russia, the strongest and most populous of the Soviet republics, emerged as the dominant leader. Already independence movements in the tiny Baltic republics of Estonia, Latvia, and Lithuania had begun the disintegration of the Soviet Union, and now other republics declared their autonomy and then coalesced loosely in a Commonwealth of Independent States.

Early in 1992, Bush and Yeltsin proclaimed a new era of "friendship and partnership" and formally declared an end to the Cold War. That struggle, according to historian Christopher Lasch, now belonged "to the age of political dinosaurs, when the earth was dominated by two overgrown empires." Future arms control proposals promised to make the world a safer place. The American victory was underscored as Yeltsin went even further than Gorbachev and abandoned the notion of nuclear parity—maintaining an arsenal similar to that of the United States—and agreed to cut back conventional Russian forces to complement the nuclear cuts. Meanwhile, the United States and its allies contemplated a new role for NATO, the North Atlantic Treaty Organization, and the extension of aid to the republics in the former Soviet Union who needed help in reorganizing their economies as free enterprise systems.

While celebrating the collapse of the Soviet Union, the United States found itself facing a vastly different situation in Europe, but one equally to its liking, at least at first. The liberalization initiated by Gorbachev in his own country quickly spread the desire for change beyond Soviet borders and soon toppled governments in most countries within the Soviet orbit. Bush spoke of a " New World Order," which he defined as "a world where the strong respect the rights of the weak," and anticipated international stability, guided by the example of the United States. Instead, the fall of communism brought an increase in disorder as the disintegration of central authority opened the way to intense political wrangling and the rekindling of ancient racial, cultural, and religious antagonisms.

The most dramatic chapter in the collapse of communism began in November 1989, when East Germany's Communist party boss announced unexpectedly that citizens of his country would be free to leave East Germany. Within hours, thousands of people gathered on both sides of the 28-mile Berlin Wall—the symbol of the Cold War that divided Berlin into east and west sectors. As the border guards stepped aside, East Germans flooded into West Berlin amidst dancing, shouting, and fireworks. All through the night noisy celebrators reveled in what one observer called the "greatest street party in the history of the world."

Within days, an outpouring of sledgehammer-wielding Germans pulverized the Berlin Wall, and soon the Communist government led by Erich Honnecker came tumbling down with it. Though people whispered of a reunified Germany, such a step still seemed impossible. Yet the idea of German reunification became "a kind of runaway freight train that nobody—East or West—seems able to contain," as a former CIA director put it. By October 1990, less than a year after the free movement of East Germans across their borders began, the two Germanys were reunited with the agreement of the U.S., Great Britain, France, and the USSR.

The fall of the Berlin Wall, bringing the sense that an epic moment in history had arrived, reverberated all over Eastern Europe. Everywhere it brought in its wake the pell-mell overthrow of Communist regimes. In Poland, the 10-year-old Solidarity movement led by Lech Walesa finally triumphed in its long struggle against Soviet domination and found itself in power, with Walesa as president. In May 1990, the Polish people went to the polls to elect a parliament in the first free election in 68 years. Governing, however, sometimes proved more difficult than leading the revolt. The nation faced enormous economic problems, and Americans had to decide just how much help they could afford to provide to keep the economy afloat.

The destruction of the Berlin Wall in November 1989 was a symbolic blow to the entire Cold War structure that had grown up in Europe in the postwar years. It touched off joyous celebrations.

In Czechoslovakia, two decades after Soviet tanks had rolled into the streets of Prague to suppress a policy of liberalization, the forces of freedom were victorious. Within a month of the Berlin Wall dismantlement, playwright Vaclav Havel became president. Like Walesa, he traveled to the United States in search of aid, and movingly addressed the United States Congress. One mark of the changed world was the sight of a European intellectual, who liked the Rolling Stones, reminding American politicians in their own chambers about the ideals of Thomas Jefferson. But then Czechoslovakia fragmented into its two main ethnic components and the delicately balanced confederation fell apart. The "domino effect," in the phrase one top Soviet official used, likewise brought new regimes in Bulgaria, Hungary, Romania, and Albania.

Yugoslavia proved to be the extreme case of resurgent ethnic hostility in the face of collapsing central authority. The Balkan region had long been a powder keg—a spark there had set off World War I—and only dictatorship had held the diverse republics together. When Slovenia and Croatia declared their independence in 1991, the fragile nation descended into chaos. The decision of the Muslim and Croatian majority in Bosnia to secede from Serbian-dominated Yugoslavia led Bosnian Serbs, backed by the Serbian republic, to embark upon a brutal siege of the city of Sarajevo and an even more ruthless "ethnic cleansing" campaign to eliminate opposition elements of newly independent Bosnia and Herzegovina.

The United States and the Middle East

The Middle East remained equally unstable, as the ancient Arab-Israeli conflict dragged on. For American policymakers, who had staunchly aided Israel for decades, the ticklish problem was to restrain both Palestinian terrorism and Israeli expansionism while bringing both sides together to negotiate a lasting peace. However, neither Reagan nor Bush could maintain the momentum for a negotiated peace that Carter had begun. The Israelis withdrew from the Sinai, as they had agreed at Camp David in 1978, but in June 1982, they invaded Lebanon in an attempt to destroy the Palestine Liberation Organization (PLO). Lebanese factions, themselves involved in a bitter civil war, sought Syrian help against the Israelis. In August, U.S. marines joined France and Italy in a peacekeeping mission to restore order and soon found themselves allied with one Lebanese faction against Syria. A year later, terrorist bombs in the American barracks killed 241 servicemen. Though President Reagan declared that maintaining American troops in Lebanon was "central to our credibility on a global scale," he soon reversed course and pulled out the last 1,600 soldiers. Later, though, the United States stationed American vessels in the troubled Persian Gulf, as the Middle East remained as turbulent as before.

In the early 1990s Secretary of State James Baker finally secured agreement from the major parties in the region to speak to one another face-to-face. Though intense squabbling continued, with one party or another walking out or failing to come to the negotiating table, the discussions themselves were a step forward. A victory in the Israeli parliamentary elections in mid-1992 for the less hawkish Yitzhak Rabin, a prime minister more willing to cease building new projects on occupied territory and more open to compromise, offered further hope for the talks.

In Bush's first term, another problem in the region drew the United States into a shooting war. When Saddam Hussein, ruler of Iraq, invaded neighboring Kuwait in August 1990 and annexed the territory, the United States took a strong stand. Earlier, between 1985 and 1990, it had provided massive military support for Iraq in the war it was waging with Iran. Angered at the Iranian practice of taking hostages, the United States provided Iraq with computers, lasers, and machine tools useful in the development of missiles. Now, however, the Iran-Iraq war had ended, and Iraq's invasion of Kuwait threatened the flow of Saudi Arabian oil to the West. Equally troubling, Saddam seemed intent on unifying Arab nations, thereby threatening Israel and dominating the region's production of oil upon which the United States was highly dependent.

A multinational coalition freed Kuwait after Iraqi leader Saddam Hussein—whose image appears on the signs at this anti-American demonstration in Baghdad—annexed the oil-rich land in 1990. The Persian Gulf War gave George Bush a quick victory, but the long-range results of American involvement were more questionable.

Saddam's invasion aroused an immediate reaction. The United Nations Security Council voted 14-0 to condemn the invasion, and a few days later, endorsed by a 13-0 vote an embargo on trade with Iraq. The American secretary of state and the Soviet foreign minister issued a joint statement condemning the attack. Working through the UN, as Truman had done in Korea, the United States implemented a blockade but all the while began planning for war.

Bush condemned Iraq's "naked aggression," likened Saddam to Hitler, and called the integrity of neighboring Saudi Arabia an essential American interest. He vowed to undo the annexation of Kuwait, and when asked by reporters what would happen, he responded, "Just wait, watch, and learn." Bush was not concerned with oil alone, but also with maintaining a semblance of stability in the Middle East and supporting Israel's security interests, which were threatened by Saddam's intentions. Bush wanted as well to demonstrate that neither he nor the United States would tolerate being pushed around.

Quickly, the United States began planning a response. Bush mobilized American reserves, including a sizable number of women, organized a multinational army of nearly half a million troops, and secured a resolution authorizing the use of force from the Senate and House. In mid-January 1991, the 28-nation alliance struck at Iraq in Operation Desert Storm with both air and ground forces.

Unlike the costly, drawn-out, and ultimately unpopular war in Vietnam, the Persian Gulf War was an engrossing spectator sport. Television footage showed "smart bombs" being guided to their targets by laser beams. Some missiles carried cameras revealing their journey from beginning to end. Briefings by General H. Norman Schwarzkopf and other members of his staff carefully released information about the military operations and orchestrated a sympathetic response.

Victory in what Saddam called the "mother of all battles" came quickly, as the alliance forces completely overwhelmed the Iraqis with sophisticated missiles, airplanes, and tanks. Bush's approval rating soared to 91 percent. This was, the *New York Times* declared in one headline, "A Short Persuasive Lesson in Warfare." The mood of euphoria in the United States soon soured, however, as Saddam retained power and used his remaining military might to put down revolts of Kurds and Shiites in Iraq. Bush's unwillingness to become bogged down in an Iraqi civil war and his eagerness to return troops home left the conflict unfinished. A year after victory, Saddam was as strong as he had been before.

The United States and Latin America

In Latin America, the Reagan and Bush administrations intervened frequently. Viewing Central America as a Cold War battlefield early in his presidency, Reagan openly opposed the left-wing guerrillas of El Salvador who fought to overthrow a repressive right-wing regime. Earlier, Jimmy Carter had cut off American aid to El Salvador's military government after four American Catholic churchwomen had been assaulted and killed and the dictatorship had done nothing in response. But he had resumed aid when the revolutionaries renewed their attacks just before he left office.

Fearful that another nation might follow the Marxist examples of Cuba and Nicaragua, the United States under Reagan hardened its position. It increased its assistance to the antirevolutionary Salvadoran government, heedless of a similar course followed years before in Vietnam. Efforts to destroy the radical Farabundo Martí National Liberation Front (FMLN) failed. Reagan rejected an FMLN offer to negotiate and for the next six years poured about $1 million a day into El Salvador. As Americans took over the economy, the CIA sought to prevent both the left wing and the far-right wing, which employed "death squads" to kill thousands of people, from gaining power.

That policy was unsuccessful. In 1989, the far-right faction, *Alianza Republicana Nacionalista* (ARENA), won Salvadoran elections and polarized the country. When the American-trained Salvadoran military murdered six Jesuit priests and two women, the United States first blamed the FMLN, then demanded an investigation after it became evident the army had ordered the massacre. Although American officials admitted in early 1990 that the FMLN could not be defeated, the fighting continued.

Nicaragua became an even bloodier battleground and one where Reagan persistently flouted international law and the U.S. Constitution when Congress refused to yield to his efforts to defeat revolutionary reformers. In 1979, revolutionaries calling themselves Sandinistas (after César Sandino, who fought in the 1920s against occupying American troops) overthrew the repressive Somoza family, which had ruled for three decades. Jimmy Carter initially extended aid to the Sandinistas and recognized the new regime, then cut off support to show his disapproval of their curbs on civil liberties and of their alleged efforts to assist rebels in El Salvador. The Republicans adopted a far stronger position. Their 1980 platform pledged to replace the Sandinistas with a "free and independent" government. Once in office, the Reagan administration charged that the Sandinistas were driving out moderate elements, welcoming Cuban and Soviet assistance, and supplying leftist guerrillas in El Salvador. In November 1981, Reagan signed a National Security directive authorizing the CIA to arm and train counterrevolutionaries known as *contras*. Although this policy violated United States neutrality laws, the training continued, and the *contras* began to attack from bases in Honduras and Costa Rica. As the Sandinistas built up their forces and secured aid from western Europe and the Soviet bloc, Nicaragua became enmeshed in a bitter civil war.

Oliver North, testifying here before a congressional committee, flouted the law in the Iran-*contra* affair. Convicted for his cavalier distortions and fabrications, North was not the only one involved in the illegal government program.

The war went badly for the *contras*. Their failures by the end of 1983 led the CIA to assume the initiative in military operations and to mine Nicaraguan harbors in violation of international law. When Congress discovered these secret missions, it cut off military aid to the *contras*. In Reagan's second term, Congress insisted on ending military aid, though humanitarian assistance to the *contras* continued. American economic sanctions meanwhile disrupted the Nicaraguan economy further and led to a crippling inflation rate, but still the Sandinistas clung to power until peaceful elections in early 1990 drove them out. President Daniel Ortega gave way to Violeta Barrios de Chamorro and her National Opposition Union. Though the Sandinistas were still represented in the bureaucracy, and the economy remained in desperate straits, the Nicaraguans were ready for democratic change, and the new regime seemed to offer the best hope of healing the wounds of the bloody civil war.

The Middle Eastern and Central American crises became entangled in the Iran-*contra* affair. In 1987, the nation discovered that the National Security Council had launched an effort to free American hostages in the Middle East by selling arms to Iran and then using the funds to aid the *contras,* in direct violation of both the law and congressional will. Commissions and congressional hearings demonstrated the chaos in the administration and cast doubt on the president's ability to govern. The subsequent trial of Oliver North, the National Security Council official responsible for the policy, focused on his distortions and falsifications before congressional committees and on his destruction of official documents that could have substantiated charges of wrongdoing. It showed further the confusion and duplicity at the top levels of government. Convicted in 1989, North received a light sentence requiring no time in prison from a judge who recognized that North was not acting entirely on his own.

Only on the tiny Caribbean island of Grenada did Reagan win a modest victory. The president ordered marines there in October 1983, after a military coup installed a government sympathetic to Fidel Castro's Cuba. Concerned about the construction of a large airfield on the island, 2,000 marines invaded the island, rescued a number of

American medical students, and claimed triumph. Though the United Nations condemned the incursion, Americans still cheered what the administration called its "rescue mission."

Likewise, Bush took credit for a similar incursion in Panama, ostensibly to protect American lives. Conjuring up memories of past imperialism, the United States invaded Panama, it said, to protect the Panama Canal, defend American citizens following a number of attacks, and stop the drug traffic. The incursion resulted in the capture of military leader Manuel Noriega, notorious for his involvement in the drug trade. Noriega was brought to the United States, tried, and in a lengthy trial, convicted of drug-trafficking charges.

The United States and South Africa

In South Africa, Americans, like people around the world, applauded the black struggle against apartheid, which grew more militant in the 1980s. Under the rigid policy of apartheid, the white minority, constituting about 15 percent of the population, segregated and suppressed the black majority and denied it voting rights. The United States declared its dislike for this systematic and ruthless segregation, written into law, but in past years had refused to take further steps to underscore its opposition. Large investments, naval ports, and a reluctance to oppose allies who still controlled African territory blocked American resistance. Then the ferment within the United States, sparked by the civil rights movement and opposition to dictatorships in Central America, brought pressure to take a stronger stand.

Under Reagan, the United States followed a policy of what it called "constructive engagement," in which it relied on talk but not economic sanctions to force an end to apartheid. By 1986, the bankruptcy of that approach was evident, and Congress imposed sanctions, including a rule prohibiting new American investments, despite Reagan's objections. The economic pressure damaged the South African economy and persuaded more than half of the 300 American firms in business there to leave.

In 1989, a new prime minister, Frederik W. DeKlerk, recognized that South Africa could no longer withstand the pressure from the United States and the rest of the world. The next year he freed the 71-year-old Nelson Mandela, the symbol of militant opposition to apartheid, after 27 years in prison and announced plans gradually to overturn apartheid. On his release from prison, Mandela made a triumphant tour of the United States, and witnessed an outpouring of support in recognition of his unflagging perseverance. Both before

Freed after 27 years in prison, South African activist Nelson Mandela led the struggle against apartheid in his own country and became a hero in the United States for his efforts. Here Mandela and his wife, Winnie, acknowledge the cheers of the crowd at a rally in New York City in June 1990.

Since the 1960 presidential campaign, televised debates have been a popular way for the candidates to reach large numbers of the American people. In the 1992 campaign, the three major candidates—Republican George Bush, Independent H. Ross Perot, and Democrat Bill Clinton—met in a series of televised debates.

and after he was freed, his eldest daughter, Maki Mandela, a graduate student in the United States, toured American campuses to generate further support. Talks in South Africa between the white government and the African National Congress aimed at creating a smooth transition to a biracial democracy, particularly after a national referendum indicated white support for the change, but fierce resistance on the part of some white elements slowed the process. Americans watched, wondering whether policy would change without the bloodbath they feared.

The Election of 1992

As the world changed, so the United States changed, and the election of 1992 reflected the national and international transformations taking place. After four years in office, George Bush sought a second term, but first had to fight off a fierce challenge from conservative journalist Patrick Buchanan. When Bush was finally renominated by the Republican party, he found himself involved in an unusual three-way race.

On the Democratic side, Governor Bill Clinton of Arkansas triumphed over a crowded field of candidates. Overcoming allegations of marital instability, marijuana use, and draft evasion, he argued that it was time for a new generation to take command. Forty-six years old, he had reached maturity in the 1960s, and stood in stark contrast to Bush, who had come of age during World War II.

The third candidate was Ross Perot, a billionaire businessman from Texas who had made a fortune in the computer data-processing field. Perot declared that he alone could pare down the federal deficit, fix the faltering economy, and provide the outside leadership the nation needed. Running independently of the two established parties, he became a serious candidate when volunteers collected enough signatures to place his name on the ballot in all 50 states. Although he pulled out of the race in July, he became a significant factor again with his reentry in the fall.

The three candidates faced a disillusioned land. A Gallup Poll reported in September that 79 percent of all Americans felt the nation was in economic decline, 65 percent believed it was in moral decline, and 19 percent declared it was in military decline. The deficit appeared to be choking both present and future public policy. Health care boasted brilliant technological advances, but was becoming prohibitively expensive and patently unfair. Crime threatened to become an national epidemic.

This campaign, unlike any in the past, was fought on television. There were three presiden-

Presidential Elections, 1980–1992

Year	Candidates	Party	Popular Vote	Electoral Vote
1980	RONALD REAGAN	Republican	43,899,248 (50.8%)	489
	Jimmy Carter	Democrat	36,481,435 (41.0%)	49
	John B. Anderson	Independent	5,719,437 (6.6%)	0
1984	RONALD REAGAN	Republican	53,428,357 (58.7%)	525
	Walter F. Mondale	Democrat	36,930,923 (40.6%)	13
1988	GEORGE BUSH	Republican	47,946,422 (53.9%)	426
	Michael Dukakis	Democrat	41,016,429 (46.1%)	112
1992	BILL CLINTON	Democrat	43,728,275 (43.2%)	357
	George Bush	Republican	38,167,416 (37.7%)	168
	Ross Perot	Independent	19,237,245 (19.0%)	0

Note: Winners' names appear in capital letters.

tial debates, involving all three candidates, but they told only part of the story. Far more important were appearances on talk shows and interview programs. Ross Perot energized his campaign with appearances on "Larry King Live." Bill Clinton used a post–Super Bowl appearance on "60 Minutes" to contain charges questioning his character, and later played his saxophone on the "Arsenio Hall Show" and appeared on MTV. This reliance on the electronic marketplace was visible evidence of the shift occurring in American politics.

At times the campaign turned nasty. In the final week, Bush tried to suggest that only he had the necessary experience to provide effective leadership in a changing world. Referring to Clinton and his running mate Al Gore, Jr., as "two bozos," he claimed that "my dog Millie knows more about foreign affairs" than his Democratic opponent. Despite such rhetoric, the contest was less ugly than Bush's victorious campaign four years before.

In the end, it became a clash of competing visions. In accepting the Republican nomination, Bush underscored his faith in the individual rather than the bureaucracy and insisted, "Government is too big and spends too much." Clinton, in contrast, claimed that the government had a necessary role to play "to make America work again."

On election day, Clinton won 43 percent of the popular vote to 38 percent for Bush and 19 percent for Perot. The electoral vote margin was even larger: 357 for Clinton, 168 for Bush, 0 for Perot. The Democrats retained control of both houses of Congress, with more women and minority members than ever before.

The president-elect moved quickly to demonstrate his intention of shifting America's course after 12 years of Republican rule. His Cabinet nominations included four women, four African-Americans, and two Latinos. He held a televised "economic summit" to explore national options, and demonstrated a keen grasp of the details of policy. In his inaugural address in early 1993, Clinton told an eager nation that "a new season of American renewal has begun." Major problems loomed ahead, but a new generation stood ready to try whatever was necessary to resolve them.

CONCLUSION

The Recent Past in Perspective

In the 1980s and early 1990s, the United States witnessed the triumph of conservatism. The assault on the welfare state, dubbed the "Reagan Revolution," involved creating a less regulated economy, whatever the implications for less fortunate

Americans. Policies inaugurated by Reagan and followed by Bush continued the trend begun by Richard Nixon in the 1970s. They reshaped the political agenda and reversed the liberal approach that had held sway since the New Deal of Franklin Roosevelt in the 1930s. In foreign affairs, Republican administrations likewise shifted course. Reagan first assumed a steel-ribbed posture toward the Soviet Union, then moved toward détente, and watched as his successor declared victory in the Cold War and enjoyed far closer relations with the former Soviet republics than Americans had known since the end of the Second World War.

There were limits to the transformation, to be sure. Such fundamental programs as Social Security and Medicare remained securely in place, accepted by all but the most implacable splinter groups. Even the most conservative presidents of the past half century could not return to a romanticized era of unbridled individualism and puny federal government. On the foreign front, despite the end of the Cold War, the nation's defense budget remained far higher than many Americans wished, and the nuclear arsenal continued to pose a threat to the human race.

Nor was the transformation beneficial to everyone. Periods of deep recession wrought havoc on the lives of blue-collar and white-collar workers alike. Middle-class Americans like David Patterson, introduced at the start of the chapter, were caught in the spiral of downward mobility that made them question their own hopes and dreams. Liberals and conservatives both worried about the mounting national debt and the ability of the economy to compete with Japan, Korea, Germany, and other countries. Countless Americans were uneasy about the growing gaps between rich and poor. They fought with one another over what rules should govern a woman's right to an abortion. Children wondered for the first time in American history whether they could hope to do better than their parents had done. Reluctantly they tried to prepare themselves to accept a scaled-down vision of the future.

In the 1980s and early 1990s, the United States sought a new stability, at home and abroad. In the process, the nation struggled to adhere to its historic values in a complex and changing world. Despite shifts in policy during the Republican years, and equally dramatic shifts when the Democrats took command, those basic values still governed, as the American people continued their centuries-old effort to live up to the promise of the American dream.

Recommended Reading

Historians have not yet had a chance to deal in detail with the developments of the immediate past, so fuller descriptions must be found in other sources. Much of the best writing about the years in this chapter appears in the newspapers and magazines of the popular press. But a number of useful treatments about selected topics provide good starting points in various areas.

General and Statistical Works

Barry Bluestone and Bennett Harrison, *The Deindustrialization of America: Plant Closings, Community Abandonment, and the Dismantling of Basic Industry* (1982); Peter Duignan and Alvin Rabushka, eds., *The United States in the 1980s* (1980); Andrew Hacker, ed., *U/S: A Statistical Portrait of the American People* (1983); Katherine S. Newman, *Falling from Grace: The Experience of Downward Mobility in the American Middle Class* (1988); Kevin P. Phillips, *The Politics of Rich and Poor: Wealth and the American Electorate in the Reagan Aftermath* (1990); Neil Postman, *Amusing Ourselves to Death: Public Discourse in the Age of Show Business* (1985); U.S. Bureau of the Census, *Statistical Abstract of the United States: 1991*; U.S. Bureau of the Census, *U.S. Census of Population, 1990.*

The Reagan Presidency

Lawrence I. Barrett, *Gambling with History: Reagan in the White House* (1983); Paul Boyer, ed., *Reagan as President: Contemporary Views of the Man, His Politics, and His Policies* (1990); Lou Cannon, *President Reagan: A Role of a Lifetime* (1991) and *Reagan* (1982); Ronnie Dugger, *On Reagan: The Man and His Presidency* (1983); Rowland Evans and Robert Novak, *The Reagan Revolution* (1981); Fred I. Greenstein, ed., *The Reagan Presidency: An Early Assessment* (1983); Haynes Johnson, *Sleepwalking Through History: America Through the Reagan Years* (1991); Richard A. Viguerie, *The New Right: We're Ready to Lead* (1981); Garry Wills, *Reagan's America: Innocents at Home* (1985).

The Bush Presidency

Colin Campbell, S.J., and Bert A. Rockman, eds., *The Bush Presidency: First Appraisals* (1991).

TIMELINE

1980	Ronald Reagan elected president
1980–1982	Recession
1981	Reagan breaks air controllers' strike
1981–1983	Tax cuts; deficit spending increases
1982	American invasion of Lebanon
1983	Reagan proposes Strategic Defense Initiative
1984	Reagan reelected
1986	Tax reform measure passed Immigration Reform and Control Act passed
1987	Iran-*contra* affair becomes public Stock market crashes Intermediate-Range Nuclear Forces Treaty signed
1988	George Bush elected president
1989	Federal bailout of savings and loan industry Fall of the Berlin Wall
1990	National debt reaches $3.1 trillion Immigration Act of 1990 passed Sandinistas driven from power in Nicaragua Nelson Mandela freed in South Africa
1990–1992	Recession
1991	Persian Gulf War Failed coup in the Soviet Union Disintegration of the Soviet Union Department of Housing and Urban Development scandal uncovered Strategic Arms Reduction Treaty (START) signed
1991–1992	Ethnic turbulence in a fragmented Yugoslavia
1992	Bill Clinton elected president Czechoslovakia splits into separate republics

Immigration

Roger Daniels, *A History of Immigration and Ethnicity in American Life* (1990); David M. Reimers, *Still the Golden Door: The Third World Comes to America* (1985); Paul James Rutledge, *The Vietnamese Experience in America* (1992); Virginia Yans-McLaughlin, ed., *Immigration Reconsidered: History, Sociology, and Politics* (1990).

Foreign Affairs

Paul Kennedy, *The Rise and Fall of the Great Powers: Economic Change and Military Conflict from 1500 to 2000* (1987); Walter LaFeber, *America, Russia, and the Cold War, 1945–1990* (6th ed., 1991), *Inevitable Revolutions: The United States in Central America* (1983), and *The American Age: United States Foreign Policy at Home and Abroad Since 1750* (1989); Sandra Mackey, *Lebanon* (1989); Robert Scheer, *With Enough Shovels: Reagan, Bush and Nuclear War* (1982); Strobe Talbott, *The Russians and Reagan* (1984); Seth P. Tillman, *The U.S. and the Middle East* (1982); Sanford J. Ungar, ed., *Estrangement: America and the World* (1985); Mary B. Vanderlaan, *Revolution and Foreign Policy in Nicaragua* (1986); Thomas W. Walker, ed., *Revolution and Counterrevolution in Nicaragua* (1991).

Fictional Accounts of the Recent Past

Tim O'Brien, *The Nuclear Age* (1985); Anne Tyler, *Dinner at the Homesick Restaurant* (1982); Tom Wolfe, *The Bonfire of the Vanities* (1987).

Appendix

Declaration of Independence in Congress, July 4, 1776

THE UNANIMOUS DECLARATION OF THE THIRTEEN UNITED STATES OF AMERICA

When, in the course of human events, it becomes necessary for one people to dissolve the political bonds which have connected them with another, and to assume, among the powers of the earth, the separate and equal station to which the laws of nature and of nature's God entitle them, a decent respect to the opinions of mankind requires that they should declare the causes which impel them to the separation.

We hold these truths to be self-evident: That all men are created equal; that they are endowed by their Creator with certain unalienable rights; that among these are life, liberty, and the pursuit of happiness; that, to secure these rights, governments are instituted among men, deriving their just powers from the consent of the governed; that whenever any form of government becomes destructive of these ends, it is the right of the people to alter or to abolish it, and to institute new government, laying its foundation on such principles, and organizing its powers in such form, as to them shall seem most likely to effect their safety and happiness. Prudence, indeed, will dictate that governments long established should not be changed for light and transient causes; and accordingly all experience hath shown that mankind are more disposed to suffer, which evils are sufferable, than to right themselves by abolishing the forms to which they are accustomed. But when a long train of abuses and usurpations, pursuing invariably the same object, evinces a design to reduce them under absolute despotism, it is their right, it is their duty, to throw off such government, and to provide new guards for their future security. Such has been the patient sufferance of these colonies; and such is now the necessity which constrains them to alter their former systems of government. The history of the present King of Great Britain is a history of repeated injuries and usurpations, all having in direct object the establishment of an absolute tyranny over these states. To prove this, let facts be submitted to a candid world.

He has refused his assent to laws the most wholesome and necessary for the public good.

He has forbidden his governors to pass laws of immediate and pressing importance, unless suspended in their operation till his assent should be obtained; and, when so suspended, he has utterly neglected to attend to them.

He has refused to pass other laws for the accommodation of large districts of people, unless those people would relinquish the right of representation in the legislature, a right inestimable to them, and formidable to tyrants only.

He has called together legislative bodies at places unusual, uncomfortable, and distant from the depository of their public records, for the sole purpose of fatiguing them into compliance with his measures.

He has dissolved representative houses repeatedly, for opposing, with manly firmness, his invasions on the rights of the people.

He has refused for a long time, after such dissolutions, to cause others to be elected; whereby the legislative powers, incapable of annihilation, have returned to the people at large for their exercise; the state remaining, in the mean time, exposed to all the dangers of invasions from without and convulsions within.

He has endeavored to prevent the population of these states; for that purpose obstructing the laws for naturalization of foreigners; refusing to pass others to encourage their migration hither, and raising the conditions of new appropriations of lands.

He has obstructed the administration of justice, by refusing his assent to laws for establishing judiciary powers.

He has made judges dependent on his will alone, for the tenure of their offices, and the amount and payment of their salaries.

He has erected a multitude of new offices, and sent hither swarms of officers to harass our people and eat out their substance.

He has kept among us, in times of peace, standing armies, without the consent of our legislatures.

He has affected to render the military independent of, and superior to, the civil power.

He has combined with others to subject us to a jurisdiction foreign to our constitution, and unacknowledged by our laws, giving his assent to their acts of pretended legislation:

For quartering large bodies of armed troops among us;

For protecting them, by a mock trial, from punishment for any murders which they should commit on the inhabitants of these states;

For cutting off our trade with all parts of the world;

For imposing taxes on us without our consent;

For depriving us, in many cases, of the benefits of trial by jury;

For transporting us beyond seas, to be tried for pretended offenses;

For abolishing the free system of English laws in a neighboring province, establishing therein an arbitrary government, and enlarging its boundaries, so as to render it at once an example and fit instrument for introducing the same absolute rule into these colonies;

For taking away our charters, abolishing our most valuable laws, and altering fundamentally the forms of our governments;

For suspending our own legislatures, and declaring themselves invested with power to legislate for us in all cases whatsoever.

He has abdicated government here, by declaring us out of his protection and waging war against us.

He has plundered our seas, ravaged our coasts, burned our towns, and destroyed the lives of our people.

He is at this time transporting large armies of foreign mercenaries to complete the works of death, desolation, and tyranny already begun with circumstances of cruelty and perfidy scarcely paralleled in the most barbarous ages, and totally unworthy the head of a civilized nation.

He has constrained our fellow-citizens, taken captive on the high seas, to bear arms against their country, to become the executioners of their friends and brethren, or to fall themselves by their hands.

He has excited domestic insurrection among us, and has endeavored to bring on the inhabitants of our frontiers the merciless Indian savages, whose known rule of warfare is an undistinguished destruction of all ages, sexes, and conditions.

In every stage of these oppressions we have petitioned for redress in the most humble terms; our repeated petitions have been answered only by repeated injury. A prince, whose character is thus marked by every act which may define a tyrant, is unfit to be the ruler of a free people.

Nor have we been wanting in our attentions to our British brethren. We have warned them, from time to time, of attempts by their legislature to extend an unwarrantable jurisdiction over us. We have reminded them of the circumstances of our emigration and settlement here. We have appealed to their native justice and magnanimity; and we have conjured them, by the ties of our common kindred, to disavow these usurpations, which would inevitably interrupt our connections and correspondence. They, too, have been deaf to the voice of justice and of consanguinity. We must, therefore, acquiesce in the necessity which denounces our separation, and hold them, as we hold the rest of mankind, enemies in war, in peace friends.

We, therefore, the representatives of the United States of America, in General Congress assembled, appealing to the Supreme Judge of the world for the rectitude of our intentions, do, in the name and by the authority of the good people of these colonies, solemnly publish and declare, that these United Colonies are, and of right ought to be, FREE AND INDEPENDENT STATES; that they are absolved from all allegiance to the British crown, and that all political connection between them and the state of Great Britain is, and ought to be, totally dissolved; and that, as free and independent states, they have full power to levy war, conclude peace, contract alliances, establish commerce, and do all other acts and things which independent states may of right do. And for the support of this declaration, with a firm reliance on the protection of Divine Providence, we mutually pledge to each other our lives, our fortunes, and our sacred honor.

*Constitution of the United States of America**

Preamble

We the people of the United States, in order to form a more perfect union, establish justice, insure domestic tranquillity, provide for the common defense, promote the general welfare, and secure the blessings of liberty to ourselves and our posterity, do ordain and establish this Constitution for the United States of America.

Article I

Section 1 All legislative powers herein granted shall be vested in a Congress of the United States, which shall consist of a Senate and a House of Representatives.

Section 2 The House of Representatives shall be composed of members chosen every second year by the people of the several States, and the electors in each State shall have the qualifications requisite for electors of the most numerous branch of the State Legislature.

No person shall be a Representative who shall not have attained to the age of twenty-five years, and been seven years a citizen of the United States, and who shall not, when elected, be an inhabitant of that State in which he shall be chosen.

Representatives and direct taxes shall be apportioned among the several States which may be included within this Union, according to their respective numbers, *which shall be determined by adding to the whole number of free persons, including those bound to service for a term of years and excluding Indians not taxed, three-fifths of all other persons.* The actual enumeration shall be made within three years after the first meeting of the Congress of the United States, and within every subsequent term of ten years, in such manner as they shall by law direct. The number of Representatives shall not exceed one for every thirty thousand, but each State shall have at least one Representative; *and until such enumeration shall be made, the State of New Hampshire shall be entitled to choose three, Massachusetts eight, Rhode Island and Providence Plantations one, Connecticut five, New York six, New Jersey four, Pennsylvania eight, Delaware one, Maryland six, Virginia ten, North Carolina five, South Carolina five, and Georgia three.*

When vacancies happen in the representation from any State, the Executive authority thereof shall issue writs of election to fill such vacancies.

The House of Representatives shall choose their Speaker and other officers; and shall have the sole power of impeachment.

Section 3 The Senate of the United States shall be composed of two Senators from each State, *chosen by the legislature thereof,* for six years; and each Senator shall have one vote.

Immediately after they shall be assembled in consequence

*The Constitution became effective March 4, 1789. Any portion of the text that had been amended appears in italics.

of the first election, they shall be divided as equally as may be into three classes. The seats of the Senators of the first class shall be vacated at the expiration of the second year, of the second class at the expiration of the fourth year, and of the third class at the expiration of the sixth year, so that one-third may be chosen every second year; *and if vacancies happen by resignation or otherwise, during the recess of the legislature of any State, the Executive thereof may make temporary appointments until the next meeting of the legislature, which shall then fill such vacancies.*

No person shall be a Senator who shall not have attained to the age of thirty years, and been nine years a citizen of the United States, and who shall not, when elected, be an inhabitant of that State for which he shall be chosen.

The Vice-President of the United States shall be President of the Senate, but shall have no vote, unless they be equally divided.

The Senate shall choose their other officers, and also a President *pro tempore,* in the absence of the Vice-President, or when he shall exercise the office of President of the United States.

The Senate shall have the sole power to try all impeachments. When sitting for that purpose, they shall be on oath or affirmation. When the President of the United States is tried, the Chief Justice shall preside; and no person shall be convicted without the concurrence of two-thirds of the members present.

Judgment in cases of impeachment shall not extend further than to removal from the office, and disqualification to hold and enjoy any office of honor, trust or profit under the United States: but the party convicted shall nevertheless by liable and subject to indictment, trial, judgment and punishment, according to law.

Section 4 The times, places and manner of holding elections for Senators and Representatives shall be prescribed in each State by the legislature thereof; but the Congress may at any time by law make or alter such regulations, except as to the places of choosing Senators.

The Congress shall assemble at least once in every year, and such meeting *shall be on the first Monday in December, unless they shall by law appoint a different day.*

Section 5 Each house shall be the judge of the elections, returns and qualifications of its own members, and a majority of each shall constitute a quorum to do business; but a smaller number may adjourn from day to day, and may be authorized to compel the attendance of absent members, in such manner, and under such penalties, as each house may provide.

Each house may determine the rules of its proceedings, punish its members for disorderly behavior, and with the concurrence of two-thirds, expel a member.

Each house shall keep a journal of its proceedings, and from time to time publish the same, excepting such parts as may in their judgment require secrecy; and the yeas and nays of the members of either house on any question shall, at the desire of one-fifth of those present, be entered on the journal.

Neither house, during the session of Congress, shall, without the consent of the other, adjourn for more than three days, nor to any other place than that in which the two houses shall be sitting.

Section 6 The Senators and Representatives shall receive a compensation for their services, to be ascertained by law and paid out of the treasury of the United States. They shall in all cases except treason, felony and breach of the peace be privileged from arrest during their attendance at the session of their respective houses, and in going to and returning from the same; and for any speech or debate in either house, they shall not be questioned in any other place.

No Senator or Representative shall, during the time for which he was elected, be appointed to any civil office under the authority of the United States, which shall have been created, or the emoluments whereof shall have been increased, during such time; and no person holding any office under the United States shall be a member of either house during his continuance in office.

Section 7 All bills for raising revenue shall originate in the House of Representatives; but the Senate may propose or concur with amendments as on other bills.

Every bill which shall have passed the House of Representatives and the Senate, shall, before it becomes a law, be presented to the President of the United States; if he approve he shall sign it, but if not he shall return it with objections to that house in which it originated, who shall enter the objections at large on their journal, and proceed to reconsider it. If after such reconsideration two-thirds of that house shall agree to pass the bill, it shall be sent, together with the objections, to the other house, by which it shall likewise be reconsidered, and, if approved by two-thirds of that house, it shall become a law. But in all such cases the votes of both houses shall be determined by yeas and nays, and the names of the persons voting for and against the bill shall be entered on the journal of each house respectively. If any bill shall not be returned by the President within ten days (Sundays excepted) after it shall have been presented to him, the same shall be a law, in like manner as if he had signed it, unless the Congress by their adjournment prevent its return, in which case it shall not be a law.

Every order, resolution, or vote to which the concurrence of the Senate and House of Representatives may be necessary (except on a question of adjournment) shall be presented to the President of the United States; and before the same shall take effect, shall be approved by him, or being disapproved by him, shall be repassed by two-thirds of the Senate and House of Representatives, according to the rules and limitations prescribed in the case of a bill.

Section 8 The Congress shall have power:

To lay and collect taxes, duties, imposts, and excises, to pay the debts and provide for the common defense and general welfare of the United States; but all duties, imposts and excises shall be uniform throughout the United States;

To borrow money on the credit of the United States;

To regulate commerce with foreign nations, and among the several States, and with the Indian tribes;

To establish an uniform rule of naturalization, and uniform laws on the subject of bankruptcies throughout the United States;

To coin money, regulate the value thereof, and of foreign coin, and fix the standard of weights and measures;

To provide for the punishment of counterfeiting the securities and current coin of the United States;

To establish post offices and post roads;

To promote the progress of science and useful arts by securing for limited times to authors and inventors the exclusive right to their respective writings and discoveries;

To constitute tribunals inferior to the Supreme Court;

To define and punish piracies and felonies committed on the high seas and offenses against the law of nations;

To declare war, grant letters of marque and reprisal, and make rules concerning captures on land and water;

To raise and support armies, but no appropriation of money to that use shall be for a longer term than two years;

To provide and maintain a navy;

To make rules for the government and regulation of the land and naval forces;

To provide for calling forth the militia to execute the laws of the Union, suppress insurrections, and repel invasions;

To provide for organizing, arming, and disciplining the militia, and for governing such part of them as may be employed in the service of the United States, reserving to the States respectively the appointment of the officers, and the authority of training the militia according to the discipline prescribed by Congress;

To exercise exclusive legislation in all cases whatsoever, over such district (not exceeding ten miles square) as may, by cession of particular States, and the acceptance of Congress, become the seat of government of the United States, and to exercise like authority over all places purchased by the consent of the legislature of the State, in which the same shall be, for erection of forts, magazines, arsenals, dockyards, and other needful buildings;—and

To make all laws which shall be necessary and proper for carrying into execution the foregoing powers, and all other powers vested by this Constitution in the government of the United States, or in any department or officer thereof.

Section 9 *The migration or importation of such persons as any of the States now existing shall think proper to admit shall not be prohibited by the Congress prior to the year 1808; but a tax or duty may be imposed on such importation, not exceeding $10 for each person.*

The privilege of the writ of habeas corpus shall not be suspended, unless when in cases of rebellion or invasion the public safety may require it.

No bill of attainder or ex post facto law shall be passed.

No capitation or other direct tax shall be laid, unless in proportion to the census or enumeration herein before directed to be taken.

No tax or duty shall be laid on articles exported from any State.

No preference shall be given by any regulation of commerce or revenue to the ports of one State over those of another; nor shall vessels bound to, or from, one State be obliged to enter, clear, or pay duties in another.

No money shall be drawn from the treasury, but in consequence of appropriations made by law; and a regular statement and account of the receipts and expenditures of all public money shall be published from time to time.

No title of nobility shall be granted by the United States: and no person holding any office of profit or trust under them, shall, without the consent of the Congress, accept of any present, emolument, office, or title, of any kind whatever, from any king, prince, or foreign state.

Section 10 No State shall enter into any treaty, alliance, or confederation; grant letters of marque and reprisal; coin money; emit bills of credit; make anything but gold and silver coin a tender in payment of debts; pass any bill of attainder, ex post facto law, or law impairing the obligation of contracts, or grant any title of nobility.

No States shall, without the consent of Congress, lay any imposts or duties on imports or exports, except what may be absolutely necessary for executing its inspection laws: and the net produce of all duties and imposts, laid by any State on imports or exports, shall be for the use of the treasury of the United States; and all such laws shall be subject to the revision and control of the Congress.

No State shall, without the consent of Congress, lay any duty of tonnage, keep troops or ships of war in time of peace, enter into any agreement or compact with another State, or with a foreign power, or engage in war, unless actually invaded, or in such imminent danger as will not admit of delay.

Article II

Section 1 The executive power shall be vested in a President of the United States of America. He shall hold his office during the term of four years, and, together with the Vice-President, chosen for the same term, be elected as follows:

Each State shall appoint, in such manner as the legislature thereof may direct, a number of electors, equal to the whole number of Senators and Representatives to which the State may be entitled in the Congress; but no Senator or Representative, or person holding an office of trust or profit under the United States, shall be appointed an elector.

The electors shall meet in their respective States, and vote by ballot for two persons, of whom one at least shall not be an inhabitant of the same State with themselves. And they shall make a list of all the persons voted for, and of the number of votes for each; which list they shall sign and certify, and transmit sealed to the seat of government of the United States, directed to the President of the Senate. The President of the Senate shall, in the presence of the Senate and House of Representatives, open all the certificates, and the votes shall then be counted. The person having the greatest number of votes shall be the President, if such number be a majority of the whole number of electors appointed; and if there be more than one who have such majority, and have an equal number of votes, then the House of Representatives shall immediately choose by ballot one of them for President; and if no person have a majority, then from the five highest on the list said house shall in like manner choose the President. But in choosing the President the votes shall be taken by States, the representation from each State having one vote; a quorum for this purpose shall consist of a member or members from two-thirds of the States, and a majority of all the States shall be necessary to a choice. In every case, after the choice of the President, the person having the greatest number of votes of the electors shall be the Vice-President. But if there should remain two or more who have equal votes, the Senate shall choose from them by ballot the Vice-President.

The Congress may determine the time of choosing the electors and the day on which they shall give their votes; which day shall be the same throughout the United States.

No person except a natural-born citizen, *or a citizen of the United States at the time of the adoption of this Constitution,* shall be eligible to the office of President; neither shall any person be eligible to that office who shall not have attained to the age of thirty-five years, and been fourteen years a resident within the United States.

In case of the removal of the President from office or of his death, resignation, or inability to discharge the powers and duties of the said office, the same shall devolve on the Vice-President, and the Congress may by law provide for the case of removal, death, resignation, or inability, both of the President and Vice-President, declaring what officer shall then act as President, and such officer shall act accordingly, until the disability be removed, or a President shall be elected.

The President shall, at stated times, receive for his services a compensation, which shall neither be increased nor diminished during the period for which he shall have been elected, and he shall not receive within that period any other emolument from the United States, or any of them.

Before he enter on the execution of his office, he shall take the following oath or affirmation:—"I do solemnly swear (or affirm) that I will faithfully execute the office of the President of the United States, and will to the best of my ability preserve, protect and defend the Constitution of the United States."

Section 2 The President shall be commander in chief of the army and navy of the United States, and of the militia of the several States, when called into the actual service of the United States; he may require the opinion, in writing, of the principal officer in each of the executive departments, upon any subject relating to the duties of their respective offices, and he shall have power to grant reprieves and pardons for offenses against the United States, except in cases of impeachment.

He shall have power, by and with the advice and consent of the Senate, to make treaties, provided two-thirds of the Senators present concur; and he shall nominate, and by and with the advice and consent of the Senate, shall appoint ambassadors, other public ministers and consuls, judges of the Supreme Court, and all other officers of the United States, whose appointments are not herein otherwise provided for, and which shall be established by law: but Congress may by law vest the appointment of such inferior officers, as they think proper, in the President alone, in the courts of law, or in the heads of departments.

The President shall have power to fill up all vacancies that may happen during the recess of the Senate, by granting commissions which shall expire at the end of their next session.

Section 3 He shall from time to time give to the Congress information of the state of the Union, and recommend to their consideration such measures as he shall judge necessary and expedient; he may, on extraordinary occasions, convene both houses, or either of them, and in case of disagreement between them, with respect to the time of adjournment, he may adjourn them to such time as he shall think proper; he shall receive ambassadors and other public ministers; he shall take care that the laws be faithfully executed, and shall commission all the officers of the United States.

Section 4 The President, Vice-President and all civil officers of the United States shall be removed from office on impeachment for, and on conviction of, treason, bribery, or other high crimes and misdemeanors.

Article III

Section 1 The judicial power of the United States shall be vested in one Supreme Court, and in such inferior courts as the Congress may from time to time ordain and establish. The judges, both of the Supreme and inferior courts, shall hold their offices during good behavior, and shall, at stated times, receive for their services a compensation which shall not be diminished during their continuance in office.

Section 2 The judicial power shall extend to all cases, in law and equity, arising under this Constitution, the laws of the United States, and treaties made, or which shall be made, under their authority—to all cases affecting ambassadors, other public ministers and consuls;—to all cases of admiralty and maritime jurisdiction;—to controversies to which the United States shall be a party;—to controversies between two or more States;—*between a State and citizens of another State;*—between citizens of different States;—between citizens of the same State claiming lands under grants of different States, and between a State, or the citizens thereof, and foreign states, citizens or subjects.

In all cases affecting ambassadors, other public ministers and consuls, and those in which a State shall be party, the Supreme Court shall have original jurisdiction. In all the other cases before mentioned, the Supreme Court shall have appellate jurisdiction, both as to law and fact, with such exceptions, and under such regulations, as the Congress shall make.

The trial of all crimes, except in cases of impeachment, shall be by jury; and such trial shall be held in the State where said crimes shall have been committed; but when not committed within any State, the trial shall be at such place or places as the Congress may by law have directed.

Section 3 Treason against the United States shall consist only in levying war against them, or in adhering to their enemies, giving them aid and comfort. No person shall be convicted of treason unless on the testimony of two witnesses to the same overt act, or on confession in open court.

The Congress shall have power to declare the punishment of treason, but no attainder of treason shall work corruption of blood, or forfeiture except during the life of the person attainted.

Article IV

Section 1 Full faith and credit shall be given in each State to the public acts, records, and judicial proceedings of every other State. And the Congress may by general laws prescribe the manner in which such acts, records, and proceedings shall be proved, and the effect thereof.

Section 2 The citizens of each State shall be entitled to all privileges and immunities of citizens in the several States.

A person charged in any State with treason, felony, or other crime, who shall flee from justice, and be found in another State, shall on demand of the executive authority of the State from which he fled, be delivered up, to be removed to the State having jurisdiction of the crime.

No person held to service or labor in one State, under the laws thereof, escaping into another, shall, in consequence of any law or regulation therein, be discharged from such service or labor, but shall be delivered up on claim of the party to whom such service or labor may be due.

Section 3 New States may be admitted by the Congress into this Union; but no new State shall be formed or erected within the jurisdiction of any other State; nor any State be formed by the junction of two or more States, or parts of States, without the consent of the legislatures of the States concerned as well as of the Congress.

The Congress shall have power to dispose of and make all needful rules and regulations respecting the territory or other property belonging to the United States; and nothing in this Constitution shall be so construed as to prejudice any claims of the United States, or of any particular State.

Section 4 The United States shall guarantee to every State in this Union a republican form of government, and shall protect each of them against invasion; and on application of the legislature, or of the executive (when the legislature cannot be convened), against domestic violence.

Article V

The Congress, whenever two-thirds of both houses shall deem it necessary, shall propose amendments to this Constitution, or, on the application of the legislatures of two-thirds of the several States, shall call a convention for proposing amendments, which, in either case, shall be valid to all intents and purposes, as part of this Constitution, when ratified by the legislatures of three-fourths of the several States, or by conventions in three-fourths thereof, as the one or the other mode of ratification may be proposed by the Congress; provided *that no amendments which may be made prior to the year one thousand eight hundred and eight shall in any manner affect the first and fourth classes in the ninth section of the first article; and* that no State, without its consent, shall be deprived of its equal suffrage in the Senate.

Article VI

All debts contracted and engagements entered into, before the adoption of this Constitution, shall be as valid against the United States under this Constitution, as under the Confederation.

This Constitution, and the laws of the United States which shall be made in pursuance thereof; and all treaties made, or which shall be made, under the authority of the United States, shall be the supreme law of the land; and the judges in every State shall be bound thereby, anything in the Constitution or laws of any State to the contrary notwithstanding.

The Senators and Representatives before mentioned, and the members of the several State legislatures, and all executive and judicial officers, both of the United States and of the several States, shall be bound by oath or affirmation to support this Constitution; but no religious test shall ever be required as a qualification to any office or public trust under the United States.

Article VII

The ratification of the conventions of nine States shall be sufficient for the establishment of this Constitution between the States so ratifying the same.

Done in Convention by the unanimous consent of the States present, the seventeenth day of September in the year of our Lord one thousand seven hundred and eighty-seven and of the Independence of the United States of America the twelfth. In witness whereof we have hereunto subscribed our names.

Amendments to the Constitution*

Amendment I [1791]

Congress shall make no law respecting an establishment of religion, or prohibiting the free exercise thereof; or abridging the freedom of speech, or of the press; or the right of the people peaceably to assemble, and to petition the government for a redress of grievances.

Amendment II [1791]

A well-regulated militia being necessary to the security of a free State, the right of the people to keep and bear arms shall not be infringed.

Amendment III [1791]

No soldier shall, in time of peace, be quartered in any house without the consent of the owner, nor in time of war, but in a manner to be prescribed by law.

Amendment IV [1791]

The right of the people to be secure in their persons, houses, papers, and effects, against unreasonable searches and seizures, shall not be violated, and no warrants shall issue but upon probable cause, supported by oath or affirmation, and particularly describing the place to be searched, and the persons or things to be seized.

Amendment V [1791]

No person shall be held to answer for a capital or otherwise infamous crime, unless on a presentment or indictment of a grand jury, except in cases arising in the land or naval forces, or in the militia, when in actual service in time of war or public danger; nor shall any person be subject for the same offense to be twice put in jeopardy of life or limb; nor shall be compelled in any criminal case to be a witness against himself, nor be deprived of life, liberty or property, without due process of law; nor shall private property be taken for public use without just compensation.

Amendment VI [1791]

In all criminal prosecutions, the accused shall enjoy the right to a speedy and public trial, by an impartial jury of the State and district wherein the crime shall have been committed, which district shall have been previously ascertained by law, and to be informed of the nature and cause of the accusation; to be confronted with the witnesses against him; to have compulsory

*The first ten amendments are known as the Bill of Rights.

process for obtaining witnesses in his favor, and to have the assistance of counsel for his defense.

Amendment VII [1791]
In suits at common law, where the value in controversy shall exceed twenty dollars, the right of trial by jury shall be preserved, and no fact tried by a jury shall be otherwise reexamined in any court of the United States, than according to the rules of the common law.

Amendment VIII [1791]
Excessive bail shall not be required, nor excessive fines imposed, nor cruel and unusual punishments inflicted.

Amendment IX [1791]
The enumeration in the Constitution, of certain rights, shall not be construed to deny or disparage others retained by the people.

Amendment X [1791]
The powers not delegated to the United States by the Constitution, nor prohibited by it to the States, are reserved to the States respectively, or to the people.

Amendment XI [1798]
The judicial power of the United States shall not be construed to extend to any suit in law or equity, commenced or prosecuted against one of the United States by citizens of another State, or by citizens or subjects of any foreign state.

Amendment XII [1804]
The electors shall meet in their respective States, and vote by ballot for President and Vice-President, one of whom, at least, shall not be an inhabitant of the same State with themselves; they shall name in their ballots the person voted for as President, and in distinct ballots the person voted for as Vice-President, and they shall make distinct lists of all persons voted for as President, and of all persons voted for as Vice-President, and of the number of votes for each, which lists they shall sign and certify, and transmit sealed to the seat of government of the United States, directed to the President of the Senate;—the President of the Senate shall, in the presence of the Senate and House of Representatives, open all the certificates and the votes shall then be counted;—the person having the greatest number of votes for President shall be the President, if such number be a majority of the whole number of electors appointed; and if no person have such majority, then from the persons having the highest numbers not exceeding three on the list of those voted for as President, the House of Representatives shall choose immediately, by ballot, the President. But in choosing the President, the votes shall be taken by States, the representation from each State having one vote; a quorum for this purpose shall consist of a member or members from two-thirds of the States, and a majority of all the States shall be necessary to a choice. And if the House of Representatives shall not choose a President whenever the right of choice shall devolve upon them, before *the fourth day of March* next following, then the Vice-President shall act as President, as in the case of the death or other constitutional disability of the President.

The person having the greatest number of votes as Vice-President shall be the Vice-President, if such number be a majority of the whole number of electors appointed; and if no person have a majority, then from the two highest numbers on the list the Senate shall choose the Vice-President; a quorum for the purpose shall consist of two-thirds of the whole number of Senators, and a majority of the whole number shall be necessary to a choice. But no person constitutionally ineligible to the office of President shall be eligible to that of Vice-President of the United States.

Amendment XIII [1865]

Section 1 Neither slavery nor involuntary servitude, except as a punishment for crime whereof the party shall have been duly convicted, shall exist within the United States, or any place subject to their jurisdiction.

Section 2 Congress shall have power to enforce this article by appropriate legislation.

Amendment XIV [1868]

Section 1 All persons born or naturalized in the United States, and subject to the jurisdiction thereof, are citizens of the United States and of the State wherein they reside. No State shall make or enforce any law which shall abridge the privileges or immunities of citizens of the United States; nor shall any State deprive any person of life, liberty, or property, without due process of law; nor deny to any person within its jurisdiction the equal protection of the laws.

Section 2 Representatives shall be apportioned among the several States according to their respective numbers, counting the whole number of persons in each State, excluding Indians not taxed. But when the right to vote at any election for the choice of Electors for President and Vice-President of the United States, Representatives in Congress, the executive and judicial officers of a State, or the members of the legislature thereof, is denied to any of the male inhabitants of such State, being twenty-one years of age and citizens of the United States, or in any way abridged, except for participation in rebellion, or other crime, the basis of representation therein shall be reduced in the proportion which the number of such male citizens shall bear to the whole number of male citizens twenty-one years of age in such State.

Section 3 No person shall be a Senator or Representative in Congress, or Elector of President and Vice-President, or hold any office, civil or military, under the United States, or under any State, who, having previously taken an oath, as a member of Congress, or as an officer of the United States, or as a member of any State legislature, or as an executive or judicial officer of any State, to support the Constitution of the United States, shall have engaged in insurrection or rebellion against the same, or given aid or comfort to the enemies thereof. Congress may, by a vote of two-thirds of each house, remove such disability.

Section 4 The validity of the public debt of the United States, authorized by law, including debts incurred for payment of pensions and bounties for services in suppressing insurrection or rebellion, shall not be questioned. But neither the United

States nor any State shall assume or pay any debt or obligation incurred in aid of insurrection or rebellion against the United States, or any claim for the loss of emanicipation of any slave; but all such debts, obligations, and claims shall be held illegal and void.

Section 5 The Congress shall have power to enforce, by appropriate legislation, the provisions of this article.

Amendment XV [1870]

Section 1 The right of citizens of the United States to vote shall not be denied or abridged by the United States or by any State on account of race, color, or previous condition of servitude.

Section 2 The Congress shall have power to enforce this article by appropriate legislation.

Amendment XVI [1913]

The Congress shall have power to lay and collect taxes on incomes, from whatever source derived, without apportionment among the several States, and without regard to any census or enumeration.

Amendment XVII [1913]

Section 1 The Senate of the United States shall be composed of two Senators from each State, elected by the people thereof, for six years; and each Senator shall have one vote. The electors in each State shall have the qualifications requisite for electors of [voters for] the most numerous branch of the State legislatures.

Section 2 When vacancies happen in the representation of any State in the Senate, the executive authority of such State shall issue writs of election to fill such vacancies: Provided that the legislature of any State may empower the executive thereof to make temporary appointments until the people fill the vacancies by election as the legislature may direct.

Section 3 The amendment shall not be so construed as to affect the election or term of any Senator chosen before it becomes valid as part of the Constitution.

Amendment XVIII [1919]

Section 1 After one year from the ratification of this article the manufacture, sale, or transportation of intoxicating liquors within, the importation thereof into, or the exportation thereof from the United States and all territory subject to the jurisdiction thereof, for beverage purposes, is hereby prohibited.

Section 2 The Congress and the several States shall have concurrent power to enforce this article by appropriate legislation.

Section 3 This article shall be inoperative unless it shall have been ratified as an amendment to the Constitution by the legislatures of the several States, as provided by the Constitution, within seven years from the date of the submission thereof to the States by the Congress.

Amendment XIX [1920]

Section 1 The right of citizens of the United States to vote shall not be denied or abridged by the United States or by any State on account of sex.

Section 2 The Congress shall have power to enforce this article by appropriate legislation.

Amendment XX [1933]

Section 1 The terms of the President and Vice-President shall end at noon on the 20th day of January, and the terms of Senators and Representatives at noon on the 3d day of January, of the years in which such terms would have ended if this article had not been ratified; and the terms of their successors shall then begin.

Section 2 The Congress shall assemble at least once in every year, and such meeting shall begin at noon on the 3d day of January, unless they shall by law appoint a different day.

Section 3 If, at the time fixed for the beginning of the term of the President, the President-elect shall have died, the Vice-President-elect shall become President. If a President shall not have been chosen before the time fixed for the beginning of his term, or if the President-elect shall have failed to qualify, then the Vice-President-elect shall act as President until a President shall have qualified, and the Congress may by law provide for the case wherein neither a President-elect nor a Vice-President-elect shall have qualified, declaring who shall then act as President, or the manner in which one who is to act shall be selected, and such persons shall act accordingly until a President or Vice-President shall have qualified.

Section 4 The Congress may by law provide for the case of the death of any of the persons from whom the House of Representatives may choose a President whenever the right of choice shall have devolved upon them, and for the case of the death of any of the persons from whom the Senate may choose a Vice-President whenever the right of choice shall have devolved upon them.

Section 5 Sections 1 and 2 shall take effect on the 15th day of October following the ratification of this article.

Section 6 This article shall be inoperative unless it shall have been ratified as an amendment to the Constitution by the legislatures of three-fourths of the several States within seven years from the date of its submission.

Amendment XXI [1933]

Section 1 The eighteenth article of amendment to the Constitution of the United States is hereby repealed.

Section 2 The transportation or importation into any State, Territory, or Possession of the United States for delivery or use therein of intoxicating liquors, in violation of the laws thereof, is hereby prohibited.

Section 3 This article shall be inoperative unless it shall have been ratified as an amendment to the Constitution by conventions in the several States, as provided in the Constitution, within seven years from the date of submission thereof to the States by the Congress.

Amendment XXII [1951]

Section 1 No person shall be elected to the office of President more than twice, and no person who has held the office of President, or acted as President, for more than two years of a term to which some other person was elected President shall be elected to the office of President more than once. But this article shall not apply to any person holding the office of President when this article was proposed by the Congress, and shall not prevent any person who may be holding the office of President, or acting as President, during the term within which this article becomes operative from holding the office of President or acting as President during the remainder of such term.

Section 2 This article shall be inoperative unless it shall have been ratified as an amendment to the Constitution by the legislatures of three-fourths of the several States within seven years from the date of its submission to the States by the Congress.

Amendment XXIII [1961]

Section 1 The District constituting the seat of Government of the United States shall appoint in such manner as the Congress may direct:

A number of electors of President and Vice-President equal to the whole number of Senators and Representatives in Congress to which the District would be entitled if it were a State, but in no event more than the least populous State; they shall be in addition to those appointed by the States, but they shall be considered for the purposes of the election of President and Vice-President, to be electors appointed by a State; and they shall meet in the District and perform such duties as provided by the twelfth article of amendment.

Section 2 The Congress shall have the power to enforce this article by appropriate legislation.

Amendment XXIV [1964]

Section 1 The right of citizens of the United States to vote in any primary or other election for President or Vice-President, for electors for President or Vice-President, or for Senator or Representative in Congress, shall not be denied or abridged by the United States or any State by reason of failure to pay any poll tax or other tax.

Section 2 The Congress shall have the power to enforce this article by appropriate legislation.

Amendment XXV [1967]

Section 1 In case of the removal of the President from office or of his death or resignation, the Vice-President shall become President.

Section 2 Whenever there is a vacancy in the office of the Vice-President, the President shall nominate a Vice-President who shall take office upon confirmation by a majority vote of both houses of Congress.

Section 3 Whenever the President transmits to the President pro tempore of the Senate and the Speaker of the House of Representatives his written declaration that he is unable to discharge the powers and duties of his office, and until he transmits to them a written declaration to the contrary, such powers and duties shall be discharged by the Vice-President as Acting President.

Section 4 Whenever the Vice-President and a majority of either the principal officers of the executive departments or of such other body as Congress may by law provide, transmit to the President pro tempore of the Senate and the Speaker of the House of Representatives their written declaration that the President is unable to discharge the powers and duties of his office, the Vice-President shall immediately assume the powers and duties of the office as Acting President.

Thereafter, when the President transmits to the President pro tempore of the Senate and the Speaker of the House of Representatives his written declaration that no inability exists, he shall resume the powers and duties of his office unless the Vice-President and a majority of either the principal officers of the executive department[s] or of such other body as Congress may by law provide, transmit within four days to the President pro tempore of the Senate and the Speaker of the House of Representatives their written declaration that the President is unable to discharge the powers and duties of his office. Thereupon Congress shall decide the issue, assembling within forty-eight hours for that purpose if not in session. If the Congress, within twenty-one days after receipt of the latter written declaration, or, if Congress is not in session, within twenty-one days after Congress is required to assemble, determines by two-thirds vote of both Houses that the President is unable to discharge the powers and duties of his office, the Vice-President shall continue to discharge the same as Acting President; otherwise, the President shall resume the powers and duties of his office.

Amendment XXVI [1971]

Section 1 The right of citizens of the United States, who are eighteen years of age or older, to vote shall not be denied or abridged by the United States or by any State on account of age.

Section 2 The Congress shall have power to enforce this article by appropriate legislation.

States of the United States

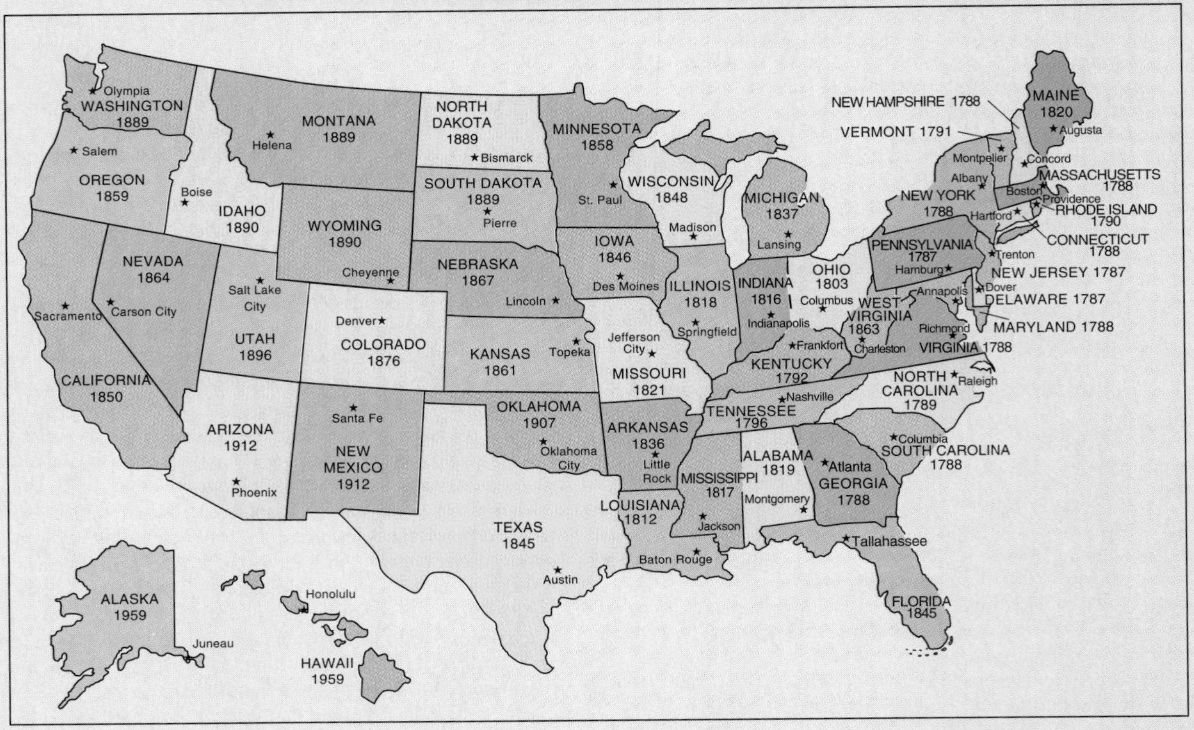

STATE	DATE OF ADMISSION	STATE	DATE OF ADMISSION
Delaware	December 7, 1787	Michigan	January 16, 1837
Pennsylvania	December 12, 1787	Florida	March 3, 1845
New Jersey	December 18, 1787	Texas	December 29, 1845
Georgia	January 2, 1788	Iowa	December 28, 1846
Connecticut	January 9, 1788	Wisconsin	May 29, 1848
Massachusetts	February 6, 1788	California	September 9, 1850
Maryland	April 28, 1788	Minnesota	May 11, 1858
South Carolina	May 23, 1788	Oregon	February 14, 1859
New Hampshire	June 21, 1788	Kansas	January 29, 1861
Virginia	June 25, 1788	West Virginia	June 19, 1863
New York	July 26, 1788	Nevada	October 31, 1864
North Carolina	November 21, 1789	Nebraska	March 1, 1867
Rhode Island	May 29, 1790	Colorado	August 1, 1876
Vermont	March 4, 1791	North Dakota	November 2, 1889
Kentucky	June 1, 1792	South Dakota	November 2, 1889
Tennessee	June 1, 1796	Montana	November 8, 1889
Ohio	March 1, 1803	Washington	November 11, 1889
Louisiana	April 30, 1812	Idaho	July 3, 1890
Indiana	December 11, 1816	Wyoming	July 10, 1890
Mississippi	December 10, 1817	Utah	January 4, 1896
Illinois	December 3, 1818	Oklahoma	November 16, 1907
Alabama	December 14, 1819	New Mexico	January 6, 1912
Maine	March 15, 1820	Arizona	February 14, 1912
Missouri	August 10, 1821	Alaska	January 3, 1959
Arkansas	June 15, 1836	Hawaii	August 21, 1959

Territorial Expansion of the United States

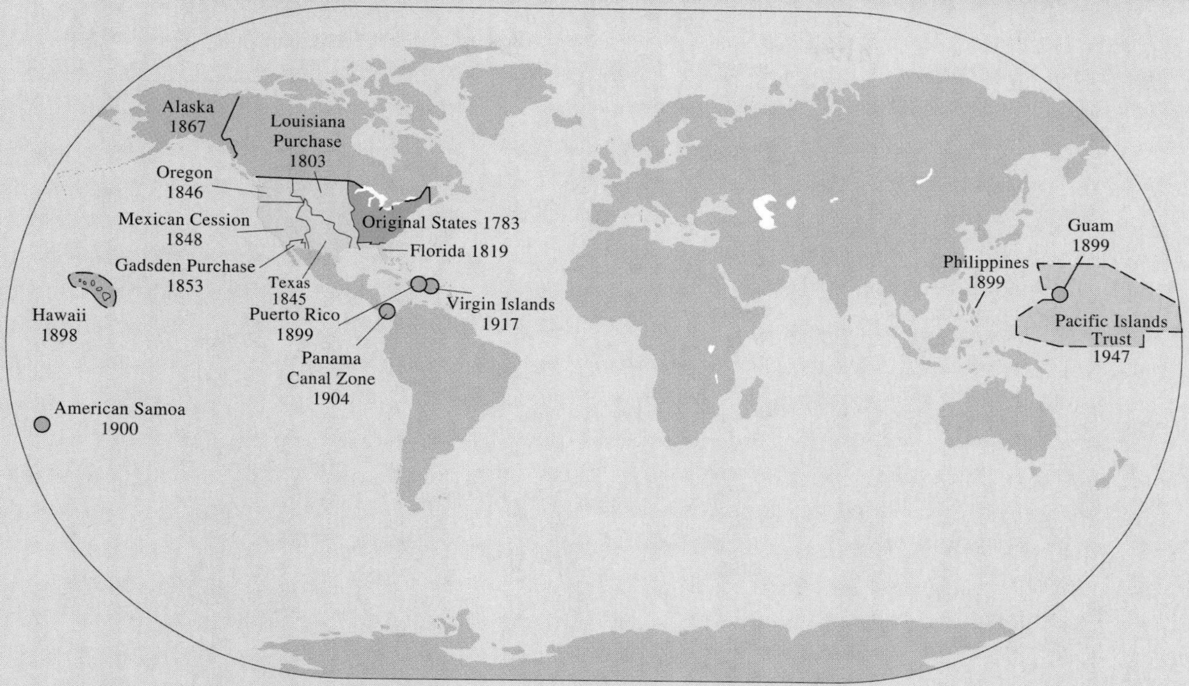

DATE	TERRITORY	AREA (SQ. MI.)	CUMULATIVE TOTAL (SQ. MI.)
1793	Original states	888,685	888,685
1803	Louisiana Purchase	827,192	1,715,877
1819	Florida	72,003	1,787,880
1845	Texas	390,143	2,178,023
1846	Oregon	285,580	2,463,603
1848	Mexican Cession	529,017	2,992,620
1853	Gadsden Purchase	29,640	3,022,260
1867	Alaska	589,757	3,612,017
1898	Hawaii	6,450	3,618,467
1899	Philippines	115,600	3,734,067
1899	Puerto Rico	3,435	3,737,502
1899	Guam	212	3,737,714
1900	American Samoa	76	3,737,790
1904	Panama Canal Zone	553	3,738,343
1917	Virgin Islands	133	3,738,476
1947	Pacific Islands Trust	8,489	3,746,965
	All others	46	3,747,011

Presidential Elections

YEAR	CANDIDATES	PARTIES	% OF POPULAR VOTE*†	ELECTORAL VOTE‡	% VOTER PARTICIPANTION†
1789	GEORGE WASHINGTON	No party designations		69	
	John Adams			34	
	Other candidates			35	
1792	GEORGE WASHINGTON	No party designations		132	
	John Adams			77	
	George Clinton			50	
	Other candidates			5	
1796	JOHN ADAMS	Federalist		71	
	Thomas Jefferson	Democratic-Republican		68	
	Thomas Pinckney	Federalist		59	
	Aaron Burr	Democratic-Republican		30	
	Other candidates			48	
1800	THOMAS JEFFERSON	Democratic-Republican		73	
	Aaron Burr	Democratic-Republican		73	
	John Adams	Federalist		65	
	Charles C. Pinckney	Federalist		64	
	John Jay	Federalist		1	
1804	THOMAS JEFFERSON	Democratic-Republican		162	
	Charles C. Pinckney	Federalist		14	
1808	JAMES MADISON	Democratic-Republican		122	
	Charles C. Pinckney	Federalist		47	
	George Clinton	Democratic-Republican		6	
1812	JAMES MADISON	Democratic-Republican		128	
	DeWitt Clinton	Federalist		89	
1816	JAMES MONROE	Democratic-Republican		183	
	Rufus King	Federalist		34	
1820	JAMES MONROE	Democratic-Republican		231	
	John Quincy Adams	Independent Republican		1	
1824	JOHN QUINCY ADAMS	Democratic-Republican	30.5	84	26.9
	Andrew Jackson	Democratic-Republican	43.1	99	
	Henry Clay	Democratic-Republican	13.2	37	
	William H. Crawford	Democratic-Republican	13.1	41	
1828	ANDREW JACKSON	Democratic	56.0	178	57.6
	John Quincy Adams	National Republican	44.0	83	
1832	ANDREW JACKSON	Democratic	54.5	219	55.4
	Henry Clay	National Republican	37.5	49	
	William Wirt	Anti-Masonic	8.0	7	
	John Floyd	Democratic		11	
1836	MARTIN VAN BUREN	Democratic	50.9	170	57.8
	William H. Harrison	Whig		73	
	Hugh L. White	Whig	49.1	26	
	Daniel Webster	Whig		14	
	W. P. Mangum	Whig		11	
1840	WILLIAM H. HARRISON	Whig	53.1	234	80.2
	Martin Van Buren	Democratic	46.9	60	
1844	JAMES K. POLK	Democratic	49.6	170	78.9
	Henry Clay	Whig	48.1	105	
	James G. Birney	Liberty	2.3	0	
1848	ZACHARY TAYLOR	Whig	47.4	163	72.7
	Lewis Cass	Democratic	42.5	127	
	Martin Van Buren	Free-Soil	10.1	0	
1852	FRANKLIN PIERCE	Democratic	50.9	254	69.6
	Winfield Scott	Whig	44.1	42	

YEAR	CANDIDATES	PARTIES	% OF POPULAR VOTE*†	ELECTORAL VOTE‡	% VOTER PARTICIPANTION†
1852	John P. Hale	Free-Soil	5.0	0	
1856	JAMES BUCHANAN	Democratic	45.3	174	78.9
	John C. Frémont	Republican	33.1	114	
	Millard Fillmore	American	21.6	8	
1860	ABRAHAM LINCOLN	Republican	39.8	180	81.2
	Stephen A. Douglas	Democratic	29.5	12	
	John C. Breckinridge	Democratic	18.1	72	
	John Bell	Constitutional Union	12.6	39	
1864	ABRAHAM LINCOLN	Republican	55.0	212	73.8
	George B. McClellan	Democratic	45.0	21	
1868	ULYSSES S. GRANT	Republican	52.7	214	78.1
	Horatio Seymour	Democratic	47.3	80	
1872	ULYSSES S. GRANT	Republican	55.6	286	71.3
	Horace Greeley	Democratic	44.0	0°—§	
1876	RUTHERFORD B. HAYES	Republican	48.0	185	81.8
	Samuel J. Tilden	Democratic	51.0	184	
1880	JAMES A. GARFIELD	Republican	48.5	214	79.4
	Winfield S. Hancock	Democratic	48.1	155	
	James B. Weaver	Greenback-Labor	3.4	0	
1884	GROVER CLEVELAND	Democratic	48.5	219	77.5
	James G. Blaine	Republican	48.2	182	
1888	BENJAMIN HARRISON	Republican	47.9	233	79.3
	Grover Cleveland	Democratic	48.6	168	
1892	GROVER CLEVELAND	Democratic	46.0	277	74.7
	Benjamin Harrison	Republican	43.0	145	
	James B. Weaver	Populist	8.5	22	
1896	WILLIAM McKINLEY	Republican	51.1	271	79.3
	William J. Bryan	Democratic	46.7	176	
1900	WILLIAM McKINLEY	Republican	51.7	292	73.2
	William J. Bryan	Democratic; Populist	45.5	155	
1904	THEODORE ROOSEVELT	Republican	56.4	336	65.2
	Alton B. Parker	Democratic	37.6	140	
	Eugene V. Debs	Socialist	3.0	0	
1908	WILLIAM H. TAFT	Republican	51.6	321	65.4
	William J. Bryan	Democratic	43.1	162	
	Eugene V. Debs	Socialist	2.8	0	
1912	WOODROW WILSON	Democratic	41.9	435	58.8
	Theodore Roosevelt	Progressive	27.4	88	
	William H. Taft	Republican	23.2	8	
	Eugene V. Debs	Socialist	6.0	0	
1916	WOODROW WILSON	Democratic	49.4	277	61.6
	Charles E. Hughes	Republican	46.2	254	
	Allan L. Benson	Socialist	3.2	0	
1920	WARREN G. HARDING	Republican	60.4	404	49.2
	James M. Cox	Democratic	34.2	127	
	Eugene V. Debs	Socialist	3.4	0	
1924	CALVIN COOLIDGE	Republican	54.0	382	48.9
	John W. Davis	Democratic	28.8	136	
	Robert M. La Follette	Progressive	16.6	13	
1928	HERBERT C. HOOVER	Republican	58.2	444	56.9
	Alfred E. Smith	Democratic	40.9	87	
1932	FRANKLIN D. ROOSEVELT	Democratic	57.4	472	56.9
	Herbert C. Hoover	Republican	39.7	59	
1936	FRANKLIN D. ROOSEVELT	Democratic	60.8	523	61.0
	Alfred M. Landon	Republican	36.5	8	
1940	FRANKLIN D. ROOSEVELT	Democratic	54.8	449	62.5

YEAR	CANDIDATES	PARTIES	% OF POPULAR VOTE*†	ELECTORAL VOTE‡	% VOTER PARTICIPANTION†
1940	Wendell L. Willkie	Republican	44.8	82	
1944	FRANKLIN D. ROOSEVELT	Democratic	53.5	432	55.9
	Thomas E. Dewey	Republican	46.0	99	
1948	HARRY S TRUMAN	Democratic	49.5	303	53.0
	Thomas E. Dewey	Republican	45.1	189	
	J. Strom Thurmond	States' Rights	2.4	39	
	Henry A. Wallace	Progressive	2.4	0	
1952	DWIGHT D. EISENHOWER	Republican	55.1	442	63.3
	Adlai E. Stevenson	Democratic	44.4	89	
1956	DWIGHT D. EISENHOWER	Republican	57.4	457	60.6
	Adlai E. Stevenson	Democratic	42.0	73	
1960	JOHN F. KENNEDY	Democratic	49.7	303	64.0
	Richard M. Nixon	Republican	49.6	219	
	Harry F. Byrd	Independent	0.7	15	
1964	LYNDON B. JOHNSON	Democratic	61.1	486	61.7
	Barry M. Goldwater	Republican	38.5	52	
1968	RICHARD M. NIXON	Republican	43.4	301	60.6
	Hubert H. Humphrey	Democratic	42.7	191	
	George C. Wallace	American Independent	13.5	46	
1972	RICHARD M. NIXON	Republican	60.7	520	55.5
	George S. McGovern	Democratic	37.5	17	
1976	JIMMY CARTER	Democratic	50.0	297	54.3
	Gerald R. Ford	Republican	48.0	240	
1980	RONALD REAGAN	Republican	50.8	489	53.0
	Jimmy Carter	Democratic	41.0	49	
	John B. Anderson	Independent	6.6	0	
1984	RONALD REAGAN	Republican	58.7	525	52.9
	Walter F. Mondale	Democratic	40.6	13	
1988	GEORGE BUSH	Republican	54.0	426	50.1
	Michael Dukakis	Democratic	46.0	111	
1992	BILL CLINTON	Democratic	43.2	357	54.0
	George Bush	Republican	37.7	168	
	H. Ross Perot	Independent	19.0	0	

*Candidates receiving less than 2.5 percent of the popular vote have been omitted. Hence the percentage of popular vote may not total 100 percent.
†Prior to 1824, most presidential electors were chosen by state legislators rather than by popular vote.
‡Before the Twelfth Amendment was passed in 1804, the electoral college voted for two presidential candidates; the runner-up became the vice-president.
§Greeley died before the electoral college met. His votes were divided among four other candidates.

Supreme Court Justices

NAME	SERVICE	APPOINTED BY...
John Jay*	1789–1795	Washington
James Wilson	1789–1798	Washington
John Blair	1789–1796	Washington
John Rutledge	1790–1791	Washington
William Cushing	1790–1810	Washington
James Iredell	1790–1799	Washington
Thomas Johnson	1791–1793	Washington
William Paterson	1793–1806	Washington
John Rutledge†	1795	Washington
Samuel Chase	1796–1811	Washington
Oliver Ellsworth	1796–1799	Washington
Bushrod Washington	1798–1829	J. Adams
Alfred Moore	1799–1804	J. Adams
John Marshall	1801–1835	J. Adams
William Johnson	1804–1834	Jefferson
Henry B. Livingston	1806–1823	Jefferson
Thomas Todd	1807–1826	Jefferson
Gabriel Duval	1811–1836	Madison
Joseph Story	1811–1845	Madison
Smith Thompson	1823–1843	Monroe
Robert Trimble	1826–1828	J. Q. Adams
John McLean	1829–1861	Jackson
Henry Baldwin	1830–1844	Jackson
James M. Wayne	1835–1867	Jackson
Roger B. Taney	1836–1864	Jackson
Philip P. Barbour	1836–1841	Jackson
John Catron	1837–1865	Van Buren
John McKinley	1837–1852	Van Buren
Peter V. Daniel	1841–1860	Van Buren
Samuel Nelson	1845–1872	Tyler
Levi Woodbury	1845–1851	Polk
Robert C. Grier	1846–1870	Polk
Benjamin R. Curtis	1851–1857	Fillmore
John A. Campbell	1853–1861	Pierce
Nathan Clifford	1858–1881	Buchanan
Noah H. Swayne	1862–1881	Lincoln
Samuel F. Miller	1862–1890	Lincoln
David Davis	1862–1877	Lincoln
Stephen J. Field	1863–1897	Lincoln
Salmon P. Chase	1864–1873	Lincoln
William Strong	1870–1880	Grant
Joseph P. Bradley	1870–1892	Grant
Ward Hunt	1873–1882	Grant
Morrison R. Waite	1874–1888	Grant
John M. Harlan	1877–1911	Hayes
William B. Woods	1880–1887	Hayes
Stanley Matthews	1881–1889	Garfield
Horace Gray	1882–1902	Arthur
Samuel Blatchford	1882–1893	Arthur
Lucious Q. C. Lamar	1888–1893	Cleveland
Melville W. Fuller	1888–1910	Cleveland
David J. Brewer	1889–1910	B. Harrison
Henry B. Brown	1890–1906	B. Harrison
George Shiras	1892–1903	B. Harrison
Howell E. Jackson	1893–1895	B. Harrison
Edward D. White	1894–1910	Cleveland
Rufus W. Peckham	1896–1909	Cleveland
Joseph McKenna	1898–1925	McKinley
Oliver W. Holmes	1902–1932	T. Roosevelt
William R. Day	1903–1922	T. Roosevelt
William H. Moody	1906–1910	T. Roosevelt
Horace H. Lurton	1910–1914	Taft
Charles E. Hughes	1910–1916	Taft
Willis Van Devanter	1910–1937	Taft
Joseph R. Lamar	1911–1916	Taft
Edward D. White	1910–1921	Taft
Mahlon Pitney	1912–1922	Taft
James C. McReynolds	1914–1941	Wilson
Louis D. Brandeis	1916–1939	Wilson
John H. Clarke	1916–1922	Wilson
William H. Taft	1921–1930	Harding
George Sutherland	1922–1938	Harding
Pierce Butler	1923–1939	Harding
Edward T. Sanford	1923–1930	Harding
Harlan F. Stone	1925–1941	Coolidge
Charles E. Hughes	1930–1941	Hoover
Owen J. Roberts	1930–1945	Hoover
Benjamin N. Cardozo	1932–1938	Hoover
Hugo L. Black	1937–1971	F. Roosevelt
Stanley F. Reed	1938–1957	F. Roosevelt
Felix Frankfurter	1939–1962	F. Roosevelt
William O. Douglas	1939–1975	F. Roosevelt
Frank Murphy	1940–1949	F. Roosevelt
Harlan F. Stone	1941–1946	F. Roosevelt
James F. Byrnes	1941–1942	F. Roosevelt
Robert H. Jackson	1941–1954	F. Roosevelt
Wiley B. Rutledge	1943–1949	F. Roosevelt
Harold H. Burton	1945–1958	Truman
Frederick M. Vinson	1946–1953	Truman
Tom C. Clark	1949–1967	Truman
Sherman Minton	1949–1956	Truman
Earl Warren	1953–1969	Eisenhower
John Marshall Harlan	1955–1971	Eisenhower
William J. Brennan, Jr.	1956–1990	Eisenhower
Charles E. Whittaker	1957–1962	Eisenhower
Potter Stewart	1958–1981	Eisenhower
Byron R. White	1962–	Kennedy
Arthur J. Goldberg	1962–1965	Kennedy
Abe Fortas	1965–1969	Johnson
Thurgood Marshall	1967–1991	Johnson
Warren E. Burger	1969–1986	Nixon
Harry A. Blackmun	1970–	Nixon
Lewis F. Powell, Jr.	1972–1988	Nixon
William H. Rehnquist	1972–1986	Nixon
John Paul Stevens	1975–	Ford
Sandra Day O'Connor	1981–	Reagan
William H. Rehnquist	1986–	Reagan
Antonin Scalia	1986–	Reagan
Anthony M. Kennedy	1988–	Reagan
David H. Souter	1990–	Bush
Clarence Thomas	1991–	Bush
Ruth Bader Ginsburg	1993–	Clinton

***Chief Justices appear in bold type.**

†Acting Chief Justice; Senate refused to confirm appointment.

Population of the United States

YEAR	NUMBER OF STATES	POPULATION	% INCREASE	POPULATION PER SQUARE MILE
1790	13	3,929,214		4.5
1800	16	5,308,483	35.1	6.1
1810	17	7,239,881	36.4	4.3
1820	23	9,638,453	33.1	5.5
1830	24	12,866,020	33.5	7.4
1840	26	17,069,453	32.7	9.8
1850	31	23,191,876	35.9	7.9
1860	33	31,443,321	35.6	10.6
1870	37	39,818,449	26.6	13.4
1880	38	50,155,783	26.0	16.9
1890	44	62,947,714	25.5	21.2
1900	45	75,994,575	20.7	25.6
1910	46	91,972,266	21.0	31.0
1920	48	105,710,620	14.9	35.6
1930	48	122,775,046	16.1	41.2
1940	48	131,669,275	7.2	44.2
1950	48	150,697,361	14.5	50.7
1960	50	179,323,175	19.0	50.6
1970	50	203,235,298	13.3	57.5
1980	50	226,545,805	11.5	64.1
1990	50	248,709,873	9.8	70.3

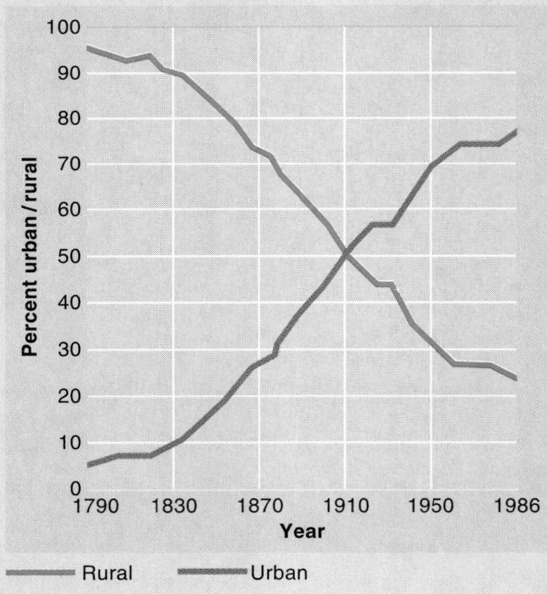

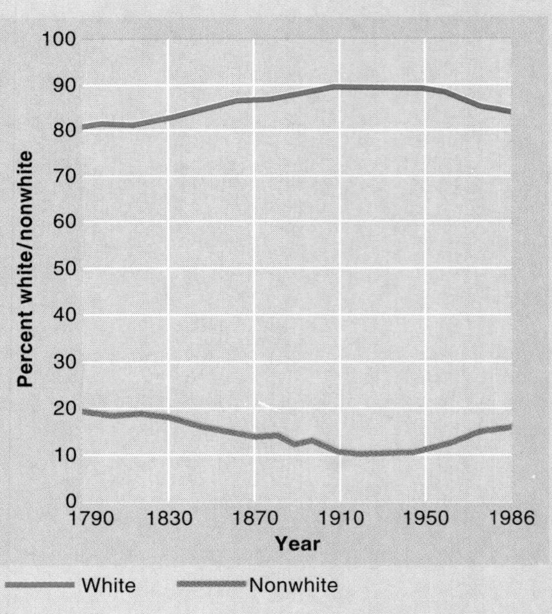

Source: U.S. Bureau of the Census estimates.

Demographic Contours of the American People

YEAR	LIFE EXPECTANCY FROM BIRTH: WHITE	LIFE EXPECTANCY FROM BIRTH: BLACK	AGE AT FIRST MARRIAGE: MALE	AGE AT FIRST MARRIAGE: FEMALE	NUMBER OF CHILDREN UNDER 5 PER 1,000 WOMEN AGE 20–44	AGE DISTRIBUTION (%): UNDER 15	AGE DISTRIBUTION (%): 15–59	AGE DISTRIBUTION (%): OVER 59
1800					1,342			
1810					1,358			
1820					1,295			
1830					1,145			
1840					1,085			
1850					923	41.5	54.3	4.1
1860					929	40.5	55.1	4.3
1870					839	39.2	55.8	5.0
1880					822	38.1	56.3	5.6
1890			26.1	22.0	716	35.5	58.0	6.2
1900	47.6	33.0	25.9	21.9	688	34.4	59.0	6.4
1910	50.3	35.6	25.1	21.6	643	32.1	61.0	6.8
1920	54.9	45.3	24.6	21.2	604	31.8	60.6	7.5
1930	61.4	48.1	24.3	21.3	511	29.4	62.1	8.5
1940	64.2	53.1	24.3	21.5	429	25.0	64.5	10.4
1950	69.1	60.8	22.8	20.3	589	26.9	61.0	12.2
1960	70.6	63.6	22.8	20.3	737	31.1	55.7	13.2
1970	71.7	64.1	22.5	20.6	530	28.5	57.4	14.1
1980	74.4	68.1	23.6	21.8	440	22.6	61.6	15.7
1989	75.9	71.7	25.3*	23.6*	377	21.7	61.4	16.9

*1987 figures.

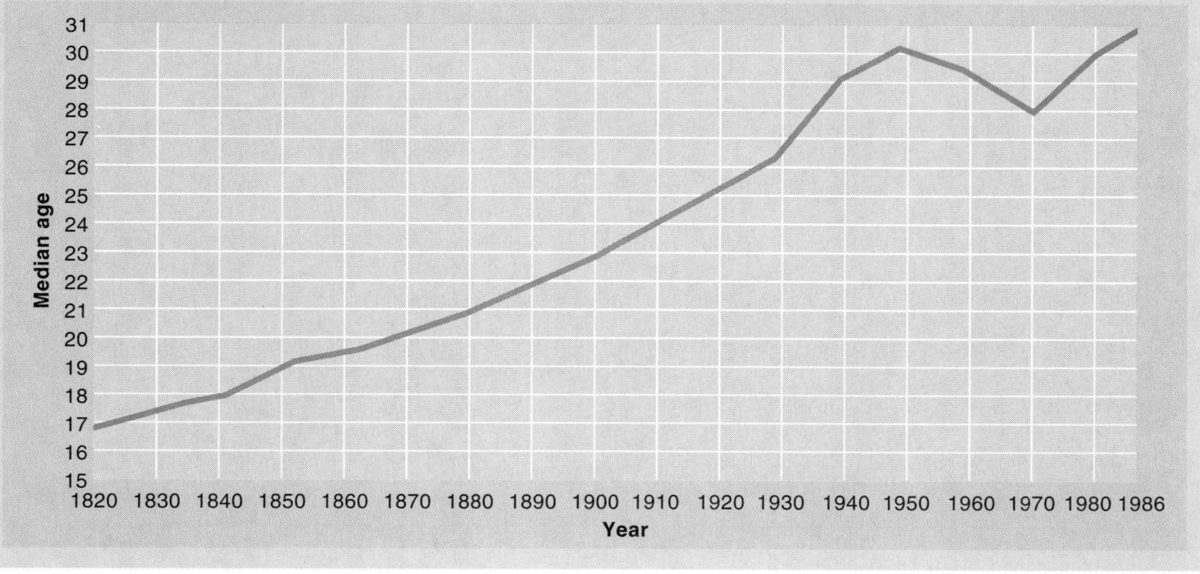

National Origins of U.S. Immigrants, 1821–1987

			EUROPE					
		TOTAL EUROPE	NORTH AND WEST	EAST AND CENTRAL	SOUTH AND OTHER	WESTERN HEMI-SPHERE	ASIA	OTHER
YEAR	TOTAL IMMIGRANTS	NO. (%)	NO. (%)	NO. (%)	NO. (%)	NO. (%)	NO. (%)	NO. (%)
1821–1830	144	99 (69.2)	96 (67.1)	—	3 (2.1)	12 (8.4)	—	32 (22.4)
1831–1840	599	496 (82.8)	490 (81.8)	—	1 (1.0)	33 (5.5)	—	70 (11.7)
1841–1850	1,713	1,599 (93.3)	1,592 (92.9)	2 (0.1)	5 (0.3)	62 (3.6)	—	53 (3.1)
1851–1860	2,598	2,453 (94.4)	2,432 (93.6)	3 (0.1)	21 (0.8)	75 (2.9)	42 (1.6)	29 (1.1)
1861–1870	2,315	2,065 (89.2)	2,032 (87.8)	12 (0.5)	21 (0.9)	167 (7.2)	65 (2.8)	19 (0.8)
1871–1880	2,812	2,272 (80.8)	2,070 (73.6)	127 (4.5)	76 (2.7)	405 (14.4)	124 (4.4)	11 (0.4)
1881–1890	5,247	4,738 (90.3)	3,778 (72.0)	624 (11.9)	331 (6.3)	425 (8.1)	68 (1.3)	16 (0.3)
1891–1900	3,688	3,559 (96.5)	1,641 (44.5)	1,210 (32.8)	704 (19.1)	41 (1.1)	70 (1.9)	18 (0.5)
1901–1910	8,795	8,136 (92.5)	1,909 (21.7)	3,914 (44.5)	2,313 (26.3)	361 (4.1)	246 (2.8)	53 (0.6)
1911–1920	5,736	4,376 (76.3)	998 (17.4)	1,916 (33.4)	1,463 (25.5)	1,141 (19.9)	195 (3.4)	23 (0.4)
1921–1930	4,107	2,477 (60.3)	1,302 (31.7)	591 (14.4)	587 (14.3)	1,516 (36.9)	99 (2.4)	16 (0.4)
1931–1940	528	348 (65.9)	205 (38.8)	58 (11.0)	85 (16.1)	160 (30.3)	15 (2.8)	5 (0.9)
1941–1950	1,035	622 (60.1)	492 (47.5)	48 (4.6)	82 (7.9)	355 (34.3)	32 (3.1)	26 (2.5)
1951–1960	2,516	1,328 (52.8)	445 (17.7)	611 (24.3)	272 (10.8)	996 (39.6)	151 (6.0)	40 (1.6)
1961–1970	3,322	1,239 (37.3)	394 (11.9)	419 (12.6)	426 (12.8)	1,579 (47.6)	445 (13.4)	58 (1.9)
1971–1980	4,384	801 (18.3)	188 (4.3)	246 (5.6)	368 (8.4)	1,929 (44.0)	1,634 (37.3)	19 (0.4)
1981–1987	4,068	446 (11.0)	156 (3.9)	199 (4.9)	91 (2.2)	1,580 (38.9)	1,902 (46.7)	140 (3.4)

Note: Numbers are given in thousands.

The American Work Force

YEAR	TOTAL NUMBER OF WORKERS	MALES AS % OF TOTAL WORKERS	FEMALES AS % OF TOTAL WORKERS	MARRIED WOMEN AS % OF FEMALE WORKERS	% OF LABOR FORCE UNEMPLOYED	% OF WORKERS IN LABOR UNIONS
1870	12,506,000	85	15	NA*	NA	NA
1880	17,392,000	85	15	NA	NA	NA
1890	23,318,000	83	17	13.9	4 (1894 = 18%)	NA
1900	29,073,000	82	18	15.4	5	3
1910	38,167,000	79	21	24.7	6	6
1920	41,614,000	79	21	23.0	5 (1921 = 12%)	12
1930	48,830,000	78	22	28.9	9 (1933 = 25%)	7
1940	53,011,000	76	24	36.4	15 (1944 = 1%)	27
1950	59,643,000	72	28	52.1	5	25
1960	69,877,000	68	32	59.9	5.4	26
1970	82,049,000	63	37	63.4	4.8	25
1980	108,544,000	58	42	59.7	7.0	23
1990	124,787,000	55	45	54.5	5.5	16

*NA = not available.

The American Farmer

YEAR	FARM POPULATION (IN THOUSANDS)	% OF TOTAL POPULATION	NUMBER OF FARMS (IN THOUSANDS)	TOTAL ACRES (IN THOUSANDS)	AVERAGE ACREAGE PER FARM
1850	NA*	NA	1,449	293,561	203
1860	NA	NA	2,044	407,213	199
1870	NA	NA	2,660	407,735	153
1880	21,973	43.8	4,009	536,082	134
1890	24,771	42.3	4,565	623,219	137
1900	29,875	41.9	5,740	841,202	147
1910	32,077	34.9	6,366	881,431	139
1920	31,974	30.1	6,454	958,677	149
1930	30,529	24.9	6,295	990,112	157
1940	30,547	23.2	6,102	1,065,114	175
1950	23,048	15.3	5,388	1,161,420	216
1960	15,635	8.7	3,962	1,176,946	297
1970	9,712	4.8	2,949	1,102,769	374
1980	6,051	2.7	2,433	1,039,000	427
1989	4,801	1.9	2,171	991,000	457

*NA = not available.

The American Economy

YEAR	GROSS NATIONAL PRODUCT (GNP) (IN $ BILLIONS)	STEEL PRODUCTION (IN SHORT TONS)	AUTOMOBILES REGISTERED	FOREIGN TRADE (IN $ BILLIONS)	
				EXPORTS	IMPORTS
1790	NA*	NA	NA	0.02	0.02
1800	NA	NA	NA	0.07	0.09
1810	NA	NA	NA	0.07	0.09
1820	NA	NA	NA	0.07	0.07
1830	NA	NA	NA	0.07	0.07
1840	NA	NA	NA	0.13	0.10
1850	NA	NA	NA	0.15	0.18
1860	NA	13,000	NA	0.40	0.36
1870	7.4†	77,000	NA	0.45	0.46
1880	11.2‡	1,397,000	NA	0.85	0.76
1890	13.1	4,779,000	NA	0.91	0.82
1900	18.7	11,227,000	8,000	1.50	0.93
1910	35.3	28,330,000	458,300	1.92	1.65
1920	91.5	46,183,000	8,131,500	8.66	5.79
1930	90.7	44,591,000	23,034,700	4.01	3.50
1940	100.0	66,983,000	27,465,800	4.03	7.43
1950	286.5	96,836,000	40,339,000	10.82	9.13
1960	506.5	99,282,000	61,682,300	19.60	15.05
1970	992.7	131,514,000	89,279,800	42.70	40.19
1980	2,631.7	111,800,000	121,600,000	220.78	244.87
1990	5,465.1	96,720,000§	144,375,000‖	394.0	495.0

*NA = not available.

†Figure is average for 1869–1878.

‡Figure is average for 1879–1888.

§Figure is for 1988.

‖Figure is for 1989.

The Federal Budget, 1940–1990

YEAR	NATIONAL DEFENSE	HUMAN RESOURCES	PHYSICAL RESOURCES	NET INTEREST	OTHER	UNDISTRIBUTED OFFSETTING RECEIPTS
1940	17.5	43.7	24.4	9.5	8.2	–3.4
1945	89.5	2.0	1.9	3.4	4.8	–1.5
1950	32.2	33.4	8.6	11.3	18.7	–4.3
1955	62.4	21.8	4.0	7.1	9.8	–5.1
1960	52.2	28.4	8.7	7.5	8.4	–5.2
1965	42.8	30.9	9.5	7.3	14.5	–5.0
1970	41.8	38.5	8.0	7.4	8.8	–4.4
1975	26.0	52.1	10.7	7.0	8.3	–4.1
1980	22.7	53.0	11.2	8.9	7.6	–3.4
1985	26.7	49.9	6.0	13.7	7.2	–3.5
1990	23.9	49.5	10.0	14.7	4.9	–2.9
1992 (est.)	20.8	52.7	10.4	13.5	5.3	–2.6

The Federal Debt

YEAR	DEBT	PER CAPITA
1790	$75,463,000	$19
1800	82,976,000	16
1810	53,173,000	7
1820	91,016,000	9
1830	48,565,000	4
1840	3,573,000	0.20
1850	63,453,000	3
1860	64,844,000	2
1870	2,436,453,000	61
1880	2,090,909,000	42
1890	1,222,397,000	19
1900	1,263,417,000	16
1910	1,146,940,000	12
1920	24,299,321,000	230
1930	16,185,310,000	132
1940	42,967,531,000	326
1950	257,357,352,000	1,708
1960	286,330,761,000	1,596
1970	370,918,707,000	1,825
1980	914,300,000,000	4,035
1990	3,206,347,000,000	12,892

Photo Credits

Part- and Chapter-Opening Illustrations

Part One *A Southeast View of the Great Town of Boston in New England in America,* colored engraving by William Burgis, probably 1731–1736. The New York Public Library, Astor, Lenox & Tilden Foundations. **Chapter 1** The French, under Jean Ribault, discovering the River of May in Florida on May 1, 1564, engraving by Theodore De Bry, 1591, after a painting by Jacques Le Moyne, who accompanied the expedition in 1564. The Granger Collection. **Chapter 2** Detail of a painting by Gerard Soest, court painter to Charles II, depicting Cecil Calvert grasping a map of Maryland held by his grandfather, the second Lord Baltimore, 1669–1670. Enoch Pratt Free Library, Baltimore. **Chapter 3** Anonymous, *Slave Deck of the Albanoz,* n.d. National Maritime Museum, Greenwich, England. **Chapter 4** Joseph Beekman Smith, *Wesley Chapel on John Street, New York City—1768* (detail), completed 1817–1844 (based on earlier sketches). Courtesy of the Old John Street United Methodist Church, New York City. **Chapter 5** *A View of the Town of Concord* (April 1775), attributed to Ralph Earle. Concord Museum, Concord, Mass.

Part Two John McRae, *Raising the Liberty Pole,* 1776. Library of Congress. **Chapter 6** William Mercer, *Battle of Princeton,* c. 1786–1790. The Historical Society of Pennsylvania, Philadelphia. **Chapter 7** First page of the U.S. Constitution. John Feingersh/Stock, Boston. **Chapter 8** George Ropes, *The Launching of the Ship* Fame, 1802. Courtesy of the Essex Institute, Salem, Mass. **Chapter 9** Thomas Coke Ruckle, *Fairview Inn or Three Mile House on Old Frederick Road* (detail), 1829(?). Collection of the Maryland Historical Society, Baltimore. **Chapter 10** B. J. Harrison, *Fair of the American Institute at Niblo's Garden,* c. 1845. Museum of the City of New York.

Part Three William Henry Jackson, *Kanesville-Missouri River Crossing,* 1856. **Chapter 11** John Antrobus, *Negro Burial,* c. 1860. The Historic New Orleans Collection, Museum/Research Center. **Chapter 12** A. Wighe, *Trial by Jury,* 1849. Museum of Art, Rhode Island School of Design, gift of Edith Jackson Green and Ellis Jackson. **Chapter 13** Albert Bierstadt, *The Rocky Mountains, Lander's Peak,* 1863. The Metropolitan Museum of Art, Rogers Fund, 1907 (07.123). **Chapter 14** Theodor Kaufmann, *On to Liberty,* 1867. The Metropolitan Museum of Art, gift of Erving and Joyce Wolf, 1982 (1982.443.3). **Chapter 15** Winslow Homer, *The Sharpshooter* (detail), 1863. Private Collection. **Chapter 16** Winslow Homer, *A Visit From the Old Mistress,* 1876. National Museum of American Art/Art Resource.

Part Four John Ferguson Weir, *Forging the Shaft,* 1874–1877. The Metropolitan Museum of Art, Purchase, Lyman G. Bloomingdale Gift, 1901. **Chapter 17** Harvey Dunn, *The Homesteader's Wife,* 1916. South Dakota Art Museum Collection, Brookings, S.D. **Chapter 18** Robert Koehler, *The Strike* (detail), 1886. Private Collection. **Chapter 19** *The Lost Bet,* chromolithograph after the painting by Joseph Klir, 1892; printed by Winter's Art Co., Chicago, 1893. The Chicago Historical Society. **Chapter 20** Rufus Zogbaum, *Dewey at Manila Bay,* 1899. Courtesy Vermont State House, Montpelier, Vt.

Part Five John Sloan, *Sixth Avenue Elevated at Third Avenue.* Collection of Whitney Museum of American Art. **Chapter 21** George Bellows, *Cliff Dwellers,* 1913. Los Angeles County Museum. **Chapter 22** Harvey Dunn, German and American Wounded After the Meuse–Argonne Offensive, 1918. Smithsonian Institution. **Chapter 23** City Activities with Dance Hall, from *America Today* by Thomas Hart Benton, 1930. Collection: The Equitable Life Assurance Society of the U.S., N.Y. **Chapter 24** "If We Would Guide by the Light of Reason We Must Let Our Minds Be Bold," from *Society Freed Through Justice,* by George Biddle, 1935–1936. Courtesy U.S. Department of Justice. **Chapter 25** World War I poster.

Part Six Billy Morrow Jackson, *Greater Downtown,* 1986. Courtesy of the artist. **Chapter 26** Edward Kienholz, *O'er the Ramparts We Watched Fascinated,* 1959. The Stephen S. Alpert Family Trust. **Chapter 27** Robert Bechtle, *'58 Rambler,* 1967. Sloan Collection, Valparaiso University Museum of Art, gift of Mrs. McCauley Conner in memory of her father, Barklie McK. Henry. **Chapter 28** Audrey Flack, *Kennedy Motorcade, November 22, 1963,* 1964. Courtesy Louis K. Meisel Gallery, New York. **Chapter 29** Norman Rockwell, *The Problem We All Live With,* original oil painting for *Look,* January 14, 1964. Printed by permission of the Estate of Norman Rockwell. Copyright © 1964 Estate of Norman Rockwell. Photograph courtesy of the Norman Rockwell Museum at Stockbridge, Mass. **Chapter 30** Billy Morrow Jackson, *Station,* 1981–1982. Courtesy Jane Haslem Gallery, Washington, D.C.

Text Illustrations *(listed by page numbers)*

9 Hopewell culture, serpentine earthworks, near Cincinnati. Cahokia Mounds Museum Society. **10** Reconstructed view of Cahokia, painted by Valerie Waldorf. Cahokia Mounds Museum Society. **11** Pottery effigy vessel from Arkansas. Museum of the American Indian, Heye Foundation, New York. **15** Drawing of the city of Loanga, at the mouth of the Congo River. Granger Collection, New York. **21** Lucas Cranach the Younger, *Epitaph of the Burgomasters of Myenburg.* The Bettmann Archive. **23** Reconstructed view of Tenochtitlán, by Ignacio Marquina. American Museum of Natural History, New York. **24** T. De Bry, Battle between the Spaniards and Indians at Cuzco, from *The Island of Pearls* (Frankfurt, 1590). Rare Book Collection, New York Public Library, Astor, Lenox & Tilden Foundations. **25** Fray Bernardo de Sahagún, woodcut of Aztecs suffering from smallpox, from *Historia de las Cosas de Nueva España,* sixteenth century. Biblioteca Medicea Laurenziana, Florence, Italy; photo Guido Sansoni. **29** George Gower, *Queen Elizabeth I* ("The Armada Portrait"). By kind permission of the Marquess of Tavistock and Trustees of Bedford Estates.

39 John White, *Secotan,* 1585–1587. Trustees of the British Museum. **40** Sidney King, conjectural mural of Jamestown, c. 1965. Courtesy Colonial National Historical Park, Jamestown, Va. **41** Adriaen Brouwer (1605/6–1638), *The Smokers.* The Metropolitan Museum of Art, Bequest of Michael Friedsam, 1931. The Friedsam Collection. **42** ABOVE: Title page of *Nova Britannia . . .* (London, 1609). BELOW: List of what New World Settlers should bring, from Edward Williams, *Virginia,* 2d ed. (London, 1605). Both, Rare Book Collection, New York Public Library, Astor, Lenox & Tilden Foundations. **43** Tobacco production, from William Tatham, *An Historical and Practical Essay on the Culture of Tobacco.* Arents Collection, New York Public Library, Astor, Lenox & Tilden Foundations. **45** Early Chesapeake architecture, crude earthfast clapboard church. Harold Wickliffe Rose Papers, Yale University Library, New Haven, Conn. **48** Anonymous portrait of John Winthrop, governor of the Massachusetts Bay Colony. American Antiquarian Society; photo Marvin Richmond. **52** Title page, William Hubbard, *The Present State of New England, Being a Narrative of the Troubles with the Indians . . .* (Boston and London, 1677). Rare Book Collection, New York Public Library, Astor, Lenox & Tilden Foundations. **53** LEFT: Richard J. Stinely, plan of Rowley, Massachusetts, from David Grayson Allen, *In English Ways* (1982). By permission of University of North Carolina Press. RIGHT: John Walker, Sr., map of Chelmsford, 1591. Public Records Office, Chelmsford, Essex, England. **54** William Boardman House, Saugus, Mass., with floor plans. Society for the Preservation of New England Antiquities; photo Marcus Whiffen. **55** Reconstructed Chesapeake planter's house. Photo Julie Roy Jeffrey. **57** Page from a New England primer. American Antiquarian Society. **61** Thomas Coram, *Mulberry Plantation.* Gibbes Art Gallery, Carolina Art Association. **64** Lenape wampum belt. Museum of the American Indian, Heye Foundation, New York. **65** Edward Hicks, *Penn's Treaty with the Indians.* National Gallery of Art, Washington, D.C.

75 LEFT: Diagram of "tight packing." National Maritime Museum, Greenwich, England. RIGHT: W. Ralph, *Negroes Just Landed from a Slave Ship,* 1808. Print Collection, New York Public Library, Astor, Lenox & Tilden Foundations. **77** Anonymous, *The Old Plantation.* Abby Aldrich Rockefeller Center for American Folk Art, Williamsburg, Va. **79** LEFT: John Singleton Copely, *Head of a Negro.* Detroit Institute of Arts, Founders Society, Gibbs-Williams Fund. RIGHT: John Greenwood, *Jersey Nanny,* 1784. Museum of Fine Arts, Boston, gift of Henry Lee Shattuck. **82** Paul Revere, engraving of King Philip. American Antiquarian Society; photo Marvin Richmond. **86** Joseph Tapping headstone. King's College Chapel Burial Ground, Boston. Photo Daniel Farber. **87** Betsy Shaw headstone, Plymouth, Mass. Photo Daniel Farber. **89** Charles A. Lawrence, *Boston's First Town House, 1657–1711,* 1930. The Bostonian Society. **92** Witch Hanging, from Ralph Gardner, *England's Grievance Discovered . . .* (London, 1655). New York Public Library, Rare Book Collection. **94** Alexander De Batz, *Desseins de Sauvages de Plusieurs Natims,* 1735. Peabody Museum, Harvard University.

103 Portraits of John Jacob Schmick and Johanna Schmick. Moravian Historical Society, Nazareth, Pa. **104** LEFT: Advertisement for recovery of a runaway indentured servant, *Pennsylvania Packet,* December 28, 1772. ABOVE: Advertisement for the sale of an Irish servant girl's time, *Pennsylvania Journal,* November 25, 1772. Both, Historical Society of Pennsylvania, Philadelphia. **108–109** Van Bergen Overmantel Homestead. New York Historical Association, Cooperstown. **111** Frontispiece of Benjamin Franklin's *Poor Richard's Almanack.* Historical Society of Pennsylvania, Philadelphia. **113** Anonymous, *The Cheney Family,* 1795. National Gallery of Art, Washington, D.C., gift of Edgar William and Bernice Chrysler Garbisch. **116** Richard J. Stinely, plot of tidewater landscape, from Rhys Isaac, *The Transformation of Virginia* (1983). By permission of University of North Carolina Press. **120** William Russell Birch, *Preparation for War to Defend Commerce* (detail), 1800. Athenaeum of Philadelphia, gift of Mrs. Charles Pearson. **125** Joseph Badger, *Jonathan Edwards.* Yale University Art Gallery, New Haven, Conn., gift of Eugene Phelps Edwards. **127** Title page of Cotton Mather sermon "Advice from Taberah," October 1711. Massachusetts Historical Society. **128** John Wollaston, *George Whitefield.* The Bettmann Archive. **130** Anonymous, *Front View of Yale College and the College Chapel, New Haven, 1786.* Yale University Art Gallery, New Haven, Conn., gift of Jess Lathrop Moss. **134** Henry Dawkins, *The Paxton Expedition,* Library Company of Philadelphia.

145 *A View of the Taking of Quebec, September 13, 1759,* printed for Robert Wilkinson & Bowles & Carver, London. Royal Ontario Museum, Toronto, Canada. **151** Anonymous American, *Patrick Henry Arguing the "Parson's Cause."* Virginia Historical Society, Richmond. **154** J. S. Barber, New Hampshire Stamp Master in Effigy, from *Interesting Events in the History of the U.S., 1829.* Metropolitan Museum of Art, New York, bequest of Charles Allen Munn. **155** Paul Revere, *A View of Part of the Town of Boston . . . 1768,* 1770. Henry Francis du

Pont Winterthur Museum, Winterthur, Del. **157** Paul Revere, *The Boston Massacre,* 1770. American Antiquarian Society. **159** *The Bostonians Paying the Excise-Man.* Colonial Williamsburg Foundation. **160** *To the Delaware Pilots . . . (signed) The Committee for Tarring and Feathering. November 27, 1773,* broadside. Rare Book Collection, New York Public Library, Astor, Lenox & Tilden Foundations. **163** Paul Revere, *The Able Doctor, or America Swallowing the Bitter Draught,* 1774. Massachusetts Historical Society, Boston. **164** LEFT: Title page, Thomas Paine's *Common Sense,* 1776. Library of Congress. RIGHT: William Sharp, *Thomas Paine,* engraved after a painting by George Romney, 1793. New-York Historical Society, New York. **166** Charles Wilson Peale, *Portrait of Benjamin Rush,* c. 1783–1786. Henry du Pont Winterthur Museum, Winterthur, Del. **167** *A Society of Patriotic Ladies at Edenton in North Carolina,* printed by R. Sayer and J. Bennett, 1775. Colonial Williamsburg Foundation, Williamsburg, Va.

179 Godefroy, *Journée de Lexington,* published in Nicholas Ponce, *Recueil d'Estampes.* Library of Congress. **185** *The Surrender of Earl Cornwallis . . . to General Washington and Count de Rochambeau,* engraving and etching by Thornton, based on a drawing by Hamilton, published in Edward Barnard, *History of England,* 1783. Library of Congress. **187** J. R. Smith, after George Romney, *Joseph Tayadaneega, Called the Brant,* 1779. Prints Division, New York Public Library, Astor, Lenox & Tilden Foundations. **188** Benjamin West, *Commissioners of the Preliminary Peace Negotiations with Great Britain,* c. 1783. Henry Francis du Pont Winterthur Museum, Winterthur, Del. **190** Anonymous, *A Real American Rifle Man,* 1780. Library of Congress. **195** Francois Xavier Habermann, *Représentation du Feu terrible à Nouvelle Yorck . . .*, 177-(?). Library of Congress. **196** John Trumbull, "The Tory's Day of Judgment," from *M'Fingal.* The Bettmann Archive. **198** Portrait of James Armistead Lafayette, 1784. Virginia Historical Society, Richmond. **199** *A Representation of the Figures Exhibited and Paraded Through the Streets of Philadelphia on Saturday the 30th of September 1780.* American Antiquarian Society; photo Marvin Richmond. **201** *La Destruction de la Statue Royale à Nouvelle Yorck (Königlichen Bilde Saule zu Neu Yorck),* 177-(?), hand-colored etching, Chez Basset. Paris. Library of Congress. **203** Samuel Hill, A.S.W. View of the State House in Boston, published in *Massachusetts Magazine,* July 1793. Stokes Collection, New York Public Library, Astor, Lenox & Tilden Foundations. **206** Anonymous portrait, traditionally said to be of Abigail Adams. New York State Historical Association, Cooperstown. **207** *The Female Patriot,* broadside, New York, May 30, 1770. Library of Congress. **208** Anonymous, *A Correct View of the Old Methodist Church in John St.* Metropolitan Museum of Art, New York, The Edward W. C. Arnold Collection of New York Prints, Maps, and Pictures; bequest of Edward W. C. Arnold, 1954. **211** *Now fitting for a Privateer,* broadside, Beverly, Mass., September 17, 1776. American Antiquarian Society; photo Marvin Richmond. **213** Currency of the Continental Congress, issued 1779. American Antiquarian Society; photo Marvin Richmond.

224 Bertrand, after Vauthier, *L'Amérique,* 181-(?). Library of Congress. **219** *Taxation Royal Tyranny,* broadside, Philadelphia, September 22, 1779. Library of Congress. **228** Anonymous, *General Daniel Shays and Colonel Job Shattuck,* 1787, published in *Bickerstaff's Boston Almanach,* 3d ed., 1787. National Portrait Gallery, Smithsonian Institution, Washington, D.C. **229** Paul Revere, silver bowl presented to General Wm. Shepard, c. 1787. Yale University Art Gallery, New Haven, Conn., Mabel Brady Garvan Collection. **231** Gilbert Stuart, *James Madison,* 1804. Mead Art Museum, Amherst College, Amherst, Mass. **232** Thomas Rossiter, *Constitutional Convention, 1787,* 186-(?). Independence National Historic Park Collection, Philadelphia. **235** Title page of Mercy Otis Warren, *Observations on the New Constitution,* 1788. Rare Books Collection, New York Public Library, Astor, Lenox & Tilden Foundations. **238** *The Federal Ship Hamilton,* from Martha Lamb, *History of New York City,* 1877. New York Public Library, Astor, Lenox & Tilden Foundations. **234** Samuel Jennings, *Liberty Displaying the Arts and Sciences,* 1792. Library Company of Philadelphia. **240** Quilt, initials C. A. C., 1853. National Gallery of Art, Washington, D.C. Index of American Design. **240** Chest; possibly made in Ohio, c. 1860. From the collection of the Henry Ford Museum and Greenfield Village, Dearborn, Michigan.

245 S. H. Gimber, after J. L. Morton, *Washington's Reception on the Bridge at Trenton in 1789,* lithograph. Library of Congress. **246** Amos Doolittle, after Peter LaCour, *Federal Hall, the Seat of Congress,* 1789. Stokes Collection, New York Public Library, Astor, Lenox & Tilden Foundations. **247** John Trumbull, *Alexander Hamilton.* Yale University Art Gallery, New Haven, Conn. **248** William Birch and Son, *Bank of the United States, in Third St., Philadelphia,* 1799. Library of Congress. **249** Jean-Antoine Houdon, *Bust of Thomas Jefferson,* 1789. New-York Historical Society, New York. **251** Attributed to Frederick Kimmelmayer, *Washington Reviewing the Western Army at Fort Cumberland, Maryland, October 18, 1794.* Metropolitan Museum of Art, New York, gift of Edgar William and Bernice Chrysler Garbisch. **252** Anonymous Chinese artist, after Barralet, *The Apotheosis of Washington,* after 1802. Peabody Museum, China Trade Gallery, Salem, Mass. **254** Joseph Wright, *George Washington,* 1790. Metropolitan Museum of Art, New York, bequest of Charles Allen Munn. **257** *Porcupine in Colors Just Betrayed.* Historical Society of Pennsylvania, Philadelphia. **259** William Winstanley, *John Adams,* 1798. Adams National Historical Site, Quincy, Mass.; photo George Dow. **260** *Cinque-têtes, or the Paris Monster,* c. 1798–1800. Huntington Library, San Marino, Cal. **263** James Van Dyke, *Aaron Burr,* 1834. New-York Historical Society, New York. **264** Textile banner celebrating Jefferson's victory, 1800. National Museum of American History, Smithsonian Institution, Washington, D.C.

271 George I. Parkyns, View of the Suburbs of Washington, D.C., c. 1800. Library of Congress. **273** Pierre L'Enfant, *Plan of the City of Washington,* 1792. New York Public Library, Astor, Lenox & Tilden Foundations. **274** Chester Harding, *John Marshall,* 1828. Boston Athenaeum. **276** Lewis and Clark, Map of the Missouri River, October 22–31, 1804. Joslyn Art Museum, Omaha, Neb., Maximilian Bodmer Collection, Internorth Art Foundation, Center for Western Studies. **281** Benjamin Henry Latrobe, *An Overseer Doing His Duty.* Maryland Historical Society. **282** Charles Bodmer, *Forest Scene on the*

Tobihanna, Alleghany Mountains, 1833. **283** Boqueto de Woiserie, *Under My Wings Everything Prospers,* view of New Orleans from the plantation of Marginy, November 1803. Chicago Historical Society. **288** John Singleton Copley, *Thomas and Sarah (Morris) Mifflin,* 1743. Historical Society of Pennsylvania, Philadelphia. **291** Pavel Petrovich Svinin, *Negro Methodist Meeting.* Metropolitan Museum of Art, New York, Rogers Fund. **293** George Ropes, *Crowninshield Wharf After the Embargo,* c. 1806. Essex Institute, Salem, Mass. **296** S. W. Fores, *The Fall of Washington, or Maddy in Full Flight,* London, 1814. Brown University Library, Providence, R.I., Anne S. K. Brown Military Collection. **297** Ambrose Louis Garneray, *The Battle of Lake Erie.* Chicago Historical Society. **302** *Portrait of Se-Quo-Yah, Cherokee,* after C. B. King, 1836–1844. National Museum of Natural History, Smithsonian Institution, Washington, D.C. **305** John L. Krimmel, *Election Day at the Statehouse,* c. 1815, Historical Society of Pennsylvania, Philadelphia. **306** Samuel F. B. Morse, *Congress Hall: Old House of Representatives,* 1821. Corcoran Gallery of Art, Washington, D.C.

320 Mary Keys, *Lockport on the Erie Canal,* 1832. Munson-Williams-Proctor Institute, Museum of Utica, N.Y. **324** Southworth and Hawes, *The George Barrell Emerson School,* c. 1840–1862. Metropolitan Museum of Art, New York, gift of I. N. Phelps Stokes, Edward S. Hawes, Alice Mary Hawes, and Marian Augusta Hawes. **326** The Manchester Print Works at Manchester, N.H., from *Gleason's Pictorial,* 1854. Library of Congress. **328** Pendleton, *Lowell, Massachusetts, 1834.* Worcester Art Museum, Worcester, Mass., Goodspeed Collection. **329** Time Table of the Lowell Mills, October 1851. Baker Library, Harvard Business School, Cambridge, Mass. **330** Anonymous, *Drawing In.* Museum of American Textile History, North Andover, Mass. **333** Photograph of the Ohio River at Cincinnati, 1848. Public Library of Cincinnati and Hamilton County, Ohio. **337** Asselineau, after John Bachman, *Panoramic View of Philadelphia,* c. 1855. Historical Society of Pennsylvania, Philadelphia. **340** "Maternal Instruction" from *Godey's Lady's Book and Magazine* (February 1845). **342** Anonymous, *The Sargent Family,* 1800. National Gallery of Art, Washington, D.C., gift of Edgar William and Bernice Chrysler Garbisch. **343** H. Knight, *The Family at Home,* 1836. Hirschl & Adler Galleries. **347** N. Currier, after L. Maurer, *Preparing for Market,* 1856. Yale University Art Gallery, New Haven, Conn., Mabel Brady Garvan Collection.

360 Mathew Brady, *Black Dockworkers,* c. 1860. National Archives. **364** Anonymous, *The Quilting Party,* after an engraving in *Gleason's Pictorial,* after 1854. Abby Aldrich Rockefeller Center for Folk Art, Williamsburg, Va. **366** Adele Petigru Allston and Robert F. W. Allston. Both, South Caroliniana Library, Columbia, S.C. **371** George Fuller, *Interior of a Slave Cabin,* January 28, 1858. Private Collection. **374** Anonymous, *Slave Market,* c. 1860. The Carnegie Museum of Art, Gift of Mrs. W. Fitch Ingersoll, 58.4. **376** Christmas on the Plantation, *Frank Leslie's Illustrated Newspaper,* December 16, 1857. New York Public Library, Astor, Lenox & Tilden Foundations. **377** Slave family of five generations, 1862, all born on plantation of J. J. Smith, Beaufort, S.C., photographed by T. H. Sullivan. Library of Congress. **381** George Fuller, *Cotton Press and Gin,* February 2, 1858, Private Collection. **383** *Horrid Massacre in Virginia,* woodcut, 1831. Library of Congress. **384** *Frederick Douglass,* c. 1855, engraved portrait by J. C. Battre from a daguerrotype. New York Public Library, Schomburg Center for Research in Black Culture. **385** Meeting in the African Church, *Frank Leslie's Illustrated Newspaper,* April 30, 1853. Library of Congress.

392 *Symptoms of Indigestion,* 1824. Library Company of Philadelphia. **393** Robert Cruickshank, *All Creation Going to the White House,* 1829. Library of Congress. **397** Old Hickory, figurehead, 1834. Museum of the City of New York. **401** LEFT: "A Drop of Hard Cider, or The Tippecanoe Roarer," songbook cover, 1840. Cincinnati Historical Society. BOTTOM: "Federal-Abolition-Whig Trap to Catch Voters In," broadside, c. 1840. Library of Congress. **405** J. Maze Burbank, *Religious Camp Meeting,* 1839. The Whaling Museum, New Bedford, Mass. **408** "Shakers Near Lebanon State of New York—Their Mode of Worship." **411** N. Currier, *The Drunkard's Progress, from the First Glass to the Grave,* 1846. Museum of the City of New York, Harry T. Peters Collection. **417** "Ye abolitionists in council—Ye orator of ye day denouncing ye Union, May, 1859," illustration reproduced in *Harper's Weekly,* May 28, 1859. Newberry Library, Chicago. **419** N. Currier, *Certificate of Marriage,* 1848. Library of Congress. **420** LEFT: E. Decker, *Elizabeth Cady Stanton.* RIGHT: *Lucretia Mott.* Both, Sophia Smith Collection, Smith College, Northampton, Mass.

429 Jon Gast, *Westward the Course of Empire . . . ,* 1872. Library of Congress. **431** Mathew Brady, *James Knox Polk,* 1849. Library of Congress. **433** Currier & Ives, *Flight of the Mexican Army at the Battle of Buena Vista, February 23, 1847.* Museum of the City of New York. **437** Lorenzo Lorain, *Oregon City,* 1857. Oregon Historical Society. **439** Emigrant wagon, c. 1848. The Granger Collection. **440** Benjamin Franklin Reinhart, *The Emigrant Train Bedding Down for the Night,* 1867. Corcoran Gallery of Art, Washington, D.C., gift of Mr. and Mrs. Lansdell K. Christie. **443** *The Rigors of the Trail . . . the End of a Long Day.* Denver Public Library, Western History Department. **446** Charles Nahl, *Saturday Night at the Mines,* 1856. Stanford University Museum of Art, gift of Mrs. Jane L. Stanford. **447** TOP: Mining, Auburn Ravine, American River, 1852. California State Library, Sacramento. **447** BOTTOM: William Henry Jackson, *Ophir City, Nevada,* c. 1875. Denver Public Library, Western History Department. **448** C. C. A. Christensen, *The Nauvoo Temple, 1844.* Brigham Young University Art Museum Collection, Provo, Utah. **451** Sacramento Street, San Francisco, 1853. Bancroft Library, University of California, Berkeley. **453** Alfred Jacob Miller, *Throwing the Lasso,* 1836. Yale University Library, New Haven, Conn., Beinecke Rare Book and Manuscript Collection. **455** Charles Christian Nahl, *The Fandango,* 1873. Crocker Art Museum, Sacramento, CA, E. B. Crocker Collection.

463 Richard Caton Woodville, *War News from Mexico,* 1848. National Institute of Design, N.Y. **467** *Caution! Colored People of Boston . . . ,* broadside, 1851. Library of Congress. **470** *The Blessings of Liberty, or How to Hook a Gentleman ob (sic) Color,* 1851. Library of Congress. **472** *Soliciting a Vote,* 1852. Library of Congress. **473** George Caleb Bingham, *Verdict of the People,* 1853–1854. Boatmen's Boneshares, Inc., St. Louis. **475** Know-Nothing Cartoon. New York Public Library, Astor,

Lenox & Tilden Foundations. **479** Gun-toting Missourians crossing into Kansas. Newberry Library, Chicago. **483** LEFT: G. G. Lange, *Rochester, New York,* 1860. Library of Congress. RIGHT: Calvert, *Sunny South,* c. 1850. The Bettmann Archive. **483** Abraham Lincoln in 1860 (left) and 1865 (right). Bettmann Archive. **484** Thomas Hovenden, *Last Moments of John Brown,* 1884. Metropolitan Museum of Art, Gift of Mr. and Mrs. Carl Stoeckel, 1897. **485** Southern Sympathizer Tarred and Feathered in Haverhill, Massachusetts, from *Frank Leslie's Illustrated Newspaper,* August 31, 1861. New York Public Library, Astor, Lenox & Tilden Foundations. **488** *The True Issue,* cartoon. Library of Congress.

495 First Michigan Regiment musters in Detroit, May 11, 1861, before taking the train to Washington. Detroit Public Library. **499** Jefferson Davis, c. 1857. Museum of the Confederacy, Richmond, Va. **500** Alexander Gardner, *Lincoln with Pinkerton and Major General McClelland at Antietam, October 1862.* Library of Congress. **502** Killed at Antietam: Horse of a Confederate Officer. **503** Field Hospital, Savage Station, Va. Library of Congress. **505** J. G. Tanner, *Engagement Between the Monitor and the Merrimac.* National Gallery of Art, Washington, D.C. **507** Advertisements for Substitute Confederate Conscriptees, Virginia Historical Society, Richmond. **510** Emancipation Day at Smith's Plantation Port Royal, S.C., from *Frank Leslie's Illustrated Newspaper,* January 24, 1863. New-York Historical Society, New York. **514** Mathew Brady, *Confederate Captives at Gettysburg.* National Archives. **515** Mathew Brady, *Burial Party at Cold Harbor, April 1965.* National Archives. **517** Currier & Ives, *The 54th Massachusetts Regiment Storming Fort Wagner, South Carolina . . . ,* 1890. Museum of the City of New York. **521** *A Relic of Pope's Retreat (Overturned Train).* Library of Congress. **522** Currier & Ives, *The Solider's Dream of Home.* Museum of the City of New York. **523** Ruins of Richmond, May 1865. Library of Congress.

531 "The Desolate Home: A Picture of the Suffering of the South," from *Frank Leslie's Illustrated Newspaper,* February 23, 1867. Library of Congress. **534** Thomas Nast, "Slavery Is Dead," from *Harper's Weekly,* January 12, 1867. Newberry Library, Chicago. **537** Burning of a Freedmen's School, *Harper's Weekly,* May 26, 1866. Library Company of Philadelphia. **540** Office of the Freedmen's Bureau, Memphis, from *Harper's Weekly,* June 2, 1866. Library of Congress. **543** Negro Home in the South: Sharecroppers. Brown Brothers. **546** Black Schoolchildren. Valentine Museum, Richmond, Va. **548** A. R. Waud, *The First Vote. Harper's Weekly,* November 16, 1867. **550** Thomas Nast, *Worse than Slavery,* n.d. Library of Congress. **552** LEFT: Currier & Ives, "Middle Age," from *The Seasons of Life,* 1868. Museum of the City of New York. RIGHT: *A Visit from the Ku Klux Klan,* 1878. The Granger Collection. **553** Thomas Nast, "This Is a White Man's Government," from *Harper's Weekly,* September 5, 1868. Library Company of Philadelphia.

567 Currier & Ives, *Winter Morning in the Country,* 1875. Metropolitan Museum of Art, New York, bequest of Adele S. Colgate. **569** George Innes, *The Lackawanna Valley,* n.d. National Gallery of Art, Washington, D.C. **570** Advertisement for a threshing machine, n.d. The Bettmann Archive. **571** W. A. Raymond, *Oregon Wheat Harvest,* c. 1880. The Bettmann Archive. **573** Solomon D. Butcher, The Rawding Family of Custer County, Nebraska, 1886. Nebraska State Historical Society, Solomon D. Butcher Collection. **575** Frederic Remington, *In a Stampede,* 1888. The Granger Collection. **576** Porter Thayer, *Mr. & Mrs. J. A. Davis in Their General Store,* West Dover, New Hampshire, c. 1890–1900. Vermont Historical Society, Montpelier. **578** Black Elk, Oglala Sioux, 1888. Smithsonian Institution. **584** Dock Workers Loading Bales of Cotton, n.d. Library of Congress. **588** *In Self-Defense, Harper's Weekly,* 1876. **591** Custer's Last Stand, from *Harper's Weekly,* January 16, 1868. New York Public Library, Astor, Lenox & Tilden Foundations. **592** Strobridge & Co., *The Purposes of the Grange: Gift for the Grangers,* 1873. Library of Congress.

603 Comstock mine, 1877. Library of Congress. **605** Strobridge & Co., *Interior of Dining Cars on the Cininnati, Hamilton & Dayton R.R.* The Granger Collection. **609** Randolph Street West from Elevated Station, 1896. Chicago Historical Society. **610** Burt G. Phillips, Woman and a Child at the Battery, c. 1907. Museum of the City of New York. **612** Trolleys on lower Broadway New York, c. 1890. Brown Brothers. **614** House in River Forest, Ill., 1893. Culver Pictures. **615** Advertisement for home washing machine and wringer, 1869. The Granger Collection. **616** Women Cyclists, Crawfordsville, Indiana. Crawfordsville District Public Library. **620** Hod Carriers. Temple University Urban Archives, Philadelphia. **621** Stetson Hat Factory, Fur-Cutting Room. Pennsylvania Historical and Museum Commission, Division of Archives and Manuscripts, Harrisburg. **627** Charles Van Schaik, Domestic Servants near Black River Falls, Wisconsin. State Historical Society of Wisconsin, Madison. **632** Surrender of Strikers to Pinkerton Detectives, from *Harper's Weekly,* July 16, 1892. New York Public Library, Astor, Lenox & Tilden Foundations.

642 Campaign poster, Harrison and Morton, 1888. Library of Congress. **646** Victoria Claflin Woodhull reading her argument before the House Judiciary Committee. The Granger Collection. **647** Frances Willard, autographed 1889. The Bettmann Archive. **648** Seymour J. Guy, *The William H. Vanderbilt Family in 1873.* Biltmore House and Gardens, Asheville, N.C. **650** Denison House Public Health Clinic, Dorchester, Boston, 1900. Schlesinger Library, Radcliffe College, Cambridge, Mass. **652** Thomas Nast, *Who Stole the People's Money.* The Granger Collection. **654** *Jane Addams.* University of Illinois at Chicago Circle, Jane Addams Memorial Collection. **656** "From the Depths," from J. Ames Mitchell, *The Silent War,* 1906. Culver Pictures. **659** LEFT: C. Graham, *The Ferris Wheel,* 1893. Chicago Historical Society. RIGHT: Detroit Photographic Co., *End of an Era,* c. 1900. Library of Congress. **661** William Jennings Bryan, 1896. Library of Congress. **662** William McKinley campaigning. The Granger Collection. **664** William Jennings Bryan campaign artifacts. Kenneth J. Moran, University of Minnesota, Duluth. **665** William McKinley campaign artifacts. Kenneth J. Moran, University of Minnesota, Duluth.

673 U.S. troops in a trench, Philippines, c. 1900. Library of Congress. **675** Pan Pacific Photo, Annexation Ceremony, Iolani Palace, Honolulu, August 13, 1898. Library of Congress. **678** Some Ships of the U.S. Fleet, *Harper's Weekly,* January 30, 1892. New York Public Library, Astor, Lenox & Tilden Foundations. **681** Decorated Mast of the USS *Maine,* Havana Harbor, 1900. The Granger Collection. **683** LEFT: W. G. Read, *Teddy's Rough Riders,* c. 1898. The Granger Collection. RIGHT: Underwood & Underwood, *Troop A, Ninth U.S. Cavalry, Famous Indian Fighters,* 1898. Library of Congress. **686** Filipino guerrillas captured at Pasay and Paranque. 1899. Library of Congress. **687** McKinley campaign poster, 1900. Culver Pictures. **689** Dalrymple, "The New Diplomacy: Theodore Roosevelt and the Big Stick," *Judge,* January 14, 1905, Library of Congress. **690** LEFT: John Barrett, Panama Canal construction scene: steam shovel railroad car. Library of Congress. RIGHT: Joseph Kippler, Jr., 1904. The Granger Collection. **692** LEFT: Grant Hamilton, "The Spanish Brute Adds Mutilation to Murder," *Judge,* July 9, 1898. Culver Pictures. RIGHT: "Liberty Halts American Butchery in the Philippines," *Life,* 1899. **693** LEFT: "Panama or Bust," *The New York Times,* 1903. RIGHT: L. C. Gregg, For President, *Atlanta Constitution,* 1904. **696** W. A. Rogers, McKinley and Uncle Sam leading charge against Boxer Rebellion, 1900. The Granger Collection. **698** Theodore Roosevelt at Portsmouth, N.H., Peace Treaty Negotiations, 1905. The Bettmann Archive.

711 John Sloan, *Backyards, Greenwich Village,* 1914. Whitney Museum of American Art, New York. **712** Lewis Hine, *Breaker Boys Working in Ewen Breaker, Pittston, Pennsylvania,* January 1911. National Archives, Records for the Children's Bureau. **715** Jessie Tarbox Beals, *Room in a Tenement Flat,* 1910. Museum of the City of New York. **717** Poster for *Tess of the Storm Country,* starring Mary Pickford, 1914. The Memory Shop, New York. **718** Lewis Hine, *Carolina Cotton Mill,* 1908. International Museum of Photography at George Eastman House, Rochester, N.Y. **719** Anonymous photographs of a tenement flat. LEFT: Before. RIGHT: After. Temple University Archives, Philadelphia. **721** Alfred Stieglitz, *The Steerage,* 1907. Collection, The Museum of Modern Art, New York, gift of Alfred Stieglitz. **724** Triangle Shirtwaist Company fire, 1911. Brown Brothers. **727** Jewish Immigrants in Galveston, Texas, c. 1909. Eugene C. Barker Texas History Center, University of Texas, Austin. **728** Dearborn Street, looking south from Randolph Street, 1909. Chicago Historical Society. **730** Theodore Roosevelt speaking in New York City, 1910. Brown Brothers. **733** Cover, *Collier's,* May 11, 1912. The Granger Collection. **735** History class, Tuskegee Institute, c. 1910. Library of Congress. **740** Suffragettes in Washington, D.C., 1913. The Bettmann Archive.

750 *Saying Goodbye,* 1917. National Archives, Records of the War Department. **753** Front page, *The New York Times,* Saturday, May 18, 1915. New York Public Library, Astor, Lenox & Tilden Foundations. **755** "Woodrow on Toast," *Punch,* August 27, 1913. Library of Congress. **758** Howard Chandler Christie, *Gee! I wish I were a man,* 1918. The Granger Collection. **760** Liberty Bond poster. The Granger Collection. **761** LEFT: "Will You Be a Free Man or Chained." Army Educational Commission, Social Hygiene Commission. RIGHT: Still from *Fit to Fight.* War Department, Commission on Training Camps. **763** Salvation Army Women in field kitchen. National Archives, U.S. Signal Corps. **764** Social Club for Black Servicemen, Newark, N.J., c. 1918. National Archives. **766** French troops in trenches on the western front. Roger-Viollet, Paris. **770** *Women in Industry,* 1917–1918. National Archives, Women's Bureau. **773** The "Big Four" in the Hotel Crillon, Paris, December 1918. The Granger Collection.

783 Ku Klux Klan, c. 1920. Library of Congress. **784** Ben Shahn, *Bartolomeo Vanzetti and Nicola Sacco,* from the Sacco-Vanzetti series of 23 paintings, 1931–1932, Tempera on paper over composition board, 10½ × 14½ inches. Collection, The Museum of Modern Art, New York, gift of Abby Aldrich Rockefeller. **787** Traffic jam, St. Louis, Missouri, 1920s. Brown Brothers. **789** Thomas Hart Benton, *Boom Town,* 1927–1928. Memorial Art Gallery of the University of Rochester (N.Y.), Marion Stratton Gould Fund. **791** TOP: George W. Bellows, *Dempsey and Firpo,* 1924. Whitney Museum of American Art, New York. BOTTOM: Ticker-tape parade for Charles Lindbergh. Culver Pictures. **792** Colgate Ribbon dental cream. By permission of the Colgate-Palmolive Company. **793** LEFT: Barbasol. By permission of Leeming Division, Pfizer, Inc. **794** John Steuart Curry, *Baptism in Kansas,* 1928. Whitney Museum of American Art. **797** Marcus Garvey. Brown Brothers. **800** Woman washing, Iowa, 1922. **801** Typists, 1922s. Bettmann Archive. **804** Harding and Coolidge, 1920. UPI/Bettmann. **809** Herbert Hoover campaigning. Bettmann Archive.

817 Hoover Dam. Culver Pictures. **819** Isaac Soyer, *Employment Agency,* 1937. Whitney Museum of American Art, New York. **821** Bonus Army shacks in flames, Anacostia Flats, 1932. National Archives, U.S. Signal Corps. **822** Franklin D. Roosevelt with miners, 1932. Wide World. **825** Depression in the Midwest: the Dust Bowl, n.d. The Bettmann Archive. **830** WPA workers widening a street, c. 1935. The Bettmann Archive. **832** Arthur Rothstein, a farmer and son during dust storm, Oklahoma, 1936. Library of Congress. **834** Secretary of Labor Frances Perkins at Carnegie Steel Plant, Pittsburgh. Brown Brothers. **836** Eleanor Roosevelt with Mary McLeod Bethune and Aubrey Williams, 1937. UPI/Bettmann. **837** Russell Lee, Mexican Carrot Workers near Santa Maria, Texas, February 1939. Library of Congress. **843** Trylon and Perisphere with General Motors Building in foreground, New York World's Fair, 1939. Courtesy Mrs. Edith Lutyens Bel Geddes. **846** *It Happened One Night,* 1934. The Museum of Modern Art/Film Stills Archive, New York. **847** *Drums Along the Mohawk,* 1939. The Museum of Modern Art/Film Stills Archive, New York. **848** Anxious kin await news of sunken sub, 1939. UPI/Bettmann Newsphotos.

856 *Ein Volk, ein Reich, ein Führer,* 1938. The Granger Collection. **860** USS *Shaw* exploding in Japanese raid on Pearl Harbor, December 7, 1941. National Archives, General Records of the Navy Department. **861** Factory workers, North American Aviation, Inglewood, California, 1942. Library of Congress. **865** Russell Lee, Japanese-Americans, Los Angeles, April 1942. Library of Congress. **867** Migrant family, Sawboro, North Carolina, July 1940. Library of Congress. **867** Women in wartime industry. **872** Collecting scrap for recycling. Library of Congress. **873** Alfred Eisenstadt, *Soldier's Farewell,* Penn Station, New York. LIFE Magazine, © 1944 Time, Inc. **874** George Strock, American war dead, Bura, New Guinea, 1943. LIFE Magazine, © 1943 Time, Inc. **879** Mass annihilation, Noordhausen, Germany, April 25, 1945. UPI/Bettmann Newsphotos. **880** President Roosevelt and General Eisenhower at Castelvetrano, Sicily, December 8, 1943. Roosevelt Library, Hyde Park, N.Y. **884** Mock-up of atomic bomb havoc displayed in an Osaka department store, 1984. Kitamura/Gamma Liaison.

896 President Truman gets an ear of corn from five-year-old Katherine Melburn, September 1948. UPI/Bettmann Newsphotos. **897** Eisenhower with delegation of Republican National Committee Women, New York, August 1952. UPI/Bettmann. **898** A. Gerasimov, *Stalin at the 6th Congress of the Russian Communist Party.* The Bettmann Archive. **899** Eisenhower and Khrushchev at Camp David. Bob Henriques/Magnum. **904** The Berlin Airlift, 1948–1949. The Bettmann Archive. **905** John Foster Dulles. UPI/Bettmann Newsphotos. **907** Heroic painting of Mao Zedong, n.d. Rene Burri/Magnum. **909** LEFT: General Douglas MacArthur returns from Korea, San Francisco, 1951. Wayne Miller/Magnum. RIGHT: Korean War, June 1953. UPI/Bettmann. **915** Atomic Bomb Test, Mururoa Atoll. ECPA/Gamma-Liaison. **916** Family in home fallout shelter. J. Edward Bailey/*Time* Magazine. **918** Alger Hiss. Elliot Erwitt/Magnum. **919** Senator Joseph McCarthy testifying, 1954. UPI/Bettmann Newsphotos.

931 McDonald's, Des Plaines, Illinois. Courtesy McDonald's Corporation, Oakbrook, Ill. **932** Cars on a highway. Erich Hartmann/Magnum. **938** Levittown, Pa., 1957. Margaret Bourke-White, LIFE Magazine, © Time, Inc. **940** ENIAC computer ready for use, 1946. Photo University of Pennsylvania, Philadelphia. **941** Mickey Mouse Club. Photofest. **942** Supermarket. George Silk/LIFE Magazine, © Time Warner, Inc. **943** Billy Graham, 1951. UPI/Bettmann. **945** Marilyn Monroe. UPI/Bettmann. **946** Harlem women, 1920s. Schomburg Collection, New York Public Library, Astor, Lenox & Tilden Foundations. **947** TOP LEFT: Secretary of Labor Frances Perkins at Carnegie Steel plant, Pittsburgh. Brown Brothers. TOP CENTER: Drill press workers, Commercial Iron Works plant, Portland, Oregon, 1943. Oregon Historical Society. TOP RIGHT: Dorothea Lange, Woman and Child, San Francisco, 1952. The Oakland Museum. BOTTOM: Hippie couple, 1960s. Ken Heyman. **951** "Dewey Defeats Truman," November 1948. UPI/Bettmann Newsphotos. **955** Jackie Robinson sliding into home plate, July 1954. UPI/Bettmann Newsphotos. **957** National Guard escorting black students, Little Rock, Ark., 1957. Burt Glinn/Magnum. **958** Martin Luther King, Jr. Bob Henriques/Magnum. **960** Workers in the broccoli fields, Edcouch, Texas, 1948. University of Louisville, Photographic Archives, Standard Oil of New Jersey Collection.

967 LEFT: Kennedy-Nixon televised debate. Wide World Photos. RIGHT: President Kennedy, the First Lady, and Robert Frost at a dinner for Nobel Prize laureates, April 1, 1962. UPI/Bettmann. **969** Lyndon B. Johnson taking oath of office, November 1963. AP/Wide World Photos. **971** Lunar landing, August 1969. NASA. **973** Immigrants becoming citizens. UPI/Bettmann Newsphotos. **978** TOP: Violence during the 1968 Democratic Convention, Chicago. UPI/Bettmann Newsphotos. BOTTOM: President Nixon. Hiroji Kubota/Magnum. **984** Gary Trudeau, *Doonesbury.* September 17, 1973. Copyright 1973. G.B. Trudeau. Reprinted with permission of Universal Press Syndicate. All rights reserved. **985** Gerald Ford. UPI/Bettmann. **986** Jimmy and Rosalynn Carter walk to his inauguration, January 1971. The White House. **989** Buddhist monk, Saigon, October 1963. UPI/Bettmann Newsphotos. **992** Helicopters evacuating troops, Vietnam. Hiroji Kubota/Magnum. **995** General Loan shooting a suspected Vietcong. AP/Wide World Photos. **996** Aftermath of Kent State shooting. © John Paul Filo. **997** Nixon in China. Sygma. **998** Brezhnev and Nixon, 1972. UPI/Bettmann Newsphotos. **999** Begin, Sadat, and Carter tour Gettysburg battlefield. Jim Moore/Gamma-Liaison.

1007 Lunch counter sit-in. Bruce Roberts/Photo Researchers. **1008** James Meredith at Ole Miss. UPI/Bettmann Newsphotos. **1009** Police with dogs, Birmingham, Alabama. Charles Moore/Black Star. **1010** March on Washington, August 1963. Robert Kelley/LIFE Magazine, © Time, Inc. **1013** Malcolm X. UPI/Bettmann Newsphotos. **1015** Motorcycle policeman escorting a school bus. Owen Franken/Gamma-Liaison. **1020** "This healthy, normal baby has a handicap . . . ." NOW Legal Defense and Education Fund. **1021** By permission of *Ms.* Magazine. **1022** Wisconsin Nurses for ERA. J. L. Atlan/Sygma. **1023** Justice Sandra Day O'Connor. Zimberoff/Sygma. **1025** Farm Workers' Union. Black Star. **1026** Chicano Power Mural, East Los Angeles housing project. Craig Aurness/Woodfin Camp & Associates. **1027** Bilingual classroom, Houston. Dan F. Connolly/Gamma-Liaison. **1029** Native American children, Wisconsin. Bob Adelman/Magnum. **1030** Native Americans at Wounded Knee, S.D., 1973. Michael Abramson/Gamma-Liaison. **1033** Student antiwar protest, Columbia University. UPI/Bettmann Newsphotos. **1036** LEFT: Joan Baez, 1964. John Launois/Black Star. RIGHT: Bob Dylan, 1963. Wide World Photos. **1037** LEFT: The Beatles. Archive Photos. RIGHT: The Supremes. Brown Brothers. **1038** Rock festival, Woodstock, New York, 1969. **1039** KKK antigay demonstration, Houston, 1985. Gamma/Liaison, Dan Connolly. **1041** Three Mile Island. Dirck Halstead/Gamma-Liaison.

1049 Jerry Falwell, 1980. UPI/Bettmann. **1051** The Reagan inauguration, 1980. Diana Walker/Gamma-Liaison. **1052** George Bush with New Orleans–area high school students, August 1988. J. David Ake/UPI/Bettmann. **1057** Los Angeles riot damage, 1992. Wide World Photos. **1067** Cuban refugee filling out a registration form for resident states. Dan Miller/Woodfin Camp & Associates. **1072** Gorbachev arriving at the Iceland Summit, October 1986. Larry Downing/Woodfin Camp & Associates. **1073** Boris Yeltsin after winning presidential election, June 1991. Reuters/Bettmann. **1074** Crowd celebrating destruction of Berlin Wall, November 1989. R. Bossu/Sygma. **1075** Anti-American demonstration, Baghdad. Chris Morris/Black Star. **1077** Oliver North. John Ficara/Woodfin Camp & Associates. **1078** Wilson and Winnie Mandela at a rally in New York City, June 1990. **1079** George Bush, Ross Perot, and Bill Clinton during televised presidential debate. Jeffrey Markowitz/Sygma.

Index